World Economic Outlook

ECONOMICS

THE IRWIN SERIES IN ECONOMICS

ECONOMICS

DAVID C. COLANDER
Middlebury College

IRWIN
Burr Ridge, Illinois
Boston, Massachusetts
Sydney, Australia

Section opener photos

Section 1 Reuters/Bettmann
Section 2 Tony Savino/The Image Works
Section 3 Photo Researchers/Rafael Macia
Section 4 Reuters/Bettmann

Senior sponsoring editor: Gary Nelson
Developmental editor: Pat McCabe
Marketing manager: Ron Bloecher
Project editor: Lynne Basler
Production manager: Irene H. Sotiroff
Designer: Laurie J. Entringer
Art manager: Kim Meriwether
Photo research coordinator: Patricia A. Seefelt
Compositor: Better Graphics, Inc.
Typeface: 10/12 Times Roman
Printer: Von Hoffmann Press

Library of Congress Cataloging-in-Publicaton Data

Colander, David C.
  Economics / David C. Colander
    p.   cm.
  Includes index.
  ISBN 0-256-10784-X; ISBN 0-256-15703-0 UPDATED EDITION
  1. Economics.   I. Title.
  HB171.5.C788   1993
  330—dc20   92–24423

Cover photo: Hans Neleman, The Image Bank

Printed in the United States of America
1 2 3 4 5 6 7 8 9 0 VH 9 8 7 6 5 4 3

To Bill Vickrey,
whose integrity, honesty, brilliance, and eccentricities
make me proud to have been his student

Preface

Why write a new introductory economics textbook? Since I am an economist, the answer must be that the expected benefits outweighed the expected costs. But that doesn't mean I had my bank balance in mind when I decided to write this book. Quite honestly, there are easier ways of earning money (my wife's a doctor). There had to be some other benefits out there. For me, those other benefits had to do with a belief about how economics should be taught—what was important and what was not.

Before I started writing this book I had done quite a bit research on economic education. As part of that research Arjo Klamer and I had surveyed and interviewed graduate students in a number of top graduate programs. Two of the most disturbing things we discovered were that economic institutions and economic literature were being given short shrift in graduate economics education. For example, in response to the question, "How important is a knowledge of economic literature to being successful as an economist?" only 10 percent of the students responded that it was very important, while 43 percent said it was unimportant. In response to the question, "How important to achieving success as an economist is having a thorough knowledge of the economy?" only 3 percent said it was very important, while 68 percent said it was unimportant.

I believe that the majority of the profession is concerned with these results. Certainly the students we interviewed were concerned. They said they believed that institutions and literature were very important. Their survey responses simply indicated their perception of how people succeed in the profession, but the current situation was not the way it should be. Almost all economists I know believe that students need to know economic literature and have a thorough knowledge of the institutions. Without the appropriate background knowledge of institutions and literature, all the technical skills in the world aren't going to provide one with the economic sensibility necessary to understand what's going on in the economy or to decide whether or not a model is relevant.

As I thought about these results and considered my own teaching, I realized that the problem was not only in graduate schools; it had filtered down to undergraduate texts. As I looked through the texts, I saw excellent discussions of technical issues and of models, but little discussion of economic sensibility. These books didn't even try to provide the intellectual context within which those models developed or the institutional context to which these models were to be applied. The standard texts had settled into teaching technique for the sake of technique and had shifted away from teaching economic sensibility.

I decided that if I were serious about playing a role in reinstituting economic sensibility and a knowledge of institutions and literature in economic education, I would have to write an introductory textbook that did that. I took it as a challenge. Meeting that challenge was what drove me to write this book; it is what kept me going when all my rational instincts told me it was too much time and too much work.

Teaching Economic Sensibility

The question I faced was: How do you incorporate economic sensibility into a textbook? Economic sensibility is more than a knowledge of modeling techniques; it is a mindset in which one's lens of the world is a latticework of ascending cost/benefit frameworks in which one is deciding on the optimal degree of rationality. Economic sensibility is an enforced reasonableness that provides insight into complicated issues; it is a perspective, not a technique. The argument I heard in favor of teaching technique was that economic sensibility could not be taught. I reject that argument. Economic sensibility may be hard to teach because it does not come naturally for most people, but it can and must be taught. The question is: How do you teach it? The answer I came to is "Enthusiastically."

Economics with Passion

I am first and foremost an economics teacher; I am excited by economics. I find economic ideas relevant, challenging, and exciting. In my lectures I try to convey that excitement, and if the lecture is going right, I can feel the excitement in my students. Then off they go to read the text. All too often when they return to class, the fire in their eyes is gone; the textbook has lulled them into complacency. Those who know me know that I can put up with many things (not quietly, but nonetheless put up with), but one of those things isn't complacency. I want students to think, to argue, to challenge, to get passionate about the ideas. I encourage this reaction from students not just because economists' ideas deserve to be treated passionately, but also because, through a combination of passion and reason, eventually students achieve economic sensibility. I decided what was missing from most textbooks was the passion. I promised myself my book would retain the passion.

Now there's no way I'm going to get passionate about Slutsky equations, phase diagrams, indifference curves, or an AS/AD model. Mathematicians may get passionate about such things, I don't. I do get passionate about the insights economics gives one into the problems we, as individuals and as society, must face: the budget deficit, TANSTAAFL, environment, and agricultural subsidies. If the techniques help in understanding the ideas fine, but if they don't, good-bye to the techniques.

Passion without Bias

While not all textbooks are written by passionless people, the conventional wisdom is that authors should hide their passion to make their books more marketable. In some ways this makes sense—often passion and ideological bias go together. Many economists' passions are ideologically linked, and if you remove the ideology, you remove the passion. Good economic sensibility cannot be—and cannot even appear to be—biased; if passion is purged in maintaining neutrality, it is purged for a good cause.

But passion and ideological bias need not go together. I believe it is possible for a passionate textbook to be reasonably objective and unbiased. And I set out to write a book that would be as unbiased as possible (but not more so) and to do so without masking my passion for economic ideas. Various techniques allow me to do this. For example, to keep the students interested in the ideas rather than focusing on technique, I present some ideas in a debate format with two passionate believers on both sides arguing the points. The debate format makes the arguments come alive; they are no longer technical issues that must be memorized; they are passionate ideas, and as the students get caught up in the debate, they think about the ideas much more deeply than they otherwise would.

A Conversational Tone

To transmit that sense of passion to the students, I needed a writing style that allowed it to come through. Quite honestly, textbookese douses passion faster than a cold shower. So this book is not written in textbookese. It's written in conversational English—I'm talking to the students. When they read the book, they will know me; they may not like me like my mother likes me, but they will know me.

The conversational tone is not a monotone; it ebbs and flows depending on the nature of the material. Sometimes, in the analytic parts, the style approaches textbookese; the important technical aspects of economics requires technical writing. When we hit those parts, I tell the students and encourage them to stick with me. But, even here I try to provide intuitive explanations that students can relate to.

The use of conversational style has two effects. First, it eliminates the sense some students have that textbooks provide the "truth." When the textbook author is a real person with peccadilloes and warts, the students won't accept what he or she says unless it makes sense to them. Approaching a textbook with a Missouri "show me" attitude stimulates true learning. Second, the conversational style keeps the students awake. If students' heads are nodding as they read a chapter, they're not learning. Now I know this book is not *Catcher in the Rye;* it's a textbook conveying sometimes complex ideas. But the excitement about economic ideas and the real world comes through.

The approach I take allows me to deal simply with complicated ideas. For example, in the book I discuss New Keynesian economics, New Classical economics, real busi-

ness cycles, strategic pricing, the theory of the second best, rent-seeking, Pareto optimality, and challenges to Pareto optimality. The conversational style conveys the essence of these complex topics to students in a nontechnical fashion without tying the students' brains up in technical tourniquets. The style allows me to relate the ideas to concrete examples rather than mathematical formulas, providing intuitive discussions of the ideas that capture the economic sensibility.

Models in Historical and Institutional Context

Discussing only the minimum of techniques necessary for the students to understand the ideas allows me more leeway to get into, and discuss, institutional and historical issues as they relate to current policy. Models without context are meaningless, and thus you'll find more historical and institutional issues in this book than in other principles books. The book has numerous maps; the discussion conveys the sense that geography, history, and psychology are important, even though it touches on them only tangentially.

One of the ways in which this historical and institutional approach shows up is in the complete coverage of the changing nature of economic systems. Socialism is undergoing enormous changes, and students are interested in what is happening and why it is happening. Their questions cannot be answered with technical models, but they can be discussed informally in a historical context. And that's what this book does.

International Focus

When I started to work on the book back in the 1980s, I decided to include a much deeper discussion of the international sectors than most textbooks did then. Now, while most books at least purport to have international coverage, this book definitely does.

In the introductory section, a full chapter, "An Introduction to the World Economy," sets the stage for the integration of international issues into the text (no other principles book has such a chapter). In the macro section, not only are international issues built into the macro model from the get-go; but an entire chapter, "The International Dimensions of Monetary and Fiscal Policy," places macro policy in an international perspective. Additionally, in the case study chapter, "Macroeconomics, Social Policy, and Economic Reasoning," international issues once again come to the fore.

In the micro section, international policy issues are fully integrated throughout. For example, "The Regulation of Markets: Antitrust and Industrial Policies" discusses not only how international issues are changing the U.S. antitrust policy, but also discusses antitrust policy in a variety of countries. And there are still a full four chapters devoted to international issues at the end of the book, providing the flexibility for professors to give even more emphasis to international issues, depending on time constraints.

The Invisible Forces

I've incorporated in the book a pedagogical device I've found useful where I want to include the social and political forces that affect reality. That device is to convey to students a picture of reality being controlled not only by the invisible hand, but also by the invisible foot (politics) and the invisible handshake (social and cultural forces). This *invisible forces* imagery lets me relate economists' abstract models to the real world; it allows me to discuss the real-world interface between economics, politics, and social forces. What makes this device effective is that students can picture these three invisible forces fighting each other to direct real-world events; that image allows them to put economic models into perspective.

Other Pedagogical Features

I hope you'll find the style and approach teachable. But a textbook needs more than style to be user-friendly, and the publisher and I have worked hard to make this the most user-friendly textbook that exists. Let's consider the in-text pedagogy.

Overall Organization

The book is divided into four sections, and the micro and macro sections are divided into subparts. This organizational structure allows the instructor to pick and choose materials for the course, whether it be for an 8-week quarter or a 16-week semester. A number of alternative outlines are presented in the Instructor's Manual to assist you in using this book effectively.

Learning Objectives

Each chapter opens with a numbered list of learning objectives. These objectives give students a sense of the chapter concepts and provide a guide to approaching the material. The numbers associated with each objective are keyed to the text discussion, allowing students to focus on the discussion with a context. The learning objective numbers are also integrated with the key points in the chapter summaries. Thus, the learning objectives provide a framework both for learning and for review.

Key Terms

The vocabulary essential to understanding economics is boldfaced within the running text at the point where the term is introduced and defined.

Marginal Definitions

The key terms are used to form a running glossary for each chapter. The boldfaced term is highlighted and again defined in the margin, permitting easy review of important terminology and concepts. (Boldfaced page numbers in the index allow for quick reference to the marginal definitions.)

Graphics

Analytical graphs are simple and straightforward so that students can easily follow what's happening. Consistent use of color allows differentiation between movements along curves and shifts of curves. Descriptive and historical data are presented in a visually attractive fashion that parallels what the students will see in the popular press. Periodic photos direct the students outside the text and into the real world. For example, almost every chapter has a margin picture of a reference source, letting students know that there's much more to economics than what's in the text.

Boxes

The text discussion is further enlivened, both visually and conceptually, by a series of boxes. These boxes serve one of two purposes. Those entitled "A Reminder" serve as a review for students; they summarize and consolidate key material. Those entitled "Added Dimension" either extend the text material or provide another perspective on it, relating the material to the real world and deepening students' understanding.

Case Studies

Economics is more than textbook discussions of models. It is applying economic reasoning to economic events, using economic knowledge to interpret articles about economics, understanding when economic reasoning is being objectively applied and when it is biased. It is a type of critical thinking, involving the use of models not because they are right, but because they are useful.

To apply economics effectively, students must have practice in doing so. For that reason this book differs from other books: it includes case studies and newspaper articles as integral parts of the text. It then discusses both the content and the perspective of those articles, giving the student some practice in going beyond the text and actually applying what they learn. Two chapters, "Macroeconomics, Social Policy, and Economic Reasoning" and "Microeconomics, Social Policy, and Economic Reasoning" are devoted entirely to these case studies.

Chapter Summaries and Key Terms List

At the end of each chapter are both a chapter summary and a key terms list. The summaries provide a review of the key points; they reflect the integrated learning strategy that organizes the pedagogical presentation of the material. Each of these points is referenced to the appropriate learning objective, making review more efficient. The page-referenced key terms list provides quick review of the terms that have been boldfaced in the text and that all students should know.

Questions for Thought and Review and Problems and Exercises

Each chapter concludes with 10 questions and 2 problems or exercises. These take the students back through the chapter. Some ask for recall, some ask the student to apply reasoning, some ask for synthesis of the material, and some ask the student to go beyond what they have learned and apply not the analysis, but the general economic reasoning process they have learned. Each question is rated for degree of difficulty. To further stimulate the students to go beyond the text, some questions send students into the library or to real world institutions for answers.

Appendixes

Appendixes that lead the students beyond the chapter material are found at the end of various chapters. These cover issues such as graphical analysis, mathematics of the Keynesian model, and indifference curves. They allow a deeper technical presentation by those faculty who want it.

Pedagogical Supplements

The supplements package that supports the text received the same careful attention to pedagogy as did the text.

The **STUDY GUIDE** enables students to review chapter content and key concepts through a variety of exercises that are integrated by the pedagogical framework of the text. Students are encouraged to practice analyzing, evaluating, and using economic information with two special types of exercises. And multiple-choice mastery tests provide practice for classroom exams. Answers are included for all activities.

The **INSTRUCTOR'S MANUAL** uses P.L.U.S. (*Professional Learning Unit Systems*) to identify which of the text *and* ancillary learning aids are available to students and instructors within a lecture outline, providing an at-a-glance menu. The lecture outline for each chapter also suggests points to emphasize, further topics for discussion, in-class exercises, and it identifies critical thinking skills. A separate section provides alternative examples and offers suggestions for drawing on other critical thinking skills, based on the chapter material. Annotated selected readings and references and a bibliography of supplementary resources round out the resources offered in this ancillary. Answers to end-of-chapter questions are provided.

The **TEST BANK** offers approximately 100 questions per chapter that are classified by learning objective, degree of difficulty, and skill. Where useful, questions contain a rationale for their answers. (Software versions on Computest3 are available.)

TEACHING TRANSPARENCIES are available for all of the important figures and tables in the text.

READY NOTES replicate, in book form, the *Teaching Transparencies* so that students may take notes and make sketches easily during lecture.

PRINCIPLES OF ECONOMICS SIMULATION SOFTWARE allows students to apply the economic theory they are learning by making decisions in a variety of economic contexts and seeing the effects of those decisions. A workbook asks students to make observations, answer questions, and complete exercises as they work through the simulations. Available for IBM or IBM-compatible PCs.

MACROVIEW is a tutorial that uses modules, with page references to the text, to help students explore key macroeconomic concepts. Students are directed to manipulate graphical or other information in a model and then to answer questions about the effects of these actions on various relationships. The software is available for IBM or IBM-compatible PCs.

MICROVIEW helps students explore key microeconomic concepts in the same way that *MACROVIEW* does.

COMPUTEST3 TEST GENERATOR allows instructors to add and edit questions; save and reload tests; create different versions of each test; attach graphics to questions and/or answers; import and export ASCII files; and select questions based on type, level of difficulty, key word, learning objective or skill level. Included on the disk is an Online Testing Program that allows the test-maker to create tests that can be taken by students using a computer. Computest3 provides password protection of saved tests and the question database and it can run on a network. Available for IBM and IBM-compatible PCs and in a MAC version.

ECONOMICS NEWSLETTER, which examines current U.S. and world economic issues and is published periodically by Richard D. Irwin, is sent to adopters.

ECONOMICS U$A, the video library, is also available to adopters. These 28 half-hour programs bring economic theory to life with a blend of historic footage, documentary sequences, interviews, and analysis.

People to Thank

A book this size is not the work of a single person, despite the fact that only one is listed as author. So many people have contributed so much to this book it is hard to know where to begin thanking them.

The initial push for the project came from a friend, Scott Stratford. He knows how important he was for this book coming into being, and I thank him. Then there were those who worked on the early drafts: Viraj Miranni, Steve Fossil, Cele Gardner, Mike Elia, and numerous other students, colleagues, and friends who worked on aspects of the book along the way. Various classes suffered through early versions of the text and told me what worked and what didn't. The book was written for them, and it could not have been written without them.

Throughout the entire process there were the numerable referees who went through the drafts and kept me on track:

Jack Adams
University of Arkansas

Stan Antoniotti
Bridgewater State College

Mahmoud P. Arya
Edison Community College

James Q. Aylsworth
Lakeland Community College

George Bohler
University of North Florida

Bijit K. Bora
Carleton College

Gerald E. Breger
Grand Rapids Junior College

Mario Cantu
Northern Virginia Community College

Tom Carroll
Central Oregon Community College

Carol A. M. Clark
Guilford College

Roy Cohn
Illinois State University

Eleanor Craig
University of Delaware

Jerry L. Crawford
Arkansas State University

Ed Dennis
Franklin Pierce College

Phillip Droke
Highline Community College

Fred Englander
Fairleigh Dickinson University

Valerie Englander
St. John's University

Sharon Erenberg
Eastern Michigan University

Rhona C. Free
Eastern Connecticut State University

Joseph Garwood
Valencia Community College

Bernard Gauci
Hollins College

Robert Gentennar
Hope College

Jack B. Goddard
Northeastern State University

Deniek Gondwee
Gettysburg College

Richard Hansen
Southeast Missouri State University

Raymond N. Harvey
Niagara County Community College

Robert Jantzen
Iona College

Walter Johnson
University of Missouri

Diane E. Kraas
Augustana College

Leonard Lardaro
University of Rhode Island

Randall Lutter
State University of New York at Buffalo

Raymond Mack
Community College of Allegheny County Boyce Campus

Drew Mattson
Anoka-Ramsey Community College

Bruce McCrea
Lansing Community College

H. Neal McKenzie
Dalton College

Debbie A. Meyer
Brookdale Community College

Craig Milnor
Clarke College

William Morgan
University of Wyoming

Mark Morlock
California State University-Chico

H. Richard Moss
Ricks College

Theodore Muzio
St. Vincent College

Hillar Neumann, Jr.
Northern State University

Maureen O'Brien
University of Minnesota–Duluth

Amar Parai
State University of New York College at Fredonia

E. Dale Peterson
Late of Mankato State University

Richard Rosenberg
University of Wisconsin

Linda Schaeffer
California State University–Fresno

Ted Scheinman
Mt. Hood Community College

Timothy Schibik
University of Southern Indiana

Dorothy Siden
Salem State College

R. J. Sidwell
Eastern Illinois University

G. Anthony Spira
University of Tennessee

Mitch Stengel
University of Michigan–Dearborn

Robert Stonebreaker
Indiana University of Pennsylvania

Frank Taylor
McLennan Community College

Wade Thomas
State University of New York College at Oneonta

Joe Turek
Illinois Benedictine College

Alejandro Velez
St. Mary's University

David Weinberg
Xavier University

Kenneth Woodward
Saddleback College

I cannot thank this group of referees enough. They corrected many of my stupid mistakes, they explained to me how a text can contribute to good teaching, and they kept me focused on combining teaching economic sensibility with economic models. They provided me with page upon page of detailed comments and suggestions for improvement. The book strongly reflects their input and is much more usable because of that input. Just before I began the final draft of the manuscript, we took another look at our plans for the book via a questionnaire. Thanks to the over 500 who responded. Those responses helped to confirm many ideas and to fine-tune the final manuscript. When the final draft was finished, it was classroom-tested by R. Asher at Bowie State University and by James Q. Aylsworth at Lakeland Community College and their students. They discovered a few mistakes and offered helpful suggestions and enthusiasm, which I gratefully accepted.

Once the manuscript takes its final form there are still an almost infinite number of jobs to be done on it. Figures must be checked, arguments checked, drafts read, reread, and reread once again. I had immense help in these undertakings: Ding Chun, George Doupsas, and Ali Mehdi worked one whole summer for me, and Chris Gemignani worked another on such projects. They did a great job.

In this entire process the people at Irwin were extremely important and helpful. One was Wendy Hagel, a sales rep at Irwin, who convinced me that Irwin was the right publisher for me. Another was Gary Nelson, the sponsoring editor, who believed in the project and saw to it that it went forward. He, more than anyone else, has kept this project on track. The book would not have been what it is without him. With his steadying influence, he has coordinated the entire process and made it work. Then there's Pat McCabe, my

development editor, who had to put up with me through the entire process. She not only did that with great aplomb; she also added important pedagogical dimensions to the book and maintained her sense of humor and belief in the book throughout a sometimes hectic and stormy process. Then there's the upper-level management at Irwin, specifically, Lew Gossage, Bill Setton, and, Jeff Sund. I had less contact with them, but I fully recognize their guiding hands. Their belief in the project and their willingness to make it possible for an antibureaucratic author to fit in with a formal publishing institution allowed the book to proceed. I thank them all enormously.

The actual production process of a four-color introductory book is complicated, and to do it on an accelerated schedule requires enormous efforts. Luckily, I had Lynne Basler as project editor directing the manuscript through the process. She did a superb job, as did all the players in the production process: Bruce Sylvester, the copy editor; Laurie Entringer, the designer who made the book look good; Michelle Oberhoffer, the photo researcher; Irene Sotiroff, production manager, who worked with Better Graphics, Inc., the typesetter and Von Hoffmann Press, the printer; and Kim Meriwether, art manager, who worked closely with EletraGraphics, Inc., on the art program.

Of course, as they did their superb job, they created more work for me, reading the galley proofs, the page proofs, and doing all the final checking that must be done in an effort to eliminate those pesky errors that occur out of nowhere. Paul Sommers went over the manuscript with his fine-tooth comb and discerning eye and caught things overlooked until then. I thank him.

After you have what you believe is a good book, the process still isn't done. You still have to get people to look at it. Ron Bloecher, Bevan O'Callaghan and John Wood started early to develop a strategy that will get the book considered. Then, there are the sales reps who are the core of a textbook publishing company. Long before this book was complete I met with many sales reps, discussing the book and learning to see it through their eyes. That process made the book much better than it otherwise would have been.

These days an introductory economics book is much more than a single book; it is an entire package, and numerous people have worked on the package. Paul Estenson and Mary Acker did the INSTRUCTOR'S MANUAL; Richard Trieff and Benjamin Shlaes did the STUDY GUIDE; and Mitch Charkiewicz, Susan Dadres, Joanne M. Dott, Eleanor R. Fapohunda, Dorinda Lynn, and Thomas A. McGahagan worked on the TEST BANK with me. They did a great job, and I thank them one and all.

Finally, there's the group of people who helped me at every stage of the process. Throughout the entire project, Helen Reiff has been my right hand, temporarily putting aside her law practice to see that justice was done to my book. Then, there's my wife, Pat, who put her medical practice on hold to give me more time to work on the book. She saw to it that Zack and Kasey, both of whom were conceived after this project was underway, and I, got the love and care we needed. My love and admiration for her remain as unbounded as ever.

As you can see, although my name is on the book, many people besides me deserve the credit. I thank them all.

Contents in Brief

Contents

3   The Economic Organization of Society   59

4   U.S. Economic Institutions   79

5   An Introduction to the World Economy   107

S E C T I O N

2
Macroeconomics

S E C T I O N

3

Microeconomics

21 Supply, Production, and Costs: I *451*

22 Supply, Production, and Costs: II *468*

23 Perfect Competition *482*

33 Work and the Labor Market 685

34 Nonwage Income: Rent, Profits, and Interest 709

SECTION 4

International Economics

35 International Trade 725

36 International Finance 746

ECONOMICS

About the Author

David Colander is the Christian A. Johnson Distinguished Professor of Economics at Middlebury College. He has authored, coauthored, or edited 19 books and over 60 articles on a wide range of economic topics.

He earned his B.A. at Columbia College and his M.Phil and Ph.D. at Columbia University. He also studied at the University of Birmingham in England and at Wilhelmsburg Gymnasium in Germany. Professor Colander has taught at Columbia College, Vassar College, and the University of Miami, as well as having been a consultant to Time-Life Films, a consultant to Congress, a Brookings Policy Fellow, and Visiting Scholar at Nuffield College, Oxford. Recently, he spent two months in Bulgaria, where he worked with former professors of political economy on how to teach Western economics.

He belongs to a variety of professional associations and has been on the Board of Directors of the History of Economic Thought Society, the Eastern Economics Association, and is on the Board of Advisors of the *Journal of Economic Perspectives*.

He is married to a pediatrician, Patrice, which is fortunate, since they have a family of five boys. In their spare time, the Colanders have designed and built their oak post-and-beam house on a ridge overlooking the Green Mountains to the east and the Adirondacks to the west. The house is located on the site of a former drive-in. (They replaced the speaker poles with fruit trees and used the I-beams from the screen as support for the second story of the carriage house and the garage. Dave's office and library are in the former projection room.)

1 INTRODUCTION

Section I is an introduction, and an introduction to an introduction seems a little funny. But other sections have introductions, so it seemed a little funny not to have an introduction to Section I; and besides, as you will see, I'm a little funny myself (which, in turn, has two interpretations; you will, I'm sure, decide which of the two is appropriate). It will, however, be a very brief introduction, consisting of questions you probably have and some answers to those questions.

SOME QUESTIONS AND ANSWERS

Why study economics?
Because it's neat and interesting and helps provide insight into events that are constantly going on around you.

Why is this book so big?
Because there's lots of important information in it and because the book is designed so your teacher can pick and choose. You'll likely not be required to read all of it, especially if you're on the quarter system. But once you start it, you'll probably read it all anyhow. (Would you believe?)

Why does this book cost so much?
To answer this question you'll have to read the book.

Will this book make me rich?
No.

Will this book make me happy?
It depends.

This book doesn't seem to be written in normal textbook style. Is this book really written by a professor?
Yes, but he is different. He misspent his youth working on cars; he married his high school sweetheart after they met again at their 20th high school reunion. Together they designed and built their own house on the site of a former drive-in theater. (They replaced the speaker poles with a fruit orchard and turned the concession stand into an office and workshop.) At the same time, his wife went back to medical school and got her MD because she was tired of being treated poorly by doctors. Their five kids make sure he doesn't get carried away in the professorial cloud.

Will the entire book be like this?
No, the introduction is just trying to rope you in. Much of the book will be hard going. Learning happens to be a difficult process: no pain, no gain. But the author isn't a sadist; he tries to make learning as pleasantly painful as possible.

What do the author's students think of him?
Weird, definitely weird—and hard. But fair, interesting, and sincerely interested in getting us to learn. (Answer written by my students.)

So there you have it. Answers to the questions that you might never have thought of if they hadn't been put in front of you. I hope they give you a sense of me and the approach I'll use in the book. There are some neat ideas in it. Let's now briefly consider what's in the first five chapters.

(continued)

A SURVEY OF THE FIRST FIVE CHAPTERS

This first section is really an introduction to the rest of the book. It gives you the background necessary to have the latter chapters make sense. Chapter 1 gives you an overview of the entire field of economics as well as an introduction to my style. Chapter 2 introduces you to supply and demand, and shows you not only the power of those two concepts, but also the limitations.

Chapter 3 tries to put supply and demand in context. It discusses the evolving economic systems and how economic forces interact with political and social forces. In it you'll see how the power of supply and demand analysis is strengthened when it's interpreted with a knowledge of economic institutions. Chapters 4 and 5 then introduce you to some of those economic institutions. Chapter 4 concentrates on domestic institutions; Chapter 5 concentrates on international institutions. Now let's get on with the show.

1

Economics and Economic Reasoning

*In my vacations, I visited the
poorest quarters of several cities and walked through one street after
another, looking at the faces of the poorest people. Next I resolved to
make as thorough a study as I could of Political Economy.*

Alfred Marshall

After reading this chapter, you should be able to:

1

State five aspects of economics.

2

Explain how to make decisions by comparing
marginal costs and marginal benefits.

3

Define opportunity cost.

4

Demonstrate opportunity cost with a
production possibility curve.

5

State the principle of increasing
opportunity cost.

6

Explain real-world events in terms of three
"invisible forces."

7

Differentiate between microeconomics and
macroeconomics.

8

Distinguish between positive economics, normative
economics, and the art of economics.

When an artist looks at the world, he sees color. When a musician looks at the world, she hears music. When an economist looks at the world, she sees a symphony of costs and benefits.[1] The economist's world might not be as colorful or as melodic as the others' worlds, but it's more practical. If you want to understand what's going on in the world that's really out there, you need to know economics.

I hardly have to convince you of this fact if you keep up with the news. Unemployment is up; inflation is down; interest rates are up; businesses are going bankrupt. . . . The list is endless. So let's say you grant me that economics is important. That still doesn't mean that it's worth studying. The real question then is: How much will you learn? I remember courses on important issues from which I learned nothing, and courses on unimportant issues from which I learned lots. Most depends on you, but part of what one learns in a course depends on the teacher and part depends on the textbook. On both these counts, you're in luck; since your teacher chose this book for your course, you must have a super teacher.[2]

WHAT ECONOMICS IS ABOUT ■ 1

To understand the economy you need to learn:

1. Some *economic terminology*.
2. Some *insights* economists have gained in thinking about economic issues.
3. Some information about *economic institutions*.
4. Some information about the *policy options* facing society today.

By no coincidence this book discusses economic terminology, economic insights, economic institutions, and policy options. You also get a bonus:

5. The book presents you with a guide to *economic reasoning*.

Let's consider each in turn.

Economic Terminology

First, there's economic terminology, which is tossed around by the general public with increasing frequency. *GDP, corporations,* and *money supply* are just a few of the terms whose meaning any educated person in modern society needs to know. If you go to a party and don't know these terms and want to seem intelligent, you'll have to nod knowingly. It's much better to actually *know* when you nod knowingly.

Two terms I want to introduce to you immediately are the *economy* and *economics.* The **economy** is the institutional structure through which individuals in a society coordinate their diverse wants or desires. **Economics** is the study of the economy. That is, economics is the study of how human beings in a society *coordinate* their wants and desires.

Economy Institutional structure through which individuals in a society coordinate their wants.

Economics The study of how human beings coordinate their wants.

---

[1] Authors are presented with a problem today. Our language has certain ambiguous words that can be interpreted as affording unequal treatment to women. For example, we use the term *man* both to describe all human beings and to describe a specific group of human beings. Similarly, we use the pronoun *he* when we mean all people. One can avoid such usage by writing *he and she* and *men and women* or *human beings,* and in much of this book these terms will be used, although every so often either the masculine or feminine term will appear. This is to see if you notice and to encourage you to think of possible sexist aspects in your own usage.

  If you are wondering whether you are sexist, consider the following riddle: A father and son are in a car accident. The father is killed and the boy is injured. When the boy is brought to the hospital, the doctor on emergency room duty says, "I can't operate on him—he's my son." How can this be? If it doesn't seem like a riddle, good; if it does, whenever you see the term *man* think *man and woman,* until the riddle is no longer a riddle.

[2] This book is written by a person, not a machine. That means that I have my quirks, my odd sense of humor, and my biases. All textbook writers do. Most textbooks have the quirks and eccentricities edited out so that all the books read and sound alike—professional but dull. I choose to sound like me—sometimes professional, sometimes playful, and sometimes stubborn. In my view, that makes the book more human and less dull. So forgive me my quirks— don't always take me too seriously—and I'll try to keep you awake when you're reading this book at 3 A.M., the morning of the exam. If you think it's a killer to read a book this long, you ought to try writing one.

One of society's largest problems is that individuals want more than is available, given the work they're willing to do. If individuals can be encouraged to work more and consume less, that problem can be reduced. Coordination often involves coercion; it involves limiting people's wants and increasing the amount of work individuals are willing to do to fulfill those wants.

Many of society's coordination problems involve scarcity. Therefore, economics is sometimes defined as the study of the allocation of scarce **resources** to satisfy individuals' wants or desires. I focus the definition on coordination rather than on scarcity to emphasize that the quantity of goods and services available depends on human action: individuals' imagination, innovativeness, and willingness to do what needs to be done.

The reality of our society is that many people would rather play than help solve society's problems. So the basic economic problem involves inspiring people to do things that other people want them to do and inspiring people not to do things that other people don't want them to do. Thus, economics is the study of how to get people to do things they're not wild about doing (such as studying) and not to do things they *are* wild about doing (such as eating all the lobster they like), so that the things some people want to do are consistent with the things other people want to do.

Economic Insights

Second, you'll learn about some general insights economists have gained into how the economy functions—how an economy seems to proceed or progress without any overall plan or coordinating agency. It's almost as if an invisible hand were directing economic traffic. These insights are called economic theory; theory ties together economists' terminology and knowledge about economic institutions.

We're so used to the economy's functioning that we may not realize how amazing it is that the economy works as well as it does. Imagine for a moment that you're a visitor from Mars. You see the U.S. economy functioning relatively well. Stores are filled with goods. Most people have jobs. So you ask, "Who's in charge of organizing and coordinating the economic activities of the 250 million people in the United States?" The answer you get is mind boggling: "No one. The invisible hand of the market does it all." Economic theory helps explain such mind-boggling phenomena.

Economic Institutions

Third, you'll learn about economic institutions: how they work and why they sometimes don't work. An **economic institution** is a physical or mental structure that significantly influences economic decisions. Corporations, governments, and cultural norms are all economic institutions. Many economic institutions have social, political, and religious dimensions. For example, your job often influences your social standing. In addition, many social institutions, such as the family, have economic functions. If any institution significantly affects economic decisions, I include it as an economic institution because you must understand that institution if you are to understand how the economy functions.

Economic institution A physical or mental structure that significantly influences economic decisions.

Since **cultural norms** may be an unfamiliar concept to you, let's consider how such norms affect economies. A cultural norm is a standard people use when they determine whether a particular activity or behavior is acceptable. For example, religious rules once held that Catholics shouldn't eat meat on Friday, so Friday became a day to eat fish. The prohibition ended in the 1960s, but the tendency to eat fish on Friday night has endured. In the United States today, more fish is consumed on Fridays than on any other day of the week. This fact can be understood only if you understand the cultural norm that lies behind it. Similarly, in the United States more hams are bought in April and more turkeys are bought in November and December than in other months; more pork is consumed per capita in Sweden than in Israel. Can you explain why?

Cultural norm A standard people use when they determine whether a particular activity or behavior is acceptable.

Besides helping you understand the economy, knowledge of economic institutions also directly benefits you. How do firms decide whom to hire? How do banks work? How does unemployment insurance work? What determines how much a Japanese car will cost you? How much does the government require your boss to deduct from your paycheck? Knowing the answers to these real-world questions will make your life easier.

Economic Policy Options

Economic policy Action to influence the course of economic events.

Fourth, you'll learn about economic policy options facing our country. An **economic policy** is an action (or inaction) taken, usually by government, to influence economic events. Examples of economic policy questions are: How should the government deal with the next recession? (Alas, we can be sure that there will be a next recession.) What should the government do about the budget deficit? Will lowering interest rates stimulate the economy? Should government allow two large companies to merge? You won't get specific answers to these questions; instead, you'll simply learn what some of the policy options are, and what advantages and disadvantages each option offers.

Economic Reasoning

Economic reasoning Making decisions on the basis of costs and benefits.

Finally, there's a bonus: learning **economic reasoning**—how to think like an economist. People trained in economics think in a certain way. They analyze everything critically; they compare the costs and the benefits of every issue and make decisions based on those costs and benefits. For example, say you're trying to decide whether protecting baby seals is a good policy or not. Economists are trained to put their emotions aside and ask: What are the costs of protecting baby seals, and what are the benefits? Thus, they are open to the argument that the benefits of allowing baby seals to be killed might exceed the costs. To think like an economist is to address almost all issues using a cost/benefit approach.

Economic reasoning, once learned, is infectious. If you're susceptible, being exposed to it will change your life. It will provide you with an explanation for everything—including issues normally considered outside the scope of economics. For example, you will use economic reasoning to decide the likelihood of getting a date for Saturday night, and who will likely pay for dinner. You'll use it to decide whether you'll read this book, whether you'll attend class, whom you will marry, and what kind of work you'll likely go into after you graduate. You'll be able to provide an economic explanation for just about everything.

A GUIDE TO ECONOMIC REASONING

If the benefits of doing something exceed the costs, do it. If the costs of doing something exceed the benefits, don't do it.

2

Let's explore economic reasoning in more detail so that you can begin to apply it as you read this book. As I just indicated, in the economic way of thinking, every choice has costs and benefits, and decisions are made by comparing the two. The rules are simple:

> *If the benefits of doing something exceed the costs, do it.*
> *If the costs of doing something exceed the benefits, don't do it.*

Marginal Costs and Marginal Benefits

Marginal cost Additional cost above what you've already incurred.

Marginal benefit Additional benefits above what you've already derived.

Economists have found that when one is considering a choice among a variety of alternatives, often it's unnecessary to look at total benefits and total costs. All one need look at are *marginal costs* and *marginal benefits*. These are key concepts in economics, and it pays to learn them early on.

Marginal means additional or incremental. So a **marginal cost** is the additional cost to you over and above the costs you have already incurred. Consider, for example, attending class. You've already paid your tuition, so the marginal (or additional) cost of going to class does not include tuition.

Similarly, with marginal benefit. The **marginal benefit** of reading this chapter is the *additional* knowledge you get from reading it. If you already knew everything in this chapter before you picked up the book, the marginal benefit of

ECONOMIC KNOWLEDGE IN ONE SENTENCE: TANSTAAFL

Once upon a time, Tanstaafl was made king of all the lands. His first act was to call his economic advisors and tell them to write up all the economic knowledge the society possessed. After years of work, they presented their monumental effort: 25 volumes, each about 400 pages long. But in the interim, King Tanstaafl had become a very busy man, what with running a kingdom of all the lands and everything. Looking at the lengthy volumes, he told his advisors to summarize their findings into one volume. Despondently, the economists returned to their desks, wondering how they could summarize what they'd been so careful to spell out. After many more years of rewriting, they were finally satisfied with their one-volume effort, and tried to make an appointment to see the king. Unfortunately, affairs of state had become even more pressing than before, and the king couldn't take the time to see them. Instead he sent word to them through an advisor that he couldn't be bothered with a whole volume, and ordered them, under threat of death (for he had become a tyrant), to reduce the work to one sentence.

The economists returned to their desks, shivering in their sandals and pondering their impossible task. Thinking about their fate if they were not successful, they decided to send out for one last meal. Unfortunately, when they were collecting money to pay for the meal, they discovered they were broke. The disgusted delivery man took the last meal back to the cook, and the economists started down the path to the beheading station. On the way, the delivery man's parting words echoed in their ears. They looked at each other and suddenly they realized the truth. "We're saved!" they screamed. "That's it! That's economic knowledge in one sentence!" They wrote the sentence down and presented it to the king, who thereafter fully understood all economic problems. (He also gave them a good meal.) The sentence?

There Ain't No Such Thing As A Free Lunch— **TANSTAAFL**

---

reading it now is zero, except that you now know you are prepared for class, whereas before you might only have suspected you were prepared.

Comparing marginal (additional) costs with marginal (additional) benefits will often tell you how you should adjust your activities to be as well off as possible. If the marginal benefit of engaging in an activity exceeds the marginal cost of doing so, you should do it. But if the marginal benefit is less than the marginal cost, you should do something else.

As an example, let's consider a discussion I might have with a student who tells me that she is too busy to attend my classes. I respond, "Think about the tuition you've spent for this class—it works out to about $30 a lecture." She answers that the book she reads for class is a book that I wrote and that I wrote it so clearly she fully understands everything. She goes on:

> I've already paid the tuition and whether I go to class or not, I can't get any of the tuition back, so the tuition doesn't enter into my marginal cost decision. The marginal cost to me isn't the tuition; it's what I could be doing with the hour instead of spending it in class. Because I value my time at $75 an hour [people who understand everything value their time highly], and even though I've heard that your lectures are super, I estimate that the marginal benefit of your class is only $50. The marginal cost, $75, exceeds the marginal benefit, $50, so I don't attend class.

I would congratulate her on her diplomacy and her economic reasoning, but tell her that I give a quiz every week, that students who miss a quiz fail the quiz, that those who fail all the quizzes fail the course, and that those who fail the course do not graduate. In short, she is underestimating the marginal benefits of attending my course. Correctly estimated, the marginal benefits of attending my class exceed the marginal costs of cutting my class. So she should attend my class.

There's much more to be said about economic reasoning, but that will come later. For now, all you need remember is that in economic thinking *all things have a cost—and a benefit*. Decisions are made on the basis of the **economic decision rule:** If benefits exceed costs, do it. If costs exceed benefits, don't do it.

Economic decision rule If benefits exceed costs, do it. If costs exceed benefits, don't do it.

Economics and Passion

Recognizing that everything has a cost is reasonable, but it's a reasonableness that many people don't like. It takes some of the passion out of life. It leads you to consider possibilities like these:

- Saving some people's lives with liver transplants might not be worth the cost. The money might be better spent on nutritional programs that would save 20 lives for every 2 lives you might save with transplants.
- Maybe we shouldn't try to eliminate all pollution, because the cost of doing so may be too high. To eliminate all pollution would be to forgo too much of some other good activity.
- Buying a stock that went up 20 percent wasn't necessarily the greatest investment if in doing so you had to forgo some other investment that would have paid you a 30 percent return.
- It might make sense for the automobile industry to save $12 per car by not installing a safety device, even though without the safety device some people will be killed.

You get the idea. This kind of reasonableness is often criticized for being cold-blooded. But, not surprisingly, economists first reason *economically;* the social and moral implications of their conclusions are integrated later.

Economists' reasonableness isn't universally appreciated. Businesses love the result; others aren't so sure, as I discovered some years back when my then girlfriend told me she was leaving me. "Why?" I asked. "Because," she responded, "you're so, so . . . reasonable. I can't stand it any more!" It took me many years after she left to learn what she already knew: There are many types of reasonableness, and not everyone thinks an economist's reasonableness is a virtue. I'll discuss such issues later; for now, let me simply warn you that, for better or worse, studying economics will lead you to view questions in a cost/benefit framework.

Opportunity Cost

Opportunity cost The benefit forgone when you do not choose a particular activity because you've decided instead to choose another activity.

3

Maurice Allais—Nobel prize, 1988, for work on efficient use of resources. © *The Nobel Foundation.*

Putting economists' cost/benefit rules into practice isn't easy. To do so, you have to be able to choose and measure the costs and benefits correctly. Economists have devised the concept of opportunity cost to help you do that. The **opportunity cost** of undertaking an activity is the benefit forgone by undertaking that activity. The benefit forgone is the benefit that you might have gained from choosing the next-best alternative. To obtain the benefit of something, you must give up (forgo) something else—namely, the next-best alternative. All activities that have a next-best alternative have an opportunity cost.

Let's consider some examples. The opportunity cost of going out once with Natalia (or Nathaniel), the most beautiful woman (attractive man) in the world, might well be losing your solid steady, Margo (Mike). The opportunity cost of cleaning up the environment might be a reduction in the money available to assist low-income individuals. The opportunity cost of having a child might be two boats, three cars, and a two-week vacation each year for five years.

Examples are endless, but let's consider two that are particularly relevant to you: your choice of courses and your decision about how much to study. Let's say you're a full-time student and at the beginning of the term you had to choose four or five courses to take. Taking one precluded taking some other, and the opportunity cost of taking an economics course may well have been not taking a course on theater. Similarly with studying, you have a limited amount of time to spend studying economics, studying some other subject, sleeping, or partying. The more time you spend on one activity, the less time you have for another. That's opportunity cost.

Notice how neatly the opportunity cost concept takes into account costs and benefits of all other options, and converts these alternative benefits into costs of the decision you're now making. This conversion helps you to compare costs and benefits and to select the activity with the largest difference between benefits and costs.

Opportunity costs' relevance isn't limited to your individual decisions. Opportunity costs are also relevant to government's decisions, which affect everyone in society. A common example is the guns-versus-butter debate. The resources that a society has are limited; therefore, its decision to use those resources to have more guns (more weapons) means that it must have less butter (fewer consumer goods). Thus, when society decides to spend $1 trillion developing a Star Wars defense system, the opportunity cost of that decision is $1 trillion not spent on fighting drugs, helping the homeless, or paying off some of the national debt.

The opportunity cost concept has endless implications. It can even be turned upon itself. For instance, it takes time to think about alternatives; that means that there's a cost to being reasonable, so it's only reasonable to be somewhat unreasonable. If you followed that argument, you've caught the economic bug. If you didn't, don't worry. Just remember the opportunity cost concept for now; I'll infect you with economic thinking in the rest of the book.

I've just gone over opportunity cost. I'm now going to go over the same concept again—only this time I'll go over it numerically and graphically. Opportunity cost can be seen numerically with a **production possibility table,** which lists a choice's opportunity cost by summarizing what alternative outputs you can achieve with your inputs. An **output** is simply a result of an activity—your grade in a course is an output. An **input** is what you put in to achieve that output. In this example, study time is an input.

Let's present the study time/grades example numerically. To do so we must be more precise. Say you have exactly 20 hours a week to devote to two courses: economics and history. (So, maybe I'm a bit optimistic.) Grades are given numerically and you know that the following relationships exist: if you study 20 hours in economics, you'll get a grade of 100, 18 hours—94, and so forth.[3]

Let's say that the best you can do in history is a 98 with 20 hours of study a week; 19 hours of study guarantee you a 96, and so on. The production possibility table in Exhibit 1(a) shows the highest combination of grades you can get with

The Production Possibility Table

Production possibility table Summarizes alternative outputs achievable with inputs.

Output The result of an activity.

Input What you put in to achieve an output.

---

[3] Throughout the book I'll be presenting numerical examples to help you understand the concepts. The numbers I choose are often arbitrary. After all, you have to choose something. As an exercise you might choose different numbers that apply to your own life and work out the argument using those numbers. For those who don't want to make up their own numbers, the study guide has examples with different numbers.

various allocations of the 20 hours available for studying the two subjects. One possibility is getting 100 in economics and 58 in history. Another is getting 70 in economics and 78 in history.

Notice that the opportunity cost of studying one subject rather than the other is embodied in the production possibility table. The information in the table comes from experience; we are assuming that you've discovered that if you transfer an hour of study from economics to history, you'll lose 3 points on your grade in economics and gain 2 points in history. Thus, the opportunity cost of a 2-point rise in your history grade is a 3-point decrease in your economics grade.

The Production Possibility Curve

Production possibility curve Graphical presentation of the opportunity cost concept which indicates the maximum combination of outputs that can be obtained from a given number of inputs.

The information in the production possibility table can also be presented graphically in a diagram. This graphical presentation of the opportunity cost concept is called the **production possibility curve.** This curve indicates the maximum combination of outputs you can obtain from a given number of inputs.

A production possibility curve is created from a production possibility table by mapping the table in a two-dimensional graph. I've taken the information from the table in Exhibit 1(a) and mapped it in Exhibit 1(b). The history grade is mapped, or plotted, on the horizontal axis; the economics grade is on the vertical axis.

As you can see from the bottom row of Exhibit 1(a), if you study economics for all 20 hours and study history for 0 hours, you'll get grades of 100 in economics and 58 in history. Point *A* in Exhibit 1(b) represents that choice. If you study history for all 20 hours and study economics for 0 hours, you'll get a 98 in history and a 40 in economics. Point *E* represents that choice. Points *B*, *C*, and *D* represent three possible choices between these two extremes.

Hours of study in history	Grade in history	Hours of study in economics	Grade in economics
20	98	0	40
19	96	1	43
18	94	2	46
17	92	3	49
16	90	4	52
15	88	5	55
14	86	6	58
13	84	7	61
12	82	8	64
11	80	9	67
10	78	10	70
9	76	11	73
8	74	12	76
7	72	13	79
6	70	14	82
5	68	15	85
4	66	16	88
3	64	17	91
2	62	18	94
1	60	19	97
0	58	20	100

(a)

(b)

EXHIBIT 1 (a and b)   **A Production Possibility Table and Curve for Grades in Economics and History**

The production possibility table (a) shows the highest combination of grades you can get with only 20 hours available for studying economics and history.

   The information in the production possibility table in (a) can be plotted on a graph, as is done in (b). The grade received in economics is on the vertical axis, and the grade received in history is on the horizontal axis.

DEALING WITH MATH ANXIETY

Knowing my students, I can see the red flags rising, the legs tensing up, the fear flooding over many of you. Here it comes—the math and the graphs.

I wish I could change things by saying to you, "Don't worry—mathematics and graphical analysis are easy." But I can't. That doesn't mean math and graphical analysis aren't easy. They are. They're wonderful tools that convey ideas neatly and efficiently. But I've had enough teaching experience to know that somewhere back in elementary school some teacher blew it and put about 40 percent of you off mathematics for life. A tool that scares you to death is not useful; it can be a hindrance, not a help, to learning. I also know that nothing your current teacher or I now can say, write, or do is going to change that for most of those 40 percent. On the other hand, I've had a little bit of luck with about 10 percent of the 40 percent (which makes 4 percent—4 out of 100 students) with pure honesty. So I'll try it on you. Here's what I tell them.

Economics is really simple. Economists know that it is, and they also know that if word got around about how simple economics is, few students would take economics. But economists are smart. They make economics seem more difficult than it is by couching simple economic ideas

in graphs. The graphs convince many students that economics is really hard, allowing economics professors to teach simple ideas that the students think are hard.

About 4 percent of my students become so mad at the thought of being duped that they overcome their math anxiety. The rest just wonder whether this teacher is for real.

If avoiding being duped means something to you, believe the preceding story; if it doesn't, don't. But whatever you do, try to follow the numerical and graphical examples carefully, because they not only cement the knowledge into your minds; they also present the ideas I'm discussing in a rigorous manner.

The ideas conveyed in the numerical and graphical examples will be explained in words—and the graphical analysis (the type of mathematical explanation most used in introductory economics) generally will simply be a more precise presentation of the accompanying discussion in words. In some economics courses, understanding the words may be enough, but in most, the exams pose the questions in graphical terms, so there's no getting around the need to understand the ideas graphically. And it is simple. (Appendix B discusses the basics of graphical analysis.)

Notice that the production possibility curve slopes downward from left to right. That means that there is an inverse relationship (a trade-off) between grades in economics and grades in history. The better the grade in economics, the worse the grade in history, and vice versa. That downward slope represents the opportunity cost concept—you get more of one benefit only if you get less of another benefit.

The production possibility curve not only represents the opportunity cost concept; it also measures the opportunity cost. For example, in Exhibit 1(b), say you want to raise your grade in history from a 94 to a 98 (move from point *D* to point *E*). The opportunity cost of doing so would be a 6-point decrease in your economics grade, from 46 to 40.

To summarize, the production possibility curve demonstrates that:

1. There is a limit to what you can achieve, given the available institutions, resources, and technology.
2. Every choice you make has an opportunity cost. You can get more of something only by giving up something else.

Increasing Marginal Opportunity Cost   I chose an unchanging trade-off in the study time/grade example because it made the initial presentation of the production possibility curve easier. Since, by assumption, you could always trade two points on your history grade for three points on your economics grade, the production possibility curve was a straight line. But is that the way we'd expect reality to be? Probably not. The production possibility curve is generally bowed outward, as in Exhibit 2(b).

Why? To make the answer more concrete, let's talk specifically about society's choice between defense spending (guns) and spending on domestic needs (butter). The information in Exhibit 2(b) is derived from the table in Exhibit 2(a).

Let's see what the shape of the curve means in terms of numbers. Let's start with society producing only butter (point *A*). Giving up a little butter (one pound)

EXHIBIT 2 (a and b)   Production Possibility Curve Table and Graph

The table in (**a**) contains information on the trade-off between the production of guns and butter. This information has been plotted on the graph in (**b**). Notice in (**b**) that as we move along the production possibility curve from *A* to *F*, trading butter for guns, we get fewer and fewer guns for each pound of butter given up. That is, the opportunity cost of choosing guns over butter increases as we increase the production of guns. This concept is called the principle of increasing marginal opportunity cost. The phenomenon occurs because some resources are better suited for the production of butter than for the production of guns, and we use the better ones first.

% resources devoted to production of guns	Number of guns	Pounds of butter	Row
0	0	15	A
20	4	14	B
40	7	12	C
60	9	9	D
80	11	5	E
100	12	0	F

(a)   (b)

initially gains us a lot of guns (4), moving us to point *B*. The next two pounds of butter we give up gains us slightly fewer guns (point *C*). If we continue to trade butter for guns, we find that at point *D* we gain almost no guns from giving up a pound of butter. The opportunity cost of choosing guns over butter increases as we increase the production of guns.

The reason the opportunity cost of guns increases as we consume more guns is that some resources are relatively better suited to producing guns, while others are relatively better suited to producing butter. Put in economists' terminology, some resources have a comparative advantage over other resources in the production of butter, while other resources have a comparative advantage in the production of guns. A resource has a **comparative advantage** in the production of a good when, compared to other resources, it's relatively better suited to producing that good than to producing another good.

When making small amounts of guns and large amounts of butter, in the production of those guns we use the resources whose comparative advantage is in the production of guns. All other resources are devoted to producing butter. Because the resources used in producing guns aren't good at producing butter, we're not giving up much butter to get those guns. As we produce more and more of a good, we must use resources whose comparative advantage is in the production of the other good—in this case, more suitable for producing butter than for producing guns. As we remove resources from the production of butter to get the same additional amount of guns, we must give up increasing amounts of butter. An alternative way of saying this is that the opportunity cost of producing guns becomes greater as the production of guns increases. As we continue to increase the production of guns, the opportunity cost of more guns becomes very high because we're using resources to produce guns that have a strong comparative advantage for producing butter.

Let's consider two more specific examples. Say the United States suddenly decides it needs more wheat. To get additional wheat, we must devote additional

Comparative advantage To be better suited to the production of one good than to the production of another good.

EXHIBIT 3 (a, b, and c)   Efficiency and Inefficiency

The production possibility curve helps us see what is meant by efficiency. At point A, in (a), all inputs are used to make 6 pounds of butter and 4 guns. This is inefficient since there is a way to obtain more of one without giving up any of the other, that is , to obtain 6 pounds of butter and 6 guns (point C) or 4 guns and 8 pounds of butter (point B). All points inside the production possibility curve are inefficient. With fixed inputs and given technology, we cannot go beyond the production possibility curve. For example, point D is unattainable.

A technological change that improves production techniques will shift the production possibility curve outward, as shown in both (b) and (c). How the curve shifts outward depends on how technology improves. For example, if we become more efficient in the production of both guns and butter, the curve will shift out as in (b). If we become more efficient in producing guns, but not in producing butter, then the curve will shift as in (c).

land to growing it. This land is less fertile than the land we're already using, so our additional output of wheat per acre of land devoted to wheat will be less. Alternatively, consider the use of relief pitchers in a baseball game. If only one relief pitcher is needed, the manager sends in the best; if he must send in a second one, then a third, and even a fourth, the likelihood of winning the game decreases.

For many of the choices society must make, opportunity costs tend to increase as we choose more and more of an item. Such a phenomenon about choice is so common, in fact, that it has acquired a name: the **principle of increasing marginal opportunity cost.** That principle states:

> *In order to get more of something, one must give up ever-increasing quantities of something else.*

In other words, initially the opportunity costs of an activity are low, but they increase the more we concentrate on that activity. Sometimes this law is called the flowerpot law, because if it didn't hold, all the world's food could be grown in a flowerpot. But it can't be. As we add more seeds to a fixed amount of soil, the output per seed decreases.

Efficiency   We like, if possible, to get as much output for as few inputs or resources as possible. That's how **productive efficiency** is defined: achieving as much output for as few inputs or resources as possible. We would like to be efficient. The production possibility curve helps us see what is meant by productive efficiency. Consider point A in Exhibit 3(a), which is inside the production possibility curve. If we are producing at point A, we are using all our resources to produce 4 guns and 6 pounds of butter. Point A represents **inefficiency,** since with the same inputs we could be getting either 4 guns and 8 pounds of butter (point B) or 6 pounds of butter and 6 guns (point C). Both points B and C represent efficiency, as long as we prefer more to less. We always want to move our production out to a point on the production possibility curve.

5

Principle of increasing marginal opportunity cost   Initial opportunity costs are low but they increase the more you concentrate on the activity.

In order to get more of something, one must give up ever-increasing quantities of something else.

Productive efficiency   Getting as much output for as few inputs as possible.

RESOURCES, INPUTS, TECHNOLOGY, AND OUTPUT

Production involves transforming *inputs* into *outputs*. For example, seeds, dirt, and labor (inputs) combine to produce wheat (output). Many introductory economics texts call inputs *resources* and divide those inputs into three resources: land, labor, and capital. Economists in the 1800s, often called *Classical economists,* discussed production as a means of transforming land, labor, and capital into outputs. Classical economists divided all inputs into those three categories because they were interested in answering the question: How is income divided among landowners, workers, and capitalists? The three divisions helped them focus on that question: landowners' income was rent, workers' income was wages, and capitalists' income was profit.

Modern advanced analysis of production doesn't follow this threefold division. Instead, the modern analysis is more abstract and tells how inputs in general are transformed into outputs in general. Modern economic theory has moved away from the traditional division because the division of income among these three groups isn't central to the questions economists are now asking.

But that leaves open the problem: What division of resources makes the most sense? The answer depends on what question you're asking. For example, in the grade example in this chapter, your time was the input, while in the guns-and-butter example the inputs were machines, nat-

ural resources, and labor. In the most abstract categorization the ultimate resources are space (represented by land), time (represented by labor), and matter (represented by capital). Thus, in one way of looking at it, the traditional distinction is still relevant. But in another way, it isn't. It directs our focus of analysis away from some important inputs. For example, one of the inputs that economists now focus on is *entrepreneurship,* the ability to organize and get something done. Entrepreneurship is an important input that's distinct from labor. Most listings of general resources today include entrepreneurship.

Here's another important point about resources. The term *resource* is often used with the qualifier *natural,* as in the phrase *natural resources.* Coal, oil, and iron are all called *natural resources.* Be careful about that qualifier *natural.* Whether something is or isn't a natural resource depends on the available technology. And technology is unnatural. For example, at one time a certain black gooey stuff was not a resource—it was something that made land unusable. When people learned that the black gooey stuff could be burned as a fuel, oil became a resource. What's considered a resource depends on technology. If solar technology is ever perfected, oil will go back to being black gooey stuff.

Why not move out farther, say to point *D?* If we could, we would, but by definition the production possibility curve represents the most output we can get from a certain combination of inputs. So point *D* is unattainable, given our resources and technology.

When technology improves, when more resources are discovered, or when the economic institutions get better at fulfilling our wants, we can get more output with the same inputs. What this means is that when technology or an economic institution improves, the entire production possibility curve shifts outward from *AB* to *CD* in Exhibit 3(b). How the production possibility curve shifts outward depends on how the technology improves. For example, say we become more efficient in producing guns, but not more efficient in producing butter. Then the production possibility curve shifts outward to *AC* in Exhibit 3(c).

Policies that costlessly shift the production possibility curve outward are the most desirable policies because they don't require us to decrease our consumption of one good to get more of another. Alas, they are the most infrequent. Improving technology and institutions and discovering more resources are not costless; generally there's an opportunity cost of doing so that must be taken into account.

Distribution and Productive Efficiency   In discussing the production possibility curve, I avoided questions of distribution: Who gets what? But such questions cannot be ignored in real-world situations. Specifically, if the method of production is tied to a particular income distribution and choosing one method will help some people but hurt others, we can't say that one method of production is efficient and the other inefficient, even if one method produces more total output than the other.

Efficiency Achieving a goal as cheaply as possible.

The term **efficiency** involves achieving a goal as cheaply as possible. The term has meaning only in regard to a specified goal. Say, for example, that we have a society of ascetics who believe that consumption is immoral. For such a society,

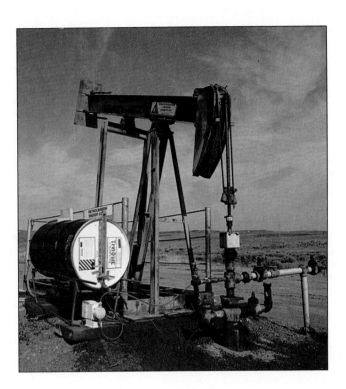

In the 1990s oil has remained an important natural resource.

producing more for less (productive efficiency) would not be efficient since consumption is not its goal. Or say that we have a society that cares that what is produced is fairly distributed. An increase in output that goes to only one person and not to anyone else would not necessarily be efficient.

In our society, however, most people prefer more to less, and many policies have relatively small distributional consequences. On the basis of the assumption that more is better than less, economists use their own kind of shorthand for such policies and talk about efficiency as identical to productive efficiency—increasing total output. But it's important to remember the assumption under which that shorthand is used: that the distributional effects that accompany the policy aren't undesirable and that we, as a society, prefer more output.

The production possibility curve represents the tough choices society must make. Not everyone recognizes these choices. For example, politicians often talk as if the production possibility curve is nonexistent. They promise voters the world, telling them, "If you elect me, you can have more of everything." When they do that, they obscure the hard choices and increase their probability of getting elected.

Economists do the opposite. They promise little except that life is tough, and they continually point out that there are no free lunches. Such reasonableness doesn't work any better with politicians than it did with my former girlfriend. Political candidates who exhibit such reasonableness seldom get elected. Economists' reasonableness has earned economics the nickname, *the dismal science*.

There's an infinite number of examples and extensions I could give, but I'll stop here, hoping that my explanation of the production possibility curve has given you a relatively painless introduction to graphical analysis and helped cement the opportunity cost concept into your memory.

The opportunity cost concept applies to all aspects of life. It embodies *economic forces*. **Economic forces** are the forces of scarcity; when there isn't enough to go around, goods must be rationed. Rationing is a structural mechanism for deter-

The Production Possibility Curves and Tough Choices

Economics and the Invisible Forces

Economic forces The forces of scarcity.

mining who gets what. For example, dormitory rooms are often rationed by lottery, and permission to register in popular classes is often rationed by a first-come, first-registered rule. The same with food: if food weren't rationed, there wouldn't be enough to go around, so it must be rationed—by charging a price for it. All scarce goods or rights must be rationed in some fashion.

Rationing reflects scarcity and economic forces. One of the important choices that a society must make is whether to allow these economic forces to operate freely and openly or to try to rein them in. When society gives relatively free rein to economic forces, economic forces become market forces. When an economic force works through the market, it's called a **market force.**

Market force An economic force working through the market.

Market forces ration by changing prices. When there's a shortage, the price goes up. When there's a surplus, the price goes down. Much of this book will be devoted to analyzing how the market works like an invisible hand, guiding economic forces to coordinate individual actions and allocate scarce resources. The **invisible hand** is the price mechanism, the rise and fall of prices that guides our actions in a market.

Invisible hand Economic forces that guide our actions.

Societies can't choose whether or not to allow economic forces to operate— economic forces are always operating. However, societies may choose whether to allow market forces to predominate. Other forces play a major role in deciding whether to let market forces operate. I'll call these other forces the **invisible handshake** (which includes social and historical forces) and the **invisible foot** (which includes political and legal forces). Economic reality is determined by a contest among these three invisible forces.

Invisible handshake Social and historical forces that guide our actions.

Invisible foot Political and legal forces that guide our actions.

6

Let's consider an example in which the invisible handshake prevents an economic force from becoming a market force: the problem of getting a date for Saturday night. If a school (or a society) has significantly more people of one sex than the other (let's say more men than women), some men may well find themselves without a date—that is, men will be in excess supply—and will have to find something else to do, say study or go to a movie by themselves. An "excess supply" person could solve the problem by paying someone to go out with him or her, but that would probably change the nature of the date in unacceptable ways. It would be revolting to the person who offered payment and to the person who was offered payment. That unacceptability is an example of the invisible handshake in action—the complex of social and cultural norms that guides and limits our activities. People don't try to buy dates because the invisible handshake prevents them from doing so. The invisible handshake makes the market solution for dating inappropriate.

Now let's consider another example in which it's the invisible foot—political and legal influences—that stops economic forces from becoming market forces. Say you decide that you can make some money delivering mail in your neighborhood. You try to establish a small business, but suddenly you experience the invisible foot in action. The U.S. Postal Service has a legal monopoly, so you'll be prohibited from delivering regular mail in competition with the post office. Economic forces—the desire to make money—led you to want to enter the business, but in this case the invisible foot squashes the invisible hand.

Often the invisible foot and invisible handshake work together against the invisible hand. For example, in the United States there aren't enough babies to satisfy all the couples who desire them. Babies born to particular sets of parents are rationed—by luck. Consider a group of parents, all of whom want babies. Those who can, have a baby; those who can't have one, but want one, try to adopt. Adoption agencies ration the available babies. Who gets a baby depends on whom people know at the adoption agency and on the desires of the birth mother, who can often specify the socioeconomic background (and many other characteristics) of the family in which she wants her baby to grow up. That's the economic force in action; it gives more power to the supplier of something that's in short supply.

THE INVISIBLE FORCES

Ideas are encapsulated in metaphors, and Adam Smith's "invisible hand" metaphor has been a central one in economics since 1776. It's a neat metaphor, but it sometimes makes economic forces seem to be the only forces guiding the direction of society. And that just ain't so.

In the 1970s and 1980s a number of modern-day economists attempted to broaden the dimensions of economic analysis. To explain what they were doing, they introduced metaphors for two other invisible forces. The term *invisible handshake* was coined by Arthur Okun, former chairman of the president's Council of Economic Advisers and an economist at the Brookings Institution, an economic think tank. Okun argued that social and historical forces—the invisible handshake—often prevented the invisible hand from working.

The term *invisible foot* was coined by Stephen Magee, chairman of the Department of Finance at the University of Texas. Magee summarized the argument of a large number of economists that individuals often use politics to get what they want, expressing this phenomenon with the invisible foot metaphor. Government action to benefit particular pressure groups is the invisible foot. By the late 1980s these two additional terms were commonly used by the group of economists who were struggling to integrate economic insights with social and political insights.

If our society allowed individuals to buy and sell babies, that economic force would be translated into a market force. The invisible hand would see to it that the quantity of babies supplied would equal the quantity of babies demanded at some price. The market, not the adoption agencies, would do the rationing.[4]

Most people, including me, find the idea of selling babies repugnant. But why? It's the strength of the invisible handshake backed up and strengthened by the invisible foot.

What is and isn't allowable differs from one society to another. For example, in Russia, until recently, private businesses were against the law, so not many people started their own businesses. In the United States until the 1970s, it was against the law to hold gold except in jewelry, so most people refrained from holding gold. Ultimately a country's laws and social norms determine whether the invisible hand will be allowed to work.

The invisible foot and invisible handshake are active in all parts of your life. The invisible foot influences many of our everyday actions. You don't compete with the post office; you don't sell body parts or addictive drugs. These actions are all against the law. But many people do sell alcohol; that's not against the law if you have a permit. The invisible handshake also influences us. You don't make profitable loans to your friends (you don't charge your friends interest); you don't charge your children for their food (parents are supposed to feed their children); many sports and media stars don't sell their autographs (some do, but many consider the practice tacky); you don't lower the wage you charge to get a job away from someone else (you're no scab). The list is long. You cannot understand economics without understanding the limitations that political and social forces—the invisible foot and the invisible handshake—place on economic actions.

In summary, what happens in a society can be seen as the reaction and interaction of these three forces: the invisible hand (economic forces), the invisible foot (political and legal forces), and the invisible handshake (social and historical forces). Economics has a role to play in sociology, history, and politics, just as sociology, history, and politics have roles to play in economics.

Economics is about the real world. Throughout this book I'll use the invisible forces analogy to talk about real-world events and the interrelationships of economics, history, sociology, and politics.

---

[4] Even though it's against the law, some babies are nonetheless "sold" on a semilegal, or what is called a gray, market. The 1990 "market price" for a healthy baby was about $30,000. If it were legal to sell babies (and if people didn't find having babies in order to sell them morally repugnant), the price would be much lower, since there would be a larger supply of babies.

WINSTON CHURCHILL AND LADY ASTOR

There are many stories about Nancy Astor, the first woman elected to Britain's Parliament. A vivacious, fearless American woman, she married into the English aristocracy and, during the 1930s and 1940s, became a bright light on the English social and political scenes, which were already quite bright. One story told about Lady Astor is that she and Winston Churchill, the unorthodox genius who had a long and distinguished political career and who was Britain's prime minister during World War II, were sitting in a pub having a theoretical discussion about morality. Churchill suggested that as a thought experiment Lady Astor ponder the question: If a man were to promise her a huge amount of money—say a million pounds—for the privilege, would she sleep with him? Lady Astor did ponder the question for a while and finally answered, yes, she would, if the money were guaranteed. Churchill then asked her if she would sleep with him for five pounds. Her response was sharp: "Of course not. What do you think I am—a prostitute?" This time Churchill won the battle of wits by answering, "We have already established that fact; we are now simply negotiating about price."

One moral that economists might draw from this story is that economic incentives, if high enough, can have a powerful influence on behavior. An equally important moral of the story is that noneconomic incentives can also be very strong. Why do most people feel it's wrong to sell sex for money—even if they would be willing to do so if the price were high enough? Keeping this second moral in mind will significantly increase your economic understanding of real-world events.

ECONOMIC TERMINOLOGY

Economic terminology needs little discussion. It simply needs learning. As terms come up in discussion, you'll begin to recognize them. Soon you'll begin to understand them, and finally you'll begin to feel comfortable using them. In this book I'm trying to describe how economics works in the real world, so I introduce you to many of the terms that occur in business and in discussions of the economy. Learning economic vocabulary, like learning German or French vocabulary, isn't fun. It's not something that's easily taught in classes. It's something that's learned by study and repetition outside the class. Learning vocabulary takes repetition and memorization, but no one ever said all learning is fun.

Whenever possible I'll integrate the introduction of new terminology into the discussion so that learning it will seem painless. In fact I've already introduced you to a number of economic terms: *opportunity cost, the invisible hand, market forces, economic forces*—just to name a few. By the end of the book I'll have introduced you to hundreds more.

ECONOMIC INSIGHTS

Economists have thought about the economy for a long time, so it's not surprising that they've developed some insights into the way it works. The problem for economics professors is that economists have developed so many insights that it's virtually impossible to present even a small portion of them. (The opportunity costs of doing so are too high.) So we must figure out shorthand methods of presenting large amounts of material. To do this, we compress the information into principles, theories, and models, all of which are shorthand methods of presenting insights, and all of which are abstract.[5] Once learned, they're applicable to a wide variety of examples. Economic insights are often embodied in an **economic model** (a simplified representation of reality).

Economic model   Simplified representation of reality.

You've already been introduced to one economic principle, the principle of increasing marginal opportunity cost, which is an insight about the relationship among outputs: In order to get more of one output, you must give up ever increasing quantities of another output. That principle can be applied to a wide variety of examples, so you need to learn only the principle, not each specific example.

---

[5] Principles differ from theories and models in how formally they're presented. Theories and models are formal; they are deduced from well-specified assumptions. Principles are informal; they are often drawn from theories or models, but their assumptions aren't as well specified.

To see the importance of principles, think back to grade school when you learned to add. You didn't memorize the sum of 147 and 138; instead you learned a principle of addition. The principle says that when adding 147 and 138, you first add $7 + 8$—which you memorized was 15—you write down the 5, carry the 1, which you add to $4 + 3$ to get 8. Then add $1 + 1 = 2$. So the answer is 285. When you know that one principle, you know how to add millions of combinations of numbers.

In the same way, knowing a theory gives you insight into a wide variety of economic phenomena, even though you don't know the particulars of each phenomenon. For example, much of economic theory deals with the *pricing mechanism* and how the market operates to coordinate *individuals' decisions*. Economists have come to the following insights:

> *When the quantity supplied is greater than the quantity demanded, price has a tendency to fall.*
> *When the quantity demanded is greater than the quantity supplied, price has a tendency to rise.*

Using these insights, economists have developed a theory of markets that leads to the further insight that, under certain conditions, the market will coordinate individuals' decisions—will allocate scarce resources *efficiently* so society moves out to its production possibility curve, not inside it. An efficient economy is one that reaps the maximum amount of outputs from the available inputs. Economists call this insight the **invisible hand theory.**

Theories and the models used to represent them are enormously efficient methods of conveying information, but they're also necessarily abstract. They rely upon simplifying assumptions, and *if you don't know the assumptions, you don't know the theory*. The result of forgetting assumptions could be similar to what happens if you forget that you're supposed to add numbers in columns. Forgetting that, yet remembering all the steps, can lead to a wildly incorrect answer. For example,

$$\begin{array}{r} 471 \\ +\ 327 \\ \hline \end{array}$$

5037 is wrong.

Knowing the assumptions of theories and models allows you to progress beyond gut reaction—and better understand the strengths and weaknesses of various economic systems.

Presenting the invisible hand theory in its full beauty is an important part of any economics course. Presenting the assumptions upon which it is based and the limitations of the invisible hand is likewise an important part of the course. I'll do both throughout the book.

All too often economic insights are presented as an abstract model—something you memorize for the exam and then forget. That's not economics and that's not learning. If you look at the history of economic thought, you'll see that economic theory, and the models in which that theory is presented, developed as a shorthand way of telling a story. These stories are important; they make the theory come alive and convey the insights that give economic theory its power. In this book I present plenty of theories and models, but they're accompanied by stories that provide the context that makes them relevant.

At times, because there's much new terminology, discussing models and theories takes up much of the presentation time and becomes a bit oppressive. That's the nature of the beast. As Albert Einstein said, "Theories should be as simple as possible, but not more so." When a theory or a model becomes oppressive, pause and think about the underlying story that the theory is meant to

The Invisible Hand Theory

When the quantity supplied is greater than the quantity demanded, price has a tendency to fall.
When the quantity demanded is greater than the quantity supplied, price has a tendency to rise.

Invisible hand theory The market will coordinate individuals' decisions.

Economic Theory and Stories

convey. That story should make sense and be concrete. If you can't translate the theory into a story, you don't understand the theory.

Microeconomics and Macroeconomics

Microeconomics The study of how individual choice is influenced by economic forces.

7

Economic theory is divided into two parts: microeconomic theory and macroeconomic theory. Microeconomic theory considers economic reasoning from the viewpoint of individuals and firms and builds up from there to an analysis of the whole economy. I'll define **microeconomics** as *the study of individual choice, and how that choice is influenced by economic forces.* Microeconomics studies such things as the pricing policies of firms, households' decisions on what to buy, and how markets allocate resources among alternative ends. Our discussions of opportunity cost and the production possibility curve were based on microeconomic theory. It is from microeconomics that the invisible hand theory comes.

As one builds up from microeconomic analysis to an analysis of the entire society, everything gets rather complicated. Many economists try to uncomplicate matters by taking a different approach—a macroeconomic approach—first looking at the aggregate, or whole, and then breaking it down into components. A micro approach would analyze a person by looking first at each individual cell and then building up. A macro approach would start with the person and then go on to his or her components—arms, legs, fingernails, feelings, and so on. Put simply, microeconomics analyzes from the parts to the whole; macroeconomics analyzes from the whole to the parts.

Neither approach is independent of the other. In recent years the analysis of macroeconomic issues—inflation, unemployment, business cycles, and growth—has used more and more microeconomic analysis to supplement it. Thus, many economists now define macroeconomics as the study of inflation, unemployment, business cycles, and growth. I'll compromise and define **macroeconomics** as *the study of inflation, unemployment, business cycles, and growth primarily from the whole to the parts—focusing on aggregate relationships and supplementing that analysis with microeconomic insights.*

Macroeconomics The study of inflation, unemployment, business cycles, and growth.

To demonstrate the relationship between micro and macro analysis, let's consider again the production possibility curve, which is based on microeconomic principles. If unemployment is high, the economy is operating inside the production possibility curve and hence is not operating efficiently. Similarly, growth shifts the production possibility curve outward. Thus, even though the production possibility curve is derived from microeconomic principles, it can be used to discuss macroeconomic issues.

ECONOMIC INSTITUTIONS

To know whether you can apply economic theory to reality, you must know about economic institutions. Economic institutions are complicated combinations of historical circumstance and economic, cultural, social, and political pressures. Economic institutions are all around you and affect your everyday life. For example, let's consider three economic institutions: schools, corporations, and cultural norms. Where you go to school determines the kind of job you'll get. Corporations determine what products are available to buy. Cultural norms determine what you identify as legitimate business activities. Understanding economic institutions requires the wisdom of experience, tempered with common sense—all combined with a desire to understand rather than to accept without question.

Economic institutions sometimes seem to operate in quite different manners than economic theory says they do. For example, economic theory says that prices are determined by supply and demand. However, a knowledge of economic institutions says that prices are set by rules of thumb—often by what are called cost-plus-markup rules. (That is, you determine what your costs are, multiply by 1.4 or 1.5, and the result is the price you set.) Economic theory says that supply and demand determine who's hired; a knowledge of economic institutions says that hiring is often done on the basis of whom you know, not by economic forces.

These apparent contradictions have two complementary explanations. First, economic theory abstracts from many issues. These issues may account for the differences. Second, there's no contradiction—economic principles are often affecting decisions from behind the scenes. For instance, supply and demand pressures determine what the price markup over cost will be. In this case the invisible handshake is guided by the invisible hand. In all cases, however, to apply economic theory to reality—to gain the full value of economic insights—you've got to have a sense of economic institutions.

The final goal of the course is to present the economic policy options facing our society today. For example, should the government restrict mergers between firms? Should it run a budget deficit? Should it do something about the international trade deficit? Should it decrease taxes?

I saved my discussion of this goal for last because there's no sense talking about policy options unless you know some economic terminology, some economic theory, and something about economic institutions. Once you know something about those, you're in a position to consider the policy options available for dealing with the economic problems our society faces.

Objective Policy Analysis

In thinking about policy, we must keep a number of points in mind. The most important is that good economic policy analysis is **objective.** Objective analysis does not say, "This is the way things should be," reflecting a goal established by the analyst. That would be **subjective** analysis. Instead it says, "This is the way the economy works, and if society (or the individual or firm for whom you're doing the analysis) wants to achieve a particular goal, this is how it might go about doing so." Objective analysis keeps your subjective views—your value judgments—separate.

Objective   Keeping one's personal views or value judgments out of an analysis.

Subjective   Allowing one's personal views or value judgments to affect one's analysis.

To make clear the distinction between objective and subjective analysis, economists have divided economics into three categories: *positive economics, normative economics,* and the *art of economics.* **Positive economics** is the study of what is, and how the economy works. It asks such questions as: How does the market for hog bellies work? How do price restrictions affect market forces? These questions fall under the heading of economic theory. **Normative economics** is the study of how the economy should be, not from the standpoint of the economist, but from the standpoint of society. The reason economics focuses on the normative question from the standpoint of society is that economists have no special expertise in saying, "This is the way things should be." Thus, in normative economics, economists try to figure out objectively what will make society better. Normative economics asks such questions as: What should the distribution of income be? What should tax policy be designed to achieve?

Positive economics   The study of what is, and how the economy works.

Normative economics   The study of how the economy should be, from society's standpoint.

The **art of economics** relates positive economics to normative economics; it is the application of the knowledge learned in positive economics to the achievement of the goals one has determined in normative economics. It looks at such questions as: To achieve a certain distribution of income, how would you go about it, given the way the economy works?[6] Most policy discussions fall under the art of economics.

Art of economics   The application of the knowledge learned in positive economics to the achievement of the goals determined in normative economics.

In each of these three branches of economics, economists separate their own value judgments from their objective analysis as much as possible. The qualifier "as much as possible" is important since some value judgments inevitably sneak in. We are products of our environment, and the questions we ask, the framework

---

[6] This three-part distinction was made back in 1896 by a famous economist, John Neville Keynes, father of John Maynard Keynes, the economist who developed macroeconomics. This distinction was instilled into modern economics by Milton Friedman and Robert Lipsey in the 1950s. They, however, downplayed the art of economics, which J. N. Keynes had seen as central to understanding the economists' role in policy.

we use, and the way we interpret empirical evidence all embody value judgments and reflect our background.

Maintaining objectivity is easiest in positive economics where one is simply trying to understand how the economy works. In positive economics one is working with abstract models. Maintaining objectivity is harder in normative economics. It's easy to jump from the way one thinks the world should be to believing that society agrees with you.

It's hardest to maintain objectivity in the art of economics because it embodies all the problems of both positive and normative economics. It's about how to achieve certain normative ends given the way the economy works, but it also adds more problems. Because noneconomic forces affect policy, to practice the art of economics one must make judgments about how these noneconomic forces work. These judgments are likely to embody one's own value judgments. So one must be exceedingly careful to be as objective as possible in practicing the art of economics.

Policy and the Invisible Forces

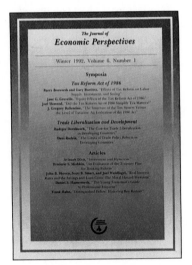

Students find the *Journal of Economic Perspectives* the most relevant of the journals published by the American Economic Association.

When you think about the policy options facing society, you'll quickly discover that the choice of policy options depends on much more than economic theory. One must take into account historical precedent plus social, cultural, and political forces. In an economics course I don't have time to analyze these forces in as much depth as I'd like. That's one reason there are separate history, political science, sociology, and anthropology courses. But I don't want to pretend that these forces don't play an important role in policy decisions. They do.

That's why I use the invisible force terminology when I cover these other issues. It allows me to integrate the other forces without explaining in depth how they work. I'll use this terminology when discussing policy and applying economic insights to policy questions. In economics we focus the analysis on the invisible hand, and much of economic theory is devoted to how the economy would operate if the invisible hand were the only force operating. But as soon as we apply theory to reality and policy, we must take into account the other invisible forces.

An example will make my point more concrete. Most economists agree that holding down or eliminating tariffs (taxes on imports) and quotas (numerical limitations on imports) makes good economic sense. They strongly advise governments to follow a policy of free trade. Do governments follow free trade policies? Almost invariably they do not. The invisible foot—politics—leads society in a different direction. If you're advising a policy maker, you need to point out that these other forces must be taken into account, and how other forces should (if they should) and can (if they can) be integrated with your recommendations.

Here's another example. Economic analysis devoid of institutional content would say that the world would be more efficient if we allowed U.S. citizenship to be bought and sold. But to advise policies that would legally allow a market for buying and selling U.S. citizenship would be to recommend a kind of efficiency that goes against historical, cultural, and social norms. The invisible handshake and the invisible foot would prevent the policies from being introduced, and any economist who proposed them would probably be banished to an ivory or other type of tower.

CONCLUSION

There's tons more that could be said by way of introducing you to economics, but an introduction must remain an introduction. As it is, this chapter should have:

1. Introduced you to economic reasoning.
2. Surveyed what we're going to cover in this book.
3. Given you an idea of my writing style and approach.

We'll be spending long hours together over the coming term, and before entering into such a commitment it's best to know your partner. While I won't know you, by the end of this book you'll know me. Maybe you won't love me as my mother does, but you'll know me.

This introduction was my opening line. I hope it also conveyed the importance and relevance that belong to economics. If it did, it has served its intended purpose. Economics is tough, but tough can be fun.

KEY POINTS

· Learning economics consists of learning: economic terminology, economic insights, economic institutions, policy options, and economic reasoning. **1**
· Economic reasoning structures all questions in a cost/benefit frame: If the benefits of doing something exceed the costs, do it. If the costs exceed the benefits, don't. **2**
· Often economic decisions can be made by comparing marginal costs and marginal benefits. **2**
· "There ain't no such thing as a free lunch" (**TANSTAAFL**) embodies the opportunity cost concept. **3**

· The production possibility curve embodies the opportunity cost concept. **4 5**
· Economic reality is controlled and directed by three invisible forces: the invisible hand, the invisible foot, and the invisible handshake. **6**
· Economics can be divided into microeconomics and macroeconomics. **7**
· Economics also can be subdivided into positive economics, normative economics, and the art of economics. **8**

KEY TERMS

art of economics *(23)*
comparative advantage *(14)*
cultural norm *(7)*
economic decision rule *(9)*
economic forces *(17)*
economic institution *(7)*
economic model *(20)*
economic policy *(8)*
economic reasoning *(8)*

economics *(6)*
economy *(6)*
efficiency *(16)*
inefficiency *(15)*
input *(11)*
invisible foot *(18)*
invisible hand *(18)*
invisible hand theory *(21)*
invisible handshake *(18)*
macroeconomics *(22)*

marginal benefit *(8)*
marginal cost *(8)*
market force *(18)*
microeconomics *(22)*
normative economics *(23)*
objective *(23)*
opportunity cost *(10)*
output *(11)*
positive economics *(23)*

principle of increasing marginal opportunity cost *(15)*
production possibility curve *(12)*
production possibility table *(11)*
productive efficiency *(15)*
subjective *(23)*

QUESTIONS FOR THOUGHT AND REVIEW

The number after each question represents the estimated degree of critical thinking required. (1 = almost none; 10 = deep thought.)

1. Design a grade production possibility table and curve that embody the principle of increasing marginal opportunity cost. *(4)*
2. What would the production possibility curve look like if there were decreasing marginal opportunity costs? Explain. Think of an example of decreasing marginal opportunity costs. *(8)*

3. Show how a production possibility curve would shift if a society became more productive in its output of widgets but less productive in its output of wadgets. *(5)*
4. List two microeconomic and two macroeconomic problems. *(2)*
5. Does economic theory prove that the free market system is best? Why? *(4)*
6. Calculate, using the best estimates you can make:
   a. Your opportunity cost of attending college.
   b. Your opportunity cost of taking this course.

c. Your opportunity cost of attending yesterday's lecture in this course. *(6)*

7. List two recent choices you made and explain why you made those choices in terms of marginal benefits and marginal costs. *(5)*

8. Individuals have two kidneys but most of us need only one. People who have lost both kidneys through accident or disease must be hooked up to a dialysis machine, which cleanses waste from their bodies. Say a person who has two good kidneys offers to sell one of them to someone whose kidney function has been totally destroyed. The seller asks $30,000 for the kidney, and the person who has lost both kidneys accepts the offer. Who benefits from the deal? Who is hurt? Should a society allow such market transactions? Why? *(9)*

9. Is a good economist always objective? Why? *(4)*

10. When all people use economic reasoning, inefficiency is impossible, because if the cost of reducing that inefficiency were greater than the benefits, the efficiency would be eliminated. Thus, if people use economic reasoning, it's impossible to be on the interior of a production possibility curve. Is this statement true or false? Why? *(8)*

PROBLEMS AND EXERCISES

1. A country has the following production possibility table:

Resources devoted to clothing	Output of clothing	Output of food
100%	20	0
80	16	5
60	12	9
40	8	12
20	4	14
0	0	15

a. Draw the country's production possibility curve.

b. What's happening to marginal opportunity costs as output of food increases?

c. Say the country gets better at the production of food. What will happen to the production possibility curve?

d. Say the country gets equally better at producing food and producing clothing. What will happen to the production possibility curve?

2. Go to two stores: a supermarket and a convenience store.

a. Write down the cost of a gallon of milk in each.

b. The prices are most likely different. Using the terminology used in this chapter, explain why that is the case and why anyone would buy milk in the store with the higher price.

c. Do the same exercise with shirts or dresses in Wal-Mart (or its equivalent) and Saks (or its equivalent).

Economics in Perspective

All too often, students study economics out of context. They're presented with sterile analysis and boring facts to memorize, and are never shown how economics fits into the large scheme of things. That's bad; it makes economics seem boring—but economics is not boring. Throughout this book, sometimes in the appendixes and sometimes in boxes, every so often I'll step back and put the analysis in perspective—giving you an idea from whence the analysis sprung and its historical context. In educational jargon, this is called *enrichment*.

I begin here with economics itself.

First, its history: In the 1500s there were few universities. Those that existed taught religion, Latin, Greek, philosophy, history, and mathematics. No economics. Then came the *Enlightenment* (about 1700) in which reasoning replaced God as the explanation of why things were the way they were. Pre-Enlightenment thinkers would answer the question, "Why am I poor?" with, "Because God wills it." Enlightenment scholars looked for a different explanation. "Because of the nature of land ownership" is one answer they found.

Such reasoned explanations required more knowledge of the way things were, and the amount of information expanded so rapidly that it had to be divided or categorized for an individual to have hope of knowing a subject. Soon philosophy was subdivided into science and philosophy. In the 1700s, the sciences were split into natural sciences and social sciences. The amount of knowledge kept increasing, and in the late 1800s and early 1900s social science itself split into subdivisions: economics, political science, history, geography, sociology, anthropology, and psychology. Many of the insights about how the economic system worked were codified in Adam Smith's *The Wealth of Nations,* written in 1776. Notice that this is before economics as a subdiscipline developed, and Adam Smith could also be classified as an anthropologist, a sociologist, a political scientist, and a social philosopher.

Throughout the 18th and 19th centuries economists such as Adam Smith, Thomas Malthus, John Stuart Mill, David Ricardo, and Karl Marx were more than economists; they were social philosophers who covered all aspects of social science. These writers were subsequently called *Classical economists*. Alfred Marshall continued in that classical tradition, and his book, *Principles of Economics,* published in the late 1800s, was written with the other social sciences much in evidence. But Marshall also changed the questions economists ask; he focused on those questions that could be asked in a graphical supply/demand framework. In doing so he began what is called *neo-classical economics*. Marshall's analysis forms the basis of much of the specifics of what's currently taught in undergraduate microeconomic courses.

In the 1930s, as economists formalized Marshall's insights, many other social science insights were removed. By the 1950s these social sciences were cemented into college curricula and organized into college departments. Economists learned economics; sociologists learned sociology.

For a while economics got lost in itself, and economists learned little else. Marshall's analysis was downplayed, and the work of more formal economists of the 1800s (such as Leon Walras, Francis Edgeworth, and Antoine Cournot) was seen as the basis of the science of economics. Economic analysis that focuses only on formal interrelationships is called *Walrasian economics*.

Thus, in the 1990s, there are two branches of neo-classical economics: Marshallian and Walrasian. The Marshallian branch sees economics as a way of thinking and integrates insights from other disciplines. The Walrasian branch sees economics as a logical science and excludes other social sciences. This book falls solidly in the Marshallian tradition. It sees economics as a way of thinking—as an engine of analysis used to understand real-world phenomena, not as a logical exercise in deductive reasoning. My strong belief is that in undergraduate school one should learn Marshallian economics; in graduate school one can learn Walrasian economics.

Marshallian economics is an art, not a science. It sees institutions as well as political and social dimensions of reality as important, and it shows you how economics ties into those dimensions.

Graphish
The Language of Graphs

A picture is worth 1,000 words. Economists, being efficient, like to present ideas in graphs, which are a type of picture. But a graph is worth 1,000 words only if the person looking at the graph knows the graphical language; *Graphish,* we'll call it. (It's a bit like English.) Graphish is usually written on graph paper. If the person doesn't know Graphish, the picture isn't worth any words and Graphish can be babble.

I have enormous sympathy for students who don't understand Graphish. A number of my students often get thrown for a loop by graphs. They understand the idea, but Graphish confuses them. This appendix is for them, and for those of you like them. It's a primer in Graphish.

Two Ways to Use Graphs

In this book I use graphs in two ways:

1. To present an economic model or theory visually: to show how two variables interrelate.
2. To present real-world data visually. To do this, I use primarily bar charts, line charts, and pie charts.

Actually, these two ways of using graphs are related. They are both ways of presenting visually the *relationship* between two things.

Graphs are built around a number line, or axis, like the one in Exhibit B1(a). The numbers are generally placed in order, equal distances from one another. That number line allows us to represent a number at an appropriate point on the line. For example, point *A* represents the number 4.

The number line in Exhibit B1(a) is drawn horizontally, but it doesn't have to be; it can also be drawn vertically, as in Exhibit B1(b).

How we divide our axes, or number lines, into intervals, is up to us. In Exhibit B1(a), I called each interval *1;* in Exhibit B1(b), I called each interval *10.* Point *A* appears after 4 intervals of 1 (starting at 0 and reading from left to right), so it represents 4. In Exhibit B1(b), where each interval represents 10, to represent 5, I place point *B* halfway in the interval between 0 and 10.

So far, so good. Graphish developed when a vertical and a horizontal number line were combined, as in Exhibit B1(c). When the number lines are put together they're called *axes.* (Each line is an axis. *Axes* is the plural of *axis.*) I now have a two-dimensional space in which *one point can represent two numbers.* (This two-dimensional space is called a *coordinate space.*) For example, point *A* in Exhibit B1(c) represents the numbers (4, 5)—4 on the horizontal number

(a)

(b)

(c)

EXHIBIT B1 (a, b, and c)   **Horizontal and Vertical Number Lines and a Coordinate System**

line and 5 on the vertical number line. Point *B* represents the numbers (1, 20). (By convention, the horizontal numbers are written first.)

Being able to represent two numbers with one point is neat because it allows the relationships between two numbers to be presented visually instead of having to be expressed verbally, which is often cumbersome. For example, say the cost of producing 6 units of something is $4 per unit and the cost of producing 10 units is $3 per unit. By putting both these points on a graph, we can visually see that producing 10 costs less per unit than does producing 6.

Another way to use graphs to present real-world data visually is to use the horizontal line to represent time. Say that we let each horizontal interval equal a year and each vertical interval equal $100 in income.

By graphing your income each year, you can obtain a visual representation of how your income has changed over time.

Graphs can be used to show any relationship between two variables. (*Variables* are what economists call the units that are measured on the horizontal and vertical axes.) As long as you remember that graphs are simply a way of presenting a relationship visually, you can keep graphs in perspective.

Using Graphs in Economic Modeling   I use graphs throughout the book as I present economic models, or simplifications of reality. A few terms are often used in describing these graphs, and we'll now go over them. Consider Exhibit B2(a), which lists the number of pens

---

EXHIBIT B2 (a ,b, c, and d)   A Table and Graphs Showing the Relationships between Price and Quantity

Price of pens (in dollars)	Quantity of pens bought per day	Row
3.00	4	A
2.50	5	B
2.00	6	C
1.50	7	D
1.00	8	E

(a)

(b)

(c)

(d)

bought per day (column 2) at various prices (column 1).

We can present the table's information in a graph by combining the pairs of numbers in the two columns of the table and representing, or plotting, them on two axes. I do that in Exhibit B2(b).

By convention, when graphing a relationship between price and quantity, economists place price on the vertical axis and quantity on the horizontal axis.

I can now connect the points, producing a line like the one in Exhibit B2(c). With this line, I interpolate the numbers between the points. That is, I make the reasonable assumption (which makes for a nice visual presentation) that the relationship between the variables is the same *between* the points as it is *at* the points. This assumption is called the *interpolation assumption*. It allows us to think of a line as a collection of points and therefore to connect the points into a line.

Even though the line in Exhibit B2(c) is straight, economists call any such line drawn on a graph a *curve*. Because it's straight, the curve in Exhibit B2(c) is called a *linear curve*. Notice that this curve starts high on the left-hand side and goes down to the right. Economists say any curve that looks like that is "downward-sloping." They also say that a *downward-sloping* curve represents an *inverse* relationship between the two variables: When one goes up, the other goes down. In this example, the line demonstrates an inverse relationship between price and quantity—that is, when the price of pens goes up, the quantity bought goes down.

Exhibit B2(d) presents a curve that really is curved. It starts low on the left-hand side and goes up to the right. Such curves are called *nonlinear curves*. Economists say any curve that goes up to the right is "upward-sloping." An *upward-sloping* curve represents a *direct* relationship between the two variables (what's measured on the horizontal and vertical lines). In a direct relationship, when one variable goes up, the other goes up too. *Downward-sloping* and *upward-sloping* are terms you need to memorize if you want to read, write, and speak Graphish, keeping graphically in your mind the image of the relationships they represent.

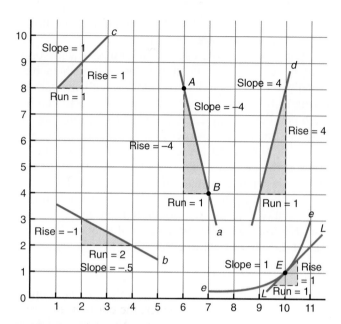

EXHIBIT B3   Slopes of Curves

Slope   One can, of course, be far more explicit about how much the curve is sloping upward or downward. To be more explicit, mathematicians define the term *slope* as the change in the value on the vertical axis divided by the change in the value on the horizontal axis. Sometimes it's presented as "rise over run":

$$\text{Slope} = \frac{\text{Rise}}{\text{Run}} = \frac{\text{Change in value on vertical axis}}{\text{Change in value on horizontal axis}}$$

Slopes of Linear Curves   In Exhibit B3 I present five linear curves and measure their slope. Let's go through an example to show how we can measure slope. To do so, we must pick two points. Let's use points A (6, 8) and B (7, 4) on curve a. Looking at these points, we see that as we move from 6 to 7 on the horizontal axis, we move from 8 to 4 on the vertical axis. So when the number on the vertical axis falls by 4, the number on the horizontal axis increases by 1. That means the slope is −4 divided by 1, or −4.

Notice that the inverse relationships represented by the two downward-sloping curves, a and b, have negative slopes and that the direct relationships represented by the two upward-sloping curves, c and d,

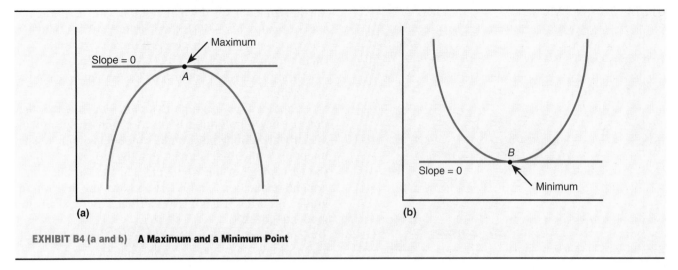

EXHIBIT B4 (a and b)   A Maximum and a Minimum Point

have positive slopes. Notice also that the flatter the curve, the smaller the numerical value of the slope; and the more vertical, or steeper, the curve, the larger the numerical value of the slope. There are two extreme cases:

1. When the curve is horizontal (flat), the slope is zero.
2. When the curve is vertical (straight up and down), the slope is infinite (larger than large).

Knowing the term *slope* and how it's measured lets us describe verbally the pictures we see visually. For example, if I say a curve has a slope of zero, you should picture in your mind a flat line; if I say "a curve with a slope of minus one," you should picture a falling line that makes a 45° angle with the horizontal and vertical axes. (It's the hypotenuse of an equilateral triangle with the axes as the other two sides.)

Slopes of Nonlinear Curves   The preceding examples were of *linear (straight) curves*. With *nonlinear curves*—the ones that really do curve—the slope of the curve is constantly changing. As a result, we must talk about the slope of the curve at a particular point, rather than the slope of the whole curve. How can a point have a slope? Well, it can't really, but it can almost, and if that's good enough for mathematicians, it's good enough for us.

Defining the slope of a nonlinear curve is a bit more difficult. The slope at a given point on a nonlinear curve is determined by the slope of a linear (or straight) line that's tangent to that curve. (A line that's tangent to a curve is a line that just touches the curve, and touches it only at one point in the immediate vicinity of that point.) In Exhibit B3 the line *LL* is tangent to the curve *ee* at point *E*. The slope of that line, and hence the slope of the curve at the one point where the line touches the curve, is +1.

Maximum and Minimum Points   Two points on a nonlinear curve deserve special mention. These points are the ones for which the slope of the curve is zero. I demonstrate those in Exhibit B4(a) and (b). (At point *A*, we're at the top of the curve so it's at a maximum point; at point *B*, we're at the bottom of the curve so it's at a minimum point.) These maximum and minimum points are often referred to by economists, and it's important to realize that the value of the slope of the curve at each of these points is zero.

There are, of course, many other types of curves, and much more can be said about the curves I've talked about. I won't do so because, for purposes of this course, we won't need to get into those refinements. I've presented as much Graphish as you need to know for this book.

Presenting Real-World Data in Graphs

The previous discussion treated the Graphish terms that economists use in presenting models, which focus on hypothetical relationships. Economists also use graphs in presenting actual economic data. Say, for example, that you want to show how exports have changed over time. Then you would place years on

(a)

(b)

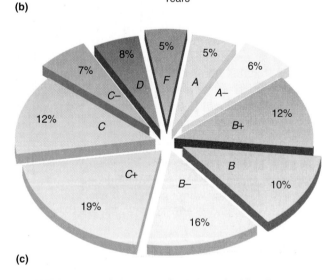

(c)

EXHIBIT B5 (a, b, and c)   **Presenting Information Visually**

the horizontal axis (by convention) and exports on the vertical axis, as in Exhibit B5(a) and (b). Having done so, you can either connect the data, as in (a), or fill in the areas under the points for that year, as in (b). The first is called a *line graph;* the second is called a *bar graph.*

Another type of graph is a *pie chart,* such as the one presented in Exhibit B5(c). A pie chart is useful in visually presenting how a total amount is divided. The uncut pie is the total amount, and the pie pieces reflect the percentage of the whole pie that the various components make up. Exhibit B5(c) shows the division of grades on a test I gave. Notice that 5 percent of the students got A's.

There are other types of graphs, but they're all variations on line and bar graphs and pie charts. Once you understand these three basic types of graphs, you shouldn't have any trouble understanding the other types.

Interpreting Graphs about the Real World   Understanding Graphish is important, because if you don't, you can easily misinterpret the meaning of graphs. For example, consider the two graphs in Exhibit B6(a) and (b). Which graph demonstrates the larger rise in income? If you said (a), you're wrong. The intervals in the vertical axes differ, and if you look carefully you'll see that the curves in both graphs represent the same combination of points. So when considering graphs, always make sure you understand the markings on the axes. Only then can you interpret the graph.

Let's now review what we've covered.

- A graph is a picture of points on a coordinate system in which the points denote relationships between numbers.
- A downward-sloping line represents an inverse relationship or a negative slope.
- An upward-sloping line represents a direct relationship or a positive slope.
- Slope is measured by rise over run, or a change of y (the number measured on the vertical axis) over a change in x (the number measured on the horizontal axis).
- The slope of a point on a nonlinear curve is measured by the rise over run of a line tangent to that point.
- At the maximum and minimum points of a nonlinear curve, the value of the slope is zero.
- In reading graphs, one must be careful to understand what's being measured on the vertical and horizontal axes.

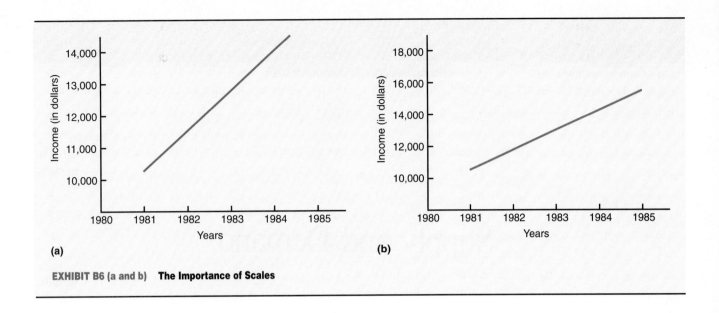

(a)

(b)

EXHIBIT B6 (a and b)   **The Importance of Scales**

2

Supply and Demand

Teach a parrot the terms supply
and demand *and you've got an economist.*

Thomas Carlyle

After reading this chapter, you should be able to:

1
State the law of demand.

2
Draw a demand curve from a demand table.

3
Distinguish a shift in demand from a
movement along the demand curve.

4
State the law of supply.

5
Draw a supply curve from a supply table.

6
Distinguish a shift in supply from a
movement along the supply curve.

7
Explain the importance of opportunity cost
and substitution to the laws of supply
and demand.

8
State the three dynamic laws of supply
and demand.

9
Work with and interpret supply
and demand curves.

Supply and demand. Supply and demand. Roll the phrase around your mouth, savor it like a good wine. *Supply* and *demand*—are the most used words in economics. And for good reason. They provide a good off-the-cuff answer for any economic question. Try it.

Why are bacon and oranges so expensive this winter? *Supply and demand.*

Why are interest rates falling? *Supply and demand.*

Why can't I find decent wool socks any more? *Supply and demand.*

The importance of the interplay of supply and demand makes it only natural that early in any economics course, you must learn about supply and demand. Let's start with demand.

DEMAND

Poets and songwriters use literary license. Take the classic song by the Rolling Stones entitled "You Can't Always Get What You Want." Whether the statement is or isn't true depends on how you define *want*. If you define *want* as "being sufficiently desirous of something so that you do what's necessary to buy the good," then in a market in which prices are flexible, you *can* always get what you want. The reason: what you want depends on what the price is. If, however, you define *want* as simply "being desirous of something," then there are many unfulfilled "wants," such as my wanting an expensive sports car. I want to own a Maserati. But, I must admit, I'm not willing to do what's necessary to own one. If I really wanted to own one, I'd mortgage everything I own, increase my income by doubling the number of hours I work, not buy anything else, and get that car. But I don't do any of those things, so there's a question of whether I really want the car. Sure, I'd want one if it cost $10,000, but from my actions it's clear that at $190,000 I don't really want it. If *want* is defined as "being sufficiently desirous of something that you will do what's necessary to buy the good," you can always get what you want, because your willingness to pay the going price for something is the only way to tell whether you really want it. What you want at a low price differs from what you want at a high price.

Prices are the tool by which the invisible hand—the market—coordinates individuals' desires and limits how much people are willing to buy—how much they really want. When goods are scarce, the market reduces people's desires for those scarce goods; as their prices go up, people buy fewer of them. As goods become abundant, their prices go down, and people want more of them. The invisible hand sees to it that what people want (do what's necessary to get) matches what's available. In doing so, the invisible hand coordinates individuals' wants. While you can't always get what you want at a low price, at some price— maybe a super-high price—you can. It isn't surprising that the Stones chose the other definition of *want;* it's unlikely that their song would have become a hit had they put in the appropriate qualifier. You can't dance to "You Can't Always Get What You Want at the Price You Want."

What makes the qualifier appropriate is the **law of demand:**

> *More of a good will be demanded the lower its price, other things constant.*

Or alternatively:

> *Less of a good will be demanded the higher its price, other things constant.*

This law is fundamental to the invisible hand's ability to coordinate individuals' desires: as prices change, people change how much of a particular good they're willing to buy.

To be clear about the meaning of the law of demand, economists differentiate the concepts *demand* and *quantity demanded.* **Demand** refers to a schedule of quantities of a good that will be bought per unit of time at various prices. **Quantity**

The Law of Demand

Law of demand Quantity of a good bought is inversely related to the good's price.

1

Demand Quantities of a good that will be bought at various prices; it is represented by the entire demand curve.

EXHIBIT 1   A Sample Demand Curve

The law of demand states that the quantity demanded of a good is inversely related to the price of that good. As the price of a good goes up, the quantity demanded goes down.

Quantity demanded Quantity of a good that buyers want to buy; it can be represented by a point on a demand curve.

Demand curve Graphical representation of how much of a good will be bought at various prices.

demanded refers to a specific amount that will be demanded per unit of time at a specific price.

In graphical terms, *demand* refers to the entire **demand curve** which tells how much of a good will be bought at various prices. *Quantity demanded* refers to a point on a demand curve, so when economists talk about movements along a demand curve, they mean changes in quantity demanded.

Exhibit 1 shows a demand curve. In graphical terms the law of demand states that the quantity demanded of a good is negatively related to that good's price, other things constant. As the price goes up, the quantity demanded goes down. As you can see in Exhibit 1, price and quantity are negatively related so the demand curve slopes downward to the right.

Just think of something you'd really like but can't afford. If the price is cut in half, you—and other consumers—become more likely to buy it. Quantity demanded goes up as price goes down.

Just to be sure you've got it, let's consider a real-world example: demand for vanity—specifically, vanity license plates. In 1989 the North Carolina state legislature increased the vanity plates' price from $30 to $40. In response, the quantity demanded fell from 60,334 at $30 a year to 31,122 at $40 a year. That's the law of demand in action.

Other things constant Holding all variables except one constant.

Other Things Constant   To understand the law of demand, you must understand the terminology used to discuss that law and the assumptions upon which that law is based. Let's first consider the phrase, "Other things constant."

Notice that in stating the law of demand, I put in a qualification: **other things constant.**[1] That's three extra words and unless they were important I wouldn't have put them in. But what does "other things constant" mean? Say that over a period of two years, the price of cars rises as the number of cars sold likewise rises. That seems to violate the law of demand, since the number of cars sold should have fallen in response to the rise in price. Looking at the data more closely, however, we see that a third factor has also changed: individuals' income has increased overall. As income increases, people buy more cars, increasing the demand for cars.

The increase in price works as the law of demand states—it decreases the number of cars bought. But in this case, income doesn't remain constant; it increases. That rise in income increases the demand for cars. That increase in demand outweighs the decrease in quantity demanded that results from a rise in

---

[1] *Other things constant* is a translation of the Latin phrase *ceteris paribus*. Sometimes economists just use *ceteris paribus* without translating it.

price, so ultimately more cars are sold. If you want to study the effect of price alone—which is what the law of demand refers to—you must make adjustments to hold income constant when you make your study. That's why the qualifying phrase *other things constant* is an important part of the law of demand.

How much somebody wants to buy a good depends on many other things besides its price. These include individuals' tastes, prices of other goods, and even the weather. Those other factors must remain constant if you're to make a valid study of the effect of an increase in the price of a good on the quantity demanded of it. In practice it's impossible to keep all other things constant, so you have to be careful when you say that when price goes up, quantity demanded goes down. It's likely to go down, but it's always possible that something besides price has changed.

Economists recognize that many things besides price affect demand. They call them **shift factors of demand.** A shift factor of demand is something, besides the good's price, that affects how much of the good is demanded. Important shift factors of demand include:

Shift factors of demand Something other than price that affects how much of a good is demanded.

1. Society's income.
2. The prices of other goods.
3. Tastes.
4. Expectations.

These aren't the only shift factors. In fact anything—except price changes—that affects demand (and many things do) is a shift factor. While economists agree these shift factors are important, they believe that no shift factor influences how much is demanded as consistently as price of the specific item does. That's what makes economists focus first on price as they try to understand the world. That's why economists make the law of demand central to their analysis.

Relative Price   A second qualification is that the law of demand refers to a good's **relative price.** The relative price of a good is the price of that good compared to the price of another good or combination of goods. For example, if the price of a compact disc is $11 and the price of an apple is 50 cents, the relative price of CDs compared to the price of apples is $11/50¢ = 22. In other words, you can buy 22 apples with one CD or one CD with 22 apples.

Relative price Price of a good compared to the price of some other good.

The actual price you pay for the goods you buy is called *the money price*. You don't say that a CD will cost 22 apples; you say that a CD will cost $11. But don't let that fool you. While the $11 may not look like a relative price, it is. It is the price of the CD compared to a composite price for all other goods. That composite price for all other goods is the price of money. What's the price of money? It's simply how much you'll pay for money. Most people will pay $1 for $1, so the price of $1 is $1. The money price of $11 means that you can trade one CD for 11 one-dollar bills.

Money is not desired for its own sake. You want dollar bills only because you can trade them for something else. You have in the back of your mind a good sense of what else you could do with that $11—what the opportunity cost of spending it on a CD is. You could buy, say, three Big Macs, a double order of fries, and a vanilla shake for $11. The opportunity cost of buying the CD is that big tray of fast food. Thus the money price of an item represents the price of that item relative to the prices of all other goods.

As long as your sense of what that opportunity cost is doesn't change, money price is a good representation of relative price. Over short periods the opportunity cost of $1 doesn't change. Over longer periods, though, because of inflation, money prices are not a good representation of relative prices. Say, for instance, that money prices (including your wage) on average go up 10 percent. (When this happens, economists say the price level has gone up by 10 percent.) Also say the money price of a CD goes up by 2 percent. Has the relative price of CDs gone up

Trygve Haavelmo—Nobel prize, 1989, for work on specifying supply and demand curves. © *The Nobel Foundation.*

EXHIBIT 2   A Demand Table

	Price (in dollars)	Cassette rentals demanded per week
A	0.50	9
B	1.00	8
C	2.00	6
D	3.00	4
E	4.00	2

or down? Since the *average* money price has gone up 10 percent and the money price of a CD has risen by 2 percent, the relative price has fallen by 8 percent. The law of demand would say that the quantity of CDs demanded would increase because the relative price has gone down, even though the money price has gone up.

The use of money prices makes life easier for members of society, but it makes life harder for economics students, who must remember that even though they see the money price of an item as an absolute number, it is actually a relative price.

7   I emphasize that the law of demand refers to relative price because the explanation for it involves demanders' ability to *substitute* some other good for that good. If a good's relative price goes up, some people will substitute some other good for it because that substitute's relative price goes down. For example, if the money price of compact discs rises and the money price of music tapes doesn't rise, individuals will substitute music tapes for CDs.

The Demand Table

As I emphasized in Chapter 1, introductory economics depends heavily on graphs and graphical analysis—translating ideas into graphs and back again into words. So let's graph the demand curve.

Exhibit 2 describes Alice's demand for renting videocassettes. In this example, the demand is for the temporary use of a videocassette. For example, at a price of $2, Alice will buy the use of six cassettes per week.

There are a number of points about the relationship between the number of videos Alice rents and the price of renting them that are worth mentioning. First, the relationship follows the law of demand: as the rental price rises, quantity demanded decreases. Second, quantity demanded has a specific *time dimension* to it. In this example it is the number of cassette rentals per week that is referred to, not the number of cassettes rented per day, hour, or year. Without the time dimension, the table wouldn't provide us with any useful information. Nine cassette rentals per year is quite a different concept from nine cassette rentals per week. Third, the cassette rentals that Alice buys are interchangeable—the ninth cassette rental doesn't significantly differ from the first, third, or any other cassette rental.

The concept of interchangeable goods causes economists significant problems in discussing real-world demand schedules because the quality of goods often differs in the real world. A pink Volkswagen is quite different from a gray Aston Martin, yet they're both cars. Luckily, in textbooks interchangeable goods cause few problems because we can pick and choose among examples. Textbook authors simply avoid examples that raise significant quality problems. However, it's only fair to point out that in the real world economists spend a great deal of time adjusting their analyses for differences in quality among goods.

Two final points are already familiar to you. Fourth, the price the table refers to is a relative price even though it is expressed as a money price, and fifth, the schedule assumes that everything else is held constant.

EXHIBIT 3   **From a Demand Table to a Demand Curve**

The demand table in Exhibit 2 is translated into a demand curve in Exhibit 3. Each point on the table corresponds to a point on the curve. For example, point *A* on the graph represents row *A* in the table: Alice demands 9 videocassette rentals at a price of 50 cents. A demand curve is constructed by plotting all points from the demand table and connecting the points by a line.

Exhibit 3 translates Exhibit 2's information into a graph. Point *A* (quantity = 9, price = $.50) is graphed first at the (9, $.50) coordinates. Next we plot points *B*, *C*, *D*, and *E* in the same manner and connect the resulting dots with a solid line. The result is the demand curve, which graphically conveys the same information that's in the demand table. Notice that the demand curve is downward sloping (from left to right), indicating that the law of demand holds in the example. When a curve slopes downward to the right, we say that there is an inverse relationship between the price and the quantity demanded.

The demand curve represents the *maximum price* that an individual will pay for various quantities of a good; the individual will happily pay less. For example, say someone offers Alice six cassette rentals at a price of $1 each (point *F* of Exhibit 3). Will she accept? Sure; she'll pay any price within the shaded area to the left of the demand curve. But if someone offers her six rentals at $3.50 each (point *G*), she won't accept. At a rental price of $3.50, she's willing to buy only three cassette rentals.

Normally economists talk about market demand curves rather than individual demand curves. A **market demand curve** is the horizontal sum of all individual demand curves. Market demand curves are what most firms are interested in. Firms don't care whether individual A or individual B buys their good; they care that *someone* buys their good.

It's a good graphical exercise to add the individual demand curves together to create a market demand curve. I do that in Exhibit 4. In it I assume that the market consists of three buyers, Alice, Bruce, and Cathy, whose demand tables are given in Exhibit 4(a). Alice and Bruce have demand tables similar to the demand tables discussed previously. At a price of $3 Alice rents four cassettes; at a price of $2 she rents six. Cathy is an all-or-nothing individual. She rents one cassette as long as the price is equal to or below $1; otherwise she rents nothing. If you plot Cathy's demand curve, it's a vertical line. However, the law of demand still holds: as price increases, quantity demanded decreases.

The quantity demanded by each demander is listed in columns 2, 3, and 4 of Exhibit 4(a). Column 5 gives total market demand; each entry is the sum of the entries in columns 2, 3, and 4. For example, at a price of $3 (row *F*), Alice

From a Demand Table to a Demand Curve

2

Individual and Market Demand Curves

Market demand curve   Horizontal sum of all individual demand curves.

EXHIBIT 4 (a and b)   From Individual Demands to a Market Demand Curve

The table (**a**) shows the demand schedules for Alice, Bruce, and Cathy. Together they make up the market for videocassette rentals. Their total quantity demanded (market demand) for videocassette rentals at each price is given in column 5. As you can see in (**b**), Alice's, Bruce's, and Cathy's demand curves can be added together to get the total market demand curve. For example, at a price of $2, Cathy demands 0, Bruce demands 3, and Alice demands 6, for a market demand of 9 (point *D*).

(1)	(2)	(3)	(4)	(5)	
Price (in dollars)	Alice	Bruce	Cathy	Market demand	
0.50	9	6	1	16	A
1.00	8	5	1	14	B
1.50	7	4	0	11	C
2.00	6	3	0	9	D
2.50	5	2	0	7	E
3.00	4	1	0	5	F
3.50	3	0	0	3	G
4.00	2	0	0	2	H

(a)

(b)

demands four cassette rentals, Bruce demands one, and Cathy demands zero, for a total market demand of five cassette rentals.

Exhibit 4(b) shows three demand curves: one each for Alice, Bruce, and Cathy. The market, or total, demand curve is the horizontal sum of the individual demand curves. To see that this is the case, notice that if we take the quantity demanded at $1 by Alice (8), Bruce (5), and Cathy (1) (row *B*, columns 2, 3, and 4), they sum to 14, which is point *B* (14, $1) on the market demand curve. We can do that for each level of price. Alternatively, we can simply add the individual quantities demanded prior to graphing (which we do in column 5 of Exhibit 4(a)) and graph that total in relation to price. Not surprisingly, we get the same total market demand curve.

In practice, of course, firms don't measure individual demand curves, so they don't sum them up in this fashion. Instead, they estimate total demand. Still, summing up individual demand curves is a useful exercise because it shows you how the market demand curve is made up of the sum (the horizontal sum, graphically speaking) of the individual demand curves, and it gives you a good sense of where market demand curves come from. It also shows you that, even if individuals don't respond to small changes in price, the market demand curve can still be smooth and downward sloping. That's because for the market, the law of demand is based on two phenomena:

1. At lower prices existing demanders buy more.
2. At lower prices new demanders (some all-or-nothing demanders like Cathy) enter the market.

Shifts in Demand versus Movement along a Given Demand Curve

As I have emphasized already, the demand curves we draw assume other things are held constant. That is, we assume the price of the good, not shift factors, is causing the demand curve to be downward sloping. To distinguish between the effects of price and the effects of shift factors on how much of a good is demanded, we need some terminology.

(a)

(b)

EXHIBIT 5 (a and b)   Shifts in Demand versus Movement along a Demand Curve

A change in price causes a movement along the demand curve. For example, in (**a**),if the price of videocassette rentals is $3.50, 3 rentals will be demanded (point *A*). If the price falls to $2, the quantity of rentals demanded will be 9 (point *B*). Thus, the fall in price brings about a movement along the demand curve, from point *A* to point *B*.

A shift factor change causes a shift in demand. For example, in (**b**), at the price of $3.50, 3 cassette rentals will be demanded (point *A*), but if income rises while price remains the same, people are willing to buy 5 cassette rentals for $3.50 instead of only 3. An increase in income causes the entire demand curve to shift outward from D_0 to D_1.

If how much is demanded is affected by price, we call that effect a change in the quantity demanded. Since a demand curve tells us how much is demanded at different prices, a change in the quantity demanded is represented graphically by a **movement along the demand curve.** If how much is demanded is affected by a shift factor, there is said to be a **shift in demand.** Since a change in a shift factor changes how much would be bought at each different price, a change in demand means that the entire demand curve shifts, to either the right or the left. Thus, a change in a shift factor causes a *shift* in demand; a change in price causes a *movement* along the demand curve. Differentiating between a shift in demand and movement along the demand curve is important but difficult, so it's useful to differentiate the two types of change graphically. I do so in Exhibit 5.

Exhibit 5(a) shows the effect of a change in the price of cassettes from $3.50 to $2. Point *A* (quantity demanded 3, price $3.50) represents the starting point. Now the price falls to $2 and the quantity demanded rises from 3 to 9, so we move along the demand curve to point *B*. Notice the demand curve (D_0) has already been drawn to demonstrate the effect that price has on quantity.

Now let's say that price of $3.50 doesn't change but income rises and, as it does, quantity demanded rises to 5. Thus, at a price of $3.50, 5 cassette rentals are demanded rather than only 3. That point is represented by point *C* in Exhibit 5(b). But if income causes a rise in quantity demanded at a price of $3.50, it will also likely cause an increase in the quantity demanded at all other prices. The demand curve will not remain where it was, but will shift to D_1 to the right of D_0. Because

3

Movement along a demand curve A change in the quantity demanded due to a change in price.

Shift in demand A shift of the entire demand curve.

of the change in income the entire demand curve has shifted. Thus, we say a change in this shift factor has caused a shift in demand.

To see if you understand, say the local theater decides to let everyone in for free. What will happen to demand for videocassettes? If your answer is there will be a shift in demand—the entire demand curve will shift inward—you've got it. Just to be sure, let's try one last example. Say tastes change: couch potatoes are out, hard bodies are in. What will happen to the demand for cassettes? The entire demand curve shifts in some more.

The difference between shifts in demand and movements along the demand curve deserves emphasis:

- A change in a shift factor causes a shift in demand (a shift of the entire demand curve).
- A change in price of a good causes a change in the quantity demanded (a movement along an existing demand curve).

SUPPLY

Factors of production Resources, or inputs, necessary to produce goods.

In one sense, supply is the mirror image of demand. Individuals control the inputs, or resources, necessary to produce goods. Such resources are often called **factors of production.** Individuals' supply of these factors to market mirrors other individuals' demand for those factors. For example, say you decide you want to rest rather than weed your garden. You hire someone to do the weeding; you demand labor. Someone else decides she would prefer more income instead of more rest; she supplies labor to you. You trade money for labor; she trades labor for money. Here supply is the mirror image of demand.

For a large number of goods, however, the supply process is more complicated than demand. As Exhibit 6 shows, for a large number of goods, there's an intermediate step in supply. Individuals supply factors of production to firms. **Firms** are organizations of individuals that transform factors of production into consumable goods. Let's consider an example. Say you're a taco technician. You supply your labor to the factor market. The taco company demands your labor (hires you). The taco company combines your labor with other inputs like meat, cheese, beans, and tables and produces many tacos (production) which it supplies to customers in the goods market. For produced goods, supply depends not only on individuals' decisions to supply factors of production; it also depends on firms' ability to produce—to transform those factors of production into consumable goods.

Firms Organizations of individuals formed to transform factors of production into consumer goods.

The supply of nonproduced goods is more direct. Individuals supply their labor in the form of services directly to the goods market. For example, an independent contractor may repair your washing machine. That contractor supplies his labor directly to you.

Thus, the analysis of the supply of produced goods has two parts: an analysis of the supply of factors of production to households and to firms, and an analysis of why firms transform those factors of production into consumable goods.

The Law of Supply

Supply Quantities that will be brought to market at various prices.

In talking about supply, the same convention exists that we used for demand. **Supply** refers to the various quantities offered for sale at various prices. **Quantity supplied** refers to a specific quantity offered for sale at a specific price.

EXHIBIT 6   Transformation of Factors of Production into Consumable Goods

Supply refers to the quantities that will be bought at various prices. When goods are simply traded, supply and demand both come from households. One household supplies the good; another household demands the good.

With produced goods, the supply process is more complicated. Households supply factors; firms demand factors and use those factors to produce goods, which are then supplied to households.

There's also a law of supply, which corresponds to the law of demand. The **law of supply** states the quantity supplied of a good is positively related to that good's price, other things constant. Specifically:

> *Law of supply: More of a good will be supplied the higher its price, other things constant.*

Or:

> *Law of supply: Less of a good will be supplied the lower its price, other things constant.*

Price regulates quantity supplied just as it regulates quantity demanded. Like the law of demand, the law of supply is fundamental to the invisible hand's (the market's) ability to coordinate individuals' actions.

The same graphical distinction holds for the terms *supply* and *quantity supplied* as did for the terms *demand* and *quantity demanded*. In graphical terms, *supply* refers to the entire supply curve because a supply curve tells us how much will be offered for sale at various prices. *Quantity supplied* refers to a point on a supply curve, so if you refer to movements along a supply curve, you're talking about changes in the quantity supplied. Notice how the supply curve in Exhibit 7 slopes upward to the right.

What accounts for the law of supply? When the price of a good rises, individuals and firms can rearrange their activities in order to supply more of that good to the market, substituting production of that good for production of other goods. Thus, the same psychological tendency of individuals that underlies the law of demand—their determination to want more for less—underlies the law of supply. Individuals and firms want the highest price they can get for the smallest possible quantity they can supply.

With firms, there's a second explanation of the law of supply. Assuming firms' costs are constant, a higher price means higher profits (the difference between a firm's revenues and its costs). The expectation of those higher profits leads it to increase output as price rises, which is what the law of supply states.

Quantity supplied Quantity of a good suppliers want to sell; it can be represented by a point on a supply curve.

Law of supply Quantity supplied of a good is directly related to the good's price.

4

EXHIBIT 7   The Supply Curve

The supply curve demonstrates graphically the law of supply, which states that the quantity supplied of a good is directly related to that good's price, other things held constant. The supply curve is upward sloping.

Other Things Constant   As with the law of demand, the first qualification of the law of supply is that it assumes other things are held constant. Thus, if the price of wheat rises and quantity supplied falls, you'll look for something else that changed—for example, a drought might have caused the drop in quantity supplied. Your expectations would go as follows: Had there been no drought, the quantity supplied would have increased in response to the rise in price, but because there was a drought, the supply decreased, which caused prices to rise.

As with the law of demand, the law of supply represents economists' off-the-cuff response to the question: What happens to quantity supplied if price rises? If the law seems to be violated, economists search for some other variable that has changed. As was the case with demand, these other variables that might change are called *shift factors*.

Relative Price   A second qualification is that the law of supply refers to *relative price*. The reason is that, like the law of demand, the law of supply is based on individuals' and firms' ability to substitute production of this good for another or vice versa. If the price of corn rises relative to the price of wheat, farmers will grow less wheat and more corn. If both prices rise by equal percentages, the relative price won't change and it won't be worthwhile to substitute one good for another.

The Supply Table

Remember Exhibit 4(a)'s demand table for cassette rentals. In Exhibit 8(a), columns 2 (Ann), 3 (Barry), and 4 (Charlie), we follow the same reasoning to construct a supply table for three hypothetical cassette suppliers. Each supplier follows the law of supply: when price rises, they supply more, or at least as much as they did at a lower price.

From a Supply Table to a Supply Curve

Exhibit 8(b) takes the information in Exhibit 8(a)'s supply table and translates it into a graph of Ann's supply curve. For instance, point C_A on Ann's supply curve corresponds to the information in column 2, row C. Point C_A is at a price of $1 and a quantity of 2. Notice that Ann's supply curve is upward sloping, meaning that price is positively related to quantity. Charlie's and Barry's supply curves are similarly derived.

The supply curve represents the set of *minimum prices* an individual seller will accept for various quantities of a good. The market's invisible hand stops suppliers from charging more than the market price. If suppliers could escape the market's invisible hand and charge a higher price, they would gladly do so. Unfortunately for them, and fortunately for consumers, a higher price encourages other suppliers to begin selling cassettes. Competing suppliers' entry into the market places a limit on the price any supplier can charge.

ADDED DIMENSION

SUPPLY, PRODUCTION, AND PROFIT

Many goods must be produced—that is, inputs must be physically transformed before they become desirable goods. Production is complicated and requires a separate analysis before it can be integrated into our analysis. In what's called *Walrasian economics* (named after famous Swiss economist Leon Walras), the problem of production is assumed away; his is an analysis of a trading economy. This is important to recognize since it's Walrasian economics that provides the logical underpinnings for supply/demand analysis. In Walrasian economics individuals have certain goods they trade; at some prices they sell, at some (lower) prices they buy. It is in this sense that supply is simply the mirror image of demand.

An easy way to see that supply is a mirror image of demand is to think about your supply of hours of work. When we talk of work, we say you're supplying hours of work at $6 per hour. But that same supply of work can be thought of as demand for leisure time. If, at $6 an hour, you choose to work 8 hours a day, you're simultaneously choosing to keep 16 hours for yourself (24 hours a day minus the 8 hours spent working). If we talk in terms of leisure, we speak of demand for leisure; if we talk of work, we speak of supply of labor. One is simply the mirror image of the other.

Another approach to economics is *Marshallian economics* (named after Alfred Marshall, a famous English economist). Marshallian economics does include an analysis of production. It relates costs of production with what firms are willing to sell. The reason production is difficult to integrate with an analysis of supply is that with many production processes, per-unit costs fall as production increases. For example, in the 1920s Henry Ford produced a lot more model T cars than either he or any of his competitors had produced before. As he produced more, costs per unit fell and the price of cars fell. Even today many businesses will tell you that if they can increase demand for their good, their per-unit costs and their price will go down. Such examples don't violate the law of supply. Costs per unit fall because of the nature of production. As the nature of production changes, the upward-sloping supply curve shifts outward.

There's another point we should mention about supply. Sometimes students get the impression from textbooks that supply and demand simply exist—that firms can't go out, find demand curves, and start supplying. That's not a realistic picture of how the economy works. Demand curves aren't there for students or firms to see. Producing goods and supplying them inevitably involves risk and uncertainty. A company like General Motors may spend $1 billion designing a certain type of car, only to find that consumers don't like its style, or that another company has produced a car consumers like better. In that case, GM suffers a large loss.

To compensate for the potential for losses, suppliers also have the potential to make a profit on goods they sell. When the price of a good is high compared to costs of the resources used in production, expected profits are high, so more producers are encouraged to take the risk. When the price of a good is low compared to the costs, fewer firms take the risk because expected profits are low. Thus, profit is a motivating force of supply in a market economy.

The market supply curve is derived from individual supply curves in precisely the same way that the demand curve was. To emphasize the symmetry in reasoning, I've made the three suppliers quite similar to the three demanders. Ann (column 2) will supply 2 at $1; if price goes up to $2 she increases her supply to 4. Barry (column 3) begins supplying at $1 and at $3 supplies 5, the most he'll supply, regardless of how high price rises. Charlie (column 4) has only two units to supply. At a price of $3.50 he'll supply that quantity; but higher prices won't get him to supply any more.

We sum horizontally the individual supply curves to get the market supply curve. In Exhibit 8(a) (column 5), we add together Ann's, Barry's, and Charlie's supply to arrive at the market supply curve, which is graphed in Exhibit 8(b). Notice each point on it corresponds to the information in columns 1 and 5 for a particular row. For example, point *H* corresponds to a price of $3.50 and a quantity of 14.

The market supply curve's upward slope is determined by two different sources: by existing suppliers supplying more and by new suppliers entering the market. Sometimes existing suppliers may not be willing to increase their quantity supplied in response to an increase in prices, but a rise in price often brings brand new suppliers into the market. For example, a rise in teachers' salaries will have little effect on the amount of teaching current teachers do, but it will increase the number of people choosing to be teachers.

Individual and Market Supply Curves

EXHIBIT 8 (a and b)   From a Supply Table to a Supply Curve

As with market demand, market supply is determined by adding all individual supplies at a given price. Three suppliers—Ann, Barry, and Charlie—make up the market of videocassette suppliers. The total market supply is the sum of their individual supplies at each price (shown in column 5 of (a).

Each of the individual supply curves and the market supply curve have been plotted in (b). Notice how the market supply curve is the horizontal sum of the individual supply curves.

(1) Price (in dollars)	(2) Ann's supply	(3) Barry's supply	(4) Charlie's supply	(5) Market supply	Row
0.00	0	0	0	0	A
0.50	1	0	0	1	B
1.00	2	1	0	3	C
1.50	3	2	0	5	D
2.00	4	3	0	7	E
2.50	5	4	0	9	F
3.00	6	5	0	11	G
3.50	7	5	2	14	H
4.00	8	5	2	15	I

(a)

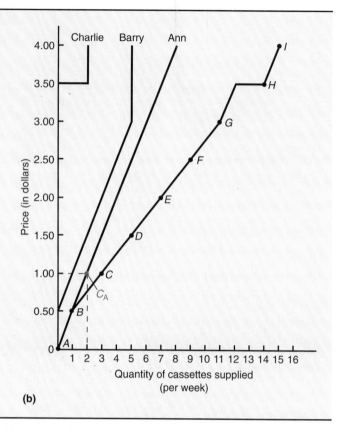

(b)

Shifts in Supply versus Movement along a Given Supply Curve

Just as there can be shifts in the demand curve resulting from shift factors, so too can there be shifts in the supply curve caused by shift factors. Important shift factors of supply include:

1. Changes in the prices of inputs used in the production of a good.
2. Changes in technology.
3. Changes in suppliers' expectations.
4. Changes in taxes and subsidies.

Shift in supply   A shift of the entire   **6**
supply curve.

Movement along a supply curve   A change in the quantity supplied due to a change in price.

These aren't all the shift factors; as was the case with demand, anything that affects supply other than price is a shift factor. Each of these shift factors will cause a **shift in supply,** whereas a change in the price causes a **movement along the supply curve.**

As with demand, it's useful to graph an example of a shift in supply and to differentiate that from a movement along the supply curve. Exhibit 9 does this. Exhibit 9(a) shows the effect of a change in the price of cassettes from $1.50 to $2.50. Point A (5, $1.50) represents the starting point. Now, for some reason, price rises to $2.50 and the quantity supplied rises to 9 (point B). Because of the price increase there's a movement along the supply curve.

Now, however, let's say that there's an improvement in technology: a new type of cassette that's cheaper to make than the existing cassette. Such an advance in technology shifts the supply curve outward to the right. Why? Because it lowers costs for each unit sold, enabling suppliers to offer more for sale at each price. An improvement in technology is shown in Exhibit 9(b). Notice that the entire supply curve shifts from S_0 to S_1, showing that for each higher price, the quantity supplied will be greater. For example, at price $1.50, 5 cassettes are supplied; but after the technological improvement, at price $1.50, 7 cassettes are supplied. The same reasoning holds for any price.

EXHIBIT 9 (a and b)   Shifts in Supply versus Movement along a Supply Curve
A change in the price of a good results in a movement along the supply curve. For example, in (**a**) if the price of videocassette rentals is $1.50, 5 cassettes would be supplied (point *A*). But if the price of cassette rentals increases for some reason, say to $2.50, suppliers would increase supply to 9 (point *B*). The change in price results in a movement along the supply curve from point *A* to point *B*.

Shift factors cause a shift in the supply curve. For example, in (**b**), at the price of $1.50, 5 cassettes would be supplied (point *A*). If some new technology were introduced, lowering the cost of producing the cassette, then suppliers would supply 7 cassettes at the price of $1.50 (point *C*). An improvement in technology results in a shift in the supply curve from S_0 to S_1.

Do we see such shifts in the supply curve often? Yes. A good example is computers. For the past 30 years, technological changes have continually shifted computers' supply curve out.

This should give you an idea of factors that shift supply, and should cement for you the difference between a shift in supply and a movement along a supply curve. But in case it didn't, here it is one more time:

Shift in supply: A change in a nonprice factor—a shift of the entire supply curve.

Movement along a supply curve: A change in the quantity supplied due to a change in price—a movement along a supply curve.

Thomas Carlyle, the English historian who dubbed economics "the dismal science," also wrote this chapter's introductory tidbit, "Teach a parrot the words *supply* and *demand* and you've got an economist." In Chapter 1, I hope I convinced you that economics is *not* dismal. In the rest of this chapter I hope to convince you that while supply and demand are important to economics, parrots don't make good economists. If students think that when they've learned the terms *supply* and *demand* they've learned economics, they're mistaken. Those terms are just labels for the ideas behind supply and demand, and it's the ideas that are important. What's relevant about supply and demand isn't the labels but how the concepts interact. For instance, what happens if quantity supplied

THE MARRIAGE OF
SUPPLY AND DEMAND

doesn't equal quantity demanded? It's in understanding the interaction of supply and demand that economics becomes interesting *and relevant*.

The First Dynamic Law of Supply and Demand

When you have a market in which neither suppliers nor demanders can organize and in which prices are free to adjust, economists have a good answer for the question: What happens if quantity supplied doesn't equal quantity demanded? If quantity supplied is greater than quantity demanded (that is, if there is **excess supply**), some suppliers won't be able to sell all their goods. Each supplier will think: Gee, if I offer to sell it for a bit less, I'll be the lucky one who sells my good; someone else will be stuck with not selling their good. But because all suppliers with excess goods will be thinking the same thing, the price in the market will fall.

The reverse is also true. Say that instead of excess supply, there's **excess demand:** quantity demanded is greater than quantity supplied. There are more demanders who want the good than there are suppliers selling the good. Let's consider what's likely to go through demanders' minds. They'll likely call long-lost friends who just happen to be sellers of that good and tell them it's good to talk to them and, by the way, don't they want to sell that . . .? Suppliers will be rather pleased that so many of their old friends have remembered them, but they'll also likely see the connection between excess demand and their friends' thoughtfulness. To stop their phones from ringing all the time, they'll likely raise their price. The reverse is true for excess supply. It's amazing how friendly suppliers become to potential demanders when there's excess supply.

Excess supply Quantity supplied is greater than quantity demanded.

Excess demand Quantity demanded is greater than quantity supplied.

First dynamic law of supply and demand When quantity demanded is **8** greater than quantity supplied, prices tend to rise; when quantity supplied is greater than quantity demanded, prices tend to fall.

This tendency for prices to rise when demand exceeds supply and for prices to fall when supply exceeds demand is a phenomenon economists call the **first dynamic law of supply and demand:**

> *When quantity demanded is greater than quantity supplied, prices tend to rise; when quantity supplied is greater than quantity demanded, prices tend to fall.*

Exhibit 10 shows the first dynamic law of supply and demand by the arrows labeled *A*. With excess supply the arrows push price down; with excess demand the arrows push price up. It's called a *dynamic law* because *dynamic* refers to change and this law refers to how prices change, not to what prices will be.

The Second Dynamic Law of Supply and Demand

How much pressure will there be for prices to rise or fall? That too will likely depend on differences between quantity supplied and quantity demanded. The greater the difference, the more pressure there is on individuals to raise or lower prices. If you're a seller (supplier) and all your old friends are calling you (there's major excess demand), you'll simply put a message on your answering machine saying, "The price has gone up 200 percent or 300 percent. If you're still interested in talking about old times, stay on the line. Otherwise, it was nice knowing you." If, however, only a couple of old friends call you (there's only minor excess demand), you'll probably raise your price only slightly. Or if you're a buyer (demander) and there's major excess supply, you'll leave the following message: "If you're trying to sell me anything, I'm broke and can only pay less than what you ask."

Second dynamic law of supply and demand The larger the difference between quantity supplied and quantity demanded, the greater the pressure for price to rise if there's excess demand or to fall if there's excess supply.

THE DYNAMIC LAWS OF SUPPLY AND DEMAND

1. When quantity demanded is greater than quantity supplied, prices tend to rise; when quantity supplied is greater than quantity demanded, prices tend to fall.
2. The larger the difference between quantity sup-

plied and quantity demanded, the faster prices will rise (if there is excess demand) or fall (if there is excess supply).
3. When quantity supplied equals quantity demanded, prices have no tendency to change.

EXHIBIT 10   The Dynamic Laws of Supply and Demand

The dynamic laws of supply and demand tell us what forces will be set in motion when the quantity supplied does not equal the quantity demanded.

Thus, the **second dynamic law of supply and demand** is:

In a market, the larger the difference between quantity supplied and quantity demanded, the greater the pressure on prices to rise (if there is excess demand) or fall (if there is excess supply).

The second dynamic law of supply and demand is demonstrated by the smaller *B* arrows in Exhibit 10. Because the difference between quantity supplied and quantity demanded is less than before, the upward and downward pressures aren't as strong.

People's tendencies to change prices exist as long as there's some difference between quantity supplied and quantity demanded. But the change in price brings the laws of supply and demand into play. As price falls, quantity supplied decreases as some suppliers leave the business (the law of supply); and as some people who originally weren't really interested in buying the good think, "Well, at this low price, maybe I do want to buy," quantity demanded increases (the law of demand). Similarly, when price rises, quantity supplied will increase (the law of supply) and quantity demanded will decrease (the law of demand).

Whenever quantity supplied and quantity demanded are unequal, price tends to change. If, however, quantity supplied and quantity demanded are equal, price will stay the same because no one will have an incentive to change it. This observation leads to the **third dynamic law of supply and demand:**

When quantity supplied equals quantity demanded, prices have no tendency to change.

The third dynamic law of supply and demand is represented by point *C* in Exhibit 10. At point *C* there's no upward or downward pressure on price.

The Third Dynamic Law of Supply and Demand

Third dynamic law of supply and demand When quantity supplied equals quantity demanded, prices don't tend to change.

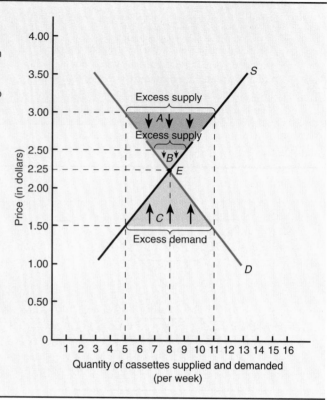

EXHIBIT 11   The Marriage of Supply and Demand

Combining supply and demand lets us see the dynamic laws of supply and demand. These laws tell us the pressures on price when there is excess demand (there is upward pressure on price) or excess supply (there is downward pressure on price). Understanding these pressures is essential to understanding how to apply economics to reality.

The Graphical Marriage of Demand and Supply

9

Exhibit 11 shows supply and demand curves for cassettes and demonstrates the operation of the dynamic laws of supply and demand. Let's consider what will happen to the price of cassettes in four cases:

1. When the price is $3;
2. When the price is $2.50;
3. When the price is $1.50;
4. When the price is $2.25.

1. When price is $3, quantity supplied is 11 and quantity demanded is only 5. Excess supply is 6. At a price of $3 individual demanders can get all they want, but most suppliers can't sell all they wish; they'll be stuck with cassettes that they'd like to sell. Suppliers will tend to offer their goods at a lower price and demanders, who see plenty of suppliers out there, will bargain harder for an even lower price. Both these forces will push the price as indicated by the *A* arrows in Exhibit 11.

2. When price falls from $3 to $2.50, the pressures are the same kind as in (1), only they're weaker, because excess supply is smaller. There aren't as many dissatisfied suppliers searching for ways to sell their cassettes. Generally, the rate at which prices fall depends on the size of the gap between quantity supplied and quantity demanded. This smaller pressure is shown by the *B* arrows in Exhibit 11.

Now let's start from the other side.

3. Say price is $1.50. The situation is now reversed. Quantity supplied is 5 and quantity demanded is 11. Excess demand is 6. Now it's demanders who can't get what they want and suppliers who are in the strong bargaining position. The pressures will be on price to rise in the direction of the *C* arrows in Exhibit 11.

4. At $2.25, price is at its equilibrium: quantity supplied equals quantity demanded. Suppliers offer to sell 8 and demanders want to buy 8, so there's no pressure on price to rise or fall. Price will tend to remain where it is (point *E* in Exhibit 11).

The concept of equilibrium appears often throughout this text. You need to understand what equilibrium is and what it isn't. The concept itself comes from physics—classical mechanics. To say something is in **equilibrium** is to say that the dynamic forces pushing on it cancel each other out. For example, a book on a desk is in equilibrium because the upward force exerted on the book by the desk equals the downward pressure exerted on the book by gravity. In supply and demand analysis, equilibrium means that the upward pressure on price is exactly offset by the downward pressure on price. **Equilibrium price** is the price toward which the invisible hand drives the market.

So much for what equilibrium is. Now let's consider what it isn't.

First, equilibrium isn't inherently good or bad. It's simply a state in which dynamic pressures offset each other. Some equilibria are awful. Say two countries are engaged in a nuclear war against each other and both sides are blown away. An equilibrium will have been reached, but there's nothing good about it.

Second, equilibrium isn't a state of the world. It's a characteristic of the framework you use to look at the world. A framework for looking at the world is called a **model.** The same situation could be seen as an equilibrium in one framework and as a disequilibrium in another. Say you're describing a car that's speeding along at 100 miles an hour. That car is changing position relative to objects on the ground. Its movement could be, and generally is, described as if it were in disequilibrium. However, if you consider this car relative to another car going 100 miles an hour, the cars could be modeled as being in equilibrium because their positions relative to each other aren't changing.

Understanding that equilibrium is a characteristic of the framework of analysis, not of the real world, is important in applying economic models to reality. For example, in the preceding description I said equilibrium occurs where supply equals demand. In a model where the invisible hand is the only force operating, that's true. In the real world, however, other forces—political and social forces—are operating. These will likely push price away from that supply/demand equilibrium. Were we to consider a model that included all these forces—political, social, and economic—equilibrium would be likely to exist where supply isn't equal to demand. In the real world, the invisible hand, foot, and handshake often work in different directions and vary in strength. For example:

· In agricultural markets, farmers use political pressure (the invisible foot) to obtain higher than supply/demand equilibrium prices. Generally they succeed so agricultural prices rise above the supply/demand equilibrium price. The laws of supply and demand assume no political pressures on prices.

· In labor markets, social pressures often offset economic pressures and prevent unemployed individuals from accepting work at lower wages than currently employed workers (the invisible handshake). Similarly, when there's a strike, social pressures prevent people who don't have jobs from taking jobs strikers have left. People who do take those jobs are called names like *scab* or *strike-breaker,* and they don't like those names. A pure supply and demand model, though, assumes everyone who wants a job will try to become a scab.

· In product markets, suppliers conspire to limit entry by other suppliers. They work hard to get Congress to establish tariffs and make restrictive regulations (the invisible foot). They also devise pricing strategies that scare off other suppliers and allow them to hold their prices higher than a supply/demand equilibrium. A pure supply and demand model assumes no conspiring at all.

Equilibrium

Equilibrium Dynamic forces affecting a concept or an object cancel each other out.

Equilibrium price Price toward which the invisible hand drives the market.

Model Framework for looking at the world.

PUBLIC CHOICE AND RENT-SEEKING ECONOMIC MODELS

Economics is a developing discipline, so the models used in one time period aren't necessarily the models used in another. In their research, economists debate which models are best and how to integrate more insights into their existing models.

Two groups of economists who've recently pushed back the frontiers of economics are the *public choice economists* and the *neo-classical political economists*. Public choice economists, led by Gordon Tullock and James Buchanan, argue that the political dimension must be part of economists' models. To integrate the political dimension, they apply economic analysis to politics and consider how economic forces affect the laws that are enacted and how, in turn, those laws affect economics. Their work was instrumental in leading to the invisible foot metaphor discussed in Chapter 1, and won James Buchanan a Nobel prize in 1986.

Neo-classical political economists share with public choice economists the view that the political dimension must be part of economists' models, and have developed a variety of formal models that significantly modify earlier models' predictions. Many of their models focus on rent seeking (how suppliers can restrict supply and thereby create rents for themselves). *Rent* is defined as an income earned when supply is restricted. For example, say a carpenter's union limits the number of people who can do carpentry. The supply of carpenters will decrease and existing carpenters will earn a higher wage that includes a rent component. Rents can be created either by using politics (the invisible foot) or by special agreements (the invisible handshake). Hence, neo-classical political economists are at the forefront of the movement to broaden economic analysis.

Although the formal analyses of both these groups haven't been adopted by the majority of economists, other economists often use their informal results and insights. Throughout this book I'll discuss these and other groups' views, but I'll focus on the mainstream model that the majority of economists use.

• In the housing rental markets, consumers often organize politically and get local government to enact rent controls (ceilings on rents that can be charged for apartments). Here's an example of government (the invisible foot) putting downward pressure on price.

If social and political forces were included in the analysis, they'd provide a counterpressure to the dynamic forces of supply and demand. The result would be an equilibrium with continual excess supply or excess demand. The invisible hand pushing toward a supply/demand equilibrium would be thwarted by other invisible forces pushing in the other direction.

A formal political/social/economic model that included all these forces simultaneously would be complicated, and economists are still working on perfecting one. Meanwhile economists, in their formal analysis, focus on a pure supply and demand model in which only the invisible hand is operating. That model lets you see clearly the economic forces at work. When economists apply the pure supply/demand model to reality, however, they discuss the effects of these other forces.

In this book I'll introduce you to both the formal model (in which only market forces are operating) and the informal model (in which all forces are operating).

Changes in Supply and Demand

To ensure that you understand the supply and demand graphs throughout the book and can apply them, let's go through three examples. Exhibit 12 deals with an increase in demand; Exhibit 13 deals with a decrease in supply.

Let's consider again the supply and demand for cassette rentals. In Exhibit 12, the supply is S_0 and initial demand is D_0. They meet at an equilibrium price of $2.25 and a quantity demanded of 8 (point A). Now say demand for cassette rentals increases from D_0 to D_1. At a price of $2.25, the quantity of cassette rentals supplied will be 8 and the quantity demanded will be 10; excess demand of 2 exists.

As the first dynamic law of supply and demand dictates, the excess demand pushes prices upward in the direction of the small arrows, decreasing the quantity demanded. As it does so, movement takes place along both the supply curve and the demand curve. The first dynamic law of supply and demand tells us that price will be pushed up.

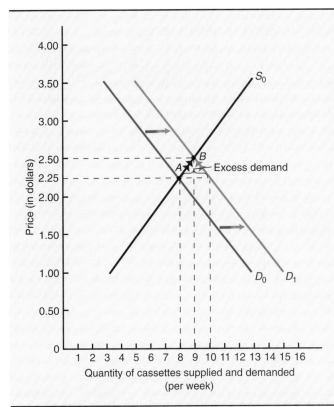

EXHIBIT 12   Example of a Shift in Demand

When there is an increase in demand (the demand curve shifts outward), there is upward pressure on the price . If there is an increase in demand from D_0 to D_1, the quantity of cassette rentals that was demanded at a price of $2.25, 8, increases to 10, but the quantity supplied remains at 8. This excess demand tends to cause prices to rise. Eventually, a new equilibrium is reached at the price of $2.50, where the quantity supplied is 9.

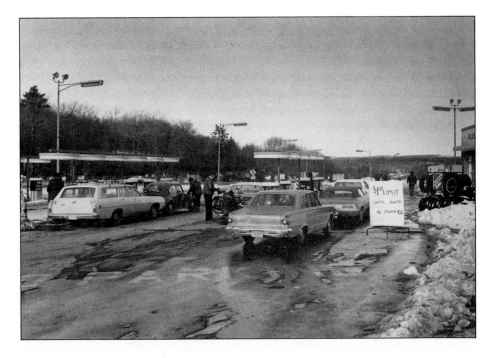

The long lines and shortages of the 1974 gas crisis are typical results of a price ceiling.   © *George Gardner/The Image Works.*

The upward push on price decreases the gap between the quantity supplied and the quantity demanded. As the gap is decreased, the upward pressure decreases, as the second dynamic law requires. But as long as that gap exists at all, price will be pushed upward until the new equilibrium price ($2.50) and new quantity (9) are reached (point *B*). At point *B* the third dynamic law of supply and demand takes hold: quantity supplied equals quantity demanded. So the market is

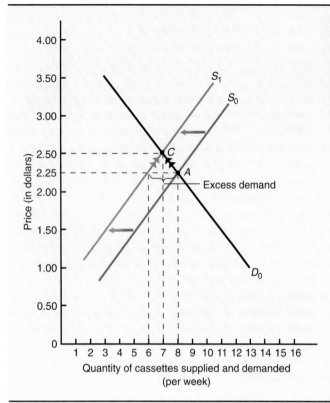

EXHIBIT 13   Example of a Shift in Supply

If supply of cassettes decreases, then the entire supply curve shifts inward to the left from S_0 to S_1. At the price of $2.25, the quantity supplied has now decreased to 6 cassettes, but the quantity demanded has remained at 8 cassettes. The excess demand tends to force the price upward. Eventually, an equilibrium is reached at the price of $2.50 and quantity 7 (point C).

in equilibrium. Notice that the adjustment is twofold: The higher price brings about equilibrium by both increasing the quantity supplied (from 8 to 9) and decreasing the quantity demanded (from 10 to 9).

Exhibit 13 begins with the same situation that we started with in Exhibit 12; the initial equilibrium quantity and price are (8, $2.25; point A). In this example, however, instead of demand increasing, let's assume supply decreases—say because some suppliers change what they like to do, and decide they will no longer supply this good. That means that the entire supply curve shifts inward to the left (from S_0 to S_1). At the initial equilibrium price of $2.25, the quantity demanded is greater than the quantity supplied. Two more cassettes are demanded than are supplied. (Excess demand = 2.)

As the dynamic laws of supply and demand require, this excess demand exerts upward pressure on price. Price is pushed in the direction of the small arrows. As the price rises, the upward pressure on price is reduced (in accord with the second dynamic law of supply and demand) but will still exist until the new equilibrium price, $2.50, and new quantity, 7, are reached. At $2.50, the quantity supplied equals the quantity demanded. The adjustment has involved a movement along the demand curve and the new supply curve. As price rises, quantity supplied is adjusted upward and quantity demanded is adjusted downward until quantity supplied equals quantity demanded where the new supply curve intersects the demand curve at point C, an equilibrium of (7, $2.50).

I leave a final example as an exercise for you. Demonstrate graphically how the price of computers could have fallen dramatically in the past 10 years, even as demand increased. (Hint: Supply has shifted even more, so even at lower prices, far more computers have been supplied than were being supplied 10 years ago.)

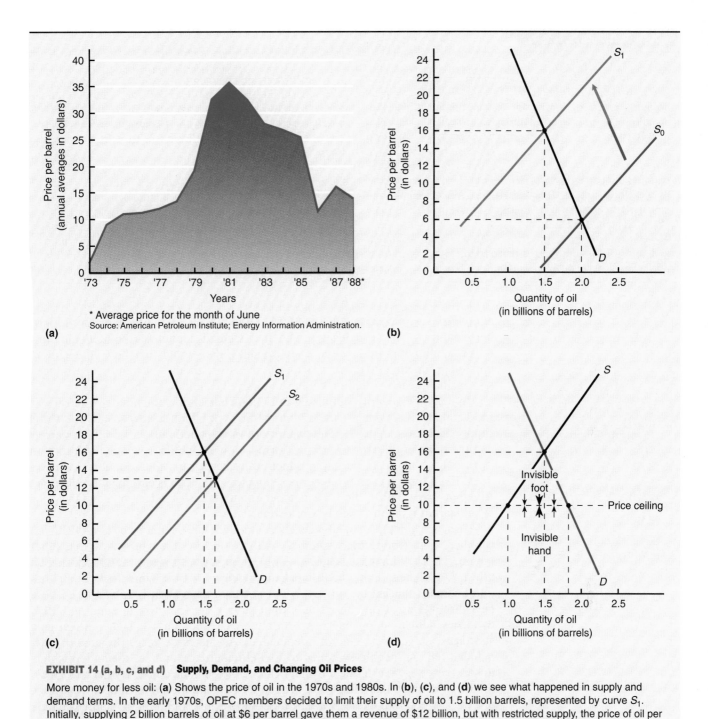

(a)

* Average price for the month of June
Source: American Petroleum Institute; Energy Information Administration.

(b)

(c)

(d)

EXHIBIT 14 (a, b, c, and d)   Supply, Demand, and Changing Oil Prices

More money for less oil: (**a**) Shows the price of oil in the 1970s and 1980s. In (**b**), (**c**), and (**d**) we see what happened in supply and demand terms. In the early 1970s, OPEC members decided to limit their supply of oil to 1.5 billion barrels, represented by curve S_1. Initially, supplying 2 billion barrels of oil at $6 per barrel gave them a revenue of $12 billion, but with restricted supply, the price of oil per barrel rose to $16, giving OPEC members a revenue of $24 billion (1.5 billion x $16). New exploration shifted the supply curve out, lowering price as in (**c**). In (**d**) we see the effect of a price ceiling.

Now that we've discussed the basic analysis and its limitations, we can apply the supply/demand model to a real-world situation.

Exhibit 14(a) shows the changes in the price of oil from 1973 to 1988. Exhibit 14(b) demonstrates the supply/demand forces associated with those changes in the period 1973–81, during which the price of oil went up substantially. Prior to the 1970s its price had been relatively stable. In the early 1970s at a series of meetings

SUPPLY AND DEMAND
IN ACTION: OIL PRICE
FLUCTUATIONS

In Chapter 1, I distinguished between an economic force and a market force. Economic forces are operative in all aspects of our lives; market forces are economic forces that are allowed to be expressed through a market. My examples in this chapter are of market forces—of goods sold in a market—but supply and demand can also be used to analyze situations in which economic, but not market, forces operate. An economist who is adept at this is Gary Becker of the University of Chicago. He has applied supply and demand analysis to a wide range of issues, even the supply of and demand for children.

Becker doesn't argue that children should be bought and sold. But he does argue that economic considerations play a large role in people's decisions on how many children

to have. In farming communities, children can be productive early in life; by age six or seven, they can work on a farm. In an advanced industrial community, children provide pleasure, but generally don't contribute productively to family income. Even getting them to help around the house can be difficult.

Becker argues that since the price of having children is lower for a farming society than for an industrial society, farming societies will have more children per family. Quantity of children demanded will be larger. And that's what we find. Developing countries that rely primarily on farming often have three, four, or more children per family. Industrial societies average fewer than two children per family.

of countries who were members of OPEC (the Organization of Petroleum Exporting Countries), some delegates who had studied economics pointed out how OPEC could get more for less. They argued if they could somehow all decide to limit oil production (to decrease supply), then even though each of them produced less, actually each would make more money. Exhibit 14(b) shows why.

Initially the quantity supplied was 2 billion barrels and the price per barrel was $6. Total OPEC revenue was $12 billion ($6 × 2 billion). Now say OPEC shifts supply back from S_0 to S_1. The quantity of oil supplied falls to 1.5 billion barrels and the price of oil rises to $16 per barrel. Now members' revenue is $24 billion ($16 × 1.5 billion). In cutting production by 25 percent they double their revenues! Even though each producer is selling less oil, each is earning more income. And that's what OPEC did. The member countries restricted supply, and the price of oil started rising drastically worldwide.

The high price provoked a reaction among a large number of non-OPEC oil suppliers (and from OPEC members who could hide their oil sales from other members). They increased their quantity of oil supplied significantly, causing an upward movement along the original supply curve. At the same time oil exploration boomed, shifting the oil supply curve back out to S_2 in Exhibit 14(c). These new discoveries of oil shifted oil's total supply curve outward, even as OPEC countries held their oil back. As supply was responding to higher prices and shortages, so too was quantity demanded. As the price rose, the quantity demanded fell. As people switched to fuel-efficient cars and set their thermostats lower, there was a resulting movement along the demand curve. By the late 1980s, the invisible hand had effectively broken OPEC's limitation on supply, and price fell to between $12 and $15 a barrel as shown in Exhibit 14(c), approximately where it would have been (after adjustment for inflation) had OPEC never organized to limit supply.

Before these adjustments occurred, the sudden jump in oil price caused political reactions within the United States. The invisible foot put downward pressure on the price of oil in the United States. It led to a **price ceiling** (a government-imposed limit on how high a price can be charged). This political pressure prevented the price of oil from rising to the full new supply/demand equilibrium. The result was an oil shortage. The quantity of oil demanded was greater than the quantity of oil supplied. There were dire predictions that people would freeze to death or wouldn't be allowed to use energy-intensive products.

Exhibit 14(d) shows how such a price ceiling will cause such shortages. The price ceiling is $10, even though the supply/demand equilibrium price is $16. Quantity supplied is 1 billion barrels, while quantity demanded is 1.8 billion barrels. The difference between quantity supplied and quantity demanded reflects

Price ceiling Government-imposed limit on how high a price may be set.

the number of people going without oil. When the invisible foot or invisible handshake prevents price from rising to the equilibrium price, the invisible hand doesn't disappear. It places upward pressure on price while the invisible foot places downward pressure on price. In this case the invisible hand won out, and the price ceilings were eliminated, allowing the price of oil to rise substantially. The rise in price eliminated the shortages.

It isn't only price ceilings that have predictable effects. **Price floors** (government-imposed limits on how low a price can be charged) also do. A price floor such as the minimum wage or a government-imposed mandatory price for milk creates a situation of excess supply. The quantity supplied exceeds the quantity demanded, and some way must be found to ration the available quantity demanded among the suppliers. We'll deal with these issues in detail later.

Price floor Government-imposed limit on how low a price may be set.

CONCLUSION

Throughout the book I'll be presenting examples of supply and demand. So I'll end this chapter here because its intended purposes have been served. What were those intended purposes? First, the discussion and examples should have exposed you to enough economic terminology and economic thinking to allow you to proceed to my more complicated examples. Second, the discussion should also have set your mind to work putting the events around you into a supply/demand framework. Doing that will give you new insights into the events that shape all our lives. Finally, this chapter should have made you wary of applying supply/demand analysis to the real world without considering the other invisible forces out there battling the invisible hand.

KEY POINTS

- The law of demand (supply): More (less) of a good will be demanded (supplied) the lower its price, other things constant. **1** **4**
- A market demand (supply) curve is the sum of all individual demand (supply) curves. **1** **4**
- A shift in quantity demanded (supplied) is a movement along the demand (supply) curve. A shift in demand (supply) is a shift of the entire demand (supply) curve. **3** **6**
- The laws of supply and demand refer to relative prices; they hold true because individuals can substitute. **7**

- When quantity demanded is greater than quantity supplied, prices tend to rise. When quantity supplied is greater than quantity demanded, prices tend to fall. **8**
- When quantity supplied equals quantity demanded, prices have no tendency to change. **8**
- When demand shifts out, the equilibrium price rises. When supply shifts out, the equilibrium price falls. **8** **9**

KEY TERMS

demand *(35)*
demand curve *(36)*
equilibrium *(51)*
equilibrium price *(51)*
excess demand *(48)*
excess supply *(48)*
factors of production *(42)*
firms *(42)*

first dynamic law of supply and demand *(48)*
law of demand *(35)*
law of supply *(43)*
market demand curve *(39)*
model *(51)*
movement along the demand curve *(41)*

movement along the supply curve *(46)*
other things constant *(36)*
price ceiling *(56)*
price floor *(57)*
quantity demanded *(35)*
quantity supplied *(42)*
relative price *(37)*

second dynamic law of supply and demand *(49)*
shift factors of demand *(37)*
shift in demand *(41)*
shift in supply *(46)*
supply *(42)*
third dynamic law of supply and demand *(49)*

QUESTIONS FOR THOUGHT AND REVIEW

The number after each question represents the estimated degree of critical thinking required. (1 = almost none; 10 = deep thought.)

1. Draw a demand curve from the following demand table. *(1)*

P	Q
37	20
47	15
57	10
67	5

2. Draw a market demand curve from the following demand table. *(1)*

P	D_1	D_2	D_3	Market demand
37	20	4	8	32
47	15	2	7	24
57	10	0	6	16
67	5	0	5	10

3. It has just been reported that eating meat is bad for your health. Using supply and demand curves, demonstrate the report's likely effect on the price and quantity of steak sold in the market. *(3)*

4. New York City has had residential rent control for many years. Using supply/demand analysis, explain what effect eliminating those controls would probably have. *(4)*

5. Draw a market supply curve from the following supply table. *(1)*

P	S_1	S_2	S_3	Market supply
37	0	4	14	18
47	0	8	16	24
57	10	12	18	40
67	10	16	20	46

6. Show, using supply and demand curves, the likely effect of a minimum wage law. If you were a worker, would you support or oppose minimum wage laws? Why? *(6)*

7. Distinguish the effect of a shift factor of demand from the effect of a change in price on the demand curve. *(3)*

8. Say the United States were to legalize the sale of certain currently illegal drugs. Using supply/demand analysis, show what effect legalization would have on the price of those drugs and on the quantity bought. *(7)*

9. Mary has just stated that normally, as price rises, supply will increase. Her teacher grimaces. Why? *(5)*

10. Supply/demand analysis states that equilibrium occurs where quantity supplied equals quantity demanded, but in U.S. agricultural markets quantity supplied almost always exceeds quantity demanded. How can this be? *(5)*

PROBLEMS AND EXERCISES

1. You're given the following individual demand tables for comic books.

Price	John	Liz	Alex
$ 2	4	36	24
4	4	32	20
6	0	28	16
8	0	24	12
10	0	20	8
12	0	16	4
14	0	12	0
16	0	8	0

   a. Determine the market demand table.
   b. Graph the individual and market demand curves.
   c. If the current market price is $4, what's total market demand? What happens to total market demand if price rises to $8?

   d. Say that an advertising campaign increases demand by 50 percent. Illustrate graphically what will happen to the individual and market demand curves.

2. Draw hypothetical supply and demand curves for tea. Show how the equilibrium price and quantity will be affected by each of the following occurrences:
   a. Bad weather wreaks havoc with the tea crop.
   b. A medical report implying tea is bad for your health is published.
   c. A technological innovation lowers the cost of producing tea.
   d. Consumers' income falls.
   e. The government imposes a $5 price ceiling on tea.
   f. The government imposes a $15 price ceiling on tea.
   g. The government imposes a $15 price floor on tea.

3

The Economic Organization of Society

In capitalism man exploits man;
in socialism it's the other way 'round.

Abba Lerner

After you read this chapter, you should be able to:

1

List three central questions that every
economy must answer.

2

Define capitalism and socialism.

3

Explain how capitalist and socialist
economies answer the three central
economic questions.

4

Give a brief overview of the history of
economic systems: how feudalism begat
mercantilism which begat capitalism, and
how capitalism and socialism continue to
evolve.

5

Explain how markets coordinate economic
decisions.

6

Explain what is meant by the phrase
"Socialism is the longest path from
capitalism to capitalism."

The scene is the People's Court in Bucharest, Romania, December 25, 1989. The newly deposed dictator of Romania, Nicolae Ceausescu, and his wife, Elena, are on trial for crimes against the state.

Judge: *What have you done for society?*

Nicolae Ceausescu: *I built hospitals.*

Judge: *What about the food shortage?*

Nicolae Ceausescu: *The people have 440 pounds of corn a year.*

Judge: *You destroyed the Romanian people and their economy.*

Elena Ceausescu: *I gave my entire life for our people.*

Judge: *We condemn the two of you to death.*

On that same day, Elena and Nicolae Ceausescu were executed by a firing squad for economic crimes against the Romanian people.

The political and economic turmoil in socialist countries have been much in the news in the 1990s. And with good reason. The Soviet Union is no more; most republics of the former Soviet Union have forsaken socialism and are struggling to introduce a market economy. These events involve some of the most far-reaching changes in the nature of economic systems that the world has seen since the 1930s—changes so major that some social scientists have called the developments "the end of history." Such a sweeping statement is more than a tad too strong, but the developments are certainly important. What's more, they provide me with a good vehicle to introduce some broader issues involving economic systems and the workings of markets. The next two chapters consider the evolution of economies and the changes that socialist economies are currently going through. In this chapter I address the evolution of economies in its broadest sweep to give you a sense of the nature of capitalism and socialism, the two most important economic systems in today's world. Then, in the final chapter of the book—after you've learned more about economic thinking and insights—I consider more explicitly the workings of a socialist economy and discuss some of the problems that led to the current upheavals in socialist countries.

ECONOMIC SYSTEMS: CAPITALISM AND SOCIALISM

Economic system Set of economic institutions that determines important economic decisions.

In Chapter 1, I discussed how an **economic system** (the set of economic institutions that determine a country's important economic decisions) works via the interaction of three invisible forces: the invisible hand (economic forces), invisible foot (political forces), and invisible handshake (social forces).

An economic system is closely tied to a political system through which people decide what their society desires. In a democracy, voting procedures determine society's will. In an autocracy, a ruling individual or group of individuals decides what society's desires are. Besides determining what a society wants, an economic system must see that individuals' decisions about what they do are coordinated with what society wants, and with what other individuals do. Coordination is necessary so that the whats that the whos want, match the whats that are available.

Before we discuss how the invisible forces operate, we need to consider what people can reasonably expect from an economic system. They can expect it to produce the goods that people want in a reasonably efficient way and to distribute those goods reasonably fairly. Put another way, people can reasonably expect that an economic system will decide:

1. *What* to produce.
2. *How* to produce it.
3. *For whom* to produce it.

These three decisions that an economic system must make are necessarily vague, because what people expect is vague. But when people feel that an economic system hasn't given them what they want, the result isn't always so vague—as the Ceausescus found out.

In making their three decisions, societies have a problem. Usually what individuals, on their own, want to do isn't consistent with what "society" wants them to do. Society would often like people to consider what's good for society and to fit what's good for themselves into what society wants them to do. For example, say society has garbage and that society determines that your neighborhood is the best place to set up a garbage dump. Even if you agree a garbage dump is needed, you probably won't want it in your neighborhood. This **NIMBY (Not In My Back Yard)** attitude has become familiar in the 1990s.

NIMBY **N**ot **I**n **M**y **B**ack **Y**ard. Phrase used by people who approve of a project but don't want it built near them.

Another area in which individual goals and social goals come into conflict is in producing and consuming goods. Individuals generally like to consume much more than they like to produce, so society has the problem of scarcity. It must provide incentives for people to produce more and consume less. It's a sure sign that an economic system isn't working when there are important things that need to be done, but many people are sitting around doing nothing because the system doesn't provide individuals incentive to do that work.

How hard is it to make the three decisions I've listed? Imagine for a moment the problem of living in a family: the fights, arguments, and questions that come up. "Do I have to do the dishes?" "Why can't I have piano lessons?" "Bobby got a new sweater. How come I didn't?" "Mom likes you best." Now multiply the size of the family by millions. The same fights, the same arguments, the same questions—only for society the problems are millions of times more complicated than for one family.

How do you solve these complicated coordination problems? Do you create an organization to tell people what to do and when to do it? Or do you let people do what they want, subject to a set of rules? The two main economic systems the world has used in the past 50 years—capitalism and socialism—answer these questions differently.

Capitalism

Capitalism is an economic system based upon private property and the market in which, in principle, individuals decide how, what, and for whom to produce. Under capitalism, individuals are encouraged to follow their own self-interest, while market forces of supply and demand are relied upon to coordinate economic activity. Distribution is to each individual according to his or her ability, effort, and inherited property.

Capitalism Economic system based on private property and the market.

Reliance upon market forces doesn't mean that political, social, and historical forces play no role in coordinating economic decisions, because the other forces influence how the market works. For a market to exist, **private property rights** (in which exclusive control over an asset or a right is given to a private individual or firm) must be allocated and defended by government. The concept of private ownership must exist and must be accepted by individuals in society. When you say, "This car is mine," it means that it is unlawful for someone else to take it. If someone takes it without your permission, he or she is subject to punishment through the legal system.

Private property rights Exclusive control of an asset or a right by a private individual or a firm.

Markets work through a system of rewards and payments. If you do something, you get paid for doing that something; if you get something, you pay for that something. How much you get is determined by how much you give. This relationship seems fair to most people. But there are instances when it doesn't seem fair. Say someone is unable to work. Should that person not get anything? How about Joe down the street who was given $10 million by his parents? Is it fair that he gets lots of toys like Corvettes and skiing trips to Aspen, and doesn't have to work, while the rest of us have to work 40 hours a week and maybe go to school at night?

We'll consider those questions about fairness in a later chapter. For now, all I want to present is the underlying concept of fairness that capitalism embodies: "Them that works, gets; them that don't, starve."[1] In capitalism, individuals are encouraged to follow their own self-interest.

In capitalist economies, individuals are free to do whatever they want as long as it's legal. The market is relied upon to see that what people want to get, and want to do, is consistent with what's available. If there's not enough of something to go around (if there's excess demand), its price goes up; if more of something needs to get done, the price given to individuals willing to do it goes up. If something isn't wanted or doesn't need to be done (if there's excess supply), its price goes down. Under capitalism, fluctuations in prices coordinate individuals' wants.

Chapters 1 and 2 told how the market works. By almost all accounts capitalism has been an extraordinarily successful economic system. Since much of this book will be devoted to explaining capitalist economies' success, and since capitalism is probably somewhat familiar to you already, let's discuss socialism first.

Socialism

Socialism Economic system based on government ownership.

2

Socialism is an economic system based upon government ownership. Under socialism individuals are encouraged to act for the society's benefit. Government planning, rather than the market, is relied upon to coordinate economic activity. Distribution is supposed to be determined by need.

Many of the countries that were socialist in the 1980s shown in Exhibit 1 are undergoing major changes. Some economists argue that socialism self-destructed because it did not offer acceptable answers to the questions an economic system must address. They claim socialism didn't provide individuals with incentives to produce enough. Soon, they say, the world will have only one economic system: capitalism. Other economists argue socialism is not dead; it is simply in a transition period during which it's redefining itself.

Because socialism is in such a state of transition, defining it precisely is difficult, so let's concentrate on what I call *traditional socialism,* socialism as it was defined in the three or four decades before 1990. Traditional socialism uses administrative control or central planning to answer the questions *what, how,* and *for whom.* In a traditional socialist economic system, government planning boards set society's goals and then give individuals directives as to how to achieve those goals. Recent reforms in countries that still have socialist economies, such as China, have reduced the government's role and increased the market's role, but even in China government planning still plays a major role in the what, how, and for whom decisions.

You can best understand the idea behind socialism by thinking about how decisions are made in a family. In most families, decisions about who gets what are determined by usually benevolent parents. When Sabin gets a new coat and his sister Sally doesn't, it's because Sabin needs a coat while Sally already has two coats that fit her and are in good condition. Victor may be slow as molasses, but from his family he still gets as much as his superefficient brother Jerry. In fact, Victor may get more than Jerry because he needs extra help.

Markets have little role in most families. In my family, when food is placed on the table we don't bid on what we want, with the highest bidder getting the food. In my family every person can eat all he or she wants, although if one child eats

---

[1] How come the professor gets to use rotten grammar but screams when he sees rotten grammar in your papers? Well, that's fairness for you. Actually, I should say a bit more about writing style. All writers are expected to know correct grammar; if they don't, they don't deserve to be called writers. Once one knows grammar, one can individualize his or her writing style, breaking the rules of grammar where the meter and flow of the writing require it. In college you're still proving that you know grammar so, in papers handed in to your teacher, you shouldn't break the rules of grammar until you've proven to the teacher that you know them.

EXHIBIT 1   Socialist Countries in Transition

This map shows the most important formerly traditional socialist economies that are now going through major transitions. China and the former USSR were the largest socialist economies, although there were a number of socialist countries in Eastern Europe, Africa, and Asia.
Source: *CIA World Fact Book.*

more than a fair share, that child gets a lecture from me on the importance of sharing—of seeing to it that everyone has already had a fair share before you take or even ask for seconds. "Be thoughtful; be considerate. Think of others first," are lessons that many families try to teach.

Socialism is an economic system that tries to organize society in the same way as these families. Socialism tries to see that individuals get what they need. Socialism tries to get individuals to take other people's needs into account and to adjust their own wants in accordance with what's available. A capitalist economy expects people to be selfish; it relies on markets and competition to direct that selfishness to the general good. In socialist economies, individuals are urged to look out for the other person; if individuals' inherent goodness won't make them consider the general good, government will make them.[2]

Let's now discuss how a socialist country and a capitalist country might make different decisions about the what, how, and for whom questions. Let's consider

---

[2] As you probably surmised, the above distinction is too sharp. Even in capitalist societies one wants people to be selfless, but not too selfless. Children in capitalist societies are generally taught to be selfless at least in dealing with friends and family. The difficulties parents and societies face is finding a midpoint between the two positions: selfless but not too selfless; selfish but not too selfish.

two goods: designer jeans and whole-wheat bread. Compared to their cost in the formerly socialist countries, in most capitalist societies designer jeans are relatively inexpensive while whole-wheat bread is relatively expensive. Why? One reason is that central planners decide that designer jeans are frivolous luxury items, so they produce few or none and charge a high price for what they do produce. Similarly, they decide that whole-wheat bread is good for people, so they produce large quantities and price it exceptionally low. Planners, not supply and demand, determine what, how, and for whom to produce.

To accomplish planners' ends—getting people to do what planners think is best—requires stronger government control than exists in capitalist countries. To maintain that control, government generally owns the means of production, such as factories and machines, and tells people where they will work and how much they will receive. In traditional socialism, individuals' choices are limited and planners' choices, not individuals' choices, determine the answers to the central economic questions.

In summary, the three principal components of a socialist economy compared to a capitalist economy are:

1. Government ownership of the means of production, rather than private ownership as in capitalism. Central planners, rather than owners of businesses, decide what to produce.

2. Allocated labor. Workers are told by a government planning board where they will work and how much they will be paid, rather than workers making individual choices of employment based on wage levels in different jobs, as in capitalism.

3. Government-determined prices. Usually high prices for luxury goods and low prices for necessities, rather than market-determined prices as in capitalism.

There are, of course, markets in traditional socialist economies. Just as in capitalist economies, individuals buy goods by going to the store. The difference between stores in the two kinds of economies is that in a socialist economy the government tells the storekeeper what goods will be offered, what price to charge, and how much of a good will be delivered to the store, while in a capitalist society, the storeowner can order as much of any good as he or she wants and can charge any price he or she wants—whatever the market will bear.

Differences between Socialism and Capitalism

The difference between socialist and capitalist economies is not that socialist economies are planned economies and capitalist economies are unplanned. Both economies involve planning. **Planning** simply involves deciding—before the production takes place—what will be produced, how to produce it, and for whom it will be produced. The differences are in who does the planning, what they try to do in planning, and how the plans are coordinated.

In capitalist countries, businesspeople do the planning. Businesspeople decide that they can sell designer jeans, Nintendo games, or economics textbooks. They target their likely customers and decide how much to produce and what price to charge. In socialist countries, government planners decide what people need and should have. In an idealized capitalist society, businesses design their plans to maximize their profit; the market is relied upon to see that individual self-interest is consistent with society's interest. In an idealized socialist society, the government designs its plans to make society better. In a capitalist economy, coordination of plans is left to the workings of the market. In a socialist economy, coordination is done by government planners. Exhibit 2 summarizes how capitalism and socialism answer the three central economic questions: how, what, and for whom.

Central economic question	Capitalism's answer	Socialism's answer
What to produce?	What firms believe people want and will make the firm a profit.	What central planners believe socially beneficial.
How to produce?	Businesspeople decide how to produce efficiently, guided by their desire to make a profit.	Central planners decide, guided by what they believe is good for the country (ideally).
For whom to produce?	Distribution according to ability and inherited wealth.	Distribution according to individual's need (as determined by central planners).

EXHIBIT 2   Capitalism's and Socialism's Answers to the Three Economic Questions

Socialism and Communism

Notice that a couple of times I've used the term *society's goals*. To determine those goals, society has established political systems. In the United States, most people believe that the best political system is **democracy,** in which society's goals are determined by representatives chosen by the people in periodic elections. An alternative political system is **autocracy,** where a small group of people not subject to elections determine society's goals. Most socialist countries have been autocratic, but that need not be the case.

Communism is a type of autocratic or state socialism in which the Communist party is the small group of people, not subject to elections, who decide what society's goals are. **Pure communism** is an economic system in which everyone is selfless; that is, every individual is concerned about society's goals instead of their own private goals. In fact, no one has a private goal. Everyone's goal is the same, so there's no conflict among goals under pure communism. In theory, as individuals become more and more willing to give up their own goals and to work for society's goals, government control will become less and less necessary until finally the state (meaning government) will wither away. Pure communism has never actually existed, but it was the stated goal of many socialist societies controlled by the Communist party. These countries have often been called *communist* rather than *socialist* by the popular press and in everyday speech.

People's resentment of autocratic control in socialist countries led to demands for democracy in the late 1980s, demands that still continue. Communists justify their political control as being a necessary part of a transition to pure communism. Communists argue that capitalist society is divided into two classes: business owners (capitalists) and workers. They argue that in reality business owners control democratic governments and that communists must take control over the government in order to stop business owners from exploiting workers. When the transition period that the communists say will take place under their control has been successfully completed, the Communist party will have served its purpose and it and the state, or government it controlled, will "wither away."

The distribution of wealth in a true communist system was to be "from each according to his ability, to each according to his need." When this ideal situation had been accomplished, the Communist party would be seen as society's savior rather than as an autocratic governing group. That ideal distribution and that ideal situation have never happened. By the late 1980s people in most socialist countries saw their communist rulers as oppressors, not saviors. Distribution was not "to each according to his needs"; it was to each according to his connections with the Communist party. People demanded democratic elections and multiparty political systems. Changes are now taking place, and economists are watching carefully to see what type of economic system these countries ultimately choose.

Communism Type of autocratic or state socialism in which a small unelected Communist party decides society's goals.

Pure communism Economic system in which everyone willingly puts the common good first.

They may have overthrown their autocratic communist political systems, but some of them may choose to maintain socialist economic systems.

Evolving Economic Systems

4

Capitalism and socialism have not existed forever. Capitalism came into existence in the mid-1700s; socialism in its traditional form came into existence in the early 1900s.

Both capitalism and socialism have changed over the years, and a look at their evolution will give us a good sense of the struggle among the invisible forces to dominate our lives. In the 1930s, during the Great Depression, capitalist countries integrated a number of what might be called *socialist institutions* with their existing institutions. Distribution was no longer, even in theory, only according to ability; need also played a role. Government's economic role in capitalist societies increased, and some of the how, what, and for whom decisions were transferred from the market to the government. For example, most capitalist nations established a welfare system and social security system providing an economic safety net for people whose incomes were inadequate for their needs.

The 1980s saw the reverse process take place, with socialism integrating some capitalist institutions with its existing institutions. Market sectors in socialist countries expanded, government's economic importance decreased, and some how, what, and for whom decisions were transferred from government to the market. Instead of being assigned jobs by the government, workers were often allowed to choose jobs themselves, and some firms were allowed to produce independently of planners' decisions. Even in cases where production decisions weren't transferred, socialist planning boards used market principles more and more in making their decisions.

The result has been a blending of economic systems and a blurring of the distinctions between capitalism and socialism. If the trend toward use of market mechanisms in socialist countries continues, in the 21st century there may be only

Soviet people happily tearing down a statue of Lenin, which they saw as a symbol of communism. *Reuters/Bettmann*

one general type of economic structure. It won't be pure socialism and it won't be pure capitalism. It will be a blend of the two.

For students of history the recent changes in economic systems are not surprising. Economic systems are in a continual state of evolution. To understand recent movements in socialist countries and to put market institutions in perspective, in the next section I briefly consider the history and nature of economic systems.

Remember the distinction between market and economic forces: Economic forces have always existed—they operate in all aspects of our lives; but market forces have not always existed. Markets are social creations societies use to coordinate individuals' actions. Markets developed, sometimes spontaneously, sometimes by design, because they offered a better life for at least some—and usually a large majority of—individuals in a society.

To understand why markets developed, it is helpful to look briefly at the history of the economic systems from which our own system descended.

Let's go back in time to the year 1000 when Europe had no nation–states as we now know them. There was no coordinated central government, no unified system of law, no national patriotism, no national defense, although there was a strong religious institution simply called the Church that fulfilled some of these roles. There were few towns; most individuals lived in walled manors or "estates." These manors "belonged to" the "lord of the manor."[3] I say "belonged to" rather than "were owned by" because most of the empires or federations at that time were not formal nation–states that could organize, administer, and regulate ownership. There were no documents or deeds giving ownership of the land to an individual. Instead there was tradition, and in normal times nobody questioned the lord's right to the land. The land "belonged to" the lord because the land "belonged to" him—that's the way it was.

Because there was no central nation–state, the manor served many functions a nation–state would have served had it existed. The lord provided protection, often within a walled area surrounding the manor house or, if the manor was large enough, a castle. He also provided administration and decided disputes. He also decided *what* would be done, *how* it would be done, and *who* would get what, but these decisions were limited. In the same way that the land belonged to the lord because that's the way it always had been, what people did and how they did it were determined by what they always had done. Tradition ruled the manor more than the lord did.

The Life of a Serf   Individuals living on the land were called *serfs*. What serfs did was determined by what their fathers had done. If the father was a farmer, the son was a farmer. A woman followed her husband and helped him do what he did. That was the way it always had been and that's the way it was—tradition again.

Most serfs were farmers, and surrounding the manor were fields of about a half acre each. Serfs were tied by tradition to their assigned plots of land; according to tradition, they could not leave those plots and had to turn over a portion of their harvest to the lord every year. How much they had to turn over varied from manor to manor, but payments of half the total harvest were not unheard of. In return, the lord provided defense and organized the life of the manor—boring as it was. Thus, there was a type of trade between the serf and the lord, but it was nonnegotiable and did not take place through a market.

---

[3] Occasionally the "lord" was a lady, but not often.

THE HISTORY OF ECONOMIC SYSTEMS

Feudal Society: Rule of the Invisible Handshake

6700 B.C.	First known coins (Iran).
3600 B.C.	First system of taxation (Mesopotamia).
2100 B.C.	First welfare system (Egypt).
2000 B.C.	Coins in general use.
2000 B.C.–500 A.D.	International trade flourishes.
301 B.C.	First wage and price controls (Emperor Diocletian of Rome).
100 B.C.	First corporation (Rome).
105 A.D.	Chinese invent paper (a cheap substance to replace parchment).
700–1400	Development of feudal estates.
1275	Development of tariffs in England.
1400–1800	End of feudal estates and development of private property and wage workers.
1600–1800	Mercantilism and state control of economic activity.
1700s	Development of paper money (France).
1750–1900	Industrial Revolution.
1760–1800	Enclosure movement in England, solidifying private property and market economy.
1776	Publication of Adam Smith's *Wealth of Nations*.
1867	Publication of Karl Marx's *Das Kapital*.
1860–1960	Development of social security and unemployment insurance (Germany).
1935–1970	Integration of socialist institutions into capitalism.
1988 onward	Socialist economies in upheaval adopt markets and capitalist institutions.

Feudalism Political system divided into small communities in which a few powerful people protect those who are loyal to them.

Problems of a Tradition-Based Society   This system, known as **feudalism,** developed about the 8th and 9th centuries and lasted until about the 15th century, though in isolated countries such as Russia it continued well into the 19th century, and in all European countries its influence lingered for hundreds of years (as late as about 140 years ago in some parts of Germany). Such a long-lived system must have done some things right, and feudalism did: it answered the what, how, and for whom questions in an acceptable way.

But a tradition-based society has problems. In a traditional society, because someone's father was a baker, the son must also be a baker, and because a woman was a homemaker, she wouldn't be allowed to be anything but a homemaker. But what if Joe Blacksmith, Jr., the son of Joe Blacksmith, Sr., is a lousy blacksmith and longs to knead dough, while Joe Baker, Jr., would be a superb blacksmith but hates making pastry? Tough. Tradition dictated who did what. In fact, tradition probably arranged things so that we will never know whether Joe Blacksmith, Jr., would have made a superb baker.

As long as a society doesn't change too much, tradition operates reasonably well, although not especially efficiently, in holding the society together. However, when a society must undergo change, tradition does not work. Change means that the things that were done before no longer need to be done, while new things do need to get done. But if no one has traditionally done these new things, then they don't get done. If the change is important but a society can't figure out some way for the new things to get done, the society falls apart. That's what happened to feudal society. It didn't change when change was required.

Some individuals in feudal society just couldn't take life on the manor, and they set off on their own. Because there was no organized police force, they were unlikely to be caught and forced to returned to the manor. Going hungry, being killed, or both, however, were frequent fates of an escaped serf. One place to which serfs could safely escape, though, was a town or city—the remains of what in Roman times had been thriving and active cities. These cities, which had been

TRADITION AND TODAY'S ECONOMY

■ n a tradition-based society, the invisible handshake (the social and cultural forces embodied in history) gives a society inertia (a tendency to resist change) which predominates over economic and political forces.

> *"Why did you do it that way?"*
>
> *"Because that's the way we've always done it."*

Tradition-based societies had markets, but those were peripheral, not central, to economic life. In feudal times what was produced, how it was produced, and for whom it was produced were primarily decided by tradition.

In today's U.S. economy, the market plays the central role in economic decisions. But that doesn't mean that tradition is dead. As I said in Chapter 1, tradition still plays a significant role in today's society, and, in many aspects of society, tradition still overwhelms the invisible hand. Consider the following:

1. The persistent view that women should be home-makers rather than factory workers, consumers rather than producers.
2. The raised eyebrows when a man is introduced as a nurse, secretary, homemaker, or member of any other profession conventionally identified as *women's work.*
3. Society's unwillingness to permit the sale of individuals or body organs.
4. Parents' willingness to care for their children without financial compensation.

Each of these tendencies reflects tradition's influence in Western society. Some are so deep-rooted that we see them as self-evident. Some of tradition's effects we like; others we don't—but we often take them for granted. Economic forces may work against these traditions, but the fact that they're still around indicates the continued strength of tradition in our market economy.

---

decimated by plagues, plundering bands, and starvation in the preceding centuries, nevertheless remained an escape hatch for runaway serfs because they relied far less on tradition than did manors. City dwellers had to live by their wits; merchants developed who lived predominantly by trading. They were middlemen; they would buy from one group and sell to another.

Trading in towns was an alternative to the traditional feudal order because trading allowed people to have an income independent of the traditional social structure. Markets broke down tradition. Initially merchants traded using *barter* (exchange of one kind of good for another): silk and spices from the Orient for wheat, flour, and artisan products in Europe. But soon a generalized purchasing power (money) developed as a medium of exchange. Money greatly expanded the possibilities of trading because its use meant that goods no longer needed to be bartered. They could be sold for money, which could then be spent to buy other goods.

In the beginning, land was not one of the goods that could be traded, but soon the feudal lord who just had to have a silk robe but had no money was saying, "Why not? I'll sell you a small piece of land so I can buy a shipment of silk." Once land became tradeable, the traditional base of the feudal society was undermined. Tradition that can be bought and sold is no longer tradition—it's just another commodity.

Toward the end of the Middle Ages, markets went from being a side show, a fair that spiced up peoples' lives, to being the main event. Over time, some traders and merchants started to amass fortunes that dwarfed those of the feudal lords. Rich traders settled down; existing towns and cities expanded and new towns were formed. As towns grew and as fortunes shifted from feudal lords to merchants, power in society shifted to the towns. And with that shift came a change in society's political and economic structure.

As these traders became stronger politically and economically, they threw their support behind a king (the strongest lord) in the hope that the king would expand their ability to trade. In doing so they made the king even stronger. Eventually, the king became so powerful that his will prevailed over the will of the

From Feudalism to Mercantilism

Mercantilism Economic system in which government doles out the rights to undertake economic activities.

other lords and even over the will of the Church. As the king consolidated his power, nation–states as we know them today evolved. *The invisible foot—government—became an active influence on economic decision making.*

As markets grew, feudalism evolved into **mercantilism** (an economic system in which the government determines the what, how, and for whom decisions by doling out the rights to undertake certain economic activities). Political rather than social forces came to control the central economic decisions. The evolution of feudal systems into mercantilism occurred in somewhat this way: As cities and their markets grew in size and power relative to the feudal manors and the traditional economy, a whole new variety of possible economic activities developed. It was only natural that individuals began to look to the king to establish a new tradition that would determine who would do what. Individuals in particular occupations organized into groups called *guilds,* which were similar to strong labor unions today. These guilds, many of which had financed and supported the king, now expected the king and his government to protect their interests. As new economic activities, such as trading companies, developed, individuals involved in these activities similarly depended on the king for the right to trade and for help in financing and organizing their activities. For example, in 1492, when Christopher Columbus had the wild idea that by sailing west he could get to the East Indies and trade for their riches, he went to Spain's Queen Isabella and King Ferdinand for financial support.

Since many traders had played and continued to play important roles in financing, establishing, and supporting the king, the king was usually happy to protect their interests. The government doled out the rights to undertake a variety of economic activities. By the late 1400s Western Europe had evolved from a feudal to a mercantilist economy.

The mercantilist period was marked by the increased role of government, which could be classified in two ways: by the way it encouraged growth and by the way it limited growth. Government legitimized and financed a variety of activities, thus encouraging growth. But government also limited economic activity in order to protect the monopolies of those it favored, thus limiting growth. So mercantilism allowed the market to operate, but it kept the market under its control. The market was not allowed to respond freely to the laws of supply and demand.

From Mercantilism to Capitalism

Capitalists Businesspeople who have acquired large amounts of money and use it to invest in businesses.

The mercantilist period saw major growth in Western Europe, but mercantilism also unleashed new tensions within society. Like feudalism, mercantilism limited entry into economic activities. It used a different form of limitation—the invisible foot (politics) rather than the invisible handshake (social and cultural tradition)—but individuals who were excluded still felt unfairly treated.

The most significant source of tension was the different roles played by craft guilds and owners of new businesses, who were called **capitalists** or industrialists. Craft guild members were artists in their own crafts: pottery, shoemaking, and the like. New business owners destroyed the art of production by devising machines to replace hand production. Machines produced goods cheaper and faster than craftsmen.[4] The result was an increase in supply and a downward pressure on the price, which was set by government. Craftsmen didn't want to be replaced by machines. They argued that machine-manufactured goods didn't have the same quality as hand-crafted goods and that the new machines would disrupt the economic and social life of the community.

Industrialists were the outsiders with a vested interest in changing the existing system. They wanted the freedom to conduct business as they saw fit. Because of the enormous cost advantage of manufactured goods over crafted goods, a few

---

[4] Throughout this section I use *men* to emphasize that these societies were strongly male-dominated. There were almost no businesswomen. In fact, a woman had to turn over her property to a man upon her marriage, and the marriage contract was written as if she were owned by her husband!

THE RISE OF MARKETS IN PERSPECTIVE

Back in the Middle Ages, markets developed spontaneously. "You have something I want; I have something you want. Let's trade" is a basic human attitude we see in all aspects of life. Even children quickly get into trading: chocolate ice cream for vanilla, two GI Joe dolls for a ride on a motor scooter. Markets institutionalize such trading by providing a place where people know they can go to trade. New markets are continually coming into existence. Today there are markets for baseball cards, pork bellies (which become bacon and pork chops), rare coins, and so on.

Throughout history societies have tried to prevent some markets from operating because they feel those markets are ethically wrong or have undesirable side effects. Societies have the power to prevent markets. They make some kinds of markets illegal. In the United States the addictive drug market, the baby market, and the sex market, to name a few, are illegal. In socialist countries, markets in a much wider range of goods (such as clothes, cars, and soft drinks) and activities (such as private business for individual profit) have been illegal.

But, even if a society prevents the market from operating, it cannot escape the dynamic laws of supply and demand. If there's excess supply, there will be downward pressure on prices; if there's excess demand, there will be upward pressure on prices. To maintain an equilibrium in which the quantity supplied does not equal the quantity demanded, a society needs a force to prevent the invisible hand from working. In the Middle Ages that strong force was religion. The Church told people that if they got too far into the market mentality—if they followed their self-interest—they'd go to Hell.

Until recently in socialist society, the state has provided the preventive force—and in their educational system socialist countries would emphasize a more communal set of values. They taught students that a member of socialist society does not try to take advantage of other human beings but, rather, lives by the philosophy "From each according to his ability; to each according to his need."

For whatever reason—some say because true socialism wasn't really tried; others say because people's self-interest is too strong—the "from each according to his ability; to each according to his need" approach didn't work in socialist countries. They have switched (some say succumbed) to greater reliance on the market.

industrialists overcame government opposition and succeeded within the mercantilist system. They earned their fortunes and became an independent political power.

Once again the economic power base shifted, and two groups competed with each other for power—this time the guilds and the industrialists. The government had to decide whether to support the industrialists (who wanted it to loosen government's power over the country's economic affairs) or the craftsmen and guilds (who argued for strong government limitations and for maintaining traditional values of workmanship). This struggle raged in the 1700s and 1800s. But during this time, governments themselves were changing. This was the Age of Revolutions and the kings' powers were being limited by democratic reform movements—revolutions supported and financed in large part by the industrialists.

The Need for Coordination in an Economy   One argument craftsmen put forward was that coordination of the economy was necessary, the government had to be involved. If government wasn't going to coordinate economic activity, who would? To answer that question, a British moral philosopher named Adam Smith developed in his famous book, *The Wealth of Nations* (1776), the concept of the invisible hand, and used it to explain how markets could coordinate the economy without the active involvement of government. Smith wrote:

> Man has almost constant occasion for the help of his brethren, and it is in vain for him to expect it from their benevolence only. He will be more likely to prevail, if he can interest their self-love in his favour, and show them that it is for their own advantage to do for him what he requires of them. Whoever offers to another a bargain of any kind proposes to do this. Give me that which I want, and you shall have that which you want, is the meaning of every such offer; and it is in this manner that we obtain from one another the far greater part of those good offices which we stand in need of. It is not from the benevolence of the butcher, the brewer, or the baker, that we expect our dinner, but from their regard to their own interest.

We address ourselves, not to their humanity but to their self-love, and never talk to them of our own necessities but of their advantages.

Smith argued that the market's invisible hand would guide suppliers' actions toward the general good. No government coordination was necessary.

With the help of economists such as Adam Smith, the industrialists' view won out. Government pulled back from its role in guiding the economy and adopted a **laissez-faire** policy, leaving coordination of the economy to the invisible hand. (*Laissez faire*, a French term, means "Let events take their course; leave things alone.")

Laissez-faire Economic policy of leaving coordination of individuals' wants to be controlled by the market.

The Industrial Revolution   The invisible hand worked; capitalism thrived. During the **Industrial Revolution,** which began about 1750 and continued through the late 1800s, machine production increased enormously, almost totally replacing hand production. The economy grew faster than ever before. Society was forever transformed. New inventions changed all aspects of life. James Watt's steam engine (1769) made manufacturing and travel easier. Eli Whitney's cotton gin (1793) changed the way cotton was processed. James Kay's flying shuttle (1733),[5] James Hargreaves's spinning jenny (1765), and Richard Arkwright's power loom (1769), combined with the steam engine, changed the way cloth was processed and the clothes people wore.

Industrial Revolution Period (1750–1900) during which technology and machines rapidly modernized industrial production.

The need to mine vast amounts of coal to provide power to run the machines changed the economic and physical landscapes. The repeating rifle changed the nature of warfare. Modern economic institutions replaced guilds. Stock markets, insurance companies, and corporations all became important. Trading was no longer financed by government; it was privately financed (although government policies, such as colonial policies giving certain companies monopoly trading

The Industrial Revolution was marked by the development of machines, such as this spinning frame, which could significantly improve productivity. © *Shaffer Archives.*

---

[5] The invention of the flying shuttle frustrated the textile industry because it enabled workers to weave so much cloth that the spinners of thread from which the cloth was woven couldn't keep up. This challenge to the textile industry was met by offering a prize to anyone who could invent something to increase the thread spinners' productivity. The prize was won when the spinning jenny was invented.

ADDED DIMENSION

THE ROLE OF ECONOMISTS IN ECONOMIC TRANSITIONS

For economics to be relevant, it must have something to say about social policy. Good economists try to be objective and recommend policies that they believe would be good for society in general rather than for any particular group in society.

Deciding what is in society's interest isn't always easy. For economists, it requires interpreting what society wants and comparing different policies, using what economists believe is society's preference. That often means proposing policies that will help some people but hurt others.

Adam Smith's "invisible hand" argument for the free working of the market and against government intervention is a good example. Smith favored a laissez–faire policy, meaning the government should not interfere with the operation of the economy. In this argument Smith and other Classical economists found themselves aligned with the industrialists or manufacturers, who wanted the right to enter into markets as they saw fit, and against the guilds and independent artisans, who wanted government to control who did what. These two groups each had different reasons for supporting laissez-faire policy, however. Industrialists supported the policy because they believed it benefited them. Sometimes they claimed policies that helped themselves actually benefited society, but they only made this argument because it helped make their case more persuasive. Economists supported the laissez-faire policy because they believed it benefited society.

It's not easy to decide which policies will benefit society when the policies you're looking at will help some people and hurt other people. It's hard to weigh a policy and decide whether the good that it will probably do outweighs the harm that it may cause. Modern economists have spent a long time struggling with this problem. Some have avoided the problem. They have refused to advocate any policy that might hurt anyone, which pretty much eliminates advocating any policy at all. Good policy-oriented economists make working judgments of what they believe is in society's interest; these working judgments determine which policies they advocate.

In reality, economists' (or anyone's) arguments for the general good of society are unlikely to have much effect on the policies of any government unless their arguments coincide with the interest of one group or another. A policy of less government involvement favored manufacturers over craftspeople. That the policy favored manufacturers or industrialists isn't the reason economists favored it (they argued that less government involvement would be good for society as a whole), but it is the reason industrialists supported laissez-faire, and the industrialists' support of laissez-faire was critical in getting the policy adopted in Britain in the late 1700s.

Once markets were established, the terms of the debate changed. Many economists stopped advocating laissez-faire policies. Good economists recognize the advantages of markets, but they also recognize the problems of markets.

rights with a country's colonies, helped in that trading). The Industrial Revolution, democracy, and capitalism all arose in the middle and late 1700s. By the 1800s they were part of the institutional landscape of Western society. Capitalism had arrived.

Capitalism was marked by significant economic growth in the Western world. But it was also marked by human abuses—18-hour work days, low wages, children as young as five years old slaving long hours in dirty, dangerous factories and mines—all to produce enormous wealth for an elite few. Such conditions and inequalities led to criticism of the capitalist or market economic system.

Welfare Capitalism

From Capitalism to ~~Socialism~~

Marx's Analysis   The best-known critic of this system was Karl Marx, a German philosopher, economist, and sociologist who wrote in the 1800s and who developed an analysis of the dynamics of change in economic systems. Marx argued that economic systems are in a constant state of change and that capitalism would not last. Workers would revolt and capitalism would be replaced by the pure communism we discussed earlier. This would begin, he predicted, with the institution of a socialist economic system.

Marx saw an economy marked by tensions among economic classes. He saw capitalism as an economic system controlled by the capitalist class (businessmen). His class analysis was that capitalist society is divided into capitalist and worker classes. He said constant tension between these economic classes causes changes in the system. The capitalist class made large profits by exploiting the **proletariat** class (working class) and extracting what he called *surplus value* from workers who, according to Marx's labor theory of value, produced all the value inherent in goods. Surplus value was the profit that, according to Marx's normative views,

Proletariat The working class (laborers, blue collar employees, and low-level office workers).

capitalists added to the price of goods. What economic analysis sees as a return to recognizing a need that society has and fulfilling it, Marx saw as exploitation.

Marx argued that this exploitation would increase as production facilities became larger and larger and as competition among capitalists decreased. At some point, he believed, exploitation would lead to a revolt by the proletariat, who would overthrow their capitalist exploiters.

By the late 1800s, some of what Marx predicted had occurred, although not in the way that he thought it would. Production moved from small to large factories. Corporations developed and classes became more distinct from one another. Workers were significantly differentiated from owners. Small firms merged and were organized into monopolies and trusts (large combinations of firms). The trusts developed ways to prevent competition among themselves and ways to limit entry of new competitors into the market. Marx was right in his predictions about these developments, but he was wrong in his prediction about society's response to them.

The Revolution That Did Not Occur   Western society's response to the problems of capitalism was not a revolt by the workers. Whereas Marx said capitalism would fall because of the exploitation of workers by the owners of business or capitalists, what actually happened was that the market economy was modified by political forces. Governments stepped in to stop the worst abuses of capitalism. The hard edges of capitalism were softened.

Evolution, not revolution, was capitalism's destiny. The democratic state did not act, as Marx argued it would, as a mere representative of the capitalist class. Competing pressure groups developed; workers gained political power which offset the economic power of businesses.

In the late 1930s and the 1940s workers dominated the political agenda. During this time capitalist economies developed an economic safety net which included government-funded programs, such as public welfare and unemployment insurance, and established an extensive set of regulations affecting all aspects of the economy. Today depressions are met with direct government policy. Antitrust laws, regulatory agencies, and social programs of government softened the hard edges of capitalism. Laws were passed prohibiting child labor, mandating a certain minimum wage, and limiting the hours of work. Capitalism became what is sometimes called **welfare capitalism,** an economic system in which the market is allowed to operate, but in which government plays key roles in determining distribution and making the *what, how,* and *for whom* decisions.

Due to these developments, government spending now accounts for about a third of all spending in the United States, and for more than half in some European countries. Were an economist from the late 1800s to return from the grave, he'd probably say socialism, not capitalism, exists in Western societies. Most modern-day economists wouldn't go that far, but they would agree that our economy today is better described as a welfare capitalist economy than as a capitalist, or even a market, economy. Because of these changes, the U.S. and Western European economies are a far cry from the competitive "capitalist" economy that Karl Marx criticized. Markets operate, but they are constrained by the other invisible forces.

The concept *capitalism* developed to denote a market system controlled by one group in society, the capitalists. Looking at Western societies today, we see that domination by one group no longer characterizes Western economies. Although in theory capitalists control corporations through their ownership of shares of stock, in practice corporations are controlled in large part by managers. There remains an elite group who control business, but "capitalist" is not a good term to describe them. Managers, not capitalists, exercise primary control over business and even their control is limited by laws or the fear of laws being passed by governments.

Welfare capitalism Economic system in which the market operates but government regulates markets significantly.

Tjalling Koopmans—Nobel prize, 1975, for work on allocation of resources.
© *The Nobel Foundation.*

Governments in turn are controlled by a variety of pressure groups. Sometimes one group is in control; at other times, another. Government policies similarly fluctuate. Sometimes they are proworker, sometimes proindustrialist, sometimes progovernment, and sometimes prosociety.

From Feudalism to Socialism

You probably noticed that I crossed out ''Socialism'' in the previous section's heading and replaced it with ''Welfare Capitalism.'' That's because capitalism did not evolve through socialism to pure communism as Marx predicted it would. But Marx's socialist ideas did take root in Russia, a society that the Industrial Revolution had in large part bypassed. Arriving at a different place and a different time than Marx predicted it would, socialism, you should not be surprised to read, arrived in a different way than Marx predicted. There was no revolution of the proletariat to establish socialism. Instead, there was World War I, which the Russians were losing, and Russia's feudal economy and government, which were crippled by the war effort. A small group of socialists overthrew the czar (Russia's king) and took over the government in 1917. They quickly pulled Russia out of the war and then set out to organize a socialist society and economy.

Russian socialists tried to adhere to Marx's ideas, but they found that Marx had concentrated on how capitalist economies operate, not on how a socialist economy should be run. Thus, Russian socialists faced a huge task with little guidance. Their most immediate problem was how to increase production so that the economy could emerge from feudalism into the modern industrial world. In Marx's analysis, capitalism was a necessary stage in the evolution toward the ideal state: The capitalists exploit the workers, but in doing so capitalists extract the necessary surplus—an amount of production in excess of what was consumed. That surplus had to be extracted in order to provide the factories and machinery upon which a socialist economic system would be built. But since there had been no capitalism in Russia, a true socialist state could not be established immediately. Instead the socialists created an economic system that they called **state socialism.** The state would see to it that people worked for the common good until they could be relied on to do so on their own.

State socialism Economic system in which government sees to it that people work for the common good rather than relying on people to do that on their own.

Socialists saw state socialism as a transition stage to pure socialism. This transition stage still exploited the workers; when Joseph Stalin took power in Russia in the late 1920s, he took the peasants' and small farmers' land and turned it into collective farms. The government then paid farmers low prices for their produce. When farmers balked at the low prices, millions of them were killed.

Simultaneously Stalin created central planning agencies which directed individuals what to produce and how to produce it, and determined for whom things would be produced. During this period *socialism* became synonymous with *central economic planning*.

Also during this time, Russia took control of a number of neighboring states and established the Union of Soviet Socialist Republics (USSR), the formal name of the Soviet Union. The Soviet Union also installed Soviet-dominated governments in a number of Eastern European countries. In 1949 most of China, under the rule of Mao Zedong, adopted Soviet-style socialist principles.

Since the late 1980s the Soviet socialist economic and political structure has fallen apart. The Soviet Union as a political state broke up, and its former republics became autonomous. Eastern European countries were released from Soviet control. Now they faced a new problem: transition from socialism to a market economy. Why did the Soviet socialist economy fall apart? Because workers lacked incentives to work; production was inefficient; consumer goods were either unavailable or of poor quality; and high Soviet officials were exploiting their positions, keeping the best jobs for themselves and moving themselves up in the waiting lists for consumer goods. In short, the parents of the socialist family (the Communist party) were no longer acting benevolently; they were taking many of the benefits for themselves.

Corporations (businesses) are technically owned by the owners of capital (shareholders). In theory at least they control corporations by electing the officers (the people who make the *what, how,* and *for whom* production decisions). In practice, however, effective control of corporations is generally in the hands of a small group of managing officers.

In the debate about the possible future evolution of capitalism, the question of who controls business decisions is likely to take center stage. Some reformers in the United States argue that the current U.S. system is wrong in both

theory and practice. They argue that corporations should reflect the need of stakeholders (all the individuals who have a stake in a corporation's activities). Stakeholders include the corporation's stockholders and officers as well as workers, customers, and the community where the corporation operates. An economy in which all stakeholders, not just shareholders, elect the officers who make the *what, how,* and *for whom* decisions would still use the market. It would still be a market economy, but it would no longer be a capitalist economy.

Recent political and economic upheavals in Eastern Europe and the Soviet Union suggest the kind of socialism these societies had tried did not work. However, that failure does not mean that socialist goals are bad; nor does it mean that no type of socialism can ever work. To overthrow socialist-dominated governments it is not necessary to accept capitalism, and many citizens of these countries are looking for an alternative to both systems. Most, however, wanted to establish market economies.

From Socialism to ?

The upheavals in the Soviet Union and Eastern Europe have left only China as a major power using a socialist economic system. But even in China there have been changes and the country is moving toward the limited use of markets. For example, in the late 1980s, Deng Xiao-ping introduced significant economic reform in China, establishing markets and introducing private property in numerous sectors of the economy. As these changes have been made, it has become harder and harder to distinguish between capitalist and socialist economies. These changes have led some socialists to modify their view that state socialism is the path from capitalism to pure communism, and instead to joke: "Socialism is the longest path from capitalism to capitalism."

As socialist economies have moved closer to becoming market economies or attempted to become full market economies, they've been confronted with problems that are new to them although commonplace in nonsocialist economies: unemployment, inflation, and an explicit acceptance of large inequities in the distribution of income. In most socialist countries *profit* (income earned in excess of costs) had been a dirty word, but since the reforms, profit making has become acceptable and individuals who earn profits have become respectable. The result of these problems and of an enormous fall in their income has been that the political and economic structure in the formerly socialist countries became volatile. Rampant political instability made it hard for market forces to operate. For example, many potential entrepreneurs believed that the government's view of profits might change and that individuals who earned large profits would again be seen as enemies of the state and could have their profits expropriated. Potential entrepreneurs feared that rather than being heroes, profit earners could be cast as the villains and be condemned for their capitalist activities. Even if that fear were removed, it was unclear what the laws were, who owned what, and what type of contracts would and would not be enforceable.

Uncertainty and lack of a stable institutional framework created economic crises in many socialist countries in the early 1990s. The former socialist countries' future is unclear. Whichever way things go, this is a grand time to be an economist. You have a ringside seat at historic changes.

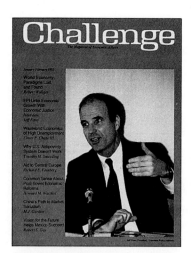

A popular economics magazine written for laypeople.

Our economic system will probably be different 30 years from now. If the debate between socialism and capitalism disappears, another debate will rise up to take its place. A new topic for debate may be: Who should be the decision makers in a market economy? In the U.S. economy in the late 1980s a handful of financiers became celebrities by reaping billions of dollars in profits for themselves. Many people came to wonder whether an economic system that so glorified greed was really desirable and in the 1990s some of those same financiers found themselves in jail, with the financial institutions they had controlled in ruins. Such widespread reactions may well lead to further evolution of the capitalist system.

Also in the 1990s Japan is the economic star. As we will discuss in Chapter 5, Japan's economy has many similarities to mercantilism. In Japan, government and industrialists work closely together and government plays a key role in the economy. Given the success of the Japanese economy, the push in the United States toward a type of mercantilism similar to Japan's is likely to be strong. And so it's safe to predict that the 1990s will see further evolution of economic systems. The lesson of history seems to be that change remains the one constant in economic systems.

ECONOMIC SYSTEMS OF THE FUTURE

KEY POINTS

- Any economic system must answer three central questions: **1**

    What to produce?
    How to produce it?
    For whom to produce it?

- In capitalism the what, how, and for whom decisions are made by the market. **2** **3**
- In socialism the what, how, and for whom decisions are made by government planning boards. **2** **3**
- Political, social, and economic forces are active in both capitalism and socialism. **3**

- Economic systems are in a constant state of evolution. **4**
- In feudalism, tradition rules; in mercantilism, the government rules; in capitalism, the market rules. **4**
- In welfare capitalism, the market, the government, and tradition each rule components of the economy. **4**
- Socialism developed in Russia and initially used a planning system. **4**
- Socialism is currently undergoing a transition; the future structure of socialist society is unclear. **5**

KEY TERMS

autocracy *(65)*	economic system *(60)*	mercantilism *(70)*	proletariat *(73)*
capitalism *(61)*	feudalism *(68)*	NIMBY *(61)*	pure communism *(65)*
capitalists *(70)*	Industrial	planning *(64)*	socialism *(62)*
communism *(65)*	Revolution *(72)*	private property	state socialism *(75)*
democracy *(65)*	laissez-faire *(72)*	rights *(61)*	welfare capitalism *(74)*

QUESTIONS FOR THOUGHT AND REVIEW

The number after each question represents the estimated degree of critical thinking required. (1 = almost none; 10 = deep thought.)

1. Is capitalism or socialism the better economic system? Why? *(9)*
2. What three questions must any economic system answer? *(2)*

3. How does socialism answer these three questions? *(3)*
4. How does capitalism answer these three questions? *(3)*
5. What arguments can you give for supporting a socialist organization of a family and a capitalist organization of the economy? *(6)*

6. Why did feudalism evolve into mercantilism? Could feudalism stage a return? Why? *(6)*
7. Why did mercantilism evolve into capitalism? Could mercantilism stage a return? Why? *(6)*
8. Some intellectuals have argued "history is ended" because of recent developments in socialist economies. Respond, basing your answer on Marx's analysis. *(7)*
9. A common joke in socialist countries in the early 1990s was that a person went into a free market store and asked how much a loaf of bread cost. "$1.00" said the clerk. "But that's outrageous. Down the street at the state-run store, it only costs a nickel." "So why don't you buy it there?" said the clerk. "Well," said the customer, "they don't have any." Using supply/demand analysis, show why this situation makes economic sense. *(4)*
10. The Heisenberg principle states that it's impossible to know the true nature of reality because in analyzing that reality, you change it. How might the Heisenberg principle apply to Marx's economic analysis? *(6)*

PROBLEMS AND EXERCISES

1. Suppose a socialist government decided to set all prices at the supply/demand equilibrium price.
   a. Show graphically what price they'd set.
   b. How would such an economy differ from a market economy?
   c. Do you think a socialist government could carry out that decision?
   d. Show graphically what would happen if it set the price too high and if it set the price too low.
   e. Which of the preceding two situations best describes what the actual situation was in socialist economies?
2. Poland, Bulgaria, and Hungary (all former socialist countries) were in the process of changing to a market economy in the early 1990s.
   a. Go to the library and find the latest information about their transitions.
   b. Explain what has happened in those countries, using the invisible hand, invisible handshake, and invisible foot metaphors.

4

U.S. Economic Institutions

The business of government is to
keep the government out of business—that is, unless business needs
government aid.

Will Rogers

After reading this chapter, you should be able to:

1

Provide a bird's-eye view of the U.S.
economy.

2

State the advantages and disadvantages of
various types of business.

3

Explain why even though households have
the ultimate power, much of the economic
decision making is done by business and
government.

4

List two general roles of government and
seven specific roles of government.

5

Go out and learn more about U.S.
economic institutions on your own.

You saw in Chapter 2 that supply and demand are the driving forces behind the invisible hand. But the invisible hand doesn't operate in an invisible world; it operates in a very real world—a world of institutions that sometimes fight against, sometimes accept, and sometimes strengthen the invisible hand. Thus, to know how the invisible hand works in practice, we need to have some sense of economic institutions and data about the U.S. economy. Let's first look at some data.

A BIRD'S-EYE VIEW OF THE U.S. ECONOMY

1

The powerful U.S. economic machine generates enormous economic activity and provides a high standard of living (compared to most other countries) for almost all its inhabitants. It also provides economic security for its citizens. Starvation is far from most people's minds. Exhibit 1 gives you an idea of what underlies the U.S. economy's strength. For example, in it you can see that the United States is a large country with a temperate climate and a wide range of natural resources. It has excellent transportation facilities and a relatively homogeneous population, most of which speaks the same language, English.

The Importance of Geographic Economic Information

5

Such geographic economic information is vitally important. To understand an economy you should know: Where are goods produced? Where are natural resources found? What natural resources does it lack? What are normal transportation routes? To keep their analyses simpler, economists often discuss economic problems without discussing geographic dimensions. But no discussion of an economy should forget that geographic dimensions of economic problems are significant. To determine whether to send my students off to the library to learn this information, I give them a quiz. I present them with two lists like those in the box on page 82. The list on the right gives twenty places in the United States. The list on the left gives a particular economic characteristic, such as an industry, product, activity, or natural condition that has been turned to economic advantage. Students are required to match the numbers with important characteristics of each area.

If you can score 15 or higher on this quiz, I'm impressed with your knowledge of economic geographic facts. If you scored lower than 15, I strongly suggest learning more geographic facts. The study guide has a number of other projects, information, and examples. An encyclopedia has even more, and your library has a wealth of information. You could spend the entire semester acquiring facts. I'm not suggesting that, but I *am* suggesting that you follow the economic news carefully and pay attention to where various *whats* are produced.

The positive attributes of the U.S. economy don't mean that the United States has no problems. Critics point out crime is rampant, drugs are omnipresent, economic resources such as oil and minerals are declining, the environment is deteriorating, the distribution of income is skewed toward the rich, and an enormous amount of economic effort goes into economic gamesmanship (real estate deals, stock market deals, deals about deals) which seems simply to reshuffle existing wealth, not to create new wealth. Internationally the U.S. economic position has deteriorated substantially since the 1950s and 1960s. In many people's eyes, Japan has replaced the United States as the world's economic leader. Rather than lending money to other countries as it had done in the 1950s and 1960s, in the 1980s the United States borrowed enormous amounts from other countries and is now the biggest debtor nation in the world. In short, the U.S. economy is great, but it's far from perfect.

A CIA publication with very up-to-date international and domestic statistics.

Diagram of the U.S. Economy

Exhibit 2 diagrams the U.S. economy. Notice it's divided up into three groups: business, households, and government. Households supply factors of production to business and are paid by business for doing so. The market where this interaction takes place is called a *factor market*. Business produces goods and services

EXHIBIT 1   CIA Information Survey on United States

GEOGRAPHY

Total area: 9,372,610 km²; land area: 9,166,600 km²; includes only the 50 states and District of Columbia

Comparative area: about three-tenths the size of Russia; about one-third the size of Africa; about one-half the size of South America (or slightly larger than Brazil); slightly smaller than China; about two and one-half times the size of Western Europe

Land boundaries: 12,248 km total; Canada 8,893 km (including 2,477 km with Alaska), Mexico 3,326 km, Cuba (US naval base at Guantánamo) 29 km

Coastline: 19,924 km

Climate: mostly temperate, but varies from tropical (Hawaii) to arctic (Alaska); arid to semiarid in west with occasional warm, dry chinook wind

Terrain: vast central plain, mountains in west, hills and low mountains in east; rugged mountains and broad river valleys in Alaska; rugged, volcanic topography in Hawaii

Natural resources: coal, copper, lead, molybdenum, phosphates, uranium, bauxite, gold, iron, mercury, nickel, potash, silver, tungsten, zinc, crude oil, natural gas, timber

Land use: arable land 20%; permanent crops NEGL%; meadows and pastures 26%; forest and woodland 29%; other 25%; includes irrigated 2%

Environment: pollution control measures improving air and water quality; acid rain; agricultural fertilizer and pesticide pollution; management of sparse natural water resources in west; desertification; tsunamis, volcanoes, and earthquake activity around Pacific Basin; continuous permafrost in northern Alaska is a major impediment to development

PEOPLE

Population: 254,521,000 (July 1991), growth rate 0.8% (1992)

Birth rate: 14 births/1,000 population (1992)

Death rate: 9 deaths/1,000 population (1992)

Net migration rate: 2 migrants/1,000 population (1992)

Infant mortality rate: 10 deaths/1,000 live births (1992)

Life expectancy at birth: 72 years male, 79 years female (1992)

Total fertility rate: 1.8 children born/woman (1992)

Ethnic divisions: white 84.1%, black 12.4%, other 3.5% (1989)

Religion: Protestant 56%, Roman Catholic 28%, Jewish 2%, other 4%, none 10% (1989)

Language: predominantly English; sizable Spanish-speaking minority

Literacy: 98% (male 97%, female 98%) age 25 and over having completed 5 or more years of schooling (1989)

Labor force: 126,867,000 (includes armed forces and unemployed); civilian labor force 125,303,000 (1991)

Organized labor: 16,568,000 members; 16.1% of total wage and salary employment which was 102,786,000 (1991)

ECONOMY

GDP: $5,673 billion, per capita $22,470; real growth rate 0.7% (1991)

Inflation rate (consumer prices): 4.2% (1991)

Unemployment rate: 6.6% (1991)

Budget: revenues $1,054 billion; expenditures $1,323 billion, including capital expenditures

Exports: $428.1 billion (f.o.b., 1991); *commodities*—capital goods, automobiles, industrial supplies and raw materials, consumer goods, agricultural products; *partners*—Western Europe 27.3%, Canada 22.1%, Japan 12.1% (1989)

Imports: $499.4 billion (c.i.f., 1990); *commodities*—crude and partly refined petroleum, machinery, automobiles, consumer goods, industrial raw materials, food and beverages; *partners*—Western Europe 21.5%, Japan 19.7%, Canada 18.8% (1989)

External debt: NA

Industrial production: growth rate 1.9% (1991)

Electricity: 776,550,000 kW capacity; 3,020,000 million kWh produced, 12,080 kWh per capita (1990)

Industries: leading industrial power in the world, highly diversified; petroleum, steel, motor vehicles, aerospace, telecommunications, chemicals, electronics, food processing, consumer goods, fishing, lumber, mining

Agriculture: accounts for 2% of GNP and 2.8% of labor force; favorable climate and soils support a wide variety of crops and livestock production; world's second-largest producer and number-one exporter of grain; surplus food producer; fish catch of 5.0 million metric tons (1988)

Illicit drugs: illicit producer of cannabis for domestic consumption with 1987 production estimated at 3,500 metric tons or about 25% of the available marijuana; ongoing eradication program aimed at small plots and greenhouses has not reduced production

Economic aid: donor—commitments, including ODA and OOF, (FY80-89), $115.7 billion

Exchange rates: *British pounds* (£) per US$—0.5171 (January 1991), 0.5603 (1990), 0.6099 (1989), 0.5614 (1988), 0.6102 (1987), 0.6817 (1986), 0.7714 (1985)

COMMUNICATIONS

Railroads: 270,312 km

Highways: 6,365,590 km, including 88,641 km expressways

Inland waterways: 41,009 km of navigable inland channels, exclusive of the Great Lakes (est.)

Pipelines: 275,800 km petroleum, 305,300 km natural gas (1985)

Ports: Anchorage, Baltimore, Beaumont, Boston, Charleston, Cleveland, Duluth, Freeport, Galveston, Hampton Roads, Honolulu, Houston, Jacksonville, Long Beach, Los Angeles, Milwaukee, Mobile, New Orleans, New York, Philadelphia, Portland (Oregon), Richmond (California), San Francisco, Savannah, Seattle, Tampa, Wilmington

Merchant marine: 396 ships (1,000 GRT or over) includes 3 passenger-cargo, 38 cargo, 25 bulk, 174 tanker, 13 tanker tug-barge, 14 liquefied gas, 129 intermodal; in addition there are 231 government-owned vessels

Civil air: 8,252 commercial multiengine transport aircraft, including 6,036 jet, 831 turboprop, 1,382 piston (Dec. 1989)

Airports: 14,177 total, 12,417 usable; 4,820 with permanent surface-runways; 63 with runways over 3,659 m; 325 with runways 2,440–3,659 m; 2,524 with runways 1,220–2,439 m

Telecommunications: 182,558,000 telephones; stations—4,892 AM, 5,200 FM (including 3,915 commercial and 1,285 public broadcasting), 7,296 TV (including 796 commercial, 300 public broadcasting, and 6,200 commercial cable); 495,000,000 radio receivers (1982); 150,000,000 TV sets (1982); satellite communications ground stations—45 Atlantic Ocean INTELSAT and 16 Pacific Ocean INTELSAT

Source: The World Factbook, 1992.

and sells them to households and government. The market where this interaction takes place is called the *goods market*.

Notice also the arrows going out and coming in for both business and households. Those arrows represent the international connection, which I'll discuss in Chapter 5.

A REMINDER

ECONOMIC GEOGRAPHY OF THE UNITED STATES

The Quiz

In the first column, I list 20 economic characteristics. In the second column, I list 20 states, cities or areas of the country. Associate the locale with the proper characteristic by printing the letter on the line.

_____ 1. excellent climate for spacecraft launching

_____ 2. major concentration of investment and banking services

_____ 3. film and TV industry

_____ 4. significant fishing and lobstering industries

_____ 5. the maple sugar state

_____ 6. concentration of textile industries

_____ 7. large gold deposits

_____ 8. major oil reserves

_____ 9. iron ore and iron extraction

_____ 10. major automobile production

_____ 11. major port for oil imports

_____ 12. tourism is a major industry, especially at Mardi Gras

_____ 13. significant irrigation farming

_____ 14. island's seasonal economy driven by summer residents and tourists

_____ 15. nearly all energy needs supplied by hydroelectric power

_____ 16. significant natural gas reserves

_____ 17. staging area for shipment of prime beef

_____ 18. concentration of lead mining

_____ 19. extensive silver mines

_____ 20. major timber production and port for shipping wood products to Japan and the Far East.

a. South Dakota
b. Utah
c. Colorado
d. Northern Minnesota
e. Florida
f. Detroit and surrounding area
g. Georgia, South Carolina, and North Carolina
h. Seattle and surrounding area
i. Houston
j. Pennsylvania and West Virginia
k. Oklahoma
l. Idaho
m. Southern California
n. Vermont
o. New York City
p. Kansas City
q. Oregon
r. New Orleans
s. Maine
t. Martha's Vineyard

Finally, consider the arrows connecting government with households and business. Government taxes business and households. It buys goods and services from business and buys labor services from households. Then with some of its tax revenue it provides services to both business and households (roads, education) and gives some of its tax revenue directly back to individuals. In doing so it redistributes income. But government also serves a second function. It oversees the interaction of business and households in the goods and factor markets. Government, of course, is not independent. The United States is a democracy so households vote to determine who shall govern.

Exhibit 2 gave you an overview of the institutional organization of the U.S. economy. Let's now consider some specifics. First look at business, second at households, and finally at government.

BUSINESS

President Calvin Coolidge once said, "The business of America is business." That's a bit of an overstatement, but business is responsible for over 80 percent of U.S. production. (Government is responsible for the other 20 percent.) In fact,

Answers: 1: e. 2: o. 3: m. 4: s. 5: n. 6: g. 7: a. 8: k. 9: d. 10: f. 11: i. 12: r. 13: l. 14: t. 15: q. 16: j. 17: p. 18: c. 19: b. 20: h.

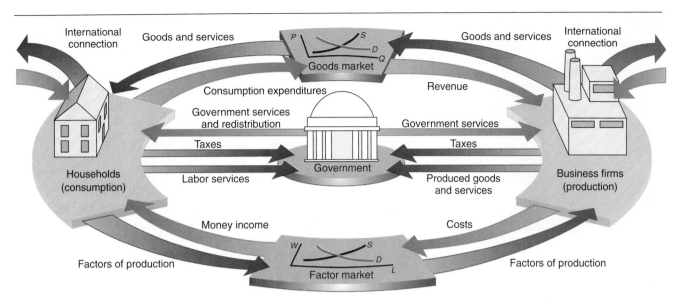

EXHIBIT 2   Diagrammatic Representation of the U.S. Economy

any time a household decides to produce something, it becomes a business. **Business** is simply the name given to private producing units in our society.

Businesses in the United States decide *what* to produce, *how* much to produce, and *for whom* to produce it. They make these central economic decisions on the basis of their own feelings, which are influenced by market incentives. Anyone who wants to can start a business, provided he or she can come up with the required cash and meet the necessary regulatory requirements. Each year about 225,000 are started.

Don't think of business as something other than people. Businesses are ultimately made up of a group of people organized together to accomplish some end. In terms of numbers, most businesses are one- or two-person operations. Home-based businesses, at least if they're part-time activities, are easy to start. All you have to do is say you're in business, and you are. If that business becomes complex enough and big enough to have employees (especially if it needs its own building), the difficulties begin. Before the business may expand its operations, a large number of licenses, permits, approvals, and forms must be obtained from various government agencies. That's why **entrepreneurship** (the ability to organize and get something done) is an important part of business. To give you a sense of what it's like to run a business, let's consider a real-world example.

In 1986 Susan and Ralph decided that it would be fun to open a kitchen shop in a prosperous Vermont town. They planned to sell kitchen utensils and light food and drink, including coffee, muffins, cheese, and wine.

They found a building, bought it, and, after getting a building permit, began remodeling. Because it was to be the home of a business, the building had to meet strict fire, electrical, and plumbing codes. Because Susan and Ralph planned to sell wine, they had to apply for a liquor license.

Their plans initially called for an upstairs store area, but state inspectors told Susan and Ralph that in a building and zone like theirs, an upstairs store was against the law. So much for upstairs.

They had to establish contacts with suppliers, get insurance, and obtain permits from the town to comply with zoning, health, and sanitation codes and regulations surrounding the sale of prepared food.

Business A private producing unit in our society.

Entrepreneurship and Business

Entrepreneurship The ability to organize and get something done.

Trials and Tribulations of Starting a Business

Wassily Leontief—Nobel prize, 1973, for work on interrelationship among sectors of the economy. © The Nobel Foundation.

Then, of course, there are taxes. Any business with employees must withhold taxes from their wages and send those taxes periodically to the various taxing authorities. This includes social security taxes, federal income taxes, and state income taxes. There are also unemployment compensation taxes, state property taxes, and sales taxes that the business, not the employees, must pay.

All this costs a lot of money. Susan and Ralph had to open a business checking account with their bank. (They couldn't run all that expense through their personal checking account because sound accounting practice requires people to keep their business checks separate from their personal checks.) They had to have some money to put in the business account. They used some of their savings, but they needed more funds. That meant they had to apply for a loan from the bank. The bank required them to present a formal business plan.

It took two years and well over $200,000 to start the business. And this was a small business. Somebody without training and background in handling forms, taxes, and bureaucratic regulations usually doesn't do well in business. To such a person, entry into business isn't free; it isn't even possible.

Consumer Sovereignty and Business

Consumer sovereignty Consumers' wishes control what business produces for sale.

Profit What's left over from total revenues after costs are subtracted.

To say that businesses decide what to produce isn't to say that **consumer sovereignty** (the consumer's wishes) doesn't reign in the United States. Businesses decide what to produce based on what they believe will sell. A key question a person in the United States should ask about starting a business is: Can I make a profit from it? **Profit** is what's left over from total revenues after all the appropriate costs have been subtracted. Businesses that guess correctly what the consumer wants generally make a profit. Businesses that guess wrong generally operate at a loss.

People are free to start businesses for whatever purposes they want. No one asks them: "What's the social value of your term paper assistance business, your Twinkies business, your fur coat business, or your textbook publishing business?" Yet the U.S. economic system is designed to channel individuals' desire to make a profit into the general good of society. That's the invisible hand at work. As long as the business doesn't violate a law and conforms to regulations, people in the United States are free to start whatever business they want, if they can get the money to finance it. That's a key difference between the U.S. market economy and a traditional socialist economy where people aren't free to start a business even if they could get the financing.

A Vermont country store, a small business like those found across the United States.

Accounting for revenues and expenditures is an important part of business. Elaborate methods of keeping track of those revenues and expenses have developed over the years. A firm's balance sheet (a statement of the firm's net worth at a point in time) is shown below. As you can see, the balance sheet is divided into assets on the left side and

---

COMPANY NAME

Balance Sheet
December 31, 1992

Assets*		Liabilities and stockholders' equity*	
Current assets	$13,859	Current liabilities	$12,675
Property, plant, and equipment	20,362	Long-term liabilities	5,843
		Stockholders' equity	15,703
		Total liabilities and	
Total assets	$34,221	stockholders' equity	$34,221

---

* Dollars in millions.

liabilities and stockholders' equity (also called *net worth*) on the right side. An *asset* is anything of value. An asset need not be a physical item. It might be a right to do something or use something. For example, landing rights are important assets of airline companies. A *liability* is an obligation. When a firm borrows money, it takes on a liability because it has an obligation to pay the money back to the lender. The totals of the two sides must be equal, since *stockholders' equity (net worth)* is defined as the difference between assets and liabilities. That is:

$$\text{Assets} = \text{Liabilities} + \text{Stockholders' equity}$$

or

$$\text{Assets} = \text{Liabilities} + (\text{Assets} - \text{Liabilities})$$

$$\text{Assets} = \text{Assets.}$$

The two sides of the equation are equal by definition. Both assets and liabilities are divided into various subcategories on a balance sheet, but at this stage, all you need to remember is the sheet's general structure.

A firm's income statement is shown below. Whereas a balance sheet measures a stock concept (a firm's position at a point in time), an income statement measures a flow concept (the amount of income and expenses passing through a company during a particular period of time). A firm's sales, or total revenue, is given at the top. Then the cost of goods sold is subtracted from total revenue. The resulting number is called *gross profit*, although many income statements don't list gross profits. Next, operating costs and fixed interest payments are subtracted, giving earnings before taxes. Finally, income taxes are subtracted, giving the firm's net income.

COMPANY NAME

Income Statement*
For the Year Ended December 31, 1992

Sales	$8,710
Cost of goods sold	5,980
Gross profit	2,730
Operating expenses	1,509
Fixed interest payment	165
Income before federal income taxes	1,056
Federal income taxes	509
Net income	$ 547

Earnings per share of common stock: $2.36
Dividends per share of common stock: $1.05

---

* Dollars in millions.

Categories of Business

Exhibit 3(a) shows a selection of various categories of U.S. businesses with their relative amount of receipts (the total income firms take in) for each category. Total receipts aren't necessarily the best indicator of the importance of various types of business to the economy. Exhibit 3(b) ranks businesses by their relative employment.

Levels of Business

Businesses in the United States are organized on a variety of levels: manufacturing firms, wholesale firms, and retail firms. For most products the manufacturer isn't the same firm as the firm that sells the product to you. Often products are sold five or six times before they reach the consumer. Thus, most firms *provide a service*—getting you the good when you want it—rather than producing the good.

The growing importance of the service sector to the economy has led some observers to say that we're in a postindustrial society. In their view, the U.S. economy today is primarily a service economy, not a production economy. So classifying the economy may or may not be helpful, but you should note how important the provision of services and the distribution of goods are to our economy.

From Manufacturer to You   To give you a sense of the path of a good from manufacturer to ultimate buyer, let's consider a hypothetical example of a window I bought from Clearview Window Corporation. Clearview bought the glass, wood, and machines needed to make the window from other companies, perhaps spending a total of $20. Those purchases all fell within what is classified as wholesale trade. Clearview Window then assembled the components (cost of assembly: $60), making Clearview's total cost of the window $80.

I needed a window for my house, so I went down to Buildright, a local building supply store, which sells both wholesale to general contractors and retail to plain people who walk in off the street. Wholesale customers get a 20 percent discount from the retail price, which is deducted at the end of the month from the total bill they've run up. These wholesale customers charge their own customers the full retail price. I'm a plain person, so when I ordered my window, Buildright told me the cost would be $200. However it didn't have the right size in stock.

Buildright stacked my order with orders from other customers and called up its Clearview distributor (who has a franchise from Clearview Window in the

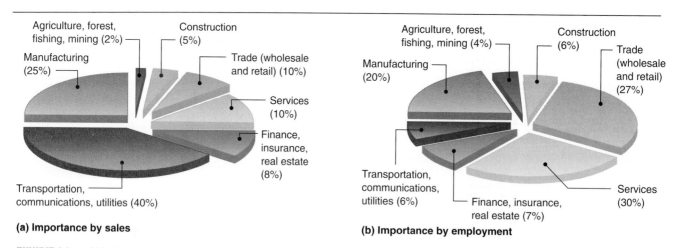

(a) Importance by sales

(b) Importance by employment

EXHIBIT 3 (a and b)   Importance and Size of Various Types of Business

The general types of business are listed here. (a) shows their relative importance by sales. (b) shows their relative importance by employment. Notice that less than half the population is involved in what most laypeople consider production—manufacturing, construction, mining, and agriculture.

Source: *Monthly Labor Review* and *Survey of Current Business*.

ADDED DIMENSION

IS THE UNITED STATES A POSTINDUSTRIAL SOCIETY?

Producing physical goods is only one of a society's economic tasks. Another task is to provide services (activities done for others). Services do not involve producing a physical good. When you get your hair cut, you buy a service, not a good. Much of the cost of the physical goods we buy actually is not a cost of producing the good, but is a cost of one of the most important services: distribution (getting the good to where the consumer is). After a good is produced, it has to get to the individuals who are going to consume it at the time they need it. If the distribution system gets botched up, it's as if the good had never been produced.

Let's consider a couple of examples. Take Christmas trees. Say you're sitting on 60,000 cut spruce trees in the Vermont mountains but an ice storm prevents you from shipping them until December 26. Guess what? You're now stuck with 60,000 spruce trees and the problem of somehow getting rid of them. Or take hot dogs. How many of us have been irked that a hot dog that cost 25¢ to fix at home costs $2 at a football game? But a hot dog at home isn't the same as a hot dog at a game. Distribution of the good is as important as production and is what you're paying the extra $1.75 for.

territory where I live) to place one big order for a number of windows, including mine. The Clearview distributor charged Buildright $140. The Clearview distributor keeps a pile of windows in stock which he replenishes from a shipment of newly made windows that come in once a month from the Clearview plant. For my window he pays about $100 plus freight.

So it costs Clearview $80 to make my window; Clearview sells it to the distributor for $100 plus freight. The distributor needs to cover his costs for storage, handling, inventory, billing, and of course he has to make a profit, so he sells the window to Buildright for $140. The owner of Buildright has to cover expenses and make a profit, so he sells me the window for $200 ($160—a 20 percent discount—if he thought I was a wholesale customer).

Producing the good is only a small component of the cost. Distribution—getting the good where it is wanted when it is wanted—makes up approximately 60 percent of the total cost of the window in this example. That large percentage is not unusual. The same story holds true for most goods you buy.

Another way to classify businesses is by size. As Exhibit 4 shows, most Americans are employed by small firms (those with fewer than 100 employees). Most

Sizes of Business

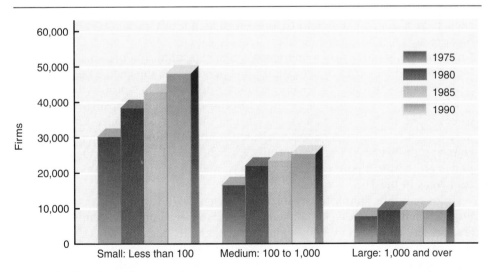

EXHIBIT 4   **Firms by number of employees**

Businesses can be classified by the number of people they employ, as shown here. Notice that small firms with fewer than 100 employees make up the largest category and have been increasing rapidly. *Source: Statistical Abstract,* 1992.

industries are composed of small firms, especially the retail trade and construction industries. The notable exception is manufacturing, which has a group of large producers, such as auto manufacturers.

In the past 20 years this predominance of small employers has increased, as is seen by comparing the 1975 and 1990 figures. The percentage of workers employed by large companies (defined as companies with over 1,000 employees) has fallen. The percentage of workers employed by moderate-size companies has increased somewhat and the percentage employed by small firms has increased substantially.

Exhibit 5 combines activity and size of firms, looking at the largest businesses in various types of activities. Notice the enormous size of some of the businesses, especially in the industrial category. General Motors has sales of well over $100 billion; Sears has sales of well over $50 billion and assets (the physical and financial property that it controls) of almost $100 billion. Compare these figures to the total output of a country like Nepal ($3.0 billion) and you have a sense of the size of some U.S. businesses.

A sector's relative size does not necessarily capture its importance to the economy. Take agriculture, for example. It's small in terms of both payroll and revenue, but if it stopped doing its job of providing our food, its importance would quickly become apparent. Similarly, the financial sector is relatively small, but modern industry couldn't function without a highly developed financial sector. Just as a missing bolt can bring a car to a sudden halt, so too can problems in one sector of the economy bring about a sudden halt to a much larger part of the economy.

Goals of Business

Nonprofit business Business whose motivation is to do good, not to make a profit.

Another way to classify businesses is by their goals. They can be either for-profit businesses or nonprofit businesses. For-profit businesses keep their earnings after they pay expenses (if there are any to keep); **nonprofit businesses** try only to make enough money to cover their expenses with their revenues. If a nonprofit business winds up with a profit, that money goes into ''reserves'' where it's saved to use in case of later losses.

The goal of a nonprofit business is to serve the community or some segment of the community. Nonprofit businesses include all government-run businesses, some hospitals, pension funds, foundations, many fund-raising organizations such as the American Cancer Society, most universities and colleges, and many museums. Working for a nonprofit organization doesn't mean working for free. Salaries are an expense of a business, and are paid by both for-profit and nonprofit firms. In fact, salaries paid to individuals managing nonprofit organizations can be higher than in for-profit organizations, and perks of the job can be fantastic.[1] But perks are classified as ''expenses'' and aren't included in ''profits.''

Why discuss the goals of business? Because the goals of business are central to economic theory and economists' insight into how economies function. In a pure capitalist country, all businesses are for-profit businesses. In a pure socialist country, all businesses are nonprofit. As I discussed in Chapter 3, the United States is far from a pure capitalist country, and nonprofit businesses play significant roles in the U.S. economy.

Not only are nonprofit organizations responsible for significant amounts of production in education and medicine, they also often control enormous assets in areas where no production takes place. For example, pension funds (funds held in trust for workers) control over 25 percent of the outstanding stock on the New York Stock Exchange. These nonprofit pension funds make decisions about

---

[1] *Perks* is short for *perquisites*. An example of a perk might be the business supplying you with a limousine and driver in New York City or Washington, D.C., an unlimited expense account, trips to Europe and the Far East, and a condo in Honolulu.

Ten largest industrial corporations	Sales	Assets
	(in millions)	
General Motors	$132,774.9	$191,012.8
Exxon	103,547.0	85,030.0
Ford Motor	100,785.6	180,545.2
Int'l Business Machines	65,096.0	86,705.0
General Electric	62,202.0	192,876.0
Mobil	57,389.0	40,561.0
Philip Morris	50,157.0	50,014.0
E.I. du Pont de Nemours	37,643.0	38,870.0
Chevron	37,464.0	33,970.0
Texaco	37,130.0	25,922.0

Ten largest retailing companies	Sales	Assets
Sears Roebuck	$ 59,101.7	$ 83,533.0
Wal-Mart Stores	55,483.8	20,565.1
Kmart	37,724.0	18,931.0
Kroger	22,144.6	4,303.1
J.C. Penney	19,085.0	13,563.0
American Stores	19,051.9	6,545.0
Dayton Hudson	17,927.0	10,337.0
Safeway	15,151.9	5,225.8
Great Atlantic & Pacific Tea Co.	11,592.5	3,212.8
May Department Stores	11,170.0	8,545.0

Ten largest diversified financial companies	Assets	Revenues
Federal Nat'l Mortgage Ass'n	$180,978.0	$ 14,559.0
American Express	175,752.0	26,961.0
Salomon	159,459.0	8,196.0
Merrill Lynch	107,024.2	13,428.3
Aetna Life & Casualty	89,928.2	17,497.2
Morgan Stanley Group	80,353.2	7,382.0
American International Group	79,835.2	18,388.6
CIGNA	69,827.0	18,582.0
Federal Home Loan Mortgage	59,502.0	4,461.0
ITT	58,764.0	21,651.0

Ten largest commercial banks	Assets	Deposits
Citicorp	$213,701.0	$144,175.0
BankAmerica Corp.	180,646.0	137,883.0
Chemical Banking Corp.	139,655.0	94,173.0
Nationsbank Corp.	118,059.3	82,726.5
J.P. Morgan & Co.	102,941.0	32,519.0
Chase Manhattan Corp.	95,862.0	67,224.0
Bankers Trust New York Corp.	72,448.0	25,071.0
Banc One Corp.	61,417.4	48,464.7
Wells Fargo & Co.	52,537.0	42,244.0
PNC Bank Corp.	51,379.9	29,469.5

EXHIBIT 5   The Largest Businesses, 1992

Source: Courtesy *Fortune* magazine, April 19, 1993 and May 31, 1993.

where to invest money and they earn very large sums of money. Thus, indirectly, the workers (whose pension funds these are) own a large share of business. In other words, many of the profits of for-profit businesses don't go to capitalists. They go to workers.

The three primary forms of business are sole proprietorships, partnerships, and corporations. Of the 18 million businesses in the United States, approximately 74 percent are sole proprietorships, 9 percent are partnerships, and 17 percent are corporations, as we see in Exhibit 6(a). In terms of total receipts, however, we get a quite different picture, with corporations far surpassing all other business forms, as Exhibit 6(b) shows. In fact, the largest 500 corporations account for 90 percent of the total receipts of all U.S. businesses.

Forms of Business

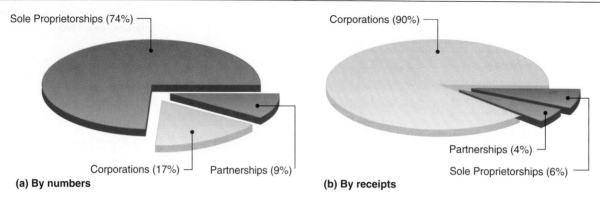

Sole Proprietorships (74%)

Corporations (90%)

Corporations (17%)   Partnerships (9%)

Partnerships (4%)

Sole Proprietorships (6%)

(a) By numbers

(b) By receipts

EXHIBIT 6 (a and b)   Forms of Business

The charts divide firms by the type of ownership. Approximately 74 percent of businesses in the United States are sole proprietorships (**a**). In terms of annual receipts, however, corporations surpass all other forms (**b**).
Source: *Statistical Abstract*, 1991.

2

Each of the different forms of business has certain advantages and disadvantages. To help you understand these three basic forms of business, let's consider each in some detail.

Sole Proprietorships and Partnerships   If you're starting a business on your own, you'll most likely start a **sole proprietorship.** They're easy to start, require minimal bureaucratic hassle, and are controlled by you, the owner. You are the business. You do what you want when you want to do it.

Sole proprietorship A business that has only one owner.

If you decide to expand, you'll likely hire a few employees. If you do, you're still a sole proprietorship; a sole proprietorship can have employees, although by definition it can have only one owner.

Let's say that you're successful and you decide to expand again, diversifying your product line as well as increasing output of your current product. At this point, you'll probably discover one of the serious disadvantages of the sole proprietorship: difficulty in raising the funds or capital necessary for expansion. Shortage of funds is one of the biggest problems facing most small businesses. To expand, the odds are that you will change to one of the other two forms of business. For instance, one way to get funds is to take on a partner and change your form of business from a sole proprietorship to a partnership.

Partnership A business with two or more owners, with each owner liable for every other owner's actions.

A **partnership** is a business with two or more owners. Like a sole proprietorship, the partnership might have no workers except the owners themselves. Payment of each partner's share of the business profits is made according to the terms of the contractual arrangement under which the partnership was established.

A partnership's advantage over a sole proprietorship is that partners can share the work and risks of business. For example, one partner might provide funds and the other partner might provide business expertise. Problems with partnerships include the fact that each partner can be held accountable for the business acts of each of the other partners, whether or not he or she authorized these acts. Say your partner contracts to buy air conditioners to sell in Alaska. Absurd as this project is, you as well as your partner are legally bound by the contract. The problem is made worse by the fact that partnerships have unlimited liability. As a result of your partner's blunders, you can lose not only what you've invested in the business but also your personal assets. Thus, you should enter into any partnership with your eyes wide open.[2]

[2] This discussion of partnerships is simplified for clarity. U.S. law allows for some types of partnership that do not have these attributes, such as Subchapter S partnerships and limited partnerships.

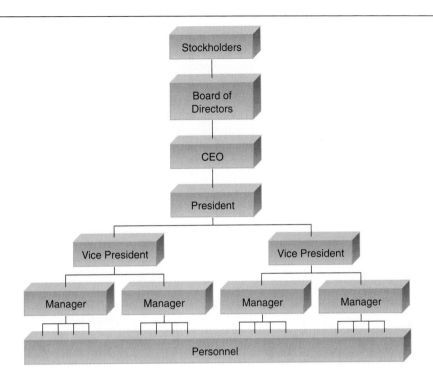

EXHIBIT 7   Typical Organization Chart of Corporation

An example of the corporate organization is given here. Persons in positions on each level of organization must report to the level above, until one gets to the Board of Directors, who are responsible to the stockholders.

Corporations   Because of the problems with partnerships and sole proprietorships, most large companies and many small companies in the United States are corporations. A **corporation** is a business that's legally owned by its stockholders, who are represented by a board of directors. Corporations are legal entities that, in law, are treated as fictitious persons. Anything a person can do in a legal sense, a corporation can. Unlike partnerships and sole proprietorships, corporations don't end with the death or retirement of one partner or the sole proprietor. Corporations have an existence independent of any of the human beings who own or manage them. When a corporation is formed, it issues **stock** (certificates of ownership in a company) which is sold or given to individuals. Proceeds of the sale of that stock make up what is called the *equity capital* of a company. Ownership of stock entitles you to vote in the election of a corporation's directors. Directors make the decisions about a company's policies; they appoint a company's president and chief executive officer (CEO), who in turn appoint lower-level officers. The CEO reports to the directors, who in turn are responsible to the stockholders. Exhibit 7 shows a typical organizational chart of a corporation.

Corporations were developed as institutions to make it easier for company owners to be separated from company management. A corporation provides **limited liability** for the owners. Whereas with the other two forms of business, owners can lose everything they possess even if they have only a small amount invested in the company, in a corporation the owners can lose only what they have invested in that corporation. If you've invested $100, you can lose only $100. In the other kinds of business, even if you've invested only $100, you could lose everything; the business's losses must be covered by the individual owners.

Say, for example, that the Happiness Company is a partnership, and that your $20 investment made you one of the company's 20,000 partners. Unfortunately, the Happiness Company doesn't produce happiness; it produces grief and it's sued for $1 billion. If the other partners are poor and you're a billionaire, you can be held responsible for the entire $1 billion loss. As you can imagine, limited liability is an important advantage that a corporation can offer.

Corporation A business legally treated as a "person" and owned by stockholders who are not liable for the actions of the corporate "person."

Stock Certificates of ownership of a firm.

Limited liability Owner of business is liable only to the extent of his or her own investment.

A corporation's stocks can be distributed among as few as three persons or among millions of stockholders. Stocks can be bought and sold either in an independent transaction between two people (an *over-the-counter* trade) or through a broker and a *stock exchange*. Appendix A provides a brief introduction to the stock market.

In corporations there is a separation of ownership and control. Most stockholders have little input into the decisions a corporation makes. Instead corporations are often controlled by their managers who often run them for their own benefit as well as for the owners'. The reason is that owners' control of management is limited.

A large percentage of most corporations' stock is not even controlled by the owners; instead it is controlled by financial institutions such as mutual funds (financial institutions that invest individuals' money for them) and by pension funds (financial institutions that hold people's money for them until it is to be paid out to them upon their retirement). Thus, ownership of corporations is another step removed from individuals. Studies have shown that 80 percent of the largest 200 corporations in the United States are essentially controlled by managers and have little effective stockholder control.

Why is the question of who controls a firm important? Because economic theory assumes business owners' goal is to maximize profits, which would be true of corporations if stockholders made the decisions. Managers don't have the same incentives to maximize profits that owners do. There's pressure on managers to maximize profits, but that pressure can often be weak or ineffective.

HOUSEHOLDS

Households Groups of individuals living together and making joint decisions.

The second classification we'll consider in this overview of U.S. economic institutions is households. **Households** (groups of individuals living together and making joint decisions) are the most powerful economic institution. They ultimately control government and business, the other two economic institutions. Households' votes in the political arena determine government policy; their decisions about supplying labor and capital determine what businesses will have available to work with; and their spending decisions or expenditures (the "votes" they cast with their dollars) determine what business will be able to sell.

While the ultimate power does in principle lie with the people and households, we, the people, have assigned much of that power to representatives. As I discussed above, corporations are only partially responsive to owners of their stocks, and much of that ownership is once removed from individuals. Ownership of 1,000 shares in a company with a total of 2 million shares isn't going to get you any influence over the corporation's activities. As a stockholder, you simply accept what the corporation does.

A major decision that corporations make independently of their stockholders concerns what to produce. True, ultimately we, the people, decide whether we will buy what business produces, but business spends a lot of money telling us what services we want, what products make us "with it," what books we want to read, and the like. Most economists believe that consumer sovereignty reigns—that we are not fooled or controlled by advertising. Still, it is an open question in some economists' minds whether we, the people, control business or the business representatives control people. There's similar debate in the political sphere of our lives. U.S. representatives and senators feel only partially responsible to voters. (They feel slightly more responsible around election time.)

Because of this assignment of power to other institutions, in many spheres of the economy households are not active producers of output but merely passive recipients of income. That's why much of the discussion of the household sector focuses on the distribution of household income. Thus, my consideration of households will be short and will focus on their income and their role as suppliers of labor.

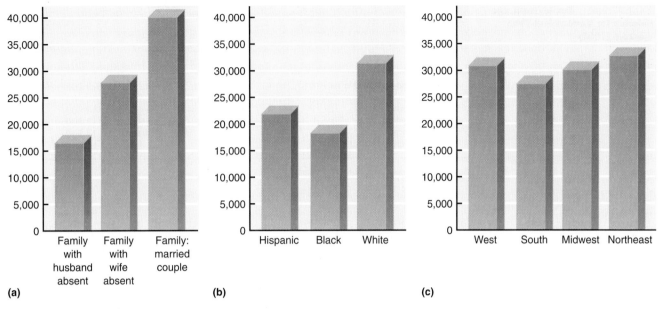

EXHIBIT 8 (a, b, and c)   Median Household Income by Type of Household, Race, and Region

These bar charts give you a sense of the distribution of income in the United States in 1990. Notice that the type of household, the race of the household, and the region where the household is located all help to determine household income.
Source: U.S. Bureau of the Census, *Current Population Reports*, 1992.

Household Types and Income

The U.S. population of about 250 million is composed of about 90 million households. Exhibit 8 looks at three ways income is divided up among households. Notice the relatively low incomes of families where the husband is absent and of black families. Because income determines how many goods and services a person will get, these two groups have fared especially poorly in the *for whom* department.

One political concern about income is: whether income is fairly (equitably, as opposed to equally) distributed, and whether all households have sufficient income. That's a tough question to answer. For now, let me simply note that the poverty level for a family of four in the United States is defined by the U.S. Department of Commerce as an income below $13,950 per year (1992 figure). By this definition 14.2 percent of all households in the United States were below the poverty level in 1991. This percentage is divided unequally between whites and blacks, with 32.7 percent of all black households below the poverty level and 11.3 percent of all white households below it.

Households as Suppliers of Labor

The largest source of household income is wages and salaries (the income households get from labor). Households supply the labor with which businesses produce and government governs. The total U.S. labor force is 120 million, about 7 percent (8 million) of whom are unemployed as of early 1993. The average U.S. work week is 41.6 hours for males and 35 hours for females.

Exhibits 9(a) and (b) divide U.S. employment by types of jobs and predict growth rates of certain job categories. Notice that many of the jobs are service jobs, since the United States has become largely a service economy. Exhibit 9(b) shows that this greater emphasis on services rather than goods is continuing. Many of the fastest-growing job categories are in service industries; many of the fastest-declining are in manufacturing and agriculture.

Other divisions of jobs show even more differences. For example, physicians earn about $150,000 per year; lawyers often earn $100,000 per year, and CEOs of

Type of job	Number of full-time workers (in thousands)		Median earnings per year	
	Female	Male	Female	Male
Managerial and professional	11,165	12,082	$29,200	$40,400
Technical, sales, and administrative support	16,084	9,844	19,000	27,000
Service occupations	4,612	4,492	12,900	17,200
Precision production	854	9,581	17,500	26,200
Machine operators	3,383	10,618	14,500	20,400
Farming, fishing, and forestry	170	1,260	11,600	14,000

Source: *Employment and Earnings,* January 1993.

large corporations often make $1,000,000 per year or more. A beginning McDonald's employee generally makes less than $10,000.

One of the biggest changes in the labor markets in the 1980s was unions' decline in importance. Labor unions are an economic institution closely associated with households. They were initially created to balance businesses' power. By organizing into unions, workers became an economic institution and gained a larger say in the production process. Unions pushed U.S. wages up relative to wages in other countries and established in the United States some of the best working conditions in the world. But unions also had a negative effect; part of businesses' response to the high U.S. wages has been to move production facilities to countries where workers receive lower wages. That's one reason the U.S. manufacturing sector has declined relative to the service sector and union membership and influence have fallen substantially. Service workers have far fewer unions, and their jobs are much more difficult to move to other countries.

People Power

An important way households influence government and business is in their cultural and ideological beliefs. Those beliefs determine what is allowable and what isn't. When those beliefs differ from the existing situation, "people power" has the potential to change the existing institutions significantly. For example, in Eastern Europe by the late 1980s people's beliefs had become so inconsistent with the existing institutions that people demanded and brought about major economic and political reforms even though there was no formal mechanism, such as free elections, for them to exert their power. People power goes beyond power people exert in elections. People in an economy have a cultural sensibility, or outlook, which limits actions of both government and business.

Households can exert people power to keep government and business in line. Do people accept the existing situation, or do they feel business or government is wrong? To keep people power on their side, U.S. businesses spend a lot of money on public service and advertisements stating that they, the businesses, are good citizens.

Because of the importance of these cultural and social limitations to business (the invisible handshake), you need some sense of which way the invisible handshake will push. While summarizing the sensibility of a country's people is impossible, it is necessary to make the attempt because it is through those sensibilities—through informal, invisible channels—that households exert much of their power on the economy. Thus, in the next section I will present my view of the sensibility of the American people.

The Social, Cultural, and Ideological Sensibilities of American People

Although, as I've pointed out, the actual U.S. economy is best described as welfare capitalism or a mixed economy due to a number of government programs designed to blunt the sharp edge of the market's forces, the American **ideology** (values held so deeply that they are not questioned) is, in word if not in deed, "let

Fastest-growing jobs	Fastest-declining jobs
Home health aides	Electrical and electronic equipment assemblers, precision
Systems analysts and computer scientists	Electrical and electronic assemblers
Personal and home care aides	Child care workers, private household
Medical assistants	Textile draw-out and winding machine operators

Source: *Monthly Labor Review*, November 1991.

the market do it.'' Like apple pie and motherhood, competition and freedom to undertake economic activities are seen as sacred. Small enterprises and entrepreneurships are especially prized, and in 1990 there were well over 11 million small business organizations.

Apple pie and motherhood have changed over the years, and so has competition. In the Great Depression of the 1930s the U.S. population's unbridled faith in the market was tested. Under President Franklin D. Roosevelt's New Deal in the 1930s, numerous government programs were developed to ease the market's harshness. Laws were passed establishing minimum prices at which goods could be sold. Labor was given the right to organize to achieve its ends; a new farm program limited price fluctuations of agricultural goods; a welfare system, including social security programs and unemployment insurance, was established. These laws and programs are generally viewed as good.

With the advent of World War II (1941–45), defense spending zoomed and government spending as a percentage of total U.S. spending increased from less than 10 percent of total U.S. income in the early 1930s to more than 50 percent of total U.S. income in 1944. After the war that percentage declined, but the march of government programs to regulate the market continued. In the decade following the war the government sector's role increased further and the economy grew rapidly. In 1946 the government took responsibility for maintaining high employment. In the 1960s and 1970s the *safety net* (a set of programs that guaranteed individuals a minimum standard of living) was expanded.

During the postwar period there developed what's called a **military-industrial complex** (a combination of defense industry firms and the U.S. armed forces, which have vested interests in keeping defense spending flowing, regardless of whether that spending is good for society). In 1991 defense spending was about $315.5 billion (approximately 22 percent of the federal government budget) but as outside threats to the United States decreased, the military-industrial complex was being squeezed and defense spending's percentage of the federal budget has been falling in the early 1990s.

The military-industrial complex is the best known of the vested interests trying to protect themselves, but it's not unique. Other groups' vested interests might also be described as complexes. For example, we could say there's a social-educational complex which protects education interests, while a health industry-welfare complex protects medical benefits. These complexes compete for government expenditures.

These developments may seem to go against the cultural and ideological support the American public gives the market. Support for the market and tolerance of vested interests seem contradictory, but people's ideological views need not be consistent, and they often aren't. A new and larger role for government in the market has been accepted by most people. They believe these programs are proper, so now government programs that restrict the market (for example, the social security system) are seen as fundamentally American as is the market.

Another important aspect of a people's sensibility is their view of morality.

Ideology Values held so deeply that they are not questioned.

Military-industrial complex Combination of defense industries and U.S. armed forces.

(a) Income   **(b) Expenditures**

EXHIBIT 10 (a and b)   Income and Expenses of State and Local Governments, 1992

The charts give you a sense of the importance of state and local government—where they get, (a), and where they spend, (b), their revenues.
Source: Survey of Current Business, January 1993.

Compared to other countries, the United States has a relatively strict standard of economic morals—activities such as direct bribery and payoffs are illegal. (In some countries, these activities aren't illegal. In numerous others, they're illegal but openly tolerated.) The U.S. government bureaucracy, while considered by many to be inefficient, is generally thought to be honest and not corrupt; moreover, by international standards it's actually efficient. Around the fringes of the standard morality there's still room for influence peddling, discreet payoffs, and trading favors, but by international standards of corruption they're small potatoes.

There's much more to be said about the cultural sensibilities of the American people, but I'll stop here. Those of you unfamiliar with U.S. cultural and social norms can best find out about them by following the newspapers and by having discussions with friends. My goal in presenting this material isn't to cover the American people's social and cultural sensibilities completely—that would take a whole book by itself—but simply to remind you how important they are: How an economy functions, what types of policies can be instituted, and what people's perceptions of the economic problems are, are all shaped by its people's social, cultural, and ideological sensibilities. The invisible handshake is an important determinant of economic events.

GOVERNMENT

4

The third major U.S. economic institution I'll consider is government. Government plays two general roles in the economy. It's both a referee (setting the rules that determine relations between businesses and households) and an actor (collecting money in taxes and spending that money on its own projects, such as defense and education). Let's first consider government's role as an actor.

Government as an Actor

The United States has a federal government system, which means we have various levels of government (federal, state, and local), each with its own powers. All levels of government combined consume about 30 percent of the country's total output and employ about 17 million individuals. The various levels of government also have a number of programs that redistribute income through taxation or through a variety of social welfare and assistance programs designed to help specific groups.

State and Local Government   State and local governments employ over 14 million people and spend almost $1 trillion a year. As you can see in Exhibit 10(a), state

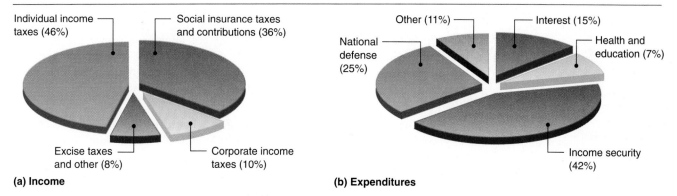

EXHIBIT 11 (a and b)   Pie Diagram of Federal Government

The pie diagrams show the sources and uses of federal government revenue.
Source: Survey of Current Business, January 1993.

and local governments get much of their income from taxes: property taxes, sales taxes, and state and local income taxes. They spend their tax revenues on administration, education (education through high school is available free in U.S. public schools), and roads, as Exhibit 10(b) shows. These activities fall within microeconomics, which we'll discuss in the microeconomics sections of this book.

Federal Government   Probably the best way to get an initial feel for the federal government and its size is to look at the various categories of its tax revenues and expenditures in Exhibit 11. Notice income taxes make up about 46 percent of the federal government's revenue, while social security taxes make up about 36 percent. That's more than 80 percent of the federal government's revenues, most of which shows up as a deduction from your paycheck. In Exhibit 11(b), notice the federal government's two largest categories of spending are defense and income maintenance, with expenditures on interest payments close behind.

Interest payments are important because the U.S. government has a large debt. **Debt** is an amount of money that one owes to others. It is a stock concept, which corresponds to the liability portion of a company's balance sheet. The U.S. government has accumulated a large debt, over $3 trillion in the early 1990s or over $12,000 per U.S. citizen. Interest must be paid on that debt, which explains why the budget's interest component is so high. The national debt has accumulated because the federal government has run almost continual budget deficits since the 1940s. A deficit is a flow concept that corresponds to the net income portion of a company's income statement. A **government budget deficit** occurs when government expenditures exceed government revenues—that is, when tax revenues fall short of budgeted expenditures and the government borrows to make up the difference. A **government budget surplus** occurs when revenues exceed expenditures.

Individuals like government programs that assist them, and they pressure politicians to provide these programs. However people don't like the taxes they have to pay for those programs, and they put pressure on politicians to lower taxes. These two pressures have resulted in the federal government's significant deficits since the 1940s.

Even if government spending made up only a small proportion of total expenditures, government would still be central to the study of economics. The reason is

Debt An amount of money one owes to others.

Government budget deficit Government expenditures exceed government revenues.

Government budget surplus Government revenues exceed government expenditures.

Government as a Referee

that in a market economy, government controls the interaction of business and households. Government sets the rules of interaction and acts as a referee, changing the rules when it sees fit. Government decides whether the invisible hand will be allowed to operate freely.

Government is involved in every interaction between households and business, in the form of laws regulating that interaction. For example, in the United States today:

1. Businesses are not free to hire and fire whomever they want. They must comply with equal opportunity and labor laws. Even closing a plant requires 60 days' notice for many kinds of firms.
2. Many working conditions are subject to government regulation: safety rules, wage rules, overtime rules, hours-of-work rules, and the like.
3. Businesses cannot meet with other businesses to agree on prices they will charge.
4. Workers in a union cannot require all workers in a firm to join the union before they are hired. In many states, they cannot require workers to join the union at all.

Most of these laws evolved over time. Up until the 1930s household members in their roles as workers and consumers had few rights. Businesses were free to hire and fire at will and, if they chose, to deceive and take advantage of consumers.

Over time, laws have changed. New laws to curb business abuses have been passed, and government agencies have been formed to enforce these laws. Now many people think the pendulum has swung too far the other way. They believe businesses are saddled with too many regulatory burdens.

One big question that I'll address throughout this book is: What referee role should the government play in an economy? For example, should government redistribute income from the rich to the poor through taxation? Should it allow a merger between two companies? Should it regulate air traffic? Should it regulate prices?

Since considering government's role will be a central element of the entire book, I'll present a few terms and roles now to establish a framework for the later chapters.

4 Economic Roles of Government   I first consider the economic roles of government. These roles tend to be somewhat less controversial than its political roles.

Providing a Stable Institutional Framework   A basic economic role of government is to provide a stable institutional framework (the set of rules determining what we can and can't do). Before people conduct business, they need to know the rules of the game and have a reasonable belief about what those rules will be in the future. The modern economy requires contractual arrangements to be made among individuals. These arrangements must be enforced if the economy is to operate effectively. Ultimately only the government can create a stable environment and enforce contracts through its legal system. Where governments don't provide a stable environment, as often happens in developing countries, economic growth is difficult; usually such economies are stagnant. Liberia in the early 1990s is an example. As two groups there fought for political control, the Liberian economy stagnated.

Almost all economists believe providing an institutional framework within which the market can operate is an important function of government. However they differ significantly as to what the rules for such a system should be. Even if the rules are currently perceived as unfair, an argument can be made for keeping them. Individuals have already made decisions based on the existing rules so it's unfair to them to change the rules in midstream. Stability of rules is a benefit to society.

Recent economic reforms in the former Soviet Union provide a good example of this point. First, the Soviets modified their rules to encourage profits and entrepreneurship. Within a year they changed the rules again, attacking entrepreneurs as profiteers and confiscating their earnings. Then they began to encourage entrepreneurship again, but the second time few entrepreneurs came forward because of fear that the rules would change once again. Then there was a conservative coup; then a reestablishment of the market. Finally the entire political structure fell apart and the Soviet Union was no more.

When rules are perceived as unfair and changing them is also perceived as unfair, which often happens, the government finds itself in the difficult position of any referee, trying to strike a balance between the two degrees of unfairness.

Promoting Effective and Workable Competition   One of the most difficult economic functions of government is its role in protecting and promoting competition. As I discussed above, U.S. ideology sees monopoly power as bad. **Monopoly power** is the ability of individuals or firms currently in business to prevent other individuals or firms from entering the same kind of business; thereby monopoly power can raise existing firms' prices. Similarly U.S. ideology sees **competition** (individuals' or firms' ability to enter freely into business activities) as good. Government's job is to promote competition and prevent monopoly power from limiting competition.

> **Monopoly power** Ability to prevent others from entering a business field, which enables a firm to raise its price.

> **Competition** Ability of individuals to freely enter into business activities.

What makes this a difficult function for government is that most individuals and firms believe that competition is far better for the other guy than it is for themselves, that their monopolies are necessary monopolies, and that competition facing them is unfair competition. For example, farmers support competition, but they also support government farm subsidies and import restrictions, which make it harder for foreign individuals to compete in the United States. Likewise firms support competition, but they also support tariffs, which protect them from foreign competition. Professionals, such as architects and engineers, support competition, but they also support professional licensing, which limits the number of competitors who can enter their field.

Correcting for Externalities   When two people freely enter into a trade or agreement, they both believe that they will benefit from that trade. But unless they're required to do so, traders are unlikely to take into account the effect that that agreement or trade may have on others. (An effect of a trade or agreement on a third party that the people who made the trade did not take into account is called an *external effect* or **externality.**) An externality can be positive (in which case society as a whole benefits even more than the two traders) or negative (in which case society as a whole benefits less than the two parties). In either case, externalities provide a potential role for government. If one's goal is to benefit society as much as possible, trades with positive externalities should be encouraged, and trades with negative externalities should be restricted.

> **Externality** Effect of a trade or agreement on third parties that people did not take into account when they entered the trade or agreement.

An example of a positive externality is education. When someone educates herself or himself, it is not only the person who is helped. All society benefits since better-educated people make better citizens and can often figure out new approaches to solving problems, solutions that benefit everyone.

An example of a negative externality is pollution. For example, when people use air conditioners, they'll probably let loose a small amount of chlorofluorocarbons, which go up into the earth's atmosphere and contribute to the destruction of the ozone layer. The ozone layer protects all living things by filtering some of the sun's ultraviolet light rays, which can contribute to cancer and other harmful or fatal conditions. Neither the firms that produce the air conditioners nor the consumers who buy them pay for the negative effect those chlorofluorocarbons have on society. This means that the destruction of the ozone layer is an externality—the result of an action that is not taken into account by traders.

When externalities exist, government has a potential role: to step in and change the rules so that actors must take into account the effect of their actions on society as a whole. I emphasize that the role is a *potential* one, because government often has difficulty dealing with externalities in such a way that society gains. For example, even if the U.S. government totally banned chlorofluorocarbons, the problem wouldn't be solved because ozone layer destruction is an international, rather than a national, problem. I also emphasize *potential* because government isn't simply an institution trying to do good. It's an institution that reflects, and is often guided by, politics and vested interests. It's not clear that given the political realities, government intervention to correct externalities would improve the situation. In later chapters I'll have a lot more to say about government's role in correcting for externalities.

Public good Good whose consumption by one individual does not prevent its consumption by other individuals.

Private good Good that, when consumed by one individual, cannot be consumed by other individuals.

Providing for Public Goods   **Public goods** are goods whose consumption by one individual does not prevent their consumption by other individuals. This means that when a supplier supplies a public good to one person, he or she supplies the good to all. In contrast, a **private good** is one that, when consumed by one individual, cannot be consumed by other individuals. An example of a private good is an apple; once I eat that apple, no one else can consume it. An example of a public good is national defense. National defense must protect all individuals in the country; it cannot protect some people but leave others unprotected.

Everyone agrees that national defense is needed. But will everyone, as individuals, supply it, or will everyone rely on someone else doing it? Self-interested people would like to enjoy the benefits of defense, while letting someone else pay for it. Because national defense is a public good, if someone else defends the country you're defended for free; you can be a **free rider.** Everyone has an incentive to be a free rider, but if everyone is a free rider, there won't be any defense. In such cases government can step in to require that everyone pay part of the cost of national defense to make sure that no one is a free rider.

Free rider Person who participates in something for free because others have paid for it.

Ensuring Economic Stability and Growth   In addition to providing general stability, government has the potential role of providing economic stability. If it's possible, most people would agree that government should prevent large fluctuations in the level of economic activity; maintain a relatively constant price level; and provide an economic environment conducive to economic growth. These aims, which became U.S. government goals in 1946 when the Employment Act was passed, are generally considered macroeconomic goals. They're justified as appropriate aims for government to pursue because they involve **macroeconomic externalities** (externalities that affect the levels of unemployment, inflation, or growth in the economy as a whole).

Macroeconomic externality Externality that affects the levels of unemployment, inflation, or growth in an economy as a whole.

Here's how a macroexternality could occur. When individuals decide how much to spend, they don't take into account the effects of their decision on others; thus, there may be too much or too little spending. Too little spending often leads to unemployment. But in making their spending decision, people don't take into account the fact that spending less might create unemployment. So their spending decision can involve a macroexternality. Similarly when people raise their price and don't consider its effect on inflation, they too might be creating a macroexternality.

FINDING MORE INFORMATION ABOUT THE ECONOMY   **ADDED DIMENSION**

No introductory book is able to provide you with all the information you should have about the economy. You should know about:

- Financial institutions, such as banks, insurance companies, and stock markets.
- The state of the economy: unemployment rates, inflation rates, and growth rates.
- The operations of business, such as advertising and assembly line production.

I'll provide general information on such topics, but you should get up-to-date specifics by following the economic news. Such current information is integral to any economics course. Where should you look? A good beginning is the following:

- Cursory: Business section of your local paper and network news on TV. A slim treatment of the economic issues, but at least it introduces you to the terms.
- One step up from cursory: *Time, Newsweek, U.S. News & World Report;* a national newspaper's business sections (*New York Times, Los Angeles Times, Washington Post*); CNN on TV.
- Reasonably thorough: *Business Week, Forbes, Fortune* magazines; "Wall Street Week" and "The McNeil–Lehrer Report" on TV.
- Excellent: *The Wall Street Journal, The Economist, The Financial Times.*

Political Roles of Government   The other group of possible roles for government, *political roles,* involves more controversial issues.

Providing for a Fair Distribution of Society's Income   The first, and probably most controversial, of these roles concerns income distribution. Many believe the government should see that the economic system is fair or at least is perceived as fair by the majority of the people in the society.

But determining what's fair is a difficult philosophical question. Let's simply consider two of the many manifestations of the fairness problem. Should the government use a **progressive tax** (a tax whose rates increase as a person's income increases) to redistribute money from the rich to the poor? (A progressive income tax schedule might tax individuals at a rate of 15 percent for income up to $20,000; at 25 percent for income between $20,000 and $40,000; and at 35 percent for every dollar earned over $40,000.) Or should government impose a **regressive tax** (a tax whose rates decrease as income rises) to redistribute money from the poor to the rich? Or should government impose a flat or **proportional tax** (a tax whose rates are constant at all income levels, say 25 percent on every dollar of income, no matter what your total annual income is) and not redistribute money? The United States has chosen a somewhat progressive income tax, while the social security tax is a proportional tax up to a specified earned income.

Another tax question government faces is: Should there be *exemptions* (items of income that aren't taxed at all)? An exemption might be granted for $2,400 of income multiplied by the number of children the taxpayer has. A single mother with five children wouldn't be taxed at all on $12,000 ($2,400 × 5) of her annual income. Or is that a *tax loophole* (a legal but unfair exemption)? Economists can tell government the effects of various types of taxes and forms of taxation, but we can't tell government what's fair. That is for the people, through the government, to decide.

Determining Demerit and Merit Goods or Activities   Another controversial role for government involves deciding what's best for people independently of their desires. The externality justification of government intervention assumes that individuals know what is best for themselves.

But what if people don't know what's best for themselves? What if they do know but don't act on that knowledge? For example, people might know that

Demerit goods or activities Things government believes are bad for you, although you may like them.

Merit goods or activities Things government believes are good for you, although you may not think so.

addictive drugs are bad for them but because of peer pressure, or because they just don't care, they may take addictive drugs anyway. Government action prohibiting such activities through law or high taxes may then be warranted. Goods or activities that are deemed bad for people even though they choose to use the goods or engage in the activities are known as **demerit goods or activities.** The addictive drug is a demerit good; using addictive drugs is a demerit activity.

Alternatively there are some activities that government believes are good for people, even if people may not choose to engage in them. For example, government may believe that going to the opera or contributing to charity is a good activity. But in the United States only a small percentage of the population goes to the opera, and not everyone in the United States contributes to charity. Similarly government may believe that whole-wheat bread is more nutritious than white bread. But many consumers prefer white bread. Activities and goods that government believes are good for you even though you may not choose to engage in the activities or consume the goods are known as **merit goods or activities,** and government support for them through subsidies or tax benefits may be warranted.

The Limits of Government Action

Economic theory doesn't say government should or shouldn't play any particular role in the economy. Those decisions depend on costs and benefits of government action. The public often perceives economic theory and economists as suggesting the best policy is a policy of laissez-faire, or government noninvolvement in the economy. Many economists do suggest a laissez-faire policy, but that suggestion is based on empirical observations of government's role in the past, not on economic theory.

Still, economists as a group generally favor less government involvement than does the general public. I suspect that the reason is that economists are taught to look below the surface at the long-run effect of government actions. They've discovered that the effects of government actions often aren't the intended effects, and that programs frequently have long-run consequences that make the problems worse, not better. Economists, both liberal and conservative, speak in the voice of reason: "Look at all the costs; look at all the benefits. Then decide whether government should or should not intervene." Political pressures often force government to act, regardless of what rational examination suggests. A good example is new air safety regulations after a plane crash. The public generally favors these overwhelmingly. Most economists I know say: "Wait. Don't act in haste. Consider the benefits and costs that would result." After careful consideration, advantages and disadvantages aren't always clear; some economists favor more regulation, some economists favor less regulation—but they all make their assessments on the basis of rational examination, not emotion.

KEY POINTS

- The invisible hand doesn't operate in an invisible world. Knowing economics requires knowing real-world information. **1 2 3 5**
- Views about government's appropriate role in the economy have changed over time. **4**
- In the United States, businesses make the what, how much, and for whom decisions. **2**
- Businesses, households, and government can be categorized in a variety of ways. **1**

- The three main forms of business are corporations, sole proprietorships, and partnerships. **2**
- Income is unequally divided among households. Whether that's bad, and whether anything should be done about it, are debatable. **3**
- Governments play two general roles in the economy: economic and political. **4**
- Government has seven possible economic roles in a capitalist society: **4**

1. Providing a stable institutional and legal structure within which markets can operate.
2. Promoting workable and effective competition.
3. Correcting for external effects of individuals' decisions.
4. Providing public goods that the market doesn't adequately supply.

5. Ensuring economic stability and growth.
6. Providing an acceptably fair distribution of society's products among its individuals.
7. Encouraging merit and discouraging demerit goods or activities.

· In deciding whether government has a role to play, economists look at the costs and benefits of a given role. ▪**4**

KEY TERMS

business *(83)*
competition *(99)*
consumer sovereignty *(84)*
corporation *(91)*
debt *(97)*
demerit goods or activities *(102)*
entrepreneurship *(83)*
externality *(99)*

free rider *(100)*
government budget deficit *(97)*
government budget surplus *(97)*
households *(92)*
ideology *(94)*
limited liability *(91)*
macroeconomic externality *(100)*

merit goods or activities *(102)*
military-industrial complex *(95)*
monopoly power *(99)*
nonprofit business *(88)*
partnership *(90)*
private good *(100)*
profit *(84)*

progressive tax *(101)*
proportional tax *(101)*
public good *(100)*
regressive tax *(101)*
sole proprietorship *(90)*
stock *(91)*

QUESTIONS FOR THOUGHT AND REVIEW

The number after each question represents the estimated degree of critical thinking required. (1 = almost none; 10 = deep thought.)

1. A market system is often said to be based on consumer sovereignty—the consumer determines what's to be produced. Yet business decides what's to be produced. Can these two views be reconciled? How? If not, why? *(5)*
2. How many kilometers of highway does the United States have? *(2)*
3. The United States is sometimes classified as a postindustrial society. What's meant by this? And, if it's an accurate classification, is it good or bad to be a postindustrial society? *(7)*
4. A nonprofit company will generally charge lower prices than a for-profit company in the same business because the nonprofit company doesn't factor a profit into its prices. True or false? Why? *(6)*

5. You're starting a software company in which you plan to sell software to your fellow students. What form of business organization would you choose? Why? *(5)*
6. The social security system is inconsistent with pure capitalism, but is almost an untouchable right of Americans. How can this be? *(6)*
7. You've set up the rules for a game and started the game, but now realize that the rules are unfair. Should you change the rules? *(6)*
8. Say the government establishes rights to pollute so that without a pollution permit you aren't allowed to emit pollutants into the air, water, or soil. Firms are allowed to buy and sell these rights. In what way will this correct for an externality? *(9)*
9. What are two general roles of government and seven specific roles? *(3)*
10. According to polls, most U.S. economists classify themselves as liberal, but they generally favor less government involvement in the economy than does the general public. Why? *(6)*

PROBLEMS AND EXERCISES

1. Go to a store in your community.
   a. Ask what limitations the owners faced in starting their business.
   b. Were these limitations necessary?
   c. Should there have been more or fewer limitations?
   d. Under what heading of reasons for government intervention would you put each of the limitations?
   e. Ask what taxes the business pays and what benefits it believes it gets for those taxes.
   f. Is it satisfied with the existing situation? Why? What would it change?

2. You've been appointed to a county counterterrorist squad. Your assignment is to work up a set of plans to stop a group of 10 terrorists the government believes are going to disrupt the economy as much as possible with explosives.
   a. List their five most likely targets in your county, city, or town.
   b. What counterterrorist action would you take?
   c. How would you advise the economy to adjust to a successful attack on each of the targets?

Trading in Stocks

Small corporations' stock is usually traded *over-the-counter,* which doesn't mean you go in a store and walk up to the counter. *Over-the-counter* is an expression representing the stock exchange on which these stocks are bought and sold. An over-the-counter share has a *bid* price and a higher *ask* price. The bid price is the price someone has offered to pay for shares; the ask price is the price a shareholder has told her brokers she wants to get for her shares. Trades are usually made at some price between the bid and ask figures, with the broker collecting a commission for arranging a trade.

Exhibit A1 shows a typical stock exchange listing. Stocks sold on the New York Stock Exchange have only one price listed. That's because the exchange has a "specialist" market-maker system, in which a particular broker markets a particular group of stocks. This specialist always stands ready to buy or sell shares of a stock at some price. The specialist sets a price and then varies it according to whether he or she is receiving more buy orders or more sell orders.

In order to buy or sell a New York Stock Exchange stock, you go to a stockbroker and say you want to buy or sell whatever stock you've decided

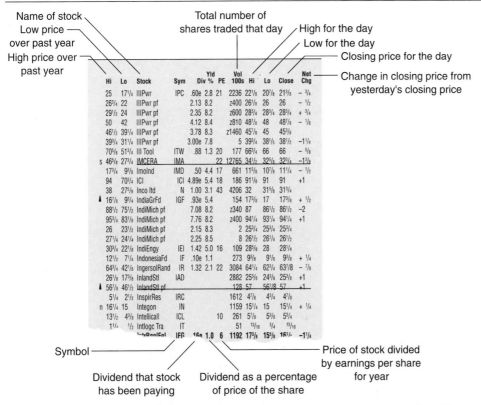

Name of stock
Low price over past year
High price over past year
Total number of shares traded that day
High for the day
Low for the day
Closing price for the day
Change in closing price from yesterday's closing price
Symbol
Dividend that stock has been paying
Dividend as a percentage of price of the share
Price of stock divided by earnings per share for year

EXHIBIT A1   Stock Quotations, New York Stock Exchange

Source: *The Wall Street Journal,* April 12, 1992. Reprinted by permission of *The Wall Street Journal* © 1992 Dow Jones & Company, Inc. All rights reserved worldwide.

Source: *The Wall Street Journal,* April 12, 1992. Reprinted by permission of *The Wall Street Journal,* © 1992 Dow Jones Company, Inc. All Rights Reserved Worldwide.

on—say Ford Motor Company. The commission you're charged for having the broker sell you the stock (sell it for you) varies. Any purchase of fewer than 100 shares of one corporation is called an *odd lot* and you'll be charged a higher commission than if you buy a 100-share lot or more.

There are a number of stock exchanges. The largest and most familiar is the New York Stock Exchange. About 47 million individuals own stock they bought on the New York Stock Exchange.

To judge how stocks as a whole are doing, a number of indexes have been developed. These include Standard and Poor's (S&P 500), the Wilshire Index, and the Dow Jones Industrial Average. The Dow Jones is the one you're most likely to hear about in the news.

When a share of a corporation's existing stock is sold on the stock exchange, corporations get no money from that sale. The sale is simply a transfer of ownership from one individual (or organization) to another. The only times a corporation gets money from the sale of stock are when it first issues the shares.

5

An Introduction
to the World Economy

*As for foreign exchange, it is
almost as romantic as young love, and quite as resistant to formulae.*

H. L. Mencken

After reading this chapter, you should be able to:

1

Explain what is meant by *the industrial
countries of the world* and *the developing
countries of the world.*

2

State where in the world various resources
are found and where goods are produced.

3

State two ways international trade differs
from domestic trade.

4

Make sense of an exchange rate table
in the newspaper.

5

Explain two important causes
of a trade deficit.

6

List five important international
economic institutions.

7

Give a brief economic history of the
European Economic Community and Japan
since the 1940s.

Once there was a time when you could proceed from a discussion of the U.S. economy to a discussion of macroeconomics and microeconomics, the two divisions of economics. No longer. International issues now must also be taken into account in just about every economic decision the United States faces. The U.S. economy is now integrated with the world economy, and we cannot reasonably discuss U.S. economic issues without discussing the role that international considerations play in these issues.

Consider the clothes on your back. Most likely they were made abroad. Similarly with the cars you drive. It's likely that half of you drive a car that was made abroad. Of course, it's often difficult to tell. Just because a car has a Japanese or German name doesn't mean that it was produced abroad. Some Japanese and German companies now have manufacturing plants in the United States and some U.S. firms have manufacturing plants abroad. When goods are produced by **multinational corporations** (corporations with substantial

Multinational corporation Corporation with substantial operations on both the production and sales sides in more than one country.

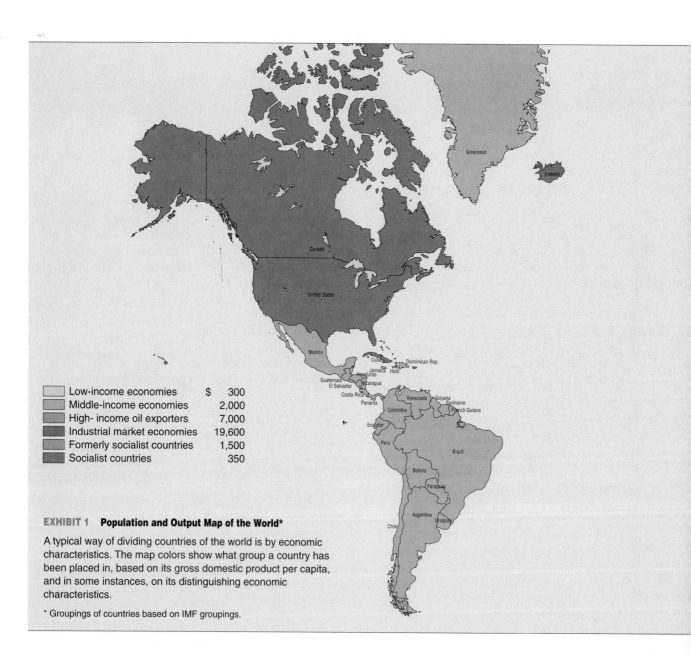

	Low-income economies	$	300
	Middle-income economies		2,000
	High- income oil exporters		7,000
	Industrial market economies		19,600
	Formerly socialist countries		1,500
	Socialist countries		350

EXHIBIT 1   Population and Output Map of the World*

A typical way of dividing countries of the world is by economic characteristics. The map colors show what group a country has been placed in, based on its gross domestic product per capita, and in some instances, on its distinguishing economic characteristics.

* Groupings of countries based on IMF groupings.

operations on both the production and sales sides in more than one country), corporate names don't always tell much about where a good is produced. As multinational corporations' importance has grown, most manufacturing decisions are made in reference to the international market, not the domestic U.S. market.

The economic focus has shifted to the world economy in finance as well as manufacturing. In 1970 the world's 10 largest banks were all headquartered in the United States. Today not even one is in the United States.

The international connection means international economic problems and the policies of other countries (European trade policy, developing countries' debt problems, questions of the United States's competitiveness, transfer of U.S. technology to China, Japanese microeconomic policy, OPEC pricing policies) all have moved to the center of the economic stage. This chapter introduces you to these issues.

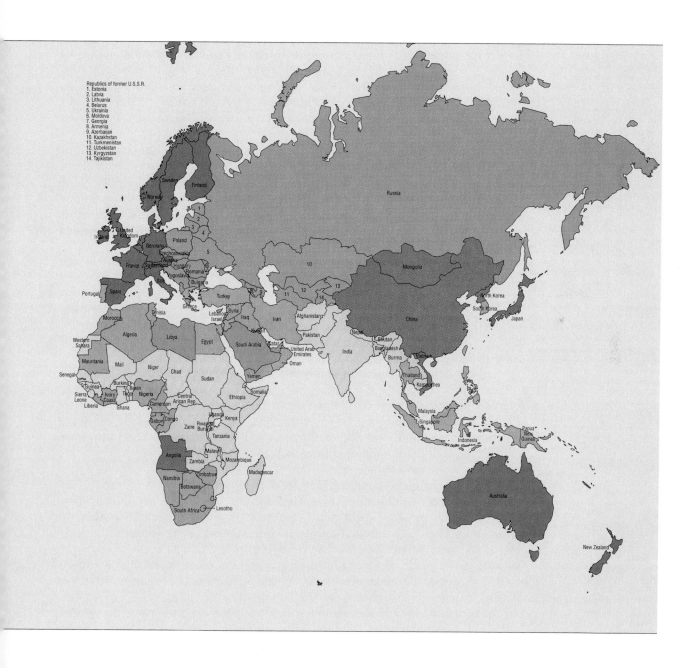

INTERNATIONAL ECONOMIC STATISTICS: AN OVERVIEW

1

Exhibit 1's map of the world is divided into categories based on per capita output (output per person) and then relevant economic characteristics. *Industrial high-income countries* (such as the United States, Germany, and Britain) have a large industrial production base. A second group of countries, such as Kuwait and Saudi Arabia, have high incomes, but don't have the industrial base. Since their high income is primarily based on oil exports, those countries are known as oil-producing high-income countries. The next two classifications, *middle-income countries* and *low-income countries* (or as they are sometimes called, *developing countries*), make up the majority of countries in the world. The final two classifications, the *formerly socialist countries* and the *socialist countries,* are in a period of flux and will probably be much in the news in the 1990s.

The above method isn't the only method of classification. An alternative method is by region: Latin American, African, Middle Eastern, Asian, European, North American, and Eastern European countries. Since geographically grouped countries often share a cultural heritage, they also often face similar problems.

None of these classifications is airtight. Each country is different from every other, so no grouping works perfectly. Exhibit 1's classification system based largely on output per person is the most commonly used, and should give you a sense of what's meant by such classifications. The next time you hear "the industrial nations of the world" or "the developing countries of the world," you should be able to close your eyes and picture the relevant group of economies on a map or, at least, have a general idea of which countries are meant.

Economic Geography

Most classifications of countries are based on a country's total output or production. Production statistics, however, don't necessarily capture a nation's importance or the strategic role it plays in the world economy. Consider Saudi Arabia. Its total output isn't particularly large, but since it's a major supplier of oil to the world, its strategic importance goes far beyond the relative size of its economy. Without its oil, many of the industrial countries of the world would come to a grinding halt. Similarly Panama's production is minuscule, but its location on a narrow isthmus between the Atlantic and Pacific Oceans and the fact that the Panama Canal runs through its territory make Panama vital to the world economy.

These examples demonstrate why we need, besides a knowledge of countries' productive capacities, a knowledge of economic geography: Where do the world's natural resources lie? Which countries control them? What are the major trade routes? How are goods shipped from one place to another?

2

Exhibit 2 locates some of the world's major energy resources and trade routes. Note the major flow of energy resources from the Middle East. You can see why the Middle East is so important to the world economy (oil and the Suez Canal). Other such resource maps would show why many countries treat South Africa with care (gold, many other alloying metals, and diamonds) and why Chile (with 27 percent of all copper) is important to the world economy.

Differing Economic Problems

The economic problems countries face are determined by a variety of factors such as countries' per capita income level. High-income countries generally face quite different problems than low-income countries. Even two countries within the same group often face different problems. For example, a significant U.S. problem is its trade deficit. As I'll discuss later in the chapter, the United States **imports** (buys goods produced in foreign countries) much more than it **exports** (sells U.S. goods to foreign countries). A significant Japanese problem is its trade surplus; Japan exports much more than it imports.

Although the identical economic insights apply to all countries, institutions differ substantially among countries. For example, many developing countries

Imports Goods and services a country buys from abroad.

Exports Goods and services a country sells abroad.

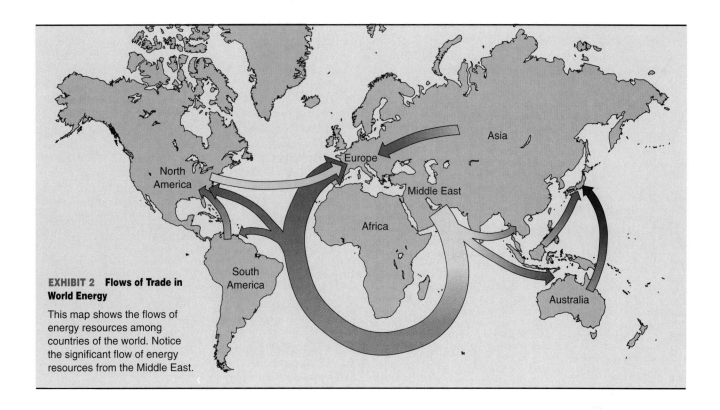

EXHIBIT 2   Flows of Trade in World Energy

This map shows the flows of energy resources among countries of the world. Notice the significant flow of energy resources from the Middle East.

have few financial institutions, so when people there want to save, there's no way for them to do so. Similarly with transportation systems. If a firm wants to ship a good from Kansas City to Seattle, it can use trucks, trains, or planes. However, if an African firm wants to ship a good from one city to another in Zaire—say from Kinshasa to Lubumbashi—it must import trucks that can travel on unpaved or even nonexistent roads.

One reason economies differ is that they produce different goods. Why? That's a question I'll explore in some detail in a later chapter on international trade. For now, I'll simply introduce you to a key term in international trade which plays a major role in what different countries produce. That term is **comparative advantage.** A country has a comparative advantage in producing a good if it can produce that good at a lower opportunity cost (forgone production of another good) than another country can. For example, say the United States can produce widgets at a cost of $4 apiece and wadgets at $4 apiece, while Korea can produce widgets at a cost of 300 won apiece and wadgets at a cost of 100 won apiece. In the United States the opportunity cost of one widget is one wadget. (Since each costs $4, the United States must reduce its production of wadgets by one to produce another widget.) In Korea the opportunity cost of a widget is three wadgets since it costs three times as much to produce a widget as it does to produce a wadget. Because the United States's opportunity cost of producing widgets is lower than Korea's, the United States is said to have a comparative advantage in producing widgets. Similarly Korea is said to have a comparative advantage in producing wadgets because its opportunity cost of wadgets is one-third of a widget while the United States' opportunity cost of wadgets is one widget. If one country has a comparative advantage in one good, the other country must necessarily have a comparative advantage in the other good. Notice how comparative advantage hinges on opportunity cost, not total cost. Even if one country can produce all

Comparative Advantage and Trade

Comparative advantage A country's ability to produce a good at a lower opportunity cost than another country can.

Economic geography isn't much covered in most economics courses because it requires learning enormous numbers of facts, and college courses aren't a good place to learn facts. College is designed to teach you how to interpret and relate facts. Unfortunately if you don't know facts, much of what you learn in college isn't going to do you much good. You'll be relating and interpreting air. The following quiz presents some facts about the world economy. On the left I list characteristics of countries or regions. On the right I list 20 countries or regions. Associate the characteristics with the country or region.

If you score 15 or better, you have a reasonably good sense of economic geography. If you don't, I strongly suggest learning more facts. The study guide has a number of other projects, information, and examples. An encyclopedia has even more, and your library has a wealth of information. You could spend the entire semester acquiring facts. I'm not suggesting that; I am suggesting following the economic news carefully, paying attention to where various commodities are produced, and picturing in your mind a map whenever you hear about an economic event.

_____ 1. former British colony, now small independent island country famous for producing rum

_____ 2. large sandy country contains world's largest known oil reserves

_____ 3. very large country with few people produces 25 percent of the world's wool

_____ 4. temperate country ideal for producing wheat, soybeans, fruits, vegetables, wine, and meat

_____ 5. small tropical country produces abundant coffee and bananas

_____ 6. has world's largest population and world's largest hydropower potential

_____ 7. second largest country in Europe; famous for wine and romance

_____ 8. former Belgian colony has vast copper mines

_____ 9. European country; exports luxury clothing, footwear, and automobiles

_____ 10. large country that has depleted many of its own resources but has enough coal to last its people for hundreds of years

_____ 11. long, narrow island; most thickly populated country in the world; exports majority of the world's electronic products

_____ 12. recently politically reunified country; one important product is steel

_____ 13. second largest country in the world; a good neighbor to the United States; leading paper exporter

_____ 14. European country for centuries politically repressed; now becoming industrialized; chemicals are one of its leading exports

_____ 15. 96 percent of its people live on 4 percent of the land; much of the world's finest cotton comes from here

_____ 16. politically and racially troubled African nation has world's largest concentration of gold

_____ 17. huge, heavily populated country eats most of what it raises but is a major tea exporter

_____ 18. large country that produces gold and diamonds; has recently undergone major political and economic changes

_____ 19. has only about 50 people per square mile but lots of trees; major timber exporter

_____ 20. sliver of a country on Europe's Atlantic coast; by far the world's largest exporter of cork

a. Australia
b. Argentina
c. Barbados
d. Canada
e. China
f. Costa Rica
g. Egypt
h. India
i. Saudi Arabia
j. Italy
k. South Africa
l. Zaire
m. Portugal
n. Sweden
o. Spain
p. France
q. United States
r. Germany
s. Japan
t. Russia

Answers: 1: c. 2: i. 3: a. 4: b. 5: f. 6: e. 7: p. 8: l. 9: j. 10: q. 11: s. 12: r. 13: d. 14: o. 15: g. 16: k. 17: h. 18: t. 19: n. 20: m.

EXHIBIT 3   Per Capita Consumption of Different Commodities, 1991

In Exhibit 3 you can see the per capita consumption of meat and poultry in various countries. Notice that the United States consumes less beef and veal than does Argentina, and its consumption of pork is small compared to all the other countries.

Source: *Statistical Abstract*, 1992.

(a)

(b)

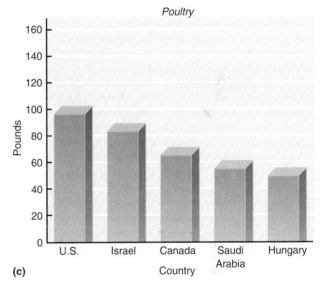

(c)

goods cheaper than another country, trade between them is still possible since the opportunity costs of various goods differ.

Countries not only produce different goods, they also consume different goods. Exhibit 3 presents per capita consumption of some foods in selected countries. Notice the differences. The United States ranks high in per capita consumption of beef and poultry, but low in consumption of pork. One reason for the differences is that goods' relative prices differ among countries. The United States and Argentina produce lots of beef, so the price of beef is low in these countries and consumption of beef is high. Germany produces lots of pigs, so the price of pork in Germany is low and Germans consume lots of pork. Such differences are consistent with economic explanations.

Other differences in consumption (and production) are explained by custom, history, and tradition. For example, Japanese traditionally eat rice with meals; Americans eat bread and potatoes. Drinking alcoholic beverages in Russia is a time-honored tradition; Muslim countries, such as Saudi Arabia, forbid consumption of alcoholic beverages. Understanding international economic issues often requires an in-depth understanding of various countries' histories and cultures. **3**

David Ricardo—An 18th-century stock-broker and economist who played a key role in the development of the theory of comparative advantage. *The Bettmann Archive.*

HOW INTERNATIONAL TRADE DIFFERS FROM DOMESTIC TRADE

Quotas Quantity limitations on imports and exports.

Tariffs Taxes on imports.

Nontariff barriers Indirect regulatory restrictions on imports and exports.

Foreign exchange market Markets in which one currency can be exchanged for another.

*Inter*national trade differs from *intra*national (domestic) trade in two ways. First, international trade involves potential barriers to the flow of inputs and outputs. Before they can be sold in the United States, international goods must be sent through U.S. Customs; that is, when they enter the United States they are inspected by U.S. officials and usually charged fees, known as *customs*. A company in Texas can produce output to sell in any U.S. state without worrying that its right to sell will be limited; a producer outside the U.S. boundary cannot. At any time a foreign producer's right to sell in the United States can be limited by government-imposed **quotas** (limitations on how much of a good can be shipped into a country), **tariffs** (taxes on imports), and **nontariff barriers** (indirect regulatory restrictions on imports and exports).

The last category, indirect regulatory restrictions on imports and exports, may be unfamiliar to you, so let's consider an example. U.S. building codes require that plywood have fewer than, say, three flaws per sheet. Canadian building codes require that plywood have fewer than, say, five flaws per sheet. The different building codes are a nontariff barrier, making trade in building materials between the United States and Canada difficult.

The second way international trade differs from domestic or intranational trade is countries' use of different currencies. When people in one country sell something to people in another, they must find a way to exchange currencies as well as goods. **Foreign exchange markets** (markets where one currency can be exchanged for another) have developed to provide this service.

How many dollars will an American have to pay to get a given amount of the currency of another country? That depends on the supply of and demand for that currency. To find what you'd have to pay, you look in the newspaper for the exchange rate set out in a foreign exchange table. Exhibit 4 shows such a table.

4

If you want shekels, you'll have to pay about 43¢ apiece. If you want Punt, one Punt will cost you $1.63. (If you're wondering what shekels and Punt are, look at Exhibit 4.)

Unless you collect currencies, the reason you want the currency of another country is that you want to buy something that country produces or an existing asset of that country. Say you want to buy a Hyundai car which costs 6,120,000

EXCHANGE RATES

Wednesday, February 19, 1992

The New York foreign exchange selling rates below apply to trading among banks in amounts of $1 million and more, as quoted at 3 p.m. Eastern time by Bankers Trust Co., Telerate Systems Inc. and other sources. Retail transactions provide fewer units of foreign currency per dollar.

	U.S.$ equiv. Wed.	U.S.$ equiv. Tues.	Currency per U.S.$ Wed.	Currency per U.S.$ Tues.
Argentina (Peso)	1.03	1.00	.97	1.00
Australia (Dollar)	.7570	.7550	1.3210	1.3245
Austria (Schilling)	.08647	.08618	11.57	11.60
Bahrain (Dinar)	2.6539	2.6525	.3768	.3770
Belgium (Franc)	.02958	.02953	33.81	33.86
Brazil (Cruzeiro)	.00069	.00069	1454.81	1438.90
Britain (Pound)	1.7540	1.7525	.5701	.5706
30-Day Forward	1.7450	1.7439	.5731	.5734
90-Day Forward	1.7287	1.7269	.5785	.5791
180-Day Forward	1.7055	1.7039	.5863	.5869
Canada (Dollar)	.8432	.8407	1.1860	1.1895
30-Day Forward	.8410	.8386	1.1890	1.1925
90-Day Forward	.8367	.8341	1.1952	1.1989
180-Day Forward	.8308	.8280	1.2036	1.2077
Czechoslovakia (Koruna)				
Commercial rate	.0353357	.0353982	28.3000	28.2500
Chile (Peso)	.002974	.002966	336.30	337.14
China (Renminbi)	.183150	.183486	5.4600	5.4500
Colombia (Peso)	.001805	.001790	553.90	558.68
Denmark (Krone)	.1570	.1568	6.3685	6.3763
Ecuador (Sucre)				
Floating rate	.000768	.000763	1301.64	1310.02
Finland (Markka)	.22239	.22241	4.4966	4.4963
France (Franc)	.17888	.17855	5.5903	5.6006
30-Day Forward	.17800	.17767	5.6180	5.6283
90-Day Forward	.17636	.17602	5.6703	5.6811
180-Day Forward	.17401	.17371	5.7468	5.7568
Germany (Mark)	.6085	.6072	1.6435	1.6470
30-Day Forward	.6057	.6045	1.6511	1.6542
90-Day Forward	.6005	.5991	1.6654	1.6692
180-Day Forward	.5929	.5917	1.6865	1.6901
Greece (Drachma)	.005282	.005266	189.33	189.89
Hong Kong (Dollar)	.12887	.12894	7.7595	7.7555
Hungary (Forint)	.0129719	.0129366	77.0900	77.3000
India (Rupiah)	.03817	.03874	26.20	25.81
Indonesia (Rupiah)	.0004975	.0004995	2010.01	2002.00
Ireland (Punt)	1.6275	1.6241	.6144	.6157
Israel (Shekel)	.4340	.4352	2.3039	2.2980
Italy (Lira)	.0008113	.0008094	1232.62	1235.42
Japan (Yen)	.007802	.007813	128.17	128.00
30-Day Forward	.007794	.007804	128.31	128.14
90-Day Forward	.007783	.007793	128.49	128.32
180-Day Forward	.007778	.007788	128.56	128.41

	U.S.$ equiv. Wed.	U.S.$ equiv. Tues.	Currency per U.S.$ Wed.	Currency per U.S.$ Tues.
Jordan (Dinar)	1.4984	1.4738	.6674	.6785
Kuwait (Dinar)	3.4247	3.4358	.2920	.2911
Lebanon (Pound)	.001138	.001138	879.00	879.00
Malaysia (Ringgit)	.3856	.3854	2.5935	2.5950
Malta (Lira)	3.1949	3.1949	.3130	.3130
Mexico (Peso)				
Floating rate	.0003267	.0003267	3061.01	3061.01
Netherland (Guilder)	.05408	.5399	1.8491	1.8522
New Zealand (Dollar)	.05425	.5415	1.8433	1.8467
Norway (Krone)	.1554	.1551	6.4367	6.4463
Pakistan (Rupee)	.0408	.0408	24.52	24.52
Peru (New Sol)	1.0466	1.0466	.96	.96
Philippines (Peso)	.03929	.03929	25.45	25.45
Poland (Zloty)	.00009462	.00009091	10569.00	11000.01
Portugal (Escudo)	.007109	.007122	140.67	140.41
Saudi Arabia (Riyal)	.26667	.26667	3.7500	3.7500
Singapore (Dollar)	.6085	.6077	1.6435	1.6455
South Africa (Rand)				
Commercial rate	.3531	.3536	2.8323	2.8278
Financial rate	.2827	.2773	3.5370	3.6060
South Korea (Won)	.0013072	.0013072	765.00	765.00
Spain (Peseta)	.009722	.009722	102.88	102.86
Sweden (Krone)	.1678	.1674	5.9609	5.9728
Switzerland (Franc)	.6727	.6720	1.4865	1.4880
30-Day Forward	.6709	.6703	1.4905	1.4919
90-Day Forward	.6673	.6667	1.4985	1.4999
180-Day Forward	.6624	.6617	1.5097	1.5112
Taiwan (Dollar)	.040364	.040388	24.77	24.76
Thailand (Baht)	.03951	.03951	25.31	25.31
Turkey (Lira)	.0001755	.0001774	5698.00	5637.01
United Arab (Dirham)	.2723	.2723	3.6725	3.6725
Uruguay (New Peso)				
Financial	.000395	.000395	2530.01	2530.01
Venezuela (Bolivar)				
Floating rate	.01586	.01558	63.04	64.20
SDR	1.37992	1.38092	.72468	.72415
ECU	1.24550	1.24600		

Special Drawing Rights (SDR) are based on exchange rates for the U.S., German, British, French, and Japanese currencies. Source: International Monetaty Fund.

European Currency Unit (ECU) is based on a basket of community currencies.

EXHIBIT 4   A Foreign Exchange Rate Table

From the exchange rate table, you learn how much a dollar is worth in other countries. For example, on this day, February 19, 1992, one dollar would buy 5.5903 French francs or 128.17 yen. The table also tells you how many dollars other currencies can buy. For example, one British pound could buy 1.754 dollars.

Source: Reprinted by permission of *The Wall Street Journal* © 1992 Dow Jones & Company, Inc. All rights reserved worldwide.

South Korean won. Looking at the table you see that the exchange rate is $1 for 765 won. Dividing 765 into 6,120,000 won tells you that you need $8,000 to buy the car. So before you can buy the Hyundai, somebody must go to a foreign exchange market with $8,000 and exchange those dollars for 6.12 million won. Only then can the car be bought in the United States. Most final buyers don't do this; the importer does it for them. But whenever a foreign good is bought, someone must trade currencies.

One reason a U.S. economics course must consider international issues early on is the U.S. **balance of trade** (the difference between the goods a country imports and the goods it exports). When imports exceed exports, a country is running a **trade deficit**; when exports exceed imports, a country is running a **trade surplus**.

Exhibit 5 shows that since the mid-1970s the United States has been running a trade deficit, which increased substantially in the late 1980s. Although it declined a bit in the early 1990s, most economists consider the trade deficit a figure to watch. In 1987 when the trade deficit was at its highest, U.S. imports were about 9 percent of its total output; exports were about 6 percent. The 3 percent difference meant the United States imported about $170 billion worth of goods more than it exported.

THE U.S. INTERNATIONAL TRADE DEFICIT

Balance of trade Difference between the goods and services a country buys from abroad and those it sells abroad.

Trade deficit Excess of goods and services bought from abroad over goods and services sold abroad.

Trade surplus Excess of goods and services sold abroad over goods and services bought from abroad.

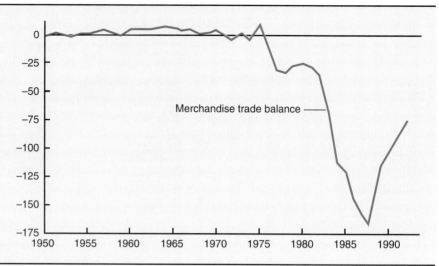

EXHIBIT 5   U.S. Trade Balance

The balance of trade is the difference between the amount of goods a country imports and the amount it sells abroad, or exports. As you can see from the graph, since the early 1980s the United States has imported many more goods than it has exported. Economists say the United States is running a trade deficit. As you can see, the trade deficit declined somewhat in the early 1990s, but it remained large.
Source: U.S. Dept. of Commerce, *Survey of Current Business.*

Debtor and Creditor Nations

Running a trade deficit isn't necessarily bad. In fact, while you're doing it, it's rather nice. If you were a country, you probably would be running a trade deficit now since, most likely, you're consuming (importing) more than you're producing (exporting). How can you do that? By living off past savings, getting support from your parents or a spouse, or borrowing. Countries have the same options. They can live off foreign aid, past savings, or loans. For example, the U.S. economy is currently financing its trade deficit by selling off assets—financial assets such as stocks and bonds, or real assets such as real estate and corporations. Since the assets of the United States total many trillions of dollars, it can continue to run trade deficits of similar size for decades to come.

The United States has not always run a trade deficit. Following World War II it ran large trade surpluses with the other countries so it was an international lender. Thus, it acquired large amounts of foreign assets. Because of the large trade deficits the United States ran in the 1980s, now the United States is a large debtor nation. The United States has borrowed more from abroad than it has lent abroad.

As the United States has gone from being a large creditor nation to being the world's biggest debtor, international considerations have been forced upon us. The cushion of being a creditor—of having a flow of interest income—has been replaced by the trials of being a debtor and having to pay out interest every year without getting anything for it.

Determinants of the Trade Deficit

In determining the size of the trade deficit two factors are important:

    1. U.S. competitiveness and the value of the dollar.
    2. The state of the U.S. economy compared to that of other countries.

Let's look at each factor.

5 **U.S. Competitiveness**   Probably the single most important issue in determining whether a country runs a trade deficit or a trade surplus is its **competitiveness** (the ability to produce goods more cheaply than other countries). Competitiveness depends upon productivity: a country's output per worker and its technological innovativeness (its ability to develop new and different products).

In the 1960s and early 1970s the United States was highly competitive. Even though U.S. workers were paid substantially more than foreign workers, U.S.

Competitiveness A country's ability to produce goods and services more cheaply than other countries.

BLACK AND GRAY MARKETS IN CURRENCY

Foreign exchange markets are a good example of supply and demand forces at work. Whenever there's excess supply or demand for something, there's incentive for suppliers and demanders to get together to eliminate the excess.

Let's consider the issue in relation to the former Soviet Union. In 1989 at the official price of 0.64 rubles per dollar, the quantity of dollars demanded far exceeded the quantity of dollars supplied. In the former Soviet Union adventurous individuals (who weren't worried about the wrath of the invisible foot—that is, about being prosecuted for violating foreign exchange laws) traded in a black market at a higher price, which in the early 1990s reached 30 rubles per dollar. A black market, which involves trades of a good that can't legally be traded, is a natural result of government price restrictions. Often the government knows that such trading goes on and chooses, for political reasons, not to enforce its own laws strictly. (There are situations like this in the United States. Here the speed limit is 55 miles per hour on many roads, but almost everyone drives at 65 miles per

hour, which police tend to accept as a fact of life.) When a black market is unofficially condoned, trading on it becomes more open and it's often called a *gray market*. Since risk of prosecution is less, upward pressure on price from the invisible foot is less; so gray market prices are usually closer to the supply/demand equilibrium than are black market prices.

The Soviet foreign exchange market became a gray market in late 1989. (The gray market price of a dollar was between 5 and 15 rubles rather than the 1.6 rubles you'd get at the official rate.) If you went to the former Soviet Union at that time, individuals would come up to you on the street and offer to trade rubles for dollars at something near the gray market price. In 1991 the Soviet Union broke apart and Russia began to let the ruble be freely tradable. Because of political and economic problems, however, the ruble's value fell enormously to well over 100 rubles to a dollar in 1992.

goods were cheaper, better, and more desired than foreign goods. In the 1950s the label MADE IN JAPAN was a sign of low-quality, cheap goods. That has changed since the late 1970s. While the United States lost its competitive edge, Japan gained one. Today MADE IN JAPAN is a sign of quality.

Japan's rise from a defeated country after World War II, with few natural resources, little land, and a devastated economy, into an international economic power that outcompetes the United States in almost every aspect of economics was an important economic story of the 1980s. One reason for Japan's rise was cultural. Another reason was the relative values of the Japanese yen and U.S. dollar. Throughout much of the 1960s, 1970s, and 1980s the yen's relative value was low. A major determinant of a country's competitiveness is the value of its currency. A currency that is low in value relative to other currencies encourages the country's exports by lowering their prices and discourages its imports by raising their prices. (In 1965, $1 bought about 305 yen; in 1992, $1 bought about 130 yen. Similarly the dollar's relatively high value during the 1960s undermined U.S. competitiveness.)

In the late 1980s the dollar's value relative to the yen fell substantially, making U.S. goods more competitive. But that fall didn't eliminate the U.S. trade deficit, and it became apparent that the problems of the United States in international competitiveness have additional causes. Moreover, the fall in the dollar's value has a downside: It means that U.S. assets are cheaper for foreigners. They can buy not only the products we make, but also the firms that make those products, the buildings within which those products are made, and the land upon which those buildings stand. In the 1990s we'll likely hear much about foreigners "buying up America."

Bertil Ohlin—Nobel prize, 1977, for work on international economics. © *The Nobel Foundation.*

The State of the U.S. Economy   A second factor in determining the trade balance is the state of the economy. The level of U.S. income affects the trade balance, and the trade balance affects the level of U.S. income. The reason for the first effect is simple. Say the United States is running a trade deficit—when U.S. income rises, the U.S. imports more, so the trade deficit increases.

The second effect—the trade balance's effect on U.S. income—isn't so simple. Say the United States has a trade deficit—when the United States imports more (or exports less), the trade deficit worsens and the rise in imports means U.S. production falls, which means U.S. citizens have less income; they spend less and U.S. income falls even more. So an increase in the trade deficit lowers income. It also works the opposite way: When the United States exports more (imports less), U.S. production rises; as U.S. production rises, U.S. citizens have more income; they spend more and U.S. income rises even more. This effect of exports on domestic income is what economists mean when they say a country has "export-led growth." A country with export-led growth has a trade surplus which stimulates growth in income.

Economists' View of Trade Restrictions

Large trade deficits often inspire politicians to call for trade restrictions prohibiting imports. Most economists, liberal and conservative alike, oppose such restrictions. The reason is that even though trade restrictions directly decrease the trade deficit, they also have negative effects on the economy that work in the opposite direction. One negative effect is that trade restrictions reduce domestic competition. When a group of U.S. producers can't compete with foreign producers—either in price or in quality—that group often pushes for trade restrictions to prevent what they call "unfair" foreign competition. U.S. producers benefit from the trade restrictions, but consumers are hurt. Prices to consumers rise and the quality of the goods they buy falls. A second negative effect is that trade restrictions bring retaliation. If one country limits imports, the other country responds; the first country responds to that . . . The result is called a *trade war*, and a trade war hurts everyone.

Such a trade war occurred in the 1930s and significantly contributed to the Great Depression of that period. To prevent trade wars, countries have entered into a variety of international agreements. The most important is the **General Agreement on Tariffs and Trade (GATT),** in which countries agree not to impose new tariffs or other trade restrictions except under certain limited conditions.

General Agreement on Tariffs and Trade (GATT) International agreement not to impose trade restrictions except under certain limited conditions.

True to form, the U.S. trade deficit of the 1980s and 1990s has brought about significant political pressure for import restrictions on foreign goods—especially Japanese goods. Supporters of trade restrictions against Japan argue that GATT isn't fair, that Japan has many more barriers to U.S. goods than the United States has barriers to Japanese goods. Japan bashing in the United States, and United States bashing in Japan, have become common, and a trade war between the two countries is a definite possibility.

INTERNATIONAL ECONOMIC POLICY AND INSTITUTIONS

Just as international trade differs from domestic trade, so does international economic policy differ from domestic economic policy. When economists talk about U.S. economic policy, they generally refer to what the U.S. federal government can do to achieve certain goals. In theory, at least, the U.S. federal government has both the power and the legal right of compulsion to make U.S. citizens do what it says. It can tax, it can redistribute income, it can regulate, and it can enforce property rights.

There is no international counterpart to a nation's federal government. Any meeting of a group of countries to discuss trade policies is voluntary. No international government has powers of compulsion. Hence, dealing with international problems must be done through negotiation, consensus, bullying, and concessions.

Governmental International Institutions

To discourage bullying and to encourage negotiation and consensus, governments have developed a variety of international institutions to promote negotiations and

INTERNATIONAL ECONOMIC INSTITUTIONS

■ he *United Nations* was founded in 1945, after World War II, in the hope of providing a place where international problems could be resolved through discussion and negotiation rather than through war.

The *World Bank* is a multilateral, international financial institution established in 1944. One of its main objectives is to provide funding to developing countries.

The *International Monetary Fund* (IMF), another international financial institution founded in 1944, lends money to developing countries in the form of "aid" packages which require recipient countries to try to reach certain economic goals.

The *Organization of Petroleum Exporting Countries* (OPEC) consists of 13 major oil-exporting countries in the Middle East, Far East, Africa, and South America. Formed in 1960, the organization promotes its member countries' joint national interests, such as preventing reductions in oil's price.

The *Organization of Economic Cooperation and Development* (OECD) was set up in 1961 to promote economic cooperation among individual countries. Its 24 members include all major industrial countries and most Western European countries. The OECD is the best source of comparative statistics for Western economies.

---

coordinate economic relations among countries. These include the United Nations (UN), General Agreement on Tariffs and Trade (GATT), World Bank, World Court, International Monetary Fund (IMF), and regional organizations such as OPEC (Organization of Petroleum Exporting Countries), OPIC (Organization of Petroleum Importing Countries), European Economic Community (EEC), and North American Free Trade Association.

These organizations have a variety of goals. For example, the **World Bank** works closely with developing countries, channeling low-interest loans to them to foster economic growth. The **IMF** is concerned with international financial arrangements. When developing countries encountered financial problems in the 1970s and had large international debts that they could not pay, the IMF helped work on repayment plans.

In addition to these formal institutions, there are informal meetings of various countries. These include **Group of Five** meetings of Japan, Germany, Britain, France, and the United States; and **Group of Seven** meetings with Japan, Germany, Britain, France, Canada, Italy, and the United States.

Since governmental membership in international organizations is voluntary, their power is limited. When the United States doesn't like a World Court ruling, it simply states that it isn't going to follow the ruling. When the United States is unhappy with what the United Nations is doing, it withholds some of its dues. Other countries do the same from time to time. Other member countries complain, but can do little to force compliance. It doesn't work that way domestically. If you decide you don't like U.S. policy and refuse to pay your taxes, you'll wind up in jail.

What keeps nations somewhat in line when it comes to international rules is a moral tradition: Countries want to (or at least want to look as if they want to) do what's "right." Countries will sometimes follow international rules to keep international opinion favorable to them. But national self-interest often overrides international scruples.

World Bank A multinational, international financial institution.

IMF A multinational, international financial institution concerned primarily about monetary issues.

Group of Five A group of five countries (Japan, Germany, Britain, France, and the United States) that meet to try to coordinate their economic policies.

Group of Seven A group of seven countries (Japan, Germany, Britain, France, Canada, Italy, and the United States) that meet to try to coordinate economic policies.

Multinational Corporations

Chapter 4 introduced you to U.S. corporations and listed the largest corporations in the United States. More and more of these and other corporations are transcending national boundaries. They have branches on both the production and sales sides throughout the world. As they do, they become multinational corporations rather than national corporations.

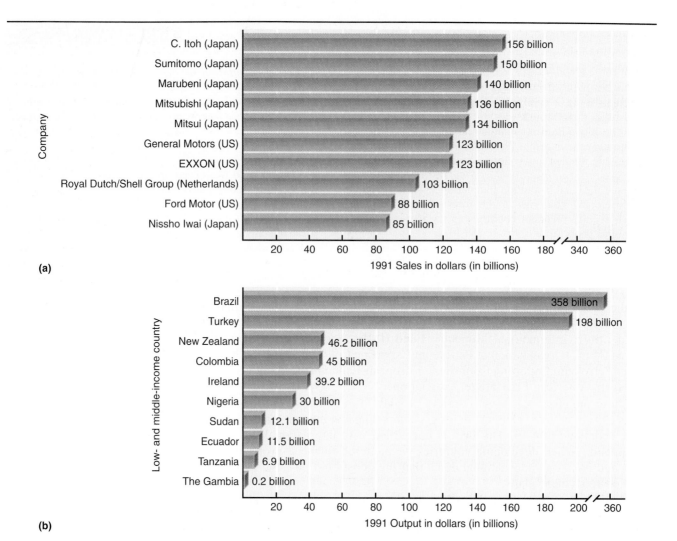

(a)

(b)

EXHIBIT 6 (a and b)   Multinational Corporations

As you can see in the charts, a number of multinational corporations are larger than the economies of some countries in terms of sales. This is important to a small country whose economy can be affected by a decision a multinational corporation might make.
Source: *The World Fact Book*, 1992.

Multinational corporations offer enormous benefits for countries. They create jobs; they bring new ideas and new technologies to a country, and they provide competition for domestic companies, keeping them on their toes. But multinational corporations also pose a number of problems for governments. One is their implications for domestic and international policy. A domestic corporation exists within a country and can be dealt with using policy measures within that country. A multinational corporation exists within many countries and there is no multinational government to regulate or control it. If it doesn't like the policies in one country—say taxes are too high or regulations too tight—it can shift its operations to other countries.

Countries often compete for these multinationals by changing their regulations to encourage companies to use them as their home base. For instance, firms might register their oil tankers in Liberia to avoid paying U.S. wages and put their funds in Bahamian banks to avoid U.S. financial disclosure laws. At times it seems that multinationals are governments unto themselves, especially in relation to poorer countries. Consider Exhibit 6(a)'s list of some large multinational corporations and their sales. Then compare it with Exhibit 6(b)'s list of some small and middle-size economies and their output. In terms of sales, a number of multinational corporations are larger than the economies of middle-size countries. This comparison is not quite accurate, since sales do not necessarily reflect power; but when a company's decisions can significantly affect what happens in a country's economy, that company has significant economic power.

When multinational corporations have such power, it is not surprising that they can sometimes dominate a country. The multinational can use its expertise and experience to direct a small country to do its bidding rather than the other way around.

Another problem multinational corporations present for governments involves multiple jurisdiction. Multinational corporations can distance themselves from questionable economic activities by setting up *dummy corporations.* A dummy corporation exists only on paper, and is actually controlled by another corporation. Sometimes when a corporation really wants to separate itself from the consequences of certain actions, it creates dummy dummy and dummy dummy dummy corporations, in which one paper corporation controls another paper corporation, which in turn controls another paper corporation. Each corporation is incorporated in a different nation, which makes it difficult, if not impossible, to trace who is actually doing what and who can be held accountable.

Before you condemn multinationals, remember: Multinationals don't have it so easy either. Customs and laws differ among countries. Trying to meet the differing laws and ambiguous limits of acceptable action in various countries is often impossible. For example, in many countries bribery is an acceptable part of doing business. If you want to get permission to sell a good, you must pay the appropriate officials *baksheesh* (as it's called in Egypt) or *la mordita* (as it's called in Mexico). In the United States such payments are called bribes and are illegal. Given these differing laws, the only way a U.S. company can do business in some foreign countries is to break U.S. laws.

Moreover, multinational corporations often work to maintain close ties among countries and to reduce international tension. If part of your company is in an Eastern European country and part in the United States, you want the two countries to be friends. So beware of making judgments about whether multinational corporations are good or bad. They're both simultaneously.

So far I've given you a brief introduction to the international economic problems the United States faces and to some of the international institutions that exist to coordinate international economic activity. In this section I introduce two of our most important rivals, the European Economic Community and Japan, giving you a brief background of their history and economic institutions.

In 1957, several governments of Europe formed the **European Economic Community (EEC)**, often called the European Common Market. In this customs union, members allow free trade among themselves to help their economies by providing a larger marketplace and more competition for their own companies. Over time the EEC has expanded from 6 countries to the 12 shown in Exhibit 7's map.

The EEC's initial goals were:

1. To remove barriers to trade among member nations;
2. To establish a single commercial policy toward nonmember countries;
3. To better coordinate member countries' economic policies;
4. To promote competitiveness with other countries.

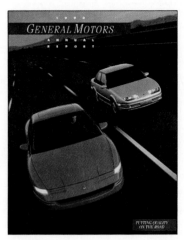

The annual report of any company generally is glossy and upbeat about the future.

WHO ARE OUR
INTERNATIONAL
COMPETITORS?

The European Economic
Community

7

European Economic Community (EEC)
A free trade union of European countries (also called *European Common Market*).

EXHIBIT 7   Map of EEC Countries

Members of the European Economic Community in 1992 include Ireland, Great Britain, Denmark, Netherlands, Belgium, Luxembourg, Germany, France, Italy, Greece, Spain, and Portugal.

Meeting those goals hasn't been easy, but the EEC has made significant progress.

Why did the countries of the EEC combine? Two primary reasons were to establish better markets for European companies and to compete better against U.S. goods. In the 1950s and 1960s when the United States was highly competitive with other countries and had a trade surplus, it could look beneficently at, and even encourage, such developments. In the 1990s, however, U.S. goods are often uncompetitive and there's a large trade deficit, so the United States finds it much harder to encourage a potential competitor; the EEC's gains likely will come at the expense of the United States.

These U.S. fears have increased as cooperation among EEC countries has grown. In 1992 all trade barriers among member nations were scheduled to be removed, and the EEC is to have a single commercial policy toward outside nations. By the year 1997 it hopes to have a single currency, the ECU if internal political problems can be resolved. The early 1990s saw significant discussions on what that commercial policy will be and whether it will be fair to the United States. Other European countries are also talking about uniting with the EEC countries and forming a larger European trading community.

The EEC makes a formidable competitor for the United States. Its combined production slightly exceeds U.S. production so it is the larger market. Moreover, the EEC has a strong international economic position, since many member countries enjoy trade surpluses while the United States has a trade deficit.

Developments in the EEC have been made even more important by recent events in Eastern Europe. Eastern European countries have changed from socialist to more market-oriented economic systems and are attempting to establish

---

The largest European Community economy is Germany. Germany has been on the losing end of two world wars and nonetheless has emerged as one of the leading economies of the world. One reason is cultural: German culture reinforces hard work and makes saving a virtue. Also, the country's coal and iron resources helped it establish a strong industrial base as long ago as the early 1900s.

After losing World War II in 1945, Germany was divided into East and West Germany. East Germany, which had a large part of the manufacturing base of prewar Germany, was controlled by a Communist government. West Germany was controlled by the victorious Allied forces, who encouraged it to set up a democratic market economy. The Allies limited West German military spending, while the United States, through the Marshall Plan (an assistance plan for Europe which the United States ran after World War II), pumped in large amounts of money to help the West German economy recover from the war. And recover it did. In the 1960s and 1970s the West German economy grew so fast that it was called an *economic miracle*.

West Germany's economic story contrasted significantly with East Germany's. East Germany grew more than any of the other Eastern bloc Communist economies, but its growth didn't match West Germany's. To prevent East Germans from emigrating to West Germany, East Germany closed its borders with West Germany in 1961 and built a wall between the two countries. Economic and political changes in East Germany at the end of the 1980s led to the introduction of a market economy in East Germany, an opening of the border, and physical destruction of the wall. In 1990 East and West Germany were reunified. The problems of reunification will likely extend through the 1990s.

The German economy is much more centralized than is the U.S. economy. Banks play a much more important role than do banks in the United States, and often control a variety of German companies. In the United States such control would be illegal. Thus, while Germany, like the United States, is a market economy, it is a different kind of market economy.

---

closer economic and political ties with the West. East and West Germany are reunified. These developments will open up new markets for which both the United States and the EEC will compete. In that competition, the EEC has both cultural and geographic advantages over the United States.

In response to the EEC's increasing strength, the United States has entered into a free trade agreement with Canada and Mexico. If all goes according to plan, by the mid-1990s all customs duties (tariffs) between these three countries will be eliminated. The United States also argued strongly against high EEC protective barriers on imports from foreign countries. Since there are no international organizations specifically designed to coordinate and facilitate international trade among trading areas, a new policy problem of the 1990s may be trade wars among "free trading" areas.

Japan is a little country with a lot of people—about 125 million, half as many people as the United States—but it fits them into 146,000 square miles, less than 4 percent of the area of the United States. Almost two-thirds of Japan is covered with forest, and much of the rest of the land has poor soil. It has almost no oil; its coal is very low grade; it must import nearly 100 percent of its petroleum and all of its iron ore (used to make steel) and bauxite (used to make aluminum). It has some copper and other minerals such as zinc, but not enough. Even with heavy forestation, it doesn't have enough lumber for domestic use and must make substantial expenditures for imported lumber.

"Japan, Inc."

Besides being small, crowded, and poorly endowed, Japan is a chain of islands and has a language that is extremely difficult to learn. These facts have tended, until very recently, to isolate it from the rest of the world. Japan broke its isolation by entering World War II, which it lost, leaving its economy in ruins.

By almost all objective analyses, then, one would expect Japan to be a poor, underdeveloped country. It isn't. Instead, it is one of the most successful and developed economies in the world. Its economic strength has earned it the nickname *Japan, Inc*. In the 1980s it set the world's standard for competitiveness. Why?

Cultural Reasons for Japan's Success

One reason is cultural. Japan has a social and cultural commitment to hard work. A second cultural trait that has helped Japan's economy is its strong tradition of saving money. These cultural traits are reinforced by social and economic institutions. Japan's educational system is much more demanding than that of the United States. Students go to school longer and are required to work harder than most American students. This imposes on children a discipline and a habit of hard work that persists in later life. Many Japanese enjoy work. Their work is their hobby as well as their job. Only in Japan will you find government-sponsored classes teaching people how not to work so hard.

The Japanese savings tradition is also encouraged by government policies that keep prices of consumer goods high, make borrowing for consumer goods comparatively expensive, and maintain a skimpy government pension system. One of the reasons the Japanese save a much higher percentage of their incomes than most other people do is that they worry about supporting themselves in their old age.

Japan as a Neomercantilist Country

Another reason for Japanese development is its government's strong role in stimulating export-led growth. Japan's economic growth is not an example of the power of the invisible hand, but of the three invisible forces working together to direct an economy toward growth. In many economists' view, the Japanese economic system is as closely related to mercantilism as to capitalism. Some have called it a **neomercantilist** economic system.

Neomercantilist Market economy guided by government.

The power of Japan's neomercantilist approach is striking. In the 1940s, with few resources and raw materials and devastated by World War II, Japanese firms, under government direction, borrowed in order to finance the purchase of raw materials from abroad. The Japanese government directed firms to allocate a large portion of output for export. They started with small products, paid workers low wages, saved their profits, and learned about international markets. Then they plowed back those savings into more raw materials, more manufacturing, and more exports. They continued this process, each time manufacturing more sophisticated products than before.

Japan put off making improvements in housing, transportation, highways, parks, cultural institutions, and public health while it directed its efforts to rebuilding and developing technology. Government policy encouraged and sheltered business.

MITI The Japanese agency which guides the Japanese economy.

The Japanese government developed an aggressive trading policy under the control of its Ministry of International Trade and Industry (**MITI**). It encouraged businesses to cooperate with one another, not to compete, in order to be more efficient. The government instituted strong tariffs that are still in force. They prohibit altogether the import of some articles that might compete with Japanese manufacturers. In short, Japan does not follow a laissez-faire policy in either the domestic or the international economy, and it is successful.

The Japanese Cooperative Spirit

This policy of government support for business is aided by labor institutions. Japan's labor market is remarkably different from that in the United States. Large companies have what are called *permanent employees*. By tradition, a man, once hired, stays with the same company for his entire working life. Women are unlikely to be permanent employees and are expected to resign their jobs when they get married. The relationship between the company

ECONOMIES THAT DON'T WORK SO WELL

F or every economy that works well, there are many more economies that aren't achieving their goals. Considering one of them helps us keep our perspective. Take Pakistan, a country of about 120,000,000 people. Pakistan is poor; the average per capita income is about $400. Its political structure is, in theory, democratic, but the army plays a major role in determining who will rule. Coups d'état (overthrows of the government) and unexplained deaths of high leaders are common. The resulting political instability keeps out most foreign investments.

Pakistan is an Islamic republic which has had significant fights with India ever since the two nations were created out of the former single British commonwealth country. The British commonwealth ''India'' was divided into ''India'' and ''Pakistan'' in 1947 after World War II. In 1971 Pakistan's internal strife led to half the country declaring its independence and forming a separate country, Bangladesh.

Pakistan's economy is primarily agricultural, although it also manufactures textiles and chemicals. One out of every 80 people has a TV; one out of every 1,000 has a car. Housing is poor for the majority of the people, and many barely get enough to eat. Income distribution is highly unequal, with a small group being very rich and a great majority being extremely poor.

Most industry has heavy government involvement and is highly inefficient. Without large tariff barriers, it could not compete. Such dependency on the government's prevention of competition breeds corruption. Most Pakistanis have little faith that their government bureaucracy will work for the benefit of society.

and the worker is close—a worker is a member of the corporate family and his social life revolves around the company. The nature of the Japanese labor market is now changing. Some women can be permanent employees and some employees move to other companies, but the traditional system still prevails.

Labor unions exist in Japan, but are organized according to industry. In the United States unions are more likely to be organized by type of skill. Organization by industry allows Japanese workers to do many different jobs within a firm. Until recently, U.S. organized workers would not work outside their specialty.

Japan's pay structure is also different from that in the United States. Japanese workers know that their bonuses, gifts, and special allowances depend on how well their company is doing. Until recently, most U.S. workers received only a wage or salary and no bonus. Another Japanese characteristic contributing to its economic success is the tradition of cooperation between unions and business; in the United States, labor and management are frequently in conflict.

Another difference is that Japan has few lawyers and is a far less litigious society than the United States. Some cynics have suggested the small number of lawyers is a major reason for Japan's great success. Businesses don't get bogged down by legal maneuvering and litigious behavior. Less cynical people downplay this issue, but they agree Japanese people's cooperative spirit contributes to Japan's success.

Inefficient Japanese Traditions   Not all Japanese institutions promote efficiency. Some Japanese institutions hinder economic progress. Take its agricultural system. Before the war, most farmland in Japan that was not owned by the government was owned by a few individuals who rented it out in small parcels to others. After the war, the big farmland holdings were broken up by the government and sold off to former tenants at low prices. The result was thousands of small farms—averaging an acre in size. Few are larger than three acres. These small farms are highly inefficient, but are kept in business by large government subsidies and tariffs on foreign agricultural products. Because of the structure of Japanese political institutions, these subsidies are almost untouchable, despite U.S. farmers' complaints about trade restrictions.

Japan, Inc., versus
the United States

Both the Japanese and U.S. economies are successful, but they differ significantly from each other. There is less competition among firms in Japan than in the United States. Japanese firms work closely with government in planning their industrial strategy. U.S. firms often see government as an opponent, not a partner. Similarly with labor and business: In Japan they generally cooperate; in the United States they generally are opponents.

The Japanese Ministry of International Trade and Industry plays a key role in determining what will be produced and who will produce it. MITI's goal has been to establish strong export-led growth, and it has succeeded. MITI also has an economic planning board that oversees many parts of the Japanese economy. Japan is no laissez-faire economy.

The differences between the U.S. and Japanese economies are large, but shouldn't be overestimated. Both economies rely on markets. In both, profit incentives motivate production.

As multinational corporations bridge the gap between these two economies, the differences (once very large) are shrinking. U.S. labor unions and firms are cooperating more, while Japanese firms and labor unions are cooperating less. The Japanese system of permanent employment in large firms is breaking down.

With both systems successful, it is difficult to say that one set of institutions is better than the other. They are merely distinct from each other. The differences reflect social, cultural, and geographical conditions in the two countries. Some people have suggested that the United States should adopt a neomercantilist system like Japan's. Maybe it should, but it is not at all clear that Japanese institutions could be transferred to the United States. What works in one country can bomb in another.

The argument that policies that work in one country cannot necessarily be translated into policies that work in another country doesn't mean Japan's experience is of no relevance to the United States. In itself, the fact that a policy works in one country means that that policy deserves consideration by other countries. That's tough for an economist with a strong distrust of government to say, but it must be said. An open mind is a necessary attribute of a good economist.

Knowing about other countries' economies helps us keep our own economy in perspective. I don't have the space here (an example of scarcity) to look at other countries' tax structures, public finances, support of education, labor markets . . . the list is endless. But as you wonder about any of the economic policies that are discussed throughout this book, take a few minutes to ask somebody from a foreign country about its economy, and go to the library and look up another country's way of handling its economy (even if you look no further than an encyclopedia). See how that country compares to the United States. Then try to explain what does or doesn't work in that country and whether it would or would not work in the United States. Doing so will make the course more meaningful and your understanding of economics stronger.

KEY POINTS

- To understand the U.S. economy, one must understand its role in the world economy. **1**
- Knowledge of the facts about the world economy is necessary to understand the world economy. **2**
- Countries can be classified in many ways, including industrial, middle-income, and low-income economies. **1**
- International trade differs from domestic trade because (1) there are potential barriers to trade and (2) countries use different currencies. **3**
- The relative value of a currency can be found in an exchange rate Table. **4**
- The U.S. trade deficit is large. It is financed by selling U.S. assets to foreign owners. **5**

- U.S. competitiveness and the state of the U.S. economy compared to other countries are important in determining the trade deficit's size. **5**
- International policy coordination must be achieved through consensus among nations. **6**
- Multinational corporations are corporations with significant operations in more than one country. **6**
- Two important international competitors to the United States are the EEC and Japan. In Japan and in many EEC nations, government plays a larger role in directing the economy than in the United States. **7**

KEY TERMS

balance of trade *(115)*
comparative advantage *(111)*
competitiveness *(116)*
European Economic Community (EEC) *(121)*
exports *(110)*

foreign exchange market *(114)*
General Agreement on Tariffs and Trade (GATT) *(118)*
Group of Five *(119)*
Group of Seven *(119)*

IMF *(119)*
imports *(110)*
MITI *(124)*
multinational corporation *(108)*
neomercantilist *(124)*
nontariff barriers *(113)*

quotas *(113)*
tariffs *(113)*
trade deficit *(115)*
trade surplus *(115)*
World Bank *(119)*

QUESTIONS FOR THOUGHT AND REVIEW

The number after each question represents the estimated degree of critical thinking required. (1 = almost none; 10 = deep thought.)

1. A good measure of a country's importance to the world economy is its area and population. True or false? Why? *(5)*
2. The United States exports wheat while Japan exports cars. Why? *(5)*
3. What are the two ways in which international trade differs from domestic trade? *(3)*
4. Find the exchange rate for Swedish krone in Exhibit 4 and also the most current rate from your newspaper. *(3)*

5. If one U.S. dollar will buy .67 Swiss francs, how many U.S. dollars will one Swiss franc buy? *(5)*
6. The U.S. economy is falling apart because the United States is the biggest debtor nation in the world. Discuss. *(7)*
7. What is likely to happen to the U.S. trade deficit if the U.S. economy grows rapidly? Why? *(5)*
8. Why do most economists oppose trade restrictions? *(5)*
9. What effect has the establishment of the EEC had on the U.S. economy? Why? *(9)*
10. Japan's successful economy is an example of the power of the invisible hand. True or false? Why? *(6)*

PROBLEMS AND EXERCISES

1. This is a library research question.
   a. What are the primary exports of Brazil, Honduras, Italy, Pakistan, and Nigeria?
   b. Which countries produce most of the world's tin, rubber, potatoes, wheat, marble, and refrigerators?
2. This is an entrepreneurial research question. You'd be amazed about the information that's out there if you use a bit of initiative.
   a. Does the largest company in your relevant geographic area (town, city, whatever) have an export division? Why or why not?
   b. If you were an advisor to the company, would you suggest expanding or contracting its export division? Why or why not?
   c. Go to a store and look at 10 products at random. How many were made in the United States? Give a probable explanation why they were produced where they were produced.

2
MACROECONOMICS

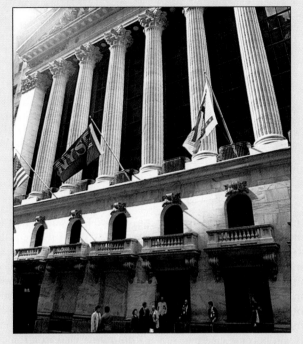

In the 1930s the U.S. economy fell into a Great Depression. Businesses collapsed and unemployment rose until 25 percent of the work force—millions of people—were out of work.

The Depression changed economics in the way it was taught and in the way economic problems were conceived. Before the 1930s economics was microeconomics (the study of partial equilibrium supply and demand). After the 1930s the study of the core of economic thinking was broken into two discrete areas: microeconomics, as before, and macroeconomics (the study of the economy in the aggregate).

The specific focus of macroeconomics is the study of unemployment, business cycles (fluctuations in the economy), growth, and inflation. While the macroeconomic theories studied have changed considerably over the past 60 years, macroeconomics' focus on those problems has remained. Thus, we'll define **macroeconomics** as *the study of the economy in the aggregate with specific focus on unemployment, inflation, business cycles, and growth.*

Macroeconomic policy debates have centered on a struggle between two groups: *Keynesian* (pronounced KAIN-sian) economists and Classical economists. Should the government run a budget deficit or a surplus? Should the government increase the money supply when a recession threatens? Should it decrease the money supply when inflation threatens? Can government prevent recessions? Keynesians generally answer one way; Classicals, another.

Each group has many variants. On the Classical side are neo-Classicals, New Classicals, and monetarists. On the Keynesian side are neo-Keynesians, New Keynesians, and post-Keynesians, just to name a few. At the introductory level we needn't concern ourselves with these various subdivisions. We'll focus on Keynesians and Classicals.

While there are many differences between Keynesians and Classicals, the fundamental policy difference is the following: Classical economists generally oppose government intervention in the economy; they favor a *laissez-faire* policy.[1] Keynesians are more likely to favor government intervention in the economy. They feel a laissez-faire policy can sometimes lead to disaster. Both views represent reasonable economic positions. The differences between them are often subtle and result from their taking a slightly different view of what government can do and a slightly different perspective on the economy.

Economic events are unlikely to resolve the differences between the two, as both sides usually have reasonable explanations of what happened. For example, Keynesians blamed the 1970s inflation on oil price hikes and commodity price increases; Classicals blamed it on the Keynesian policies of government deficits and expansionary monetary policy. In the 1980s, Keynesians claimed economic expansion during the Reagan presidency was caused by Keynesian-type policies (the large deficits Reagan ran); Classicals claimed that it was due to supply-side incentive effects of the Reagan tax cut. In the 1990s Keynesians claimed the recession of 1991–92 demonstrated the failure of supply-side policies; Classicals claimed it was caused by too few supply-side policies. All these explanations are defensible.

To understand these policy debates you have to know macroeconomic terminology, macroeconomic theory, and macroeconomic institutions, combined with a sense of the history of the debate.

---

[1] "Laissez-faire" (introduced to you in Chapter 3) is a French expression meaning "Leave things alone; let them go on without interference."

Part 1, Macroeconomic Problems, introduces you to the macroeconomic problems, terminology, and statistics used in tracking the economy's macroeconomic performance.

Part 2, Macroeconomic Theory: The Basics provides the background you need to understand macroeconomic theory sufficiently so that you can understand the policy debates that have been going on for the last 50 years and continue unabated. In these chapters the terms of the debate between Keynesians and Classicals will become clear.

Part 3, Monetary and Financial Institutions, discusses the financial sector and shows you how that sector fits into the macroeconomic landscape. It gives you a sense of the nuts and bolts of macroeconomic policy and the financial institutions in the economy.

Part 4, Extensions of Macroeconomic Thinking, brings you up to date on recent theoretical developments. It's not required to understand recent policy debates, but it's certainly helpful, especially if you're trying to understand some of the nuances (the fine points) of those debates.

Part 5, Macroeconomic Policy Debates, discusses the art of macroeconomic policy. It applies the terminology, theory, and knowledge of institutions that you'll have gained from earlier chapters. It includes case studies that bridge the gap between the general discussions in the text and real-life policies.

1 Macroeconomic Problems

CHAPTER

6

Economic Growth, Business Cycles, Unemployment, and Inflation

CHAPTER

7

National Income Accounting

6

Economic Growth, Business Cycles, Unemployment, and Inflation

Remember that there is nothing stable in human affairs; therefore avoid undue elation in prosperity, or undue depression in adversity.

Socrates

After reading this chapter, you should be able to:

1

Summarize relevant statistics about growth, business cycles, unemployment, and inflation.

2

Name some causes of growth.

3

List four phases of the business cycle.

4

Relate the target rate of unemployment to potential income.

5

Explain how unemployment is measured and state some microeconomic categories of unemployment.

6

Distinguish a real concept from a nominal concept.

7

Define inflation and differentiate between cost-push and demand-pull inflation and expected and unexpected inflation.

8

State two important costs of inflation.

Robert Solow—Nobel prize, 1987, for work on economic growth. © *The Nobel Foundation.*

Like people, the economy has moods. Sometimes it's in wonderful shape—it's expansive; at other times, it's depressed. Like people whose moods are often associated with specific problems (headaches, sore back, an itch), the economy's moods are associated with various problems.

Macroeconomics is the study of the aggregate moods of the economy, with specific focus on problems associated with those moods—the problems of growth, business cycles, unemployment, and inflation. These four problems are the central concern of macroeconomics. The macroeconomic theory we'll consider is designed to explain how supply and demand in the aggregate interact to create these problems. The macroeconomic policy controversies we'll consider concern these four problems. So it's only appropriate that in this first chapter we consider an overview of these problems, their causes, their consequences, and the debate about what to do about them. It introduces you to some of the terms we'll be using and gives you a sense of the interrelationship of these problems. Just how are business cycles and growth related to inflation and unemployment? The chapter won't answer all your questions (if it did, we wouldn't need the other chapters), but it will provide you with a framework for the remaining chapters.

We'll start with the problems of growth and business cycles because it was the Great Depression of the 1930s—a severe business cycle—that led to the creation of macroeconomics as a course of study separate from microeconomics.

GROWTH AND BUSINESS CYCLES

Generally the U.S. economy is growing or expanding. Economic activity—the production of goods and services (output)—is increasing. When people produce and sell their goods, they earn income, so when an economy is growing, both total output and total income are increasing. Such growth gives most people more this year than they had last year. Since most of us prefer more to less, growth is easy to take.

1   The U.S. Department of Commerce traced U.S. economic growth in output since about 1890 and discovered on average output of goods and services grew about 3.5 percent per year. This 3.5 percent growth rate is sometimes called the *secular trend growth rate.* The rate at which the actual output grows in any one year fluctuates, but on average, the U.S. economy has been growing at that long-term trend.[1] When economists talk about economic growth, they generally mean this long-term growth trend of output of 3.5 percent per year.

Causes of Growth

Economic growth (per capita) allows everyone, on average, in society to have more. Thus, it isn't surprising that most governments are generally searching for policies that will allow them to grow. Indeed, one reason market economies have been so successful is that they have consistently channeled individual efforts toward production and growth. Individuals feel a sense of accomplishment in making things grow and, if sufficient economic incentives and resources exist, individuals' actions can lead to a continually growing economy.

2   But sufficient economic incentives and resources cannot be taken as givens. Economic growth depends upon people saving and investing rather than consuming their income. Investing now helps create machines that in the future can be used to produce more output with less effort. Growth also depends upon technological change—finding new, better ways to do things. For instance, when Nicholas Alpert discovered canning (the ability to store food in a vacuum so it wouldn't spoil), the economic possibilities of society expanded enormously. The combination of investing in machines and technological change plays a central role in the growth of any economy.

Economic growth also depends on people. More people generally produce more output than fewer people do. There are a couple of qualifications, however. First, there must not be so many people that they are significantly interfering with

---

[1] Since population has also been growing, at about 2.5 percent per year, per capita growth (growth per person) has been less than 3.5 percent—about 1 percent per year.

A per capita growth rate of 1 percent per year means on average people will be able to consume 1 percent more per year. Most of you, I suspect, are hoping to do better than that, and most of you will do better, both because you're in college studying economics (so you'll do better than average) and because most individuals in their working years can expect to consume slightly more each year than they did the previous year. Since income also tends to increase with age up to retirement, and ends completely at death, a specific individual's income, and hence his or her consumption, will generally increase by more than the per capita growth in income.

So, if the future is like the past, you can look forward to a rate of increase in consumption significantly above average.

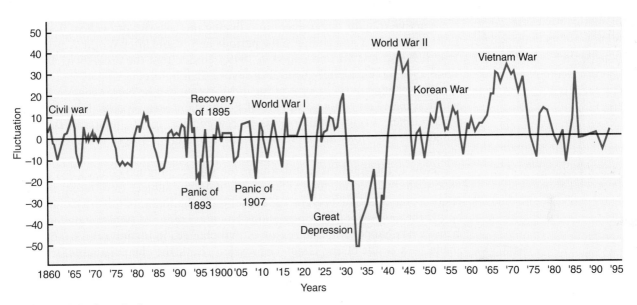

EXHIBIT 1   U.S. Business Cycles

Business cycles have always been a part of the U.S. economic scene.

Source: Courtesy of Ameritrust Co., Cleveland, Ohio, and update by author.

each other's activities. And second, the people must choose to work. If people don't have an incentive to work, there won't be much output, regardless of how many people there are.

There are, of course, many other causes of growth. Nonetheless, this brief introduction should identify some growth issues to keep in the back of your mind as we consider other goals, because policies that sometimes seem to help alleviate other problems, like unemployment or inflation, can have negative effects on growth.

While the secular, or long-term, trend is a 3.5 percent increase in total output, there are numerous fluctuations around that trend. Sometimes total output is above the trend; at other times total output is below the trend. Such a short-term fluctuation of output around the long-term trend is called a **business cycle.** Thus, a business cycle is the upward or downward movement of economic activity that occurs around the growth trend. Exhibit 1 graphs the fluctuations in the U.S. economy since 1860.

Until the late 1930s, economists took such cycles as facts of life. They had no convincing theory to explain why business cycles occurred, nor did they have policy suggestions to smooth them out. In fact, they felt that any attempt to smooth them through government intervention would make the situation worse.

Since the 1940s, however, many economists have not taken business cycles as facts of life. They have hotly debated the nature and causes of business cycles and

Causes of Business Cycles

Business cycle The upward or downward movement of economic activity that occurs around the growth trend.

of the underlying growth. Classical economists argue that fluctuations are to be expected in a market economy. Indeed, it would be strange if fluctuations did not occur when individuals are free to decide what they want to do. We should simply accept these fluctuations as we do the seasons of the year. If you have no policy to deal with some occurrence, you might as well accept that occurrence. Keynesian economists argue that fluctuations can and should be controlled. They argue that *expansions* (the part of the business cycle above the long-term trend) and *contractions* (the part of the cycle below the long-term trend) are symptoms of underlying problems of the economy, which should be dealt with. Which of these two views is correct is still a matter of debate.

If prolonged contractions (recessions) are a type of cold the economy catches, the Great Depression of the 1930s was double pneumonia. The Great Depression led to changes in the U.S. economy's structure. The new structure included a more active role for government in reducing the severity of cyclical fluctuations. Look at Exhibit 1 and compare the periods before and after World War II. (World War II began in 1941 and ended in 1945.) Notice that the downturns and panics since 1945 have generally been less severe than before.

This change in the nature of business cycles can be better seen in Exhibit 2, which is based on National Bureau of Economic Research data. Notice that since 1945 business cycles' duration has increased, but, more important, the average length of expansions has increased while the average length of contractions has decreased.

How to interpret these statistics is the subject of much controversy. As is the case with much economic evidence, the data are subject to different interpretations. Some economists argue the reduction in fluctuations' severity is an illusion.

If the severity of the fluctuations has been reduced (which most economists believe has happened), one reason is that changes in institutional structure were made as a result of the Great Depression. Both the financial structure and the government taxing and spending structure were changed, giving the government a more important role in stabilizing the economy. Considering that stronger government role is a key element of macroeconomics.

The Phases of the Business Cycle

Much research has gone into measuring business cycles and setting official reference dates for the beginnings and ends of contractions and expansions. As a result of this research, business cycles have been divided into phases and an explicit terminology has been developed. The National Bureau of Economic Research announces the government's official dates of contractions and expansions. In the postwar era (since mid-1945), the average business expansion has lasted about 48 months. A major expansion occurred from 1983 until 1991, when the U.S. economy fell into a recession, where it remained through the beginning of 1992.

Business cycles have varying durations and intensities, but economists have developed a terminology to describe all business cycles and just about any

EXHIBIT 2   Duration of Business Cycles, Pre-World War II and Post-World War II (in Months)

Cycles	Pre–World War II (1845–1945)	Post–World War II (1945–1992)
Number	22	10
Average duration (trough to trough)	50	56
Length of longest cycle	99 (1870–79)	118 (1961–70)
Length of shortest cycle	28 (1919–21)	28 (1980–82)
Average length of expansions	29	48
Length of shortest expansion	10 (1919–20)	12 (1980–81)
Length of longest expansion	80 (1938–45)	106 (1961–69)
Average length of recessions	21	11
Length of shortest recession	7 (1918–19)	6 (1980)
Length of longest recession	65 (1873–79)	17 (1981–82)

Source: *Survey of Current Business* and Economic Report of the President, 1993.

position we might find ourself in on the business cycle. Since this terminology is often used by the press it is helpful to go over it. We do so in reference to Exhibit 3 which gives you a visual picture of a business cycle.

Let's start at the top. The top of a cycle is called the *peak*. A very high peak, representing a big jump in output, is called a **boom.** (That's when the economy is doing great. Most everyone who wants a job has one and everyone is happy.) Eventually an expansion peaks. (At least, in the past, they always have.) When the economy starts to fall from that peak, there's a **downturn** in business activity. If that downturn persists for more than two consecutive quarters of the year, that downturn becomes a **recession.** (In a recession the economy isn't doing so great; many people are unemployed and a number of people are depressed.)

A large recession is called a **depression.** There is no formal line indicating when a recession becomes a depression. In general, a depression is much longer and more severe than a recession. This ambiguity allows some economists to joke, "When your neighbor is unemployed, it's a recession; when you're unemployed, it's a depression." If pushed for something more specific, I'd say that if unemployment exceeds 12 percent for more than a year, the economy is in a depression.

Boom A very high business cycle peak.

Downturn The economy falling from its peak.

Recession Downturn lasting for more than two consecutive quarters of the year.

Depression A large recession.

When I first went to college, I thought that there were facts and there were theories, and that theories were tested by comparing them to the facts. Alas, my college professors delighted in twisting any neat divisions I made, and my neat distinction between fact and theory is one of the things that bit the dust.

The difficulty is that facts are simply empirical observations. What is a fact depends on who is doing the observing. Economic facts (data) must often be collected through more complicated methods than simple observation. Numbers must be collected (presenting first the collector and then the viewer with possible errors). Numbers must be combined, and often subsets of numbers must be chosen (opening up the possibility of more errors). Finally numbers must be interpreted.

Much of the debate in economics is conducted in the statistical trenches: looking at the data and attempting to pull out "facts" from that data. The "fact" that business cycles' peaks and troughs were reduced after World War II was pretty much accepted as a fact until Christina Romer, an economist at Princeton, re-analyzed the data and came up with a different conclusion. She found that no postwar change in business cycles had occurred. Many economists disagreed with her findings, but whether she was right or wrong is not the important point. The important point is that after she presented her new interpretation, the "fact" was in dispute, and no longer a fact. The moral: Beware of "facts."

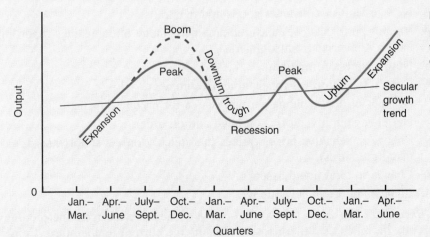

EXHIBIT 3 Business Cycle Phases

Economists have many terms that describe the position of the economy on the business cycle. Some of them are given in this exhibit.

Upturn The economy coming out of a trough.

Expansion An upturn lasting two consecutive quarters of the year.

The bottom of a recession or depression is called the *trough*. When the economy comes out of the trough, economists say it's in an **upturn.** If an upturn lasts two consecutive quarters of the year, it's called an **expansion,** which leads us back up to the peak. And so it goes.

This terminology is important because if you're going to talk about the state of the economy, you need the terminology to do it. Why are businesses so interested in the state of the economy? They want to be able to predict whether it's going into a contraction or an expansion. Making the right prediction can determine whether the business will be profitable or not. That's why a large amount of economists' activity goes into trying to predict the future course of the economy.

Leading and Coincidental Indicators

Unemployment rate The percentage of people in the labor force who can't find a job.

Capacity utilization rate Rate at which factories and machines are operating compared to the rate at which they could be used.

Target rate of unemployment Lowest sustainable rate of unemployment economists believe is possible under existing conditions.

4

Potential output Output that would materialize at the target rate of unemployment and the target level of capacity utilization.

Coincidental indicator A type of economic thermometer.

Leading indicator A type of economic barometer.

Two measures that economists use to determine where the economy is on the business cycle are the **unemployment rate** (the percentage of people in the labor force who can't find a job) and the **capacity utilization rate** (the rate at which factories and machines are operating compared to the rate at which they could be used). Generally economists feel that 5–6 percent unemployment and 80–85 percent capacity utilization are about as much as we should expect from the economy. Therefore, they use them as targets. Thus the **target rate of unemployment** is defined as the lowest sustainable rate of unemployment economists believe is possible under existing conditions. To push the economy beyond that would be like driving your car 90 miles an hour. True, the marks on your speedometer might go up to 130, but 90 is a more realistic top speed. Beyond 120 (assuming that's where your car is red-lined), the engine is likely to blow up (unless you have a Maserati).

Economists translate the target unemployment rate and target capacity utilization rate into the level of output with which those rates will be associated. That level of output is called **potential output** (or *potential income,* because, as I mentioned, output creates income). Potential output is the output that would materialize at the target rate of unemployment and the target level of capacity utilization. Potential output grows at the secular (long-term) trend rate of 3.5 percent per year. When the economy is in a downturn or recession, actual output is below potential output. When the economy is in a boom, actual output is above potential output.

Economists have developed a set of leading and **coincidental indicators** that, as their labels suggest, give us a good idea of when a recession is about to occur and when the economy is in one. **Leading indicators** tell us what's likely to happen 12 to 15 months from now, much as a barometer gives us a clue about tomorrow's weather. They include:

1. Average workweek for production workers in manufacturing.
2. Layoff rate in manufacturing.
3. New orders for consumer goods and materials.
4. Vendor performance, measured as a percentage of companies reporting slower deliveries from suppliers.
5. New business formation.
6. Contracts and orders for plant and equipment.
7. Number of new building permits issued for private housing units.
8. Net change in inventories on hand and on order.
9. Change in sensitive prices (prices that quickly reflect supply and demand pressures).
10. Change in total liquid assets.
11. Changes in the money supply.

Coincidental indicators tell us what phase of the business cycle the economy is currently in, much as a thermometer tells us the current temperature. Coincident indicators are:

1. Number of employees on nonagricultural payrolls.
2. Personal income minus transfer payments (welfare, social security, war veterans' benefits, and so on).
3. Industrial production.
4. Manufacturing and trade sales volume.

Economists use leading indicators in making forecasts about the economy. Leading indicators are called *indicators,* not *predictors,* because they're only rough approximations of what's likely to happen in the future. For example, before you can build a house, a building permit must be applied for. Usually this occurs six to nine months before the actual start of construction. By looking at the number of building permits that have been issued, you can predict how much building is likely to begin in six months or so. But the prediction might be wrong, since getting a building permit does not require someone to actually build. Business economists spend much of their time and effort delving deeper into these indicators, trying to see what they are really telling us, as opposed to what they seem to be telling us. Business economists joke that the leading indicators have predicted six of the past two recessions.

Sifting through the data to find clues in new statistical series is drudgery detective work, but it's the backbone of business economists' work. Just as TV detectives' antics don't reflect what most detectives do, economists' brief appearances on the TV news don't reflect what economists do.

Business cycles and growth are directly related to unemployment in the U.S. economy. When an economy is growing and is in an expansion, unemployment is usually falling; when an economy is in a downturn, unemployment is usually rising. That's why the unemployment rate is an indicator of the business cycle.

UNEMPLOYMENT

The relationship between the business cycle and unemployment is obvious to most people, but often the seemingly obvious hides important insights. Just why are the business cycle and growth related to unemployment? True, income must fall in a recession, but, logically, unemployment need not result. A different result could be that everyone's income falls. Looking at the problem historically, we see unemployment has not always been a problem associated with business cycles.

Unemployment became a problem about the time of the Industrial Revolution. In pre-industrial farming societies, unemployment wasn't a problem; there was always work to be done and all had their assigned tasks. The reason is that pre-industrial farmers didn't receive wages—they received net revenue (the income left after all costs had been paid). That means the average amount they netted per hour (the equivalent of a wage) was flexible. In good years they had a high income per hour; in bad years they had a low income per hour.

The flexibility in people's net income per hour meant that when there were fluctuations in economic activity, people's income rose or fell, but they kept on working. Low income was a problem, but, since people didn't become unemployed, **cyclical unemployment** (unemployment resulting from fluctuations in economic activity) was not a problem.

Cyclical unemployment Unemployment resulting from fluctuations in economic activity.

While cyclical unemployment did not exist in pre-industrial society, **structural unemployment** (unemployment resulting from changes in the economy itself) did. For example, say demand for a product falls because of technological change. Some unemployment would likely result; that unemployment would be called *structural unemployment.* But structural unemployment wasn't much of a problem for government, or at least people did not consider it government's problem. The reason is that unemployment of family members was dealt with internally, by the family. If someone in the family had income, that person would share it with unemployed family members.

Structural unemployment Unemployment resulting from changes in the economy itself.

The Industrial Revolution changed the nature of work and introduced unemployment as a problem for society. This is because the Industrial Revolution was accompanied by a shift to wage labor and to a division of responsibilities. Some

CAPITALISM, THE FEAR OF
HUNGER, AND THE DUTCH
DISEASE

U sing "the fear of hunger" to see that people work may sound rather mean, but looked at from a societal view it can be "kind." For example, consider the socialist countries that wiped out the fear of unemployment. All people were guaranteed a job. (In fact, all people were required by law to have one.) By law, unemployment was eliminated. But this created other problems. People would show up at work but not really work. After all, they couldn't be fired. The results were shoddy products, shortages, and general dissatisfaction. As one cynical citizen said, "We pretend to work and they pretend to pay us." These negative consequences of eliminating unemployment were a significant reason why people pushed for the elimination or modification of socialism. They said, "If this is the result of eliminating unemployment, bring back unemployment." And the formerly socialist countries have done that with a vengeance in the early 1990s.

I use the term *fear of hunger* rather than *fear of unemployment* to emphasize that if people can expect a good income even if they lose their jobs, the fear of unemployment loses some of its bite. For example, in European countries like the Netherlands people were guaranteed almost as much income if they had no job as they would have earned if they did have a job. The result: the unemployment rate rose and the Dutch economy stagnated. The effect of such high support payments to people who didn't work acquired a name: *the Dutch disease*.

No one argues that unemployment or the fear of hunger is good. But many do argue that going too far in eliminating it has such negative effects on growth that unemployment is the better of two bads.

individuals (capitalists) took on ownership of the means of production and *hired* others to work for them, paying them a wage per hour. This change in the nature of production marked a significant change in the nature of the unemployment problem.

First, it created the possibility of cyclical unemployment. With wages set at a certain level, when economic activity fell, workers' income per hour did not fall. Instead, when slack periods occurred, factories would lay off or fire some workers. That isn't what happened on the farm; when a slack period occurred on the farm, the income per hour of all workers fell and few were laid off.

Second, the Industrial Revolution was accompanied by a change in how families dealt with unemployment. Whereas in pre-industrial farm economies individuals or families took responsibility for their own slack periods, in a capitalist industrial society factory owners didn't take responsibility for their workers in slack periods. The pink slip (a common name for the notice workers get telling them they are laid off) and the problem of unemployment were born in the Industrial Revolution.

Without wage income, unemployed workers were in a pickle. They couldn't pay their rent, they couldn't eat, they couldn't put clothes on their backs. So what was previously a family problem became a social problem. Not surprisingly, it was at that time—the late 1700s—that economists began paying more attention to the problem of unemployment.

Initially, economists and society still did not view unemployment as a societal problem. It was the individual's problem. If people were unemployed, it was their own fault; hunger, or at least the fear of hunger, would drive people to find other jobs relatively quickly. Thus, early capitalism didn't have an unemployment problem; it had an unemployment solution: the fear of hunger.

As capitalism evolved into welfare capitalism, the hunger solution decreased in importance. Capitalist societies no longer saw the fear of hunger as an acceptable answer to unemployment. Social welfare programs such as unemployment insurance and assistance to the poor were developed to help deal with unemployment.

In the Employment Act of 1946, the U.S. government specifically took responsibility for unemployment. The act assigned government the responsibility of creating an economic climate in which just about everyone who wanted a job could have one—a situation that economists defined as **full employment.** It was government's responsibility to offset cyclical fluctuations and thereby prevent cyclical unemployment and to somehow deal with structural unemployment.

Full employment Nearly everyone who wants a job has one.

Initially government regarded 2 percent unemployment as a condition of full employment. Two percent became the target rate of unemployment. The 2 percent was made up of **frictional unemployment** (unemployment caused by people quitting a job just long enough to look for and find another one) and of a few "unemployables," such as alcoholics and drug addicts, along with a certain amount of necessary structural unemployment resulting when the structure of the economy changed. Thus, any unemployment higher than 2 percent was considered either unnecessary structural or cyclical unemployment and was now government's responsibility; frictional and necessary structural unemployment were still the individual's problem.

Frictional unemployment People have left their jobs to look for and find other jobs.

Macroeconomics developed as a separate field and focused on how to combat cyclical unemployment. As you will see in coming chapters, government believed it could offset cyclical unemployment and achieve full employment by seeing to it that there was sufficient aggregate demand.

By the 1950s government had given up its view that 2 percent unemployment was consistent with full employment. It raised its target rate of unemployment to 3 percent, then to 4 percent, then to 5 percent. By the 1970s and early 1980s government raised it further, to 6.5 percent unemployment. In the late 1980s and early 1990s the target rate of unemployment was reduced to a bit over 5 percent.

Why these changing definitions of *full employment?* One reason is that in the 1970s and early 1980s a low inflation rate, which also was a government goal, seemed to be incompatible with a low unemployment rate. I'll talk about this incompatibility later when I discuss "stagflation." A second reason is demographics: Different age groups have different unemployment rates, and as the population's age structure changes, so does the target unemployment rate.

A third reason is our economy's changing social and institutional structure. These social and institutional changes affected the nature of the unemployment problem. For example, in the post–World War II period, family wealth increased substantially and borrowing became easier than before, giving many unemployed individuals a bit more leeway before they were forced to find a job. For instance, more family wealth meant that upon graduation from high school or college, children who couldn't find the job they wanted could live at home and be supported by their parents for a year or two.

Another example of how changing institutions changed the unemployment problem is women's expanding role in the economy. In the 1950s the traditional view that "woman's place is in the home" remained strong. Usually only one family member—the man—had a job. If he lost his job, no money came in. In the 1970s to 1990s, more and more women entered the work force so that today over 60 percent of all families are two-earner families. In a two-earner family, if one person loses a job, the family doesn't face immediate starvation. The other person's income carries the family over.

Government institutions also changed. Programs like unemployment insurance and public welfare were created to reduce suffering associated with unemployment. But in doing so, these programs changed the way people responded to unemployment. People in the 1990s are more picky about what jobs they take than they were in the 1920s and 1930s. People don't just want any job, they want a *fulfilling* job with a decent wage. As people have become choosier about jobs, a debate has raged over the extent of government's responsibility for unemployment.

Differing views of individuals' responsibility and society's responsibility lead to different views on whether somebody is actually unemployed. Understanding this point will help clarify some theoretical differences covered in upcoming chapters.

Whose Responsibility
Is Unemployment?

ADDED DIMENSION   CATEGORIES OF UNEMPLOYMENT

A good sense of the differing types of unemployment and the differing social views that unemployment embodies can be conveyed through three examples of unemployed individuals. As you read the following stories, ask yourself which category of unemployment each individual falls into.

Example 1: Joe is listed as unemployed and collects unemployment insurance. He's had various jobs in the past and was laid off from his last one. He spent a few weeks on household projects, believing he would be called back by his most recent employer—but he wasn't. He's grown to like being on his own schedule. He's living on his unemployment insurance (while it lasts, which usually isn't more than six months), his savings, and money he picks up by being paid cash under the table working a few hours now and then at construction sites. The Unemployment Compensation office requires him to make at least an attempt to find work, and he's turned up a few prospects. However some were back-breaking laboring jobs and one would have required him to move to a distant city, so he's avoided accepting regular work. Joe knows the unemployment payments won't last forever. When they're used up, he plans to increase his under-the-table activity. Then, when he gets good and ready, he'll really look for a job.

Example 2: Flo is a middle-aged, small-town housewife. She worked before her marriage, but when she and her husband started their family she quit her job to be a full-time housewife and mother. She never questioned her family values of hard work, independence, belief in free enterprise, and scorn of government handouts. When her youngest child left the nest, she decided to finish the college education she'd only just started when she married. After getting her degree, she looked for a job, but found the market for middle-aged women with no recent experience was depressed—and depressing. The state employment office where she sought listings recognized her abilities and gave her a temporary job in that very office. Because she was a "temp," however, she was the first to be laid off when the

state legislature cut the local office budget—but she'd worked long enough to be eligible for unemployment insurance.

She hesitated about applying, since handouts were against her principles. On the other hand, while working there she'd seen plenty of people, including her friends, applying for benefits after work histories even slimmer than hers. She decided to take the benefits. While they lasted, she found family finances on almost as sound a footing as when she was working. Although she was bringing in less money, net family income didn't suffer much since she didn't have social security withheld nor did she have the commuting and clothing expenses of going to a daily job.

Example 3: Tom had a good job at a manufacturing plant where he'd worked up to a wage of $450 a week. Occasionally he was laid off, but only a few weeks, and then he'd be called back. In 1989 the plant was bought by an out-of-state corporation which laid off half the work force and put in automated equipment. Tom, an older worker with comparatively high wages, was one of the first to go, and he wasn't called back. He had a wife, three children, a car payment, and a mortgage. He looked for other work but couldn't find anything paying close to what he'd been getting. Tom used up his unemployment insurance and his savings. He sold the house and moved his family into a trailer. Finally he heard that there were a lot of jobs in Massachusetts 800 miles away. He moved there, found a job, and began sending money home every week. Then the Massachusetts economy faltered. Tom was laid off again, and his unemployment insurance ran out again. Relying on his $100,000 life insurance policy, he figured he was worth more to his family dead than alive, so he killed himself.

As these three examples suggest, unemployment encompasses a wide range of cases. Unemployment is anything but a one-dimensional problem, so it's not surprising that people's views of how to deal with it differ.

There we'll compare and contrast Classical economists' and Keynesian economists' views. Classical economists take the position that, generally, individuals should be responsible for finding jobs. They emphasize that an individual can always find *some* job at *some* wage rate, even if it's only selling apples on the street for 40¢ apiece. Given this view of individual responsibility, unemployment is impossible. If a person isn't working, that's his or her choice; the person simply isn't looking hard enough for a job. For an economist with this view, almost all unemployment is actually frictional unemployment.

Keynesian economists tend to say society owes a person a job commensurate with the individual's training or past job experience. They further argue that the job should be close enough to home so a person doesn't have to move. Given this view, frictional unemployment is only a small part of total unemployment. Structural and cyclical unemployment are far more common.

Which of these two views most people hold depends partly on the general state of the economy. The more people are unemployed, the more tempting it is to see unemployment as a structural or cyclical problem. To see it in either of those ways puts more of the blame on society and less on unemployed individuals. In

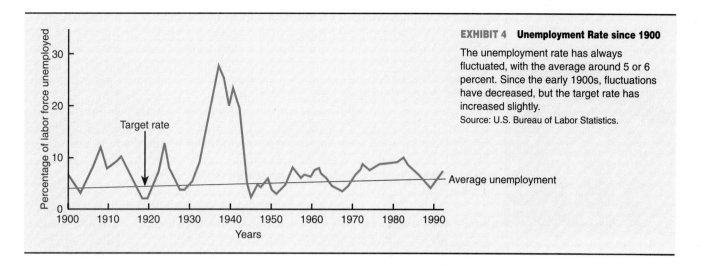

the Great Depression of the 1930s, with up to 25 percent of the population unemployed, views about unemployment changed. Most people came to see it as society's and not the individual's problem.

Keynesian economics was born in the Great Depression. In the 1950s and 1960s, as Keynesian economics expanded to include a majority of macroeconomists, the Keynesian view of unemployment also became the view of the majority of the population.

But in the 1970s and 1980s that view started to change. In Britain, for example, Prime Minister Margaret Thatcher stated specifically that unemployment was not a societal problem; it was an individual problem. Similar views were expressed in the United States. By 1990 an increasing number of people followed the Classical view and saw unemployment as an individual responsibility. In 1991 the pendulum swung back; as the economy fell into recession, the Keynesian view was once again gaining.

How Is Unemployment Measured?

When there's debate about what the unemployment problem is, it isn't surprising that there's also a debate about how to measure it. When talking about unemployment, economists usually refer to the "unemployment rate" published by the U.S. Department of Labor's Bureau of Labor Statistics (BLS). Fluctuations in the official unemployment rate since 1900 appear in Exhibit 4. In it you can see that during World War II (1941–45) unemployment fell from the high rates of the 1930s depression to an extremely low rate, only 1.2 percent. You can also see that while the rate started back up in the 1950s, reaching 4 or 5 percent, it remained that low up until the 1970s, when the rate began gradually to rise again. After peaking in the early 1980s it began to descend again. In 1990 it was about 5 percent; then in 1991 the economy fell into recession and unemployment rates rose to about 7 percent in 1992 and 1993.

Calculating the Unemployment Rate   The U.S. unemployment rate is determined by dividing the number of unemployed individuals by the number of people in the civilian labor force. To determine the civilian labor force, start with the total population and subtract from that all persons incapable of working, such as inmates of institutions and people under 16 years of age. From that figure another subtraction is made—the number of people not in the labor force, including homemakers, students, retirees, the voluntarily idle, and the disabled. The result is the potential work force, which is about 50 percent of the total population. We then subtract about 2 million individuals who are in the armed forces, to arrive at a civilian labor force. Today the civilian labor force is about 127 million as you can see in Exhibit 5.

The *Monthly Labor Review*, a Department of Labor publication, is one of the best sources of labor statistics.

To determine the number of unemployed individuals, we subtract from the civilian labor force all those employed during a given week. The Bureau of Labor Statistics defines people as "employed" if they work at a paid job for more than 15 hours a week or if they are unpaid workers in an enterprise operated by a family member. The BLS's definition of *employed* includes all those who were temporarily absent from their jobs that week because of illness, bad weather, vacation, labor–management dispute, or personal reasons, whether or not they were paid by their employers for the time off. By subtracting the total of employed people from the total labor force, we get the number of unemployed individuals. In 1991 it was about 8,500,000. Dividing this number by the labor force (127,000,000) gives us an unemployment rate of 6.7 percent.

BLS measures unemployment using a number of assumptions that have been the source of debate. For example, people may be staying at home and not looking for a job because they feel they don't have a chance to find one. Some Keynesian economists believe these individuals should be considered unemployed. Moreover they question whether part-time workers should be classified as employed.

The Keynesian argument is that there is a lack of decent jobs and of affordable transportation to get to the jobs that do exist, resulting in a high degree of discouragement so that many people have simply stopped trying. Because BLS statisticians define these people as voluntarily idle and do not count them as unemployed, Keynesians argue that the BLS undercounts unemployment significantly.

The Classical argument about unemployment is that being without a job often is voluntary. People say they are looking for a job, but they're not really looking. Many are working "off the books"; others are simply vacationing. Some Classicals contend that the way the BLS measures unemployment exaggerates the number of those who are truly unemployed.

So is the official unemployment rate too high or too low? The definition of *unemployment* involves value judgments. Both the Keynesian and the Classical arguments are defensible. But both sides agree the unemployment measure is imperfect, missing many people who should be included and including many people who should not be counted. This means that official unemployment figures must be carefully interpreted and modified in the light of other information, such as number of people employed, part-time employment, and your own perspective on the problem. In short, measuring and interpreting the unemployment rate (like measuring and interpreting most economic statistics) is an art, not a science.

Despite problems, the unemployment rate statistic still gives us useful information about changes in the economy. The measurement problems themselves

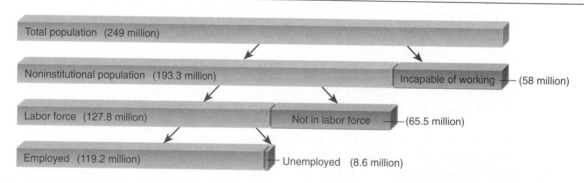

EXHIBIT 5   Unemployment/Employment Figures (in millions)*

This exhibit shows you how the unemployment rate is calculated. Notice that the labor force is not the entire population.
* Based on September 1991 employment/unemployment figures.
Source: *Economic Bulletin Board,* June 1993.

are little changed from year to year, so in comparing one year to another, those problems are not an issue. Keynesian and Classical economists agree that a changing unemployment rate generally tells us something about the economy. That's why the unemployment rate is used as a leading indicator.

Right after World War II economists talked about achieving full employment so that everyone who wanted a job could have one. But, over time, economists increased their perceptions of the level of unemployment consistent with full employment. As this happened, the concept *full employment* no longer seemed an appropriate description of the lowest achievable rate of unemployment. So economists replaced it with other concepts that were more consistent with economic reality. The concept we'll use in this book is the *target rate of unemployment,* which is defined as the lowest sustainable rate of unemployment economists believe possible under existing conditions.

As I've said, the target rate of unemployment changes over time. In the early 1990s most economists believe 5.5 percent is a reasonable target rate. If the economy were to have lower unemployment, they believe the result would be accelerating inflation—too much demand compared to available supply. With more unemployment, economists see the economy going into a downturn or a recession—too much supply compared to available demand. That's why in 1991 and 1992 when the economy had 7 percent unemployment, they believed that the economy was in recession. When the economy is in neither boom nor bust, economists expect about 5.5 percent unemployment (the target rate).

The target unemployment rate is used as a reference point for the economy. It establishes potential income (the income in the economy at the target rate of unemployment and target level of capacity utilization). To determine what effect changes in the unemployment rate will have on income, we use **Okun's rule of thumb,** which states that a 1 percent change in the unemployment rate will cause income to change in the opposite direction by 2.5 percent. For example, if unemployment rises from 5 percent to 6 percent, total output of $5 trillion will fall by 2.5 percent, or $125 billion, to $4.875 trillion. In terms of numbers of workers, a 1 percent increase in the unemployment rate means about 1,200,000 additional people are out of work.

Full Employment and the Target Rate of Unemployment

4

Unemployment and Potential Income

4

Okun's rule of thumb A 1 percent change in the unemployment rate will cause income in the economy to change in the opposite direction by 2.5 percent.

Arthur Okun—the economist for whom Okun's rule of thumb is named. *UPI Bettmann.*

ADDED DIMENSION

FROM FULL EMPLOYMENT TO
THE TARGET RATE OF
UNEMPLOYMENT

A s I emphasized in Chapter 1, good economists attempt to remain neutral and objective. It isn't always easy, especially when the language we use is often biased. (Think back to the puzzle about the doctor in Chapter 1. Have you solved it yet?)

This problem has proved to be a difficult one for economists in their attempt to find an alternative to the concept, *full employment*. An early contender was the *natural rate of unemployment*. Economists have often used the term *natural* to describe economic concepts. For example, they've talked about "natural" rights and a "natural" rate of interest. The problem with this usage is that what's natural to one person isn't necessarily natural to another. The term *natural* often conveys a sense of "that's the way it should be." However, in describing as "natural" the rate of unemployment that an economy can achieve, economists weren't making any value judgments about whether 5.5 percent unemployment is what should, or should not, be. They simply were saying that given the institutions in the economy, that is what is achievable. So a number of economists objected to the use of the term *natural*.

As an alternative a number of economists started to use the term, *nonaccelerating inflation rate of unemployment (NAIRU)*, but even users of this term agreed it was a horrendous term. And so most avoided its use and shifted to the relatively neutral term, *target rate of unemployment*.

The target rate of unemployment is the rate that one believes is attainable without causing accelerating inflation. It is not determined theoretically; it is determined empirically. Economists look at what seems to be achievable and is historically normal, adjust that for structural and demographic changes they believe are occurring, and come up with the target rate of unemployment.

These figures are rough, but they give you a sense of the implications of a change. For example, say unemployment falls .2 percent, from 5.5 to 5.3 percent. That means about 240,000 more people have jobs and that income will be $25 billion higher than otherwise would have occurred if the increase holds for the entire year. Notice I said "will be $25 billion higher than otherwise would have occurred" rather than simply saying "will increase by $25 billion." As we discussed in the growth section, generally the economy is growing as a result of increases in productivity or increases in the number of people choosing to work. Changes in either of these can cause income and employment to grow, even if there's no change in the unemployment rate. We must point this out because in the 1980s the number of people choosing to work increased substantially, significantly increasing the labor participation rate. Income and employment grew even when the unemployment rate was unchanged, and sometimes even when it rose.

Because labor force participation rates fluctuate, what happens to actual income depends more on what happens to employment than on what happens to unemployment. When the labor participation rate changes, an increase in unemployment doesn't necessarily mean a decrease in employment and income.

Microeconomic Categories of Unemployment

In the post–World War II period unemployment was seen primarily as cyclical unemployment, and the focus of macroeconomic policy was on how to eliminate that unemployment through a specific set of macroeconomic policies: monetary and fiscal policies, which I'll discuss in Part 2. Understanding monetary and fiscal policies is important, but in the 1990s it's not enough. Unemployment has many dimensions, so different types of unemployment are susceptible to different types of policies. Today's view is that you don't use a sledge hammer to pound in finishing nails, and you don't use macro policies to deal with certain types of unemployment; instead you use micro policies. To determine where microeconomic policies are appropriate as a supplement to macroeconomic policies, economists break unemployment down into a number of categories and analyze each category separately. These categories include how people become unemployed, demographic characteristics, duration of unemployment, and industry. (See Exhibit 6.)

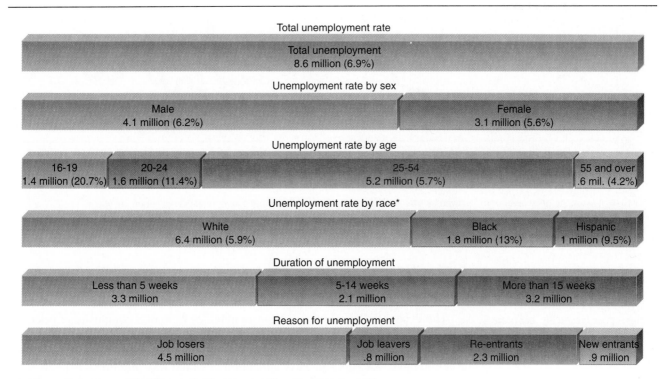

Total unemployment rate

Total unemployment
8.6 million (6.9%)

Unemployment rate by sex

Male
4.1 million (6.2%)

Female
3.1 million (5.6%)

Unemployment rate by age

16-19
1.4 million (20.7%)

20-24
1.6 million (11.4%)

25-54
5.2 million (5.7%)

55 and over
.6 mil. (4.2%)

Unemployment rate by race*

White
6.4 million (5.9%)

Black
1.8 million (13%)

Hispanic
1 million (9.5%)

Duration of unemployment

Less than 5 weeks
3.3 million

5-14 weeks
2.1 million

More than 15 weeks
3.2 million

Reason for unemployment

Job losers
4.5 million

Job leavers
.8 million

Re-entrants
2.3 million

New entrants
.9 million

EXHIBIT 6   Unemployment by Microeconomic Subcategories, First Quarter, 1993

Unemployment isn't all the same. This exhibit gives you a sense of some of the subcategories of unemployment.
* Figures adjusted to include estimates of the number of Hispanics.
Source: *Economic Bulletin Board*, June 1993.

Inflation is a continual rise in the price level. The price level is an index of all prices in the economy. Even when inflation isn't roaring and inflation itself isn't a problem, the fear of inflation guides macroeconomic policy. Fear of inflation prevents governments from expanding the economy and reducing unemployment. It prevents governments from using macroeconomic policies to lower interest rates. It gets some political parties booted out of office. (Democrat Jimmy Carter lost his bid for a second U.S. presidential term in part because of high inflation at the time.) It gets others elected. (Republican George Bush won the U.S. presidency in 1988 in part because of low inflation in the late 1980s.)

A one-time rise in the price level is not inflation. Unfortunately, it's often hard to tell if a one-time rise in the price level is going to stop, so the distinction blurs in practice, but we must understand the distinction. If the price level goes up 10 percent in a month, but then remains constant, the economy doesn't have an inflation problem. Inflation is an *ongoing rise* in the price level.

From 1800 until World War II the U.S. inflation rate fluctuated, as we see in Exhibit 7(a), which shows historical movements of the price level. Since World War II the price level has continually risen, which means the inflation rate (the measure of the change in prices over time) has been positive, as can be seen in Exhibit 7(b). The rate at which the price level rises fluctuates, but the movement has been consistently upward.

Since inflation is a sustained rise in the general price level, one must first determine what the general price level was at a given time and then decide how much it has changed. Because there are a number of different ways of doing this, there are a number of different measures of the price level. The most often used are the Producer Price Index, the GDP deflator, and the Consumer Price Index. Each has certain advantages and disadvantages.

INFLATION

Inflation   Continual rise in the price level.

7

1

Measurement of Inflation

(a)

(b)

EXHIBIT 7 (a and b)   Price Level and Inflation

Until 1940, rises in the price level were followed by falls in the price level, keeping the price level relatively constant, as you can see in (**a**).
Since the 1940s, inflation has almost always been positive, as you can see in (**b**), which means that the price level has been continually rising.
Source: U.S. Dept. of Commerce.

Producer Price Index (PPI) Composite of prices of certain raw materials.

The **Producer Price Index (PPI)** is an index or ratio of a composite of prices of a number of important raw materials, such as steel, relative to a composite of the prices of those raw materials in a base year. It does not correctly measure actual inflation, but it does give an early indication of which way inflation will likely head since many of the prices that make it up are the prices used as inputs in the production of other goods.

GDP deflator Index of the price level of aggregate output or the average price of the components in GDP relative to a base year.

The total output deflator, or **GDP deflator** (gross domestic product deflator), is an index of the price level of aggregate output or the average price of the components in total output or GDP relative to a base year.[2] It's the inflation index economists generally favor because it includes the widest number of goods. Unfortunately, since it's difficult to compute, it's published only quarterly and with a fairly substantial lag. (That is, by the time the figures come out, the period the figures measure has been over for quite a while.)

Consumer Price Index (CPI) Index of inflation measuring prices of a fixed "basket" of consumer goods, weighted according to each component's share of an average consumer's expenditures.

Published monthly, the **Consumer Price Index (CPI)** is the index of inflation most often used in news reports about the economy. As opposed to measuring the prices of all goods, it measures the prices of a fixed "basket" of goods that consumers buy, weighting each component of the basket according to its share of an average consumer's expenditures. Exhibit 8 shows the relative percentages. As you see, housing, transportation, and food make up the largest percentages of the CPI. To give you an idea of what effect the rise in price of a component of the CPI will have on the CPI as a whole, let's say food prices rise 10 percent in a year and all other prices remain constant. Since food is about 20 percent of the total, the CPI will rise 20% × 10% = 2%. The CPI and GDP deflator indices roughly equal each other when averaged over an entire year.

Measuring changes in prices over time is difficult. One of the most vexing price indexing problems is how to include quality changes. For example, say 1993 cars have a new style and, unlike 1992 models, provide airbags as a standard feature. They cost 5 percent more. Has the price of cars really gone up 5 percent, or is the 5 percent simply the cost of improving cars' design and equipment? There are ways to answer these questions, but none are totally satisfactory. With significant changes in goods' quality occurring every year, most economists don't worry about small amounts of inflation (1 or 2 percent), because it's not even certain such small changes actually represent inflation.

---

[2] We'll discuss why total output is called GDP in the next chapter.

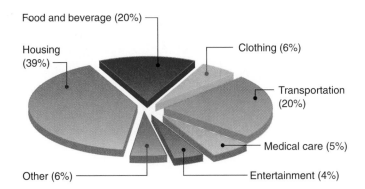

Food and beverage (20%)

Housing (39%)

Clothing (6%)

Transportation (20%)

Medical care (5%)

Other (6%)

Entertainment (4%)

EXHIBIT 8   Composition of CPI

The Consumer Price index is determined by looking at the prices of the categories listed in this exhibit. These categories represent the rough percentages of people's expenditures. In reality, there are Consumer Price Indexes for two population groups: (1) for all urban consumers (the urban CPI)—about 80 percent of the U.S. population—and (2) for urban wage earners and clerical workers (the wage-earner CPI)—about 32 percent of the U.S. population. The numbers that compose the CPI are collected at 85 separate locations and include prices from over 57,000 housing units and 19,000 business establishments.
Source: Bureau of Labor Statistics, *CPI Detailed Reports,* 1993.

One important way in which inflation indices are used is to separate changes in real output from changes in nominal output. **Real output** is the total amount of goods and services produced adjusted for price level changes. It is the measure of output that would exist if the price level had remained constant. **Nominal output** is output as measured. For example, say total output rises from $4 trillion to $5 trillion. Nominal output has risen by

$$\frac{\$5 \text{ trillion} - \$4 \text{ trillion}}{\$4 \text{ trillion}} = \frac{\$1 \text{ trillion}}{\$4 \text{ trillion}} = 25\%.$$

Let's say, however, the price level has risen 20 percent, from 100 percent to 120 percent. Real output (nominal output adjusted for inflation) hasn't risen by 25 percent; it has risen by less than nominal output has increased. To determine how much less, we must adjust the nominal figures to account for inflation. This is called *deflating* the nominal figures. To deflate we divide the most recent nominal figure, $5 trillion, by the price index of 120 percent (or 1.2):

$$\frac{\$5 \text{ trillion}}{1.2} = \$4.167 \text{ trillion}.$$

That $4.167 trillion is the measure of output that would have existed if the price level had not changed. What output would have been if the price level had remained constant is the definition of real output so $4.167 trillion is the measure of real output. Real output has increased from $4 trillion to $4.167 trillion, or by $167 billion.

When you consider price indices, you mustn't lose sight of the forest for the trees. Keep in mind the general distinction between real and nominal GDP. The concepts *real* and *nominal* and the process of adjusting from nominal to real by dividing the nominal amount by a price index will come up again and again. So whenever you see the word *real,* remember:

The "real" amount is the nominal amount divided by the price index. It is the nominal amount adjusted for inflation.

Inflation results when more people on average raise their prices than lower their prices. Thus, to explain why inflation occurs we must explain why people raise prices. The logical answer is that they believe that in doing so they can get a larger slice of the total output pie for themselves.

Real and Nominal Concepts

Real output   Output adjusted for price level changes; the level of output that would exist if the price level remained constant.

Nominal output   Output as measured before adjustments for changes in the price level.

6

The "real" amount is the nominal amount divided by the price index. It is the nominal amount adjusted for inflation.

Why Does Inflation Occur?

EXHIBIT 9 (a and b)   Demand-Pull and Cost-Push Inflation

In demand-pull inflation, shown in (**a**), prices are rising because of increases in demand. Such inflation is usually associated with shortages. In cost-push inflation, shown in (**b**), prices rise because of increases in supply prices or leftward shifts in supply.

Demand-pull inflation Economy at or above full employment with excess demand.

7

Cost-push inflation Economy below full employment with prices rising even though there are no shortages of goods or workers.

Think back to Chapter 2's discussion of the dynamic laws of supply and demand. There we saw that a gap between the quantity demanded and the quantity supplied leads to upward pressure on price. Exhibit 9(a) demonstrates this. If price is initially P_0 and demand rises from D_0 to D_1, there will be upward pressure on the good's price. When the majority of markets in the economy experience increases in demand, we say there's demand-pull pressure, and the inflation that results is called **demand-pull inflation.**

When demand is high, price increases enlarge a person's share. Demand-pull inflations are generally characterized by shortages of goods and shortages of workers. Because there's excess demand, firms know that if they raise their prices, they'll still be able to sell their goods, and workers know if they raise their wages, they will still get hired.

Exhibit 9(b) shows a second possible explanation why people might raise their price. Say one group of individuals ($0A$) figured out a way to limit the quantity supplied to Q_a. To do so, they must keep suppliers AB out of the market through some type of legal or social pressure. If they succeed, price rises from P_0 to P_1 as supply shifts to the left. When a significant proportion of markets (or one very important market, such as the labor market or the oil market) experience restrictions on supply, we say that there is cost-push pressure. The resulting inflation is called **cost-push inflation.**

In cost-push inflation, because there is no excess demand (there may actually be excess supply), firms are not sure there will be sufficient demand to sell off their goods and all workers are not sure that after raising their wage they will all be hired, but the ones who actually do the pushing are fairly sure they won't be the ones who can't sell off their goods or the ones fired. A classic cost-push example occurred in the 1970s when OPEC raised its price on oil, triggering cost-push inflation.

The demand-pull/cost-push distinction is helpful as long as one remembers that it must be used with care. The price level is always determined by both demand pressures and cost pressures. In all inflations, both demand-pull and cost-push pressures play a role. As Alfred Marshall (the 19th-century English economist who originated supply and demand analysis) said, it is impossible to separate the roles of supply and demand in influencing price, just as it is impossible to separate which blade of the scissors is cutting a sheet of paper. Both sides always play a role.

To see the difficulty, let's consider the OPEC oil price rise. What would have happened if all prices rose but total quantity demanded did not rise? The result would have been unemployment, a fall in production, and a decrease in the demand for oil. Prices, on average, wouldn't have continued to rise as demand fell. But prices on average *did* continue to rise because total demand did not stay constant—it rose significantly for reasons that we'll discuss in later chapters. So some economists called it demand-pull inflation rather than cost-push inflation. Since inflation is an ongoing rise in prices and, in any ongoing rise, both demand and supply play a role, the cost-push/demand-pull distinction must be used carefully.

A second helpful distinction is between expected and unexpected inflation. **Expected inflation** is inflation people expect to occur. **Unexpected inflation** surprises people.

To see why this expected/unexpected distinction is important, remember when an individual sets a price (for goods or labor) he or she is actually setting a relative price—relative to some price level that they expect to exist out there. The dynamic laws of supply and demand affect relative prices, not nominal prices. Now let's say everyone suddenly expects the price level to rise 10 percent. Let's also say that all individual sellers want a 1/2 percent raise in their relative price. They're not greedy; they just want a little bit more than what they're currently getting.

The reason expectations of inflation are important is the relative price increase people want must be tacked onto the inflation they expect. When people expect a 10 percent inflation, in order to have a one-half of 1 percent rise in their relative price, they have to raise their money price by 10½ percent—10 percent to keep up and 1/2 percent to get ahead. Ten percent of the inflation is caused by expectations of inflation; 1/2 percent of the inflation is caused by cost-push pressures. The cost-push/demand-pull distinction concerns what causes the 1/2 percent pressure. The expected/unexpected distinction refers to the cause of that 10 percent inflation. Thus, whether or not inflation is expected makes a big difference in individuals' behavior. If people expect inflation, they'll raise their prices to get ahead or to keep up. They won't do that for unexpected inflation, because of course they don't know unexpected inflation is coming.

Since prices and wages are often set for periods of two months to three years ahead, whether inflation is expected can play an important role in the inflation process. In the early 1970s people didn't expect the high inflation rates that did occur. When inflation hit, people just tried to keep up with it. By the end of the 1970s people expected more inflation than actually occurred and raised their prices—and, in doing so, caused the inflation rate to increase.

Expectations of inflation play an important role in any ongoing inflation. They can snowball a small inflationary pressure into an accelerating large inflation. Individuals keep raising their prices because they expect inflation, and inflation keeps on growing because individuals keep raising their prices. That's why expectations of inflation are of central concern to economic policy makers.

Inflation has costs, but not the costs that noneconomists often associate with it. Specifically inflation doesn't make the nation poorer. True, whenever prices go up somebody (the person paying the higher price) is worse off, but the person to whom the higher price is paid is better off. The two offset each other. So inflation does not make the society on average any poorer. Inflation does, however, redistribute income from people who cannot or do not raise their prices to people who can and do raise their prices. This often creates feelings of injustice about the economic system. Thus, inflation can have significant distributional effects.

Expected and Unexpected Inflation

Expected inflation Inflation people expect to occur.

Unexpected inflation Inflation that surprises people.

Costs of Inflation

8   A second cost of inflation is its effect on the information content of prices. Consider an individual who laments the high cost of housing, pointing out that it has doubled in 10 years! But if inflation averaged 7 percent a year over the past 10 years, a doubling of housing prices should be expected. In fact, with 7 percent inflation, on average *all* prices double every 10 years. That means the individual's wages have probably also doubled, so he or she is no better off and no worse off than 10 years ago. The price of housing relative to other goods, which is the relevant price for making decisions, hasn't changed. When there's inflation it's hard for people to know what is and what isn't a relative price. People's minds aren't computers, so inflation reduces the amount of information that prices can convey and causes people to make choices that do not reflect relative prices.

Despite these costs, inflation is usually accepted by governments as long as it stays at a low rate. What scares economists is inflationary pressures above and beyond expectations of inflation (for example, if the money supply is increasing at a fast rate). In that case, expectations of higher inflation can cause inflation to build up and compound itself. A 3 percent inflation becomes a 6 percent inflation, which in turn becomes a 12 percent inflation. Once inflation hits 5 percent or 6 percent, it's definitely no longer a little thing. Inflation of 10 percent or more is significant. Once it hits triple digits—100 percent or more—it's a **hyperinflation.**

Hyperinflation Inflation of 100 percent or more per year.

The United States has been either relatively lucky or wise because it has not experienced hyperinflation since the Civil War (1861–65). Other countries, such as Brazil, Israel, and Argentina, have not been so lucky (or have not followed policies as wise as the United States has). These countries have frequently had hyperinflations. But even with inflations at these levels, economies have continued to operate and, in many cases, continued to do well.

In a hyperinflation people try to spend their money quickly, but they still use the money. Let's say the U.S. price level is increasing 1 percent a day, which is a yearly inflation rate of about 4,000 percent.[3] Is an expected decrease in value of 1 percent per day going to cause you to stop using dollars? Probably not, unless you have a good alternative. You will, however, avoid putting your money into savings accounts unless that savings account somehow compensates you for the expected inflation (the expected fall in the value of the dollar) and you will try to ensure your wage *is* adjusted for inflation. In a hyperinflation, wages, the prices firms receive, and individual savings are all in some way adjusted for inflation. Hyperinflations lead to economic institutions with built-in expectations of inflation. For example, usually in a hyperinflation the government issues indexed bonds whose value keeps pace with inflation.

Once these adjustments have been made, substantial inflations will not destroy an economy, but they certainly are not good for it. Such inflations tend to break down confidence in the monetary system, the economy, and the government.

THE INTERRELATIONSHIP OF GROWTH, INFLATION, AND UNEMPLOYMENT

In this chapter, we've talked about growth, inflation, and unemployment. Now let's address their interrelationship. If the government could attack inflation without worrying about unemployment or growth, it probably would have solved the problem of inflation by now. Unfortunately, solving inflation often worsens unemployment and slows growth. When the government tries to stop inflation, it often causes a recession. Similarly, reducing unemployment by stimulating growth tends to increase inflation. To the degree that inflation and unemployment are opposite sides of the coin, the opportunity cost of reducing unemployment is

---

[3] Why about 4,000 percent and not 365 percent? Because of compounding. In the second day the increase is on the initial price level *and* the 1 percent rise in price level that occurred the first day. When you carry out this compounding for all 365 days, you get almost 4,000 percent.

inflation. The government must make a trade-off between low unemployment and slow growth on the one hand and inflation on the other. Opportunity costs must be faced in macro as well as in micro.

KEY POINTS

- The secular trend growth rate of the economy is 3.5 percent. Fluctuations around the secular trend growth rate are called *business cycles*. **1**
- Two important causes of growth are appropriate economic incentives and people. **2**
- Phases of the business cycle include peak, trough, upturn, and downturn. **3**
- The target rate of unemployment is the lowest sustainable rate of unemployment possible under existing institutions. It's associated with an economy's potential income. The lower the target rate of unemployment, the higher an economy's potential income. **4**
- The microeconomic approach to unemployment

- subdivides unemployment into categories and looks at those individual components. **5**
- A real concept is a nominal concept adjusted for inflation. **6**
- Inflation is a continual rise in the price level. Both cost-push and demand-pull pressures play a role in any inflation. **7**
- Expectations of inflation can provide pressure for an inflation to continue even when other causes don't exist. **7**
- For inflation to continue, it must be accompanied by an increase in the money supply. **7**
- Two important costs of inflation are an equity cost and an information cost. **8**

KEY TERMS

boom *(139)*
business cycles *(137)*
capacity utilization rate *(140)*
coincidental indicators *(140)*
Consumer Price Index (CPI) *(150)*
cost-push inflation *(152)*
cyclical unemployment *(141)*

demand-pull inflation *(152)*
depression *(139)*
downturn *(139)*
expansion *(140)*
expected inflation *(153)*
frictional unemployment *(143)*
full employment *(143)*
GDP deflator *(150)*
hyperinflation *(154)*

inflation *(149)*
leading indicators *(140)*
nominal output *(151)*
Okun's rule of thumb *(147)*
potential output *(140)*
Producer Price Index (PPI) *(150)*
real output *(151)*
recession *(139)*

structural unemployment *(141)*
target rate of unemployment *(140)*
unemployment rate *(140)*
unexpected inflation *(153)*
upturn *(140)*

QUESTIONS FOR THOUGHT AND REVIEW

The number after each question represents the estimated degree of critical thinking required. (1 = almost none; 10 = deep thought.)

1. An economist has just made an argument that rules should be followed because they're rules. Which kind of economist is this person: Keynesian or Classical? Why? (*This question uses material from the section introduction.*) *(7)*
2. If unemployment fell to 1.2 percent in World War II, why can't it be reduced to 1.2 percent in the 1990s? *(8)*
3. The index of leading indicators has predicted all past recessions. Nonetheless it's not especially useful for predicting recessions. Explain. *(7)*
4. Distinguish between structural unemployment and cyclical unemployment. *(3)*

5. Does the unemployment rate underestimate or overestimate the unemployment problem? Explain. *(5)*
6. If unemployment rises 2 percent, what will likely happen to income in the United States? *(7)*
7. Why are expectations central to understanding inflation? *(5)*
8. Inflation, on average, makes people neither richer nor poorer. Therefore it has no cost. True or false? Explain. *(7)*
9. Who would be more likely to see a psychiatrist: a Keynesian economist or a Classical economist? Why? (*This question uses material from the section introduction.*) *(8)*
10. Would you expect that inflation would generally be associated with low unemployment? Why? *(7)*

PROBLEMS AND EXERCISES

1. The following questions require library research.
   a. What are the current unemployment rate, capacity utilization rate, and rate of inflation? What do you predict they will be next year?
   b. Find some predictions for each of these figures for next year.
   c. Are these predictions consistent with your predictions? Why?
   d. In what position on the business cycle does the economy currently find itself?
2. The following questions concern statistics and economic institutions.

   a. Go to the local unemployment office and ask to see the form people fill out to collect unemployment insurance. What are the eligibility criteria?
   b. A friend shows you a newspaper article saying unemployment increased but output also increased. He says that this doesn't make sense, it must be a mistake. What do you tell your friend?
   c. Inflation rose 5 percent; real output rose 2 percent. What would you expect to happen to nominal output?
   d. Real output rose 3 percent and nominal output rose 7 percent. What happened to inflation?

7

National Income Accounting

The government is very keen on amassing statistics. . . . They collect them, add them, raise them to the nth power, take the cube root and prepare wonderful diagrams. But you must never forget that every one of these figures comes in the first instance from the village watchman, who just puts down what he damn pleases.

Sir Josiah Stamp (head of Britain's revenue department in the late 19th century)

After reading this chapter, you should be able to:

1
State why national income accounting is important.

2
Define GDP, GNP, NDP, NNP, and NI.

3
Calculate GDP in a simple example, avoiding double counting.

4
Explain why GDP = $C + I + G + (X - M)$.

5
Distinguish between real and nominal values.

6
State some limitations of national income accounting.

Before you can talk about macroeconomics in depth, you need to be introduced to some terminology used in macroeconomics. That terminology can be divided into two parts. The first part deals with national income accounting, which was specifically developed to handle macroeconomic aggregate concepts (concepts embodying a number of components). Examples include total consumption, total income, and the price level.

The second part distinguishes between real and nominal (or money) concepts. As we discussed in an earlier chapter, **real concepts** are concepts adjusted for inflation; **nominal concepts** are concepts specified in monetary terms with no adjustment for inflation. Real and nominal concepts are used to differentiate and compare goods and actions over time.

Real concepts Economic concepts adjusted for inflation.

Nominal concepts Economic concepts specified in monetary terms with no adjustment for inflation.

NATIONAL INCOME ACCOUNTING

Simon Kuznets—Nobel prize, 1971, for work on national accounting. © The Nobel Foundation.

1

National income accounting A set of rules and definitions for measuring economic activity in the aggregate economy.

In the 1930s it was impossible for macroeconomics to exist in the form we know it today because many aggregate concepts of macroeconomics we now take for granted either had not yet been formulated or were so poorly formulated that it was useless to talk rigorously about them. This lack of aggregate terminology was consistent with the Classical economists' lack of interest in the aggregate approach in the 1930s; they preferred to focus on microeconomics.

With the advent of Keynesian macroeconomics in the mid-1930s, development of a terminology to describe macroeconomic aggregates became crucial. Measurement is a necessary step toward rigor. A group of Keynesian economists set out to develop an aggregate terminology and to measure the aggregate concepts they defined, so that people would have concrete terms to use when talking about macroeconomic problems. Their work (for which two of them, Simon Kuznets and Richard Stone, received the Nobel prize) is called **national income accounting** (a set of rules and definitions to use in measuring activity in the aggregate economy—that is, in the economy as a whole). To talk about the aggregate economy without knowing the concepts of national income accounting is equivalent to talking about cricket without knowing what a wicket is, or to talk about rock music without knowing U2.

National income accounting provides a way of measuring total, or aggregate, economic production. National income accounting also breaks down aggregate economic production into subaggregates (such as consumption, investment, and personal income) and defines the relationship among these subaggregates. In short, national income accounting enables us to measure and analyze how much the nation is producing and consuming.

Learning national income accounting is necessary. Before you play Chopin, you must learn to play scales, and before you fiddle with the aggregate economy, you must learn national income accounting.

Measuring Total Economic Output of Goods and Services

2

Gross domestic product (GDP) Aggregate final output of residents and businesses in an economy in a one-year period.

A firm generally measures how busy it is by how much it produces. To talk about how well the aggregate economy is doing, national income accounting uses a corresponding concept, aggregate output, which goes under the name **gross domestic product (GDP).**

GDP is the total market value of all final goods and services produced in an economy in a one-year period. It's probably the single most-used economic measure. When economists, journalists, and other analysts talk about the economy, they continually discuss GDP: how much it has increased or decreased, and what it's likely to do. In deciding whether a change in GDP means a growth in output, we must take account of inflation (the rise in prices of goods on average). If we don't, we won't know whether output has really risen.

Gross National Product and Gross Domestic Product

Up until 1992 the United States (unlike the rest of the world) used gross national product as its primary measure of aggregate output. Economic issues are becoming internationalized and national income accounting has been affected by that internationalization. In 1992 the

United States followed the rest of the world and switched to gross domestic product as its primary measure of aggregate output.

Whereas *gross domestic product* measures the economic activity that occurs *within a country*, **gross national product (GNP)** measures the economic activity of all the people and businesses *of a country*. So the economic activity of U.S. citizens working abroad is counted in U.S. GNP but isn't counted in U.S. GDP. Similarly for the foreign economic activity of U.S. companies. However the income of a Mexican or German person or business working in the United States isn't counted in U.S. GNP but is counted in U.S. GDP. Thus, GDP describes the economic output within the physical borders of a country while GNP describes the economic output produced by the citizens of a country. To move from GDP to GNP one must add **net foreign factor income** to GDP. Net foreign factor income is defined as the income from foreign domestic factor sources minus foreign factor incomes earned domestically.

For many countries there's a significant difference between GNP and GDP, but for the United States there isn't because the foreign output of U.S. businesses and people for the most part offsets the output of foreign businesses and people within the United States. So for the United States, GNP doesn't significantly differ from GDP.

Gross national product (GNP) Aggregate final output of citizens and businesses of an economy in a one-year period.

Net foreign factor income Difference between GDP and GNP.

Calculating GDP

Aggregate final output (GDP) consists of millions of different services and products: apples, oranges, computers, haircuts, financial advice. . . . To arrive at total output, somehow we've got to add them all together into a composite measure. Say we produced 7 oranges plus 6 apples plus 12 computers. We have not produced 25 comapplorgs. You can't add apples and oranges and computers. You can only add like things (things that are measured in the same units). For example, 2 apples + 4 apples = 6 apples. If we want to add unlike things, we must convert them into like things. We do that by multiplying each good by its *price*. Economists call this *weighting* the importance of each good by its price. For example, if you have 4 pigs and 4 horses and you price pigs at $200 each and horses at $400 each, the horses are weighted as being twice as important as pigs.

Multiplying the quantity of each good by its market price changes the terms in which we discuss each good from a quantity of a specific product to a *value* measure of that good. For example, when we multiply 6 apples by their price, 25¢ each, we get $1.50; $1.50 is a value measure. Once all goods are expressed in that value measure, they can be added together.

Take the example of seven oranges and six apples. (For simplicity let's forget the computers, haircuts, and financial advice.) If the oranges cost 50¢ each, their total value is $3.50; if the apples cost 25¢ each, their total value is $1.50. Their values are expressed in identical measures, so we can add them together. When we do so, we don't get 13 orples; we get $5 worth of apples and oranges.

If we follow that same procedure with all the final goods and services produced in the economy in the entire year, multiplying the quantity produced by the price per unit, we have all the economy's outputs expressed in units of value. If we then add up all these units of value, we have that year's gross domestic product.

There are two important aspects to remember about GDP. First, GDP represents a flow (an amount per year), not a stock (a stable amount at a particular moment of time). Second, GDP refers to the market value of *final* output. Let's consider these statements separately.

GDP Is a Flow Concept   In economics it's important to distinguish between flows and stock. Say a student just out of college tells you she earns $8,000. You'd probably think, "Wow! She's got a low-paying job!" That's because you implicitly assume she means $8,000 per year. If you later learned that she earns $8,000 per week, you'd quickly change your mind. The confusion occurred because how much you

Sir Richard Stone—Nobel prize, 1984, for work on national accounting. © *The Nobel Foundation.*

earn is a *flow* concept; it has meaning only when a time period is associated with it: so much per week, per month, per year. A *stock* concept is the amount of something at a given point in time. No time interval is associated with it. Your weight is a stock concept. You weigh 150 pounds; you don't weigh 150 pounds per week.

GDP is a flow concept, the amount of total final output a country produces per year. The *per year* is often left unstated, but it is important to keep in your mind that it's essential. GDP is usually reported quarterly or every three months, but it is reported on an *annualized basis,* meaning the U.S. Department of Commerce, which compiles GDP figures, uses quarterly figures to predict total output for the whole year.

GDP Measures Final Output   As a student in my first economics class I was asked to tell how to calculate GDP. I said, "Add up the value of the goods and services produced by all the companies in the United States to arrive at GDP." I was wrong (which is why I remember it). Many goods produced by one firm are sold to other firms, which use those goods to make something else. GDP doesn't measure total transactions in an economy; it measures *final output.* When one firm sells products to another firm for use in production of yet another good, the first firm's products aren't considered final output. They're **intermediate products** (products used as inputs in some other product). To count intermediate goods as well as final goods as part of GDP would be to double count them.

> **Intermediate products** Products of one firm used as inputs in some other product.

If we did not eliminate intermediate goods, a change in organization would look like a change in output. Say one firm that produced steel merged with a firm that produced cars. Both together then produce exactly what each did separately before the merger. Final output hasn't changed, nor has intermediate output. The only difference is that the intermediate output of steel is now internal to the firm. Using only firms' sales of goods to final consumers (and not sales to other firms) in one's measure of GDP prevents mere changes in organization from affecting the measure of output. Double counting would significantly overestimate final output.

3 **Two Ways of Eliminating Intermediate Goods**   There are two ways to eliminate intermediate goods from the measure of GDP. One is to calculate only final output (goods sold to consumers). To do so, firms would have to separate goods they sold to consumers from intermediate goods used to produce other goods. For example,

This 17th-century engraving by Rembrandt, "The Money Lender," shows that careful bookkeeping and accounting have been around for a long time.
Bleichroeder Print Collection, Baker Library, Harvard Business School.

each firm would report how much of its product it sold to consumers and how much it sold to other producers for use that year in production of other goods; one would eliminate the latter to exclude double counting.

A second way to eliminate double counting is to follow the **value added** approach. Value added is the increase in value that a firm contributes to a product or service. Value added is calculated by subtracting from the value of sales the cost of materials that a firm uses to produce a good or service. For instance, if a firm buys $100 worth of thread and $10,000 worth of cloth and uses them in making a thousand pairs of jeans which are sold for $20,000, the firm's value added is not $20,000; it is $9,900 ($20,000 in sales minus the $10,100 in intermediate goods that the firm bought). Exhibit 1 provides another example.

Value added The increase in value that a firm contributes to a product or service; calculated by subtracting from the value of sales the cost of materials a firm uses to produce a good or service.

Say we want to measure the contribution to GDP made by a vendor who sells 200 ice cream cones at $2.50 each (they're good cones) for total sales of $500. The vendor bought his cones and ice cream from a middleperson at a cost of $400, who in turn paid the cone factory and ice cream maker a total of $250. The farmer who sold the cream to the factory got $100. Adding up all these transactions, we get $1,250, but that includes intermediate goods. Either by counting only the final value of the vendor's sales, $500, or by adding the value added at each stage of production (column III), we eliminate intermediate sales and arrive at the street vendor's contribution to GDP of $500.

Value added is calculated by subtracting the cost of materials from the value of sales, leaving only the value added at each stage of production. The aggregate value added at each stage of production is, by definition, precisely equal to the value of final sales, since it excludes all intermediate products. In Exhibit 1, the equality of the value added approach and the final-sales approach can be seen by comparing the vendor's final sales of $500 (row 4, column II) with the $500 value added (row 5, column III).

Calculating GDP: Some Examples   To make sure you understand what value added is and what makes up GDP, let's consider some sample transactions and determine what value they add and whether they should be included in GDP. Let's first consider second-hand sales: When you sell your two-year-old car, how much value has been added? The answer is none. The sale involves no current output, so there's no value added. If, however, you sold the car to a used car dealer for $2,000 and he resold it for $2,500, $500 of value has been added—the used-car dealer's efforts transferred the car from someone who didn't want it to someone who did. I point this out to remind you that GDP is not only a measure of the production of goods; it is a measure of the production of goods *and services*.

Now let's consider a financial transaction. Say you sell a bond (with a face value of $1,000) that you bought last year. You sell it for $1,200 and pay $100 commission to the dealer through whom you sell it. What value is added to final output? You might be tempted to say that $200 of value has been added, since the value of the bond has increased by $200. GDP, however, refers only to value that is added as the result of production, not to changes in the values of financial assets. Therefore the price at which you buy or sell the bond is irrelevant to the question at hand. The only value that is added by the sale is the transfer of that

Participants	I Cost of materials	II Value of sales	III Value added	Row
Farmer	$ 0	$ 100	$100	1
Cone factory and ice cream maker	100	250	150	2
Middleperson (final sales)	250	400	150	3
Vendor	400	500	100	4
Totals		$1,250	$500	5

EXHIBIT 1   Value Added Approach Eliminates Double Counting

bond from someone who doesn't want it to someone who does. Thus, the only value added as a result of economic activity is the dealer's commission, $100. The remaining $1,100 (the $1,200 you got for the bond minus the $100 commission you paid) is a transfer of an asset from one individual to another, but such transfers do not enter into GDP calculations. Only production of goods and services enters into GDP.

Let's consider a different type of financial transaction: The government pays an individual social security benefits. What value is added? Clearly no production has taken place, but money has been transferred. As in the case of the bond, only the cost of transferring it—not the amount that gets transferred—is included in GDP. This is accomplished by including in GDP government expenditures on goods and services, but not the value of government transfers. Thus, social security payments, welfare payments, and veterans' benefits do not enter into calculations of GDP. That's why the government can have a $1.2 trillion budget but only $450 billion ($1.2 trillion minus $750 billion of transfer payments) is included in GDP.

Finally let's consider the work of a house-spouse. How much value does it add to economic activity in a year? Clearly if the house-spouse is any good at what he or she does, a lot of value is added. Taking care of the house and children is hard work. Estimates of the yearly value of a house-spouse's services are often in the $35,000 to $45,000 range. Even though much value is added and hence, in principle, house-spouse services should be part of GDP, by convention a house-spouse contributes nothing to GDP. GDP measures only *market activities;* since house-spouses are not paid, their value added is not included in GDP. This leads to some problems in measurement. For example, suppose a woman divorces her house-spouse and then hires him to continue cleaning her house for $20,000 per year. Then he will be contributing $20,000 value added. That, since it is a market transaction, is included in GDP.

The house-spouse example shows that the GDP measure has some problems. There are other areas in which it also has problems, but since this is an economics text, not an accounting text, I won't go into those problems. Numerous decisions about how to handle various types of transactions had to be made to get a workable measure. Some of those decisions could have gone the other way, but, overall, the terminology of national income accounting is a model of consistency. It focuses on measuring final market output for the entire economy.

TWO METHODS OF CALCULATING GDP

The National Income Accounting Identity

National income accounting identity
The relationship between output and income whereby one equals the other.

GDP can be calculated in two ways: the expenditures method and the income method. This is because of the *national income accounting identity*.

National income accounting is a form of accounting to which you were introduced in Chapter 4. Accounting is a way of keeping track of things. It is based on certain identities; for a firm, its cost plus profit equals revenues because they are identical to revenues. National income accounting is no different. It too is based on an identity. By definition, whenever a good or service (output) is produced, somebody receives an income for producing it. This relationship between output and income, the **national income accounting identity,** can be seen in Exhibit 2, which illustrates the circular flow of income in an economy.[1]

In Exhibit 2 we see that as firms produce goods, they create income in the form of wages, rents, interest, and profits (the top flow). Consumers either spend or save their income. Their spending comes back to the firms in the form of consumption (consumers buy firms' output) or, if they save their income, in the

---

[1] An *identity* is a statement of equality that's "true by definition." In algebra an identity is sometimes written as a triple equal sign ($\equiv$). It is more equal than simply equal. How something can be more equal than equal is beyond me, too, but I'm no mathematician.

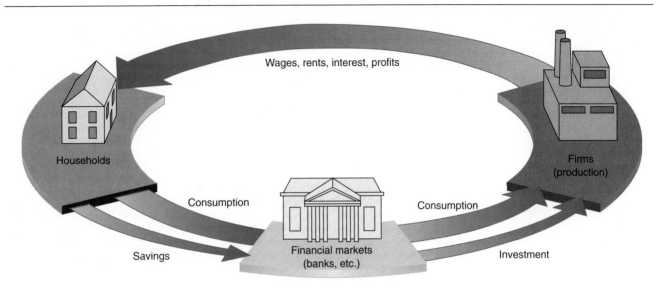

EXHIBIT 2   The Circular Flow

One of the most important insights about the aggregate economy is that it is a circular flow in which output and input are interrelated. Households' expenditures (consumption and savings) are firms' income; firms' expenditures (wages, rent, etc.) are households' income.

form of investment (firms borrow the savings and buy other firms' output), assuming financial markets can translate that savings into investment.

The value of the wages, rents, interest, and profits (the flow along the top in Exhibit 2) equals the value of goods bought (the flow along the bottom). How are these values kept exactly equal? That's the secret of double entry bookkeeping: output must always equal income.

Profit is defined as what remains after all other income (wages, rent, and interest) is paid out. For example, say a firm has a total output of $800 and that it paid $400 in wages, $200 in rent, and $100 in interest. The firm's profit is determined by subtracting that income paid out from the value of total output. Profit equals $800 − $700 = $100. That profit is the income of the owners of the firm. All income (determined by adding profits to wages, rent, and interest) equals $800, which, not surprisingly, equals the value of the output.

The accounting identity even works if a firm incurs a loss. Say that instead of paying $400 in wages, the firm paid $700, along with its other payments of $200 in rent and $100 in interest. Total output is still $800, but total income, excluding profits, is now $1,000. *Profits* are still defined as total output minus income paid out in wages, rent, and interest. Profits in this example are negative: $800 − $1,000 = (−$200). There's a *loss* of $200. Adding that loss to other income ($1,000 + (−$200)) gives total income of $800—which is identical to the firm's total output of $800.

The national income accounting identity (Total output = Total income) allows us to calculate GDP either by adding up all values of final outputs (the *expenditures approach*) or by adding up the values of all earnings or income (the *income approach*).   **4**

As with most issues in accounting, there are certain conceptual difficulties in applying seemingly reasonable definitions. In this instance the difficulty is what to do when two economies are interrelated with individuals and businesses of one country producing in another country so that a distinction must be made between GDP and GNP. Although, by definition, expenditures must equal income, there's a question of whose income whose expenditures must equal. If all figures were collected in terms of domestic income and output, there would be no problem, but in the United States as of 1992 the output side is presented as domestic output (the

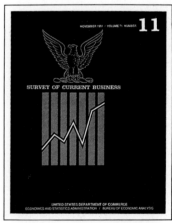

The *Survey of Current Business,* a Department of Commerce publication, is one of the best sources of GDP figures.

NATIONAL INCOME
ACCOUNTING AND DOUBLE
ENTRY BOOKKEEPING

The key to all accounting, including national income accounting, is double entry book-keeping, a system of financial record keeping invented in Italy and attributed to Luigi Pacioli (1494). Double entry bookkeeping is based on redundancy. It requires that accounting terms be defined in such a way that the cost side of the ledger is kept exactly equal to the income side. Since they're exactly equal, in theory one need calculate only one of the two sides, but in practice both sides are calculated, so the accountant can check his or her work. If both sides independently add up to the same figure, it's likely that no mistake was made.

In the national income accounts kept by the U.S. Department of Commerce, the two sides of the ledger are the expenditure accounts and the income accounts. Every entry on one side of the accounts has an offsetting entry on the other side. Whenever production (an increase in output) takes place on the expenditure side, there is a simultaneous increase in income entered on the income side.

As discussed in Chapter 4, in balance sheet accounting (accounting measuring the assets and liabilities of an individual, firm, or country) assets equal liabilities plus net worth. Net worth plays the swing role in balance sheet accounting that profits play in income accounting. *Net worth* is defined as the amount that remains when liabilities are subtracted from assets:

$$\text{Net worth} = \text{Assets} - \text{Liabilities}.$$

Net worth is recorded on the liabilities side of the ledger. Adding liabilities and net worth, we have

$$\text{Assets} = \text{Liabilities} + \text{Net worth}.$$

Substituting in for net worth, we have

$$\text{Assets} = \text{Liabilities} + (\text{Assets} - \text{Liabilities})$$

or

$$\text{Assets} = \text{Assets}.$$

Since by substituting we can get the same term on both sides of the equation, the statement "Assets = Liabilities + Net worth" is true by definition.

In national income accounting, profit plays the swing role. Profits are what is left after all other forms of income are accounted for. *Profits* are defined as the difference between total output and other income and are counted as income. So we have

$$\text{Output} = \text{Other income} + \text{Profits}$$

$$\text{Profits} = \text{Output} - \text{Other income}.$$

Substituting in for profits gives

$$\text{Output} = \text{Other income} + \text{Output} - \text{Other income}.$$

Therefore,

$$\text{Output} = \text{Output}.$$

output of firms and residents of the United States) while the input side is still presented as national income (the income of U.S. citizens and firms). These two differ by net foreign factor income. As we've discussed, in the particular case of the United States the difference is minimal, but, conceptually, it's important to keep the distinction in mind so that with either the expenditures approach or the income approach one arrives at the same result.

Let's consider these two approaches in detail.

The Expenditures Approach

Exhibit 3 gives the categories of expenditures normally used in the expenditures approach to calculating U.S. GDP: personal consumption expenditures, government purchases, gross private investment, and net exports. All expenditures fall into one or another of these four divisions, so by adding up these four categories, we get total expenditures on U.S. goods and services minus U.S. residents' expenditures on foreign goods. By definition, in national income accounting those expenditures on U.S. goods and services equal the total amount of production of goods and services (GDP).

GDP, first quarter, 1993	Dollars (in billions)		% of GDP
Personal consumption expenditures (C)	4,097		69%
Durable goods		481	
Nondurable goods		1,291	
Services		2,325	
Gross private investment (I)	770		13
Fixed investment		766	
Change in business inventories		4	
Net exports of goods and services (X − M)	−30		−0.5
Exports		636	
Imports		667	
Government purchases of goods and services (G)	1,115		18.5
Federal		449	
State and local		666	
	5,952		100%

EXHIBIT 3   GDP via the Expenditures Approach, 1992

Source: *Economic Bulletin Board*, July 1993.

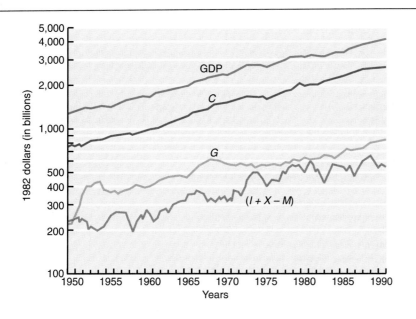

EXHIBIT 4   Movements of U.S. GDP since 1950

This exhibit demonstrates the approximate movement of GDP and its components since 1950. As you can see, gross private investment fluctuates the most over the years, and GDP tends to rise overall each year. (The numbers are for GNP, but for the United States, GDP and GNP are sufficiently close so that one can approximate the other.)
Source: *Survey of Current Business.*

Gross domestic product is equal to the sum of these four categories of expenditures:

$$GDP = C + I + G + (X - M)$$

where

C = Consumption
I = Investment
G = Government expenditures
$(X - M)$ = Net exports.

Exhibit 4 demonstrates movements in U.S. GDP and its component parts since 1950. As you can see, the individual parts fluctuate in relative importance. Of the components, investment fluctuates most; personal consumption expenditures fluctuate least. Let's consider each component in turn.

Consumption Expenditure (C)   All goods and services bought by households are lumped together under "consumption." This huge category includes such purchases as your visit to the dentist, college tuition, and the new car you buy. Consumption is the largest category in GDP, accounting for about 69 percent of

EXHIBIT 5   Breakdown of Consumer Expenditures, 1992

EXHIBIT 5   **Breakdown of Consumer Expenditures, 1992**

	Dollars (in billions)		% of Expenditures
Durable goods	481		12%
Motor vehicles and parts		204	
Furniture and household equipment		181	
Other		96	
Nondurable goods	1,291		31
Food		631	
Clothing		222	
Gasoline and oil		105	
Fuel oil		13	
Other nondurable goods		320	
Services	2,325		57
Housing		600	
Household operation		228	
Transportation		155	
Medical care		635	
Other		707	
	4,097		100%

Source: *Economic Bulletin Board*, July 1993.

EXHIBIT 6   **Gross Private Investment, 1992**

	Dollars (in billions)			% of Investment
Fixed investment	766			
Nonresidential		548		71%
Structures			168	
Producers' durable equipment			380	
Residential		218		28
Single-family structures			118	
Multifamily structures			13	
Producers' durable equipment			7	
Other			80	
Change in business inventory	4			1
Subtotal gross investment	770			100%
Depreciation	657			
Net investment	113			

Source: *Survey of Current Business*, January 1993.

Durable goods Goods expected to last more than one year.

Nondurable goods Goods expected to last less than one year.

the total. Being so large, consumption is normally broken down into subcategories: durable consumer goods, nondurable consumer goods, and services. **Durable goods** are defined as goods expected to last more than one year. (Why one year? Because one year, although arbitrary, is a reasonable cutoff point.) Durables include cars and household appliances. **Nondurable goods** are goods that last less than one year. The food you eat and the movie tickets you buy fall under this heading. Services are activities done for another person (cutting hair, teaching, and mowing a lawn). They are a form of economic activity, but they do not involve production or sale of goods. Exhibit 5 breaks down these subcategories of consumer expenditures into subsubcategories.

Gross and Net Private Investment *(I)*   Investment is expenditures by firms or households on goods, often called *capital goods,* that are used over and over to make products or provide services. Housing, tractors, steel mills, and wine barrels are examples. Thus, when economists speak of investment they don't mean the kind of activity taking place when individuals buy stocks or bonds—economists consider that saving, not investing. Gross private investment, the third largest category, makes up about 14 percent of GDP. Exhibit 6 breaks down gross private investment into two subcategories: fixed investment and change in business inventory. Fixed investment is, by far, the larger component. It includes investments in residential and nonresidential buildings and in equipment.

Change in business inventory ("inventory investment" for short) is a different form of investment. It's the increase or decrease in the value of the stocks of inventory that businesses have on hand. Notice I said "increases in the *value* of inventory." Say a car dealership normally keeps 50 cars in stock. Its inventory is 50 cars. In 1993 it increases its stock of cars to 55. Its inventory investment for 1993 is 5 cars times their value. If inventory remains constant from one year to the next, there's no inventory investment. If inventories fall, inventory investment is negative.

Inventory investment is highly volatile. Drawing implications from an increase in inventory investment is difficult, because a change in inventory investment can mean two different things. When firms expect to sell a lot, they usually produce significant amounts for inventory, so an increase in inventory investment may signal expected high sales. But inventory can also increase because goods the firm produces aren't selling. In that case, an increase in inventory investment signals low sales. Those five extra cars are just sitting on the dealer's lot. Thus, economists keep a close eye on inventory investment as well as on why inventory investment has changed.

Sooner or later, assets such as plants and equipment wear out. Economists call this wearing out process **depreciation** (the decrease in an asset's value). Depreciation is part of the cost of producing a good; it is the amount by which plants and equipment decrease in value as they grow older. Much of each year's private investment involves expenditures to replace assets that have worn out. For example, as you drive your car, it wears out. A car with 80,000 miles on it is worth less than the same type of car with only 1,000 miles on it. The difference in value is attributed to depreciation.

Depreciation Decrease in an asset's value.

To differentiate between total or gross investment and the new investment that's above and beyond replacement investment, economists use the term **net private investment** (gross investment minus depreciation). In 1992 gross investment was $770 billion and depreciation was $657 billion, so net investment was $113 billion. Economists pay close attention to net private investment because it gives an estimate of the increase in the country's productive capacity.

Net private investment Gross investment minus depreciation.

Government Purchases (G)   Government purchases are divided into federal expenditures and state and local expenditures. In macroeconomics the main focus is on the federal government because only the federal government is directly concerned with the aggregate economy. This doesn't mean state and local government expenditures don't affect the economy; they do, as do any expenditures. It simply means that state and local governments generally don't take that effect into account since each is relatively small compared to the total economy.

Government uses its tax revenue to build bridges, buy copying machines, print application forms, pay the president, and meet innumerable other expenses. Many of these government goods and services are paid for from general tax revenue and are provided free to consumers of the goods or services. As a result, they have no price at which to value them. By convention, economists value these goods and services at cost. Thus, if the federal government spends $300 billion on defense, government spending on defense is valued at $300 billion.

Total government purchases (the second-largest component of GDP) account for about 19 percent of GDP. Exhibit 7 breaks down purchases by various levels of government.

Notice state and local governments make more purchases than does the federal government, and federal government expenditures total $449 billion. Each year the federal government budget (about $1.2 trillion) is much larger than these federal government purchases of $449 billion that enter into GDP. The reason is

EXHIBIT 7   **Breakdown of Government Purchases**

	Dollars (in billions)	% of Total
State and local government expenditures (1992)	665.7	60%
Goods, durable and nondurable	95.5	
Services	477	
Structures	93.2	
Federal government expenditures (1992)	449.1	40
National defense	315.5	
Nondefense	133.7	
Total	1114.8	100%

Source: *Survey of Current Business*, January 1993.

Transfer payments Payments to individuals by the federal government that aren't payment for a good or service.

the remaining part of the federal government budget involves **transfer payments** (payments made to individuals that *aren't* payment for a good or service). Since they're simply a transfer, not a purchase of a good or service, they don't contribute to GDP. The largest of these transfers is social security payments.

Net Exports $(X - M)$ Some goods and services produced in the United States (such as wheat, computers, and U.S. vacations) are bought by people in foreign countries. Other goods and services (such as French champagne and taxi rides in London) are bought from foreign countries by U.S. residents. If these exports and imports are equal, they net out and make no contribution to GDP. If the value of what the United States sells to foreign countries is greater than what it buys from foreign countries, the United States is producing more than it is spending. In this case net exports (exports minus imports) are positive, and the difference between exports and imports must be added to GDP, since the increase represents net foreign expenditure on U.S.-produced goods. It's U.S. production bought by foreigners, but U.S. production nonetheless.

If the United States buys more from foreign countries than it sells, imports exceed exports, so net exports are negative. In this case, U.S. spending is more than U.S. production. Since GDP measures production, not spending, the excess of imports over exports must be subtracted from U.S. GDP. If it weren't subtracted, we couldn't measure production by measuring expenditures. To some degree, imports and exports offset each other. However, as I said in Chapter 5, in the United States in the early 1990s imports have significantly exceeded exports.

Exhibit 8 presents U.S. exports and imports. In the first quarter of 1993 exports were $184.9 billion; imports were $197.8 billion; so net exports were −$12.9 billion.

Summing Up the Components   Now that we've gone through the components, let's put them all together. Exhibit 9 shows rough estimates of the relative sizes of the components for six countries.

Net domestic product GDP adjusted to take account of depreciation.

GDP and NDP   In the discussion of investment, I differentiated gross investment from net investment. Gross investment minus depreciation equals net investment. Economists have created another aggregate term, **net domestic product (NDP),** to reflect the adjustment to investment because of depreciation. NDP is the sum of consumption expenditures, government expenditures, net foreign expenditures, and net investment (gross investment − depreciation). Thus,

$$GDP = C + I + G + (X - M)$$

$$NDP = C + (\text{net } I) + G + (X - M).$$

NDP takes depreciation into account, and depreciation is a cost of producing goods; so NDP is actually preferable to GDP as the expression of a country's domestic output. However, measuring true depreciation (the actual decrease in an asset's value) is difficult because asset values fluctuate. In fact, it's so difficult

EXHIBIT 8   Net Exports, 1992

	Dollars (in billions)	% of Total exports or imports
Exports	636	
Merchandise	445	70%
Services	191	30
Imports	667	
Merchandise	544	82
Services	123	18
Net exports	−30	

EXHIBIT 8   Net Exports, 1992

Source: *Economic Bulletin Board*, July 1993.

EXHIBIT 9   **Breakdown of GDP for Selected Countries**

Country	Nominal GDP, 1990 (U.S. $ in billions)	Personal consumption (% of GDP)	Gross private investment (% of GDP)	Government expenditures (% of GDP)	Exports (% of GDP)	Imports (− % of GDP)
Brazil	388	63	22	12	8	−5
Germany	1157	53	20	20	28	−21
Japan	2115	58	29	11	13	−11
Pakistan	43	72	19	13	11	−15
Tunisia	10	82	18	15	33	−48
Tanzania	6	84	18	12	6	−20

that in the real world accountants don't try to measure true depreciation, but instead use a number of conventional rules of thumb that yield an accepted figure. In recognition of this reality, economists call the adjustment made to GDP to arrive at NDP the *capital consumption allowance* rather than *depreciation*. Since estimating depreciation is difficult, GDP rather than NDP is generally used in discussions.

The alternative way of calculating GDP is the income approach. **Domestic income** (DI) has four components: compensation to employees, rents, interest, and profits. Total domestic income equals NDP, not GDP. Why? Because of depreciation, which is a cost, not an income to anyone. As I stated previously, an economy's domestic income must be separated from an economy's **national income** (NI) (the total income earned by citizens and businesses of a country). Domestic income corresponds to domestic product; national income corresponds to national product. When the United States shifted from GNP to GDP as its primary measure of economic output, it would have been reasonable also to shift to domestic as opposed to national income concepts. Alas, it did not; the primary income statistics reported in the United States are still national income statistics.

To move from domestic income to national income one must add net foreign factor income to domestic income. For the United States in the 1990s, net foreign factor income has been minimal so there's not a lot of difference between the two concepts, but since the primary income figures reported by the U.S. government are national income figures, I discuss the breakdown of national income rather than domestic income, leaving you to make the adjustments to domestic income concepts by subtracting net foreign factor income from national income concepts.

The Income Approach

Domestic income (DI) Total income earned by residents and businesses in a country.

National income (NI) Total income earned by citizens and businesses of a country.

Compensation to Employees   Compensation to employees (the largest component of national income) consists of wages and salaries paid to individuals, along with fringe benefits and government taxes for social security and unemployment insurance. As you can see in Exhibit 10, compensation to employees made up about 74 percent of national income in 1992.

EXHIBIT 10   Components of National Income, 1992

	Dollars (in billions)		% of national income
Compensation to employees	3,525		74%
Rents	5		0
Net interest	415		9
Profits	798		7
Proprietors' income		404	9
Corporate profits		394	8
National income	4,743		100%

Source: *Economic Bulletin Board*, July 1993.

Rents   Rents are the income from property received by households. Rents received by firms are not included because a firm's rents are simply another source of income to the firm and hence are classified as profits. In 1990 rents were negative, which means that the depreciation owners took on buildings exceeded the income they earned from those buildings.

Interest   Interest is the income private businesses pay to households that have lent the businesses money, generally by purchasing bonds issued by the businesses. (Interest received by firms doesn't show up in this category for the same reason that rents received by firms don't show up in the *rent* category.) Interest payments by government and households aren't included in national income since by convention they're assumed not to flow from the production of goods and services. In 1990 net interest was 11 percent of national income.

Profits   Profits are the amount that is left after compensation to employees, rents, and interest have been paid out.[2] Profits are normally divided into two categories: profits of unincorporated businesses and proprietors' income or profits of incorporated businesses. Both require some discussion. In an earlier chapter, I pointed out that in most unincorporated businesses, the owner works for the business. The amount that is left over after paying interest, rent, and compensation to employees is both a compensation for the owner's work (valued at his or her opportunity cost of working elsewhere) and the owner's profit. Thus, if a gift shop owner earns $30,000 a year after paying wages, interest, and rent, and she could have earned $20,000 working elsewhere, her compensation is $20,000 and her profits are $10,000. Tabulation of the national income data doesn't show this separation and, by convention, the entire amount ($30,000 in the example) is included as "profit."

As I also discussed in Chapter 4, corporations are fictitious legal entities. For purposes of calculating national income, they can have no income; all income in national income accounting must be attributed to households.

Corporate profits are, in reality, either paid out to stockholders in *dividends* (payments to the holders of a company's stock), in which case they are considered household income; or are not distributed to stockholders but are instead held within the firm as corporate retained earnings. For national income accounting purposes, these retained earnings are undistributed profits, which must be attributed to households. That's what is done. In the national income accounts all undistributed profit is attributed to households. To do so the U.S. Department of Commerce simply adds all undistributed profits to household income. In 1992 corporate profits were about $394 billion (8% of national income).

---

[2] As we discussed earlier, the national income accounts use accounting profits which must be distinguished from economic profits, which are calculated on the basis of opportunity costs.

The sum of compensation to employees, rents, interest, and profits is supposed to equal national income. However, if you added the four components together, you would find national income does not quite equal net national product. To make the two equal, one must add indirect business taxes to national income. National income *plus* indirect business taxes equals NNP.

Indirect business taxes include sales taxes (a general tax on sales), excise taxes (a sales tax on a particular item or group of items), business property taxes, customs duties, and license fees. These taxes are ultimately paid by households, since according to national income accounting, households ultimately receive all the income. How are they paid for by households? Either the firm raises its prices to include the tax or its earnings fall by the amount of the tax. In either case, households pay. When firms add the cost of taxes to their price, households pay the higher prices. When firms subtract the cost of taxes from their earnings, households pay by receiving lower wages or lower dividends (or both) from those firms. But it is firms, not households, that make the actual payment of these taxes, so to go from national income to **net national product** (GNP adjusted for depreciation) by adding up the components of household income, indirect business taxes must be added back to national (or household) income. That means

$$NNP = NI + \text{Indirect business taxes.}$$

Two other often-used concepts deserving mention are personal income and disposable personal income. (These can be either national or domestic concepts. Since the United States still reports them as national concepts, I follow that convention here.)

Personal Income National income measures the income individuals receive for doing productive work. Individuals receive other income that they do not directly earn (for example, social security payments, welfare payments, food stamps, and veterans' benefits). These payments from government to individuals are not part of national income, but they are available to spend.

Similarly in national income accounting, individuals are attributed income that they do not actually receive. This income includes undistributed corporate profits (retained earnings), employers' contributions to the social security system, and corporate income taxes.

If we add to national income the amounts of such payments that households receive, and subtract from national income the amounts attributed to households but not actually received by them, we arrive at **personal income (PI):**

$$PI = NI + \text{Transfer payments from government}$$
$$- \text{Corporate retained earnings}$$
$$- \text{Corporate income taxes}$$
$$- \text{Social security taxes.}$$

Disposable Personal Income We've accounted for most taxes, but not all. There's still personal income taxes and payroll taxes, which are subtracted from individuals' paychecks or paid directly by self-employed individuals. Personal income taxes and payroll taxes show up on employees' paycheck stubs, but employees don't actually get the money; the government does. Subtracting these personal income taxes from personal income, we arrive at **disposable personal income:**

$$PI - \text{Personal taxes} = \text{Disposable personal income.}$$

Disposable personal income is what people have readily available to spend. Thus, economists follow disposable personal income carefully.

From GDP to Disposable Personal Income Exhibit 11 reviews the steps involved in moving from GDP to disposable personal income for the United States. Going through these steps should give you a good sense of the relationships among the concepts we've discussed.

National Income and Net National Product: Adjustments for Indirect Business Taxes

2

Net national product GNP adjusted for depreciation.

Other National Income Terms

Personal income (PI) National income plus net transfer payments from government minus amounts attributed but not received.

Disposable personal income Personal income minus personal income taxes and payroll taxes.

GDP, GNP, NDP, AND NNP: A
REVIEW

We've covered a lot of definitions quickly, so a review is in order. GDP (the total output of the residents of a society) can be measured in two ways: the expenditures approach and the income approach.

Using the expenditures approach,

$$GDP = C + I + G + (X - M).$$

Much investment is replacement investment—it is made to cover depreciation, and is a cost of production. When one subtracts depreciation from GDP, one arrives at NDP:

$$NDP = GDP - Depreciation.$$

To move from net domestic product to net national product one must add net foreign factor income (foreign earnings of citizens minus domestic earnings of foreigners) to net domestic product:

$$NNP = NDP + Net\ foreign\ factor\ income.$$

The income approach adds up compensation to employees, rent, interest, and profits to arrive at national income:

$$NI = Compensation\ to\ employees + Rent$$
$$+ Interest + Profits.$$

One then adds indirect taxes (which businesses pay on behalf of households) to national income to arrive at NNP:

$$NNP = NI + Indirect\ business\ taxes.$$

Adding depreciation to NNP, we arrive at GNP:

$$GNP = NNP + Depreciation.$$

Finally, subtracting net foreign factor income,

$$GDP = GNP - Net\ foreign\ factor\ income.$$

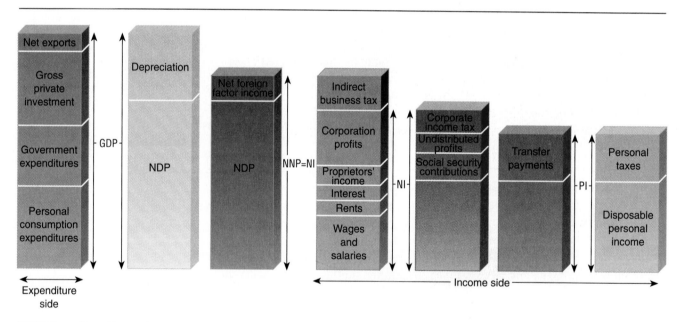

EXHIBIT 11   **From GDP to Disposable Personal Income**

Here are the steps involved in moving from GDP to disposable personal income.

USING GDP FIGURES

Now that we've worked our way through two methods of calculating GDP, let's consider what it's used for and what it tells us. The most important way GDP figures are used is to make comparisons of one country's production with another country's and of one year's production with another year's.

Most countries use somewhat similar measures to calculate GDP. Thus, we can compare various countries' GDP levels and get a sense of their economic size and power.

Comparing GDP among Countries

Per capita GDP is another measure often used to compare various nations' income. To arrive at per capita GDP, we divide GDP by the country's total population. Doing so gives you a sense of the relative standards of living of the people in various countries.

If you look up some of these measures, some of the comparisons should give you cause to wonder. For example, Bangladesh has per capita GDP of only about $180, compared to U.S. per capita GDP of about $22,000. How do people in Bangladesh live? In answering that question, remember GDP measures market transactions. In poor countries, individuals often grow their own food (subsistence farming), build their own shelter, and make their own clothes. None of those activities are market activities, and while they're sometimes estimated and included in GDP, they often aren't estimated accurately. They certainly aren't estimated at the value of what these activities would cost in the United States. Also, remember GDP is an aggregate measure that values activities at the market price in that society. The relative prices of the products and services a consumer buys often differ substantially among countries. In New York City $900 a month gets you only a small studio apartment. In Haiti $900 a month might get you a mansion with four servants. Thus, GDP can be a poor measure of the relative living standards in various countries.

To avoid this problem in comparing per capita GDP, economists often calculate a different concept, *purchasing power parity,* which adjusts for the different relative prices among countries before making comparisons.

A second way in which the GDP concept is used is to compare one year with another.

Economic Welfare over Time

Last chapter, when we talked about growth in the economy, we were really talking about growth in total output or GDP. Similarly when we talked about contractions and expansions, it was in reference to GDP.

Using GDP figures to compare the economy's performance over time is much better than relying merely on our perceptions. Most of us have heard the phrase, *the good old days.* Generally we hear it from our parents or grandparents, who are lamenting the state of the nation or economy. In comparing today to yesterday, they always seem to picture the past with greener grass, an easier life, and happier times. Compared to the good old days, today always comes out a poor second.

Our parents and grandparents may be right when they look back at particular events in their own lives, but if society were to follow such reasoning, it would conclude that all of history has been just one long downhill slide, worsening every year. In actuality, perceptions of the good old days are likely to be biased. It's easy to remember the nice things of yesterday while forgetting its harsh realities. Relying on past perception is not an especially helpful way of making accurate comparisons.

A preferable way is to rely on data that are not changed by emotion or anything else. Looking at GDP over time provides a way of using data to make comparisons over time. For example, say we compare U.S. GDP in 1932 ($58 billion) to GDP in 1992 ($5,952 billion). Would it be correct to conclude the economy had grown 95 times larger? No. As we discussed in the last chapter, GDP figures aren't affected by emotions, but they are affected by inflation. To make comparisons over time, we can't confine ourselves to a simple look at what has happened to GDP.

In our earlier discussion of supply and demand, I spent quite a bit of space distinguishing between a rise in the price level and a change in relative prices. That's because the distinction is important. A similar important distinction economists make is in comparing output levels over time. Suppose prices of all goods and hence the price level (remember, the price level includes wages) go up 25 percent in one year, but outputs of all goods remain constant. GDP will have risen 25 percent, but will society be any better off? No. To compare GDP over time, you must distinguish between increases in GDP due to inflation and increases in GDP that represent real increases in production and income.

Real and Nominal GDP

Nominal GDP   GDP calculated at existing prices.

Real GDP   Nominal GDP adjusted for inflation.

As I stated last chapter, to separate increases in GDP caused by inflation from increases in GDP that represent real increases in production and income, economists distinguish between **nominal GDP** (GDP calculated at existing prices) and **real GDP** (nominal GDP adjusted for inflation). This distinction is sufficiently important to warrant repetition in this chapter. To adjust nominal output for inflation we create a price index (a measure of how much the price level has risen from one year to the next) and divide nominal GDP by that price index.[3]

For example, say the price level rises 10 percent (from a price index of 1 to a price index of 1.1) and nominal GDP rises from $4 trillion to $4.6 trillion. Ten percent of that rise in nominal GDP represents the 10 percent rise in the price level. If you divide nominal GDP, $4.6 trillion, by the new price level index, 1.1, you get $4.18 trillion (the amount GDP would have been if the price level had not risen). That $4.18 trillion is called real GDP. To decide whether production has increased or decreased over time, we simply compare the real income. In this example, real income has risen from $4 trillion to $4.18 trillion, so we can conclude that the real economy has grown by 18/400, or 4.5 percent.

Real GDP is what is important to a society because it measures what is *really* produced. Considering nominal GDP instead of real GDP can distort what's really happening. Let's say the U.S. price level doubled tomorrow. Nominal GDP would also double, but would the United States be better off? No.

We'll use the distinction between real and nominal continually in this course, so to firm up the concepts in your mind, let's go through another example. Consider Somalia in 1987 and 1988, when nominal GDP rose from 159 billion to 268 billion (measured in their local currency units) while the GDP deflator rose from 100 percent to 173.5 percent. Dividing nominal GDP in 1988 by the GDP deflator, we see *real GDP* fell by over 2 percent. So not only did Somalia's economy not grow; it actually shrank.

SOME LIMITATIONS OF NATIONAL INCOME ACCOUNTING

The quotation at this chapter's start pointed out that statistics can be misleading. I want to reiterate that here. Before you can work with statistics, you need to know how they are collected and the problems they have. If you don't, the results can be disastrous. Here's a possible scenario: A student who isn't careful looks at the data and discovers an almost perfect relationship between imports and investment occurring in a Latin American country. Whenever capital goods imports go up, investment of capital goods goes up by an equal proportion. The student develops a thesis based on that insight, only to learn after submitting the thesis that no data on investments are available for that country. Instead of gathering actual data, the foreign country's statisticians estimate investment by assuming it to be a constant percentage of imports. Since many investment goods are imported, this is reasonable, but the estimate is not a reasonable basis for an economic policy. It would be back to the drawing board for the student, whose thesis would be useless because the student didn't know how the country's statistics had been collected.

If you ever work in business as an economist, statistics will be your life's blood. Much of what economists do is based on knowing, interpreting, and drawing inferences from statistics. Statistics must be treated carefully. They don't always measure what they seem to measure. Though U.S. national income accounting statistics are among the most accurate in the world, they still have serious limitations.

---

[3] Now you know why the total output deflator is called the *GDP deflator*. It is an index of the rise in prices of the goods and services that make up GDP.

THE COLANDER HAPPINESS INDEX

The only way economists can determine how happy people are is to ask them if they're happy and then develop a happiness index. I've done so in some of my classes by giving them a numerical measure for degrees of happiness:

Ecstatic	5
Very happy	4
Happy	3
Somewhat unhappy	2
Depressed	1

Each student writes down the number that most closely represents his or her average state of happiness for the past year. The average of those calculations forms the "Colander happiness index" for the class—usually between 3 and 3.2. My students are essentially reasonably happy.

In fact, when other economists have taken a type of happiness poll elsewhere, results have been fairly consistent—even in poor countries. Except in times of crisis, people on average are reasonably happy, regardless of their income level, their wealth, or the state of the economy where they live.* I interpret this as meaning there's some level of income below which we'll be unhappy because we're starving, but above that level more output for a society doesn't mean more happiness for a society.

Now this stability of happiness could mean that economics, economic progress, and growth don't matter, that they're irrelevant to happiness. But we economists are naturally loath to give it such an interpretation. Instead, economists slide over such problems and poll people as to how many prefer a higher income to a lower income. I've also conducted these polls and have yet to find an individual who says he or she prefers less income to more income. (If I found one, of course, I'd volunteer to relieve that person of some income, which would make us both happier.)

The fact that everyone, or almost everyone, prefers more output, but that more output or an increase in income doesn't make everyone happier is not really a contradiction. I know from watching *Star Trek* (and from reading Lord Tennyson) that it's in striving that human beings acquire happiness. Without striving, the human being is but an empty shell. But enough; if this discussion continues, it will, heaven forbid, turn from economics to philosophy.

---

* I've given the test to students in Vermont, New York, and Great Britain, and each time the results have been similar. However when I gave the test to students in Florida at the University of Miami and to students in Bulgaria, the results were different. In Miami they came up consistently higher for each category. Four students actually checked "ecstatic." I'm not precisely sure what this Florida factor signifies. In Bulgaria, the results were lower (a 2.8 average). Bulgaria was undergoing a wrenching economic change and many incomes had been cut by two-thirds, so this low result was explainable.

GDP Measures Market Activity Not Welfare

The first, and most important, limitation to remember is that GDP does not measure happiness nor does it measure economic welfare. GDP measures economic (market) activity. Real GDP could rise and economic welfare could fall. For example, say some Martians came down and let loose a million Martian burglars in the United States just to see what would happen. GDP would be likely to rise as individuals bought guns and locks and spent millions of dollars on protecting their property and replacing stolen items. At the same time, however, welfare would fall.

Welfare is a complicated concept. The economy's goal should not be to increase output for the sake of increasing output, but to make people better off or at least happier. But a pure happiness measure is impossible. Economists have struggled with the concept of welfare and have decided that the best they can do is to concentrate their analysis on economic activity, leaving others to consider how economic activity relates to happiness. I should warn you, however, that there is no neat correlation between increases in GDP and increases in happiness. You can see that in the above box.

Measurement Errors

GDP figures are supposed to measure all economic activity, but they do not. Illegal drug sales, under-the-counter sales of goods to avoid income and sales taxes, work performed and paid for in cash to avoid income tax, nonreported sales, and prostitution are all market activities, yet none of them is included in GDP figures. Estimates of the underground, nonmeasured economy's importance range from 3 to 20 percent of GDP in the United States and as high as 40 percent in Italy. That is, if measured U.S. GDP is $6 trillion, inclusion of the underground, nonmeasured activity would raise it to between $6.18 trillion and $7.2 trillion. If we were able to halt underground activity and direct those efforts to the above-ground economy, GDP would rise significantly. For instance, if we legalized prostitution and marijuana sales and quadrupled tax-collection mechanisms, GDP would rise. But that rise in GDP wouldn't necessarily make us better off.

A second type of measurement error occurs in adjusting GDP figures for inflation. Measurement of inflation involves numerous arbitrary decisions about changes in quality of goods. For example, if the price of a Toyota goes up 5 percent from 1993 ($20,000) to 1994 ($21,000), that's certainly a 5 percent rise in price. But what if the 1994 Toyota has a "new improved" 16-valve engine? Can you say that the price of cars has risen 5 percent, or should you adjust for the improvement in quality? And if you adjust, how do you adjust? The people who keep track of the price indices used to measure inflation will be the first to tell you there's no one right answer. How that question, and a million other similar questions involved in measuring inflation, is answered can lead to significant differences in estimates of inflation and hence in estimates of real GDP growth. One recent study for Canada argued inflation could be either 5.4 or 15 percent, depending on how the inflation index was calculated! Which inflation figure one chose would make a big difference in one's estimate of how the economy was doing. Similarly every five years the United States switches base years (in 1992, it switched from 1982 to 1987), and when it does many of the statistics change.

Misinterpretation of Subcategories

A third limitation of national income accounting concerns possible misinterpretation of the components. In setting up the accounts, a large number of arbitrary decisions had to be made: What to include in "investment"? What to include in "consumption"? How to treat government expenditures? The decisions that were made were, for the most part, reasonable, but they weren't the only ones that could have been made. Once made, however, they influence our interpretations of events. For example, when we see that investment rises, we normally think that our future productive capacity is rising, but remember that investment includes housing investment, which does not increase our future productive capacity. In fact, some types of consumption (say purchases of personal computers by people who will become computer-literate and use their knowledge and skills to be more productive than they were before they owned computers) increase our productive capacity more than some types of "investment."

GDP Is Worth Using Despite Its Limitations

By pointing out these problems, economists are not suggesting that national income accounting statistics should be thrown out. Far from it; measurement is necessary and the GDP measurements and categories have made it possible to think and talk about the aggregate economy. I wouldn't have devoted an entire chapter of this book to national income accounting if I didn't believe it was important. I am simply arguing that national income accounting concepts should be used with sophistication, with an awareness of their weaknesses as well as their strengths.

Used with that awareness, national income accounting is a powerful tool; one wouldn't want to be an economist without it. For those of you who aren't planning to be economists, it's still a good idea for you to understand the concepts of national income accounting. If you do, the business section of the newspaper will no longer seem like Greek to you. You'll be a more informed citizen and will be better able to make up your own mind about macroeconomic debates.

The U.S. government has issued over $250 billion worth of cash. That's about $1,000 for every man, woman, and child. Now ask yourself how much cash you're carrying on you. Add to that the amounts banks and businesses keep, and divide that by the number of people in the United States. The number economists get when they do that calculation is way below the total amount of cash the United States has issued. So what happens to the extra cash?

Let's switch for a minute to a Miami safehouse being raided by drug enforcement officers. They find $50 million in cash. That's what most economists believe happens to much of the extra cash: It goes underground. An underground economy lurks below the real economy.

The underground economy consists of two components: (1) the production and distribution of illegal goods and services and (2) the nonreporting of legal economic activity.

Illegal activity such as selling illegal drugs and prostitution generates huge amounts of cash. (Most people who buy an illegal good or service would prefer not to have the transaction appear on their monthly credit card statements.) This presents a problem for a big-time illegal business. It must explain to the Internal Revenue Service (IRS) where all that money came from. That's where money laundering comes in. Money laundering is simply making illegally gained income look as if it came from a legal business. Any business through which lots of cash moves is a good front for money laundering. Laundromats move lots of cash, which is where the term *money laundering* came from. The mob bought laundromats and claimed a much higher income from the laundromats than it actually received. The mob thus "laundered" the excess money. Today money laundering is much more sophisticated. It involves billions of dollars and international transactions in three or four different countries, but the purpose is the same: making illegally earned money look legal.

The second part of the illegal economy involves deliberately failing to report income in order to escape paying taxes on it. When people work "off the books," when restaurants don't ring up cash sales, when waiters forget to declare tips on their tax returns, they reduce their tax payments and make it look as if they have less income and as if the economy has less production than it actually does.

How important is the underground economy? That's tough to say; it is, after all, underground. A U.S. Department of Commerce economist estimated it at 1.5 percent of the total U.S. economy. The IRS estimates the underground economy at about 10 percent of the total U.S. economy; some economists estimate it as high as 15 or 20 percent. In other countries, such as Sweden, where the tax rate is higher than in the United States, estimates of the underground economy's size range as high as 30 percent of the aboveground economy.

KEY POINTS

- National income accounting is the terminology used to talk about the aggregate economy. **1**
- GDP measures aggregate final output of an economy. It's a flow, not a stock, measure of market activity. **2**
- Intermediate goods can be eliminated from GDP in two ways:
  1. By measuring only final sales.
  2. By measuring only value added. **3**
- National income is directly related to national output. Whenever there's output, there's income. **2**
- GDP is divided up into four types of expenditures:

  $$GDP = C + I + G + (X - M).$$ **2** **4**

- NDP = GDP − Depreciation. **2**
- NNP = NDP + Net foreign factor income. **2**
- NNP = NI + Indirect business taxes. **2**
- NI = Compensation to employees + Rent + Interest + Profit. **2**
- To compare income over time, we must adjust for price-level changes. After adjusting for inflation, nominal measures are changed to "real" measures. The real amount is the nominal amount divided by the price index. **5**
- National income accounting concepts are powerful tools for understanding macroeconomics, but we must recognize their limitations. **6**

KEY TERMS

depreciation *(167)*
disposable personal
  income *(171)*
domestic income
  (DI) *(169)*
durable goods *(166)*
gross domestic product
  (GDP) *(158)*
gross national product
  (GNP) *(159)*

intermediate
  products *(160)*
national income
  (NI) *(169)*
national income account-
  ing *(158)*
national income accounting
  identity *(162)*
net domestic product
  (NDP) *(168)*

net foreign factor
  income *(159)*
net national product
  (NNP) *(171)*
net private
  investment *(167)*
nominal concepts *(158)*
nominal GDP *(174)*

nondurable goods *(166)*
personal income
  (PI) *(171)*
real concepts *(158)*
real GDP *(174)*
transfer payments *(168)*
value added *(161)*

QUESTIONS FOR THOUGHT AND REVIEW

The number after each question represents the estimated degree of critical thinking required. (1 = almost none; 10 = deep thought.)

1. What's the relationship between a stock concept and a flow concept? Give an example that hasn't already been given in this chapter. *(5)*
2. A company sells 1,000 desks for $400 each. Of these, it sells 750 to other companies and 250 to individuals. What is that company's contribution to GDP? *(4)*
3. The United States is considering introducing a value added tax. What tax rate on value added is needed to get the same increase in revenue as is gotten from an income tax with a rate of 15 percent? Why? *(8)*
4. If the United States introduces universal child care, what will likely happen to GDP? What are the welfare implications of that rise? *(5)*
5. You've been given the following data:

Transfer payments	$ 72
Interest paid by consumers	4
Net exports	4
Indirect business taxes	47
Net foreign factor income	2
Corporate income tax	64
Contribution for social insurance	35

Personal tax and nontax payments	91
Undistributed corporate profits	51
Gross private investment	185
Government purchases	195
Personal consumption	500
Depreciation	59

On the basis of these data calculate GDP, GNP, NNP, NDP, NI, personal income, and disposable personal income. *(6)*

6. Rent is $400, investment is $100, interest is $200, savings are $75, profits are −$200, wages are $4,000, and consumption is $3,000. Assuming net foreign factor income and indirect business taxes are zero, what is the level of NDP? *(5)*
7. Economists normally talk about GDP even though they know NDP is a better measure of economic activity. Why? *(3)*
8. How does personal income differ from national income? *(3)*
9. What is the difference between national personal income and domestic personal income? *(4)*
10. If society's goal is to make society happier, and higher GDP isn't closely associated with society being happier, why do economists even talk about GDP? *(9)*

PROBLEMS AND EXERCISES

1. Given the following data about the economy:

Consumption	$700
Investment	500
Corporate income tax	215
Proprietors' income	250
Government expenditure	300
Profits	250
Wages	700
Net exports	275
Rents	25
Depreciation	25
Indirect business taxes	100
Undistributed corporate profits	60
Net foreign factor income	− 3
Interest	150
Social security contribution	0
Transfer payments	0
Personal taxes	165

   a. Calculate GDP and GNP with both the expenditures approach and the income approach.

   b. Calculate NDP, NNP, NI, and domestic income.

   c. Calculate PI.

   d. Calculate disposable personal income.

2. There are three firms in an economy: A, B, and C. Firm A buys $250 worth of goods from firm B and $200 worth of goods from firm C and produces 200 units of output which it sells at $5 per unit. Firm B buys $100 worth of goods from firm A and $150 worth of goods from firm C and produces 300 units of output which it sells at $7 per unit. Firm C buys $50 worth of goods from firm A and nothing from firm B. It produces output worth $1,000. All other products are sold to consumers.

   a. Calculate GDP.

   b. If a value added tax (a tax on the total value added of each firm) of 10 percent is introduced, how much revenue will the government get?

   c. How much would government get if it introduced a 10 percent income tax?

   d. How much would government get if it introduced a 10 percent sales tax on final output?

Macroeconomic Theory
The Basics

CHAPTER

8

The Classical School and the Macroeconomic Debate

CHAPTER

9

The Keynesian Model of the Aggregate Economy

CHAPTER

10

The Complete Keynesian Multiplier Model and Fiscal Policy

8

The Classical School and the Macroeconomic Debate

An economist's "lag" may be a politician's catastrophe.
George Schultze

After reading this chapter, you should be able to:

1
Explain who the Classicals are.

2
Discuss the reasoning behind Say's law.

3
Interpret the quantity theory of money.

4
Differentiate aggregate supply and demand
from partial equilibrium supply
and demand.

5
Summarize Keynes's attack
on the Classicals.

6
Explain how Classical thinking changed in
response to Keynes's attack.

The Great Depression of the 1930s marked a significant change in U.S. economic institutions and ideology. In the depression not only the deadbeat up the street was unemployed, so were your brother, your mother, your uncle—the hardworking backbone of America. These people wanted to work and if the market wasn't creating jobs for them, the market system was at fault.

During the depression, the popular view of government's proper role in the economy changed considerably. Before, the predominant ideology was laissez-faire: keep the government out of the economy. After the depression most people believed that government must have a role in regulating the economy.

Economists who generally oppose government intervention fall under the heading, **Classical economists.** Those who generally favor government intervention in the aggregate economy are known as **Keynesian economists.** This chapter presents the Classical views on macroeconomic issues. We'll also take a quick look at Keynesian economists' criticisms of Classical views.

Classical economists Economists who generally oppose government intervention in the economy.

Keynesian economists Economists who generally favor government intervention in the aggregate economy.

THE EMERGENCE OF CLASSICAL ECONOMICS

Classical economics began in the late 1700s and early 1800s as economists developed the ideas in Adam Smith's seminal work, *An Inquiry into the Nature and Causes of the Wealth of Nations*. The essence of Classical economics' approach to problems was laissez-faire: The market, left to its own devices, was self-adjusting. Wages and prices would adjust to eliminate unemployment. Classicals recognized that in the short run there might be temporary problems, but their analysis focused on the long run.

1

When the Great Depression hit and unemployment became a problem, most Classical economists avoided the issue (as economists, and most people, tend to do when they don't have a good answer). When pushed by curious students to explain how, if the market's invisible hand was so wonderful, the invisible hand could have allowed the depression and its 25 percent unemployment, Classical economists drew supply-and-demand-for-labor curves like those in Exhibit 1.

They explained, "Unemployment results when workers hold their wage too high (that is, they won't take the lower wages offered) above the equilibrium level. Other forces (government policies and economic institutions such as labor unions) can operate to prevent the invisible hand from working its magic." For example, in Exhibit 1, the equilibrium wage is W_e. If the wage is held at W_1 for some reason, quantity of labor supplied is S_1 and quantity of labor demanded is D_1. The difference between the two ($S_1 - D_1$) is unemployment.

Adam Smith, a moral philosopher, whose book, *The Wealth of Nations,* is seen as the beginning of modern economics. *The Bettmann Archives.*

F or hundreds of years, economists have debated questions such as "How much government intervention into the market should there be?" and "What form should the intervention take?" although the groups debating were not always called what they are today. These questions are still being debated today. Thus, considering the historical debate between Keynesians and Classicals that occurred in the 1930s and 1940s is of more than historical interest; it is of direct interest in the 1990s. Both Classicals and Keynesians are still around—although both now have prefixes—"New"—associated with them. In the 1990s the central debate in macroeconomics is between New Keynesians and New Classicals.

The *New* prefix is not the only prefix that's been used. In the 1960s and 70s the prefix *neo* was assigned to Keynesians and Classicals of the time, and the central macroeconomic debate was between neo-Classicals and neo-Keynesians. (*Neo* is Latin for *new*.) Then in the 1980s neo-Keynesian and neo-Classical ideas lost favor, and the *neo* was replaced with *New*. (It was a better solution than *new new* or *neo-new*.) Why the change? Because ideas evolved and people needed some way to distinguish among the changing ideas. (It was like managing to tell All-New Improved Tide from Tide, New Tide, and New and Improved Tide in the supermarket.) But even as ideas change, some underlying ideas remain the same.

Unless one is interested in the history of economic thought, it isn't important to keep these prefixes in mind, nor is it important to know the technical specifics of the debates between various groups of Classicals and Keynesians. What's important is to keep in mind that the central, unchanging debate between Classicals and Keynesians is continuing: How much should the government intervene in the macroeconomy? Keynesians generally favor intervention; Classicals generally oppose intervention.

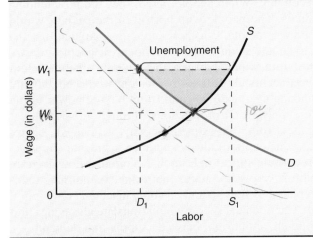

EXHIBIT 1   Unemployment in the Classical Model

If social or political forces hold the wage above the equilibrium wage (at W_1 rather than W_e), the result will be unemployment of $S_1 - D_1$. To eliminate that unemployment, the wage must fall.

Their policy prescription followed from their analysis: The solution to unemployment was to eliminate labor unions and government policies that held wages too high. If these things happened, the wage rate would fall, and unemployment would be eliminated.

Laymen weren't pleased with this argument. (Remember, economists don't try to present pleasing arguments—only arguments they believe are correct.) But laymen couldn't point to anything wrong with it. It made sense, but it wasn't satisfying. People thought, "Gee, Uncle Joe, who's unemployed, would take a job at half the going wage. But he can't find one—there just aren't enough jobs to go around at any wage."

Most lay people had a different explanation. The popular lay explanation of the depression was that there was an oversupply of goods which had glutted the market. All that was needed to eliminate unemployment was for government to hire the unemployed, even if it were only to dig ditches and fill them back up. The people who got the new jobs would spend their money, creating even more jobs. Pretty soon, the United States would be out of the depression.

Say's Law

Classical economists argued against this lay view. They argued that money to hire those people would have to come from somewhere. It would have to be borrowed. Such borrowing would use money that would have financed private economic activity and jobs; hence, such borrowing would reduce private economic activity. The net effect would mean no increase in the total number of jobs. In short, the Classicals were saying an oversupply of goods was impossible.

2   This Classical argument was first made by a French businessman, Jean Baptiste Say, although it was a British stockbroker, David Ricardo, who made it famous. Say's argument went as follows: People work and supply goods to the market because they want other goods. Thus, the very fact that they supply goods means they have income to demand goods of equal value. This idea is normally stated as follows:

Say's law: *Supply creates its own demand.*

Say's law is central to the Classical vision of the economy. It says that there can never be a general glut of goods on the market; aggregate demand will always be sufficient to buy what is supplied.

Not all Classical economists initially accepted Say's law. The most spirited argument against it was put forward by Thomas Malthus, a preacher.[1] Malthus argued that when people saved, part of their income would be lost to the economy and that there wouldn't be as much aggregate demand out there as aggregate supply. According to Malthus, Say's law did not necessarily hold true.

Say and Ricardo rejected Malthus's argument. They argued that people's savings were not lost to the economy. When people saved, they did it by lending their savings to other individuals. The people who borrowed the savings would spend what they borrowed on investments. Classical economists argued that the interest rate would fluctuate to equate savings and investment. If people's desire to save increased, the interest rate would fall and the quantity of investment would increase. So any savings seemingly lost to the system would be actually translated into investment, making aggregate demand (total buying power in the economy) equal to aggregate supply (total production), through either a direct route (consumption) or an indirect route (investment by way of savings). Aggregate demand (investment plus consumption) always equaled aggregate supply.

The direct route and indirect route appear in Exhibit 2, a circular flow diagram similar to last chapter's Exhibit 2. Say's law states that total expenditures (consumption plus investment), depicted by flows *b* and *c,* would just equal production or income, depicted by flow *a*. The financial sector would translate all savings into investment to maintain a continual equilibrium between supply and demand.

Say's law became a tenet of Classical economics. It didn't say that unemployment could never exist—there could be lots of little pockets of unemployment in various industries if wages didn't adjust. It did say that whatever unemployment existed was a microeconomic, relative wage–price problem and, if wages and prices were allowed to adjust, unemployment would go away on its own.

In terms of the discussion of unemployment in an earlier chapter, Classical economists agreed that *frictional* and *structural unemployment* could exist, but they did not agree that *cyclical unemployment* could be caused by a shortage of aggregate demand.

Say's law: Supply creates its own demand.

---

[1] As was pointed out earlier, Thomas Malthus is most famous for the Malthusian doctrine which stated that population grows much faster than food production so the future of mankind is starvation. It was the Malthusian doctrine that earned economics the name of *the dismal science*.

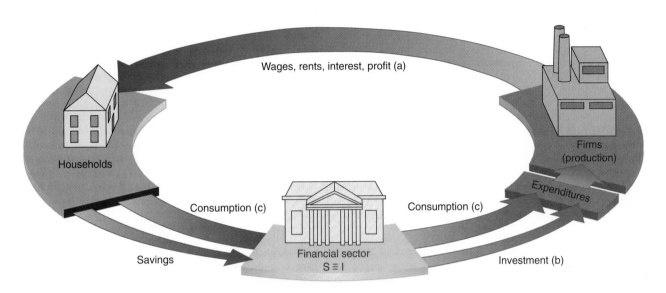

Wages, rents, interest, profit (a)

Households

Firms (production)

Expenditures

Consumption (c)

Financial sector
$S \equiv I$

Consumption (c)

Savings

Investment (b)

EXHIBIT 2   The Equality of Production (Aggregate Supply) and Expenditures (Aggregate Demand)

According to Say's law, aggregate production always was at the full employment level. Any funds that escaped from the circular flow into the financial sector (savings) would be brought back into the circular flow by the financial sector in the form of investment. Thus, the financial sector was assumed to keep savings always equal to investment.

THE TREASURY VIEW, LLOYD GEORGE, AND KEYNES

The Great Depression descended on Britain in the 1920s, before it hit the United States. Therefore many debates about what to do about it occurred first in Britain. British Chancellor of the Exchequer Winston Churchill (a Conservative Party member who later became prime minister) followed the advice of his Treasury Department, which was composed of Classical economists. They advised him that Britain should go back on the gold standard (a monetary system that fixes a currency's price relative to gold and other currencies). All countries that use gold to value their currency have *fixed currency exchange rates*. For example, if 1 British pound = 1 ounce of gold and 1 U.S. dollar = 1/2 ounce of gold, then 1 British pound = 2 U.S. dollars = 1 ounce of gold.

Churchill followed the Classical economists' advice and returned the pound to the gold standard from which Britain, and all other countries, had departed during World War I. He set a high value on the pound relative to other currencies. As a result, British wages and prices were high relative to those in other countries. Foreign imports were cheap, which was good. British exports were expensive and uncompetitive abroad, which was not good. Unemployment in Britain was high, which was bad. The British Treasury Department's advice on how to eliminate unemployment boiled down to "Keep a stiff upper lip. British wages and prices will eventually fall, or foreign wages and prices will rise."

Regardless of the argument's economic merits, its political merits were dubious. Lloyd George (leader of the opposition Liberal party) advocated a massive government hiring program to eliminate unemployment. Keynes (a prominent advisor to the Liberal party, who had, before Lloyd George's proposals, been seen as a Classical economist) modified his economic analysis in part to justify that shift. That was the beginning of the Keynesian approach to macroeconomics.

Needless to say, many of the Classicals were not very pleased with Keynes's shift, and they saw his economic analysis as opportunism. His shifting position led to a well-known joke about economists: If you ask five economists a question, you will get five different answers; if you ask Keynes a question you will get six different answers.

However, stiff upper lips can carry politicians only so far, and soon thereafter the British Conservative party was also advocating public works programs to help end the depression. Politics often plays a key role in directing economic thinking.

Source: This account is based on Peter Clarke's book, *The Keynesian Revolution in the Making 1924–1936* (Oxford, England: Oxford University Press, 1988).

That was the state of the debate in the 1930s when a well-known economist, John Maynard Keynes, came along and said that Classical economists were all wrong. He argued that lowering wages wouldn't necessarily solve unemployment and that supply doesn't necessarily create its own demand. Keynes's argument fit the popular lay argument and led to activist government policies. Keynes argued that laissez-faire wasn't the right policy and that government needed to intervene in the economy. But hold it! Talking about Keynes is getting ahead of our story. We mention this much about him here simply to establish some context in which the Classical argument developed.

The Quantity Theory of Money

Money A medium of exchange that individuals use to buy goods.

Quantity theory of money Price level varies in response to variations in the money supply.

Equation of exchange $MV = PQ$

3

Classical economists buttressed their Say's law analysis of the aggregate economy with the quantity theory of money. We will discuss money in much more detail in later chapters. For now all you need have is a general sense of what **money** is: It is a medium of exchange (such as dollar bills) that individuals use to buy goods. Thus, the quantity of money is the amount of the medium of exchange in the economy. In its simplest terms, the **quantity theory of money** says that the price level varies in response to changes in the quantity of money. In other words, changes in the price level are caused by changes in the money supply. If the money supply goes up 20 percent, prices go up 20 percent. If money supply goes down 5 percent, prices go down 5 percent.

The Classical quantity of theory of money centers around the **equation of exchange:**

$$MV = PQ$$

where:

> M = Quantity of money
> V = Velocity
> P = Price level
> Q = Quantity of real goods sold.

Q is the real output of the economy (real GDP). P is the price level, so PQ is the economy's nominal output (nominal GDP) (the quantity of goods valued at whatever price level exists at the time). Remember, real GDP equals nominal GDP divided by (deflated by) the price level; while nominal GDP equals nominal income.

Velocity of money Average number of times the same dollar gets spent in a year.

V, the **velocity of money,** is the number of times per year, on average, a dollar goes around to generate a dollar's worth of income. Put another way, velocity is the amount of income per year generated by a dollar of money. MV also equals nominal output. Thus, if there's $100 of money in the economy and velocity is 20,

Classical economists strongly favored using gold for money since it placed limits on the quantity of money available. Policy fights about the quantity of money have been around a long time, as can be seen in this hand-colored etching, "The Blessings of Paper Money, or King a Bad Subject." *Bleichroeder Print Collection, Baker Library, Harvard Business School.*

ADDED DIMENSION

CLASSICAL ECONOMISTS AND
THE VEIL OF MONEY

■ he veil-of-money assumption developed early in Classical economic thought. The predecessors of the Classicals were mercantilists, who had argued that the wealth of nations depended on a nation's store of gold, which was then used as money. (Remember, during this time the international financial system was on a gold standard.)

Countries with balance of payments deficits paid for those deficits with gold, which decreased their money supply. Countries with balance of payments surpluses received gold, which increased their money supply. Mercantilists encouraged countries to protect their gold supplies with tariffs so their gold supplies (their money) wouldn't go into foreign hands.

Adam Smith called his book *The Wealth of Nations* because he argued that the wealth of nations did not depend on the amount of gold or money a country had; it depended on the real output of the country's economy. More money (gold) without more goods would only cause inflation. (This is only simple arithmetic according to the quantity theory of money.) Classical economists argued that a country didn't have to worry about a balance of payments deficit and losing gold. A balance of payments deficit would decrease the money supply and hence the price level. A country's exports would be cheaper, which would tend to eliminate the balance of payments deficit.

Smith, and Classical economists following him, argued that money and the price level were simply veils over the real economy and the veil of money had to be removed for us to understand the workings of the real economy. The quantity theory of money was a simple way of presenting that insight.

GDP is $2,000. We can calculate *V* by dividing nominal GDP by the money supply. In the United States in 1990, GDP was approximately $5.5 trillion, *M* was approximately $825 billion, so velocity was GDP/M = 6.67, meaning each dollar in the economy circulated enough to support approximately $6.67 in total income.

The equation of exchange is a *tautology,* meaning it's true by definition. What changes it from a tautology to a theory are certain assumptions the Classicals made about the variables in the equation of exchange.

First, Classical economists assumed velocity remains constant. They argued that money is spent only so fast; how fast is determined by the economy's institutional structure, such as how close to stores individuals live, how people are paid (weekly, bi-weekly, or monthly), and what sources of credit are available (can you go to the store and buy something on credit; that is, buy something without handing over cash?). This institutional structure changes slowly, they argued, so velocity won't fluctuate very much. Next year, velocity will be approximately the same as this year.

If velocity remains constant, the quantity theory can be used to predict how much nominal GDP will grow if we know how much the money supply grows. For example, if the money supply goes up 6 percent, using the quantity theory a Classical economist would predict that nominal GDP will go up by 6 percent.

The second Classical assumption concerned *Q,* real output. Classical economists assumed that *Q* was independent of the money supply. That is, the Classicals thought *Q* was **autonomous,** meaning real output was determined by forces outside the quantity theory.

This Classical assumption is sometimes called the **veil-of-money assumption,** which holds that real output is not influenced by changes in the money supply. Classical economists argued that in order to understand what is happening in the real economy, you must lift the veil of money.

This veil-of-money assumption made analyzing the economy a lot easier than it would have been had the financial and real sectors been interrelated and had real economic activity been influenced by financial changes. It allowed Classical economists to separate two puzzles: how the real economy works and how the price level and financial sector work. Instead of having two different jigsaw

Autonomous Determined by forces outside the model.

Veil-of-money assumption Real output isn't influenced by changes in money supply.

puzzles all mixed up, each puzzle could be worked separately. They could analyze what happens in the real economy (in the production of real goods and services) separately from what happens to the money supply and price level. Classical economists recognized that there were interconnections between the real and financial sectors, but they argued that most of these interconnections involved short-run considerations. Classical economists were primarily interested in the long run.

In the long run there is a strong intuitive reason why the real and nominal economies are separate. Say one day you walk into work and your salary has doubled—but all prices also have doubled. What difference will these changes make in your behavior? Since no relative price has changed, it seems fair to say that your behavior won't be affected very much. That's what the Classical economists were saying with the veil-of-money assumption.

With both V (velocity) and Q (quantity or output) unaffected by changes in M (money supply), the only thing that can change is P (price level). Classical economists said that M and P would change by equivalent percentages.

The final assumption of the Classical quantity theory was the *direction of causation*. Classical economists argued that changes in the money supply caused changes in the price level: In the quantity theory of money equation the direction of causation went from left to right,

$$MV \Rightarrow PQ,$$

not the other way around. Thus, when a Classical economist was asked to predict what would happen to inflation, he or she would ask what's happening to the money supply's growth rate. If the money supply were continually increasing at an 8 percent rate, the Classical economist's prediction would be that inflation would be 8 percent.

We've covered a lot of ground in the last few pages, so let's briefly summarize how we went from the equation of exchange to the quantity theory. We start with the equation of exchange:

$$MV = PQ.$$

To that we add three assumptions:

1. Velocity is constant.
2. Real output is independent of the money supply.
3. Causation goes from money supply to prices.

The result is the quantity theory of money.

Friederich von Hayek—Nobel prize, 1974, for work on interdependence of institutional, social, and economic phenomena. © *The Nobel Foundation.*

AGGREGATE SUPPLY AND DEMAND

We can show the Classical arguments graphically, with aggregate supply and demand curves. The **aggregate supply curve** (*AS*) represents the graphical relationship between the price level and the total amount of real output supplied in an economy. The **aggregate demand curve** (*AD*) represents the graphical relationship between the price level and the total amount of output demanded in an economy.

The Classical Theory in Terms of Aggregate Supply and Demand

4

In aggregate supply and demand analysis, the price level is on the vertical axis and GDP (real output) is on the horizontal axis, as shown in Exhibit 3(a). The Classical propositions show up in the shape of the aggregate supply and demand curves. Let's first consider the aggregate supply curve.

What shape will it have? The veil-of-money assumption states that real output is independent of the price level: as the price level changes, real output doesn't change. Say that initially the price level is P_1 and real output is Q^*. Point A represents this combination. Now say the price level rises to P_2. Because the

EXHIBIT 3 (a and b)   The Long-Run Classical Model

In the Classical model, the aggregate supply curve is perfectly vertical. It determines the level of aggregate demand (Say's law) and output, as in (**a**). Notice that aggregate demand plays a passive role in the Classical model. It is assumed always to equal aggregate supply (in this example at a real income of 100).

The quantity of money determines the price level, and only the price level. The velocity is related to the slope of the velocity line in (**b**). If the velocity were 12 rather than 6, the total nominal income of 1,200 could be supported by a money supply of 100 rather than a nominal income of 600.

price level does not affect real output, when the price level rises from P_1 to P_2, real output does not change. So point B is also on the aggregate supply curve. By going through this same reasoning you can deduce that the aggregate supply curve must be perfectly vertical because a vertical aggregate supply means output is independent of the price level. Exhibit 3(a) shows a perfectly vertical Classical aggregate supply curve.

Now that we know the shape, let's ask, "At what level of real output will the aggregate supply be?" The answer depends on what people want to supply to the market. Classical economists argued that as long as individuals have free choice about what amount of labor and other resources to supply to the market, and as long as relative wages and prices can fluctuate, whatever level individuals choose to supply must be the *full-employment level*. Remember, the full-employment level is the economy's potential level of income. Thus, assuming flexible wages and prices, Q^* is the full-employment level of output.

The next question is "Will there be enough aggregate demand to buy up the aggregate supply?" Say's law answers that question: Supply creates its own demand, so *whatever* point we are at on the aggregate supply curve, the quantity of aggregate demand will equal the quantity of aggregate supply! So Say's law tells us we needn't worry about demand. It will be at whatever level is supplied. Thus, Classical economists had no separate analysis of aggregate demand. It was simply assumed to equal aggregate supply via Say's law. If the price level of output rises, people's nominal income (wages, interest, rents, and profits) rises just enough to buy that output.

If supply creates its own demand regardless of what the price level is, aggregate supply and aggregate demand do not determine the price level: Aggregate supply equals aggregate demand at all price levels. And that's exactly what Classical economists argued. They argued that real forces do not determine the

Aggregate supply curve Relationship between price level and the total amount of output supplied in an economy.

Aggregate demand curve Relationship between price level and the total amount of output demanded in an economy.

price level. Monetary forces determine the price level. According to the Classical's quantity theory of money, the price level is determined by the money supply.

Exhibit 3(b) graphs the relationship between the money supply and price level that is determined by the quantity theory of money. Say the money supply is $200 and velocity is 6 so total nominal income, PQ, is $1,200. Since we're assuming in part (a) that real output Q^* is 100, the price level must be 12. If the money supply decreases to $100, velocity remains the same and nominal income falls to $600. Real output remains unchanged at 100 while price level falls to 6. In the Classical model the quantity of money determines the price level and only the price level.

Classical theory avoids the question of how the economy would adjust if the quantity of aggregate supply did not equal the quantity of aggregate demand. Since, by assumption, aggregate supply creates its own aggregate demand, the aggregate economy is assumed always to be in equilibrium, and there is no need for disequilibrium analysis.

Unemployment in the Classical Model

Notice that unemployment can't be caused by a shortage of aggregate demand in the pure Classical model. But unemployment would be possible if structural rigidities held the wage rate above the equilibrium rate. Such a possibility was shown in Exhibit 1, where wages were too high in relation to prices. Classical economists explained unemployment primarily in this way.

Unemployment in the pure Classical model is caused by wages relative to prices; it's not a price level problem. That's why unemployment doesn't show up in the aggregate supply/aggregate demand analysis, which assumes that all relative prices (including wages) adjust to keep individual markets in equilibrium. If the wage rate remained too high, Classical economists agreed that structural unemployment could exist. That structural unemployment would simply shift back the aggregate supply curve. But since supply creates its own demand, it also shifts back the aggregate demand curve, and the aggregate economy stays in equilibrium. Structural unemployment isn't caused by a shortage of aggregate demand; it's caused by wage rates that are too high.

Classical economists' solution to unemployment followed from their analysis. Since the cause of unemployment is wages that are too high, the solution is to reduce wages. Classical economists recognized that this "reduce the wage rate" solution to unemployment was politically unpopular and was, at best, a long-run solution. But their analysis led to this policy. "Have faith," they said. "Eventually wages will fall and the economy will come out of the depression."

A Problem with the Classical Model

As long as the economy was operating smoothly, the above Classical analysis of the aggregate economy met no serious opposition. But the prolonged depression of the 1930s changed individuals' views about what focus economics should take. The Classical "have faith" solution was no longer acceptable. With a 25 percent unemployment rate, everyone was interested in the short run, not the long run. John Maynard Keynes put that concern most eloquently: "In the long run we're all dead."

Keynes played a major role in the development of macroeconomic thinking in the 1930s. In effect, he said, "Let's forget the long run and focus on the short run." He stopped asking whether the economy would eventually get out of the depression on its own, and he started asking what short-run forces were causing the depression and what could society do to escape it. By taking this approach he created the field of macroeconomics, and at the same time he forced major changes in Classical economics.

In response to Keynes's challenge, Classical economists added an analysis of the short run to their analysis of the long run. They adjusted their long-run Classical model (Exhibit 3) into a more realistic short-run Classical aggregate supply/aggregate demand model (often simply called the *Classical model,* which we'll call it here). Even though, from now on, most of our discussion will be about

CLASSICAL ECONOMISTS AND AGGREGATE SUPPLY/AGGREGATE DEMAND ANALYSIS   ADDED DIMENSION

C lassical economists before 1936 wouldn't have put their analysis in an aggregate supply/aggregate demand framework. Their arguments were generally informal arguments with political and social as well as economic dimensions. Graphical analysis forced them to specify their arguments in two dimensions although Classical economists believed the issues had far more than two dimensions.

For example, the aggregate supply/aggregate demand analysis has no time dimension and most Classical economists of that era were careful to state that their analysis was *long run,* an analysis of where the economy was eventually heading, not where it was at any particular moment. They agreed that in the short run there could be many problems, but they didn't analyze them. They considered short-term problems too complex to deal with.

In the 1930s the center for Classical economists was England's London School of Economics (LSE). When word got to the LSE students that Keynes, up north in Cambridge, England, was working on a model focusing on demand for output as a whole, they were incredulous. One student at that time recalled:

> We had heard that some very strange things were happening in Cambridge. We couldn't quite make out what it was, something about the elasticity of demand for output as a whole, and we knew that was nonsense, because we were brought up properly on Marshall, and we knew all about elasticity and demand curves.* We knew that if you drew a demand curve you had to assume all the other prices were fixed; otherwise you wouldn't know what the demand curve

for this item was. If you were to draw a demand curve for another item (for example, say you wanted to look at the Consumer Surplus which you could enjoy from being able to buy some item for less than you would have been willing to pay), it was your duty to wipe out the first demand curve because the first one was allowing the price to vary. You had to have the prices fixed for everything else if you were going to draw a demand curve. Knowing this, we knew that demand curves and demand and elasticity referred only to partial analysis; and yet, somehow in Cambridge they must have known that and still, very perversely, they were talking about elasticity of demand for output as a whole. (from an interview with economist Abba Lerner)

The LSE students decided to clear up the confusion; they got in touch with the Cambridge students and agreed to meet once a week at Bishop's Stortford, a town chosen because it's about halfway between London and Cambridge on the railway line. The meetings were to continue until one side or the other won the argument. The result was that many of the LSE students, such as James Meade (who later won a Nobel prize in economics) and Abba Lerner (who's quoted here and who eventually became a key exponent of Keynes's theories) were converted to Keynesian economics. They believed it was both possible and necessary to talk about the demand for output as a whole. In doing so, they gave up Say's law.

---

* *Elasticity* (a term used to describe demand curves) measures the percent change in quantity in response to a percent change in price.

the short-run model, it's important to remember the short-run model that is presented in Exhibit 5 and that what is now called *the Classical model* developed in response to Keynes's criticism of the "pure" long-run model.

The best way to understand the short-run Classical aggregate supply/ aggregate demand model is to briefly consider Keynes's attack on it. Although his attack on the Classical view was multifaceted, its essence can be simply stated: The Classical model worked too neatly since everything was always in equilibrium. He asked, what if, for some reason, everything wasn't in equilibrium? What if there was an aggregate disequilibrium? What if the quantity of aggregate supply exceeded the quantity of aggregate demand, as shown in Exhibit 4?

In that case, Keynes pointed out, if the veil-of-money assumption were true and there were a dichotomy between the real and monetary sectors (as the long-run Classical model assumed), the aggregate demand curve, as well as the aggregate supply curve, would be perfectly vertical because a change in the wage and price level could not affect the real economy. In that case there would be no way a fall in the wage and price level would bring about an equilibrium between the two. By assumption, changes in the price level (which would include a fall in the wage level) would have no effect on either the quantity demanded or the quantity supplied, since no relative prices would have changed. Keynes wrote:

> [I]f competition between unemployed workers always led to a very great reduction of the money-wage, there would be a violent instability in the price-level. Moreover, there might be no position of stable equilibrium except in conditions consistent with full employment; since the wage-unit might have to fall without limit.

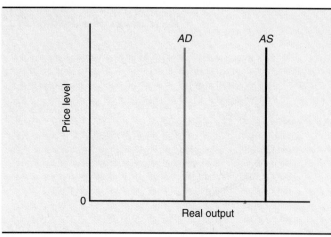

EXHIBIT 4   Keynes's Challenge to the Classical Story

Keynes argued that if the price level were only a veil and did not affect the real economy, there was no way in which a fall in the price level could bring about an aggregate equilibrium. Both the *AS* and *AD* curves would be perfectly vertical, and they would never intersect.

In short, he argued that if the veil-of-money assumption were true and money did not affect the real economy, changes in the price level would only happen if the money supply were changed and would not bring about equilibrium.

Notice that in his argument Keynes shifted the analysis here from the long run to the short run. He argued that you can't simply assume the long run will arrive without explaining how short-run adjustment forces drive the economy to the long-run equilibrium. Somehow there must be a short-run **disequilibrium adjustment story** to explain how you get to the long run. The original Classical model lacked that story. It was always in equilibrium. That was the essence of Keynes's attack.

To have an adequate disequilibrium adjustment story (a story of how the economy adjusts from disequilibrium to equilibrium), Classical economists needed first to answer two questions: How could an economy get out of equilibrium? And second, how could it get back into equilibrium? The formal discussion of their answers to these questions is quite analytic, but luckily, understanding the analytics is not necessary to understand their argument. So we will stick with an intuitive explanation. (I present a slightly more formal treatment in an appendix.)

Disequilibrium adjustment story An explanation of how short-run adjustment forces drive the economy to long-run equilibrium.

THE CLASSICAL DISEQUILIBRIUM ADJUSTMENT STORY

6

In response to Keynes's arguments, Classicals agreed that the veil-of-money assumption held true only in the long run. They said that in the short run, changes in the price level could occur independently of changes in the money supply and those changes in the price level could affect the aggregate quantity demanded. Specifically a fall in the price level would increase the aggregate quantity demanded. For example, the fall in the price level would make people who held money richer. (If you have $100 cash and the price level falls by half, that $100 can buy twice as much as before.) Also the fall in price level would lower the price of a country's exports and increase the price of its imports. These effects would mean that a *fall in the price level would increase the aggregate quantity demanded.* Thus, the short-run aggregate demand curve would be downward sloping and there would be a **law of aggregate demand** that would parallel the law of demand for individual markets to which you were introduced in Chapter 2.

Law of aggregate demand As price level falls, aggregate quantity demanded will increase.

The second part of their disequilibrium story was that *aggregate supply would remain fixed, regardless of what happened to demand, and that it would not be affected by changes in the price level.* This meant that there is no Classical law of aggregate supply. The Classical aggregate supply curve is perfectly vertical.

Classical economists argued that suppliers are price takers, meaning they produce the full-employment level of output and offer it for sale on the market at whatever price it brings. Aggregate supply remains at the full-employment level, *even if excess supply exists.* According to the Classical model, suppliers, faced with disequilibrium, simply raise or lower the prices they charge and the wages

ADDED DIMENSION

PRICE LEVEL VERSUS RELATIVE
PRICE/WAGE CHANGES

The Classical arguments about the effect of price level changes on quantity of aggregate demand provide a method for the aggregate economy to achieve equilibrium if the wage and price levels both change by equal percentages, moving together so there are no domestic relative price changes. If the wage rate (the average wage workers receive) changes at a different rate than the price level, that difference provides another disequilibrium adjustment mechanism—a relative wage/price adjustment mechanism. For example, let's say that when there is unemployment, the wage level falls but the price level does not. That fall in the wage level increases the return to entrepreneurial effort, making it worthwhile for businesses to expand, thereby increasing employment.

The aggregate supply and demand analysis in this book abstracts from such relative wage/price issues. It assumes wages and prices move together. That assumption focuses the analysis on the relationship between aggregate supply and aggregate demand and on how disequilibriums between the two will be resolved. You should remember that other relative price adjustments can also occur. If they do, the analysis will be modified but not fundamentally altered.

they pay, keeping output constant. That's what an unchanging vertical aggregate supply curve implies: Changes in the price level make no difference to quantity supplied. In the Classical aggregate analysis, all adjustment is done by movements along the aggregate demand curve. Classicals maintained the assumption that aggregate supply would not shift.

The assumptions that aggregate supply is perfectly vertical and that it doesn't shift are important to the Classicals' theory of disequilibrium adjustment in the short run. They eliminate the need to consider any interconnection between the aggregate quantity demanded and the aggregate quantity supplied. Aggregate supply remains fixed at full employment.

As you will see, Keynes specifically challenged this Classical version of adjustment. He argued that, faced with excess supply, firms will decrease production. As they do, the aggregate supply curve will shift back, which will cause the aggregate demand curve to shift back. But once again I'm getting ahead of the story. I consider Keynes's view of the disequilibrium adjustment process in the next chapter. At this point, simply remember the Classical aggregate supply is unchanging; it remains fixed at full employment, regardless of whether there's excess supply or excess demand.

To give you a good sense of the Classical theory of aggregate disequilibrium, let's go through the example in Exhibit 5. In it, say the price level (P_1) is too high for aggregate supply (AS) and demand (AD) to be in equilibrium. In response, the price level falls. This fall in the price level makes individuals richer, which increases aggregate quantity demanded. That price level fall (shown by the arrows along the AS curve) also lowers the relative price of the country's exports and raises the relative price of imports, further increasing aggregate quantity demanded. Thus, in response to the fall in the price level, the aggregate quantity demanded increases along arrow A, until the aggregate economy is once again in equilibrium at P_0 (the law of aggregate demand).

The Law of Aggregate Demand and the Classical Explanation of Aggregate Disequilibrium Adjustment

Classical economists recognized that in the real world, the price and wage levels weren't going to fall to anywhere near the level necessary to bring about equilibrium. So in practical terms, they agreed that their model did not provide a workable solution for how to escape the depression. But the model pointed to a culprit: wage and price rigidities which were preventing the Classical price level adjustment mechanism from operating.

In the Classical view the depression of the 1930s was lasting so long because social and political forces prevented the law of aggregate demand (the price level adjustment system) from operating. Thus, their solution to the depression was the

Classicals' View of the Great Depression

EXHIBIT 5   The Classical AS/AD Model

At price level P_1, the quantity of aggregate supply, Q_S, exceeds the quantity of aggregate demand, Q_D, so the price level begins to fall. This fall in the price level will cause the quantity of aggregate demand to increase through its effect on the holders of money and through its effect on the price of exports and imports. As these effects take hold, eventually an equilibrium is reached at the price level P_0 and aggregate output Q_S.

laissez-faire solution: to stop the measures Congress was passing to hold up wages and prices; to break up labor unions; and to let the wage–price level fall. That's where their theory led.

THE POLICY DEBATE

By the late 1930s many Classical economists were giving up their policy prescriptions. Politicians weren't listening to them; Classical economists sensed it was not the time to push their ideas. For example, in Britain by the 1930s all three of the country's political parties (the Liberal party, the Labor party, and the Conservative party) had abandoned support of a laissez-faire policy. Each party was offering a competing government-organized program to fight unemployment.

Many students weren't listening to them, either: Students wanted to discuss policies to end the depression. They didn't want to hear about the long run. For example, when Canadian exchange student Robert Bryce came back to Harvard after studying at Britain's Cambridge University where Keynes was a professor, his fellow students asked him to organize seminars to discuss the ideas he'd heard Keynes propound. (It was through Bryce's Harvard seminars that Keynes's ideas were transmitted to the United States.) When students organize their own seminars, you know they're interested.

One more reason why Classical economists were giving up their policy prescriptions is that economists are people too. Despite their training, economists are often compassionate people; their gut feelings were the same as the general population's: There must be a better way. Thus, during the depression some Classical economists advocated a variety of policies that didn't follow from their theory.[2]

THE RISE OF KEYNESIAN ECONOMICS

We've just looked at the state of economics as it was when John Maynard Keynes responded to popular demand for an alternative policy to laissez-faire. In his book, *The General Theory of Employment, Interest, and Money,* he gave people both an alternative explanation of the depression and a suggestion of what to do about it that didn't rely upon cutting wages.

While there were many dimensions to Keynes's ideas, their essence was that Say's law (supply creates its own demand) was wrong. Keynes argued that

---

[2] For example, in the 1930s A. C. Pigou supported government programs to end unemployment, as did Henry Simons, an important American Classical economist at the University of Chicago.

Thomas Malthus was right—general gluts could exist (and certainly did exist in the 1930s).

Keynes (a shrewd investor who was extremely active in the financial sector) argued that the financial sector didn't work the way Say's law assumed it did. It didn't translate savings into investment fast enough to prevent a general glut in output. According to Keynes, the level of savings did not determine the level of investment. Instead the level of investment would change the level of income and thereby change the level of savings. Let's consider an example. Say that a large portion of the people in the U.S. economy suddenly decide to save more and consume less. Consumption demand would decrease and savings would increase. If those savings were not immediately transferred into investment (as the Classicals assumed they would be), investment demand would not increase by enough to offset the fall in consumption demand and aggregate demand would fall. There would be excess supply. Faced with this excess supply, firms would cut back production, which would decrease income. People would be laid off. As people's incomes fell, their desire to consume and their desire to save would decrease. (When you're laid off you don't save.) Eventually income would fall far enough so that once again savings and investment would be in equilibrium, but that equilibrium could be at a lower income level at a point below full employment. In short, what Keynes argued was that the economy could get stuck in a rut.

Once the economy got stuck in a rut with a glut, it had no way out. The government had to do something to pull the economy out of the rut. Keynes and his followers presented a set of models and arguments to explain their views. Those models, which were aggregate models, became the central macroeconomic models.

Keynesian ideas spread like wildfire among the younger economists. By the 1950s Keynesian economics became accepted by most of the profession. It was taught everywhere in the United States. A terminology developed: national income accounting, which was closely tied to Keynesian concepts. As the terminology became generally used, Keynesian economics became as deeply embedded—and as little thought about—as Say's law had been earlier. That's one of the main reasons why Keynesian economics is not the end of the story, and why in the 1970s there was a *New Classical* resurgence.

Yet back in the 1950s and 1960s Keynesian economics was gaining popular support. The policies that came to be associated with Keynesian economics were monetary policy and fiscal policy. *Monetary policy* meant varying the money supply to affect the level of spending in the economy. *Fiscal policy* meant varying the government budget deficit or surplus (by varying government expenditures and taxes) to control the level of spending. Together they were supposed to provide a steering wheel by which economists could control the economy, keeping it free of business cycles.

In the next two chapters we'll see how all this works.

Classical economic philosophy still lives in conservative journals, such as the *Cato Journal*.

KEY POINTS

- In the early 1900s Classical economics focused on partial equilibrium microeconomics. It explained unemployment in microeconomic terms: Unemployment was caused by too high a wage level. **1**
- Pure Classical economic analysis of the aggregate economy centered on two propositions: Say's law and the quantity theory of money. **2 3**
- The quantity theory of money determines the price level, and Say's law sees to it that the ag-

gregate economy is always in equilibrium at full employment. **2 3**
- Aggregate supply is the relationship between price level and total amount of output supplied. **4**
- Aggregate demand is the relationship between price level and total amount of output demanded. **4**
- The partial equilibrium adjustment story doesn't work with aggregate supply and aggregate de-

mand because it works only for relative prices. **4**
· In the long-run Classical model aggregate demand isn't considered. It's simply assumed to exist at a level equal to aggregate supply. **6**
· In the short-run Classical model the aggregate supply curve is perfectly vertical but aggregate demand is downward sloping because of the law of aggregate demand. **6**

· The law of aggregate demand is explained by the effect of a change in the price level on money holders and on prices of imports and exports. **6**
· The law of aggregate demand provided a theoretical, but not a practical or political, way to achieve aggregate equilibrium. **5**
· By the late 1930s many economists were giving up the Classical view and becoming Keynesian economists who opposed laissez-faire. **5**

KEY TERMS

aggregate demand
  curve *(190)*
aggregate supply
  curve *(190)*
autonomous *(189)*
Classical
  economists *(184)*

disequilibrium adjustment
  story *(194)*
equation of ex-
  change *(188)*
Keynesian econo-
  mists *(184)*

law of aggregate
  demand *(184)*
money *(188)*
quantity theory of
  money *(188)*
Say's law *(186)*

veil-of-money
  assumption *(189)*
velocity of money *(188)*

QUESTIONS FOR THOUGHT AND REVIEW

The number after each question represents the estimated degree of critical thinking required. (1 = almost none; 10 = deep thought.)

1. What is the central difference between Keynesian and Classical economists? *(2)*
2. Explain how lowering the wage level will decrease unemployment if the price level doesn't change when the wage is lowered. *(5)*
3. Explain how lowering the wage level will decrease unemployment if the price level is flexible and changes when the wage is lowered. *(7)*
4. What three assumptions turn the equation of exchange into the quantity theory of money? *(3)*
5. Assuming the quantity theory of money held true, what would happen if a country on a gold standard ran a balance of payments surplus? *(5)*

6. A popular proposal to end the depression in the 1930s was to create a new money with coupons on it. If the money weren't used within a specific period of time, the coupons would be worthless. Would that proposal help eliminate unemployment, given the Classical analysis? How? *(8)*
7. Why were Classical economists hesitant about using aggregate supply/aggregate demand analysis? *(6)*
8. If a country had a flexible exchange rate rather than a fixed exchange rate, how would the Classical short-run adjustment argument change? *(8)*
9. Classical economists saw the depression as a political problem, not an economic problem. Why? *(6)*
10. How would the Classical economists' model change if suppliers based quantity supplied on expected aggregate demand? *(8)*

PROBLEMS AND EXERCISES

1. Assume the money supply is $500, the velocity of money is 8, and the price level is 2. Using the quantity theory of money:
   a. Determine the level of real output.
   b. Determine the level of nominal output.
   c. Assuming velocity remains constant, what will happen if the money supply rises 20 percent?
   d. If the government established price controls and also raised the money supply 20 percent, what would happen?
   e. How would you judge whether the assumption of fixed velocity is reasonable?

2. The classical analysis of the economy rests on wage and price stability.
   a. Ask a local business what it would do to prices if demand for its product fell 10 percent.
   b. Ask a local business how it determines wages. What would it do to wages if unemployment in the community were 8 percent? 10 percent?
   c. Draw an aggregate supply and demand curve. Demonstrate the Classical equilibrium. Now say that demand decreases 10 percent. Using the insights you gained in parts (*a*) and (*b*) and *AS* and *AD* curves, explain how the economy will likely adjust.

The Argument between Keynes and the Classics

The previous discussion summarizes the argument between Keynes and the Classics. This Appendix goes deeper into the underlying assumptions of the Classical model and discusses the difference between Keynes and the Classics with specific reference to the underlying assumptions of the *AS* and *AD* curves.

The formal presentation of the Keynesian and Classical disequilibrium adjustment mechanisms involves understanding the underlying assumptions of supply and demand. Forgetting those underlying assumptions can cause confusion. Your immediate reaction to the question, "How could the economy get back into equilibrium once it got out of equilibrium?" might well have been to draw the aggregate supply and aggregate demand curves in just the way you drew the partial equilibrium (microeconomic) supply and demand curves, and to use the same **partial equilibrium analysis** of adjustment that you used in Chapter 2. That won't do, and the Classicals knew it wouldn't do. That's why they used Say's law and the quantity theory of money, and not supply and demand, when they talked about the aggregate economy.

How Aggregate Supply and Demand Differ from Partial Equilibrium Supply and Demand

Aggregate supply and demand curves are based upon the relationship between the *price level* and the *aggregate quantity of goods* supplied and demanded (real GDP). The partial equilibrium adjustment mechanism doesn't apply to macroeconomic aggregate supply and demand curves. There is no reason why a higher price level (remember the price level includes the wage level) need bring about a higher aggregate quantity of goods supplied or decrease the aggregate quantity demanded. There are no extra profits to be made since if the price level rises, the firms' costs go up just as much as the price of its goods goes up.

The laws of supply and demand discussed in Chapter 2 are about relative prices. Those laws are based upon the effect that changes in relative prices have upon quantity supplied and quantity demanded of that particular good. These laws don't necessarily hold for aggregate supply or aggregate demand.

To assume that the laws of supply and demand hold true in the aggregate is to fall prey to the **fallacy of composition** (the false assumption that what's true for a part will also be true for the whole) that the aggregate equals the sum of its parts. Sometimes this may be true, but sometimes it may not.

The preceding argument is abstract. Let's specifically consider the problem in the aggregate disequilibrium adjustment story that doesn't exist in the partial equilibrium adjustment story.

Let's first review how the partial equilibrium adjustment mechanism works. Say we have the partial equilibrium supply and demand curves in Exhibit A1(a) and the relative price is P_1, above the equilibrium price. Excess supply is $Q_s - Q_D$. The dynamic law of supply says that in response to this excess supply, suppliers will decrease the quantity supplied; we move along the supply curve in the direction of the arrow B. As the relative price falls, demanders will increase the quantity they demand, and as they do we also move along the arrow A. Both these forces push us closer to equilibrium. Eventually, according to the dynamic law of supply and demand, we reach equilibrium at price P_e and quantity demanded Q_e.

For that partial equilibrium adjustment story to work, the supply and demand curves must be independent. As we move along one curve, the other curve must remain constant rather than shift. If that were not the case, the final equilibrium wouldn't be (Q_e, P_e); it would be some other equilibrium that existed after the curves shifted. That's why "all other things constant" was a central assumption of the laws of supply and demand.

When talking about the aggregate economy, you *cannot* assume all other things constant. When we talk about aggregate supply and demand, the partial equi-

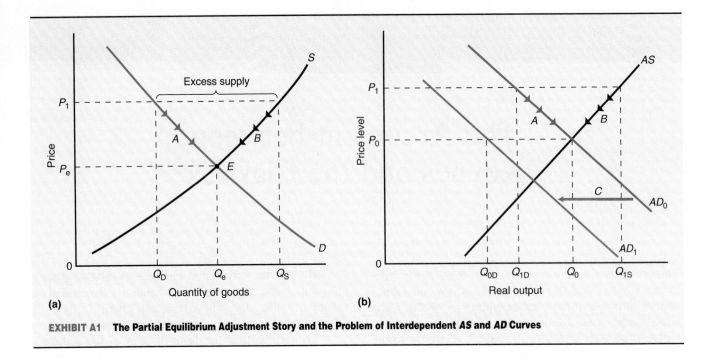

EXHIBIT A1   The Partial Equilibrium Adjustment Story and the Problem of Interdependent *AS* and *AD* Curves

librium adjustment story doesn't work because *aggregate supply and aggregate demand are not independent*. Specifically, a movement along the aggregate supply curve will cause the aggregate demand curve to shift. Why? Because as we move back along an aggregate supply curve, people are being laid off and profits are falling. Income (one of the variables a demand curve holds constant) falls, shifting the aggregate demand curve back. So either a *movement along*, or a *shift of*, the aggregate supply curve causes a *shift* of the aggregate demand curve.

The problem of interdependent aggregate supply and aggregate demand curves is shown in Exhibit A1(b). Let's begin in disequilibrium at price level P_1 where quantity supplied is Q_{1S} and quantity demanded is Q_{1D}. Now we start moving back along the *AS* curve (arrow *B*) and along the *AD* curve (arrow *A*), for the same reasons as we did in the partial equilibrium case. So far, so good. It looks as if the economy is moving toward equilibrium. However, as the quantity of aggregate supply falls, income falls, which causes demand to *decrease*, shifting the *AD* curve back from AD_0 to AD_1. As we move toward equilibrium along the *AS* curve, the aggregate demand curve shifts back (arrow *C*), and with it the equilibrium price and quantity fall. What initially looked like the equilibrium price, P_0, will not be the equilibrium price. In fact, it's unclear where the final equilibrium will be, or whether there will be one. It's like a horse with a carrot dangling two feet ahead of its nose. The horse chases the carrot, but whenever the horse moves, the carrot moves too.

A Short-Run Classical Aggregate Supply/Aggregate Demand Analysis

As we've discussed, in response to Keynes's criticisms, Classical economists modified their model from a long-run model of the aggregate economy always in equilibrium to a short-run model that allowed for disequilibrium and that had a disequilibrium adjustment mechanism. This short-run model is sometimes called the *Classical model*.[1]

In the short-run Classical model, the aggregate supply curve is, as before, perfectly vertical. The reasoning is the same as before: the price level doesn't affect producers' decisions about what to supply. What differs in this short-run Classical model from the long-run Classical model is the aggregate demand curve. In response to Keynes's criticism, Classical economists developed a number of explanations of why the aggregate demand curve might be downward sloping and how aggregate disequilibrium adjustment

---

[1] As I stated at the beginning of this chapter, we must recognize that this more realistic Classical analysis developed partially in response to Keynes's criticism. Keynes characterized the Classical economists in the manner described in the preceding section, and forced them to respond to his characterization. I say "partially" because some Classical economists, like Keynes's colleague, D. H. Robertson, objected to his characterization of Classical economics. They argued that they had developed complicated theories of short-run dynamic disequilibrium adjustment to complement the long-run Classical theory. The disagreement between Robertson and Keynes carried over into their personal lives, straining and almost ending their friendship. In the 1990s as historians of economic thought have reconsidered the work of Robertson, many have been impressed. They agree that his analysis did solve some of the problems, and it forms a historical basis for some New Classical ideas we'll consider in a later chapter.

could occur. Thus, there's a Classical law of aggregate demand that corresponds to the partial equilibrium law of demand in Chapter 2. The law of aggregate demand states that as the price level falls, the aggregate quantity demanded will increase. That sounds similar to the partial equilibrium law of demand, but the reasoning underlying it is quite different.

Explanations of the Law of Aggregate Demand

The basis of the partial equilibrium law of demand is that people substitute one good for another when the price of one increases relative to another. This doesn't apply with the law of aggregate demand. Because aggregate demand is total output, there are no other goods to substitute for; and since aggregate demand is determined by the price level, there are no relative prices to consider. To explain the shape of the aggregate demand curve, something else is needed. Classical economists provided three justifications: the Pigou effect, the Keynes effect, and the international effect. Each of these effects makes the aggregate demand curve downward sloping and thereby provides mechanisms through which the price level affects the total quantity demanded.

The Pigou Effect   A. C. Pigou was one of the leading Classical economists in the 1920s and 1930s. He had been one of Keynes's teachers. (Keynes called him *the Prof.*) In response to Keynes's criticisms he developed an argument that came to be known as the *Pigou effect.* The **Pigou effect** explains the law of aggregate demand as follows: Say the price level falls; that fall will increase the value of money since each dollar will buy more than it would at a higher price level. Therefore you could say that the real money supply (the money supply divided by the price level) has increased. As the real money supply rises, Pigou and the Classicals argued, the quantity of aggregate goods demanded increases until it has increased enough to equal aggregate supply.

To see how this occurs, let's consider an example. Assume the economy experiences a recession—there is an excess supply of workers and goods. The wage and price levels begin to fall. That fall in the price level increases the value of the dollars in people's pockets, making them richer. Because they're richer, they spend more—the quantity demanded increases. With this adjustment mechanism, the Classicals had an answer to how an aggregate disequilibrium could be eliminated. The Pigou effect states that a fall in the *price level* increases the quantity of aggregate demand by making the holders of cash (*real balances*) richer. As they become richer they spend more and the quantity of aggregate demand increases.

The Keynes Effect   Another explanation of the law of aggregate demand (quantity of aggregate demand increases as price level falls) is called the *Keynes effect* because it was Keynes (the economist criticizing Classical economists) who worked out the effect for them. (It was like a game of chess in which your opponent helps you with a move.) According to the **Keynes effect,** a decrease in the price level will increase the real money supply. This increase in the real money supply will lower interest rates which will increase investment. Why? Because at lower interest rates businesses will find it cheaper to borrow and hence will undertake more investment projects.[2]

Since investment is one component of aggregate demand, the quantity of aggregate demand will increase when the price level falls. The Keynes effect is another reason why the Classical aggregate demand curve slopes downward to the right.

The International Effect   The Keynes effect and the Pigou effect hold for a closed economy—an economy without international trade. As soon as we allow for international trade there's another reason why the aggregate demand curve slopes downward: the **international effect,** which works as follows: Given a fixed exchange rate (which most countries had at the time, since they were on the gold standard, which uses fixed exchange rates), when the price level in a country goes down, the price of its exports decreases relative to the price of foreign goods, so exports increase. Similarly for imports, when the price level in a country falls, the relative price of its imports rises, so imports decrease.

For example, say the price level in the United States falls 50 percent. That means that a hamburger that previously cost $2 now will cost $1. Of course, people's incomes also fall, so a person who before had earned $400 per week now earns only $200 per week. However, a fall in the U.S. price level does not affect the price of imports. That means French perfume that previously cost $80 an ounce will still cost $80 an ounce. Since you're now earning only $200 a week, the relative price of French perfume to you will have doubled, and by the law of demand you'll consume less French perfume. You'll substitute American perfume. As the U.S. price level falls, U.S. residents substitute American goods for foreign goods, increasing the quantity of U.S. goods demanded.

The effect is the opposite with exports. Foreigners' income won't have fallen, but the price of U.S. wheat will have declined. So by the law of de-

---

[2] The Keynes effect can't be fully developed here because it depends on issues which themselves won't be fully developed until later chapters. I present it here for completeness, because it is one of the explanations of the downward-sloping aggregate demand curve.

mand foreigners will buy more U.S. wheat than before. As the U.S. price level falls, foreign residents substitute American goods for their own goods, increasing the quantity of U.S. goods demanded.

Both of these effects increase aggregate quantity demanded for U.S. goods. Thus, the international effect of a price level change is a third reason why the aggregate demand curve slopes downward.

How important the international effect is depends on how important international trade is to a country. If the country trades very little and has a flexible exchange rate, the international effect will be small. If the country trades a large amount and has fixed exchange rates, the international effect will be large.

If you reflect upon the international effect, you'll see a relationship between it and the reasoning underlying the partial equilibrium downward-sloping demand curve. Internationally, a country's price level is a relative price. If economists open the analysis to include goods from other countries, a country's overall price level can be equated to the price for a single good—just the opposite of the case of a country's economy examined by itself. In an international context, aggregate supply and demand are partial equilibrium curves and can be compared to the laws of supply and demand for a single good. So it isn't surprising that the international effect contributes to a downward-sloping aggregate demand curve.

No Law of Aggregate Supply

As we discussed in the text, there is no Classical law of aggregate supply. The Classical aggregate supply curve is perfectly vertical. Classical economists argued that suppliers are price takers. (They produce the full-employment level of output and offer it for sale on the market at whatever price it may bring.) Aggregate supply remains at the full-employment level, *even if excess supply exists*. According to the Classical model, suppliers, faced with disequilibrium, simply raise or lower the prices they charge and the wages they pay, keeping output constant. That's what an unchanging vertical aggregate supply curve implies: Changes in price level make no difference to quantity supplied. In the Classical aggregate analysis, all adjustment is done by movements along the aggregate demand curve. Classicals maintained the assumption that aggregate supply would not shift.

Are Classical Disequilibrium Adjustment Assumptions Reasonable?

The questions to ask yourself are:

1. Is the assumption about an unchanging supply reasonable?
2. What would happen if aggregate supply did not remain fixed?
3. How strong would you expect the Pigou, Keynes, and international effects to be?
4. Are there some other effects that might change the adjustment process?

Keynes asked these questions and came up with an alternative explanation of aggregate disequilibrium adjustment, as we'll see in the next chapter.

9

The Keynesian Model of the Aggregate Economy

Keynes stirred the stale economic frog pond to its depth.
Gottfried Haberler

After reading this chapter, you should be able to:

1

Summarize the Keynesian story of how a
recession occurs.

2

Tell the Keynesian story using the
Keynesian aggregate production/aggregate
expenditure model.

3

Use the Keynesian equation to determine
equilibrium income.

4

Explain the multiplier process.

5

Tell that Keynesian story using aggregate
supply and demand curves.

6

Differentiate between Keynesian and
Classical views of the economy.

Although Keynes developed some of the analysis of how the price level adjusts to bring about aggregate equilibrium, price level adjustment is not central to Keynes's argument, and he did not focus on it. Instead he focused on the *income adjustment mechanism,* an aggregate adjustment mechanism that has nothing to do with price level.

1

Income adjustment mechanism A mechanism by which the aggregate economy arrives at equilibrium through shifts of aggregate supply and demand, rather than through changes in the price level.

The **income adjustment mechanism** is an alternative mechanism by which aggregate equilibrium can be achieved. It is a mechanism by which the aggregate economy arrives at equilibrium through *shifts* in production, income, and savings (shifts of aggregate supply and aggregate demand), rather than through changes in the price level (*movements along* the aggregate demand curve). Thus, as we shall see, the income adjustment mechanism focuses on the interconnection between aggregate supply and demand, not movements along aggregate supply and demand.

Keynes focused on the income adjustment mechanism for two reasons:

1. He felt that the price level adjustment mechanism of the Classical aggregate supply/aggregate demand analysis, if it worked at all, worked too slowly for political and social forces to accept. Keynes felt the price level adjustment mechanism was, at best, only of theoretical importance. In response to the classical argument that the price adjustment mechanism would work in the long run, he quipped, ''In the long run we're all dead.''

    Yes, he agreed, there were some theoretical issues raised by the price level adjustment mechanism, but he argued that those issues weren't especially important during the depression. Social pressures (the invisible handshake) wouldn't let prices and wages fall fast enough for the Classical price level adjustment mechanism to work. And even if the social pressures were overcome, political pressures (the invisible foot) would stop the fall in the price level, if it started. In the United States, for example, as the wage and price levels began to fall in the 1930s, in response to strong political pressure from people being hurt by that fall, the government passed minimum wage and ''fair price'' legislation which made it illegal for many firms to lower wages and prices. So the issue—how would the economy adjust if price and wage levels were flexible—was relevant only for academic debate.

2. Keynes felt that in the aggregate, changes in the wage and price level could not produce effects strong enough to maintain the economy at a full-employment equilibrium. To say theoretically that an adjustment force exists is one

John Maynard Keynes, a multitalented policy and theoretical economist, whose book, *The General Theory,* is seen as the beginning of modern macroeconomics. *Bettmann Newsphotos.*

When Keynes said, "In the long run we're all dead," he didn't mean that we can forget the long run. What he meant was that if the long run is sufficiently long so that short-run forces do not let it come about, then for all practical purposes there is no long run. In that case, the short-run problem must be focused on.

Keynes's view of the political and social forces of the time was that voters would not be satisfied waiting for market forces to bring about full employment. Keynes felt that if something were not done in the short run to alleviate unemployment, voters would opt for fascism (as had the Germans) or communism (as had the Russians). He saw both alternatives as undesirable. For him, what would happen in the long run was academic.

Classicals, on the other hand, argued that the short-run problems were not as bad as Keynes made them out to be so short-run problems should not be focused on to the exclusion of long-run problems. Modern day Classicals argue that today we are living in Keynes's long run, so that his long-run problems are our short-run problems.

IN THE LONG RUN WE'RE ALL DEAD

thing; to say it is strong enough to achieve aggregate equilibrium is another. Keynes argued that long before the price level adjustment mechanism would achieve equilibrium, the income adjustment force would have already done so. Thus, he argued that theoretically Classical economists were wrong.

For much of Keynes's book, *The General Theory of Employment, Interest, and Money,* in which he developed the Keynesian model, he put aside that second, academic, reason because the first (the real-world reason) was sufficient reason not to consider wage and price level flexibility. Thus, in the simple Keynesian model that we'll discuss in this chapter and the next, wage and price levels are assumed institutionally fixed, leaving the model free to concentrate on what Keynes considered to be the most important dynamic adjustment force: the income adjustment force.

This assumption would later come back and haunt Keynesian economists. While wages and prices are slow to adjust downward, they are not so slow to adjust upward. In the 1970s the wage and price levels rose continuously and inflation became the economy's biggest problem. Many Classical economists blamed this inflation on Keynesian policies based on a model that assumed the wage and price level fixed. This led to a resurgence of Classical analysis.

THE
GENERAL THEORY
OF
EMPLOYMENT INTEREST
AND MONEY

BY
JOHN MAYNARD KEYNES
FELLOW OF KING'S COLLEGE, CAMBRIDGE

NEW YORK
HARCOURT, BRACE & WORLD, INC.

The General Theory—the book that created macroeconomics as a separate subject.

THE KEYNESIAN MODEL

To understand the Keynesian model, it is helpful to put it in perspective. Keynes was educated in Classical economics. In the late 1920s he had written a two-volume book, *The Treatise on Money,* which was meant to be an extension of the Classical model. But as soon as he had finished writing it, he decided it was fundamentally wrong. In the next few years he struggled to escape from what he felt was the confining Classical model.

Eventually he did escape, but only by specifically forsaking the Classical assumption that the economy will always be at full employment and hence at its potential or full-employment level of income. Keynes argued that the aggregate levels of income and employment would be determined by what was happening in the economy. They were not phenomena that could be assumed. Thus, Keynes's model focuses on how the equilibrium levels of income and employment in the economy are achieved. Let's now turn to a formal presentation of the Keynesian model.

According to the Classical model, supply (production) creates demand (expenditure), which is the equivalent of saying there will always be demand to buy up all that is produced (Say's law), and therefore the economy will always be at its full-employment or potential level of income. Keynes escaped that model by looking separately at expenditure and production decisions. He examined two separate questions: How are production decisions made and how are expenditure decisions made? After considering these questions separately, he considered how those production and expenditure decisions are related.

We'll start, as Keynes did, by looking separately at production and expenditure decisions.

Aggregate Production in the Keynesian Model

2

Aggregate production The total amount of production (and hence income) in an economy.

Aggregate production is the total amount of production of all goods and services in every industry in an economy. It is at the center of the Keynesian model. Production creates an equal amount of income so income and production are always equal. In turn, income affects aggregate expenditures (or aggregate demand). Aggregate production creates an equal amount of income but does not necessarily create an equal level of aggregate quantity demanded. Unlike Classical economists who believed in Say's law and believed that equilibrium would always be at full employment, Keynes believed that disequilibrium was possible and that the expenditures people planned to make would not necessarily exactly equal production. A difference between the two would start an adjustment process that would bring about an aggregate equilibrium which would not necessarily be at full employment. His model was designed to determine what would happen if the expenditures people planned to make did not equal production.

Graphically, aggregate production is represented by a 45° line of a graph with real income in dollars measured on the horizontal axis and production measured in dollars on the vertical axis (Exhibit 1). By definition, production creates an amount of income equal to the amount of production or output, so this aggregate production curve can also be called an *aggregate income curve*. At all points on the aggregate production curve, income equals production. That is why the aggregate production curve is the 45° line—because that is the only line at which income equals production. For example, consider the exhibit's point *A*, where income (measured on the horizontal axis) is $4,000 and production (measured on the vertical axis) is also $4,000. That is true only on the 45° line. Keynes believed that production could expand until it hit a capacity constraint at potential income (line *B*).

Aggregate Expenditures in the Keynesian Model

Aggregate expenditures Total level of expenditures in an economy; equals $C + I + G + (X - M)$.

Aggregate expenditures consist of consumption (spending by consumers), investment (spending by business), spending by government, and net foreign spending on U.S. goods (the difference between U.S. exports and U.S. imports). These four components were presented in our earlier discussion of national income accounting, which isn't surprising since the national income accounts were designed around the Keynesian model. We now consider each of those components more carefully.

Disposable income (Y_d) Income left over after paying taxes ($Y_d = Y - T$).

Consumption   The largest component of expenditures is consumption. While various things affect the level of consumption expenditures, it is most affected by disposable income. **Disposable income** is that part of income left after paying taxes which, in the simple Keynesian model, are assumed to be a constant amount.

The assumed relationship between consumption and disposable income is reasonable: Most of us look at our disposable income, and then determine how much of it we will spend. Thus in the Keynesian model the central relationship is between consumer spending and disposable income.

Let's consider the consumption decisions of an individual who earned $12,000 and paid $2,000 in taxes last year. That leaves $10,000 in disposable income. Assume $9,000 goes to consumption and $1,000 goes to savings. If next year this person's disposable income rises to $12,000, we would expect consumption also to increase to, say, $10,600. If disposable income fell to $8,000, consumption would fall to $7,400. Exhibit 2 shows a consumer's entire hypothesized relationship between disposable income and consumption. Notice that when disposable income is zero, we still assume the person consumes. How? By borrowing or dipping into previous savings. Consumption that would exist at a zero level of

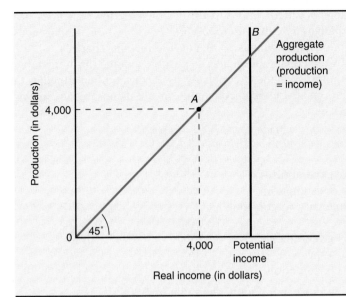

EXHIBIT 1   The Aggregate Production Curve

Since, by definition, output equals income, on each point of the aggregate production curve income must equal production. This equality holds true only on the 45° line.

EXHIBIT 2   Consumption Related to Disposable Income

(1) Disposable income (Y_d)	(2) Change in disposable income (ΔY_d)	(3) Consumption (C)	(4) Change in consumption (ΔC)	Row
0	—	1,000	—	A
1,000	1,000	1,800	800	B
2,000	1,000	2,600	800	C
3,000	1,000	3,400	800	D
4,000	1,000	4,200	800	E
5,000	1,000	5,000	800	F
6,000	1,000	5,800	800	G
7,000	1,000	6,600	800	H
8,000	1,000	7,400	800	I
9,000	1,000	8,200	800	J
10,000	1,000	9,000	800	K
11,000	1,000	9,800	800	L
12,000	1,000	10,600	800	M
13,000	1,000	11,400	800	N
14,000	1,000	12,200	800	O
15,000	1,000	13,000	800	P

disposable income is called **autonomous consumption** (consumption that's un-affected by a change in disposable income). It includes those expenditures a person would make even if he or she were unemployed.

Autonomous consumption (C_0) Consumption that's unaffected by changes in disposable income.

Notice that as disposable income rises, consumption also rises, but not by as much as disposable income. The relationship between changes in disposable income and changes in consumption is shown in columns 2 and 4. The numbers in these columns can be derived from columns 1 and 3. Each entry in column 2 represents the difference between the corresponding entry in column 1 and the entry in the previous row of column 1. Similarly each entry in column 4 is the difference between the corresponding entry in column 3 and the entry in the previous row of column 3. For example, as disposable income rises from $10,000 to $11,000, the change in disposable income is $1,000. Similarly as consumption rises from $9,000 to $9,800, the change in consumption is $800.

Since much of Keynes's analysis focuses on changes in expenditures that occur in response to changes in income, it is important to distinguish that portion of consumption that changes in response to changes in income from that portion

Endogenous consumption (bY_d) Consumption that changes as disposable income changes.

Consumption function A functional representation of the relation between consumption and disposable income ($C = C_0 + bY_d$).

that does not. As previously stated, that portion of consumption that does not change when income changes is called *antonomous consumption*. **Endogenous consumption** is consumption that changes as disposable income changes.

The relationship between consumption and disposable income (as in the table in our example) can be expressed more concisely as a **consumption function** (a representation of the relationship between consumption and disposable income as a mathematical function):

$$C = C_0 + b(Y - T) = C_0 + bY_d$$

where

C = consumption expenditures
C_0 = autonomous consumption
b = marginal propensity to consume
Y = gross income
T = taxes paid to government
Y_d = disposable income = $Y - T$
bY_d = endogenous consumption.

The consumption function corresponding to the table in Exhibit 2 is

$$C = \$1,000 + .8Y_d.$$

Notice that if you substitute the data from any row in the table in Exhibit 2, both sides of the consumption function are equal. For example, in row C of Exhibit 2, we see that consumption (C) = $2,600. Since disposable income (Y_d) = $2000 we can calculate the right side of the equation: $1,000 + .8($2,000) = $2,600. So the two sides are equal.

The Marginal Propensity to Consume   There is one part of the consumption function we haven't talked about yet: the letter b (.8 in the numerical example). The letter b is the marginal propensity to consume. Keynes was interested in what would happen to consumption spending as disposable income changed. He argued that when disposable income fell by, say $1,000, consumption would fall by somewhat less than that amount ($800 in the example). He defined **marginal propensity to consume (mpc),** as the relationship between a *change* in consumption, ΔC, that resulted from a *change* in disposable income, ΔY_d. (The Greek letter Δ, or delta, which corresponds to the letter D in our alphabet, is commonly used to designate *change in*.) In mathematical notation, marginal propensity to consume is represented by the symbol b:

Marginal propensity to consume (mpc) The relationship between the change in consumption and change in disposable income (b).

$$b = \text{mpc} = \frac{\text{Change in consumption}}{\text{Change in disposable income}} = \frac{\Delta C}{\Delta Y_d}.$$

Using the data in Exhibit 2, let's determine the level of b (the mpc) by dividing a change in consumption by a corresponding change in disposable income:

$$b = \frac{\Delta C}{\Delta Y_d} = \frac{\$800}{\$1,000} = .8.$$

Based on figures for consumption and disposable income for Britain at the time, Keynes estimated that the mpc was between .8 and .9. That estimate is not central to his argument, as long as the mpc remains between zero and one.

Graphing the Consumption Function   Now that we're familiar with the components and terminology used with the consumption function, let's see how to graph it. Exhibit 3 graphs the particular consumption function given by

$$C = \$1,000 + .8Y_d.$$

Notice that at zero disposable income, consumption is $1,000. This is the autonomous portion of consumption.

The consumption function's slope tells us how much consumption changes with a particular change in disposable income. In other words, slope, b, graphi-

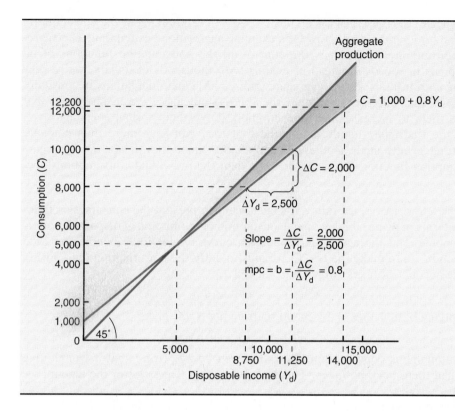

EXHIBIT 3   Graph of Consumption Function

The consumption function graphed here represents the function derived from the information in Exhibit 2. It has a slope of .8, the mpc, and an intercept of 1,000, the level of autonomous consumption. The shaded area is savings, the difference between income and consumption.

cally represents the marginal propensity to consume for a particular consumption function.

The apc and the mpc   Besides the marginal propensity to consume there's one other term you need to know, both because we'll use it in the future and because it will help cement your understanding of mpc. That term is the **average propensity to consume (apc),** defined as consumption divided by disposable income:

Average propensity to consume (apc)
Consumption divided by disposable income.

$$\text{apc} = \frac{\text{Consumption}}{\text{Disposable income}} = \frac{C}{Y_d}.$$

For example, if disposable income is 400, and consumption is 370, apc = 370/400 = .925. Alternatively if disposable income is 500 and consumption is 450, apc = .9.

Notice that the apc changes as income changes. That makes it different from mpc. (By assumption mpc is constant at all levels of income.) The reason is the constant term, C_0, in the consumption function. (The subscript $_0$ is used throughout the book to indicate what a term such as C will equal when the variable it depends on—in this case, Y_d—is zero.) The relationship between apc and mpc is given by

$$\text{apc} = \frac{C_0}{Y_d} + \text{mpc}.$$

As long as autonomous consumption, C_0, is positive, apc is greater than mpc. Only when $C_0 = 0$ are mpc and apc equal.

The differences between apc and mpc are important to remember; apc refers to consumption divided by disposable income:

$$\text{apc} = \frac{C}{Y_d};$$

mpc refers to the *change in* consumption over the *change in* disposable income:

$$\text{mpc} = \frac{\Delta C}{\Delta Y_d}.$$

The Aggregate Consumption Function   Thus far we've been looking at the consumption function for an individual. Now let's examine aggregate consumption. The aggregate consumption function is the sum of all the consumption functions of all individuals in society. Instead of dealing with thousands of dollars, we're now dealing with trillions. In the aggregate, many individual fluctuations in consumption offset each other. For example, the Smith family may have an emergency that causes them to increase their consumption above their normal spending level, while the Rodriguez family might find that they can save more than planned. Offsetting events such as these occur all the time; they make the aggregate consumption function much more stable than the individual consumption functions.

Disposable Income, Income, and Taxes   It's customary to present the consumption function in terms of disposable income. Consumption is a function of disposable (after-tax) income. But the aggregate production curve relates total income and total production, so to make the two fit we must modify the consumption relationship to take account of taxes, which we will call T_0:

$$C = C_0 + b(Y - T_0).$$

Multiplying both Y and T_0 by b and rearranging terms gives

$$C = (C_0 - bT_0) + bY.$$

Autonomous consumption, C_0, is lowered by bT_0 from what it would have been had there been no taxes. This isn't surprising. Taxes lower the amount we spend.

It is customary, too, to assume initially that taxes are zero to avoid this complication, and we'll follow this simplification. This means that disposable income and income are identical, so consumption is a function of income. Since

$$C = C_0 + bY_d \text{ and } Y_d = Y \text{ (because } T_0 = 0)$$
$$C = C_0 + bY.$$

In the next chapter when we consider government spending and taxes in detail, we will relax this assumption.

Consumption and Savings   What people don't consume, they save. Since the aggregate production curve tells us the income that people have, and the consumption function tells us how much they spend, the difference between the two is how much they save. The amount of savings is shown by the shaded area in Exhibit 3. There is no savings at income level $5,000, where expenditures equal income (where the consumption function crosses the aggregate production curve). At lower levels of income, savings is negative; at higher levels of income, savings is positive.

Savings, the mps, and the aps   You know from the circular flow diagram that when all individuals spend all their income (which they derive from production), the aggregate economy is in equilibrium. *Injections* into the system will equal *withdrawals* from the system. In this simple Keynesian model, savings represent withdrawals; autonomous expenditures represent injections.

The circular flow diagram expresses the national income identity: aggregate income equals aggregate output. Keynes asked: (1) does aggregate expenditure always equal aggregate production? and (2) if not, what will happen in the economy to bring them into equilibrium? Since individuals save some of their income, expenditures and income need not be equal. The question is: Are the savings translated back into expenditures? If they aren't, injections will not equal withdrawals and income will have to change. Thus, in the hypothesized relationship, and in the economy, savings play an important role. What people don't consume, they save. Specifically,

Savings = Disposable income − Consumption.

EXHIBIT 4 (a, b, and c)   **Savings Table, Savings Function, and Consumption Function**

The information in the table (**a**) can be translated into a graph. That is done in (**b**). In (**c**) you can see the relationship between the savings curve in (**b**) and the difference between the consumption function and the aggregate production curve.

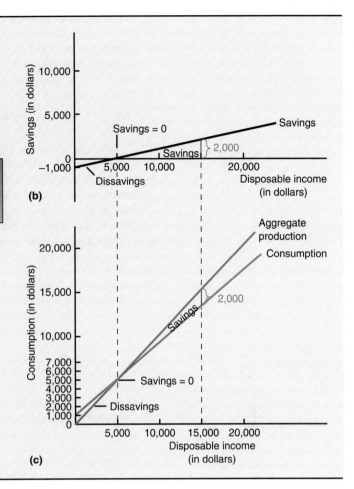

(1) Disposable income (Y_d)	(2) Change in disposable income (ΔY_d)	(3) Savings (S)	(4) Change in savings (ΔS)	Row
0	—	−1,000	—	A
1,000	1,000	−800	200	B
2,000	1,000	−600	200	C
3,000	1,000	−400	200	D
4,000	1,000	−200	200	E
5,000	1,000	0	200	F
6,000	1,000	200	200	G
7,000	1,000	400	200	H
8,000	1,000	600	200	I
9,000	1,000	800	200	J
10,000	1,000	1,000	200	K
11,000	1,000	1,200	200	L
12,000	1,000	1,400	200	M
13,000	1,000	1,600	200	N
14,000	1,000	1,800	200	O
15,000	1,000	2,000	200	P

(a)

(b)

(c)

If savings is translated back into expenditures, no adjustment is necessary. If savings is not translated back into expenditures, the aggregate economy will not be in equilibrium.

As with consumption, we can use a savings table and savings function to show the relationship between savings and income. Exhibit 4 presents the savings table and graph of the savings function corresponding to the relationships for consumption in Exhibits 2 and 3.

You can see that the amount saved increases as income increases—the higher the level of income, the higher the level of savings. For example, as income goes up from $10,000 to $11,000 (rows K and L of column 1), savings rises from $1,000 to $1,200 (rows K and L of column 3).

Column 2 shows the change in disposable income and column 4 shows the change in savings that occurs as income increases from one row to another. In the example, the change in disposable income was $1,000 and the change in savings was $200.

Just as we defined mpc and apc with the consumption function, so too can we define **marginal propensity to save (mps)** and **average propensity to save (aps).**

The mps is the percentage saved from an additional dollar of disposable income:

$$mps = \frac{\Delta S}{\Delta Y_d}.$$

The aps is savings divided by disposable income:

$$aps = \frac{S}{Y_d}.$$

Marginal propensity to save (mps) The percentage saved from an additional dollar of disposable income.

Average propensity to save (aps) Savings divided by disposable income.

The aps changes with disposable income. If disposable income is $10,000, the aps = 1,000/10,000 = .1. If disposable income is $15,000, savings is $2,000, so aps = 2,000/15,000 = 0.133.

Exhibit 4(b) graphs the savings function. Notice that it is an upward-sloping function whose slope equals the mps and whose intercept (the point where it crosses the vertical axis) is negative. In this example it is −$1,000.

The consumption function and the savings function are related. Exhibit 4(c) shows the consumption function presented earlier. By extending the income levels between the two graphs you can see that the distance between the consumption function and the production curve equals the distance between the horizontal axis and the savings function. Each function provides us with the same information because savings is the mirror image of consumption. What isn't consumed is saved.

When we add up the marginal propensity to consume and the marginal propensity to save, we arrive at 1:

$$\text{mpc} + \text{mps} = 1.$$

In our example, this works. Since mpc = .8 and mps = .2, the sum equals 1. The same holds true for the apc and aps:

$$\text{aps} + \text{apc} = 1.$$

Investment Expenditures by business on plants and equipment.

Investment   The second component of aggregate expenditures is **investment** (expenditures by businesses on plants and equipment). To keep his model simple, Keynes assumed investment depends on the "animal spirits of investors." In other words, investment is *autonomous*; it's independent of the level of disposable income and is determined outside the model. Investment is represented by

$$I = I_0.$$

Exhibit 5(a) relates society's income and investment. It represents the amount all firms invest at each level of income. As you can see, the amount of investment doesn't change in response to income changes. Exhibit 5(b) graphs the relationship between investment and income. The relationship is simply the function $I = 1,000$. Notice that the investment function is a perfectly horizontal line. That means the investment function's slope is zero. When income is $0, investment is $1,000; when income is $5,000, investment is still $1,000. That's because in order to keep the model simple, investment is assumed to be independent of income; that's the meaning of a graphical zero slope.

Just as autonomous consumption can change, so can autonomous investment. Keynes believed investment could shift around a lot, just as he believed the consumption function was capable of shifting. As we'll see shortly, it was precisely those sudden, unexpected shifts in investment spending that Keynes saw as the cause of booms as well as recessions. He also believed investment would be influenced by other variables such as the interest rate, but he didn't include these other influences in the simple model.

Government Expenditures   To keep this first look at the Keynesian model simple, let's also assume government spending is autonomous. That is, it does not change as income changes. Therefore the general equation for government spending would be

$$G = G_0$$

which is represented graphically as a horizontal line, just like the investment function.

Net Exports   When people in the United States spend their income on foreign imports (M), the expenditures are lost to the U.S. economy. However when foreigners spend their income on U.S. exports (X), that spending adds to U.S.

(1) Investment $I = I_0$	(2) Disposable income (Y_d)	(3) Change in investment (ΔI)	(4) Change in income (Y_d)	Row
1,000	0	–	–	A
1,000	1,000	0	1,000	B
1,000	2,000	0	1,000	C
1,000	3,000	0	1,000	D
1,000	4,000	0	1,000	E
1,000	5,000	0	1,000	F
1,000	6,000	0	1,000	G
1,000	7,000	0	1,000	H
1,000	8,000	0	1,000	I
1,000	9,000	0	1,000	J
1,000	10,000	0	1,000	K
1,000	11,000	0	1,000	L
1,000	12,000	0	1,000	M
1,000	13,000	0	1,000	N
1,000	14,000	0	1,000	O
1,000	15,000	0	1,000	P

(a)

(b)

EXHIBIT 5 (a and b)   Investment Schedule and Investment Curve

In the table in **(a)** you can see that the amount of investment does not change with changes in income. It is autonomous—determined outside of the model. That's why there is no change in investment as income changes. Because investment is not affected by changes in income, the investment curve graphed in **(b)** will have a slope of zero.

expenditures. The common convention is to subtract imports from exports and to talk about net exports $(X - M)$. When net exports are positive, exports exceed imports; when net exports are negative, imports exceed exports.

Again, to keep the Keynesian model simple at this point, we assume net exports are autonomous—net exports do not change as income changes. The equation is

$$X - M = X_0 - M_0.$$

Since they are autonomous, net exports are graphically represented by a horizontal line, just like the graphs of investment and government spending. To keep the analysis simple, we will assume that net exports are also constant at $1,000.

Aggregate Expenditures   *Aggregate expenditures* (AE) is the summation of all four components of expenditures:

Aggregate expenditures $= C + I + G + (X - M).$

Exhibit 6(a) lists the values of each expenditure at a different level of income, or production, as discussed in the preceding several sections. The summation of expenditures, aggregate expenditures, is in column 5. Notice that, by assumption in our example, the only endogenous expenditure that changes as income changes is consumption.

As you can see in Exhibit 6(b), the aggregate expenditures curve is the graphical sum of all four expenditures curves, and it has the same slope, mpc = 0.8, as the consumption function. Notice that the aggregate expenditures curve crosses the vertical axis at a point that's the sum of all four autonomous expenditures: $C_0 + I_0 + G_0 + (X_0 - M_0) = \$4,000$. A good exercise to help you visualize the relationships involved here is to compare the data in the columns in the table with points on the graphs to see how they correspond.

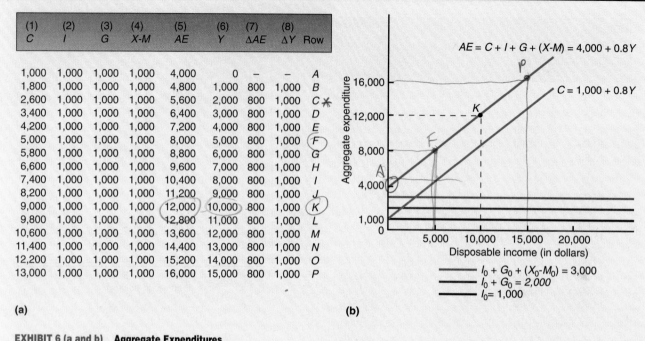

(1) C	(2) I	(3) G	(4) X-M	(5) AE	(6) Y	(7) ΔAE	(8) ΔY	Row
1,000	1,000	1,000	1,000	4,000	0	–	–	A
1,800	1,000	1,000	1,000	4,800	1,000	800	1,000	B
2,600	1,000	1,000	1,000	5,600	2,000	800	1,000	C
3,400	1,000	1,000	1,000	6,400	3,000	800	1,000	D
4,200	1,000	1,000	1,000	7,200	4,000	800	1,000	E
5,000	1,000	1,000	1,000	8,000	5,000	800	1,000	F
5,800	1,000	1,000	1,000	8,800	6,000	800	1,000	G
6,600	1,000	1,000	1,000	9,600	7,000	800	1,000	H
7,400	1,000	1,000	1,000	10,400	8,000	800	1,000	I
8,200	1,000	1,000	1,000	11,200	9,000	800	1,000	J
9,000	1,000	1,000	1,000	12,000	10,000	800	1,000	K
9,800	1,000	1,000	1,000	12,800	11,000	800	1,000	L
10,600	1,000	1,000	1,000	13,600	12,000	800	1,000	M
11,400	1,000	1,000	1,000	14,400	13,000	800	1,000	N
12,200	1,000	1,000	1,000	15,200	14,000	800	1,000	O
13,000	1,000	1,000	1,000	16,000	15,000	800	1,000	P

(a)

$AE = C + I + G + (X\text{-}M) = 4{,}000 + 0.8Y$

$C = 1{,}000 + 0.8Y$

Aggregate expenditure

Disposable income (in dollars)

$I_0 + G_0 + (X_0\text{-}M_0) = 3{,}000$
$I_0 + G_0 = 2{,}000$
$I_0 = 1{,}000$

(b)

EXHIBIT 6 (a and b)   Aggregate Expenditures

Aggregate expenditures are the sum of all the components of expenditures. These can be added numerically in the table, as they are in (a) or graphically, as they are in (b). Notice that the table and the graph correspond. For example, in row *K* of the table, aggregate expenditures are $12,000, just as they are at point *K*, which graphs expenditures at income $10,000.

DETERMINING THE LEVEL OF AGGREGATE INCOME

Now that we've developed the graphical framework (the aggregate production/ aggregate expenditure, or AP/AE, framework), we can put the two together and see how the level of aggregate income is determined in the Keynesian model. We begin by representing a different aggregate expenditures curve [$C + I + G + (X - M)$] and the aggregate production curve on the same graph, as in Exhibit 7.

The aggregate production curve is the 45° line. It tells you the level of aggregate production and also the level of aggregate income since, by definition, income equals production. Expenditures, which do not necessarily equal production or income, are represented by the aggregate expenditures curve. Let's now take a closer look at the relationship between the *AE* and *AP* curves.

Let's first say that income is $12,000. As you can see, at income of $12,000, expenditures are $11,400. Aggregate income exceeds aggregate expenditures. This is true for any income level above $10,000. Similarly at all income levels below $10,000, aggregate production is less than aggregate expenditures. For example, at a production level of $8,000, aggregate expenditures are $8,600.

The only income level at which aggregate production equals aggregate expenditures is $10,000. Since we know that in equilibrium aggregate expenditures must equal aggregate production, $10,000 is the equilibrium level of income in the economy. It is the level of income at which neither producers nor consumers have any reason to change what they are doing. At any other level of income, since there is either a shortage or a surplus of goods, there will be incentive to change. Thus, you can use the aggregate production curve and the aggregate expenditures curve to determine the level of income at which the economy will be in equilibrium.

Solving for Equilibrium Graphically

Let's go through another example. Say the consumption function is

$$C = \$400 + .75Y.$$

Government spending is $200. Investment is $100 and net exports are $50. What is

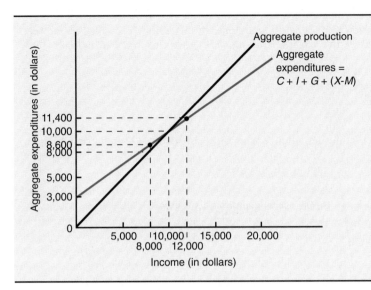

EXHIBIT 7   Comparing AE to AP

The aggregate expenditures curve intersects the aggregate production curve at $10,000; therefore, this is the equilibrium level of income in the economy. Above $10,000, aggregate production exceeds aggregate expenditures. Below $10,000, aggregate expenditures exceed aggregate production.

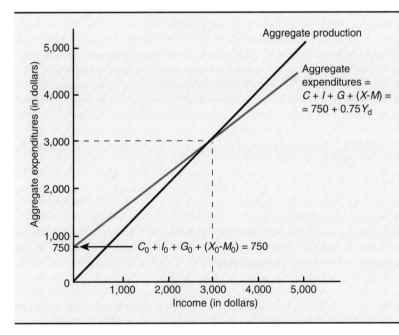

EXHIBIT 8   Solving for Equilibrium Graphically

The aggregate expenditures curve combines consumption, government spending, investment, and net exports. Equilibrium occurs where the aggregate expenditures curve intersects the aggregate production curve.

the equilibrium level of income in this economy? Exhibit 8 shows the aggregate expenditures curve and the aggregate production curve that go with these numbers. In it you can see that the equilibrium income is $3,000. This is the only income level where aggregate expenditures equal aggregate production.

Another way to determine the level of income in the Keynesian model (a way that's useful to know) is through the **Keynesian equation,**

$$Y = \left[\frac{1}{(1-b)}\right][C_0 + I_0 + G_0 + (X_0 - M_0)],$$

which shows the relationship between autonomous expenditures and the equilibrium level of income. The Keynesian equation does not come out of thin air. It comes from combining the set of equations underlying the graphical presentation of the Keynesian model into the two brackets. (The Keynesian equation is derived in the accompanying box.)

Determining the Level of Aggregate Income with the Keynesian Equation

Keynesian equation Equation showing the relationship between autonomous expenditures and the equilibrium level of income.

3

The Keynesian equation is derived by combining the equations presented in the text algebraically to arrive at the equation for income. Rewriting the expenditures relationships, we have:

$$C = C_0 + bY$$
$$I = I_0$$
$$G = G_0$$
$$(X - M) = (X_0 - M_0).$$

Aggregate production, by definition, equals aggregate income (Y) and, in equilibrium, aggregate income must equal the four components of aggregate expenditures. Beginning with the national income accounting identity, we have

$$Y = C + I + G + (X - M).$$

Substituting the terms from the first four equations, we have

$$Y = C_0 + bY + I_0 + G_0 + X_0 - M_0.$$

Subtracting bY from both sides,

$$Y - bY = C_0 + I_0 + G_0 + X_0 - M_0.$$

To arrive at the Keynesian equation we factor out Y:

$$Y(1 - b) = C_0 + I_0 + G_0 + (X_0 - M_0).$$

Now solve for Y by dividing both sides by $(1 - b)$:

$$\overset{multiplier}{Y = [1/(1 - b)]} \overset{autonomous\ expenditure}{[C_0 + I_0 + G_0 + (X_0 - M_0)]}$$

This is the Keynesian equation. It embodies all the equations that went into the Keynesian model. When we combine a group of related equations into a single equation, as we did here, that single equation is called a *reduced-form equation*.

What numbers do we substitute? The numbers in the right-hand bracket are simply the sum of all autonomous expenditures. Added up, they tell us the total aggregate autonomous expenditure in the economy.

Now let's consider the left-hand bracket. As you can see, the aggregate autonomous expenditure is multiplied by the term $[1/(1 - b)]$, which, not surprisingly, is called the *multiplier*. Once you know the value of b (marginal propensity to consume), you can calculate the multiplier by reducing $[1/(1 - b)]$ to a simple number. For example, if $b = .8$, the multiplier is

4

$$1/(1 - .8) = 1/.2 = 5.$$

Multiplier A number that tells the magnified effect of a shift in autonomous expenditures on income $[1/(1 - b)]$.

The **multiplier** tells you the relationship between autonomous expenditures and income. For example, if autonomous expenditures are \$4,000 and the multiplier is 5, equilibrium income in the economy will be \$20,000.

Let's see how the equation works by considering our previous example. In it the mpc (b) was .75. Subtracting .75 from 1 gives .25. Dividing 1 by .25 gives 4. (Remember, doing that is asking how many 1/4ths there are in 1.) So our first term is 4. In that example autonomous consumption (C_0) was \$400; investment (I_0) was \$100; government spending (G_0) was \$200; and net exports ($X_0 - M_0$) were \$50. Adding these up gives \$750. The Keynesian equation tells us to multiply this total autonomous expenditures, \$750, by 4. Doing so gives $4 \times \$750 = \$3,000$, the same answer we got graphically.

The Keynesian equation gives you a simple way to determine equilibrium income in the Keynesian model. You determine the multiplier $[1/(1 - b)]$ and multiply it by the sum of all autonomous expenditures.

Five different marginal propensities to consume and the multiplier associated with each are shown in Exhibit 9. Notice as mpc increases, the multiplier increases. Knowing the multiplier associated with each marginal propensity to consume gives you an easy way to determine equilibrium income in the economy.

mpc = b	multiplier = $1/(1 - b)$
.5	2
.75	4
.8	5
.9	10
.95	20

EXHIBIT 9   Marginal Propensities to Consume and Multipliers

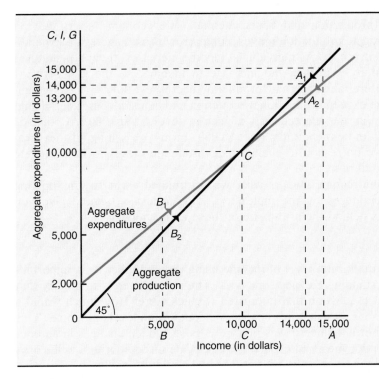

EXHIBIT 10   The Income Adjustment Mechanism

At income levels A and B, the economy is in disequilibrium. Depending on which direction the disequilibrium goes, it generates increases or decreases in production and expenditures until the economy reaches income level C, where aggregate expenditures equal aggregate production.

Let's look at one more example of the multiplier. Say that the mpc is .8 but that autonomous expenditures are $4,500 instead of $4,000. What is the level of income? Multiplying the sum of autonomous expenditures, $4,500, by 5 tells us that income is $22,500. With a multiplier of 5, income rises by $2,500 because of an increase in autonomous expenditures of $500.

The preceding discussion provides a technical method of determining equilibrium income in the Keynesian model. But it doesn't help us understand what the model means for the economy and what forces are operating to ensure that the income level we determined is the equilibrium income level. For it to be the equilibrium level of income, there must be adjustment forces that push the economy toward that equilibrium whenever the economy is not in equilibrium. Let's now discuss those forces. Let's ask what happens when the macroeconomy is in disequilibrium—when aggregate production does not equal aggregate expenditures. Exhibit 10 shows us.

Let's first consider the economy at income level A where aggregate production equals $15,000 and aggregate expenditure equals $14,000. Since production exceeds expenditures by $1,000 at income level A, firms can't sell all they produce; inventories pile up. In response, firms make an adjustment. They decrease aggregate production and hence income. As businesses slow production, the economy moves inward along the aggregate production curve as shown by

A Closer Look at the Income Adjustment Mechanism

arrow A_1. As income falls, the gap between aggregate production and aggregate expenditures decreases. For example, say businesses decrease aggregate production to $14,000. Aggregate income also falls to $14,000, which causes aggregate expenditures to fall, as indicated by arrow A_2, to $13,200. There's still a gap, but it's been reduced by $200, from $1,000 to $800.

Since a gap still remains, income keeps falling. A good exercise is to go through two more steps. With each step, the economy moves closer to equilibrium.

Now let's consider the economy at income level B ($5,000). Here production is less than expenditures. Firms find their inventory is running down. (Their investment in inventory is far less than they'd planned.) In response, they increase aggregate production and hence income. The economy starts into an expansion as aggregate production moves along arrow B_2 and aggregate expenditures move along arrow B_1. As individuals' income increases, their expenditures also increase, but by less than the increase in income, so the gap between aggregate expenditures and aggregate production decreases. But as long as expenditures and income exceed production, production and hence income keep rising.

Finally, let's consider the economy at income level C, $10,000. At point C, income is $10,000 and expenditures are $10,000. Firms are selling all they produce, so they have no reason to change their production levels. The aggregate economy is in equilibrium.

The equilibrium income level is what we determined earlier by multiplying autonomous expenditures by the multiplier. This discussion should give you insight into what's behind the arithmetic of those earlier models.

SHIFTS IN AUTONOMOUS EXPENDITURES

Determining the equilibrium level of income using the multiplier is an important first step in understanding Keynes's analysis. The second step is to modify that analysis to answer a question that interested Keynes more: How much would a change in autonomous expenditures change the equilibrium level of income? This second step is important since it was precisely those sudden changes in autonomous expenditures Keynes said caused the aggregate disequilibrium, and it was these sudden changes he said the Classical model couldn't handle.

Because Keynes felt autonomous expenditures were subject to sudden shifts, I was careful to point out *autonomous* meant "determined outside the model and not affected by income." Autonomous expenditures can, and do, shift for a variety of other reasons. When they do, the adjustment process is continually being called into play. Let's consider some reasons autonomous expenditures shift.

Shifts in Autonomous Consumption

For example, autonomous consumption can shift because of natural disaster (which causes people on average to consume more), but the most important reason it shifts is due to changes in people's expectations about the future. When consumers are confident, the consumption function shifts up. When consumers are scared about the future (as happened in late 1991 and early 1992) the consumption function shifts down. The aggregate expenditures curve shifts up or down accordingly.

Because autonomous consumption shifts around so much, economists measure consumer confidence carefully. These measurements play a large role in economists' estimates of what is likely to happen in the economy.

Shifts in the Investment Function

Another expenditure Keynes believed was continually shifting was the investment function. Reasons the investment function shifts include:

1. Changes in interest rates.
2. Changes in expectations.
3. Technological developments.

Changes in Interest Rates   Keynes believed the interest rate was determined by supply and demand for money, not, as the Classicals believed, by supply and demand for investment. However, Keynes argued the interest rate helped to determine the amount of investment and hence aggregate expenditures. He agreed with the Classicals that as interest rates fall, investment tends to rise. Since the interest rate is the cost of borrowing, when it's cheaper to borrow, you borrow and invest more.

Classical economists believed that interest rate changes would be sufficient to adjust the level of investment so that aggregate expenditures would always equal aggregate production. They believed that because they believed in Say's law. When people saved, financial markets translated that savings into investment, thereby keeping the economy at full employment. Keynes, on the other hand, believed that if for some reason the supply and demand for money caused the interest rate to fall, the lower interest rate would stimulate investments, which in turn would shift up the investment function, the aggregate expenditures function, and equilibrium income. This relationship is the basis of the Keynes effect discussed in the previous chapter.

Notice, however, the difference between the Keynesian view and the Classical view. In the Keynesian view, the monetary sector and real sector are connected; the interest rate is determined in the monetary sector, and that interest rate affects the real sector. In the Classical model, the interest rate is determined in the real sector. It reflects real, not monetary, forces.

Franco Modigliani—Nobel prize, 1985, for work on the theory of consumption.
© *The Nobel Foundation.*

Changes in Expectations   Keynes saw expectations of future sales and profits as the most important determinant of investment demand. When businesspeople expect sales to be good, they invest a lot; when they expect sales to be poor, they cut back on investment.

Keynes believed these expectations could be highly unstable. They were based on rumors, beliefs about future tax policy, and world events. To convey a sense of unpredictability to the expectations he called them *animal spirits.*

For Keynes, unpredictability was not irrationality. Some things in life, he argued, are unpredictable. What future demand for your product would be was one of these things. Thus, basing your decision on rumors and guesses was the best you could do; it wasn't irrational.

Technological Developments   A third major cause of shifts in the investment function is technological developments. When a new technology develops, it makes the old technology obsolete. Firms using that old technology find they can't compete; to keep up they must invest in the new technology. Some economists define periods in economic history by technological development and the investment resulting from that technological development. For example, the 1880s was the railroad period.

A recent major technological advance is the computer revolution beginning in the 1960s. In the 1990s the biotechnological revolution could dwarf the effects of the computer revolution. These technological advances open up new opportunities and generate large amounts of investment by making past investment obsolete. As investment increases, aggregate expenditures and aggregate income increase.

In the same way that private expenditures can shift, so too can government expenditures. During a war, government expenditures can increase significantly. In peacetime, government defense expenditures can fall. As we'll see in the next chapter, government's desire to affect the level of income is another reason government expenditures can change.

Even if expenditures within a country are stable, outside expenditures often are not. A war or a shift in political alignments can totally change flows of exports and imports. For example, World Wars I and II brought U.S. trade with Germany to a

Shifts in Government Expenditures

Shifts in Autonomous Imports and Exports

halt but significantly increased U.S. exports to other countries. The U.S. economy boomed. The depression in Europe in the middle and late 1920s cut back on European imports from the United States, significantly decreasing U.S. exports and further pushing the U.S. economy into a recession. In the 1990s the events in the former Soviet Union lowered U.S. exports and lowered Eastern European countries' exports even more. We already know from history that exchange rates and tariff policies impact both imports and exports. All these changes show up as shifts in the autonomous expenditures curve.

Shifts in Autonomous Expenditures and Keynes's Model

To give you a sense of how Keynes saw his model working, let's say that for some reason there is a shock to the economy, decreasing aggregate expenditures so that aggregate production is greater than aggregate expenditures. Suppliers can't sell all they produce. Their reaction, Keynes argued, would be to lay off workers and cut profits. That response would solve the problem if only one firm was in disequilibrium, but wouldn't solve the problem if all firms were in disequilibrium. When *all* producers respond in this fashion, aggregate income, and hence aggregate expenditures, will also fall. The suppliers' cutback will simply start a vicious cycle, which is multiplied. As the laid-off workers cut their expenditures, producers will cut back production, laying off more workers. The economy will enter into a downward spiral with aggregate production and expenditures chasing each other. The result will be an economic depression.

Will the downward spiral ever end? Keynes argued that eventually it would; fired individuals will dip into savings and not cut their expenditures by the full amount of their decrease in income. Because they do, as income falls, aggregate production and aggregate expenditures will get closer and closer together, and at some level of income aggregate production will equal aggregate expenditures. The algebraic and geometric models we considered in this chapter tell us how much income must fall to bring the economy to aggregate equilibrium.

Shifts in Autonomous Expenditures and the Multiplier   Shifts in autonomous expenditures were important to Keynes. They are what creates *aggregate* disequilibrium. But they are not what distinguishes Keynes from the Classicals. It's what happens next as a response to that shift that distinguishes the two. The Classicals said that the price level adjustment would bring the economy back into equilibrium. If, as Keynes argued was the case, the price level was institutionally fixed, the Classicals believed that shift would have no secondary effect and that the economy would remain in a kind of permanent disequilibrium.

The essence of the Keynesian revolution was his belief that the Classicals were dead wrong about the economy remaining in a permanent disequilibrium if the price level were fixed. Keynes argued that a disequilibrium would start the multiplier process in which both production and income would fall. As that happened, the economy would fall into an under–full-employment equilibrium.

Keynes further argued that a fixed price level assumption was not the issue. He argued that the income adjustment process worked very quickly and had a powerful effect, while the price level adjustment process worked slowly and had a weak effect. He agreed that the price level adjustment mechanism might work if a disequilibrium continued into the long run, but he argued it would never have a chance to work because the income adjustment process would have eliminated that disequilibrium. For Keynes, the fixed price assumption was only a simplifying assumption; it was not a necessity, as long as the price level didn't adjust almost instantaneously.

The Income Adjustment Process: An Example   The income adjustment process is directly related to the multiplier. The reason is that any initial shock (a change in autonomous aggregate expenditures) is *multiplied* in the adjustment process. Let's see how this works in Exhibit 11's example, which will also serve as a review of the Keynesian model. In this example, let's say trade negotiations between the

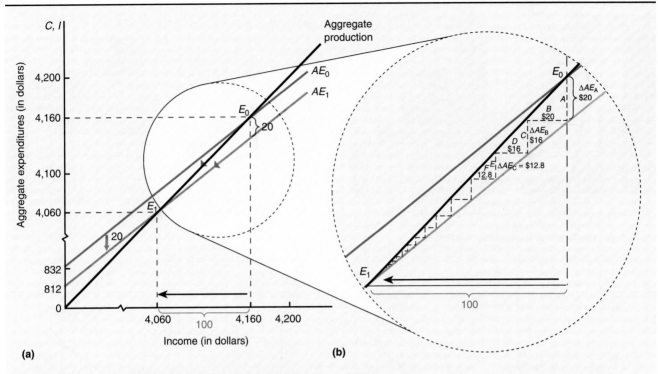

EXHIBIT 11 (a and b)   Shifts in the Aggregate Expenditures Curve

Graph (**a**) shows the effect of a shift of the aggregate expenditures curve. When exports decrease by $20, the aggregate expenditures curve shifts downward from AE_0 to AE_1. In response, income falls by a multiple of the shift, in this case by $100.

Graph (**b**) shows the multiplier process under a microscope. In it the adjustment process is broken into discrete steps. For example, when income falls by 20 (shift B), expenditure falls by (16) (shift C). In response to that fall of expenditures, producers reduce output by 16, which decreases income by 16 (shift D). The lower income causes expenditures to fall further (shift E) and the process continues.

United States and other countries have fallen apart and U.S. exports decrease by $20. This is shown in the AE curve's downward shift from AE_0 to AE_1.

How far must income fall until equilibrium is reached? To answer that question, we need to know the initial shock, $\Delta X = -20$, and the size of the multiplier, $[1/(1 - b)]$. In this example, mpc = .8 so the multiplier is 5. That means the final decrease in income that brings about equilibrium is $100 (five times as large as the initial shock of $20).

Exhibit 11(b), a blowup of the circled area in Exhibit 11(a), shows the detailed steps of the adjustment process so you can see how it works. Initially autonomous expenditures fell by $20 (shift A), causing firms to decrease production by $20 (shift B). But that decrease in income caused expenditures to decrease by another $16 (0.8 × $20) (shift C). Again firms respond by cutting production, this time by $16 (shift D). Again income falls (shift E) causing production to fall (shift F). The process continues again and again (the remaining steps) until equilibrium income falls by $100, five times the amount of the initial shock. The mpc tells how much closer at each step aggregate expenditures will be to aggregate production. You can see this adjustment process in Exhibit 12, which shows the first steps with multipliers of various sizes.

Learning to work with the Keynesian model requires practice, so in Exhibit 13(a) and (b) I present two different expenditures functions and two different shifts in autonomous expenditures. Below each model is the equation representing how much aggregate income changes in terms of the multiplier and the components of autonomous expenditures. As you see, this equation calculates how much the shift will be, while the graph determines it in a visual way.

FURTHER EXAMPLES OF THE KEYNESIAN MODEL

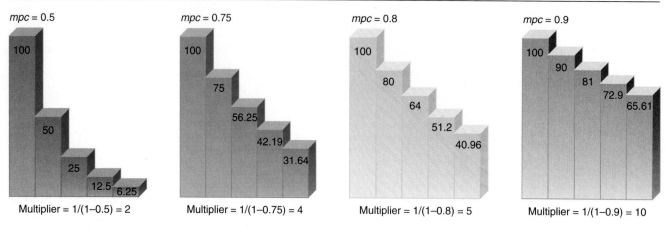

EXHIBIT 12   The First Five Steps of Four Multipliers

The larger the marginal propensity to consume, the more steps are required before the shifts become small.

(a)   **(b)**

EXHIBIT 13 (a and b)   Two Different Expenditure Functions and Two Different Shifts in Autonomous Expenditures

The steeper the slope of the *AE* curve, the greater the effect on equilibrium income. In (**a**) the slope of the *AE* curve is .75 and a shift of $30 causes a shift in income of $120. In (**b**), the slope of the *AE* curve is .66 and a shift of $30 causes a shift in income of $90.

As a final example, let's see how Keynes used his model to explain the 1930s depression. He argued the following: In 1929 there was a financial crash which continued into the 1930s. Financial markets were a mess. Businesspeople became scared, so they decreased investment; consumers became scared, so they decreased autonomous consumption and increased savings. The result was a sudden large shift downward in the aggregate expenditures curve.

Businesspeople responded by decreasing output which decreased income and started a downward spiral. This downward spiral confirmed business's fears. The

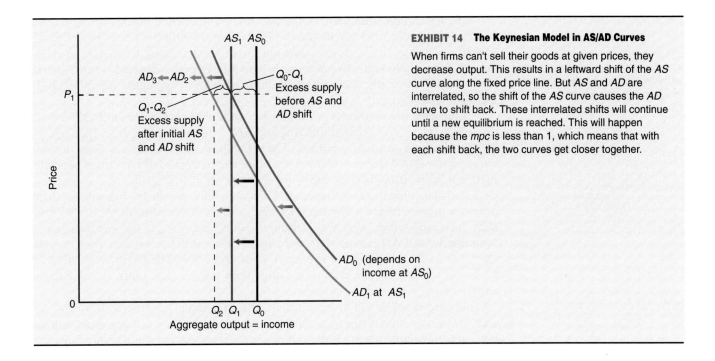

EXHIBIT 14   The Keynesian Model in AS/AD Curves

When firms can't sell their goods at given prices, they decrease output. This results in a leftward shift of the *AS* curve along the fixed price line. But *AS* and *AD* are interrelated, so the shift of the *AS* curve causes the *AD* curve to shift back. These interrelated shifts will continue until a new equilibrium is reached. This will happen because the *mpc* is less than 1, which means that with each shift back, the two curves get closer together.

decreased output further decreased income and expenditures. The process continued until eventually the economy settled at a low-income equilibrium, far below the potential, or full-employment, level of income.

The process that Keynes argued played an important role in bringing about the depression is sometimes called the **paradox of thrift.** Individuals attempted to save more but in doing so caused income to decrease, and they ended up saving less.

Paradox of thrift Individuals attempting to save more cause income to decrease; thereby they end up saving less.

The Keynesian explanation of the depression and of how the aggregate economy adjusted is quite different than the Classical explanation. To see this difference, let's consider what the Keynesian model would be like if it were presented in aggregate supply/aggregate demand curves.

The Keynesian Model in Aggregate Supply/Aggregate Demand Graphs

Exhibit 14 shows the Keynesian view of the economy using an aggregate supply/aggregate demand graph. Let's say we find ourselves in aggregate disequilibrium with the price level fixed at P_1 so production is greater than expenditures, or (expressed in aggregate supply and aggregate demand terms) the quantity of aggregate supply is greater than the quantity of aggregate demand. In the Keynesian model, the price level cannot adjust because it is, in the short run, institutionally determined. Thus, we can draw a fixed price level line, P_1, which captures the institutional reality of fixed prices. *That line is not an AS curve.* An aggregate supply curve is the quantity suppliers want to supply given a price level. Drawing a flat supply curve presupposes that the price level is free to fluctuate if individuals want it to. Keynes said that it was not free to fluctuate. Instead the fixed price line is a line that reflects an institutional constraint on price level adjustment. It is a combination of relevant points on a shifting aggregate supply curve.

In the Classical model, if the price level can't adjust, the economy is stuck in a type of permanent disequilibrium. Production remains at the potential output level, but people are not buying the goods.

Keynes argued that that isn't how the world works. He said that if firms couldn't sell their goods at the existing prices, they would cut production, shifting the aggregate supply curve back from AS_0 to AS_1, to eliminate the excess supply at the existing price level.

Effective demand Demand that exists after suppliers cut production in response to aggregate supply exceeding demand.

But, he argued, that shift *would not* bring about equilibrium. As aggregate supply shifts back, workers' income will fall. Therefore the shift back in aggregate supply will cause the aggregate demand curve to shift back from AD_0 to AD_1. What Keynes called *effective demand* would fall. **Effective demand** is the demand that exists after suppliers cut production in response to aggregate supply exceeding aggregate demand.

Comparing the two shifts in Exhibit 14, we see that at price level P_1 the initial difference $(Q_0 - Q_1)$ between the AS_0 and AD_0 is more than the difference $(Q_1 - Q_2)$ between AS_1 and AD_1 curves. The AD curve shifts back less than the AS curve shifts. Why? Because of an assumption Keynes made. He assumed people's marginal propensity to consume—the decrease in spending that accompanies a decrease in income—is less than one. As income falls, people try to maintain their previous income level by dipping into their savings so spending decreases by less than does production, which by definition equals income. As income decreases, both the AS and AD curves *shift,* but *the AS curve shifts more than does the AD curve, so as income falls, the two move closer together.* The fall in production to Q_1 is not the end of the story since after both curves shift there is still excess supply of $Q_1 - Q_2$.

Because there is still disequilibrium, the adjustment continues. Both the AS and AD curves shift further and further to the left. As they do, aggregate supply and aggregate demand get closer and closer together, and at some level of income they are once again in equilibrium, $AS = AD$, at price level P_1. Thus, in response to a negative shock the Keynesian model ultimately leads to an aggregate supply/aggregate demand equilibrium at an income level below potential or full-employment equilibrium. Nevertheless, given fixed wages and prices, the aggregate economy gravitates toward this equilibrium.

Keynes called this progressive shifting of the AS and AD curves the *income adjustment mechanism.* He said it would work far faster than the price level adjustment mechanism. Because this income adjustment worked so fast, as a first approach to understanding a recession, a model focusing on changes in income level was far more useful than one focusing on changes in prices. That's why he developed his new model.

Notice the difference between the Keynesian and Classical views of aggregate supply. Keynes believed the aggregate supply curve would shift around depending on what producers expected demand to be. Aggregate equilibrium would be brought about by *shifts of* the aggregate supply and aggregate demand curves with the price level remaining constant. As you saw in the last chapter, Classical economists assumed that the aggregate supply curve was stable at the full-employment income level. Equilibrium was brought about by changes in the price level—by *movements along* the aggregate supply and aggregate demand curves. This is the main difference in how the Keynesians and Classicals saw aggregate equilibrium achieved. The Classical model assumes firms would not respond to excess supply by cutting production and shifting supply. The quantity supplied would remain at Q_0 and the supply curve, AS_0, would remain fixed; it would not shift back to AS_1 and beyond. According to the Classicals, firms would simply wait for prices to fall, even if the fall in the price level took a long time to operate.

The Relationship between the AS/AD Model and the AE/AP Model

The *AE/AP* model and the *AS/AD* model are directly related. Shifts in the AS curve are represented by movements along the aggregate production curve (the 45° line). In the Keynesian *AE/AP* model, it is easy to lose sight of aggregate supply because it passively follows aggregate demand. A justification for treating aggregate supply passively is that Keynes was interested in the chase between aggregate supply and aggregate demand. Since the Classicals didn't have an analysis of aggregate demand, he focused on aggregate demand. Keynes's passive treatment of aggregate supply caused some confusion among macroeconomists and led to some of them mistakenly calling Keynes's model a *demand-based*

EXHIBIT 15 (a and b)   The Relationship between the AS/AD Model and the AE/AP Model

In these exhibits you can see the equivalency of the AS/AD dynamics and the AP/AE dynamics. Notice that a movement along the AE curve corresponds to a shift of the AD curve, and a movement along the AP curve corresponds to a shift of the AS curve. When AE equals AP, as it does at $4,012, the AS and AD curves will stop shifting. © David Colander.

model. That's incorrect; it is a short-run model of both aggregate demand and aggregate supply.

So that you don't confuse the Keynesian concept of aggregate supply (which is simply total production and is unrelated to the price level) with the Classical concept of aggregate supply (which relates aggregate quantity supplied to the price level), economists call the Keynesian concept *aggregate production* rather than *aggregate supply*. Similarly economists call the Keynesian concept of aggregate demand *aggregate expenditures* rather than *aggregate demand*. The Keynesian model looks at the relationship between aggregate production and aggregate expenditures.

Keep in mind, however, that when we talk about changes in aggregate production and aggregate expenditures, we are talking about shifts of the aggregate supply and aggregate demand curves, not movement along these curves. Exhibit 15(a) demonstrates this relationship, considering the effect of a fall in exports of $20 when the multiplier is 2. As you can see, that fall in exports of $20 will cause income to fall $40, from $4,052 to $4,012.

Exhibit 15(b) shows that same adjustment in aggregate supply and demand curves. Notice here that the price level remains fixed and the *AS* and *AD* curves shift back. Each *shift back* of the *AS* curve in Exhibit 15(b) is equivalent to a *movement along* the aggregate production curve in Exhibit 15(a). Similarly each shift back of the *AD* curve is equivalent to a movement along the aggregate expenditures curve. When the *AE* and *AP* curves intersect, so do the *AS* and *AD* curves.

DIFFERENCES BETWEEN THE KEYNESIAN AND CLASSICAL VIEWS

6

We've now made it through the basic Keynesian model. There are a lot of terms and curves there, but I don't want to let those terms and curves get in the way of the ideas. Classical economists said that in a perfectly competitive market economy with a flexible wage and price level, unemployment could not exist. Thus, the existence of unemployment was evidence that the economy was not competitive. The answer to unemployment was to make the economy competitive.

Keynesian economists agreed that in a perfectly competitive market economy, unemployment could not exist, but they argued that a perfectly competitive economy was impossible. In the absence of perfectly flexible wages and prices, they said that unemployment was caused by a shortage of aggregate demand which started a multiplier process that magnified the initial shift into a much larger shift. After the shifts, the economy would arrive at an aggregate income equilibrium below full-employment equilibrium.

Keynes said cutting wages (the Classical solution to the depression in a competitive economy) wouldn't help much because in response to those wage cuts, firms would simply cut prices. Cutting prices would begin the price adjustment mechanism which would stimulate aggregate demand a bit, but nowhere near enough to solve the problem. Long before the problem was solved by any real-world mechanism relying on a change in the price level, the income adjustment mechanism would shift aggregate supply and aggregate demand and bring about an under–full-employment equilibrium.

At this equilibrium, because there were unemployed resources, there would still be some downward pressure on the price level. And eventually that downward pressure might break down the social and political forces that held the price level constant, thereby moving the economy toward a Classical long-run full-employment equilibrium, but those pressures were weak. Long before these pressures worked, most likely, another shock would have hit the economy and moved the economy to a new short-run equilibrium. In Keynes's view the economy jumped from one short-run equilibrium to another. Those jumps are the business cycles discussed in the first chapter of this section.

When I first studied the Keynesian model, I remember the point at which I finally understood it. Before that point, it was a complicated mathematical set of equations. After that point, it was obvious. I hope that you've made it to that point where the model is obvious. But, beware. When I present New Classical ideas, you'll see that the obvious will no longer seem so obvious.

KEY POINTS

- Keynes focused on the income adjustment mechanism rather than the price level adjustment mechanism because he felt it was more powerful. He felt the Classical price adjustment mechanism was too weak to bring about an aggregate equilibrium. **1**
- The Keynesian model is made up of the aggregate production curve and the aggregate expenditure curve. In equilibrium, planned aggregate production must equal planned aggregate expenditures. **2**
- Aggregate expenditures (AE) is made up of consumption, investment, government spending, and net exports: **2**

$$AE = C + I + G + (X - M).$$

- Consumption depends upon the level of income; the mpc tells us the change in consumption that occurs with a change in income. **2**
- Savings is the mirror image of consumption. When planned aggregate production equals planned aggregate expenditures, planned savings equals planned investment. **2**

- Investment doesn't depend upon the level of income. Shifts in investment or shifts in autonomous consumption can be the initial shock that begins the multiplier process. **2**
- Keynes believed a business cycle is caused by (1) a shock creating a small disequilibrium and (2) the multiplier, which expands that initial shock to a much larger decrease or increase in production and income. The multiplier is the income adjustment mechanism. **2 4**
- The Keynesian equation is **3**

$$Y = \left[\frac{1}{(1 - b)}\right][C_0 + I_0 + G_0 + (X_0 - M_0)].$$

- The multiplier tells us how much a change in autonomous expenditures will change income. **4**
- Keynesians see aggregate equilibrium occurring in shifts of the aggregate supply and aggregate demand curves. Classicals see aggregate equilibrium occurring by movements along the aggregate supply and aggregate demand curves. **5 6**

KEY TERMS

aggregate expenditures *(206)*	average propensity to save (aps) *(211)*	endogenous consumption *(208)*	marginal propensity to consume (mpc) *(208)*
aggregate production *(206)*	consumption function *(208)*	income adjustment mechanism *(204)*	marginal propensity to save (mps) *(211)*
autonomous consumption *(207)*	disposable income *(206)*	investment *(212)*	multiplier *(216)*
average propensity to consume (apc) *(209)*	effective demand *(224)*	Keynesian equation *(215)*	paradox of thrift *(223)*

QUESTIONS FOR THOUGHT AND REVIEW

The number after each question represents the estimated degree of critical thinking required. (1 = almost none; 10 = deep thought.)

1. If there were only three individuals in an economy, would you expect aggregate production to differ from aggregate expenditures? Why or why not? *(5)*
2. If savings were instantaneously translated into investment, what would be the multiplier's size? What would be the level of antonomous expenditures? *(7)*
3. Name some other forces that might cause shocks to aggregate expenditures. *(2)*
4. Mr. Whammo has just invented a magic pill. Take it and it transports you anywhere. Explain his invention's effects on the economy. *(10)*
5. The marginal propensity to consume is .8. Autonomous expenditures are $4,200. What is the level of income in the economy? Demonstrate graphically. *(3)*

6. The marginal propensity to save is .33 and autonomous expenditures have just fallen by $20. What will likely happen to income? *(5)*
7. The marginal propensity to save is .5 and autonomous expenditures have just risen $200. The economy is at its potential level of income. What will likely happen to income? Why? *(9)*
8. Derive the multiplier if the economy has a government expenditures function $G = G_0 + gY$ instead of $G = G_0$. *(8)*
9. Some people have argued that Keynesian economics is appropriate for contractions and Classical economics is appropriate for expansions. Explain why they might be correct. *(8)*
10. How would the Keynesian model change if wages were constant but prices were flexible? *(9)*

PROBLEMS AND EXERCISES

1. Congratulations. You've been appointed economic advisor to Happyland. Your research assistant says the country's mpc is .8 and autonomous investment has just risen by 20.

   a. What will happen to income?

   b. Your research assistant comes in and says he's sorry but the mpc wasn't .8; it was .5. How does your answer change?

   c. He runs in again and says exports have fallen by 10 and investment has risen by 10. How does your answer change?

   d. You now have to present your analysis to the president, who wants to see it all graphically. Naturally you oblige.

2. Congratulations again. You've just been appointed economic advisor to Examland. The mpc is .6; investment is $1,000; government spending is $8,000; autonomous consumption is $10,000; and net exports are $1,000.

   a. What is the level of income in the country?

   b. Net exports increase by $2,000. What will happen to income?

   c. What will happen to unemployment? (Remember Okun's law.)

   d. You've just learned the mps changed from .4 to .5. How will this information change your answers in a, b, and c?

   a. $Y = \left(\frac{1}{1-.6}\right)(10,000 + 1000 + 8000 + 1000) + (2.5)(20,000)$
   $= 50,000$

   b. $2.5 \times 2000 = +5000$

   c. -4%

   d. mul $= 2$, $\therefore$ $40,000 / 4000 / -4\%$

   ─────────────────────────────

   Okin's Law (Rule of Thumb)

   1% chg in unemployment $\Rightarrow 2.5\%$ chg in economy in opp direct.

   $+1\% = -2.5\%$

   $-1\% = +2.5\%$

10

The Complete Keynesian Multiplier Model and Fiscal Policy

Keynes said some things that were new and some things that were true. Unfortunately, the things that were new weren't true and the things that were true weren't new.

Frank Knight

After reading this chapter, you should be able to:

1

Explain expansionary and contractionary fiscal policies.

2

Demonstrate fiscal policy using words, graphs, and the Keynesian equation.

3

Distinguish a structural deficit from a passive deficit.

4

Explain how the trade balance affects income and is affected by income.

5

List six problems with fiscal policy and explain how those problems limit its use.

6

Describe how automatic stabilizers work.

The discussion in the previous chapter highlighted the Keynesian story of: (1) how aggregate income is determined and (2) how small shifts in aggregate expenditure could be multiplied into larger fluctuations in aggregate production and aggregate income. Together these two stories form the Keynesian explanation of why there can be equilibrium at an income level below the full-employment income level and why income in the economy fluctuates.

The Keynesian model was not designed only to understand why fluctuations (booms and busts) occur in the economy; it was also designed to suggest *policies* to deal with the depression, policies that would get the economy out of its under–full-employment equilibrium. Keynes offered an alternative to the Classical laissez-faire policy.

Keynes's initial policy proposals were for public works (for the government to spend more without collecting more taxes to pay for the spending or, in other words, to run a deficit by spending more). Keynesians soon broadened that policy to include: (1) another way to stimulate the economy—by reducing taxes, (2) a way to slow down the economy when it was called for—by decreasing government spending or increasing taxes, and (3) policies to change the money supply as a way of controlling the economy.

We'll see Keynesian policy affecting money in later chapters. In this chapter, we consider government policies that change the level of government spending and taxes as a way of affecting the economy.

FISCAL POLICY

Fiscal policy The policy of changing the level of either government spending or taxes to stimulate or slow down the economy.

■ 1

Policy aimed at changing the level of either government spending or taxes to stimulate or slow down the economy is known as **fiscal policy.** Or, looking at that another way, fiscal policy is the manipulation of the government budget deficit or surplus to influence the level of aggregate income (or GDP) in the economy. If aggregate income is too low (actual income is below target income), the appropriate fiscal policy is *expansionary fiscal policy:* increase the deficit, or reduce a surplus, which means the government spends more or takes in less. If aggregate income is too high (actual income is above target income), the appropriate fiscal policy is *contractionary fiscal policy:* reduce the deficit, or increase a surplus, which means the government takes in more in taxes or spends less.

Keynesians considered fiscal policy the steering wheel for the aggregate economy. They said Classical economists with their laissez-faire policy were trying to drive an economy without any steering wheel. If that were the case, is it any wonder the economy crashed?

In the 1930s everyone agreed that income was too low and that if fiscal policy worked, the appropriate fiscal policy was expansionary. Keynesians advocated that governments run deficits. That advocacy made Keynesian economics the center of political debate at the time. Keynesians were accused of being communists, of looking for a way to destroy the U.S. economy, because they advocated running a deficit. In the late 1940s and early 1950s, textbooks that included the Keynesian model were subject to vehement attack; university presidents and trustees were pressured to fire any professor who used a "Keynesian" text. Much has changed since then. By the 1960s and 1970s fiscal policy was a well-established tool of most governments, and Keynesian economics had become mainstream economics. Such was the influence of the Keynesian model.

The Story of Keynesian Fiscal Policy

Let's start this discussion with the story of fiscal policy for an economy in a depression. What caused that depression? As we saw in the last chapter, when people got scared and cut back their spending, the multiplier took over and expanded that small negative shock into a full-blown depression. In a depression, aggregate production and aggregate expenditures are equal, but at a level of income and production far below the potential level of income—below full employment of all productive resources.

Seeing this low level of income and understanding the Keynesian model of the previous chapter, you should be led to the following insight: If somehow you can

THE ECONOMIC STEERING WHEEL

Our economic system is frequently put to shame in being displayed before an imaginary visitor from a strange planet. It is time to reverse the procedure. Imagine yourself instead in a Buck Rogers interplanetary adventure, looking at a highway in a City of Tomorrow. The highway is wide and straight, and its edges are turned up so that it is almost impossible for a car to run off the road. What appears to be a runaway car is speeding along the road and veering off to one side. As it approaches the rising edge of the highway, its front wheels are turned so that it gets back onto the road and goes off at an angle, making for the other side, where the wheels are turned again. This happens many times, the car zigzagging but keeping on the highway until it is out of sight. You are wondering how long it will take for it to crash, when another car appears which behaves in the same fashion. When it comes near you it stops with a jerk. A door is opened, and an occupant asks whether you would like a lift. You look into the car and before you can control yourself you cry out, "Why, there's no steering wheel."

"Of course we have no steering wheel," says one of the occupants rather crossly. "Just think how it would cramp the front seat. It's worse than an old-fashioned gearshift lever and it's dangerous. Suppose we have a steering wheel and somebody held on to it when we reached a curb. He would prevent the automatic turning of the wheel, and the car would surely be overturned. And besides, we believe in democracy and cannot give anyone the extreme authority of life and death over all the occupants of the car. That would be dictatorship."

"Down with dictatorship," chorus the other occupants of the car.

"If you are worried about the way the car goes from side to side," continues the first speaker, "forget it. We have wonderful brakes so that collisions are prevented nine times out of ten. On our better roads the curb is so effective that one can travel hundreds of miles without going off the road once. We have a very efficient system of carrying survivors of wrecks to nearby hospitals and for rapidly

sweeping the remnants from the road to deposit them on nearby fields as a reminder to man of the inevitability of death."

You look around to see the piles of wrecks and burned-out automobiles as the man in the car continues. "Impressive, isn't it? But things are going to improve. See those men marking and photographing the tracks of the car that preceded us? They are going to take those pictures into their laboratories and pictures of our tracks, too, to analyze the cyclical characteristics of the curves, their degree of regularity, the average distance from turn to turn, the amplitude of the swings, and so on. When they have come to an agreement on their true nature we may know whether something can be done about it. At present they are disputing whether this cyclical movement is due to the type of road surface or to its shape or whether it is due to the length of the car or the kind of rubber in the tires or to the weather. Some of them think that it will be impossible to avoid having cycles unless we go back to the horse and buggy, but we can't do that because we believe in Progress. Well, want a ride?"

The dilemma between saving your skin and humoring the lunatics is resolved by your awakening from the nightmare, and you feel glad that the inhabitants of your own planet are a little more reasonable. But are they as reasonable about other things as they are about the desirability of steering their automobiles? Do they not behave exactly like the men in the nightmare when it comes to operating their economic system? Do they not allow their economic automobile to bounce from depression to inflation in wide and uncontrolled arcs? Through their failure to steer away from unemployment and idle factories are they not just as guilty of public injury and insecurity as the mad motorists of Mars?

Source: Abba Lerner, "The Economic Steering Wheel," first published in *The University Review*, vol. 7, no. 4 (June 1941), pp. 257–65 (now NEW LETTERS), June 1941. Used by permission.

generate a countershock (a jolt in the opposite direction of the shift in autonomous expenditure that started the depression), you can get the multiplier working in reverse, expanding the economy in the same way the initial shock and multiplier had contracted it. You need a countershock to motivate people to spend, and as they increase their spending, society will be better off. But each individual, acting in her own interest, has no incentive to spend more. Each individual would reason: If I spend more, I'll be worse off. Theoretically, my additional spending might help society, but the positive effect would be so diluted that, in terms of my own situation, I don't see how my increased spending is going to benefit me.

For example, if a grocery store clerk increased her shopping expenditures by $100, only about $25 of that expenditure would go into food, so if her store is one of five stores selling various articles in the area where she shops, only $5 would go to her store. If she were one of 20 employees, her $5 represents only an additional 25¢ spending per employee at the store. If she were about to lose her job, her $100 spending wouldn't save it. However, if *all* individuals, or a large proportion of all individuals, increased their spending by $100 each, spending at her store would rise considerably and her job would likely be saved.

One of the subthemes of this book is that economic thought and policy are more complicated than an introductory book must necessarily make it seem. "Keynesian policy" is a good case in point. In the early 1930s, before Keynes wrote *The General Theory*, he was advocating public works programs and deficits as a way to get the British economy out of the depression. He came upon what we now call the *Keynesian theory* as he tried to explain to Classical economists why he supported deficits. After arriving at his new theory, however, he spent little time advocating fiscal policy and, in fact, never mentions fiscal policy in *The General Theory*, the book that presents his theory. The book's primary policy recommendation is the need to socialize investments—for the government to take over the investment decisions from private individuals. When one of his followers, Abba Lerner, advocated expansionary fiscal policy at a seminar Keynes attended, Keynes strongly objected, leading Evsey Domar, another Keynesian follower, to whisper to a friend, "Keynes should read *The General Theory*."

What's going on here? There are many interpretations, but the one I find most convincing is the one presented by historian Peter Clarke. He argues that after finishing *The General Theory*, Keynes turned his interest from a policy revolution to a theoretical revolution. He believed he had found a serious flaw in Classical economic theory. The Classicals assumed full employment, but did not show how the economy could move to that equilibrium from a disequilibrium. That's when Keynes's interest changed from a policy to a theoretical revolution.

His followers, such as Lerner, carried out the policy implications of his theory. Why did Keynes sometimes oppose these policy implications? Because he was also a student of politics and he recognized economic theory can often lead to politically unacceptable policies. In a letter to a friend he later said Lerner was right in his logic, but he hoped the opposition didn't discover what Lerner was saying. Keynes was more than an economist; he was a politician as well.

How do you simultaneously get all or most individuals to spend more than they want to? In the 1930s government found it wasn't easy. President Franklin Roosevelt went on radio to calm people's fears ("We have nothing to fear but fear itself") and to encourage people to spend to create more jobs.

According to the Keynesian model, these admonitions could have worked if they had generated sufficient initial spending; that initial increase would have generated some more spending which, in turn, would have generated even more spending. But these admonitions didn't work. The Keynesian model offered expansionary fiscal policy as an alternative.

With fiscal policy government could provide the needed increased spending by decreasing taxes, increasing government spending, or both. Fiscal policy would provide the initial expansionary spending, increasing individuals' incomes. As individuals' incomes increased, they would spend more. As they spent more, the multiplier process would take over and expand the effect of the initial spending.

Keynesians argued that fiscal policy—the policy of government changing its spending and taxing to influence production and income levels in the economy—was the missing steering wheel of the economy.

Thus, both cutting taxes and increasing government expenditures are expansionary fiscal policy. The government provides the initial expansionary shock, and then the multiplier takes hold and expands the economy.

There is nothing special about government's ability to stimulate the economy with additional spending. If a group of individuals wanted to—and had spending power large enough to make a difference—they could do so, but private individuals don't have the incentive to do so. Their spending helps mainly other people and has only a small feedback on themselves. Unless they're altruistic, they don't take into account the effect of their spending on the aggregate spending stream and hence on aggregate income.

The significantly different effects when everyone does something rather than when only one person does it play an important role in economics. This difference has a number of names: the public goods problem, the tragedy of the commons, and the multiperson dilemma.

The problem is neatly seen by considering a football game. If everyone is standing, and you sit down, you can't see. Everyone is better off standing. No one has an incentive to sit down. However, if somehow all individuals could be enticed to sit down, all individuals would be even better off. Sitting down is a public good—a good that benefits others—but one that nobody on his or her own will do. Keynes argued that, in times of depression, spending is a public good because it benefits everyone, so government should spend.

Now that you've got the idea of fiscal policy, let's consider how fiscal policy works in the Keynesian equation developed in the previous chapter.

$$\Delta Y = [1/(1 - b)][\Delta C_0 + \Delta I_0 + \Delta G_0 - b\Delta T_0 + \Delta(X_0 - M_0)].$$

This equation tells you how much income will change, ΔY, in response to a change in any component of autonomous expenditures. (If it isn't familiar, I'm afraid it's review time.)

Fiscal policy operates by shifting government expenditures (ΔG_0) or taxes ($b\Delta T_0$). This causes an initial shift which will be increased by the multiplier $[1/(1 - b)]$ times that initial shift. For example, say $mpc = .75$ so the multiplier is 4. Say government increases its expenditures by \$100. Income will rise by \$400 (4 × \$100).

Fiscal Policy in
the Keynesian Model

2

The Differential Effect of Cutting Taxes and Increasing Government Spending   The government can also increase income by decreasing taxes. However, to increase income by the same amount, you need to cut taxes by more than you need to expand government spending. To see why, let's return to the Keynesian model. For simplicity we assume all autonomous expenditures except government spending and taxes remain constant. (In other words, $\Delta C_0 = 0$, $\Delta I_0 = 0$, and $\Delta(X_0 - M_0) = 0$.) This leaves only ΔG_0 and $b\Delta T_0$ as the autonomous changes. We'll look at the effect of government spending and the effect of taxes separately:

change in government spending	change in taxes
$\Delta Y = \dfrac{1}{(1 - b)}\Delta G_0$	$\Delta Y = \dfrac{1}{(1 - b)}(-b\Delta T_0)$

As you can see, two things about the change in taxes make it different from a change in government spending:

1. There is a minus sign associated with taxes.
2. ΔT_0 is reduced by the amount of the fraction b whereas ΔG_0 is not.

The minus sign associated with taxes tells us that a change in taxes works in the opposite direction from a change in government spending. The reasoning for the minus sign with taxes is intuitively obvious. An *in*crease in taxes reduces expenditures as does a *de*crease in government expenditures. That's all the negative sign tells us.

The b associated with the change in taxes is intuitively more complicated, but it does have an intuitive explanation. The explanation is that changes in taxes affect aggregate income indirectly through the consumption function:

$$C = C_0 + b(Y - T_0).$$

To see this, say government cuts taxes by \$100. That has no direct effect on expenditures. But it does increase disposable income by \$100, which in turn

Lawrence Klein—Nobel prize, 1980, for work on Keynesian macroeconomic modeling. © The Nobel Foundation.

2

Recessionary gap The difference between equilibrium income and potential income when potential income exceeds equilibrium income.

increases individuals' consumption by $75. That $75 has a multiplied effect on the economy. The other $25 goes immediately into savings.

So even though taxes aren't listed as an expenditure, when the government cuts taxes, it increases people's disposable income which, in turn, increases individuals' consumption, shifting the aggregate expenditures curve up. Alternatively an increase in taxes shifts the aggregate expenditures curve down. Because taxes affect the economy through disposable income (not directly through expenditure), the effects of the same amounts of change in government expenditures and in taxes don't totally offset each other. The expenditure function shifts down less because of taxes than the expenditure function shifts up because of an equal amount of government expenditures. So if government increases expenditures and taxes equally, there will be a slightly expansionary effect on the economy. (At one time the differential effect between taxes and government expenditures was considered important for policy. Today it's considered rather unimportant because of the economy's unpredictability and political limitations on the use of fiscal policy, as we'll discuss later in this chapter.)

Exhibit 1 graphs the way fiscal policy works. An increase in government expenditures (or a decrease in taxes) shifts the aggregate expenditures curve up as in Exhibit 1(a); a decrease in government expenditures (or an increase in taxes) shifts the aggregate expenditures curve down as in Exhibit 1(b). In both cases, notice income changes by a multiple of the change in government expenditure. That's the multiplier in action.

Controlling the Level of Income with Fiscal Policy   Having determined how an increase in government spending can shift the aggregate expenditures curve, let's now consider how government can control the level of aggregate income in the economy with fiscal policy.

Fighting Recession: Expansionary Fiscal Policy   Let's first consider the case where the economy is in a recession (Exhibit 2). Initially the economy is at equilibrium at income level $1,000 which is below potential income ($1,180). When equilibrium income is below potential income, this difference is called a **recessionary gap.** If everything goes as it should in the Keynesian story, this is what happens. The government recognizes this recessionary gap in aggregate income of, say, $180 and responds by increasing government expenditures by $60. This shifts the AE curve from AE_0 upward to AE_1, increasing aggregate income to the full-potential aggregate income level. Such government action is called *expansionary fiscal policy*.

Businesses that receive government contracts hire the workers who have been laid off by other firms and open new plants; income increases by $60. But the process doesn't stop there. At this point, the multiplier process sets in. As the newly employed workers spend more, other businesses find that their demand increases. They hire more workers, who spend an additional $40 (since their mpc = .67). This increases income further. The same process occurs again and again. By the time the process has ended, income has risen by $180 and is back at $1,180, the potential level of income.

How did the government economists know to increase spending by $60? They knew by backward induction. They empirically estimated that the slope of the aggregate expenditures curve was .67, which meant that the multiplier was $1/(1 - .67) = 1/.33 = 3$. They divided the multiplier, 3, into the recessionary gap, $180, and determined that if they increased spending by $60, income would increase by $180.

2   **Fighting Inflation: Contractionary Fiscal Policy**   Keynes devised and developed his model around a depression. However in principle there's no reason why fiscal policy can't work in reverse (decreasing expenditures that are too high), given the assumptions of the model. You might think that it's impossible for income to be

(a)   **(b)**

EXHIBIT 1 (a and b)   Fiscal Policy

The government can use fiscal policy as a tool to shift the *AE* curve. An increase in government spending or a decrease in taxes (**a**) shifts the *AE* curve upward by ΔG_0 or by $-b\Delta T_0$. A decrease in government spending or an increase in taxes (**b**) shifts the *AE* curve down by $-\Delta G_0$ or by $b\Delta T_0$. Income changes by a multiple of the change in taxes or spending.

EXHIBIT 2   Fighting a Recession

If the economy is below its potential income level, the government can increase its expenditures to stimulate the economy. The multiplier process takes over and expands the initial shock of the additional spending until actual income equals potential income.

too high, and that, instead, at higher incomes everyone is better off. This is not always the case. Expenditures are "too high" when instead of causing real income to increase, they cause inflationary pressure. If there's inflationary pressure, people on average want to raise their prices, which either causes shortages if wages and prices are fixed (can't be raised) or inflation if wages and prices are not fixed. When this is the case, the aggregate supply curve cannot shift out any further so there is excess demand and demand-pull inflation, as Exhibit 3 shows.

EXHIBIT 3   Excess Demand and Demand-Pull Inflation

Once the *AS* curve shifts out to potential income, it cannot shift out any more. If the quantity of aggregate demand (AD_0) exceeds the quantity of aggregate supply (AS_0) at that fixed price level, there will be excess demand of Q_D-Q_S and demand-pull inflation.

Inflationary gap   The difference between equilibrium income and potential income when equilibrium income exceeds potential income.

$$\Delta Y = \frac{1}{1-b}(-b\Delta T_0)$$

$$\frac{\Delta Y}{5} = -.8\,\Delta T_0$$

$$\frac{\Delta Y}{-.8 \times 5} = \Delta T_0$$

$$\frac{-1000}{-4} = \Delta T_0$$

$$250 = \Delta T_0$$

Fiscal Policy and the Structural Deficit

Remember from the previous chapter, the Keynesian model is a *fixed price* model that tells a story about a chase between aggregate supply and demand. For that chase to occur, aggregate supply must be below potential output. Once the quantity of aggregate demand shifts up beyond potential output, the fixed price assumption is no longer relevant and inflation occurs. Whenever equilibrium income exceeds potential income, there's said to be an **inflationary gap.** When there's an inflationary gap, expenditures are too high. To prevent inflation, Keynesians believe that the government should exercise contractionary fiscal policy (cutting government spending or raising taxes).

Exhibit 4 shows a numerical example of contractionary fiscal policy at work. Potential income is $4,000, *mpc* = .8, but the equilibrium level of income is $5,000. Thus, there is an inflationary gap of $1,000, which causes upward pressure on wages and prices with no additional output resulting.

This case calls for contractionary fiscal policy. The government increases taxes by $250, shifting the *AE* curve from AE_0 to AE_1, which decreases the equilibrium level of income by $1,000, back to $4,000, the potential level of income. The government has offset the expansionary shock with contractionary fiscal policy.

How did the government know to increase taxes by $250? Again, by backward induction. The multiplier, [1/(1 − *b*)], is 5, but the government knows that not all the tax increase will decrease expenditures since people will reduce their savings in order to hold their expenditures up. Expenditures will initially fall by the *mpc* multiplied by the increased taxes, or (.8 × $250) = $200, and then the multiplier will operate on that $200. Since the multiplier is 5, the total decrease will be (5 × $200) = $1,000. As you can see, once the government knows the multiplier and the inflationary or recessionary gap, it can determine what fiscal policy it should use to achieve the potential level of income.

Our preceding two examples made some simplifying assumptions to ease your introduction to fiscal policy. One assumption was that the size of the deficit was independent of income. In the real world, the size of the deficit is not independent of income. In the real world, a large portion of government tax revenues depends on income. The model we have been using assumes taxes are autonomous when, in fact, as income increases, tax revenues increase, while as income falls, tax revenues fall. Specifically, as opposed to being autonomous, a large portion of

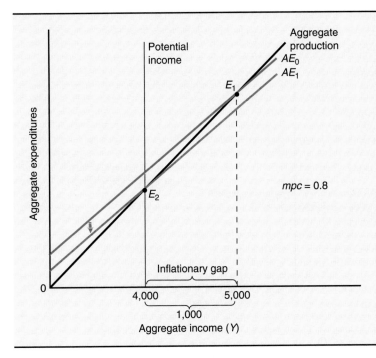

EXHIBIT 4   **Fighting Inflation**

When equilibrium income exceeds potential income, the economy has an inflationary gap. There will be either shortages, or inflation, or both. In this case, contractionary fiscal policy, shifting the *AE* curve downward, is called for.

taxes is **endogenous** (determined inside the model). Endogenous taxes are that portion of taxes that are dependent on the level of income in the economy. A more realistic tax function that incorporates endogenous taxes is

$$T = T_0 + tY$$

where

T_0 = autonomous taxes
t = tax rate per dollar of income
Y = income.

Let's consider how this relationship affects the analysis.

Exhibit 5(a), a table of government expenditures and taxes at various income levels, gives us the information needed to calculate the tax function. To do so, we see that each time income changes by $20, taxes change by $5, or by .25$Y$. So tax rate ($t$) is .25.

Autonomous taxes are determined by calculating what tax revenues would be if income were zero. To do so, we extend the table back to income level zero and determine if income were zero, tax revenue would be $17.50. So the tax function associated with this table is

$$T = \$17.50 + .25Y.$$

All tax revenues other than $17.50 are endogenous. As you can see, government tax revenues increase as aggregate income increases. This means that the government budget deficit (the difference between government expenditures and government tax revenue) decreases as aggregate income increases. For example, if aggregate income goes up by $20, government revenues go up by $5 while government expenditures remain constant, so the government budget deficit falls when income increases.

Exhibit 5(b) graphs the information in the table. Government expenditures do not change relative to aggregate income; therefore *G* has zero slope and intersects the vertical axis at *G* = $100. Regardless of what income is, government expenditure is $100; it is autonomous.[1] The government tax function, however, slopes

Endogenous Determined inside the model.

---

[1] Actually government spending is not totally autonomous either. Some government spending, especially government transfer payments (which do not show up in the government expenditure function), depends on income, but that dependence is relatively small and can be assumed away for now.

EXHIBIT 5 (a and b)   Government Expenditures and Taxes

A characteristic of most economies is that as income changes, tax revenues change in the same direction. In the example given in **(a)**, as income rises by $20, say from $310 to $330, tax revenues increase by $5, from $95 to $100. This lowers the government budget deficit.

The relationships in **(a)** are presented graphically in **(b)**. The government expenditures curve is unaffected by changes in income. Thus its slope is zero. The government tax curve is upward-sloping, so as income increases, taxes increase. The shaded areas represent the government budget deficit or surplus.

Y	G	T	Deficit (–) or surplus (+)	Row
$250	$100	$80	$–20	A
270	100	85	–15	B
290	100	90	–10	C
310	100	95	–5	D
330	100	100	0	E
350	100	105	+5	F
370	100	110	+10	G

(a)

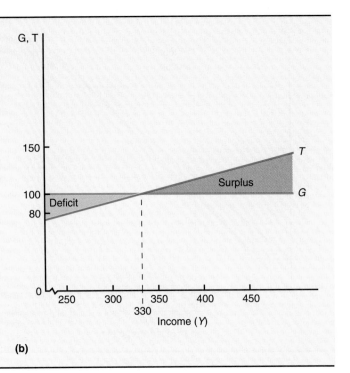

(b)

upward, reflecting the fact that tax revenues increase with aggregate income. Since the government's major revenue sources are taxes related to income, when income rises, more income is subject to income tax, so government tax revenues rise. When income falls, tax revenues fall.

The difference between government revenues and government expenditures (the shaded area) is the budget surplus or deficit. As you can see, at low levels of income the government has a deficit. At high levels of income the deficit is reduced and, if expenditures don't change, the deficit can become a surplus.

Fiscal policy shifts either the tax curve or the government spending curve. Expansionary fiscal policy shifts the tax curve down or the government spending curve up, causing the deficit to be larger. Contractionary fiscal policy shifts the tax curve up or the government spending curve down, causing the deficit to be smaller.

Including endogenous government taxes modifies the Keynesian equation. (This chapter's appendix presents a complete model including endogenous government taxes.) Specifically it reduces the multiplier's size by the effect of the endogenous taxes. As opposed to being $[1/(1 - b)]$, the multiplier becomes $[1/(1 - b + bt)]$. Thus, for example, say mpc (b) is .75 and the tax rate is .25. With a zero tax rate, the multiplier would be $1/(1 - .75) = 4$. When the tax rate equals .25, the multiplier is 2.3:

$$1/[1 - .75 + (.75 \times .25)] = 1/(1 - .75 + .188) = 1/.438 = 2.28.$$

The multiplier decreases from 4 to 2.3.

What's the general reasoning behind this decrease in the multiplier? When there's an income tax, in each round of the multiplier there will be an additional withdrawal from the flow of income. Withdrawals make the multiplier smaller and the aggregate expenditures curve flatter.

Structural and Passive Deficits

3 Because the size of the government budget deficit depends on the level of income and also affects the level of income, it's difficult to talk unambiguously about fiscal policy. Is the government running a deficit to stimulate the economy? Or is the deficit simply the result of a fall in the level of aggregate income?

To differentiate between these two cases, economists use a reference income level at which to judge fiscal policy. That reference income level is their estimate of the economy's potential level of income. They then ask: Would the economy have a deficit if it were at its potential level of income? The portion of the deficit that would exist even if the economy were at its potential level of income is called a **structural deficit.** If an economy is operating below its potential, the actual deficit will be larger than the structural deficit. The portion of the deficit that exists because the economy is operating below its potential level of output is called a **passive deficit.** Economists believe that an economy can eliminate a passive deficit through growth in income, whereas it can't grow out of a structural deficit. Because the economy can't grow out of structural deficits, they are of more concern to policy makers than are passive deficits.

In reality there is significant debate about what an economy's potential income level is, and hence there is disagreement about what percentage of a deficit is structural and what part is passive. Nonetheless, the distinction is often used and is important to remember.

Structural deficit A deficit that would exist even if the economy were at its potential level of income.

Passive deficit The portion of the deficit that exists because the economy is operating below its potential level of income.

To see whether you follow the analysis, let's consider an example.

You have the following information about the economy:

An Example

$$\text{Actual income} = \$3,000$$
$$\text{Potential income} = \$3,400$$
$$\text{mpc} = .6$$
$$\text{Tax rate} = .15$$
$$\text{Current budget deficit} = \$100.$$

The government wants you to prescribe a policy that will increase aggregate income to its potential level. What do you prescribe?

To answer the question you work backward, determining that there is a recessionary gap of $3,400 - \$3,000 = \$400$. You then calculate the multiplier as follows:

$$1/(1 - b + bt) = 1/[1 - .6 + (.6 \times .15)] = 1/(1 - .6 + .09) = 1/.49 = 2.$$

Dividing the multiplier, 2, into the recessionary gap of $400 gives $200, so your proposal should be to increase government expenditures by $200 which in turn would increase the deficit from $100 to $300.

However you should point out that once income increases, the actual deficit won't increase by $200. Since income increases by $400, and the tax rate is 15 percent, tax revenues will rise by $60 so the final deficit will not be $300, but will be $300 - \$60 = \$240$.

Of that initial $100 deficit, $60 was a passive deficit and $40 was a structural deficit. The final $240 deficit is all structural (a deficit that growth can't eliminate) since after the policy has been implemented the economy is at its potential level of output.

Once there was a time when development of the Keynesian model stopped with the addition of endogenous government taxes. International issues did not need to be considered because their role was minor. No longer. The balance of trade (net exports) has become an important policy issue for the U.S. economy. In the late 1980s and early 1990s the U.S. economy experienced large balance of trade deficits. (Net exports have been negative.) Thus, any exposition of the Keynesian model must include an analysis of net exports and the effect of fiscal policy on the trade deficit. So we'll now consider our second simplifying assumption.

The previous chapter introduced net exports to the Keynesian model with a simplification that doesn't accord with reality. There we assumed that both exports and imports were autonomous. While that assumption is approximately true for exports, it is not for imports.

NET EXPORTS AND THE COMPLETE KEYNESIAN MULTIPLIER MODEL

So the previous chapter's equation for exports ($X = X_0$) is reasonable, but imports are more realistically given by

$$M = M_0 + mY$$

where

M_0 = autonomous imports
m = marginal propensity to import.

So net exports ($X - M$) equals

$$(X - M) = X_0 - M_0 - mY.$$

4   This equation tells us that the level of imports depends on the level of income. That means that net exports is endogenous: *when income changes, imports will change; hence net exports ($X - M$) will change.* When U.S. income goes up, the amount of foreign products we buy goes up and so imports go up. When U.S. income goes down, the amount of foreign products we buy goes down; we import less. The **marginal propensity to import** (*mpm* or simply *m*) tells us what the change in imports will be if there's a change in income.[2] The importance of this relationship between imports and income was demonstrated in 1991 and 1992 when the U.S. economy went into recession. Imports fell and the trade deficit decreased from over $100 billion to about $70 billion.

But this is not the only relationship between net exports and income. The Keynesian model tells us that a change in the trade balance affects income. It follows that, like the government budget deficit, net exports has a dual relationship with income. First, it affects net income—a trade surplus can stimulate an economy; a trade deficit can slow it down. Second, net exports—the U.S. trade balance—is in turn affected by income.

Taking this second relationship between income and net exports into account adds another withdrawal from each round of the multiplier process. It reduces the multiplier's size. Specifically, as opposed to being $[1/(1 - b + bt)]$, the multiplier becomes $[1/(1 - b + bt + m)]$. Using our earlier example, if $b = .75$ and $t = .25$, in the absence of imports depending on income ($m = 0$), the multiplier would be 2.3 as we calculated previously. With endogenous imports and a marginal propensity to import of .1, the multiplier in the Keynesian equation is once again modified. Specifically it becomes

$$\frac{1}{[1 - .75 + .75(.25) + .1]} = \frac{1}{(1 - .75 + .188 + .1)} = \frac{1}{.538} = 1.86.$$

The size of the multiplier falls from 2.3 to 1.86. The effect of any change in exogenous expenditures is reduced as some of that change is absorbed in the international economy.

The implication of the first relationship could be seen in the late 1980s when U.S. net exports were significantly negative—imports exceeded exports by $150 billion a year. The large trade deficit made aggregate expenditures on U.S. goods lower than they otherwise would have been. Had that been the only effect on aggregate expenditures, income would have fallen (net exports affecting income), and the U.S. balance of trade deficit would have fallen (income affecting net exports). But that wasn't the only effect on aggregate expenditures. Simultaneously the U.S. government was running a deficit of approximately $150 billion, which made aggregate expenditures higher than they otherwise would have been. The deficit pushed income up (the deficit affecting income), which would have increased tax revenue and decreased the deficit (income affecting the deficit).

These effects were occurring at the same time. The United States had twin deficits: a government budget deficit and a balance of trade deficit. The twin deficit effects canceled out.

Marginal propensity to import The percent change in imports associated with a percent change in income.

---

[2] For example, if the *mpm* is .1 and income rises by $20, imports will rise by $2. (.1 × $20 = $2.)

The fact that income affects the trade deficit presents yet another effect policy makers must take into account. They must worry about what happens to imports and the trade balance as they conduct fiscal policy to achieve domestic goals.

Now that we've become familiar with each component, we're ready to put them all together into the **complete Keynesian equation:**[3]

$$Y = \frac{1}{(1 - b + bt + m)} \times (C_0 + I_0 + G_0 - bT_0 + X_0 - M_0).$$

Notice that both the tax rate (t), and the marginal propensity to import (m), have a plus sign and thus reduce the multiplier's size. They are withdrawals from the income stream, like the marginal propensity to save.

Most relationships economists are interested in concern the effect of changes in exogenous expenditures on changes in income. Thus the complete Keynesian equation is often presented in terms of changes in autonomous expenditures and income:

$$\Delta Y = \frac{1}{(1 - b + bt + m)} \times [\Delta C_0 + \Delta I_0 + \Delta G_0 - b\Delta T_0 + \Delta(X_0 - M_0)].$$

This equation can be used to determine the effect of policy initiatives on income. For example, say the government runs a successful export drive. If exogenous exports increase by 20, what will happen? Income will rise by $[1/(1 - b + bt + m)] \times 20$. Given b, t, and m, you can calculate how much that will cause U.S. income to rise and what effect that rise would have on the trade deficit and government budget deficit.

A Numerical Example Let's consider an example to show you how the model is applied. Let's say that income is $3,000 and potential income is $3,500. The government wants to know what policy it should follow to increase income from $3,000 to $3,500, which it has determined is the level of potential income. First, the economist will estimate the values of b, m, and t by statistical analysis so that he or she can determine the multiplier. Let's say the economist estimates $b = .9$, $m = .2$, and $t = .22$. Substituting these numbers into the formula for the multiplier,

$$\frac{1}{(1 - b + bt + m)},$$

the economist would estimate the multiplier to be

$$\frac{1}{1 - .9 + .9(.22) + .2} = \frac{1}{.5} = 2.$$

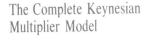

Having determined that the multiplier is 2 and that potential income exceeds current income by $500, the economist divides that $500 by 2 to determine the amount exogenous expenditures must increase: $250.

The economist's next step is estimating what's likely to happen to those autonomous expenditures that the government doesn't control, such as autonomous exports, imports, and investment. Let's say the economist determines that those autonomous factors will rise by $200. Subtracting that $200 from the needed increase in autonomous expenditures gives ($250 − $200) = $50. An additional $50 of autonomous expenditures is needed. This increase can be achieved by expansionary fiscal policy: either increasing government expenditures by $50 or

The Complete Keynesian Multiplier Model

2

Complete Keynesian equation The equation relating income and autonomous expenditures when income tax and changing imports are taken into account.

---

[3] This equation is called a *reduced-form equation*. It embodies all the relationships we've just discussed. It is derived formally in this chapter's appendix.

The real-world models economists use are far more complicated than this one. Real-world models incorporate the monetary sector and many more interrelationships. Nonetheless the *multiplier model*, as the simple Keynesian model is sometimes called, gives you a good sense both of macroeconomic modeling and of some key relationships in the Keynesian approach to the aggregate economy.

decreasing taxes by $55.56.[4] Either would increase income by $100, which combined with the effect of the $200 shifts in other exogenous expenditures (which increased income by $400) would equal the $500 increase in equilibrium income needed for the economy to achieve the potential level of income.

The economist might also be asked what effect the policy would have on the trade deficit. To answer that question, she would look at the marginal propensity to import, which is .2. Expansionary fiscal policy would increase income by 100 and hence increase the trade deficit by $(.2 \times 100) = 20$ from what it otherwise would have been.

To see whether you can work with this model, say what policy you would propose to eliminate a trade deficit of 10.[5]

Countercyclical Policy and Fine-Tuning The essence of fiscal policy is government changing its taxes and its spending to offset any deviation that would occur in other autonomous expenditures, thereby keeping the economy at its potential level of income.

If government can act fast enough, and change its taxes and spending in a *countercyclical* way, depressions can be prevented. A fiscal policy in which the government offsets any shock that would create a business cycle is called **countercyclical fiscal policy.** Such countercyclical policy designed to keep the economy always at its potential level of income is called **fine-tuning.**

Countercyclical fiscal policy A fiscal policy in which the government offsets any shock that would create a business cycle.

Fine-tuning Countercyclical fiscal policy designed to keep the economy at its potential level of income.

A Real-World Example

To give you an idea of how fiscal policy works in the real world, we'll look at a couple of examples. Let's first consider what happened in World War II.

The depression in the United States continued through the 1930s. However by the beginning of the 1940s it was no longer the focus of U.S. policy as the war in Europe (which had started in 1939) and in the Pacific (where it had started somewhat earlier) became more and more the central issue, especially after December 7, 1941, when Japan attacked the United States by bombing Pearl Harbor in Hawaii. At that point the United States entered the war against Japan and soon thereafter entered the war against Germany.

Fighting a war costs money, so economists' attention turned to how to raise that money. Taxes went up enormously, but government expenditures rose far more. The result can be seen in Exhibit 6(a), which tabulates GNP, the deficit, and unemployment data for 1937–46. As you can see, the deficit increased greatly and income rose by more than the deficit. Exhibit 6(b) shows the Keynesian multiplier model which describes those effects. As predicted, the U.S. economy expanded enormously in response to the expansionary fiscal policy that accompanied the war. (The wartime expansion was accompanied by wage and price controls and a large increase in the money supply, so we must be careful about drawing too strong an inference from this expansion.)

It might seem from the example of World War II, when the U.S. economy expanded sharply, that wars are good for the economy. They certainly do bring about expansionary policy, increase GDP, and decrease unemployment. But remember, GDP is *not* welfare and a decrease in unemployment is not necessarily good. In World War II people went without basic necessities; production of guns and bombs increased but production of butter decreased. Many people were killed or permanently disabled, which decreases unemployment but can hardly be called a good way to expand the economy and lower unemployment.

---

[4] Remember, the taxes' initial effect is multiplied by the *mpc*. The tax decrease must be large enough to compensate. To arrive at how much to cut taxes, divide the needed government expenditure stimulus by *mpc* (in this case, 50/.9 = 55.56).

[5] The correct answer is to run contractionary fiscal policy, decreasing government expenditure by 25, which would decrease income by 50 and imports by 10. I chose this example to demonstrate that international goals can, and often do, conflict with domestic goals. To achieve the desired trade balance with fiscal policy, the government would have to give up achieving its potential income.

EXHIBIT 6 (a and b)   War Finance: Expansionary Fiscal Policy

During wars, government budget deficits have risen significantly. As they have, unemployment has fallen and GNP has risen enormously. You can see the effect in the table in (**a**), which presents the U.S. government budget deficit and unemployment rate during World War II. The graph in (**b**) shows that this is what would be predicted by the Keynesian model.

Year	GNP (billions of dollars)	Deficit (billions of dollars)	Unemployment rate
1937	90	−2.8	14.3
1938	84	−1.0	19.0
1939	90	−2.9	17.2
1940	99	−2.7	14.6
1941	124	−4.8	9.9
1942	157	−19.4	4.7
1943	191	−53.8	1.9
1944	210	−46.1	1.2
1945	211	−45.0	1.9
1946	208	−18.2	3.9

(a)

(b)

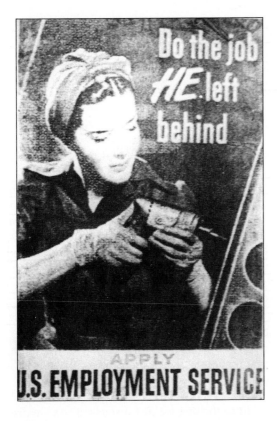

During World War II unemployment fell enormously, and the government issued many posters to get women to work. After the war, the government issued many posters to get women to give up their jobs for "their men."   © *James L. Shaffer.*

As a second example of how economists think about fiscal policy, let's look into the future to the middle and late 1990s when the revenue that the U.S. government gets from social security taxes is predicted to be much higher than expenditures on social security benefits paid out to people. Economists have pointed out that, in the absence of any change in policy, U.S. fiscal policy will likely turn highly contractionary. Using the simple Keynesian model, they have predicted that that surplus will slow down the economy and push it into a period of slow growth and recession.

PROBLEMS WITH FISCAL POLICY

Fiscal policy sounds so easy—and in the model it is. If there's a contraction in the economy, the government runs an expansionary fiscal policy; if there's inflation, the government runs a contractionary fiscal policy, keeping the economy at the desired level of income.

In reality, that's not the way it is. A number of important problems arise, which makes the actual practice of fiscal policy difficult. These problems don't mean that the model is wrong; they simply mean that for fiscal policy to work, the policy conclusions drawn from the model must be modified to reflect the real-world problems. Let's consider how the reality might not fit the model. The model assumes:

1. The government knows what the situation is (for instance, the size of *mpc*, *mpm*, and other exogenous variables). In reality, the government must estimate them.
2. The government knows the economy's potential income level (the highest level of income that doesn't cause inflation). In reality, the government may not know what this level is.
3. The government has flexibility in changing spending and taxes. In reality, government cannot change them quickly.
4. Financing the deficit doesn't have any offsetting effect. In reality, it often does.
5. The size of the government debt doesn't matter. In reality, the size of the government debt often does matter.
6. Fiscal policy doesn't negatively affect other government goals. In reality, it often does.

Let's consider each a bit further.

Knowing What the Situation Is

All our examples used numbers that were chosen arbitrarily. In reality, the numbers used in the model must be estimated since data upon which estimates can be made aren't always available. Most economic data are published quarterly, and it usually takes six to nine months of data to indicate, with any degree of confidence, the state of the economy and which way it is heading. Thus, we could be halfway into a recession before we even knew it was happening. (Data are already three months old when published; then we need two or three quarters of such data before they compose a useful body of information to work with.)

In an attempt to deal with this problem, the government relies on large macroeconomic models and leading indicators to predict what the economy will be like six months or a year from now. As part of the input to these complex models, the government must predict economic factors such as the *mpc* and *mpm*. These predictions are imprecise so the forecasts are imprecise. Economic forecasting is still an art, not a science.

Economists' data problems limit the use of fiscal policy for fine-tuning. There's little sense in recommending expansionary or contractionary policy until you know what policy is called for.

Knowing the Level of Potential Income

This problem is related to the one we just discussed. As we discussed earlier, the target level of employment and the potential level of income are not easy concepts to define. At one time it was thought 3 percent unemployment meant full employment. Some time later it was generally thought 6 percent unemployment meant full employment. About that time economists stopped calling the potential level of income the *full-employment* level of income.

Any variation in potential income can make an enormous difference in the policy prescription that could be recommended. To see how big a difference, let's translate a 1 percent change in unemployment into a change in income. According to Okun's law, the general rule of thumb economists use to translate changes in the unemployment rate into changes in income is that a 1 percent fall in the unemployment rate equals a 2.5 percent increase in income. Thus, in 1992 with income at about $6 trillion, a 1 percent fall in the unemployment rate would have increased income $150 billion.

Now let's say one economist believes 6 percent is the long-run achievable target unemployment level, while another believes it's 4.5 percent. That's a 1.5 percent difference. Since a 1 percent decrease in the unemployment rate means an increase of about $150 billion in national income, their views of the income level we should target differ by over $225 billion (1.5 × $150 = $225). Yet both views are reasonable. Looking at the same economy (the same data) one economist may call for expansionary fiscal policy while the other may call for contractionary fiscal policy.

In practice, differences in estimates of potential income often lead to different policy recommendations. Empirical estimates suggest that the size of the multiplier is between 2 and 3. Let's compromise and call it 2.5. That means autonomous expenditures must be predicted to shift either up or down by more than $90 billion before an economist who believes the target unemployment rate is 4.5 percent would agree in policy recommendation with an economist who believes the rate is 6 percent. Since almost all fluctuations in autonomous investment and autonomous consumption are less than this amount, there's no generally agreed upon policy prescription for most fluctuations. Some economists will call for expansionary policy; some will call for contractionary policy; and the government decision makers won't have any clear-cut policy to follow.

You might wonder why the range of potential income estimates is so large. Why not simply see whether the economy has inflation at the existing unemployment and income levels? Would that it were so easy. Inflation is a complicated process. Seeds of inflation are often sown years before inflation results. The main problem is that establishing a close link between the level of economic activity and inflation is a complicated statistical challenge to economists, one that has not yet been satisfactorily met. That leads to enormous debate as to what the causes are.

Economists believe that outside some range (perhaps 4 percent unemployment on the low side and 8 percent on the high side) too much spending causes inflation and too little spending causes a recession. That 4 to 8 percent range is so large that in most cases the U.S. economy is in an ambiguous state where some economists are calling for expansionary policy and others are calling for contractionary policy.

Once the economy reaches the edge of the range or falls outside it, the economists' policy prescription becomes clearer. For example, in the depression, when this Keynesian model was developed, unemployment was 25 percent—well outside the range. Should the economy ever go into such a depression again, economists' policy prescriptions will be clear. The call will be for expansionary fiscal policy. Most times the economy is within the ambiguous range so there are disagreements among economists.

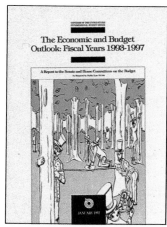

The CBO Report—*The Economic and Budget Outlook* is one of the many government publications that discusses macroeconomic policy options.

The Government's Flexibility in Changing Taxes and Spending

For argument's sake, let's say economists agree that contractionary policy is needed and that's what they advise the government. Will the government implement it? And, if so, will it implement contractionary fiscal policy at the right time? The answer to both questions is: probably not. There are also problems with implementing economists' calls for expansionary fiscal policy. Even if economists are unanimous in calling for expansionary fiscal policy, putting fiscal policy in place takes time and has serious implementation problems.

Numerous political and institutional realities in the United States today make the task of implementing fiscal policy difficult. Government spending and taxes cannot be changed instantaneously. New taxes and new spending must be legislated. It takes time for the government to pass a bill. Politicians face intense political pressures; their other goals may conflict with the goals of fiscal policy. For example, few members of Congress who hope to be reelected would vote to raise taxes in an election year. Similarly few members would vote to slash defense spending when military contractors are a major source of employment in their districts, even when there's little to defend against. Squabbles between Congress and president may delay initiating appropriate fiscal policy for months, even years. By the time the fiscal policy is implemented, what may have once been the right fiscal policy may have ceased to be right and some other policy may have become right.

Imagine trying to steer a car at 60 miles an hour when there's a five-second delay between the time you turn the steering wheel and the time the car's wheels turn. Imagining that situation will give you a good sense of how fiscal policy works in the real world.

Financing the Deficit Doesn't Have Offsetting Effects

Given the assumptions on which the Keynesian model is based, a Classical economist would say it's logically correct. But the Classical economist would then quickly add that the assumptions are wrong.

Classicals argue that the government financing of a deficit will offset the deficit's expansionary effect. Classical economists say that the Keynesian model assumes savings and investment are unequal, and that the government can increase its expenditures without at the same time causing a decrease in private expenditures. Classical economists object to that assumption. They believe the interest rate equilibrates savings and investment. They argue that when the government sells bonds to finance the deficit, that sale of bonds will crowd out private investment. **Crowding out** occurs as follows: When the government runs a deficit, it must sell bonds to finance that deficit. To get people to buy and hold the bonds, the government must make them attractive. That means the interest rate the bonds pay must be higher than it otherwise would have been. This tends to push up the interest rate, which makes it more expensive for private businesses to borrow, so they reduce their borrowing and their investment. That private investment is crowded out by expansionary fiscal policy.

Crowding out The offsetting effect on private expenditures caused by the government's sale of bonds to finance expansionary fiscal policy.

The crowding out effect also works in reverse on contractionary fiscal policy. Say the government runs a surplus. That surplus will slow the economy via the multiplier effect. But it also means the Treasury can buy back some of its outstanding bonds, which will have a tendency to push bond prices up and interest rates down. Lower interest rates will stimulate investment which, in turn, will have an offsetting expansionary effect on the economy. So when we include financing the deficit in our consideration of fiscal policy, the net multiplier effect is reduced.

How large this financing offset to fiscal policy will be is a matter of debate. Classicals see the crowding out effect as relatively large, in many cases almost completely negating the effect of expansionary fiscal policy. Keynesians see it as relatively small, as long as the economy is in a recession or operating below its potential income level. The empirical evidence is mixed and has not resolved the debate. Both sides see some crowding out occurring as the debt is financed by selling bonds. The closer to the potential income level the economy is, the more crowding out is likely to occur.

Size of the Government Debt Doesn't Matter

There is no inherent reason why the adoption of Keynesian policies should have caused the government to run deficits year after year and hence to incur ever-increasing debt. Keynesian policy is consistent with running deficits some years and surpluses other years. In practice, the introduction of Keynesian policy has been accompanied by many deficits and few surpluses, and by a large increase in government debt. If that increase in government debt hurts the economy, one can oppose Keynesian policy, even if one believes that policy might otherwise be beneficial.

FIGHTING THE VIETNAM
INFLATION

One time economists were united in their views on appropriate fiscal policy was during the Vietnam War, from the early 1960s until 1975, when the economy was pushed to its limits. About 1965, President Lyndon B. Johnson's economic advisors started to argue strongly that a tax increase was needed to slow the economy and decrease inflationary pressures. President Johnson wouldn't hear of it. He felt a tax increase would be political suicide. Finally in mid-1968, after Johnson had decided not to run for reelection, a temporary income tax increase was passed. By then, however, many economists felt that the seeds of the 1970s inflation had already been sown.

There are two reasons why Keynesian policy has led to an increase in government debt. First, early Keynesian economists favored large increases in government spending as well as favoring the government's using fiscal policy. These early Keynesians employed the Keynesian economic model to justify increasing spending without increasing taxes. A second reason is political. Politically it's much easier for government to increase spending and decrease taxes than to decrease spending and increase taxes. Due to political pressure, expansionary fiscal policy has predominated over contractionary fiscal policy.

Whether debt is a problem is an important and complicated issue as we'll see in a later chapter devoted entirely to the question. For now, all you need remember is that if one believes that the debt is harmful, then there might be a reason not to conduct expansionary fiscal policy, even when the model calls for it.

An economy has many goals, so it's not surprising that those goals often conflict. Achieving potential income is only one of those goals. In an earlier example in this chapter, we saw those conflicts. When the government ran expansionary fiscal policy, the balance of trade deficit grew. As the economy expands and income rises, exports remain constant but imports rise. If a nation's international considerations do not allow a balance of trade deficit to become larger, as is true in many countries, those governments cannot run expansionary fiscal policies—unless they can somehow prevent this balance of trade deficit from becoming larger.

So where do these six problems leave fiscal policy? While they don't eliminate it, they restrict its usefulness. Fiscal policy is a sledgehammer, not an instrument for fine-tuning. When the economy goes into a depression, the appropriate fiscal policy is clear. Similarly when the economy has a hyperinflation, the appropriate policy is clear. But in less extreme cases, there will be debate on what the appropriate fiscal policy is—a debate economic theory can't answer conclusively.

Economists quickly recognized the political problems with instituting direct countercyclical fiscal policy. To avoid these problems they suggested policies that built fiscal policy into U.S. institutions so that it would be put into effect without any political decisions being necessary. They called a built-in fiscal policy an **automatic stabilizer,** which is any government program or policy that will counteract the business cycle without any new government action. Automatic stabilizers include welfare payments, unemployment insurance, and the income tax system.

To see how automatic stabilizers work, consider the unemployment insurance system. When the economy is slowing down or is in a recession, the unemployment rate will rise. When people lose their jobs, they will reduce their consumption, starting the multiplier process, which decreases income. Unemployment insurance immediately helps offset the decrease in individuals' incomes as the government pays benefits to the unemployed. Thus, the budget deficit increases, and part of the fall in income is stopped without any explicit act by the government. Automatic stabilizers also work in reverse. When income increases, they decrease the size of the deficit.

Fiscal Policy Doesn't
Negatively Affect Other
Government Goals

Fiscal Policy in Practice:
Summary of the Problems

Building Keynesian
Policies into Institutions

6

Automatic stabilizer Any government program or policy that will counteract the business cycle without any new government action.

EXHIBIT 7 **Decrease in Fluctuations in the Economy**

One of the arguments in favor of Keynesian economics is that since it was introduced into the U.S. economy, fluctuations in the economy have decreased.

Source: Federal Reserve Historical Charts and Economic Report of the President.

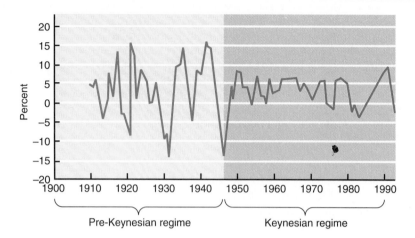

Another automatic stabilizer is our income tax system. Earlier in this chapter we said that tax revenue fluctuates as income fluctuates and that this makes the deficit hard to predict. When the economy expands unexpectedly, the budget deficit is lower than originally expected; when the economy contracts unexpectedly, the budget deficit is higher than expected. Let's go through the reasoning why. When the economy is strong, people have more income and thus pay higher taxes. This increase in tax revenue reduces expenditures from what they would have been, and moderates the economy's growth. When the economy goes into a recession, the opposite occurs.

Automatic stabilizers may seem like the solution to the economic woes we have discussed, but they, too, have their shortcomings. One problem is that when the economy is first starting to climb out of a recession, automatic stabilizers will slow the process, rather than help it along, for the same reason they slow the contractionary process. As income increases, automatic stabilizers increase government taxes and decrease government spending, and as they do, the discretionary policy's expansionary effects are decreased.

Despite these problems, most Keynesians believe automatic stabilizers have played an important role in reducing fluctuations in our economy. They point to the kind of data we see in Exhibit 7, which they say show a significant decrease in fluctuations in the economy. Other economists aren't so sure; they argue the apparent decrease in fluctuations is an optical illusion. As usual, economic data are sufficiently ambiguous to give both sides strong arguments. The verdict is still out.

Fiscal Policy in Perspective

By now you should be able to think in terms of the Keynesian model and see how disequilibriums between aggregate production and aggregate expenditures can be resolved by adjustments in aggregate income. But beware. The Keynesian model is only a model. It's a tool, a crutch, to help you see certain relationships. It does so by obscuring others, including interest rate adjustment, price level adjustment, and supply incentive effects.

Consideration of these aspects led to significant changes in macroeconomic thinking over the years. Classical economics rose like a phoenix from the ashes and re-emerged, first as monetarism and then as New Classical economics, as we'll see in later chapters. These modern Classical economists challenged the way Keynesian economists think about expansionary effects of fiscal policy, and won many converts. Nevertheless the Keynesian model is how many economists still think about the aggregate economy. Therefore, it is useful to know this model, as long as you keep in mind that it is only a first approximation to analyzing what happens in the economy.

KEY POINTS

- Fiscal policy is the manipulation of the government budget deficit or surplus to influence the level of income in the economy. **1**
- Fiscal policy works by providing a deliberate countershock to offset unexpected shocks to the economy. **2**
- Expansionary fiscal policy is represented graphically as an upward shift of the aggregate expenditures curve. **2**
- Contractionary fiscal policy is represented graphically as a downward shift of the aggregate expenditures curve. **2**
- The effect of fiscal policy can be determined by using the Keynesian equation. **2**
- The size of the deficit or surplus influences the level of income in the economy, but is also influenced by it. **3**

- The size of the trade balance (net exports) influences the level of income in the economy but is also influenced by it. **4**
- Fiscal policy is affected by the following problems, among others: **5**

  1. Lack of knowledge of what policy is called for.
  2. Government's inability to respond quickly enough.
  3. Government debt.

- Keynesian fiscal policy is now built into U.S. economic institutions through automatic stabilizers. **6**

KEY TERMS

automatic stabilizer *(247)*
complete Keynesian equation *(241)*
countercyclical fiscal policy *(242)*

crowding out *(246)*
endogenous *(237)*
fine-tuning *(242)*
fiscal policy *(230)*

inflationary gap *(236)*
marginal propensity to import *(240)*

passive deficit *(239)*
recessionary gap *(234)*
structural deficit *(239)*

QUESTIONS FOR THOUGHT AND REVIEW

The number after each question represents the estimated degree of critical thinking required. (1 = almost none; 10 = deep thought.)

1. Explain how Franklin D. Roosevelt's statement, "We have nothing to fear but fear itself," pertains to macroeconomic policy. *(4)*
2. Congratulations! You've just been appointed chairman of the Council of Economic Advisers in Textland. The *mpc* is .8; all nonconsumption expenditures and taxes are exogenous. There is a recessionary gap of $400, which the government wants to eliminate by changing taxes. What policy would you suggest? *(4)*
3. Your research assistant comes running in and tells you that instead of changing taxes, the government wants to achieve the same result by increasing expenditures. What policy would you recommend now? *(4)*
4. Your research assistant has a worried look on her face. "What's the problem?" you ask. "I goofed," she confesses. "I thought taxes were exogenous when actually there's a marginal tax rate of .1." Before she can utter another word, you say, "No problem. I'll simply recalculate my answers to Questions 2 and 3 and change them before I send them in." What are your corrected answers? *(5)*

5. She still has a pained expression. "What's wrong?" you ask. "You didn't let me finish," she says. "Not only was there a marginal tax rate of .1; there's also an *mpm* of .2." Again you interrupt to make sure she doesn't feel guilty. Again you say, "No problem," and recalculate your answers to Question 5 to account for the new information. What are your new answers? *(5)*
6. That pained look is still there, but this time you don't interrupt. You let her finish. She says, "And they want to see the answers graphically." You do the right thing. *(4)*
7. Two economists are debating whether the normal rate of unemployment is 4 or 6 percent. Mr. A believes it's 4 percent; Ms B believes it's 6 percent. One says the structural deficit is $40 billion; the other says it is $20 billion. Which one says which? Why? *(5)*
8. What is the current state of U.S. fiscal policy? Would you advise the United States to change its fiscal policy? Why? *(7)*
9. If interest rates have no effect on investment, what percentage of crowding out will there be? *(5)*
10. A country has a balance of trade deficit and a recessionary gap. Advise it how to eliminate both. *(9)*

PROBLEMS AND EXERCISES

1. Congratulations. You've just been appointed economic advisor to Dreamland. The president wants your advice on how to reduce unemployment from 8 to 6 percent. Income is $40,000, *mpc* is .5, *mpm* is .1, and marginal tax rate is .2

   a. Advise her.

   b. She wants to know what would happen to her formerly balanced budget if she follows your advice. You naturally tell her.

   c. Now she wants to know what will happen to her formerly zero trade deficit. You tell her.

   d. Hearing your answers, she tells you that your policy is unacceptable. She wants to reduce unemployment and to keep both the trade and the government budget in balance. How do you respond?

2. Condolences. You've been fired from your job in Dreamland, but you found another job in a neighboring Fantasyland. Its economy is almost the same as Dreamland's but you must rely on your research assistant for the specific numbers. He says income is $50,000, *mpc* is .5, *mpm* is .1, marginal tax rate is .25, and the president wants to lower unemployment from 8 to 6 percent.

   a. Advise him.

   b. Your research assistant comes in and says "Sorry, I meant that the *mpc* is .66, *mpm* is .15, and marginal tax rate is .2." You redo your calculations.

   c. You're just about to see the president when your research assistant comes running, saying "Sorry, sorry, I meant that the *mpc* is .75, *mpm* is zero, and marginal tax rate is .1." Redo your calculations.

The Algebraic Keynesian Model

I've kept math to a minimum in the text, but many of the ideas and issues can be neatly seen mathematically. In this Appendix I briefly go through the issues mathematically. The basic Keynesian model consists of the following equations:

(1) $C = C_0 + bY_d$

(2) $Y_d = Y - T$

(3) $I = I_0$

(4) $G = G_0$

(5) $T = T_0 + tY$

(6) $X = X_0$

(7) $M = M_0 + mY$

(8) $C + I + G + (X - M) = Y.$

Equation (1) is the consumption function. C_0 is autonomous consumption; bY_d is the *mpc* multiplied by disposable income.

Equation (2) defines disposable income as a function of real income minus taxes.

Equation (3) is the investment function. I_0 is autonomous investment.

Equation (4) is the government expenditures function. G_0 is autonomous spending.

Equation (5) is the tax function. Taxes are composed of two parts. The autonomous component, T_0, is unaffected by income. The endogenous portion of taxes is tY. The tax rate is represented by t.

Equation (6) is the exogenous export function.

Equation (7) is the import function. Imports are composed of two parts. M_0 is the autonomous portion. The endogenous portion is mY. The marginal propensity to import is represented by m.

Equation (8) is the national income accounting identity: Total expenditures = income.

To use this model meaningfully, we must combine all these equations into a single equation, called a *reduced-form equation*, which will neatly show the effect of various shifts on the equilibrium level of income. To do so we first substitute Equation (5) into Equation (2) and then Equation (2) into Equation (1):

(1a) $C = C_0 + b(Y - T).$

We then substitute (1a), (3), (4), (5), (6), and (7) into Equation (8), giving

$$C_0 + b(Y - T_0 - tY) + I_0 + G_0 + (X_0 - M_0) - mY = Y.$$

Removing the parentheses,

$$C_0 + bY - bT_0 - btY + I_0 + G_0 + (X_0 - M_0) - mY = Y.$$

Moving all of the Y terms to the right side,

$$C_0 - bT_0 + I_0 + G_0 + (X_0 - M_0) = Y - bY + btY + mY.$$

Factoring out Y on the right side,

$$C_0 - bT_0 + I_0 + G_0 + (X_0 - M_0) = Y(1 - b + bt + m).$$

Dividing by $(1 - b + bt + m)$ gives

$$[C_0 - bT_0 + I_0 + G_0 + (X_0 - M_0)][1/(1 - b + bt + m)] = Y.$$

$1/(1 - b + bt + m)$ is the multiplier for a simple Keynesian model with endogenous taxes and endogenous imports.

Thus, the general structure of the reduced form equation is

$Y =$ (multiplier)(autonomous expenditures).

When we discuss changes in autonomous expenditures, the general form is

$\Delta Y =$ (multiplier)(Δ autonomous expenditures).

To see whether you follow the argument, let's try a numerical example. Say you want to increase income (Y) by 100. Assume $b = .8$, $t = .2$, and $m = .04$. Substituting in these numbers lets us determine the multiplier: $1/[1 - .8 + .8(.2) + .04] = 2.5$.

We can now determine how much to change autonomous expenditure to affect income. For example, to increase income by 100, we must increase autonomous expenditure by 40 (100/2.5).

3

Monetary and Financial Institutions

CHAPTER

11

Financial Institutions

CHAPTER

12

Money and Banking

CHAPTER

13

The Federal Reserve System and Monetary Policy

11

Financial Institutions

*Finance is a means of assuring the
flow of capital. Historically it has also been a means for guiding that
flow. In the first case, it is a mechanism in aid of the industrial
system as we know it. In the second, it is a power controlling it.*

Adolf A. Berle, Jr.

After reading this chapter, you should be able to:

1

Explain how financial assets can be created
by an agreement between two people.

2

List four types of financial institutions.

3

Distinguish a primary financial market from
a secondary financial market.

4

List three money market assets and two
capital market assets.

5

Roughly determine the present value of an
amount of money at a future date.

6

Explain why, when interest rates fall, bond
prices rise—and vice versa.

7

Differentiate the Classical and Keynesian
views of the financial sector.

Markets make specialization and trade possible and thereby make the economy far more efficient than it otherwise would be. But the efficient use of markets requires a financial sector that facilitates and lubricates those trades.

In thinking about the economy, students often focus on the *real* economy: producing real goods or services such as shoes, operas, automobiles, and textbooks. That's an incomplete view of the economy. The financial sector plays a central role in organizing and coordinating our economy; it makes modern economic society possible. A car won't run without oil; a modern economy won't operate without a financial sector.

In thinking about the financial sector's role, remember the following insight. *For every real transaction there is a financial transaction that mirrors it.* For example, when you buy an apple, the person selling the apple is buying 35¢ from you by spending his apple. The financial transaction is the transfer of 35¢; the real transaction is the transfer of the apple.

For larger items the financial transaction lying behind the real transaction can be somewhat complicated. When you buy a house, you'll probably pay for part of that house with a mortgage, which requires that you borrow money from a bank. The bank, in turn, borrows from individuals the money it lends to you. Similarly, when you buy a car, or even a book, on credit. There's a financial transaction reflecting every real transaction. The financial sector is important for the real sector. If the financial sector doesn't work, the real sector doesn't work. All trade involves both the real sector and the financial sector. Thus in this book I don't have a separate section on the steel sector or even the computer sector of the economy, but I do have a separate section on the financial sector of the economy.

FINANCIAL ASSETS AND FINANCIAL LIABILITIES

1

Financial asset   Asset such as a stock or bond whose benefit to the owner depends on the issuer of the asset meeting certain obligations.

Financial liability   Obligation assumed by the issuer of a financial asset which gives a financial asset its value.

To understand the financial sector and its relation to the real sector, you must understand: (1) what financial assets are, (2) how financial institutions work, (3) what financial markets are, and (4) how they work.

An *asset* is something that provides its owner with expected future benefits. There are two types of assets: real assets and financial assets. Real assets are assets such as houses or machinery whose services provide direct benefits to their owners, either now or in the future. A house is a real asset—you can live in it. A machine is a real asset—you can produce goods with it. **Financial assets** are assets, such as stocks or bonds, whose benefit to the owner depends on the issuer of the asset meeting certain obligations. These obligations are called **financial liabilities.** *Every financial asset has a corresponding financial liability;* it's that financial liability that gives the financial asset its value. In the case of bonds, for example, a company's agreement to pay interest and repay the principal gives bonds their value. If the company goes bankrupt and reneges on its liability to pay interest and repay the principal, the asset becomes worthless. The corresponding liability gives the financial asset its value.

The financial liability created by a financial asset can be either an *equity liability* or a *debt liability*. An example of an equity liability is a share of stock that a firm issues. It is a liability of the firm; it gives the holder ownership rights which are spelled out in the financial asset. An equity liability, such as a stock, usually conveys a general right to dividends, but only if the company's board of directors decides to pay them.

A debt liability conveys no ownership right. It's a type of loan. An example of a debt liability is a bond that a firm issues. The bond is a liability of the firm but an asset of the individual who holds the bond. A debt liability, such as a bond, usually conveys legal rights to interest payments and repayment of principal.

Real assets are created by real economic activity. For example, a house or a machine must be built. Financial assets are created whenever somebody takes on a financial liability. For example, say I promise to pay you $1,000,000,000 in the future. You now have a financial asset and I have a financial liability. Understanding that financial assets can be created by a simple agreement of two people is fundamentally important to understanding how the financial sector works.

A **financial institution** is a business whose primary activity is buying, selling, or holding financial assets. For example, some financial institutions (depository institutions and investment intermediaries) sell promises to pay in the future. These promises can be their own promises or someone else's promises. When you open a savings account in a bank, the bank is selling you its own promise that you can withdraw your money, plus interest, at some unspecified time in the future. Such financial institutions are called **depository institutions.** When you buy a government bond or security from a firm, it's also selling you a promise to pay in the future. But in this case, it's a third party's promise. So a securities firm is a financial institution that sells third parties' promises to pay. It's a type of investment intermediary.

As financial institutions sell financial assets, they channel savings from savers (individuals who give other people money now in return for promises to pay it back with interest later) to borrowers (investors or consumers who get the money now in return for their promise to pay it and the interest later).

As economists use the term, *to save* is to buy a financial asset. *To invest* (in economic terminology) is to buy real, not financial, assets that you hope will yield a return in the future.[1] How do you get funds to invest if you don't already have them? You borrow them. That means you create a financial asset which you sell to someone else who saves.

Some financial institutions also hold and store individuals' financial assets. Such financial institutions are called **contractual intermediaries** because they intermediate (serve as a go-between) between savers and investors. For example, a pension fund is a financial institution that holds individuals' savings and pays back those savings plus interest after the individuals retire. In doing so it uses individuals' savings to buy financial assets from people and firms who want to borrow. Similarly, a commercial bank is a financial institution that holds an individual's cash in the form of checking deposits; it distributes that cash to others when that individual tells it to. A checking deposit is a financial asset of an individual and a financial liability of the bank.

Exhibit 1 lists four types of financial institutions and shows the percentage of total U.S. financial assets each holds along with the sources and uses of funds for each. Although financial brokers hold no financial assets, they're important because they facilitate buying and selling such assets. Let's consider each grouping separately.

Depository institutions (by far the largest category) are financial institutions whose primary financial liability is deposits in checking accounts. They hold approximately 47 percent of all the financial assets in the United States. This category includes commercial banks, savings banks, savings and loan associations (S&Ls), and credit unions. The primary financial liability of each is deposits. For example, the amount in your checking account or savings account is a financial asset for you and a financial liability for the bank holding your deposit. Banks make money by lending your deposits (primarily in the form of business and commercial loans), charging the borrower a higher interest rate than they pay the depositor. Those loans from banks to borrowers are financial assets of the bank and financial liabilities of the borrower.

Laws governing financial institutions have changed significantly in the 1980s and 1990s. In the 1970s each financial institution was restricted to specific types of financial transactions. Savings banks and S&Ls handled savings accounts and mortgages; they were not allowed to issue checking accounts. Commercial banks were not allowed to hold or sell stock; they did, however, issue checking accounts. These restrictions allowed us to make sharp, clear distinctions among financial institutions. Changes in the laws have eliminated many of these re-

FINANCIAL INSTITUTIONS

Financial institution Business whose primary activity is buying, selling, or holding financial assets.

Depository institution Financial institution whose primary financial liability is deposits in checking or savings accounts.

Contractual intermediary A financial institution that holds and stores individuals' financial assets.

2

Depository Institutions

---

[1] This terminology isn't the terminology most lay people use. When a person buys a stock, in economic terms that person is saving, though most lay people call that *investing*.

EXHIBIT 1   List of Financial Institutions

Financial Institutions	% of Total Financial Assets	Primary Assets (Uses of Funds)	Primary Liabilities (Sources of Funds)
Depository institutions:			
Commercial banks	32	Business and consumer loans, mortgages, U.S. government securities, and municipal bonds	Checkable deposits and savings deposits
Savings and loan associations	10	Mortgages	Savings deposits (and checkable deposits)
Mutual savings banks	3	Mortgages	Savings deposits (and checkable deposits)
Credit unions	2	Consumer loans	Savings deposits (and checkable deposits)
Contractual intermediaries:			Employer and employee contributions
Pension funds	19	Corporate bonds and stock	
Life insurance companies	13	Corporate bonds and mortgages	Policy premiums
Fire and casualty insurance companies	5	Municipal bonds, corporate bonds and stock, and U.S. government securities	Policy premiums
Investment intermediaries:			
Money market mutual funds	6	Money market instruments	Shares
Mutual funds	5	Stocks and bonds	Shares
Finance companies	5	Consumer and business loans	Commercial paper, stocks, and bonds
Financial brokers:			
Investment banks	0	None	None
Brokerage houses	0	None	None

Source: Federal Reserve System.

ADDED DIMENSION

DO FINANCIAL ASSETS MAKE SOCIETY RICHER?

Financial assets are neat. You can call them into existence simply by getting someone to accept your IOU. *Remember, every financial asset has a corresponding financial liability equal to it.* So when you say a country has $1 trillion of financial assets, you're also saying that the country has $1 trillion of financial liabilities. An optimist would say a country is rich. A pessimist would say it's poor. An economist would say that financial assets and financial liabilities are simply opposite sides of the ledger and don't indicate whether a country is rich or poor.

To find out whether a country is rich or poor, you must look at its *real assets*. If financial assets increase the economy's efficiency and thereby increase the amount of real assets, they make society better off. This is most economists' view of financial assets. If, however, they decrease the efficiency of the economy (as some economists have suggested some financial assets do because they focus productive effort on financial gamesmanship), financial assets make society worse off.

The same correspondence between a financial asset and its liability exists when a financial asset's value changes. Say stock prices fall significantly. Is society poorer? Clearly the people who own the stock are poorer, but the people who might want to buy stock in the future are richer since the price of assets has fallen. So in a pure accounting sense, society is neither richer nor poorer when the prices of stocks rise or fall.

But there are ways in which changes in the value of financial assets might signify that society is richer or poorer. For example, the changes in the values of financial assets might *reflect* (rather than cause) real changes. If suddenly a company finds a cure for cancer, its stock price will rise and society will be richer. But the rise in the price of the stock doesn't cause society to be richer. It reflects the discovery that made society richer. Society would be richer because of the discovery even if the stock's price didn't rise.

There's significant debate about how well the stock market reflects real changes in the economy. Classical economists believe it closely reflects real changes; Keynesian economists believe it doesn't. But both sides agree that it is the changes in the real economy, not the changes in the price of financial assets, that underlie what makes an economy richer or poorer.

strictions, blurring the distinction between the various types of financial institutions. Now all depository institutions can issue checking accounts. In the 1990s many more changes are likely.

Some differences remain that reflect their history. Commercial banks' primary assets are loans, and their loans include business loans, mortgages, and consumer loans. Savings banks' and S&Ls' primary assets are the same kind as those of commercial banks, but their loans are primarily mortgage loans.

The most important contractual intermediaries are insurance companies and pension funds. These institutions promise, for a fee, to pay an individual a certain amount of money in the future, either when some event happens (a fire or death) or, in the case of pension funds and some kinds of life insurance, when the individual reaches a certain age or dies. Insurance policies and pensions are a form of individual savings. Contractual intermediaries manage those savings. As the average age of the U.S. population increases, as it will throughout the 1990s, the share of assets held by these contractual intermediaries will increase.

Contractual Intermediaries

Investment intermediaries provide a mechanism through which small savers pool funds to invest in a variety of financial assets rather than in just one or two. An example of how pooling works can be seen by considering a mutual fund company, which is one type of investment intermediary. A mutual fund enables a small saver to diversify (spread out) his or her savings (for a fee, of course) so that if something goes wrong with one financial asset, small savers will not lose all their savings. In the case of mutual funds, savers buy shares in that fund which, in turn, holds shares or bonds of many different companies. When a fund holds many different companies' shares or bonds, it spreads the risk so a saver won't lose everything if one company goes broke. Such spreading of risks by holding many different types of financial assets is called **diversification.**

Investment Intermediaries

A finance company is another type of investment intermediary. Finance companies make loans to individuals and businesses, as do banks, but instead of holding deposits, as banks do, finance companies borrow the money they lend. They borrow from individuals by selling them bonds and commercial paper. **Bonds** are promissory notes specifying that a certain amount of money plus interest will be paid back in the future. **Commercial paper** is a short-term promissory note that a certain amount of money plus interest will be paid back on demand. Finance companies charge borrowers higher interest than banks do, in part because their cost of funds (the interest rate they pay) is higher than banks' cost of funds. (The interest rate banks pay on savings and checking accounts is the cost of their funds.) As was the case with depository institutions, a finance company's profit is the difference between the interest rate it charges on its loans and the interest rate it pays for the funds it borrows.

Diversification Spreading, and therefore lowering, risk by holding shares or bonds of many different companies.

Bonds Promissory notes that a certain amount of money plus interest will be paid back in the future.

Commercial paper Short-term promissory note that a certain amount of money plus interest will be paid back on demand.

Why do people go to finance companies if finance companies charge higher interest than banks? Because of convenience and because finance companies' loan qualifications are easier to meet than banks'.

Securities firms are of two main types: investment banks and brokerage houses. Investment banks assist companies in selling financial assets such as stocks and bonds. They provide advice, expertise, and the sales force to sell the stocks or bonds. They handle such things as *mergers* and *takeovers* of companies. A merger is when two or more companies join to form one new company. A takeover occurs when one company buys out another company. Investment banks do not hold individuals' deposits and do not make loans to consumers. That's why in Exhibit 1 they have zero assets and hence zero liabilities. They are nonetheless financial institutions because they assist others in buying and selling financial assets.

Financial Brokers

Brokerage houses assist individuals in selling previously issued financial assets. Brokerage houses create a secondary market in financial assets, as we'll

Secondary financial market Market in which previously issued financial assets can be bought and sold.

FINANCIAL MARKETS

Financial market Institution that brings buyers and sellers of assets together.

Primary and Secondary Financial Markets

Primary financial market A market where newly-issued financial assets are sold.

3

The Wall Street Journal—Must reading material for businesspeople; only the editorial page is highly conservative.

Liquidity Ability to turn an asset into cash quickly.

see shortly. A **secondary financial market** is a market in which previously issued financial assets can be bought and sold.

A financial market is a market where financial assets and financial liabilities are bought and sold. The stock market, the bond market, and bank activities are all examples of financial markets.

Financial institutions buy and sell financial assets in financial markets. Sometimes these markets are actual places, like the New York Stock Exchange, but generally a market simply exists in the form of a broker's Rolodex files, computer networks, telephone lines, and lists of people who sometimes want to buy and sell. When individuals want to sell, they call their broker and their broker calls potential buyers; when individuals want to buy, the broker calls potential sellers. A market is an institution that brings buyers and sellers together; a **financial market** is an institution (the Rolodex cards and the telephone) that brings buyers and sellers of financial assets together.

There are various types of financial markets. A **primary financial market** is a market in which newly issued financial assets are sold. These markets transfer savings to borrowers who want to invest (buy real assets). Sellers in this market include *venture capital firms* (which sell part ownerships in new companies) and *investment banks* (which sell new stock and new bonds for existing companies). Whereas investment banks only assist firms in selling their stock, venture capital firms often are partnerships that invest their own money in return for part ownership of a new firm.

Many new businesses will turn to venture capital firms for financing because only established firms can sell stock through an investment bank. Risks are enormous for venture capital firms since most new businesses fail. But potential gains are huge. A company that's already established will most likely use an investment bank to get additional funds. Investment banks know people and institutions who buy stocks; with a new stock offering they use those contacts. They telephone these leads to try to *place* (sell) the new issue.

Generally new offerings are too large for one investment bank to sell. So it contracts with other investment banks and brokerage houses to sell portions of the new stock or bond issue. Exhibit 2 shows an advertisement announcing a stock offering. In this advertisement, the investment bank, Oppenheimer & Co., Inc., announces it's selling 1,500,000 shares of stock for Alliance Pharmaceutical Corp. at $11 per share. Oppenheimer also has subcontracted with all the other investment banks and brokerage houses listed to assist in the sale.

There are many different types of buyers for newly issued financial assets. They include rich individuals and financial institutions, such as life insurance companies, pension funds, and mutual funds.

A secondary financial market transfers existing financial assets from one saver to another. (Remember, in economics, when an individual buys a financial asset such as a stock or bond, he or she is a saver. In economics, investment occurs only when savings are used to buy items such as machines or a factory.) A transfer on a secondary market does not represent any new savings; it is savings for one person and dissavings for another. One cancels out the other. The New York Stock Exchange is probably the best-known secondary financial market. It transfers stocks from one stockholder to another.

The secondary market does, however, have an important role to play in new savings. The existence of a secondary market lets the individual buyer of a financial asset know that she can resell it, transferring the asset back into cash at whatever price the secondary market sets. This ability to turn an asset into cash quickly is called **liquidity.** Secondary markets provide liquidity for financial asset holders and thereby encourage them to hold financial assets. If no secondary

EXHIBIT 2   An Advertisement Annoucing a Stock Offering

This announcement is neither an offer to sell nor a solicitation of an offer to buy these securities. The offer is made only by the Prospectus.

New Issue/July 18, 1989

1,500,000 Shares

Common Stock

Price $11 Per Share

Copies of the Prospectus may be obtained from the undersigned only in States where the undersigned may legally offer these securities in compliance with the securities laws thereof.

Oppenheimer & Co., Inc.

Drexel Burnham Lambert
Incorporated

Hambrecht & Quist

Kidder, Peabody & Co.
Incorporated

Montgomery Securities   Paine Webber Incorporated   Prudential–Bache Capital Funding

Shearson Lehman Hutton Inc.

Wertheim Schroder & Co.
Incorporated

Allen & Company
Incorporated

Thomson McKinnon Securities Inc.

Bateman Eichler, Hill Richards
Incorporated

Boettcher & Company, Inc.

Brean Murray, Foster Securities Inc.   Cowen & Co.   Furman Selz Mager Dietz & Birney
Incorporated

Hayes & Griffith, Inc.   Ladenburg, Thalmann & Co. Inc.   Ragen MacKenzie

Raymond James & Associates, Inc.   Rosenkrantz Lyon & Ross
Incorporated   Rothschild Inc.

Stifel, Nicolaus & Company   Sutro & Co.   Swartwood, Hesse Inc.   Tucker Anthony
Incorporated   *Incorporated*   *Incorporated*

Courtesy Oppenheimer & Co., Inc., World Financial Center, New York, NY.

The floor of the New York Stock Exchange is often a hectic place. *UPI/Bettmann.*

market existed, most people would hesitate to buy a stock or a 30-year bond. What if they needed their money in, say, 10 years? Or 10 weeks?

Besides the organized secondary financial markets we often hear about—the New York Stock Exchange, AMEX (American Stock Exchange), and Chicago Mercantile Exchange—there are informal *over-the-counter* markets. Over-the-counter markets work like the primary financial markets: Brokers know of other individuals interested in buying what's for sale. Buying and selling takes place over the phone with the broker acting as an intermediary.

Money Markets and Capital Markets

Money markets Markets in which financial assets with maturity of less than one year are bought and sold.

Capital market Market in which financial assets with maturity of more than one year are bought and sold.

Financial markets can also be divided into two other categories: **money markets** (in which financial assets having a maturity of less than one year are bought and sold) and **capital markets** (in which financial assets having a maturity of more than one year are bought and sold). (*Maturity* refers to the date the issuer must pay back the money that was borrowed plus any remaining interest, as agreed when the asset was issued.) For example, say the U.S. government issues an IOU (sometimes called a *Treasury bill*) that comes due in three months. This will be sold in the money market because its maturity is less than a year. Or say the government or a corporation issues an IOU that comes due in 20 years. This IOU, which is called a *bond,* will be sold in a capital market.

TYPES OF FINANCIAL ASSETS

Now that you've been introduced to financial institutions and markets, we can consider some specific financial assets. Financial assets are generally divided into money market assets and capital market assets. Exhibit 3 lists some of the most important money market assets and the amounts invested in them since 1970. Notice how the relative importance of various assets changes over time. Let's briefly consider several.

	1970	1980	1990
Negotiable bank certificates of deposit (large denomination)	25	259	543
Commercial paper	33	124	557
U.S. Treasury bills	81	216	527
Repurchase agreements	3	59	144
Eurodollars	2	55	92
Federal funds	20	55	61
Bankers' acceptances	7	55	52

EXHIBIT 3   Principal Money Market Instruments: Amount Outstanding, 1970–1990 *(Billions of Dollars, End of Year)*

Source: Federal Reserve Bank.

Money Market Assets

Money market assets are financial assets that mature in less than one year. They usually pay lower interest rates than do longer-term capital assets because they offer the buyer more liquidity. A general rule of thumb is: The more liquid the asset, the lower the return. As in the over-the-counter market, money market and capital market transactions are made over the phone lines using computers. Newly issued money market assets are sold through an investment bank or a securities dealer.

Some of the most important money market assets are negotiable CDs, U.S. Treasury bills, and commercial paper.

Negotiable CDs   CD is short for *certificate of deposit*. Think of it as a large amount of savings you agree to hold in an account at the bank for a specified period of time. But what if you need cash before the time is up? That's where the "negotiable" comes in. (Not all CDs are negotiable.) You can sell a negotiable CD in a secondary market and get cash for it if you need cash. The new owner can either sell it again on the secondary market or simply withdraw the money from the bank that issued it, including interest, when the required time is up (when the CD matures).

CD (certificate of deposit) A piece of paper certifying that you have a sum of money in a savings account in the bank for a specified period of time.

Commercial Paper   Why borrow from a bank if you can borrow directly from the public? Why not cut out the middleman? Large corporations often do precisely that. The borrowings are called *commercial paper*. Commercial paper is a short-term IOU of a large corporation. Commercial paper pays a higher interest rate than U.S. Treasury bills, but a lower interest rate than banks would charge the corporation. The same reasoning holds for a person who buys commercial paper. Commercial paper generally pays a higher interest rate than a CD, which is why people are willing to lend directly to the firm. Since the bank is an intermediary between the lender of funds and the borrower, the process of lending directly and not going through a financial intermediary is called **disintermediation.**

Disintermediation Borrowing directly from an individual without going through an intermediary bank.

U.S. Treasury Bills   These are U.S. government IOUs that mature in less than a year. Since it's unlikely the U.S. government will go broke, IOUs of the U.S. government are very secure so U.S. Treasury bills need pay a relatively low rate of interest.

Where do these government IOUs come from? Think back to the discussion of fiscal policy in which the government spent more than it took in in revenues. That deficit must be financed by borrowing. Selling U.S. Treasury bills is one way the U.S. government borrows money.

EXHIBIT 4   Principal Capital Market Instruments: Amount Outstanding, 1970–1990 (Billions of Dollars, End of Year)

	1970	1980	1990
Corporate stocks (market value)	906	1634	4165
Residential mortgages	353	1098	2924
U.S. government securities (marketable long-term)	160	407	1653
Corporate bonds	167	366	987
Commercial and farm mortgages	115	351	846
Bank commercial loans	314	331	815
Consumer loans	143	374	809
State and local government bonds	144	288	640
U.S. government agency securities	51	193	412

Source: Federal Reserve System.

EXHIBIT 5   A Stock Certificate

Stock certificates generally look impressive to make holders think they have something valuable. Recently there has been a move to replace certificates with computer entries, but somehow a computer entry doesn't give one a feeling of real value. Most people care about such things; large companies, that hold much of the stock on the exchange, don't. They prefer computer entries.

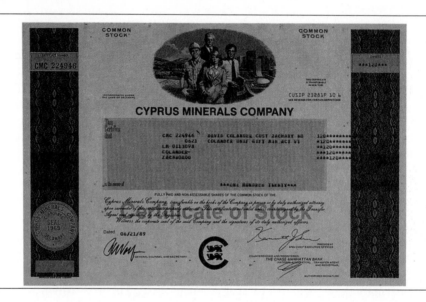

Differences among Money Market Assets Money market assets differ slightly from each other. For example, Treasury bills are safer than commercial paper and pay slightly lower interest. For the most part, however, they are interchangeable, and the interest rates paid on them tend to increase or decrease together.

Capital Market Assets

Capital market assets have a maturity of over one year. Exhibit 4 shows the important capital market instruments and the amounts invested in them since 1970. As you can see, the most important are stocks, bonds, and mortgages. Since mortgages are discussed later in this chapter, we'll focus here on stocks and bonds.

Stock Ownership right to a company.

Stocks A **stock** is a partial ownership right to a company. The stock owner has the right to vote on company policy, although generally, for smaller shareholders, this right doesn't convey much power. A stockholder can however attend the firm's stockholder meeting and ask questions of firm officers. Exhibit 5 shows a stock certificate certifying that the holder (who's named on the certificate's face) owns a specified number of shares in the firm—in this case, 120 shares of Cyprus Minerals. This is a valuable certificate, printed on special paper, which will last indefinitely without turning yellow or crumbling away. If the stock certificate is lost or stolen, the owner's investment will still be safe because no one can sell a stock certificate unless the owner has endorsed it on the back (somewhat like a check), which she should not do until the moment she's ready to sell it or confer it as a gift. If a stock certificate is lost or destroyed, the owner can get another one

THE DOW

Of all the current economic institutions, perhaps the one you hear most about is Wall Street. Wall Street is a real street in New York City, but the term *Wall Street* is often used to refer to the entire financial sector. Probably the most important institution on Wall Street is the New York Stock Exchange, where ownership rights in corporations are traded. These ownership rights are called *stocks*. Stocks are also called *shares*, because they represent the share of a business the stockholder owns. While individuals who own stocks are chiefly interested in the price of shares they own, they also want to know the general movement of prices in the market as a whole.

A measure indicating this is the *Dow Jones Industrial Average*, commonly called *the Dow*. The Dow Jones average was created in 1884 when newsman Charles Dow (founder of *The Wall Street Journal*) chose a group of what he felt were representative stocks and began reporting their prices as typical of general movements in the market. Initially he chose 12 stocks, added up their prices, divided the total by 12, and arrived at an average price per share.

Unfortunately for the statistician, the financial people who manage the firms represented by the stocks do funny things with stocks, such as splitting stocks or issuing stock dividends. A *stock split* occurs when the company decides to give each owner extra shares—say two shares for each one the owner already has. A stock dividend means that instead of using money to pay you the earnings on your shares, the company gives you one or more additional shares of stock. Stock splits and stock dividends, both of which increase the number of shares in the market, lower the price of all the company's shares but do not make the owners worse off, because the people own more shares. Often, in fact, owners are made better off, because the price of the shares soon starts to rise again.

But after stock splits and stock dividends of any of the stocks comprising the Dow average, dividing by 12 no longer gives us a representative measure of what happened to the average price. Statisticians did some fancy adjusting, and now, even though the number of stocks included in the Dow has risen from 12 to 30, the divisor used is less than 2. So to compute the Dow Jones Industrial Average, you simply add the prices of the following 30 big, well-known companies, and divide by a number slightly less than 2.

Dow Jones Industrial Stocks

Alcoa	Goodyear Tire and Rubber
Allied Signal	IBM
American Express	International Paper
AT&T	McDonald's
Bethlehem Steel	Merck
Boeing Co.	Minnesota M&M
Caterpillar, Inc.	J. P. Morgan
Chevron	Philip Morris
Coca-Cola	Procter & Gamble
Disney	Sears, Roebuck
Du Pont	Texaco
Eastman Kodak	Union Carbide
Exxon	United Technologies
General Electric	Westinghouse
General Motors	Woolworth

There are many other measures of the market, such as the NASDAQ 500 and Wilshire 5000. But the Dow Jones average is most used. Most TV news programs include a few spoken words or message flashed on the screen: "The Dow Jones Average is down 5.63 for the day," or "Dow— + 26.9."

The divergent interests of debtors and creditors are nicely captured in this late 19th-century drawing by W. W. Chenery. *Bleichroeder Print Collection, Baker Library, Harvard Business School.*

Capital gains and losses aren't limited to stock. They can occur with any asset—financial or real. A capital gain or loss is simply the change in the value of an asset.

Noneconomists often call capital gains and losses *paper gains and losses* because no money transfers hands as the gain or loss occurs. Often you'll hear, "Oh, it's only a paper loss [or paper gain]," as if somehow a capital loss wasn't quite as bad as a loss that has to be paid for in money. It's the same for a "paper gain," which they feel isn't as good as a gain that puts money in your pocket.

Economists don't use the "paper" terminology. They emphasize the opportunity cost concept. When you have a capital gain, you have the option of realizing that gain by selling the asset for the increased price. The opportunity cost of not selling that asset is the price of that asset including the capital gain. Say the price of a share of Cyprus Minerals goes from $21 to $30. If you sell the share, you get $9 (minus transaction costs) in your pocket. If you don't sell the share, the cost of not selling the share is $30. If you didn't sell the share at $21, the cost of not selling it was only $21. Thus, using the opportunity cost framework, a capital gain or loss is as real as any other gain or loss.

from the company because the company keeps a list of its owners (the people who own stock) and their addresses, but the owner must pay a fee.

The owner of a stock can sell it at any time she pleases, provided someone wants to buy it. She will get whatever the going price is at the moment her sale is closed, minus a commission to the broker. Or she can keep it, hoping that its price will go up and it will be worth more. If the company is paying dividends (periodic payments to owners of its stock), every three months she gets a check for those dividends. She doesn't have to do anything to get these checks—the company mails them automatically to "the shareholder of record."

Stocks have no maturity date. The money you paid for them never has to be paid back to you. Stocks require no periodic payments to you every year. So it's possible to buy a stock and get nothing for it. So why would anyone buy a stock? Because with it comes ownership rights—all the company's income that isn't paid out to factors of production belongs to the stockholders. For example, say you own one share of the million shares Cyprus Minerals has issued, and after paying all costs and debts due, Cyprus Minerals has $6 million in after-tax profits. Your percentage of that $6 million is $6. This $6 can be paid out to stockholders in dividends. Or the company can retain the $6 (which would then be called *retained earnings*), in which case the stock's value will likely increase because the firm can invest the retained earnings and earn more profit. (An increase in the value of a stock is called a *capital gain*.) The company's board of directors decides which option the company will follow.

Notice that a share of stock gives you the right to a percentage of the company's profits this year and all future years. Because it does, the price of a stock depends upon investors' opinions of a company's prospects. A company with excellent prospects sells for a high price; a company whose prospects are dim sells for a low price. What's high? What's low? That depends. A rough rule of thumb is to take a multiple of the company's earnings (its *earnings per share*) to determine the price a person would be willing to pay for a share. For instance, "10 times earnings" means a share is selling for 10 times the company's annual earnings divided by the number of shares outstanding. If Cyprus Minerals in our previous example was expected to continue earning $6 a share, and stock buyers applied the 10-times-earnings rule of thumb, the stock would sell for $60 a share.

An average company stock sells for somewhere around 10 times earnings. (This average price/earnings ratio fluctuates somewhat over time.) A company with excellent future prospects might sell for 20 or 30 times earnings. A company with poor prospects might sell for merely 2 or 3 times earnings. The price/earnings ratio for a company is reported in the newspaper stock tables.

Harry Markovitz—Nobel prize, 1990, for work on financial economics. © *The Nobel Foundation.*

EXHIBIT 6   A Bond

Like stocks, bonds are generally impressive pieces of paper.

Bonds   A bond is a promise of the bond-issuer to pay interest of a certain amount at specified intervals (usually annually) to the bondholder and to pay the bond's face value when the bond matures. Bonds are different from stocks. They generally have a maturity date when borrowers pay back the money. Exhibit 6 shows an unregistered bond.

Attached to some bonds are a series of coupons. Each coupon has a date on it. Usually coupons are dated six months apart. When the date comes, say February 1, the owner (or whoever has possession of the bond) "clips the coupon." There's nothing mysterious about clipping coupons. You take some scissors and cut off the coupon and send it to the company's agent, who sends you a check for the coupon's value.

A coupon's value depends on a bond's face value and its coupon rate (the interest rate stated on the bond). Exhibit 6's bond has a face value of $5,000 and a coupon rate of 12.75 percent per year. That means that by cashing the coupons promptly, the bondholder receives $637.50 each year in the form of two $318.75 payments. Upon delivering the bond to the issuer when the bond matures, the holder receives $5,000.

Printed on the bond is the *maturity date,* October 1, 2002. There's no sense hanging onto that bond after October 1, 2002, because after that its interest is all used up. You can easily tell when that happens, even if you forget to keep track of the date, because in October 2002, you will have clipped the last coupon.

When you cash a bond like this upon maturity, you mail it (registered, insured, return receipt requested) to the *paying agent,* a bank whose name and address are shown in tiny type somewhere on the bond. (In Exhibit 6, it's the Chemical Bank.) You write a letter saying that this is your bond and you want to cash it in. You include your social security number (which the bank needs to report the transaction to the IRS), and in a few days the bank mails you a check. That's it. Because this bond is "unregistered," there is no owner's name on it. When the bond matures, anyone who gets hold of it can turn to the issuing company and get cash for it. Hence it's wise to keep such bonds in a safety-deposit box.

EXHIBIT 7   A BOND TABLE

This exhibit gives you the meaning of each of the entries in a bond table. ("cv" means a bond that is convertible, into a stock; therefore its value depends on the price of the stock as well as the interest rate)

Name of bond, along with coupon rate

The net interest rate that would be received on the bond if one paid the closing price

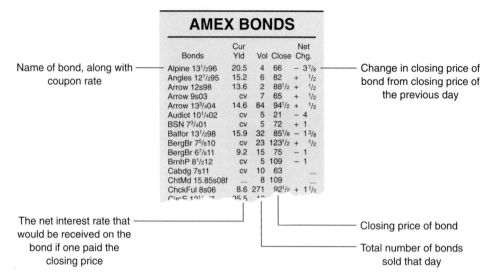

Change in closing price of bond from closing price of the previous day

Closing price of bond

Total number of bonds sold that day

If you need the money from the bond before the maturity date, you'll enter into the secondary bond market. Call your bond broker and ask what your bond is selling for. The broker will quote you a price (which might be more or less than $5,000, depending on supply and demand for that bond). If you accept the current price, you send the bond to the broker, who'll send you the price quoted.

Generally when bonds are issued, their coupon rate is close to the market interest rate prevailing in the economy for bonds of similar risk. These bonds sell *at par* (at their face value). If market interest rates rise, the future stream of income becomes worth less and the bond sells at a discount (at less than its face value). If the market interest rate falls, the future stream of income becomes worth more and the bond sells at a premium (at more than its face value).

Exhibit 7 shows a bond table. Let's see what it tells us. Alpine bonds, the first bond issue on the list, pay a coupon rate of $13\frac{1}{2}$ percent annual interest and come due in 1996. They currently sell for $66 for every $100 of their par value (the value stated on the bond), which means that their yield (the net interest rate you get if you buy the bond at the closing price) is $20\frac{1}{2}$ percent. Each year you get $13.50 from the bond that cost you $66. Dividing $13.50 by $66 gives $20\frac{1}{2}$ percent.

At the time this bond table appeared, $20\frac{1}{2}$ percent was higher than the interest rate on most bonds in the United States. That suggests there were fears Alpine might default on the bonds. Notice some other bonds in the table are selling at premiums. They were issued with a face value of $100, but their current prices are over $100. If you sell a ''BrnhP'' bond for $109 but paid only $100 for it, you make a gain of $9 on the sale price, but the new owner's yield or net annual interest per dollar is lower than the $8\frac{1}{2}$ percent stated for these bonds. That's because $8\frac{1}{2}$ percent of $100 is $8.50, but $8.50 as a percentage of $109 is only 7.8 percent. This 7.8 percent is the bond's yield.

THE VALUE OF A FINANCIAL ASSET

To understand financial assets, you must understand how financial asset prices are determined. Why does an average share of stock sell for 10 times earnings? How come bond prices rise as market interest rates fall, and fall as market interest rates rise? In answering such questions, the first point to recognize is that $1 today is not equal to $1 next year. Why? Because if I have $1 today I can invest it and earn interest (say 10 percent per year), and next year I will have $1.10, not $1. So if the annual interest rate is 10 percent, $1.10 next year is worth $1 today or,

To determine what a bond will sell for, first remember a bond is a flow of payments over time. Its selling price depends on how much those payments are worth. If it's unlikely those payments will continue (for example, if the company issuing the bond is close to bankruptcy, the bond isn't worth much), this *risk* plays an important role in determining the bond's price.

A second factor in determining a bond's price is the current interest rate in the economy. If the interest rate today (for bonds of similar riskiness) is higher than the bond's coupon rate (which generally represents the interest rate that existed when the bond was originally issued), a bond will sell for less than its face value on the secondary market. Why? Because if it sold at its face value, it would make more sense for people to buy newly issued bonds paying higher interest rates. When a bond sells for less than its face value, its yield (the rate of return you receive per dollar of purchase price per year from a bond) increases. For example, say there's a one-year 5 percent coupon bond with $100 face value, and this bond is selling for $50. For $50 you'll get a $5 payment (5 percent of $100). That comes out to a 10 percent yield.

If the interest rate is lower than the coupon rate, bonds will sell for more than their face value. Why? Because at its face value, the bond is much more desirable than newly issued bonds. The market value of the bond will rise until the yield on the bond equals the interest rate on similar newly issued bonds. Only then will the buyer be indifferent between the old and new bonds.

Because of this relationship between interest rates and bond prices, generally whenever market interest rates rise, bond prices fall; whenever market interest rates fall, bond prices rise. Thus, the interest rate in the economy plays an important role in determining a bond's price on the secondary market.

alternatively, $1 next year is worth roughly 91 cents today. A dollar two years in the future is worth even less today, and dollars 30 years in the future are worth very little today.

Present Value and Interest Rate

How much less $1 in the future is worth today depends on the interest rate. If the interest rate is close to zero, $1 is worth only a little bit less; if the interest rate is 5 percent, $1 is worth quite a bit less. The higher the interest rate, the less a dollar is worth in the future. How do I know? Because I pulled out my handy business calculator and pressed in the numbers to calculate the **present value** (the value now of income payments in the future).

Present value Value now of income payments in the future.

Exhibit 8 graphically displays, for three different annual interest rates, how much a given amount of money at various lengths of time in the future is worth now. Notice that: (1) the higher the interest rate, the less a given amount of money in the future is worth now and (2) how quickly the present value falls at higher annual interest rates. At 15 percent interest, $100 thirty years from now is currently worth $1.51, as shown in Exhibit 8(c).

The present value reasoning also works in reverse. You can determine the future value of a given amount of money today. Say you have $100 now. If you earn 8 percent annual interest on it, it will be $215.89 in 10 years and $466.10 in 20 years. The higher the interest rate and the longer the time frame, the greater the future value will be.

Most of you, I suspect, don't have business calculators. For people who don't, there are bond tables to tell you present values of future dollars. A table or a calculator is extremely helpful in determining the price a bond should sell for. That's because a bond consists of a stream of income payments over a number of years *and* the repayment of the face value of the bond. Each year's interest payment and the eventual repayment of the face value must be calculated separately and then the results added together.

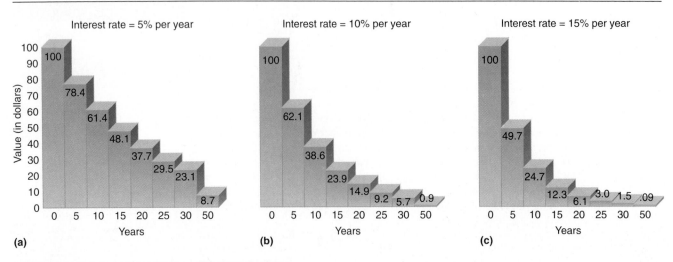

EXHIBIT 8 (a, b, and c)   Present Value of Money in the Future

The present value of money in the future declines as the interest rate increases. Notice how once the interest rate hits 10% or more, (**b**), (**c**), money 50 years in the future is close to worthless.

William Sharpe—Nobel prize, 1990, for work on financial economics. © *The Nobel Foundation.*

Asset Prices, Interest Rates, and the Economy

All financial assets can be broken down into promises to pay certain amounts at certain times in the future or, if the financial asset is a share of stock, not a promise but an expectation of such payment. So all financial assets (stocks or bonds) can be valued. You simply calculate the present value of all expected future payments. For example, say a share of stock is earning $1 per share and is expected to do so long into the future. If the interest rate is 10 percent, the present value of that future stream of expected earnings is $10. With this knowledge, let's return to our question, ''Why do stocks generally sell for 10 times earnings?'' We now have an answer. It's because that's roughly what the present value formula says they should sell for.

There is, however, a proviso to the preceding reasoning. If promises to pay aren't trustworthy, you don't put the amount that's promised into your calculation; you put in the amount you expect. That's why when a company or a country looks as if it's going to default on loans or stop paying dividends, the value of its bonds and stock will fall considerably. For example, in the late 1980s many people thought Brazil would default on its bonds. That expectation caused the price of Brazilian bonds to fall to about 30¢ on the dollar.

This chapter isn't meant to cover the intricacies of valuation over time. That's done in a finance course. The point of this chapter is to help you understand the relationship between interest rates and asset prices. Increases in interest rates (because they make future flows of income coming from an asset worth less now) make financial asset prices fall. Decreases in interest rates (because they make the future flow of income coming from an asset worth more now) make financial asset prices rise.

Since a slight change in interest rates can lead to a large change in asset prices, many individuals speculate on what's going to happen to interest rates and switch their investments from one type of financial asset to another, causing potential problems for the macroeconomy. So understanding how assets are valued is fundamental to understanding the macroeconomic debate.

LEADING YOU THROUGH TWO FINANCIAL TRANSACTIONS

We've covered a lot of material quickly so the institutions discussed may be a bit of a blur in your mind. To get a better idea of how these financial markets work, let's follow two transactions you'll likely make in your lifetime and see how they work their way through the financial system.

You want to drive. The law requires you to have insurance, so you go to two or three insurance companies, get quotes of their rates, and choose the one offering the lowest rate. Say it costs you $800 for the year. You write a check for $800 and hand the check to the insurance agent who keeps a commission (let's say $80) and then sends her check for $720 to the insurance company. The insurance company has $720 more sitting in the bank than it had before you paid your insurance premium.

The insurance company earns income in two ways: (1) in the difference between the money it takes in payments and the claims it pays out and (2) in the interest it makes on its financial assets. What does the company use to buy these financial assets? It has payments from its customers (your $720, for example) available because payments come in long before claims are paid out.

Because earnings on financial assets are an important source of an insurance company's income, your $720 doesn't stay in the insurance company's bank for long. The insurance company has a financial assets division which chooses financial assets it believes have the highest returns for the risk the asset involves. Bond salesmen telephone the financial assets division offering to sell bonds. Similarly, developers who want to build shopping malls or ski resorts go to the financial assets division, offering an opportunity to participate (really asking to borrow money).

The financial assets division might decide to lend your $720 (along with $10 million more) to a mall developer who builds in suburban locations. The division transfers the $720 to the mall developer and receives a four-year, 12 percent promissory note (a promise to pay the $720 back in four years along with $86.40 per year in interest payments). The promissory note is a financial asset of the insurance company and a financial liability of the developer. When the developer spends the money, the $720 leaves the financial sector and re-enters the spending stream in the real economy. At that point it becomes investment in the economic sense.

Buying a House

Most people, when they buy a house, don't go out and plop down the thousands of dollars it costs. Instead they go to a bank or similar financial institution, and borrow a large portion of the price, taking out a mortgage on the house. A **mortgage** is simply a special name for a secured loan on real estate. By mortgaging her house, a person is creating a financial liability for herself and a financial asset for someone else. This financial asset is secured by the house. If the person defaults on the loan, the mortgage holder (who, as you will see, may or may not be the bank) can foreclose on the mortgage and take title to the house.

Mortgage A special name for a secured loan on real estate.

The funds available in banks come primarily from depositors who keep their savings in the bank in the form of savings accounts or checking accounts. Balances in these accounts are often small, but with lots of depositors they add up and provide banks with money to lend out. If you're planning to buy a house, you'll most likely go to a bank.

The bank's loan officer will have you fill in a lengthy form and the bank will send an appraiser out to the house to assess its value. The appraiser asks questions about the house: Does it meet the electrical code? What kind of pipes does it have? What kind of windows does it have? All this information about you and the house is transferred onto a master form that the loan officer uses to decide whether to make the loan. (Contrary to what many lay people believe, in normal times a loan officer wants to make the loan. Remember, a bank's profits are the difference between what it pays in interest and what it receives in interest; it needs to make loans to make profits. So he or she often looks at hazy answers on the form and puts an interpretation on them that's favorable to making the loan.)

In two weeks or so, depending on how busy the bank is, you hear back that the loan is approved for, say, $80,000 at 9 percent interest and two points. A point is 1 percent of the loan; it is a charge the bank makes for the loan. So two points means the bank is charging you $1,600 for making you a loan of $80,000 at 9 percent interest. (And you wondered why the bank was anxious to make you a loan!) The bank credits your account with $78,400, which allows you to write a check to the seller of the house at a meeting called the *closing*.

The bank gets a lot of money in deposits, but generally it doesn't have anywhere near enough deposits to cover all the mortgages it would like to make. So the process doesn't stop there. Instead the bank generally sells your mortgage on the secondary market to Fannie Mae (the Federal National Mortgage Association) or Ginnie Mae (the Government National Mortgage Association), which pay, say, $80,400 for the $80,000 mortgage. They're buying your mortgage (which you paid $1,600 in points to be allowed to get) for $400 more than its amount. The bank makes money both ways: when it makes the loan and when it sells the loan.

Fannie Mae and Ginnie Mae are nonprofit companies organized by the government to encourage home ownership. They do this by easing the flow of savings into mortgages. They take your mortgage and a number of similar ones from different areas and make them into a bond package: a $100,000,000 bond fund secured by a group of mortgages. (Remember the long forms and the questions the appraiser asked? Those forms and answers allow Fannie Mae and Ginnie Mae to classify the mortgage and put it in a group with similar mortgages.) They then sell shares in that bond fund to some other institution that gives Fannie Mae and Ginnie Mae money in return. The Maes use that money to buy more mortgages, thereby channeling more savings into financing home ownership.

Who buys Fannie Mae and Ginnie Mae bonds? Let's go back and consider our insurance company. If the insurance company hadn't made the loan to the developer, the company might have decided the Ginnie Mae bonds were the best investment it could make. So who knows? Your insurance company may hold the mortgage to your house.

You, of course, don't know any of this. You simply keep making your mortgage payments to the bank which, for a fee, forwards it to Ginnie Mae, which uses it to pay the interest on the bond it sold to the insurance company.

Summary

We could go through other transactions, but these two should give you a sense of how real-world financial transactions work their way through financial institutions. Financial institutions make money by the fees and commissions they charge for buying and selling loans, and on the difference between the interest they pay to get the money and the interest they receive when they lend the money out.

WHY FINANCIAL INSTITUTIONS ARE IMPORTANT FOR MACROECONOMICS

Now that you have a sense of the financial sector, let's briefly consider how it fits into the macroeconomic models and debates discussed in earlier chapters. The debate was between Classicals who believed government should follow a laissez-faire policy and Keynesians who believed government should take an activist role in controlling the aggregate economy with policies such as fiscal policy.

The Classical View of the Financial Sector

Classical economists see the financial sector operating relatively smoothly. It is like a mirror that reflects the real sector, and as long as government doesn't disturb that mirror the financial sector won't be a problem. That's why Classical economists said that savings will be translated into investment relatively smoothly and that the Keynesian problem of insufficient demand wouldn't arise. Say's law is based on a smoothly working financial sector.

Exhibit 9 shows the Classical view of the financial market. The supply of savings is upward sloping, and the demand for investment is downward sloping. The interest rate adjusts to maintain savings equal to investment at the full-employment level of income.

Because Classicals see the financial sector working smoothly, they generally oppose any meddling with the financial system (last-ditch loans to companies about to go out of business, credit controls, limitation on interest rates, and other government involvement in financial markets).

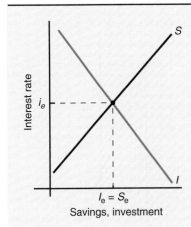

EXHIBIT 9   The Classical View of the Financial Sector

Classical economists see the financial market working smoothly so that savings and investment would always be equal. If they weren't, the interest rate would change so they were equal. Since savings always equal investment, there can be no Keynesian-type multiplier process.

Keynesian economists see the financial sector differently. While they also see the financial sector as a mirror, often it's more like a reflecting pond with waves. These waves in the financial sector can have serious repercussions in the real sector. Specifically Keynesians do not believe that the financial market efficiently translates savings into investment. Sometimes, because the financial sector isn't working correctly, there's too much savings; sometimes there's too little savings. When the financial sector fails to translate savings back into investment, the quantity of aggregate supply differs from the quantity of aggregate demand. When this occurs, the multiplier process starts, causing unwanted business cycles. Put simply Keynesians believe the financial sector can get messed up, and when it gets messed up it messes up the real economy too.

The Keynesian view of financial markets can best be seen in Exhibit 10. In it you can see that the supply of savings is relatively vertical—the interest rate doesn't have much effect on it. Similarly with the demand for investment. Keynes argued that investment was not a simple decision based on interest rates but was a difficult decision based on expectations of the future and gut feelings. Why are the shapes of these curves important? Because those shapes tell us how much the interest rate must change to bring the financial market back into equilibrium. If the curves are relatively vertical (as Keynesians believe) and there's a shift in demand for investment from I_0 to I_1, the interest rate must change enormously (from i_0 to i_1) to bring the economy back into equilibrium. Such large interest rate fluctuations would cause serious problems in the financial sector.

If a change in the interest rate doesn't bring about equilibrium in the savings/investment market, what does? Changes in income. Since saving often doesn't equal investment, the result is income fluctuations in the real economy. Those fluctuations change income and hence savings. Equilibrium between savings and investment is brought about by the savings curve shifting (shown in Exhibit 10 as the shift from S_0 to S_1) as income falls from Y_0 to Y_1.

If the interest rate isn't determined in the savings/investment market in the Keynesian model, where is it determined? Keynesians believe it's determined in the money market, by people's demand for highly liquid assets and the supply of those liquid assets, specifically money. This means that a change in the money supply could affect interest rates and could play a role in equilibrating savings and investment.

We'll discuss these questions more in later chapters. Before we do, we'll take a much closer look at how one particular financial institution—banks—and one particular financial asset—money—fit into the macroeconomic landscape.

The Keynesian View of the Financial Sector

EXHIBIT 10   The Keynesian View of the Financial Sector

Keynesians see financial markets working in fits and starts and often staying in disequilibrium for long periods of time. If the interest rate adjusts, it does so slowly. Before the interest rate adjusts to bring savings and investment into equilibrium, the multiplier process would be set in motion, causing income to shift and the savings curve to shift. Shifts in the savings curve, not changes in the interest rate, bring about equilibrium in the Keynesian model.

KEY POINTS

- Every financial asset has a corresponding financial liability. **1**
- Financial institutions buy, sell, or hold financial assets. **2**
- Primary financial markets sell newly issued financial assets. Secondary financial markets transfer existing financial assets from one individual to another. **3**
- Financial assets with a maturity of less than one year (such as negotiable CDs and commercial paper) are sold in money markets. Financial assets with a maturity of over one year (such as bonds and mortgages) are sold on capital markets. They usually pay a higher rate of return than money market assets because they are less liquid. **4**

- Bonds pay a fixed interest on an investment each year until maturity, at which point the face value is paid. **4**
- Stocks have no maturity date, pay no interest, and do not return your original investment, but they give you ownership rights to a company and, thus, its profits. **4**
- Present value is the current value of a future amount of money. As the interest rate rises, the present value of a future amount of money falls. **5** **6**
- Classicals believe the financial market works efficiently; Keynesians believe it often gets messed up. **7**

KEY TERMS

bonds *(259)*
CD (certificate of deposit) *(263)*
capital market *(262)*
commercial paper *(259)*
contractual intermediary *(257)*

depository institution *(257)*
disintermediation *(263)*
diversification *(259)*
financial asset *(256)*
financial institution *(257)*
financial liability *(256)*

financial market *(260)*
liquidity *(260)*
money market *(262)*
mortgage *(271)*
present value *(269)*
primary financial market *(260)*

secondary financial market *(260)*
stock *(264)*

QUESTIONS FOR THOUGHT AND REVIEW

The number after each question represents the estimated degree of critical thinking required. (1 = almost none; 10 = deep thought.)

1. Is the cash in your pocketbook or wallet a real or a financial asset? Why? *(3)*
2. If financial institutions don't produce any tangible real assets, why are they considered a vital part of the U.S. economy? *(4)*
3. Which market, the primary or secondary, contributes more to the production of tangible real assets? Explain why. *(4)*
4. Why do money market assets generally yield lower interest payments than capital assets? *(3)*
5. Suppose that in 1990 you bought a newly issued bond with a $10,000 face value, a coupon rate of 9 percent, and a maturity date of 2020. How much interest would it pay each year? If the interest rate in the economy is 8 percent, would the bond be likely to sell for more or less than $10,000? *(4)*
6. Consider a company whose stock sells for $24 a share, has about $2 million in annual earnings, and has a million shares outstanding. What's that firm's price/earnings ratio? *(3)*
7. If a bond with a $5,000 face value and a 7.5 percent coupon rate is selling on the secondary bond market for $4,000, what can you say about the interest rate in the economy? *(2)*
8. A presidential candidate favors little government intervention in the economy. Would Classicals or Keynesians be more likely to support his candidacy? Why? *(3)*
9. How might a Keynesian economist explain a stock market crash? *(5)*
10. How might a Classical economist explain a stock market crash? *(9)*

PROBLEMS AND EXERCISES

1. A bond has a face value of $10,000 and a coupon rate of 10 percent. It is issued in 1991 and matures in 2001.
   a. How much does the bond pay annually?
   b. If the bond is currently selling for $9,000, what is its yield?
   c. If the interest rate in the economy rises, what will happen to the bond's price? Why?

2. Go to a local bank.
   a. Ask for a loan application. Inquire if you will be eligible for a loan.
   b. Ask why or why not.
   c. Find out how many different types of accounts they have and how these accounts differ.
   d. Ask if they will cash a $1,000 out-of-state check. If so, how long will it take for them to do so?

12

Money and Banking

> *The process by which banks create money is so simple that the mind is repelled.*
> John Kenneth Galbraith

After reading this chapter, you should be able to:

1
Explain what money is.

2
Enumerate the three functions of money.

3
State the alternative definitions of money and their primary components.

4
Explain how banks create money.

5
Calculate both the simple and the complex money multiplier.

6
Explain how a financial panic can occur and the potential problem with government guarantees to prevent such panics.

The financial institutions and assets discussed in the previous chapter are many and complicated. Each has its own peculiarities and interrelationships with the economy. Absorbing as my overview of them was, I suspect you've had enough, and if I tried to present in its entirety, the debate between Keynesians and Classicals about the financial sector that was introduced at the end of the last chapter, I would soon send you into a mental institution or at least into art history or sociology.

So instead, to simplify, I will follow the usual practice and focus on one of a group of the most important financial assets, which collectively are called *money*, and on a single financial institution, banks, which directly affect money.

At this point you're probably saying, "I know what money is; it's cash—the dollar bills I carry around." In one sense you're right; each is money. But in another sense you're wrong. Money is much more than cash. In fact a number of short-term financial assets are included as money. To see why, let's consider the definition and uses of money and then see which financial assets meet that definition.

The definition is as follows: **Money** is a highly liquid financial asset that's generally accepted in exchange for other goods and is used as a reference in valuing other goods. Consider the dollar bill that you know is money. Look at it; it states on it that it is a *Federal Reserve Note*, which means that it is an IOU (a liability) of the **Federal Reserve Bank** (the **Fed**), which is the U.S. central bank. (We'll discuss the Fed in depth in the next chapter, but at this point all you need know is that the Fed's liabilities serve as cash in the United States.)

From the previous chapter we know what a liquid financial asset is. It's an asset that can be quickly exchanged for another good. But the definition of money also requires that these financial assets are generally accepted in exchange for other goods and are used as a reference in valuing other goods. This definition says money serves three functions:

1. It serves as a medium of exchange.
2. It serves as a unit of account.
3. It serves as a store of wealth.

To get a better understanding of what money is, let's consider each in turn.

Money as a Medium of Exchange   The easiest way to understand money's medium-of-exchange use is to imagine what an economy would be like without money. Say you want something to eat at a restaurant. Without money you'd have to barter with the restaurant owner for your meal. *Barter* is a direct exchange of goods and/or services. You might suggest bartering one of your papers or the shirt in the sack

THE DEFINITION AND FUNCTIONS OF MONEY

Money A financial asset that makes the real economy function smoothly by serving as a medium of exchange, a unit of account, and a store of wealth.

Federal Reserve Bank (Fed) The central bank of the United States. Its liabilities serve as cash.

Functions of Money

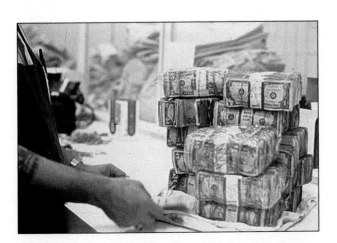

Lots of Money. *Federal Reserve Bank of Boston.*

that you'd be forced to carry with you to trade for things you want. Not liking to carry big sacks around, you'd probably decide to fix your own meal and forgo eating out. Bartering is simply too difficult.

The use of money as a medium of exchange makes it possible to trade real goods and services without bartering. It facilitates exchange by reducing the cost of trading. Instead of carrying around a sack full of goods, all you need to carry around is a billfold full of money. You go into the restaurant and pay for your meal with money; the restaurant owner can spend (trade) that money for anything she wants.

Money doesn't have to have any inherent value to function as a medium of exchange. All that's necessary is that everyone believes that other people will accept it in exchange for their goods. This neat social convention makes the economy more efficient.

That social convention depends on there not being too much or too little money. If there's too much money compared to the goods and services offered at existing prices, the goods and services will sell out, and money won't buy you anything. The social convention will break down, or prices will rise. If there's too little money compared to the goods and services offered at the existing prices, there will be a shortage of money and people will have to resort to barter, or prices will fall.

In order to maintain money's usefulness and to prevent large fluctuations in the price level, the money issuer, which in the United States is the Federal Reserve Bank, or Fed, must issue neither too much nor too little money. (As I stated previously, the Fed is the central bank of the United States; its liabilities serve as money for the U.S. economy.) People accept money in payment and agree to hold money because they believe the Fed will issue neither too little nor too much money. This explains why the Fed doesn't freely issue large amounts of money. To issue money without restraint would destroy the social convention that gives money its value.

Money as a Unit of Account   A second use of money is as a unit of account. Throughout the book we've emphasized that money prices are actually relative prices. A nominal price, say 25¢, for a pencil conveys the information of a relative price: 1 pencil = $\frac{1}{4}$ of 1 dollar or $\frac{1}{6}$ of a hamburger because money is both our unit of account and our medium of exchange. When you think of 25¢, you think of $\frac{1}{4}$ of a dollar and of what a dollar will buy. The 25¢ a pencil costs only has meaning relative to the information you've stored in your mind about what it can buy. If a hamburger costs \$1.50, you can compare hamburgers and pencils (1 pencil = $\frac{1}{6}$ of a hamburger) without making the relative price calculations explicit.

Having a unit of account makes life much easier. For example, say we had no unit of account and you had to remember the relative prices of all goods. For instance, with three goods you'd have to memorize that an airplane ticket to Miami costs 6 lobster dinners in Boston or 4 pairs of running shoes, which makes a pair of shoes worth $1\frac{1}{2}$ lobster dinners.

Memorizing even a few relationships is hard enough, so it isn't surprising that societies began using a single unit of account. If you don't have a single unit of account, to know the relative prices of all combinations of just 20 goods you need to remember over a million relative prices. If you have a single unit of account, you need know only 20 prices. A single unit of account saves our limited memories and helps us make reasonable decisions based on relative costs.

Money is a useful unit of account only as long as its value relative to other prices doesn't change too quickly. That's because it's not only used as a unit of account at a point in time. It's also a unit of account *over time*. Money is a standard of deferred payment. The value of payments that will be made in the future (such as the college loan payments many of you will be making in the future) are determined by the future value of money. A hyperinflation would significantly reduce the value of what you have to pay back. So a hyperinflation

ADDED DIMENSION

CHARACTERISTICS
OF A GOOD MONEY

The characteristics of a good money are that its supply be relatively constant, that it be limited in supply (sand wouldn't make good money), that it be difficult to counterfeit, that it be divisible (have you ever tried to spend half a horse?), that it be durable (raspberries wouldn't make good money), and that it be relatively small and light compared to its value (watermelon wouldn't make good money either). All these characteristics were reasonably (but not perfectly) embodied in gold. Many other goods have served as units of account (shells, wampum, rocks, cattle, horses, silver), but gold historically became the most important money, and in the 17th and 18th centuries gold was synonymous with money.

But gold has flaws as money. It's relatively heavy, easy to counterfeit with coins made only partly of gold, and, when new gold fields are discovered, subject to fluctuations in supply. These flaws led to gold's replacement by paper currency backed only by trust that the government would keep its commitment to limit its supply.

Paper money can be a good money if somehow people can trust the government to limit its supply and guarantee that its supply will be limited in the future. That trust has not always been well placed.

would help you, right? Actually, probably not—because a hyperinflation would also rapidly destroy money's usefulness as a unit of account and thereby destroy the U.S. economy.

In a hyperinflation all prices rise so our frame of reference is lost. Is 25¢ for a pencil high or low? If the price level changed 33,000 percent (as it did in 1988 in Nicaragua) or over 100,000 percent (as it did in 1989 in Argentina), 25¢ for a pencil would definitely be low, but would $100 be low? Without a lot of calculations we can't answer that question. A relatively stable unit of account makes it easy to answer.

The unit-of-account usefulness of a money also requires that prices don't change too quickly. If the government printed money to pay all its expenses, money's relative price would fall quickly (an increase in supply lowers price), which is another way of saying that the price level would explode and the unit-of-account function of money would be seriously undermined. Maintaining the unit-of-account usefulness of money is a second reason government doesn't pay all its bills by printing money.

Given the advantages to society of having a unit of account, it's not surprising that a monetary unit of account develops even in societies with no government. For example, in a prisoner of war camp during World War II, prisoners had no money, so they used cigarettes as their unit of account. Everything traded was given a price in cigarettes. The exchange rates on December 1, 1944, were:

  1 bar of soap: 2 cigarettes
  1 candy bar: 4 cigarettes
  1 razor blade: 6 cigarettes
  1 can of fruit: 8 cigarettes
  1 can of cookies: 20 cigarettes

As you can see, all prices were in cigarettes. If candy bars rose to 6 cigarettes and the normal price was 4 cigarettes, you'd know the price of candy bars was high.

Money as a Store of Wealth   In an earlier chapter, we saw that financial assets serve as a store of wealth. Whenever you save, you forgo consumption now so that you can consume in the future. To bridge the gap between now and the future, you must acquire a financial asset. This is true even if you squirrel away cash under the mattress. In that case, the financial asset you've acquired is simply the cash itself. Money is a financial asset. (It's simply a bond that pays no interest.) So a third use of money is as a store of wealth. As long as money is serving as a medium of exchange, it automatically also serves as a store of wealth. The restaurant owner can accept your money and hold it for as long as she wants

UNFUNNY MONEY

RIO DE JANEIRO—"Take a banana," says Italo Gasparini, the director of the Brazilian Central Bank's currency department. "What does it cost? One hundred cruzados? Is that cheap or expensive? I don't know. Do you know?"

Nobody knows. Inflation is so high that it perplexes everyone. A television set costing 20,000 cruzados at the beginning of this year now costs 190,000 (about $320). Rents have been leaping more than 800% a year. A newspaper may double in price overnight. The 10-cruzado bank note, worth nearly a dollar two years ago, is now routinely discarded as trash.

The bank note's disgrace upsets Mr. Gasparini. He recently returned from a ceremony launching the 10,000-cruzado note. When planning the note eight months ago, he hoped it would be worth about $50. It buys $17. Because the ceremony started late, people joked that he would have to present a 20,000-cruzado note. Already, he is preparing a 50,000 bill for March and a 100,000 for May. Without any illusions.

"It's impossible to keep up," he says.

On Verge of Catastrophe

After years of high inflation, Brazil is on the verge of an uncontrollable price spiral that could plunge the West's eighth-largest economy, and the developing world's largest debtor, into chaos. Inflation this year will top 900%, compared with 365% in 1987. And it is still accelerating.

So far, nevertheless, Brazilians have muddled through with a mixture of submission and adaptability. They can manage another year, optimists believe, even if inflation stays at about the November monthly rate of 26.9%—an annual rate close to 2,000%. A tenuous so-called pact among the government, businessmen and labor unions is trying to hold inflation at that high level.

Widespread Indexation

Muddling through is facilitated by thorough indexing of the economy. Salaries climb along with prices, although in the public sector they have lagged at least 30% this year and sparked the strikes. Companies and well-heeled individuals rely on the "overnight"—that is, 24-hour deposits in treasury bonds available in all banks and paying a yield tied to inflation.

Despite the inflation, some people continue to make money. One is Edison Dytz, a retired army colonel who a year ago opened a small computer store in Brasilia, the capital. He keeps his inventory low, buying about six computers at a time. As soon as he has any funds, he puts them in the "overnight." He bought his premises because rents rise so sharply. With interest rates prohibitive, he avoids debt. He keeps his budget not in cruzados but in OTNs, a commonly traded bond whose value rises monthly at about the rate of inflation.

How the unpredictable President Sarney deals with all this in his last year of office is anybody's guess. The best that optimists hope for is more muddling through as things gradually worsen. The worst that could happen—and all see the danger increasing—is illustrated by Mr. Gasparini, the Central Bank official. He turns to a wall poster showing how money evolved: from the exchange of fish and grain, through fashioned objects, to precious metal, coins and then bills. "This evolution could go into reverse here," he says.

before she spends it. (But had you paid her in fish, she'd be wise not to hold it more than a few hours.)

Money's usefulness as a store of wealth also depends upon how well it maintains its value. If prices are going up 100,000 percent per year, the value of a stated amount of money is shrinking fast. People want to spend their money as quickly as possible before prices rise any more. Thus, once again, money's usefulness as a social convention depends upon the government not issuing too much money.

Even if prices aren't rising, you might wonder why people would hold money which pays no interest, rather than holding a government bond which does pay interest. The reason is that money is more easily translated into other goods than are bonds. Since money is also the medium of exchange, it can be spent instantaneously (as long as there's a shop open nearby). Our ability to spend money for goods makes money worthwhile to hold even if it doesn't pay interest.

Alternative Definitions of Money

According to the definition of *money,* what people believe is money is a determining factor in deciding whether a financial asset is money. What is money depends on what people will accept as money; consequently it's difficult to define *money*

ADDED DIMENSION

NOW ACCOUNTS AND MONEY MARKET ACCOUNTS

At one time the only checking accounts were those of commercial banks. You put your money in a commercial bank and wrote a check. Then savings banks (banks allowed only to have savings accounts) started allowing individuals to write *n*egotiable *o*rders of *w*ithdrawals on their savings accounts (NOW accounts). So if you held $10,000 in a savings account you could write an IOU to someone and the savings bank promised to pay it. That IOU looked like a check and for all practical purposes it was a check. But unlike a checking account, NOW accounts paid interest on depositors' balances. Many people started shifting from checking accounts to NOW accounts, and soon commercial banks complained of unfair competition by savings banks. These complaints led to commercial banks being allowed to pay interest on their checking accounts.

Mutual funds saw how nicely NOW accounts worked and decided to imitate them. Individuals who kept their money stored with a mutual fund were allowed to write IOUs based on their deposits (up to three IOUs per month, each for a minimum of, say, $500). The mutual fund invested depositors' money in the money market (short-term bills, commercial paper, and CDs). Hence, accounts with mutual funds are called *money market accounts*. These accounts pay slightly higher interest than savings banks accounts, and, like the NOW account, are close to a checking account.

So today people have a choice of depository institutions, which is nice for people, but tough for textbook writers and students who have to learn more divisions.

unambiguously. A number of different financial assets serve some of the functions of money and thus have claims to being called *money*. To handle this ambiguity, economists have defined different concepts of money and have called them M_1, M_2, and L. Each is a reasonable concept of money. Let's consider their components.

M_1 M_1 consists of cash in the hands of the public and checking account balances. Clearly, cash in the hands of the public (the dollar bills and coins you carry around with you) are money, but how about your checking account deposits? The reason they're included in this definition of money is that just about anything you can do with cash, you can do with a check. You can store your wealth in your checking account; you can use a check as a medium of exchange (indeed, for some transactions you have no choice but to use a check), and your checking account balance is denominated in the same unit of account (dollars) as is cash. If it looks like money, acts like money, and functions as money, it's a good bet it's money. Indeed, checking account deposits are included in all definitions of money.

The same arguments can be made about traveler's checks. (Some advertisements even claim that traveler's checks are better than money because you can get them replaced.) Currency, checking account deposits, and traveler's checks make up the components of M_1, the narrowest definition of money. Exhibit 1 presents the relative sizes of M_1's components.

M_2 M_2 is made up of M_1 plus savings deposits, small-denomination time deposits, and money market mutual fund shares, along with some esoteric financial instruments that won't concern us here. The relative sizes of the components of M_2 are given in Exhibit 1. (The esoteric instruments are classified as "Other.")

The money in savings accounts (savings deposits) is counted as money because it is readily spendable—all you need do is go to the bank and draw it out. Small-denomination time deposits are also called *certificates of deposit (CDs)*.

M_2's components include more financial assets than M_1, some of which don't quite meet all the requirements of being called money. But all the components are highly liquid and play an important role in providing reserves for commercial banks. What makes the M_2 definition important is that economic research has shown that M_2 is the definition of money most closely correlated with the price level and economic activity.

M_1 Component of money supply consisting of cash in the hands of the public plus checking accounts and traveler's checks.

M_2 Component of the money supply consisting of M_1 plus other relatively liquid assets.

Savings deposits (30%)
Money market mutual funds (10%)
Other (2%)
Currency (30%)
Checking accounts (69%)
Small-denomination time deposits (32%)
M_1 (26%)
Travelers' checks (1%)
Components of M_2
Components of M_1

EXHIBIT 1   Components of M₂ and M₁

The two most-used definitions of the money supply are M_1 and M_2. The primary components of M_1 are cash and checking accounts. M_2 includes all of M_1, plus savings accounts and time deposits.
Source: *Federal Reserve Bulletin*, February 1992.

Beyond M₂: L   The same type of argument can be made for a wide variety of short-term financial assets (assets whose maturity is less than one year). They all have some of the attributes of money. They're liquid and can be "spent" relatively easily. For that reason they're included in some definitions of money. There are definitions for M_3, M_4, and beyond. Most economists concern themselves only with the first two definitions (M_1 and M_2) and the broadest definition, which is called L (for *liquidity*). The **L** definition of money includes almost all short-term assets.

L The broadest definition of the money supply consisting of almost all short-term financial assets.

Distinguishing between Money and Credit   You might have thought that credit cards would be included in one of the definitions of *money*. But we didn't include them. In fact, credit cards are nowhere to be seen in a list of financial assets. Credit cards aren't a financial liability of the bank that issues them. Instead credit cards create a liability for their holders (money owed to the company or bank that issued the card) and the banks have a financial asset as a result.

Let's consider how a credit card works. You go into a store and buy something with your credit card. You have a real asset—the thing you bought. The store has a financial asset—an account receivable. The store sells that financial asset to the bank (for a fee, of course) and gets cash in return. Either the bank collects cash when you pay off your financial liability or, if you don't pay it off, the bank earns interest on its financial asset (usually at a high rate, about 18 percent per year).

This distinction between credit and money should be kept in mind. Money is a financial asset of individuals and a financial liability of banks. Credit is savings made available to be borrowed. Credit is not an asset.

Credit cards and credit impact the amount of money people hold. When credit is instantly available (as it is with a credit card) there's less need to hold money. (If you didn't have a credit card, you'd carry a lot more cash.) Liquidity is less valuable to people. So credit and credit cards do make a difference in how much money people hold, but because they are not financial assets, they are not money.

Now that we've considered what money is, both in theory and in practice, let's consider the banking system's role in creating money.

Banks are financial institutions that borrow from people (take in deposits) and use the money they borrow to make loans to other individuals. Banks make a profit by charging a higher interest on the money they lend out than they pay for the money they borrow.

Banking is generally analyzed from the perspective of **asset management** (how a bank handles its loans and other assets) and **liability management** (how a bank attracts deposits and what it pays for them). When banks offer people ''free checking'' and special money market accounts paying 6.8 percent, they do so after carefully considering the costs of those liabilities to them.

To think of banks as borrowers as well as lenders may seem a bit unusual, but borrowing is what they do. When you keep money in a savings account or a checking account, the bank is borrowing from you, paying you a zero (or low) interest rate and lending your money to other people at a high interest rate. Much of banks' borrowing is short-term borrowing, meaning banks must pay the money back to the lender either on demand (as in the case of checking accounts or savings accounts) or within a specific period of time (as in the case of certificates of deposit).

In the United States, banks operate in a regulated environment. They have limits on what kind of loans they can make and what type of borrowing they're allowed to do. The primary regulator of the money supply in the United States is the Federal Reserve Bank (the Fed), which we'll consider in detail in the next chapter.

BANKS AND THE CREATION OF MONEY

Asset management A bank's handling of loans and other assets.

Liability management How a bank attracts deposits and what it pays for them.

How Banks Create Money

How do banks create money? As John Kenneth Galbraith's epigram at the start of this chapter suggested, the process is simple—so simple it seems almost mystical to many.

The key to understanding how banks create money is to remember the nature of financial assets: Financial assets can be created from nothing as long as an offsetting financial liability is simultaneously created. Since money is any financial asset that serves the function of money, money can be created rather easily. Seeing how dollar bills are created is the easiest way to begin examining the process. Dollar bills are IOUs of the Fed that serve the three functions of money. So whenever the Fed issues an IOU, it creates money.[1] Similarly other banks create money by creating financial assets that serve the functions of money. As we saw when we considered the definition of *money,* bank checking accounts serve those functions, so they are money, just as cash is.

The First Step in the Creation of Money   To see how banks create money, let's consider what would happen if you were given a freshly printed $100 bill. Remember, the Fed created that $100 bill simply by printing it. The $100 bill is a $100 financial asset of yours and a financial liability of the Fed, which issued it.

If the process of creating money stopped there, it wouldn't be particularly mysterious. But it doesn't stop there. Let's consider what happens next as you use that money.

The Second Step in the Creation of Money   Say you decide to put the $100 bill in your checking account. To make the analysis easier, let's assume that your bank is a branch of the country's only bank, Big Bank. All money deposited in branch banks goes into Big Bank. After you make your deposit, Big Bank is holding $100

---

[1] As we'll see in the next chapter, dollar bills aren't the Fed's only IOUs.

cash for you, and you have $100 more in your checking account. You can spend it whenever you want simply by writing a check. So Big Bank is performing a service for you (holding your money and keeping track of your expenditures) for free. Neat, huh? Big Bank must be run by a bunch of nice people.

But wait. You and I know that bankers, while they may be nice, aren't as nice as all that. There's no such thing as a free lunch. Let's see why the bank is being so nice.

Banking and Goldsmiths   To see why banks are so nice, let's go way back in history to when banks first developed.[2] At that time, gold was used for money and people carried around gold to make their payments. But gold is rather heavy, so if they had to make a big purchase, it was difficult to pay for the purchase. Moreover carrying around a lot of gold left them vulnerable to being robbed by the likes of Robin Hood. So they looked for a place to store their gold until they needed some of it.

From Gold to Gold Receipts   The natural place to store gold was the goldsmith shop, which already had a vault. For a small fee, the goldsmith shop would hold your gold, giving you a receipt for it. Whenever you needed your gold, you'd go to the goldsmith and exchange the receipt for gold.

Pretty soon most people kept their gold at the goldsmith's, and they began to wonder: Why go through the bother of getting my gold out to buy something when all that happens is that the seller takes the gold I pay and puts it right back into the goldsmith's vault? That's two extra trips.

Consequently people began using the receipts the goldsmith gave them to certify that they had deposited $100 worth (or whatever) of gold in his vault. At that point gold was no longer the only money—gold receipts were also money. However, as long as the total amount in the gold receipts directly represented the total amount of gold, it was still reasonable to say, since the receipts were 100 percent backed by gold, that gold was the money supply.

Once this process of using the receipts rather than the gold became generally accepted, the goldsmith found that he had substantial amounts of gold in his vault. All that gold, just sitting there! On a normal day only 1 percent of the gold was claimed by ''depositors'' and had to be given out. Usually on the same day an amount at least equal to that 1 percent came in from other depositors. What a waste! Gold sitting around doing nothing! So when a good friend came in, needing a loan, the goldsmith said, ''Sure, I'll lend you some gold receipts as long as you pay me some interest.'' When the goldsmith made this loan, he created more gold receipts than he had covered in gold in his vault. He created money.

Pretty soon the goldsmith realized he could earn more from the interest he received on loans than he could earn from goldsmithing. So he stopped goldsmithing and went full-time into making loans of gold receipts. At that point the number of gold receipts outstanding significantly exceeded the amount of gold in the goldsmith's vaults. But not to worry; since everyone was willing to accept gold receipts rather than gold, the goldsmith had plenty of gold for those few who wanted actual gold.

It was, however, no longer accurate to say that gold was the country's money or currency. Gold receipts were the money. They met the definition of *money*. These gold receipts were backed partially by gold and partially by people's trust that the goldsmiths would pay off their deposits on demand. The goldsmith shops had become banks.

---

[2] The banking history reported here is, according to historians, apocryphal (more myth than reality). But it so nicely makes the point that I repeat it anyhow.

Banking Is Profitable   The banking business was very profitable for goldsmiths. Soon other people started competing with them, offering to hold gold for free. After all, if they could store gold, they could make a profit on the loans to other people (with the first people's money). Some even offered to pay people to store their gold.

The goldsmith story is directly relevant to banks. People store their cash in banks and the banks issue receipts—checking accounts—which become a second form of money. When people place their cash in banks and use their receipts from the bank as money, those receipts also become money because they meet the definition of *money:* They serve as a medium of exchange, a unit of account, and a store of wealth. So money includes both cash that people hold and their deposits in the bank.

Which brings us back to why banks hold your cash for free. They do it, not because they're nice, but because when you deposit cash in the bank, your deposit allows banks to make profitable loans they otherwise couldn't make.

With that background, let's go back to your $100, which the bank is now holding for you. You have a checking account balance of $100 and the bank has $100 cash. As long as other people are willing to accept your check in payment for $100 worth of goods, your check is as good as money. In fact it *is* money in the same way gold receipts were money. But when you deposit $100, no money has been created yet. The form of the money has simply been changed from cash to a checking account or demand deposit.

Now let's say Big Bank lends out 90 percent of the cash you deposit, keeping only 10 percent as **reserves** on hand—that is, enough money to manage the normal cash inflows and outflows. This 10 percent is the **reserve ratio** (the ratio of cash to deposits a bank keeps as a reserve against withdrawals of cash). So, like the goldsmith, Big Bank lends out $90 to someone who needs a loan. That person the bank loaned the money to now has $90 cash and you have $100 in a demand deposit, so now there's $190 of money, rather than just $100 of money. The $10 in cash the bank holds in reserve isn't counted as money since the bank must keep it as reserves and may not use it as long as it's backing loans. Only cash held by the public is counted as money. By making the loan, the bank has created $90 in money.

Of course, no one borrows money just to hold it. The borrower spends the money, say on a new sweater, and the sweater store owner now has the $90 in cash. The store owner doesn't want to hold it either. She'll deposit it back into the bank. Since there's only one bank, Big Bank discovers that the $90 it has loaned out is once again in its coffers. The money operates like a boomerang: Big Bank loans $90 out and gets the $90 back again.

The same process occurs again. The bank doesn't make any money holding $90, so it lends out $81, keeping $9 (10 percent of $90) in reserve. The story repeats and repeats itself, with a slightly smaller amount coming back to the bank each time. At each step in the process money (in the form of checking account deposits) is being created.

Determining How Many Demand Deposits Will Be Created   What's the total amount of demand deposits that will ultimately be created from your $100? To answer that question, we continue the process over and over: 100 + 90 + 81 + 72.9 + 65.6 + 59 + 53.1 + 47.8 + 43.0 + 38.7 + 34.9. Adding up these numbers gives us $686. Adding up $686 plus the numbers from the next 20 rounds gives us $961.08.

As you can see, that's a lot of adding. Luckily there's an easier way. Mathematicians have shown that you can determine the amount of money that will eventually be created by such a process by multiplying the initial $100 in money that was found and deposited by $1/r$, where r is the reserve ratio (the percentage banks keep out of each round). In this case the reserve ratio is 10 percent.

The Money Multiplier

Reserves   The amount of cash a bank keeps on hand to manage normal inflows and outflows.

Reserve ratio   The ratio of cash to deposits a bank keeps as a reserve against cash withdrawals.

Dividing,

$$1/r = 1/.10 = 10$$

so the amount of demand deposits that will ultimately be created by the process is

$$(10 \times \$100) = \$1,000.$$

The \$1,000 is in the form of checking account deposits (demand deposits). The entire \$100 in cash that you were given, and which started the whole process, is in the bank as reserves.

Simple money multiplier The measure of the amount of money ultimately created per dollar deposited by the banking system when people hold no cash. It equals $1/r$ where r is the percentage of deposits the bank keeps as reserves.

5

Calculating the Money Multiplier   The ratio $1/r$ is called the **simple money multiplier.** It tells us how much money will ultimately be created by the banking system from an initial inflow of money. In our example, $1/.10 = 10$. Had the bank kept out 20 percent each time, the money multiplier would have been $1/.20 = 5$. If the reserve ratio were 5 percent, the money multiplier would have been $1/.05 = 20$. The higher the reserve ratio, the smaller the money multiplier, and the less money will be created.

To test whether you've got the process down pat, ask yourself what would happen if each person held some of his or her money in the form of cash at each stage of the process. If you said that it would reduce the amount of money that would be created, you've got it. If that wasn't your answer, a review is probably in order.

How did we know that people holding money would reduce the money multiplier? We noticed that money held as cash reduced the amount banks can loan out in the same way a higher reserve requirement does. So the money multiplier must be smaller. To see this, let's consider that \$100 you were given, only this time assume at each round people hold 20 percent of what they receive, depositing only 80 percent in the bank. Instead of depositing \$100, the person would deposit only \$80. The bank keeps 10 percent of this \$80, which is \$8, and lends out \$72. Eighty percent of \$72 is \$57.60, which the borrower deposits back in the bank. The bank then keeps 10 percent of that \$57.60, or \$5.76, and lends out \$51.84. Individuals keep 20 percent of that \$51.84 as cash, or \$10.37, depositing \$41.47 back in the bank. Of that \$41.47 deposit, the bank then lends out \$37.32 (90 percent of \$41.47). Each amount the bank lends out increases the money supply.

Following this same reasoning, the total money created after 10 rounds will be:

r = % depos kept as reserves
c = % of cash people keep

$$80 + 57.60 + 41.47 + 29.86 + 21.49 + 15.48 + 11.15 + 8.02 + 5.78 + 4.16$$

which equals \$275. To that amount we must add the cash that people hold which ultimately will equal \$75, with the bank holding \$25. So \$350 is the approximate amount of money that will be created when banks hold 10 percent as reserves and people hold cash equal to 20 percent of what they receive.

5

Complex money multiplier The measure of the amount of money created per dollar deposited in the banking system when people hold cash: $(1 + c)/(r + c)$.

Again, that's a lot of addition, and mathematicians have found a simple formula to determine the money multiplier when people hold cash. It's $(1 + c)/(r + c)$. The formula $(1 + c)/(r + c)$ is called the **complex money multiplier.**

Before we substitute in, it's important to call your attention to the definition of c. It's not the 20 percent that we just used—that was the ratio of the money people kept to the total money they received. It's the ratio of money people hold as cash to the money people hold as demand deposits. The two ratios are, however, related. If people deposit in the bank 80 percent of the money they receive, they're keeping 25 percent of the money they deposit. For example, if they receive \$100 and keep \$20, they're depositing \$80.

The ratio of cash to money they receive is

$$20/100 = 20\%.$$

ADDED DIMENSION

THE COMPLEX MONEY
MULTIPLIER AND RECENT
REFORMS IN BANKING

L ife keeps getting tougher. In the old days (as recently as the 1980s) economics students only had to learn the simple money multiplier. Recent reforms in the U.S. banking system have made that impossible. The Depository Institutions Deregulation Act of 1980 extended the reserve requirement to a wide variety of financial institutions besides banks but it also lowered the reserve requirement for most deposits. In the 1990s the average reserve requirement for all types of bank deposits is about 2 percent. (The reserve requirement on checking accounts is between 3 and 12 percent.)

If you insert that low average ratio into the simple money multiplier you get a multiplier of 50! The real-world money multiplier is much lower than that because of people's holding of cash; the ratio of money people hold as cash, c, is over .4. (For each person in the United States there's about $1,000 in cash. Don't ask me where that cash is, but according to the data it's out there.) Thus, despite the fact that it makes for a more complex multiplier, these holdings must be included in the story. Otherwise you won't have a sense of how the real-world system works.

Measuring c (the ratio of cash to money they deposit), we get

$$c = 20/80 = 25\%.$$

So in our example, $c = .25$ and $r = .1$.

With the complex money multiplier we can calculate precisely how much the money multiplier would be when people hold cash. Say banks hold 10 percent of the loans in reserve ($r = .10$ percent) and individuals hold as cash 20 percent of the amount they deposit ($c = .25$). Substituting the numbers into the formula gives

$$(1 + .25)/(.1 + .25) = 3.57.$$

When people hold 20 percent of their money as cash, and banks hold 10 percent of their deposits as reserves, the complex money multiplier is 3.57. So in our example, from that initial $100, $357 in money would be created. (Notice by carrying the math out 10 rounds, we got $350, which is close to this figure.)

Faith as the Backing of Our Money Supply

The creation of money and the money multiplier are easy to understand if you remember that money (the financial asset created) is offset by an equal amount of financial liabilities of the bank. The bank owes its depositors the amount in their checking accounts. Its financial liabilities to depositors, in turn, are secured by the loans (the bank's financial assets) and by the financial liabilities of people to whom the loans were made. Promises to pay underlie any modern financial system.

The initial money in the story about the goldsmiths was gold, but it quickly became apparent that it was far more reasonable to use gold certificates as money. Therefore gold certificates backed by gold soon replaced gold itself as the money supply. Then, as goldsmiths made more loans than they had gold, the gold certificates were no longer backed by gold. They were backed by promises to get gold if the person wanted gold in exchange for the gold certificate. Eventually the percentage of gold supposedly backing the money became so small that it was clear to everyone that the promises, not the gold, underlay the money supply.

The same holds true with banks. Initially cash (Federal Reserve IOUs) was backed by gold, and banks' demand deposits were in turn backed by Federal Reserve IOUs. But by the 1930s the percentage of gold backing money grew so small that even the illusion of the money being backed by anything but promises was removed. All that backs the modern money supply are banks' promises to pay.

Creation of Money Using T-Accounts

You've already been introduced to the basis of financial accounting: the T-account presentation of balance sheets. The balance sheet is made up of assets on one side and liabilities and net worth on the other. By definition the two sides are equal; they balance (just as the T-account must).

EXHIBIT 2

TEXTLAND BANK
Balance Sheet
December 31, 1992

Assets		Liabilities and net worth	
Cash	$ 30,000	Demand deposits	$150,000
Loans	300,000	Net worth	350,000
Property	170,000		
Total assets	$500,000	Total liabilities and net worth	$500,000

To cement the money creation process in your mind, let's discuss how banks create money using transactions that affect the balance sheet. Exhibit 2 shows the initial balance sheet of an imaginary Textland Bank, which we assume is the only bank in the country. As you can see, Textland has $500,000 in assets: $30,000 in cash, $300,000 in loans, and $170,000 in property. On the liabilities side, it has $150,000 in demand deposits and $350,000 in net worth. The two sides of the balance sheet are equal.

The first thing to notice about this balance sheet is that if all holders of checking accounts (demand deposits) wanted their cash, the bank couldn't give it to them. The cash it holds is only a portion—20 percent—of the total deposits:

$$\$30,000/\$150,000 = .20.$$

Banks rely upon statistical averages and assume that not all people will want their money at the same time. Let's assume Textland Bank has decided 20 percent is an appropriate reserve ratio.

Now let's say that John Finder finds $10,000 in cash. He keeps some of that cash and deposits the rest into Textland Bank. Let's assume in general that people's ratio of cash to demand deposits is 30 percent, which means that ratio of cash to total money received is 23 percent.[3]

So John keeps 23 percent of each dollar he finds and deposits 77 percent of it in the bank. Thus, John Finder deposits $7,700 in the bank and keeps $2,300. After he does so, what will happen to the money supply? The first step is seen in Transaction 1, which shows the effect of John Finder's deposit on the bank's account. The bank gains $7,700 in cash, but its liabilities also increase by $7,700, so, as you can see, the two sides of the balance sheet are still equal. At this point no additional money has been created; $7,700 cash has simply been changed to a $7,700 demand deposit.

Transaction 1

Assets			Liabilities and Net Worth		
Cash (beginning balance)	$30,000		Demand deposits (beginning balance)	$150,000	
Cash from John	7,700		John's deposit	7,700	
Total cash		$ 37,700	Total demand deposits		$157,700
Loans		300,000	Net worth		350,000
Property		170,000			
Total assets		$507,700	Total liabilities and net worth		$507,700

Now let's assume the bank uses a reserve ratio of 20 percent, meaning it lends out 80 percent of what it takes in. Therefore it lends out $80\% \times \$7,700 = \$6,160$ to

---

[3] If c is the ratio of cash to deposits (c = cash/deposits), the ratio of cash to total amount received is [cash/(deposits + cash)]. If we divide both numerator and denominator by cash, we have

$$(cash/cash)/[(deposits/cash) + (cash/cash)] = 1/[(1/c) + 1].$$

Substituting in c = 30 percent, we have

$$1/[(1/.3) + 1] = 1/(3.33 + 1) = 1/4.33 = .23 \text{ or } 23\%.$$

Fred Baker, keeping 20 percent × $7,700 = $1,540 in reserve. The change in the bank's balance sheet is seen in Transaction 2. This step creates $6,160 in money. Why? Because John Finder still has $7,700 in his checking account and $2,300 in cash, while Fred Baker has $6,160 cash, so, combining John's checking account balance with Fred's cash, the public has $16,160 in money. As you can see, loans have increased by $6,160 and cash in Textland Bank has decreased by $6,160.

Transaction 2

Assets			Liabilities and Net Worth	
Cash (after Trans. 1)	$ 37,700		Demand deposits (after Trans. 1)	$157,700
Cash given to Fred	6,160		Net worth	350,000
Total cash		$ 31,540		
Loans (beginning balance)	300,000			
Loan to Fred	6,160			
Total loans		306,160		
Property		170,000	Total liabilities and net worth	$507,700
Total assets		$507,700		

Fred Baker didn't borrow the money to hold onto it. He spends most of it buying a new oven from Mary Builder. Fred and Mary hold some of their money in the form of cash. We assume the public holds 23 percent of their money balance in the form of cash, so of that $6,160, $4,743 (77% × $6,160 = $4,743) will work its way back as bank deposits. In our story, after getting paid, Mary Builder deposits the $4,743 into Textland Bank (the only bank according to our assumptions). Textland's balance sheet now looks like Transaction 3.

Transaction 3

Assets			Liabilities and Net Worth	
Cash (after Trans. 2)	$31,540		Demand deposits	$157,700
Cash from Mary	4,743		Mary's deposit	4,743
Total cash		$ 36,283	Total demand deposits	$162,443
Loans		306,160	Net worth	350,000
Property		170,000		
Total assets		$512,443	Total liabilities and net worth	$512,443

The public has $3,717 in cash ($2,300 held by John Finder and $1,417 held by Fred Baker); Mary Builder has a demand deposit of $4,743; and John Finder has a demand deposit of $7,700. So there's still $16,160 worth of money in the system. But Textland Bank has excess reserves of $3,794, since it must keep only $949 of Mary's $4,743 deposit as reserves:

$$80\% \times \$4743 = \$3794.$$

So the bank is looking to make a loan.

Now the process occurs again. Exhibit 3 shows the effects of the process for 10 rounds, starting with the initial $10,000. Each time it lends the money out, 77 percent of what it lends comes back to the bank like a boomerang and serves as reserves for more loans. After 10 rounds we reach a point where the public holds $5,961 in cash and total demand deposits are up to $19,949. Adding these two gives us a total money supply of $25,910. This is approaching the $26,000 we'd arrived at using the complex money multiplier:

$$[(1 + c)/(r + c)](\$10,000) = [(1 + .3)/(.2 + .3)](\$10,000)$$

$$= 2.6(\$10,000) = \$26,000.$$

If we carried it out for a few more rounds, we'd actually reach what the formula predicted.

EXHIBIT 3   The Money-Creating Process

Bank Gets	Bank Keeps (Reserve Ratio: 20%)	Bank Loans (80%) = Person Borrows	Demand Deposits (77% of What Person Gets)	Person Keeps (23% of What Person Gets)
			7,700	2,300
7,700	1,540	6,160	4,743	1,417
4,743	949	3,794	2,921	873
2,921	584	2,337	1,799	538
1,799	360	1,439	1,108	331
1,108	222	886	682	204
682	136	546	420	126
420	84	336	259	77
259	52	207	159	48
159	32	127	98	29
98	20	78	60	18
	3,979		19,949	+ 5,961

Total money created (after 10 rounds)   =   25,910

Note the $10,000 in currency notes is held jointly by the bank and the public. After 10 rounds the bank holds $3,979 in cash and the public holds $5,961 in cash. Thus, a total of $9,940 (approaching $10,000) is held in cash. However, the money supply, which includes both cash and checking account deposits, has been increased to almost $26,000. The additional money is in the form of checking account deposits.

In summary, the process of money creation isn't difficult to understand as long as you remember that money is simply a bank's financial liability held by the public. Whenever banks create financial liabilities for themselves, they create financial assets for individuals, and those financial assets are money.

REGULATION OF BANKS AND THE FINANCIAL SECTOR

You just saw how easy it is to create money. The banking system and money make the economy operate more efficiently, but they also present potential problems. For example, say that for some reason suddenly there's an increase in money (that is, in promises to pay) without any corresponding increase in real goods and services. As the money supply increases without an increase in real goods to buy with that money, more money is chasing the same number of goods. Aggregate demand exceeds aggregate supply. The result will be a fall in the value of money (inflation), meaning real trade will be more complicated. Alternatively if there's an increase in real goods but not a corresponding increase in money, there will be a shortage of money, which will hamper the economy. Either the price level will fall (deflation) or there will be a recession.

Societies have continually experienced these problems and the financial history of the world is filled with stories of financial upheavals and monetary problems. For example, there are numerous instances of private financial firms who have promised the world, but their promises have been nothing but hot air. One instance occurred in the 1800s in the United States, when banks were allowed to issue their own notes (their own promises to pay). These notes served as part of the U.S. money supply. Sharp financial operators soon got into the process and created banks out in the boonies called *wildcat banks* because they were situated in places where only a wildcat would go. These wildcat banks issued notes even though they had no deposits, hoping that no one would cash the notes in. Many such banks defaulted on their promises, leaving holders of the notes with only worthless pieces of paper. Merchants quickly caught on, and soon they began checking in a "book of notes" which listed whether the notes the buyer was offering were probably good or not.

Another problem that can develop in the banking system is a financial panic. Banking and financial systems are based on promises and trust. People put their cash into other financial assets (such as demand deposits) and believe that these demand deposits are as good as cash. In normal times, demand deposits really are as good as cash. When times get bad, people become concerned about the financial firms' ability to keep those promises and they call upon the firms to redeem the promises. But banks have only their reserves (a small percentage of their total deposits) to give depositors. Most of the depositors' money is loaned out and cannot be gotten back quickly, even though the banks have promised depositors that their deposits will be given back "on demand." Put another way, banks borrow short and lend long.

When a lot of depositors lose faith in a bank and, all at one time, call on the bank to keep its promises, the bank cannot do so. The result is that the bank fails when depositors lose faith, even though the bank might be financially sound for the long run. Fear underlies financial panics and can undermine financial institutions.

Anatomy of a Financial Panic

6

To prevent such panics, the U.S. government has guaranteed the obligations of various financial institutions. Guaranteeing programs include the Federal Deposit Insurance Corporation (FDIC), Federal Savings and Loan Insurance Corporation (FSLIC), and a variety of government-guaranteed bonds. These guarantees work as follows: The financial institutions pay a small premium for each dollar of deposit to the government-organized insurance company. That company puts the premium into a fund used to bail out banks experiencing a run on deposits. These guarantees have two effects:

Government Policy to Prevent Panic

1. They prevent the unwarranted fear that causes financial crises. Depositors know that the government will see that they can get their cash back even if the bank fails. This knowledge stops them from responding to a rumor and trying to get their money out of a suspect financial institution before anyone else does.

2. They prevent warranted fears. Why should people worry about whether or not a financial institution is making reasonable loans on the basis of their deposits if the government guarantees the financial institutions' promises to pay regardless of what kind of loans the institutions make?

Guarantees prevent unwarranted fears. The illusion upon which banks depend (that people can get their money in the short run, even though it's only in the long run that they can *all* get it) can be met by temporary loans from the government. Guarantees can prevent unwarranted fears from becoming financial panics. The guarantee makes the illusion a reality. If people can indeed get their money in the

The Benefits and Problems of Guarantees

Merton Miller—Nobel prize, 1990, for work on financial economics. © *The Nobel Foundation.*

long run, seeing to it that this illusion *is* reality isn't expensive to the government. As long as the bank has sufficient long-term assets to cover its deposits, the government will be repaid its temporary loan.

Unfortunately covering the unwarranted fear can also mean preventing the warranted fear from putting an effective restraint or discipline on banks' lending policies. If deposits are guaranteed, why should depositors worry whether banks have adequate loans to cover their deposits in the long run? Thus, when there's a bigger illusion than the short-run/long-run illusion, and depositors can't get their money in the long run (that is, their fears were warranted), guaranteeing deposits can be expensive indeed. The U.S. government found this out in the late 1980s in connection with its guarantees of federal savings and loan institutions' deposits.

The Savings and Loan Fiasco of the Late 1980s and Early 1990s As we said, the United States has guaranteed the deposits of a variety of financial institutions, including savings and loan institutions (S&Ls). S&Ls had developed as institutions to hold savings and invest those savings back into the community. Up until 1980, S&Ls were heavily regulated by the government and weren't allowed to invest in anything except private residential mortgages, which generally are relatively safe investments. The only place S&Ls were allowed to get their funds from was their depositors' savings accounts. During the period when S&Ls were heavily regulated, the U.S. government began to guarantee S&L deposits.

In 1982 financial institutions were deregulated, and S&Ls were allowed to invest in anything they wished and to compete for funds with commercial banks by issuing interest-bearing checking accounts (called *NOW accounts*) and negotiable CDs. They did so. They paid high interest on their deposits and, to justify that high interest, they invested in high-interest financial assets such as high-risk junk (low-grade) bonds and commercial real estate. Unfortunately S&Ls didn't have the management capability to assess the risks, and they made billions of dollars worth of bad loans which would never be paid back. During the 1980s the U.S. economy also changed. Banking policies that had made sense in the late 1970s and early 1980s no longer made sense in the mid-1980s. The result was the savings and loan fiasco of the late 1980s and early 1990s. Many S&Ls failed and didn't have enough money to pay back depositors. The U.S. government, which had guaranteed those deposits, had to bail out the S&Ls by paying the depositors.

The cost of this government bailout, which is required by the guarantees, will be hundreds of billions of dollars. In fact, because of the complexity and vast number of the deals so many S&Ls made, it will probably be years before the government actually knows the final cost.

How Could the Savings and Loan Fiasco Happen? How, you ask, can banks make so many bad loans that they don't have enough money to pay back depositors? Part of the answer is fraud—banks made loans to friends that they knew were more like gifts than like loans. Part of the answer is that it doesn't take many bad loans to pull a bank under. Remember, banks take deposits in and lend those deposits out, hoping to make a profit from the **spread** (the difference between their costs and the interest they pay out, and the interest they take in minus bad loans). If, on average, more loans go bad than expected and the banks' costs are higher than expected, banks' profit can evaporate, leaving a loss. When that happens deposits must be covered by the banks' net worth, which is small—about 1 percent of total deposits—so there isn't much room for many bad loans. As was just pointed out, the S&Ls paid high interest rates and made many risky loans.

Another part of the answer is that it isn't hard to make a bad loan. Making loans is inherently risky. A person walks in with a grand idea for a mall—all she needs is a $10,000,000 loan. The mall is needed by the community and will be worth $30,000,000 once it's built. She has investors willing to put up $2,000,000 of

Spread The difference between a bank's costs of funds and the interest it receives on lending out those funds.

their own money and she's willing to pay 12 percent interest and give the mall as collateral. She's built successful malls before. So the bank makes the loan. The building starts, only to have the builder discover there's stone ledge beneath the site. Blasting is required—costs go up 12 percent. A builders' strike delays construction—costs go up 4 percent. When things are ready to proceed once the strike is settled, it rains daily, slowing construction—costs go up another 8 percent. The economy goes into a recession and one store that had promised to rent space in the mall pulls out. Let's say the store that pulled out was an ''anchor'' store (that is, the mall relied on that store's presence to attract large numbers of shoppers, who would then wander around and shop in the mall's smaller stores). Now the major industry in town shuts down. The mall's finished value falls 40 percent. You get the picture. Making loans requires taking chances and, when you take chances, once in a while you lose. S&Ls bet that there would be no recession. When a recession started, they lost their bet, and a number of their loans went bad.

The last part of the answer is the government guarantee. Had the government not guaranteed the S&L's deposits, depositors (not the government) would have incurred the loss. They likely would have become alarmed as they saw troubles coming to their S&Ls and would have withdrawn their money before the situation became a disaster. But they didn't watch carefully and had no reason to be alarmed, because they knew the government had guaranteed their deposits (at least, up to $100,000).

Should the government have guaranteed S&L deposits? That's an open question. The guarantees did serve their purpose; they prevented unwarranted runs on S&Ls. (That is, depositors didn't all run to the bank at the same time and ask to withdraw their money in cash.) But the guarantee program had serious flaws. If the government were going to guarantee deposits, it should have charged banks

Semiautonomous government banks, called Federal Reserve banks, all issue their own publications discussing issues related to money and banking.   The *Economic Review* is published by the Federal Reserve bank in Atlanta.

This 18th-century etching by Robert Goez, "The Speculator," captures a popular view of financial activities. It shows a man reduced to rags by bad speculation.   *Bleichroeder Print Collection, Baker Library, Harvard Business School.*

much higher fees. Government then would have had enough money to cover the losses resulting from bad loans. Or government should have maintained a strong regulatory presence, limiting the risks the S&Ls undertook.

The S&L crisis didn't answer the debate between the two goals: avoiding unwarranted fears while not limiting warranted fears. Keynesians blame the crisis on the bank deregulation that let S&Ls make risky loans and investments. They claimed the S&Ls' crisis showed the need for regulation. Classicals blame government guarantees that stopped the market forces from operating. As usual, both Keynesians and Classicals have reasonable arguments.

KEY POINTS

- Money is a useful financial instrument. **1**
- Money serves as a unit of account, a medium of exchange, and a store of wealth. **2**
- There are various definitions of money: M_1, M_2, and L. **3**
- Since money is what people believe money to be, creating money out of thin air is easy. How banks create money out of thin air is easily understood if you remember that money is simply a financial liability of a bank. **4**
- The simple money multiplier is $1/r$. **5**
- The complex money multiplier is $(1 + c)/(r + c)$. **5**
- Financial panics are based on fear. They can be prevented by government, but only at a cost. **6**

KEY TERMS

asset management *(283)*
complex money multiplier *(286)*
Federal Reserve Bank (Fed) *(277)*
L *(282)*
liability management *(283)*
M_1 *(281)*
M_2 *(281)*
money *(277)*
reserve ratio *(285)*
reserves *(285)*
simple money multiplier *(286)*
spread *(292)*

QUESTIONS FOR THOUGHT AND REVIEW

The number after each question represents the estimated degree of critical thinking required. (1 = almost none; 10 = deep thought.)

1. Money is to the economy as oil is to an engine. Explain. *(4)*
2. List the three functions of money. *(1)*
3. Why doesn't the government pay for all its goods simply by printing money? *(4)*
4. What are two components of M_2 that are not components of M_1? *(1)*
5. Assuming individuals hold no cash, calculate the simple money multiplier for each of the following reserve requirements: 5%, 10%, 20%, 25%, 50%, 75%, 100%. *(3)*
6. Assuming individuals hold 20% of their money in the form of cash, recalculate the money multipliers from Question 5. *(5)*
7. If dollar bills (Federal Reserve notes) are backed by nothing but promises and are in real terms worthless, why do people accept them? *(4)*
8. If the U.S. government were to raise the reserve requirement to 100 percent, what would likely happen to the interest rate banks pay? Why? *(6)*
9. What was the cause of the S&L crisis? What role did government guarantees play in that crisis? *(6)*
10. Is the current U.S. banking system susceptible to panic? If so, how might a panic occur? *(5)*

PROBLEMS AND EXERCISES

1. While Jon is walking to school one morning, a helicopter flying overhead drops a $100 bill. Not knowing how to return it, Jon keeps the money and deposits it in his bank. (No one in this economy holds cash.) If the bank keeps 5 percent of its money in reserves:
    a. How much money can the bank now lend out?
    b. After this initial transaction, by how much is the money in the economy changed?
    c. What's the money multiplier?
    d. How much money will eventually be created by the banking system from Jon's $100?
2. Assume that there's only one bank in the country, that the reserve requirement is 10 percent, and that people deposit 80 percent of the money they receive into their bank accounts. The bank begins with $20,000 cash, $225,000 in loans, $105,000 in physical assets, $200,000 in demand deposits, and $150,000 in net worth.
    a. An immigrant comes into the country and deposits $10,000 in a bank. Show this deposit's effect on the bank's balance sheet.
    b. The bank keeps enough of this money to satisfy its reserve requirement and loans out the rest to Ms Entrepreneur. Show the effect on the bank's balance sheet.
    c. Ms Entrepreneur uses the money to pay Mr. Carpenter, who deposits 80 percent of what he gets in the bank. Show the effect on the bank's balance sheet.
    d. Show the bank's balance sheet after the money multiplier is all through multiplying.

13

The Federal Reserve System and Monetary Policy

There have been three great inventions since the beginning of time: fire, the wheel and central banking.

Will Rogers

After reading this chapter, you should be able to:

1

Recount a brief history of the Fed.

2

State what monetary policy is.

3

List the three tools of monetary policy and explain how they work.

4

Go through the effect of an open market operation on a bank, using T-accounts.

5

Explain how monetary policy works in the Keynesian model.

6

Explain how monetary policy works in the Classical model.

7

List five problems often encountered in conducting monetary policy.

The preceding chapter ended with a discussion of financial panics which can occur when people lose faith in one financial asset and want to shift to another. Financial panics are no stranger to banking. In the 1800s the United States suffered a financial panic every 20 years or so. Initially a few people would suddenly fear they wouldn't be able to get their money out of their bank. They'd run down to the bank to get it. Others would see them getting their money and would do likewise. This was referred to as *a run on the bank*. As a result, their bank would have to close. If a bank closed, people would worry about other banks closing, and they'd run to *their* banks. That process could spread uncontrollably; banks would close and there would be a general financial panic. These panics led to considerable debate about what government should do to regulate and control the banking system.

Much of the initial debate about the U.S. banking industry concerned whether there should be a central bank (a bank that could make loans to other banks in times of crisis and could limit those banks' expansionary loans at other times). Supporters of a central bank argued that a central bank would create financial stability. Opponents argued that it would cause recessions and favor industrial interests over farming interests.

Initially central bank supporters predominated, and it wasn't long before the Bank of the United States, the first central U.S. bank chartered by the U.S. government, was established. Debates about the bank were rancorous and in 1811 its charter was not renewed. It went out of existence.

Five years later, in 1816, the political forces changed and the Second Bank of the United States was chartered. Its attempt to stop the inflationary spiral of 1817 and 1818 caused a depression. The bank was blamed. Political forces once again changed, and in 1832 the Second Bank was dismantled.

The next hundred years were marked by periodic financial crises and recessions—every 10 or 20 years. These crises led to arguments that the country needed a central bank to help prevent future crises, but when a particular crisis

HISTORY AND STRUCTURE OF THE FEDERAL RESERVE SYSTEM

1

The issue of regulating banks has been at the forefront of economic policy discussions for centuries as can be seen in this 18th- or 19th-century English print of unknown origin, "The Bank Restriction Barometer." *Bleichroeder Print Collection, Baker Library, Harvard Business School.*

ended, the argument would fade away. In 1907, however, there was a major financial panic. In response the government established the Federal Reserve Bank (the Fed) in 1913. The Federal Reserve Bank has remained in existence ever since and is now the United States central bank.

The Fed Is a Central Bank

Central bank   A banker's bank; it conducts monetary policy and supervises the financial system.

2

Monetary policy   Policy that influences the economy through changes in the money supply and available credit.

A **central bank** is a type of bankers' bank. If banks need to borrow money, they go to the central bank, just as when you need to borrow money, you go to a neighborhood bank. If there's a financial panic and a run on banks, the central bank is there to make loans to the banks until the panic goes away. Since its IOUs are cash, simply by issuing an IOU it can create money. A central bank's duties also include assisting government with its financial affairs. A central bank serves as a financial advisor to government. As is often the case with financial advisors, the government sometimes doesn't like the advice and doesn't follow it.

Besides being a bankers' bank and a financial advisor, the Fed also conducts monetary policy for the government. **Monetary policy** is a policy of influencing the economy through changes in the money supply and credit availability in the economy. Monetary policy is one of the two main macroeconomic tools (the other is fiscal policy) by which government attempts to control the aggregate economy. Unlike fiscal policy, which is controlled by the government directly, monetary policy is controlled by the Fed.

Historical Influences in the Federal Reserve Bank's Structure

In many countries, such as Germany, Great Britain, and France, the central bank is a part of their government, just as this country's Department of the Treasury and the Department of Commerce are part of the U.S. government. In the United States the central bank is not part of the government in the same way as in some European countries. Because of political infighting about how much autonomy the central bank should have in controlling the economy, the Federal Reserve Bank was created as a semi-autonomous organization. The bank is privately owned by the member banks. However, member banks have few privileges of ownership. For example, the Board of Governors of the Federal Reserve is appointed by the U.S. president, not by the owners. Also almost all the profits of the Fed go to the government, not to the owners. In short, the Fed is owned by the member banks in form only. In practice the Fed is an agency of the U.S. federal government.

Although it is an agency of the federal government, the Fed has much more independence than most agencies. Once appointed, Fed governors cannot be removed from office, nor can they be reappointed; their terms are 14 years. Because they cannot be removed and because they have little incentive to try to get reappointed, they feel little political pressure. If the president doesn't like what they do, tough luck, until their appointments expire or one of them decides to resign or retire.

There are seven officers of the Federal Reserve Bank; they are called the Governors of the Federal Reserve. In practice, since pay at the Federal Reserve is much lower than at private banks and consulting firms, many appointees stay less than 14 years. When your job resumé includes ''Governor of the Federal Reserve,'' private organizations are eager to hire you and pay you five or six times as much as you earned at the Fed. This means that none of the Federal Reserve Governors are hard up for a job. So while at the Federal Reserve they can pretty much follow the policies they believe are best without being concerned about political retaliation, even if their terms aren't for life.

The president appoints one of the seven members to be chairman of the Board of Governors for a four-year term. The chairman has enormous influence and power, and is often called the second most powerful person in the United States. This is a bit of an exaggeration, but the chairman's statements are more widely reported in the financial press than any other government official's.

The Fed's general structure reflects its political history. Exhibit 1 demonstrates that structure. Notice in Exhibit 1(a) most component banks are in the East and Midwest. The South and West have only three banks: Atlanta, Dallas, and

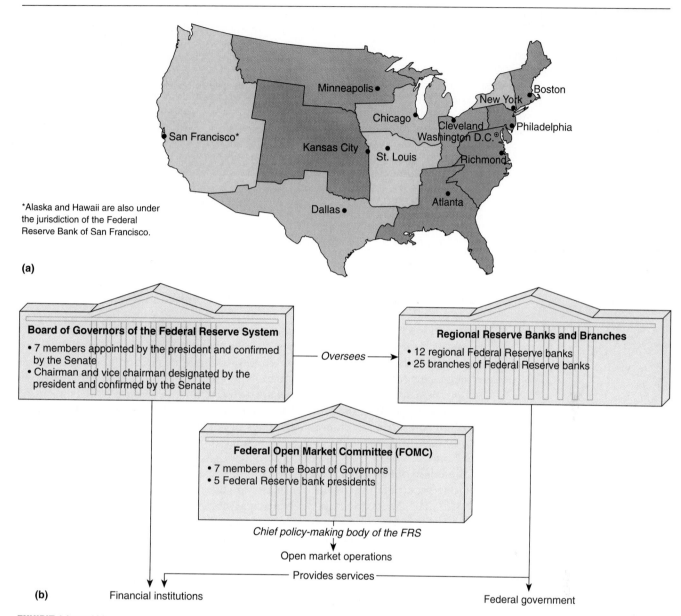

(a)

*Alaska and Hawaii are also under the jurisdiction of the Federal Reserve Bank of San Francisco.

(b)

EXHIBIT 1 (a and b)   The Federal Reserve System

The Federal Reserve System is composed of 12 regional banks. It is run by the Board of Governors. The FOMC is the most important policy-making body

Source: The Federal Reserve System.

San Francisco. The reason is that in 1913 when the Fed was established, the West and South were smaller and less important economically than the rest of the country, so fewer banks were established there.

As these regions grew, the original structure remained because no one wanted to go through the political wrangling restructuring would bring about. Instead, the southern and western regional Feds established a number of branches to handle their banking needs.

In legislation establishing the Fed, Congress gave it six explicit functions:

1. Conducting monetary policy (influencing the supply of money and credit in the economy).

2. Supervising and regulating financial institutions.

3. Serving as a lender of last resort to financial institutions.

4. Providing banking services to the U.S. government.
5. Issuing coin and currency.
6. Providing financial services to commercial banks, savings and loan associations, savings banks, and credit unions.

Of these the most important policy is monetary policy.

MONETARY POLICY

2

Monetary policy is probably the most used policy in macroeconomics. The Fed conducts and controls it, whereas fiscal policy is conducted directly by the government. Both policies are directed toward the same end: influencing the level of aggregate economic activity, hopefully in a beneficial manner. (In many other countries institutional arrangements are different and the central bank is a part of government, so both monetary and fiscal policy are directly conducted by the government, albeit by different branches of government.)

Actual decisions about monetary policy are made by the Federal Open Market Committee (FOMC), the Fed's chief policy-making body. All seven members of the Board of Governors, together with the president of the New York Fed and a rotating group of four of the presidents of the other regional banks, sit on the FOMC. The financial press and business community follow their discussions closely. There are even Fed watchers whose sole occupation is to follow what the Fed is doing and to tell people what it will likely do.

Tools of Monetary Policy

3

The three tools of monetary policy are:

1. Changing the reserve requirement.
2. Changing the discount rate.
3. Open market operations.

Let's discuss each in turn.

Changing the Reserve Requirement   Earlier you saw how the total amount of money created from a given amount of cash depends on the percentage of deposits that a bank keeps in reserves (the bank's reserve ratio). These reserves are IOUs of the Fed—either vault cash or deposits at the Fed. By law, the Fed controls the percentage of deposits banks keep in reserve by controlling the reserve requirement of all U.S. banks. The percentage the Federal Reserve System sets as the minimum amount of reserves a bank must have is called the **reserve requirement.**

Reserve requirement Minimum ratio of reserves to deposits that a bank must have.

Required Reserves and Excess Reserves   The amount banks keep in reserve depends partly on Federal Reserve requirements and partly on how much banks feel they need for safety (the cash they need to keep on hand at any time to give depositors who claim some of their deposits in the form of cash). The amount most banks need for safety is much smaller than what the Fed requires. For them, it's the Fed's reserve requirement that determines the amount they hold as reserves.

Banks hold as little in reserves as possible. Why? Because reserves earn no interest for a bank. And we all know that banks are in business to earn profits. How much is as little as possible? That depends on the type of liabilities the bank has. In April 1992 required reserves for large banks for their checking accounts (also called *demand deposits*) were about 10 percent. The reserve requirement for savings accounts and time deposits that mature in less than one-half year was 3 percent. The reserve ratio for many other of the banking system's liabilities was even lower, making the reserve requirement for total liabilities about 2 percent.

In 1991 total reserves were about $53 billion and required reserves were about $52 billion. This means excess reserves (reserves in excess of requirements) were about $1 billion. Thus, the reserve requirement plays a central role in how much money banks have to lend out.

One of the best sources of financial statistics, the *Federal Reserve Bulletin*.

The Reserve Requirement and the Money Supply   By changing the reserve requirements, the Fed can increase or decrease the money supply. If the Fed increases the reserve requirement, it contracts the money supply; banks have to keep more reserves so they have less money to lend out; the decreased money multiplier (the multiple contraction of deposits occurring in deposits in response to a change in reserves) further contracts the money supply. If the Fed decreases the reserve requirement, it expands the money supply; banks have more money to lend out; the money multiplier further expands the money supply. The Fed has seldom used changes in the reserve requirement to control the money supply, but in April 1992 it lowered the reserve requirement on large banks from 12 to 10 percent in an attempt to expand the money supply.

The total effect on the money supply of changing the reserve requirement can be determined by thinking back to the money multiplier, which (if individuals hold no cash), as you saw last chapter, should equal $(1/r)$—1 divided by the percentage of each dollar deposit that banks hold in reserves. When people hold no cash, at a reserve requirement of 25 percent, the money multiplier will be 4 so $1,000,000 in cash will support a $4,000,000 money supply. With a 10 percent reserve requirement, the money multiplier will be 10. With a 20 percent reserve requirement, the money multiplier will be 5.

When people hold cash, the ratio of money people hold as cash relative to deposits also helps to determine the money multiplier which becomes

$$[(1+c)/(r+c)].$$

In reality that ratio is about 0.4 ($c = .4$) and the average reserve requirement for demand deposits is about .1 ($r = .1$). So the realistic money multiplier for demand deposits is

$$(1+0.4)/(0.1+0.4) = 1.4/0.5 = 2.8.$$

A $100 increase of reserves will cause a $280 increase in demand deposits. For other deposits the reserve requirement is much lower, so the money multiplier is larger for those.

What do you do if you're a bank and you come up short of reserves? The Fed funds option is one solution, as the accompanying box says. The bank can borrow from another bank that has excess reserves. But if the entire banking system is short of reserves, that option won't work since there's no one to borrow from. Another option is to stop making new loans and to keep as reserves the proceeds of loans that are paid off. Still another option is to sell Treasury bonds to get the needed reserves. (Banks often hold some of their assets in Treasury bonds so that they can get additional reserves relatively easily if they need them.) These Treasury bonds are sometimes called *secondary reserves*. They do not count as bank reserves—only IOUs of the Fed count as reserves. But Treasury bonds can be easily sold and transferred into cash which does count as reserves. Banks use all these options.

THE FED FUNDS MARKET

lthough banks find it difficult to be both fully loaned out and to stay within the reserve requirement (which is determined by biweekly averages), they've developed ways to manage. Say your bank didn't make as many loans as it expected to so that it has a surplus of reserves (excess reserves). Say also that another bank has made a few loans it didn't expect to make so it has a shortage of reserves. The bank with surplus reserves can lend money to the bank with a shortage—and it can lend it overnight. At the end of a day, a bank will look at its balances and see whether it has a shortage or surplus of reserves. If it has a surplus, it will call a federal funds (''Fed funds'') dealer to learn the interest rate for Fed funds. Say the rate is 6 percent. The bank will then agree to lend its excess reserves overnight to the other

bank for the daily equivalent of 6 percent per year. It's all simply done electronically, so there's no need actually to transfer funds. In the morning the money (plus overnight interest) is returned. The one-day interest rate is low, but when you're dealing with millions or billions, it adds up.

The market in which banks lend and borrow reserves (the *federal funds market*) is highly efficient. When money is tight (most banks have shortages of reserves), the Fed funds rate is high; when money is loose (most banks have excess reserves), the rate is low. Generally, large city banks are borrowers of Fed funds; small country banks are lenders of Fed funds.

Economists keep a close eye on the Fed funds rate in determining the state of monetary policy.

Discount rate Rate of interest the Fed charges on loans it makes to banks.

Changing the Discount Rate A second tool of monetary policy concerns another alternative banks have if they are short of reserves. A bank can also go to its bank (the Federal Reserve, the banker's bank) and take out a loan.

The **discount rate** is the rate of interest the Fed charges for those loans. An increase in the discount rate makes it more expensive for banks to borrow from the Fed. A discount rate decrease makes it less expensive for banks to borrow. Therefore changing the discount rate is a second way the Fed can expand or contract the money supply.

On the surface, the reasoning seems straightforward. A discount rate decrease lowers the bank's cost and allows it to borrow more from the Fed. More reserves (IOUs of the Fed) are in the system so the money supply increases and the interest rates banks charge customers fall. An increase in the discount rate works in the opposite way.

In practice, however, the way the discount rate works is more complicated. The discount rate that the Fed charges is usually much lower than competing interest rates, such as the Fed funds rate that the banks would pay if they didn't borrow from the Fed. Thus, based on pure economic costs, banks should borrow lots of money from the Fed. But the invisible handshake is at work here, and the Fed discourages banks from using this option. It's a bit like having your parents lend you money. They'll lend you money, probably at a zero interest rate, but they may frown upon it and lecture you if you borrow from them. As a result, you use them only as a last resort. Similarly most banks borrow from the Fed only as a last resort.

Banks generally are very responsive to the Fed's desires. They know that the Fed controls the auditors of the banks, and if a bank borrows too often, the Fed may well suggest the auditors make a special visit to the bank to see why it needs to borrow. With such ''moral suasion,'' the actual discount rate is not the determinant; the Fed's reproach is.

Nonetheless, the changes in the discount rate affect the money supply as we'd expect them to. The reason is that the Fed uses the discount rate as a signal to banks: An increase in the discount rate signals that the Fed wants money tightened; a decrease signals that the Fed wants the money supply expanded. Banks usually respond appropriately.

Open Market Operations Changes in discount rate and reserve requirement are not used in day-to-day Fed operations. They're used mainly for major changes. For

The Federal Reserve banks process millions of checks every day through automated machines, such as this one. *Federal Reserve Bank of Boston.*

day-to-day operations, the Fed uses a third tool: **open market operations**—the Fed's buying and selling government securities (the only type of asset the Fed is allowed by law to hold in any appreciable quantity). These open market operations are the primary tool of monetary policy.

Open market operations The Fed's buying and selling government securities.

When the Fed buys a Treasury bill or bond, it pays for it with its IOU. This IOU doesn't have to be a written piece of paper. It may be simply a computer entry credited to the bank's account, say $1 billion. As you saw in Chapter 12, an IOU of the Fed is money.

Because the IOU the Fed uses to buy a government security serves as reserves to the banking system, with the simple act of buying a Treasury bond and paying for it with its IOU the Fed can increase the money supply (since this creates reserves for the bank). To increase the money supply, the Fed goes to the bond market, buys a bond, and pays for it with its IOU. The individual or firm who sold the bond now has an IOU of the Fed. When the individual or firm deposits the IOU in a bank, presto! The reserves of the banking system are increased. If the Fed buys $1,000,000 worth of bonds, it increases reserves by $1,000,000 and the total money supply by $1,000,000 times the money multiplier.

When the Fed sells Treasury bonds, it collects back some of its IOUs, reducing banking system reserves and decreasing the money supply. Thus,

> *To expand the money supply, the Fed buys bonds.*
> *To contract the money supply, the Fed sells bonds.*

To expand the money supply, the Fed buys bonds.
To contract the money supply, the Fed sells bonds.

Open market operations are the Fed's most-used tool in controlling the money supply. Periodically the Open Market Committee looks at trading in the financial markets and decides what its open market operations will be and whether it wants to expand or contract the money supply.

4

Let's go through an example using T-accounts. Say there's only one bank, Textland Bank, with branches all over the country. Textland is fully loaned out at a 10 percent reserve requirement. For simplicity, assume people hold no cash. Exhibit 2 shows Textland's initial balance sheet.

Now say the Fed sells $10,000 worth of Treasury bonds to individuals. The person who buys them pays with a check to the Fed for $10,000. The Fed, in turn, presents that check to the bank, getting $10,000 in cash from the bank. This step is shown in Transaction 1.

EXHIBIT 2

TEXTLAND BANK
Balance Sheet
December 31, 1993

Assets		Liabilities and net worth	
Cash (reserves)	$ 300,000	Demand deposits	$3,000,000
Loans	2,000,000	Net worth	1,000,000
Treasury bonds	400,000		
Property	1,300,000		
Total assets	$4,000,000	Total liabilities and net worth . . .	$4,000,000

Textland Bank Balance Sheet
Transaction 1

Assets			Liabilities and net worth	
Cash (reserves)	$ 300,000		Demand deposits	$3,000,000
Payment to Fed (person's Treasury purchase)	(10,000)		Deposit for cash (person's check) . .	(10,000)
Total cash		$ 290,000	Total deposits	$2,990,000
Loans		2,000,000	Net worth	1,000,000
Treasury bonds		400,000		
Property		1,300,000		
Total assets		$3,990,000	Total liabilities and net worth	$3,990,000

As you can see, bank reserves are now $290,000, which is too low to meet requirements on demand deposits of $2,990,000. With a 10 percent reserve requirement, $2,990,000 in deposits would require $(1/10) \times \$2,990,000 = \$299,000$, so the bank is $9,000 short of reserves. It must figure out a way to meet its reserve requirement. Let's say that it calls in $9,000 of its loans. After doing so it has assets of $299,000 in cash and $2,990,000 in demand deposits, so it looks as if the bank has met its reserve requirement.

If the bank could meet its reserve requirement that way, its balance sheet would be as shown in Transaction 2. Loans would decrease by $9,000 and cash would increase by the $9,000 necessary to meet the reserve requirement.

Textland Bank Balance Sheet
Transaction 2

Assets			Liabilities and net worth	
Cash (reserves)	$ 290,000		Demand deposits	$2,990,000
Loans (repaid)	9,000		Net worth	1,000,000
Total cash		$ 299,000		
Loans	2,000,000			
Loans called in	(9,000)			
Total loans		1,991,000		
Treasury bonds		400,000		
Property		1,300,000		
Total assets		$3,990,000	Total liabilities and net worth	$3,990,000

Unfortunately for the bank, meeting its reserve requirement isn't that easy. That $9,000 in cash had to come from somewhere. Most likely, the person who paid off the loans in cash did it partly by running down her checking account, borrowing all the cash she could from others, and using whatever other options she had. Since by assumption in this example, people don't hold cash, the banking system was initially fully loaned out, and Textland Bank was the only bank, the only cash in the economy was in Textland Bank's vaults! So that $9,000 in cash had to come from its vaults. Calling in the loans cannot directly solve its reserve problem. It still has reserves of only $290,000.

But calling in its loans did *indirectly* help solve the problem. Calling in loans decreased investment which, because it decreased aggregate demand, decreased the income in the economy. (If you're not sure why this is the case, think back to the Keynesian model.) That decrease in income decreases the amount of demand deposits people want to hold. As demand deposits decrease, the bank's need for reserves decreases.

Contraction of the money supply in this example works in the opposite way to an expansion of the money supply discussed in the last chapter. Banks keep trying to meet their reserve requirement by getting cash, only to find that for the banking system as a whole the total cash is limited. Thus, the banking system as a whole must continue to call in loans until that decline in loans causes income to fall sufficiently to cause demand deposits to fall to a level that can be supported by the smaller reserves. In this example, with a money multiplier of 10, when demand deposits have fallen by $100,000 to $2,900,000, total reserves available to the system ($290,000) will be sufficient to meet the reserve requirement.

Think back to the discussion of the Fed's structure. Recall the FOMC is the Fed's chief policy-making body. Now you know why. It decides on open market operations, and open market operations are the Fed's chief tool for controlling the economy.

Both Keynesians and Classicals agree that monetary policy is important, but they differ in how they see monetary policy affecting the economy, and in their recommendations to government about how to conduct monetary policy. These differences will become more apparent when we discuss macro policy in later chapters, but to provide a good foundation for those later discussions, let's now briefly consider these differences.

How Monetary Policy Works

Monetary Policy in the Keynesian Model   In Keynesian terms, monetary policy can be seen as an alternative method of shifting the aggregate expenditures curve up or down, thereby controlling the level of income in the economy. Let's see how.

In Exhibit 3(a) we see that when the Fed decreases the money supply (uses contractionary monetary policy), it increases the interest rate. Exhibit 3(b) shows the effect of that increased interest rate on investment. As you can see, because the demand for investment is downward sloping, as discussed in an earlier chapter, the rise in interest rate decreases the quantity of investment.

A decrease in investment starts the multiplier process and decreases income by a multiple of the amount that investment decreased. Exhibit 3(c) shows the effect of a fall in investment on income. The fall in investment causes income to fall. Thus, *contractionary* monetary policy tends to *decrease* the money supply, *increase* the interest rate, *decrease* investment, and *decrease* income and output:

contractionary monetary policy

$$M \downarrow \rightarrow i \uparrow \rightarrow I \downarrow \rightarrow Y \downarrow$$

Expansionary monetary policy works in the opposite manner, as Exhibit 3(d) shows. *Expansionary* monetary policy tends to *increase* the money supply, *decrease* the interest rate, *increase* investment, and *increase* income and output:

expansionary monetary policy

$$M \uparrow \rightarrow i \downarrow \rightarrow I \uparrow \rightarrow Y \uparrow$$

The preceding discussion of how monetary policy works in theory is helpful, but it probably isn't very intuitive. Let's go through the reasoning again, only this time focusing on trying to provide an intuitive feel for what is happening. Say the

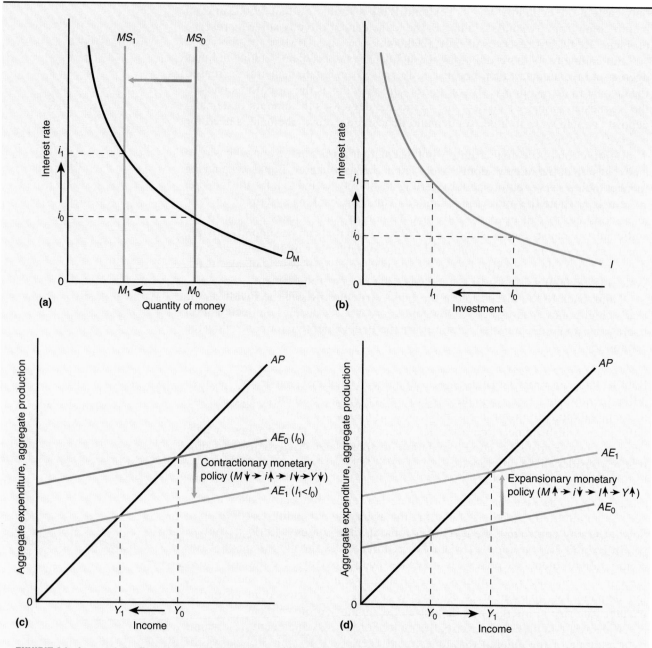

(a)

(b)

(c)

(d)

EXHIBIT 3 (a, b, c, and d)   **Expansionary and Contractionary Monetary Policy and the Aggregate Expenditures Curve**

With a decrease in the money supply, the interest rate will rise from i_0 to i_1 (**a**). The rise in the interest rate results in a decrease in investment from I_0 to I_1 (**b**). The fall in investment shifts the aggregate expenditures curve from AE_0 to AE_1. Income decreases from Y_0 to Y_1 (**c**), which decreases savings sufficiently so that savings equal investment. (**d**) shows expansionary monetary policy working the opposite way. It shifts the aggregate expenditures curve upward, from AE_0 to AE_1. Income increases from Y_0 to Y_1.

Fed uses open market operations. As the Fed either injects or pulls out reserves, it influences the amount of money banks have to lend and the interest rate at which they can lend it. When banks have more reserves than required, they want to lend. (That's how they make their profit.) To get people to borrow more from them, banks will decrease the interest rate they charge on loans. So expansionary monetary policy tends to decrease the interest rate banks charge their customers; contractionary policy tends to increase the interest rate banks charge customers. Expansionary monetary policy increases the amount of money banks have to

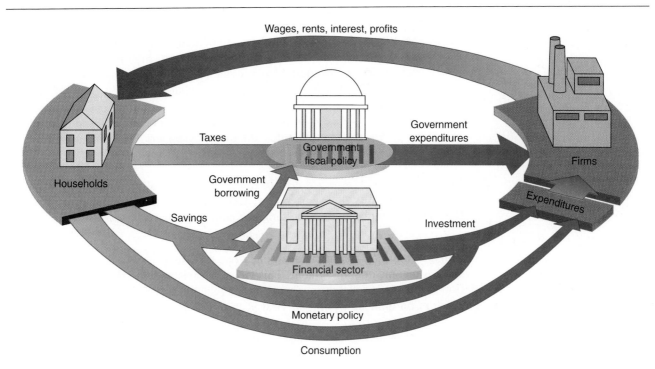

EXHIBIT 4   Keynesian Monetary Policy in the Circular Flow

If monetary and fiscal policy are needed, it is because the financial sector is, in some ways, clogged and is not correctly translating savings into investment. Monetary policy works to unclog the financial sector. Fiscal policy provides an alternative route for savings around the financial sector. A government deficit absorbs excess savings and translates it back into the spending stream. A surplus supplements the shortage of savings and reduces the flow back into the spending stream.

lend, which tends to increase investment. Contractionary monetary policy decreases the amount of money banks have to lend, which tends to decrease investment.

Keynesian Monetary Policy in the Circular Flow   Exhibit 4's familiar circular flow diagram shows how monetary policy works in the Keynesian model. In the Keynesian view monetary policy works inside the financial sector to help equate the flow of savings with investment. When the economy is operating at too low a level of income and when savings exceeds investment, in the absence of monetary policy, income will fall. Expansionary monetary policy tries to channel more savings into investment so the fall in income is stopped. It does so by increasing the available credit, lowering the interest rate, and increasing investment and hence income.

Contractionary monetary policy is called for when savings is smaller than investment and the economy is operating at too high a level of income, causing inflationary pressures. In this case, monetary policy tries to restrict the flow of savings in investment. Thus, to control the economy, Keynesians tend to favor an activist monetary policy with the Fed taking an active role in controlling the interest rate.

The Keynesian Emphasis on the Interest Rate   Because Keynesians see monetary policy working through the effect of interest rates on investment, they focus on the interest rate in judging monetary policy. They interpret a rising interest rate as a tightening of monetary policy. They interpret a falling interest rate as a loosening of monetary policy.

Keynesians believe the Fed should target interest rates in setting monetary policy. For example, if the interest rate is currently 6 percent and the Fed wants to loosen monetary policy, it should buy bonds until the interest rate falls to $5\frac{3}{4}$

percent. If it wants to tighten monetary policy, it should sell bonds to make the interest rate go up to, say, $6\frac{1}{2}$ percent.

In the 1950s the early Keynesians advocated keeping the interest rate low. More recently Keynesians have advocated keeping the interest rate low enough to foster growth, but high enough to prevent inflationary pressures. As you can imagine, it's a fine line between the two so whatever policy the Fed chooses usually has critics.

Discussions of whether interest rates are too high or too low and the effect of monetary policy on interest rates fill our newspapers' financial pages. These articles reflect the Keynesian focus on monetary policy.

6 Monetary Policy in the Classical Model   In the Classical model, monetary policy is best seen in the quantity theory of money. Expansionary monetary policy increases M (the money supply) and in the long run simply increases P (price level):

$$MV = PQ.$$

Thus, in the long run monetary policy has no effect on real economic variables such as income or employment. This view is consistent with the Classical proposition that there is a dichotomy between the real and nominal sectors. The Classical position on monetary policy is best seen in this theory.

The Classical Emphasis on Money Supply   The quantity theory of money framework, and the long-run relationship between money and prices that Classicals emphasize lead them to focus on the money supply as the key variable in judging whether monetary policy is tight or loose. A large increase in the money supply indicates expansionary monetary policy; a large decrease in the money supply indicates contractionary monetary policy.

"Steady-as-You-Go" Policy   Because of the Classicals' focus on the long run, they favor a "steady-as-you-go" monetary policy, increasing the money supply just enough each year to allow for the normal real growth in the economy. That increase is to be maintained regardless of the state of the economy. Following that rule, Classicals claim, is most likely to provide the stable financial setting necessary for a market economy to operate. Thus, Classicals oppose the Keynesian policy of an activist monetary policy.

The reason for their steady-as-you-go policy proposal is that, in the short run, Classical economists are much less certain about the workings of monetary policy. They argue that in the short run it operates in numerous ways that are too hard to analyze because they're constantly changing. How long monetary policy takes to work; by what channels it influences the real economy; and how, in the short run, it will influence prices versus real income—all this is unknowable. But what is knowable is that monetary policy will have some unknown strong effect in the short run and will raise the price level in the long run.

Classicals don't believe that monetary policy can ease or hinder the link between savings and investment because they believe the financial markets are already coordinating the flow from savings into investment as well as possible. True, sometimes savings and investment might get screwed up a bit, but monetary policy, with its uncertain effect, will likely screw it up even more. Moreover, Classicals believe that since politicians focus on short-run effects, political pressures will generally be toward increasing the money supply. In the long run these increases in the money supply will lead to an increase in the price level, so a Keynesian activist monetary policy that does not follow a predetermined rule will have an undesirable effect on inflation.

Real and Nominal Interest Rates   In support of their argument that the money supply rather than the interest rate should be considered in judging the looseness or tightness of monetary policy, Classicals point out the distinction between real and nominal interest rates. **Nominal interest rates** are the rates you actually see and pay. When a bank pays 7 percent interest, that 7 percent is a nominal interest rate. **Real interest rates** are rates adjusted for expected inflation.

For example, say you get 7 percent interest from the bank, but the price level goes up 7 percent. At the end of the year you have $107 instead of $100, but you're no better off than before, because the price level has risen—on average, things cost 7 percent more. What you would have paid $100 for last year now costs $107. (That's the definition of *inflation*.) Had the price level remained constant, and had you received 0 percent interest, you'd be in the equivalent position to receiving 7 percent interest on your $100 when the price level rises by 7 percent. That 0 percent is the *real interest rate*. It is the interest rate you would expect to receive if the price level remains constant.

The real interest rate cannot be observed because it depends on expected inflation, which cannot be directly observed. To calculate the real interest rate, you must subtract what you believe to be the expected rate of inflation from the nominal interest rate. For example, if the nominal interest rate is 7 percent and expected inflation is 4 percent, the real interest rate is 3 percent. Alternatively, the relationship between real and nominal interest rates is important both for your study of economics and for your own personal finances.

Nominal interest rate = Real interest rate + Expected inflation rate.

Real and Nominal Interest Rates and Monetary Policy   What does this distinction between nominal and real interest rates mean for monetary policy? It supports the Classical argument against using monetary policy to control the economy because it adds yet another uncertainty to the effect of monetary policy. Keynesians said that expansionary monetary policy lowers the interest rate and contractionary monetary policy increases the interest rate. However, if the expansionary monetary policy leads to expectation of increased inflation, Classicals point out expansionary monetary policy can increase nominal interest rates (the ones you see). Why? Because of expectations of increasing inflation.

The distinction between nominal and real interest rates strengthens the Classical case that the best monetary policy is an unchanging policy. In the short run, the effects of monetary policy's effects are too uncertain; in the long run, they simply lead to changes in the price level.

Given the ambiguity of the short-run effect and the negative effect of the long run, monetary policy should not be used to influence the economy. Instead, according to Classical economists, the economy should be governed by a specific rule that sets the money supply at a predetermined level and either holds it there or increases it at a constant rate.

Earlier, after discussing fiscal policy's structure and mechanics, I presented the problems with using fiscal policy. Now that you've been through the structure and mechanics of monetary policy, let's consider the problem with using it too.

Knowing What Policy to Use   To use monetary policy effectively, you must know the potential level of income. Otherwise you won't know whether to use expansionary or contractionary monetary policy. Let's consider an example: mid-1991. The economy seemed to be coming out of a recession. The Fed had to figure out whether to use expansionary monetary policy to speed up and guarantee the recovery, or use contractionary monetary policy and make sure inflation didn't start up again. Initially the Fed tried to fight inflation, only to discover that the economy wasn't coming out of the recession. In early 1992 the Fed switched from contractionary to expansionary monetary policy.

Nominal interest rate   Interest rates you actually see and pay.

Real interest rates   Nominal interest rates adjusted for expected inflation.

Nominal interest rate = Real interest rate + Expected inflation rate

Problems in the Conduct of Monetary Policy

7

Monetary base Vault cash plus reserves banks have on deposit at the Fed.

James Tobin—Nobel prize, 1981, for work on the interrelationship between money and the real economy. © *The Nobel Foundation.*

Understanding the Policy You're Using To use monetary policy effectively, you must know whether the monetary policy you're using is expansionary or contractionary. You might think that's rather easy, but it isn't. In our consideration of monetary policy tools you saw that the Fed doesn't directly control the money supply. It indirectly controls it, generally through open market operations. It controls what's called the **monetary base** (the vault cash and reserves banks have at the Fed). Then the money multiplier determines the amounts of M_1, M_2, and other monetary measures in the economy.

That money multiplier is influenced by the amount of cash that people hold as well as the lending process at the bank. Neither of those is the stable number that we used in calculating the money multipliers. They change from day to day and week to week so even if you control the monetary base, you can never be sure exactly what will happen to M_1 and M_2 in the short run. Moreover, the effects on M_1 and M_2 are sometimes different; one measure is telling you that you're expanding the money supply and the other measure is telling you you're contracting it.

And then, of course, there are changes in the interest rate—the measure of monetary policy that Keynesians focus on. If interest rates rise, is it because of expected inflation (which is adding an inflation premium to the nominal interest rate) or is it the real interest rate that is going up? There is frequent debate over which it is. Combined, these measurement problems make the Fed often wonder not only about what policy it should follow, but what policy it is following.

Lags in Monetary Policy Monetary policy, like fiscal policy, takes time to work its way through the economic system. The Fed can change the money supply or interest rates; people don't have to borrow, however. An increased money supply may simply lead to excess reserves and have no influence on income. This problem can be especially difficult in a recession.

For example, in the 1930s the Fed increased banks' reserves, but the money supply fell by about 25 percent. This led early Keynesians to focus on fiscal policy rather than monetary policy as a way of expanding the economy. They likened expansionary monetary policy to pushing on a string. The same problem exists with using contractionary monetary policy. Banks have been very good at figuring out ways to circumvent cuts in the money supply, making the intended results of contractionary monetary policy difficult to achieve.

Political Pressure While the Fed is partially insulated from political pressure by its structure, it's not totally insulated. Presidents place enormous pressure on the Fed to use expansionary monetary policy (especially during an election year) and blame the Fed for any recession. When interest rates rise, the Fed takes the pressure, and if any members of the Board of Governors are politically aligned with the president, they find it difficult to persist in contractionary policy when the economy is in a recession.

Conflicting International Goals Monetary policy is not conducted in a vacuum. It is conducted in an international arena and must be coordinated with other governments' monetary policy. Similarly, as we'll see a little later, monetary policy affects the exchange rate and trade balance. Often the desired monetary policy for its international effects is the opposite of the desired monetary policy for its domestic effects.

CONCLUSION AND A LOOK AHEAD

I could continue with a discussion of the problems of using monetary policy, but the above should give you a good sense that conducting monetary policy is not a piece of cake. It takes not only a sense of the theory; it also takes a feel for the economy. In short the conduct of monetary policy is not a science. It does not allow the Fed to steer the economy as it might steer a car. It does work well enough to allow the Fed to *influence* the economy—much as an expert rodeo rider rides a bronco bull.

This chapter is not the end of our discussion of monetary policy. We'll see more of monetary policy when we discuss how to conduct macroeconomic policy in the next section. There you'll learn how monetary policy works in practice, the central role it plays in understanding inflation, and how it is integrated with fiscal policy. Before we turn to those issues, however, it is helpful to consider more deeply some of the theoretical and policy debates about macroeconomic policy. That is what we do in the next chapter.

KEY POINTS

- The Fed is a central bank; it determines monetary policy for the United States.   **1**
- Monetary policy influences the economy through changes in the money supply and credit availability.
- The three tools of monetary policy are:
    1. Changing the reserve requirement.
    2. Changing the discount rate.
    3. Open market operations.   **3**
- A change in reserves changes the money supply by the change in reserves times the money multiplier.   **3**
- Open market operations is the Fed's most important tool:

    To expand the money supply, the Fed buys bonds.

    To contract the money supply, the Fed sells bonds.   **4**

- In the Keynesian model, contractionary monetary policy works as follows:

$$M \downarrow \rightarrow i \uparrow \rightarrow I \downarrow \rightarrow Y \downarrow.$$

Expansionary monetary policy works as follows: **5**

$$M \uparrow \rightarrow i \downarrow \rightarrow I \uparrow \rightarrow Y \uparrow.$$

- As an indicator of monetary policy, Keynesians focus on interest rates; Classicals focus on money supply.   **5** **6**
- Classical economists see the short-run effects of monetary policy as ambiguous. They favor a long-run monetary rule.   **6**
- Problems of monetary policy include knowing what policy to use, knowing what policy you are using, lags, political pressure, and conflicting international goals.   **7**

KEY TERMS

central bank *(298)*
discount rate *(302)*
monetary base *(310)*

monetary policy *(298)*
nominal interest
   rate *(309)*

open market
   operations *(303)*

real interest rates *(309)*
reserve requirement *(300)*

QUESTIONS FOR THOUGHT AND REVIEW

The number after each question represents the estimated degree of critical thinking required. (1 = almost none; 10 = deep thought.)

1. Is the Fed a private or a public agency? *(5)*
2. Why are there few regional Fed banks in the western part of the United States? *(2)*
3. The Fed wants to change the reserve requirement in order to increase the money supply (which is currently 4,000) by 200. The money multiplier is 3. What's the current reserve requirement and how should the Fed change it? *(6)*
4. The Fed wants to increase the money supply (which is currently 4,000) by 200. Assume that for each 1 percent the discount rate falls, banks borrow an additional 20. If instead of changing the reserve requirement, the Fed decides to change the discount rate, how much should the Fed change the rate to increase the money supply by 200? *(6)*

5. The Fed wants to increase the money supply (which is currently 4,000) by 200. Only now it decides to use open market operations. What should it do to achieve the desired change? *(6)*

6. You can lead a horse to water, but you can't make it drink. How might this adage be relevant to expansionary (as opposed to contractionary) monetary policy? *(7)*

7. The interest rate has just fallen. How might Classical and Keynesian economists draw different implications from that event? *(7)*

8. Investment increases by 20 for each interest rate drop of 1 percent. The income multiplier is 3. If the money multiplier is 4, and each change of 5 in the money supply changes the interest rate by 1 percent, what open market policy would you recommend to increase income by 240? *(6)*

9. If the nominal interest rate is 6 percent and inflation is 5 percent, what's the real interest rate? *(3)*

10. "The effects of open market operations are somewhat like a stone cast in a pond." After the splash, discuss the first three ripples. *(4)*

PROBLEMS AND EXERCISES

1. Suppose the Fed decides it needs to pursue an expansionary policy. Assume people hold no cash, the reserve requirement is 20 percent, and there are no excess reserves.
   a. Show how the Fed would increase the money supply by $2 million by changing the reserve requirement.
   b. Show how the Fed would increase the money supply by $2 million through open market operations.

2. Suppose the Fed decides that it needs to pursue a contractionary policy. It wants to decrease the money supply by $2 million. Assume people hold 25 percent of their money in the form of cash balances, the reserve requirement is 20 percent, and there are no excess reserves.
   a. Show how the Fed would decrease the money supply by $2 million by changing the reserve requirement.
   b. Show how the Fed would decrease the money supply by $2 million through open market operations.
   c. Go to your local bank and find out how much excess reserves they hold. Recalculate (a) and (b) assuming all banks held that amount in excess reserves.

Keynesian and Classical Theories of Interest and Their Implications for Monetary Policy

To understand the theoretical differences between Keynesian and Classical economists' theories of monetary policy, we must understand their alternative theories of interest. Keynesians believe the interest rate is primarily a monetary phenomenon so they have a monetary theory of the rate of interest. For Keynesians the interest rate is determined by the supply and demand for money. Classicals believe the interest rate is a real phenomenon so they have a real theory of the rate of interest. In an earlier chapter you were introduced to the Keynesian and Classical theories of the interest rate. This appendix further develops their theories and discusses their implications for conducting monetary policy.

The Keynesian Supply and Demand for Money Theory of the Interest Rate

As we saw in the last chapter, money is a financial asset people want to hold. But how much do they want to hold? It shouldn't surprise you that economists' answer is that it depends upon the supply and demand for money.

The Supply of Money The Fed determines the money supply by setting the amount of reserves in the system. Then the total amount of money in the economy is determined by the reserve requirement and the money multiplier. Here we'll assume that the Fed can perfectly determine the amount of money supplied to the economy and that that amount of money supplied isn't influenced by the interest rate. That makes the supply of money perfectly vertical as in Exhibit A1.

The Demand for Money As we saw in the last chapter, people want to hold money because it's useful to them as a medium of exchange and as a store of wealth. But

holding money isn't costless. *Money pays lower interest than other financial assets.* So how much money people want to hold depends on the interest rate on those other financial assets. The higher the interest rate on other financial assets, the greater the opportunity cost of holding money and the lower the quantity of money demanded. At lower interest rates, quantity of money demanded is larger because the opportunity cost of holding money is lower. Demand for money as a function of the interest rate is shown by the curve D_M in Exhibit A1.

The Keynesian theory of interest comes from combining the supply of money with the demand for money as in Exhibit A1. The interest rate is determined where the quantity of money supplied equals the quantity of money demanded (i_e). If the supply of money increases, say from M_0 to M_1 as in Exhibit A1(b), the interest rate will fall from i_0. If the demand for money increases, the interest rate will rise. Keynes argued that in the short run the money market determines the interest rate.

The Classical Savings Investment Theory of the Interest Rate

The supply and demand for money isn't the only market that plays a role in determining the interest rate. The Classical view is that the interest rate is determined by the supply of savings and the demand for those savings for investment purposes. Money doesn't affect the interest rate so it doesn't affect the real economy. It only affects the price level. So the best monetary policy is a policy that provides stability of the price level. It's a long-run policy that emphasizes a constant predetermined growth rate of the money supply.

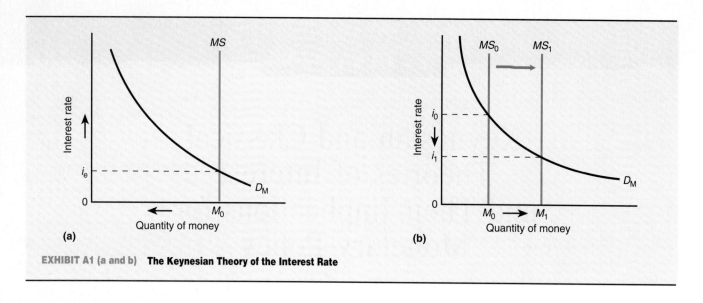

EXHIBIT A1 (a and b)   The Keynesian Theory of the Interest Rate

Implications of Keynesian and Classical Theories for Monetary Policy

In the Classical model, interest rate fluctuations keep savings equal to investment at the full-employment level of income. Changes in the interest rate equilibrate the savings/investment market. That's not the way it works in Keynes's model. Income fluctuations, not interest rate fluctuations, bring the savings/ investment market into equilibrium. This happens in the following way: Income fluctuates, which causes savings to fluctuate. That fluctuation in savings brings the savings/investment market into equilibrium. So in Keynes's model the real economy is affected by money. In the Classical model money only affects the price level.

The implication of the Keynesian theory of interest for monetary policy is it's necessary to maintain an *active* discretionary monetary policy to keep the interest rate at a level that will maintain a savings/ investment equilibrium at the target level of income. Classicals believe in a monetary rule.

4
Extensions of Macroeconomic Thinking

14

The Evolution of
Macroeconomic Thinking

*Economics is a science of thinking
in terms of models joined to the art of choosing models which are
relevant to the contemporary world.*

J. M. Keynes

After reading this chapter, you should be able to:

1

List three groups of Classical economists
and three groups of Keynesian economists.

2

Explain why monetarists are included under
the Classical heading.

3

Define crowding out and state why it is
important.

4

State the two New Classical arguments
against the Keynesians.

5

Explain what *rational expectations* means
and why it is important.

6

Differentiate supply-side economics from
New Classical economics.

7

Explain the Keynesian/New Classical
flip-flop in their views of the government
budget deficit.

Way back in Chapter 1, we admitted that macroeconomics is still evolving. Today macroeconomics has come a long way from the simple Keynesian model and its derivatives. The last chapter introduced you to the first step in that evolution: the integration of monetary policy into the Keynesian model. That integration was formalized into a model called the IS/LM model (the *I*nvestment = *S*avings/*L*iquidity = *M*oney model). The **IS/LM** model formally ties together the Keynesian theory of the interest rate with the Keynesian theory of the determination of income. Keynesians who use the IS/LM model are called **neo-Keynesians** (Keynesian economists who have formally integrated money into the Keynesian model with the IS/LM model).

An important reason why Keynesians integrated money into their model was that a group of Classicals had been attacking the simple Keynesian model which had *not* integrated money into the model. This group of Classicals so emphasized money that they're often called **monetarists** (Classical economists who strongly focus on money and a modified quantity theory of money model). In the 1960s macroeconomics was primarily a debate between neo-Keynesians and monetarists.

In the 1970s the Keynesian model was modified again to include not only the effect of interest rates but also the effect of changing prices. The new model was called a *flexible-price IS/LM model*. This flexible-price IS/LM model was a far cry from the simple Keynesian model that was the focus of my earlier presentation of Keynesian economics.

As often happens with a structure that has been gerrymandered to fit changing needs, the resulting flexible-price IS/LM model wasn't only cumbersome, it was also inadequate. Most economists believed this, but they also believed the flexible-price IS/LM model was the best they had. Without something better, you go with what you've got.

Then in the middle and late 1970s and early 1980s macroeconomics experienced what some economists considered a revolution. The neo-Keynesian IS/LM model and monetarist quantity theory models were dropped by one group of economists, including Robert Lucas (University of Chicago), Robert Barro (Harvard University), and Thomas Sargent (University of Minnesota), and replaced with a new model. Although this new model was much more formal (meaning it had a lot of fancy equations) than the old Classical model, it had enough similarities to the Classical model to be called the *New Classical model,* and the group of economists who used it was called *New Classicals.*

A central element of the New Classical model was that it was based on **micro foundations**—that is, it "built up" from individuals' decisions to aggregate results. Thus, a **New Classical economist** is one whose views are similar to those of a Classical or a monetarist economist, but who uses a much more formal model based on micro foundations.

The New Classical challenge to the neo-Keynesian model provoked a variety of responses by Keynesians. One group argues that the neo-Keynesian model is still the best, and that the New Classical arguments are so far-fetched they don't deserve a response. One neo-Keynesian (Nobel prize winner Robert Solow) said, "If someone comes up and tells you he is Napoleon, you don't start debating with him about tactics at Waterloo."

Another group of Keynesians generally called *New Keynesians* agree with the New Classicals that the neo-Keynesian model needed to be dropped. But they don't believe the New Classical model represents the way the economy works. Using the same general micro foundations model as the New Classicals, they developed a new, highly formal model which comes to Keynesian conclusions much like those of the simple Keynesian model presented in this book. Their model showed that Keynesian insights and policy had a theoretical basis, even in a model with micro foundations. Thus a **New Keynesian economist** is an economist whose views are similar to those of Keynesians and neo-Keynesians, but who

---

IS/LM (*Investment = Savings/Liquidity = Money*) A model that formally ties together the Keynesian theory of the interest rate with the Keynesian theory of the determination of income.

Neo-Keynesians Keynesian economists who have formally integrated money into the Keynesian model with the *IS/LM* model.

2

Monetarists Classical economists who strongly focus on the importance of money.

Micro foundations An analysis of individuals' decisions used to build up a theory of aggregate results.

New Classical economist Economist whose views are similar to those of Classicals or monetarists but who uses a much more formal model based on micro foundations.

New Keynesian economist An economist whose views are similar to those of Keynesians and neo-Keynesians, but who uses a much more formal model based on micro foundations.

(the 1940s and 1950s)

(the 1960s and 1970s)

(the 1980s and 1990s)

EXHIBIT 1   The Evolution of Keynesian and Classical Thinking

Over time the names of the groups involved in the debate about macroeconomics have changed, but the central issue at debate has remained. Classicals, monetarists, and New Classicals tend to favor laissez-faire. Keynesians of all flavors tend to favor activist policy.

uses a much more formal model based on micro foundations. Exhibit 1 summarizes this evolution.

This continuing evolution of models and renaming of groups creates a difficult situation for textbooks. In the 1990s there are at least six competing models: Classical, Keynesian, neo-Keynesian, monetarist, New Classical, and New Keynesian. Each has nuances and subtleties of its own, and there's no way anyone can learn those distinctions in a short time. But the names are used relatively often, so it's helpful to know in a general way what the various groups believe. That's what I try to show in this chapter. I present the flavor and sense of that evolution and those debates.

I begin the discussion of the evolution by introducing you to monetarist thinking and the important role monetarists had in forcing Keynesians to expand their macroeconomic model to include money (and hence to become neo-Keynesians). I then summarize New Classicals' and New Keynesians' views. I conclude with a general discussion of the Keynesian/Classical policy debates which transcends all the *neo*s and *new*s.

MONETARISTS AND THE NEO-KEYNESIAN RESPONSE

Classical economists didn't die out with the advent of Keynesian economics. They did, however, become almost invisible for a while as Keynesian economics and the Keynesian model swept the field. The group of economists who maintained the Classical view was led by Milton Friedman. In analyzing the aggregate economy, Friedman and his followers focused on the quantity theory of money which, as you saw in Chapter 8, stated that the money supply affected the price level and had little predictable effect on employment or output.

Friedman argued that: (1) in the long run, the quantity of money and prices move together, (2) there is a dichotomy between the real and nominal sector, and (3) Say's law (supply creates its own demand) generally holds true. Thus, Friedman maintained the Classical view of the economy. Friedman and his associates pointed out, forcefully and correctly, that money mattered and that macroeconomics must focus on monetary policy as well as fiscal policy. As stated before, because of their focus on monetary policy, this reincarnation of Classical thought became known as monetarism, and supporters became known as monetarists.

Keynesians soon agreed that money did indeed matter. They reread Keynes's writings that dealt with money and realized that the Keynesian position had always been that money mattered. They agreed that some early Keynesians who had focused exclusively on fiscal policy were wrong; early Keynesians had misinterpreted Keynes. In response Keynesians added money to the Keynesian model, along the lines explained in the last chapter. As that happened, the Keynesian model came to be called the *neo-Keynesian model.*

It was then that the distinction between the Keynesian theory of the interest rate (determined in the money market by supply and demand for money) and the Classical theory of the interest rate (determined in the savings/investment market)

THE KEEPER OF THE
CLASSICAL FAITH: MILTON
FRIEDMAN

B y most accounts Milton Friedman was a headstrong student. He didn't simply accept the truths his teachers laid out. If he didn't agree, he argued strongly for his own belief. He was very bright and his ideas were generally logical and convincing. He needed to be both persistent and intelligent to maintain and promote his views in spite of strong opposition.

Throughout the Keynesian years of the 1950s and 1960s, Friedman stood up and argued the Classical viewpoint of economics. He kept Classical economics alive. He was such a strong advocate of the quantity theory of money that during this period, Classical economics was called monetarism. Friedman was the leader of the monetarists.

Friedman argued that fiscal policy simply didn't work. It led to expansions in government's size. He also opposed an activist monetary policy. The effects of monetary policy, he said, were too variable for it to be useful in guiding the economy. He called for a steady growth in the money supply and argued consistently for a laissez-faire policy by government.

He has made his mark in both microeconomics and macroeconomics. In the 1970s his ideas caught hold and helped spawn the New Classical school of economics. He was awarded the Nobel prize in economics in 1976.

made its way into the textbooks. In the 1960s Keynesians argued that the primary difference between themselves and monetarists was that the monetarists believed *that only* money mattered, while Keynesians believed *only that* money mattered.

Crowding Out

3

Crowding out The offset to fiscal policy that occurs due to the decrease in investment caused by financing the deficit.

These debates between monetarists and Keynesians aren't the subject of introductory economics, but one aspect of the debates sheds important light on the workings of monetary and fiscal policy and on the differences and similarities of economists' views. That aspect is **crowding out** (the offset to fiscal policy that occurs due to financing the deficit).

We briefly discussed crowding out earlier, but it's now time for a more complete discussion. Monetarists argued that expansionary fiscal policy (increasing the deficit) is effective only if it's accompanied by expansionary monetary policy (increasing the money supply). If the money supply weren't increased, there would be a rise in the interest rate, which would choke off private investment. This decrease in private investment would offset the expansionary effect of the increased deficit. To see why this might occur, let's look more closely at expansionary fiscal policy.

Let's first ask what *expansionary fiscal policy* means. The answer should be at the tip of your tongue. It means government increases spending or decreases taxes to stimulate the economy; it increases the deficit.

When government runs a deficit, it spends more money than it collects in taxes but it doesn't spend more money than it has. It pays for everything it buys. How? The same way you would if you ran a deficit. It borrows the money by selling government bonds on the open market. So when the government runs a deficit, it must borrow the amount of the deficit—it must sell bonds.

To handle these financing problems, the U.S. Department of the Treasury has an entire division devoted to debt management. When past bonds come due, the Treasury must refinance the debt; when the deficit increases, the Treasury must sell new bonds. If the government runs a surplus, the Treasury can pay off some past debt by buying back some bonds.

If this discussion of the Treasury selling bonds caused you to recall the Fed's conduct of monetary policy and open market operations, that's good. (If not, you should probably go back and review the last chapter.) It's through the bond market that monetary policy and fiscal policies are interconnected. The Fed conducts monetary policy by buying and selling government bonds (open market operations).

Let's now consider how the connection between monetary policy and fiscal policy works. We'll start with the government running expansionary fiscal policy.

EXHIBIT 2 (a and b)   A Schematic Representation of Crowding Out

An increase in government spending will expand income through the multiplier as in the top portion in (**a**). However it will also cause interest rates to rise and thereby cause investment to decrease, which will tend to decrease income, as shown in the bottom portion of (**a**). This is called *crowding out*. The net effect of fiscal policy depends on the degree of crowding out that takes place. When there is complete crowding out , as there is in (**b**), the effect of fiscal policy will be totally offset.

We know that running a deficit is expansionary and that it will start the income multiplier process in motion. However, to finance a deficit the Treasury must sell government bonds.

What will be the effect of selling those bonds? To get people to buy and hold the bonds, the government must make them attractive. That means the interest rate the bonds pay must be higher than it otherwise would have been. Thus, when the government runs a deficit, it must finance that deficit by selling bonds, which tends to push up the interest rate. This rise in the interest rate decreases private investment, because it is more costly to borrow. This decrease in private investment has a contractionary effect on the economy which works in the opposite direction of the expansionary fiscal policy. Hence the name *crowding out*. Increased government spending crowds out private spending. Exhibit 2(a) shows the interconnection. The top arrows represent the direct effect of increased spending. The bottom arrows represent the effects of financing that increased spending. They work in the opposite direction.

Monetarists argued that crowding out would totally offset the expansionary effect so that expansionary fiscal policy would have no net effect on the economy other than to replace (crowd out) private investment with government spending.

The view of complete crowding out is shown in the Keynesian model in Exhibit 2(b). Income in the economy is Y_0 and government has decided to expand that income to Y_1 by increasing its spending by ΔG.

If financing were not an issue, expansionary fiscal policy would shift up aggregate expenditures from AE_0 to AE_1, increasing income from Y_0 to Y_1. Financing the deficit, however, increases interest rates and decreases investment by ΔI, which shifts the AE curve all the way back to AE_2. Income falls back to Y_0. Because of crowding out, there is no net expansionary effect on fiscal policy.

If such crowding out occurs, the only way fiscal policy could have an effect would be if the Fed increased the money supply simultaneously with the expansionary fiscal policy. Let's consider how that works.

Say government is again using expansionary fiscal policy, only this time the Fed buys the bonds necessary to finance the deficit. This is called **monetizing the**

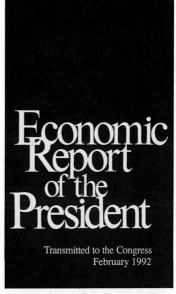

Economic Report of the President—Every year the President's Council of Economic Advisers issues an annual report that discusses the state of the economy.

Monetizing the Deficit

ADDED DIMENSION

THE TREASURY ACCORD

T o give you an idea of how early Keynesian economics focused on fiscal policy, let's consider one of the important policy fights of the late 1940s and early 1950s. During World War II, the U.S. government ran enormous deficits to finance the war effort. The Treasury and Fed agreed, in what was known as the *Treasury Accord,* that the Fed would assist in the war effort by holding the interest rate constant. How did the Fed do that? With open market operations. It bought bonds whenever the interest rate started to rise. (If it isn't clear to you how this Fed policy could hold the interest rate constant, review Chapter 13.)

The Treasury Accord eliminated an independent monetary policy by requiring the Fed to buy bonds, making monetary policy totally subservient to fiscal policy. During the war, almost all economists felt the Accord was reasonable. After the war, the Accord was continued, and independent monetary policy was prevented. Keynesians argued that this was the way it should be. Monetarists objected, arguing that monetary policy was too important to be held subservient to fiscal policy. Monetarists said that maintaining the Accord would lead to significant inflation.

In 1951, six years after the end of the war, the Fed broke the Accord. Since then there have been two tools of macro policy: monetary policy and fiscal policy.

Monetizing the deficit The Fed buying the U.S. bonds necessary to finance the deficit.

Accommodating monetary policy A monetary policy in which the Fed increases the money supply so that no crowding out accompanies expansionary fiscal policy.

deficit because the deficit is being financed with newly printed money. For example, say government increases the deficit by \$10 billion and the Fed simultaneously buys up \$10 billion in bonds in open market operations. If this happens, there's no need for the interest rates on the bonds to rise to get people to hold the additional bonds. People don't have to hold any additional bonds. The Fed is holding them.

Since crowding out is caused by the rise in interest rates necessary to get people to hold the increased debt required by the deficit, in this example there would be no crowding out. Or, more precisely, the crowding out would be offset by expansionary monetary policy. A monetary policy that offsets the crowding out side effect of expansionary fiscal policy is called an **accommodating monetary policy.** Monetarists say that expansionary fiscal policy works only if there is accommodating monetary policy.

If you think back to the description of expansionary fiscal policy in the Keynesian model, you'll see the description fits. Expansionary monetary policy works by lowering the interest rate (i.e., the Fed buys bonds, which decreases the supply of bonds, which means the interest rate doesn't have to be so high to get people to hold these bonds). The fall in the interest rate increases investment, which increases income by a multiple of the increase in investment. When the Fed buys the additional government debt necessary to finance the deficit (as it does when it monetizes the debt), the monetary policy affects the economy in the same way. But instead of the interest rate falling, it merely doesn't rise. So if the Fed monetizes the debt, crowding out is eliminated and the full multiplier effect predicted by the Keynesian model occurs.

The Neo-Keynesian Response and the Compromise View on Crowding Out

Neo-Keynesians soon agreed that crowding out could occur, but they argued that it wouldn't necessarily be 100 percent offset. Since, according to Keynesians, financial markets were often in disequilibrium, there was often excess savings out there which could be tapped with only a slight rise in the interest rates. In such cases, little crowding out occurred, and expansionary fiscal policy had a strong effect even without accommodating monetary policy.

Eventually a compromise was reached between neo-Keynesians and monetarists. That compromise was that some crowding out would occur whenever fiscal policy was used, but that it wasn't complete crowding out.

Exhibit 3 shows the compromise view of the effect of expansionary fiscal policy. As before, income in the economy is initially at Y_0 and the government has decided to expand income to Y_P by increasing its spending from G_0 to G_1. In the absence of any crowding out, the policy would effectively shift the AE_0 curve to

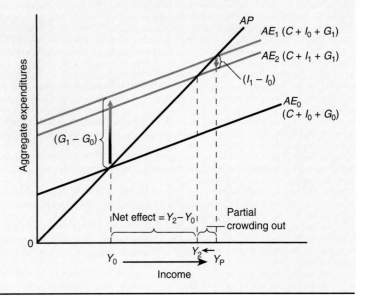

EXHIBIT 3   Partial Crowding Out

Where there is partial crowding out, an increase in government spending will still have an expansionary effect, but the effect will be smaller than it otherwise would have been.

AE_1. However, financing the deficit causes investment to fall from I_0 to I_1, which shifts the AE curve back down from AE_1 to AE_2. Since the downward shift in investment isn't enough to offset completely the expansionary fiscal policy, income increases (to Y_2), but not by as much as predicted by the multiplier. In the compromise view, crowding out decreases the expansionary effect of a government deficit, but it doesn't completely offset it. How much crowding out offsets the expansionary effect of fiscal policy is a matter of debate. Monetarists believe more crowding out occurs; neo-Keynesians believe less occurs.

Most economists today accept this compromise view of crowding out and the interrelationship of monetary and fiscal policy. In this compromise each side agrees that both fiscal and monetary policies matter, although they differ on how much and in what way they matter.

The difference about crowding out is not the only difference between neo-Keynesians and monetarists. A second difference concerns the effectiveness of both fiscal and monetary policy as tools for guiding the economy. Specifically, neo-Keynesians maintain that monetary policy should be used in combination with fiscal policy to steer the economy; they favor an *activist* monetary and fiscal policy.

Monetarists maintain that fiscal policy is weak and, given the political problems of using it, not a relevant policy tool. They further maintain that although monetary policy is powerful, it's unpredictable in the short run. So even though monetary policy is powerful, it cannot, and should not, be used to control the level of output in the economy. Thus, paradoxically, monetarists favor a *laissez-faire* monetary policy.

Monetarists believe that in the long run money affects only the price level. Since the short-run effects are unpredictable and in the long run only the price level is affected, monetarists say that monetary policy should follow a **monetary rule** (a prescribed monetary policy that's to be followed regardless of what's happening in the economy). They argue that:

1. The money supply should be increased by a determined percentage, say 3 percent per year, to allow for changes in productivity and real growth.
2. Monetary policy should not be used in the short run to try to steer the economy.

Monetarists believe that monetary policy should be used only to achieve long-run

The Activism/Laissez-Faire Debate

Monetary rule A prescribed monetary policy to be followed regardless of what is happening in the economy.

objectives, the most important of which is price stability. Keynesians believe that short-run monetary policy can be used to achieve other objectives.

We'll look at some examples of how these differences work out in practice in later chapters. For now the most important things to remember are: (1) monetarists are the 1960s reincarnation of the original Classical economists and (2) monetarists believe that the government should follow a monetary rule.

NEW CLASSICAL ECONOMICS AND THE NEW KEYNESIAN RESPONSE

The 1970s marked a truce between monetarists and neo-Keynesians. They agreed to disagree. But a new debate emerged with the development of New Classical economics. New Classicals argued that the Keynesian model wasn't the correct one to represent the economy because:

1. It was ad hoc macroeconomics. Macroeconomics should, they argued, have micro foundations—that is, it should be built up from microeconomic principles. For example, rather than simply assuming the wage level or price level constant, a macroeconomic model should use microeconomic principles to show whether holding wages and prices (which make up the wage and price levels) constant is in individuals' interest. New Classicals argued that it was in firms' and individuals' interest to move their wages and prices up or down depending on supply and demand conditions. Therefore their assumption of flexible wages and prices was more logical than the Keynesian assumption of fixed wages and prices.

■4

2. Keynesian models were not consistent with the assumption that individuals exercised rational expectations. **Rational expectations** are expectations about the future based on the best information available now. New Classicals argue that the assumption of individual rationality is central to economists' microeconomic approach to understanding economic reality. They argue that Keynesians, in their model, assume individuals are irrational.

Rational expectations The proposition that people, not only economists, will expect that the best estimate of what the economic model predicts will happen.

The Debate between New Classicals and New Keynesians

New Classical theory caught on in the late 1970s and early 1980s for a variety of reasons. First, it was consistent with economic events of the 1970s, specifically high inflation. Whereas Keynesian economics had little to say about inflation, New Classical economics explained why there was inflation and what could be done about it. Second, New Classical economics was consistent with the change in the U.S. political climate. President Reagan's election in 1980 marked a shift in the country's political mood away from the activism of the preceding decades and toward a more laissez-faire position.

A third reason why New Classical economics caught on was a simple desire for change on the part of researchers. Scientists, like everyone else, are subject to flights of fancy and fads. (New Classicals argue that Keynesian economics was simply a fad and that New Classical economics was a return to traditional Classical economics.) Working on a new theory is exciting and offers good prospects for interesting dissertations and journal articles so young economists have a strong incentive to adopt new theories.

Whatever the reasons, New Classical views caught on like wildfire in the economics profession. For a while in the early 1980s it looked as if all macroeconomics would change and become New Classical economics. But that didn't happen. Instead a group of Keynesians developed a set of models that reintroduced Keynesian economic ideas into New Classical models. These models are quite different from neo-Keynesian models described in the previous section, and they've become known as *New Keynesian models*. Economists who developed and use the New Keynesian models became known as *New Keynesians*.

The New Classical/New Keynesian theoretical debates are complicated and will not be discussed here. It is important, however, to discuss their ideas because those ideas have had a significant effect on the way economists think about, and discuss, policy.

The essence of the New Classical policy argument is the following: Say the government uses an activist monetary and fiscal policy. People aren't stupid; they'll soon come to expect that activist monetary and fiscal policy will be used and, in response, will change their behavior. But if they change their behavior, the government's estimates of what is going to be the effect of policy, based on past experience, will be wrong.

Let's consider an example. Say everyone knows government will run expansionary fiscal policy if the economy is in a recession. In the absence of any expected policy response by government, people would have lowered their prices when they saw a recession coming. Expecting government expansionary policy, however, they won't lower their prices. Thus, an activist policy creates its own problems, which can be avoided by establishing a set of rules that limit government's policy responses.

As we can see from this discussion, the key element of New Classical ideas about policy is that you must consider the effects of policy on people's behavior and that those effects place a limit on the type of policies that can be followed. Specifically, the fact that the economy is falling into a recession is not a sufficient reason for the government to run expansionary monetary and fiscal policies. Some New Classicals went further than that, arguing that if all people have rational expectations and the economy is competitive, there's no room for any activist monetary policy.

New Keynesians generally agree with this New Classical argument about expectations. But they argue that it doesn't rule out activist monetary and fiscal policies in all instances. They argue that many fluctuations in the economy are due to a collective irrationality, which leaves room for government to correct that irrationality.

A good way to see how New Classical and New Keynesian ideas have affected macroeconomic policy, or at least thinking about macroeconomic policy, is the discussion of macroeconomic policy in the 1990 *Economic Report of the President*. There's little or no discussion of an activist fiscal policy and sizes of multipliers. Instead the central theme of its description of fiscal policy is, "Fiscal policy should move toward *credible, systematic* policies that would promote strong noninflationary growth" (p. 77).

Similarly with the report's discussion of monetary policy. A key statement of principle for monetary policy is:

> Monetary policy needs to maintain credibility, because credibility helps ensure that the goals of policy will be attained during a period of dynamic economic and financial developments. Policy credibility is enhanced by building a record of achievement of the stated goals of policy and by consistently following stated policy principles.

I suspect the redundancy in those descriptions is by design. The economists writing the report wanted to emphasize that one cannot think of macroeconomic policy without thinking about what effect expectations of macroeconomic policy will have. The policy must be credible, systematic, and consistent. All these statements emphasize that you cannot think of policy choices in one time period as not affecting individuals' behavior in another time period.

An analogy to raising a child might make the point clear. Say that the child is crying in a restaurant. Do you hand out a piece of candy to stop the crying or do you maintain your "no candy" rule? Looking only at the one situation, it might make sense to give the candy, but doing so will undermine your credibility and consistency, and therefore has an additional cost. This emphasis on credibility is the primary effect New Classical/New Keynesian work has had on macroeconomic policy. In conducting macroeconomic policy, one must consider the effect that expectations of that policy will have on the economy generally, and not only in a particular case.

The Effect of New Classical and New Keynesian Ideas on Real-World Macroeconomic Policy

5

Michael Boskin—Chairman of the Council of Economic Advisers under President Bush in the early 1990s. *Reuters/Bettmann.*

New Classicals and New Keynesians also agree that in practice credibility is hard to achieve. The 1990 *Economic Report of the President* summarizes the problem nicely:

> Policy credibility is clearly useful to have, but achieving it may not be easy. Simply announcing a change in policy does not make it believable. Credibility depends in part on the plausibility and consistency of the announced policy in the context of the overall economic environment and other policies. Credibility probably depends most importantly on a track record of following the stated principles of policy.

Most economists can agree with this statement. New Keynesians' and New Classicals' disagreement concerns what policy is plausible and hence what policy can be credible.

The New Classical/New Keynesian debate and its focus on credibility are part of a larger policy debate between Classicals and Keynesians. When it comes to assessing what real-world policies can be credible, the *neo* and *New* prefixes become irrelevant. Keynesians, neo-Keynesians, and New Keynesians take one position on real-world policy; Classicals, monetarists, and New Classicals take another. Let's turn to those differing positions.

THE KEYNESIAN/CLASSICAL POLICY DEBATE

Debates about economic theory often mask debates about economic policy. Economists use theories to guide their reasoning, but before they can translate the results of a theory into a policy prescription, they must add a sense of institutions and history, adjusting the model to fit reality. Keynesians and Classicals differ not only in the theoretical models they prefer, but also, and probably more importantly, in their sense of institutions and history.

The Classical View of Government Policy

As you saw in earlier chapters, Classicals have a profound distrust of government and the political process. They tend to believe that even if theoretically the government might be able to help solve a recession, there's a serious question whether, given the political process, it will do so. Politics will often guide government to do something quite different than "further the general good." In the Classical view, real-world government intervention is more likely to do harm than good.

The classical view of government as a tool that individuals use to enrich themselves has been around for a long time, as can be seen in this 19th-century lithograph. *Bleichroeder Print Collection, Baker Library, Harvard Business School.*

Classicals see democratic government as being significantly controlled by special interest groups. While, in theory, government might be an expression of the will of the people, in practice it's not. Thus, government is not a legitimate method of correcting problems in the economy. True, government sometimes does good, but this is the exception. Overall the costs of government action outweigh the benefits.

In the Classical view, politicians often are guided by politics, not by society's best interest. Therefore any policy that increases the government's role is highly suspect and should be avoided. New Classical models reflect this view and focus on a model that highlights a laissez-faire policy for government.

Keynesians tend to have more faith in government not only being able to recognize what's wrong, but also in being willing to work to correct it. Thus, for a Keynesian it's worthwhile to talk about a model that highlights an activist role for government.

The Keynesian View of Government Policy

Keynesians tend to see government as an expression of the will of the people. Thus, they see it as a legitimate method of correcting problems in the economy. True, government is sometimes misled by interest groups who direct government to do their own bidding rather than follow the general interest, but this is simply a cost of government. In the Keynesian view, generally the benefits of government outweigh the costs.

Notice that these differences between Keynesians and Classicals are based on judgment calls requiring a knowledge of the workings of the market and the social institutions that tie our country together. They're judgments upon which reasonable individuals may differ—between the two extremes are innumerable shades of Keynesians and Classicals. There's no objective way of deciding which group is right or wrong.

Who's Right on Policy?

Little of the theoretical or policy debate between the New Classicals and New Keynesians filters down to the lay public. The theoretical arguments are too hard for most journalists to capture in the available space, and the policy arguments are too general for a good article. But journalists' incentives are to write articles. (That's what they get paid for.) And so they search out policy controversies to write about. One debate they have discussed is the one between supply-side and Keynesian economics. Since supply-side economics is partially related to New Classical economics, it is appropriate to consider that debate now.

Supply-Side Economics and the Keynesian/Classical Debate

6

Supply-side economics developed not in the economics profession, but in the popular press, in Jude Wanniski's book *The Way the World Works*. Wanniski, a former newspaper reporter, prides himself on never having taken an economics course. He bases his arguments on some ideas of economist Arthur Laffer, who argued that the U.S. economy's problem was that tax rates were too high and that if rates were cut, the economy would expand.

Differences between Supply-Side and Keynesian Explanations of How a Tax Cut Stimulates the Economy   At first glance Wanniski's supply-side argument may look very much like a Keynesian argument for fiscal policy in which cutting taxes stimulates the economy via the multiplier effect. But there's an important difference between the Keynesian and supply-side views. The supply-side explanation of how the tax cut would stimulate the economy is by microeconomic incentives. It focuses on tax rates, not tax revenues.

The supply-side argument goes as follows: If the government cuts tax rates, people will have greater incentive to work, to save, and to invest. As they do all these things, output will increase. (The aggregate supply curve, and hence potential income, will shift out.) Since supply creates its own demand, aggregate

EXHIBIT 4 (a and b)   Keynesian and Supply-Side Explanations of a Tax Cut

In the supply-side explanation of how a tax cut stimulates the economy, shown in (a) (1), an outward shift of the AS curve, leads to (2), an increase in aggregate demand. Supply leads demand. The Keynesian explanation shown in (b) has demand leading supply—the AD curve shifts outward from AD_0 to AD_1, resulting in an inflationary gap if the economy is at its potential income.

demand will also increase. The economy will expand because of greater incentives to work. Exhibit 4(a) shows the supply-side view. A decrease in taxes directly shifts the AS curve out and, since supply creates its own demand, also shifts the demand curve out. Since, in the supply-side view, aggregate supply is the best estimate of potential income, the tax cut increases potential income too.

The Keynesian explanation of the effect of a cut in taxes differs. The Keynesian theoretical explanation holds that a tax cut increases aggregate demand. If the level of potential income is greater than the actual level of income, producers will increase output, which further increases aggregate demand. In the Keynesian view the tax cut doesn't affect potential income. Exhibit 4(b) shows the Keynesian view. The economy is initially at potential income. The tax cut shifts aggregate demand, but not aggregate supply, because aggregate supply can't increase beyond potential income. The result will be either shortages or inflation.

The Keynesian explanation of a tax cut's effect is the multiplier process: In it, *demand* leads *supply* and potential income is unaffected. In the supply-side explanation, *supply* leads *demand* and potential income is increased.

The differences are important because in the early 1980s when this debate was raging, inflation was serious and many economists, both Keynesian and Classical, felt that the economy was operating at its potential income. If that were true, the Keynesian view of the tax cut would suggest that the tax cut would cause inflation; the supply-side view was that it wouldn't cause inflation, because the tax cut would increase individuals' incentives to work and thereby increase potential output.

We see the theoretical difference between the two explanations by considering the following thought experiment: Say the government replaced the income tax (a tax in which the total amount a person pays changes with the amount of income she earns) with a poll tax (a tax in which the total amount an individual pays is constant regardless of his income). Say also that the poll tax generated as much revenue as the income tax. What would be the effect on the aggregate economy? Supply-siders would say that aggregate output would increase enormously since the reward to additional work would be increased significantly. For supply-siders, a cut in tax rates, not a cut in tax revenues, is what stimulates the economy.

A Keynesian would say that a shift from an income tax to a poll tax would have no effect on the economy. Why? Because tax revenues wouldn't change; only the method of assessing the taxes would change. In the Keynesian model, it is the amount of tax collected, not the tax rate, that affects the economy. A change in the tax rates, tax revenue remaining constant, would have no effect.

In reality, tax revenues are almost invariably changed by changing tax rates, so which way a tax cut works is difficult to discover, which is why there is so much debate about which side is right.

Professional Economists' View of Supply-Side Economics   Most economists, Classical as well as Keynesian, at first put down supply-side arguments as being politically motivated. All economists agreed that there were supply-side effects on incentives to save and on labor supply or effort, but they argued that for the aggregate economy these incentive effects were primarily long-run effects that take two to four years to have much effect. That time period was longer than the one-year horizon that is the focus of macroeconomic policy. So most economists dismissed the supply-side arguments.

Politically, and in the popular press, however, supply-side economics became a catch phrase associated with the political push to cut taxes. In much of the popular press supply-siders were equated with Classicals and were seen as the opposition to Keynesians.

How could such a thing happen? If you think textbook writers must condense, think of the plight of a reporter who must say everything in 300 words. As one reporter told me after I complained, "They're both against Keynesians, right? Then they're the same."

Supply-Side Policy and Classical Policy   When the press reports again and again that you believe a particular proposition, often you do begin to believe it. I suspect many Classical economists simply grew tired of pointing out distinctions, so they accepted the supply-side label. This acceptance of the supply-side label by Classicals was made easier by the fading of the debate about the workings of tax cuts. (It wasn't resolved; it just faded away.) The supply-side label came to mean simply someone who opposes Keynesians and gives a strong emphasis to incentive ■6 effects. Most Classicals could live with that, and so in the 1980s more and more of them accepted the supply-side label.

The major difference between a supply-side and a Classical economist is that the typical supply-sider is more *activist* than a Classical economist. Supply-side activism differs from Keynesian activism, which focuses on regulating and controlling the market. Supply-siders believe the government should *actively* foster market incentives and promote a promarket political agenda. Government policy should be designed to strengthen desired incentives. Classicals believe that such activism, even in favor of the market, will often make things worse. They favor a laissez-faire policy.

Historically, as we saw in earlier chapters, Classical economists opposed budget deficits while Keynesian economists supported them. Both positions were simplifications—but reasonable simplifications. The 1980s changed that as many New Classicals put forward a view of the deficit quite outside the Classical tradition. New Classicals said that deficits didn't matter. This switch occurred about the time that many Keynesians were arguing that the government budget deficit was too large and should be reduced. Thus, the 1980s saw Classicals and Keynesians flip-flop their positions on the budget deficit.

New Classical and Keynesian Flip-Flopping Views of the Deficit

Why the New Classicals Flipped   One reason for the New Classical switch in position ■7 was the rediscovery of a theoretical argument for ignoring the effects of deficits.

Ricardian equivalence theorem Proposition that it makes no difference whether government spending is financed by taxes or by a deficit.

That argument was called the *Ricardian equivalence theorem,* named for David Ricardo, an early Classical economist who first developed the argument. The **Ricardian equivalence theorem** states that it makes no difference whether government spending is financed by taxes or by a deficit. The effect of an increase in government spending is the same in either case: a transfer of resources from the private sector to the government and *no* net effect on the aggregate economy.

The reasoning for the Ricardian equivalence theorem is based on rational expectations. If the government runs a deficit, some time in the future that deficit must be paid off—meaning some time in the future, taxes will be higher than if there were no deficit. Rational individuals will take those future taxes into account in their decisions and will spend less now, just as they would have spent less on themselves now if current taxes had been raised. So individuals with rational expectations will be unaffected by a government deficit.

Earlier Classical economists didn't emphasize the Ricardian equivalence theorem because they saw it as primarily a *theoretical* argument of little practical relevance. They opposed deficits because of their concern that government would waste the money. New Classicals focused more on formal theory, so they gave this argument more weight.

7   A second reason for the flip-flop was a change in the political realities. Even for those New Classicals who didn't believe that tax cut incentives would stimulate the economy or didn't believe in the Ricardian equivalence theorem, there was a major reason to support tax cuts. Tax cuts would limit new government programs. It was as if you had a spendthrift spouse who spent money faster than you could earn it. You've tried many strategies to get the spouse to stop spending, but nothing has worked. So you adopt the final strategy: earn less money and spend it immediately yourself so the bills pile up higher and higher and your spouse won't have anything to spend. That will stop the spouse's spending.

Thus, some New Classicals supported supply-side tax cuts because of the limitation cuts placed on government social programs. And it worked. In the 1980s large cuts occurred in many social programs—cuts many had previously believed were impossible.

The New Classical support for tax cuts also helped to put in office presidential candidates who opposed government activism (primarily Republicans) and helped to keep out of office presidential candidates in favor of government activism (primarily Democrats).

7   **Why the Keynesians Flipped**   The argument that one didn't have to worry about deficits was at the center of the Keynesian policy revolution. Indeed, because he made that argument, Alvin Hansen, a Harvard economist who was instrumental in introducing Keynesian economics to the United States in the late 1930s, had been called a radical communist. Most 1930s Classical economists opposed Keynesianism precisely because it led to deficits. A balanced budget placed a constraint on government that was consistent with Classicals' judgment about governments.

Part of the early Keynesians' support of the federal deficit was based upon the political position that allowing budget deficits would allow an expansion of government programs. By the 1980s government programs had expanded about as much as was politically feasible, so that reason to favor deficits ended.

Many Keynesians also felt that the large deficit was forcing government to hold down the economy with its other tool, monetary policy. Heavy reliance on monetary policy to slow the U.S. economy in the 1980s and 1990s, while government ran large deficits, is one reason Keynesians have argued for a more contractionary fiscal policy. They believed that a more contractionary fiscal policy would allow the Fed to run a more expansionary monetary policy, lowering interest rates, increasing investment, and increasing growth. In short, crowding out would be reduced. Thus, even though Keynesians supported a more expansionary aggregate policy than Classicals, they criticized the monetary/fiscal mix: They

ADDED DIMENSION

THE THEORETICAL DIFFERENCE BETWEEN NEW CLASSICAL AND NEW KEYNESIAN MODELS

There is an old French saying which, translated, says, "The more things change, the more they remain the same." It's appropriate for the New Keynesian/New Classical debate. In the latest interchanges between New Classicals and New Keynesians, the Keynesian/Classical debate has come almost full circle. Now, almost 60 years after Keynes first challenged the Classical view, we see the same debate about aggregate supply and its relation to aggregate demand at the center of the contest.

New Classicals see aggregate supply creating demand (Say's law). If there's disequilibrium between quantity of aggregate supply and quantity of aggregate demand, suppliers will *not* cut back output more than desired. Instead they'll cut wages and prices. A fall in wage and price levels will bring the economy back to equilibrium at full employment—the market clearing assumption. How? Via the Keynes effect, the Pigou effect, and the international effect explained in the appendix to the chapter on Keynesian theory.

New Keynesians see the aggregate supply curve as shifting in response to shifts in demand. A shift in aggregate supply causes a further shift in aggregate demand, which causes an even further shift in aggregate supply and so on. The multiplier process begins. Ultimately, as the multiplier process works itself out, equilibrium is reached at an equilibrium income level, which is below potential income. Individuals are responding to excess demand in an individually rational way. What's individually rational is collectively irrational. It leads to an under–full-employment equilibrium. In a New Keynesian equilibrium, the quantity of aggregate supply equals the quantity of aggregate demand, but neither is at the desired level.

The Keynesian multiplier process is caused by the difference between individually rational expectations and what would be collectively rational if all individuals could get together and agree to hold output higher than what's in their individual interest. If everyone knew everyone else were going to lower price, everyone *would* lower price. New Keynesians argue that it's collectively rational to lower price, but it is not individually rational. Because individuals follow their individual interest, they do not lower their price in response to excess supply. Instead they lower production, causing shocks to the system which are multiplied. It is that multiplication that fiscal policy and monetary policy are designed to offset.

It's not unreasonable to ask which model is right. I can't answer that question. Empirically neither model has shown conclusively that it's right. The evidence is vague and difficult to interpret. All we can observe is income. Supply, demand, and equilibrium are all theoretical constructs which are not directly observable. Both models are reasonable ways of approaching a complicated reality. Thus, the more pertinent question is which model is more useful. That depends on what problem you're addressing. If you know both models and understand what each predicts, you can choose the most reasonable one for the particular problem at hand. When you have a complicated reality, it's not surprising that you have debates about how best to describe it and interpret what's happening.

Classicals emphasize shifting aggregate supply and the aggregate price adjustment mechanism. They argue that the economy is best modeled as if it were perfectly competitive and always in a supply-demand equilibrium.

Keynesians tend to see the economy in continuous supply-demand disequilibrium—the wage and price adjustment mechanism is too weak or too slow to maintain equilibrium so the economy must rely, at least in part, on the income adjustment multiplier process. That's the central difference between Keynesian and Classical models.

---

supported a somewhat less expansionary fiscal policy but a much more expansionary monetary policy. They believed if the deficit was reduced, a stronger stimulus to the economy could come from monetary policy without generating inflation.

Not all Keynesians flip-flopped, but enough of them did so that it was no longer an acceptable simplification to say that Keynesians generally supported deficits and expansionary fiscal policy. So in the 1990s we find both Classicals and Keynesians divided in their views of the deficit. I'll talk more about this in a later chapter.

Because of these recent shifts in policy prescriptions and views of the economy, the 1990s is a difficult period for journalists and textbook writers. There's no neat division between Classical and Keynesian views on macroeconomic policy.

As we get into real policy debates, the water gets muddy and the clear-cut positions exemplified in the models fall apart. Nevertheless you may consider yourself quite economically literate if you understand the following distinctions after your study of the Classical and Keynesian theoretical models covered in this chapter:

THE BOTTOM LINE OF MACRO THEORY

1. You should know the basic Keynesian and Classical views and be able to differentiate what view each side is likely to take on an issue.

2. You should be familiar with the two Classical propositions and how those propositions influence the Classical views of how the economy works.

3. You should be familiar with the Keynesian multiplier model and how it influences the Keynesian view of how the economy works.

4. You should be able to talk about monetary and fiscal policy, Classicals' and Keynesians' views of monetary and fiscal policy, and the problems both sides say result from using them.

5. You should be aware of Keynesians' and Classicals' recent positions on policy, and know some of the political influences that led them to take those positions.

If, a year from now, you remember those five things, you'll be more informed about macroeconomics than 99.5 percent of the population—which won't be bad for having taken only an introductory course.

KEY POINTS

- Macroeconomic theory continues to evolve. **1**
- The monetarist/Neo-Keynesian debate concerned crowding out and activism versus laissez-faire. **2** **3**
- When the central bank buys sufficient government bonds to finance the deficit, it monetizes the deficit. **3**
- New Classicals opposed Keynesian economics as ad hoc economics and as being inconsistent with the assumption that people have rational expectations. **4**
- Both New Classicals and New Keynesians agree

that a policy's credibility is central to its success. **5**
- The policy debate between Keynesians and Classicals is primarily a debate over activism versus laissez-faire. **5**
- Supply-side economists are somewhat more activist than are other Classical economists, but they favor a government promarket incentives activism. **6**
- In the 1980s Keynesians and Classicals flip-flopped in their views of the deficit. **7**

KEY TERMS

accommodating monetary policy *(322)*
crowding out *(320)*
IS/LM (*I*nvestment = *S*avings/*L*iquidity = *M*oney) *(318)*

micro foundations *(318)*
monetarists *(318)*
monetary rule *(323)*
monetizing the deficit *(322)*

neo-Keynesians *(318)*
New Classical economist *(318)*
New Keynesian economist *(318)*

rational expectations *(324)*
Ricardian equivalence theorem *(330)*

QUESTIONS FOR THOUGHT AND REVIEW

The number after each question represents the estimated degree of critical thinking required. (1 = almost none; 10 = deep thought.)

1. Identify whether Keynesian or Classical economists might have said the following:
   a. It's important not to be ad hoc in one's assumptions.

   b. Don't give Johnny an ice cream cone. It's against the rules.
   c. Come on, Johnny's sick. Let's give him an ice cream cone just this once. *(4)*
2. List three groups of Keynesians and three groups of Classicals. Identify each group's main ideas. *(2)*
3. The economy has just gone into a recession. What

would a Classical advise the government to do? State two arguments a Classical would use to defend that advice. *(5)*

4. The economy has just gone into a recession. What would a Keynesian advise the government to do? State four arguments a Keynesian would use to defend that advice. *(5)*

5. Demonstrate crowding out graphically. Would passing a law holding the interest rate constant eliminate crowding out? *(6)*

6. Name the two central propositions of New Classical economics. What are the New Keynesian arguments against them? *(4)*

7. The government changes its income tax system from the current system to a poll tax system. Explain the effect on you (or, if you don't work, on a friend of yours who does). *(6)*

8. What implications does your answer to Question 7 have for the debate between supply-siders and Keynesians? *(5)*

9. Supply-siders favor the creation of free enterprise zones (areas of the economy with no government regulation). Give the likely Classical and Keynesian positions on free enterprise zones. *(5)*

10. Deficits make no difference to what happens in the real economy. True or false? Why? *(9)*

PROBLEMS AND EXERCISES

1. Interview your teacher about her or his views on macro policy.
   a. Classify the teacher as a Classical, a Keynesian, or something else. (Not all economists are Keynesians or Classicals. There are Institutionalists, radicals, and many other types.)
   b. If you can classify the teacher as a Classical or Keynesian, can you more specifically classify him or her as a neo, new, or some other type of Classical or Keynesian? (There are many others such as Post Keynesians and Austrian Classicals.)

2. Do the same thing with your parents, spouse, or significant other, only this time determine where you would place them on the basis of their views since they most likely won't have any idea of how to even pronounce the terms.

15

Inflation and the Phillips Curve Trade-Off

The first few months or year of inflation, like the first few drinks, seem just fine. Everyone has more money to spend and prices aren't rising quite as fast as the money that's available. The hangover comes when prices start to catch up.

Milton Friedman

After reading this chapter, you should be able to:

1

Explain why sustained high inflation is inevitably accompanied by a roughly equal increase in the money supply and expectations of inflation.

2

Differentiate between long-run and short-run Phillips curves.

3

Outline the Classical theory of inflation.

4

Outline the Keynesian theory of inflation.

5

Distinguish the Keynesian and Classical views of the Phillips curve trade-off.

6

Explain why a Keynesian would be more likely to support an incomes policy than a Classical economist would.

Inflation and its relationship to unemployment were introduced earlier. Now that we've worked our way through macroeconomic theory and financial institutions, we're ready to consider these issues again and discuss the problems societies have had in trying to cope with inflation.

Inflation is a continuous rise in the price level. All economists agree on that. They also agree (1) that high inflation rates are inevitably accompanied by a roughly proportional increase in the money supply and (2) that high inflation rates are associated with expectations of inflation of approximately that rate. Thus, most economists accept that when inflation is really high, say 40 percent, the money supply will be increasing by about 40 percent, and people will be expecting approximately 40 percent inflation.[1] Why do these rough equalities hold? Let's consider the money supply and inflation first.

Say, for example, that the U.S. money supply growth rate is 40 percent. What will likely happen? From the equation of exchange ($MV = PY$), you can deduce that something else must also change. Assuming velocity, V, isn't decreasing enormously and real output isn't increasing enormously, that 40 percent increase in the money supply must be accompanied by a rise in the price level of about 40 percent. Otherwise there will be a shortage of goods. Alternatively say prices are rising at a 40 percent rate but the money supply isn't growing at all. Unless velocity is increasing by 40 percent a year, firms will be unable to sell their goods at the higher prices because the amount of money people are spending won't buy the goods that firms are offering to sell at those higher prices. Given the shortage of aggregate demand, firms will be forced to stop increasing their prices.

Notice that so far we've said nothing about what's causing what to increase, which clearly is something policymakers would like to know. Determining the cause of inflation is important in determining how to fight it.

To distinguish cases in which price increases cause the money supply increases from cases in which money supply increases cause the price increases, inflation is divided into **cost-push inflation** (price increases cause money supply increases) and **demand-pull inflation** (money supply increases cause price increases).

In an ongoing inflation it's often impossible to distinguish whether it's cost-push or demand-pull. The reason is expectations of inflation. Say money supply is expected to increase. Firms will expect demand for their good to increase and will raise prices on the basis of that expectation. Then, even though price increases may come before money supply increases, it's the expected increase in the money supply that causes prices to rise. However, regardless of whether prices are being pulled by the money supply or are pushing the money supply, all economists agree that for substantial inflation to continue the money supply must rise.

The second relationship that most economists agree exists is between inflation and expectations of inflation. The relationship is based on common sense. For example, if inflation is currently 20 percent, assuming no major change in policy, it is reasonable to expect that it will remain about 20 percent. So people's natural tendency is to base their expectations on what is or has recently been. Expectations based on what has been in the past are called **adaptive expectations.**

Adaptive expectations aren't the only reasonable type. People likely will also base their expectations of inflation on their understanding of the economy, economists' predictions of inflation, and their own past experience. For example, if the money supply is increasing substantially, many economists will predict high inflation. To the degree that people believe economists, people will expect high

INFLATION

Inflation   A continuous rise in the price level.

The Money Supply
and Inflation

Cost-push inflation   Inflation where price increases cause money supply increases.

Demand-pull inflation   Inflation where money supply increases cause price increases.

Inflation and Expectations of Inflation

Adaptive expectations   Expectations of the future based on what has been in the past.

---

[1] Where economists disagree is on what causes what to increase. Is inflation causing the money supply to increase, or are increases in the money supply causing inflation? We'll address these issues shortly.

There have been periods when it wasn't difficult to distinguish between cost-push and demand-pull inflations. For example, during the post–World War II period, which began in late 1945, there was large pent-up demand. Because of shortages of goods during the war, people had saved up buying power. After the war most economists were expecting strong inflationary pressures from demand-pull forces. And that's what happened. There was general agreement that the period's inflation was demand-pull inflation.

But in the early 1970s that stored-up buying power didn't exist. Then there was a significant supply shock—oil prices rose substantially, placing cost-push pressure on prices. That's why most economists call the inflation of the early 1970s cost-push inflation.

inflation, even though it's not yet high. So the relationship between current inflation and expectations of future inflation is not perfect.

But, on average, most economists agree that expectations of inflation approximately equal the amount of inflation in the economy.

Inflation and Unemployment: The Phillips Curve Trade-Off

Perhaps the most vexing dilemma policy makers face in dealing with inflation is the inflation/unemployment policy dilemma: Whenever they try to fight inflation, unemployment seems to increase, and whenever they try to fight unemployment, inflation seems to increase. It is captured graphically in a curve, shown in Exhibit 1(b), called the short-run Phillips curve. In it, unemployment is measured on the horizontal axis; inflation is on the vertical axis. The Phillips curve shows us what combinations of inflation and unemployment are possible. It tells us that when unemployment is low, say 4 percent, inflation tends to be high, say 4 percent (point *A* on the short-run Phillips curve). It also tells us that if we want to lower inflation, say to 1 percent, we must be willing to accept high unemployment, say 7 percent (point *B* in Exhibit 1(b)).

Phillips curve A representation of the relation between inflation and unemployment.

The **Phillips curve** was initially a representation of historical inflation and unemployment data. As economists looked at unemployment and inflation data over time, they noticed that there seemed to be a trade-off between inflation and unemployment. When unemployment was high, inflation was low; when unemployment was low, inflation was high. That empirical relationship seemed rather stable in the 1950s and 1960s. Exhibit 1(a) shows this empirical relationship for the United States for the years 1954–68, when it became built into the way economists looked at the economy.

Because it seemed to represent a relatively stable trade-off, in the 1960s the Phillips curve played a central role in discussions of macroeconomic policy. Republicans (often advised by Classical economists) generally favored contractionary monetary and fiscal policy, which maintained high unemployment and low inflation (a point like *B* in Exhibit 1(b)). Democrats (often advised by Keynesian economists) generally favored expansionary monetary and fiscal policies which brought about low unemployment but high inflation (a point like *A* in Exhibit 1(b)).

The Breakdown of the Short-Run Phillips Curve   In the early 1970s the empirical short-run Phillips curve relationship seemed to break down. When one looked at the data, there no longer seemed to be a trade-off between unemployment and inflation. Instead in the 1970s, when unemployment was high, inflation was also high. Exhibit 2 shows the empirical relationship between inflation and unemployment from 1961 to 1981. Notice that the relatively stable relationship up until 1969 breaks down in the 1970s. In the 1970s there doesn't seem to be any trade-off between inflation and unemployment at all. Something clearly changed in the 1970s.

To discover what changed, economists devoted much thought to explaining the theory underlying the Phillips curve. What caused inflation? How would inflation interact with unemployment if people acted in certain reasonable ways?

Milton Friedman—Nobel prize, 1976, for work on monetary theory. © *The Nobel Foundation.*

(a)   **(b)**

EXHIBIT 1 (a and b)   The Phillips Curve Trade-Off

Analyzing the empirical relationship between unemployment and inflation from 1954 to 1968—shown in (**a**)—led economists to believe there was the relatively stable Phillips curve which, for policy choices, could be represented by the smooth Phillips curve in (**b**). Source: Economic Report of the President.

EXHIBIT 2   The Breakdown of the Phillips Curve Relationship, 1961–1981

In the 1970s the empirical Phillips curve relationship between inflation and unemployment broke down, leading many economists to question the existence of any Phillips curve relationship that allowed policy makers to choose between inflation and unemployment.

As economists thought about these problems, they developed and refined their theories and models of both inflation and unemployment.

 The Distinction between the Short-Run and Long-Run Phillips Curves   As views of the Phillips curve changed, economists began distinguishing between a short-run Phillips curve and a long-run Phillips curve. The key element of that distinction is based on **expectations of inflation** (the rise in the price level that the average person expects). On each point on the **short-run Phillips curve,** expectations of inflation are constant. At each point on the **long-run Phillips curve,** expectations of inflation equal actual inflation. Economists used this distinction to explain why the short-run Phillips curve relationship broke down in the 1970s.

The reasons expectations are so central to the Phillips curve is seen by considering an individual's decision about what wage or price to set. Say you expect 0 percent inflation and you want a 2 percent wage or price increase. You'll raise your wage or price by 2 percent. Now say you expect 20 percent inflation and you want a 2 percent real wage increase. To get it, you must increase your wage by 22 percent. If everyone expects 20 percent inflation, everyone will raise their wage or price by 20 percent just to keep up.

2

Expectations of inflation   The rise in the price level that the average person expects.

Short-run Phillips curve   A curve showing the trade-off between inflation and unemployment when expectations of inflation are constant.

Long-run Phillips curve   Curve showing the trade-off (or complete lack thereof) when expectations of inflation equal actual inflation.

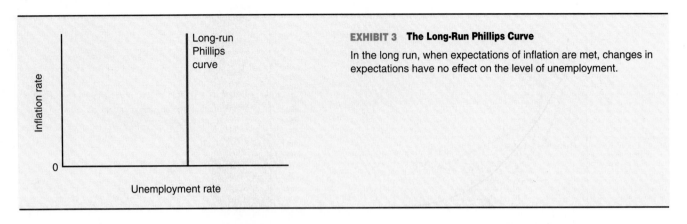

EXHIBIT 3   The Long-Run Phillips Curve

In the long run, when expectations of inflation are met, changes in expectations have no effect on the level of unemployment.

This means that expectations of inflation play a significant role in inflation. When expectations of inflation are higher, the same level of unemployment will be associated with a higher rate of inflation. To capture this relationship, it makes sense to assume that the short-run Phillips curve moves up or down as expectations of inflation change.

The Shape of the Long-Run Phillips Curve   To determine what the long-run Phillips curve would look like, economists asked themselves: What difference should expectations of inflation make to the target level of unemployment? Their answer was none. If people expect 20 percent inflation and are raising their wages and prices 20 percent on average, the situation is just the same as if they expect 4 percent inflation and are raising their wages and prices 4 percent on average. People aren't fooled by expected inflation. Thus, economists theorized that the long-run Phillips curve would be a vertical line, as in Exhibit 3. As you can see, in the long run, when expectations of inflation are fully built into people's wage- and price-setting decisions, there's no trade-off between inflation and unemployment.

This vertical long-run Phillips curve fits the empirical data for the 1970s and provides an explanation for why the short-run trade-off broke down. To see this, let's consider the years 1964 and 1970. Unemployment in both years was approximately 5 percent, but inflation in 1970 was over 5 percent while inflation in 1964 was less than 2 percent. Why the difference? Consider what happened in the interim: Inflation was consistently rising so it's reasonable to assume that expectations of inflation were higher in 1970 than in 1964. Expectations of inflation explain the difference. When expectations are higher, actual inflation at each level of unemployment will be higher.

Moving from a Short-Run to a Long-Run Phillips Curve   We can see how an economy moves from a short-run to a long-run Phillips curve by examining Exhibit 4. Say, for example, that initially the economy is at point A. Expected inflation is zero, unemployment is 5.5 percent, and the relevant short-run Phillips curve is PC_1, which has zero expected inflation. Now, say that the government expands aggregate demand with expansionary monetary policy. This causes unemployment to fall to 4 percent and inflation to rise to 6 percent (point B). We move along the initial short-run Phillips curve, PC_1.

But point B isn't a long-run equilibrium because expectations of inflation (0 percent) do not equal actual inflation (6 percent). Since actual inflation exceeds expected inflation, expectations of inflation will rise. As those expectations rise, PC_1, which assumes zero expected inflation, is no longer relevant; the relevant short-run Phillips curve will shift up. We can state this as a general rule. Whenever actual inflation exceeds expected inflation, we can predict that expectations will rise and the short-run Phillips curve will shift up. It will continue shifting up until expected inflation equals actual inflation. This occurs at point C on PC_2,

EXHIBIT 4   The Long-Run and the Short-Run Phillips Curve

When the economy is at point *B*, actual inflation, 6 percent, exceeds expected inflation, 0 percent. Because actual exceeds expected, expectations of inflation will rise, shifting the short-run Phillips curve up in the direction of *PC₂*. It will continue shifting up until expected inflation once again equals actual inflation. The long-run Phillips curve is such that at all points expected inflation equals actual inflation,

which assumes 6 percent expected inflation. On PC_2, when inflation is 6 percent (point *C*), unemployment isn't 4 percent; it's 5.5 percent. Since at points *A* and *C* actual inflation equals expected inflation, *A* and *C* are both on the long-run Phillips curve. By connecting *A* and *C* and all other points at which expected inflation equals actual inflation, you arrive at the long-run Phillips curve, which, as you can see, is a vertical line.

Thus, while in the short run there is a trade-off between inflation and unemployment, in the long run there is no trade-off: The unemployment rate cannot be changed by accepting more inflation.

By the 1980s most economists accepted the view that there was a short-run trade-off but no long-run trade-off. Once again, however, economists' beliefs were challenged by empirical observation. As unemployment decreased from 7 percent in 1986 to about 5 percent in 1989, inflation increased, but there were no signs of accelerating inflation, even though expectations had had time to adjust. Then in 1990 and 1991 as unemployment rose, inflation fell. This led some economists to argue that a long-run trade-off between inflation and unemployment was returning. Because of these new observations, the inflation/unemployment trade-off is likely to be much in debate in the 1990s.

Most economists accept the existence of a short-run Phillips curve and the rough equality between expectations of inflation, increases in the money supply, and the actual rate of inflation. In a theory, however, one must blur out a number of aspects of reality to focus on those aspects one believes are most important. That's what Keynesians and Classicals do with their theories of inflation.

THEORIES OF INFLATION AND THE PHILLIPS CURVE TRADE-OFF

Keynesians blur the relationship between inflation and money in order to focus on the institutional process of setting prices and cost-push pressures as the underlying causes of the inflationary process. According to Keynesians, the money supply increases with inflation but these increases aren't the cause of inflation; the money supply increases occur because government tries to see that inflation (the rise in the price level) doesn't lead to unemployment and cost-push pressures. When government increases aggregate demand to see that the price increases don't lead to unemployment, it ratifies the inflation. According to Keynesians, money supply increases are a necessary, but not a causal, link in the inflation process.

Classicals blur the price-setting process and the cost-push pressures in order to focus on demand-pull pressure and the relationship between increases in the money supply and inflation. When Classicals see inflation they see the government increasing the money supply. Both theories shed light on inflation. Let's now consider them a bit more carefully.

The Classical Theory of Inflation

3

The Classical theory of inflation can be summed up in one sentence: *Inflation is everywhere and always a monetary phenomenon.* If the money supply doesn't rise, the price level won't rise. Forget all the other stuff. It obscures the connection between money and inflation. (As I discussed in the last chapter, this focus on money is why Classicals were called *monetarists* in the 1960s and 1970s.)

The Quantity Theory of Money and Inflation

That connection between money and inflation is relatively simple and can be seen in the quantity theory: When the money supply rises, prices go up; if the money supply doesn't continue to rise, inflation won't continue. Consider the quantity theory of money:

$$MV = PQ.$$

Classicals assume velocity, V, and real output, Q, are relatively constant. They also consider the price level, P, relatively flexible. According to Classical theory, any inflation is caused by demand-pull pressures—which are generated by increases in the money supply. Therefore,

$$\Delta M \to \Delta P.$$

Lawrence Davidson, a Classical economist at the St. Louis Federal Reserve Bank, summarizes that view:

> Monetarists (another name for Classical economists) also believe that there are numerous sources of price change, yet only changes in money growth can permanently alter the rate of inflation. Therefore, we expect that non-monetary factors will sometimes affect short-term measured inflation rates. If these non-monetary sources of measured inflation arise unexpectedly over time, and if they only temporarily affect the inflation rate, then the only lasting, predictable, and controllable source of inflation would be monetary growth. ("Inflation Misinformation and Monetary Policy," *St. Louis Federal Reserve Bank Review,* 1982, p. 21.)

Classical Modifications of the Quantity Theory

The quantity theory of money embodies the central element of the Classical theory of inflation. There are many modifications which explain why the connection between money and inflation in the short

The Classical view that printing money causes inflation is seen in the 18th-century satirical drawing by James Gilray of William Pitt spewing paper money out of his mouth while gold coins are locked up in his stomach. *Bleichroeder Print Collection, Baker Library, Harvard Business School.*

MIDAS, Transmuting all into GOLD PAPER.

run isn't perfectly tight. One important modification is that Classicals believe that people are often fooled into thinking an increase in nominal demand caused by an increase in the money supply is actually an increase in real demand. The result will be a short-run expansionary effect on the real economy, as suggested in this chapter's opening quotation from Milton Friedman.

Let's consider an example. In 1971 the Fed increased the money supply significantly; as a result income rose and unemployment fell. In response in 1972 inflation fell slightly, as did unemployment. However, in 1973 and 1974 both inflation and unemployment rose substantially. Here's an example of expansionary monetary policy increasing real output as prices are slow to respond to increases in aggregate demand. But in the long run the expansionary monetary policy caused inflation. Classical economists also believe that people can be fooled in the opposite direction—thinking that a decrease in nominal demand is actually a decrease in real demand. This makes it difficult to stop an ongoing inflation because the initial short-run effect is on real output. The effect on inflation occurs in the long run.

Let's consider an example, again from the 1970s, when significant inflation—10 percent—became built into the economy. In late 1979 and the early 1980s the Fed decreased the money supply growth significantly. This led to a leap in unemployment from 7 to 10 percent, but initially no decrease in inflation. By 1984, however, inflation had fallen to about 4 percent, and it remained low throughout the 1980s.

There are many alternative ways in which short-run Classical theory of inflation makes adjustments for changes in velocity, real output, and expectations, but the core of their theory is inevitably that *inflation is everywhere and always a monetary phenomenon*. That core connection between money and inflation is pleasant for students because it makes it possible to present succinctly the Classical view.

The Classical View of the Phillips Curve Trade-Off

The Classical view of the trade-off centers around the **natural rate of unemployment** (the rate of unemployment to which the economy naturally gravitates).[2] This natural rate of unemployment is independent of the inflation rate and expectations of inflation. It is the unemployment rate that will exist in long-run equilibrium when expectations of inflation equal the actual level of inflation. The long-run Phillips curve is vertical at this natural rate of unemployment.

Unemployment rates below the natural unemployment rate would lead to actual inflation higher than expected inflation, which would bring about a future increase in expectations of inflation, and an upward shift of the short-run Phillips curve. This Classical view is shown in Exhibit 5.

At unemployment rates to the left of the long-run Phillips curve (unemployment rates below the natural rate), actual inflation is above expectations of inflation so the short-run Phillips curve will shift upward (shown by the upward arrows in Exhibit 5). To the right of the long-run Phillips curve (at unemployment rates higher than the natural rate), actual inflation is below expectations of inflation and the short-run Phillips curve will shift downward (shown by the downward arrows in the exhibit). Maintaining an unemployment rate below the natural rate would cause an ever-increasing acceleration of inflation. Such an accelerating inflation is unsustainable because it destroys the benefits of money. It would cause hyperinflation and a breakdown of the economy. Eventually the government must give up its attempt to lower the unemployment rate below the natural rate. But even after giving up its attempt to achieve an unemployment rate below the natural rate, the government will have left a legacy of high inflation. The

The St. Louis Fed Journal has consistently presented the monetarist view of economic policy.

5

Natural rate of unemployment Classical term for the unemployment rate in long-run equilibrium when expectations of inflation equal the actual level of inflation.

---

[2] The natural rate concept is the Classical equivalent of what this book calls the *target rate of unemployment*. The Keynesian equivalent for the target rate is the *nonaccelerating inflation rate of unemployment* (NAIRU).

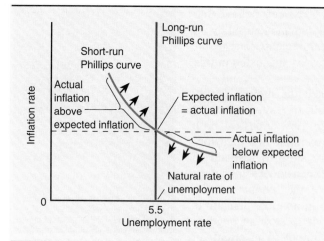

Stagflation   Combination of high inflation and high unemployment.

combination of high and accelerating inflation and high unemployment is known as **stagflation.**

Exhibit 6 graphs the Classical explanation of how stagflation occurs. Say the economy starts at an equilibrium of zero actual inflation, zero expected inflation, and 5.5 percent unemployment, which, let's suppose, happens to be the natural rate of unemployment. Now government comes along and expands the economy with expansionary monetary or fiscal policy to point A on the short-run Phillips curve so that there will be 3 percent inflation and 4 percent unemployment. The 3 percent actual inflation exceeds 0 percent expected inflation, which causes a shift up in expectations of inflation. This increase in expectations causes the short-run Phillips curve to shift up from PC_1 to PC_2.

After expectations of inflation have shifted up fully, instead of being able to achieve 4 percent unemployment with a 3 percent inflation rate, it would take a 6 percent inflation rate to maintain unemployment at 4 percent (point B). Let's say the government is willing to accept 6 percent inflation and uses expansionary monetary or fiscal policy to try to maintain unemployment at 4 percent, which is 1.5 percent below the natural rate. Expectations of inflation would shift up to 6 percent and the short-run Phillips curve would shift up to PC_3. Now the government finds that to keep the economy at 4 percent unemployment would require an even more expansionary policy and an inflation rate of 9 percent (point C). And even that 9 percent is only temporary; as long as the unemployment rate is less than the natural rate, actual inflation will be above expected inflation, the short-run Phillips curve will be shifting up, and inflation will be accelerating.

That's what Classicals said happened in the 1970s. Government, following Keynesians' advice, expanded the economy and reduced unemployment below the natural rate, causing expectations of inflation to rise and the short-run Phillips curve to shift up. Inflation stopped rising only when the government accepted the natural rate of unemployment as inevitable. In the Classical view, government expansionary policy caused stagflation.

The Keynesian Theory of Inflation

Keynesians would agree with much of what the Classicals have to say but believe that they aren't focusing on the important institutional and structural aspects of inflation. Keynesians argue that when firms and individuals set prices, they do not take into account the effect of their pricing decisions on the price level. Since generally firms, rather than consumers, set prices, those prices quickly adjust upward in response to an increase in demand, but are much slower to adjust downward in response to a decrease in demand.

The revenue firms receive is divided among profits, wages, and rent. All this income is ultimately paid to individual owners of the factors of production. Firms are simply intermediaries between individuals as owners of the factors of produc-

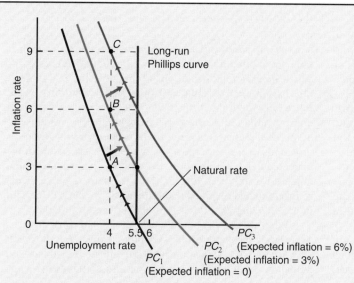

EXHIBIT 6   The Classical Explanation of Stagflation

When the government utilizes expansionary monetary or fiscal policy in an attempt to lower unemployment below the natural rate, expectations of inflation exceed actual inflation and the short-run Phillips curve shifts upward. Inflation continually increases until government gives up its attempt to do the impossible.

tion and individuals as consumers. Keynesians argue that given the institutional structure of our economy, it's often easier for firms to increase wages, profits, and rents to keep the peace with their employees and other factors of production than it is to try to hold those costs down. Firms then pay for that increase by raising the prices they charge consumers. That works as long as, in response to the rising price level, the government increases the money supply so that the demand is there to buy the goods at the higher prices.

Let's consider an example: A zuka firm is happy with its competitive position in the zuka market. It expects 0 percent inflation. Productivity (output of zukas per unit input) is increasing 2 percent, the same as the increase in productivity in the economy as a whole, so the firm can hold its nominal price of zukas constant even if it increases wages by 2 percent. Since the price level isn't expected to change, holding the price of zukas constant should maintain the firm's share of the zuka market. The firm offers workers a 2 percent increase.

The firm meets its workers to discuss the 2 percent offer. At that meeting it becomes clear to the firm that its workers will push for a 4 percent pay increase. What should the firm do? In a highly competitive market in which supply and demand forces alone determine wages and prices, there's no question what it would do; it would increase wages only 2 percent and hold its price constant. Real-world firms, however, often meet workers' demands under the expectation that other firms will do so too. Meeting these demands helps maintain morale and prevents turnover of key workers. This occurs whether or not there are unions. The result is an upward push on nominal wages and prices.

This upward push on nominal wages and prices can exist only if the labor and product markets are not highly competitive. In a highly competitive market, even small amounts of unemployment and excess supply would cause wages and prices to fall. Keynesians believe that most real-world markets are not highly competitive in this fashion. While they agree that some competition exists, they argue that in most sectors of the economy, competition works slowly. The invisible handshake, as well as the invisible hand, influences wages and prices. The result is that even when there is substantial unemployment and considerable excess supply of goods, existing workers can still put an upward push on nominal wages, and existing firms can put an upward push on nominal prices.

The Insider/Outsider Model and Inflation   To get a better picture of how existing workers can push up wages despite substantial unemployment, let's consider a Keynesian model which divides the economy into insiders and outsiders. Insiders are work-

THE DISTRIBUTIONAL EFFECTS OF INFLATION

If inflation is a distributional fight, who wins and who loses? The winners are people who can raise their wages or prices and still keep their jobs and sell their labor or goods. The losers are people who can't.

The composition of these groups changes over time. For example, at one time people on social security and pensions lost out during inflations since social security and pensions were, on the whole, set at fixed rates. Inflation lowered recipients' real income. But social security payments and many pensions are now indexed (automatically adjusted to compensate for inflation) so their recipients are no longer losers. Their real income became independent of inflation.

Similarly, it's sometimes said that bond holders are hurt by inflation, since the value of the money with which the bonds are redeemed falls during inflation. That's true, but whether bond holders lose depends on how the interest rate on bonds adjusts to the expected inflation rate. In recent years the nominal interest rate has adjusted quickly

to expectations of inflation. When that happens it is unclear how much bond holders have lost. If nominal interest rates adjust quickly to expectations of inflation, the real interest rate may remain as high as it otherwise would have been. For example, in the 1950s bond holders received 2 percent interest; inflation was low so 2 percent interest was close to a 2 percent real interest rate. In the early 1970s interest rates on bonds were 8 percent, in large part because people expected 6 percent inflation. Six percent compensated bond holders for inflation, leaving them the same 2 percent real return they had received in the 1950s. So we must be careful in generalizing about distributional effects of inflation.

What we can say about the distributional consequences of inflation is that people who don't expect inflation and who are tied in to fixed contracts denominated in unindexed monetary values will likely lose in an inflation. However, these people are rational and probably won't let it happen again. They'll be prepared for a subsequent inflation.

ers who have good jobs with excellent long-run prospects, and current business owners. Both receive above-equilibrium wages, profits, and rents. If the world were competitive, their wages, profits, and rents would be pushed down to the equilibrium level. To prevent this from happening, Keynesians argue, insiders develop sociological and institutional barriers that prevent outsiders from competing those above-equilibrium wages, profits, and rents away. Because of those barriers, outsiders (often minorities) must take dead-end, low-paying jobs or attempt to undertake marginal businesses that pay little return for many hours worked. Even when outsiders do find better jobs or business opportunities, they are first to be fired and their businesses are the first to suffer in a recession. Thus, outsiders have much higher unemployment rates than insiders. For example, in the United States blacks tend to be outsiders; black unemployment rates are generally twice as high as white unemployment rates for the same age groups.

In short, Keynesians see an economic system that's only partially competitive. In their view, the invisible hand is often thwarted by other invisible forces. Such partially competitive economies are often characterized by insiders' monopolies. Imperfect competition allows workers (and firms) to raise nominal wages (and prices) even as unemployment (and excess supply of goods) exists. Then, as other insiders do likewise, the price level rises. This increase in the price level lowers workers' real wage. In response, workers further raise their nominal wages to protect their real wages. The result is an ongoing chase in which the insiders protect their real wage, while outsiders suffer. (If the ideas of *nominal* and *real* are unclear to you, a review of earlier chapters may be in order.)

Within this imperfectly competitive system, both wages and prices develop their own inertia which often takes on a life of its own. Keynesians believe that to understand inflation you must understand the psychology of the individuals with wage- and price-setting power, including both firms and organizations of workers.

Thus, Keynesians see the nominal wage- and price-setting process as generating inflation. As one group pushes up its nominal wage or price, another group responds by doing the same. More groups follow until finally the first group finds its relative wage or price hasn't increased. Then the entire process starts again. Once the nominal wage and price levels have risen, government has two options: It can either ratify the increase by increasing the money supply, thereby accepting the inflation; or it can refuse to ratify it, causing unemployment.

The Role of Unemployment in Keynesian Theories of Inflation   What role does unemployment play in the inflation process for Keynesians? They see the fear of unemployment as a way of "disciplining" workers to accept lower pay. The reality that there are a number of unemployed people out there waiting to take the jobs of employed workers who ask for too high a wage increase helps prevent existing workers from raising their wage. Thus, unemployment helps fight inflation. But unemployment is not a complete retardant of inflation because many workers and firms have insulated themselves from unemployment through implicit or explicit contracts providing them with job and market security regardless of the level of unemployment. This means that the unemployment costs of fighting inflation are borne heavily by minorities and other outsiders. Insiders are more protected and have less to fear from unemployment.

The Keynesian View of the Phillips Curve Trade-Off   As I've stated, Keynesians see an   **5** economy of imperfectly competitive markets. Keynesians believe that, in the short run, social forces (the invisible handshake, which creates a type of implicit contract between buyers and sellers) and explicit contracts play a large role in price determination. Because of these social forces, there is no reason that, in the short run, expected inflation must precisely equal actual inflation. Keynesians argue that if the economy is kept close to the existing level of inflation (say within 2 or 3 percent), these social forces can hold inflationary expectations in check at their existing level and prevent them from being built into higher inflationary demands, and thereby shifting up the short-run Phillips curve. Thus, within a limited range of inflation rates around the actual inflation rate, many Keynesians believe that the short-run Phillips curve can be relatively stable, and not shift up even though actual inflation exceeds expected inflation. They argue that the trade-off existing up to 1969 was not an illusion and that that relationship did exist in the late 1980s. There can be a long-run trade-off between inflation and unemployment, as there was up until 1969. In a sense Keynesians are saying that the long run never comes.

The reason many Keynesians believe there can be a long-run trade-off between inflation and unemployment is not that they believe people are irrational; it is that they believe people are reasonable. Keynesians argue that, given the cost of rationality, it would be unreasonable for most people to make explicit calculations about inflation's effect on their incomes. People have a general feeling, but that is all they have. Consequently people's calculations about their relative wage and prices based on the price level are inexact. Three or four percent inflation per year is about .008 percent per day, meaning that $1,000 will lose about 8¢ in value each day. That 8¢ is hardly noticeable. Price indices are more inexact than that. Therefore, say many Keynesians, low inflation levels (2 or 3 percent) will be accepted by individuals without leading them to immediate increases in their nominal wages or prices.

Keynesians argue that people will rationally respond quite differently to a 2 percent decrease in their real wage caused by a 2 percent decrease in their nominal wage than they would to a 2 percent decrease in their real wage caused by a 2 percent increase in the price level. This argument accounts for the Keynesian explanation of the reasonably stable trade-off that existed before 1969.

How then do these Keynesians explain the 1970s? The answer is that the economy experienced a combination of unfortunate events, including oil price shocks and overly expansionary government policies. These events caused inflation to exceed what psychologists called the *just-noticeable difference*.

The **just-noticeable difference** is the threshold where our senses realize that something has changed. For example, say it gets 3°F warmer; most people won't notice. But if it gets 10°F warmer, most people will notice. Thus, the just-noticeable difference is a change of somewhere between 3°F and 10°F. Keynesians argue that in the 1970s inflation exceeded that threshold. As it did, inflation became built into people's expectations and everyone who previously had wanted

Just-noticeable difference   A threshold below which our senses don't recognize that something has changed.

DIETING AND FIGHTING
INFLATION

The debate on what to do about inflation has an analogy to dieting. Fasting will cause you to lose about a pound a day. Want to lose 30 pounds? A Classical dietitian would say, "Fast. Thirty pounds equals 105,000 calories. When you've managed to complete a period in which you've eaten 105,000 fewer calories than are necessary to maintain your present weight, you'll have lost 30 pounds." A Keynesian dietitian would offer a variety of diets or would explore your soul to discover why you want to overeat, and would perhaps suggest a liquid protein plan. The Keynesian diet would also involve your taking in 105,000 fewer calories than if you'd continued to overeat. But, Keynesians argue, you can't stick with a diet unless you've discovered what makes you want to overeat.

a 4 percent wage hike now asked for a 9 percent hike, while firms that wanted a 3 percent price increase raised their prices by 8 percent to account for the expected higher price level due to inflation. The entire short-run Phillips curve shifted up, as suggested by the Classicals. But that happened only because the economy was pushed too far; it doesn't negate the existence of a continuing trade-off between inflation and unemployment within certain limits.

Thus, there is a central difference between the Keynesian and Classical views of the Phillips curve. The Keynesian view allows that within a limited range there is a long-run trade-off between inflation and unemployment. That's why Keynesians generally support a more expansionary policy than do Classical economists and also why they support more activist monetary and fiscal policies. In the Keynesian view, government macroeconomic policy can do good; in the Classical view, it cannot.

Similarities and Differences between Keynesian and Classical Theories

The preceding discussion highlighted differences between Keynesian and Classical theories of inflation. Keynesians see inflation as an institutional phenomenon; Classicals see it as a monetary phenomenon.

The distinction between the Keynesian and Classical theories of inflation comes out most clearly when we consider the effects of a supply-price shock, such as a sudden increase in the price of oil. Keynesians see such a supply-price shock as a cost-push pressure, likely to lead to significant inflationary pressures as people try to maintain their relative income at their previous level.

Classical economists see a supply-price shock as simply a relative price change. They argue that as long as the government does not increase the money supply, other relative prices will fall and there will be little inflationary pressure from a supply-price shock. So they advocate maintaining a monetary rule and not increasing the money supply to accommodate higher prices.

These differences between the theories shouldn't obscure the similarities. Once the economy reaches its potential output, both Keynesians and Classicals see inflation as an excess demand phenomenon: too much money chasing too few goods. The differences in views occur when the economy is not at its potential output. Keynesians believe inflation is still possible; Classicals believe it is not.

KEYNESIAN AND
CLASSICAL POLICIES TO
FIGHT STAGFLATION

The two different theories of inflation lead to two different sets of policies to fight inflation and the unemployment/inflation dilemma. Classicals say to stop inflation one must reduce the rate of growth of the money supply. Control the money supply and you will control inflation.

Keynesians agree that controlling the money supply will ultimately control inflation, but they argue that it will do so in an inefficient and unfair manner. They argue that tight monetary policy usually causes unemployment among those least able to handle it. Keynesians ask, "Why should this group bear the cost of fighting inflation?" Their argument is that putting a brick wall in front of a speeding car will stop the car, but that doesn't mean that's how you should stop a car. Instead Keynesians are more likely to favor the use of supplemental policies in conjunc-

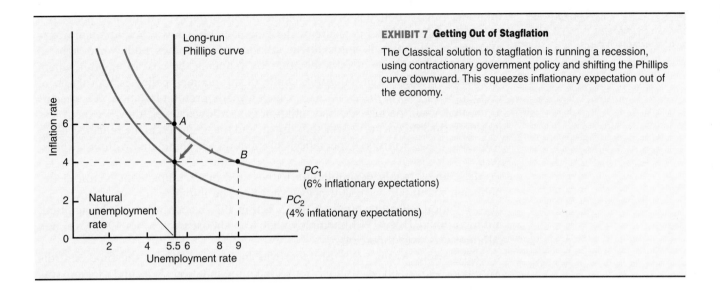

EXHIBIT 7 Getting Out of Stagflation

The Classical solution to stagflation is running a recession, using contractionary government policy and shifting the Phillips curve downward. This squeezes inflationary expectation out of the economy.

tion with contractionary monetary policy. Let's consider both views more carefully.

One way to escape a stagflation is embodied in the Classical analysis of the natural rate of unemployment. If you got into the problem by actual inflation exceeding expected inflation because you tried to hold unemployment below the natural rate, you can get out of inflation by having actual inflation below expected inflation. To do that you must maintain the unemployment rate higher than the natural rate. In essence you run a planned recession. Exhibit 7 graphs this method of getting out of stagflation.

Say that initially the economy was in equilibrium at 6 percent inflation and 5.5 percent unemployment, and that the natural rate of unemployment was 5.5 percent (point *A*). Say that the government runs contractionary aggregate policy so that the unemployment rate increases to 9 percent and inflation falls to 4 percent (point *B*). As expectations of inflation fall, the short-run Phillips curve shifts down from PC_1 (6 percent inflationary expectation) to PC_2 (4 percent inflationary expectation).

As long as the actual unemployment rate remains above the natural rate of unemployment, the Phillips curve trade-off will keep falling as expectations of inflation keep falling in response to lower-than-expected inflation. If government policies hold unemployment above the natural rate, eventually expectations of inflation will fall to zero. At that point the government can stop squeezing inflation out of the economy and it can be allowed to return to the natural rate of unemployment. This is the Classical solution to stagflation: contractionary monetary and fiscal policies squeezing the inflationary expectation out of the economy. True, it involves suffering, but the economy must atone for the expansionary sins of the Keynesians.

For Classicals, however, since people's expectations are rational and the rate of increase in the money supply determines the rate of inflation, the suffering need not be that great if the government is firm. If a strict monetary rule can be adopted and people can know that no matter what, the government won't exceed the monetary growth rate specified in the rule, expectations of inflation will fall quickly.

Inducing a recession to rid the economy of expected inflation isn't a pleasant policy so it isn't surprising that a Keynesian alternative has often been tried. The Keynesian alternative is to use a supplemental policy that directly holds down

The Classical Approach to Fighting Stagflation

6

The Keynesian Approach to Fighting Stagflation

Incomes policy A policy placing direct pressure on individuals to hold down their nominal wages and prices.

6

inflation. Such a policy is often called an *incomes policy*. An **incomes policy** is a policy that places direct pressure on individuals to hold down their nominal wages and prices. Because it holds down inflation, an incomes policy can help to eliminate expectations of inflation, thereby reducing the cost in unemployment necessary to fight inflation. An example of an incomes policy is a program of temporary *wage and price controls,* which directly prohibit inflation. Keynesians argue that when people see that inflation is at a lower level, they'll expect less inflation, the Phillips curve will shift down, and the controls can be repealed. With wage and price controls, expectations of inflation are eliminated without a recession.

It seems a highly desirable alternative, and in 1971 President Nixon, a Republican, instituted wage and price controls. The initial results were encouraging—inflation fell substantially in 1972. But in 1973 as controls were being lifted, inflation jumped. By 1974 unemployment was almost back to its 1972 level and inflation was over 8 percent.

What went wrong? One problem was bad timing. About the time controls were removed, an oil price shock generated more inflation. A second problem was that the fall in the inflation rate allowed aggregate policy to be more expansionary than it otherwise would have been. In 1972 and 1973 unemployment decreased. This suggests expansionary monetary and fiscal policies. Temporary wage and price controls can only temporarily hold down inflation. If controls are expected to have a long-run effect, they must be long-run controls—but no one expected the 1971–74 wage and price controls to be long run. Thus, temporary controls change nothing in the underlying reality. Using controls often tempts government to be too expansionary.

It's unclear what the inflation rate in the absence of these controls would have been. Supporters of temporary wage and price controls argue that the controls stopped a bad situation from getting worse. Opponents of temporary price controls as a way to reduce expectations of inflation argue that inevitably such price controls will be used to camouflage expansionary policy and thus should be avoided.

CONCLUSION

The Classical and Keynesian views of inflation and the Phillips curve trade-off reflect two consistent worldviews. Keynesians see a world in which sociological and institutional factors interact with market forces, keeping the economy in a perpetual disequilibrium when considered in an economic framework. Classicals see a world in which market forces predominate. They consider institutional and sociological factors insignificant and view the overall economy as one in continual equilibrium. These two worldviews carry over to their analyses of the central policy issue facing most governments as they decide on their monetary and fiscal policies: the trade-off between inflation and unemployment.

These different worldviews are why there are major disagreements about policy. Classicals believe the best policy is laissez-faire; Keynesians believe an activist policy is needed. Given their contrasting worldviews, the debate will likely continue for a long time.

KEY POINTS

- High inflation is inevitably accompanied by roughly proportional increases in the money supply and expectations of inflation.   **1**
- The short-run Phillips curve differs from the long-run Phillips curve because on the long-run Phillips curve expected inflation must equal actual inflation.   **2**

- The Classical theory of inflation blurs out the institutional process of setting prices and focuses on the relation between money and inflation.   **3**
- The Keynesian theory of inflation blurs out the relationship between inflation and money and focuses on the institutional process of setting prices.   **4**

- In the Classical theory of inflation, the only equilibrium is on the long-run Phillips curve. **5**
- In the Keynesian theory of inflation, a short-run Phillips curve trade-off can persist into the long run as long as inflation doesn't exceed a certain range. **5**

- Classicals argue that the only way to stop inflation is to stop increasing the money supply. Keynesians argue that supplemental policies (such as an incomes policy) are needed. **6**

KEY TERMS

adaptive
  expectations *(335)*
cost-push inflation *(335)*
demand-pull
  inflation *(335)*
expectations of
  inflation *(337)*

incomes policy *(348)*
inflation *(335)*
just-noticeable
  difference *(345)*
long-run Phillips
  curve *(337)*

natural rate of
  unemployment *(341)*
Phillips curve *(336)*

short-run Phillips
  curve *(337)*
stagflation *(342)*

QUESTIONS FOR THOUGHT AND REVIEW

The number after each question represents the estimated degree of critical thinking required. (1 = almost none; 10 = deep thought.)

1. Distinguish cost-push from demand-pull inflation. *(2)*
2. Draw a short-run and a long-run Phillips curve. *(2)*
3. How would a Keynesian explain the relatively stable inflation/unemployment trade-off existing before 1969? *(5)*
4. How would a Classical economist explain the relatively stable inflation/unemployment trade-off existing before 1969? *(9)*
5. What policy implications would a Classical draw from the quotation at the beginning of the chapter? *(4)*
6. What policy implications would a Keynesian draw from the quotation at the beginning of the chapter? *(6)*
7. What implication does the insider/outsider view of the economy have for macroeconomic policy? *(6)*
8. What arguments would a Classical economist give in opposing an incomes policy? *(3)*
9. Demonstrate graphically how an induced recession will eliminate stagflation. *(4)*
10. The Phillips curve is nothing but a figment of economists' imagination. True or false? *(9)*

PROBLEMS AND EXERCISES

1. People's perception of inflation often differs from actual inflation.
   a. List five goods that you buy relatively frequently.
   b. Looking in old newspapers (found in the library on microfiche) locate sale prices for these goods since 1950, finding one price every five years or so. Determine the average price rise of each of these five goods from 1950 until today.
   c. Compare that price rise with the rise in the Consumer Price Index.
2. Congratulations. You've just been appointed finance minister of Inflationland. Inflation has been ongoing for the past five years at 5 percent. The target rate of unemployment, 5 percent, is also the actual rate.
   a. Demonstrate the economy's likely position on both short-run and long-run Phillips curves.
   b. The president tells you she wants to be reelected. Devise a monetary policy strategy for her that might help her accomplish her goal.
   c. Demonstrate that strategy graphically, including the likely long-run consequences.

Macroeconomic Policy Debates

16

International Dimensions of Monetary and Fiscal Policies

*The actual rate of exchange is
largely governed by the expected behavior of the country's
monetary authority.*

Dennis Robertson

After reading this chapter, you should be able to:

1

Explain why there is significant debate
about what U.S. international goals
should be.

2

Explain the effects of exchange rates on
income, growth, and inflation.

3

Explain the paths through which monetary
policy affects exchange rates
and the trade balance.

4

Explain the paths through which fiscal
policy affects exchange rates
and the trade balance.

5

Summarize the reasons why governments
try to coordinate their monetary
and fiscal policies.

In the 1990s it's impossible to talk about macroeconomic policy without talking about international issues. That's what we do in this chapter: We discuss the effect that monetary and fiscal policies have on international macroeconomic goals plus the effect that certain international phenomena have on domestic macroeconomic goals of low inflation, low unemployment, and high growth.

The discussion in this chapter is not totally new to you. Earlier chapters have introduced you to many international concepts and touched upon the international dimensions of fiscal and monetary policies. But now it's time to put those discussions together and consider the issues more carefully. This discussion will provide you with the necessary international base for understanding the macroeconomic policy you'll be reading about in the newspapers. In later chapters we'll consider international trade and international finance in more depth.

THE AMBIGUOUS INTERNATIONAL GOALS OF MACROECONOMIC POLICY

1

Macroeconomics' international goals are less straightforward than its domestic goals. There is general agreement about the domestic goals of macroeconomic policy: We want low inflation, low unemployment, and high growth. There's far less agreement on what a country's international goals should be.

Most economists agree that the international goal of U.S. macroeconomic policy is to maintain the U.S. position in the world economy. But there's enormous debate about what achieving that goal means. Do we want a high or a low exchange rate? Do we want a balance of trade surplus? Or would it be better to have a balance of trade deficit? Or should we not even pay attention to the balance of trade? Let's consider the exchange rate goal first.

The Exchange Rate Goal

An **exchange rate** is the rate at which one country's currency can be traded for another country's currency.

Exchange rate The rate at which one country's currency can be traded for another country's currency.

Fixed exchange rate Exchange rates are set and governments are committed to buying and selling currencies at a fixed rate.

Flexible exchange rate The exchange rate is set by market forces (supply and demand for a country's currency).

Partially flexible exchange rate Government sometimes buys and sells currencies to influence the price directly; at other times government simply accepts the exchange rate determined by supply and demand forces.

Fixed and Flexible Exchange Rates   Countries can have fixed exchange rates, flexible exchange rates, or a partially flexible exchange rate. With a **fixed exchange rate,** the exchange rates are set and governments are committed to buying and selling currencies at a fixed rate. With a **flexible exchange rate,** the exchange rate is set by market forces (supply and demand for a country's currency). With a **partially flexible exchange rate,** the government sometimes buys and sells currencies to influence the price directly, and at other times the government simply accepts the exchange rate determined by supply and demand forces. In the 1990s the United States uses a partially flexible exchange rate.

In this chapter, to keep the analysis at a manageable level, I assume that the country in question has a flexible exchange rate—thus, it accepts that its exchange rate will be determined by the forces of supply and demand. But that doesn't mean that the country can't indirectly influence the exchange rate—through monetary and fiscal policies' effects on the economy and on supply and demand for dollars. It is that indirect effect that we focus on in this chapter. In the chapter on international finance I extend the analysis to include a country's ability to affect exchange rates directly.

2   Do Countries Want a High or a Low Exchange Rate?   There is a debate over whether a country should have a high or a low exchange rate. A high exchange rate for the dollar makes foreign currencies cheaper, lowering the price of imports. Lowering import prices places competitive pressure on U.S. firms and helps to hold down inflation. All of this benefits U.S. residents' living standard. But a high exchange rate encourages imports and discourages exports. In doing so, it can cause a balance of trade deficit which can exert a contractionary effect on the economy by decreasing aggregate demand for U.S. output. So a high exchange rate also has a cost to U.S. residents.

A low exchange rate has the opposite effect. It makes imports more expensive and exports cheaper, and it can contribute to inflationary pressure. But, by encouraging exports and discouraging imports, it can cause a balance of trade surplus and exert an expansionary effect on the economy.

Thus, depending on the state of the economy, there are arguments for both high and low exchange rates. Hence there's often a divergence of views about what the exchange rate goal should be. Because of that divergence of views, many economists argue that a country should have no exchange rate policy because exchange rates are market-determined prices that are best left to the market. These economists question whether the government should even worry about the effect of monetary policy and fiscal policy on exchange rates. According to them, government should simply accept whatever exchange rate exists and not consider it in its conduct of monetary and fiscal policies.

A deficit in the **trade balance** (the difference between imports and exports) means that as a country we're consuming more than we're producing. Imports exceed exports, so we're consuming more than we could if we didn't run a deficit. A surplus in the trade balance means that exports exceed imports—we're producing more than we're consuming. Since consuming more than we otherwise could is kind of nice, it might seem that a trade deficit is preferred to a trade surplus.

But wait. A trade deficit isn't without costs, and a trade surplus isn't without benefits. We pay for a trade deficit by selling off U.S. assets to foreigners—by selling U.S. companies, factories, land, and buildings to foreigners, or selling them financial assets such as U.S. dollars, stocks, and bonds. All the future interest and profits on these assets will go to foreigners, not U.S. citizens. That means eventually, some time in the future, we will have to produce more than we consume so we can pay them *their* profit and interest on *their* assets. Thus, while in the short run a trade deficit is nice, in the long run it presents problems.

As long as a country can borrow, or sell assets, a country can have a trade deficit. But if a country runs a trade deficit year after year, eventually the long run will arrive and the country will run out of assets to sell and run out of other countries from whom to borrow. When that happens, the trade deficit problem must be faced.

The debate about whether a trade deficit should be of concern to policy makers involves whether these long-run effects should be anticipated and faced before they happen.

Opinions differ greatly. Some say not to worry. We should accept what's happening and not concern ourselves about a trade deficit. These "not-to-worry" economists argue that the trade deficit will end when U.S. citizens don't want to borrow from foreigners any more and foreigners don't want to buy any more of our assets. They argue that the inflow of financial capital (money coming into the United States to buy our assets) from foreigners is financing new investment which will make the U.S. economy strong enough in the long run to reverse the trade deficit without serious disruption to the U.S. economy. So why deal with the trade deficit now when it will take care of itself in the future?

Others argue that, yes, the trade deficit will eventually take care of itself, but the economic distress accompanying the trade deficit taking care of itself will be great. By dealing with the problem now, the United States can avoid a highly unpleasant solution in the future.

Both views are reasonable, which is why there's no consensus on what a country's trade balance goal should be.

In the real world when there's debate about a goal, that goal generally gets far less weight than goals about which there's general agreement. Since there's general agreement about a country's domestic goals (low inflation, low unemployment, and high growth), domestic goals generally dominate the U.S. political agenda.

Even if there weren't uncertainty about a country's international goals, do-

The Trade Balance Goal

Trade balance The difference between a country's exports and its imports.

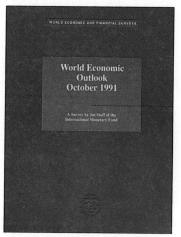

World Economic Outlook—This IMF publication provides useful economic surveys of problems facing the world economy.

International versus Domestic Goals

mestic goals would likely dominate the political agenda. The reason is that inflation, unemployment, and growth affect a country's citizens directly. Trade deficits and exchange rates affect them indirectly—and in politics, indirect effects take a back seat.

Often a country responds to an international goal only when the international community forces it to do so. For example, when a developing country can't borrow any more money from other countries, it reluctantly makes resolving its trade deficit a key goal. Similarly when other countries threatened to limit Japanese imports, Japan took steps to increase the value of the yen and decrease its trade surplus. When a country is forced to face certain economic facts, international goals can become its primary goals. As countries become more economically integrated, these pressures from other countries become more important.

THE EFFECTS OF MONETARY AND FISCAL POLICIES ON INTERNATIONAL GOALS

To say that achieving international goals is not the determining factor in the choice of macroeconomic policies isn't to say that economists don't consider the effect of monetary and fiscal policies on international goals. They watch these carefully. For example, the United States ran trade deficits through much of the 1980s, and by the late 1980s other countries were placing heavy pressure on the United States to do something. You can understand U.S. macroeconomic policy during that period only if you understand the international pressure the United States was under. To follow the debates about macroeconomic policy, you must be familiar with how monetary and fiscal policies affect the exchange rate and the trade balance. Those effects often can significantly influence the choice of policies. We begin by considering the effect of monetary policy.

Monetary Policy's Effect on Exchange Rates

Monetary policy affects exchange rates in three ways: (1) through its effect on the interest rate, (2) through its effect on income, and (3) through its effect on price levels and inflation.

The Effect on Exchange Rates via Interest Rates   Expansionary monetary policy pushes down the U.S. interest rate, which decreases the financial capital inflow into the United States, pushes down the value of the dollar, and decreases the U.S. exchange rate via the interest rate path. Contractionary monetary policy does the opposite. It raises the U.S. interest rate, which tends to bring in financial capital flows from abroad, increases the value of the dollar, and increases the U.S. exchange rate.

To see why these effects take place, consider a person in Japan in the late 1980s when the Japanese interest rate was about 2 or 3 percent. He or she reasoned, "Why should I earn only 2 or 3 percent return in Japan? I'll save (buy some financial assets) in the United States where I'll earn 8 percent." If the U.S. interest rate goes up due to contraction in the money supply, other things equal, the advantage of holding one's financial assets in the United States will become even greater and more people will want to save here. People in Japan hold yen, not dollars, so in order to save in the United States they must buy dollars. Thus, a rise in U.S. interest rates increases demand for dollars and, in terms of yen, pushes the U.S. exchange rate up.

It's important to recognize that it's the relative interest rates that govern the flow of financial capital. In the early 1990s Japan tightened its money supply, raising interest rates there to 6 percent. This relative increase in the Japanese interest rate decreased demand for dollars and thus lowered the U.S. exchange rate.

The Effect on Exchange Rates via Income   Monetary policy also affects income in a country. As money supply rises, income expands; when money supply falls,

James Meade—Nobel prize, 1977, for his contributions to international economic theory. © The Nobel Foundation.

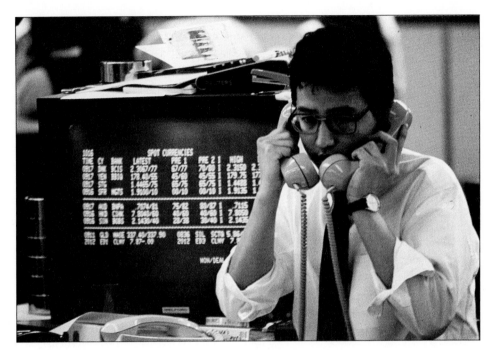

For international trade to take place, currencies must be convertible into other currencies. Here we see a Japanese currency trader taking bids on buying and selling currencies. *Fujifotos/The Image Works.*

income contracts.[1] This effect on income provides another way the money supply affects the exchange rate. As we saw earlier, when income rises, imports rise while exports are unaffected. To buy U.S. products, foreigners need U.S. dollars which they must buy with their own currency. So when U.S. imports rise, the supply of dollars to the foreign exchange market increases as U.S. citizens sell dollars to buy foreign currencies to pay for those imports. This effect through income and imports provides a second path through which monetary policy affects the exchange rate: Expansionary monetary policy causes U.S. income to rise, imports to rise, and the U.S. exchange rate to fall via the income path. Contractionary monetary policy causes U.S. income to fall, imports to fall, and the U.S. exchange rate to rise via the income path.

The Effect on Exchange Rates via Prices   A third way in which monetary policy can affect exchange rates is through its effect on prices in a country. Expansionary monetary policy pushes the U.S. price level up. As the U.S. price level rises relative to foreign prices, U.S. exports become more expensive, and goods the United States imports become cheaper, decreasing U.S. competitiveness. This increases demand for foreign currencies and decreases demand for dollars. Thus, via the price path, expansionary monetary policy pushes down the dollar's value for the same reason that an expansion in income pushes it down.

Contractionary monetary policy pushes the U.S. price level down. As the U.S. price level goes down relative to foreign prices, U.S. exports become more competitive and the goods the United States imports become more expensive. Thus, contractionary policy pushes the value of the dollar up via the price path.

The Net Effect of Monetary Policy on Exchange Rates   Notice that all these effects of monetary policy on exchange rates are in the same direction. Expansionary monetary policy pushes a country's exchange rate down; contractionary mone-

---

[1] When there's inflation, it's the rate of money supply growth relative to the rate of inflation that's important. If inflation is 10 percent and money supply growth is 10 percent, the rate of increase in the real money supply is zero. If money supply growth falls to, say, 5 percent while inflation stays at 10 percent, there will be a contractionary effect on the real economy.

tary policy pushes a country's exchange rate up. Summarizing these effects, we have the following relationships for expansionary and contractionary monetary policy:

Expansionary policy

Contractionary policy

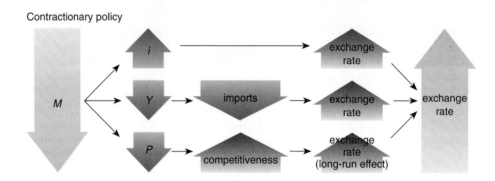

There are, of course, many provisos to the relationship between monetary policy and the exchange rate. For example, as the price of imports goes up, there is some inflationary pressure from that rise in price and hence some pressure for the price level to rise as well as fall. Monetary policy affects exchange rates in subtle ways, but if an economist had to give a quick answer to what effect monetary policy would have on exchange rates it would be:

1. *Expansionary monetary policy lowers exchange rates. It decreases the relative value of a country's currency.*

2. *Contractionary monetary policy increases exchange rates. It increases the relative value of a country's currency.*

Monetary Policy's Effect on the Trade Balance

When a country's international trade balance is negative (in deficit), the country is importing more than it is exporting. When a country's international trade balance is positive, the country is exporting more than it is importing.

Monetary policy affects the trade balance in three ways: through income, through the price level, and through the exchange rate.

The Effect on the Trade Balance via Income

Expansionary monetary policy increases income. When income rises, imports rise, while exports are unaffected. As imports rise, the trade balance shifts in the direction of deficit. So, via the income path, expansionary monetary policy shifts the trade balance toward a deficit.

Contractionary policy works in the opposite direction. It decreases income. When income falls, imports fall, while exports are unaffected, so the trade balance shifts in the direction of surplus. Thus, via the income path, expansionary monetary policy increases the trade deficit; contractionary monetary policy decreases the trade deficit.

The Effect on the Trade Balance via the Price Level   A second way monetary policy affects the trade balance is through its effect on a country's price level. Expansionary monetary policy pushes a country's price level up. This decreases its competitiveness and increases a trade deficit. So, via the price path, expansionary monetary policy increases a trade deficit.

Contractionary monetary policy works in the opposite direction. It tends to push a country's price level down; this fall makes exports more competitive and imports less competitive. Both these effects tend to decrease a trade deficit. So, via the price path, contractionary monetary policy decreases a trade deficit.

Monetary policy's effect on the price level is a long-run, not a short-run, effect. It often takes a year for changes in the money supply to affect prices and another year or two for changes in prices to affect imports and exports. Thus, the price path is a long-run effect. Price level changes don't significantly affect the trade balance in the short run.

The Effect on the Trade Balance via Exchange Rates   A third path through which expansionary monetary policy influences the trade balance is the exchange rate. Expansionary U.S. monetary policy decreases the interest rate which tends to push the dollar exchange rate down, increasing U.S. competitiveness. This decreases a trade deficit and hence works in a direction opposite to the effects of income changes and price level changes on the trade balance. Like the price effect, the exchange rate path on the trade balance is a long-run effect. This path doesn't have a significant effect in the short run.

Contractionary monetary policy works in the opposite direction. It raises the exchange rate, increasing the relative price of U.S. exports and lowering the relative price of imports into the United States. Both effects tend to increase a trade deficit.

The Net Effect of Monetary Policy on the Trade Balance   Since the effects are not all in the same direction, talking about the net effect of monetary policy on the trade balance is a bit more ambiguous than talking about its net effect on a country's exchange rate. However, only one of these paths—the income path—is a short-run effect. Thus, in the short run the net effect of monetary policy is relatively clear: Expansionary monetary policy tends to increase a trade deficit; contractionary monetary policy tends to decrease it. Since, in the long run, the price path effect and the exchange rate effect tend to offset each other, the short-run effects of monetary policy through the income path often carry over to the long-run effect.

Summarizing these three relationships, we have the following relationships for expansionary and contractionary monetary policy:

Expansionary policy

Contractionary policy

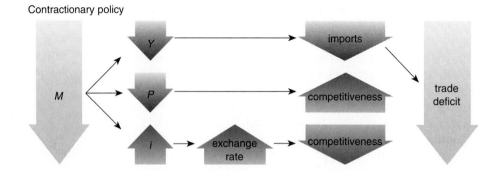

1. Expansionary monetary policy makes a trade deficit larger.

2. Contractionary monetary policy makes a trade deficit smaller.

Fiscal Policy's Effect on Exchange Rates

While many complications can enter the trade balance picture, most economists would summarize monetary policy's short-run effect on the trade balance as follows:

1. *Expansionary monetary policy makes a trade deficit larger.*

2. *Contractionary monetary policy makes a trade deficit smaller.*

Now we'll consider fiscal policy's effect on exchange rates. Fiscal policy, like monetary policy, affects exchange rates via three paths: via income, via price, and via interest rates. Let's begin with its effect through income.

The Effect on Exchange Rates via Income   Expansionary fiscal policy expands income and therefore increases imports, increasing the trade deficit and lowering the exchange rate. Contractionary fiscal policy contracts income, thereby decreasing imports and increasing the exchange rate. These effects of expansionary and contractionary fiscal policies via the income path are similar to the effects of monetary policy, so if it's not intuitively clear to you why the effect is what it is, it may be worthwhile to review the slightly more complete discussion of monetary policy's effect presented previously.

The Effect on Exchange Rates via Prices   Let's turn to the effect of fiscal policy through prices. Expansionary fiscal policy increases aggregate demand and increases prices of a country's exports; hence it decreases the competitiveness of a country's exports, which pushes down the exchange rate. Contractionary fiscal policy works in the opposite direction. These are the same effects that monetary policy had. And, as was the case with monetary policy, the price path is a long-run, not a short-run, effect.

The Effect on Exchange Rates via Interest Rates   Fiscal policy's effect on the exchange rate via the interest rate path is different from monetary policy's effect. Let's first consider the effect of expansionary fiscal policy. Whereas expansionary monetary policy lowers the interest rate, expansionary fiscal policy raises interest rates because the government sells bonds to finance that deficit. The higher U.S. interest rate causes foreign capital to flow into the United States, which pushes up the U.S. exchange rate. Therefore expansionary fiscal policy's effect on exchange rates via the interest rate effect is to push up a country's exchange rate.

Contractionary fiscal policy decreases interest rates since it means that the number of bonds that must be sold to finance a deficit decreases. Lower U.S. interest rates cause capital to flow out of the United States, which pushes down the U.S. exchange rate.

The Net Effect of Fiscal Policy on Exchange Rates   Of these three effects, the interest rate effect and the income effect are both short-run effects. These two work in opposite directions to each other so the net effect of fiscal policy on the exchange rate is ambiguous. Let's summarize these three effects.

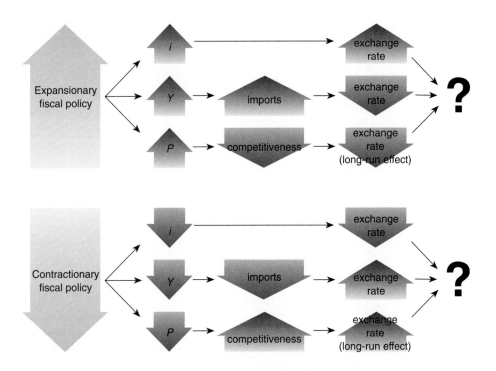

Thus, it's unclear what the effect of expansionary or contractionary fiscal policy will be on exchange rates.

Fiscal policy works on the trade deficit primarily through its effects on income and prices. (Since fiscal policy's effect on the exchange rate is unclear, there is no need to consider its effect through exchange rates.)

Fiscal Policy's Effect on the Trade Deficit

The Effect via Income   Let's begin looking at the income path. As with expansionary monetary policy, expansionary fiscal policy increases income. This higher income increases imports, which increases the size of the trade deficit.

Contractionary fiscal policy decreases income and decreases imports. Hence it decreases the size of a trade deficit. These are the same effects as those of monetary policy.

The Effect via the Price Path   The effect via the price route is also similar to effects of monetary policy. Expansionary fiscal policy pushes up the price level, increasing the price of a country's exports and decreasing its competitiveness. Hence it increases the trade deficit.

Contractionary fiscal policy pushes down the price level, decreasing the price of a country's exports, increasing its competitiveness, and decreasing the trade deficit. This effect via price is a long-run effect, as it is with monetary policy.

The Net Effect of Fiscal Policy on the Trade Deficit   Since these two effects work in the same direction, fiscal policy's net effect on the trade balance is clear:

Expansionary fiscal policy increases a trade deficit.

Contractionary fiscal policy decreases a trade deficit.

Summarizing these two effects schematically, we have:

Expansionary fiscal policy increases a trade deficit.

Contractionary fiscal policy decreases a trade deficit.

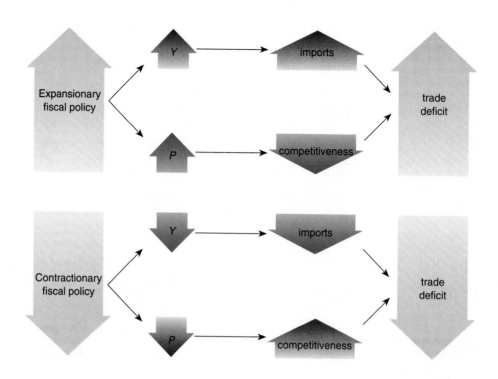

Exhibit 1 summarizes the primary net short-run effects of both expansionary monetary and fiscal policies on international goals. (The effects of contractionary policy work in the opposite direction.)

INTERNATIONAL PHENOMENA AND DOMESTIC GOALS

So far, we've focused on the effect of monetary and fiscal policies on international goals. But often the effect is the other way around: International phenomena change and have significant influences on the domestic economy and achieving domestic goals.

For example, say that Japan ran contractionary monetary policy. That would increase the Japanese exchange rate and increase Japan's trade surplus, which means it would decrease the U.S. exchange rate and increase the U.S. trade deficit, both of which would affect U.S. domestic goals. So the monetary and fiscal policies of other countries can have significant effects on the U.S. domestic economy. This has led to significant pressure for countries to coordinate their economic policies.

International Monetary and Fiscal Coordination

Unless forced to do so because of international pressures, most countries don't let international goals guide their macroeconomic policy. But for every effect that monetary and fiscal policies have on a country's exchange rates and trade balance, there's an equal and opposite effect on the combination of other countries' exchange rates and trade balances. When one country's exchange rate goes up, by definition another country's exchange rate must go down. Similarly when one country's balance of trade is in surplus, another's must be in deficit. This interconnection means that other countries' fiscal and monetary policies affect the United States, while U.S. fiscal and monetary policies affect other countries, so pressure to coordinate policies is considerable.

Because of this interdependence, many economists argue that all countries must work together to coordinate their monetary and fiscal policies. For example, if Japan has a trade surplus and the United States has a trade deficit, the United States can run contractionary monetary policy or Japan can use expansionary monetary policy to help expand U.S. exports to Japan and thereby reduce the U.S. trade deficit. Why would Japan do something like that? Because, if it

EXHIBIT 1   The Effect of Expansionary Monetary and Fiscal Policy on International Goals

In the short run, expansionary monetary policy tends to increase a trade deficit and decrease the exchange rate. Expansionary fiscal policy tends to increase the trade deficit. Its effect on the exchange rate is ambiguous.

The world has become much more interdependent in recent years. In this picture you see cars made in Germany being unloaded for sale in the United States. © *David Wells/The Image Works.*

doesn't, the United States might threaten to limit Japanese exports to the United States. So Japan must take U.S. desires into account in conducting its monetary and fiscal policies.

Coordination, of course, works both ways. If other countries are to take the U.S. economy's needs into account, the United States must take other countries' needs into account in determining its goals. Say, for example, the U.S. economy is going into a recession. This domestic problem calls for expansionary monetary policy. But expansionary monetary policy will increase U.S. income and U.S. imports and lower the value of the dollar. Say that, internationally, the United States has agreed that it must work toward eliminating the U.S. trade deficit in the short run. Does it forsake its domestic goals? Or does it forsake its international commitment?

There's no one right answer to those questions. It depends on political judgments (how long until the next election?), judgments about what foreign countries can do if the United States doesn't meet its international commitments, and similar judgments by foreign countries about the United States. The result is lots of international economic parleys (generally in rather pleasant surroundings) to discuss these issues. Nicely worded communiques are issued, which say, in

Coordination Is a Two-Way Street

effect, that each country will do what's best for the world economy as long as it's also best for itself.

Crowding Out and International Considerations

As a final topic in this chapter, let's reconsider the issue of *crowding out* that we considered in an earlier chapter, only this time we'll take into account international considerations. Say a government is running a budget deficit, and that the central bank has decided it won't accommodate the deficit. This happened in the 1980s with the Fed and the U.S. government. What will be the result? The basic idea of crowding out is that the budget deficit will cause the interest rate to go up. But wait. There's another way to avoid the crowding out that results from financing the deficit: Foreigners could buy the debt at the existing interest rate. This is called *internationalizing the debt,* and is what happened to the U.S. economy in the late 1980s.

In the 1980s there were massive inflows of financial capital from abroad. These inflows held down the U.S. interest rate even as the federal government ran large budget deficits. Thus, those large deficits didn't push up interest rates because foreigners, not U.S. citizens, were buying U.S. debt.

But, as we discussed, internationalization of the U.S. debt is not costless. While it helps in the short run, it presents problems in the long run. Foreign ownership of U.S. debt means that the United States must pay foreigners interest each year on that debt. To do so the United States must export more than it imports, which means that the United States must consume less than it produces at some time in the future, to pay for the trade deficits it's running now.

As you can see, the issues become complicated quickly.

CONCLUSION

This brief chapter in no way exhausted the international topics. Countries use many policies to effect their international goals. But this chapter has, I hope, made you very aware of the international dimensions of our economic goals, and of how monetary and fiscal policies affect those goals. That awareness is necessary to discuss the real-world macroeconomic policies that we turn to in the next chapter.

KEY POINTS

- The international goals of a country are often in dispute. **1**
- A fall in the value of a country's currency will tend to increase income, growth, and inflation. **2**
- Expansionary monetary policy tends to lower a country's exchange rate and increase its trade deficit. **3**
- Contractionary fiscal policy has an ambiguous effect on a country's exchange rate but tends to decrease its trade deficit. **4**
- For every effect that monetary and fiscal policies have on a country's exchange rate and trade balance, there is an equal and opposite effect on the combination of foreign countries' exchange rates and trade balances. **5**
- International capital inflows can reduce crowding out. **5**

KEY TERMS

exchange rate *(354)*
fixed exchange rate *(354)*

flexible exchange rate *(354)*

partially flexible exchange rate *(354)*

trade balance *(355)*

PROBLEMS AND EXERCISES

1. Draw the schematics to show the effect of contractionary fiscal policy on exchange rates.

2. Draw the schematics to show the effect of expansionary monetary policy on the trade deficit.

QUESTIONS FOR THOUGHT AND REVIEW

The number after each question represents the estimated degree of critical thinking required. (1 = almost none; 10 = deep thought.)

1. Look up the current U.S. exchange rate relative to the yen. Would you suggest raising it or lowering it? Why? *(7)*
2. Look up the current U.S. trade balance. Would you suggest raising it or lowering it? Why? *(7)*
3. What effect on the U.S. trade deficit and exchange rate would result if Japan ran an expansionary monetary policy? *(4)*
4. What would be the effect on the U.S. trade deficit and the U.S. exchange rate if Japan ran a contractionary fiscal policy? *(4)*
5. If New Classicals are correct and expansionary monetary policy immediately increases inflationary expectations and the price level, how might the effect of monetary policy on the exchange rate be different than that presented in this chapter? *(9)*
6. What effect will a combination of expansionary fiscal policy and contractionary monetary policy have on the exchange rate? *(5)*
7. How would a Classical economist differ from a Keynesian economist in their policies for dealing with an oil price shock? Why? *(8)*
8. Is the United States justified in complaining of Japan's use of an export-led growth policy? Why? *(8)*
9. What effect would you expect a fall in the price of oil to have on the U.S. economy? Why? *(6)*
10. Can there be a rise in the international price level? Why? *(9)*

17

Using Monetary and Fiscal Policies to Achieve Macroeconomic Goals

The worst episodes of recent monetary history—the great inflations—have been marked by the subjection of central bankers to overriding political pressures.

R. S. Sayers

After reading this chapter, you should be able to:

1

Summarize the conflicting goals of macro policy.

2

Explain why macroeconomic policy is an art, not a science.

3

State the main points of agreement between Keynesians and Classicals.

4

State the main points of disagreement between Keynesians and Classicals.

5

Summarize macroeconomic policy since the 1940s.

6

Take a hypothetical situation and develop a reasonable macroeconomic strategy for dealing with that situation.

In earlier chapters I introduced you to the terminology, the institutions, and the theory, of the macroeconomy. It's now time to put it all together.

- What should government do if the economy seems to be falling into a recession?
- What should government do if inflation seems to be increasing?
- What should government do if the economy seems to be falling into a recession but simultaneously inflation seems to be increasing?
- What should government do if there's a large trade deficit at the same time that it's worried about a recession?
- What should government do if its currency's value is falling and there's concern about inflation?

Policymakers face these and similar questions every day. In this chapter, using the theory and insights we developed in previous chapters, we'll try to come to grips with these difficult real-world issues.

The first section provides some context for discussing these questions by considering the conflicting goals and macroeconomic policy. It summarizes and reviews similarities and differences between Keynesians and Classicals from earlier chapters. The second section reviews important episodes in the history of macroeconomic policy, showing you how things worked out in real-world cases. The final section presents you with some hypothetical cases and shows how the understanding you've gained in earlier chapters can let you function as an economic advisor to a government.

One reason why macroeconomic policy is so complicated is that it involves conflicting goals. As we saw in the chapter on inflation, domestically the low inflation goal often conflicts with the low unemployment/high growth goal. And as we saw in the previous chapter, international trade balance and exchange rate goals often conflict with one another and with domestic goals. Thus, the government finds itself and the economy on a tightrope. The government is continually trying to be expansionary, but not too expansionary. Too expansionary a policy will accelerate inflation and expand trade deficits. But government also knows that if it's too contractionary, it will cause a recession.

To maintain the economy on this tightrope, governments have monetary and fiscal policies to use as a balance bar. If the economy seems to be falling into inflation, governments can use contractionary monetary and fiscal policies; if it seems to be falling into recession, they can use expansionary monetary and fiscal policies. If they face both problems simultaneously, they must rely on **prayer policy** (you do what you do and you pray that it will work the way you hope it will) to supplement monetary and fiscal policies.

In thinking about these goals, we must recognize that there are limits to what can be achieved with macroeconomic policy. Economists might tell governments that they're asking for too much. These governments are like a person who asks his doctor for a health program that will enable him to run a four-minute mile, forget about a training program, and eat anything he wants. Some things just can't be done, and it's important for governments to recognize the inevitable limitations and trade-offs, at least with the monetary and fiscal policy tools currently available. Good economists are continually pointing out those limits.

But, like a patient who doesn't like to hear there are limits, governments often go to other advisors who offer more upbeat advice; and economists are often put in the position of the stick in the mud who sees only problems, not potentials.

This stick-in-the-mud image isn't appropriate. We economists are often dynamic, innovative, positive sorts of people (would you believe?) who've just been cast in a difficult role of pointing out that there are no free lunches.

What makes economists' stick-in-the-mud role so difficult is that the trade-

THE ART OF MACROECONOMIC POLICY

1

Prayer policy You do what you do and pray that it will work.

The Limits of Macroeconomic Policy

2

offs are often uncertain, meaning that once in a while the "promise-them-every-thing" advisors turn out to be right. Here's an example. In 1984 and 1985 most economists were convinced that there was serious concern about inflationary pressures. Based on this concern, they warned against too expansionary monetary and fiscal policies. They kept predicting higher inflation than occurred. But due in part to some unexpected falls in the prices of oil and raw materials, that inflation didn't occur even though government listened instead to a set of "full-speed-ahead" advisors. Because the inflation didn't occur the advisors who said "Full speed ahead" could point to this period and correctly say that they were right.

With policy effects so uncertain, most economists are hesitant to make unambiguous predictions about policy. But they do have a sense of the effects of certain policies and the trade-offs each involves. Exhibit 1 summarizes those trade-offs.

Keynesian and Classical Styles of Macroeconomic Policy

Art of macro policy The way macro policy is conducted in the real world, not in textbook models.

The trade-offs presented in Exhibit 1 must be interpreted carefully. When conducting real-world macroeconomic policy, economists are very aware that economic relationships aren't certain and that conducting macroeconomic policy is an art, not a science. In practicing the **art of macro policy,** Keynesians and Classicals have different styles, and before we talk about some real-world episodes, it's helpful to review their positions on the art of using monetary and fiscal policies.

Similarities and Differences between Keynesians and Classicals on Fiscal Policy

4 Keynesians see expansionary fiscal policy as having a short-run stimulative effect on the economy. It increases real income, reduces unemployment, and, if potential income is exceeded, can cause inflation. Classicals see expansionary fiscal policy as having far less effect on real income and unemployment, and are divided

---

EXHIBIT 1   Macroeconomic Policy Dilemmas

	Option	Advantages	Disadvantages
Monetary policy	Expansionary monetary policy	1. Interest rates may fall. 2. Economy may grow. 3. Decreases unemployment.	1. Inflation may worsen. 2. Exchange rate may fall. 3. Capital outflow. 4. Trade deficit may increase.
	Contractionary monetary policy	1. Exchange rate may rise. 2. Helps fight inflation. 3. Trade deficit may decrease. 4. Capital inflow.	1. Risks recession. 2. Increases unemployment. 3. Slows growth. 4. May help cause short-run political problems.
Fiscal policy	Expansionary fiscal policy (borrow and spend)	1. Maybe growth will continue. 2. May help solve short-run political problems. 3. Decreases unemployment.	1. Budget deficit worsens. 2. Hurts country's ability to borrow in the future. 3. Trade deficit may increase. 4. Upward pressure on interest rates.
	Contractionary fiscal policy (reduce deficit)	1. May help fight inflation. 2. May allow a better monetary/fiscal mix. 3. Trade deficit may decrease.	1. Risks recession. 2. Increases unemployment. 3. Slows growth. 4. May help cause short-run political problems.

on their view of its effect on inflation. The monetarist school of Classical thought says the deficit isn't important for inflation; some New Classicals say that the deficit doesn't make any difference, since people with rational expectations offset any effect of the deficit. But the majority Classical position is that expansionary fiscal policy can contribute to inflationary pressures because it increases aggregate demand. According to the majority Classical position, expansionary fiscal policy causes aggregate demand to rise since aggregate supply doesn't change. The result is inflation.

These theoretical differences between Keynesians and Classicals and among different subgroups of Classical economists on the expansionary effect of fiscal policy aren't too important in practice, since, in the real world, fiscal policy is a difficult tool to use. The reason is political problems. A country's fiscal policy generally reflects political considerations as much or more than economic stabilization considerations. Due to these political considerations, governments usually lean toward expansionary fiscal policy, regardless of economists' advice.

If expansionary aggregate policy (a deficit) is needed, fiscal policy generally turns expansionary. Tax cuts or spending increases are politically popular, and if the need for a tax cut or increased spending is recognized in time, usually we can count on expansionary fiscal policy.

Turning the other way—contractionary fiscal policy—isn't so easy. When the U.S. president says, "Read my lips: No new taxes," and the U.S. Congress says, "No cuts in government programs," it's rather difficult to have contractionary fiscal policy. The fiscal policy steering wheel is consistently being pulled toward expansion. Fiscal policy still has an effect, but what that fiscal policy is isn't determined by macroeconomic considerations.

Both Keynesians and Classicals agree about the political difficulties of using fiscal policy. Thus, much of the debate about what types of macroeconomic policy to use generally focuses on monetary policy.

The majority Keynesian and Classical views on monetary policy agree that expansionary monetary policy can stimulate the economy in the short run (although some New Classicals argue that people with rational expectations will immediately push up prices, so expansionary monetary policy can only cause inflation, even in the short run). But Keynesians and Classicals disagree about the long run. Classicals tend to see the long-run effect of monetary policy as exclusively on inflation; Keynesians believe that inflationary monetary policy is dependent on how close the economy is to its potential income. Because of this difference, Keynesians tend to advocate more activist policies while Classicals tend to advocate more laissez-faire policies.

Theoretically these differences show up in their views on the aggregate supply curve. Keynesians see the aggregate supply curve as dependent upon expected demand. Thus, an increase in nominal demand can increase real output. Classicals see aggregate supply as independent of expected aggregate demand. Unless expansionary monetary policy fools suppliers into thinking there's been an increase in real demand, it can only cause inflation.

Most Keynesians and Classicals agree that in the short run, expansionary monetary policy can stimulate growth and keep the economy out of a recession. But it can do so only at the cost of creating inflationary pressure. That inflationary pressure leads to increased rates of inflation in the long run, as it breaks down institutional constraints on firms raising wages and prices and as it is built into expectations. Therefore the initial inflationary side effects of expansionary monetary policy are often hidden. This hiding of costs creates enormous political pressure for expansionary monetary policy. With politicians' short-run time horizon, a push for expansionary monetary policy is almost inevitable, especially around election time.

The debate about whether or not to use expansionary monetary policy arises because of disagreement about whether moderate expansionary pressures will

102d Congress, 2d Session

Economic Indicators

FEBRUARY 1992

(Includes data available as of March 6, 1992)

Prepared for the Joint Economic Committee by the Council of Economic Advisers

UNITED STATES
GOVERNMENT PRINTING OFFICE
WASHINGTON : 1992

This Commerce Department report provides up-to-date macroeconomic information.

Similarities and Differences between Keynesians and Classicals on Monetary Policy

4

always lead to inflation in the long run. Keynesians believe that low and moderate rates of inflation can sometimes stimulate growth in the economy without leading to accelerating inflation. Classicals believe that even low rates of inflation will stimulate growth only in the short run. After the short-run high, the inflation will become built into expectations and will lead to accelerating inflation. This difference in views means that there's a range of inflation and unemployment where it's not clear whether expansionary or contractionary monetary policy should be used. The economy is often in this range. On the one hand, to use expansionary policy in that range is to take a chance that inflationary expectations will get built into expectations and institutions. On the other hand, to use contractionary policy can lead to a slow-growth, high-unemployment economy.

Agreement about Macroeconomic Policy

1. Expansionary monetary and fiscal policies have short-run stimulative effects on income.
2. Expansionary monetary and fiscal policies have potential long-run inflation effects.
3. Monetary policy is politically easier to use than fiscal policy.
4. Expansionary monetary and fiscal policies tend to increase a trade deficit.
5. Expansionary monetary policy places downward pressure on the exchange rate.
6. Expansionary fiscal policy has an ambiguous effect on the exchange rate.

Amid these debates between Keynesians and Classicals we shouldn't lose sight of the convergence of views. There's more agreement about policy than disagreement. Both Keynesians and Classicals generally agree that:

1. *Expansionary monetary and fiscal policies have short-run stimulative effects on income.*
2. *Expansionary monetary and fiscal policies have potential long-run inflation effects.*
3. *Monetary policy is politically easier to use than fiscal policy.*
4. *Expansionary monetary and fiscal policies tend to increase a trade deficit.*
5. *Expansionary monetary policy places downward pressure on the exchange rate.*
6. *Expansionary fiscal policy has an ambiguous effect on the exchange rate.*

In the actual conduct of policy, these agreements often mean that various economists' advice is similar, whether they're Keynesian or Classical.

Let's now turn to macroeconomic policy over the past 50 years. As you read it, try to determine which periods reflect Keynesian advice, which reflect Classical advice, and which reflect consensus advice.

A BRIEF HISTORY OF POST-WORLD WAR II MACROECONOMIC POLICY

5

New Deal President Franklin Roosevelt's name for his practical "do-something" approach to economic policy.

Keynesian economics developed in the 1930s during the depression. This early work in the United States was primarily theoretical, and during the depression Keynesian economists didn't have significant input into policy. President Franklin Roosevelt opposed deficits (and hence the use of expansionary fiscal policy). Moreover he didn't like Keynes, whom he met during one of Keynes's visits to the United States. The Fed had a number of Keynesian advisors but, at the time, monetary policy wasn't the focus of Keynesian economics.

Nonetheless the U.S. government was running deficits and starting public works programs as part of Roosevelt's **New Deal.** These programs, however, reflected the New Deal's practical "do something" approach to policy rather than the influence of Keynesian (or Classical) economics.

The first half of the 1940s brought World War II. U.S. government spending increased enormously; U.S. taxes increased to very high rates. (The top rate was over 90 percent on high incomes.) But the increase in spending was so large that the U.S. government started running wartime deficits significantly larger than anything it had run in the depression. In response the U.S. economy boomed. Economic activity expanded enormously. Much of the production, however, was used for the war effort; consumption goods were in short supply. To keep the resulting inflationary pressures in check, wage and price controls were instituted.

The 1949 Recession

During the war, the combination of price controls and high wartime government expenditures led to low unemployment and low inflation. The U.S. economy came out of World War II operating at capacity output. The major economic questions of the immediate postwar period were: (1) how to convert the economy from wartime to peacetime production without falling back into a depression and (2) how to eliminate price controls without generating a large inflation. Both questions were successfully answered.

Soon after the war ended, price controls were lifted. The results were positive: While inflation picked up, it remained low, even as aggregate demand remained high.

The economy also avoided a recession or depression, at least initially—partly due to pent-up demand. Despite high tax rates, aggregate demand remained high as people spent some of their forced wartime savings. Their increased consumption offset much of the decrease in government spending. In spring 1948 the high wartime income tax rates were cut, giving the economy an additional expansionary push. But that push didn't offset the contractionary effect of the further decline in government spending and the economy started to fall into a recession by the end of 1949.

That recession was short-lived because in 1950 the Korean War started, the United States got involved in it, and government spending jumped due to rearmament. The economy quickly came out of the recession. Thus, in this first postwar recession we see fiscal policy working. But the fiscal policy (changes in government spending) was not implemented for stabilization purposes. Instead it reflected wartime and political needs. Monetary policy during this period was limited by the **Treasury Accord of 1952,** which required the Fed to hold the interest rate on government bonds constant. The economy continued strong through the Korean War.

Treasury Accord of 1952   An agreement between the Fed and U.S. Department of the Treasury in which the Fed agreed to hold the interest rate on government bonds constant.

The 1953–1954 Recession

In the summer of 1953 the Korean War ended and government expenditures decreased. Consumer confidence fell. To try to prevent a recession, the Fed, which had won its independence in the Treasury Accord of 1952, loosened monetary policy. The expansionary monetary policy didn't work (or at least it wasn't enough), and industrial production fell almost 10 percent from July 1953 to May 1954. No specific expansionary fiscal policy was implemented, but automatic stabilizers, such as unemployment insurance, helped slow output's fall. By the end of 1954 consumer confidence was picking up and sales were increasing. By mid-1955 the economy was moving into a boom and the concern turned from recession to inflation.

The 1955–1956 Inflation

To fight this inflation, the Fed tightened the money supply, increasing the reserve requirement and raising the discount rate. It hoped that the tightened money supply would stop the inflation, but not stop real output from growing or cause unemployment to increase. These hopes weren't met. The contractionary monetary policy did slow inflation, but it also decreased real output. By 1957 that decrease had become significant, and the concern changed from inflation to unemployment and recession.

The 1957–1958 Recession

The tight monetary policy of 1956 hit the capital goods industry especially hard; business investment dropped 16 percent and consumers' expenditures for durable items fell almost as much. This decline was worsened by the end of a Middle East Crisis (such crises have been almost continual since World War II), which caused U.S. exports to decrease. (During the crisis, U.S. exports had boomed as foreign countries bought food and goods from the United States to stockpile them for a potential war.) During this period the Fed was still concerned about inflation. This was the time when the inflation/unemployment Phillips curve trade-off became part of economists' lexicon.

Faced with this dual problem, the Fed had to choose which problem to fight. Initially it chose to fight inflation; it didn't loosen monetary policy significantly. But in late 1958 and early 1959 the Fed reversed itself and moved toward a more expansionary monetary policy, causing interest rates to fall. Combined with a large increase in mortgages guaranteed by the Federal Housing Administration and the Veterans' Administration, this expansionary monetary policy worked. By mid-1959 the economy was in a boom. Once again the policy concern changed and inflation, not unemployment, became the focus of policymakers' concern.

The 1960 Inflation and Recession

To fight the inflation, the Fed used contractionary monetary policy and decreased the money supply. Again, the results were the same. Contractionary monetary policy slowed the inflation, but it also brought the economy into recession.

Industrial production fell during the second half of 1960 and into the first part of 1961. Unemployment increased substantially. This was one of the few times that the economy had fallen into a recession during a presidential election. Many observers believe that the recession played a significant role in Richard Nixon's defeat by John F. Kennedy.

The Sustained Expansion of the 1960s

Partly because of the 1950s experience in fighting inflation and partly because of a change in policy advisors from Classical economists advising Republicans to Keynesian economists advising Democrats, in the 1960s the focus of monetary and fiscal policies changed from inflation and toward avoiding a recession. (John F. Kennedy's administration marked the first time that strong Keynesians were in key positions on the Council of Economic Advisers.[1]) The result was that generally up until 1969 monetary policy was expansionary. The economy remained in a sustained expansion through much of the 1960s.

During the early 1960s fiscal policy was also somewhat expansionary. Then in 1966–67 it became highly expansionary as the government attempted to fight a large war in Vietnam while simultaneously maintaining domestic progress by programs such as President Lyndon Johnson's War on Poverty. By 1966 most economists, Keynesian as well as Classical, had concluded that significant inflationary pressures were developing and that both monetary and fiscal policies needed tightening. Politically the government didn't want to hear such advice. It's true that monetary policy was tightened for about six months in 1966, but then it was loosened again until 1969, by which time inflation had picked up significantly. Fiscal policy was even less responsive to economists' advice, and, for political reasons, fiscal policy remained highly stimulative until 1968, when the government instituted a 10 percent income tax surcharge.

This 1968 tax increase and 1969 tight monetary policy both worked to slow down the economy. But about that same time, government war spending decreased. The result was a more contractionary fiscal policy than desired. Combined with a highly contractionary monetary policy, this contractionary fiscal policy led to a sudden braking of the economy.

The braking brought about by this combination caused interest rates to rise to their highest levels in decades, leading to the 1969–70 recession. With this recession, the sustained expansion of the 1960s ended, as did economists' hopes of eliminating the business cycle with fine-tuning of monetary and fiscal policies.

The 1969 Recession and the 1970–1973 Boom

Wage and price controls Legal limitations on the prices and wages that can be set.

Faced with a substantial economic downturn in 1969, the Fed acted relatively fast to reverse its policy to fight the recession. Since inflation hadn't yet responded to the tight monetary policy of 1969, fighting the recession required forgetting about using monetary policy to meet its inflation goals (which weren't being met anyway). Instead, to meet the inflation goals, the government instituted partial **wage and price controls** (legal limit on prices and wages).

Wage and price controls began in August 1971. The combination of price controls and expansionary monetary policy worked. In 1972 economic output increased significantly and inflation stayed low. In November 1972 President Nixon was reelected by a large majority. This significant monetary expansion right before a presidential election led some people to believe that Nixon and his economic advisors had learned a lesson from their 1960 election loss when, as

---

[1] Actually, during Harry S Truman's presidency (1945–1953) economists sympathetic to Keynes were on the council, but they were primarily Roosevelt New Dealers rather than Keynesian economists.

mentioned before, the economy went into a recession right before the election. Right before a presidential election, you never use contractionary monetary or fiscal policies if you want to win.

Soon after the 1972 election, wage and price controls were loosened. Finally in 1973 they were dismantled. The result was a significant increase in inflation which, by 1973, had reached 9 percent.

How much of this inflation was due to the removal of price controls and the expansionary monetary policy, and how much was due to exogenous supply price shocks, is a matter of debate between Keynesians and Classicals. Classicals argue that the inflation was primarily caused by the removal of price controls and the expansionary monetary policy. Keynesians disagree, pointing out that three **supply price shocks** hit the economy during this period.

The first supply price shock concerned import prices. In 1972 and 1973 the U.S. economy had a fixed exchange rate with other major currencies, which meant that the U.S. government was committed to buying and selling currencies to maintain that fixed exchange rate whenever the quantity of dollars demanded didn't equal the quantity of dollars supplied. In 1971 the dollar was valued at a high relative exchange rate, imports significantly exceeded exports and the United States had a significant balance of trade deficit. In response to that deficit, the United States and other countries agreed that the dollar would be devalued by 12 percent in December 1971. This raised import prices by 12 percent, causing a supply price shock.

The second supply price shock—the poor grain harvest of 1972—pushed up food prices. The third supply price shock—the Arab oil embargo—limited oil shipments to the United States and tripled the price of oil. Combined, these three supply price shocks caused significant inflationary pressure. They presented the Fed with a dilemma: either (1) expand the money supply, ratify the supply shock inflation, and allow other prices to rise in response, thereby avoiding a recession but building inflation into the economy, or (2) don't expand the money supply, trying to prevent the supply price shocks from being built into expectations of inflation and risk recession.

Initially the Fed expanded the money supply, but in 1973 it decided that it must do something about the inflation. It significantly tightened the money supply. The economy responded predictably and went into a recession.

Supply price shock A shock that causes a rise in nominal wages and prices.

Herbert Stein—Chairman of the Council of Economic Advisers under President Nixon.   *UPI/Bettmann.*

The 1973–1975 Recession

The result of the tight monetary policy in 1973 was a severe recession, not only in the United States but in all major industrialized countries, as decreased U.S. imports had contractionary effects on foreign countries' exports. Inflation was reduced, but it remained high by historical standards. This recession lasted well into 1975, when the focus of policy once again shifted from concern about inflation to concern about the recession.

That concern led to an expansionary fiscal policy (a large 1975 tax cut) and expansionary monetary policy. Combined, these policies helped pull the economy out of the recession. Inflation, however, which had remained very high during the recession, became even higher, causing the Fed serious concern over which problem it should be fighting. Despite this concern, through the late 1970s the Fed maintained an expansionary monetary policy.

The 1980–1982 Recession-Expansion-Recession

In October 1979, however, the Fed abruptly changed its focus from recession to inflation. At that point it also stopped focusing on interest rate targets as a measure of monetary policy and announced that, henceforth, it would focus on the money supply, not interest rates, as a measure of monetary policy.

The result was an enormous increase in interest rates, which rose to more than 20 percent, and a sudden decrease in the money supply. In the short run these policies had few effects upon inflation which, partly due to a second oil-price shock, had reached double digits in late 1979 and early 1980. But they significantly affected real output. In response to these measures the U.S. economy went into a large contraction. Industrial production fell by well over 10 percent.

In May 1980 the Fed moderated its policy and backed off on its highly contractionary policy. In response, business activity picked up and by November 1980 the economy was in a major expansion. The expansion didn't take place soon enough for President Jimmy Carter. He was voted out of office partly because the public blamed him for the period's **stagflation** (simultaneous high inflation and high unemployment).

After the election, once again, the concern changed from recession to inflation; the Fed tightened the money supply significantly. Again the interest rate rose to almost 20 percent, causing large decreases in spending on housing and consumer durables. By June 1981 the economy was deep into a recession. By November 1982, 12 million people were unemployed. The term *stagflation* was used with increasing frequency.

In response to this recession, both fiscal policy and monetary policy turned expansionary. On the fiscal policy side, in 1981 the United States enacted a major cut in income tax rates, although some of the effects of the cut were offset by increased social security taxes that kicked in about this same time. Simultaneously the Fed loosened monetary policy and backed away from its strict monetary rule. Since then the Fed has used an eclectic mix of money supply targets and interest rate targets.

Stagflation Simultaneous high inflation and high unemployment.

The 1983–1990 Expansion

Combined, these expansionary policies helped pull the economy out of the recession. The 1981–82 recession, unlike the earlier one in 1980, had a major impact on inflationary expectations, and by the mid-1980s it was clear that the double-digit inflation and expectations of an exploding inflation rate had ended. Exactly why this sudden decrease in inflation and inflationary expectations occurred is a matter of debate. Traditional Classical economists attributed it primarily to tight monetary policy which convinced people the Fed was serious about fighting inflation and established its credibility. Supply-side Classical economists attributed it to cuts in the income tax rates which had stimulated supply and led to significant growth. Keynesian economists attributed the reduced inflation to negative supply price shocks during this period: Oil prices fell, food and raw material prices fell, and labor relations were relatively smooth. All three explanations (traditional Classical, supply-side Classical, and Keynesian) probably capture part of the truth.

Whatever the cause, throughout this period employment was increasing substantially, inflation stayed low, and the U.S. economy seemed strong. But there were problems. The banking and financial system significantly overextended itself during this period, resulting in hundreds of billions of dollars of government-guaranteed loans which came due in 1989 and 1990. Additionally both the U.S. trade deficit and government budget deficit remained high, creating serious potential long-term problems.

So the debate remained about this period: Was it a time of sustained positive growth, or was it merely a time in which a group of yuppies and rich people became richer while creating serious long-term problems for the United States?

The 1990 Recession

In fall 1990 the string of good luck seemed to end. Due to a Middle East military conflict, oil prices rose substantially, causing significant inflationary pressures.

The consensus view going into the 1990s was that fiscal policy was expansionary, not for macroeconomic reasons, but for political reasons. This was unlikely to change significantly so monetary policy had to provide the contractionary effect. In 1990 by both measures (interest rates and money supply) the Fed was being relatively contractionary, and there was significant debate about whether it should loosen up to prevent a recession. Whichever policy it followed would cause problems.

In September 1990 the G-7 countries met and decided to coordinate their monetary policies. All would maintain relatively contractionary policy, so that the 1974 experience wouldn't be repeated—they would come down on the side of fighting inflation. Many economists felt that this would be the path to a serious recession, which would lead the Fed and other countries' central banks to change their policies from contractionary to expansionary, as they had in the past.

The United States had an even stronger reason to maintain contractionary policy. The country already had a significant trade balance deficit which was expected to worsen due to rising prices of oil imports.

The policy most economists advocated for the United States was reducing the deficit by tightening up somewhat on fiscal policy, but not too much—for fear of furthering recessionary pressures. This contractionary fiscal policy was meant to be counteracted by expansionary monetary policy. The combination of policies would lower the interest rate some, decreasing the value of the dollar, which, in the long run, would stimulate U.S. exports.

The Fed worked behind the scenes to achieve these goals, arguing that the economy could go a lot more smoothly if fiscal policy would become slightly more contractionary. It offered to loosen up on monetary policy, but only if Congress and the president made some movements toward tightening up the deficit—to make fiscal policies more contractionary.

By the end of summer 1990 the president and Congress hadn't made any progress in eliminating the deficit, which actually had become larger because the government was taking in less than the expected amount of revenue, thanks to a slowdown in the U.S. economy.

In October the deficit was reduced somewhat. In response the Fed eased monetary policy slightly, but, for fear of inflation, didn't ease up significantly. Once again the Fed and other central banks had to decide whether to accommodate and possibly trigger accelerating inflation, or to hold the line and possibly cause a recession. They tried to find a middle road: running expansionary, but not too expansionary, policy. It didn't work. In fall 1990 the economy went into recession. Unemployment increased from 5.1 to 7 percent and real GDP fell. In response the Fed's concern turned to fighting the recession, although initially that response was muted because it didn't want to rekindle inflation.

The recession lingered on through all of 1991 despite signs that it was ending. When it was clear that the recession was lingering on into early 1992, the Fed forgot about inflation and its desire for tighter fiscal policy before it would institute a looser monetary policy. Despite the government's increasing budget deficit, the Fed loosened monetary policy significantly. Interest rates fell to their lowest level in 30 years. Their fall pushed down the U.S. exchange rate and that decrease, combined with the recession, lowered the U.S. foreign trade deficit. But most economists felt that the trade deficit would increase again when the economy came out of the recession.

The history of macroeconomic policy since the 1930s should have given you a sense of the changing focus of macroeconomic policy, the political difficulties of using the fiscal policy tool, and the shifting back and forth over concern about inflation and recession. A natural reaction to that history is that, in hindsight, the handling of monetary and fiscal policy leaves much to be desired. Fiscal policy has often had the wrong effects at the right time, or the right effects at the wrong time, but it has seldom had the right effect at the right time. There wasn't much discussion of fiscal policy in this history because it hasn't been used much to try to direct the economy. That's why much of this history concerned monetary policy.

In its conduct of monetary policy, the Fed has seemed to switch goals from one moment to the next and to continually go too far in both directions. The result has been a stop-go set of policies, causing the economy to alternate between inflationary booms and recessions. This leads modern Classical economists to argue that the Fed's policies have lacked credibility. Keynesians emphasize, however, that such an assessment can only be made with hindsight. Given the

Assessment of Policy

he discussion of economic policy history touched only briefly on the politics of the decisions, but as you read through it I hope you were thinking of who was in office. If you didn't, it might be helpful to reconsider that history, taking into account the following information about the presidents and their parties, the chairmen of the Council of Economic Advisers and their political classifications, and the chairmen of the Fed and their political affiliations.

Thinking about this information should convince you that while, in theory, the differences between Classicals and Keynesians are substantial, in practice they are often blurred by politics.

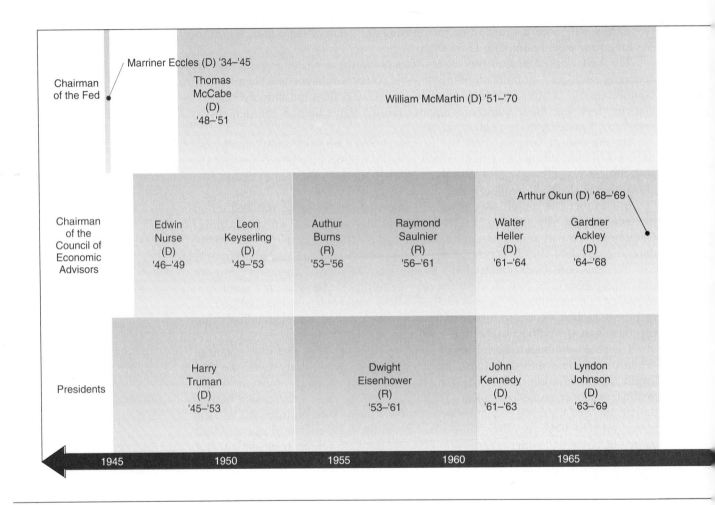

knowledge available to policymakers and the political and institutional constraints under which they operate, many Keynesians believe that the past 50 years, while not pretty, are representative of about as good a macroeconomic policy as can be expected. In short, macroeconomics is an art, and art isn't always pretty or neat.

CONGRATULATIONS!
YOU ARE NOW
A POLICY ADVISOR   **6**

Now that we've been through the history of macroeconomic policy, let's switch gears and consider two hypothetical examples that raise some of the same issues. Only this time you don't have hindsight to assist you.

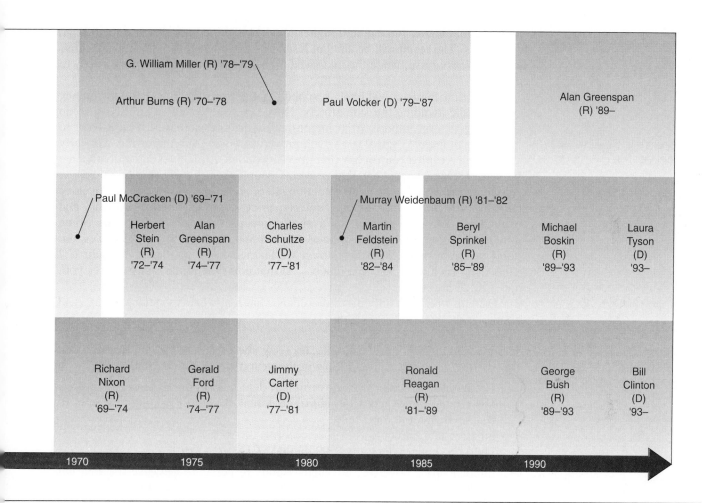

In the first example, you've been appointed head of the Xanadu central bank. You have the following information about the economy: Monetary Policy in Xanadu

The current interest rate is 10 percent.
The unemployment rate is 8 percent.
The government is running a budget deficit of 1 billion xanadi (the Xanadu currency), which is 2 percent of its GDP.
The country has a trade deficit of 2 billion xanadi.
Inflation is 6 percent.
Your central bank has almost no international reserves so you can do little to affect the exchange rate in the market.

Prime Minister Xorcist, who appointed you, is running for reelection. He tells you that, to win, he must lower the unemployment rate and reduce the interest rate. He also remembers from the introductory economics course he took with you when you were teaching at Xanadu U. that increasing the money supply will accomplish these goals.

How do you respond? You tell him that yes, in the short run expansionary monetary policy will accomplish his goals, but that it will have some side effects. Specifically it will likely increase the trade deficit, push down Xanadu's exchange rate, and boost inflation.

"Why?" he asks. First, you tell him that imports depend upon income, so when income increases, imports will increase so the trade deficit will worsen. Then you explain that lower interest rates will mean fewer people will want to hold their money in xanadi (Xanadu's currency). That will lower demand for xanadi while higher income and higher imports will increase demand for foreign currencies. The result will be a fall in Xanadu's exchange rate. This fall will cause import prices to rise, while the increased money supply will contribute directly to inflation.

The prime minister will likely respond that he wants you to expand the money supply while avoiding the side effects. How can you do that? You'll have to do something to stop imports from increasing as income increases. You'll have to introduce an **import control law** which prevents people from importing. Similarly you'll need a **capital control law** that prevents people from investing abroad and a **foreign exchange control law** that prevents people from buying foreign currency. And of course you'll have to do something to prevent inflation, which means price controls. In short, with import controls, price controls, capital controls, and exchange controls, you can for a short time prevent the effects. The prime minister tells you, "But those policies will be unpopular!" You answer, "Yes, but don't you remember the other lesson we learned in economics at Xanadu U.? There's no such thing as a free lunch." At that point the prime minister fires you, and you go into exile.

Dealing with such difficult trade-offs is what real-world monetary policy is all about.

Import control law A law preventing people from importing.

Capital control law A law preventing people from investing abroad.

Foreign exchange control law A law preventing people from buying foreign currency.

A Potential Monetary Crisis

In our second hypothetical example, let's say you've entered a time machine that transports you to the United States in the year 1998. Here you find:

6

- There is $2 trillion of U.S. government debt held by foreigners.
- The United States has a foreign trade deficit of about $200 billion a year.
- Unemployment is 6 percent.
- Inflation is 4 percent.
- The U.S. budget deficit is $500 billion. (180 bil - 200 bil)

Interest rates, however, are high—about 10 percent—because the Fed has been using contractionary monetary policy. Despite these problems, the U.S. economy is going along relatively smoothly.

The day you arrive, however, a new book, *The U.S. Economic Crash of 2000,* is published. It's a best-seller. Suddenly foreigners no longer want to hold the $2 trillion of government debt. Since the U.S. budget deficit is $500 billion, that means that $2.5 trillion of U.S. government debt will be coming onto the market and will need buyers in the United States. For the United States to find holders for that debt, its interest rate will have to rise enormously—say from 10 percent to 20 or 30 percent. The Fed says it can't allow interest rates to go that high and asks what to do. You suggest the Fed buy more government bonds (monetizing part of the debt) and open up its discount window, letting banks borrow money to buy more of that debt. You also advise the government to finally do something about the budget deficit. But with foreigners selling U.S. bonds, even eliminating the deficit won't necessarily hold the interest rate down.

Still you've made some progress. Combined, those two actions—buying more government bonds and decreasing the discount rate—might mean that the interest rate rises only to 15 percent, not to 20 or 30 percent. But even that much progress comes at a cost. The expansionary monetary policy would bring about enormous inflationary pressures in the U.S. economy.

This hypothetical isn't so hypothetical. The potential for such an event has increased in the past decade as more and more U.S. debt becomes held by foreign investors. Most foreigners can easily change from holding dollar-denominated assets to holding assets denominated in another currency, which has led to the possibility of "runs" on financial assets in a country.

Fear about the U.S. economy's stability could lead to a rush to sell U.S. debt. The U.S. exchange rate would fall precipitously and, as it did, import prices would go up. Such runs could create financial havoc in the same way that runs on some banks created financial havoc in the depression. The Fed could undertake the policies you recommend, but there's no guarantee those policies will be enough. The question is whether the international financial system, which has no equivalent to a central bank (although the International Monetary Fund has some attributes of a central bank), is up to dealing with such problems.

All economists agree the potential for the problem is there. Whether the problem will ever materialize is debatable. Some economists believe the large sales of U.S. financial assets to foreigners, which characterized the late 1980s and early 1990s, will slowly taper off and the United States will slide out of the problem. Others believe that an international financial panic will arise suddenly. There will be no soft landing. They argue that in the 1980s the U.S. economy jumped out of a 20th-story window. Each year it passed one or two floors. As it passed each floor on the way down, the "not-to-worry" advocates kept pointing out how right they were—because nothing had happened. And they were right— for 19 of the 20 stories. It's the ground floor that's the problem.

Even if one agrees with the 20th-story–window analogy, one can believe that the political chances of doing anything to prevent the hard landing are roughly the same as a person successfully deciding in midair that maybe it would be best not to have jumped. About all one can do, policywise, is hope one hits a big leafy tree to break the fall, or that the fire department will be down there with a net.

Actually there's some chance of that. Other countries' economies are tied to the U.S. economy. If the United States goes splat, they go splat too. Because they know that, some reassurance is provided us. Those on the first floor of the building have an incentive to build a net.

CONCLUSION

As you can see, real-world monetary and fiscal policies are not cut and dried. Working with these policies is an art, not a science, and involves politics and psychology as well as economics. But the messiness of real-world policy doesn't mean that one can forget the simplified theories and relationships of economic models. Far from it. Real-world policy problems require a much deeper understanding of the models so that one can see through the messiness and design a policy consistent with the general principles embodied in those models.

KEY POINTS

- The goals of macro policy often conflict with one another. **1 2**
- Keynesians tend to favor activist policy; Classicals tend to favor laissez-faire policy. **1 4**
- Keynesian and Classical economists agree about many aspects of macroeconomic policy. **3**
- Monetary policy has been used far more often than fiscal policy over the past 50 years. **5**

- Monetary policy has been characterized by stop-go measures as the Fed's concern has shifted from inflation to recession. **5**
- Often short-run solutions to problems create even worse long-run problems. **5**
- Macroeconomic policy is an art, not a science. **6**

KEY TERMS

art of macro policy *(368)*
capital control law *(378)*
foreign exchange control law *(378)*

import control law *(378)*
New Deal *(370)*
prayer policy *(367)*
stagflation *(374)*

supply price shock *(373)*
Treasury Accord of 1952 *(371)*

wage and price controls *(372)*

PROBLEMS AND EXERCISES

1. In the library, research one of the Fed's responses to a recession discussed in this chapter.
   a. Would you have done anything differently?
   b. If you would have, what would be the possible negative effects of your actions?
   c. Who was president, Fed chairman, and chairman of the Council of Economic Advisers during the recession you looked at? Give their political affiliations.
   d. If individuals from the opposite party were in office during that recession, how might the responses have been different?

2. Find the current unemployment, inflation, and growth rates.
   a. What fiscal policy is government using to deal with the problems?
   b. What monetary policy is government using?
   c. Who is currently president, Fed chairman, and chairman of the Council of Economic Advisers? What are their political affiliations?
   d. How might the responses be different if individuals from another party were in power?

QUESTIONS FOR THOUGHT AND REVIEW

The number after each question represents the estimated degree of critical thinking required. (1 = almost none; 10 = deep thought.)

1. Keynesians and Classicals are in direct opposition on macroeconomic policy. True or false? Why? *(5)*
2. The experience with price controls during World War II demonstrates that price controls work. True or false? Why? *(7)*
3. The experience of the New Deal suggests that economists' theoretical debates have little effect on government's real-world policies. True or false? Why? *(7)*
4. Demonstrate, using aggregate supply and demand curves, what happened in the 1969 recession. *(5)*
5. The experience with price controls in 1971–74 demon-

strates that price controls don't work. True or false? Why? *(7)*
6. Give three possible explanations for the increase in inflation in the 1970s. *(3)*
7. Give three possible explanations for the 1983–90 decrease in inflation. *(6)*
8. How might the policy advice given to Prime Minister Xorcist have changed if he hadn't needed to run for reelection for three more years? *(6)*
9. What is the current state of the U.S. economy, and what policies would you advise government to use? *(10)*
10. The U.S. economy is headed toward doom. True or false? Why? *(10)*

18

Deficits and Debt

*Any government, like any family,
can for a year spend a little more than it earns. But you and I know
that a continuance of that habit means the poorhouse.*

Franklin D. Roosevelt

After reading this chapter, you should be able to:

1

Define the terms *deficit* and *debt*.

2

State why economists focus on financial
health rather than on deficits.

3

Explain why, in an expanding economy, a
government can run a limited, but
continual, deficit without serious concern
about the consequences.

4

Differentiate between a real deficit and a
nominal deficit.

5

Explain why, even though the real budget
deficit of the United States is much lower
than the nominal deficit, there is still reason
for concern about the deficit.

6

Explain why there are alternative
reasonable views about the deficit.

In our discussion of macroeconomic policies and problems, two concepts come up continually: deficits and debt. Is the U.S. budget deficit something we have to worry about? Is the $4 trillion U.S. government debt going to be an unbearable burden on our grandchildren? These and similar questions are sufficiently important to warrant a separate chapter that explores the government budget deficit and debt.

Before we begin the exploration, let's briefly consider the definitions. A **deficit** is a shortfall of revenues under payments; it is a flow concept. If your income (revenues) is $20,000 per year and your expenditures (payments) are $30,000 per year, you are running a deficit. If revenues exceed payments, you are running a surplus. This means that a *government budget deficit* occurs when government expenditures exceed government revenues.

Debt is accumulated deficits minus accumulated surpluses; it is a stock concept. For example, say you've spent $30,000 a year for 10 years and have had annual income of $20,000 for 10 years. So you've had a deficit of $10,000 per year. At the end of 10 years, you will have accumulated a debt of $100,000:

$$10 \times \$10,000 = \$100,000.$$

(Spending more than you have in income means that you need to borrow the extra $10,000 per year from someone, so in later years much of your expenditure will be on interest on your previous debt.)

Deficit A shortfall of incoming revenue under outgoing payments.

■**1**

Debt Accumulated deficits minus accumulated surpluses.

U.S. GOVERNMENT DEFICITS AND DEBT: THE HISTORICAL RECORD

Let's begin with a consideration of the historical record of deficits in the United States. Exhibit 1(a) graphs the U.S. budget deficits since 1945. As you can see, for many years the U.S. budget has been significantly in deficit. But that hasn't always been the case. Before the 1940s the U.S. government would run a budget surplus sometimes (mainly in peacetime) and a budget deficit at other times (mainly during wartime). After World War II—that is, after 1945—that changed, and since that time the United States has run consistent deficits.

Because debt is accumulated deficits, and the United States has a continual deficit every year, you would expect United States debt to have increased substantially since World War II. Exhibit 1(b) shows that is indeed the case.

Policy Regimes, the Deficit, and the Debt

Policy regime The general set of rules, whether explicit or implicit, governing the monetary and fiscal policies a country follows.

Why was there a change after World War II? A reason many economists suggest is the change in macroeconomic **policy regimes**—the general set of rules that governs the monetary and fiscal policies that a country follows—that occurred after World War II.

The big difference in policy regimes before and after World War II was the introduction of Keynesian economics and its use of discretionary fiscal policy. Before World War II, Classical economics dictated that government budget deficits were bad and that, except in wartime, they should be avoided. And that was the policy the U.S. government followed. That was changed by Keynesian economics which prescribed deficits to stimulate the economy and achieve a higher level of output. According to Keynesian economics, deficits were not necessarily bad. You had to look at the state of the economy to decide whether a deficit was good or bad. Because Keynesian economics removed the stigma connected with deficits, some economists argue that government budget deficits are the result of Keynesian policies. Others argue that view is too simplistic. They point out that Keynesian economics never said that all deficits are good—it only said that deficits aren't necessarily bad, and when the economy is in a recession deficits might actually be good.

The argument that Keynesian economics accounts for the deficit is weakened by the fact that in the 1980s when there was a second change in policy regimes—Keynesian economics was discarded and replaced with a Classical supply-side economic policy regime—the deficit did not end. In fact, the deficit grew. The New Classical supply-side policy regime has led to an even larger deficit than existed in the Keynesian policy regime. The new Classical supply-side regime

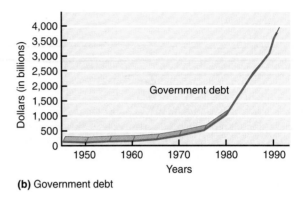

(a) Government deficits

(b) Government debt

EXHIBIT 1 (a and b)   U.S. Budget Deficits and Debt

Since the end of World War II, the U.S. government has run consistent deficits. These deficits increased substantially in the 1980s and early 1990s. The result has been a large rise in government debt held by the public. (This exhibit excludes debt held by public agencies.)
Source: Economic Report of the President.

focuses on the need for tax cuts whenever they can possibly be implemented. This supply-side Classical focus on tax cuts as the key to economic prosperity with little concern about the deficit is why you are now likely to see role reversals—Keynesians arguing against a deficit and Classicals arguing in favor of government running a deficit!

Differing groups of economists' changing views of deficits have had little impact on the lay public's view about deficits and debt. The lay public doesn't like either. In response, politicians say that they too don't like deficits and debt and that they're greatly concerned about the deficit problems.

In the 1980s political concern about the deficit grew so large that Congress passed the **Gramm-Rudman-Hollings Act** establishing mandatory deficit targets for the United States. This act was designed to eliminate deficits by 1991. When it became clear that it would not achieve its goals, it was supplemented by the **Deficit Reduction Act of 1990,** a law placing spending limits on government. For

Politics and the Deficit

Gramm-Rudman-Hollings Act   A law establishing mandatory deficit targets for the United States.

Deficit Reduction Act of 1990   A law establishing spending limits for government.

This lithograph, entitled "Legislative assault (on the budget)" appeared in a French newspaper in 1835.
Bleichroeder Print Collection, Baker Library, Harvard Business School.

ADDED DIMENSION THE GRAMM-RUDMAN-HOLLINGS ACT AND THE DEFICIT REDUCTION ACT OF 1990

In December 1985 Congress passed the Balanced Budget and Emergency Deficit Control Act, commonly known as the Gramm-Rudman-Hollings Act. It required government to balance the budget by 1991. Specifically it set limits for the deficit's size and provided that if the limits weren't met, mandatory across-the-board cutbacks would be instituted in most nonexempt programs. (Interest payments, social security, and a number of other social programs were exempt.) These mandatory cutbacks were to be made in order to achieve the deficit goals.

The act attempted to make government face up to the difficult decisions of what programs should be cut, or what taxes should be raised. Most politicians favored deficit reduction but weren't willing to make the compromises necessary actually to cut the deficit.

The act pushed politicians to cut the deficit. In 1990 a summit between Congress and the president was designed to confront the deficit and to avoid the mandatory cuts required by the Gramm-Rudman-Hollings law. So that law did serve its intended purpose.

But, by specifying the limits in terms of the deficit—and not in terms of the government's financial health—the law led to the budget gimmicks and accounting tricks. These gimmicks and tricks reduced the deficit but did nothing (or actually made things worse) for the government's overall financial health.

In 1990 it became clear that the Gramm-Rudman-Hollings Act's goal of eliminating the deficit by 1991 would not be met. So a new law was passed—the Deficit Reduction Act of 1990. Under this act the president and Congress agreed to hold down spending and to once again balance the budget sometime in the future. Then the economy fell into recession, and each side competed with the other in offering tax cuts that would further increase the deficit.

Given the political realities, most people believed that this act would be as ineffective as Gramm-Rudman-Hollings and that it would be a long time in the future before the U.S. budget would be balanced.

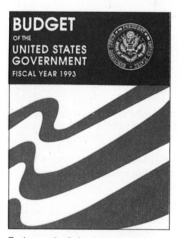

Each year the federal government publishes its budget, which details its spending programs.

some politicians, these laws were not strong enough. They suggested a balanced budget amendment to the U.S. Constitution that would make it unconstitutional for the government to run a deficit. Support for such an amendment grew in the early 1990s as budget deficits reached $400 billion. Even economists who support that balanced budget amendment agree that the reason for not running a budget deficit is not the immediate economic consequences of a deficit. The reason is political. They believe that a balanced budget requirement would work like a lock on the refrigerator and that the political structure of the United States lacks self-control in spending, and hence needs that lock. If you unlock a refrigerator, people without self-control will grow fat. Similarly, without the discipline of a mandatory balanced budget, government and politicians without self-control won't make the hard choices. Instead they'll say, "We can have both guns and butter. We'll pay for them by running a deficit."

Judging by events since the 1940s, there's substance to the political argument that most democracies lack self-control in spending and taxing decisions. Most political observers agree that democracy tends to put off hard decisions. People want lots of things from government, but nobody wants to pay for things in taxes. Running a deficit (buy now, pay later) allows democracies to put off the paying and hence to put off the hard choices.[1]

ECONOMISTS' WAY OF LOOKING AT DEFICITS AND DEBT

Where do economists come out in the debate about the deficit? On most sides of the issue. But the reasons for their differences are quite unlike the reasons lay people and politicians differ. Why? Because there are a number of technical aspects behind the deficits and debt that most economists understand, and most lay people (and politicians) don't. Thus, to understand economists' views on deficits and debt, you've got to understand these technical aspects behind applying those definitions. We'll now examine these technical aspects and see how understanding them changes our ideas about problems deficits and debt pose for society.

---

[1] The fact that democracy has problems doesn't mean that some other form of government is preferable to democracy. As Winston Churchill said, democracy is the worst form of government, except for all the other forms.

The definitions of *deficits* and *debt* are simple, but their simplicity hides important aspects that will help you understand current debates about deficits and debt. Thus, it's necessary to look carefully at some ambiguities in the definitions. Let's start with deficits.

Deficits are a shortfall of revenues compared to expenditures. So whether you have a deficit depends on what you include as a revenue and what you include as an expenditure. How you make these decisions can make an enormous difference in whether you have a deficit.

For example, consider the problem of a firm with revenues of $8,000 but no expenses except a $10,000 machine expected to last five years. Should the firm charge the $10,000 to this year's expenditures? Should it split the $10,000 evenly among the five years? Or should the firm use some other approach? Which method the firm chooses makes a big difference in whether its current budget will be in surplus or deficit.

This accounting issue is central to the debate about whether we should be concerned about the U.S. budget deficit. Say, for example, that government promises to pay an individual $1,000 ten years from now. How should government treat that promise? Since the obligation is incurred now, should government count as an expense now an amount that, if saved, would allow government to pay that $1,000 later? Or should government not count it as an expenditure until it actually pays out the money?

The same ambiguity surrounds revenues. For example, say you're holding government bonds valued at $100,000, which pay $10,000 interest per year, while you're spending $10,000 per year. You might think your budget is balanced. But what if the market value of the bonds (the amount you can sell them for) rises from $100,000 to $120,000? Should you count that $20,000 rise in value of the bonds as a revenue? Using an opportunity cost approach which economists use, a person holding bonds should count the rise in the bond's market value as revenue, which means that your income for the year is $30,000, not $10,000. Similarly the government that issued the bond should count the rise in the market value of the bond it issued as an expenditure and count the fall in the market value of a bond it issued as income.[2]

Many such questions must be answered before we can determine whether a budget is in deficit or surplus. Some questions have no right or wrong answer. For others there are right or wrong answers that vary with the question being asked. For still others, an economist's "right way" is an accountant's "wrong way." In short, there are many ways to measure expenditures and receipts so there are many ways to measure deficits.

To say that there are many ways to measure deficits is not to say that all ways are correct. If you pretend to have income that you don't have, that's wrong by all standards. Similarly if you're inconsistent; it would be wrong sometimes to measure an income flow one way and sometimes another. Standard accounting practices rule out a number of "creative," but improper, approaches to measuring deficits. But even eliminating these, there remain numerous reasonable ways of defining deficits, which accounts for much of the debate about them.

The point of the previous discussion is that deficits are simply a summary measure of a budget. As a summary, a deficit figure reduces a complicated set of accounting relationships down to one figure. To understand whether that one summary measure is something to worry about, you've got to understand the accounting

---

[2] Since a fixed rate bond's price varies inversely with the interest rate in the economy, a rise in the interest rate creates an income for bond issuers and an expense for bond holders. Reviewing the reasons why in relation to the present value formula is a good exercise.

procedures used to arrive at it. Only then can you make an informed judgment about whether a deficit is something to worry about.

The Need to Judge Debt relative to Assets

Debt is accumulated deficits. If you spend $1,000 more than you earn for each of three years, you'll end up with a $3,000 debt. (To make things simple, we assume that spending includes paying interest on the debt.)

Debt is also a summary measure of a country's financial situation. As a summary measure, debt has even more problems than deficit. Unlike a deficit (which is the difference between outflows and inflows and hence provides at least a full summary measure), debt by itself is only half of a picture. The other half of the debt picture is assets. For a country, assets include its skilled work force, its natural resources, its factories, its housing stock, and its holdings of foreign assets. For a government, assets include the buildings and land it owns but, more importantly, it includes a portion of the assets of the people in the country, since government gets a portion of those earnings of all assets in tax revenue.

To get an idea why the addition of assets is necessary to complete the debt picture, consider two governments: one has debt of $3 trillion and assets of $500 trillion; the other has $1 trillion in debt but only $1 trillion in assets. Which is in a better position? The government with more debt is, because its debt is significantly exceeded by its assets. The example's point is simple: To judge a country's debt, you must view its debt in relation to its assets.

Arbitrariness in Defining Debt

Like income and revenues, assets and debt are subject to varying definitions. Say, for example, that an 18-year-old is due to inherit $1 million at age 21. Should that expected future asset be counted as an asset now? Or say that the government buys an aircraft for $1 billion and discovers that it doesn't fly. What value should the government place on that aircraft? Or say that a country owes $1 billion, due to be paid 10 years from now, but inflation is ongoing at 100 percent per year. The inflation will reduce the value of the debt when it comes due by so much that its current real value will be $1 million—the approximate present value of $1 billion in 10 years with 100 percent inflation. It will be like paying $1 million today. Should the country list the debt as a $1 billion debt or a $1 million debt?

As was the case with income, revenues, and deficits, there's no unique answer to how assets and debts should be valued. So even after you take assets into account, you still have to be careful when deciding whether or not to be concerned about debt.

Difference between Individual and Government Debt

Another important fact about debt is that all debt is not the same. In particular, government debt is different than an individual's debt. There are three reasons for this.

First, government is ongoing. There's no real need for government ever to pay back its debt. An individual's lifespan is limited; when a person dies, there's inevitably an accounting of assets and debt to determine whether anything is left to go to heirs. Before any part of a person's estate is passed on, all debts must be paid. The government, however, doesn't ever have to make an accounting.

Second, government has an option for paying off a debt that individuals don't have. Specifically it can pay off a debt by creating money. As long as people will accept a country's currency, a country can always exchange its interest-bearing debt for money (non–interest-bearing debt). By doing so, it pays off its debt.

Third, much of a government debt is **internal government debt** (government debt owed to its own citizens). Paying interest on the debt involves a redistribution among citizens of the country, but it does not involve a net reduction in income of the average citizen. For example, say that a country has a $3 trillion debt, all of which is internal debt. Say also that the government pays $300 billion interest on its debt each year. That means the government must collect $300 billion in taxes so people are $300 billion poorer; but it pays out $300 billion in

Internal government debt Government debt owed to its own citizens.

(a)

(b)

EXHIBIT 2 (a and b)   U.S. Deficits and Debt relative to GDP

The size of the deficits and the size of the debt look somewhat different when considered relative to the GDP. Notice specifically how the total debt to GDP declined substantially from the 1950s to the 1980s and how it has increased in the 1980s and 1990s.
Source: Economic Report of the President and Historical Statistics.

interest to them, so on average, people in the country are neither richer nor poorer because of the debt.[3]

External government debt (government debt owed to individuals in foreign countries) is different, being more like an individual's debt. Paying interest on it involves a net reduction in domestic income. U.S. taxpayers will be poorer; foreign holders of U.S. bonds will be richer.

These three differences between government debt and individual debt must be continually kept in mind when considering governments' debt problems.

Let's now apply some of these insights. In Exhibits 1(a) and (b) we saw that U.S. government debt and deficits have been increasing since World War II. Let's now consider the question from a slightly different perspective taking into account government's ability to handle debt and deficits. That different perspective is to look at deficits and debt relative to GDP, as in Exhibits 2(a) and (b). As you can see, relative to GDP recent deficits look much smaller. As a percentage of GDP, deficits haven't shown the same alarming trend as when they're considered in absolute terms. And it's the same with debt. Relative to GDP, debt has not been continually increasing. Instead, from after World War II to the 1970s and from 1988 to 1990, the debt/GDP ratio actually decreased.

Why measure deficits and debt relative to GDP? Because the ability to pay off a deficit depends upon a nation's productive capacity. Government's ability to bring in revenue depends upon GDP. So GDP serves the same function for government as income does for an individual. It provides a measure of how much debt, and how large a deficit, government can handle.

Considering deficits and debt relative to GDP should ease our concern about the large U.S. deficit and growing U.S. debt. Although the absolute size of the deficits is much larger today than earlier, their relative importance compared to GDP is not. Similarly for debt. Though the debt has been increasing continuously, the problem it presents hasn't necessarily increased.

Considering debt relative to GDP is still not quite sufficient. Economists are also concerned about the interest rate paid on the debt. How much of a burden a given amount of debt imposes depends on the interest rate that must be paid on that debt. The interest rate on debt times the total debt is the **debt service** a country

External government debt Government debt owed to individuals in foreign countries.

Deficits, Debt, and Debt Service relative to GDP

Debt service The interest rate on debt times the total debt.

---

[3] There are, of course, distributional effects. The people who pay the taxes are not necessarily the same people who receive the interest.

Interest
GDP

EXHIBIT 3   Federal Interest Payments relative to GDP

Interest payments as a percentage of GDP remained relatively constant until the 1970s, after which they rose significantly due to high interest rates and large increases in debt. In the late 1980s, they fell as GDP increased, but with the recession in the 1990s they rose substantially again, even as interest rates fell.

must pay each year. Money spent on debt service cannot be spent on buying new goods and services.

Over the past 50 years, the interest rate has fluctuated considerably; when it has risen, the debt service has increased; when it has fallen, debt service has decreased. Exhibit 3 shows the federal interest rate payments relative to GDP. This ratio increased substantially in World War II and then again in the 1970s and early 1980s. In the late 1980s it declined slightly, but then in the early 1990s it rose again. Thus, this measure of the debt problem suggests that it is more of a problem than the debt/GDP measure, but less of a problem than when we simply looked at debt.

Let's now turn to a consideration of how growth in GDP reduces problems posed by deficits and debt service.

Two Ways GDP Growth Reduces Problems Posed by Deficits

GDP can grow either because there's *real* growth or because there's *inflationary* growth. Both types of growth play major roles in economists' assessment of deficits. So we must consider how both types of GDP growth affect deficits and debt.

Real Growth and the Deficit   When a society experiences real growth, it becomes richer, and, being richer, it can handle more debt. Real growth in the United States has averaged about 2.5 percent per year, which means that U.S. debt can grow at a rate of 2.5 percent without increasing the debt/GDP ratio. But for debt to grow, government must run a deficit, so a constant debt/GDP ratio in a growing economy is consistent with a continual deficit. How much of a deficit are we talking about? U.S. federal government debt is about $3.6 trillion and GDP is about $6 trillion, so the government debt/GDP ratio is about 60 percent. A real growth rate of 2.5 percent means that real GDP is growing at about $150 billion per year. That means that government can run a deficit of $90 billion a year without increasing the debt/GDP ratio:

$$60\% \times \$150 \text{ billion} = \$90 \text{ billion.}$$

Of course, for those who believe that total U.S. government debt is already too large relative to GDP, this argument (that the debt/GDP ratio is remaining constant) is unsatisfying. They'd prefer the debt/GDP ratio to fall.

Is the current U.S. debt/GDP ratio too high? That's a difficult question. The United States can afford its current debt, in the sense that it can afford to pay the interest on that debt. In fact, it could afford a much higher debt/GDP ratio since U.S. government bonds are still considered one of the safest assets in the world. No one is worried about the U.S. government defaulting. So technically the current debt can be handled and can probably be increased by trillions of dollars without problem. But, of course, that debt requires interest to be paid on it. In

1992 the U.S. government paid out approximately $200 billion in interest. A larger debt would require even higher interest payments. The $200 billion in interest payment is government revenue that can't be spent on defense or welfare; it's a payment for past expenditures. Ultimately the interest payments are the burden of the debt. That's what people mean when they say a deficit is burdening future generations. That burden is the interest payments future generations will have to make to the holders of U.S. debt.[4]

Summarizing: Real growth makes it possible for a country to run a deficit without increasing the debt/GDP ratio. Since that ratio is a key ratio for judging economists' concern about debt, real growth lessens concern about the deficit.

We now turn to inflation's effect on deficits and debt.

Inflation, Debt, and the Real Deficit   Inflation's subtle effect on deficits and debt requires careful consideration. The first key point is that *inflation wipes out debt*. How much does it wipe out? Consider an example. Say a country has a $2 trillion debt and inflation is 4 percent per year. That means that the real value of all assets denominated in dollars is declining by 4 percent each year. If you had $100 and there's 4 percent inflation in a year, that $100 will be worth 4 percent less at the end of the year—the equivalent of $96 had there been no inflation. By the same reasoning, when there's inflation the value of the debt is declining 4 percent each year. Four percent of $2 trillion is $80 billion, so with an outstanding debt of $2 trillion, 4 percent inflation will eliminate $80 billion of the debt each year.

The larger the debt and the larger the inflation, the more debt will be eliminated with inflation. For example, with 10 percent inflation and a $2 trillion debt, $200 billion of the debt will be eliminated by inflation each year. With 4 percent inflation and a $4 trillion debt, $160 billion of the debt will be eliminated.

If inflation is wiping out debt, and the deficit is equal to the increases in debt from one year to the next, inflation also affects the deficit. Economists take this into account by defining two types of deficits: a nominal deficit and a real deficit.

A **nominal deficit** is the deficit determined by looking at the difference between expenditures and receipts. It's what most people think of when they think of the budget deficit; it is the value that is generally reported.

A **real deficit** is the nominal deficit adjusted for inflation's effect on the debt. It is the nominal deficit *minus* the decrease in the value of the government's total outstanding debts due to inflation. Thus, to calculate the *real* deficit one must know the nominal deficit, the rate of inflation, and the total outstanding government debt. Let's consider some examples.

In our first example, assume:

Nominal deficit = $100 billion
Inflation = 4%
Total debt = $2 trillion.

The definition of *real deficit* states:

Real deficit = Nominal deficit − (Inflation × Total debt).

Substituting in the numbers gives us

Real deficit = $100 billion − (4% × $2 trillion)
= $100 billion − $80 billion
= $20 billion.

Nominal deficit The deficit determined by looking at the difference between expenditures and receipts.

Real deficit The nominal deficit adjusted for inflation's effect on the debt.

Real deficit = Nominal deficit − (Inflation × Total debt).

[4] This statement about the burden of the debt doesn't contradict my earlier statement that government's internal debt doesn't directly decrease income in a country. With internal debt, those interest payments are paid to someone in the country. Thus, the burden of the debt isn't the loss of income to society. The burden is the prior commitment of government revenue to paying interest on government bonds. If collecting those tax revenues necessary to pay off bond holders has negative incentive effects and reduces income, then the debt indirectly lowers income in the economy.

Though the nominal deficit is $100 billion, the real deficit is only $20 billion.

In our second example, assume:

Nominal deficit = $100 billion
Inflation = 10%
Total debt = $2 trillion.

The only change from the first example is the inflation rate. But look what happens to the real deficit.

$$\text{Real deficit} = \$100 \text{ billion} - (10\% \times \$2 \text{ trillion})$$
$$= \$100 \text{ billion} - \$200 \text{ billion}$$
$$= -\$100 \text{ billion}.$$

In this case, the country is not running a real deficit. After adjusting for inflation the $100 billion nominal deficit becomes a $-$100 billion deficit (a $100 billion real surplus)!

In our third example, assume:

Nominal deficit = $100 billion
Inflation = 4%
Total debt = $4 trillion.

In this example we've changed both the inflation rate and the amount of total debt. Now see what happens:

$$\text{Real deficit} = \$100 \text{ billion} - (4\% \times \$4 \text{ trillion}) = -\$60 \text{ billion}.$$

The $100 billion deficit becomes a $60 billion surplus. As you can see, the real deficit can differ significantly from the nominal deficit.

Inflation, Debt, and Deficits   This distinction between the nominal deficit and the real deficit is not an illusion. Inflation wipes out debt, and that fact must be considered when evaluating the effect of a deficit. Inflation is an important reason why the U.S. debt/GDP ratio declined in the postwar period. When inflation increases, the debt/GDP ratio can decrease even when the nominal deficit is large.

You may be somewhat hesitant to accept the preceding argument about how inflation eliminates debt and can change a nominal deficit into a real surplus. The first time I was presented with the argument, I was dubious. Somehow, inflation as a way of reducing debt's burden sounds too good to be true. If you are hesitant, it's with good reason. While the argument that inflation wipes out debt is correct, your fears are not groundless. Inflation is not a costless answer to eliminating debt.

To see that it isn't, let's carefully consider how inflation eliminates the debt. Say you bought U.S. bonds having a 4 percent annual interest rate with the expectation that the price level would remain constant. That's not a bad return; in each year you expect $4 for each $100 you loaned the government, and as each bond matures you expect to get $100 back. Now let's say that inflation is 6 percent per year. For each year of the loan the dollars with which the government pays you back are worth 6 percent less than the dollars you loaned the government, so instead of getting 4 percent more, you're losing 2 percent—the 4 percent interest you get minus the 6 percent inflation.

For you (the holder of debt) inflation isn't a costless way to eliminate a debt. It's very costly to creditors, who lose what the government gains. The government's gain from an inflation is the bond holder's loss from inflation. So the effect of inflation on debt is no illusion; it is simply a transfer of money from bond holders to the government.

Nominal and Real Interest Rates and Deficits   Such transfers of income do not make bond holders (creditors) very happy. Yes, the government's real debt is being reduced by inflation, but it's being reduced by bond holders' losses. And bond holders aren't helpless people. What can they do about it? For the fixed interest rate bonds they already hold, they can do nothing. When they bought the bonds, the contract was set. But they can do something about future bonds. The next time a bond salesman suggests buying government bonds, purchasers will likely take any expected inflation into account. Instead of buying a bond with a 4 percent interest rate, they won't buy a bond unless it offers, say, 10 percent interest—4 percent real interest and 6 percent to compensate them for the 6 percent expected inflation.

Expectations of inflation push up the nominal interest rate and cause bond holders to demand an inflation premium on their bonds. Expected future inflation causes the real interest rate to be different from the nominal interest rate. Thus, in the absence of inflation the nominal interest rate might be 4 percent. With 6 percent inflation, the nominal interest rate might be 10 percent: 4 percent real interest rate plus 6 percent expected inflation.

If the nominal interest rate is 6 percent higher than the real interest rate, bond holders have fully adjusted their 6 percent expectations of inflation into their bond purchases. In this case they won't lose if there's 6 percent inflation. Bond holders do not lose when they expect inflation and build that expectation into their financial dealings. But if bond holders don't lose when they expect inflation and make a full adjustment for it, government can't win.

To see that with full interest rate adjustment for inflation, creditors don't lose, it is helpful to divide the government's deficit into two components: a spending-on-current-needs component and a debt service component.

Let's say the government has a total debt of $2 trillion, total expenditures of $500 billion, and a nominal deficit of $100 billion. Let's also assume that initially there's no expected inflation. Because there's no expected inflation, the 4 percent nominal interest rate will also be the real interest rate and the nominal deficit will equal the real deficit. This means that the government is paying $80 billion a year in interest ($2 trillion debt × 4 percent interest). The debt service component of the deficit is $80 billion, leaving $420 billion to finance spending on current needs.

Now assume that there's a 6 percent inflation but the interest rate remains 4 percent. That 6 percent inflation decreases real debt by $120 billion (6 percent × $2 trillion). Using the real deficit formula, you can calculate that the government is actually running a real surplus of $20 billion:

$$\text{Real deficit} = \$100 \text{ billion} - (6\% \times \$2 \text{ trillion})$$
$$= \$100 \text{ billion} - \$120 \text{ billion}$$
$$= -\$20 \text{ billion}.$$

But what happens if the 6 percent inflation were fully expected? In that case, the nominal interest rate on the debt, assuming it's all short term, will rise from 4 to 10 percent to account for the expected inflation. Debt service will be $200 billion (10 percent × $2 trillion), $120 billion more than government would have had to pay had there been no inflation adjustment to the interest rate. That $120 billion increase in the debt service expenditures just equals the $120 billion that the inflation wiped out.

This $120 billion increase in the debt service component of the deficit decreases the $420 billion current-spending component of the budget to $300 billion. So when nominal interest rates go up, simply in order to maintain the nominal deficit at its current level government must either reduce spending on current needs or it must raise taxes and collect more in revenues. It's paying extra interest to bond holders to compensate them for their loss.

This distinction between nominal and real is necessary to make a judgment about a given nominal deficit. When there's high expected inflation and a large debt, much of the nominal deficit is a debt service component which is simply offsetting the decrease in the debt that the inflation is bringing about.

This insight into debt is directly relevant to the budget situation in the United States. For example, back in 1990 the nominal U.S. deficit was about $220 billion

With Full Adjustment in Expectations, Creditors Don't Lose

ere's a proposal that some economists have suggested could significantly reduce the nominal U.S. deficit. Currently most bonds are fixed-interest bonds. They pay back a stated number of dollars in a given period. For example, at 10 percent interest a $1,000 five-year bond pays $100 interest each year for five years, and pays back another $1,000 at the end of five years.

Some economists have proposed the following: make the amount that is to be paid back, the $1,000, indexed to inflation. Thus, if price level rises 40 percent, the amount paid back would be $1,400 rather than $1,000. Bonds that pay back an amount dependent on inflation are called *indexed bonds*.

Let's now ask: What would happen if the United States were to issue indexed bonds? Since bond holders are compensated for inflation, the interest on bonds would fall. If 5 percent inflation were the expected rate and the nominal interest rate were 7 percent, the real interest rate would be 2 percent—so the interest rate on bonds would be 2 instead of 7 percent, U.S. debt service would fall from about $200 billion to between $50 billion and $60 billion, and the measured U.S. deficit would decrease significantly.

Most economists oppose having the government issue indexed bonds. Yes, they agree, it would lower the measured deficit, but it would not change real U.S. debt. At the same time, indexing would introduce new complexities of government finance as the inflation index came under even more scrutiny because so much money would be riding on it.

Whether or not you favor the proposal, it is a superb proposal from an academic perspective. It helps us recognize the difference between real and nominal deficits.

while the real deficit was $60 billion. But that low real deficit was not costless to the government. When inflationary expectations were much lower, as they were in the 1950s, government paid 3 or 4 percent on its bonds. In 1990 it paid 8 or 9 percent, which is about 5 percent more than it paid in the 1950s. With its $2.75 trillion debt, the United States was paying about $140 billion more in interest than it would have had to pay if no inflation had been expected and the nominal interest rate had been 3 rather than 8 percent. That reduced the amount it could spend on current services by $140 billion. This means that much of the 1990 nominal U.S. deficit existed because of the rise in debt service necessary to compensate bond holders for the expected inflation.

Summary to This Point

We've covered a lot of material, so before we move on let's review four important points:

1. Deficits are summary measures of the state of the economy. They are dependent on the accounting procedures used.
2. It is the financial health of the economy, not the deficit, that we should be concerned with.
3. Deficits and debt should be viewed relative to GDP to determine their importance.
4. The real deficit is the nominal deficit adjusted for the inflation reduction in the real debt:

Real deficit = Nominal deficit − (Expected inflation × Debt).

Some Reasons for Concern about the U.S. Government Budget Deficit

Considering real deficits rather than nominal deficits and viewing the deficit and debt relative to GDP should have lessened your concern about the size of the U.S. deficit. Given inflation, the real deficit is lower than the nominal deficit, and given real growth we can stand an increase in total debt without the burden becoming intolerable.

But, as with most issues in economics, we must think about "on the other hand." The most important "on the other hand" concerns how future commitments are calculated in the U.S. budget and the accounting gimmicks used to make the nominal deficit seem low. To see how these work, let's consider the accounting system used by the U.S. government budget.

The U.S. Budget Does Not Include Many Government Obligations   The U.S. government uses a **cash flow accounting system.** When it spends or collects money, these outflows or inflows show up on the budget. When the government doesn't have a cash inflow or outflow, nothing shows up on the budget. This cash flow accounting system leads to a number of important aspects of the budget and the deficit.

First, a number of obligations government incurs do not show up as part of the deficit. One such obligation is federal loan guarantees, such as guarantees on student loans, pensions, and deposits in banks. Since no cash is spent when these guarantees are made, they don't show up as an expenditure.

Just how important these can be became apparent in 1989 when numerous savings and loan associations went bankrupt and the Federal Savings and Loan Insurance Corporation (FSLIC, the organization that guarantees S&L deposits) was called upon to meet its obligation. The cost to government will likely be well over $300 billion—all from off-budget obligations that never showed up in the government budget when they were incurred! So here we have a case of government incurring a huge obligation that never showed up as an expense at the time it was incurred.

The FSLIC doesn't have the United States's only outstanding obligation that doesn't appear in the budget. There are also obligations of the FDIC (Federal Deposit Insurance Corporation), a government organization that guarantees bank deposits, Penny Benny (Pension Benefit Guarantee Corporation), a government organization that guarantees pension payments by firms through pension benefits insurance, and others. Through these programs the U.S. government has guaranteed trillions of dollars of obligations out there, meaning that even if it had a real deficit of zero, its overall financial health might still be questionable.

The Government Uses Accounting Tricks to Make the Deficit Look Smaller   Of even more concern is the way in which the U.S. government met its obligation to bail out the savings and loan corporations. What it did not do is admit to the obligation and enter it into the books as an expense. Entering the S&L bailout on the books would have increased the nominal deficit and made it look as if the government weren't reducing the deficit—but the government was committed to reducing the deficit.

Instead the government increased insurance fees on savings and loans institutions slightly and counted those fees as additional current revenue. These fees were no way near enough to cover the cost of the S&L bailout. To cover most of the costs, the government sold special bonds. But these expenditures were *not* counted as expenditures so they didn't increase the deficit in 1989 or 1990. Instead they were called **off-budget expenditures** (expenditures of money that are not to be counted as expenditures in the budget).

So here's what happened with the S&L bailout. The fees increased current revenues; the expenditures weren't entered on the books. As it worked out, incurring a multibillion obligation in 1989 *lowered* the measured budget deficit for 1989!

Were this FSLIC action an isolated incident, it could be shaken off. It's much like failing a quiz: It might be no problem if the reason you failed the quiz was that your child or your father was sick that day: not to worry, because it was an isolated incident. But if you failed a quiz because you did no studying, failing is much more important. It suggests that unless you start studying you will likely fail all your other quizzes. The FSLIC fiasco was the government equivalent to not studying.

The U.S. government has often dealt with its budgetary problems with gimmicks to make the deficit look smaller than it is. Thus, many economists argue that the government has serious financial health problems that are hidden by the accounting procedures it uses. And it has those problems even if its real deficit is zero or in surplus.

Cash flow accounting system An accounting system entering expenses and revenues only when cash is received or paid out.

Off-budget expenditure An expenditure that is not counted in the budget as an expenditure.

The Social Security Retirement System

Let's consider the old-age retirement portion of the social security system as another example of how the government's financial health may be questionable even when its budget is not in deficit. According to some observers, that system has a built-in financial problem that will likely explode some time about the year 2020.

Funded pension system One in which money is collected and invested in a special fund from which payments are made.

Unfunded pension system One in which pensions are paid from current revenues.

Funded and Unfunded Retirement Systems   Pension systems can be either funded or unfunded. A **funded pension system** is one in which money is collected and invested in a special fund from which pension payments are made. An **unfunded pension system** is one in which pensions are paid from current revenues.

The social security system, which provides pensions for a large majority of the U.S. population, is largely an *unfunded* pension system. Until recently most of the social security taxes that the government collected as part of that pension system were not invested in a special fund to be used to pay out benefits when the person retires or otherwise becomes eligible to receive benefits. Instead to a large degree the government paid social security benefits from current tax revenue.

An unfunded pension system is not necessarily unsound. In an ongoing system there will always be revenue coming in and payments going out. There are always current workers around to support a system that pays the aged. The benefit of the unfunded system is that it allows the system initially to pay out more than people have paid in. The problem with an unfunded system is that there's no trust fund of assets earning interest to cover future payments.

A Potential Problem with Unfunded Systems   As long as the population's age distribution, the annual death rate, and the number of people working do not change much, an unfunded system presents no problem. But an unfunded system does present a potential problem if the amount paid in and the amount paid out fluctuate.

To see this, say we have only three groups of people: workers, the retired elderly, and the very young (who aren't yet working). Now suddenly we start a pension program. We use the money that we collect from the workers to pay pensions to the elderly retired people. This group of elderly people have paid nothing in, because they retired before the system started up. In short, this group gets benefits without having paid anything into the system. In the next generation, the elderly die, the workers become elderly, and the young become workers. The new group of elderly get paid by the new workers. As long as the three groups remain at equivalent relative sizes, the process works neatly—each generation will get paid when its time comes.

But let's consider what happens when there's a "baby boom" and one group suddenly has a large number of children in a short period of time. In this case, the sizes of the generations are no longer equal. Initially things work out well. The baby boom young become workers, and there are lots of them relative to the elderly. There's plenty of money coming in and comparatively little going out. This allows for an increase in payments to the elderly, or a decrease in the taxes paid by the working group, or both.

But what happens in the next generation when the baby boom workers become elderly? Then, assuming the baby boomers have a "normal" number of children, rather than the larger numbers of children their own parents had, the number of people collecting benefits becomes larger but the number of workers contributing to the system becomes smaller. In this case, payments per person must decrease, contributions coming in per worker must increase, or some combination of the two must occur. None of these alternatives is particularly pleasant.

This example doesn't come out of nowhere. It represents the current situation in the U.S. social security system. From 1946 through the late 1960s there was a baby boom, and these baby boomers are currently in the labor force. They'll start retiring in large numbers in the early 2000s and when they do, the number of workers per retiree will decrease dramatically, so that in 2020 there will be about

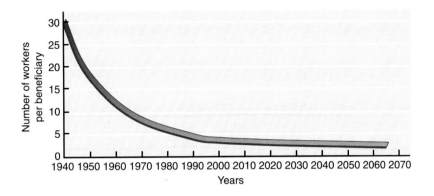

EXHIBIT 4   Projection of Workers Compared with Social Security Retirees

The number of workers per retiree declined considerably from 1940 to 1990, and it will continue to decline until about 2010.This will be the "crunch" period for social security.
Source: Social Security Administration.

2.5 workers per retiree instead of more than 15 workers per retiree as in the 1950s and 1960s. Exhibit 4 shows these unpleasant projections.

There are a number of ways to avoid these unpleasant alternatives. One way is to partially fund the system. With a partially funded pension system, some of the money paid in by the baby boom generation is put in a trust fund (when the proportion of workers to elderly is high). That trust fund and the interest it earns is used to pay part of the benefits of the elderly when the proportion of workers to elderly is low.

A second way is to vary the retirement age so that a large group of workers retires later and a small group of workers retires earlier. After age 65, people in each age group die off faster than people in younger age groups. This means that if the retirement age were raised, there would be fewer people to collect benefits than there are when the retirement age is 65. This higher retirement age would help keep the ratio of workers to elderly roughly equal, again eliminating the mismatch of revenue coming in with payments going out.

Social Security and the Budget Deficit   In the 1970s and 1980s economists pointed out that this problem would be occurring. In response the government made a number of changes. The retirement age was moved up slightly and, most important, there was a large increase in the rate of social security or FICA (Federal Insurance Contribution Act) contributions. This tax increase was to create a large trust fund that would provide significant budget surpluses in the 1980s and 1990s. These surpluses could be used to make the payments coming due in the 2000s without requiring huge tax increases or massive borrowing at that future time. Thus, in 1990, $70 billion more in social security taxes was collected than was paid out. Therefore it seems as if the supplemental trust fund solution is the one the government is following.

Unfortunately that tax increase is not resulting in government surpluses. Instead the government is running large current deficits, so it is financing the trust fund with government bonds (promises to pay). (The only asset the trust fund is allowed to hold is government bonds.) But the social security system has already promised to pay anyway. So the only difference the trust fund makes is that with the "trust fund" the government has issued pieces of paper (bonds) as backing for that promise.

An Alternative   Let's look at another possible solution to the social security problem. Say that the retirement age at which people become eligible to receive social security payments were raised in increments so that in 2010 the retirement age at which they could get full benefits would be 70. (It's now about 65.)[5] Then say that

---

[5] Government pension systems were started by the 19th-century German leader Otto von Bismarck. He reportedly chose 65 as the retirement age because his advisors told him that vital statistics for the country showed most people died before age 65.

the current social security tax rates were lowered 10 percent. This combination of policies would increase the current budget deficit, but would significantly improve the U.S. financial picture because future commitments would have been so significantly lowered that there would be no need to collect as much current social security tax revenue. So here's a case in which the deficit would increase, but the United States would be in better financial shape.

THE DEFICIT DEBATE:
WOLVES, PUSSYCATS,
OR TERMITES   **6**

Charles Schultze—Chairman of the
Council of Economic Advisers under
President Carter. *UPI/Bettmann.*

Three Alternative Views
of the Deficit

The accounting used in the social security system is only one of the U.S. government's many problem accounting areas. That's why economists emphasize that it's the financial health of the economy that's important, not the deficit. But economists also recognize that the measured deficit will be at the center of the debate about government spending and taxes, so they take positions on the deficit and its meaning to the economy.

Charles Schultze (chairman of the Council of Economic Advisers in the Carter administration and currently an economist at the Brookings Institution) has divided economists' views about the deficit and its relationship to the economy's financial health into three groups:

1. The wolf-at-the-door group, who believe the deficit will bring about imminent doom.
2. The domesticated-pussycat group, who believe the deficit doesn't matter.
3. The termites-in-the-basement group, who believe the deficit will cause serious problems in the long run.

Few economists belong to the wolf-at-the-door group. A small but vocal group of economists comprise the domesticated pussycats. They include both liberal Keynesian economists who feel the economy needs more expansion and conservative Classical economists who believe deficits don't influence behavior and hence make no difference to the real economy. The largest group of economists belong to the termites-in-the-basement group.

Three alternative views about the deficit are demonstrated in an exchange between William Proxmire, Robert Eisner, Robert Solow, and Franco Modigliani. Proxmire is a retired politician. Eisner, Solow, and Modigliani are well-known economists.

'WIZARDS' SAY FORGET THE
DEFICIT—DON'T LISTEN

William Proxmire
U.S. Senator
Washington, D.C.

Now some eminent economists are telling Congress and the administration to forget the deficit and the $2.6 trillion national debt. These objects of our deepest concern don't matter, they say. When people of the stature of Robert Eisner, a former president of the American Economic Association, whisper these seductive words, it's going to be hard for members of Congress to resist. And when the view is echoed by such Wall Street wizards as John Gutfreund and Peter

Bernstein, it's like a teen-ager being told by her revered family doctor that smoking doesn't really threaten her health—it might even relax her and ease tensions.

After more than 30 years in the Senate, I cannot think of a more alluring or dangerous philosophy for a member of Congress than the economic gospel according to Mr. Eisner. How irresistible it would be if a congressman could justify voting for increased spending and cutting taxes because it's good, hard economic sense.

The two most painful actions a member of Congress can take are first, a vote to cut popular spending programs and, second—and even more painful—a vote to increase

taxes. But if these economic and Wall Street gurus are right, every day of a congressman's service in this debt-ridden government can be Christmas. A few years ago the so-called supply-side economists promised that a cut in taxes, even without a corresponding reduction in spending, would permit the country to grow its way out of deficits and debt. A trillion and a half dollars of additional national debt has made the supply siders a laugh.

Now we're told by Mr. Eisner that the $155 billion deficit for 1988 is a mirage. In the Eisner view, expenditures on roads, aircraft carriers and fighter planes are not really spending. They're investments. Mr. Eisner claims that when we include state and local surpluses, and then allow for inflation, the government at all levels is running an Eisner surplus. Mr. Eisner computes that surplus at $42 billion for 1988. Right now, in his view, Congress isn't spending enough—it's taxing too much. According to him, this surplus is a serious drag on the economy. So come on Congress, spend more. Tax less. The deficit is not big enough. It's not even a deficit.

What's wrong with this Eisner analysis? Plenty. First, buying a highway or a warship is indeed an investment. It's also something else. It's a cost. When this kind of investment is made with borrowed money, it can be an exacting and painful cost.

Here's "an investment" that rarely pays a tangible cash return to the government. Take the federal government's biggest spender, the military: 85% of its expenditure is for military personnel, including retired pay, operations and maintenance, and procurement. None of these expenditures yield a penny of return to the government. In fact, military procurement, far from being an investment representing a source of future income, creates an "asset"—an aircraft carrier, for example, that will, once constructed, cost tens of billions of dollars to operate throughout its useful life in addition to its original cost. Some investment.

Overwhelmingly, government "investment" is of the same "wasting-asset" kind. Yes indeed, government expenditures may constitute useful services, often services to be consumed for years to come. During those years the government that borrows to "buy" the investment—the building or highway—must pay interest on its borrowing. It must maintain and operate its public asset.

As time goes on, the government must rehabilitate or replace the public asset or terminate the service it provides. Certainly the present government accounting system of counting all expenditures as outlay without offsetting credit for their future value is crude. But it is also roughly accurate and fair. This follows because every year Americans live off past government "investments" as well as buy "investments" that provide government services for the future. One could argue that, by failing to maintain the pace of highway building and other capital construction, recent congresses have been accumulating bigger deficits than reported. On this basis, I could as easily contend that the true federal deficit is $300 billion for 1988 as Mr. Eisner can argue that it is not a deficit at all, but a surplus.

The simplest, most obvious evidence that the federal government is living beyond its means is the colossal new burden of an immensely expanded national debt that now commands $155 billion a year in interest. That interest is both the fastest growing cost of government and the one cost that must be paid on time, in full. Interest and interest alone can not be cut, stretched out or reduced. It is a grim, unavoidable reminder of debt that all the sophistries of the brightest on Wall Street and academia cannot diminish.

The Eisner argument should be very appealing to your 19-year-old son who wants you to buy him a $30,000 Porsche. His pitch to you goes like this: "We're not really and truly going into debt when we spring for this Porsche. This isn't debt. This is an investment. Look, we can finance it over five years. You'll pay only about $45,000 total. I know you think I'm nuts, Dad, but this is the way the former president of the American Economic Association and the brightest guys on Wall Street see it. So how about it, Daddio? Let's get with it."

The Wall Street Journal, September 7, 1989. Reprinted by permission of THE WALL STREET JOURNAL © 1989 Dow Jones & Company, Inc. All rights reserved worldwide.

DEFICIT ISN'T TOO TAXING

Robert Eisner
Professor of Economics
Northwestern University
Evanston, Ill.

Re William Proxmire's Feb. 3 editorial-page article " 'Wizards' Say Forget the Deficit—Don't Listen": Despite his alarm, deficits—at least as they are conventionally measured—may not be bad for the economy. Mr. Proxmire taxes me—forgive the expression—for pointing out that by meaningful measure the official 1988 budget deficit of $155 billion was actually a real surplus of $42 billion. The calculations, though, are simple and illuminating.

- Apply standard business accounting practices to the federal budget and include as expenses or costs only the depreciation of capital, not capital expenditures. Substituting a reasonable estimate of depreciation for the more than $200 billion of federal investment spending (Office of Management and Budget estimate) would knock some $70 billion off the deficit, reducing it to $85 billion.
- Recognize that deficits are significant because they add to debt but what matters then is the real debt, adjusted for inflation. With inflation running at 3.6%, there was an "inflation tax" of some $72 billion on the $2 trillion of Treasury debt held by the public. Counting this inflation tax reduces the deficit to $13 billion.
- In terms of impact on the economy, we are interested in all of government, not just Washington. State and local governments over the past fiscal year ran a surplus of some $55 billion—not unrelated to $108 billion of federal grants in aid that amounted to more than two-thirds of the official federal deficit. If we add the plus $55 billion to the minus $13 billion we reach that real government budget surplus of $42 billion.

The critical issue—however we measure the budget—is what it does to the economy. Republicans since the days of Franklin D. Roosevelt have been denouncing Democratic budget deficits. Democrats have tried to have a field day denouncing the Reagan deficits that began in 1982. (They are in fact now much less, running some 3% of gross national product while they were more than 6% of GNP a few years ago.) Few politicians have been inspired to face the facts.

Despite recent record deficits, the sky has not fallen. Rather, the economy moved from deep recession and 10.7% unemployment to more than six years of sustained recovery. Unemployment fell by half. Corporate profits and the stock market soared. Business investment grew smartly.

All this indeed occurred not in spite of the budget deficits but in large part because of them. Government spending in excess of what it took from the public in taxes fueled aggregate demand, private and public, so that we were able to purchase more and more of what our productive economy could offer.

This is not to argue, contrary to Mr. Proxmire's charge, that there should be no limit to deficits. They can be too large if they bring us to the point where we are trying to buy more than can possibly be produced, a point that, despite our relative prosperity, we have hardly yet reached. And this is not to argue for wasteful government spending—or any other kind of wasteful spending. It makes a difference whether a person borrows to finance a gambling binge in Las Vegas or to buy a house or pay for his child's education. It makes a dif-

ference whether a firm borrows to finance productive capital expenditures or frivolous extravagance.

It is vitally important that in addition to maintaining current prosperity—it hardly makes sense to slow down the economy now because it might slow down later—we invest adequately in the future. I see no reason to second-guess household and business decisions on how much to save and invest as long as the economy is prosperous. But by far the greatest portion of investment in the future is by its nature public. Private productivity and our future well-being depend critically on public investment in human capital—in education, training and health, in basic research, in our vast tangible infrastructure of roads, bridges and airports, and in the protection of natural resources of land, water and air.

This is where Mr. Proxmire's counsel and all the near-hysteria about our mismeasured budget deficits, can lead us seriously astray. Our 13-year-olds score last in international comparisons on tests of math and science ability. Much of a generation grows up semiliterate or illiterate and crazed by drugs. Workers spend hours on choked highways and busi-

ness travelers spend hours waiting for clearance to land at or fly to our congested airports.

Yet our "education president" is told that there is little or no more money to be invested in education, that the war to end the scourge of drugs will have to be fought on a shoestring, that there is virtually no room for new expenditures of any kind because "the deficit" must be brought down to some arbitrary target.

I am not telling "Daddio" to borrow to buy his 19-year-old son a $30,000 Porsche—although something that will give service for five years is properly considered an investment. But worthwhile public investment does have a payoff to the economy in higher productivity and national income. And indeed out of this higher income flows increased government revenues, even if Mr. Bush keeps that famous pledge to lip readers.

Who's Right?

The Proxmire letter is typical of many intelligent lay people's view of the deficit. Proxmire attacks the adjustments that almost all economists believe should be made to the deficit. He represents the wolf-at-the-door view, which few economists endorse.

Eisner's response represents the domesticated-pussycat view held primarily by liberal Keynesian economists (of whom Eisner is one) and conservative supply-side and Classical economists, although their reasons for holding that view are quite different from those of liberal Keynesians. Liberal Keynesians believe that it is important to stimulate the economy by running a deficit. As long as the economy needs stimulation, deficits don't matter. Supply-side economists and Classical economists who fall into this group of domesticated pussycats believe that deficits don't influence the economy, period: Since people are rational and fully discount expected future tax payments that the deficit would entail, deficits make no difference to the economy.

The termites-in-the-basement view in the Solow/Modigliani letter represents the ideas of the majority of economists. They see the deficit gnawing away at the structure of the economy. They agree that the deficit per se doesn't matter, but they believe that the economy's underlying health isn't good and that it needs to be treated. Superficial cover-up work that makes the deficit look smaller, but doesn't deal with the underlying health problems, won't treat the disease.

William Proxmire—Former senator from Wisconsin who chaired the Senate Budget Committee. *UPI/Bettmann.*

CUTTING DEFICIT IS OUR ONLY ACCEPTABLE COURSE

Franco Modigliani
Robert Solow
Professors of Economics
M.I.T., Cambridge, Mass.

To the Editor:

It is unfortunate that Prof. Robert Eisner, whose contributions have made him a leading member of the economics profession, has now chosen to devote much of his attention to a contrary campaign in favor of more government expenditure and bigger deficits. Does he have a point?

Many of the arguments in "Let's Stop Worrying About the Budget Deficit" (letter, Feb. 19) are perfectly acceptable; for example, his assertion that any expenditure that primarily benefits future generations might be paid out of deficits without damaging them. The same goes for his assertion that the deficit, as measured in the budget, has numerous shortcomings. He calls attention to some that go in the direction of exaggerating the deficit (though one could argue with his specific corrections).

But he fails to mention others going in the opposite direction. Of these the most conspicuous is the treatment of Social Security; as a pension system it should not be included in the budget. It is running a surplus of some $50 billion (which should be devoted to capital formation to meet the coming bulge in the population of old relative to young). Hence, if Social Security were properly taken out of the budget, the deficit would be $50 billion larger.

But his argument is faulty on other grounds. The first is his concern that reducing the deficit at this time is likely "to slow the economy and hence bring less investment." This preoccupation must be regarded as entirely misplaced under conditions of high demand pressure and high interest rates.

Even more serious is Mr. Eisner's failure to come to grips with the fact that, since the beginning of the huge fiscal deficits in 1982, national savings (inclusive of durable goods accumulation) have plummeted from a comparatively low level of around 10 percent in the 1960's and 70's to a distressingly low one of around 5 percent in recent years. Though net national saving may not be exactly measured, there is no ground to doubt the trend. Only the large increase in capital imports (the trade deficit) has made it possible nearly to maintain the level of investment.

Professor Eisner seems to agree about some proper concern over our presumed growing debt to the rest of the world. But what he fails to realize is that none of his proposed solutions will reduce the trade deficit, unless we free resources to be used for more net exports. This requires that we either cut the deficit or cut investment. Failure to do so under conditions of full, if not overfull, employment would threaten to overload the economy, courting the risk of serious inflation.

Most thoughtful people agree that cutting investment is the last thing we should consider, and no one in his right mind thinks we should push output at the risk of inflation. This leaves cutting the deficit as the only acceptable option.

Reprinted by courtesy of Franco Modigliani and Robert Solow from a letter in the *New York Times* of March 12, 1989.

KEY POINTS

- A deficit is a shortfall of incoming revenues over outgoing payments; debt is accumulated deficits. **1**
- The deficit is a summary measure of a budget. Whether a deficit is a problem depends on the budgeting procedures that measure it. **2**
- A country's debt must be judged in relation to its assets. **2**
- To judge the importance of deficits and debt, economists look at them relative to GDP. **3**

- A real deficit is nominal deficit adjusted for the effect of inflation. **4**
- When expectations of inflation have fully adjusted, inflation involves no transfer from creditors to debtors. **4**
- The U.S. government often deals with its deficit problem with gimmicks. **5**
- There are various reasonable views about the U.S. budget deficit. **6**

QUESTIONS FOR THOUGHT AND REVIEW

The number after each question represents the estimated degree of critical thinking required. (1 = almost none; 10 = deep thought.)

1. Your income is $40,000 per year; your expenditures are $45,000. $10,000 of your $45,000 expenditure is for tuition. Is your budget in deficit or surplus? Why? *(6)*
2. "The deficit should be of concern." What additional information do you need to undertake a reasonable discussion of that statement? *(5)*

3. "The debt should be of concern." What additional information do you need to undertake a reasonable discussion of that statement? *(5)*
4. Inflation is 20 percent. Debt is $2 trillion. The nominal deficit is $300 billion. What is the real deficit? *(2)*
5. How would your answer to Question 4 differ if you knew that expected inflation was 15 percent? *(5)*
6. If the government were to issue inflation-adjusted bonds, the deficit would fall. Would you suggest such a policy? Why? *(6)*

7. State the arguments of the pussycat view of the deficit. *(6)*
8. State the arguments of the wolf-at-the-door view of the deficit. *(6)*
9. State the arguments of the termites-in-the-basement view of the deficit. *(6)*
10. In what sense is the social security trust fund an accounting gimmick? *(7)*

PROBLEMS AND EXERCISES

1. Calculate the real deficit in the following cases.
   a. Inflation is 10 percent. Debt is $3 trillion. Nominal deficit is $220 billion.
   b. Inflation is 2 percent. Debt is $1 trillion. Nominal deficit is $50 billion.
   c. Inflation is −4 percent. (Price level is falling.) Debt is $500 billion. Nominal deficit is $30 billion.
2. Using the latest figures available from your library, calculate the real budget deficit for the United States, Britain, France, Brazil, and Nigeria.

KEY TERMS

cash flow accounting system *(393)*
debt *(382)*
debt service *(387)*
deficit *(382)*
Deficit Reduction Act of 1990 *(383)*

external government debt *(387)*
funded pension system *(394)*
Gramm-Rudman-Hollings Act *(383)*

internal government debt *(386)*
nominal deficit *(389)*
off-budget expenditure *(393)*

policy regime *(382)*
real deficit *(389)*
unfunded pension system *(394)*

19

Macroeconomics, Social Policy, and Economic Reasoning

> *Economists are not solely that*
> *but also human beings, and their own values undoubtedly*
> *affect their economics.*
>
> Milton Friedman

After reading this chapter, you should be able to:

1

Read economic articles with a more
discerning eye.

2

Explain why nonmainstream economists
often use a less formal analysis than
mainstream economists.

3

Explain why radical economists often use a
class-oriented approach.

4

Explain why international considerations
are especially important for developing
countries.

5

Predict what will happen in the economy as
well as some economists predict.

6

Be on the lookout for positive and negative
spin in economic writing.

By now you should have a good sense of macroeconomic theory, policy, and institutions. This chapter puts that theory and knowledge to work, following some real-life events and discussing real-world articles—the type you see every day in newspapers and magazines. By considering these, not only will you get a deserved break from me, you will also get some practice in translating the economic knowledge you've gained in the classroom into the real world.

The chapter is organized around three selections of economic writing about macroeconomic events. The selections were chosen to reflect the type of reading you'll likely be doing (if I've infected you with the economic bug) once you're out of the course. After presenting the selections I consider their arguments and reasoning, showing my view of how they apply macroeconomic reasoning and how seriously they should be taken. Views about applying macroeconomic reasoning differ, even among experts, so my discussion should be seen as a jumping-off point for you or your professor to consider these, or similar, articles. Interpretation is an art, not a science.

CASE STUDY 1

Heterodox economist An economist who does not accept that the mainstream economic model is the appropriate way to analyze the economy.

Mainstream economist An economist who analyzes the world in a manner similar to that presented in this book.

Interpretation and Discussion 🔳

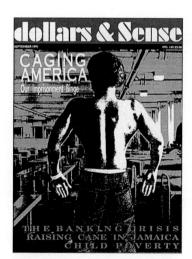

Dollars & Sense—An economic magazine that interprets current economic events from a socialist perspective.

🔳

Our first case study is an article that appeared in *Dollars & Sense,* a journal that, according to its title page, offers "interpretations of current economics from a socialist perspective." Interpreted, that means that you can expect the journal's writers to be sympathetic to a liberal or radical view and unsympathetic to a conservative view. The selection itself considers the macroeconomic policies followed by the Peruvian government in 1985 and 1986. It shows that macroeconomic principles apply not only to the U.S. economy, but to economies worldwide. Published in July 1989, it was written by a **heterodox economist** at Occidental College in California who has lived in Peru and who specializes in the Peruvian economy. A heterodox economist is one who doesn't accept the basic underlying model used by a majority of economists. Economists who do accept that model are called **mainstream economists.**

First, turn the page and read Case Study 1, "Peru's Failed Experiment." Below we'll discuss the article's perspective. Then we'll consider the content and how well the events reflect the theory you've learned.

Perspective   Although this article appeared in a socialist magazine, there's nothing necessarily socialist about it. It's a relatively objective assessment of a set of macroeconomic policies being applied to a small developing country. This objectivity reflects the author's economic training. Economists are taught to remain objective in their analyses, regardless of their political views. How objective they remain depends, of course, on where they're writing and what role they're playing. The journal in which this article appeared is designed for use in teaching. In teaching, objectivity is highly valued.

The article isn't meant to persuade you that one way of looking at the economy or some set of policies is better than another. It's meant to summarize and to provide insight into what happened. Had the author been playing a different role (say writing a platform for a political candidate or writing for a political party), his writing wouldn't have been so objective. He would have been trying to convince—to present one particular viewpoint as effectively as possible. That's why it's important to determine the author's goal when interpreting any economics article. When the goal of the writing is to sell a particular viewpoint, the economist will not necessarily be objective; the reader must supply the objectivity.

The article's objective analysis does, however, reflect a radical perspective. Unlike mainstream economists, radical economists often use a class-oriented analysis. They are much much more willing to talk about conflict between workers and capitalists and to include political and social issues in their analysis. Had I been presenting a radical macroeconomic theory in the earlier chapters rather than a mainstream economic theory, my discussion of why the economy fluctuates would have focused more on distributional fights between capitalists and

HETERODOX ECONOMICS

Throughout this book, I consistently present mainstream economic theory—the economic theory used by the majority of economists in the United States. There's much diversity of thought in mainstream economics (Keynesians and Classicals, for example), but all mainstream economists view the economy through a roughly similar set of lenses: Economic incentives are important, supply and demand forces are central to our understanding of the economy, and the market system is the best way to organize an economy.

Not all economists are mainstream. Sizable minorities called *heterodox economists* exist. They approach economics quite differently than do mainstream economists. For instance, *radical economists* (economists who don't believe the current set of market economic institutions is morally acceptable) generally view the economy as a political struggle among classes. Whereas the mainstream analysis focuses on equilibrium, the radical approach focuses on change and tensions in society. Well-known radical economists include Samuel Bowles, Herbert Gintis, and Howard Sherman. A second group of heterodox economists is *Institutionalists*. They focus much more on the role of institutions in shaping the economy than do mainstream economists. They're generally liberal in their politics. Well-known institutionalists include Marc Tool, Warren Samuels, and John Adams.

A third group of heterodox economists is *public choice advocates*. They use the mainstream supply and demand approach, but apply it much more broadly than do mainstream economists. Specifically they see government decisions as reflecting economic forces rather than attempts by government to do good. Well-known public choice economists include Gordon Tullock, James Buchanan, and Robert Tollison.

My approach to economics, while definitely mainstream, has been significantly affected by each of these three groups of heterodox economists. They've led me to consider the mainstream model critically and to incorporate social and cultural forces and influences when considering things economic. (For a further discussion of heterodox economists see Harry Landreth and David Colander, *History of Economic Theory*, Boston: Houghton Mifflin, 1989.)

workers and their different savings propensities. According to one important branch of radical theory, when profits are high, because capitalists save a large portion of their income aggregate demand will be too low, and the economy goes into a recession; then government must run a deficit to bail out the economy. Mainstream economists agree that such distributional effects exist, but they consider them too small to worry about. Mainstream economists focus on fluctuations in business investment and consumers' spending decisions, not on differences in people's marginal propensity to consume.

A second characteristic of heterodox or nonmainstream economists of all types is that their analyses tend to be less formal than mainstream analysis. *Less formal* doesn't mean better or worse. There are advantages and disadvantages to formality, but *less formal* does mean that there's more potential for ambiguity in interpretation. It's easy to say whether the logic in a formal model is right or wrong. It's much harder to say whether the logic in an informal model is right or wrong because it's often hard to see precisely what the logic is. The advantage of an informal model is that it can include many more variables and can be made more realistic, so you can talk better about the real world. Nonmainstream economists often want to talk about the real world, which is why they use informal models.

Often, after I discuss the mainstream and nonmainstream approaches, some student asks which is right. I respond with a story told by a former colleague of mine, Abba Lerner; the story goes as follows:

> "But look," the rabbi's wife remonstrated, "when one party to the dispute presented their case to you, you said, 'You are quite right,' and then when the other party presented their case you again said, 'You are quite right.' Surely they cannot both be right?" To which the Rabbi answered, "My dear, you are quite right!"

The moral of the story is that there's nothing necessarily inconsistent between radical, mainstream, and heterodox economists' approaches.[1] They are simply

---

[1] Many economists, both mainstream and heterodox, will likely object to this statement. They, like the rabbi's wife, believe that someone must be right and someone wrong. I, like the rabbi, agree with them.

CASE STUDY 1

PERU'S FAILED EXPERIMENT

Manuel Pastor

In July 1985, newly elected President Alan García initiated a dramatically different approach to the problems of debt and stabilization within Peru. Stating that "the foreign debt cannot be paid off by any of our countries," and criticizing private international bankers for their insistence on loan repayment. García announced that Peru would begin limiting debt service to 10% of export earnings. Rejecting the regressive "free market" program of the previous government, he instead tried to implement a social democratic model in which the government would reactivate the economy by increasing government spending and mandating higher wages, while leaving investment decisions in private hands.

Despite a cut-off of credit by angered international bankers, the initial results were spectacular. In 1986, inflation dropped, real wages rose, and Peru achieved the highest growth rate in the region. García was riding high. The next year, however, despite continued economic growth and further increases in the real wage, the economy began to deteriorate. Inflation doubled and the government's foreign exchange reserves plummeted, restricting the country's capacity to import. By 1988, Peru had slipped into full-blown recession and hyperinflation.

What went so right—and what went so wrong? While García-backers were quick to blame the decline on the credit boycott, the roots of García's failure lie in the social democratic model itself. His demise underlines the policy constraints facing small third world countries.

Beyond Orthodoxy

The shift in Peruvian economic policy in 1985 was part of a larger Latin American movement away from the "orthodox" economic prescriptions of the International Monetary Fund (IMF). In 1983 and 1984, virtually every debt-ridden Latin American country adopted IMF programs that required cuts in government budgets and real wages as well as currency devaluation. The results were severe: accelerating inflation, stagnant output, and falling living standards.

In late 1985 and early 1986, Argentina and Brazil began experimenting with a new set of "heterodox" economic policies. Where orthodoxy prescribed the shrinking of local economies to free up foreign exchange to repay debts, heterodoxy called for limits on debt repayment and an expansionary strategy designed to stimulate the economy into growing out of stagnation and debt. Policymakers proposed to sidestep the obvious hazard along such a path—inflation—through direct controls on wages and prices.

As in Brazil and Argentina, the rejection of orthodoxy in Peru was connected to the seeming failure of conservative economic measures. Under conservative President Fernando Belaunde Terry (1980–1985), the country suffered the effects of the global recession of the early 1980s. Between 1980 and 1983, Peru's export revenues slipped 25%, and in 1983, the country suffered a 12% plunge in real national output (GDP). With a foreign debt of $12 billion and 1982 debt service payments consuming nearly half of export earnings, the economy was squeezed.

The conservative government responded with a series of IMF programs that reduced government deficits and improved the trade balance. They also brought a doubling of the inflation rate, high unemployment, and a 40% fall in real wages between 1982 and 1985.

The Peruvian electorate overwhelmingly rejected orthodoxy in the 1985 presidential elections. Belaunde finished a distant third behind both García's American Popular Revolutionary Alliance (APRA) and a coalition of parties that stood to APRA's left. A nationalist, multi-class coalition, APRA was widely perceived at the time as the progressive middle ground between Belaunde and *Sendero Luminoso*, the "Shining Path" guerrilla group. Once in power, García adopted the new heterodox theories and brought them to the testing ground.

While García's now-famous vow to limit debt-service to 10% of export earnings attracted the most attention in the North American press, several other features of his economic program were equally important. To restrain inflation, García called for price controls, including government controls on the exchange rate. To stimulate investment, he reduced interest rates, lowering firms' borrowing costs. To revitalize local demand, he mandated increases in the minimum wage, gave substantial wage hikes in the public sector, and expanded peasant incomes through the provision of low- (and often no-) interest loans (a measure also designed to erode *Sendero's* political support in the countryside). Lastly, he increased direct government stimulation of the economy by reducing taxes and increasing subsidies.

Though many of its policies were prolabor, APRA's economic and political strategy relied on a process called *concertación:* the attempt to strike a social compact with domestic capitalists. García and his advisers believed that long-run growth could only be achieved with domestic investment, which would reduce Peru's reliance on imports and enhance its export capacity. Pessimistic about the state's ability to efficiently undertake such investment, APRA essentially allowed local capitalists to remain in control of investment.

Once in power, APRA began a dialogue with the country's largest capitalists and took a variety of measures to allay business leaders' fears of what they saw as creeping socialism. While encouraging wages to rise, García protected profit margins by lowering interest costs and freezing prices on goods provided to businesses by public enterprises such as the state-owned electric company. He also reduced public investment to expand the private sector's investment opportunities.

As an economic package, APRA's heterodox program was a fairly risky proposition. Real wage hikes and an increased government deficit were to expand demand while debt-service limits freed up sufficient foreign exchange to allow the country to import and grow. The growth would produce inflationary pressure and rising imports, draining the crucial supplies of foreign exchange. But price controls would restrain inflation in the short run, and, just in the nick of time, the *concertación* process would yield new capitalist investment, shoring up both export and domestic industries and covering the country's foreign exchange needs . . . or at least that was the plan.

Inflation Gets Hyped

The IMF, piqued by Peru's decision to stop repaying Fund loans, predicted economic disaster, but the first year of heterodoxy brought high growth, a halving of the inflation rate, a 30% rise in real wages—and a 20% increase in private investment. As expected, the government deficit rose, nearly doubling as a percentage of GDP, and the trade balance shifted from surplus to deficit due to increased imports. The import boom also depleted the government's foreign-exchange holdings, but limits on debt-service payments and stricter controls on profit repatriation by multinationals prevented an immediate foreign-exchange crisis.

While rising deficits and falling reserves were part of APRA's heterodox plan, capital flight was not. Members of the upper and middle classes, skeptical of the government's ability to control inflation, sought to protect their savings by "dollarizing"—converting *intis,* the local currency, to dollars in the free market and often shipping them to private accounts abroad. The demand for dollars drove the market value of the *inti* far below its official value, triggering fears that the government would soon devalue the official exchange rate, further accelerating inflation by increasing import costs. This fear pushed dollar demand even higher, creating an explosive, self-perpetuating inflationary cycle.

Against this backdrop of capital flight, negotiations between the government and the large capitalists dissolved in rancor. Government officials (particularly García himself) became convinced that firms were investing few of the extraordinarily high profits made in the 1986 growth boom, instead shipping their earnings abroad.

In July 1987, García took action, announcing the nationalization of the domestic banking system. The official rationale was to "democratize credit," altering the existing pattern in which large capitalists who controlled the banks gave themselves loans, neglecting the needs of smaller firms. But the real goal of the nationalization seems to have been to both curb dollar demand in the free market by forcing all exchange operations into a state-controlled financial system and to cut off credit to the large capitalists who were frustrating García during the *concertación* negotiations. The bank nationalization triggered an open war between the government and local capital, signaling the end of the APRA's multi-class alliance and marking the beginning of the slow collapse of the heterodox model.

Still, as 1987 drew to a close, economic indicators gave reason for hope. GDP grew at an impressive 6.9%, real wages posted another 10% gain, and private fixed investment increased dramatically, suggesting that private investors were behaving better than García believed when he nationalized the banking system.

But trouble loomed. Inflation had doubled, the government's deficit had increased, and the trade balance had worsened. By 1988, the economy was in shambles. The monthly inflation rate for just the month of September exceeded 100%, and real wages and GDP were falling swiftly. García's popularity slipped to all-time lows, and there was open talk of a military coup.

Looking Ahead

Surveying the ashes of what seemed such a promising program, it is tempting to lay blame at the doorstep of the international banking system. After all, international bankers responded to García's "10% limit" with a credit boycott partly intended to prevent the "Peruvian example" from gaining ground among other Latin American debtors. As a result, new long-term funds from private international lenders to Peru's public sector fell from a yearly average of over $500 million during the Belaunde years to zero, a dramatic shift for the small, Andean country.

Such a response was, of course, not surprising; banks were not likely to lend to a government making such a public splash about "banker imperialism." Anticipating the credit cutoff, Peru needed to either adjust to living from its own resources or generate more export earnings to finance necessary imports. Instead, García ignored exports and went on a growth-induced import binge, straining already weakened foreign-exchange reserves. Worst of all, García only managed to reduce debt service to around 20% of exports—no better than Belaunde's last years, when the orthodox President was able to quietly restrict debt service and maintain access to external credit.

The opportunism of Peruvian capitalists was similarly predictable. Despite García's efforts at *concertación,* local capitalists remained wary of a government that would promote high wages, challenge the IMF, and extend state control over the economy. With inflation rising and foreign dollar-accounts beckoning, local capitalists took their profits and ran, a process exacerbated by García's move to nationalize the banks.

To be sure, more technical policy mistakes also played a role in García's demise. The heterodox team probably accelerated the economy too quickly and failed to devalue the *inti* in line with the market exchange rate, both of which encouraged an excessive level of imports. While the heterodox team actually cut real government spending, collapsing tax revenues and growing losses in the state sector produced an increase in the public-sector deficit, leaving the government too cash-strapped to step up public investment when Peruvian capitalists abandoned the social democratic project.

But ultimately García's failure was not rooted in technical matters. For his social democratic model to work, he needed to both maintain access to international credit and garner the active support of capitalists and workers. The debt service limits were intended to generate "new" foreign exchange simply by reducing debt service payments. A small country like Peru, however, is too easily isolated to take such bold action. To succeed, what Peru needed was the umbrella of a region-wide debtors' cartel.

Meanwhile, García's vision of a cross-class alliance was rendered near impossible by Peru's extreme economic inequality and political polarization. The state sought to win the support of workers and peasants through higher wages and more rural credit, but did not provide them a real role in policymaking. Through *concertación,* García tried to obtain the loyalty of capitalists, offering his program as the only alternative to *Sendero* anarchy. Capitalists quickly turned against him when they saw their profits threatened by inflation, leaving the government with support from neither capitalists nor workers.

The resulting political vacuum has benefited both the right and the left, both of which hope to build momentum in the November municipal elections for the April 1990 presidential campaign. For now, the threats of a military coup have subsided, with military officers preferring to allow García's rule to die a natural death at the polls. Rightist forces, headed by ex-President Belaunde and author Mario Vargas Llosa, are proposing a rather vague retreat from state involvement in the economy. In practice, this would free limitations on big business and put the country back under the direction of the IMF.

On the left, the ex-mayor of Lima, Alfonso Barrantes, presides over a diverse and fractious coalition that spans the non-*Sendero* left and includes many parties that oppose Barrantes' relatively moderate politics but recognize that his immense personal popularity may be their key to taking power. The left's program calls for some nationalization, workers' organization into producer and consumer cooperatives, and increased public investment in agriculture, but offers few specifics on how to end hyperinflation.

Due to both the current weakness of the Peruvian state and the apparent reluctance of the Soviet Union to fund new leftist experiments in the third world, most of the Peruvian left believes that a transition to state socialism is unlikely. As a result, even a new leftist government would likely employ some market-oriented policies to politically and economically integrate local capital and reinitiate discussions with international organizations such as the World Bank and the International Monetary Fund.

This strategy, however, might produce the same social democratic contradictions that plagued the García experience. And if the left chooses to restrict debt service—as they surely will—international finance will remain limited, prolonging the current recession. Complicating matters politically are a military determined to prevent a leftist accession to power and a guerrilla insurgency equally determined to "deepen the contradictions" until the urban centers collapse.

The limited options for the Peruvian left highlight how a hostile imperialist world system and resistant local elites impose policy constraints on small, debt-ridden, third world governments. While policymakers, politicians, and academic observers attempt to absorb the lessons of García's efforts to push past these constraints, the Peruvian people are left with raging inflation, falling real wages, and the likelihood of a future marked by continuing economic and social crisis.

Manuel Pastor, DOLLARS AND SENSE, Somerville, MA, July/August 1989. Used by permission.

different ways of looking at the same event. Which approach is most useful depends on what issues and events one is analyzing. The class analysis used by radicals is often more appropriate to developing countries such as Peru than it is to the United States, and in analyzing developing countries many mainstream economists also include class fights in their approach.

4 Content Let's now move to the content. The selection considers the macroeconomic problems of Peru, a small developing country in Latin America. Peru's size significantly affects the problems it faces and the policies it can use. Notice the importance of international issues throughout the analysis. International concerns dominate in the choice of macroeconomic policies: Will the policy cause money to flow out of the country? Will the policy help Peru maintain its relationship with its international creditors? How will the policy affect imports and exchange rates? For most countries these international issues play an even larger role in determining policy than they do in the United States, although with the increasing interdependence of the U.S. economy with the world economy and its increasing international debt, the analysis in the United States is focusing more and more on international issues.

The importance of international issues can be seen in the effects of the policies followed by García's predecessor. Those contractionary (monetary and fiscal) policies, which the International Monetary Fund (IMF) required the country to follow in order to get a loan, led to high inflation, high unemployment, a 40 percent fall in real wages (money wages adjusted for changes in the price level), and an improved trade balance. The policy was called **conditionality.**

The resulting high unemployment and improved trade balance nicely fit the theory presented in the chapters on macroeconomic theory. Contractionary policies cause income to decrease and imports to fall. But how about the inflation? Why should contractionary policies cause inflation to rise? The reason is that the policy mandated by the IMF also included a large currency devaluation which significantly pushed up the price of imports. This devaluation could occur with tight monetary policy because Peru, like most developing countries, had a **nonconvertible currency**—the government rather than the market determined the exchange rate without regard to supply and demand forces. International currency movements were directly controlled by the government.

Since Peru imported a large number of the goods it consumed, this devaluation pushed up inflation in the short run and pushed down real wages. That was expected; the mainstream model accepts that such effects can occur in the short run. In the long run, however, the contractionary monetary policy should have contained the inflation. For García's predecessor, however, there was no long run. People focused on the short-run effects and voted him out of office. This long-run/short-run difference in the effect of policies is at the heart of many of the difficulties of applying standard economic policies. Often policies that help in the long run hurt in the short run. But a policy that works only in the long run may never be given a chance to work.

Now let's look at the particular macroeconomic policy followed by García in 1985. When he became president, Peru had a large international debt but a positive trade balance. It also had accelerating inflation, stagnant output, and falling living standards.

García's policies involved much stronger government control: highly expansionary monetary and fiscal policies combined with government wage and price controls and control over the exchange rate.

The wage and price controls weren't designed, however, to hold wages constant at their existing levels. They allowed one final major increase in the minimum wage and in public sector wages without a corresponding increase in allowable prices. This was likely done to maintain his political support among workers.

Raising wages while holding prices constant significantly squeezes profits, but initially the profit squeeze was prevented by reduced government taxes on businesses, increased subsidies, and a major decrease in the interest rate. The first two policies further contributed to the large government deficits; the third led to the enormously expansionary monetary policy.

There's almost no disagreement among economists of any persuasion about what the effects of such expansionary macroeconomic policy will be: large inflationary pressure which will undermine any attempts at control. The questions are: (1) When will these pent-up pressures become unmanageable? (2) Can something be done to eliminate the inflation pressure before the pressures destroy the price controls? Thus, the disagreement among economists concerns the short run, not the long run.

Notice that initially the effect of the expansionary policy was not inflation. It was an increase in real income. This is consistent with most countries' experience with expansionary macroeconomic policy. In the short run, expansionary macroeconomic policy can stimulate the aggregate economy. If accompanied by wage and price controls, it almost certainly can. And that's what happened in Peru. In the short run inflation was cut by half; real wages went up by 30 percent. The effect on the trade balance was equally predictable. The trade balance went from surplus to deficit as income rose. The reason: Imports increase as income increases. However, Peru started with a trade balance in surplus, so it had some leeway here.

Conditionality The International Monetary Fund policy of requiring contractionary monetary and fiscal policies as a condition for a loan.

Nonconvertible currency A currency whose price is determined by government decree, without regard to supply and demand forces.

Jan Tinbergen—Nobel prize, 1969, for work in statistical methods applying economic theories. © *The Nobel Foundation.*

President García's rule ended in 1990 with the Peruvian economy in a state of chaos. In the elections of 1990, a Japanese immigrant, Alberto Fujimori, was elected president. Fujimori tried to reverse García's policies and implement a set of market-oriented reforms, but was rebuffed by the legislature. In 1992, with the implicit support of the Peruvian army, he suspended the Peruvian constitution, temporarily ending democracy, in an attempt to gain the power to implement his market reforms and to eliminate terrorism. The future of the Peruvian economic and political structure remained highly uncertain and President García is in exile.

By 1988, however, the policy's long-run effects became apparent. Inflation accelerated as capitalists, expecting the inflation, tried to avoid losing from it and transferred their domestic assets into foreign assets. García's response, a nationalization of the banks, led to a breakdown of the political coalition supporting him. Ultimately he was done in by the long-run effects of his expansionary policies.

Thus, Peru provides us with a case study in which the short-run effects of contractionary policy got one politician chased out of office while the long-run effects of expansionary policy got the other politician chased out. Conducting macroeconomic policy is like walking on a tightrope.

The long-run/short-run problems exist in all countries. In the United States where politicians serve for limited periods, the difference between the long-run and short-run effects of policies often plays an important role in determining macroeconomic policy. Politicians try to give the economy a short-run boost before an election, and leave office before the long-run effects set in. Politicians have little incentive to consider the long-run consequences of policy, and that is why economists often criticize real-world macroeconomic policy.

Perhaps the central lesson to take away from this case study is the political dimension of any macroeconomic problem. It's likely that García's economic advisors predicted the eventual failure of his policy and supported a less expansionary policy. With less expansionary monetary and fiscal policies, the plan would have worked better. But his economic advisors were probably overruled. Politically, to keep the coalition together, García was forced toward more and more expansion. When political considerations dominate policies, economists' role in policy is often reduced to that of an observer and predictor of future disasters.

CASE STUDY 2

In one Sherlock Holmes story the clue is the dog that did not bark. The economy is often as much a mystery as one of Sherlock Holmes's cases; the clues about what is to come are often as obscure as the hound's silence. Case Study 2 is a report of such silence and economists' attempt to interpret it. The article was written in October 1989 by a reporter, not an economist. As you read it, ask yourself, "What is the reporter's incentive in writing this article? What about the economists she interviews? What do they base their information on? Is the conclusion the article comes to sound? Are the differences among economists discernible?"

Interpretation and Discussion

Detectives spend most of their time watching and waiting; so do business economists who forecast the future direction of the economy. Most economic theories involve relationships among variables that take one to five years to work their way through the economy. Economists know that in shorter time spans there are too many random blips—too much uncertainty—for economists, or anyone, to say much that is specific. In the very short run, many economic relationships that will occur even in the short run are overwhelmed by other, often random, events. But that doesn't mean that a knowledge of economics isn't relevant. Economics includes an understanding of economic institutions and how they operate. That

CASE STUDY 2

LEADING INDEX OF ECONOMY CLIMBS 0.3%

By Hilary Stout

WASHINGTON—The economy's slow, methodical growth is likely to continue into next year, the government's chief economic forecasting gauge suggests, although pockets of weakness still worry some economists.

The index of leading indicators, a composite of 11 statistics designed to foretell economic activity six to nine months hence, made its best showing since April, climbing 0.3% in August, the Commerce Department reported.

The increase—the second in as many months—suggests the economy is on "a pattern of slow but stable growth," said Gordon Richards, an economist at the National Association of Manufacturers.

In July, the index rose a revised 0.1%, originally estimated at a 0.2% increase. All the figures are adjusted for seasonal changes.

Five of the indicators pushed the index up; they included stock prices, building permits and factory orders for consumer goods, which were driven by a surge in automobile demand.

But some economists believe the economy is exhibiting enough weakness to keep alive the threat of recession. Among the leading indicators, an index of consumer expectations dropped significantly. Plant and equipment orders also fell. And the average work week shrank.

"Basically we don't see any strong sector of the economy, and we see several that are weak," said David Levy, a partner in Levy Economic Forecasts, Chappaqua, N.Y. "We believe the economy is going to have a very close brush with recession this year or early next, and the critical factor deciding whether it will drop (into a recession) or manage to avoid it is going to be Federal Reserve policy."

The Fed policy-making committee is due to meet this week to set monetary policy for the next several weeks. After pushing up interest rates

from March 1988 to March 1989 to head off inflation, the Fed let rates slip a few times this summer. But lately it has held them steady, waiting to see just where the economy is headed. Many analysts believe the central bank won't make any further changes in policy for now, amid signs that inflation is tapering while growth continues.

"I have to think the Fed is quite pleased with themselves at this point," said Daniel Van Dyke, head of the economic forecasting group at Bank of America in San Francisco.

The index showed that the weakest area of the economy is clearly manufacturing. For example, the prices of raw materials declined, making a negative contribution to the index. "That's good news for inflation but indicates there is slack in the industrial commodity area," noted Richard Peterson, senior vice president at Continental Bank in Chicago. Economists also said they expected August's boost in the factory orders component to drop back after orders for cars—brought on by sales incentives and new models—subside.

Many economists don't take the leading indicators index seriously as a forecasting gauge, reading it as an indication of current activity. Nevertheless, the numerous monthly declines in the index this year had triggered fears that the economy was edging toward a recession.

After the latest report, however, Lawrence Hunter, deputy chief economist for the U.S. Chamber of Commerce, contended that the leading indicators "show that the economic slowdown should come to an end in the fourth quarter," and "the real gross national product should rise throughout 1990."

Statistics Released in the Week Ended Sept. 29

	Total	Change (from prior period)
Money supply		
M1 Week ended		
Sept. 18 (in billions)	$ 790.8	− $1.8
M2 Week ended		
Sept. 18 (in billions)	$3,158.2	+ $3.9
M3 Week ended		
Sept. 18 (in billions)	$4,017.8	− $0.5
Durable goods orders		
August (in billions)	$ 126.74	+ 3.8%

Leading indicators		
August, index	144.4%	− 0.3%
Auto sales		
Sept. 11–20		
vs. year ago	211,966	− 10.2%
Farm prices		
August index	143%	− 0.7%
New jobless claims		
Week ended Sept. 16	319,000	+ 2.6%

Statistics to Be Released This Week

Purchasing management survey (Mon.)
September
Construction spending (Mon.)
August
New-home sales (Tues.)
August
Factory orders (Tues.)
August
New-car sales (Wed.)
September
Chain store sales (Thurs.)
September
Money supply (Thurs.)
September 25
Unemployment rate (Fri.)
September
Consumer installment credit (Fri.)
August

LEADING INDICATORS

Here are the net contributions of the components of the Commerce Department's index of leading indicators. After various adjustments, they produced a 0.3% rise in the index for August and a 0.1% rise in July.

	August 1989	July 1989
Workweek	− .07	.00
Unemployment claims	.19	− .08
Orders for consumer goods . .	.58	− .26
Slower deliveries	− .08	− .03
Plant and equipment orders .	− .16	.09
Building permits	.10	− .06
Durable order backlog	− .19	.02
Materials prices	− .20	− .30
Stock prices	.24	.14
Money supply	.20	.24
Consumer expectations	− .39	.26

The seasonally adjusted index numbers (1982 = 100) for August, and the change from July, are:

Index of leading indicators	144.4	0.3
Index of coincident indicators	133.9	0.4
Index of lagging indicators	122.3	0.9

The ratio of coincident to lagging indicators was 1.09, down from 1.10 in July.

The Wall Street Journal, October 2, 1989. Reprinted by permission of THE WALL STREET JOURNAL © 1989 Dow Jones & Company, Inc. All rights reserved worldwide.

knowledge can be useful in interpreting data and events. When people ask, ''What's going to happen to the economy?'' they generally don't want to know what's going to happen in one or two years; they want to know what's going to happen tomorrow, next week, or next month. Thus, when answering reporters' questions, economists are generally relying on their knowledge of economic institutions as much, or more, than they're relying on their knowledge of economic theory.

Perspective   Most economic reporters aren't trained economists; often they've had a course or two in economics but economic training isn't required. They report; they don't interpret.

A reporter's job is to report about the news that people want to know about and to write articles that people want to read. Reporters are assigned a beat and their job is to report the events that happen on that beat. Even when little is happening, economic reporters must write something. An article stating simply, ''Nothing significant happened this week'' is unlikely to sell many newspapers or endear its writer to the editor. Instead economic reporters resort to what one of my teachers called ''barking at straws.''

Such barking at straws fills up much of even the best newspapers' articles about the economy. Some articles sound as if they say something significant, but they don't say much at all. Like clockwork, you can expect to see an article about the economy after each new economic statistic comes out, even though movements in these short-run statistics are as likely to be caused by some extraneous event as they are to reflect something significant.

This article is, I suspect, a reporter's attempt to write an interesting article about nothing happening. It appeared in *The Wall Street Journal* in a space that once a week looks at the forecasts for the economy.[2]

The article is an example of the best economic reporting. I chose an example of the best to emphasize that it is not the fault of the reporter that the many articles about economics in the newspapers say little or nothing. It's that there's little or nothing to say.

Content   Economists follow economic events and statistics carefully. They also recognize that there are many different interpretations to the clues those events and statistics provide. Generally a new statistic adds more questions about where the economy is heading than it answers.

So what should an economist reply when a reporter asks about some short-run trend? Most economists answer the best they can. But they almost all admit that their very short-run predictions are based more on a knowledge of economic data, and how one set of data often leads (precedes in time) another set, rather than on the theories discussed in this book. For example, an increase in building permits and factory orders usually leads to an increase in income, so economists look at increases in those statistics and forecast that income will go up.

Now that isn't very heavy theory; it doesn't take a Ph.D. in economics to figure out that increases in building permits and factory orders will likely lead to increases in income, and that is why I don't spend more time in this book discussing short-term relationships of leading indicators and economic activity.

While an in-depth discussion is left for classes on economic forecasting, a few comments are appropriate here. Forecasting is a serious study in its own right. Finding and interpreting clues isn't easy. Analyzing these clues and their relationship to the economy often becomes highly sophisticated. There's much discussion among business economists about what group of indicators should be the index of leading indicators.

---

[2] *The Wall Street Journal* has a reputation as a conservative, almost reactionary, newspaper. On the editorial pages, that reputation is earned. The rest of the newspaper is, however, quite different. It portrays a wide diversity of views and is committed to objective reporting.

This electronic sign in the center of New York City tallies up the effect of deficits on the U.S. government's debt.

The difficulty of predicting the economy is increased by three complications. Notice that:

1. The report of leading indicators was significantly revised months after it was first issued. This often happens and makes forecasting more tricky. The clues might not be what they at first appear to be.

2. Economists know that what will happen in the economy depends on what policy the government follows. Thus, all predictions must be hedged with qualifying statements about what policy will be. When predictions depend on unknown policy responses, those predictions can never be certain.

3. Finally, there's the operation of a type of **Heisenberg principle** (a principle of quantum physics stating that observation changes what is observed and therefore knowledge is necessarily limited). Economists' predictions affect what people expect and what people expect affects what happens. Thus, economists are not simply observers. What they say (their predictions) affects what happens in the economy. Their predictions can become self-fulfilling prophecies, and they can never know what the economy would be like independent of their predictions.

Heisenberg principle The act of looking at something changes its nature.

Combined, these three complications create a situation in which even the most informed predictions about the economy are often wrong.

Moving away from forecasting, let's consider what the article tells us about macroeconomic policy. Notice that there's much discussion of how the data will affect Fed policy, but not a single mention of fiscal policy. That's telling. Political realities have made discretionary fiscal policy an unusable tool in the short run. Fiscal policy has an effect, but fiscal policy is generally determined by political goals, not macroeconomic goals.

That's not the case with monetary policy. Notice the continual mention of Federal Reserve policy and economists' discussion about how the Fed will react. In order to predict what will happen in the economy, simply looking at how events will affect the economy isn't enough. Instead you must predict how an event will affect Fed policy and how that policy will affect the economy. This indirect path of influence often makes for some seemingly paradoxical predictions. Say, for instance, that the indicators had been stronger—definitely pointing to a growing economy. That might cause some economists to predict that the economy will experience a slowdown. Why? Because a growing economy could lead the Fed to institute contractionary monetary policy in order to offset possible inflationary pressures. The contractionary monetary policy would cause interest rates to rise, which would slow down the economy.

Alternatively say statistics came in showing that the money supply fell. Remember that a fall in the money supply is associated with an increase in interest rates. So you might expect that if the money supply falls, interest rates will rise. But reality is more complicated; the Fed doesn't control the money supply directly. The Fed discovers how its open market operations (its policy of buying or selling bonds) has affected the money supply at the same time as others do. It might well react to that fall in the money supply by increasing the money supply more than it would have otherwise, so interest rates would be expected to fall, not rise. As you can see, to apply economic theory to reality you must have a good understanding of the institutional and political realities.

In summary, predicting the economy in the short run is a crapshoot. Most academic economists avoid making short-run predictions, or if they do make predictions, they couch them in uncertainty, leaving themselves an out. Economists who have mastered the art of predicting have generally mastered the art of saying, "What will happen is what will happen, unless, of course, it doesn't happen." When you're predicting what is almost impossible to predict, that's not a bad way to go.

CASE STUDY 3

The period 1981–88 (the Reagan years) was important in shaping modern macroeconomics. In response to a highly restrictive monetary policy exercised in 1981 and 1982, inflation came down substantially in 1983, but the short-run cost of that decrease in inflation was high unemployment. In 1982 the economy fell into the worst recession since the Great Depression of the 1930s.

The following selection from the 1986 Economic Report of the President concerns the Reagan policies for that year. The Economic Report of the President is a political, not an academic, document issued yearly by the president's Council of Economic Advisers. This 1986 report discussed events in 1985 and the last part of 1984 plus proposed policies for 1986.

CASE STUDY 3

INFLATION, DISINFLATION, AND THE STATE OF THE MACROECONOMY

The American economy is now in the fourth year of a robust expansion that has increased employment by more than 9 million, sustained the greatest advance in business fixed investment of any comparable period in the postwar era, while inflation has remained at less than a third of the rate prevailing when the Administration took office. Interest rates are at the lowest levels of this decade. Long-term interest rates, in particular, have declined 5 percentage points from their peaks in 1981, and home mortgage rates are down by 7 percentage points. Worldwide confidence in the vitality of the U.S. economy has been restored, as is reflected in the unprecedented inflow of foreign investment and the substantial appreciation of the dollar since 1980. The outlook is favorable for continuation of a healthy expansion. After slowing in the second half of 1984, economic activity is again accelerating. The recent moderate decline in the dollar bodes well for an eventual improvement in the trade balance. A modest and temporary acceleration of inflation is possible in 1986. But with appropriate economic policies, lower inflation, and ultimately price stability are achievable goals for an economy that continues to grow and to generate opportunities for all Americans.

Despite the impressive progress of the U.S. economy, important problems remain. Although the 3.8 percentage point decline in the unemployment rate since November 1982 far exceeds the average decline for a comparable period in earlier postwar expansions, the total unemployment rate remains high by postwar standards. Federal spending consumes an unprecedentedly large share of gross national product (GNP) for a peacetime period, diverting resources that could be more productively employed in the private sector. Determined efforts and politically difficult decisions will be required to bring Federal spending into line with revenues and thereby reduce the fiscal deficit. Inflation, now in abeyance, could be reignited by excessive monetary growth. Alternatively, a sudden move to sharply lower money growth could push the economy once again into recession.

Two central themes dominate this Report and, not coincidentally, the Administration's approach to economic policy. First, the private enterprise, free market system is generally the best mechanism to organize efficient and full employment of the economy's resources and to generate genuine opportunity and rising living standards for all. To assist the private sector, the government should limit itself to providing essential public services and should avoid blunting or distorting economic incentives by high or uneven tax rates and by unnecessary or inappropriate regulation.

Second, economic performance is seriously injured by the macroeconomic instability inevitably associated with cycles of inflation and disinflation. Such injury was reflected in the relatively sluggish economic growth of the 1970s. It was most acute and most apparent when rising inflation confronted efforts to reduce inflation by lowering monetary growth: in 1969–70, in 1974–75, briefly in late 1979 and early 1980, and finally on a more persistent basis in 1981–82. In each confrontation, the

outcome was a recession; in two cases, a severe and prolonged recession.

Even now, the consequences of earlier inflation and disinflation are still felt in the problems afflicting the American economy. The present level of unemployment is partly the heritage of past inflation and necessary actions to control it. Problems in agriculture, in industry, and in international trade are related to fluctuations in commodity prices, asset values, and the value of the dollar that, in turn, are linked to the process of inflation and disinflation and to the economic policies that underlie that process. Problems of the credit system—of borrowers, lenders, and government insurance agencies—derive partly from sharp, unexpected move-

ments in interest rates, asset values, and income levels that accompany the inflation–disinflation process.

The healthy overall performance of the U.S. economy may be small comfort to those affected by its remaining problems. But with time and with appropriate policies, these remaining problems can be corrected. The cure, however, does not lie in policies that would reignite inflation and once again inflict its debilitating effects on the American economy. Rather, the cure lies with policies that will enhance private incentives for growth, while maintaining a stable macroeconomic environment.

Economic Report of the President, 1986.

Interpretation and Discussion

This selection presents President Reagan's economic advisors' view of the 1984–85 expansion out of the 1982–83 recession. Unlike our first selection (in which objectivity was the writer's goal), The Economic Report of the President is a political document designed to cast events and the policies of the Reagan economic advisors in a favorable light. This doesn't mean that what the passage has to say isn't true; it only means that the chosen viewpoint will likely highlight certain aspects of reality while obscuring other less favorable interpretations. In 1984–85 the economy was coming out of the 1983 recession, as seen in Exhibit 1, so President Reagan's advisors had much to be positive about.

Perspective   Let's look for some examples where favorable light is placed on the events. First, notice that the report emphasizes what happened to employment (it increased substantially) rather than what happened to unemployment. From 1980 to 1986 labor force participation increased, as the number of women in the labor force rose dramatically. When labor force participation increases, both unemployment and employment can increase at the same time. In the period the report addresses, unemployment was falling, but was still high by historical standards. Employment, however, was rising substantially. Focusing on employment rather than unemployment gives a positive spin to the data; it directs the reader away from the still-high unemployment. (In the 1990s *spin control* has become a popular term to describe attempts to interpret events to the interpreter's greatest advantage.)

EXHIBIT 1   **Facts on the U.S. Economy, 1980–1988**

	GNP (in billions of $)	Net exports (in billions of $)	Inflation rate	Labor force (in millions)	Unemployment rate
1980	2,732	+32.1	13.5%	107	7.1%
1981	3,052	+33.9	10.3	109	7.6
1982	3,166	+26.3	6.2	110	9.7
1983	3,405	−6.1	3.2	112	9.6
1984	3,772	−58.9	4.3	114	7.5
1985	4,014	−78.0	3.6	116	7.2
1986	4,240	−104.4	1.9	118	7.2
1987	4,526	−123.0	3.6	120	6.2
1988	4,861	−93.2	4.1	122	5.5

Source: Council of Economic Advisers.

Another passage that casts events in a good light is the discussion of interest rates. When the council was writing the report, nominal interest rates were declining but were still high. Real interest rates were very high by historical standards—a fact the council doesn't mention. It discusses only the change in nominal interest rates rather than real interest rates.

A third example of positive spin is seen in what is not discussed. As Exhibit 1 suggests, the economy in 1984 was emerging from a severe recession. The budget deficit had increased significantly as automatic stabilizers kicked in. These automatic stabilizers had kept expenditures high and reduced tax revenue. The deficit was made even higher when taxes were cut by the Economic Recovery Tax Act of 1981. That deficit played a key role in the macroeconomic events of the time and in the political and economic discussions. Keynesian economists claimed it was the deficit that pulled the economy out of the recession. Yet the article's only mention of the deficit is a statement that the deficit will need to be brought into line by holding down spending. The possibility of increasing taxes is not discussed because that was not part of President Reagan's political agenda.

A fourth example of putting events in a positive light is the statement, "Worldwide confidence in the vitality of the U.S. economy . . . is reflected in the unprecedented inflow of foreign investment." That foreign investment was the mirror image of the large U.S. trade deficit beginning at that time. An alternative interpretation of that flow of foreign investment into the United States is that *in this time period the U.S. is selling off its assets to finance its trade deficit*. That inflow of foreign investment was caused in large part by the high real interest rates resulting from the large U.S. budget deficit combined with the tight money policy of the time. But to say that would have given negative spin to the interpretation. When reading political documents, it's important to find a zero spin position between different interpretations of the same issue.

Content   The preceding discussion of spin control shouldn't obscure the fact that the Reagan administration's economic policies were a success in the following sense: During the Reagan years the economy experienced one of the longest peacetime expansions since World War II. When the economy is doing well, not much spin control is needed to convince people that your policies are shrewd.

In economics it's almost impossible to prove that certain policies caused certain outcomes. Too many other things invariably change. Thus, there was significant debate about what the Reagan policy was, whether some other policies would have been even more successful, and whether the policies would have long-run negative effects. To consider these issues, let's look at what those policies were.

The 1981 tax cut was directed at high-income individuals. Designed to lower marginal tax rates to encourage supply incentive effects, it was an application of the supply-side economics discussed in an earlier chapter. Keynesians claimed that the supply incentive effects were minimal; they argued that the deficit resulting from the tax incentive, together with looser monetary policy, fueled the recovery. Thus, according to Keynesians, Reagan's policy succeeded because it was a Keynesian policy.

Supply-side Classical economists whose position is reflected in this report disagreed; they argued that the lower tax rates worked through the supply side, fueling the recovery by giving people incentives to produce more. This debate between Keynesians and Classicals was not settled when this report was written in 1985, and is still not settled in the 1990s. The empirical evidence is ambiguous.

You can tell that the report's authors are Classical economists by their emphasis on free enterprise and laissez-faire. They blame economic instability on previous government policies. They don't see economic instability inherent in the private economy. Thus, they blame existing unemployment on "past inflation and necessary actions to control it."

This report has very little discussion of what type of fiscal policy to use. In part that is because Classical economists are doing the writing, but it is also due to the acceptance that politics, not economic goals, will govern the size of the government budget deficit. That's why more and more of the responsibility for controlling the economy has shifted to the Fed and monetary policy.

Despite the report's Classical political overtones, it contains much that a Keynesian economist could agree with. For example, the council argues that "excessive" monetary growth could ignite inflation and that sharply lower money growth could push the economy into recession. Keynesians would be in general agreement with those views.

Similarly most Keynesians would agree that economic performance is seriously injured by macroeconomic instability. Where Keynesians and Classicals would disagree is in what is "excessive monetary growth" and what causes macroeconomic instability. Keynesians argue that the aggregate economy is inherently unstable and that discretionary monetary policy reduces that instability. Most Classicals argue that discretionary policy decreases the stability, and that a monetary rule is needed.

In assessing this report, we have the benefit of hindsight, and in that assessment the report comes out reasonably well. Specifically the economic expansion that began in 1983 continued through 1989 without generating significant inflation. Many Keynesian economists had expected a downturn in economic activity or an increase in inflation in the late 1980s. They were wrong. Neither that downturn nor a rise in inflation occurred in the 1980s. Thus, in one sense the economic report was vindicated. However, throughout the period the federal budget deficit and U.S. trade deficit remained high, allowing Keynesians to claim that it was the government deficit that fueled the expansion, and that Reagan had simply bought economic expansion for the present by mortgaging the future. They claimed that the recession of the early 1990s was the long-run consequence of the policies of the 1980s.

One area where the report was probably mistaken is in the problem with the credit system, which the council attributed to "sharp unexpected movements in interest rates." If this were true one would have expected that ending the sharp unexpected changes in interest rates would alleviate the problem. But even though those sharp unexpected movements didn't occur in the late 1980s, the private credit system and government insurance agencies that guarantee that system were severely battered as numerous S&Ls and other financial institutions defaulted, costing the government hundreds of billions of dollars. So the debate goes on.

CONCLUSION

As you can see, as soon as we start getting into real-world situations, the neat models you learned in earlier chapters don't fit so well, but that doesn't mean they're useless. Far from it. Keeping those models in the back of your mind gives logic and structure to a set of economic events and views that would otherwise be gobbledygook to you. You simply must apply them with insight and a knowledge of political and social economic institutions.

I hope that by going through these three selections in some detail, I prepared you for using the macroeconomics you've learned to interpret the everyday economic events that influence your life. It's in applying macroeconomics to those real-world events that economics changes from a course you must complete to a hobby and avocation which can give you pleasure and understanding for the rest of your life.

KEY POINTS

- Interpreting economics articles is an art, not a science. **1**
- Two different types of economic writing are the informative and the persuasive. **1**
- Informative writing attempts to be objective; persuasive writing does not. **1**
- It's important to distinguish a writer's goal when you're interpreting an article. **1**
- Different groups of economists often use different approaches. **2** **3**
- International considerations play a central role in the macro policies of small developing countries. **4**

- Implementing macroeconomic policies often brings about a long-run/short-run dilemma. **5**
- Short-run movements in the macroeconomy are often random. They can be explained but not predicted. **5**
- In the short run, economic interrelationships are complicated and can move contrary to economic theories' predictions. **5**
- The same economic set of events can be given two reasonable, contradictory interpretations. **6**

KEY TERMS

conditionality *(407)*
Heisenberg
  principle *(411)*

heterodox
  economist *(402)*

mainstream
  economist *(402)*

nonconvertible
  currency *(407)*

QUESTIONS FOR THOUGHT AND REVIEW

The number after each question represents the estimated degree of critical thinking required. (1 = almost none; 10 = deep thought.)

1. In the first case study Manuel Pastor discusses the IMF's "orthodox economic prescriptions." What were they and why didn't they work in Peru? *(8)*
2. Our discussion of macroeconomic theory suggested that contractionary macro policy puts downward pressure on inflation. The first case study suggests that contractionary macroeconomic policy causes inflation to rise. Explain the apparent contradiction. *(7)*
3. When interpreting an economics article, why is it important to determine the writer's goals? *(4)*
4. The long-run/short-run dilemma is central to understanding how the invisible foot and invisible hand interact. Explain the dilemma and its implications for policy. *(6)*

5. Most newspaper articles about the future direction of the economy are the equivalent of astrology columns. True or false? Why? *(6)*
6. In the 1990s Brazil introduced a plan to stop hyperinflation. Was that plan successful? Why or why not? (Requires library research.) *(8)*
7. Define *conditionality* and state why it is important. *(9)*
8. You've just read that the interest rate has fallen. Does this suggest expansionary monetary policy? Why? *(5)*
9. As what kind of economist would you classify your professor? Analyze one of your professor's lectures in terms of content and perspective. *(9)*
10. As what kind of economist would you classify yourself? Analyze one of your views in terms of content and perspective. *(10)*

PROBLEMS AND EXERCISES

1. Read the introduction of the most recent *Economic Report of the President* and analyze its content and perspective.

2. Find a recent newspaper report on the state of the economy and analyze its content and perspective.

MICROECONOMICS

In my vacations, I visited the poorest quarters of several cities and walked through one street after another, looking at the faces of the poorest people. Next I resolved to make as thorough a study as I could of Political Economy.

tant in real life. (5) Burn the mathematics. (6) If you can't succeed in (4), burn (3). This last I did often. (From a letter from Marshall to A. L. Bowley, reprinted in A. C. Pigou, *Memorials of Alfred Marshall, p. 427.*)

You may remember having already seen this quotation from Alfred Marshall. It began the first chapter. I chose this beginning for two reasons. First, it gives what I believe to be the best reason to study economics. Second, the quotation is from a hero of mine, one of the economic giants of all times. His *Principles of Economics* was economists' bible in the late 1800s and early 1900s. How important was Marshall? It was Marshall who first used the supply and demand curves as an engine of analysis.

I repeat this quotation here in the introduction to the microeconomics section because for Marshall economics was microeconomics, and it is his vision of economics that underlies this book's approach to microeconomics. For Marshall, economics was an art that was meant to be applied— used to explain why things were the way they were, and what we could do about them. He had little use for esoteric theory that didn't lead to a direct application to a real-world problem. Reflecting on the state of economics in 1906, Marshall wrote to a friend:

I had a growing feeling in the later years of my work at the subject that a good mathematical theorem dealing with economic hypotheses was very unlikely to be good economics: and I went more and more on the rules—(1) Use mathematics as a shorthand language, rather than as an engine of inquiry. (2) Keep to them until you have done. (3) Translate into English. (4) Then illustrate by examples that are impor-

Marshall didn't feel this way about mathematical economics because he couldn't do mathematics. He was trained as a formal mathematician, and he was a good one. But, for him, mathematics wasn't economics, and the real world was too messy to have applied to it much of the fancy mathematical economic work that some of his fellow economists were doing. Marshall recognized the influence of all three invisible forces and believed that all three had to be taken into account in applying economic reasoning to reality.

Since 1906 when Marshall wrote this letter, the economics profession has moved away from its Marshallian roots. The profession has found other heroes, who have created a mathematical foundation for economics that's both impressive and stultifying. Mathematical economics that has only the slightest connection to the real world has overwhelmed much of the real-world economics that Marshall followed. That's sad.

Not to worry. You won't see such highfalutin mathematical economics in these microeconomic chapters. The chapters follow the Marshallian methodology and present the minimum of formal theory necessary to apply the concepts of economics to the real world, and then they do just that; they start talking about real-world issues.

Part 1 presents that minimum of theory necessary to understand the economic way of thinking. It introduces you to the foundations of economic reasoning and the basic market structures. But even in these theoretical chapters the focus is on intuition and putting the economic approach to problems into perspective rather than on presenting technique for the sake of technique. Part 2 shows how economists use the tools developed in Part 1 to approach real-world problems. It gives you a sense of what competition in the real world is like as well as how economists integrate economic reasoning with real-world institutions and normative issues to give insight into what's happening, and how they come up with policy proposals. It will explain why economists differ. Finally, Part 3 considers the distribution of income and factor markets: why you earn what you earn, and what you might be able to do about it. It won't tell you how to get rich (you'll have to wait for the sequel for that), but it will give you new insights into perplexing problems.

1

Microeconomic Theory
The Basics

20

Individual Choice
and Demand

*The theory of economics must
begin with a correct theory of consumption.*
Stanley Jevons

After reading this chapter, you should be able to:

1

Discuss the principle of diminishing
marginal utility.

2

Summarize economists' analysis
of rational choice.

3

Explain how marginal utility accounts for
the law of demand.

4

Explain why economists can believe there
are many explanations of individual choice,
but nonetheless focus on self-interest.

5

Define the concept *price elasticity of
demand* and explain how it is used to
describe points on a demand curve.

6

Explain the importance of substitution in
determining the elasticity of demand.

No analysis is more important to economics than the analysis of individual choice. It is the foundation of economic reasoning and it gives economics much of its power.

We touched on the analysis of individual choice in Chapters 1 and 2. Chapter 1 introduced you to examples of economic reasoning using individual choice. In Chapter 2 you were introduced to the law of demand: The quantity demanded increases as the price decreases. In this chapter we extend that analysis and explore the formal reasoning that underlies individual choice theory and the law of demand. This formal economic analysis of choice centers on self-interest: People do what they do because doing so is in their interest. The first part of this chapter shows you that foundation and leads you through some exercises to make sure you understand the reasoning. The second part of the chapter relates that analysis to the real world, giving you a sense of when the model is useful and when it's not. Finally the third part of the chapter introduces you to elasticity, a term economists use to describe demand curves.

As you go through this chapter, think back to Chapter 1, which set out the goals for this book. One goal was to get you to think like an economist. This chapter, which formally develops the reasoning process behind economists' cost/benefit approach to problems, examines the underpinnings of how to think like an economist.

INDIVIDUAL CHOICE, SELF-INTEREST, AND ECONOMIC REASONING

Why do people do what they do? There are many explanations. Freudian psychology tells us we do what we do because of an internal fight between the id, ego, and superego plus some hangups people have about their bodies. Other psychologists tell us it's a search for approval by our peers; we want to be OK. Economists agree that these are important reasons, but argue that if we want an analysis that's simple enough to apply to problems, these heavy psychological explanations are likely to get us all mixed up. At least to start with, we need an easier underlying psychological foundation. And economists have one—self-interest. People do what they do because it's in their self-interest.

Economists' analysis of individual choice doesn't deny that most of us have our peccadillos. Each individual is unique and often strange. That's obvious in what we buy. On certain items we're penny-pinchers; on others we're big spenders. For example, how many of you or your parents clip coupons to save 40¢ on cereal but then spend $20 on a haircut? How many save 50¢ a pound by buying a low grade of meat but then spend $10 on a bottle of wine, $40 on dinner at a restaurant, or $30 for a concert ticket?

But through it all comes a certain rationality. People are doing what they're doing because they see it in their self-interest to do that; it's only rational to do so. Thus, a good beginning in understanding individual choice is to focus on the rational part of people's behavior. That's why economists start their analysis of individual choice with a relatively simple, but powerful, underlying psychological foundation.

Using that simple theory, two things determine what people do: the pleasure people get from doing or consuming something, and the price of doing or consuming that something. Price is the market's tool to bring the quantity supplied equal to the quantity demanded. Changes in price provide incentives for people to change what they're doing. Through those incentives the invisible hand guides us all. Thus, to understand economics you must understand how price affects our choices. That's why we focus on the effect of price on the quantity demanded. We want to understand the way in which a change in price will affect what we do.

In summary, economists' theory of rational choice is a simple, but powerful, theory that shows how these two things—pleasure and price—are related.

Jeremy Bentham, the 19th-century economist and philosopher who strongly advocated utilitarianism. *The Bettmann Archives.*

Let's start with an analysis of what we buy. Why do we buy what we buy? Economists' analysis of individual choice starts with the proposition that individuals try to get as much pleasure as possible out of life. To analyze the choice formally we must measure pleasure.

How does one measure pleasure? I don't know the answer to that, but back in the 1800s economists thought that eventually they would be able to measure pleasure by measuring brain waves. In the expectation of this discovery they even developed a measure of pleasure which they called a *util*. They predicted that someday a machine that could measure utils would be developed. Not surprisingly they called this machine a *utilometer*. This utilometer was to be connected to people's heads and an economist would read it as people went through their daily activities. Eating broccoli might give 10 utils; eating a hot fudge sundae might give 10,000 utils. (OK, so I'm a chocoholic.)

Eventually these 19th-century economists gave up hope of developing a utilometer, but economists use the term **utility** as a quaint, shorthand term for the pleasure or satisfaction that one expects to get from consuming a good or service. (And you thought that economists didn't have a sense of humor.) Utility serves as the basis of economists' analysis of individual choice.

In discussing utility economists initially used what are called *cardinal measures*. (An example of a cardinal measure is anything that can be measured by an actual number.) But no economist today believes that these actual numbers given to utility have meaning. Economists have gone to great lengths to show that only ordinal measures are necessary. To have an ordinal measure all you need is a ranking of goods that people reveal when they choose one good over another. (That means you can say "John is cuter than Bob," but you don't need to say how much cuter.)

It's important to keep in the back of your mind that economists don't need to measure utils, especially if you're going on in economics, but it's not important to keep it in the front of your mind. In introductory economics there's nothing quite as useful as a good old util. It gives one real numbers to work with, rather than all kinds of fancy measure theories. So here's the deal: I'll use real numbers in discussing utility and you promise that you'll remember they're not really needed. (If you don't accept this deal, see Appendix A where I go through the same analysis without using cardinal measures.)

In thinking about utility, it's important to distinguish between *total utility* and *marginal utility*. **Total utility** refers to the total satisfaction one gets from one's consumption of a product. **Marginal utility** refers to the satisfaction one gets from the consumption of an incremental or additional product above and beyond what one has consumed up to that point. For example, eating a whole pound of Beluga caviar might give you 4,700 utils (units of utility).[1] Consuming the first 15 ounces may have given you 4,697 utils. Consuming the last ounce of caviar might give you an additional 3 utils. The 4,700 is total utility; the 3 is the marginal utility of eating that last ounce of caviar.

An example of the relationship between total utility and marginal utility is given in Exhibit 1. Let's say that the marginal utility of the first slice of pizza is 14, and since you've eaten only one slice, the total utility is also 14. Let's also say that the marginal utility of the second slice of pizza is 12, which means that the total utility of two slices of pizza is 26 (14 + 12). Similarly for the third, fourth, and fifth slices of pizza, whose marginal utilities are 10, 8, and 6, respectively. If we add the

UTILITARIAN FOUNDATIONS OF INDIVIDUAL CHOICE

Measuring Pleasure

Utility A measure of the pleasure or satisfaction one gets from consuming a good or service.

Cardinal and Ordinal Utility

The Relationship between Total Utility and Marginal Utility

Total utility The satisfaction one gets from one's entire consumption of a product.

Marginal utility The satisfaction one gets from the consumption of an incremental or additional product above and beyond what one has consumed until that point.

---

[1] We choose specific numbers to make the examples more understandable and to make the points we want to make. A useful exercise is for you to choose different numbers and reason your way through the same analysis.

Number of pizza slices	Total utility	Marginal utility		
1	14		14	A
2	26		12	B
3	36		10	C
4	44		8	D
5	50		6	E
6	54		4	F
7	56		2	G
8	56		0	H
9	54		−2	I

(a)   (b)   (c)

EXHIBIT 1 (a, b, and c)   Marginal and Total Utility

Marginal utility tends to decrease as consumption of a good increases. Notice how the information in the table (**a**) can be presented graphically in two different ways. The two different ways are, however, related. The downward slope of the marginal utility curve (**c**) is reflected in the total utility curve being bowed downward in (**b**). Notice that marginal utility relates to changes in quantity so the *MU* line is graphed at the halfway point. For example, in (**c**), between 7 and 8, *MU* becomes zero.

marginal utilities you get from eating each of these five slices, we arrive at the total utility of your eating those five pieces of pizza. We do so in row E, column 2, of Exhibit 1(a).

The relationship between total and marginal utility can also be seen graphically. In Exhibit 1(b) we graph total utility (column 2 of Exhibit 1(a)) on the vertical axis and number of slices of pizza (column 1 of Exhibit 1(a)) on the horizontal axis. As you can see, total utility increases up to seven slices of pizza; after eight slices it starts decreasing—after eight pieces of pizza you're so stuffed that you can't stand to look at another slice.

In Exhibit 1(c) we graph marginal utility (column 3 of Exhibit 1(a)) on the vertical axis and slices of pizza (column 1) on the horizontal axis. Notice how marginal utility decreases while total utility increases. When total utility stops increasing (between 7 and 8 slices), marginal utility is zero. Beyond this point total utility would decrease and marginal utility would be negative. An additional slice of pizza will actually make you worse off.

Diminishing Marginal Utility

1

Diminishing marginal utility The marginal utility that a person gets from each additional unit of a good decreases with each unit consumed after some point.

Now let's consider the shapes of these curves a bit more carefully: What are they telling us about people's choices? As we've drawn the curves, the marginal utility that a person gets from each additional slice of pizza decreases with each slice of pizza eaten. Economists believe that the shapes of these curves accurately describe the pattern of people's enjoyment. They have given this principle a name: **diminishing marginal utility.** As individuals increase their consumption of a good, at some point consuming another unit of the product will simply not yield as much additional pleasure as did consuming the preceding unit.

Consider, for example, that late-night craving for a double cheese and pepperoni pizza. You order one and bite into it. Ah, pleasure! But if you've ordered a large pizza and you're eating it all by yourself, your additional pleasure is going to decrease with each additional slice that you consume. In other words you get fewer utils from each additional slice of pizza that you consume. That's the principle of diminishing marginal utility:

As you consume more of an item, x, beyond some point the additional units of consumption will yield fewer utils than the previous units.

In general X $\uparrow$ $\to$ MU$_x$ $\downarrow$ (X $\downarrow$ $\to$ MU$_x$ $\uparrow$).

As you consume more of an item, x, beyond some point the additional units of consumption will yield fewer utils than the previous units.

In general
$$X \uparrow \to MU_x \downarrow (X \downarrow \to MU_x \uparrow).$$

Notice that the principle of diminishing marginal utility does not say that you don't enjoy consuming more of a good; it simply states that as you consume more of the good, you enjoy the additional units less than you did the initial units. A fourth slice of pizza still tastes good, but it doesn't match the taste of the third slice. At some point, however, marginal utility can become negative. Say you had two large pizzas and only two hours in which to eat them. Eating the last slice could be pure torture. But in most situations you have the option *not* to consume any more of a good. When consuming a good becomes torture (meaning its utility is negative), you simply don't consume any more of it. If you eat a slice of pizza (or consume an additional unit of any other good), that's a good indication that its marginal utility is still positive.

The discussion of utility is important in economics because the marginal utility you get from a good plays a central role in determining how much you're willing to pay for it and hence how much of the good you demand. *Marginal utility and the price you will pay are related.* Given the price of a good, the higher the marginal utility you receive from a good, the more you are willing to buy of that good. Similarly, given the price, the lower the marginal utility you receive from a good, the less you're willing to buy of it.

Remembering that it's *marginal utility,* not total utility, that's related to price is important, because it helps explain a phenomenon that might otherwise be quite confusing. An illustration of that phenomenon is the diamond/water paradox, which stumped economists in the 1800s.

From Utility to Demand

The diamond/water paradox is: "Why is water, which is so useful and necessary, so cheap when diamonds, which are so useless and unnecessary, so expensive?"

If you remember the difference between total utility and marginal utility, you'll have no problem explaining the paradox. The answer goes as follows:

> Water gives us an enormous amount of total utility (without it we'd die), but because it is relatively abundant (in the United States anyway), its marginal utility is small because of the principle of diminishing marginal utility. It is marginal, not total, utility that determines what we're willing to pay for a good. Diamonds don't give us much total utility (they are, after all, only pretty stones), but because they're scarcer than water, their marginal utility is high, so we're willing to pay a lot for them. Given the extensive amount of water, we aren't willing to pay much for water, whose total utility is high but whose marginal utility is low. Of course, if you were stuck in a desert, where water was as scarce as diamonds, the marginal utility of water would rise enormously. You would probably trade all your diamonds for a gallon of water.

The Diamond/Water Paradox

The diamond/water paradox is an introduction to economists' analysis of rational choice which underlies the law of demand. The analysis of rational choice is the analysis of how individuals choose goods in order to maximize total utility, and how maximizing total utility can be accomplished by considering marginal utility. That analysis begins with the premise that rational individuals want as much satisfaction as they can get from their available income. How do they achieve that?

Let's start by considering a number of choices. (Answer each choice as you read it.)

Rational Choice and Marginal Utility

Choice 1:   Between a $1 slice of pizza giving you 41 utils and a $1 hero sandwich that gives you 30 utils.

Choice 2:   Between a Maserati at $170,000 that gives you 120,000 utils and a Yugo at $5,000 that gives you 20,000 utils.

Choice 3:   Between reading an additional chapter in this book that gives you an additional 200 utils at a cost of one hour of your time, and reading an additional chapter in psychology that gives you an additional 100 utils at a cost of 40 minutes of your time. (Psychology is easier but less fulfilling than economics.)

Choice 4:   Between having a date with that awesome guy Jerry, which gives you 2,000 utils and costs you $70, and taking out plain Jeff, which gives you 200 utils and costs you $10.

The correct choices, in terms of marginal utility, are: (1) the pizza, (2) the Yugo, (3) a chapter of this book, and (4) Jerry.

If you answered all four correctly, either you're lucky or you have a good understanding of the principle of rational choice. Now let's explore the principle of rational choice more thoroughly by considering each of the four examples.

Choice 1   Since the slice of pizza and the hero both cost $1, and the pizza gives you more utils than the hero, the pizza is the rational choice. If you spend $1 on the hero rather than the pizza, you're losing 11 utils and not making yourself as happy as you could be. You're being irrational. Any choice (for the same amount of money) that doesn't give you as many utils as possible is an irrational choice.

But now let's say that the price of heroes falls to 50¢ so that you can buy two heroes for the same price you previously had to pay for only one. Let's also say that two heroes would give you 56 utils (not $2 \times 30 = 60$—remember the principle of diminishing marginal utility). Which would now be the more rational choice? The two heroes, because their 56 utils are 15 more than you would get from that dollar spent on one slice of pizza.

Another way of thinking about your choice is to recognize that essentially what you're doing in your choices is buying utils. Obviously what you want to do is to buy utils as cheaply as possible, so you make those choices that have the lowest cost per util. Let's see how this way of thinking about it works by considering our second choice.

Choice 2   The Maserati costs $170,000 and we get 120,000 utils from it. Per dollar spent we get

$$\frac{120,000 \text{ utils}}{\$170,000} = .71 \text{ utils.}$$

This means that one util costs about $1.43 ($1 divided by .71 = $1.42). With the Yugo, for each dollar spent we get

$$\frac{20,000 \text{ utils}}{\$5,000} = 4 \text{ utils}$$

so a util costs 25¢. ($1 divided by 4 = $.25.) The cost per util is lower for the Yugo than for the Maserati, so we choose the Yugo. Since the cost per util is determined by dividing $1 by the marginal utility per dollar, to say something has the lowest cost per util is to say that it has the highest marginal utility per dollar.

Choice 3   Here the two alternatives have a cost in time, not money. The analysis, however, is the same. You calculate the marginal utility (number of utils) of the choice facing you, and divide that by the cost of the activity; that gives you the marginal utility per dollar. Then choose the activity that has the highest MU per dollar or lowest cost per util. When you do that, you see that this chapter gives you $3\frac{1}{3}$ utils per minute ($200/60 = 3\frac{1}{3}$), while the psychology chapter gives you $2\frac{1}{2}$ utils per minute. So you choose to read another chapter in this book.[2]

Choice 4   Taking out Jerry gives you $28\frac{1}{2}$ utils per dollar ($2,000/\$70$), while taking out Jeff gives you 20 utils per dollar ($200/\$10$). So you choose to take out Jerry.

The basic **principle of rational choice** is as follows: *Spend your money on those goods that give you the most marginal utility (MU) per dollar.* The principle of rational choice is important enough for us to emphasize.[3]

Principle of rational choice   Spend your money on those goods that give you the most marginal utility per dollar.

If $\dfrac{MU_x}{P_x} > \dfrac{MU_y}{P_y}$, *choose to consume an additional unit of good x.*

If $\dfrac{MU_x}{P_x} < \dfrac{MU_y}{P_y}$, *choose to consume an additional unit of good y.*

If $\dfrac{MU_x}{P_x} = \dfrac{MU_y}{P_y}$, *you're maximizing utility; you cannot increase your utility by adjusting your choices.*

If $\dfrac{MU_x}{P_x} > \dfrac{MU_y}{P_y}$, *choose to consume an additional unit of good x.*

If $\dfrac{MU_x}{P_x} < \dfrac{MU_y}{P_y}$, *choose to consume an additional unit of good y.*

If $\dfrac{MU_x}{P_x} = \dfrac{MU_y}{P_y}$, *you're maximizing utility; you cannot increase your utility by adjusting your choices.*

By substituting the marginal utilities and prices of goods into these formulas, you can always decide which good it makes more sense to consume. Consume the one with the highest marginal utility per dollar.

Let's apply these formulas by substituting in the numbers from one of our previous examples: the choice between the Maserati and the Yugo. The marginal utility of the Maserati was 120,000; the price was $170,000. The marginal utility of the Yugo was 20,000; the price was $5,000. Substituting,

$$\frac{20,000}{\$5,000} = 4 \text{ utils per \$} > \frac{120,000}{\$170,000} = .7 \text{ utils per \$}.$$

So choose the Yugo.

In each of the previous four examples, there was a clear winner. If in the examples you had been maximizing utility and hence were in equilibrium, there couldn't have been a clear winner. Why? As you make choices, it's important to remember the principle of diminishing marginal utility: As we consume more of an item, the marginal utility we get from the last unit consumed decreases. Conversely as we consume *less* of an item, the marginal utility we get from the last unit consumed *increases*. (The principle of diminishing marginal utility operates in reverse.)

The principle of rational choice tells you to keep adjusting your spending if the marginal utility per dollar (MU/P) of two goods differs. The only time you don't adjust your spending is when there is no clear winner. When you've maximized utility, the ratios of the marginal utility to price of the two goods are equal. This insight accounts for the third formula in the principle of rational choice:

If $\dfrac{MU_x}{P_x} = \dfrac{MU_y}{P_y}$, *you're maximizing utility; you're in equilibrium.*

Rational Choice and Maximizing Utility

Rational Choice and Simultaneous Decisions

So far in discussing our examples, we've considered each of the four choices separately. But in real life, choices aren't so neatly separated. Say you were presented with all four choices simultaneously. If you make all four of the decisions given in the examples, are you being rational? The answer is no. Why? The pizza gives you 46 utils per dollar; taking out Jerry gives you 28 utils per dollar; and the Yugo gives you only 4 utils per dollar. You aren't being rational; you aren't maximizing your utility. It would clearly make sense to dump the Yugo

---

[2] As I've pointed out before, we choose the numbers to make the points we want to make. A good exercise for you is to choose different numbers that reflect your estimate of the marginal utility you get from choice, and see what your rational choices are. And remember our deal.

[3] The symbol > means "greater than." The symbol < means "less than."

EXHIBIT 2   **Maximizing Utility**

Big Macs (P = $2)				Ice Cream (P = $1)			
Q	TU	MU	MU/P	Q	TU	MU	MU/P
0	0			0	0		
		20	10			29	29
1	20			1	29		
		14	7			17	17
2	34			2	46		
		10	5			7	7
3	44			3	53		
		3	1.5			2	2
4	47			4	55		
		0	0			1	1
5	47			5	56		
		−5	−2.5			0	0
6	42			6	56		
		−10	−5			−4	−4
7	32			7	52		

and take out Jerry on pizza binges instead (assuming, of course, that he'll go out with you without your Yugo).

But what about the fourth choice: studying psychology or economics? We can't compare the costs of studying to the costs of the other goods because, as I noted earlier, the costs of the two studying alternatives are expressed in terms of time, not money. If we can assign a money value to the time, however, we can make the comparison. Let's say you can earn $6 per hour, so the value of your time is 10¢ per minute. This allows us to think about the two alternatives in terms of dollars and cents. Since a chapter in economics takes an hour to read, the cost in money of reading a chapter is 60 minutes × 10¢ = $6. Similarly the cost of the 40 minutes you'd take to read the psychology chapter is $4.

With these values we can compare our studying decisions with our other decisions. The value in utils per dollar of reading a chapter of this book is

$$\frac{200}{\$6} = 33\frac{1}{3} \text{ utils per dollar.}$$

So forget about dating Jerry with its value of 28 utils per dollar. Your rational choice is to study this chapter while stuffing yourself with pizza.

But wait. Remember that, according to the principle of diminishing marginal utility, as you consume more of something, the marginal utility you get from it falls. So as you consume more pizza and spend more time reading this book, the marginal utilities of these activities will fall. Thus, as you vary your consumption, the marginal utilities you get from the goods are changing.

When do you stop varying your consumption? When you maximize utility—when the marginal utility per dollar spent on each choice is equal. Achieving equilibrium by maximizing utility (juggling one's choices, adding a bit more of one and subtracting a bit less of another) requires more information than I've so far presented. We need to know the marginal utility of alternative amounts of consumption for each choice and how much income we have to spend on all those items. With that information we can choose among alternatives.

An Example of Rational Choice   In Exhibit 2 we consider an example in which we have the necessary information to make simultaneous decisions. In this example, we have $7 to spend on ice cream cones and Big Macs. The choice is between ice cream at $1 a cone and Big Macs at $2 apiece. In the exhibit you can see the principle of diminishing marginal utility in action. The marginal utility (MU) we get from either good decreases as we consume more of it. Marginal utility (MU) becomes negative after five Big Macs or six ice cream cones.

The key columns for your decision are the MU/P columns. They tell you the MU per dollar spent on each of the items. By following the rule that we choose the good with the higher marginal utility per dollar, we can quickly determine the optimal choice.

Let's start by considering what we'd do with our first $2. Clearly we'd only eat ice cream. Doing so would give us 29 + 17 = 46 utils, compared to 10 utils if we spent the $2 on a Big Mac. How about our next $2? Again the choice is clear; the 10 utils per dollar from the Big Mac are plainly better than the 7 utils per dollar we can get from ice cream cones. So we buy one Big Mac and two ice cream cones with our first $4.

Now let's consider our fifth and sixth dollars. The MU/P for a second Big Mac is 7. The MU/P for a third ice cream cone is also 7, so we could spend the fifth dollar on either—if McDonald's will sell us half a Big Mac. We ask them if they will, and they tell us no, so we must make a choice between either two additional ice cream cones or another Big Mac for our fifth and sixth dollar. Since the marginal utility per dollar of the fourth ice cream cone is only 2, it makes sense to spend our fifth and sixth dollar on another Big Mac. So now we're up to two Big Macs and two ice cream cones and we have one more dollar to spend.

Now how about our last dollar? If we spend it on a third ice cream cone we get 7 additional utils. If McDonald's maintains its position and only sells whole Big Macs, this is our sole choice since we only have a dollar and Big Macs sell for $2. But let's say that McDonald's wants the sale and this time offers to sell us half a Big Mac for $1. Would we take it? The answer is no. The next Big Mac gives us only 5 utils per dollar whereas the third ice cream cone gives us 7 utils per dollar. So we spend the seventh dollar on a third ice cream cone.

With these choices we've arrived at equilibrium—we're maximizing total utility. Our total utility is 34 from two Big Macs and 53 utils from the three ice cream cones, making a total of 87 utils.

Why do these two choices make sense? Because they give us the most utility per dollar and hence the highest total utility. These choices make the marginal utility per dollar equal as between the last Big Mac and the last ice cream cone. The marginal utility per dollar we get from our last Big Mac is

$$\frac{MU}{P} = \frac{14}{\$2} = 7.$$

The marginal utility per dollar we get from our last ice cream cone is

$$\frac{MU}{P} = \frac{7}{\$1} = 7.$$

The marginal utility per dollar of each choice is equal, so we know we can't do any better. For any other choice we would get less total utility, so we could increase our total utility by switching to one of these two choices.

The General Principle of Rational Choice   Our example involved only two goods, but the reasoning can be extended to the choice among many goods. Our analysis of rational choice has shown us that the principle of rational choice among many goods is simply an extension of the basic principle of rational choice applied to two goods. That general principle for maximizing utility is to equate, as closely as possible, the marginal utility per dollar of the activities or goods being considered.

When $\dfrac{MU_x}{P_x} > \dfrac{MU_z}{P_z}$, *consume more of good* x.

$\dfrac{MU_y}{P_y} > \dfrac{MU_z}{P_z}$, *consume more of good* y.

Stop adjusting your consumption when the marginal utilities per dollar are equal.

$\dfrac{MU_x}{P_x} > \dfrac{MU_z}{P_z}$, consume more of good x.

$\dfrac{MU_y}{P_y} > \dfrac{MU_z}{P_z}$, consume more of good y.

Choose goods and activities so that the marginal utilities per dollar of the goods consumed are equal:

$$\frac{MU_x}{P_x} = \frac{MU_y}{P_y}.$$

So the general principle of rational choice is this:

Choose goods and activities so that the marginal utilities per dollar of the goods consumed are equal:

$$\frac{MU_x}{P_x} = \frac{MU_y}{P_y}.$$

When this principle is met, the consumer is in equilibrium; the marginal cost per util is equal for all goods and the consumer is as well off as it is possible to be.

Notice that the rule does not say that the rational consumer should consume a good until its marginal utility reaches zero. The reason is that the consumer doesn't have enough money to buy all she wants. She faces an income constraint and does the best she can under that constraint—that is, she maximizes utility. To buy more goods she has to work more, so she should work until the marginal value of another dollar earned just equals the marginal value of another dollar spent. According to economists' analysis of rational choice, a person's choice of how much to work is made simultaneously with the person's decision of how much to consume. So when you say you want a Porsche but can't afford one, economists ask whether you're working two jobs and saving all your money to buy a Porsche. If you aren't, you're demonstrating that you don't really want a Porsche, given what you would have to do to get it.

Marginal Utility and the Law of Demand

3

Now that you know the basic rule for maximizing utility, let's bring in the law of demand and see how it relates to marginal utility. The law of demand says that the quantity demanded of a good depends inversely on the relative price of that good. Accordingly when the price of a good goes up, the quantity we consume of it goes down.

Now let's consider the law of demand in relation to our marginal utility rule. When the price of a good goes up, the marginal utility *per dollar* we get from that good goes down. So when the price of a good goes up, if we were initially in equilibrium, we no longer are. Therefore we lower our consumption of that good. The principle of rational choice shows us formally that following the law of demand is the rational thing to do.

Let's see how. If

$$\frac{MU_x}{P_x} = \frac{MU_y}{P_y}$$

and the price of good y goes up, then

$$\frac{MU_x}{P_x} > \frac{MU_y}{P_y}.$$

Our condition for maximizing utility is no longer satisfied. Consider the preceding example, in which we were in equilibrium with 87 utils (34 from two Big Macs and 53 from three ice cream cones) with the principle of rational choice fulfilled:

$$\begin{array}{cc} \text{Big Mac} & \text{ice cream} \\ \dfrac{14 \text{ marginal utils}}{\$2} = \dfrac{7 \text{ marginal utils}}{\$1} = 7. \end{array}$$

If the price of an ice cream cone rises from \$1 to \$2, the marginal utility per dollar for one Big Mac (whose price hasn't changed) exceeds the marginal utility per dollar of ice cream cones:

$$\begin{array}{cc} \text{Big Mac} & \text{ice cream} \\ \dfrac{14}{\$2} > \dfrac{7}{\$2}. \end{array}$$

To satisfy our condition for maximizing utility so that our choice will be rational, we must somehow raise the marginal utility we get from the good whose relative price has risen and lower the MU we get from a good whose relative price has

INCOME AND SUBSTITUTION EFFECTS

In the discussion of the law of demand I didn't say precisely how much the quantity demanded would decrease with a price rise. I didn't because of a certain ambiguity that arises when one talks about changes in nominal prices. To understand the cause of this ambiguity, notice that with $7 we can no longer consume two big Macs and three ice cream cones. We've got to cut back for two reasons: First, we're poorer due to the rise in price. This is called the *income effect*. Second is the change in the *relative* prices. The price of ice cream has risen relative to the price of Big Macs. This is called a *substitution effect*. Technically the law of demand is based only upon the substitution effect.

To separate the two effects let's assume that somebody compensates us for the rise in price of ice cream cones. Since it would cost $10 [(2 × $2 = $4) + (3 × $2 = $6)] to buy what $7 bought previously, we'll assume that someone gives us an extra $3 to compensate us for the rise in price. This eliminates the income effect. We now have $10 so we can buy two Big Macs and the three ice cream cones as we did before. If we do so, our total utility is once again 87 (34

utils from two Big Macs and 53 utils from three ice cream cones). But will we do so?

We see that Big Macs give us more MU per dollar. What happens if we exchange an ice cream cone for an additional Big Mac so instead of buying three ice cream cones and two Big Macs, we buy three Big Macs and two ice cream cones? The MU per dollar of Big Macs falls from 7 to 5 and the MU per dollar of the ice cream cone (whose price is now $2) rises from 3.5 to 8.5. Our total utility rises to 44 from three Big Macs and 46 from two ice cream cones, for a total of 90 utils rather than the previous 87. We've increased our total utility by shifting our consumption out of ice cream, the good whose price has risen. The price of ice cream went up and, even though we were given more money so we could buy the same amount as before, we did not; we bought fewer ice cream cones. That's the substitution effect in action: It tells us that when the relative price of a good goes up, the quantity purchased of that good decreases, *even if you're given money to compensate you for the rise.*

---

fallen. Following the principle of diminishing marginal utility, we can increase marginal utility only by *decreasing* our consumption of the good whose price has risen. As we consume fewer ice cream cones and more Big Macs, the marginal utility of ice cream rises and the marginal utility of a Big Mac falls.

This example can be extended to a general rule: If the price of a good rises, you'll increase your total utility by consuming less of it. When the price of a good goes up, consumption of that good must go down. Our marginal utility rule underlies the law of demand:

3

Law of demand: The quantity demanded of a good will rise the lower its price, other things constant.

Or alternatively

The quantity demanded of a good will fall the higher its price, other things constant.

This discussion of marginal utility and rational choice shows the relationship between marginal utility and the price we're willing to pay. When MU is high, as it is with diamonds, the price we're willing to pay is high. When marginal utility is low, as it is with water, the price we're willing to pay is low. Since our demand for a good is an expression of our willingness to pay for it, quantity demanded is related to marginal utility.

Economists agree that other forces besides price and marginal utility play a role in determining what people demand. Many of these forces fall under the general category of *tastes*. What determines tastes?

Ask yourself what you ate today. Was it health food? Pizza? Foie gras? Whatever it was, it was probably not the most efficient way to satisfy your nutritional needs. The most efficient way to do that would be to eat only soybean mush and vitamin supplements at a cost of about $200 per year. That's less than one-tenth of what the average individual today spends on food per year.

Most of us turn up our noses at soybean mush. Why? Because tastes are important. The economic theory of individual choice doesn't directly analyze individuals' tastes; it simply assumes that they're given. Thus, before you apply

The quantity demanded of a good will rise the lower its price, other things constant.

The quantity demanded of a good will fall the higher its price, other things constant.

Tastes and Individual Choice

the analysis you must be sure that this simplifying assumption isn't going to hurt your understanding of the issues.

I point this out because some economists have been guilty of forgetting their simplifying assumption. An example of this is that some economists in the 1800s thought that society's economic needs eventually would be fully satisfied and that we would enter a golden age of affluence where all our material wants would be satisfied. They thought there would be surpluses of everything. Clearly that hasn't happened. Somehow it seems that whenever a need is satisfied, it's replaced by yet another want, which soon becomes another need. Compact disc players, VCRs, and color TVs are examples. As recently as the 1970s these were luxuries or not yet invented. Now, more and more, Americans consider them necessities. As more goods become available our tastes for goods increases.

There are, of course, examples of wants being temporarily satisfied, as a U.S. company on a small island in the Caribbean is reported to have discovered. Employees weren't showing up for work. The company sent in a team of efficiency experts who discovered the cause of their problem: The firm had recently raised wages, and workers had decided they could get all they wanted (warm weather, a gorgeous beach, plenty of food, and a little bit of spending money) by showing up for work once, maybe twice, a week. Such a situation was clearly not good for business, but the firm found a solution. It sent in thousands of Sears catalogs, and suddenly the workers were no longer satisfied with what they already had. They wanted more and went back to work to get it. When they were presented with new possibilities, their wants increased. Companies know that tastes aren't constant, and they spend significant amounts of money in advertising to make consumers have a taste for their goods. It works, too.

Tastes are also important in explaining differences in consumption between countries. For example, in Japan one wouldn't consider having a meal without rice. Rice has a ceremonial, almost mystical value there. In many parts of the United States supper means meat and potatoes. In Germany carp (a large goldfish) is a delicacy; in the United States many people consider carp inedible. In Korea Spam is considered a gourmet food; in the United States it's looked down upon. In the United States corn is a desirable vegetable; in parts of Europe until recently it was pig food. (After World War II, the United States sent shiploads of corn to Europe to help the people in war-devastated countries. The corn rotted. Europeans couldn't bring themselves to eat pig food, even when they were hungry and the corn was free.) Clearly tastes—as well as other factors such as income—are an important determinant of demand.

To understand tastes you have to know both psychology and economics, and know how they interrelate. So any analysis of tastes is left to upper-level economics courses.

To say we don't analyze tastes in the core of economic theory doesn't mean that we don't take them into account. Think back to Chapter 2 when we distinguished shifts in demand (the entire demand schedule shifts) from movements along the demand curve. Those movements along the demand curve were the effect of price. Tastes were one of the shift factors of demand. So economists can include tastes in their analysis; a change in tastes makes the demand curve shift.

Individual Choice Theory in Context

We began this chapter with a discussion of the simplifying nature of the economists' analysis of rational choice. Now that you've been through it, you may be wondering if it's all that simple. In any case, I'm sure most of you would agree that it's complicated enough. When we're talking about formal analysis, I'm in total agreement.

4 But if you're talking about informal analysis and applying the analysis to the real world, most economists would also agree that this theory of choice is in no way acceptable. Economists believe that there's more to life than maximizing utility. We believe in love, anger, and doing crazy things just for the sake of doing crazy things. We're real people. But, we argue, simplicity has its virtue and often people hide their selfish motivations. Few people like to go around and say, "I did this because I'm a selfish, calculating person who cares primarily about myself." Instead they usually emphasize other motives. "Society conditioned me to do it"; "I'm doing this to achieve fairness"; "It's my upbringing." And they're probably partially right, but often they hide and obscure their selfish motives in their psychological explanations. The beauty of economists' simple psychological assumption is that it cuts through many obfuscations (that's an obfuscating word meaning smokescreens) and, in doing so, it often captures a part of reality that others miss. Let's consider a couple of examples.

Why does government have restrictions on who's allowed to practice law? The typical layperson's answer is that these restrictions exist to protect the public. The economists' answer is that many of the restrictions do little to protect the public. Instead their primary function is to restrict the number of lawyers and thereby increase the marginal utility of existing lawyers and the price they can charge.

Why do people pollute? The layperson's answer is that people haven't been educated about the importance of the environment. The economists' answer is that people aren't paying enough for their polluting activities.

Why do museum directors almost always want to increase the size of their collections? The layperson's (and museum directors') answer is that they're out to preserve our artistic heritage. The economists' answer is that it often has more to do with maximizing the utility of the museum staff. (Economist William Grampp recently made this argument in a book about the economics of art. He buttressed his argument by pointing out that more than half of museums' art is in storage and not accessible to the public. Acquiring more art will simply lead to more going into storage.)

Now in no way am I claiming that the economic answer based on pure self-interest is always the correct one. But I am arguing that approaching problems by asking the question, "What's in it for the people making the decisions?" is a useful approach that will give you more insight into what's going on than many other approaches. It gets people to ask tough, rather than easy, questions. After you've asked the tough questions, then you can see how to modify the conclusions by looking deeply into the real-world institutions.

All too often students think of economics and economic reasoning as establishment reasoning. That's not true. Economic reasoning can be extremely subversive to existing establishments. But whatever it is, it is not subversive in order to be subversive, or proestablishment to be proestablishment. It's simply a logical application of a simple idea—individual choice theory—to a variety of problems.

Now that we've examined the foundations of the law of demand, it's time to talk about a term economists use to describe demand: **price elasticity of demand** (or often just *elasticity of demand*). It's a measure of the percent change in quantity of a good demanded divided by the percent change in the price of that good. Price elasticity of demand is an important concept, so let's write it down formally:

$$E_{\mathrm{d}} = \frac{\dfrac{\Delta Q}{Q}}{\dfrac{\Delta P}{P}} = \frac{\text{Percent change in quantity}}{\text{Percent change in price}}.$$

Let's consider an example. Say the price of a good goes up by 10 percent and in response the quantity demanded falls by 20 percent. The price elasticity of demand would be -2. Notice that I said -2. This follows because whenever price goes up, quantity demanded falls. This inverse relationship is deeply engrained in every economist's mind. But negative numbers are a pain, especially when you're comparing two negative numbers, say -2 and -4. Which is larger? (The answer is -2.) To avoid this confusion, generally economists talk about elasticity as a positive number and remember that it's actually negative. (Those of you who

ELASTICITY OF DEMAND

Price elasticity of demand A measure of the percent change in the quantity demanded divided by the percent change in the price.

remember some math can think of the definition of elasticity as being an absolute value, rather than a simple number.) We'll follow that convention in this book, which means that you've got to remember that the elasticity of demand is actually negative even though we talk about it as positive.

Elasticity and the Effect of a Price Increase on Total Revenue

Elasticity is a useful way of describing the effect of price on quantity. It tells what will happen to total revenue (the receipts people get from selling their products) if they change their price by some percentage. For example, when college officials consider raising tuition rates, they want to know if it will increase total revenue.

Total revenue is calculated by multiplying price times quantity. Elasticity tells us what happens to both price and quantity and hence what happens to total revenue. If price goes up by 10 percent and if in response quantity goes down by 10 percent, the elasticity of demand (E_d) will be 1. What does that tell us about total revenue? It tells us that total revenue isn't going to change since the increase in revenue caused by the rise in price will be offset by a decline in revenue caused by a decrease in quantity demanded.

How about if $E_d = 2$? That means that if price goes up by 10 percent, quantity will decrease by 20 percent. So what will happen to total revenue in this case? It's going to fall since the percent change in quantity will be bigger than the percent change in price.

How about if $E_d = 1/10$? That means the percent decrease in quantity will be one-tenth of the percent increase in price. Here total revenue will increase with a rise in price.

Now let's try some real-world examples. Let's start with the tuition example. Say that raising tuition by 10 percent will decrease the number of students by only 1 percent. What's the elasticity? The percent change in quantity is 1 percent; the percent change in price is 10 percent. Dividing the percent change in quantity by the percent change in price, we have an elasticity of .1. That's a low elasticity, so raising tuition will increase the college's total revenue.

But if a 10 percent rise in tuition will decrease the enrollment by 25 percent, the elasticity will be large (2.5). In response to an increase in tuition the college's total revenue will significantly decrease. When you have an elastic demand you should hesitate to increase price. (To make sure you're following the argument, explain the likely effect an elastic demand will have on lowering tuition.)

As another example, recall the vanity license plates that we used to illustrate the law of demand in Chapter 2. A rise in the price of vanity plates of 33 percent, from $30 to $40, decreased the quantity demanded about 50 percent, from 60,334 to 31,122, so the elasticity was about 50%/33% = 1.5. The percent decrease in quantity exceeded the percent increase in price so total revenue fell from

$$\$30 \times 60,334 = \$1,810,020$$

to

$$\$40 \times 31,122 = \$1,244,880.$$

Elasticity and the Demand Curve

Let's now see how to calculate the elasticity in the area around a point on a demand curve. In Exhibit 3 we do so for a hypothetical demand curve facing a college.

Say it's thinking of raising tuition from $900 to $945, an increase of 5 percent (45/900). Doing so will cause it to move along the demand curve from point A to point B. Extending lines down to the quantity axis we can see that this will cause enrollment to fall from 300 to 255, a decrease of 15 percent (45/300). Remembering that elasticity is defined as the percent change in quantity divided by the percent change in price, we can now calculate the elasticity of the demand curve in the vicinity of points A and B. It's 15%/5% = 3.

In thinking about elasticity, a common mistake that students make is to say *elasticity* but think *slope*. Remember that elasticity isn't the same as slope. Slope tells us what will happen to quantity demanded when price changes. In Exhibit 3

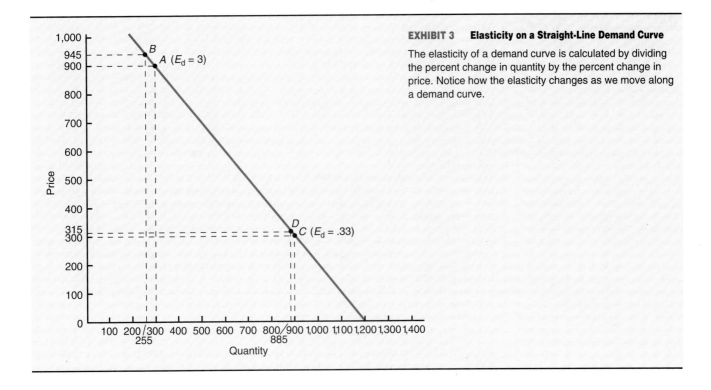

EXHIBIT 3   **Elasticity on a Straight-Line Demand Curve**

The elasticity of a demand curve is calculated by dividing the percent change in quantity by the percent change in price. Notice how the elasticity changes as we move along a demand curve.

the slope of the demand curve is −1. And since it's a straight line, its slope is −1 at every point on that demand curve. That isn't the case for elasticity. Elasticity changes at each point on a straight-line demand curve. To demonstrate, let's say that instead of starting at point A, we started at point C. Once again the president raises tuition by 5 percent. Extending our lines down to the quantity axis, we can see that quantity will decrease from 900 to 885, a decrease of 15/900 = 1.67%. So the elasticity is approximately (15/900)/(15/300) = .33.

In the preceding discussion of calculating elasticity everything worked out nicely. The math works out nicely too as long as one is talking about very small changes. As soon as the changes get bigger, however, calculating percent change in a totally unambiguous fashion is impossible. Say price falls from $5 to $4. Calculated in reference to $5, that's a 20 percent change; calculated in reference to the new price, $4, that's a 25 percent change. Which is the correct reference point? An argument could be made for either. In our preceding calculations we chose the initial price and the initial quantity as our reference point. That's the conventional thing to do when you're just using numbers. It's not the conventional thing to do when you're calculating the elasticity in reference to a demand curve.

As was previously mentioned, with a straight-line demand curve, elasticity changes at each point on that demand curve. The questions economists are usually asked about demand elasticities (such as "What will happen if we lower price by 10 percent?") concern what will happen over a range of points on the demand curve. That's the question we asked in our first example in Exhibit 3. There we were talking about a range of points on the demand curve. Because elasticity changes over the demand curve, at the initial price of 900 and quantity of 300, the elasticity was 3. At the new price of 945 and the new quantity of 255, the elasticity was (45/255)/(45/945) = 3.71. That's as exact a measure as we can give of elasticity over a range of points on a demand curve. It's somewhere between 3 and 3.71.

Obviously having a range of answers is a bit difficult. To avoid this problem when calculating elasticity of a section of a demand curve, most economists follow some averaging convention.

Calculating Elasticity: A Complication

A REMINDER

SLOPE AND ELASTICITY:
ANOTHER WAY TO
CALCULATE ELASTICITY

The elasticity formula is

$$E_d = \frac{\frac{\Delta Q}{Q}}{\frac{\Delta P}{P}}.$$

By algebraically manipulating this formula a bit, we can show how elasticity is related to slope.* Specifically

$$E_d = \frac{1}{\text{Slope}} \times \frac{P}{Q}.$$

This equation tells us that elasticity is related to slope, but it's not the slope. It's the inverse of the slope (1/slope) multiplied by P/Q. Thus, if we know the slope of a demand curve, the price, and the quantity, we can immediately determine the elasticity of demand at a given point on the curve.

* How did we move from one to another? By using some laws of algebra and remembering that the definition of slope is $\Delta P/\Delta Q$. If you try to derive the formulas, remember that in algebra dividing by a number is the same as multiplying by its inverse.

Average Elasticity over a Range   The convention I prefer is to calculate the elasticity of the two extreme points of the range (points *A* and *B* in Exhibit 3) and to average them by dividing by 2. Thus, the average elasticity for the range between *A* and *B* is

$$\text{Average } E_d = \frac{3 + 3.71}{2} = \frac{6.71}{2} = 3.35.$$

Arc elasticity The average elasticity of a range of points on a demand curve.

Arc Elasticity   The way most economists prefer to calculate elasticity over a range of points is called the *arc elasticity method*. **Arc elasticity** is the average elasticity of a range of points on a demand curve. It's calculated in the following manner: Instead of dividing the changes in price and quantity by one end point or the other, you add both end points and divide them by 2. Doing so using the facts in our previous example gives

$$\text{Arc } E_d = \frac{\frac{45}{(255 + 300)/2}}{\frac{45}{(900 + 945)/2}} = 3.32.$$

To be totally frank, economists' methods of estimating real-world demand curves aren't good enough to cause worry about the small difference in measuring average elasticity in different ways. Because of statistical problems with the data, our estimates are rough and ready and can easily vary by say 20 or even 40 percent up or down. Thus, while economists give specific elasticities for demand curves, we interpret those numbers loosely.

Some Conventions about Elasticity

In our example you may have noticed that when elasticity of demand was greater than 1 (when it was 3), total revenue fell when price rose. When elasticity of demand was less than 1 (when it was 1/3), total revenue rose when price rose. It's also true that when elasticity equals 1, total revenue won't change with a rise in price.

Elastic and Inelastic Demand Curves   These relationships hold generally and have led to the following conventions:

Elastic Percent change in quantity is greater than percent change in price, $E_d > 1$.

- If E_d is greater than 1, a rise in price lowers total revenue. (Price and total revenue move in opposite directions.) The demand curve in that price range is described as **elastic.** When demand is elastic, the percent change in quantity is greater than the percent change in price.

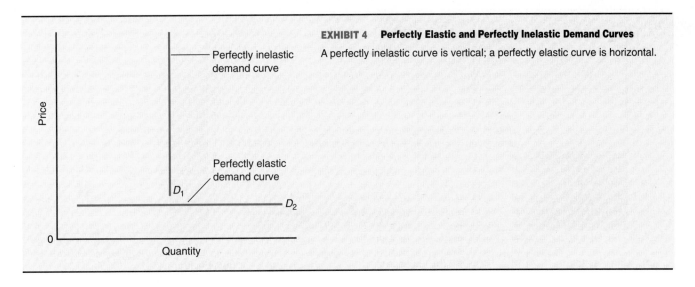

EXHIBIT 4   Perfectly Elastic and Perfectly Inelastic Demand Curves

A perfectly inelastic curve is vertical; a perfectly elastic curve is horizontal.

- If E_d is equal to 1, a rise in price leaves total revenue unchanged. The demand curve is described as having **unitary elasticity.** When demand is unit elastic, the percent change in quantity equals the percent change in price.
- If E_d is less than 1, a rise in price increases total revenue. (Price and total revenue move in the same direction.) The demand in that price range is described as **inelastic.** When demand is inelastic, the percent change in quantity is less than the percent change in price.

Unitary elasticity Percent change in quantity equals percent change in price, $E_d = 1$.

Inelastic Percent change in quantity is less than percent change in price, $E_d < 1$.

Perfectly Elastic and Inelastic Demand Curves   Economists have developed terminology other than *elastic* and *inelastic* to describe two special cases: the case in which the demand curve is perfectly flat (slope $= 0$) and the case in which the demand curve is perfectly vertical (slope $=$ infinity). When the demand curve is perfectly flat, the elasticity is infinite. Economists describe such a curve as **perfectly elastic.** When the demand curve is perfectly vertical, the elasticity is 0. Economists describe such a demand curve as **perfectly inelastic.** If one raises price with a perfectly elastic demand curve, total revenue falls to zero; and if one raises price with a perfectly inelastic demand curve, total revenue increases proportionately. A perfectly elastic (D_2) and a perfectly inelastic (D_1) demand curve are demonstrated in Exhibit 4.

Perfectly elastic Percent change in price equals zero, $E_d =$ infinity.

Perfectly inelastic Percent change in quantity equals zero, $E_d = 0$.

Now that we've got our elastic, inelastic, and unit elasticity terminology down, let's consider more carefully the relationship between elasticity and total revenue.

The relationship between elasticity and total revenue is no mystery. There's a very logical reason why they are related, which can most neatly be seen by recognizing that total revenue ($P \times Q$) is represented by the area under the demand curve at that price and quantity. For example, at point A on demand curve D_1 in Exhibit 5(a), the total revenue at price \$4 and quantity 6 is the area designated by the A and B rectangles, \$24.

If we increase price to \$5, quantity demanded decreases to 5, so total revenue is now \$25. Total revenue has increased slightly, so the demand curve at point A is slightly inelastic, but close to unit elasticity. The new total revenue is represented by the A and C rectangles. The difference between the old total revenue (A and B) and the new total revenue (A and C) is the difference between the rectangles B and C. Comparing these rectangles provides us with a visual method of estimating elasticities. Comparing the size of these two rectangles, let's see what happens to total revenue.

In Exhibit 5(b) we consider an inelastic point; in Exhibit 5(c) we consider a highly elastic point. Whereas in Exhibit 5(b) the slope of the demand curve is the same as in Exhibit 5(a), we're at a different point on the demand curve (point B). If

Elasticity and Total Revenue: A Closer Look

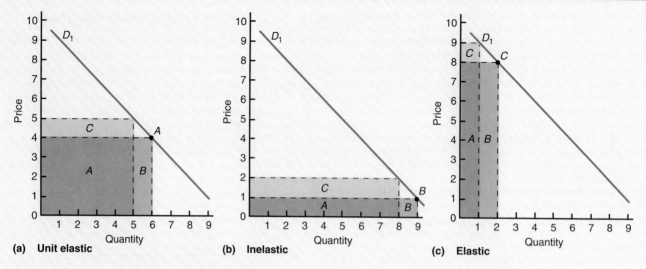

EXHIBIT 5 (a, b, and c)   Elasticity and Total Revenue

Total revenue is measured by the rectangle one gets by extending lines from the demand curve to the price and quantity axes. The change in total revenue resulting from a change in price can be estimated by comparing the size of the before and after rectangles. If price is being raised, total revenue increases by rectangle C and decreases by rectangle B. As you can see, the effect of a $1 price rise on total revenue differs significantly at different points on a demand curve. (**a**) shows an almost unitary elastic point, (**b**) shows an inelastic point and (**c**) shows an elastic point.

we raise our price from $1 to $2, quantity demanded falls from 9 to 8. The gained area (rectangle C) is much greater than the lost area (rectangle B). In other words, total revenue increases significantly, so the demand curve at point B is highly inelastic.

In Exhibit 5(c) the demand curve is again the same, but we're at still another point, C. If we raise our price from $8 to $9, quantity demanded falls from 2 to 1. The gained area (rectangle C) is much smaller than the lost area (rectangle B). In other words, total revenue decreases significantly, so the demand curve at point C is highly elastic.

Notice that the elasticity of a straight-line demand curve changes as you move along that demand curve. The way in which elasticity changes and its relationship to total revenue can be seen in Exhibit 6.

When output is zero, total revenue is zero; similarly when price is zero, total revenue is zero. That accounts for the two end points of the total revenue curve in Exhibit 6(b). Let's say we start at a price of zero, where demand is very inelastic. As we increase price (decrease quantity demanded), total revenue increases significantly, a fact that accounts for the steep slope of the total revenue curve. As we continue to do so, the increases in total revenue become smaller until finally, after output of Q_0, total revenue actually starts decreasing. It continues decreasing at a faster and faster rate until finally, at zero output, total revenue is zero. These relationships are summarized in Exhibit 6(c).

The Influence of Substitution on the Elasticity of Demand

6

Now that you know how to measure elasticity of demand, let's consider some of the factors that are likely to make demand more or less elastic. The influence of these factors can be summed up in one word: *substitution*. As a general rule, *the more substitutes a good has, the more elastic is its demand.*

The reasoning is as follows: If a good has substitutes, a price rise for that good will cause the demander to shift consumption to those substitute goods. When a satisfactory substitute for a good is available, a rise in that good's price will have a large effect on the quantity demanded, and the demand curve will tend to be elastic. For example, I think a Whopper is a satisfactory substitute for a Big Mac; if most people agree with me, the demand for Big Macs is very elastic.

(a)

(b)

EXHIBIT 6 (a, b, and c)   How Total Revenue Changes

Total revenue is at a maximum when elasticity equals one. When demand is elastic, total revenue increases with a decrease in price. When demand is inelastic, total revenue decreases with a decrease in price.

Elasticity of point on demand curve	Change in total revenue as price increases
Elastic $E_d > 1$	TR ↓
Unit Elastic $E_d = 1$	TR constant
Inelastic $E_d < 1$	TR ↑

(c)

The number of substitutes a good has is affected by several factors:

1. The larger the time interval considered, or the longer the run, the more elastic is the demand curve for the goods.
2. The less a good is a necessity, the more elastic is its demand curve.
3. The more specifically a good is defined, the more elastic is its demand curve.

These three reasons are derivatives of the substitution factor. Let's consider each to see why.

1. There are more substitutes in the long run than in the short run. That's because the long run provides more options for change. For example, let's consider the World War II period when the price of rubber went up considerably. In the short run, there were few substitutes; the demand for rubber was inelastic. In the long run, however, the rise in the price of rubber stimulated research for alternatives. Many alternatives were found. Today automobile tires, which were all made of rubber at the time World War II broke out, are almost entirely made from synthetic materials. In the long run, the demand curve was very elastic.

2. Necessities, by definition, tend to have fewer substitutes than do luxuries. Insulin for a diabetic is a necessity; the demand is highly inelastic. Chocolate ecstasy cake, however, is a luxury. A variety of other luxuries can be substituted for it (for example, cheesecake, a ball game, or a book).

3. If the good we're talking about is broadly defined (say, transportation), there aren't many substitutes and the demand will be inelastic. If you want to get from *A* to *B,* you need transportation. If the definition of the good is narrowed (say, to "transportation by bus"), there are more substitutes. Instead of taking a bus you can walk, ride your bicycle, or drive your car. In that case the demand curve is more elastic.

Let's consider how some of the substitution factors affect a specific decision.

EXHIBIT 7   Short-Run and Long-Run Elasticities of Demand

| | Price Elasticity | |
Product	Short run	Long run
Radio and television repair	0.47	3.84
Tobacco products	0.46	1.89
Electricity (for household consumption)	0.13	1.89
Stationery	0.47	0.56
Medical care and hospitalization insurance	0.31	0.92
Intercity bus trips	0.20	2.17
Toys (nondurable)	0.30	1.02
Movies/motion pictures	0.87	3.67
Foreign travel by U.S. residents	0.14	1.77

Source: Hendrik S. Houthakker and Lester D. Taylor, *Consumer Demand in the United States: Analyses and Projections* 2nd ed. (Cambridge, Mass.: Harvard University Press, 1970). Used by permission.

Let's say you've been hired by two governments (the city of Washington, D.C., and the U.S. government) to advise them about the effect that raising the gas tax by 10 percent will have on tax revenues.

In your report to the two governments, you would point out that in the short run the demand curve would be less elastic than in the long run, since people aren't going to trade in their gas-guzzling cars for fuel-efficient cars immediately in response to a 10 percent rise in gas taxes—partly because they can't afford to, partly because they don't want to, and partly because not that many fuel-efficient cars are available to buy at the moment. In the long run, however, when the time comes that they would ordinarily trade, they're likely to switch to cars that are more fuel-efficient than their old cars, and to switch as much as they can to forms of transportation that are more fuel-efficient than cars. Then the demand will be far more elastic.

The second point you'd note is that gasoline is generally considered a necessity, although not all driving is necessary. However, since gasoline is only a small part of what it costs to drive a car, the demand will probably tend to be inelastic.

As for the third factor (how broadly defined the good we're talking about is) you have to be careful. It makes your recommendations for the government of the city of Washington, D.C., and the U.S. government quite different from each other. For the U.S. government, which is interested in the demand for gasoline in the entire United States, gasoline has a relatively inelastic demand. The general rule of thumb is that a 1¢ rise in tax will raise tax revenues by $1 billion. That inelasticity can't be carried over to the demand for gasoline in a city such as Washington, D.C. Because of the city's size, people in Washington have a choice. A large proportion of the people who buy gas in Washington could as easily buy gas in Maryland or Virginia. Gasoline in Washington is a narrowly defined good and therefore has a quite *elastic* demand. A rise in price will mean a large fall in the quantity of gas demanded.

I mention this point because in August 1980 someone forgot about it when the city of Washington raised the tax on a gallon of gasoline by 8¢, a rise at that time of about 5 percent. In response monthly gasoline sales in Washington fell from 16 million gallons to 11 million gallons, a 40 percent decrease! The demand for gas in Washington was not inelastic, as it was for the United States as a whole; it was very elastic ($E_d = 8$). Washingtonians went elsewhere to buy gas. Within four months the city had repealed the tax increase.

The fact that smaller geographic areas have more elastic demands limits how highly state and local governments can tax goods relative to their neighboring localities or states. Where there are differences, new stores open all along the border and existing stores expand to entice people to come over that border and save on taxes. For example, the liquor tax is higher in Vermont than in New Hampshire, so it isn't surprising that right across the border from Vermont, New Hampshire has a large number of liquor stores. Here's one final example: If you

While price elasticity is the elasticity that economists most often talk about, elasticity is a general concept that relates percent changes in something with percent changes in something else.

One frequently used elasticity is *cross elasticity of demand* (the percent change in quantity of one good divided by the percent change in price of another good). An example of where cross elasticity might be important is a hot dog and ketchup. The price of hot dogs can influence the demand for ketchup. (Notice we used ''demand,'' not ''quantity demanded,'' to emphasize that in response to a change in anything but the price of that good, the entire demand curve shifts; there's no movement along the demand curve.)

Another commonly used elasticity term is *income elasticity of demand*, the percent change in demand that will result from a percent change in income.

$$E_{\mathrm{I}} = \frac{\text{Percent change in demand}}{\text{Percent change in income}}.$$

As an example, say your income goes up by 100 percent and your demand for Big Macs goes up by 50 percent. Your income elasticity for Big Macs would be

$$\frac{50\%}{100\%} = \frac{1}{2}.$$

The following table presents income elasticities measured for some groups of goods.

| | Income Elasticity | |
Commodity	Short run	Long run
Motion pictures	.81	3.41
Foreign travel	.24	3.09
Household electricity	.14	1.94
Intercity bus transportation	.17	1.89
Tobacco products	.21	0.86
Radio and TV repairs	.64	5.20
Food produced and consumed on farms	−.61	—
Furniture	2.60	0.53
Jewelry and watches	1.00	1.64

Source: Hendrik S. Houthakker and Lester D. Taylor, *Consumer Demand in the United States: Analyses and Projections*, 2nd ed. (Cambridge, Mass.: Harvard University Press, 1970).

In the short run, people often save increases in income, so most goods, other than impulse-bought goods, have low income elasticities. To avoid this problem economists generally focus on long-run income elasticities. Notice that some goods have long-run income elasticities less than 1, which means that their consumption doesn't keep pace with rises in income. These tend to be relative necessities (goods that are necessities compared to other goods). Other goods have long-run elasticities greater than 1; their consumption more than keeps pace with rises in income. They tend to be relative luxuries.

look at license plates in Janzen Beach, Oregon (right across the Washington state border) you'll see mostly Washington license plates. Why? If you answered that it likely has something to do with differential sales taxes in Washington and Oregon, you've got the idea.

Exhibit 7 presents additional examples of elasticity of demand. Notice that, as expected, different estimates are provided for the short- and long-run elasticities of each good. Also notice that the estimates are for the entire United States; if one were doing estimates for a specific region in the United States, the estimates could be expected to show more elasticity.

Taking an example from Exhibit 7, notice that the long-run demand for movies is elastic. If movie theaters raise their prices, it's relatively easy for individuals simply to stay home and watch television. Thus, intuitively we consider movies to have close substitutes, so we would expect the demand to be relatively elastic.

As a second example, in the short run the demand for electricity is highly inelastic. People either have electrical appliances or they don't. In the long run, however, it becomes elastic since people can shift to gas for cooking and oil for heating, and can buy more energy-efficient appliances.

As an exercise, you might see if you can explain why each of the other goods listed in the table has the elasticity of demand reported.

Individual and Market Demand Elasticity

In thinking about demand elasticity, keep in mind the point made in Chapter 2: The market demand curve is made up of the horizontal summation of individual demand curves, and some individuals have highly inelastic demands and others have highly elastic demands. A slight rise in the price of a good will cause some people to stop buying the good; the slight increase won't affect other people's demand for the good at all. Demand elasticity is influenced both by how many people drop out totally and by how much an existing consumer marginally changes his or her quantity demanded.

If a firm can somehow separate the people with less elastic demand from those with more elastic demand, it can charge more to the individuals with inelastic demands and less to individuals with elastic demands. We see examples of firms trying to do just that throughout the economy. Let's consider three:

1. Airlines' Saturday stay-over specials. If you stay over a Saturday night, usually you can get a much lower airline fare than if you don't. The reason is that businesspeople have inelastic demands and don't like to stay over Saturday nights, while pleasure travelers have more elastic demands. By requiring individuals to stay over Saturday night, airlines can separate out businesspeople and charge them more.

2. The phenomenon of selling new cars. Most new cars don't sell at the listed price. They sell at a discount. Salespeople are trained to separate out comparison shoppers (who have more elastic demands) from impulse buyers (who have inelastic demands). By not listing the selling price of cars so that the discount can be worked out in individual negotiations, salespeople can charge more to customers who have inelastic demands.

3. The almost-continual-sale phenomenon. Some items, such as washing machines, go on sale rather often. Why don't suppliers sell them at a low price all the time? Because some buyers whose washing machines break down have

Stores conduct short-run sales in order to price discriminate. *Nancy Anne Dawe.*

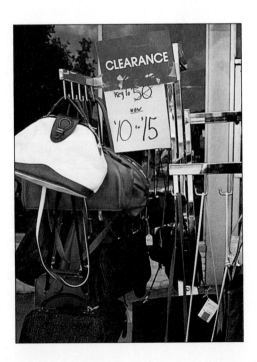

inelastic demand. They can't wait so they'll pay the "unreduced" price. Others have elastic demands; they can wait for the sale. By running sales (even though they're frequent sales), sellers can separate demanders with inelastic demand curves from demanders with elastic demand curves.

CONCLUSION

That's the end of our introduction to individual choice theory. There was a lot to learn, but I hope that the facts and applications that were combined with it made it more palatable. Whether it was or was not palatable, it's a necessary chapter. Economists are continually thinking about, empirically measuring, and applying the analysis and terminology in this chapter. Their conversations are dotted with *elastic, inelastic,* and applications of the principle of rational choice.

An economist friend, Arjo Klamer, and I did a survey in which we asked economics graduate students whether they often applied the principle of rational choice in their daily lives. They overwhelmingly answered yes. A few students wrote, "Doesn't everyone?" Even those graduate economics students who didn't like the principle of rational choice and the selfishness it implied about human nature still applied the principle of rational choice in analyzing real-world events. Their comments included, "Yes, I am brainwashed." and "Very often in spite of myself."

One of the goals of the book set forth in Chapter 1 is to get you to think like an economist. If I were to choose one principle that's central to thinking like an economist, the principle of rational choice would be it. Look at the world around you and apply the principle: Look for some phenomenon that doesn't seem as if it could have been a rational choice and then think harder because, from some perspective, it will have an explanation that accords with the principle of rational choice.

The fact that the principle of rational choice can explain everything doesn't mean that it's the best explanation imaginable. It's important to look at as many different explanations as possible, empirically testing when possible to choose among alternative explanations and, when it's impossible to test, keeping in the back of your mind various alternative explanations. Some economists believe that the principle of rational choice provides the best explanation of almost all events. Other economists believe that social and political factors must be built into the explanations of almost all events. But all economists in some way use the principle of rational choice in approaching problems. That's why this chapter is so important.

KEY POINTS

- The principle of diminishing marginal utility is: **1**

    As you consume more of an item, the additional units of consumption will yield fewer utils than the first units.

- The principle of rational choice is: **2**

    If $\dfrac{MU_x}{P_x} > \dfrac{MU_y}{P_y}$, choose to consume more of good x.

    If $\dfrac{MU_x}{P_x} < \dfrac{MU_y}{P_y}$, choose to consume more of good y.

    If $\dfrac{MU_x}{P_x} = \dfrac{MU_y}{P_y}$, you're maximizing utility; you're indifferent between good x and good y.

- The law of demand can be derived from the principle of rational choice. **3 4**
- Economists describe demand curves by their elasticity. **5**
- If one raises price and has: an elastic demand curve, total revenue falls; an inelastic demand curve, total revenue rises; a unitary elastic demand curve, total revenue is unchanged. **5**
- The more substitutes a good has, the more elastic its demand curve. **6**

KEY TERMS

arc elasticity *(438)*
diminishing marginal
  utility *(426)*
elastic *(438)*

inelastic *(439)*
marginal utility *(425)*
perfectly elastic *(439)*
perfectly inelastic *(439)*

price elasticity of
  demand *(435)*
principle of rational
  choice *(429)*

total utility *(425)*
unitary elasticity *(439)*
utility *(425)*

QUESTIONS FOR THOUGHT AND REVIEW

The number after each question represents the estimated degree of critical thinking required. (1 = almost none; 10 = deep thought.)

1. How would the world be different than it is if the principle of diminishing marginal utility seldom held true? *(8)*

2. It is sometimes said that an economist is a person who knows the price of everything but the value of nothing. Is this statement true or false? Why? *(9)*

3. Assign a measure of utility to the study you are putting into your various courses. Do your study habits follow the principle of rational choice? *(6)*

4. The marginal utility of your consumption of widgets is 40; it changes by 2 with each change in widgets consumed. The marginal utility of your consumption of wadgets is also 40 but changes by 3 with each change in wadgets consumed. The price of widgets is $2 and the price of wadgets is $3. How many widgets and wadgets should you consume? *(4)*

5. What key psychological assumptions do economists make in their theory of individual choice? *(7)*

6. Explain your motivation for four personal decisions you have made in the past year, using economists' model of individual choice. *(7)*

7. Determine the elasticity of demand if, in response to an increase in price of 10 percent, quantity decreased by 20 percent. Would it be elastic or inelastic? *(3)*

8. A firm has just increased its price by 5 percent over last year's price, and it found that quantity sold remained the same. The firm comes to you and wants to know its elasticity of demand. How would you calculate it? What additional information would you search for before you did your calculation? *(7)*

9. Why would an economist be more hesitant about making an elasticity estimate of the effect of an increase in price of 1 percent rather than an increase in price of 50 percent? *(6)*

10. Demand for college education is generally considered to be highly inelastic. What does this suggest about tuition increases in the future? Why don't colleges raise tuition by amounts even greater than they already do? *(9)*

PROBLEMS AND EXERCISES

1. *a.* The following table gives the price and total utils of three goods: A, B, and C.

Good	Price	1	2	3	4	5	6	7	8
A	$10	200	380	530	630	680	700	630	430
B	$2	20	34	46	56	64	72	78	82
C	$6	50	60	70	80	90	100	90	80

Total utility

As closely as possible, determine how much of the three goods you would buy with $20. Explain why you chose what you did.

b. The following table gives the marginal utility of John's consumption of three goods: A, B, and C.

Units of consumption	MU of A	MU of B	MU of C
1	20	25	45
2	18	20	30
3	16	15	24
4	14	10	18
5	12	8	15
6	10	6	12

(1) Good A costs $2 per unit, good B costs $1, and good C costs $3. How many units of each should a consumer with $12 buy to maximize his or her utility?

(2) How will the answer change if the price of B rises to $2?

(3) How about if the price of C is 50¢ but the other prices are as in part (1)?

2. As your annual income increases from $50,000 to $55,000 your quantity of meat demanded increases from 300 to 350 pounds.

a. Calculate your income elasticity of demand for meat.

b. What additional information would you want to have to ensure that your answer is correct?

c. If your income falls to $25,000, what would you predict would happen to your quantity of meat demanded?

Indifference Curve Analysis

As I stated in the chapter, analyzing individual choice using cardinal utility (giving utility actual numbers) is unnecessary. In the chapter, I asked you to make a deal with me: You'd remember that cardinal utility is unnecessary and I'd use cardinal numbers. This appendix is for those who didn't accept my deal (and for those whose professors want them to get some practice in graphish). It presents an example of a more formal analysis of individual choice.

Sophie's Choice

Sophie is a junk food devotee. She lives on two goods: chocolate bars, which cost $1 each, and cans of soda, which sell for 50¢ apiece. Sophie is trying to get as much pleasure as possible, given her income. Alternatively expressed, Sophie is trying to maximize her utility, given an income constraint.

By translating this statement of Sophie's choice into graphs, I can demonstrate the principle of individual choice without ever mentioning any specific amount of utility.

The graph we'll use will have chocolate bars on the vertical axis and cans of soda on the horizontal axis, as in Exhibit A1.

Graphing the Income Constraint

Let's begin by asking: How can we translate her income constraint (the $10 maximum she has to spend) into graphish? The easiest way to do that is to ask what would happen if she spent her $10 all on chocolate bars or all on cans of soda. Since a chocolate bar costs $1, if she spends it all on chocolate bars she can get 10 bars (point A in Exhibit A1). If she spends it all on cans of soda, she can get 20 cans of soda (point B). This gives us two points.

But what if she wants some combination of soda and chocolate bars? If we draw a line between points A and B, we'll have a graphical picture of her income constraint and can answer that question because that

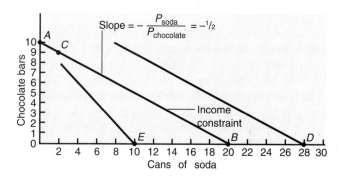

EXHIBIT A1   Graphing the Income Constraint

line shows us the various combinations she can buy. The line is her income constraint in graphish.

To see that it is, say Sophie is spending all her money on chocolate bars. She then decides to buy one fewer chocolate bar. That gives her $1 to spend on soda, which, since those cans cost 50¢ each, allows her to buy 2 cans. Point C (9 chocolate bars and 2 cans of soda) represents that decision. Notice how point C is on the income constraint. Repeat this exercise from various starting points until you're comfortable with the fact that the line does indeed represent the various combinations of soda and chocolate bars Sophie can buy with the $10. It's a line with a slope of −1/2 and intersects the chocolate bar axis at 10 and the cans-of-soda axis at 20.

To be sure that you've got it, ask yourself what would happen to the income constraint if Sophie got another $4 to spend on the two goods. Going through the same reasoning should lead you to the conclusion that the income constraint willl shift to the right so that it will intersect the cans-of-soda axis at 28 (point D), but its slope won't change. (I started the new line for you.) Make sure you can explain why.

Now how about if the price of a can of soda goes up to $1? What happens to the income line? (This is a question many people miss.) If you said the income line becomes steeper, shifting in along the cans-of-soda axis to point *E* while remaining anchored along the chocolate bar axis until the slope equals −1, you've got it. If you didn't say that, go through the same reasoning we went through at first (if Sophie buys only cans of soda . . .) and then draw the new line. You'll see it becomes steeper. Put another way, the absolute value of the slope of the curve is the ratio of the price of cans of soda to the price of chocolate bars; the absolute value of the slope becomes greater with a rise in the price of cans of soda.

Graphing the Indifference Curve

Now let's consider the second part of Sophie's choice: the pleasure part. Sophie is trying to get as much pleasure as she can from her $10. How do we deal with this in graphish?

To see, let's go through a thought experiment. Say Sophie had 14 chocolate bars and 4 cans of soda (point *A* in Exhibit A2). Let's ask her, "Say you didn't know the price of either good and we took away 4 of those chocolate bars (so you had 10). How many cans of soda would we have to give you so that you would be just as happy as before we took away the 4 chocolate bars?"

Since she's got lots of chocolate bars and few cans of soda, her answer is probably "Not too many; say, 1 can of soda." This means that she would be just as happy to have 10 chocolate bars and 5 cans of soda (point *B*) as she would to have 14 chocolate bars and 4 cans of soda (point *A*). Connect those points and you have the beginning of a "just-as-happy" curve. But that doesn't sound impressive enough, so, following economists' terminology, we'll call it an *indifference curve.* She's indifferent between points *A* and *B*.

If you continue our thought experiment, you'll get a set of combinations of chocolate bars and cans of soda like that shown in the table in Exhibit A2.

If you plot each of these combinations of points on the graph in Exhibit A2 and connect all these points, you have one of Sophie's indifference curves: a curve representing combinations of cans of soda and chocolate bars among which Sophie is indifferent.

Let's consider the shape of this curve. First, it's downward sloping. That's reasonable; it simply says that if you take something away from Sophie, you've got to give her something in return if you want to keep her indifferent between what she had before and what she has now.

Second, it's bowed inward. That's because as Sophie gets more and more of something, it takes fewer and fewer of something else to compensate for the loss of a good she incurred in order to get more of the other good. The underlying reasoning is similar to that in our discussion of the law of diminishing marginal utility, but notice we haven't even mentioned utility. Technically the reasoning for the indifference

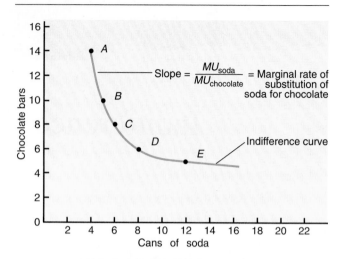

Chocolate bars	Cans of soda	
14	4	*A*
10	5	*B*
8	6	*C*
6	8	*D*
5	12	*E*

EXHIBIT A2   Sophie's Indifference Curve

curve being bowed inward is called *the law of diminishing marginal rate of substitution.* It tells us that as you get more and more of a good, if some of that good is taken away, then the marginal addition of another good you need to keep you on your indifference curve gets less and less.

Even more technically one can say that the absolute value of the slope of the indifference curve equals the ratio of the marginal utility of cans of soda to the marginal utility of chocolate bars:

$$\text{Slope} = \left| \frac{MU_{soda}}{MU_{chocolate}} \right| = \frac{\text{Marginal rate}}{\text{of substitution.}}$$

That ratio equals the marginal rate of substitution of cans of soda for chocolate bars. Let's consider an example. Say that in Exhibit A2 Sophie is at point *A* and that the marginal utility she gets from an increase from 4 to 5 cans of soda is 10. Since we know that she was willing to give up 4 chocolate bars to get that 1 can of soda (and thereby move from point *A* to point *B*), that 10 must equal the loss of utility she gets from the loss of 4 chocolate bars out of the 14 she originally had. So the marginal rate of substitution of cans of soda for chocolate bars between points *A* and *B* must be 4. That's the absolute value of the slope of that curve. Therefore her MU of a chocolate bar must be about 2.5 (10 for 4 chocolate bars).

One can continue this same reasoning, starting with various combinations of goods. If you do so, you can get a whole group of indifference curves like that

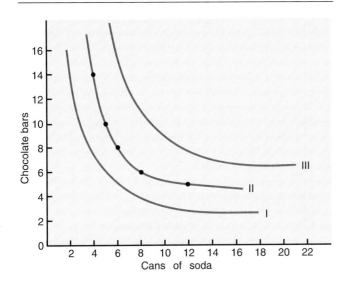

EXHIBIT A3   **A Group of Indifference Curves**

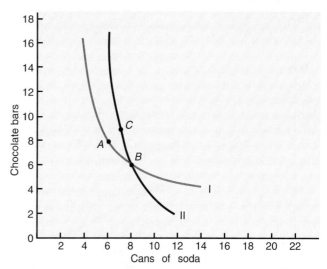

EXHIBIT A4   **Why Indifference Curves Cross**

in Exhibit A3. Each curve represents a different level of happiness. Thus, Sophie is better off if she's on Curve II than if she's on Curve I and even better off if she's on Curve III. Her goal in life is to get out to the furthest indifference curve she can.

To see whether you've followed the reasoning, ask yourself the following question: "Assuming Sophie prefers more of a good to less (which seems reasonable), can any two of Sophie's indifference curves cross each other as the ones in Exhibit A4 do?"

The answer is no, no, no! Why? Because they're indifference curves. If the curves were to cross, the "prefer-more-to-less" principle would be violated. Say we start at point *A:* Sophie has 8 chocolate bars and 6 cans of soda. We know that since *A* (8 chocolate bars and 6 sodas) and *B* (6 chocolate bars and 8 cans of soda) are on the same indifference curve, Sophie is indifferent between *A* and *B.* Similarly with points *B* and *C:* Sophie would just as soon have 9 chocolate bars and 7 cans of soda as she would 6 chocolate bars and 8 cans of soda.

It follows by logical deduction that point *A* must be indifferent to *C.* But consider points *A* and *C* carefully. At point *C*, Sophie has 7 cans of soda and 9 chocolate bars. At point *A* she has 6 cans of soda and 8 chocolate bars. At point *C* she has more of both goods than she has at point *A*, so to say she's indifferent between these two points violates the "prefer-more-to-less" criterion. Ergo (that's Latin, meaning "therefore") two indifference curves cannot intersect. That's why we drew the group of indifference curves in Exhibit A3 such that they did not intersect.

Combining Indifference Curves and Income Constraint

Now let's put the income constraint and the indifference curves together and ask how many chocolate

bars and cans of soda Sophie will buy if she has $10, given the psychological makeup described by the indifference curves in Exhibit A3.

To answer that question, we must put the income line of Exhibit A1 and the indifference curves of Exhibit A3 together, as we do in Exhibit A5.

As we discussed, Sophie's problem is to get to as high an indifference curve as possible, given her income constraint. Let's first ask if she should move to point *A* (8 chocolate bars and 10 cans of soda). That looks like a good point. But you should quickly recognize that she can't get to point *A;* her income line won't let her. (She doesn't have enough money.) Well then, how about point *B* (7 chocolate bars and 6 cans of soda)? She can afford that combination; it's on her income constraint. The problem with point *B* is the following: She'd rather be at point *C* since point *C* has more chocolate bars and the same amount of soda (8 chocolate bars and 6 cans of soda). But, you say, she can't reach point *C.* Yes, that's true, but she can reach point *D.* And, by the definition of indifference curve, she's indifferent between point *C* and point *D,* so point *D* (6 chocolate bars and 8 cans of soda), which she can reach given her income constraint, is preferred to point *B.*

The same reasoning holds for all other points. The reason is that the combination of chocolate bars and cans of soda represented by point *D* is the best she can do. It is the point where the indifference curve and the income line are tangent—the point at which the slope of the income line ($-P_s/MU_c$) equals the slope of the indifference curve ($-MU_s/MU_c$). Equating those slopes gives $P_s/P_c = MU_s/MU_c$ or

$$MU_c/P_c = MU_s/P_s.$$

This equation, you may remember from the chapter, is the equilibrium condition of our principle of rational

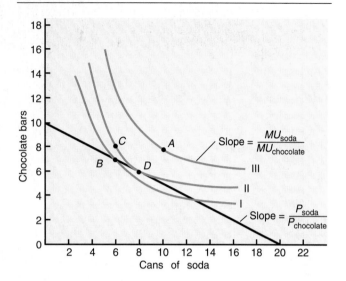

EXHIBIT A5   Combining Indifference Curves and Income Constraint

(a)

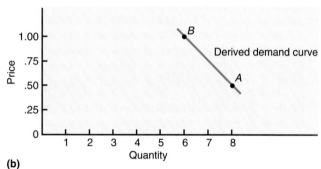

(b)

EXHIBIT A6 (a and b)   From Indifference Curves to Demand Curves

choice. So by our graphish analysis we arrived at the same conclusion we arrived at in the chapter, only this time we did it without mentioning cardinal utility. This means that even without a utilometer, economists' principle of rational choice is internally logical.

Deriving a Demand Curve from the Indifference Curve

Not only can one derive the principle of rational choice with indifference curve/income line analysis, one can also derive a demand curve. To do so, ask yourself what a demand curve is. It's the quantity of a good that a person will buy at various prices. Since the income line gives us the relative price of a good, and the point of tangency of the indifference curve gives us the quantity that a person would buy at that price, we can derive a demand curve from the indifference curves and income lines. To derive a demand curve we go through a set of thought experiments asking how many cans of soda Sophie would buy at various prices. We'll go through one of those experiments.

We start with the analysis we used before when Sophie started with $10 and chose to buy 8 cans of soda when the price of a can of soda was 50¢ (point A in Exhibit A6(a). That analysis provides us with one point on the demand curve. I represent that by point A in Exhibit A6(b). At a price of 50¢, Sophie buys 8 cans of soda.

Now say the price of a can of soda rises to $1. That rotates the income line in, from income line 1 to income line 2 as in Exhibit A6(a). She can't buy as much as she could before. But we can determine how much she'll buy by the same reasoning we used previously. She'll choose a point at which her lower indifference curve is tangent to her new income line. As you can

see, she'll choose point B, which means that she buys 6 cans of soda when the price of a can of soda is $1. Graphing that point (6 cans of soda at $1 each) on our price/quantity axis in Exhibit A6(b), we have another point on our demand curve, point B. Connect these two together and you can see we're getting a downward-sloping demand curve, just as the law of demand said we would. To make sure you understand, continue the analysis for a couple of additional changes. You'll see that the demand curve you derive will be downward-sloping.

There's much more one can do with indifference curves. One can distinguish income effects and substitution effects. (Remember, when the price of a can of soda rose, Sophie was worse off. So to be as well off as before, as is required by the substitution effect, she'd have to be compensated for that rise in price by an offsetting fall in the price of chocolate bars.) But let's make a deal. You tentatively believe me when I say that all kinds of stuff can be done with indifference curves and income constraints, and I'll leave the further demonstration and the proofs for you to experience in the intermediate microeconomics courses.

21

Supply, Production, and Costs

I

*Production is not the application
of tools to materials, but logic to work.*

Peter Drucker

After reading this chapter, you should be able to:

1

Explain why opportunity costs underlie the
law of supply.

2

Define and use the elasticity
of supply concept.

3

Distinguish between the long run and the
short run.

4

State the law of diminishing marginal
productivity and explain its role in
determining the shape of short-run
cost curves.

5

Distinguish the various kinds of cost curves
and describe the relationships among them.

6

Explain why the marginal cost curve always
goes through the minimum point of an
average cost curve.

The ability of Western market economies to supply material goods and services to members of their societies makes them the envy of many other societies and is one of the strongest arguments for using the market as a means of organizing society. Somehow markets are able to channel individuals' imagination, creativity, and drive into the production of material goods and services that other people want. They do this by giving people incentives to supply goods and services to the market.

Ultimately all supply comes from individuals. Individuals control the factors of production such as land, labor, and capital. Why do individuals supply these factors to the market? Because they want something in return. This means that industry's ability to supply goods is dependent on individuals' willingness to supply the factors of production they control. This connection became obvious in the formerly socialist countries in the late 1980s and early 1990s when consumer goods were unavailable. People in those countries stopped working (supplying their labor). They reasoned: Why supply our labor if there's nothing to get in return?

The analysis of supply is more complicated than the analysis of demand. In the supply process, people first offer the factors of production they control to the market. Then the factors are transformed by firms, such as GM or IBM, into goods that consumers want.

Complications are a pain for textbook writers; we want to make the analysis simple for you. (Really we do.) So what we do is to separate out the analysis of the supply of factors of production (considered in detail in later chapters) from the supply of produced goods. This allows us to assume that the prices of factors of production are constant in our analysis of the supply of produced goods, which simplifies the analysis enormously. There's no problem with doing this as long as you remember that behind any produced goods are individuals' factor supplies. Ultimately people, not firms, are responsible for supply.

Even with the analysis so simplified, there's still a lot to cover—so much, in fact, that we devote two chapters (this chapter and the next)—to considering production, costs, and supply. In this chapter I introduce you to the production process and short-run cost analysis. Then, in the next chapter, I focus on long-run costs and how cost analysis is used in the real world.

SUPPLY, OPPORTUNITY COST, AND REAL PEOPLE

To emphasize the reality that people, not firms, are responsible for supply, let's talk briefly about individuals' decisions to supply factors of production. How do you decide how much labor, capital, or land to supply? The answer lies in the opportunity cost to you of keeping the factor for yourself. Let's use the most relevant example for most of you—your labor.

Opportunity Costs and the Law of Supply

1

Opportunity cost The forgone benefit of the next-best alternative.

How much labor will you supply to the market? Think about it using the economic reasoning that is becoming second nature to you (I hope). The answer I'm sure you've arrived at is that it depends on how much you value your leisure, because leisure is what you're forgoing when you work. An hour of leisure is the **opportunity cost** (the forgone pleasure of the next-best alternative) of an hour of work. The same holds true for anything else you supply. Supply ultimately depends on the opportunity cost of the supplier.

Let's consider another example: housing. I'm rewriting this chapter in Bulgaria where there are few hotels. If there are no hotels, where does one stay, you ask? In people's houses. A number of Bulgarians have determined that given the right price they're willing to provide visitors with rooms in their houses. The higher the price, the more rooms that are supplied. (The same holds true around college campuses and in places that have special events.) As the price rises, the quantity of a factor supplied to a market expands.

What this means is that ultimately there's a law of supply, just as there's a law of demand. The law of supply is:

Some "goods" are actually "bads" because of the costs associated with holding them (for example, garbage, old tires, and broken cars). The opportunity cost of having them is negative. In that case more people want to get rid of the good than want to hold the good, so the good has a negative price.

Whether something has a positive or negative price depends on supply and demand. If it were discovered that garbage made an excellent fuel, people would pay for garbage. If everyone wanted to be a doctor, instead of paying doctors to treat them, people would pay to be allowed to doctor someone. If you could convince people that work is fun, they would pay you to allow them to work for you. Supply and demand determine the price of goods, but underlying supply and demand are social mores, technology, people's tastes, and the availability and usefulness of resources.

EXHIBIT 1   Supply of Factors of Production

The supply curve of a factor of production is upward sloping. This follows from the law of supply: When the price of a good increases, the quantity of that good supplied will increase.

When the price of a good increases, the quantity of that good supplied will increase.

It tells us that the supply curve will be upward sloping as in Exhibit 1.

Like the shape of demand curves, supply curves' shape is described by the concept of elasticity. **Price elasticity of supply** is the percent change in quantity supplied divided by the percent change in price. In common sense terms, it measures the relative responsiveness of quantity supplied evoked by a change in price. Because the supply curve slopes upward, the elasticity of supply is positive so you don't need to use the convention of remembering, but not using, the minus sign, as you had to with the elasticity of demand:

$$E_s = \frac{\frac{\Delta Q}{Q}}{\frac{\Delta P}{P}} = \frac{\text{Percent change in quantity}}{\text{Percent change in price}}.$$

Let's consider an example. Say that the quantity of housing supplied to the rental market in an area increases 20 percent when the price goes up 10 percent. The elasticity of supply would be 2.

Terminology Used to Describe Elasticity of Supply   The same terminology is used to describe elasticity of supply as is used to describe elasticity of demand:

If the percent increase in quantity supplied is less than the percent change in price, the elasticity of supply is less than 1 and the supply is said to be *inelastic.*

When the price of a good increases, the quantity of that good supplied will increase.

Elasticity of Supply

Price elasticity of supply The percent change in quantity supplied divided by the percent change in price.

There's an easy way to estimate the elasticity of any supply curve. You simply extend it (or a line tangent to it, if it's curved) to one of the axes, as in the accompanying graph. The point at which this extension intersects the axes indicates the elasticity of the supply curve:

- If the extension intersects the vertical (price) axis, as does S_1, the supply curve has an elasticity greater than 1; it is elastic.
- If the extension intersects the horizontal (quantity) axis, as does S_2, the supply curve has an elasticity less than 1; it is inelastic.
- If the extension intersects the two axes at the origin, the supply curve has an elasticity of 1; it has unit elasticity.

Why does this little trick work? Consider the definition of elasticity of supply:

$$E_s = \frac{1}{\text{Slope}} \times \frac{P}{Q}.$$

Look now at a straight-line curve with unit elasticity. Its slope is given by P/Q. But

$$\frac{1}{\text{Slope}} \times \frac{P}{Q} = \frac{1}{\frac{P}{Q}} \times \frac{P}{Q} = \frac{Q}{P} \times \frac{P}{Q} = 1$$

so if there's unit elasticity, the two terms cancel, no matter what the slope.

The same line of argument holds for a supply curve intersecting the horizontal axis. Its slope is given by $P/(Q-a)$ where a is the quantity bought at a zero price ($a > 0$). Calculating E_s, we have

$$E_s = \frac{1}{\left(\frac{P}{Q-a}\right)} \times \frac{P}{Q} = \frac{Q-a}{P} \times \frac{P}{Q} = \frac{Q-a}{Q} = 1 - \frac{a}{Q}.$$

Since a is positive,

$$E_s = 1 - \frac{a}{Q} < 1.$$

In other words, all points on such a supply curve are inelastic.

- A supply curve that is perfectly vertical (i.e., for which quantity supplied does not change in response to a change in price) is called *perfectly inelastic*.
- If the percent increase in the quantity supplied equals the percent increase in the price, the elasticity of supply is equal to 1 and the supply has *unit elasticity*.
- If the percent increase in the quantity supplied exceeds the percent change in price, the elasticity of supply is greater than 1 and the supply is *elastic*.

VALUE ADDED AND THE CALCULATION OF TOTAL PRODUCTION

T his book (like all economics textbooks) treats production as if it were a one-stage process—as if a single firm transformed a factor of production into a consumer good. Economists write like that to keep the analysis manageable. (Believe me, it's complicated enough.) But you should keep in mind that reality is more complicated. Most goods go through a variety of stages of production.

For example, consider the production of desks. One firm transforms raw materials into usable raw materials (iron ore into steel); another firm transforms usable raw materials into more usable inputs (steel into steel rods, bolts, and nuts); another firm transforms those inputs into desks, which it sells wholesale to a general distributor, which then sells them to a retailer, which sells them to consumers. Many goods go through five or six stages of production and distribution. As a result, if you added up all the sales of all the firms you would overstate how much total production was taking place.

To figure out how much total production is actually taking place, economists use the concept *value added*. **Value added** is the contribution that each stage of production makes to the final value of a good. A firm's value added is determined by subtracting from the firm's total output the

cost of the inputs bought from other firms. For example, if a desk assembly firm spends $4,000 of its revenue on component parts and sells its output for $6,000, its value added is $2,000, or $33\frac{1}{3}$ percent of its revenue.

When you add up all the stages of production, the value added of all the firms involved must equal 100 percent, and no more, of the total output. When I discuss "a firm's" production of a good in this book, to relate that discussion to reality, you should think of that firm as a composite firm consisting of all the firms contributing to the production and distribution of that product.

Why is it important to remember that there are these various stages of production? Because it brings home to you how complicated producing a good is. If any one of those stages gets messed up, the good doesn't get to the consumer. Producing a better mousetrap isn't enough. The firm must also be able to get it out to consumers and let them know that it's a better mousetrap. The standard economic model doesn't bring home this point. But if you're ever planning to go into business for yourself, you'd better remember it. Many people's dreams of supplying a better product to the market have been squashed by this reality.

· A supply curve that's perfectly horizontal (i.e., for which there's an infinite, or larger than imaginable, quantity response to a change in price) is called *perfectly elastic*.

Value added Contribution made to the final value of a good at each stage of production.

The Influence of Substitution on the Elasticity of Supply   Just as was the case with elasticity of demand, the most important determinant of elasticity of supply is the number of substitutes for the good. If substitution is easy, the supply will be elastic; if substitution is difficult, the supply will be inelastic.

There's a difference, however. Many supplied goods are produced, so we must take into account how easy it is to substitute for existing goods by producing more. And before we can do that we need to talk about the production process in detail.

To make sure you have the general idea, however, let's go through a couple of examples to check whether you can intuitively determine elasticity of supply. Let's first consider land. There's a fixed amount of it; you can't make more of it (at least not easily) so land is very inelastic in supply. (The supply curve is close to vertical.) Now how about ball-point pens? It's relatively easy to make another pen, so it seems reasonable that the supply of pens will be quite elastic (close to horizontal). As a third example, think about the supply of your labor. How many more hours would you supply if your wage went up by various percentages? Based on that information determine what your elasticity of labor supply is. (For doing economics mine is very inelastic.)

Ronald Coase—Nobel prize, 1991, for work on the theory of firms and markets. © *The Nobel Foundation.*

With examples like housing and labor, the law of supply is rather intuitive. These goods already exist and their supply to the market depends on people's opportunity costs of keeping them for themselves and for supplying them to the market. But many of the things we buy (such as VCRs, cars, and jackets) don't automatically exist; they must be produced. The supply of such goods depends upon production. So let's now consider production and see how production relates to supply.

THE PRODUCTION PROCESS

The Role of the Firm in Production

Firm Economic institution that transforms factors of production into consumer goods.

The Long Run and the Short Run

Long-run decision A decision in which the firm can choose among all possible production techniques.

Short-run decision Firm is constrained in regard to what production decisions it can make.

3

Production Tables and Production Functions

Production table A table showing the output that will result from various combinations of factors of production or inputs.

Modern production often involves quite different technology than production formerly did. In this picture we see the status display board in the network operations center of the Illinois Bell Telephone Company. © Cameramann/ The Image Works.

A key concept in production is the firm. A **firm** is an economic institution that transforms factors of production into consumer goods. A firm (a) organizes factors of production, (b) produces goods, and/or (c) sells produced goods to individuals.

In Chapter 4 we talked about the myriad firms that exist in real life. They include sole proprietorships, partnerships, corporations, for-profit firms, non-profit firms, and cooperatives. These various firms are the production organizations that translate factors of production into consumer goods.

The production process is generally broken down into a *long-run* planning decision, in which a firm chooses the least expensive method of producing from among all possible methods, and a *short-run* adjustment decision, in which a firm adjusts its long-run planning decision to reflect new information.

In a **long-run decision** a firm chooses among all possible production techniques. This means that it can choose the size of the plant it wants, the type of machines it wants, and the location it wants. In a **short-run decision** the firm has fewer options; it is constrained in regard to what production decisions it can make.

The terms *long run* and *short run* do not necessarily refer to specific periods of time independent of the nature of the production process. They refer to the degree of flexibility the firm has in changing the level of output. In the long run, by definition, the firm can vary the inputs as much as it wants. In the long run all inputs are variable. In the short run some of the flexibility that existed in the long run no longer exists. In the short run some inputs are so costly to adjust that they are treated as fixed. So in the long run all inputs are variable; in the short run some inputs are fixed.

How a firm combines factors of production to produce consumer goods can be presented in a **production table** (a table showing the output resulting from various combinations of factors of production or inputs).

Real-world production tables are complicated. They often involve hundreds of inputs, hundreds of outputs, and millions of possible combinations of inputs and outputs. Studying these various combinations and determining which is best requires expertise and experience. Business schools devote entire courses to it

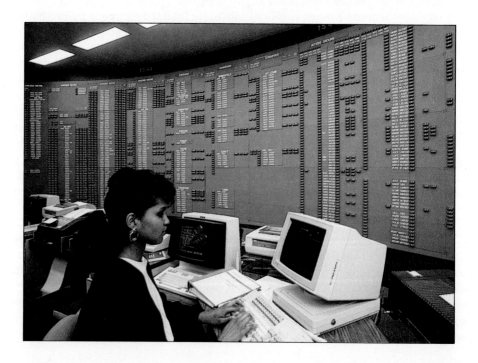

(operations research and production analysis); engineering schools devote entire specialties to it (managerial engineering).

Studying the problems and answering the questions that surround the production relationship make up much of what a firm does: What combination of outputs should it produce? What characteristics should those outputs have? What combination of inputs should it use? What combination of techniques should it use? What new techniques should it explore? To answer these questions, the managers of a firm look at a production table.

Production tables are so complicated that in introductory economics we concentrate on short-run production analysis in which one of the factors is fixed. Doing so allows us to capture some important technical relationships of production without getting too tied up in numbers. The relevant part of a production table of widgets appears in Exhibit 2(c).[1] In it the number of the assumed fixed inputs (machines) has already been determined. Columns 1 and 2 of the table tell us how output varies as the variable input (the number of workers) changes. For example, you can see that with 3 workers the firm can produce 17 units of output. Column 3

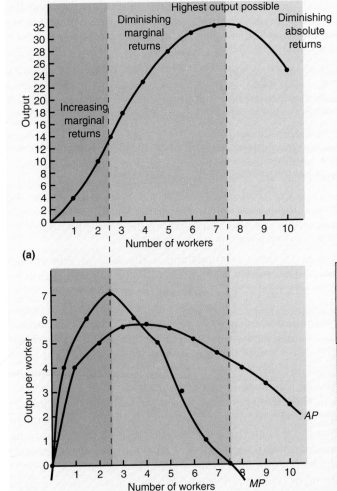

(a)

(b)

(c)

EXHIBIT 2 (a, b, and c)   A Production Table and Production Function

The production function in (a) is a graph of the production table in (c). Its shape reflects the underlying production technology. The graph in (b) shows the marginal and average product. Notice how when marginal product is increasing, the production function is bowed upward; when marginal product is decreasing, the production function is bowed downward; and when marginal product is zero, the production function is at its highest point.

Number of workers	Total ouput	Marginal product (change in total output)	Average product (total product/ number of workers)	
1	4	4	4	Increasing marginal returns
2	10	6	5	
3	17	7	5.7	
4	23	6	5.8	Diminishing marginal returns
5	28	5	5.6	
6	31	3	5.2	
7	32	1	4.6	
8	32	0	4	Diminishing absolute returns
9	30	-2	3.3	
10	25	-5	2.5	

---

[1] What's a widget? It's a wonderful little gadget that's the opposite of a wadget. (No one knows what they look like or what they are used for.) Why discuss widgets? For the same reason that scientists discuss fruit flies—their production process is simple, unlike most real-world production processes.

Marginal product Additional output you get from an additional input, other inputs constant.

Average product Total output divided by the quantity of the variable input.

Production function Equation that describes the relationships between inputs and outputs, telling the maximum amount of output that can be derived from a given number of inputs.

The Law of Diminishing Marginal Productivity

Law of diminishing marginal productivity As more and more of an input is added to an existing fixed input, eventually the additional output one gets from that additional input will fall.

tells us workers' **marginal product** (the additional output that will be forthcoming from an additional worker, other inputs constant). Column 4 tells us workers' **average product** (output per worker).

It is important to distinguish marginal product from average product. Workers' average product is the total output divided by the number of workers. For example, let's consider the case of five workers. Total output is 28 so average product is 5.6 (28 divided by 5). To find the marginal product we must ask how much additional output will be forthcoming if we change the number of workers. For example, if we change from 4 to 5 workers, the additional worker's marginal product will be 5; if we change from 5 to 6, the additional worker's marginal product will be 3. That's why the marginal products are written between the lines.

The information in a production table is often summarized in a production function. A **production function** is a curve that describes the relationship between the inputs (factors of production) and outputs. Specifically, the production function tells the maximum amount of output that can be derived from a given number of inputs. Exhibit 2(a) is the production function that displays the information in the production table in Exhibit 2(c). The number of workers is on the horizontal axis and the output of widgets is on the vertical axis.

Exhibit 2(b) graphs the workers' average and marginal productivities from the production function in Exhibit 2(a). (Alternatively you can determine those graphs by plotting columns 3 and 4 from the table in Exhibit 2(c).) Notice that both marginal and average productivities are initially increasing, but that eventually they both decrease. Between seven and eight workers, the marginal productivity actually becomes negative.

This means that initially this production function exhibits increasing marginal productivity and then it exhibits *diminishing marginal productivity*. Eventually it exhibits negative marginal productivity.

The same information can be gathered from Exhibit 2(a), but it's a bit harder to interpret.[2] Notice that initially the production function is bowed upward. Where it's bowed upward there is increasing marginal productivity, as you can see if you extend a line down to Exhibit 2(b). Then, between 2.5 and 7.5 workers, the production function is bowed downward but is still rising. In this range there's diminishing marginal productivity, as you can see by extending a line down to Exhibit 2(b). Finally there's negative marginal productivity.

The most important area of these relationships is the area of diminishing marginal productivity. Why? Because that's the most likely area for a firm to operate in. For example, if it's in the first range and marginal productivity is increasing, a firm can increase its existing workers' output by hiring more workers; it will have a strong incentive to do so and get out of that range. Similarly if hiring an additional worker actually cuts total output (as it does when marginal productivity is negative), the firm would be crazy to hire that worker. So it stays out of that range. This means that the most relevant part of the production function is that part exhibiting diminishing marginal productivity.

This range of the relationship between fixed and variable inputs is so important that economists have formulated a law that describes what happens in production processes when they reach this range—when more and more of one input is added to a fixed amount of another input. It's called the **law of diminishing marginal productivity,** which states that as more and more of a variable input is added to an existing fixed input, eventually the additional output one gets from that additional input is going to fall.

As I stated in the introductory chapter, the law of diminishing marginal productivity is sometimes called *the flower pot law* because if it didn't hold true, the world's entire food supply could be grown in one flower pot. In the absence of diminishing marginal productivity, one could take a flower pot and keep adding

---

[2] Technically the marginal productivity curve is a graph of the slope of the total product curve.

THE HISTORY OF THE LAW OF DIMINISHING MARGINAL PRODUCTIVITY

▪hen economists were first formulating their analysis of production, farming was the most important economic activity and most individuals worked on the land. Economists devised their analysis of production to help them structure their ideas about what would happen to total production as the population grew and hence the number of workers increased. In thinking about this issue, they came up with the law of diminishing marginal productivity, which describes what will happen if more and more of a flexible input (labor) is added to a fixed input (land).

The law of diminishing marginal productivity states that eventually, when more and more of a variable input is added to a fixed input, the additional output that results from that additional input decreases.

Initially the law of diminishing marginal productivity was the basis of some gloom-and-doom predictions, which prompted writer Thomas Carlyle to call economics *the dismal science*. The gloom-and-doom predictions were that since the amount of land is fixed, as the population grows, with more workers working the fixed amount of land, eventually the point of diminishing marginal productivity will be reached and the amount of food available per person will decline. Starvation will result, decreasing the population to the subsistence level of output per person. If given any more wages, workers will have more kids and reduce the output per person again to subsistence. This was known as the *iron law of wages:*

Diminishing marginal productivity combined with human beings' uncontrolled sexual drive will result in increases in the supply of labor so that average output and wages will decrease to the subsistence level.

For most Western economies the gloom-and-doom predictions have not come true. Even the originator of the predictions, Thomas Malthus, eliminated them from later editions of *An Essay on Population,* the book in which he first propounded them. Similarly the iron law of wages was soon dropped.

It was not because the law of diminishing marginal productivity doesn't hold true that the gloom-and-doom predictions were dropped. Rather they were dropped because technological changes overwhelmed the law of diminishing marginal productivity. Over time fewer and fewer individuals have been able to grow more and more output on a smaller amount of land.

While in the United States gloom-and-doom predictions have been overtaken by events, in many developing countries the law of diminishing marginal productivity is very much in effect. In many developing countries output per individual is decreasing, often to the subsistence level or even below it. Economists in some developing countries believe that not only has the point of diminishing marginal productivity set in, but the point of input saturation has been reached: Output, rather than merely not increasing with additional inputs, actually decreases, and the marginal productivity of additional workers is negative.

seeds to it, getting more and more food per seed until one had enough to feed the world. In reality, however, a given flower pot is capable of producing only so much food no matter how many seeds you add to it. At some point, as you add more and more seeds, each additional seed will produce less food than did the seed before it. Eventually the pot reaches a stage of diminishing absolute productivity in which the total output, not simply the output per unit of input, decreases as inputs are increased.

Probably in a firm far more discussion is about costs than about anything else. Invariably costs are too high and the firm is trying to figure out ways to lower costs. But the concept *costs* is ambiguous; there are many different types of costs and it's important to know these different types. Let's consider some of the most important categories of costs in reference to Exhibit 3, which gives a table of costs associated with making between 4 and 32 pairs of earrings.

Fixed costs are costs that are spent and cannot be changed in the period of time under consideration. There are no fixed costs in the long run since all inputs are variable and hence their costs are variable. In the short run, however, a number of costs will be fixed. For example, say you make earrings. You buy a machine for working with silver, but suddenly there's no demand for silver earrings. Assuming that machine can't be modified and used for other purposes, the money you spent on it is a fixed cost.

Fixed costs are shown in column 2 of Exhibit 3. Notice that fixed costs remain the same ($50) regardless of the level of production. As you can see, it doesn't matter whether output is 15 or 20; fixed costs are always $50.

THE COSTS OF PRODUCTION

Fixed Costs, Variable Costs, and Total Costs

Fixed costs Costs that are spent and cannot be changed in the period of time under consideration.

EXHIBIT 3   The Cost of Producing Earrings

1 Output	2 Fixed costs (FC)	3 Variable costs (VC)	4 Total costs (TC) (FC + VC)	5 Marginal costs (MC) (change in total costs)	6 Average fixed costs (AFC) FC/Output	7 Average variable costs (AVC) VC/Output	8 Average total costs (ATC) AFC + AVC
4	50	50	100		12.50	12.50	25.00
				10			
5	50	60	110		10.00	12.00	22.00
10	50	100	150		5.00	10.00	15.00
				6			
11	50	106	156		4.54	9.64	14.18
17	50	150	200		2.94	8.82	11.76
				7			
18	50	157	207		2.78	8.72	11.50
21	50	182	232		2.38	8.67	11.05
23	50	200	250		2.17	8.70	10.87
				10			
24	50	210	260		2.08	8.75	10.83
28	50	250	300		1.79	8.93	10.72
				15			
29	50	265	315		1.72	9.14	10.86
32	50	350	400		1.56	10.94	12.50

Variable costs The costs of variable inputs; they change as output changes.

Besides buying the machine, the silversmith must also hire workers. These workers are the earring maker's **variable costs.** Variable costs are costs that change as output changes. The earring maker's variable costs are shown in column 3. Notice that as output increases, variable costs increase. For example, when she produces 11 pairs of earrings, variable costs are $106; when she produces 17, variable costs rise to $150.

Total cost Sum of the fixed and variable costs.

All costs are either fixed or variable in the standard model so the sum of her fixed and variable costs equals her **total cost,**

$$TC = FC + VC.$$

The earring maker's total costs are presented in column 4. Each entry in column 4 is the sum of the entries in columns 2 and 3 in the same row. For example, to produce 17 pairs of earrings, fixed costs are $50 and variable costs are $150 so total cost is $200.

Average Total Cost, Average Fixed Cost, and Average Variable Cost

Total cost, fixed cost, and variable cost are important, but much of firms' discussion is of average cost. So the next distinction we want to make is between total cost and average cost. To arrive at the earring maker's average cost, we simply divide the total amount of whatever cost we're talking about by the quantity produced. Each of the three costs we've discussed has a corresponding average cost.

Average total cost (often called average cost) Total cost divided by the quantity produced.

For example, **average total cost (often called *average cost*)** equals total cost divided by the quantity produced. Thus,

$$ATC = TC/Q.$$

Average fixed cost Fixed cost divided by quantity produced.

Average fixed cost equals fixed cost divided by quantity produced:

$$AFC = FC/Q.$$

Average variable cost Variable cost divided by quantity produced.

Average variable cost equals variable cost divided by quantity produced:

$$AVC = VC/Q.$$

EXHIBIT 4 Total Cost Curves

Total fixed costs are always constant; they don't change with output. All other total costs increase with output. As output gets high the rate of increase has a tendency to increase.

Average fixed cost and average variable cost are shown in columns 6 and 7. The most important average cost concept, average total cost, is shown in column 8. Average total cost can also be thought of as the sum of average fixed cost and average variable cost:

$$ATC = AFC + AVC.$$

As you can see, the average total cost of producing 17 pairs of earrings is $11.76. It can be calculated by dividing total cost ($200) by output (17).

All these costs are important to our earring maker, but they are not the most important cost she considers in her decision as to how many pairs of earrings to produce. That distinction goes to marginal cost, which appears in column 5.[3] **Marginal cost** is the increased (decreased) total cost of increasing (or decreasing) the level of output by one unit. Let's find marginal cost by considering what happens if our earring maker increases production by one unit—from 10 to 11. Looking again at Exhibit 3, we see that the total cost rises from $150 to $156. In this case the marginal cost of producing the eleventh unit is $6.

The marginal cost concept is extremely important to economic reasoning. But before we get into that, it is important to see how these cost concepts can be presented graphically. It's important for two reasons: First, graphs reinforce your understanding of the cost concepts; and, second, one of the most efficient ways of testing whether you understand the cost concepts is with graphs. So let's say that our earring maker is a visually oriented person who asks you (an economics consultant) to show her what all those numbers in the table in Exhibit 3 mean.

To do so, you first draw a graph, putting quantity on the horizontal axis and a dollar measure of various costs on the vertical axis. In this graphical presentation we will focus on average cost curves because that's what economists generally do. But, for completeness, we will also briefly discuss total cost curves, which, since they are directly related to average cost curves, provide the same information.

Total Cost Curves   Exhibit 4 graphs the total cost, total fixed cost, and total variable cost of all the levels of output given in Exhibit 3.[4] Thus, the total cost curve is determined by plotting the entries in column 1 and the corresponding entries in

Marginal Cost

Marginal cost The cost of changing the level of output by one unit.

Graphing Cost Curves

---

[3] Since only selected output levels are shown, not all entries have marginal costs. For a marginal cost to exist, there must be a marginal change, a change by only one unit.

[4] To keep the presentation simple, we focus only on the most important part of the total cost curve, that part that follows the simplest rules. Other areas of the total cost curve can be bowed downward rather than bowed upward.

EXHIBIT 5   Per Unit Output Cost Curves

The average fixed cost curve is downward sloping; the average variable cost curve and average total cost curve are U-shaped.

column 4. For example, point *L* corresponds to a quantity of 10 and a total cost of $150. Notice that the curve is upward sloping: Increasing output increases total cost.

The total fixed cost curve is determined by plotting column 1 and column 2 on the graph. The total variable cost curve is determined by plotting column 1 and column 3.

As you can see, the total variable cost curve has the same shape as the total cost curve: Increasing output increases variable cost. This isn't surprising, since the total cost curve is the vertical summation of total fixed cost and total variable cost. For example, at output 10, total fixed cost equals $50 (point *M*); total variable cost equals $100 (point *O*); and total cost equals $150 (point *L*).

Average and Marginal Cost Curves   In Exhibit 5, I present the average fixed cost curve, average total cost curve (or average cost curve, as it's generally called), average variable cost curve, and marginal cost curve associated with the cost figures in Exhibit 3. Each point on the four curves represents a combination of two corresponding entries in Exhibit 3. Points on the average variable cost curve are determined by plotting the entries in column 1 and the corresponding entries in column 7. Points on the average fixed cost curve are determined by entries in column 1 and the corresponding entries in column 6. Points on the average total cost curve are determined by entries in column 1 and the corresponding entries in column 8. Finally the marginal cost curve is determined by plotting the entries in column 1 and the corresponding entries in column 5. As was the case with the total cost curves, all our earring maker need do is look at this graph to find the various costs associated with different levels of output.

One reason the graphical visualization of cost curves is important is that the graphs of the curves give us a good sense of what happens to costs as we change output.

Sliding-Board Shape of the Average Fixed Cost Curve   Let's start our consideration with average fixed cost. Average fixed cost is decreasing throughout; the average fixed cost curve looks like a child's sliding board: It starts out with a steep decline; then it becomes flatter and flatter. What this tells us about production is straightforward: As output increases, the same fixed cost can be spread over a wider range of output, so average fixed cost falls. Average fixed cost initially falls quickly but then falls more and more slowly. As the denominator gets bigger while the numerator stays the same, the increase has a smaller and smaller effect.

The Law of Diminishing Marginal Productivity and the U-Shape of the Average and Marginal Cost Curves   Let's now move on to the average and marginal cost curves. Why do they have the shapes they do? Or expressed another way, how does our analysis of production relate to our analysis of costs? You may have already gotten an idea of how production and costs relate if you remembered Exhibit 2 and recognized the output numbers that we presented there were the same output numbers that we used in the cost analysis. The reason they were the same is that the cost analysis is of that earlier production analysis. The laws governing costs are the same laws governing productivity that we just saw in our consideration of production.

When output is increased in the short run, it can only be done by increasing the variable input. But as more and more of a variable input is added to a fixed input, the law of diminishing marginal productivity enters in. Marginal and average productivities fall. The key insight here is that when marginal productivity falls, marginal cost must rise, and when average productivity of the variable input falls, average variable cost must rise. So to say that productivity falls is the equivalent to saying that cost rises.

It follows that if eventually the law of diminishing marginal productivity holds true, then eventually both the marginal cost curve and the average cost curve must be upward sloping. And, indeed, in our examples they are. It's also generally held that at low levels of production marginal and average productivities are increasing. This means that marginal cost and average variable cost are initially falling. If they're falling initially and rising eventually, at some point they must be neither rising nor falling. This means that both the marginal cost curve and the average variable cost curve are U-shaped.

The average total cost curve is the vertical summation of the average fixed cost curve and the average variable cost curve, so it's always higher than both of them. As you can see in Exhibit 5, the average total cost curve has the same general U-shape as the average variable cost curve, but its low point is to the right of the low point for the average variable cost curve. We'll discuss why after we cover the shape of the average variable cost curve.

Average total cost initially falls faster and then rises more slowly than average variable cost. If one increased output enormously, the average variable cost curve and the average total cost curve would almost meet. Average total cost is of key importance to our earring maker. She wants to keep it low.

The Relationship between the Marginal Productivity and Marginal Cost Curves   In Exhibit 6(a) I redraw the marginal cost curve and average variable cost curve presented in Exhibit 5. Notice their U-shape; initially costs are falling. Then there's some minimum point. After that, costs are rising.

In Exhibit 6(b) I graph the average and marginal productivity curves that we first developed in Exhibit 2(c), although this time I relate average and marginal productivities to output, rather than to the number of workers. Thus, we know that the average product of two workers is 5, and that two workers can produce an output of 10 so when output is 10, the worker's average productivity is 5. Point *A* corresponds to an output of 10 and average productivity of 5.

Now let's compare the graphs in (a) and in (b). If you look at the two graphs carefully, you'll see that one is simply the mirror image of the other. The minimum point of the average variable cost curve (output = 21) is at the same level of output as the maximum point of the average productivity curve; the minimum point of the marginal cost curve (output = 12) is for the same level of output as the

(a)

(b)

EXHIBIT 6 (a and b) The Relationship between Productivity and Costs

The shapes of the cost curves are mirror-image reflections of the shape of the corresponding productivity curves. When one is increasing, the other is decreasing; when one is at a minimum, the other is at a maximum.

maximum point on the marginal productivity curve. When the productivity curves are falling, the corresponding cost curves are rising. Why is that the case? Because as productivity falls, costs per unit increase; and as productivity increases, costs per unit decrease.

The Relationship between the Marginal Cost and Average Cost Curves   Now that we've considered the shapes of each cost curve, let's consider some of the important relationships among them—specifically the relationships between the marginal cost curve on the one hand and the average variable cost and average total cost curves on the other. These relationships are shown graphically for a different production process in Exhibit 7.

Let's first look at the relationship between marginal cost and average total cost. In areas *A* and *B* at output below 5, even though marginal cost is rising, average total cost is falling. Why? Because in areas *A* and *B* the marginal cost curve is below the average total cost curve. At point *B,* where average total cost is at its lowest, the marginal cost curve intersects the average total cost curve. In area *C,* above output 5, where average total cost is rising, the marginal cost curve is above the ATC curve.

6   The positioning of the marginal cost curve is not happenstance. The position of marginal cost relative to average total cost tells us whether average total cost is rising or falling.

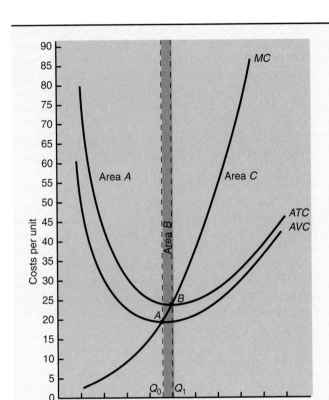

EXHIBIT 7   Relationship of Marginal Cost Curve to Average Variable Cost and Average Total Cost Curves

The marginal cost curve goes through the minimum point of both the average variable cost curve and the average total cost curve. Thus there is a small range where average total costs are falling and average variable costs are rising.

If MC > ATC, then ATC is rising.
If MC = ATC, then ATC is at its low point.
If MC < ATC, then ATC is falling.

If MC > ATC, then ATC is rising.
If MC = ATC, then ATC is at its low point.
If MC < ATC, then ATC is falling.

To understand why this is, think of it in terms of your grade point average. If you have a B average and you get a C on the next test (that is, your marginal grade is a C), your grade point average will fall below a B. Your marginal grade is below your average grade, so your average grade is falling. If you get a C+ on the next exam (that is, your marginal grade is a C+), *even though your marginal grade has risen from a C to a C+,* your grade point average will fall. Why? Because your marginal grade is still below your average grade. To make sure you understand the concept, explain the next two cases:

1. If your marginal grade is above your average grade, your average grade will rise.
2. If your marginal grade and average grade are equal, the average grade will remain unchanged.

Marginal and average reflect a general relationship that also holds for marginal cost and average variable cost.

If MC > AVC, then AVC is rising.
If MC = AVC, then AVC is at its low point.
If MC < AVC, then AVC is falling.

If MC > AVC, then AVC is rising.
If MC = AVC, then AVC is at its low point.
If MC < AVC, then AVC is falling.

This relationship is best seen in area B of Exhibit 7 when output is between Q_0 and Q_1. In this area the marginal cost curve is above the average variable cost curve, so average variable cost is rising; but the MC curve is below the average total cost curve, so average total cost is falling.

The intuitive explanation for what is represented in this area is that average total cost includes average variable cost, but it also includes average fixed cost, which is falling. As long as short-run marginal cost is only slightly above average variable cost, the average total cost will continue to fall. Put another way: Once marginal cost is above average variable cost, as long as average variable cost doesn't rise by more than average fixed cost falls, average total cost will still fall.

At this point I'm going to cut off the chapter, not because we're finished with the subject, but because there's only so much that anyone can absorb in one chapter. It's time for a break.

Those of you who are married should go out and give your spouse a big kiss; tell him or her that the opportunity cost of being away for another minute was so high that you couldn't control yourself. Those of you with kids, go out and read them a Dr. Seuss book. (My favorite is about Horton.) Let's face it—Seuss is a better writer than I, and if you've been conscientious about this course, you may not have paid your kids enough attention. Those of you with significant others, go out and do something significant. Those of you with parents bearing the cost of this education, give them a call and tell them that you appreciate their expenditure on your education. Think of the opportunity cost of that education to them; it's not peanuts. We'll return to the grind in the next chapter.

INTERMISSION

Dr. Seuss books are often more interesting than economics books.

KEY POINTS

- No one is going to supply a good to the market unless the price he will get for that good exceeds the opportunity cost of that good. **1**
- Price elasticity of supply is the percent change in quantity divided by the percent change in price. **2**
- In the long run a firm can choose among all possible production techniques; in the short run it is constrained in its choices. **3**
- The law of diminishing marginal productivity states that as more and more of a variable input

is added to a fixed input, the additional output the firm gets will eventually be decreasing. **4**
- Costs are generally divided into fixed costs, variable costs, and total costs. **5**
- The average variable cost curve and marginal cost curve are mirror images of the average product curve and the marginal product curve, respectively. **4**
- If MC > ATC, then ATC is rising.
  If MC = ATC, then ATC is constant.
  If MC < ATC, then ATC is falling. **6**

KEY TERMS

average fixed cost *(460)*
average product *(458)*
average total cost *(460)*
average variable
  cost *(460)*
firm *(456)*

fixed costs *(459)*
law of diminishing mar-
  ginal productivity *(458)*
long-run decision *(456)*
marginal cost *(461)*
marginal product *(458)*

opportunity cost *(452)*
price elasticity of
  supply *(453)*
production function *(458)*
production table *(456)*
short-run decision *(456)*

total cost *(460)*
value added *(455)*
variable costs *(460)*

QUESTIONS FOR THOUGHT AND REVIEW

The number after each question represents the estimated degree of critical thinking required. (1 = almost none; 10 = deep thought.)

1. State the law of supply and explain how it relates to opportunity cost.   *(5)*
2. If the supply curve is perfectly inelastic, what is the opportunity cost of the supplier?   *(6)*
3. "There is no long run; there are only short and shorter runs." Evaluate that statement.   *(8)*
4. What is the difference between marginal product and average product?   *(3)*
5. If average product is falling, what is happening to short-run average variable cost?   *(3)*
6. If marginal cost is increasing, what do we know about average cost?   *(4)*

7. If average productivity falls, will marginal cost necessarily rise? How about average cost?   *(4)*
8. Say that neither labor nor machines are fixed but that there is a 50 percent quick order premium paid to both workers and machines for delivery of them in the short run. Once you buy them, they cannot be returned, however. What do your short-run marginal cost and short-run average total cost curves look like?   *(9)*
9. If machines were variable and labor fixed, how would the general shapes of the short-run average cost curve and marginal cost curve change?   *(6)*
10. If you increase production to an infinitely large level, the average variable cost and the average total cost will merge. Why?   *(4)*

PROBLEMS AND EXERCISES

1. Find and graph the TC, AFC, AVC, AC, and MC from the following table.

Units	FC	VC
0	100	0
1	100	40
2	100	60
3	100	70
4	100	85
5	100	130

2. An economic consultant is presented with the following table on average productivity and asked to derive a table for average variable costs. The price of labor is $15 per hour.

Labor	TP
1	5
2	15
3	30
4	36
5	40

   a. Help him do so.
   b. Show that the graph of the average productivity curve and average variable cost curve are mirror images of each other.

Supply, Production, and Costs

II

*Economic efficiency consists of
making things that are worth more than they cost.*

J. M. Clark

After reading this chapter, you should be able to:

1

Distinguish technical efficiency from
economic efficiency.

2

Explain how economies of scale influence
the shape of long-run cost curves and how
diminishing marginal productivity influences
the shape of short-run cost curves.

3

Differentiate diminishing marginal
productivity from diseconomies of scale.

4

State the envelope relationship between
short-run cost curves and long-run
cost curves.

5

Explain the central role of opportunity
costs in all supply decisions.

6

Discuss some of the problems of using cost
analysis in the real world.

7

Apply the marginal cost concept to
decisions facing you.

Welcome back. I hope you've reestablished your relationship with the real world and are ready to return, with renewed vigor, to the world of economics. When we took our intermission last chapter we had worked our way through the various short-run costs. That short run is a time period in which some inputs are fixed. A key determinant of the shape of the short-run cost curve is marginal productivity. If those last two sentences don't ring some bells and create images of cost curves dancing in your head, you may have been intermissioning before intermission, so a review of the last chapter is in order. If those bells are ringing, then we can continue and consider firms' long-run decisions and the determinants of the long-run cost curves. We'll do that in the first part of this chapter. Then in the second part we'll talk about applying cost analysis to the real world.

MAKING LONG-RUN PRODUCTION DECISIONS

In the long run firms have many more options than they do in the short run. They can change any input they want. Plant size is not given; neither is the technology available given.

To make their long-run decisions, firms look at the costs of the various inputs and the technologies available for combining those inputs and then decide which combination offers the lowest cost. Say you're opening a hamburger stand. One decision you'll have to make is what type of stove to buy. You'll quickly discover that many different types are available.

Some use more gas than others but cost less to buy; some are electric; some are self-cleaning and hence use less labor; some are big; some are little; some use microwaves; some use convection. Some have long-term guarantees; some have no guarantees. Each has a colorful brochure telling you how wonderful it is. After studying the various detailed specifications and aspects of the production technology, you choose the stove that has the combination of characteristics that you believe best fits your needs.

Next you decide on workers. Do you want older workers, younger workers, part-time workers, experienced workers . . . ? You get the idea: Even simple production decisions involve complicated questions. These decisions are made on the basis of the expected costs, and expected usefulness, of inputs.

Technical Efficiency and Economic Efficiency

One important distinction to keep in mind in considering firms' long-run production decisions is the distinction between technical efficiency and economic efficiency. The production process transforms inputs into outputs. Any firm will want to choose a technically efficient production process. **Technical efficiency** in production means that as few inputs as possible are used to produce a given output.

Technical efficiency A situation in which as few inputs as possible are used to produce a given output.

Many different production processes can be technically efficient. For example, say you know that to produce 100 tons of wheat you can use 10 workers and 1 acre or use 1 worker and 100 acres. Which of these two production techniques is more efficient? Both can be technically efficient since neither involves the use of more of both inputs than the other technique. But that doesn't mean that both are equally efficient. That question can't be answered unless you know the relative costs of the two inputs. If an acre of land rents for $1,000,000 and each worker costs $10 a day, our answer likely will be different than if land rents for $40 an acre and each worker costs $100 a day. This is no longer a technical question; this is an economic question whose answer depends upon the costs of production. Which of the variety of technically efficient methods of production is *economically efficient?* The **economically efficient** method of production is that method that produces a given level of output at the lowest possible cost.

In long-run production decisions, firms will look at all available production technologies and choose the technology that, given the available inputs and their prices, is the economically efficient way to produce. These choices will reflect the prices of the various factors of production. Those prices, in turn, will reflect the factors' relative scarcities.

Economically efficient Using the method of production that produces a given level of output at the lowest possible cost.

Consider the use of land by firms in the United States and in Japan. The United States has large amounts of land (10 acres) per person, so the price of land is lower than in Japan, which has only .78 acre per person. An acre of rural land in the United States might cost about $700; in Japan it costs about $17,000. Because of this difference in price of inputs, production techniques use land much more intensively in Japan than in the United States. Similarly with China: Labor is more abundant so production techniques are more labor-intensive than in the United States. Whereas China would utilize hundreds of people to build a road, primarily using human labor, the United States would use three or four people along with three machines. Both countries are being economically efficient, but because costs of inputs differ, the economically efficient method of production differs. Thus, the economically efficient method of production is that technically efficient method of production that has the lowest cost.

Determinants of the Shape of the Long-Run Cost Curve In the last chapter we saw that the law of diminishing marginal productivity accounted for the shape of the short-run cost curve. That followed since we kept adding more of a variable input to a fixed input. The law of diminishing marginal productivity doesn't apply to the long run since in the long run all inputs are variable. The most important determinants of what is economically efficient in the long run are economies and diseconomies of scale. Let's consider each of these in turn and see what effect they will have on the shape of the long-run average cost curve.

Economies of Scale When the per-unit output cost of all inputs decreases as output increases, we say that there are **economies of scale** in production. For example, if producing 40,000 VCRs costs the firm $16,000,000 ($400 each), but producing 200,000 VCRs costs the firm $40,000,000 ($200 each), there are significant economies of scale associated with choosing to produce 200,000 rather than 40,000.

In real-world production processes, at low levels of production economies of scale are extremely important. The reason is that many production techniques are indivisible—they must be used at a certain minimum level before they begin to become useful. For example, say you want to produce a pound of steel. You can't just build a mini blast furnace, stick in some coke and iron ore, and come out with your single pound of steel. Technology requires that technically efficient blast furnaces be of a minimum size with a production capacity that is measured in tons per hour, not pounds per hour. The cost of the blast furnace is said to be an **indivisible set-up cost** (the cost of an indivisible input for which a certain minimum amount of production must be undertaken before the input becomes economically feasible to use).

Indivisible set-up costs are important because they create many real-world economies of scale: As output increases, the costs per unit of output decrease. As an example, consider this book. Setting the type for it is an indivisible set-up cost; it is a cost that must be incurred if any production is to take place, but it is not a cost that increases with the number of books produced. That means that the more copies of the book that are produced, the lower the typesetting cost per book. That's why it costs more per book to produce a textbook for an upper-level, low-enrollment course than it does for a lower-level, high-enrollment course. The same amount of work goes into both (both need to be written, edited, and set into type), and the printing costs differ only slightly.

The actual print run costs of printing a book are only about $1 to $8 per book. The other costs are indivisible set-up costs. Because of these indivisible set-up costs, large economies of scale are possible in printing books. Prices of produced goods, including books, reflect their costs of production. As you move to upper-level academic courses, you'll likely discover that the books are smaller and less colorful but cost as much as, or more than, this introductory text.

In the long-run planning decisions about the cost of producing this book, the expected number of copies to be sold was an important element. That figure

---

Economies of scale A decrease in per-unit cost as a result of an increase in output.

Indivisible set-up cost The cost of an indivisible input for which a certain minimum amount of production must be undertaken before the input becomes economically feasible to use.

The normal production run of a U.S. automobile is 200,000 units per year. Why is it so high? Because of indivisible set-up costs. In order to reduce those indivisible set-up costs to an acceptable level, the production level per year must equal at least 200,000 or the car is considered an economic failure. The Pontiac Fiero, a sporty two-seater, was dropped in 1988 because it didn't sell well enough to sustain that production level.

But what is an indivisible set-up cost depends on the structure of production. Japanese companies structure production differently from U.S. companies and have a much lower level of indivisible set-up costs. For example, at just about the same time as Pontiac dropped the Fiero, a Japanese company, Mazda, entered the market with the Miata, another sporty two-seater. Because Mazda's assembly line is designed to handle different sizes and shapes of vehicles (which permits economies of scope discussed later in the text), its minimum profitable production level for the Miata is about 30,000, not 200,000. This alternative structure of production made it possible for the Miata to do well in a market that buys a total of about 40,000 two-seater sports coupes annually.

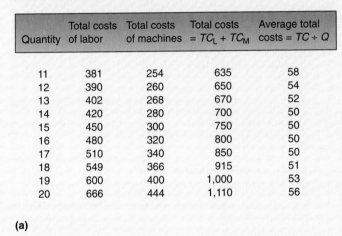

Quantity	Total costs of labor	Total costs of machines	Total costs $= TC_L + TC_M$	Average total costs $= TC \div Q$
11	381	254	635	58
12	390	260	650	54
13	402	268	670	52
14	420	280	700	50
15	450	300	750	50
16	480	320	800	50
17	510	340	850	50
18	549	366	915	51
19	600	400	1,000	53
20	666	444	1,110	56

(a)

(b)

EXHIBIT 1 (a and b)   A Typical Long-Run Average Total Cost Table and Curve

In the long run average costs initially fall because of economies of scale; then they are constant for a while, and finally they tend to rise due to diseconomies of scale.

influenced the number of books produced, which in turn affected the expected cost per unit. This will be the case any time there are economies of scale. With economies of scale, cost per unit of a small production run is higher than cost per unit of a large production run.

Exhibit 1(a) demonstrates a normal long-run production table; Exhibit 1(b) shows the related typical shape of a long-run average cost curve. (Notice that there are no fixed costs. That's because we're in the long run so all costs are variable.) Economies of scale account for the downward-sloping part. Cost per unit of output is decreasing.

Because of the importance of economies of scale, businesspeople often talk of a minimum level of production. What they mean by **minimum level of production** is that, given the price at which they expect to be able to sell a good, the indivisible set-up costs are so high that production runs of less than a certain size don't make economic sense. Thus, the minimum level of production is the amount of production that spreads set-up costs out sufficiently for a firm to undertake production profitably.

Minimum level of production The amount of production run that spreads out set-up costs sufficiently for a firm to undertake production profitably.

Diseconomies of Scale   Notice that on the right side of the graph the long-run average cost curve is upward sloping. Average cost is increasing. When the per-unit cost

We've covered a lot of costs and cost curves quickly so a review is in order. First, let's list the cost concepts and their definitions.

1. Marginal cost: the additional cost resulting from a one-unit change in output.
2. Total cost: all costs.
3. Average total cost: total cost divided by total output (TC/Q).
4. Fixed cost: cost that is already spent and cannot be recovered. (It exists only in the short run.)
5. Average fixed cost: fixed cost divided by total output (FC/Q).
6. Variable cost: cost of variable inputs. Variable cost does not include fixed cost.
7. Average variable cost: variable cost divided by total output (VC/Q).

Each of these costs can be represented by a curve. A number of these curves have specific relationships to the other cost curves.

1. MC: MC intersects AVC and ATC at their minimum points.
2. If MC > AVC, then AVC is rising. If MC < AVC, then AVC is falling.
3. If MC > ATC, then ATC is rising. If MC < ATC, then ATC is falling.
4. ATC: a U-shaped curve.
5. AVC: a U-shaped curve lower than the ATC, with the minimum point slightly to the left.
6. AFC: a sliding-board–shaped curve that starts high, initially decreases rapidly, and then decreases slowly.
7. The long-run ATC curve is a U-shaped curve which forms an envelope around the various short-run ATC curves.

Diseconomies of scale An increase in per-unit cost as a result of an increase in output.

of all inputs increases as a result of an increase in output, we say that there are **diseconomies of scale** in production. For example, if producing 200,000 VCRs costs the firm $40,000,000 ($200 each) and producing 400,000 VCRs costs the firm $100,000,000 ($250 each), there are diseconomies of scale associated with choosing to produce 400,000 rather than 200,000. Diseconomies of scale usually, but not always, start occurring as firms get large.

Diseconomies of scale could not occur if production relationships were only technical relationships. If that were the case, the same technical process could be used over and over again at the same cost. In reality, however, production relationships have social dimensions, which introduce the potential for important diseconomies of scale into the production process in two ways:

1. As the size of the firm increases, monitoring costs generally increase.
2. As the size of the firm increases, team spirit or morale generally decreases.

Monitoring costs Costs incurred by the organizer of production in seeing to it that employees do what they are supposed to.

Monitoring costs are the costs incurred by the organizer of production in seeing to it that the employees do what they're supposed to do. If you're producing something yourself, the job gets done the way you want it done; monitoring costs are zero. However as the scale of production increases, you have to hire people to help you produce. This means that if the job is to be done the way you want it done, you have to monitor (supervise) your employees' performance. The cost of monitoring can increase significantly as output increases; it's a major contributor to diseconomies of scale. Most big firms have several layers of bureaucracy devoted simply to monitoring others. The job of middle managers is, to a large extent, monitoring.

Team spirit The feelings of friendship and being part of a team that bring out people's best effort.

The other social dimension that can contribute to diseconomies of scale is the loss of **team spirit** (the feelings of friendship and being part of a team that bring out people's best efforts). Most types of production are highly dependent on team spirit. When that team spirit or morale is lost, production slows considerably. A

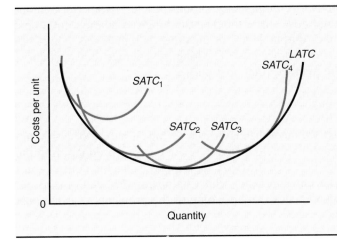

EXHIBIT 2   **Envelope of Short-Run Average Total Cost Curves**
The long-run average total cost curve is an envelope of the short-run average total cost curves. Each short-run average total cost curve touches the long-run average total cost curve at only one point.

good example is the former Soviet Union in its earlier transition from capitalism to socialism and its ongoing transition from socialism to capitalism. During both transitions, people lost faith in the system, and whatever team spirit had existed before fell apart and production decreased by 25 percent or more.

Some large firms manage to solve these problems and thus avoid diseconomies of scale. But as a firm's size increases, it's much harder to maintain that team spirit effectively and to monitor employees. So, often these problems of monitoring and loss of team spirit limit the size of firms. They underlie diseconomies of scale in which relatively less output is produced for a given increase in inputs, so that per-unit costs of output increase.

The Importance of Economies and Diseconomies of Scale   Economies and diseconomies of scale play important roles in real-world long-run production decisions. Economies of scale underlie firms' attempts to expand their market either at home or abroad. If they can make and sell more at lower per-unit costs, they will make more profits. Diseconomies of scale prevent a firm from expanding and can lead corporate raiders to buy the firm and break it up in the hope that the smaller production units will be more efficient, thus eliminating some of the diseconomies of scale.

The long-run and the short-run average cost curves have the same U-shape. But it's important to remember that the reasons why they have this U-shape are quite different. The assumption of initially increasing and then eventually diminishing marginal productivity (as a variable input is added to a fixed input) accounts for the shape of the short-run average cost curve. Economies and diseconomies of scale account for the shape of the long-run average cost curve.

Since in the long run all inputs are flexible, while in the short run some inputs are not flexible, long-run cost will always be less than or equal to short-run cost. To see this, let's consider a firm that had planned to produce 100 but now adjusts its plan to produce more than 100. We know that in the long run the firm chooses the lowest-cost method of production. In the short run it faces an additional constraint: All expansion must be done using only the variable input. That constraint must increase average cost (or at least not decrease it) compared to what average cost would have been had the firm planned to produce that level to begin with. If it didn't, the firm would have chosen that new combination of inputs in the long run. Additional constraints increase cost. This relationship between long-run and short-run average total costs is known as the **envelope relationship,** shown in Exhibit 2.

The Relationship between Short-Run Average Total Cost and Long-Run Average Total Cost

4

Envelope relationship Relationship explaining that at the planned output level, short-run average total cost equals long-run average total cost, but at all other points, short-run average total cost is higher than long-run average total cost.

Why it's called an *envelope relationship* should be clear from the exhibit. Each short-run average total cost curve touches the long-run average total cost curve at one, and only one, output level; at all other output levels, short-run average cost exceeds long-run average cost. The long-run average total cost curve is an envelope of short-run average total cost curves.

COSTS, ENTREPRENEURIAL ACTIVITY, AND THE SUPPLY DECISION

In this chapter and the last we have discussed the technical nature of costs and production. In the next chapter we will formally relate costs of production to the supply of goods. As a bridge between the two chapters, let's conclude this chapter with a consideration of the entrepreneur, who establishes the relationship between costs and the supply decision, and of some of the problems of using cost analysis in the real world.

Price Must Be Expected to Exceed Cost for a Good to Be Supplied

5

In thinking about the connection between cost and supply, one fundamental insight is that the revenue received for a good must be greater than the planned cost of producing it. Otherwise why would anyone supply it? The difference between the expected price of a good and the expected average total cost of producing it (the good's opportunity cost) is the supplier's expected economic profit per unit. It's profit that underlies the dynamics of production in a market economy.

Entrepreneur Visionary individual who makes production happen; she visualizes demand and makes things happen.

An **entrepreneur** is an individual who sees an opportunity to sell an item at a price higher than the average cost of producing it. The entrepreneur is the organizer of production and the one who visualizes the demand and convinces the individuals who own the factors of production that they want to produce that good. Similarly the entrepreneur also must convince demanders that what the entrepreneur is producing is what the demanders want. Cost enters into these decisions as a cutoff. Entrepreneurs who don't cover their cost generally don't stay in business.

The Entrepreneur and Supply

Cost curves do not become supply curves through some magic process. To move from cost to supply, entrepreneurial initiative is needed. The entrepreneur analyzes costs and supplies output. An entrepreneur must organize people to do something that he or she wants them to do. He or she must be a psychologist, a cheerleader, a boss, a confessor, and an engineer, to name just a few of the skills an entrepreneur needs. It's these dynamic, driven individuals who underlie supply and who instigate production. They're people who get other people off their behinds.

By allowing entrepreneurs to earn profit, market economies encourage people to channel their drive into supplying material goods. Entrepreneurs create production and hence supply. Without entrepreneurs there would be little supply because there would be no one to recognize and act on demand potential.

The greater the difference between price and average total cost, the greater the entrepreneur's incentive to tackle the organizational problems and supply the good. That insight underlies the dynamic laws of supply discussed in Chapter 2.

USING COST ANALYSIS IN THE REAL WORLD

6

All too often students walk away from an introductory economics course thinking that cost analysis is a relatively easy topic. Memorize the names, shapes, and relationships of the curves, and you're home free. In the textbook model, that's right. In real life, it's not, because actual production processes are marked by:

PROFILES OF TWO ENTREPRENEURS

William Lear

William Lear was an inventor extraordinaire. After completing eighth grade he quit school to go to work as a mechanic. In the early 1920s he invented the automobile radio. He failed to get financial backing for his invention, however, and sold it to Motorola.

In 1934 he developed a frequency amplifier that could be used in any radio set and which lowered the cost of radios significantly. Selling that invention to RCA made him a millionaire. During World War II he developed an automatic pilot device which made it possible for planes to take off, fly, and land even when visibility was zero. Similar systems are still in use today.

In 1962 he wanted to develop a small, low-price jet aircraft. His company, Lear, Inc. (which by then was being run by corporate managers), wouldn't go along with his idea, so he left the company and started again. In 1965 the Lear Jet was born, the fastest and cheapest small jet that then existed. Next he turned his ingenuity to audiotape and developed the first eight-track tape system.

Lear lived for inventing. He made things work, not only inventing them but also bringing them into production. After production of his inventions got underway, he often found himself at odds with the organization he'd created.

He died in 1978 while working on a turboprop plane which was meant once again to revolutionize small plane transportation.

Steven Jobs

Together with Stephen Wozniak, Steven Jobs invented the personal computer. Jobs was an adopted child and a loner who hated school. He attended after-school lectures at Hewlett-Packard, an electronics firm. At one lecture he asked the president of H-P to give him some parts for a school project. The president gave him both the parts and a summer job. At that job he met Stephen Wozniak, a dropout from the University of California at Berkeley who (on his own time) was perfecting a "blue box" which allowed individuals to make illegal, free long-distance phone calls. They first collaborated on selling these devices.

Jobs entered college in 1972, but soon dropped out. However he hung around the campus practicing meditation. In 1974 he went to India in search of spiritual enlightenment. Not finding it, he went back to Palo Alto, California, saw Wozniak again, and convinced him to work with him in perfecting and marketing a PC. Wozniak did the engineering; Jobs handled the marketing. To obtain financing, they sold Jobs's Volkswagen microbus for $1,300 and begged credit from an electronic supplier. Their product, the Apple I, was a success. It was soon followed by the Apple II.

By the 1980s Apple was a tremendous success. Wozniak voluntarily left the firm and Jobs was ousted in a 1985 power struggle. Everyday management of a major company was not their domain. Both left, but they left rich. Jobs used his many contacts to create the "Next" Computer System, designed specifically for universities. Whether he will be successful the second time around remains to be seen.

1. economies of scope
2. learning by doing and technological change
3. many dimensions
4. unmeasured costs
5. joint costs
6. indivisible costs
7. uncertainty
8. asymmetries
9. multiple planning and adjustment periods with many different short runs.

The general model provides a nice framework with which to approach production, but before the model can be really applied it must be expanded to incorporate these complications. Alas, in introductory economics we don't have time to discuss these complications in detail, but we do have time to give you a sense of their importance. We'll do so by briefly considering four qualifications.

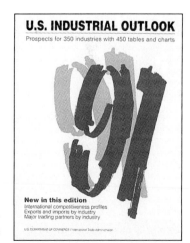

U.S. Industrial Outlook—This Commerce Department publication provides large amounts of information about real-world industries.

Economies of Scope

The cost of production of one product often depends on what other products a firm is producing. When the costs of producing products are interdependent, so that it's less costly for a firm to produce one good when it's already producing

Production then—The nature of production has changed considerably in the last 60 years. This picture shows a 1933 production line in which people did the work as the goods moved along the line. *UPI/ Bettmann.*

Economies of scope The costs of producing products are interdependent so that producing one good lowers the cost of producing another.

another, economists say that there are **economies of scope** in the production of the two goods. For example, once a firm has set up a large marketing department to sell cereal, the department might be able to use its expertise in marketing a different product—say, dog food. A firm that sells gasoline can simultaneously use its gas station attendants to sell soda, milk, and incidentals. The minimarts so common along our highways and neighborhood streets developed because gasoline companies became aware of economies of scope.

Economies of scope play an important role in firms' decisions of what combination of goods to produce. They look for both economies of scope and economies of scale. When you read about firms' mergers think about whether the combination of their products will generate economies of scope. Many otherwise unexplainable mergers between seemingly incompatible firms can be explained by economies of scope.

Learning by Doing and Technological Change

The production terminology that we've been discussing is central to the standard economic models. In the real world, however, other terms and concepts are also important. The production techniques available to real-world firms are constantly changing because of *learning by doing* and *technological change*. These changes occur over time and cannot be accurately predicted.

Unlike events in the standard economic model, all events in the real world are influenced by the past. That's why learning by doing is important in the real world, but isn't a part of the standard economic model. **Learning by doing** simply means that as we do something, we learn what works and what doesn't, and over time we become more proficient at it. Practice may not make perfect, but it certainly makes better and more efficient. Many firms estimate that output per unit input will increase by 1 or 2 percent a year, even if no changes in inputs or technologies occur, as employees learn by doing.

Learning by doing Becoming more proficient at doing something by actually doing it; in the process, learning what works and what doesn't.

The concept of learning by doing emphasizes the importance of the past in trying to predict performance. Let's say a firm is deciding between two applicants for the job of managing its restaurant. One was a highly successful student but has never run a restaurant; the other was an OK student who has run a restaurant that

Production now—The nature of production has changed considerably in the last 60 years. This picture shows a modern production line. Robots do much of the work. © *Keystone/The Image Works.*

failed. Which one does the firm hire? The answer is unclear. The first applicant may be brighter, but the lack of experience will likely mean that the person won't be hired. Businesses give enormous weight to experience. So this firm may reason that in failing, the second applicant will have learned lessons that make her the better candidate. U.S. firms faced such a choice when they were invited to expand into the new market economies of Eastern Europe in the early 1990s. Should they hire the former communist managers who had failed to produce efficiently, or should they hire the reformers? (Generally they decided on the former communist managers, hoping they had learned by failing.)

Technological change offers an increase in the known range of production techniques. Technological change provides brand new ways of producing goods. For example, at one point automobile tires were made from rubber, clothing was made from cotton and wool, and buildings were made of wood. As a result of technological change, many tires are now made from petroleum distillates, much clothing is made from synthetic fibers (which in turn are made from petroleum distillates), and many buildings are constructed from steel.

Technological change An increase in the range of production techniques that provides new ways of producing goods.

Technological change can fundamentally alter the nature of production cost. Say, for instance, that physicists discovered a new method of cold fusion (combining atoms to produce energy). That discovery would greatly reduce the need for oil and other increasingly scarce and expensive sources of energy, and it would have far-reaching effects on the costs of production of almost all goods. Other possibilities for technological change with significant effects exist in the new field of genetic engineering.

Technological changes that are far less drastic in their consequences are occurring every day. A new fertilizer is developed that increases crop yield per acre; a new machine is designed that does the work of two people. These technological changes can lower costs enormously. Whenever technological change (or learning by doing) occurs, the cost curve shifts.

Many Dimensions

The only dimension in the standard model is the level of output. Many, if not most, decisions that firms make are not the one-dimensional decisions of the actories run by numbers. Numbers to calculate profit and losses; to analyze the costs of new products; and to chart corporate strategy. But a lot of managers are relying on the wrong numbers.

As they adopt new manufacturing techniques like computer-aided design, just-in-time stock management, and total quality control, many firms are discovering that their existing account systems also need dragging into the 1990s. Unless the bean-counters join the manufacturing revolution, traditional cost accounting will have little place in the factory of the future.

The two previous paragraphs introduced an article in *The Economist* (March 3, 1990, p. 61) describing a conference on strategic manufacturing. This conference focused on managerial or cost accounting (the application of cost analysis to managerial decisions). Unlike *financial accounting* (which involves keeping track of income, assets, and liabilities), managerial accounting is used to help managers determine the cost of producing products and plan future investment. It's the direct application of microeconomics to production.

In the 1980s and 1990s there has been an enormous change in cost accounting. The leaders of this change—such as Robert Kaplan of the Harvard Business School—argue that cost accounting systems based on traditional concepts of fixed and variable costs lead firms consistently to make the wrong decisions. They argue that in today's manufacturing, direct labor costs have fallen substantially—in many industries to only 2 or 3 percent of the total cost—and overhead costs have risen substantially. This change in costs facing firms requires a much more careful division among types of overhead costs and a recognition that what should and should not be assigned as a cost to a particular product differs with each decision.

These developments in managerial accounting require an even deeper understanding of costs than accountants have previously needed. As one firm's director of manufacturing was quoted in *The Economist* article, "Unless management accountants move fast [to incorporate these new concepts], they will be almost without use to the manufacturing manager of 1995."

standard model, such as "Should we produce more or less?" They're multidimensional questions like "Should we change the quality? Should we change the wrapper? Should we improve our shipping speed? Should we increase our inventory?" Each of these questions relates to a different dimension of the production decision and each has its own marginal costs. Thus, there isn't just one marginal cost; there are 10 or 20 of them. Good economic decisions take all relevant margins into account.

The reason that the standard model is important is that each of these questions can be analyzed using the same reasoning used in the standard model. But you must remember, *in applying the analysis, it's the reasoning, not the specific model, that's important.*

Unmeasured Costs

If one were to ask, "In what area of decision making do businesses most often fail to use economic insights?" the answer most economists would give is costs. The relevant costs are generally not the costs you'll find in a firm's accounts.

Why the difference? Economists operate conceptually; they include in costs exactly what their theory says they should. Accountants who have to measure firms' costs in practice and provide the actual dollar figures take a much more pragmatic approach; their concepts of costs must reflect only those costs that are reasonably precisely measurable.

Economists Include Opportunity Cost   Let's take a few examples. First, say that a business produces 1,000 widgets that sell at $3 each for a total revenue of $3,000. To produce these widgets the business had to buy $1,000 worth of widgetgoo, which the owner has hand-shaped into widgets. An accountant would say that the total cost of producing 1,000 widgets was $1,000 and that the firm's profit was $2,000. That's because an accountant uses explicit costs that can be measured. Thus,

Accounting profit Definition of *profit* used by accountants that states profit is total revenue minus explicit measurable costs.

$$\text{Accounting profit} = \textit{Total revenue} - \textit{Explicit measurable costs.}$$

Economic profit is different. An economist, looking at that same example, would point out that the accountant's calculation doesn't take into account the time and effort that the owner put into making the widgets. While a person's time involves no explicit cost in money, it does involve an *opportunity cost,* the forgone income that the owner could have made by spending that time working in another job. If the business takes 400 hours of the person's time and the person could have earned $6 an hour working for someone else, then the person is forgoing $2,400 in income. Economists include that implicit cost in their concept of cost. When that implicit cost is included, what looks like a $2,000 profit becomes a $400 economic loss.

Economic profit = *Implicit and explicit revenues − Implicit and explicit costs.*

> **Economic profit** Definition of *profit* used by economists that states profit is total implicit and explicit revenues minus total implicit and explicit costs.

Economic Depreciation versus Accounting Depreciation   Now let's take a second example. Say a firm buys a machine for $10,000 that's meant to last 10 years, but after one year, machines like that become in short supply so instead of falling, its value rises to $12,000. An accountant, looking at the firm's costs that year, would use **historical cost** (what the machine cost in terms of money actually spent) depreciated at, say, 10 percent per year, so the machine's cost for each of its 10 years of existence would be $1,000. An economist would say that since the value of the machine is rising, the machine has no cost; in fact, it provides a revenue of $2,000 to the firm. The standard model avoids such messy, real-world issues of measuring costs and instead assumes that all costs are measurable in a single time period.

> **Historical cost** Cost in terms of money actually spent.

I suspect that even with its simplifications, the standard model has been more than enough to learn in an introductory course. Learning the standard model, however, only provides you with the rudiments of cost analysis, in the same way that learning the rules of mechanics only provides you with the basics of mechanical engineering. In addition to a knowledge of the laws of mechanics, building a machine requires years of experience. Similarly for economics and cost analysis. Introductory economics provides you with a superb framework for starting to think about real-world cost measurement, but it can't make you an expert cost analyst.

The Standard Model as a Framework

Let's now consider two examples of cost considerations in everyday life. Let's first consider an example of an incorrect decision often made by individuals that they would not make if they correctly specified cost; and, second, let's consider an example of a firm's pricing policy that makes sense if one understands marginal cost.

Cost Considerations in Everyday Life: Two Examples

An Individual's Decision about Which of Two Stocks to Sell   Say you bought two stocks: one at $100, one at $10. You have a chance to sell either stock at $50. Which should you sell? Many people would answer that you should sell the stock you bought at $10 because you'll make a profit of $40, and if you sell the $100 stock, you'll sustain a loss of $50. But that reasoning is wrong. After you spent the money to buy the two stocks in the first place, that expenditure became a fixed cost and shouldn't enter into your decision about which stock to sell. You make a profit or loss when the price of the shares goes up or down, not when you sell the stock. Since you have the options of selling, the market valuation of the stock at each moment in time is used to determine your profit, not the valuation of the stock when you sell it.

7

The economist's answer to the question of which of the two stocks you should sell is "It depends on what you expect to happen to the price of the stocks in the future." Decisions should not be based on the past, except to the degree that the past can be used to predict the future. Variations of this "mistake" occur all the time in business. Firms often set their prices based on invoice costs of the goods they sell, not on the current replacement or opportunity costs.

A Firm's Pricing Policy Based on Marginal Cost   Let's consider another example of cost and the many dimensions of output. Electric utilities often argue that they should be allowed to charge higher rates for electricity used during times of peak demand and lower rates during off-peak times. Many people argue against such a pricing policy because they believe that a firm's prices should be based on its costs. They argue that the costs of producing electricity are the same at 7 P.M. as at 4:30 A.M. and the utility should charge the same price at all times.

Understanding marginal cost and recognizing that output has multiple dimensions sheds a different light on the issue. The cost of supplying electricity consists primarily of the overhead cost that must be incurred to build facilities large enough to meet demand in the peak period. After that capacity is built, the marginal cost of supplying electricity at any point other than at the peak load is low. However the marginal cost of supplying peak load power is high. By setting different rates for peak and off-peak usage, electric companies are actually reflecting their cost structure. Economists generally support "peak load pricing" because it's based on the relevant marginal cost.

CONCLUSION AND A LOOK AHEAD

We've come to the end of our discussion of production, cost, and supply. The two chapters we spent on them weren't easy; there's tons of material here, and, quite frankly, it will likely require at least two or three reads and careful attention to your professor's lecture before your mind can absorb it. So if you're planning to sleep through a lecture, the ones on these chapters aren't the ones for that.

These chapters, in combination with our discussion of individual choice, will provide the framework for most of the later chapters, which really do get into interesting real-world issues. But you've got to know the basics to truly understand those issues. So, now that you've come to the end of these two chapters, unless you really feel comfortable with the analysis, it's probably time to review them from the beginning. (Sorry, but remember, there's no such thing as a free lunch.)

KEY POINTS

- An economically efficient production process must be technically efficient, but a technically efficient process need not be economically efficient. **1**
- Production is a social, as well as a technical, phenomenon; that's why concepts like team spirit are important. **2**
- The long-run average total cost curve is U-shaped. Economies of scale initially cause average total cost to decrease; diseconomies eventually cause average total cost to increase. **2 3**

- There is an envelope relationship between short-run average cost curves and long-run average cost curves. **4**
- An entrepreneur is an individual who sees an opportunity to sell an item at a price higher than the average cost of producing it. **5**
- Once one starts applying cost analysis to the real world, one must include a variety of other dimensions of costs that the standard model does not cover. **6 7**

KEY TERMS

accounting profit *(478)*
diseconomies of scale *(472)*
economic profit *(479)*
economically efficient *(469)*

economies of scale *(470)*
economies of scope *(476)*
entrepreneur *(474)*
envelope relationship *(473)*
historical cost *(479)*

indivisible set-up cost *(470)*
learning by doing *(476)*
minimum level of production *(471)*

monitoring costs *(472)*
team spirit *(472)*
technical efficiency *(469)*
technological change *(477)*

QUESTIONS FOR THOUGHT AND REVIEW

The number after each question represents the estimated degree of critical thinking required. (1 = almost none; 10 = deep thought.)

1. Distinguish technical efficiency from economic efficiency. *(2)*
2. A student has just written on an exam how in the long run fixed cost will make the average total cost curve slope downward. Why will the professor mark it incorrect? *(3)*
3. What inputs do you use in studying this book? What would the long-run average total cost and marginal cost curves for studying look like? Why? *(8)*
4. Why could diseconomies of scale never occur if production relationships were only technical relationships? *(7)*
5. When economist Jacob Viner first developed the envelope relationship, he told his draftsman to make sure that (1) all the marginal cost curves went through both the minimum point of the short-run average cost curve and (2) the point where the short-run average total cost curve was tangent to the long-run average total cost curve. The draftsman told him it couldn't be done. Viner told him to do it anyhow. Why was the draftsman right? *(8)*
6. What is the role of the entrepreneur in translating cost of production into supply? *(4)*
7. Your average total cost is 40; the price you receive for the good is 12. Should you keep on producing the good? Why? *(5)*
8. A student has just written on an exam that learning by doing will mean that the cost curve is downward sloping. Why did her teacher mark it wrong? *(6)*
9. Distinguish economic profit from accounting profit. *(3)*
10. If you were describing the marginal cost of an additional car driving on a road, what costs would you look at? What is the likely shape of the marginal cost curve? *(9)*

PROBLEMS AND EXERCISES

1. Visit a nearby company and ask it what would happen to its per-unit costs if sales increased by 10 percent. Try to figure out how its answer relates to the concepts in the last two chapters, remembering especially the discussion about using cost analysis in the real world.
2. Find out the total budget of your college or university. (It often takes a bit of sleuthing, but almost all college and university budgets are in the public record.) Find out the number of students. What is the total cost per student? What is the relevant marginal cost of an additional student?

   Now say you're on a planning committee charged with eliminating an expected 2 percent budget deficit next year. Using the budget figures, make some suggestions. Have a college administrator (preferably the treasurer or comptroller) come in to your class and react to those suggestions. Explain why presidents of universities and colleges don't last long.

23

Perfect Competition

*There's no resting place for an
enterprise in a competitive economy.*
Alfred P. Sloan

After reading this chapter, you should be able to:

1

List the seven conditions for perfect
competition.

2

Demonstrate why the marginal cost curve is
the supply curve for a perfectly
competitive firm.

3

Explain why producing an output at which
marginal cost equals price maximizes total
profit for a perfect competitor.

4

Determine the output and profit of a perfect
competitor graphically and numerically.

5

Explain why perfectly competitive firms
make zero economic profit in the long run.

6

Use supply and demand curves to discuss
real-world events.

7

Discuss the Pareto optimal criterion and
state three criticisms of it.

In physics when you study the laws of gravity, you initially study what would happen in a vacuum. Perfect vacuums don't exist, but talking about what would happen if you dropped an object in a perfect vacuum makes the analysis easier. So too with economics. Our equivalent of a perfect vacuum is perfect competition. In perfect competition the invisible hand of the market operates unimpeded. In this chapter we'll consider how perfectly competitive markets work and see how the cost analysis developed in the previous chapter can be applied.

A **perfectly competitive** market is a market in which economic forces operate unimpeded. For a market to be called *perfectly competitive*, it must meet some stringent conditions:

1. Buyers and sellers are price takers.
2. The number of firms is large.
3. There are no barriers to entry.
4. Firms' products are homogeneous (identical).
5. Exit and entry are instantaneous and costless.
6. There is complete information.
7. Selling firms are profit-maximizing entrepreneurial firms.

These conditions are needed to ensure that economic forces operate instantaneously and are unimpeded by other invisible or visible forces. For example, say that there weren't a large number of firms. The few firms in the industry would then have an incentive to get together and limit output so they could get a higher price. They would stop the invisible hand from working. Similarly for the other conditions although the reasoning why they're necessary can get rather complicated.

To give you a sense of these conditions, let's consider them a bit more carefully.

1. *Both buyers and sellers are price takers.* A **price taker** is a firm or individual who takes the market price as given. When you buy, say, toothpaste, you go to the store and find that the price of toothpaste is, say $1.38 for the medium-size tube; you're a price taker. The firm, however, is a price maker since it set the price at $1.38. So even though the toothpaste industry is highly competitive, it's not a perfectly competitive market. In a perfectly competitive market, supply and demand determine the price; both firms and consumers take the market price as given.

2. *The number of firms is large.* It's almost self-explanatory to say that the number of firms is large. *Large* means sufficiently large so that any one firm's output compared to the market output is imperceptible, and what one firm does has no influence on what other firms do.

3. *No barriers to entry.* **Barriers to entry** are anything that prevents other firms from entering a market. They might be legal barriers such as exist when firms acquire a patent to produce a certain product. Barriers might be technological, such as exist when the minimum efficient scale of production allows only one firm to produce at the lowest average total cost. Or barriers might be created by social forces, such as when bankers will lend only to certain types of people and not to other types. Perfect competition can have no barriers to entry.

4. *Homogeneous product.* A **homogeneous product** is a product such that each firm's output is indistinguishable from any other firm's output. Corn bought by the bushel is homogeneous. One kernel is indistinguishable from every other kernel. On the other hand, you can buy 30 different brands of many goods—soft drinks, for instance: Pepsi, Coke, 7-Up, and so on. Each is slightly different from the other and thus not homogeneous.

Commodity, currency, and stock exchanges provide the closest real world analogue to competitive markets.
© *David Wells/The Image Works.*

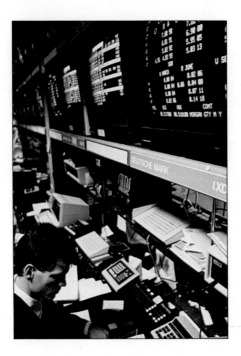

5. *Instantaneous exit and entry.* Say all the grocery stores in your neighborhood raised their prices by 30 percent without their costs having gone up. What would happen in the next week or month? Probably nothing, other than customers getting mad. You'd still shop there until a new store opened in a convenient place with more reasonable prices. In a perfectly competitive market, the new store would open immediately upon hearing that the prices in the existing stores had gone up. It wouldn't wait a week, or even an hour.

6. *Complete information.* In a perfectly competitive market, not only would the store open up immediately; you'd also know about it instantaneously. So too would other firms. Similarly if any firm experienced a technological breakthrough, all firms would know about it and would be able to use the same technology instantaneously.

7. *Profit-maximizing entrepreneurial firms.* Firms can have many goals and be organized in a variety of ways. For perfect competition to exist, firms' goals must be profit and only profit, and the people who make the decisions must receive only profits and no other form of income from the firms.

The Necessary Conditions and the Definition of Supply

These are strict, but necessary, conditions for a perfectly competitive market to exist. Combined they create an environment in which each firm, following its own self-interest, will offer goods to the market in a predictable way. If these conditions hold, we can talk formally about the supply of a produced good. If they aren't met, then our formal definition of supply of produced goods dissolves; we can still talk *in*formally about supply of produced goods and cost conditions, but we cannot use our formal concept of supply and how it relates to costs. This follows from the definition of **supply:**

Supply A schedule of quantities of goods that will be offered to the market at various prices.

> Supply is a schedule of quantities of goods that will be offered to the market at various prices.

This definition requires the supplier to be a price taker (our first condition). In almost all other market structures (frameworks within which firms interact economically) firms are not price takers; they are price makers and the question "How much should I supply, given a price?" will not be asked. Instead the question asked is "Given a demand curve, how much should I produce and what

EXHIBIT 1 (a and b)   Market Demand Curve versus Individual Firm Demand Curve

Even though the demand curve for the market is downward sloping, the perceived demand curve of an individual firm is perfectly elastic because each firm is so small relative to the market.

price should I charge?'' In other market structures the supplier sets the quantity and price, based on costs, at whatever level is best for it.[1]

The second condition—that the number of firms is large—is necessary so that firms have no ability to *collude* (to operate in concert so that they can get more for themselves). Conditions 3 through 6 are closely related to the first two; they make it impossible for any firm to forget that there are hundreds of other firms out there just waiting to supply a good if it doesn't. Condition 7 lets us specify a firm's goals. If we didn't know the goals, we wouldn't know how firms would react when faced with the given price.

What's nice about these conditions is that they allow us to formally relate supply to the cost concept that we developed in the last chapter: marginal cost. If the conditions hold, a firm's supply curve will be that portion of the firm's short-run marginal cost curve above the average variable cost curve, as we'll see shortly.

Of course, as later chapters will reveal, even if we can't technically specify a supply function, and even if the conditions for perfect competition don't fully exist, supply forces are still strong and many of the insights of the competitive model carry over. That's why it's important to know that competitive model well.

Now that we've considered the competitive supply curve for the firm let's turn our attention to the competitive demand curve for the firm. Here we must recognize that the demand curve for the industry is downward sloping as in Exhibit 1(a), but the perceived demand curve for the firm is perfectly elastic as in Exhibit 1(b). (Remember, I told you those terms would be important.)

Why the difference? It's a difference in perception. Each firm in a competitive industry is so small that it perceives its own demand curve as perfectly elastic even though the demand curve for the industry is downward sloping. Think of it as removing one piece of sand from a beach. Does that lower the level of the beach?

Demand Curves for the Firm and the Industry

---
[1] A firm's ability to set price doesn't mean that it can choose just any price it pleases. Other market structures can be highly competitive, so the range of prices a firm can charge and still stay in business is often limited. Such highly competitive firms are not perfectly competitive because they still set price, rather than supply a certain quantity and accept whatever price they get.

Price = MR	Quantity produced	Marginal cost
35.00	0	
35		28
35.00	1	24.00
35		20
35.00	2	18.00
35		16
35.00	3	15.00
35		14
35.00	4	13.00
35		12
35.00	5	15.00
35		17
35.00	6	20.00
35		22
35.00	7	26.00
35		30
35.00	8	35.00
35		40
35.00	9	47.00
35		54
35.00	10	61.00
35		68

(a)

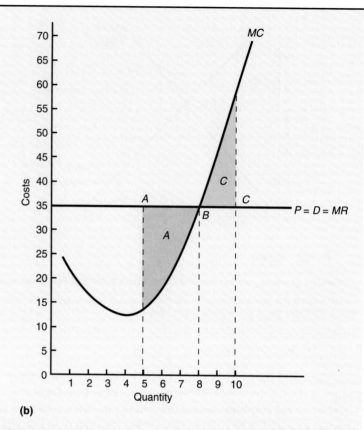

(b)

EXHIBIT 2 (a and b)　Marginal Cost, Marginal Revenue, and Price

The profit-maximizing output for a firm occurs where marginal cost equals marginal revenue. Since for a competitive firm $P = MR$, its profit maximizing output is where $MC = P$. At any other output it is forgoing profit.

For all practical, and even most impractical, purposes, we can assume it doesn't. Similarly for a perfectly competitive firm: Its demand curve is perfectly elastic even though the demand curve for the market is downward sloping.

This difference in perception is extremely important. It means that firms will increase their output in response to an increase in demand even though that increase in output will cause price to fall and can make all firms collectively worse off. But, since by the assumptions of perfect competition, they don't organize collectively, each firm follows its self-interest. Let's now consider that self-interest in more detail.

PROFIT MAXIMIZATION AND EQUILIBRIUM OF A COMPETITIVE FIRM

Marginal cost The change in cost associated with a change in quantity.

Marginal revenue The change in revenue associated with a change in quantity.

The goal of a firm is to maximize profits—to get as much for itself as possible. To do so, it should produce where **marginal cost** (the change in total cost associated with a change in quantity) equals **marginal revenue** (the change in total revenue associated with a change in quantity). Any other output level will yield lower profits. Thus, the marginal cost curve is a competitive firm's supply curve because, given a price, the firm can do no better (its profits are the highest possible) than producing the quantity at which marginal cost equals price which in turn equals marginal revenue.

To see that this is the case, consider Exhibit 2(a), which lists both marginal cost and marginal revenue. The information in Exhibit 2(a) is generally presented graphically as we do in Exhibit 2(b).

A firm is interested in maximizing profit, so in its decision about what quantity to produce it will continually ask the question: What will changes in quantity do to profit? Profit is the difference between total revenue and total cost. What happens to profit in response to a change in output is determined by *marginal revenue* (MR) and *marginal cost* (MC). That's why marginal revenue and marginal cost are key concepts in determining the profit-maximizing or loss-minimizing level of output of any firm.

To emphasize the importance of MR and MC, those are the only cost and revenue figures I show in Exhibit 2. Notice that I don't list profit at all. This is because to calculate profit you must know average total cost (ATC). But you don't need to know what ATC is to determine the profit-maximizing output. All you need know is MC and MR. When marginal revenue and marginal cost are equal, the firm is maximizing profit. You only need ATC if you want to know what that level of profit will be.

Since MC and MR are so important, let's look at them more carefully.

Let's first consider marginal revenue (the additional revenue the firm gets from selling another unit of output). For a competitive firm marginal revenue is simple to determine—it's the price it gets for the good. For example, if the firm increases output from 2 to 3, the price it receives for each additional unit sold is $35 so its marginal revenue is $35, the price of the good. At a price of $35 it can sell as much as it wants. So:

Marginal Revenue

For a competitive firm, MR = *P*.

Marginal revenue is given in column 1 of Exhibit 2(a). As you can see, MR equals $35 for all levels of output. But that's what we saw in Exhibit 1 which showed that the demand curve for a perfect competitor is perfectly elastic and equal to its marginal revenue curve.

Now let's move on to marginal cost. I'll be brief since I discussed marginal cost in detail in an earlier chapter. Marginal cost is that change in cost that accompanies a change in output. Exhibit 2(a) shows marginal cost in column 3. Notice that initially in this example, marginal cost is falling, but by the fifth unit of output, it's increasing. This is consistent with our discussion in earlier chapters. Notice also that there are numbers in the shaded rows of the marginal revenue and marginal cost columns. That's because marginal concepts tell us what happens when there's a change in something, so marginal concepts are best defined between numbers. The numbers in the unshaded rows are the marginal costs and marginal revenues at those particular outputs. So the marginal cost of increasing output from 1 to 2 is 20, and the marginal cost of increasing output from 2 to 3 is 16. The marginal cost right at 2 is 18 (between 20 and 16).

Marginal Cost

I just stated that to maximize profit a firm should produce where marginal cost equals marginal revenue. Looking at Exhibit 2 we see that a firm following that rule should produce at an output of 8 where MC = MR = 35. Now let me try to convince you that 8 is indeed the profit-maximizing output. To do so, let's consider three different possible quantities the firm might look at.

Profit Maximization: MC=MR

Let's say that initially it decides to produce 5, placing it at point *A* in Exhibit 2(b). At output *A*, the firm gets $35 for each widget and its marginal cost is $15. We don't yet know the firm's profit (the difference between its total revenue and its total cost), but we do know what effect changing output will have on profit. For example, say the firm increases production by another unit. Its revenue will rise by $35. (In other words, its marginal revenue is $35.) Its marginal cost is $20. So if it increases production by one unit, profit increases by $15 (the difference between MR, $35, and MC, $20), so at an output of 5 it makes sense (meaning the firm can increase its profit) to increase output. This reasoning holds true as long as the marginal cost is below the marginal revenue. The blue shaded area (*A*) represents the entire increase in profit the firm can get by increasing output.

Now let's say that the firm decides to produce 10 widgets, placing it at point *C*. Here the firm gets $35 for each widget, but the marginal cost of producing the last one is $61. If the firm decreases production by one unit, its cost decreases by

$61 and its revenue decreases by $35. Profit increases by $26 ($61 − $35 = $26), so at point *C*, it makes sense to decrease output. This reasoning holds true as long as the marginal cost is above the marginal revenue. The red shaded area (*C*) represents the increase in profits the firm can get by decreasing output.

At point *B* the firm gets $35 for each widget, and its marginal cost is $35. If it increases output by one unit, its cost will rise by $47 and its revenue will increase by $35, so its profit falls by $12. If the firm decreases output by one unit, its cost falls by $26 and its revenue falls by $35, so its profit falls by $9. Either increasing or decreasing production will decrease profit, so point *B*, at an output of 8, where marginal cost equals marginal revenue (price), is the **profit-maximizing condition for a perfectly competitive firm.** This leads us to the following conclusion:

Profit-maximizing conditions for a competitive firm   MR = P = MC

The profit-maximizing condition of a competitive firm is MC = MR = *P*.

You should commit this profit-maximizing condition to memory. You should also be sure that you understand the intuition behind it. If marginal revenue isn't equal to marginal cost, a firm obviously can increase profit by changing output. If that isn't obvious, the marginal benefit of an additional hour of thinking about this condition will exceed the marginal cost (whatever it is), meaning that you should . . . right, you guessed it . . . study some more.

The Marginal Cost Curve Is the Supply Curve

Now let's consider again the definition of the supply curve as a schedule of quantities of goods that will be offered to the market at various prices. Notice that the marginal cost curve fits that definition. It tells how much the firm will supply at a given price. If the price is $35, we showed that the firm would supply 8. If the price had been $20, the firm would have supplied 6; if the price had been $61, the firm would have supplied 10. Because the marginal cost curve tells us how much of a produced good a firm will supply at a given price, the marginal cost curve *is* the firm's supply curve.[2] The MC curve tells the competitive firm how much it should produce at a given price.

2

The Broader Importance of the MR = MC Equilibrium Condition

This marginal revenue = marginal cost equilibrium condition is simple, but it's enormously powerful. As we'll see, it carries over to other market structures. If you replace revenue with benefits, it also forms the basis of economic reasoning. With whom should you go out? What's the marginal benefit? What's the marginal cost? Should you marry Pat? What's the marginal benefit? What's the marginal cost? As we discussed in Chapter 1, thinking like an economist requires thinking in these marginal terms and applying this marginal reasoning to a wide variety of activities. Understanding this condition is to economics what understanding gravity is to physics. It gives you a sense of if, how, and why prices and quantities will move.

Economic Profit, Accounting Profit, and Normal Profit

In earlier chapters I have emphasized that the concept of *cost* that economists use isn't necessarily cost as measured by accountants, but is instead *opportunity cost* (the value of forgone opportunities) of using an input in its next-best alternative use. The meaning of the MR = MC equilibrium condition must be interpreted in reference to this definition.

The goal of a competitive firm is to maximize profit (the residual left over after all the factors of production have been paid). *Profit* is defined:

Profit = Total revenue − Total costs.

A profit-maximizing firm tries to hold down cost and get as much as it can for the goods it sells. A firm whose goal is profit maximization can be analyzed as an independent entity, analogous to the individual in consumer theory, but instead of maximizing utility as the individual does, the firm maximizes profit. Because profits are the difference between total revenue and total cost, the fact that there

---

[2] As you'll see, the marginal cost curve is the firm's supply curve only if price exceeds average variable cost.

Accountants' concept			Economists' concept		
Total revenue		$1,000	Total revenue		$1,000
Costs			Explicit costs		
Labor	$100		Labor	$100	
Materials	600		Materials	600	
Rent	80		Rent	80	
Total costs		780	Total explicit costs		780
Accounting profit		$ 220	Implicit costs		
			Owner's salary	100	
			Normal profit	80	
			Total implicit costs		180
			Total costs		960
			Economic profits		$ 40

EXHIBIT 3   Accountants' versus Economists' Concepts of Profit

are two alternative concepts of cost means that there are two alternative concepts of profit: accounting profit and economic profit. **Accounting profit** is the profit one arrives at using the accountants' definition of cost. **Economic profit** is the profit one arrives at using the economists' definition of cost. In this discussion of the competitive firm, we're interested in *economic* profit.

Unfortunately, as we discussed in the last chapter, in applying the analysis to the real world often there's no measure of economic profit. Accountants do the measuring and economists are stuck with using accountants' measurements and trying to relate the unmeasured economic profit to the measured accounting profit. In doing so, economists have found that accountants consistently leave out one cost that economists believe should be included: the implicit cost of owners of business. This includes the implicit interest that owners could have gotten on the funds had they invested those funds in another business (the opportunity cost of capital) and the wages they could have earned if they had spent their time working as employees for someone else as opposed to managing their own business (the opportunity cost of their time).

Exhibit 3 gives an example that distinguishes the accountants' and the economists' concepts of cost and profit. Notice that the economists' costs include implicit costs. Thus, economists' profits are lower than accountants' profits. Because accounting profits leave out these two costs, accounting profits are often higher than economic profits, which do include these costs. To distinguish between the two, economists sometimes call implicit costs *normal profits*. **Normal profits** are the returns to the owners of business for the opportunity cost of their implicit inputs. To an economist, normal profits are actually included as a cost and are not included in *economic profit*. As we'll see later, a competitive firm earns normal profits (a normal return to the work and capital its owner puts in), but it does not earn economic profit in the long run.

I've spent great effort emphasizing that all you need to know is MC and MR to determine profit-maximizing output. Now that you know that let's turn our attention to profit. How do we determine profit? Notice that when you talk about maximizing profit, you're talking about maximizing *total profit*, not profit per unit. Profit per unit would be maximized at a much lower output level than is total profit. Firms don't care about profit per unit; as long as an increase in output will increase total profits, a profit-maximizing firm should increase output. That's difficult to intuit, so let's consider a concrete example. Say two people are selling T-shirts that cost $4 each. One sells 2 T-shirts at a price of $6 each and makes a profit per shirt of $2. His total profit is $4. The second person sells the T-shirts at $5 each, making a profit per unit of only $1 but selling 8. Her total profit is $8, twice as much as the fellow who had the $2 profit per unit. In this case $5 (the price with the lower profit per unit), not $6, yields more total profit.

Accounting profit Profit defined according to accountants' definition of cost.

Economic profit Profit defined according to economists' definition of cost.

Normal profits The returns to the owners of business for the opportunity cost of their implicit inputs.

Setting MC = MR Maximizes Total Profit

Most real-world firms do not have profit as their only goal. The reason is that in the real world the decision maker's income is part of the cost of production. For example, a paid manager has an incentive to hold down costs, but has little incentive to hold down his income which, for the firm, is a cost. Alternatively say that a firm is a worker-managed firm. If workers receive a share of the profits, they'll push for higher profits but they'll also see to it that in the process of maximizing profits they don't hurt their own interests—maximizing their wages.

A manager-managed firm will push for high profit, but will see to it that it doesn't achieve those profits by hurting the manager's interests. Managers' pay will be high. In short, real-world firms will hold down the costs of factors of production *except* the cost of the decision maker.

In real life this problem of the lack of incentives to hold down costs is important. For example, firms' managerial expenses often balloon even as firms are cutting "costs." Similarly CEOs and other high-ranking officers of the firm often have enormously high salaries. How and why the lack of incentives to hold down costs affects the economy is best seen by first considering the nature of an economy with incentives to hold down all costs. That's why we use as our standard model the profit-maximizing firm.*

---

* *Standard model* means the model that economists use as our basis of reasoning; from it, we branch out.

Determining Profit and Loss

In the discussion of the firm's choice of output, given price, I carefully presented only marginal cost and price. We talked about maximizing profit, but nowhere did I mention what profit, average total cost, average variable cost, or average fixed cost is. I mentioned only marginal cost and price to emphasize that marginal cost is all that's needed to determine a competitive firm's supply curve (and a competitive firm is the only firm that has a supply curve) and the output that will maximize profit.

Determining Profit from a Table of Costs   The $P = \text{MR} = \text{MC}$ condition tells us how much output a competitive firm should produce to maximize profit. It does not tell us what level of profit the firm makes. The level of profit is determined by total revenue minus total cost. Exhibit 4 expands Exhibit 2(a) and presents a table of costs with all the costs relevant to the firm. Going through each of the columns and reminding yourself of the definition of each is a good review of the last chapter. If the definitions don't come to mind immediately, you need a review. [I pause here to allow you to review; if you don't know the definitions of MC, AVC, ATC, FC, and AFC, go back and reread the previous two chapters.]

Pause

The firm is interested in maximizing profit. Looking at Exhibit 4, you can quickly see that the profit-maximizing position is 8, as it was before, since at an output of 8, total profit is highest.

The maximum profit the firm can earn is $81, which we calculated by subtracting total cost of $199 from total revenue of $280. Notice also that average total cost is lowest at an output of about 7 and the average variable cost is lowest at an output of about 6.[3] Thus, the profit-maximizing position (which is 8), *is not* necessarily a position that minimizes either average variable cost or average total cost. It is only the position that maximizes total profit.

4   **Determining Profit from a Graph**   These relationships can be seen in a graph. In Exhibit 5(a) I add the average total cost and average variable cost curves to the graph of marginal cost and price first presented in Exhibit 2. Notice that the marginal cost curve goes through the lowest points of both average cost curves. (If you don't

---

[3] I say "about 6" and "about 7" because the table gives only whole numbers. The actual minimum point occurs at 5.55 for average variable cost and 6.55 for average total cost. The nearest whole numbers to these are 6 and 7.

EXHIBIT 4   Costs Relevant to a Firm

Price = Marginal revenue	1 Quantity produced	2 Total fixed cost	3 Average fixed cost	4 Total variable cost	5 Average variable cost	6 Total cost	7 Average total cost	8 Marginal cost	9 Total revenue	10 Total profit
$35.00	0	$40.00	—	0	—	$ 40.00	—		0	$ − 40.00
35								$28		
35.00	1	40.00	$40.00	$ 28.00	$28.00	68.00	$68.00	24.00	$ 35.00	− 33.00
35								20		
35.00	2	40.00	20.00	48.00	24.00	88.00	44.00	18.00	70.00	− 18.00
35								16		
35.00	3	40.00	13.33	64.00	21.33	104.00	34.67	15.00	105.00	1.00
35								14		
35.00	4	40.00	10.00	78.00	19.50	118.00	29.50	13.00	140.00	22.00
35								12		
35.00	5	40.00	8.00	90.00	18.00	130.00	26.00	15.00	175.00	45.00
35								17		
35.00	6	40.00	6.67	107.00	17.83	147.00	24.50	20.00	210.00	63.00
35								22		
35.00	7	40.00	5.71	129.00	18.43	169.00	24.14	26.00	245.00	76.00
35								30		
35.00	8	40.00	5.00	159.00	19.88	199.00	24.88	35.00	280.00	81.00
35								40		
35.00	9	40.00	4.44	199.00	22.11	239.00	26.56	47.00	315.00	76.00
35								54		
35.00	10	40.00	4.00	253.00	25.30	293.00	29.30	61.00	350.00	57.00

know why, it would be a good idea to go back again and review the previous chapter.)

The way you find profit graphically is first to find the point where MC = MR (point *A*). That intersection determines the quantity the firm will produce if it wants to maximize profit. Why? Because the vertical distance between a point on the marginal cost curve and a point on the marginal revenue curve represents the additional profit the firm can make by increasing output. For example, if it's producing 7, its marginal cost is $26 and its marginal revenue is $35. By increasing output it can increase profit by $5 (from $76 to $81). So to maximize profit it must see that there is no distance between the two curves—it must see where they intersect.

After having determined that quantity, drop a vertical line down to the horizontal axis and see what average total cost is at that output level (point *B*). Doing so determines the profit per unit at the profit-maximizing output because it's the distance between the price the firm receives (its average revenue) and its average cost. Since the firm will earn that profit on each unit sold, you next extend a line back to the vertical axis (point *C*). That tells us the total quantity the firm will sell. Next go up the price axis to the price that for a competitive firm is the marginal revenue (point *D*). That gives us the shaded rectangle, *ABCD*, which is the total profit earned by the firm (the total quantity times the profit per unit).

Notice that at the profit-maximizing position, the profit per unit isn't at its highest because average total cost is *not* at its minimum point. Profit per unit of output would be highest at point *E*. A common mistake that students make is to draw a line up from point *E* when they are finding profits. That is wrong. It is important to remember: *To determine maximum profit you must first determine what output the firm will choose to produce by seeing where MC equals MR and then dropping a line down to the ATC curve.* Only then can you determine what maximum profit will be.

Notice also that as the curves in Exhibit 5(a) are drawn, ATC at the profit-maximizing position is below the price, and the firm makes a profit per unit of a little over $10. The choice of short-run average total cost curves was arbitrary and doesn't affect the firm's profit-maximizing condition: MC = MR. It could have

EXHIBIT 5 (a, b, and c)   Determining Profits Graphically

The profit-maximizing output depends *only* on where the *MC* and *MR* curves intersect. The total amount of profit or loss that a firm makes depends on the price it receives and its average total cost of producing the profit-maximizing output. This exhibit shows the case of (a) a profit, (b) zero profit, and (c) a loss.

been assumed that fixed cost was higher, which would have shifted the ATC curve up. In Exhibit 5(b) it's assumed that fixed cost is $81 higher than in Exhibit 5(a). Instead of $40, it's $121. The appropriate average total cost curve for a fixed cost of $121 is drawn in Exhibit 5(b). Notice that in this case economic profit is zero and the marginal cost curve intersects the minimum point of the average total cost curve at an output of 8 and a price of $35. In this case the firm is making zero economic profit. (Remember, although economic profit is zero, all resources, including entrepreneurs, are being paid their opportunity cost, so they're getting a normal return.)

In Exhibit 5(c) fixed cost is much higher—$169. Profit-maximizing output is still 8, but now at an output of 8, the firm is making an economic loss of $6 on each unit sold, since its average total cost is $41. The loss is given by the shaded rectangle. In this case, the profit-maximizing condition is actually a loss-minimizing condition. So MC = MR = *P* is both a profit-maximizing condition and a loss-minimization condition.

I draw these three cases to emphasize to you that determining the profit-maximizing output level doesn't depend on fixed cost or average total cost. It depends only on where marginal cost equals price.

Total Revenue and Total Cost

Throughout this chapter we've emphasized the determination of profit by equating marginal cost and price. That focuses the analysis on the relevant issues since marginal changes highlight the relevant considerations in choosing the profit-maximizing output. An alternative method to see how the firm maximizes profit, which helps distinguish between profit per unit and total profit, is to look at total revenue and total cost, as Exhibit 6 does. In it we plot the firm's total revenue and total cost curves (columns 9 and 6 of Exhibit 4). The total revenue curve is a straight line; each additional good sold increases revenue by the same amount, $35. The total cost curve is bowed upward at most quantities, reflecting the changing marginal cost at different levels of output. The firm's profit is repre-

The profit-maximizing output level can also be seen by considering the total cost curve and the total revenue curve. Profit is maximized at the output where total revenue exceeds total cost by the largest amount. This occurs at an output of 8.

sented by the distance between the total revenue curve and the total cost curve. For example, at output 5, the firm makes $45 in profit.

Total profit is maximized where the vertical distance between total revenue and total cost is greatest. In this example total profit is maximized at output 8, just as in the alternative approach. At that output marginal revenue (the slope of the total revenue curve) and marginal cost (the slope of the total cost curve) are equal.

Earlier I stated the supply curve of a competitive firm is its marginal cost curve. More specifically, as mentioned in footnote 2, the supply curve is the part of the marginal cost curve that is above the average variable cost curve. Considering why this is the case should help the analysis stick in your mind.

Let's consider Exhibit 7 (a reproduction of Exhibit 5(c)) and the firm's decision at various prices. At a price of $35, it's incurring a loss of $6 per unit. If it's making a loss, why doesn't it shut down? The answer lies in the fixed costs. There's no use crying over spilt milk. In the short run a firm knows it must pay these fixed costs regardless of whether or not it produces. The firm only considers the costs it can save by stopping production, and those costs are its variable costs. As long as a firm is covering its variable costs, it pays to keep on producing. By producing, its loss is $48; if it stopped producing, its loss would be all the fixed costs ($169). So it makes a smaller loss by producing.

However once the price falls below average variable costs (below $17.80) it will pay to shut down (point *A* in Exhibit 7). In that case the firm's loss from producing would be more than $169 and it would do better to simply stop producing temporarily and save the variable cost. Thus, the point at which MC equals AVC is the **shutdown point** (that point at which the firm will gain more by temporarily shutting down than it will by staying in business). When price falls below the shutdown point, the average variable costs the firm can save by shutting down exceed the price it would get for selling the good. When price is above average variable cost, in the short run a firm should keep on producing even though it's making a loss. As long as a firm's total revenue is covering its total variable cost, temporarily producing at a loss is the firm's best strategy because it's making less of a loss than it would make if it were to shut down.

The Shutdown Point

Shutdown point Point at which the firm will gain more by shutting down than it will by staying in business.

EXHIBIT 7 The Shutdown Decision

A firm should continue to produce as long as price exceeds average variable cost. Once price falls below that, it will do better by temporarily shutting down and saving the variable costs.

LONG-RUN COMPETITIVE EQUILIBRIUM

5

Zero profit condition Requirement that in the long-run competitive equilibrium zero profits exist.

The analysis of the competitive firm consists of two parts: the short-run analysis just presented and a long-run analysis. The essence of the long-run analysis is that profits and losses are inconsistent with long-run equilibrium. In the long run only the zero profit equilibrium (Exhibit 5(b)) is possible. The requirement that in the long run zero profits exist is called the **zero profit condition.**

Why is that the case, and how does it come about? Let's say that the average firm in an industry is making an economic profit. Because entry is open to anyone, the existence of profit will entice new firms to enter, putting downward pressure on the price due to the increase in output. The price will continue to fall until no new firms have an incentive to enter, which means that the average firm in the industry is not making a profit. Only at zero profit does entry stop.

Now let's say that the average firm in the industry is making a loss. It will stay in business in the short run, as long as the price it receives exceeds the AVC, but in the long run, as its machines wear out and as its fixed costs become variable, it will get out of the business.

As some firms get out of business, the price will rise. So when firms are making a loss there is pressure for the price in that industry to rise. Price will continue to rise until firms are no longer making a loss.

Summarizing: In the long run only one of the three total average cost curve positions is an equilibrium—the one in which there is neither an economic profit nor an economic loss (the position in which long-run average total cost equals the price, which equals marginal cost). This is known as the *zero profit condition*. It defines the long-run equilibrium of a competitive industry.

We should point out once again that *zero profit* does not mean that the entrepreneur doesn't get anything for her efforts. The entrepreneur is an input like any other input. In order to stay in the business she must receive her opportunity cost or normal profit (the amount she would have received in the next-best alternative). That normal profit is built into the costs.

Another aspect of the zero profit position deserves mention. What if one firm has superefficient workers or machinery? Won't the firm make a profit in the long run? The answer is, again, no. Other firms will see the value of those workers or machines and will bid up the price of any specialized input until all profits are eliminated. As we'll discuss later, those inputs receive what are called *rents* to their specialized ability. A **rent** is an income received by a specialized factor of production. For example, say the average worker receives $400 per week but

Rent An income received by a specialized factor of production.

T he two previous chapters emphasized that it is vital to choose the relevant costs to the decision at hand. Discussing the shutdown decision gives us a chance to demonstrate the importance of those choices. Say the firm leases a large computer which it needs to operate. The rental cost of that computer is a fixed cost for most decisions, if, as long as the firm keeps the computer, the rent must be paid whether or not the computer is used. However if the firm can end the rental contract at any time, and, thereby, save the rental cost, the computer is not a fixed cost. But neither is it your normal variable cost. Since the firm can end the rental contract and save the cost only if it shuts down, that rental cost of the computer is an *indivisible set-up cost*. For the shutdown decision, the computer cost is a variable cost. For other decisions about changing quantity, it's a fixed cost.

The moral: The relevant cost can change with the decision at hand, so when you apply the analysis to real-world situations, be sure to think carefully about what is the *relevant cost*.

Sarah, because she's such a good worker, receives $600. So $200 of the $600 she receives is a rent to her specialized ability.

Remember, the costs that we use in our marginal cost curve analysis are *opportunity costs* (the amount that the input would be paid in its next-best option). Thus, if the profits exist because of specialized inputs, they'll be squeezed out by rents; if the profits exist because of a sudden increase in demand, they'll be squeezed out by new entry. For example, say that a restaurant opens and does wonderfully because it has a super chef. The restaurant makes a large profit, but it will also discover that other restaurants will be offering to hire this super chef at double or triple her current wage. Either the first restaurant matches those offers, losing its above-normal profit, or it loses the chef, losing its above-normal profits. One way or the other, the restaurant is squeezed.

The zero profit condition is enormously powerful; it makes the analysis of competitive markets far more applicable to the real world than can a strict application of the assumption of perfect competition. If economic profit is being made, firms will enter and compete that profit away. Price will be pushed down to cost of production as long as there are no barriers to entry. As we'll see in later chapters, in their analysis of whether markets are competitive many economists focus primarily on whether barriers to entry exist.

Most of the preceding discussion has focused on firm supply and demand analysis. Now let's consider supply and demand in an industry. We've already discussed industry demand. Even though the firm's demand curve is perfectly elastic, the industry demand curve is downward sloping.

The Supply and Demand Curves for the Industry

How about the industry supply curve? We previously demonstrated that the supply curve for a competitive firm is that firm's marginal cost curve (above the average variable cost curve). To move from individual firms' marginal cost curves or supply curves to the **market supply curve,** we must sum up all the firms' marginal cost curves horizontally and take account of any changes in input prices that might occur. As we sum them up, the market supply curve becomes more elastic than the individual supply curves. This means that there is a larger quantity-supplied response to an increase in price for the entire market than there is for an existing individual firm. The reason is that the supply response comes from two sources:

Market supply curve Horizontal sum of all the firms' marginal cost curves, taking account of any changes in input prices that might occur.

1. Increase in output of existing firms.
2. Entrance of new firms into the market.

To arrive at the market supply curve we cannot simply add all the individual firms' supply curves together. When there are industry-wide changes in demand, factor prices are likely to change, which would force costs up or down for each individual firm. For example, if there were an increase in demand for the industry's output that pushed up the price of that industry's input, there would be an upward shift in each of the individual firms' marginal cost (their supply curves) and the market supply curve would be less elastic than the horizontal summation of the individual firms' supply curves. In the extreme case where all firms in an industry are competitively supplying a perfectly inelastic resource or factor input, the market supply would be perfectly inelastic. Any increase in demand would increase the price of that factor. Costs would rise in response to the increase in demand; output would not.

As a check on whether you understand the ideas behind summing up supply curves, consider the following case: There are constant returns to scale but diminishing marginal product. Input prices are fixed. What does the market supply curve look like? If you answered "perfectly elastic," you've got it! You recognized that constant returns to scale and fixed input prices mean that an infinite number of firms can enter at the market price, so output can expand without limit at the existing price. If you didn't get it, a review probably is in order.

SUPPLY AND DEMAND TOGETHER

An Increase in Demand

Now that we've been through the bases of the competitive supply and demand curves, we're ready to consider the two together and to see how adjustment will likely take place in the firm and in the market.

First, in Exhibit 8(a) and (b), let's consider a market that's in equilibrium, but that suddenly experiences an increase in demand. Exhibit 8(a) shows the market reaction. Exhibit 8(b) shows a representative firm's reaction. Originally market equilibrium occurs at a price of $7 and market supply of 700 thousand units (point A in (a)), with each firm producing 10 units (point A in (b)). Firms are making zero profit because they're in long-run equilibrium. If demand increases from D_0 to D_1, the firms will see the market price increasing and will increase their output until they're once again at a position where MC $= P$. This occurs at point B at a market output of 900 thousand units in (a) and at a firm output of 12 in (b). In the short run the existing firms make an economic profit (the shaded area in Exhibit 8(b)). Price has risen to $9 but average cost is only $7.10 so if the price remains $9 the firm is making a profit of $1.90 per unit. But price cannot remain at $9 since each firm will have an incentive to expand and new firms will have an incentive to enter the market. This will push the price down.

As existing firms expand and new firms enter, there is a movement along the long-run market supply curve. Output increases and market price falls. Eventually the new long-run market equilibrium is reached. If there are no specialized inputs at that new long-run equilibrium, the price will fall back to the original price, $7. The entry of new firms or expansion of existing firms will provide the additional output. The final equilibrium will be at a higher output but the same price. If there had been specialized inputs, or if there were diseconomies of scale, the costs to the firms would have risen and the new equilibrium price would have been higher. Then the long-run supply curve would not have been perfectly elastic; it would have been upward sloping.[4]

Notice that in the long-run equilibrium once again there is zero profit being made. Long-run equilibrium is defined by zero economic profit. Notice also that the long-run supply curve is much less elastic than the short-run supply curve. That's because output changes are much less costly in the short run than in the long run. *In the short run, the price does more of the adjusting. In the long run, more of the adjustment is done by quantity.*

---

[4] To check your understanding, ask yourself the following question: What if there had been economies of scale? If you answered, "There couldn't have been," you're really into economic thinking. (For those of you who aren't all that heavily into economic thinking, the reason is that if there had been economies of scale, the market structure would not have been perfectly competitive. One firm would have kept expanding and expanding, and as it did, its costs would have kept falling.)

(a)   Market   **(b)   Firm**

EXHIBIT 8 (a and b)   Market Response to an Increase in Demand

Faced with an increase in demand which it sees as an increase in price and hence profits, a competitive firm will respond by increasing output (from A to B) in order to maximize profit. A firm's response is shown in (**b**); the market reponse is shown in (**a**). As all firms increase output and as new firms enter, price will fall until all profit is competed away. Thus the long-run supply curve will be perfectly elastic as is S_{LR} in (**a**). The final equilibrium will be at the original price but a higher output. The original firms return to their original output (A) but since there are more firms in the market, the market output increases to (C).

Next, in Exhibit 9 let's consider the effect of a technological improvement available to all firms. The initial equilibrium is at point A. The technological improvement lowers the marginal cost (from MC_0 to MC_1) and the average cost (from AC_0 to AC_1) for all firms. In the short run existing firms make a profit equal to the distance between the market price and their average cost. As firms expand output and as new firms enter, this profit is competed away and the market price is forced down, causing existing firms to cut back output to point B and finally to point C. Price falls from P_0 to P_1 to P_2 and quantity increases from Q_0 to Q_1 to Q_2, as shown in Exhibit 9(b).

As before, the increase in output eventually does not come from a movement along the short-run marginal cost curve, but instead comes from the entry of new firms or expansion by existing firms—movement along the long-run marginal cost curve.

A Technological Improvement

Now in Exhibit 10 let's consider a market that suddenly experiences a decrease in demand. Only this time let's also take into account the possibility of specialized inputs. Market equilibrium initially occurs at a price of $7 and market supply of 700,000 units, with each firm providing 10 units (point A in both (a) and (b)). Initially firms are in long-run equilibrium so there is no economic profit. Now suddenly demand decreases from D_0 to D_1. In the short run total output falls to 560,000 units and market price falls to $5 (point B).

As the price falls to $5, firms cut output and average total cost rises to $7.40, so individual firms will experience losses, as shown in the shaded region of Exhibit 10(a). In response firms will lower their output to the level where MC equals the new lower price (point B), so now each firm produces only 8 units. Those firms for whom price falls below average variable cost will exit the market.

As firms exit, there is a movement along the long-run market supply curve in Exhibit 10(b), which is more elastic than the short-run supply, but is not perfectly

A Decrease in Demand

EXHIBIT 9 (a and b) Market Response to a Technological Improvement

A technological improvement will shift the *AC* and *MC* curves down, creating short-run profits. As existing firms expand output and as new firms enter, this profit will be competed away until the price has once again fallen to equal average total costs (initially point *B* in the short run) and ultimately point *C* in the long run.

EXHIBIT 10 (a and b) Market with Specialized Inputs Response to a Decrease in Demand

Faced with a decrease in demand which it sees as a fall in price and hence profit, a competitive firm will respond by decreasing output in order to minimize losses. Firm output and market output will fall. In (**b**) we see the market response: as all firms decrease output, the demand for specialized inputs will fall, causing the firm's cost in (**a**) to fall from AC_0 to AC_1. The long-run equilibrium price will be lower than the original price, and the long-run supply curve S_{LR} will be upward sloping, rather than perfectly elastic.

elastic. The reason is that as output decreases, the demand for, and hence the price of, specialized inputs will fall, decreasing marginal cost and average cost. Eventually a new long-run market equilibrium at a price of $6 (point *C*) will be reached at a lower quantity and lower price than the original equilibrium, but at a lower quantity and higher price than the short-run equilibrium.

**Other Examples
in the Real World**

The perfectly competitive model and the reasoning underlying it are extremely powerful. With them you have a simple model to use as a first approach to predict the effect of, or to explain why, an event occurred in the real world. For example,

EXHIBIT 11 (a, b, and c) Three Real-World Examples

Supply-demand analysis can be applied to a wide variety of real-world examples. This exhibit shows three, but there are many more. As you experience life today, a good exercise is to put on your supply-demand glasses and to interpret everything you see in a supply-demand framework.

consider the following events, all of which were reported in the newspapers during the month when this chapter was written:

1. Raspberry harvest is double what was predicted.
2. Owners of the Ames chain of department stores decide to close over 100 stores after experiencing two years of losses.
3. Tourism in Vietnam is only half of what was projected.

Exhibit 11 (a, b, and c) shows these three cases. Let's briefly go through how each of them fits in with the perfectly competitive story.

In the first, the supply increases enormously so the supply curve shifts out from S_0 to S_1. In response the price of raspberries is expected to fall. The newspaper reported that the price fell from 50¢ a pound to 25¢ a pound, as shown in Exhibit 11(a), so the event is consistent with the model.

In the second example (Exhibit 11(b)), we see a shutdown decision evolving into a long-run decision to stop producing. Initially Ames saw the losses it was suffering as temporary. It was covering average variable cost so it continued producing even while it was making a loss. So in the two years prior to the shutdown decision, Ames's cost curves look like those in Exhibit 11(b). Since price exceeded average variable cost, Ames continued to produce even though it was making a loss.

But after two years of losses Ames's perspective changed. The company moved from the short run to the long run. Ames began to believe that the demand wasn't temporarily low, but that it was permanently low. It began to ask: What costs are truly fixed and what costs are simply indivisible costs that we can save if we close down completely, selling our buildings and reducing our overhead? Since in the long run all costs are variable, the ATC became its relevant AVC. Ames recognized that demand had fallen below these long-run average costs. At that point, it shut down those stores for which $P <$ AVC.

The third case is an example of a fall in demand. Because demand fell from D_0 to D_1, as shown in Exhibit 11(c), we would expect that the price of tourist services in Vietnam fell—which it did. Vietnamese hotels were cutting prices by 25 percent and Vietnam was offering special tourist packages with reduced rates.

There are hundreds of other real-world examples to which the perfectly competitive model adds insight. That's one reason why it's important to keep it in the back of your mind.

PERFECT COMPETITION, PARETO OPTIMALITY, AND JUDGING ECONOMIC SYSTEMS

Two other related reasons why perfect competition is important are that:

1. It provides an understanding of how the invisible hand works to guide self-interest into society's interest; and
2. It provides a benchmark by which to judge economic systems.

Pareto optimal criterion No person can be made better off without another being made worse off.

7

From our earlier discussions you should have an informal sense of how the invisible hand translates self-interest into society's interest, but we haven't yet discussed that issue formally. Unfortunately a formal sense of how the invisible hand guides self-interest into society's interest is not easy to provide, nor is it easy even to define what is meant by *society's interest*. As economists struggled with these issues, eventually they posed the following question: Can one show that a perfectly competitive equilibrium meets the **Pareto optimal criterion** that no person can be made better off without another being made worse off? This problem is one that many economists have worked on, but it was only in 1959 that Gerard Debreu succeeded in formally proving that a competitive economy met the Pareto optimal criterion under a specific set of conditions. For his work he was given a Nobel prize in 1983.

Let's briefly consider what Debreu proved. He showed that if there were a complete set of markets (a market for every possible good) now and in the future, and if all market transactions had no side effects on anyone not involved in those transactions, then if the economy were perfectly competitive, the invisible hand would guide the economy to a Pareto optimal result. In this case the supply curve (which represents the marginal cost to the individual supplier) would represent the marginal cost to society while the demand curve would represent the marginal benefit to society. In a supply/demand equilibrium, not only would an individual be as well off as he or she possibly could be, given where he or she started from, so too would society. A perfectly competitive market equilibrium would be Pareto optimal.

A Geometric Representation of the Welfare Loss of Deviations from Perfect Competition

Debreu's formal proof allows economists to use perfect competition as a benchmark. Since perfect competition is Pareto optimal, then any deviation from perfect competition would represent a welfare loss to society. Exhibit 12 considers an example, showing the welfare loss of a deviation from equilibrium.

As was stated earlier, the demand curve represents the marginal benefit to society; the supply curve represents the marginal cost to society. If that's the case at the competitive equilibrium, the marginal benefit equals the marginal cost and society is in a Pareto optimal position. Since the demand curve slopes downward and the supply curve slopes upward, many people are doing quite well in this competitive equilibrium. They would have been willing to pay a lot more for the good, and to supply the good at a much lower price than they actually end up doing in a competitive equilibrium. They get a surplus. Nor surprisingly, economists have developed names for the benefits consumers and producers get. Those names are *consumer surplus* and *producer surplus*. **Consumer surplus** is the difference between what consumers would have been wiling to pay and what they actually pay. In Exhibit 12 at a competitive equilibrium consumer surplus is the triangle composed of areas *A*, *B*, and *C*. **Producer surplus** is the difference between the price at which producers would have been willing to supply a good and the price they actually receive. In Exhibit 12 it's the triangle composed of areas *D*, *E*, and *F*. The competitive equilibrium maximizes producer and consumer surpluses.

Consumer surplus The difference between what consumers would have been willing to pay and what they actually pay.

Producer surplus The difference between the price at which producers would have been willing to supply a good and the price they actually receive.

Now let's say that someone places a restriction on the quantity supplied at Q_r. The price that demanders pay now rises to P_r and some consumer surplus is

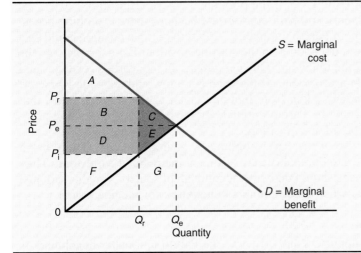

transferred to producer surplus. Those suppliers who are lucky enough to sell in the market receive price P_r even though they'd be willing to supply that quantity at price P_i. Producers who leave the market lose the rectangle represented by the areas E and G but gain back area G, the opportunity cost of their inputs, as they use those inputs in other pursuits, leaving E as a net loss. Producers still in the market benefit by area B. But that benefit comes at the cost of consumers who are hurt by that same area B. The restriction causes a transfer of benefits from consumers to producers. Consumers who leave the market are hurt by the triangle represented by the area C.

Notice that this transfer from consumer to producer surplus is not a total wash. The triangular area composed of areas C and E represents benefits that the excluded producers and excluded consumers won't get. That triangle is the welfare cost of a restriction on the market—the welfare cost of a deviation from perfect competition.

Because of its welfare implications, perfect competition has been used as a benchmark by which to judge the cost of deviating from competition. For example, as we'll see in later chapters, antitrust legislation is often designed to make markets more competitive, and the costs of government restrictions are often measured by their deviation from a competitive equilibrium.

Gerard Debreu—Nobel prize, 1983, for work on competitive equilibrium theory.
© *The Nobel Foundation.*

The Pareto optimality benchmark has been the subject of much controversy. Critics offer a number of criticisms of using perfect competition as a benchmark:

Criticism of the Pareto Optimality Benchmark

1. The **Nirvana criticism:** A perfectly competitive equilibrium is highly unstable. It's usually in some person's interest to restrict entry by others, and, when a market is close to a competitive equilibrium, it is in few people's interest to stop such restrictions.

    To compare reality to a situation that cannot occur (i.e., to Nirvana) is an unfair and unhelpful comparison because it leads to attempts to achieve the unachievable. A better benchmark would be a comparison with workable competition—a state of competition that one might reasonably hope could exist.

    Nirvana criticism Comparing reality to a situation that cannot occur.

2. The **second-best criticism:** The conditions leading to the conclusion that perfect competition leads to a Pareto optimality are so restrictive that they are never even closely met in reality. If the economy deviates in hundreds of ways from perfect competition, how are we to know whether a movement toward a competitive equilibrium in one of those ways will make the economy closer to perfect competition?

    Second-best criticism If the economy is not currently at the competitive equilibrium, it is not at all clear that particular moves toward a competitive equilibrium will be in society's interest.

Normative criticism The desirability of a Pareto optimal position depends on the desirability of the starting position. If one objects to the starting position, one will also likely object to the Pareto optimal position.

3. The **normative criticism:** Even if the previous two criticisms didn't exist, the competitive benchmark still isn't appropriate because there is nothing necessarily wonderful about Pareto optimality. A Pareto optimal position could be a horrendous position, depending on the starting position. For example, say the starting position is the following: One person has all the world's revenues and all the other people are starving. If that rich person would be made worse off by having some money taken from him and given to the starving poor, that starting position would be Pareto optimal. By most people's normative criteria, it would also be a lousy position.

    Critics of the use of the Pareto optimality goal argue that society has a variety of goals. Pareto optimality may be one of them, but it's only one. They argue that economists should take into account all of society's goals—not just Pareto optimality—when determining a benchmark for judging policies.

The Importance of the Competitive Model for All Economists

The Free Market—An economic magazine that interprets current economic events from a libertarian perspective.

The debate between supporters and critics of the Pareto optimality benchmark is an ongoing one. Supporters argue that it's the appropriate benchmark, and that competitive equilibrium achieves Pareto optimality. Critics contend that Pareto optimality is just one of many of society's goals. But even critics agree that the forces the perfectly competitive model describes—the pressure on prices to gravitate toward costs of production and the pressure for prices to change as long as supply and demand are not in equilibrium—are strong and show themselves in a variety of real-world markets. Even critics of Pareto optimality believe there is a purpose in studying perfect competition. So, for all economists, it's absolutely necessary that everybody trained in economics understands the perfectly competitive model.

CONCLUSION

We've come to the end of the presentation of perfect competition. It was tough going, but if you went through it carefully, it will serve you well, both as a basis for later chapters and as a reference point for how real-world economies work. But like many good things, a complete understanding of the chapter doesn't come easy.

KEY POINTS

• The necessary conditions for perfect competition are that buyers and sellers be price takers, the number of firms be large, there be no barriers to entry, firms' products be homogeneous (identical), exit and entry be instantaneous and costless, there be complete information, and sellers be profit-maximizing entrepreneurial firms. **1**

• The supply curve of a competitive firm is its

marginal cost curve. Only competitive firms have supply curves. **2**

• The profit-maximizing position of a competitive firm is where marginal revenue equals marginal cost. **3**

• In the short run, competitive firms can make a profit or loss. In the long run, they make zero profits. **4 5**

• The shutdown price for a perfectly competitive

firm is a price below the minimum point of the average variable cost curve. **4**

· The Pareto optimal criterion is that no one can be made better off without another being made worse off. **7**

· Three criticisms of the Pareto optimality benchmark include the Nirvana criticism, the second-best criticism, and the normative criticism. **7**

KEY TERMS

accounting profit *(489)*
barriers to entry *(483)*
consumer surplus *(500)*
economic profit *(489)*
homogeneous
  product *(483)*
marginal cost *(486)*
marginal revenue *(486)*

market supply
  curve *(495)*
Nirvana criticism *(501)*
normal profits *(489)*
normative criticism *(502)*
Pareto optimal
  criterion *(500)*

perfectly
  competitive *(483)*
price taker *(483)*
producer surplus *(500)*
profit-maximizing
  condition *(488)*
rent *(494)*

second-best
  criticism *(501)*
shutdown point *(493)*
supply *(484)*
zero profit
  condition *(494)*

QUESTIONS FOR THOUGHT AND REVIEW

The number after each question represents the estimated degree of critical thinking required. (1 = almost none; 10 = deep thought.)

1. If a firm is owned by its workers but otherwise meets all the qualifications for a perfectly competitive firm, will its price and output decisions differ from the price and output decisions of a perfectly competitive firm? Why? *(9)*

2. A profit-maximizing firm has an average total cost of $4 but gets a price of $3 for each good it sells. What would you advise it to do? *(3)*

3. How would your answer to Question 2 differ if you knew the average variable cost were $3.50? *(4)*

4. You're thinking of buying one of two firms. One has a profit margin of $8 per unit; the other has a profit margin of $4 per unit. Which should you buy? Why? *(4)*

5. Say that half of the cost of producing wheat is the rental cost of land (a fixed cost) and half is the cost of labor and machines (a variable cost). If the average total cost of producing wheat is $8 and the price of wheat is $6, what would you advise a farmer to do? ("Grow something else" is not allowed.) *(5)*

6. If marginal cost is four times the quantity produced and the price is $20, how much should the firm produce? Why? *(3)*

7. State what is wrong with each of the graphs. *(3)*

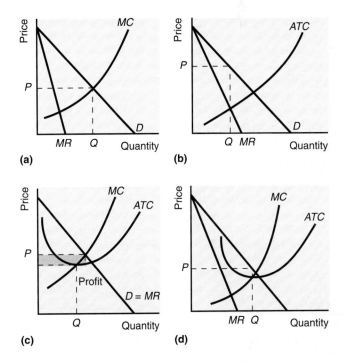

(a)

(b)

(c)

(d)

8. Find three events in the newspaper that can be explained or interpreted with supply/demand analysis. *(7)*

9. Show graphically the welfare loss that would occur if government established a requirement that everyone consume 10 percent more beets than he or she is currently consuming. *(9)*

10. If one can show that the welfare loss in Question 9 is small—say $\frac{1}{2}$ of 1 percent of the cost of the beets—and that eating beets makes people healthy, would you support a beet-eating requirement? Why? *(9)*

PROBLEMS AND EXERCISES

1. *a.* Based on the following table, what is the profit-
maximizing output?

Output	Price	Total costs
0	$10	$ 30
1	10	40
2	10	45
3	10	48
4	10	55
5	10	65
6	10	80
7	10	100
8	10	140
9	10	220
10	10	340

b. How would your answer change if, in response to an
increase in demand, the price of the good increased
to $15?

2. Economan has been infected by the free enterprise bug.
He sets up a firm on extraterrestrial affairs. The rent of
the building is $4,000, the cost of the two secretaries is
$40,000, and the cost of electricity and gas comes to
$5,000. There's a great demand for his information, and
after profits his total revenue amounts to $100,000. By
working in the firm, though, Economan forfeits the
$50,000 he could earn by working for the Friendly
Space Agency and the $4,000 he could have earned as
interest had he saved his funds instead of putting them
in this business. Is he making a profit or loss by an accountant's definitions of profit and loss? How about by
an economist's definition?

Wednesday March 27

24, 25, 26, 27, 28, part of 30

Chapters covered on next test.

Monopoly is business at the end of its journey.
Henry Demarest Lloyd

After reading this chapter, you should be able to:

1

Summarize how and why the decisions facing a monopolist differ from the collective decisions of competing firms.

2

Explain why MC = MR maximizes total profit for a monopolist.

3

Determine a monopolist's price, output, and profit graphically and numerically.

4

Show why a perfectly price-discriminating monopolist will produce the same output as a perfect competitor.

5

Show graphically the welfare loss from monopoly and explain why it may underestimate people's view of the loss from monopoly.

6

State three important barriers to entry.

7

Explain why economists generally favor having government charge for monopolies.

Monopoly A market structure in which one firm makes up the entire market.

In the previous chapter we considered perfect competition. We now move to the other end of the spectrum: monopoly. **Monopoly** is a market structure in which one firm makes up the entire market. It is the polar opposite to competition. It is a market structure in which the firm faces no competitive pressure from other firms.

Monopolies exist because of barriers to entry into a market that prevent competition. These can be legal barriers (as in the case where a firm has a patent that prevents other firms from entering), sociological barriers where entry is prevented by the invisible handshake, or natural barriers where the firm has a unique ability to produce what other firms can't duplicate.

1   A key question we want to answer in this chapter is: How does a monopolist's decision differ from the collective decision of competing firms (i.e., from the competitive solution)? Answering that question brings out a key difference between a competitive firm and a monopoly. Since a competitive firm is too small to affect the price, it does not take into account the effect of its output decision on the price it receives. A competitive firm's marginal revenue (the additional revenue it receives from selling an additional unit of output) is its price. Since a monopolistic firm's output decision can affect price, it does take that effect into account; its marginal revenue is not its price. A monopolistic firm will reason: "If I increase production, the price I can get for each unit sold will fall, so I had better be careful about how much I increase production."

Let's consider an example. Say your drawings in the margins of this book are seen by a traveling art critic who decides you're the greatest thing since Rembrandt or at least since Andy Warhol. Carefully he tears each page out of the book, mounts them on special paper, and numbers them: Doodle Number 1 (Doodle While Contemplating Demand), Doodle Number 2 (Doodle While Contemplating Production), and so on.

Doodle Number 27: Contemplating Costs

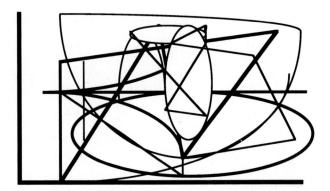

All told, he has 100. He figures, with the right advertising and if you're a hit on the art circuit, he'll have a monopoly in your doodles. He plans to sell them for $20,000 each: He gets 50 percent, you get 50 percent. That's $1 million for you. You tell him, "Hey, man! I can doodle my way through the entire book. I'll get you 500 doodles. Then I get $5 million and you get $5 million."

The art critic has a pained look on his face. He says, "You've been doodling when you should have been studying. Your doodles are worth $20,000 each only if they're rare. If there are 500, they're worth $1,000 each. And if it becomes known that you can turn them out that fast, they'll be worth nothing, I won't be able to limit quantity at all, and my monopoly will be lost. So obviously we must figure out some way that you won't doodle any more—and study instead. Oh, by the way, did you know that the price of an artist's work goes up significantly when he or she dies? Hmm." At that point you decide to forget doodling and to start studying, and to remember always that increasing production doesn't necessarily make suppliers better off.

As we saw in the last chapter, competitive firms do not take advantage of that insight. Each individual competitive firm, responding to its self-interest, is not doing what is in the interest of the firms collectively. In competitive markets, as

1	2	3	4	5	6	7	8
Quantity	Price	Total revenue	Marginal revenue	Total cost	Marginal cost	Average total cost	Profit
0	36	0	—	47			−47
			33		1		
1	33	33	30	48	1.5	48.00	−15
			27		2		
2	30	60	24	50	3	25.00	10
			21		4		
3	27	81	18	54	6	18.00	27
			15		8		
4	24	96	12	62	12	15.50	34
			9		16		
5	21	105	6	78	20	15.60	27
			3		24		
6	18	108	0	102	32	17.00	6
			−3		40		
7	15	105	−6	142	48	20.29	−37
			−9		56		
8	12	96	−12	198	68	24.75	−102
			−15		80		
9	9	81	−18	278	90	30.89	−197

EXHIBIT 1   Monopolistic Profit Maximization

one supplier is pitted against another the demanders benefit. In monopolistic markets, the firm faces no competitors and does what is in its best interest. Monopolists see to it that the monopolists, not the demanders, benefit.

How much should the monopolistic firm choose to produce if it wants to maximize profit? To answer that we have to consider more carefully the effect that changing output has on the monopoly. That's what we do in this section. First, we consider a numerical example; then we consider that same example graphically. The relevant information for our example is presented in Exhibit 1.

A MODEL OF MONOPOLY

Exhibit 1 shows the price, total revenue, marginal revenue, total cost, marginal cost, average total cost, and profit at various levels of production. It's similar to the table in Exhibit 4 of the last chapter where we determined a competitive firm's output. The big difference is that marginal revenue changes as output changes and is not equal to the price. Why? First, let's remember the definition of marginal revenue. **Marginal revenue** is the change in total revenue that occurs as a firm changes its output. In this example, if a monopolist increases output from 4 to 5 by lowering its price from $24 to $21, its revenue increases from $96 to $105, so marginal revenue is $9. That $9 can be divided into two elements: the $21 the firm got for selling another unit minus the $3 per unit fall in the price that occurred on the other four units as the firm had to lower its price in order to sell the additional unit. That's $21 − $12 = $9.

Determining the Monopolist's Price and Output Numerically

As you can tell from the table, profits are highest ($34) at 4 units of output at a price of $24. At 3 units of output and a price of $27, the firm has total revenue of $81 and total cost of $54, yielding a profit of $27. At 5 units of output and a price of $21, the firm has a total revenue of $105 and a total cost of $78, also for a profit of $27. Thirty-four dollars is the highest profit it can make, which the firm does when it produces 4 units. This is its profit-maximizing level.

Marginal revenue The change in total revenue that occurs as a firm changes its output.

As you can see in the table, at that profit-maximizing output of 4 units, marginal revenue equals marginal cost, just as it did for the competitive firms. This is the general rule that any firm should follow to maximize profit: Produce at an output level at which MC = MR. What's different is that for a monopolist marginal revenue does not equal price; marginal revenue is below price.

If you think about it, it makes sense that the point where marginal revenue equals marginal cost determines the profit-maximizing output. If the firm increases output beyond the quantity (4) where MC = MR, the additional revenue it

EXHIBIT 2 Determining the Monopolist's Price and Output Graphically

The profit-maximizing output is determined where the *MC* curve intersects the *MR* curve. To determine the price at which *MC* = *MR* the monopolist would charge, one first finds that output and then extends a line to the demand curve, in this case finding a price of 24. This price is higher than the competitive price, $20.50, but the quantity, 5, is lower than the competitor's quantity, 5.17.

gets ($9) is below the additional cost it incurs ($16). If it decreases output to 3 from 4 where MC = MR, the revenue it loses ($15) exceeds the additional cost it saves ($8).

Determining the Monopolist's Price and Output Graphically
2

Marginal revenue curve Graphical measure of the change in revenue that occurs in response to a change in price.

The monopolist's output decision can also be seen graphically. Exhibit 2 graphs the table's information into a demand curve, a marginal revenue curve, and a marginal cost curve. The marginal cost curve is a graph of the change in the firm's cost as it changes output. It's the same curve as we saw in our discussion of perfect competition. The **marginal revenue curve** is a graph of the change in total revenue. It is graphed by plotting and connecting the points given by quantity and marginal revenue in Exhibit 1. The marginal revenue curve tells us the change in total revenue when there is a change in price.

The marginal revenue curve is new, so let's consider it a bit more carefully. It tells us the additional revenue the firm will get by expanding output. It is a downward-sloping curve that begins at the same point as the demand curve but then decreases faster. In this example marginal revenue is positive up until the firm produces six units; then marginal revenue is negative; after six units the firm's total revenue decreases when it increases output.

Notice specifically the relationship between the demand curve (which is the average revenue curve) and the marginal revenue curve. Since the demand curve is downward sloping, the marginal revenue curve is below the average revenue curve. (Remember, if the average curve is falling, the marginal curve must be below it.)

Having plotted these curves, let's ask the same questions as we did before: What output should the monopolist produce, and what price should it charge? To answer those questions the key curves to look at are the marginal cost curve and the marginal revenue curve.

We can tell from the graph what will happen to profit by looking at the positions of the marginal revenue curve and the marginal cost curve at the output and price we're considering. At the output where the demand curve intersects the marginal cost curve, marginal cost is significantly above the marginal revenue curve. Whenever that's the case, profits will increase when output is reduced since the saving in cost (the area under the marginal cost curve) is greater than the lost revenue (the area under the marginal revenue curve). So when the demand curve intersects the marginal cost curve it definitely pays for the firm to restrict output.

A TRICK IN GRAPHING THE MARGINAL REVENUE CURVE

Here's a trick to help you graph the marginal revenue curve. *MR* is a line that starts at the same point on the price axis as does a linear demand curve, but that intersects the quantity axis at a point half the distance from where the demand curve intersects the quantity axis. (If the demand curve isn't linear, you can use the same trick if you use lines tangent to the curved demand curve.) So you can extend the demand curve to the two axes and measure halfway on the quantity axis, and draw a line from where the demand curve intersects the price axis to that halfway mark. That line is the marginal revenue curve.

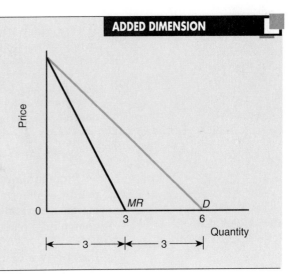

If restricting output a little bit helps that much, how about if the monopolist restricts output some more, to 4 units? Since marginal cost exceeds marginal revenue, doing so makes sense. Well then, how about decreasing output by another unit, from 4 to 3? If you look at the graph, you'll see that doing so doesn't make sense since at all output levels below 4, marginal revenue is above marginal cost. That means that the lost revenue from reducing output will exceed the saving from reducing marginal cost.

MR = MC Determines the Profit-Maximizing Output for a Monopolist From the preceding discussion you should have a good sense of what determines whether the monopolist's profit will rise or fall with a change in output, and what output it should choose. You simply compare the marginal revenue curve to the marginal cost curve at the different output levels being considered. In the first two cases the marginal revenue was below the marginal cost, so it made sense to reduce production. In the third case, the marginal revenue was equal to marginal cost, and it did not make sense to reduce production. So the monopolist should produce at the output level where MC = MR. As you can see, the output the monopolist chooses is 4 units, the same output that we determined numerically. This leads to the following insights:

> *If MR > MC, the monopolist gains profit by increasing output.*
> *If MR < MC, the monopolist gains profit by decreasing output.*
> *If MC = MR, the monopolist is maximizing profit.*

This **MR = MC** is the profit-maximizing rule for a monopolist.

Determining the Price a Monopolist Will Charge The MR = MC condition determines the quantity a monopolist produces; in turn that quantity determines the price the firm will charge. Since the demand curve tells us what consumers will pay for a given quantity, to find the price a monopolist will charge you must extend the quantity line up to the demand curve. We do so in Exhibit 2 and see that the profit-maximizing output level is 4, which allows a monopolist to charge a price of $24.

Comparing a Monopolist's and a Perfectly Competitive Firm's Outputs and Prices For a competitive firm the summations of firms' marginal cost curves is the supply curve. The competitive level of output would be at 5.17 at a price of $20.50, as Exhibit 2 shows. The monopolist's output was 4 and its price was $24. So, if a monopolistic market can be made competitive, you can see that output is lower and price is higher in a monopoly than in a competitive market. The reason is that the monopolist takes into account the effect restricting output has on price.

If MR > MC, the monopolist gains profit by increasing output.
If MR < MC, the monopolist gains profit by decreasing output.
If MC = MR, the monopolist is maximizing profit.

MR = MC The profit-maximizing rule for a monopolist.

In comparing monopoly and competition, it's important to remember the definition of a supply curve: It's the quantity that will be supplied at various prices. A supply curve shows the quantity response of *price takers*.

A monopolist is not a price taker; hence it cannot have a supply curve. A monopolist looks at its marginal cost, looks at its demand schedule, and decides what price to charge based on the intersection of its marginal revenue and marginal cost curves. It chooses output and price in a way that gives it the highest possible profit.

Equilibrium output for the monopolist, like equilibrium output for the competitor, is determined by the MC = MR condition, but because the monopolist's marginal revenue is below its price, its equilibrium output is different from a competitive market.

Example   We've covered a lot of material quickly, so it's probably helpful to go through an example slowly and carefully to review the reasoning process. Here's the problem:

Say that a monopolist with marginal cost curve *MC* faces a demand curve *D* in Exhibit 3(a). Determine the price and output the monopolist would choose.

The first step is to draw the marginal revenue curve, since we know that a monopolist's profit-maximizing output level is determined where MC = MR. We do that in Exhibit 3(b), remembering the trick of extending our demand curve back to the vertical and horizontal axes and then bisecting the horizontal axis.

The second step is to determine where MC = MR. Having found that point, we extend a line up to the demand curve and down to the quantity axis to determine the output the monopolist chooses, Q_M. We do this in Exhibit 3(c).

Finally we see where the quantity line intersects the demand curve. Then we extend a horizontal line from that point to the price axis, as in Exhibit 3(d). This determines the price the monopolist will charge, P_M.

PROFITS AND MONOPOLY

So far we've talked about the output and pricing decisions of a monopolist. We haven't said anything about whether the monopolist makes a profit.[1] As was the case with the perfect competitor, that can be determined only by comparing average total cost to price. So before we can determine profit, we need to add another curve: the average total cost curve. As we saw with a perfect competitor, it's important to follow the correct sequence when finding profit.

- First, determine the output the monopolist will produce by the intersection of the marginal cost and marginal revenue curves.
- Second, determine the price the monopolist will charge for that output.
- Third, determine average cost at that level of output.
- Fourth, determine the monopolist's profit (loss) by comparing AR (= *P*) to average total cost.

If price exceeds average cost at the output it chooses, the monopolist will make a profit. If price equals average cost, the monopolist will make no profit (but it will make a normal return). If price is less than average cost, the monopolist will incur a loss: Total cost exceeds total revenue.

An Example of a Monopolist Making a Profit

I consider the case of a profit in Exhibit 4(a), (b), and (c), going through the steps slowly. The monopolist's demand curve, marginal cost, and average total cost curve are presented in Exhibit 4(a). Our first step is to determine output, which we do by drawing the marginal revenue curve and finding the output level at which marginal cost equals marginal revenue. From that point draw a vertical line to the

---

[1] Remember the distinction between economic profit and accounting profit. This chapter's discussion of profit considers economic profit.

(a)   **(b)**   **(c)**   **(d)**

EXHIBIT 3 (a, b, c, and d)   Finding the Monopolist's Price and Output

Determining a monopolist's, price and output can be tricky. In this exhibit we go through the steps slowly to help you see how to do it.

(a)   **(b)**   **(c)**

EXHIBIT 4 (a, b, and c)   Monopolist Makes a Profit

After one has determined a monopolist's price and output decision, one can determine the profit by extending lines from points A and B to the price axis. The resulting rectangle represents the monopolist's profit.

horizontal (quantity) axis. That intersection tells us the monopolist's output, Q_M in Exhibit 4(b). The second step is to find what price the monopolist will charge at that output. We do so by extending the vertical line to the demand curve (point A) and then extending a horizontal line over to the price axis. Doing so gives price, P_M. Our third step is to determine the average cost at that price. We do so by seeing where our vertical line at the chosen output intersects the average total cost curve (point B). That tells us the monopolist's average cost at its chosen output.

To determine profit, we extend lines from where the quantity line intersects the demand curve (point A) and the average total cost curve (point B) to the price axis in Exhibit 4(c). The resulting shaded rectangle represents the monopolist's profit.

In Exhibit 5(a) and (b) we consider two other average total cost curves to show you that a monopolist may make a loss or no profit as well as an economic profit. In Exhibit 5(a) the monopolist is making zero profit; in Exhibit 5(b) it's making a loss. So clearly in the short run a monopolist can be making either a profit or a loss, or it can be breaking even.

An Example of a Monopolist Breaking Even and Making a Loss

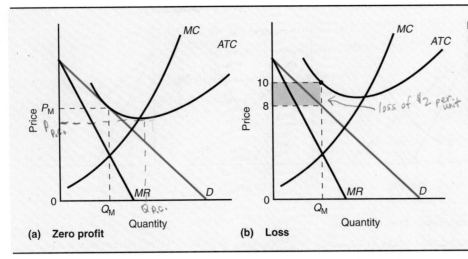

EXHIBIT 5 (a, and b)   Two Other Monopoly Cases

Depending on where the *ATC* curve falls, a monopolist can break even or make a loss in the short run. In the long run, a monopolist who is making a loss will get out of business.

(a) **Zero profit**

(b) **Loss**

A Monopolist with a Zero Marginal Cost

As an exercise, let's consider what a monopolist that has no cost of production will charge and what its profit will be. This case is presented in Exhibit 6. Its marginal cost is zero and is coincidental with (lies on top of) the horizontal axis. The marginal revenue curve intersects that marginal cost at Q_M. The price the monopolist charges is P_M. Total revenue is given by the shaded area. Assuming fixed costs are also zero, and since by assumption there is no cost, total revenue is equal to profit.

As a review of the elasticity concept, ask yourself what is the elasticity at that point. If you said it's 1, you're right. If not, I'm sorry to say, you'd better review the discussion of elasticity in the chapter on demand before the next exam. I pause for you to review.

Now that you're back, I've got another question for you. Will the elasticity at the price that the normal monopolist charges be elastic (greater than 1) or inelastic (less than 1)? If you answered without hesitation that it's always elastic, you're in good shape on elasticity. If not, you've had your warnings. Remember, life is tough; no one ever said that learning difficult concepts is easy.

The Price-Discriminating Monopolist

Price discriminate To charge different prices to different individuals.

Consumer surplus The additional amount that consumers would be willing to pay for a product above what they actually pay.

The better to cement into your mind your understanding of the profit-maximizing condition MC = MR, let's consider what would happen if our monopolist suddenly gained the ability to **price discriminate**—to charge different prices to different individuals or groups of individuals (for example, students as compared to businesspeople). This means that individuals high up on the demand curve could be charged a high price; individuals low on the demand curve could be charged a lower price without affecting the price charged to other individuals.

A firm that price discriminates captures demanders' **consumer surplus** (the difference between the price demanders would have been willing to pay and the price they must actually pay). A normal monopolist, by assumption, must charge all individuals the same price. Thus, it's giving a good deal to some individuals who would have been willing to pay more. If a monopolist can price discriminate, it doesn't have to give any demanders a good deal. It can extract the maximum consumer surplus from each demander.

A Normal Monopolist versus a Price-Discriminating Monopolist   Exhibit 7(a) graphs the decisions facing a normal monopolist. A normal monopolist will choose to produce 50 units at a price of $16 and a cost per unit of $7, making a profit of $450, the shaded rectangle. The shaded triangle is the remaining consumer surplus.

The perfectly price-discriminating monopolist is able to charge a different price to each customer. When she sells more, she doesn't have to lower her price

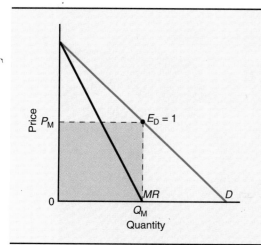

EXHIBIT 6   A Monopolist with Zero Marginal Cost

When a monopolist has a zero marginal cost, it produces an output at which the *MR* curve intersects the quantity axis and charges a price P_M. At the corresponding point on its demand curve, the elasticity is 1 because that maximizes total revenue.

(a)   *(b)*

EXHIBIT 7 (a and b)   A Normal versus a Perfectly Price-Discriminating Monopolist

If a monopolist can perfectly discriminate among buyers and can charge them all as much as they are willing to pay, her marginal revenue curve will equal its demand curve. She will produce at the same output level as does a competitive firm. On average, however, she will charge a much higher price than would a competitive firm.

to other customers willing to pay high prices. So she can extract the full consumer surplus. Since she doesn't have to lower her price to sell more, her marginal revenue isn't the same as the normal monopolist's. Since she doesn't need to lower the price for other customers when she sells more, her marginal revenue is the same as her average revenue (total revenue divided by quantity), which is simply her demand curve. So, for a perfectly price-discriminating monopolist: $P = AR = MR$.

In Exhibit 7(b) we consider the decision facing a price-discriminating monopolist. For a price-discriminating monopolist, we find that she will produce at an output of 70, a far higher output than the normal monopolist's, and will make a profit of $700, the shaded region, almost twice the profit of the normal monopolist. Both her profit and her output are higher than a normal monopolist's. She produces the same output that a perfectly competitive industry would have. There is no monopolistic restriction on output.

Price Discrimination in the Real World   The price discrimination just discussed is mainly of theoretical interest. It's presented to bring home the point that a price-discriminating monopolist will have an output more like a competitive firm than will a normal monopolist. In the real world it's highly unlikely that a monopolist will be able to charge everyone a different price. However, as discussed in the chapter on

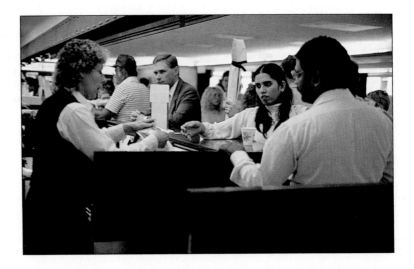

demand, price discrimination occurs all the time. There I pointed out the following examples:

1. *All airline Super Saver fares include Saturday night stayovers.*
    This is a method of price discrimination. Businesspeople who have highly inelastic demands generally aren't willing to stay over a Saturday night, so they're charged a high price while tourists and leisure travelers who have a far more elastic demand curve and who are willing to stay over a Saturday night are charged a low price.

2. *Automobiles are seldom sold at list price.*
    Once again we have an example of price discrimination. Salespeople can size up the customer and determine the customer's elasticity. People who haven't done the research and don't know that selling at 10 percent off list is normal (i.e., people with inelastic demands) pay higher prices than people who search out all the alternatives (people with elastic demand).

    Now that you've analyzed price-discriminating monopolies, you should understand them better. To see whether you do, try to provide a price discrimination explanation for the following:

3. Theaters have Monday/Tuesday night special rates.
4. Retail tire companies run special sales about half the time.
5. Restaurants generally make most of their profit on alcoholic drinks and just break even on food.

THE WELFARE LOSS FROM MONOPOLY

In the previous two sections, two conclusions should have started you thinking. The first is that there is no necessary reason why a monopolist must make a profit. The second is that if a monopolist is a price discriminator (which means it makes more profit than a normal monopoly), then its output is closer to the competitive output. From these two conclusions we can reason that profits aren't the primary reason that the economic model we're using sees monopoly as bad. If not because of profits, then why does the economic model see monopoly as bad?

A Partial Equilibrium Presentation of the Welfare Loss

5

One reason can be seen by looking more carefully at the normal monopolist's equilibrium in Exhibit 8. A monopolist produces at Q_M at price P_M; a competitive market produces a higher quantity Q_C at a lower price P_C. Now let's consider what the benefits to society would be if the monopolist would increase output. The cost to society of increasing output from Q_M to Q_C is measured by the area under the marginal cost curve, the shaded area labeled A. This cost is the opportunity cost of the resources—the value of the resources in their next-best use. The benefit to society of increasing output from Q_M to Q_C is the area under the demand curve between those two quantities: areas A, B, and D. (Area C is

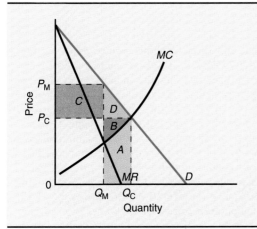

EXHIBIT 8 The Welfare Loss from Monopoly

The welfare loss of a monopolist is represented by the triangles *B* and *D*. The rectangle *C* is a transfer from consumer surplus to the monopolist. The area *A* represents the opportunity cost of diverted resources. This is not a loss to society since the resources will be used in producing other goods.

neither a gain nor a loss to society. It represents a transfer of income from the monopolist to the consumer that would occur if there were a fall in price. Since both monopolist and consumer are members of society, the gain and loss net out.)

The triangular areas *B* and *D* are the net gain to society of eliminating monopoly. Thus, these triangular areas are also a measure of the welfare loss to society from the existence of monopoly. Thinking about consumer surplus (which we discussed previously) may help you to see what's going on here. As defined before, consumer surplus is the additional amount consumers would have been willing to pay for a good, but didn't have to. In a competitive market consumers would have received the areas *C* and *D* as part of their consumer surplus. But they didn't. The monopoly extracts *C* from them as its profit (that's a redistributional effect) so the consumer loses, but the monopolist gains. But the triangle *D* is lost to society; the consumer loses it but the monopolist doesn't get it. It's the cost of the monopoly restriction. The same argument can be made about the triangle *B*, only this time replace *consumer* with *producer*. *B* is the lost producer surplus.

As discussed in the previous chapter, this area designated by *B* and *D* is often called the *deadweight loss* or **welfare loss triangle;** it is a geometric representation of the welfare cost in terms of misallocated resources that are caused by monopoly. That welfare cost of monopoly is one of the reasons economists oppose monopoly. That cost can be summarized as follows: Because monopolies distort relative prices, people's decisions don't reflect the true cost to society. Price doesn't equal marginal cost. Because price doesn't equal marginal cost, people's choices are distorted; they choose to consume less of the monopolist's output and more of some other output than they would if there were competitive markets. That distinction means that the marginal cost of increasing output is lower than the marginal benefit of increasing output, so there's a welfare loss.

Welfare loss triangle Geometric representation of the welfare cost in terms of the resource misallocation caused by monopoly.

If the welfare loss from monopoly is large, it would seemingly make sense for the government to enter into the market and prevent monopoly. If, on the other hand, the welfare loss from monopoly is small, it would make sense for the government not to worry about monopoly. Thus, the size of the welfare loss from monopoly and other restrictions on supply is an important economic question.

To answer this question economists have spent a fair amount of time trying to measure the welfare loss from monopoly. Almost all measurements of that welfare loss as a percentage of GDP have been rather small. One early attempt was made by Arnold Harberger (which is why welfare triangles are sometimes called *Harberger triangles*). Harberger estimated the demand elasticities for a variety of goods produced by monopolies and thereby estimated the welfare loss from monopoly. He found that the welfare loss from monopoly was only about $\frac{1}{2}$ of 1 percent of total GDP. Later estimates have differed slightly from the Harberger estimates and have shown monopoly to be more of a problem, but they too have

Measuring the Welfare Loss from Monopoly

THE SECOND BEST AND SOME QUALIFICATIONS TO THE WELFARE LOSS

he welfare loss argument just presented requires an addendum. The loss shown in the partial equilibrium diagram is caused by relative prices being changed from competitive prices by a monopolist. But what if monopoly already exists in some other sectors and existing prices aren't competitive prices? When a monopolist changes relative prices, will that cause a similar welfare loss? The answer depends on how the demands are interrelated and whether the new complete set of relative prices is closer to the competitive set of prices than is the old set of relative prices. Such issues were briefly introduced in the last chapter. They are called *second-best issues*. Second-best issues are issues related to determining the welfare loss due to restrictions on output if the rest of the world isn't characterized by perfect competition. In general second-best questions can only be answered by using a complicated set of equations—such a complicated set that when I was in graduate school I could hardly work my way through them, so there's no way I'm going to foist them on you.

There's one case, however, that captures the essence of the argument and shows whether you're following the problem raised by second-best issues. Say that *all* the markets in an economy, except one, are monopolistic, and the prices in these monopolistic markets are 10 percent higher than the competitive price. Now say that the one competitive price rises by 10 percent, while all other prices remain constant. Now all markets are equally monopolized. Will the monopolization of that last market create a welfare loss? The answer is no. In fact it will create a welfare gain, since the rise in the last competitive price toward a monopolistic price must make the overall relative prices closer to the relative competitive prices. If all prices exceed the competitive prices by 10 percent, the monopolistic relative prices are identical to the competitive relative prices.

The preceding argument was worked out way back in 1926 by a brilliant mathematical economist named Frank Ramsey. Because of his work, the name *Ramsey rule* has been given to the argument that if all prices rise by an equal percentage, it's like no relative price having risen at all, and hence there's no welfare loss.

been relatively small. Thus, at least from the welfare loss point of view, it would seem that while monopolies are a problem, they aren't an enormous problem to society when compared to issues such as unemployment or drugs.

Government Policy and Monopoly

The empirical estimates of the welfare loss due to monopoly suggest that monopolies are a relatively minor problem. But society has consistently been concerned about monopoly. Public dislike for monopolies has forced government to create laws preventing monopoly. It seems that the public opposes monopoly much more vehemently than one would expect it to, based on the measurement of the welfare loss from monopoly.

There are two explanations for this difference between the layperson's view of monopoly (he or she doesn't like monopoly) and the view that follows from empirical work based on the standard economic model (monopoly isn't much of a problem). One explanation is that society is wrong, that if society understood the economic model, it wouldn't be as concerned about monopoly as it is. A second explanation is that the monopolistic model isn't capturing some of people's normative arguments against monopoly. Both explanations have some validity.

Most economists would agree that the lay public often expresses a knee-jerk reaction to monopoly, not a reasoned judgment. Knee-jerk reactions are often wrong so the argument that society is wrong to be so concerned about monopoly has a ring of truth. Knee-jerk reactions often don't hold true when subjected to careful scrutiny.

But, as discussed in the previous chapter, there are questions whether the economists' competitive equilibrium is an appropriate benchmark from which to judge welfare. The competitive benchmark doesn't take into account income distributional effects and issues of fairness. The public's judgments about real-world events do take these additional welfare considerations into account. Therefore the second explanation—that the monopolistic model isn't capturing some of people's normative arguments against monopoly—is also reasonable.

These two explanations aren't necessarily contradictory. They can complement one another. In certain instances the public might oppose monopoly because it doesn't understand the costs of monopoly, while in other instances it might

John Hicks—Nobel prize, 1972, for work on welfare implications of markets.
© *The Nobel Foundation.*

dislike monopoly based on broader normative criteria that the standard model doesn't capture.

The economist's job is to help separate these two views. Doing so makes the analysis of monopoly a more complicated undertaking than simply drawing and understanding welfare triangle losses.

The standard model of monopoly just presented is elegant, but, like many things elegant, it hides some issues, and these issues could help explain the difference between the standard model of monopoly (which suggests monopoly isn't much of a problem) and the public's dislike of monopoly.

A BROADER VIEW OF MONOPOLY

6

One issue the standard model of monopoly hides is: What prevents other firms from entering the monopolist's market? You should be able to answer that question relatively quickly. If a monopolist exists, it must exist due to some type of **barrier to entry** (a social, political, or economic impediment that prevents firms from entering the market). Three important barriers to entry are natural ability, increasing returns to scale, and government restrictions. In the absence of barriers to entry the monopoly would face competition from other firms, which would erode its monopoly.

Barrier to entry A social, political, or economic impediment that prevents firms from entering a market.

This recognition is one of the main reasons why economists generally support free international trade and oppose tariffs. Tariffs are a barrier to entry to foreign firms and thus provide monopoly power to U.S. firms, allowing them to charge the consumer more than they otherwise could.

Types of Barriers to Entry and the Public's View of Monopoly

Studying how these barriers to entry are established, and what the costs of establishing them are, enriches the standard model and lets us distinguish different types of monopoly. For example, a barrier to entry might exist because a firm is better at producing a good than anyone else. It has unique qualities that make it more efficient than all other firms. The barrier to entry in this case is the firm's ability.

Such monopolies based on ability usually don't provoke the public's ire. Often in the public's mind such monopolies are "just monopolies." The standard economic model doesn't distinguish between a "just" and an "unjust" monopoly. The just/unjust distinction raises the question of whether a firm has acquired a monopoly based on its ability or based on certain unfair positions such as initially pricing low to force competitive companies out of business but then pricing high. Many public debates over monopoly focus on such normative issues, about which the economists' standard model has nothing to say.

An alternative reason why a barrier to entry might exist is that there are significant economies of scale. If sufficiently large economies of scale exist, it would be inefficient to have two producers since if each produced half of the output, neither could take advantage of the economies of scale. Monopolies that exist because economies of scale create a barrier to entry are called **natural monopolies.**

Natural monopolies Monopolies that exist because economies of scale create a barrier to entry.

A third reason monopolies can exist is that they're created by government. The support of laissez-faire by Classical economists such as Adam Smith and their opposition to monopoly arose in large part in reaction to those government-created monopolies, not in reaction to any formal analysis of welfare loss from monopoly.

Normative Views of Monopoly

Many laypeople's views of government-created monopoly reflect the same normative judgments that Classical economists made. Classical economists considered, and much of the lay public considers, such monopolies unfair and inconsistent with liberty. Monopolies prevent people from being free to enter whatever business they want and are undesirable on normative grounds. In this view, government-created monopolies are simply wrong.

Patent A legal protection of a technical innovation that gives the person holding the patent a monopoly on using that innovation.

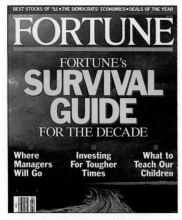

Fortune—A business magazine that closely follows real-world business activities.

Public choice economists Economists who integrate an economic analysis of politics with their analysis of the economy.

Rent seeking Attempting to influence the structure of economic institutions in order to create rents for oneself.

Rent-seeking loss from monopoly Waste caused by people spending money trying to get government to give them a monopoly.

Tullock rectangle Graphical measure of rent-seeking loss from monopoly that results when potential monopolists spend resources to gain monopoly. The waste equals the entire profit of the monopoly.

This normative argument against government-created monopoly doesn't extend to all types of government-created monopolies. The public accepts certain types of government-created monopoly that it believes have overriding social value. An example is patents. A **patent** is a legal protection of a technical innovation which gives the person holding the patent a monopoly on using that innovation. To encourage research and development of new products, government gives out patents for a wide variety of innovations, such as genetic engineering, Xerox machines, and cans that can be opened without a can opener.

A second normative argument against monopoly is that the public doesn't like the income distributional effects of monopoly. Although, as we saw in our discussion of monopoly, monopolists do not always earn an economic profit, they often do, which means that the existence of monopoly might transfer income in a way that the public (whose normative views help determine society's policy toward monopoly) doesn't like. This distributional effect of monopoly based on normative views of who deserves income is another reason many laypeople oppose monopoly: They believe it transfers income from "deserving" consumers to "undeserving" monopolists.

A third normative reason people oppose government-created monopoly that isn't captured by the standard model of monopoly is that the possibility of government-created monopoly encourages people to spend a lot of their time in political pursuits trying to get the government to favor them with a monopoly, and less time doing "productive" things.

This third normative argument against monopoly has been integrated into the standard model of monopoly by a group of political economists called **public choice economists** (economists who integrate an economic analysis of politics with their analysis of the economy). Public choice economists argue that if the government doesn't charge for a monopoly, individuals will spend large amounts of money in **rent seeking** (attempting to influence the structure of economic institutions in order to create rents for themselves). They do so by lobbying and otherwise trying to persuade government to give them the monopoly. Public choice economists further argue that the resources people spend on trying to get their monopoly is a waste of resources (that's the normative judgment) and that this waste is much larger than the traditionally incurred welfare loss from monopoly. Public choice economists argue that if there is competition for monopolies, people will spend up to the total expected amount of profit from a monopoly.

The **rent-seeking loss from monopoly** is shown in Exhibit 9. The possible profits from monopoly create a desire for monopoly and lead potential monopolists to spend resources to gain that monopoly. The resources spent are a waste (unless they serve other purposes) and hence, according to these economists who analyze rent seeking, the welfare cost of monopoly is not only the Harberger triangle, it's also the Tullock rectangle, so-named for Gordon Tullock who first made this argument back in 1967. That **Tullock rectangle** equals the entire profit of the monopolist, and its size often dwarfs the Harberger welfare triangle. According to Tullock, monopolists spend all their profits on rent seeking.

Each of these arguments probably plays a role in the public's dislike of monopoly. As you can see, these real-world arguments blend normative judgments with objective analysis, making it difficult to arrive at definite conclusions. Most real-world problems require this blending, making applied economic analysis difficult. The economist must interpret the normative judgments about what people want to achieve and explain how public policy can be designed to achieve those desired ends.

Let's now consider how economic theory might be used to analyze monopoly and to suggest some alternative policies. We first look at a debate about charging for monopolies. Then we look at a more specific example involving AIDS and AZT.

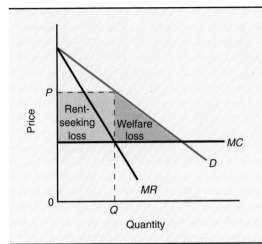

EXHIBIT 9   The Rent-Seeking Loss from Monopoly

If monopolies compete and spend money to achieve their monopoly profits, there will be an additional waste of resources to society, which will approximately equal the total expected profits. Thus rent-seeking analysis sees a second loss to society from monopoly.

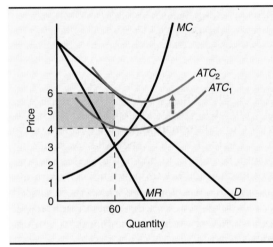

EXHIBIT 10   Selling Monopoly Rights

If the government charges a fixed fee for a monopoly, it will not affect the price, but will raise the fixed costs and hence reduce the profit. (The shaded area).

Should the government charge for a monopoly that it gives out? One group argues that if the government charges, it will increase the monopolist's cost, and hence its price, so the government shouldn't charge. The other side's normative argument is that it's only fair to charge a monopolist. Let's now see where economists come out in this debate.

The first question an economist will ask is how the government will charge for the monopoly. Let's say that, if it is to charge, it will auction off the monopoly right to the highest bidder. In Exhibit 10, if the expected profits are $120, we can predict that the bidding for the monopoly right will approach that $120 economic profit. (Remember, economic profit considers the entrepreneur's effort as a cost.)

Let's say a firm buys a monopoly to sell hot dogs on the thruway, paying $119.99 for that monopoly. The $119.99 is a cost that some people say will push up the monopolist's price. Let's now consider how the economic model says this cost will affect the firm's decision on how many hot dogs to sell and what to charge for them. The economic model directs us to ask the following question: "What does the expenditure of $119.99 do to marginal cost or marginal revenue?" The answer is that it doesn't affect marginal cost or marginal revenue so it doesn't affect the quantity or the price that the monopolist charges because both of those are determined only by where marginal cost and marginal revenue intersect.

Should Government Charge Firms if It Gives Them a Monopoly Right?

7

In the discussion about the hot dog monopoly, I was careful to specify a bid of $119.99, not $120. That still left a whole penny of economic profit. Normal profit is sufficient to keep a monopoly in a market, but, assuming a monopoly is already making a normal profit, some expected economic profit is needed to get it to enter a new market. So some small above-normal profit has to be left to the monopolist to get it to enter the business. Clearly a penny isn't enough, but it's enough to make the point to you: Disequilibrium adjustment from equilibrium requires the expectation of economic profit.

In real life often there's great uncertainty about the value of a monopoly right. Individuals have differing views of what the monopoly is worth, and depending on the actual auction and the interdynamics during the bidding, the bid for a monopoly right will be higher or lower than the actual profit.

Often it's higher because of what's called the *winner's curse*. The person who wins at the auction is the person who values the monopoly right most highly, which means that the average bidder's estimate of the value of the monopoly right was lower than the amount the winner paid. If people on average are right, that means the winner paid too much and will make a loss on operating the monopoly. That's why her victory imposes the winner's curse.

A good example of the winner's curse is Donald Trump's and Merv Griffin's bidding on Resorts International and the Taj Mahal Casino. Both men figured the expected profit too high and both their businesses got into serious financial trouble, much to these tycoons' embarrassment.

What *does* it affect? It increases fixed cost (which is why the change has no effect on marginal cost), and in doing so it shifts up the average total cost curve to a point where the monopolist makes almost no profit. Thus, according to the economic model, the result of an auction for a monopoly is to transfer most of the monopoly profit from the monopolist to the government. It will not raise price and therefore, in regard to the two arguments posed at the beginning of this section, the economist would come out in favor of charging the full value for a monopoly. Charging for a monopoly has an additional advantage. To the degree that it eliminates profit from the monopoly, it reduces rent-seeking expenditures to get that monopoly. So in this case economic analysis supports charging for a monopoly, if you're going to have a monopoly.

AIDS, AZT, and Monopoly

As a final example of how knowledge of economics helps deal with real-world monopoly problems, let's consider the problem of AIDS and the medicinal drug AZT. AZT is believed to slow the onset of AIDS. The drug was developed by Burroughs Wellcome, which has a patent on it. That patent gives Burroughs Wellcome a monopoly. Patents are given on medicine to encourage firms to find cures for various diseases. The monopoly the patent gives them lets them charge a high price so that the firms can expect to make a profit from their research. Whether such patents are in the public interest isn't an issue since the patent has already been issued.

What is an issue is what to do about AZT. Currently demand for AZT is highly inelastic, so the price Burroughs Wellcome can charge is high even though its marginal cost of producing it is low. Whether Burroughs Wellcome is making a profit on AZT depends on its cost of development. But since that cost is already spent, that's irrelevant to the current marginal cost; development cost affects Burroughs Wellcome's ATC curve, not its marginal cost curve. Thus, Burroughs Wellcome is charging an enormously high price for a drug that may help save people's lives and that costs Burroughs Wellcome a very small amount to produce.

What, if anything, should the government do? Some people have suggested that the government come in and regulate the price Burroughs Wellcome charges, requiring the firm to charge only its marginal cost. Doing so would make the marginal cost of producing AZT equal to the price people pay, which would make society better off. But most economists have a problem with that policy. They point out that doing so will have significant disincentive effects on drug companies. One reason drug companies spend billions of dollars for drug research is their expectation that they'll be able to make large profits if they're successful. If drug companies expect the government to come in and take away their monopoly when they're successful, they won't search for cures. So forcing Burroughs Wellcome to charge a low price for AZT would help AIDS victims, but it would hurt people suffering from diseases that are currently being researched and that might be researched in the future in the expectation of profits. So there's a strong argument not to regulate.

But the thought of people dying when a cheap cure—or at least a partially effective treatment—is available is repulsive to me and to many others. Indeed, Burroughs Wellcome has felt the pressure and has made AZT available to HIV-positive children (children infected with the AIDS virus but not yet suffering from actual AIDS) at a much lower price than it does to others (an example of price discrimination). In 1989 it lowered the price of AZT for everyone by 20 percent. An alternative policy suggested by economic theory is for the government to buy the patent from Burroughs Wellcome and allow anyone to make AZT so the price would approach its marginal cost. Admittedly this would be expensive. It would cause negative incentive effects, and the government would have to increase taxes to cover the buy out's costs. But this approach would avoid the problem of the regulatory approach and achieve the same ends. However, it would also introduce new problems, such as determining which patents the government should buy.

Whether such a buy-out policy makes sense remains to be seen, but in debating such issues the power of the simple monopoly model becomes apparent.

CONCLUSION

We've come to the end of the presentation of the formal models of perfect competition and monopoly. Working through the models takes a lot of effort, but, as my health club instructor used to say, "No pain, no gain." In an earlier chapter, I quoted Einstein: "A theory should be as simple as possible, but not more so." This chapter's analysis isn't simple; it takes repetition, working through models, and doing thought experiments to get it down pat. But it's as simple as possible. Even so, it's extremely easy to make a foolish mistake, as I did in my Ph.D. oral examination when I was outlining an argument on the blackboard. ["*What* did you say the output would be for this monopolist, Mr. Colander?"] As I learned then, it takes long hours of working through the models again and again to get them right.

KEY POINTS

- The price a monopolist charges is higher than that of a competitive market due to the restriction of output; a monopolist can make a profit in the long run.   **1**
- A monopolist's profit-maximizing output is where marginal revenue equals marginal cost.   **2**
- To determine a monopolist's profit, first determine its output (where MC = MR). Then determine its price and average total cost at that output level.   **3**
- A perfectly price-discriminating monopolist sells more and makes a higher profit than a normal monopolist.   **4**

- The welfare loss to society from monopoly, as measured by Harberger and others, is relatively small. Normative measures of the welfare cost can increase that loss significantly.   **5**
- The public often opposes monopoly, based on normative reasons that the economic model doesn't capture.   **5**
- Three important barriers to entry are natural ability, increasing returns to scale, and government restrictions.   **6**
- Selling rights to monopoly will eliminate profit to a degree and reduce the time and money spent on rent seeking.   **7**

KEY TERMS

barrier to entry *(517)*
consumer surplus *(512)*
marginal revenue *(507)*
marginal revenue
  curve *(508)*

monopoly *(506)*
MR = MC *(509)*
natural monopolies *(517)*
patent *(518)*
price discriminate *(512)*

public choice
  economists *(518)*
rent seeking *(518)*
rent-seeking loss from
  monopoly *(518)*

Tullock rectangle *(518)*
welfare loss
  triangle *(515)*

QUESTIONS FOR THOUGHT AND REVIEW

*The number after each question represents the estimated
degree of critical thinking required. (1 = almost none;
10 = deep thought.)*

1. Demonstrate graphically the profit-maximizing positions for a perfect competitor and a monopolist. How do they differ? *(3)*
2. Monopolists differ from perfect competitors because monopolists make a profit. True or false? Why? *(4)*
3. Explain the effects on college education of the development of a teaching machine which you plug into a student's brain and the student understands everything. How would your answer differ if a college could monopolize production of this machine? *(9)*
4. Say you place a lump sum tax on a monopolist. How will that affect her output and pricing decisions? *(4)*
5. A monopolist is selling fish. But if the fish don't sell, they rot. What will be the likely elasticity at the point on the demand curve at which the monopolist sets the price? *(6)*
6. Provide a price discrimination argument for the exis-

tence of the three unexplained examples of price discrimination in the text. *(6)*
7. Will the welfare loss from a monopolist with a perfectly elastic marginal cost curve be greater or less than the welfare loss from a monopolist with an upward-sloping marginal cost curve? *(5)*
8. Copyrights provide authors with a monopoly. What effect would eliminating copyrights have on the price and output of textbooks? Should copyrights be eliminated? *(8)*
9. Some authors believe that they should get a fee whenever someone borrows their books from the library. What effect would such a fee have on the price and quantity of books demanded? Why? Should such fees be charged? *(8)*
10. If people had to pay for monopoly, they would buy less monopoly, so the Tullock rectangle overestimates the rent-seeking loss from monopoly. True or false? Why? *(9)*

PROBLEMS AND EXERCISES

1. A monopolist with a linear demand curve finds that it can sell two units at $12 each or 12 units at $2 each. Its fixed cost is $20 and its marginal cost is constant at $3 per unit.
   a. Draw the MC, ATC, MR, and demand curves for this monopolist.
   b. At what output level would the monopolist produce?
   c. At what output level would a perfectly competitive firm produce?
2. State what's wrong with the following graphs:

(c)   Quantity

(d)   Quantity

(a)   Quantity

(b)   Quantity

25

Monopolistic Competition, Oligopoly, and Strategic Pricing

*Competition, you know, is a lot
like chastity. It is widely praised, but alas, too little practiced.*
Carol Tucker

After reading this chapter, you should be able to:

1

Interpret a concentration ratio and a Herfindahl index for two- and four-digit industries.

2

List the four distinguishing characteristics of monopolistic competition.

3

Demonstrate graphically the equilibrium of a monopolistic competitor.

4

State why an oligopoly has a strong desire to form a cartel.

5

Explain why the contestable market theory would lead to determining competitiveness by performance rather than structure.

6

Summarize the important elements of various market structures.

Market structure The physical characteristics of the market within which firms interact.

As soon as economists start talking about real-world competition, market structure becomes a focus of the discussion. **Market structure** is the physical characteristics of the market within which firms interact. It involves the number of firms in the market, the barriers to entry, and the communication among firms. Monopoly and competition are the two polar cases of market structure that economists generally focus on. Real-world markets generally fall in between, and it is useful to introduce briefly two market structures between perfect competition and monopoly: monopolistic competition and oligopoly. They not only provide you with a sense of how the models can apply to the real world; they also help cement the concepts learned in the last chapter into your mind.

Monopolistic competition A market structure in which many firms sell differentiated products.

Oligopoly A market structure with a few interdependent firms.

Perfect competition has an almost infinite number of firms; monopoly has one firm. Monopolistic competition and oligopoly fall between these two extremes. **Monopolistic competition** is a market structure in which there are many firms selling differentiated products. Because there are many firms, any one firm's decision is independent of other firms' decisions. Monopolistic competition falls closer to perfect competition; it has many firms, but not an uncountable number. **Oligopoly** is a market structure in which there are a few interdependent firms. Oligopoly falls closer to monopoly; it has only a few firms, but more than one firm. The top of Exhibit 1 shows the spectrum of market structures. The bottom estimates how the relative importance of each market structure in the U.S. economy has changed.

THE PROBLEMS OF DETERMINING MARKET STRUCTURE

Estimates such as those in Exhibit 1 must be treated with care. Defining an industry is a complicated task—inevitably numerous arbitrary decisions must be made. Similarly, defining the relevant market of a given industry is complicated. For example, there are over 16,000 banks in the United States, and banking is considered reasonably competitive. However there may be only one or two banks in a particular small town so there will be a monopoly or oligopoly with respect to banks in that town. Is the United States or the town the relevant market? The same argument exists when we think of international competition. Many firms sell in international markets and, while a group of firms may compose an oligopoly in the United States, the international market might be more accurately characterized by monopolistic competition.

Another dimension of the definitional problem concerns deciding what is to be included in an industry. If you define the industry as "the transportation industry," there are many firms. If you define it as "the automobile industry," there are fewer firms; if you define it as "the sports car industry," there are still fewer firms. Similarly with the geographic dimension of industry. There's more competition in the global market than in the local market. The narrower the definition, the fewer the firms.

Standard Industrial Classification Manual—This Commerce Department publication provides full information about SIC codes.

Classifying Industries

Standard Industrial Code (SIC) System for classifying industries.

Two-digit industry SIC designation for broadly defined industries.

To convey a sense of how specifically one is defining an industry, economists have developed a classification system of industries called a **Standard Industrial Code (SIC)**. A **two-digit industry** is a broadly defined industry. For example, "furniture and fixtures" is a two-digit industry and is denoted by the number 25. All subdivisions of that broad grouping use the same first two numbers and then add more numbers to identify the particular subdivision. For example, "metal household furniture" is a subdivision of the furniture and fixtures industry and is denoted by the number 2514.

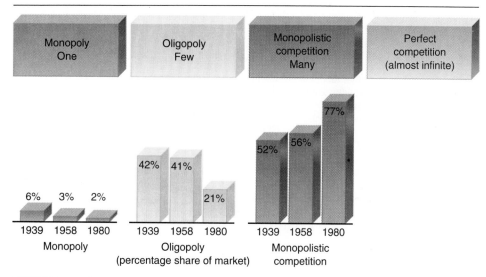

EXHIBIT 1 **The Spectrum of Market Structures**

There are many types of market structures, ranging from a market with one firm (monopoly) to a market with an almost infinite number of firms (perfect competition). Real-world markets generally fall between the two. Oligopoly is a market structure with a few *interdependent* firms. Monopolistic competition is a market structure in which there are more firms and their decisions are *independent*. The lower part of the exhibit shows that the relative importance of the different market structures has varied over time. Notice that monopolistic competition accounts for over 75 percent of the markets in the United States. Notice also, that monopoly is rare and perfect competition is nonexistent.
Source: Adapted from William G. Shepard, "Causes of Increased Competition in the U.S. Economy, 1939-1980," *Review of Economics and Statistics*, November 1982, pp. 613-26.

When economists talk about industry structure, they generally talk about **four-digit industries** in the United States. This is a convention. Economists are often called upon to give expert testimony in court cases, and if an economist wants to argue that an industry is more competitive than its opponents say it is, he or she challenges this convention of using a four-digit classification of industry, asserting that the classification is arbitrary (which it is) and that the relevant market should be the two-digit classification. Exhibit 2 presents various two- and four-digit industry groupings to give you an idea of what's included in each.

To measure industry structure economists use one of two methods: the concentration ratio or a Herfindahl index (sometimes called the *Herfindahl-Hirshman index* or the *HHI*).

A **concentration ratio** is the percentage of the total industry output that the top firms of the industry have. The higher the ratio, the closer to an oligopolistic or monopolistic type of market structure. The Herfindahl index is an index of the squares of the market shares of all the firms in the industry. Generally if one index is high, so is the other. Exhibit 3 presents the four-firm concentration ratio and the Herfindahl index of selected industries.

Concentration Ratios   The most commonly used concentration ratio is the four-firm concentration ratio. For example, a four-firm concentration ratio of 60 tells you that the top four firms in the industry produce 60 percent of the industry's output. The classification of industries as monopolistically competitive or oligopolistic that you saw in Exhibit 1 was organized in large part around concentration ratios. If the four-firm concentration ratio was below 40 percent, the presumption was that the industry was monopolistically competitive. If the four-firm concentration ratio was between 40 and 60 percent, the presumption was that it was oligopolistic. If the four-firm concentration ratio was greater than 60 percent, the industry was considered monopolistic.

Four-digit industry SIC designation for a specific type of industry within a more broadly defined industry.

Determining Industry Structure

Concentration ratio The percentage of industry output that a specific number of the largest firms have.

1

EXHIBIT 2   Two-Digit and Four-Digit Industry Groups

Two-digit industries

20	Food and kindred products
21	Tobacco manufactures
22	Textile mill products
23	Apparel and other fabricated textile products
24	Lumber and wood products, except furniture
25	Furniture and fixtures
26	Paper and allied products
27	Printing and publishing
28	Chemicals and allied products
29	Petroleum and coal products
30	Rubber and misc. plastic products

Four-digit industries (subdivisions of furniture and fixtures)

2511	Wood household furniture, excluding upholstered
2512	Upholstered household furniture
2514	Metal household furniture
2515	Mattresses and bedsprings (including folding and dual-purpose beds)
2517	Wood TV and radio cabinets
2519	Household furniture

EXHIBIT 3   Concentration Ratios and the Herfindahl Index

Industry	Four-firm concentration ratio	Herfindahl index
Meat packing	29	325
Canned fruit and vegetables	21	214
Cereal breakfast foods	86	NA
Women's and misses' dresses	6	24
Book publishing	17	190
Greeting card publishing	84	2840
Soap and detergent	60	1306
Men's footwear	28	378
Women's footwear	38	492
Bolts, nuts, rivets, and washers	13	102
Computing equipment	43	793
Radio and TV sets	49	751
Burial caskets	52	1247

The Herfindahl Index   The concentration ratio measure has problems (as do all measures). For example, say an industry has a four-firm concentration ratio of 51 percent. That doesn't tell us whether one firm has 48 percent and the next three firms each have 1 percent of the market, or whether the top four firms each have 12 or 13 percent. Yet those industries' structures are quite different from each other. Nor does the concentration ratio differentiate between industries with different numbers of firms beyond four.

To avoid these problems, an alternative definition of *market structure* has been designed—the **Herfindahl index.** It's calculated by adding the squared value of the market shares of all the firms in the industry. For example, say that 10 firms in the industry each have 10 percent of the market:

$$\text{Herfindahl index} = 10^2 + 10^2 + 10^2 + 10^2 + 10^2 + 10^2 + 10^2 + 10^2 + 10^2 + 10^2 = 1,000.$$

Two advantages of the Herfindahl index are that it takes into account all firms in an industry, and it gives extra weight to a single firm that has an especially large share of the market. For example, let's consider two industries with four-firm concentration ratios of 51 percent. In the first industry the top firm has a 48 percent market share and the next three each have a 1 percent share. In the second industry the top three firms have a 13 percent share, and the fourth has a

Herfindahl index A method used by economists to classify how competitive an industry is.

FOREIGN COMPETITIVE OLIGOPOLIES

Market structures change over time. Take, for instance, the automobile industry, which has always been used as the classic oligopoly model. Starting in the 1970s, however, foreign auto makers have made large inroads into the U.S. market and have added new competition to it. Foreign companies such as Honda, Nissan, and Toyota have entered the U.S. market as seen in the accompanying pie chart which lists major automobile companies and their market share.

As you can see, the four-firm concentration ratio is about 75 percent, so the industry is still classified as an oligopoly. GM still considers what Ford and Chrysler's reactions will be, but with the addition of foreign competition, there are getting to be too many firms for one firm to consider the reactions of all the other firms. The auto industry is becoming more monopolistically competitive.

Such change in industry structure is to be expected. Monopoly and oligopoly allow firms to make above-normal profits. Above-normal profits invite entry, and unless there are entry barriers, the result will likely be a breakdown in that monopoly or oligopoly.

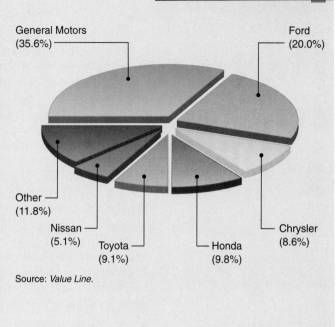

Source: *Value Line.*

12 percent share. Let's further assume that there are 49 other firms in the industry, each with a 1 percent share of the market.

The Herfindahl index of the first is

$$(48)^2 + (1)^2 \ldots + (1)^2 = 48^2 + 52 = 2304 + 52 = 2356.$$

The Herfindahl index of the second is

$$(13)^2 + (13)^2 + (13)^2 + (12)^2 + (1)^2 + \ldots + (1)^2 = 169 + 169 + 169 + 144 + 49 = 700.$$

As you can see, in certain instances the Herfindahl index gives a different view of the two industries' structures than we get from the concentration ratio method.

The Herfindahl index is important because it is used as a rule of thumb by the U.S. Department of Justice in determining whether an industry is sufficiently competitive to allow a merger between two large firms in the industry. If the Herfindahl index is less than 1000, the Department of Justice assumes the industry is sufficiently competitive, and it doesn't look more closely at the merger. We'll discuss this in more detail in the next chapter.

Conglomerate Firms and Bigness

Neither the four-firm concentration ratio nor the Herfindahl index gives us a picture of corporations' bigness. That's because many corporations are **conglomerates** (companies that span a variety of unrelated industries). For example, a conglomerate might produce both shoes and automobiles.

Conglomerate A large corporation whose activities span various unrelated industries.

To see that concentration ratios are not an index of bigness, say there were only 11 firms in the entire United States, each with a 9 percent share of each industry. Both indices would classify the U.S. economy as reasonably competitive, but many people would seriously doubt whether that were the case. Little work has been done on classifying conglomerates or in determining whether they have any effect on an industry's competitiveness.

The Importance of Classifying Industry Structure

Now that we've talked about the classifications of industries, we need to ask why it's important to classify them in market structures such as monopolistic competition and oligopoly. The reason is that the greater the number of sellers, the greater the likelihood that an industry is competitive.

In terms of formal modeling it's important to classify industries because the number of firms in an industry plays an important role in determining whether firms explicitly take other firms' actions into account. In monopolistic competition there are so many firms that individual firms *do not* explicitly take into account rival firms' likely responses to their decisions. In oligopoly there are fewer firms and each firm explicitly takes into account other firms' expected reaction to its decisions. Taking explicit account of a rival's expected response to a decision you are making is called **strategic decision making.** In oligopolies all decisions, including pricing decisions, are strategic decisions. Thus, one distinguishes between monopolistic competition and oligopoly by whether or not they explicitly take into account competitors' reactions to their decisions.

Why is the distinction important? Because it determines whether economists can model and predict the price and output of an industry. Nonstrategic decision making can be predicted relatively accurately if individuals behave rationally. Strategic decision making is much more difficult to predict, even if people behave rationally. Consistent with this distinction, economists' model of monopolistic competition has a definite prediction. A model of monopolistic competition will tell us: Here's how much will be produced and here's how much will be charged. Economists' model of oligopoly doesn't have a definite prediction. There are no unique price and output decisions at which an oligopoly will rationally arrive; there are a variety of rational oligopoly decisions.

> **Strategic decision making** Taking explicit account of a rival's expected response to a decision you are making.

MONOPOLISTIC COMPETITION   ▨2

The four distinguishing characteristics of monopolistic competition are:

1. Many sellers in a highly competitive market.
2. Differentiated products, but firms still act independently.
3. Multiple dimensions of competition.
4. Easy entry of new firms in the long run so there are no long-run profits.

Let's consider each in turn.

Many Sellers

When there are a few sellers, it's reasonable to explicitly take into account your competitors' reaction to the price you set. When there are many sellers, it isn't. In monopolistic competition one doesn't take into account rivals' reactions. Here's an example. There are many types of soap: Ivory, Irish Spring, Yardley's Old English, and so on. So when Ivory decides to run a sale, it won't spend a lot of time thinking of Old English's reaction. There are so many firms that one firm can't concern itself with the reaction of any specific firm. The soap industry is characterized by monopolistic competition. On the other hand, there are only a few major automobile firms, so when GM sets its price, it will explicitly consider what Ford's reaction may be. If GM raises its price, will Ford go along and also raise price? Or will it hold its price at its current level and try to sell its cars on the basis of lower prices? The automobile industry is an oligopoly.

The fact that there are many sellers in monopolistic competition also makes collusion difficult, since when there are many firms, getting all of them to act as one is difficult. Monopolistically competitive firms act independently.

Product Differentiation

The "many sellers" characteristic gives monopolistic competition its competitive aspect. Product differentiation gives it its monopolistic aspect. In a monopolistically competitive market, the goods that are sold aren't homogeneous as in perfect competition; they are differentiated slightly. Irish Spring soap is slightly different from Ivory which in turn is slightly different from Yardley's Old English.

So in one sense each firm has a monopoly in the good it sells. But that monopoly is fleeting; it is based upon advertising to let people know, and to convince them, that one firm's good is different from the goods of competitors. The good may or may not really be different. Bleach differs little from one brand to another, yet buying Clorox makes many people feel "safe" that they're getting pure bleach. I generally don't buy it; I buy generic bleach. Ketchup, on the other hand, while made from the same basic ingredients no matter what the brand, differs among types (in my view). I buy only Heinz and would never think of getting any other type—to me, other types aren't true ketchup.

Because a monopolistic competitor has some monopoly power, advertising to increase that monopoly power (and hence increase the firm's profits) makes sense as long as the marginal benefit of advertising exceeds the marginal cost. Despite the fact that their goods are similar but differentiated, to fit the monopolistically competitive model, firms must make their decisions as if they had no effect on other firms; they must not act strategically or interdependently; that would make the industry an oligopoly.

In perfect competition, price is the only dimension on which firms compete; in monopolistic competition, competition takes many forms. Product differentiation reflects firms' attempt to compete on perceived quality; advertising is another form competition takes. Other dimensions of competition include service and distribution outlets. These multiple dimensions of competition make it much harder to analyze a specific industry, but these alternative methods of competition follow the same general decision rules as price competition:

Multiple Dimensions of Competition

- Compare marginal costs and marginal benefits.
- Change that dimension of competition until marginal costs equal marginal benefits.

The last condition for a market to be considered monopolistically competitive is that entry must be relatively easy and there must be no significant barriers to entry. The absence of barriers to entry means that there can be no long-run economic profits; in monopolistic competition if there were long-run economic profits, other firms would enter. Barriers to entry create the potential for long-run economic profit and prevent competitive pressures from pushing price down to cost. When no barriers to entry exist, firms enter until no economic profit exists.

Ease of Entry of New Firms in the Long Run

Although a full analysis of the multiple dimensions of monopolistic competition cannot be compressed into a two-dimensional graph, a good introduction to monopolistic competition can be gained by considering it within the standard two-dimensional graph.

Graphical Representation of Monopolistic Competition

Gasoline stations watch the competition carefully and their prices often move together. © *Harriet Gan/The Image Works.*

EXHIBIT 4 (a, b, and c) Monopolistic Competition

In (a) you can see that a monopolistically competitive firm prices in the same manner as a monopolist. It sets price where marginal revenue equals marginal cost. In (b) you can see that the monopolistic competitor is not only a monopolist but also a competitor. Competition means zero economic profit in the long run. Economic profits are determined by the average total cost (*ATC*) curve. At equilibrium, *ATC* must be equal to price. It will be equal to price only if the *ATC* curve is tangent to the demand curve at the output the firm chooses. In (c) you can see that the existence of profits would set adjustments in motion that would eliminate those profits.

To do so we simply consider the four propositions of monopolistic competition and see what implication they have for our curves. First, we recognize that the firm has some monopoly power; therefore a monopolistic competitor faces a downward-sloping demand curve. The downward-sloping demand curve means that in making decisions about prices, the monopolistic competitor will, as will a monopolist, use a marginal revenue curve that is below price. So at its profit-maximizing output, marginal cost will be less than price (not equal to price as it would be for a perfect competitor). We consider that case in Exhibit 4(a).

The monopolistic competitor faces the demand curve *D*, marginal revenue curve *MR*, and marginal cost curve *MC*. This demand curve is its portion of the total market demand curve. Using the MC = MR rule discussed in the last chapter, you can see that the firm will choose output level Q_e (because that's the level of output at which marginal revenue intersects marginal cost). Having determined output, we extend a dotted line up to the demand curve and see that the firm will set a price equal to P_e. This price exceeds marginal cost. So far all we've done is to reproduce the monopolist's decision.

Where does the competition come in? Competition means zero economic profit in the long run. (If there's profit a new competitor will enter the market, decreasing the existing firms' demand [shifting it to the left].) In long-run equilibrium a perfect competitor makes only a normal profit. Economic profits are determined by ATC, not by MC, so the competition part of monopolistic competition tells us where the average total cost must be at the long-run equilibrium output. It must be equal to price, and it will be equal to price only if the ATC curve is tangent to the demand curve at the output the firm chooses. We add that average total cost curve to the MC, MR, and demand curves in Exhibit 4(b). Profit or loss, I hope you remember, is determined by the difference between price and average total cost at the quantity the firm chooses.

To give this condition a little more intuitive meaning, say, for instance, that the average cost curve shifts down—to ATC_2 (as in Exhibit 4(c)) rather than ATC_1. After the shift the firm would be making profit of the shaded rectangle. This profit would set two adjustments in motion. First, it would attract new entrants. Some of the firm's customers would defect and its portion of the market demand

(a)   **Perfect competition**   (b)   **Monopolistic competition**

EXHIBIT 5 (a and b)   A Comparison of Perfect and Monopolistic Competition

The perfect competitor perceives its demand curve as perfectly elastic, and zero economic profit means that it produces at the minimum of the *ATC* curve, as represented in (**a**). A monopolistic competitor, on the other hand, faces a downward-sloping demand curve and produces where marginal cost equals marginal revenue, as represented in (**b**). The *ATC* curve is tangent to the demand curve at that level, which is *not* at the minimum point of the *ATC* curve. The monopolistic competitor produces Q_m at price P_m. A perfect competitor with the same marginal cost curve would produce Q_c at price P_c.

curve would decrease, shifting its demand curve back in the direction of D_2. Second, to try to protect its profits the firm would likely increase expenditures on product differentiation and advertising to offset that entry. (There would be an All New, Really New, Widget Campaign.) These expenditures would shift its average total cost curve up from ATC_2 to ATC_3. These two adjustments would continue until the profits disappeared and the new demand curve was once again tangent to the average cost curve. At that point the price is P_2. A monopolistically competitive firm can make no long-run economic profit.

If both the monopolistic competitor and the perfect competitor make zero economic profit in the long run, it might seem that, in the long run at least, they're identical. They aren't, however. The perfect competitor perceives its demand curve as perfectly elastic and the zero economic profit condition means that it produces at the minimum of the average total cost curve where the marginal cost curve equals price. We demonstrate that case in Exhibit 5(a).

Comparing Monopolistic Competition with Perfect Competition

The monopolistic competitor faces a downward-sloping demand curve. It produces where the marginal cost curve equals the marginal revenue curve, and not where MC equals price. In equilibrium, price exceeds marginal cost. The average total cost curve of a monopolistic competitor is tangent to the demand curve at that output level, which cannot be at the minimum point of the average total cost curve since the demand curve is sloping downward. The minimum point of the average total cost curve (where a perfect competitor produces) is at a higher output (Q_c) than that of the monopolistic competitor (Q_m). I demonstrate the monopolistically competitive equilibrium in Exhibit 5(b) to allow you to compare monopolistic competition with perfect competition.

As you can see, the difference between a monopolist and a monopolistic competitor is in the position of the average total cost curve in long-run equilibrium. For a monopolist, the average total cost curve can be, but need not be, at a position below price so that the monopolist makes a long-run economic profit. The average total cost curve of a monopolistic competitor must be tangent to the demand curve at the price and output chosen by the monopolistic competitor. No long-run economic profit is possible.

The difference between a perfect competitor and a monopolistic competitor is that the perfect competitor in long-run equilibrium produces at a point where MC = P = ATC. At that point ATC is at its minimum.

A monopolistic competitor produces at a point where MC = MR. Price is higher than marginal cost. For a monopolistic competitor in long-run equilibrium

$$(P = \text{ATC}) \geq (\text{MC} = \text{MR}).$$

At that point ATC is *not* at its minimum.

What does this distinction between a monopolistically competitive industry and a perfectly competitive industry mean in practice? It means that for a monopolistic competitor, since increasing output lowers average cost, increasing market share is a relevant concern. If only the monopolistic competitor could expand its market, it could do better. For a perfect competitor, increasing output offers no benefit in the form of lower average cost. A perfect competitor would have no concern about market share (the firm's percentage of total sales in the market).

Advertising and Monopolistic Competition

While firms in a perfectly competitive market have no incentive to advertise (since they can sell all they want at the market price), monopolistic competitors have a strong incentive. That's because their products are differentiated from the others; advertising plays an important role in providing that differentiation.

A primary goal of advertising is to shift the firm's demand curve to the right to increase demand for its product. That allows the firm to sell more, to charge a higher price, or to enjoy a combination of the two. It is advantageous to the firm if the marginal revenue of advertising exceeds the marginal cost of advertising. Advertising has two effects: It shifts the demand curve out, and it shifts the average total cost curve up.

When many firms are advertising, the advertising might be done less to shift the demand curve out than to keep the demand curve where it is, to stop demanders from shifting to a competitor's product. In either case, firms advertise to move the demand curve further out than where it would be if the firms weren't advertising. Advertising is often designed to increase the firm's market share. Market share is especially important when there are economies of scale.

Advertising and Economies of Scale   Advertising shifts the average total cost curve up, but where there are economies of scale in production, advertising can result in lower average total costs, as Exhibit 6 shows. In it we see that advertising shifts the ATC curve upward from ATC_1 to ATC_2. (Advertising on television can cost over \$1 million per minute.) However, since more consumers hear about the product, the firm can increase output, say from Q_1 to Q_2. In such a case, cost per unit declines from C_1 to C_2, because of economies of scale. The lower cost from economies of scale more than offsets the cost of advertising.

Does Advertising Help or Hinder Us?   Our perception of products (the degree of trust we put in them) is significantly influenced by advertising. Think of the following pairs of goods:

Rolex	Timex
Cheerios	Oat Circles
Clorox bleach	basic bleach

Each of these names conveys a sense of what it is and how much trust we put in the product, and that determines how much we're willing to pay for it. For example, most people would pay more for Cheerios than for Oat Circles. Each year firms spend more than \$125 billion on advertising. That advertising increases firms' costs but it also differentiates their products.

Are we as consumers better off or worse off with differentiated products? That's difficult to say. There's a certain waste in much of the differentiation that

EXHIBIT 6 Advertising and Economies of Scale

Advertising shifts the average total cost curve up from ATC_1 to ATC_2, as shown here. Since more consumers hear about the product, the producer can increase output from Q_1 to Q_2. In the example, even though the average cost curve shifts up, the firm's cost per unit falls from C_1 to C_2.

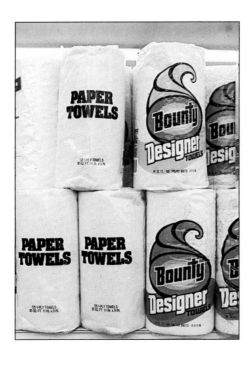

Enormous amounts of product differentiation occur in the aggregate economy. Firms spend large amounts of money to convince people that their product is better. © *Mark Antman/The Image Works.*

occurs. It shows up in the graph by the fact that monopolistic competitors don't produce at the minimum point of their average total cost curve. But there's also a sense of trust that we get from buying names we know and in having goods that are slightly different from one another. I'm a sophisticated consumer who knows that there's little difference between Clorox Bleach and a no-name store brand of bleach, or between generic aspirin and Bayer aspirin. Yet sometimes I buy Clorox Bleach and Bayer aspirin even though they cost more.

Edward Chamberlin, one of the originators of the description of monopolistic competition, believed that the difference between the cost of a perfect competitor and the cost of a monopolistic competitor was the cost of what he called "differentness."[1] If consumers are willing to pay that cost, then it's not a waste but, rather, it's a benefit to them.

---

[1] About the same time as Chamberlin developed his theory of monopolistic competition, Joan Robinson, a Cambridge, England, economist, developed a theory of imperfect competition. Her theory is similar to Chamberlin's and the two economists are generally seen as the originators of the idea.

One must be careful about drawing any implications from this analysis. Average total cost for a monopolistically competitive firm includes advertising and costs of differentiating a product. Whether we as consumers are better off with as much differentiation as we have, or whether we'd all be better off if all firms produced a generic product at a lower cost, is debatable.

OLIGOPOLY

The central element of oligopoly is that there are a small number of firms in an industry so that, in any decision it makes, each firm must take into account the expected reaction of other firms. Oligopolistic firms are mutually interdependent and therefore use strategic decision making.

Most industries in the United States have some oligopolistic elements. If you ask almost any businessperson whether he or she directly takes into account rivals' likely response, the answer you'll get is "In certain cases, yes; in others, no."

Most retail stores that you deal with are oligopolistic in your neighborhood or town, although by national standards they may be quite competitive. For example, how many grocery stores do you shop at? Do you think they keep track of what their competitors are doing? You bet. They keep a close eye on their competitors' prices and set their own accordingly.

Models of Oligopoly Behavior

No single general model of oligopoly behavior exists. The reason is that there are many possible ways in which an oligopolist can decide on pricing and output strategy, and there are no compelling grounds to characterize any of them as *the* oligopoly strategy. Although there are five or six formal models, I'll focus on two informal models of oligopoly behavior that give you insight into real-world problems rather than exercise your reasoning and modeling abilities as my earlier discussion did. The two models we'll consider are the cartel model and the contestable markets model. These two models, combined with Appendix A's case study of pricing by a jewelry firm, should give you a sense of how real-world oligopolistic pricing takes place.

Why, you ask, can't economists develop a simple formal model of oligopoly? The reason lies in the interdependence of oligopolists. Since there are so few competitors, what one firm does specifically influences what other firms do, so an oligopolist's plan must always be a contingency or strategic plan. If my competitors act one way, I'll do X, but if they act another way, I'll do Y. Strategic interactions have a variety of potential outcomes rather than a single outcome such as shown in the formal models we discussed. An oligopolist spends enormous amounts of time guessing what its competitors will do, and it develops a strategy of how it will act, depending on what its competitors do.

The Cartel Model   A **cartel** (sometimes called a *trust*) is a combination of firms that acts as if it were a single firm; a cartel is a shared monopoly. If oligopolies can limit entry by other firms, they have a strong incentive to cartelize the industry and to act as a monopolist would, restricting output to a level that maximizes profit to the combination of firms. Thus, the **cartel model of oligopoly** is a model that assumes that oligopolies act as if they were monopolists that have assigned output quotas to individual member firms of the oligopoly so that total output is consistent with joint profit maximization. All firms follow a uniform pricing policy which serves their collective interest. Since a monopolist makes the most profit that can be squeezed from a market, the cartelization strategy is the best an oligopoly can do. That strategy requires each oligopolist to hold its production below what would be in its own interest were it not to collude with the others. Such explicit formal collusion is against the law in the United States, but informal collusion is allowed and oligopolies have developed a variety of methods to collude implicitly. Thus, the cartel model has some relevance.

There are problems with it, however. For example, various firms' interests often differ, so it isn't clear what the collective interest of the firms in the industry is. In many cases a single firm, often the largest or dominant firm, takes the lead in pricing and output decisions, and the other firms (which are often called *fringe firms*) follow suit, even though they might have preferred to adopt a different strategy. In other cases the various firms meet, sometimes only by happenchance, at the golf course or at a trade association gathering, and arrive at a collective decision. In the United States meetings for this purpose are illegal, but they do occur. In yet other cases the firms just happen to come to a collective decision, even though they have never met. Such collective decisions are known as **implicit collusion.**

Implicit Price Collusion   Implicit price collusion, in which firms just happen to charge the same price but didn't meet to discuss price strategy, isn't against the law. Oligopolies often operate as close to the fine edge of the law as they can. For example, many oligopolistic industries allow a price leader to set the price, and then the others follow suit. The airline and steel industries take that route. Firms just happen to charge the same price or very close to the same price.

It isn't only in major industries that you see such implicit collusion. In small towns, you'll notice that most independent carpenters charge the same price. There's no explicit collusion, but were a carpenter to offer to work for less than the others, the invisible handshake wouldn't be extended to her at morning coffee.

Or let's take another example: the Miami fish market where sport fishermen sell their catch at the dock. When I lived in Miami I often went to the docks to buy fresh fish. There were about 20 stands, all charging the same price. Price fluctuated, but it was by subtle agreement, and close to the end of the day the word would go out that the price could be reduced.

I got to know some of the sellers and asked them why they priced like that when it would be in their individual interest to set their own price. Their answer: "We like our boat and don't want it burned." They may have been talking in hyperbole, but the invisible handshake plays an important role in stabilizing prices in an oligopoly.

Why Are Prices Sticky?   Informal collusion happens all the time in U.S. businesses. One characteristic of informal collusive behavior is that prices tend to be sticky. They don't change frequently and so the existence of informal collusion is an important reason why prices are sticky. But it's not the only reason.

Another reason is that firms don't collude, but they have certain expectations of other firms' reactions, which changes their perceived demand curves. Specifically they perceive a kinked demand curve (not kinky, but kinked) facing them. This kinked demand curve is used especially to explain why firms seldom use lower-price strategies to increase sales.

Cartel   A combination of firms that acts like a single firm.

Cartel model of oligopoly   Model that assumes that oligopolies act as if they were a single monopoly.

Implicit collusion   Multiple firms making the same pricing decisions even though they have not consulted with one another.

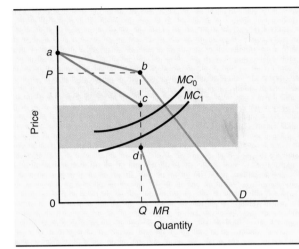

EXHIBIT 7   The Kinked Demand Curve

One explanation of why prices are sticky is that firms face a kinked demand curve. Say a firm is producing output Q at price P. If it tries to raise its price, other firms will not follow, so the demand curve is very elastic. If the firm decides to decrease its price, all other firms will immediately follow suit, so demand is less elastic, as represented by the red segment beginning at b. The corresponding MR curve is discontinuous. Shifts in marginal costs between c and d (the shaded area) will not change the price or the output that maximizes profits.

Let's go through the reasoning behind the kinked demand curve. If a firm increases its price, and the firm believes that other firms won't go along, its perceived demand curve for increasing price will be very elastic. It will lose lots of business to the other firms that haven't raised their price. The relevant portions of its demand curve and its marginal revenue curve are shown in blue in Exhibit 7.

The kinked demand curve assumes, however, that the firm's perception of how other firms would respond if it decreased its price is different. It assumes that all other firms would immediately match that decrease, so it would gain very few, if any, additional sales. A large fall in price would result in only a small increase in sales, so its demand is very inelastic. This inelastic portion of the demand curve and the corresponding marginal revenue curve are shown in red in Exhibit 7.

Notice that when you put these two curves together you get a rather strange demand curve (it's kinked) and an even stranger marginal revenue curve (one with a gap). I didn't make a mistake in drawing the curves; that's the way they come out given the assumptions. When there's a kink in the demand curve there has to be a gap in the marginal revenue curve.

If firms do indeed perceive their demand curves as kinked at the market price, we have another explanation of why prices tend to be sticky. Shifts in marginal cost in the shaded area (such as MC_0 to MC_1) will not change the firm's profit maximization position. A large shift in marginal cost is required before firms will change their price.

I should emphasize that the kinked demand curve is not a theory of oligopoly pricing. It does not say why the original price is what it is; the kinked demand curve is simply a theory of sticky prices.

The Contestable Market Model   A second model of oligopoly is the *contestable market model*. The **contestable market model** is a model of oligopoly in which barriers to entry and barriers to exit, not the structure of the industry, determine a firm's price and output decisions. Thus, it places the emphasis on entry and exit conditions and says that the price that an oligopoly will charge will exceed the cost of production, and be dependent only on the entry and exit barriers to new firms. The higher the barriers, the more the price exceeds cost. If there are no barriers to entry or exit, the price an oligopolist sets will be equivalent to the competitive price.

Contestable market model of oligopoly A model that bases pricing and output decisions on entry and exit conditions, not on market structure.

5

Comparison of the Contestable Market Model and the Cartel Model   Because of the importance of the invisible handshake in determining strategies of oligopolies, no one "oligopolistic model" exists. The stronger the ability of oligopolies to collude (i.e., the more the invisible handshake can prevent entry), the closer to a monopolist solution the oligopoly can reach. The weaker the invisible handshake and the harder it is to prevent new entry, the closer to the competitive solution the oligopoly solution is. That's as explicit as one can be.

There are two extremes that an oligopoly model can take: (1) the cartel model in which an oligopoly sets a monopoly price and (2) the contestable market model in which an oligopoly with no barriers to entry sets a competitive price. Thus, we can say that an oligopoly's price will be somewhere between the competitive price and the monopolistic price. Other models of oligopolies give results in between these two.

Much of what happens in oligopoly pricing is highly dependent on the specific legal structure within which firms interact. In Japan, where large firms are specifically allowed to collude, we see Japanese goods selling for a much higher price than those same Japanese goods sell in the United States. For example, you may well pay twice as much for a Japanese television in Japan as you would in the United States. From the behavior of Japanese firms, we get a sense of what pricing strategy U.S. oligopolists would follow in the absence of the restrictions placed on them by law.

Notice that both the cartel model and the contestable market model use strategic pricing decisions. They set their price based upon the expected reactions of other firms, which means that strategic pricing is a central characteristic of oligopoly. Let's now see how a specific consideration of strategic pricing decisions shows that the cartel model and the contestable market model are related.

Strategic Pricing and Oligopoly

New Entry as a Limit on the Cartelization Strategy

One of the things that limits oligopolies from acting as a cartel is the threat from outside competition, competition from a firm that's a potential competitor but isn't part of the social network and therefore doesn't care about the invisible handshake pressure. Often this outside competitor is much larger than the firms in the oligopoly. For example, small-town banks have a tendency to collude (implicitly, of course), offering lower interest to savers and charging higher interest to borrowers than big banks charge, even though their average costs aren't significantly higher. When I ask small-town banks why this is, they tell me that my perceptions are faulty and that I should mind my own business. But if a big bank, which could care less about increasing the wealth of a small-town banker, enters the town and establishes a branch office, interest rates to savers seem to go up and interest rates to borrowers seem to go down. The big bank can add significant competition—competition that couldn't come from within the town.

On a national scale, the outside competition often comes from international firms. For example, implicit collusion among U.S. automobile firms led to foreign firms' entry into the U.S. automobile market. There are many such examples of this outside competition breaking down cartels with no barriers to entry. Thus, a cartel with no barriers to entry faces a long-run demand curve that's very elastic. This means that its price will be very close to its marginal cost and average cost. This is the same prediction that came from the contestable market theory.

Price Wars

Whenever there's strategic decision making there's the possibility of a war. Price wars are the result of strategic pricing decisions gone wild. Thus, in any oligopoly it's possible that firms can enter into a price war where prices fall below average total cost. The reasons for such wars are varied. Since oligopolistic firms know their competitors, they can personally dislike them; sometimes a firm's goal can be simply to drive a disliked competitor out of business, even if that process hurts the firm itself. Passion and anger play roles in oligopoly pricing because interpersonal and interfirm relations are important. Alternatively a firm might impersonally push the price down temporarily to drive the other firm out of business, whereupon it can charge an even higher price because potential entrants

ADDED DIMENSION GAME THEORY AND OLIGOPOLY

The lack of ability to come to an explicit conclusion about what price and quantity an oligopoly will choose doesn't mean that economic reasoning and principles don't apply to oligopoly. They do. Most oligopolistic strategic decision making is carried out with the implicit or explicit use of *game theory* (the application of economic principles to interdependent situations). Game theory is economic reasoning applied to decision making.

To give you a sense of game theory, I'll present a well-known game called the *prisoner's dilemma* and show how game theory works. The standard prisoner's dilemma can be seen in the following example: Two suspects are caught and are interrogated separately. Each prisoner is offered the following options:

- If neither prisoner confesses, each will be given a 6-month sentence on a minor charge.
- If one prisoner confesses and the other does not, the one who confesses will go free and the other will be given a 10-year sentence.

- If they both confess, they'll each get a 5-year sentence.

What strategy will they choose? If the invisible handshake is weak, and neither can count on the other not to confess, the optimal strategy (the one that maximizes expected benefits) will be for each to confess, because each must assume the other will do the same. Confessing is the rational thing for each prisoner to do. That's why it's called the *prisoner's dilemma*. Trust gets one out of the prisoner's dilemma. If the prisoners can trust one another, the optimal strategy is not to confess, and they both get only a light sentence. But trust is a hard commodity to come by without an explicit enforcement mechanism.

What does the prisoner's dilemma have to do with oligopoly theory? It shows the problems oligopolists have in coordinating their strategies where enforcement and gaining information about competitors' policies are difficult.

know that the existing firm will drive them out if they try to enter. It's this continual possibility that strategies can change that makes oligopoly prices so hard to predict.

Oligopoly Models, Structure, and Performance

The fourfold division of markets that I've considered so far has all been based on the structure of the markets. By *structure* I mean the number, size, and interrelationship of firms in an industry. A monopoly (one firm) is the least competitive; perfectly competitive industries (an almost infinite number of firms) are the most competitive. Classification by structure is easy for students to learn and accords nicely with intuition. The cartelization model fits best with this classification system because it assumes the structure of the market (the number of firms) is directly related to the price a firm charges. It predicts that oligopolies charge higher prices than do monopolistic competitors.

The contestable market model gives far less weight to market structure. According to it, markets that look structurally highly oligopolistic could actually be highly competitive—much more so than markets that structurally look less competitive. This contestable market model view of judging markets by performance, not structure, has had many reincarnations. Close relatives of it have previously been called the *barriers-to-entry* model, the *stay-out pricing* model, and the *limit-pricing* model. These models provide a view of competition that doesn't depend on market structure.

To see the implications of the contestable market approach, let's consider an oligopoly with a four-firm concentration ratio of 60 percent and a Herfindahl index of 1500. Using the structural approach we would say that, because of the multiplicity of oligopoly models, we're not quite sure what price firms in this industry would charge, but that it seems reasonable to assume that there would be some implicit collusion and that the price would be closer to a monopolist price than to a competitive price. If that same market had a four-firm concentration ratio of 30 percent and a Herfindahl index of 700, the industry would be more likely to have a competitive price.

	Monopoly	Oligopoly	Monopolistic competition	Perfect competition
Number of firms	1	Few	Many	Almost infinite
Pricing decisions	$MC = MR$	Strategic pricing, between monopoly and perfect competition	$MC = MR$	$MC = MR = P$
Output decisions	Most output restriction	Output somewhat restricted	Output restricted somewhat by product differentiation	No outut restriction
Interdependence	Only firm in market, not concerned about competitors	Interdependent strategic pricing and output decision	Each firm acts independently	Each firm acts independently
Profit	Possibility of long-run economic profit	Some long-run economic profit possible	No long-run economic profit possible	No long-run economic profit possible

EXHIBIT 8   A Comparison of Various Market Structures

This table captures the central differences among various market structures.

A contestable market model advocate would disagree. She would argue that barriers to entry and exit are what's important. If no significant barriers to entry exist in the first case but significant barriers to entry exist in the second case, the second case would be more monopolistic than the first. An example is the Miami fish market mentioned earlier, where there were 20 sellers (none with a large percentage of the market) and significant barriers to entry. (Only fishermen from the pier were allowed to sell fish there and the slots at the pier were limited.) Because of those entry limitations the pricing and output decisions would be close to the monopolistic price. If you took that same structure but had free entry, you'd get much closer to competitive decisions.

As I presented the two views, I emphasized the differences in order to make the distinction clear. However I must also point out that there's a similarity in the two views. Often barriers to entry are the reason there are only a few firms in an industry. And when there are many firms, that suggests that there are few barriers to entry. In such situations, which make up the majority of cases, the two approaches come to the same conclusion.

As you can see, the real world gets very complicated very quickly. I'll show you just how complicated in the next chapter. But don't let the complicated real world get you down on the theories presented here. It's precisely because the real world is so complicated that we need some framework, like the one presented in this chapter. That framework lets us focus on specific, hopefully the most important, issues. Because the framework is so important, as a conclusion to this chapter I summarize the primary market structures in a final exhibit, Exhibit 8.

CONCLUSION

6

KEY POINTS

- Industries are classified by SIC code, and industry structures are measured by concentration ratios and Herfindahl indexes. **1**
- Conglomerates operate in a variety of different industries. Industry concentration measures do not assess the bigness of these conglomerates. **1**
- In monopolistic competition firms act independently; in an oligopoly they take account of each other's actions. **2 6**
- Monopolistic competitors differ from perfect competitors in that the former face a downward-sloping demand curve. **3 6**

- A monopolistic competitor differs from a monopolist in that a monopolistic competitor makes zero long-run economic profit in long-run equilibrium. **3 6**
- An oligopolist's price will be somewhere between the competitive price and the monopolistic price. **4 6**
- A contestable market theory of oligopoly judges an industry's competitiveness more by performance and barriers to entry than by structure. **5**

KEY TERMS

cartel *(535)*
cartel model of
  oligopoly *(535)*
concentration ratio *(525)*
conglomerate *(527)*

contestable market model
  of oligopoly *(536)*
four-digit industry *(525)*
Herfindahl index *(526)*
implicit collusion *(535)*

market structure *(524)*
monopolistic
  competition *(524)*
oligopoly *(524)*

Standard Industrial Code
  (SIC) *(524)*
strategic decision
  making *(528)*
two-digit industry *(524)*

QUESTIONS FOR THOUGHT AND REVIEW

The number after each question represents the estimated degree of critical thinking required. (1 = almost none; 10 = deep thought.) Questions 1 and 2 require library research.

1. You're working for a company that buys up other companies. The company assigns you to find out whether the college textbook publishing industry is highly concentrated. Is it or isn't it? *(8)*
2. Now your company tells you to find the SIC codes for the following industries: (a) motor vehicles and car bodies, (b) robes and nightgowns, (c) chewing gum. You do what you are asked. *(6)*
3. Which industry is more highly concentrated: one with a Herfindahl index of 1200 or one with a four-firm concentration ratio of 55 percent? *(6)*
4. Does the product differentiation in monopolistic competition make us better or worse off? Why? *(8)*
5.

Q	P
20	2
18	4
16	6
14	8
12	10
10	12

If a monopolistic competitor has a constant marginal cost of 6 and the accompanying demand table, what output will it choose? *(5)*
6. In Question 5, what will be the monopolistic competitor's average fixed cost at the output it chooses? Why? *(8)*
7. What did Adam Smith mean when he wrote, "Seldom do businessmen of the same trade get together but that it results in some detriment to the general public"? *(6)*
8. Private colleges of the same caliber generally charge roughly the same tuition. Would you characterize these colleges as a cartel type of oligopoly? *(9)*
9. What are some of the barriers to entry in the restaurant industry? In the automobile industry? *(5)*
10. At your college store, what markup is added to textbooks? Does that markup signify a barrier to entry? *(6)*

PROBLEMS AND EXERCISES

1. A firm is convinced that if it lowers its price, no other firm in the industry will change price; however it believes that if it raises its price, all other firms will match its increase. The current price is $8 and its marginal cost is constant at $8.
   a. Sketch the general shape of the firm's MR, MC, and demand curves. *Kinked demand curves*
   b. If the marginal cost falls to $6, what would you predict would happen to price?
   c. If the marginal cost rises to $10, what would you predict would happen to price?
   d. Do a survey of five or six firms in your area. Ask them how they believe other firms would respond to their increasing and decreasing price. Based on that survey, discuss the relevance of this kinked demand model compared to the one presented in the book.

2. You're the manager of a firm that has constant marginal cost of $6. Fixed cost is zero. The market structure is monopolistically competitive. You're faced with the following demand curve:

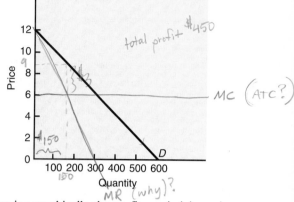

total profit $450

MC (ATC?)

MR (why)?

   a. Determine graphically the profit-maximizing price and output for your firm in the short run. Demonstrate what profit or loss you'll be making.
   b. Do the same for the long run.
   c. Thanks to a technological innovation you have zero marginal cost. Demonstrate the new profit-maximizing price and output in the short run. Demonstrate graphically the short-run profit at that new profit-maximizing output.

A Case Study

Once one gets to real-life situations, one sees that most pricing is done according to rules of thumb that exist in each industry. These rules of thumb base prices upon costs. This appendix considers the pricing strategy of a real-world retail firm and discusses how it fits into our model.

Setting Retail Prices

Most goods go through a variety of stages before they're finally sold to you, the consumer. The good is produced by a company; then it's often sold through a wholesaler to retail outlets who sell it to you. Thus, the stages are:

Manufacturer → Wholesaler → Retailer → Consumer.

Manufacturers' outlet stores supposedly eliminate the wholesaler and retailer, but in fact they've become simply a new type of discount retailing.

When you talk about pricing of a retail good, you actually have to divide it up into its parts. How does the manufacturer price? How does the wholesaler price? How does the retailer price? Most of our previous discussion was mainly relevant to pricing by manufacturers. In this section we focus on pricing by wholesalers and retailers.

Neither wholesalers nor retailers have a cost of physical production. They simply buy a product and sell that same product. Their value added is their getting the product from the manufacturer to the individuals who want it.

Cost Markup Pricing

How do these firms price? Most businesses price according to rules of thumb. They add on a percentage markup over their cost to determine their selling price. These markups have evolved over time. The percentage markup is influenced by supply and demand factors so that, if entry is free, the returns to wholesaling and retailing in the long run are normal returns—

enough to cover costs and wages plus a return to the firm's inputs. Thus, the markup varies considerably among industries. In supermarkets, because of high volume relative to inventory, the markup is low—often below 10 percent. In jewelry, where inventory is high relative to volume, the markup is high—60 to 100 percent. These markups aren't fixed; they change according to supply and demand pressures. If a good isn't selling, a firm will lower its markup. If a firm wants to take an aggressive expansion stance, it will lower its markup and expand its market share.

To give you an idea of how markups work, let's consider the pricing policy of a small jewelry store. It follows what's known as a *modified Hamilton markup* as shown in the following table.

Wholesale cost	Markup
0–$25	100%
$25–$50	66
$50–$100	60
$100–$200	55
$200–$300	50
$300–$1,000	40
$1,000–special order	20

Notice that the markup falls as the price rises. That's justified because direct selling cost (salesperson's time) is as high (or higher) on a $2 item as on a $200 item. Repairs, which are sent out to a jeweler who specializes in that work, are priced at cost because they bring in customers. Thus, for repairs there is no markup. New sales cover all overhead: direct and indirect costs.

While the formula markup is set, it's not fixed in stone. When wholesale prices are rising, the owner will recalculate prices on old inventory to the latest price. He'll also walk around town, looking into competitors' windows, checking their prices, and matching his prices to theirs. Notice that in doing so he's taking supply and demand into account and serving the function of an auctioneer because he knows if his goods are priced significantly higher than competitors', he'll lose sales. If his prices are lower than theirs, he'll check his markup policy to see that he hasn't made a mistake.

When goods don't sell in a year's time, he'll lower the price on them every week until they do sell. Again the forces of supply and demand are at work.

He doesn't stock expensive items (those selling for over $1,000), but he has a supplier who'll send them to him in a day. To these items he adds only a 20 percent markup because they don't contribute to his inventory costs (and this price keeps them competitive with those at the other jewelry stores in town).

He never runs a sale. He says, "It's bad for business because people will simply wait for a sale." He's disdainful of jewelry stores that do run so-called sales when what they, in fact, do is bring in a whole new set of merchandise marked up at a 250 percent rate and sell it at "half price," bringing the actual price down close to his own normal marked-up price. Such sales aren't really sales, but are simply advertising gimmicks which he feels lower the quality of the store holding the sale and hurt total sales in the long run. (Were I to ask the other stores, I'd hear a different view.) This case isn't unique. If you went to most retail stores you'd find a similar rule-of-thumb pricing procedure.

What's relevant about the markup rules of thumb that most firms use in pricing is that they aren't inconsistent with our models. The rules develop so as to reflect the forces of supply and demand, and they change over time. To understand the economy a blend of institutional and theoretical knowledge is required.

2
Microeconomic
Policy Debates

26

Competition in the Real World

It is ridiculous to call this an industry. This is rat eat rat; dog eat dog. I'll kill 'em, and I'm going to kill 'em before they kill me. You're talking about the American way of survival of the fittest.

Ray Kroc (founder of McDonald's)

After reading this chapter, you should be able to:

1

Define the monitoring problem and state its implications for economics.

2

Explain how corporate takeovers can improve firms' efficiency.

3

Discuss why competition should be seen as a process, not a state.

4

Show graphically what a natural monopoly is.

5

List three ways in which firms protect their monopoly.

6

State the condition that determines how much monopoly a firm will buy.

7

Apply economic reasoning to real-world events.

In earlier chapters we've seen some nice, neat models, but as I discussed in the last chapter, these models don't fit reality very well. Real-world markets aren't perfectly monopolistic; they aren't perfectly competitive either. They're somewhere between the two. The monopolistic competition and oligopoly models in that last chapter come closer to reality and capture some of the "in-between" markets, but, like any abstract discussion, they too, lose dimensions of the real-world problem. In this chapter I remedy that shortcoming and give you a sense of what real-world firms, markets, and competition are like.

THE GOALS OF REAL-WORLD FIRMS

Maybe the best place to start is with the assumption that firms are profit maximizers. There's a certain reasonableness to this assumption; firms definitely are concerned about profit, but are they trying to maximize profit? The answer is: It depends. The first insight is that if firms are profit maximizers, they aren't just concerned with short-run profit; most are concerned with long-run profit. Thus, even if they can, they may not take full advantage of a potential monopolistic situation now, in order to strengthen their long-run position. For example, many stores have liberal return policies: "If you don't like it, you can return it for a full refund." Similarly many firms spend millions of dollars improving their reputations. Most firms want to be known as "good citizens." Such expenditures on reputation and goodwill can increase long-run profit, but reduce short-run profit. These policies are inconsistent with short-run profit maximization; they aren't inconsistent with long-run profit or wealth maximization.

The Problem with Profit Maximization

A second insight into how real-world firms differ from the model is that the decision makers' income is often a cost of the firm. Most real-world production doesn't take place in owner-operated businesses; it takes place in large corporations with eight or nine levels of management, thousands of stockholders whose stock is often held in trust for them, and a board of directors chosen by management overseeing the company by meeting two or three times a year. Signing a proxy statement is as close as most stockowners get to directing "their company" to maximize profit.

Why is the structure of the firm important to the analysis? Because economic theory tells us that, unless someone is seeing to it that they do, self-interested decision makers have little incentive to hold down their pay. But their pay is a cost of the firm. And if their pay isn't held down, the firm's profit will be lower than otherwise. Most firms manage to put some pressure on managers to make at least a predesignated level of profit. (If you ask managers, they'll tell you that they face enormous pressure.) So the profit motive certainly plays a role—but to say that profit plays a role is not to say that firms maximize profit. Having dealt with many companies, I'll go out on a limb and say that there are enormous wastes and inefficiencies in many U.S. businesses.

This structure presents a problem in applying the model to the real world. The general economic model assumes individuals are utility maximizers—that they're self-seeking. Then in the standard model of the firm the assumption is made that firms, composed of self-seeking individuals, are profit-seeking firms without explaining how self-seeking individuals who manage real-world corporations will find it in their interest to maximize profit. Economists recognize this problem; it's an example of the **monitoring problem** introduced in an earlier chapter.

The general monitoring problem is that employees' incentives differ from the owner's incentives, and it's costly to see that the employee does the owner's bidding. The monitoring problem is now a central problem focused on by economists who specialize in industrial organization. They study internal structures of firms and look for an **incentive-compatible contract** which managers can be given. An incentive-compatible contract is one in which the incentives of each of the two parties to the contract correspond as closely as possible. The incentive structure is such that the firm's goals and the manager's goals match. The specific monitoring problem relevant to firm structure is that often owners find it too costly to

Monitoring problem Employees' self-interest often differs from the owner's interest, which forces the owner to monitor the employee.

■ **1**

Incentive-compatible contract An agreement in which the incentives and goals of both parties match as closely as possible.

Chief executive	Company	'92 total pay in millions
1. Thomas F. Frist, Jr.	Hosp. Corp. of America	$127.0
2. Sanford I. Weill	Primerica	67.6
3. Charles Lazarus	Toys 'R' Us	64.2
4. Leon C. Hirsch	U.S. Surgical	62.2
5. Stephen A. Wynn	Mirage Resorts	38.0
6. Anthony J. F. O'Reilly	H. J. Heinz	36.9
7. Martin J. Wygod	Medco Containment	30.2
8. William A. Anders	General Dynamics	29.0
9. Ronald K. Richey	Torchmark	26.6
10. Louis F. Bantle	UST Inc.	24.6

Source: Reprinted from the April 26, 1993, issue of *Business Week* by special permission. © 1992 by McGraw Hill, Inc.

monitor the managers to ensure that managers do what's in the owners' interest. And self-interested managers are only interested in maximizing profit if the structure of the firm requires them to do so.

When appropriate monitoring doesn't take place, high-level managers can pay themselves very well. U.S. managers are very well paid as can be seen in Exhibit 1; many receive multimillion-dollar salaries. But are these multimillion-dollar salaries too high? That's a difficult question. One way to get an idea about an answer is to compare U.S. managers' salaries with those in Japan, where the structure of control of firms is different. Banks in Japan have significant control and they closely monitor performance. The result is that in Japan high-level managers on average earn less than one-fifth of what their U.S. counterparts make, while wages of low-level workers are comparable to those of low-level workers in the United States. Given Japanese companies' success in competing with U.S. companies, this suggests that high managerial pay in the United States reflects a monitoring problem.

What Do Real-World Firms Maximize?

If firms don't maximize profit, what do they maximize? What are their goals? The answer again is: It depends. Real-world firms often have a set of complicated goals that reflect the organization structure and incentives built into the system. Clearly profit is one of their goals. Firms spend a lot of time designing incentives to get managers to focus on profit. But often other intermediate goals become the focus of firms. For example, many real-world firms focus on growth in sales; at other times they institute a cost reduction program to increase long-run profit. At still other times they may simply take it easy and not push hard at all, enjoying the position they find themselves in—being what Joan Robinson (a British economist who studied intermediate market structures and who developed the reasoning behind marginal revenue curves) called **lazy monopolists,** a term descriptive of many, but not all, real-world corporations.

Lazy monopolist Firm that does not push for efficiency, but merely enjoys the position it is already in.

The Lazy Monopolist and X-Inefficiency

Lazy monopolists see to it that they make enough profit so that the stockholders aren't squealing; they don't push as hard as they can to hold their costs down. They do their job as inefficiently as is consistent with their keeping their jobs. The result is what economists call **X-inefficiency** (firms operating far less efficiently than they could technically). Such firms have monopoly positions, but they don't make large monopoly profits. Instead their costs rise because of inefficiency and they simply make a normal level of profit.

X-inefficiency Operating a firm far less efficiently than it could be operated technically.

The standard model avoids dealing with the monitoring problem by assuming that the owner of the firm makes all the decisions. The owners of firms who receive the profit, and only the profit, would like to see that all the firm's costs are held down. Unfortunately very few real-world firms operate that way. In reality owners seldom make operating decisions. They hire or appoint managers to make

EXHIBIT 2   True Cost Efficiency and the Lazy Monopolist

A monopolist producing efficiently would have costs C_M and would produce at price P_M and quantity Q_M. A lazy monopolist, on the the other hand, would let costs rise until the minimum level of profit is reached, at C_{LM}. Profit for the monopolist is represented by the entire shaded area, whereas profit for the lazy monopolist is squeezed down to area B.

those decisions. The managers they hire don't have that same incentive to hold costs down. Therefore it isn't surprising to many economists that managers' pay is usually high and that high-level managers see to it that they have "perks" such as chauffeurs, jet planes, ritzy offices, and assistants to do as much of their work as possible.

The equilibrium of a lazy monopolist is presented in Exhibit 2. A monopolist would produce at price P_M and quantity Q_M. Average total cost would be C_M, so the monopolist's profit would be the entire shaded rectangle (areas A and B). The lazy monopolist would allow cost to increase until the firm reached its normal level of profit. In Exhibit 2, cost rises to C_{LM}. The profit of the lazy monopolist is area B. The remainder of the potential profit is eaten up in cost inefficiencies.

What places a limit on firms' laziness is the degree of competitive pressures they face. All economic institutions must have sufficient revenue coming in to cover costs so all economic institutions have a limit on how lazy and inefficient they can get—a limit imposed by their monopoly position. They can translate the monopoly profit into X-inefficiency, thereby benefiting the managers and workers in the firm, but once they've done so, they can't be more inefficient. They would go out of business.

How Competition Limits the Lazy Monopolist   If all individuals in the industry are lazy, then laziness becomes the norm and competitive pressures don't reduce their profits. Laziness is relative, not absolute. But if a new firm comes in all gung-ho and hard working, or if an industry is opened up to international competition, the lazy monopolists can be squeezed, and they must undertake massive restructuring to make themselves competitive. Many U.S. firms have been undergoing such restructuring in order to make themselves internationally competitive.

2

A second way in which competitive pressure is placed on a lazy monopolist is by a **corporate takeover** in which another firm or a group of individuals issues a tender offer (that is, offers to buy up the stock of a company to gain control and to install its own managers). Usually such tender offers are financed by large amounts of debt, which means that if they're successful, the firm will need to make large profits just to cover the interest payments on the debt.

Corporate takeover Purchase of a firm by another firm or individual.

Managers don't like takeovers because a takeover may mean losing their jobs and the perks that go along with the jobs, so they'll often restructure the company on their own. Such restructuring frequently means incurring large amounts of debt to finance a large payment to stockholders. These payments place more pressure on management to operate efficiently. Thus, the threat of a corporate takeover provides competitive pressure on firms.

Were profit not a motive at all, one would expect the lazy monopolist syndrome to take precedence. Thus, it's not surprising that nonprofit organizations often display these lazy monopolist tendencies. For example, some colleges, schools, libraries, jails, and nonprofit hospitals have a number of rules and ways of doing things that, upon reflection, benefit the employees of the institution rather than the customers. For example, at most colleges students aren't polled as to what time they would prefer classes to meet; instead the professors and administrators decide when they want to teach. I leave it to you to figure out whether your college exhibits these tendencies and whether you'd prefer that your college, library, or hospital change to a for-profit institution. Studying these incentive-compatible problems is what management courses are all about.

Motivations for Efficiency Other Than the Profit Incentive   I'm not going to discuss management theory here other than to stimulate your thinking about the problem. However I'd be remiss in presenting you this broad outline of the monitoring problem without mentioning that the drive for profit isn't the only drive that pushes for efficiency. Some individuals derive pleasure from efficiently run organizations. Such individuals don't need to be monitored. Thus, if administrators are well intentioned, they'll hold down costs even if they aren't profit maximizers. In such cases monitoring (creating an organization and structure that gives people profit incentives) can actually reduce efficiency! It's amazing to some economists how some nonprofit organizations operate as efficiently as they do—some libraries and colleges fall into that category. Their success is built on their employees' pride in their jobs, not on their profit motive.

Most economists don't deny that such inherently efficient individuals exist, and that most people derive some pleasure from efficiency, but they believe that it's hard to maintain that push for efficiency year in, year out, when some of your colleagues are lazy monopolists enjoying the fruits of your efficiency. Most people derive some pleasure from efficiency, but, based on their observation of people's actions, economists believe that holding down costs without the profit motive takes stronger willpower than most people have.

Herbert Simon—Nobel prize, 1978, for work on the importance of institutions and process to economic theory. © *The Nobel Foundation.*

Even if all the assumptions for perfect competition could hold true, it's unlikely that real-world markets would be perfectly competitive. The reason is that perfect competition assumes that individuals accept a competitive institutional structure, even though there are generally significant gains to be made by changing that structure. The simple fact is that *self-seeking individuals don't like competition for themselves* (although they do like it for others), and when competitive pressures get strong and the invisible hand's push turns to shove, individuals often shove back, using either social or political means. That's why you can only understand real-world competition if you understand how the three invisible forces (the invisible hand, foot, and handshake) push against each other to create real-world economic institutions. **Real-world competition** should be seen as a process—a fight between the forces of monopolization and the forces of competition.

Let's consider some examples. During the depression of the 1930s competition was pushing down prices and wages. What was the result? Individuals socially condemned firms for unfair competition, and numerous laws were passed to prevent "unfair" competition. Unions were strengthened politically and given monopoly powers so they could resist the pressure to push down wages. The Robinson-Patman Act was passed, which made it illegal for many firms to lower prices!

As another example, consider agricultural markets, which have many of the conditions for almost perfect competition. To my knowledge not one country in the world allows a competitive agricultural market to exist! As you'll see in later

THE FIGHT BETWEEN COMPETITIVE AND MONOPOLISTIC FIRMS

3

Real-world competition   A fight between the forces of monopolization and the forces of competition.

How Monopolistic Forces Triumph over Perfect Competition

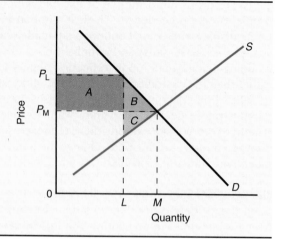

EXHIBIT 3   Movement Away from Competitive Markets

In the case where suppliers of *OL* can restrict suppliers of *LM* from entering the market, they can raise the price of the good from P_M to P_L, giving the suppliers of *OL* area *A* in additional income. The suppliers kept out of the market lose area *C* in income. The demanders, on the other hand, lose both areas *A* and *B*, giving them strong incentive to fight collusion. Often the costs of organizing for demanders are higher than the costs for the suppliers, so demanders accept the market restrictions.

chapters, the United States has a myriad of laws, regulations, and programs that prevent agricultural markets from working competitively. U.S. agricultural markets are characterized by price supports, acreage limitations, and quota systems. Thus, where perfectly competitive markets could exist, they aren't allowed to. An almost infinite number of other examples can be found. Our laws and social mores simply do not allow perfect competition to work because government emphasizes other social goals besides efficiency. When competition negatively affects these other goals (which may or may not be goals that most people in society hold), government prevents competition from operating.

Economic Insights and Real-World Competition

The nonexistence of perfectly competitive markets *should not* make you think that economics is irrelevant to the real world. Far from it. In fact, the movement away from perfectly competitive markets could have been predicted by economic theory! Consider Exhibit 3. Competitive markets will exist only if suppliers or demanders don't collude. If the suppliers producing *OL* can get together and restrict entry, preventing suppliers who would produce *LM* from entering the industry, the remaining suppliers can raise their price from P_M to P_L, giving them the shaded area, *A,* in additional income. If the cost of their colluding and preventing entry is less than that amount, economic theory predicts that these individuals will collude. The suppliers kept out of the market lose only area *C* so they don't have much incentive to fight the restrictions on entry. The demanders lose the areas *A* plus *B* so they have a strong incentive to fight. However, often their cost of organizing a protest is higher than the suppliers' cost, so the demanders accept the restrictions.

Suppliers introducing restrictions on entry seldom claim that the reason for the restrictions on entry is to increase their incomes. Usually they couch the argument for restrictions in terms of the general good but, while their reasons are debatable, the net effect of restricting entry into a market is to increase suppliers' income to the detriment of demanders. I'll consider the cases of licensing doctors and lawyers in a later chapter. For now, all I want to point out is that economic theory predicts that there will be strong pressures away from perfectly competitive markets in the real world.

How Competitive Forces Triumph over Monopoly

Don't think that because perfect competition doesn't exist, competition doesn't exist. In the real world, competition is fierce; the invisible hand is no weakling. It holds its own against the other invisible forces.

Competition is so strong that it makes the other extreme (perfect monopolies) as rare as perfect competition. For a monopoly to exist, other firms must be prevented from entering the market. In reality it's almost impossible to prevent entry, and therefore it's almost impossible for perfect monopoly to exist. Monopoly profits send out signals to other firms. Those signals cause competition from other firms who want to get some of that profit for themselves. To get some of that profit, they break down the monopoly through political or economic means. If the monopoly is a legal monopoly, high profit will lead potential competitors to lobby to change the law underpinning that monopoly. If the law can't be changed—say the monopolist has a **patent** (a legal right to be the sole supplier of a good)— potential competitors will generally get around the obstacle by developing a slightly different product or by working on a new technology that avoids the monopoly but satisfies the relevant need.

Patent A legal right to be the sole supplier of a good.

Say, for example, that you've just discovered the proverbial better mousetrap. You patent it and prepare to enjoy the life of a monopolist. But to patent your mousetrap, you must submit the technical drawings of how your better mousetrap works to the patent office. That gives all potential competitors (some of whom have better financing and already existing distribution systems) a chance to study your idea and see if they can think of a slightly different way (a way sufficiently different to avoid being accused of infringing on your patent) to achieve the same end. They often succeed—so often, in fact, that many firms don't apply for patents on new products because the information in the patent application spells out what's unique about the product. That information can help competitors more than the monopoly provided by the patent hurts competitors. Instead many firms try to establish an initial presence in the market and rely on inertia to protect what little monopoly profit they can extract.

Going to the patent office isn't the only way competitors gather information about competing products. Firms routinely buy other firms' products, disassemble them, figure out what's special about them, and then copy them within the limits of the law. This process is called **reverse engineering.**

Reverse engineering Dismantling a product in order to gain information about its makeup.

Variations on reverse engineering and cloning go on in all industries. Consider the clothing industry. One firm I know of directs its secretaries to go to top department stores on their lunch hour and to buy the latest fashions that they like. The secretaries bring the clothes back and that afternoon the seamstresses and tailors dismantle each garment into its component parts, make a pattern of each part, and sew the original up again. The next day the secretary who chose that garment returns it to the department store, saying "I don't really like it."

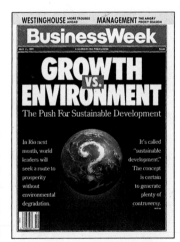

Business Week—A weekly business magazine that reports on business and economic trends.

Meanwhile the firm has express-mailed the patterns to its Hong Kong office, and two weeks later its shipment of garments comes in—garments that are almost, but not perfectly, identical to the ones the secretaries bought. The firm sells this shipment to other department stores at half the cost of the original.

Another example is the production of textbooks. This text (and every other text) was written only after a careful examination of all other successful—and a few of the not-so-successful—competitors. Then the publisher and I tried to determine what we liked and didn't like in the competitors' books; reviewers were asked what they liked and disliked in them too. Not until I had all that information did I sit down and write this book. There were lots of things the reviewers and I didn't like in the competitors' books, so this book significantly differs from those books. But many new books are clones of existing successful books. They have similar sections and the similar discussions in slightly different words. Success breeds competition.

If you ask businesspeople, they'll tell you that competition is fierce and that profit opportunities are fleeting—which is a good sign that competition does indeed exist in the U.S. economy.

Certain industries enjoy strong economies of scale so average costs are continually falling. Such industries are called **natural monopolies** because it is less costly for one firm to operate than for more than one firm to operate. I demonstrate that in Exhibit 4.

Natural Monopolies and Competition

EXHIBIT 4   Efficiency and Regulation of Natural Monopolies

This graph shows the average cost curve for a natural monopoly. One firm producing Q_1 would have average cost of C_1. If total production remains at Q_1 and another firm enters the market, sharing quantity produced, each firm would produce $Q_{1/2}$ goods at average cost C_2. If three firms each produced $Q_{1/3}$, the average cost for each would be C_3. In a case of a natural monopoly, as the number of firms in the industry increases, the average cost of producing a fixed number of units increases.

Natural monopoly Industry with strong economies of scale so the average cost is continually falling.

4

If one firm produces Q_1, its cost per unit is C_1. If two firms each produce half that amount, $Q_{1/2}$, so that their total production is Q_1, the cost per unit will be C_2, which is significantly higher than C_1. In cases of natural monopoly, as the number of firms in the industry increases, the average cost of producing a fixed number of units increases. For example, if there were three firms in the industry and they each had a third of the market, each firm would have average cost C_3. It follows that in the case of natural monopoly even if a single firm makes some monopoly profit, the price it charges may still be lower than the price two firms making no profit would charge.

Fair Price Doesn't Necessarily Mean Low Price

If the natural monopoly has a relatively inelastic demand over the range of the production, it will have an incentive to charge a high price (at which price the demand will no longer be inelastic) and will make substantial profit.

Examples of natural monopoly are local telephone service and electric utilities. But even in these cases of natural monopoly, competition works in other ways. High monopoly profits generate research on alternative ways of supplying the product, such as sending TV signals through electrical lines or sending phone messages by satellite. When this competition doesn't work fast enough, people direct their efforts toward government and political pressure is brought to bear either to control the monopoly through regulation or to break up the monopoly.

In the past the pressure to regulate these natural monopolies has been stronger than competitive pressure to lower prices. Firms have been given the exclusive right to operate in the industry but, in return, they've had to agree to have the price they charge and the services they provide regulated by regulatory boards. Regulatory boards control the price that natural monopolies charge so it will be a ''fair price'' which they generally define as a price that includes all costs plus a normal return on capital investment (a normal profit, but no excess profit). Most states have a number of regulatory boards.

When firms are allowed to pass on all cost increases to earn a normal profit on those costs, they have little or no incentive to hold down costs. In such cases, X-inefficiency develops with a passion, and such monopolies look for capital-intensive projects that will increase their rate bases. To fight such tendencies, regulatory boards must screen every cost and determine which costs are appropriate and which aren't—an almost impossible job. For example, nuclear power is an extremely capital-intensive method of producing electric power, and regulated electric companies favored nuclear power plants until they were told that some nuclear power plant construction costs could not be passed on.

Once regulation gets so specific that it's scrutinizing every cost, the regulatory process becomes extremely bureaucratic, which itself increases the cost.

Moreover to regulate effectively, the regulators must have independent information and must have a sophisticated understanding of economics, cost accounting, and engineering. Often regulatory boards are made up of volunteer laypeople who start with little expertise; they are exhausted or co-opted by the political infighting they have had to endure by the time they develop some of the expertise they need. As is often the case in economics, there's no easy answer to the problem.

Because of the problems with regulation, some economists argue that even in the case of natural monopoly, no regulation is desirable, and that society would be better off relying on direct competitive forces. They argue that regulated monopolies inevitably inflate their costs so much and are so inefficient and lazy that a monopoly right should never be granted.

How Firms Protect Their Monopolies   The image I've presented of competition being **5** engendered by profits is a useful one. It shows how a market economy adjusts to ever-changing technology and demands in the real world. Competition is a dynamic, not a static, force.

Firms do not sit idly by and accept competition. They fight it. How do monopolies fight real-world competition? By spending money on maintaining their monopoly. By advertising. By lobbying. By producing products that are difficult to copy. By not taking full advantage of their monopoly position, which means charging a low price which discourages entry. Often firms could make higher short-run profits by charging a higher price, but they forgo the short-run profits in order to strengthen their long-run position in the industry.

Cost-Benefit Analysis of Creating and Maintaining Monopolies   Preventing real-world com- **6** petition costs money. Monopolies are expensive to create and maintain. Economic theory predicts that if firms have to spend money on creating and protecting their monopoly, they're going to ''buy'' less monopoly than if it were free. How much will they buy? They will buy monopoly until the marginal cost of monopoly equals the marginal benefit. Thus, they'll reason:

- Does it make sense for us to hire a lobbyist to fight against this law which will reduce our monopoly power? Here is the probability that a lobbyist will be effective; here is the marginal cost; and here is the marginal benefit.
- Does it make sense for us to buy this machine? If we do, we'll be the only one to have it and are likely to get this much business. Here is the marginal cost and here is the marginal benefit.
- Does it make sense for us to advertise to further our market penetration? Here are the likely various marginal benefits; here are the likely marginal costs.

By now you should be getting my drift, but in case you're not, let me pound it into your head. The standard models of monopoly and perfect competition don't fit reality well. But the reasoning process they're meant to teach (how self-seeking individuals try to structure real-world institutions based upon a decision rule relating marginal benefit and marginal cost) is a useful way to look at many real-world problems. It provides insights and often clarifies events that would otherwise be unintelligible. That doesn't mean that it will explain everything; some people aren't self-seeking. But considering how the self-seeking view of human nature explains reality is often helpful. It's how economists look at the world.

ECONOMIC REASONING AND THE REAL WORLD

Every market is different. The differences are in the particular problems it faces, the dimensions that competition takes, and its options in dealing with its problems. Generalizations can be made, but these generalizations necessarily give an unworldly quality to the discussion. Thus, to supplement the general discussion, **7** it's helpful to consider specific case studies showing examples of particular markets and their problems.

TWO CASE STUDIES

In the remainder of this chapter I'll consider two case studies of real-world markets. Economic knowledge comes from combining a sense of such case studies with the generalized understanding conveyed in the formal models.

Case Study 1: Competition in the Biotech Industry

The first case study, about a new drug company, appeared in an article in *The Wall Street Journal*. I reprint it in its entirety to give you a sense of the type of articles you'll find in business newspapers and to show you what a business reporter, limited to 2,500 words, felt was important to include in her discussion of the firm and industry.

AMGEN, CLEARED TO SELL KIDNEY-PATIENT DRUG, STILL FACES BIG HURDLES

By Rhonda L. Rundle

Thousand Oaks, Calif.—After nine years of painstaking research, punctured dreams, and a string of recent setbacks, Amgen Inc. has approval to sell the hottest new drug in the biotechnology field.

Now comes the hard part.

First of all, Amgen must master a bagful of new tricks to transform itself from biotech boutique into a commercial drug company, selling to kidney patients a new anemia drug called EPO. Nuts-and-bolts decisions like setting prices and production schedules are still alien to Amgen, built mainly on the brainpower and 80-hour workweeks of eager young scientists.

But Amgen can't slowly feel its way. The tiny niche it has carefully tried to carve out is under attack. A rival EPO maker is closing in on its once-comfortable lead. And, in a measure of the kinds of trouble Amgen has gotten itself into in its short life, the company is even vulnerable to competition from its marketing partner.

In bitter and distracting legal battles, Amgen is fighting both that partner and its main competitor. Amgen's falling out with the marketing partner has already had the effect of delaying the drug's approval by over two months. And Amgen's refusal to settle a dispute with the competitor over patent rights could backfire by ultimately opening the field to many others. These struggles consume precious dollars and management time—

even though almost few people outside Amgen think the company can do better than draw.

Judgment Challenged

Thus Amgen's situation seems at least partly of its own making. "There's a deep sense of moral righteousness at Amgen that blinds them," says Robert Kupor, a biotechnology analyst at Kidder, Peabody & Co. A few people are even starting to ask whether Amgen management has the mature business judgment needed to steer the company into adulthood.

Amgen's chief executive officer, Gordon Binder, dismisses such critics. "The only thing we've lost so far is two months," he says.

Such doubts were unimaginable just a few months ago, when Amgen was being hailed as biotech's next superstar. The chief reason was EPO, or erythropoietin, a drug aimed now at the nation's 100,000 kidney-dialysis patients, but ultimately perhaps at many others, including some AIDS patients. Estimates of the anemia fighter's first-year sales are in the $100 million range, but some analysts think they could eventually top $1 billion annually, making EPO one of the most commercially successful drugs ever. Yesterday's FDA approval gives only Amgen, not its rivals, the right to sell the drug in the U.S. Among other things, the decision was a blow to Amgen's marketing partner, the Ortho Pharmaceutical unit of Johnson & Johnson.

Beyond this promise, Amgen management was until recently being praised for its entrepreneurial spirit and business sense. By cultivating relations with regulators and physicians, the company seemed to show that it had learned from the mistakes

of Genentech Inc., which stumbled last year in its transition from biotech start-up to commercial drug company.

Following a Pioneer

That would be fitting. It was Genentech's initial success a decade ago that inspired two Silicon Valley venture capitalists to start a biotech company. They recruited George B. Rathmann, a Princeton-trained chemist with a knack for creating freewheeling, productive research environments. A tall, burly man with "a mind like a Cray computer," in a former employee's words, Mr. Rathmann had a charismatic style that helped Amgen hire top scientists. He also could raise money—so well that, while working earlier at Abbott Laboratories, he had been nicknamed Golden Throat. In 1981, Amgen raised $19 million in a private offering, unprecedented for a biotech company.

The early going was tough. Within two years, Amgen was on the brink of a bankruptcy filing as the funds ran out. A hot turn in the market for technology stocks saved it, as Amgen found underwriters, raced to file with regulators, and went public at $18 a share. By just a few weeks, it beat a crash in technology stocks.

The collapse was followed by Amgen's first scientific flop—a chicken growth hormone. It didn't work down on the farm. Amgen's share price plunged as low as $3.75. (Its share closed yesterday in over-the-counter trading at $41, up $.875 on FDA approval of EPO.)

Then came a big break. In 1983 an Amgen scientific team led by Fu-Kuen Lin cloned the gene for human EPO, a protein made in the kidneys that stimulates production of red blood cells. Given to people with kidney disease, it can sharply reduce or even eliminate their need for blood transfusions. And it may be broadly useful against anemia that is due to cancer therapies or to the AZT treatment of AIDS patients.

In early 1986, with EPO still unproven in human tests, Mr. Rathmann presented a bet-the-company plan to the board. He wanted to stake a huge chunk of Amgen's modest cash reserves on a $20 million plant to produce EPO. The gamble had to be taken, he argued, to stay ahead in the race to bring EPO to market.

The competitive threat turned out to be keener than Amgen knew. Early one morning in July 1987, a securities analyst tracked Mr. Rathmann down at Amgen's Boulder, Colo., office to tell him that another company had been awarded the first EPO patent.

At Amgen, there was disbelief. It had filed its application more than two years ahead of its rival, Genetics Institute Inc., based in Cambridge, Mass. But for technical reasons the two documents had been reviewed by different sections of the patent office. Genetics Institute's patent application covered the EPO molecule itself, while Amgen's covered a process for making the substance. Amgen received its own patent three months later.

The result is a legal battle. Amgen sued Genetics Institute for patent infringement in federal court in Massachusetts. Genetics Institute filed a counterclaim, then offered to cross-license, the usual remedy adopted in such disputes. Amgen refused.

Amgen executives insist a principle is at stake: Their company was first to clone the EPO gene, so it should reap the rewards. "This is what U.S. patent laws are all about; otherwise, forget rewarding innovation for small entrepreneurs," Mr. Rathmann argues.

But some analysts fear that Amgen's judgment is clouded by emotional ties to its first big product. They note that the 61-year-old Mr. Rathmann became teary-eyed during questioning about EPO at a legal hearing last year.

Other Amgen veterans feel equally possessive of EPO. It was developed when the company was still so small everyone knew everyone else, including spouses and children. Mr. and Mrs. Rathmann held picnics at their beachfront home in Ventura. EPO was truly a family affair.

When Amgen fell behind on its schedule to file an FDA license application, EPO team members leased five motel rooms to allow round-the-clock work. Ninety-three days later, their 19,578-page document was done. That morning weary workers tied yellow ribbons and a banner on the trees at corporate headquarters proclaiming: "The Simi Valley hostages are free."

Still, Genetics Institute claims that it conceived the recombinant process for making EPO ahead of Amgen. And the longer Amgen holds out for exclusive rights, the tougher terms Genetics Institute will demand, Kidder Peabody's Mr. Kupor believes. The courts could impose their own profit-sharing formula, or worse, open the door to all EPO makers by nullifying both patents. The trial is scheduled to begin in early August in federal court in Boston. Genetics Institute is backed by a cash-rich joint venture to which it has licensed the drug, Chugai-Upjohn Inc., formed by Chugai Pharmaceutical Co., Tokyo, and Upjohn Co., Kalamazoo, Mich.

The patent mess seemed like a minor blemish on Amgen's record until the marketing-partner rift surfaced in January. Johnson & Johnson's Ortho unit sued to block EPO approval until a contractual dispute was resolved. Ortho claims Amgen violated their 1985 license agreement by failing to submit to the FDA Ortho's clinical data for patients in the early stages of kidney disease. Under the agreement, Amgen sold to Ortho all rights to the drug except those for kidney patients who require regular dialysis. (J&J already sells EPO in Europe.)

Amgen management, surprised by the suit, apparently underestimated its importance. No judge would allow a commercial squabble to prevent patients from receiving EPO, Amgen believed. As the injunction hearing began in Wilmington,

Del., on March 17, Amgen and the FDA were discussing dates for an imminent news conference to announce EPO approval.

But Johnson & Johnson produced scores of documents and other evidence to support its claims. Attorneys for the drug giant portrayed Amgen as capricious and sneaky. Busy making final plans for EPO's launch, Amgen executives were caught off guard by Johnson & Johnson's carefully laid offense.

The court ruled for Ortho, ordering Amgen to amend its FDA application to include Ortho's data. Amgen's stock price, which had soared more than 50% in the preceding four months, backed off a bit.

Amgen maintains that it never intended to split the kidney-disease market with Johnson & Johnson. The fledgling biotech concern tended to use "dialysis" as a synonym for "chronic renal disease" and naively agreed to inclusion of the shorter term in the agreement, officials assert.

Two years after it signed that marketing agreement, Amgen was surprised to learn that Ortho's initial EPO tests weren't for anemias associated with cancer or AIDS therapy—huge potential markets that Amgen had signed away to Ortho—but for a tiny group of "pre-dialysis" patients with kidney problems. Amgen worried that Ortho, backed by its parent's powerful marketing forces, was seeking to invade turf Amgen thought it had reserved.

The reasoning is that nephrologists, the doctors who are the drug's real target customers, treat both pre-dialysis and dialysis patients. If Ortho should win patients in the early stages of kidney disease, their doctors might never switch brands, worries Kathleen Wiltsey, Amgen's EPO marketing director. "This is a fight for life," she says.

Whatever the merits, Amgen clearly miscalculated the strength of Ortho's case, the FDA's response, and public reaction. The FDA, criticized by the Delaware court for favorable treatment of Amgen, pulled back and began moving more cautiously. When the FDA did grant approval yesterday, it authorized EPO for chronic renal failure, not merely for dialysis patients; the effect was to perpetuate the Amgen-Ortho struggle. The next round has already begun in private arbitration talks. Amgen expects a hearing to take place this summer or early fall. The proceedings could force Amgen to allow Ortho to jointly market Epogen, Mr. Binder, Amgen's chief executive officer, said yesterday.

The approval delay eroded Amgen's prized head start over its EPO rivals. Last summer, some analysts estimated Amgen's lead at 18 months, long enough to establish trademark loyalty for its Epogen brand of EPO. Now, estimates of its lead have shrunk to six months or less.

"We've made up the lion's share of their head start," boasts a Chugai-Upjohn spokesman. While the FDA approval came with so-called orphan-drug status, which confers a seven-year marketing monopoly, the agency also said that didn't rule out the pos-

sibility of granting the same status to Chugai-Upjohn's slightly different version of EPO.

All this complicates the outlook for EPO sales. But a more immediate question is who will pay for the drug. The annual cost for a typical kidney-dialysis patient will be between $4,000 and $8,000 a year, Amgen said yesterday. Amgen is lobbying to make sure that Medicare, which now covers roughly 90% of kidney-dialysis costs for the nation's roughly 100,000 dialysis patients, will cover most EPO costs.

Meanwhile, Amgen has been hemorrhaging financially without EPO revenue to offset the heavy launch costs. It lost nearly $9 million in its fourth quarter ended March 31. (For all of fiscal '89 it had a loss of $8.2 million on revenue of $78.1 million.) The company needs cash to continue developing its next big drug, an immune-system booster for chemotherapy patients. (The drug, gran-

ulocyte colony-stimulating factor, or G-CSF, could be ready to market late in 1990.)

Change at the Top

These problems are no longer primarily Mr. Rathmann's. He resigned as president and chief executive last October, telling astonished employees that with EPO approval near he wanted to get back to his family. Mr. Binder, now in charge, had been the chief financial officer. Harry F. Hixson, a scientist and longtime Rathmann associate, now holds the No. 2 position, with the title of president and chief operating officer.

Whether the soft-spoken Mr. Binder is the man to lead Amgen through the battles ahead remains to be seen, but some shareholders are getting impatient. Says one major holder, "I just wish these biotech companies would grow up."

Discussion

What does this case study tell us about competition in U.S. businesses? Let's consider:

1. There's no way one would call the drug industry *perfectly competitive,* but the example shows that competition—"brutal competition"—exists. That competition isn't primarily price competition. Indeed the article doesn't even discuss pricing strategies. (They exist, but the article doesn't discuss them.) Instead, the competition takes place in other dimensions: speed of supply; being first in the market; gaining legal rights.

2. A firm's success depends on much more than producing a better mousetrap cheaper. It depends upon handling relationships with other firms, legal knowledge, and finance. When one talks about inefficiency, one need not be referring to physical production. One might also be talking about inefficiency in public relations or financial affairs.

3. Of all the inputs for firms, skilled labor and financial capital provide the most trouble. Amgen had, and has, the skilled labor. The same story for similar firms might have focused on the problem of keeping skilled workers working for them. But Amgen had the normal finance problems. Unlike many other small companies, it overcame them, beating the crash in technology stock and coming up with the necessary financial capital when it was on the brink of bankruptcy.

4. The difference between wild success and total bankruptcy for a firm can be minute. Luck as well as skill plays a role in any business success.

5. The needs of a firm evolve over time. Often the person who organizes a company is not the best person to run it. The two stages require different skills and interests. Having the right type of person in charge at the right time is a key element in a company's success.

6. Legal monopolies from patents are of limited value. Notice that a competitor

has a slightly different version of the same drug which it may be allowed to sell in direct competition.

7. The company has to do more than sell the drug to doctors. It must see to it that Medicaid will pay for it. A failure on that front could mean failure of the company.

Where does economics fit into all this? Everywhere.

· In the initial choice about what research to do, Amgen chose a research focus that had a large potential demand—$100 million to $1 billion isn't small potatoes. Most likely that decision was made on the basis of marginal cost and marginal benefit.

· How the legal and financial battles come out will play a big role in Amgen's pricing strategy. If it's comfortable with its monopoly, Amgen will likely follow a high price strategy; if it's uncomfortable with it, Amgen will follow a much lower price strategy to keep other firms out on the basis of price.

· In this case economic theory doesn't say which of these two strategies will most benefit the consumer. Clearly in the short run, the low-price strategy will make consumers better off, but in the long run, expected high returns to research lead to further research and development of new drugs. If Amgen and other research-oriented companies fail to make a profit, less research will be done in the future.

· Economic analysis was used to decide what type of financing to use.

· In deciding when to negotiate with his rivals and when not to, the president might not have made the economic, reasonable decision. The article suggests that he let his emotions cloud his judgment. (Interpret *emotional* as deciding at a point where marginal cost does not equal marginal benefit.) Businesspeople are judged on how economic-based their judgments are.

Were we to look more deeply into the decisions Amgen made, we'd see more instances of economics. The point is that microeconomics concerns rational, reasonable decision making, and it is that aspect of microeconomics that enters into all levels of business.

The second case study also comes from *The Wall Street Journal*. The story it tells is not as technical as the biotech case study, but it nonetheless presents important insights into the workings of markets and competition.

Case Study 2: Competition in the Casket Industry

INDEPENDENT COFFIN SELLERS FIGHT ESTABLISHED INDUSTRY

By John R. Emshwiller

Loma Linda, Calif.—When looking for a small business to start, Sheralee and Kyle Nyswonger thought about a florist shop or a hair salon. "But there was one of those on every corner," says the 26-year-old Mrs. Nyswonger. "We thought we should do something really different."

So they opened a store to sell

coffins to the public. Their nine-month-old Hillmark Casket Gallery undersells funeral homes, the traditional retailers of coffins, by an average of 30% to 40%, says Mrs. Nyswonger, the store's manager.

On the face of it, the Nyswongers found a potential gold mine. Wholesale coffin sales exceed $800 million a year, and the nation's 22,000 funeral homes typically charge three to four times the wholesale prices. After decades of attacks by muckraking journalists and government regulators, the funeral industry hardly has a reputation as a haven of consumer bargains. What better opportunity to slash prices and clean up?

But as the Nyswongers and other would-be coffin retailers have learned, a new company bucking the longstanding practices of an established industry may have its work cut out for it. The funeral industry has come up with some potent tactics for keeping outsiders out.

Just recently, for instance, Hillmark lost a customer after a local funeral home told the family it would roughly double its funeral-service charges to more than $2,000 if the family brought in a coffin from the outside, says Mrs. Nyswonger.

More critically, the Nyswongers have had trouble simply getting coffins to sell. The world's biggest coffin maker, Batesville Casket Co. of Batesville, Ind., turned them away. Batesville will gladly sell to any licensed funeral director in the nation and plants a tree in a national forest every time someone is buried in a Batesville coffin. But the company's policy is to reject every non-funeral director who calls. Many other major coffin manufacturers sell only to funeral homes.

"We have a system of distribution [about 16,000 funeral homes] that demands a certain loyalty or the system will fall apart," says Robert C. Smith, vice president for investor relations of Hillenbrand Industries, which owns Batesville Casket.

Inland Casket Manufacturing Co., a local coffin maker, agreed to supply Hillmark, but then changed its mind because local funeral directors were threatening to stop buying from it, says Mrs. Nyswonger. Peter Fishering, vice president of Inland Casket, declines to comment.

'Handling' Fees

But such threats aren't unusual, says Ronald Hast, a Los Angeles funeral-home owner and publisher of Mortuary Management, a national trade magazine. "If a casket company is selling to a maverick, funeral directors won't buy from it," says Mr. Hast. "I guess you call that a boycott."

In addition to threatening such boycotts, funeral homes tack on "casket-handling" fees of as much as $1,000 for customers using a coffin bought from a "third party" retailer.

Defending such practices, funeral-industry officials say they have a right to do business with whomever they choose. They contend the handling fee is to recover legitimate overhead expenses normally included in the coffin price.

But the Federal Trade Commission is investigating whether coffin-handling fees violate 1984 federal regulations aimed at increasing competition and consumer choice in the funeral business. The commission has been gathering evidence about possible anti-competitive effects of handling fees, which "seem to have put some casket retailers out of business," says Carol Jennings, an FTC staff attorney. "This is a very controversial issue."

'Pre-Need' Buying

Spurred by the 1984 FTC rule that barred funeral homes from refusing to handle merchandise bought elsewhere, an estimated several dozen non-funeral-home vendors have started selling coffins in recent years. Most of these are cemeteries that sell coffins on a "pre-need" basis as an outgrowth of selling cemetery plots in advance.

But a small coffin maker in Chicago opened a retail outlet there, and another group, which says it got the idea from Hillmark, is considering starting a store in San Francisco.

Many of the new vendors have encountered obstacles, and the problems aren't limited to coffin makers. A local trucking company, Inland Valley Transportation Co. (no relation to the coffin maker), delivered one coffin to a local mortuary for Hillmark, but then stopped doing business with the retailer. It turned out the trucking company also did work for the mortuary. An Inland Valley official "told me the mortuary had said he could ship our caskets or their bodies," Mrs. Nyswonger recalls.

Ron Bredelis, Inland Valley's owner, confirms that he refused to handle any deliveries for Hillmark after the first one, but denies he was pressured into dropping the retailer. "It was just too controversial with funeral directors," he says.

No Identifying Marks

Resistance is so great that for fear of retaliation, Mrs. Nyswonger declines to identify her current coffin suppliers. "I've told them to leave all identifying marks off the caskets," she adds. She says one local funeral director who visited Hillmark demanded so insistently to know the identity of the firm's suppliers that she had to call the sheriff to get him to leave. (The U.S. has an estimated 400 coffin makers.)

Some local funeral directors argue that without knowing Hillmark's suppliers, it is impossible to tell whether the retailer really is selling at a discount. "Just comparing a blue casket to a blue casket is unfair," says Dennis Butler, owner of Watson-Butler Family Mortuary in Riverside, Calif.

Besides imposing coffin-handling fees, some local funeral directors are requiring customers to sign waivers absolving the funeral home of any liability if they choose a Hillmark coffin. "Suppose the bottom falls out," says Mr. Butler, the funeral-home owner.

Yet even funeral directors admit there is a certain generic quality to coffins. "How many ways can you change a box?" asks one director. As the funeral-home industry commonly uses the coffin price to cover much of the overhead, a retailer such as Hillmark can sell coffins for lower prices, adds Tom Johnson, president of Pierce Brothers Mortuaries in Los Angeles.

Casket Giveaway

Hillmark customers believe they are saving money. Mitsue Mobley of Redlands, Calif., says she paid about $600 at Hillmark for her late husband's coffin, half the price of a similar coffin at a mortuary she visited.

Thus, even with obstacles, the company survives. Mrs. Nyswonger says Hillmark's first-year revenue will be about $250,000. (Hillmark also sells cremation urns and grave markers and does floral arrangements.)

Hillmark's marketing efforts have ranged from newspaper ads to a Christmastime coffin giveaway, the latter on the theory that a death during that season would be extra tough financially on families already strapped by holiday spending. However, most of the company's customers have come from "word of mouth," says Mrs. Nyswonger.

For all the problems they have encountered, the Nyswongers were optimistic enough to open a second coffin store near here recently. Unlike the first outlet, which is in an out-of-the-way office strip next to a freeway, the new store is on a corner in downtown Santa Ana. It has two big picture windows with coffins always on display, says Mrs. Nyswonger. "You drive down Main Street and you can't miss it."

Discussion   What does this case study tell us about real-world competition and monopoly?

1. It shows how important the invisible handshake can be. Even in a market with 400 producers of coffins and 22,000 funeral homes, the price markup on coffins can be 300 to 400 percent and producers feel enormous pressure not to deviate from the current practices of the industry.

2. It shows how hard it is to judge competition in a particular market. Funeral homes contend that they assign much of their overhead cost to the price of coffins. If coffin prices were to fall, funeral homes might simply tack on the charges elsewhere, and the consumer would be no better off.

    Why do they do that, you ask? Without specifically analyzing the issue, it's impossible to be definite, but a likely reason is price discrimination. Remember, a monopolist can increase its profits by price discrimination. Funeral homes aren't allowed to price discriminate in the fees they charge. However by charging a set amount for specific types of funerals but a high markup on coffins, they can accomplish the same ends indirectly. They can sell individuals with inelastic demands ("Nothing's too good for my dear departed Joshua.") the $8,000 coffin (marked up from $2,000) at a $6,000 profit. They sell the $800 coffin (marked up from $200) for a $600 profit to individuals with elastic demands. ("Joshua always loved a bargain. Don't you have anything cheaper than a pine box? Maybe cardboard? He'd love that.")

    By adding the markup to the coffin, the funeral home has charged the person with the inelastic demand $5,400 more for the funeral than it has charged the person with the elastic demand.

3. It shows how industries can protect their monopoly. By threatening to take away business from a trucking company that carried a competitor's coffins, the industry prevented the competitor firm from using that trucking company.

4. Finally it shows that despite obstacles, competition works. The competitive coffin firm is expanding.

A market environment fosters individuals who are trying to break into new markets. Where do they look? Not at the flower industry (where there's significant competition and a store on every block), but at the coffin industry (where there are high profits). Individuals looking for situations of high profits are the backbone of the competitive process.

Dying is an expensive proposition, in part because the casket industry tends to be a closed monopoly maintained by funeral homes. © *Bob Daemmrich/The Image Works.*

CASE STUDY UPDATES

The two case studies presented in this chapter were written in 1989. The continuations of the case studies tell us a lot about the competitive process. Take the Hillmark Casket Gallery Case Study. It shows the tough side of the competitive process. Selling inexpensive caskets was a great idea—right? Well, if you look for the Hillmark Casket Gallery in Loma Linda, you won't find it anymore; the best information I could get was that it shut down sometime in 1991, even though the recession of the early 1990s should have been good for the cut-rate casket business. It seems that the funeral industry monopoly won, which isn't unexpected. Many small businesses with great ideas don't make it through the first five years.

The story does not end there, however. The problems of entrepreneurs, such as Hillmark, caught the eyes of regulators. In 1992 the Federal Trade Commission studied the problem and had rules pending that would make it illegal for funeral homes to charge extra when a customer buys a casket from a separate retailer. And in California, a bill was introduced into the legislature that would strip the state funeral regulatory board (which the legislature believed reflected the interests of funeral homes) of many of its powers, and would redistribute them to other state regulatory boards. If these political–institutional changes are made, and it seems likely that they will be, companies like Hillmark are much more likely to succeed in the future. Of course, it will be too late for Hillmark. (The former owner of Hillmark is, however, considering a restraint of trade lawsuit.)

The update of the Amgen story shows the other side of the competitive process. The price of their stock rose dramatically in the early 1990s as EPO came on the market and they developed a new drug, Neupogen, that stimulates white blood cell production. Sales doubled and large growth was predicted through the early 1990s.

And how about the court cases? Amgen won the case with the Genetics Institute. One part of the Johnson & Johnson case was settled in arbitration, and the other two thirds of the case was still pending in late 1992.

Figuring out where economic reasoning fits into this article is much easier than with the previous article.

- The article directly shows how competition works.
- It shows how existing firms try to prevent competition through a variety of methods in an effort to protect their monopoly profit.
- And finally it shows how potential profit leads new firms to try to figure out ways to break down those methods of protecting monopoly.

COMPETITION AND STUDYING DYNAMIC ECONOMIC PROCESSES

The studies presented here are but two of the millions of unfolding stories out there in the economy. Newspapers are an unending source of case studies. They report stories of monopoly and competition every day, showing how multidimensional competitive and monopolistic pressures are.

The competition and monopoly stories have no end. Both are continuous processes. Monopolies create competition. Then out of the competitive struggle monopolies emerge, only to be beaten down by competition.

Studying economics is also an unending process. The study doesn't stop with reading the textbook. By keeping your eyes and ears open, and following the economic news, you'll find that your understanding of how real-world markets work is deepened year after year.

KEY POINTS

- The goals of real-world firms are many. Profit plays a role, but the actual goals depend upon the incentive structure embodied in the organizational structure of the firm. **1**
- Competition limits the amount of X-inefficiency in a firm. **2**

- The competitive process involves a continual fight between monopolization and competition. **3**
- In a natural monopoly, because of economies of scale it is cheaper for one firm to produce a good than for two or more firms to produce it. **4**

· Firms protect their monopolies by such means as advertising, lobbying, and producing products that are difficult for other firms to copy. **5**

· Firms will spend money on monopolization until the marginal cost equals the marginal benefit. **6**

· Case studies provide insight into how economic theory relates to the real world. **7**

KEY TERMS

corporate takeover *(550)*
incentive-compatible
  contract *(548)*

lazy monopolist *(549)*
monitoring problem *(548)*
natural monopoly *(553–554)*

patent *(553)*
real-world
  competition *(551)*

reverse engineering *(553)*
X-inefficiency *(549)*

QUESTIONS FOR THOUGHT AND REVIEW

The number after each question represents the estimated degree of critical thinking required. (1 = almost none; 10 = deep thought.)

1. Are managers and high-level company officials paid high salaries because they're worth it to the firm, or because they're simply extracting profit from the company to give themselves? How would you tell whether you're correct? *(9)*

2. Some have argued that competition will eliminate X-inefficiency from firms. Will it? Why? *(7)*

3. Nonprofit colleges must be operating relatively efficiently. Otherwise for-profit colleges would develop and force existing colleges out of business. True or false? Why? *(9)*

4. Competition is a process, not a state, so there can be no such thing as monopoly. True or false? Why? *(8)*

5. If it were easier for demanders to collude than for suppliers to collude, there would often be shortages of goods. True or false? Why? *(9)*

6. If it were easier for demanders to collude than for suppliers to collude, the price of goods would be lower than the competitive price. True or false? Why? *(9)*

7. Monopolies are bad; patents give firms monopoly; therefore patents are bad. True or false? Why? *(7)*

8. Natural monopolies should be broken up to improve competition. True or false? Why? *(6)*

9. Technically competent firms will succeed. True or false? Why? *(6)*

10. Would you expect the funeral home industry to be competitive? Why or why not? *(8)*

PROBLEMS AND EXERCISES

1. Econocompany is under investigation by the U.S. Department of Justice for violating antitrust laws. The government decides that Econocompany has a natural monopoly and that if it is to keep its business, it must sell at a price equal to marginal cost. Econocompany says that it can't do that and hires you to explain to the government why it can't. You do so in reference to the following graph.

2. Demonstrate graphically the net gain to producers and the net loss to consumers if suppliers are able to restrict their output to Q_r in the following graph. Demonstrate the net deadweight loss to society.

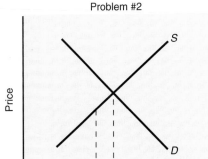

MC cant cover costs

Problem #1

Problem #2

27

The Regulation of Markets
Antitrust and Industrial Policies

*We have always known that
heedless self-interest was bad morals; we now know that it is bad
economics.*

Franklin Delano Roosevelt

After reading this chapter, you should be able to:

1

Explain the difference between the
structure and the performance methods of
judging competition.

2

Give a brief history of U.S. antitrust policy.

3

State the resolution of the IBM and AT&T
antitrust cases.

4

Differentiate among horizontal, vertical,
and conglomerate mergers.

5

List five reasons why unrelated firms would
want to merge.

6

Define the term *industrial policy*.

7

Give two arguments for and two against an
activist industrial policy.

Antitrust policy is the government's policy toward the competitive process. It's the government's rulebook for carrying out its role as referee.[1] In volleyball, for instance, such a rulebook would answer such questions as: When should a foul be called? When has a person caught and thrown rather than hit the ball over the net? In business a referee is needed for such questions as: When can two companies merge? What competitive practices are legal? When is a company too big? To what extent is it fair for two companies to coordinate their pricing policies? When is a market sufficiently competitive or too monopolistic?

The United States has seen wide swings in economists' prescriptions concerning such questions, depending on which of the two views of competition has held sway. The two competing views are:

1. **Judgment by performance:** We should judge the competitiveness of markets by the *performance* (behavior) of firms in that market.
2. **Judgment by structure:** We should judge the competitiveness of markets by the *structure* of the industry.

Both views can be defended, but in refereeing the actions of businesses government can use only one of the two at any given time.

To show how the U.S. government has applied these two views of competition in refereeing the economy, this chapter considers government's application of antitrust laws to regulate business. It then considers how recent structural changes in the economy are altering the government's role as economic referee.

Although U.S. ideology has always been strongly in favor of laissez-faire and government noninvolvement in business, there has simultaneously been a populist (pro-people) sensibility which fears bigness and monopoly. These fears of bigness and monopoly burst forth in the late 1800s as many firms were merging or organizing together to form trusts or cartels. As I stated two chapters ago, a trust or cartel is a combination of firms in which the firms haven't actually merged, but nonetheless act essentially as a single entity. A trust sets common prices and governs the output of individual member firms. A trust can, and often does, act like a monopolist.

In the 1870s and 1880s trusts were forming in a number of industries, including railroads, steel, tobacco, and oil. Some of these trusts' actions are typified by John D. Rockefeller's Standard Oil. Standard Oil demanded that railroads give it kickbacks on freight rates. These payments allowed Standard Oil to set lower prices for its products than other companies which had to pay the railroads' full price on freight. Standard Oil thus could sell at lower prices than its competitors. If prices had remained low, this would have had a positive effect on consumers and a negative effect on Standard Oil's competitors. But prices didn't remain low. By 1882 Standard Oil had driven many of its competitors out of business, and the writing was on the wall for those competitors who remained. At that time Standard Oil created a trust and "invited" its few surviving competitors to join. Then Standard Oil Trust used the monopoly power it had gained to close down refineries, raise prices, and limit the production of oil. The price of oil rose from a competitive level to a monopolistic level, and the consumer ended up suffering as well as Standard Oil's competitors.

Public outrage against trusts like Standard Oil's was high. The organizers of the trusts were widely known as *robber barons* because of their exploitation of natural resources and their other unethical behavior. The trusts were seen as making enormous profits, preventing competition, and, in general, bullying everyone in sight. In response the U.S. government passed the **Sherman Antitrust Act** of 1890.

Antitrust policy Government's policy toward the competitive process.

Judgment by performance View that competitiveness of markets should be judged by the behavior of firms in that market.

Judgment by structure View that competitiveness of markets should be judged by the structure of the industry.

1

HISTORY OF U.S. ANTITRUST LAWS

2

The Sherman Antitrust Act

Sherman Antitrust Act Law passed by U.S. Congress in 1890 to attempt to regulate the competitive process.

---

[1] As discussed earlier, the government has two roles: It's an actor, but it's also a referee.

SIMPLE TOOLS AND
COMPLICATED PROBLEMS

■ hope the previous chapters have conveyed the complexity of real-world problems and the simplicity of the tools and concepts economists use to deal with those problems. Some of my colleagues advise me against presenting the tools and the reality in such stark contrast. They argue, "No reasonable person will ever knowingly grapple with real-world problems if he or she recognizes the disparity between the simplicity of our tools and the complexity of reality. Give the students something that will make them feel more powerful."

That's not my way; I argue that our tools, while simple, are strong if they're used conceptually and aren't pushed to answer questions they can't answer. There's nothing wrong with studying a problem and arriving at the conclusion "It depends." The world would be a better place if more people recognized that the most appropriate answer to many economic policy questions is "It depends."

My debate with my academic colleagues will continue, probably indefinitely, but I must concede one point to them: The last thing politicians want to hear from their economic advisors is "It depends." If all you have to say to politicians is "It depends," you might as well not say anything. Other far less reasonable advisors (like lawyers and members of special interest groups) present politicians with arguments based on weaker tools (in my view), but their advice tends to be specific—to tell the politicians "Do this" or "Do that." They recognize that policy decisions must be made by politicians who don't have the background or time to weigh the competing arguments and decide on their own. Politicians want their economic advisors not only to provide them with objective analysis but also to weigh the evidence and tell them what to do, given the economists' knowledge of their (the politicians') value judgments. Most politicians would agree with Harry Truman, who wanted only one-armed economists—those who cannot say, "On the one hand, . . . but on the other hand . . ."

George Stigler—Nobel prize, 1982, for work on government regulation of the economy. © *The Nobel Foundation.*

The Sherman Act contained two main sections:

Section 1: Every contract, combination in the form of trust or otherwise, or conspiracy in restraint of trade or commerce among the several States, or with foreign nations, is hereby declared to be illegal. . . .

Section 2: Every person who shall monopolize, or attempt to monopolize, or combine or conspire with any other person or persons, to monopolize any part of the trade or commerce among the several States, or with foreign nations, shall be deemed guilty of a misdemeanor, and, on conviction thereof, shall be punished by a fine not exceeding five thousand dollars, or by imprisonment not exceeding one year, or by both said punishments, in the discretion of the court.

The Sherman Act was meant to be as sweeping and broad as its language sounds. After all, it was passed in response to a public outcry against trusts. But if you look at it carefully, in some respects it is vague and weak. For example, offenses under Section 2 are only misdemeanors, not felonies.[2] It's unclear what constitutes "restraint of trade." Moreover although the act prohibits monopolization, it does not explicitly prohibit monopolies. In short, with the Sherman Act Congress passed the buck to the courts, letting them decide U.S. antitrust policy.[3]

The following story summarizes the courts' role in antitrust policy. Three umpires are describing their job. The youngest of the three says, "I call them as I see them." The middle-aged umpire says, "No, that's not what an umpire does. An umpire calls them the way they are." The senior umpire says, "You're both wrong. They're nothing until I call them." And that's how it is with the courts and monopoly. Whether a firm is behaving monopolistically isn't known until the court makes its decision.

---

[2] Under federal law, a misdemeanor is any misconduct punishable by only a fine or by a jail sentence of a year or less. A felony requires a sentence of more than a year.

[3] Subsequent amendments to the Sherman Act have strengthened it. For example, offenses under Section 2 are now felonies, not misdemeanors.

As Congress was passing the Sherman Act, economists too were debating the implications of trusts and whether it was in the public interest to restrict them. Part of the debate concerned whether the mergers reflected technological changes in production and expanding transportation systems which made increased economies of scale more important (in which case restricting trusts might not be in the public interest since doing so might prevent taking advantage of economies of scale) or whether trusts simply represented attempts at monopolization to restrict output and generate monopoly profits (in which case restricting trusts would more likely be in the public interest since doing so would reduce monopoly).

A second part of the debate concerned how fast economic forces would operate and how fragile competition was. Some economists argued that competition was strong and that it would limit the profit trusts and monopolies made and force them to charge the competitive price (in which case restricting trusts might not be in the public interest). These economists were reflecting the performance viewpoint—that competition should be relied on to break down the monopolies. They argued that bigness doesn't imply the absence of market competition and that the government's role should merely be to make sure that no significant barriers to entry to new firms are created.

Other economists, reflecting the structure viewpoint, argued that competition was fragile and that competition wouldn't operate unless there were a large number of small firms. They argued that trusts and monopolies (even if they don't charge monopolistic prices) are bad, that the trusts should be broken up by government, and that laws should not allow new monopolies or trusts to be formed. However the debate was for the courts, not economists, to settle.

In 1911 the U.S. Supreme Court established its interpretation of the Sherman Act by handing down its opinions in cases involving Standard Oil and the American Tobacco Company. The Court determined that both companies were structural monopolies; each company controlled 90 percent of its market. However the Court decided that the monopolistic structure of the markets did not violate the Sherman Antitrust Act. A company's violation of the act was determined not by the structure of the industry but by the particular firm's performance—that is, by whether or not the firm engaged in "unfair business practices." This judgment by performance, not judgment by structure, is often called the *abuse theory* because a firm is legally considered a monopoly only if it commits monopolistic abuses.

In these two cases the distinction was academic. Both Standard Oil and American Tobacco were judged guilty (very guilty) of unfair business practices and were broken up. But the academic distinction played an important role in determining the industrial structure of the United States. It allowed structural monopolies to continue to exist, but it prohibited them from using certain monopolistic practices, such as demanding kickbacks.

In 1920 this structure/performance distinction was important in a case involving U.S. Steel. Here the Supreme Court ruled that while U.S. Steel was a structural monopoly, it was not a monopoly in performance. That is, the firm had not used unfair business practices to become a monopolist and thus was not in violation of antitrust law. U.S. Steel was not required to break up into a group of smaller companies as Standard Oil had been.

In an attempt to give more guidance to the courts and to provide for more vigorous enforcement of the antitrust provisions, in 1914 Congress passed the Clayton Antitrust Act and the Federal Trade Commission Act.

The **Clayton Antitrust Act** declared that four specific monopolistic practices were illegal when their effect was to lessen competition:

1. Price discrimination; that is, selling identical goods to different customers at different prices.

The Standard Oil and American Tobacco Cases: Judging Market Competitiveness by Performance

The Clayton Act and the Federal Trade Commission Act

Clayton Antitrust Act Law passed by U.S. Congress in 1914 making four specific monopolistic practices illegal.

2. Tie-in contracts in which the buyer must agree to deal exclusively with one seller and not to purchase goods from competing sellers.

3. Interlocking directorships in which memberships of boards of directors of two or more firms are almost identical.

4. Buying stock in a competitor's company when the purpose of buying that stock is to reduce competition.

Federal Trade Commission Act Law passed by U.S. Congress in 1914 making it illegal for firms to engage in certain unfair or deceptive practices.

In establishing the Federal Trade Commission (FTC) in 1914, Congress gave it the power to regulate competition and police markets. The **Federal Trade Commission Act** made it illegal for firms to use "unfair methods of competition" and to engage in "unfair or deceptive acts or practices," whether or not those actions had any impact on competition. Other than that broad mandate, Congress gave the FTC little direction as to what rules it was to use to regulate trade and police markets. As a result, for more than 20 years the commission was rather ineffective. In 1938, however, it was given the job of preventing false and deceptive advertising, which remains one of its primary roles.

The ALCOA Case: Judging Market Competitiveness by Structure

Judgment by performance was the primary criterion governing U.S. antitrust policy until 1945, when the U.S. courts changed their interpretation of the law. This occurred in the ALCOA (Aluminum Corporation of America) case in 1945. In the ALCOA case, the company was found guilty of violating the antitrust statutes even though the Court did not rule that ALCOA had been guilty of unfair practices. What ALCOA had done was to use its knowledge of the market to expand its capacity before any competitors had a chance to enter the market. In addition it had kept its prices low to prevent potential entry by competitors. It showed no signs of exploiting its monopoly power to charge high prices or to force competing firms out of business. Thus, on performance standards, it was not violating the law. But in the ALCOA case, the structure of the market, not the company's performance, was used to determine whether ALCOA was in violation of antitrust law.

Judging Markets by Structure and Performance: The Reality

Judgment by structure seems unfair on a gut level. After all, in economics the purpose of competition is to motivate firms to produce better goods than their competitors are producing, and to do so at lower cost. If a firm is competing so successfully that all the other firms leave the industry, the successful firm will be a monopolist, and on the basis of judgment by structure will be guilty of antitrust violations. Under the judgment by structure criterion, a firm is breaking the law if it does what it's supposed to be doing: producing the best product it can at the lowest possible cost.

Supporters of the judgment by structure criterion recognize this problem, but they nonetheless favor the structure criterion. An important reason for this is practicality.

Contextual Judgments and the Capabilities of the Courts Judgment by performance requires that each action of a firm must be analyzed on a case-by-case basis. Doing that is enormously time-consuming and expensive. In some interpretations, actions of a firm might be considered appropriate competitive behavior; in other interpretations, the same actions might be considered inappropriate. For example, say that IBM were to require that all maintenance to its computers be done by IBM technicians. Is IBM doing that to strengthen its monopoly power or to ensure proper maintenance? The answer depends on the context of the action.

But judging each case contextually is beyond the courts' capabilities. There are so many firms and so many actions that the courts can't judge all industries on their performance. They must devise a way to limit the issues they look at. In order to apply the performance criteria reasonably, the Supreme Court must set out certain guidelines to tell firms in what situations the Court will take a closer look at their performance. Because the available information concerns structure, those guidelines inevitably refer to market structure, even though it is firms' performance that will ultimately be judged. So even though judging by structure may have problems, it is necessary.

It's very much like the procedure college admissions offices use in deciding which applicants to accept. They judge applicants on their "total performance," not just on their quantitative scores on standardized tests. However they often use a certain quantitative score as a cutoff point in order to reduce applications to a manageable number. Applicants below the cutoff point are automatically rejected; applicants above it are considered one by one.

Another argument in favor of judging competitiveness by structure is that structure can be a predictor of future performance. Advocates of the structure criterion argue that a monopolist may be pricing low now, but that it is, after all, a monopolist, and it won't price low in the future. The low price will eliminate competition now, but once the competition is gone, the firm will not be able to resist the temptation to use its monopoly power.

Determining the Relevant Market and Industry   Supporters of the performance criterion admit that this standard has problems, but they point out that the structure criterion also has problems. As you saw in an earlier chapter, it's difficult to determine the relevant market (local, national, or international) and the relevant industry (two-digit or four-digit SIC code) necessary to identify the structural competitiveness of any industry. Such questions have been the center of many antitrust court cases. For example, in the ALCOA case, the company argued that metals such as copper and steel were interchangeable with aluminum and that therefore the relevant industry to consider was the metals industry. If the Court had chosen the U.S. metals industry, and not the aluminum industry, as the relevant industry, ALCOA wouldn't have been found to have a monopoly. The Court decided, however, that aluminum had sufficiently unique properties to constitute its own market. Since it determined that ALCOA had 90 percent of the aluminum market, ALCOA was declared a monopoly and was broken up.

The arguments in the Du Pont case (1956) again centered around the definition of *industry*. There the Supreme Court found that Du Pont was innocent of monopolizing the production of cellophane even though Du Pont was the only producer of cellophane. The Court reasoned that the relevant industry was not the cellophane industry but, rather, the flexible wrap industry, which also included aluminum foil and wax paper. Du Pont did not have a monopoly of the flexible wrap industry and thus, the Court said, was not in violation of the antitrust laws.

Similar ambiguities exist with the decision about the relevant market. In the Pabst Brewing case (1966) the definition of the market played a key role. Pabst wanted to merge with the Blatz Brewing Company. On a national scale both companies were relatively small, accounting together for about 4.5 percent of beer sales in the United States as a whole. Pabst argued that the United States was the relevant market. The Court, however, decided that Wisconsin, where Pabst had its headquarters, was the relevant market, and since the two firms held a 24 percent share of that market the merger was not allowed.

What should one make of this debate? The bottom line is that both structure and performance criteria have ambiguities, and in the real world there are no definitive criteria for judging whether a firm has violated the antitrust statutes. A firm isn't at fault or in the clear until the courts make the call.

Two important cases were decided in the 1980s. We'll consider them in a bit more detail than the older cases to provide a sense of how antitrust law affects companies today. One case involved IBM; the other involved AT&T.

Recent Antitrust Cases

3

The IBM Case   In 1969 the U.S. Department of Justice sued IBM for violating the antitrust laws. The department argued that the company had a 72 percent share of the general purpose electronic digital computing industry, and that it had acquired that market share because of unfair business practices such as bundling of hardware, software, and maintenance services at a single price (that is, requiring customers to buy all three together). If you wanted IBM equipment (hardware), you also had to take IBM service and software whether you wanted them or not. When you bought an IBM you bought everything so other companies had little chance to compete. Moreover the department argued that IBM constantly redesigned its computers, making it impossible for other companies to keep up and compete fairly on the sale of any IBM mainframe–compatible item.

IBM argued that the relevant market was broader, that it included all types of computers such as military computers, programmable calculators, and other information-processing products. It further claimed that its so-called unfair practices were simply a reflection of efficient computer technology. Fast-moving technological developments required it to continually redesign its products merely to provide its customers with the latest, best equipment. And, it said, the only way to provide the best level of service to its customers was to include its maintenance services in the price of its products.

The case dragged on for 13 years. IBM spent over $100 million on its defense. The company constructed an entire building just to house the documents in the case. The case never went to court. In January 1982 the government withdrew its lawsuit for three reasons:

1. In the 13 years since the court case had been brought, significant competition had developed in certain parts of the computer industry—specifically, the personal computer part. Apple, DEC, and others became serious competitors. Moreover a number of Japanese companies were making major inroads into the market. This strengthened IBM's contention about which was the relevant market.

2. In the 13 years since the case had been brought, the political climate had changed considerably. When the lawsuit had been started, Richard Nixon was president of the United States. By 1982 Ronald Reagan was president and he maintained a hands-off attitude toward antitrust questions. His appointees interpreted antitrust laws as less restrictive to business than their predecessors had.

3. In the 13 years since the case had been brought, the U.S. view of antitrust had changed from a U.S.-oriented view to an international view. Japanese firms were beating many U.S. firms in developing new products and in producing existing products cheaper and better. Some economists argued that one of the reasons for that success was the joint research and support that the Japanese government gave private firms through **MITI** (the Ministry of Industry and Trade), a government organization which helps business coordinate policies. Guided by MITI, Japanese firms can form cartels and effectively coordinate their policies, thus developing international markets and increasing international market share. In contrast, these economists argued, U.S. firms have been shackled by U.S. antitrust policy. IBM is one of the few U.S. companies that was internationally successful, and here was the U.S. government prosecuting it for its success.

MITI A Japanese government organization that helps business coordinate policies.

The AT&T Case The other major antitrust case of the 1980s, the AT&T case, demonstrates another aspect of U.S. antitrust policy and shows how technological change plays an important role in competition and questions of industrial market structure.

Up until 1982 AT&T was what was called a *regulated monopoly*. It had the exclusive right to provide telephone service in the United States. AT&T controlled most of the telecommunications market: long-distance and local telephone service and the production of telephones themselves as well as other communications equipment. Why was it given that right? Because it was felt that economies of scale made supplying telephone service a **natural monopoly** (an industry in which significant economies of scale make the existence of more than one firm inefficient). Telephone service required lines to be brought into every house; those lines had to be buried underground or strung overhead on poles and connected to all other houses. It made little sense to have seven or eight companies stringing competing lines. Moreover a decision was made that universal telephone service was desired and AT&T was required to provide universal service. Unregulated companies likely would have practiced *cream skimming* (providing service to low-cost areas and avoiding high-cost areas).

In return for its monopoly, AT&T was subjected to regulatory control by the Federal Communications Commission and by state utility commissions. This government regulation was designed to limit the company's profit to a fair level and prevent it from abusing its monopoly.

Under AT&T's monopoly, phone service in the United States was the best and cheapest in the world, although some believed it could and should have been even cheaper. Some economists argued that AT&T's guarantee of a "fair" return on its investment gave it a strong incentive to act as a lazy monopolist and to invest heavily, thereby increasing costs. If a company knows it can pass on its costs to customers (and add on a profit margin as well), it has little incentive to hold down costs. But even if service was more expensive than it needed to be, on the whole most agreed that the system worked well.

In the 1970s, however, technological changes fundamentally altered the nature of the long-distance telephone industry. The development of satellite transmission and fiber optics made cable connections obsolete, so long-distance telephone service was no longer a natural monopoly. In fact, significant competition began to develop, and AT&T's new competitors claimed that they weren't being allowed reasonable access to the AT&T-controlled local telephone network. AT&T charged competing firms high fees for access to all their local lines, fees that competitors argued were unfair.

The issue was complicated by the fact that the regulatory commissions, in an attempt to see that everyone had low-cost local service, had set local charges low and long-distance rates high. As long as AT&T controlled both local and long-distance calling, AT&T didn't worry about this. But when competitors began to undercharge AT&T on long-distance service, the rate-setting system (which implicitly subsidized local service with AT&T's long-distance profits) concerned AT&T greatly. AT&T's high access charges were an attempt to see that the competitors used some of their own profits to help subsidize local rates.

As a result of these claims and counterclaims, the Department of Justice introduced an antitrust suit against AT&T in 1978, alleging that potential competitors were not being allowed reasonable access to AT&T's local telephone network. The case had merit, but so did AT&T's defense: that the problem was in the setting of rates for local and long-distance calls. As is now usual for any contested antitrust case, the case went on and on and no conclusion was in sight.

Then in January 1982 (on the same day the IBM case ended) AT&T and the Department of Justice announced that they had settled the case and that AT&T had agreed to be broken up. Specifically, AT&T agreed that by January 1, 1984, it would divest itself of 22 local operating companies (known as the *baby bells*) which accounted for $87 billion of AT&T's $136 billion in assets. Exhibit 1 shows the structure of AT&T before and after divestiture. You can see that AT&T ("Ma Bell") kept its long-distance telephone service, its manufacturing division (the Western Electric Company), and its research facilities (Bell Laboratories). In return AT&T was subject to far less regulation than before. After the settlement AT&T could enter any unregulated business it desired, such as data transmission and computers.

The result of this settlement was an enormous upheaval in the telephone industry. Local rates for phone service went up twofold or even threefold while

Natural monopoly An industry in which significant economies of scale make the existence of more than one firm inefficient.

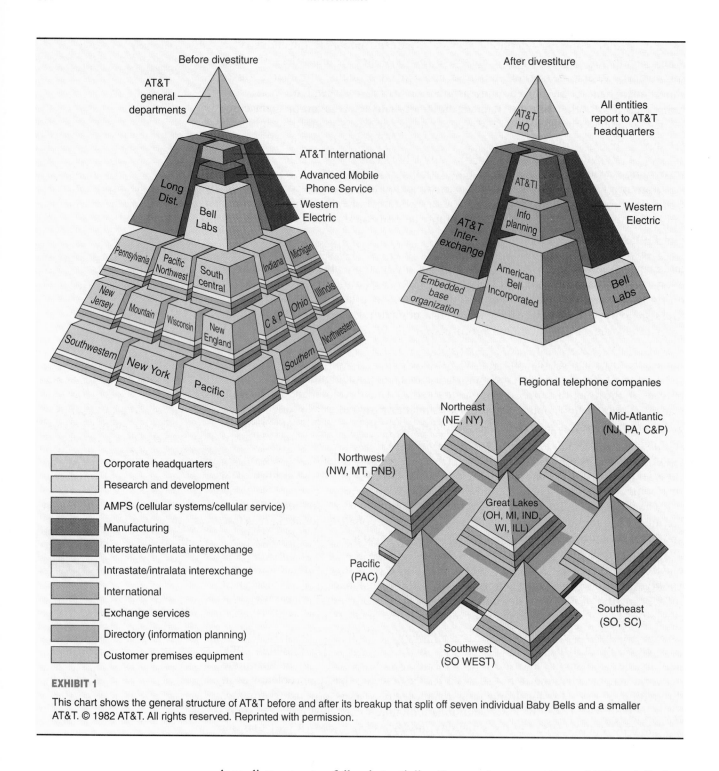

Before divestiture

AT&T general departments — AT&T International — Advanced Mobile Phone Service — Western Electric

Long Dist.   Bell Labs

Pennsylvania   Pacific Northwest   South central   Indiana   Michigan

New Jersey   Mountain   Wisconsin   New England   C & P   Ohio   Illinois

Southwestern   New York   Pacific   Southern   Northwestern

After divestiture

All entities report to AT&T headquarters

AT&T HQ

AT&TI
Info planning
AT&T Inter-exchange
American Bell Incorporated
Embedded base organization
Western Electric
Bell Labs

Legend:
- Corporate headquarters
- Research and development
- AMPS (cellular systems/cellular service)
- Manufacturing
- Interstate/interlata interexchange
- Intrastate/intralata interexchange
- International
- Exchange services
- Directory (information planning)
- Customer premises equipment

Regional telephone companies

Northeast (NE, NY)   Mid-Atlantic (NJ, PA, C&P)
Northwest (NW, MT, PNB)
Great Lakes (OH, MI, IND, WI, ILL)
Pacific (PAC)
Southeast (SO, SC)
Southwest (SO WEST)

EXHIBIT 1

This chart shows the general structure of AT&T before and after its breakup that split off seven individual Baby Bells and a smaller AT&T. © 1982 AT&T. All rights reserved. Reprinted with permission.

long-distance rates fell substantially. Two major competitors, MCI and Sprint, developed and competition for long-distance business became frenzied. Because individual customers were now responsible for supplying their own phones, the telephone supply industry became highly competitive as cheap phones flooded the market. In the early 1990s it's still unclear what the telecommunications industry's final structure will be.

Assessment of Antitrust Policy

Economic scholars' overall assessment of antitrust policy is mixed. In certain cases, such as the IBM case, most agree that antitrust prosecution went too far. But most believe that other decisions (as in the 1911 Standard Oil and American Tobacco cases) set a healthy precedent by encouraging a more competitive U.S.

business environment. Almost all agree that antitrust enforcement has not reduced the size of firms below the minimally efficient level, the level at which a firm can take full advantage of economies of scale. But they are mixed in their judgments as to whether the enforcement was needed. Performance advocates generally believe that it was not, while structural advocates generally believe that it was.

In the late 1980s and early 1990s there was not a lot of activity on the antitrust front, but nonetheless changes in industrial structure were prominent in the news. Much of that discussion was about takeovers and acquisitions of one firm by another. Most of these takeovers and acquisitions did not violate current U.S. antitrust laws because of the type of merger that they were. Thus, it's important to consider the various subcategories and types of mergers that are possible in order to put recent merger activity into perspective.

MERGERS, ACQUISITIONS, AND TAKEOVERS

Acquisitions and Takeovers

The term **merger** is a general term meaning the combination of two firms. The picture it conveys is of two firms combining to form one firm. That picture isn't appropriate for many mergers. For example, often the firm buying another company is essentially what's called a *shell corporation,* which exists primarily to buy up other firms. When a shell corporation buys another firm, the combination, while technically a merger, is called a **takeover** to emphasize that little true merging is taking place. Such takeovers change the control over the firm, but do not affect market concentration.

Merger Combination of two firms.

Takeover Purchase of a firm by another firm that then takes direct control over its operations.

Another term often used in place of *merger* is *acquisition.* In an **acquisition,** two firms merge by one firm buying out another. It is a merger, but it is not a merger of equals and the acquiring firm may not take over direct control of the acquired firm's operations. In a merger of equals, neither firm takes over the other, and it's not clear who'll be in charge after the merger.

Acquisition A company buys another company; the buyer actually controls the resulting venture, but does not necessarily exercise direct control.

Takeovers and acquisitions are said to be *friendly* or *hostile.* A friendly takeover is one in which one corporation is willing to be acquired by the other. A **hostile takeover** is one in which the firm being taken over doesn't want to be taken over. How can that happen? Remember our earlier discussion of corporations. Corporations are owned by stockholders, but are managed by a different group of individuals. The two groups' interests do not necessarily coincide. When it is said that a corporation doesn't want to be taken over, that means that the corporation's managers don't want the company to be taken over. In a hostile takeover the management of each corporation presents its side to the shareholders of both corporations. The shareholders of the corporation that is the takeover target ultimately decide whether or not to sell their shares. If enough shareholders sell, the takeover succeeds.

Hostile takeover A merger in which one company buys another that does not want to be bought.

In one form of hostile takeover (known as *double Pac Man*) two firms try to swallow each other; or alternatively the target of a hostile takeover bid tries to make itself unpalatable—the *poison pill* strategy. In the poison pill strategy, the firm that doesn't want to be taken over agrees before the merger to do something stupid if it's taken over so that this firm is no longer desirable to potential taking-over firms. For example, say that Stubborn, Inc., doesn't want to be taken over. So Stubborn borrows billions of dollars and uses that money to buy some company worth about half what Stubborn pays for it. That's a stupid move. After that move Stubborn isn't a desirable firm to be taken over. (So it wasn't so stupid, right?) Of course, after Stubborn isn't taken over, it's stuck with the company it paid too much for, and it's also stuck with the interest it has to pay on the multibillion dollar loan it took out. Stubborn has provided itself with a poison pill to keep invaders away, but it has to live with the poison pill itself. (So maybe it was a stupid move after all.)

In other cases the takeover company doesn't really want to take over the other company. Instead it's hoping for *greenmail* (a payment from the potential victim to halt the takeover bid).

The specific nature of a merger is of interest to people working for the corporations involved. It determines whether employees will move up or down in the corporate pecking order, or even whether they'll keep their jobs at all. When a firm is threatened by a hostile takeover, top management is likely to hunt for another firm, a friendly one that will be a "white knight" coming to the rescue. The white knight firm, it is hoped, will keep all the management employees in their jobs. When their jobs are at stake, it is often questionable whether management searches out that firm that will pay shareholders the best price. Management's interest is likely to be in keeping their jobs, not in making money for the shareholders.

Strategies have been developed to protect shareholders from management's interest overriding shareholders' interest. One such strategy is the *golden parachute*. The board of directors of the corporation provides that if the corporation should be acquired by another corporation, people holding top management jobs are guaranteed large payments of money—as high as $40 or $50 million in some cases. This is a golden parachute. It means that management can feel comfortable when the corporation is approached by a potential buyer and will make decisions based on the shareholders' interests, not on whether management jobs will be left undisturbed.

Golden parachutes afford shareholders some assurance that if their firm receives an acquisition or takeover offer, management will consider it. Golden parachutes protect top management because either they'll keep their jobs or, if they lose their jobs, their pain will be soothed by compensation in big bucks. Golden parachutes do nothing for low-level management and ordinary workers, who may suffer demotions or layoffs after two firms have merged.

All this financial gamesmanship has led some to believe that the government should enact laws restricting takeovers, not because of their effect on concentration and competition, but because of their effect on managerial incentives. The disadvantage of takeovers for the economy is that managers spend too much time playing the takeover game and too little time overseeing the truly productive activities of the firm. But many economists oppose the passage of such legislation, arguing that fear of a takeover keeps managers on their toes—adding competitive pressure to the economy. To prevent takeovers would be to eliminate that competitive pressure.

Mergers

Horizontal merger Companies in the same industry merging together.

Vertical merger A combination of two companies, one being a buyer of products the other company supplies.

Conglomerate merger Combination of unrelated businesses.

Mergers are also classified by the type of businesses that are merging. Two companies in the same industry merging is a **horizontal merger.** A firm merging with the supplier of one of its inputs is a **vertical merger.** Two firms in unrelated industries merging is a **conglomerate merger.**

Horizontal Mergers Most U.S. antitrust policy has concerned horizontal mergers. The creation of Standard Oil which I discussed earlier is an example of a horizontal merger. Since the passage of the Cellar-Kefauver Act of 1950, almost all mergers of companies with substantial market shares in the same industry have been prohibited, even though enforcement was loosened in the 1980s. For example, in 1986 the FTC blocked a proposed merger between Coca-Cola and 7UP because the market share after the merger would have been 80 percent.

Exactly what is considered substantial market share has changed over time. The general guideline government used in the 1970s and early 1980s was that in highly concentrated industries the government would challenge all mergers involving the following combinations of market share:

Acquiring firm	Acquired firm
4%	4% or more
10%	2% or more
15%	1% or more

For less-concentrated industries, the guidelines used slightly different percentages. In 1982 the Department of Justice changed the guidelines and began looking at all mergers in which the Herfindahl index, after the merger, would be above 1000. Unless one of the merging firms was on the verge of bankruptcy, such horizontal mergers among the largest firms in an industry were supposedly prohibited, but enforcement became lax in the late 1980s because President Reagan's appointees generally opposed antitrust enforcement. President Bush, Reagan's successor, chose appointees who weren't as opposed to antitrust enforcement, and a stricter set of guidelines was developing in the early 1990s.

Vertical Mergers   As I stated before, a vertical merger is a combination of two companies that are involved in different phases of producing a product, one company being a buyer of products the other company supplies. For example, if a computer company merges with an electronic chip company, a vertical merger has taken place. Similarly if a clothes manufacturer buys a retail boutique, that's a vertical merger. If either of the merged firms is able to limit access of other buyers or sellers to the market, such a merger is in violation of the Clayton Act.

A famous vertical merger case is the Du Pont/General Motors case (1961), in which Du Pont was required to sell its 23 percent share of General Motors because Du Pont was a major supplier to the automobile industry. The Supreme Court felt Du Pont's ownership share of GM was restricting competition. Similarly in the Brown Shoe/Kinney Shoe case (1962), Brown Shoe, primarily a wholesaler, was forbidden to buy Kinney Shoe, which was a chain of shoe retailers.

In most of the 1980s the U.S. government would challenge any vertical merger in which the supplying firm had a 10 percent market share or more and the buyer company purchased 6 percent or more of the market. This rule was loosened some as the 1980s progressed, although still, in the early 1990s, new guidelines have not yet replaced it.

Conglomerate Mergers   A third type of merger is a conglomerate merger. Conglomerate mergers occur when two relatively unrelated businesses merge. Conglomerate mergers are generally approved by the U.S. antitrust laws under the assumption that they do not significantly restrict competition. Thus, when GM bought Electronic Data Systems Corporation in 1984, no antitrust action was taken to prevent the merger because the two firms were unrelated.

Why would two unrelated firms want to merge? Or why would one want to be bought out by another? There are five general reasons: **5**

1. *To achieve economies of scope.* Although the businesses are unrelated, some overlap is almost inevitable, so economies of scope are likely. For example, one firm's technical or marketing expertise may be helpful to the other firm, or the conglomerate's increased size may give it better bargaining power with its suppliers.

2. *To get a good buy.* Firms are always on the lookout for good buys. If a firm believes that another firm's stock is significantly undervalued, it can buy that stock at its low price and then sell it at a profit later when the stock is no longer undervalued.

3. *To diversify.* Many industries have a cyclical nature. In some parts of the business cycle they do poorly; in other parts of the business cycle they do just fine. Buying an unrelated company allows a firm to diversify and thereby to even out the cyclical fluctuation in its profits.

4. *To ward off a takeover bid.* Firms are always susceptible to being bought out by someone else. Sometimes they prevent an unwanted buyout by merging with another firm in order to become so large that they're indigestible. For example, in 1989 Time, Inc., merged with Warner Communications to reduce the likelihood that Time would be taken over by a third firm, Paramount.

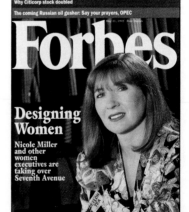

A business magazine that closely follows major mergers and acquisitions.

EXHIBIT 2 **Mergers in the United States since 1892**

The number of mergers in the United States has fluctuated substantially in the last 100 years.
Source: *Statistical Abstract of the U.S., 1991*, the Federal Trade Commission, and *Mergers and Acquisitions*, 1993.

5. *To strengthen their political-economic influence.* The bigger you are, the more influence you have. Individuals who run companies like to have and use influence. Merging can increase their net influence considerably.

Recent Merger Activity and Deacquisitions

Exhibit 2 presents the number of mergers in the United States each year since 1892. As you can see, mergers rose significantly in the last part of the 1980s. One reason is that mergers became a fad—the thing to do. Also relatively low share prices made companies a good deal. Companies' best investment was buying another company. Mergers were an especially good deal for the investment bankers who arrange the deals for a fee, and they worked hard selling the merger idea to companies. If they could persuade major companies to merge, the investment bankers stood to earn millions of dollars. It's not surprising that they pushed such deals and worked hard to find ways to finance them.

The fact that a large number of mergers took place in the late 1980s doesn't mean that the U.S. economy was seeing an overall growth in the size of companies. That's because many recent huge takeovers have been followed by **deacquisitions.** To pay off the debt it incurred to finance a takeover, a company may sell parts of the business it has bought. This is deacquisition.

Deacquisition One company's sale of parts of another company it has bought.

For example, in 1990 Kohlberg, Kravis, Roberts, and Co. (KKR) bought RJR Nabisco. KKR raised the $24.5 billion purchase price mainly by selling high-yield, high-risk bonds (commonly called *junk bonds*). Issuing these junk bonds meant that KKR had to commit itself to pay large amounts of interest on them. But the earnings Nabisco brought KKR were less than the interest KKR needed to pay off the bondholders. The only way KKR could meet the obligation was to sell off parts of Nabisco (hoping, of course, to get more for those parts than it had paid for the whole company). Among Nabisco's well-known products were Oreos, Life Savers, Chips Ahoy, and Ritz Crackers, as well as Camel, Salem, Winston, and Vantage cigarettes. Today many of those brands are no longer produced by RJR Nabisco. Instead they're produced and marketed by the various firms that bought the various pieces of the Nabisco company. So the net effect of this takeover is likely to be a decrease in overall concentration in the economy, although, depending on whether existing firms or new firms bought out the various Nabisco divisions, there may be an increase in concentration in particular industries.

Assessment of Mergers and Acquisitions

We've introduced a lot of terms in this section and, ideally, started you thinking about the issues involved in deciding on a merger and acquisition policy. This chapter does not arrive at definite conclusions, and in this it reflects the economics profession, which has no one position on what policy the United States should follow toward mergers.

But the economics profession's failure to come to an undivided view on mergers isn't necessarily a failing of economists. Mergers have both costs and benefits, and reasonable people will assess them differently.

Among Nabisco's most valuable assets were its trademark brand names. ("Little girls are pretty and nice but I like Oreos.")

The nature of competition is changing in the United States. Ten or 20 years ago, when people talked about competition, they meant competition among U.S. firms. Now, however, they often mean competition between U.S. companies and foreign firms that either have started producing here in the United States or are exporting to the United States. The reason for this is the internationalization of the U.S. economy. The large U.S. trade deficit of the 1980s was accompanied by large amounts of foreign investment in the United States. Foreign firms have strengthened their manufacturing positions here. For example, about 50 percent of the firms in the stone, clay, and glass industry in the United States are foreign-owned. Most of the large firms in the tire industry (such as Firestone, General Tire, and Armstrong) are foreign-owned. Burger King is foreign-owned. The U.S. chemical industry is 50 percent foreign-owned. There are many other examples.

Of course the process goes the other way too. U.S. firms are more and more becoming **multinationals,** with production facilities and a marketing force in one or more other countries. Just as foreign firms are investing in the United States, U.S. firms are investing in foreign countries. You can now get a McDonald's hamburger just about anywhere in the world, including China and Russia. Walt Disney has theme parks in Japan and France. More and more firms are acquiring an international perspective in which the U.S. economy is simply becoming one market in an international economy, rather than an entire market.

The internationalization of the U.S. economy adds to competition by broadening the market and adding potential producers of a variety of goods. In the 1960s the U.S. auto industry was dominated by the Big Three: Ford, GM, and Chrysler. Today those companies face fierce competition from foreign firms such as Toyota, Nissan, Honda, and Hyundai.

Foreign competition has played an important role in holding down U.S. prices, and thereby holding down U.S. wages. Foreign competition has changed the relative bargaining strengths of workers and management of corporations. In the 1960s workers were in a relatively strong position. They could threaten to strike if they didn't get the wage increases they wanted. Generally management met their demands.

The internationalization of the U.S. economy has changed that situation. If U.S. firms don't produce cheaply enough, foreign firms will replace them. Similarly in the 1990s many U.S. firms have become multinational firms and can realistically threaten to move their production to another country. That threat gives them a much stronger bargaining position with U.S. labor. The internationalization of the U.S. economy has been furthered with the recent free trade agreement with Mexico and Canada. Since labor costs account for more than

INTERNATIONAL COMPETITION, INDUSTRIAL POLICY, AND ANTITRUST POLICY

Multinationals Firms with production facilities and a marketing force in two or more countries.

60 percent of the value added of most products, foreign competition and the internationalization of U.S. firms have helped keep inflationary pressure in the United States lower than it would otherwise have been.

Because of this internationalization of competition, the political climate in the United States is changing. More and more, U.S. antitrust policymakers see the international market as the relevant market. The policy focus of government is shifting from "Is U.S. industry internally competitive so that it does not take advantage of the consumer?" to "Is U.S. industry internationally competitive so that it can compete effectively in the world economy?"

Antitrust Policy in Other Countries

Other countries' approaches toward antitrust are a likely harbinger of future U.S. antitrust policy. The reason is that other countries, because almost all of them are smaller than the United States, have consistently seen the international market as the relevant market and have designed their antitrust laws accordingly. Their domestic markets were simply too small to take advantage of economies of scale.

What's interesting about other countries' antitrust laws is how weak they are compared to U.S. laws. No other country forces companies to break up for antitrust violations, although some push for price rollbacks in cases of extreme monopolization. Even when the United States has tried to export its stringent antitrust laws, as it did during its military occupation of Germany and Japan after World War II, those laws were repealed by those nations soon after the occupation ended.

One important reason other countries oppose antitrust regulation is that they recognize the importance of economies of scale. In many countries that have only small markets, the minimum efficient production level requires high concentration. A second reason is their history. Most countries don't have the same populist worldview that exists in the United States. The ideological and cultural underpinning of strong antitrust laws (individualistic competition based on small producers) fits in nicely with the American populist worldview. In the United States many people believe that bigness is bad. That belief is not as prevalent in other countries. A third reason that other countries don't have strong antitrust laws is cultural. In the United States government and business are often seen as enemies of each other. In cultures such as Japan's or Germany's government and business are seen as allies, working together to increase exports and compete internationally.

From Antitrust Policy to Industrial Policy

As the U.S. economy becomes more and more internationalized, its approach to antitrust policy will likely be less confrontational and more supportive of the idea of allowing businesses to cooperate rather than compete with each other, so that they can better compete internationally. International competition will be relied upon more heavily than domestic competition to provide competitive pressures on U.S. firms. Government will likely allow mergers and cartels that will strengthen the United States internationally and will actively encourage cooperation among U.S. firms. These changes have already begun. For example, in 1989 the U.S. government allowed major U.S. computer companies to organize jointly to form a chip research company so that they, as a group, could better compete with Japanese companies. Previously any such activity would have been seen as a direct violation of the antitrust laws. Even though this consortium broke down in 1990, the fact that government allowed it to form is significant. It signals a major change in U.S. antitrust policy; and more of these exemptions can be expected in the future. In 1991 IBM and Apple announced that they were going to work together and share technology and information with the support of the U.S. government. Whether this change in policy toward business will increase U.S. competitiveness remains to be seen.

ANTITRUST AGENCIES IN SOME
OTHER COUNTRIES

Britain: British Monopoly Commission

While it has the power to recommend structural reorganization, the British Monopoly Commission generally has not done so. Instead it has pushed for price reductions in certain industries. After World War II a number of major industries were nationalized, putting the government in direct control of prices, but many of these industries have been privatized in the past few years.

Japan: Fair Trade Commission

The Japanese Fair Trade Commission is weak and subordinated to MITI and other government agencies. In retailing small firms continue to dominate with the support of government. But the 1980s saw the beginnings of a retailing system with large stores, like the system in the United States. The Fair Trade Commission may take a role in suppressing that development.

Germany: Federal Cartel Office

The Federal Cartel Office is relatively small. Often it allows and even encourages cartels. It does have the authority to push for price reductions if it determines that the cartel has abused its power.

France: Commission on Competition

The Commission on Competition has been very weak and has often advocated mergers. In the 1960s France actively promoted large-scale mergers and during that period the government nationalized large industries without hearing objections from the Commission on Competition.

European Economic Community

In 1992 the EEC's rules officially took precedence over member nations' local rules but it will be late in the 1990s before any practical interpretation of the rules' implications will emerge. One possibility is what happened with the European Coal and Steel Commission. Under that commission, mergers were limited in theory, but in practice none were disallowed. Another possibility is that the expansion of the market in 1992 will probably generate significant merger activity, and since the economies of scale argument will no longer apply, a stronger antitrust policy emerges.

In the 1980s and 1990s the rallying cry for many politicians has been that the U.S. economy needs an industrial policy. An **industrial policy** is the formal policy that government takes toward business. In actual fact the United States has always had, and always will have, an industrial policy. What these politicians are calling for is an *activist industrial policy* under which the government would work directly with businesses, providing funds, background research, and encouragement to specific industries in order to keep the United States internationally competitive.

The Example of Japan's MITI   Advocates of an activist U.S. industrial policy point to Japan's Ministry of International Trade and Industry (MITI) as an example of how an activist industrial policy would work. MITI is generally credited with engineering Japan's phenomenal economic growth over the past 40 years. MITI worked closely with Japanese companies to improve their competitiveness. The ministry provided money and research, and saw to it that companies focused on international, rather than domestic, competition. It smoothed the flow of capital to certain industries it wanted to promote, such as the electronics industry. It did this by taking such measures as consulting with banks and encouraging loans. MITI would say, "So-and-So is a good company" and that statement was a code to banks that they should approve So-and-So's loan application.

Activist Industrial Policy

Industrial policy Government's formal policy toward business.

Tokyo—from inside its two office towers in Kasumigaseki, the Government center near the Imperial Palace here, the Ministry of International Trade and Industry looks more like a decrepit insurance agency than the mastermind of a high-tech miracle. Paper is piled everywhere. Employees sit elbow-to-elbow at battered gray desks that seem to date from the American occupation. Some of them do. Conferences with visitors take place on fraying couches hemmed in by filing cabinets.

There is a central computer system, but it is hardly at everyone's fingertips: Even in the information processing section, which oversees the world's second-largest computer industry, a few workers prop Toshiba laptop computers on their desks.

But appearances aside, the ministry remains the repository of much of Japan's best young talent. Ambitious throngs from the senior class

Source: The *New York Times*, July 9, 1989, Business Section. Copyright © 1989 by The New York Times Company. Reprinted by permission.

of the University of Tokyo, Japan's single-school equivalent of the Ivy League, compete each year for entry-level slots at the ministry. From early on, they are given enormous responsibility and are rarely shy about using it. A semiconductor industry executive recently fumed to a reporter that he had spent a morning at the ministry being lectured about his business by a "condescending, arrogant little bureaucrat" young enough to be his son.

The ministry is 40 years old this year, and such complaints go back to its beginning. In its early days, it placed strict import quotas on everything from cars to computers and forced foreign companies to license critical technologies to Japanese partners if they wanted to invest directly in Japan. It used state-managed banks to funnel funds into automobiles, petrochemicals and steel. And it allocated scarce foreign exchange and rebuilt industrial groups into "keiretsu," related companies with interlocking stock ownership, usually including a trading company and a bank.

The ministry's better-known role, as the hidden hand behind Japan Inc., started in the 1960's. Wielding "administrative guidance" notices and organizing consortiums of companies, it navigated the oil crises, merged steel companies and began Japan's thrust into high technology.

Not everyone views its power as benign. In a controversial new book, "The Enigma of Japanese Power," Karel Van Wolferen, a Tokyo journalist, argues that it is a premier blackmailer, collecting information about corporate wrongdoing and threatening companies with "exposure if they do not follow MITI's directions."

Not surprisingly, the ministry disagrees, saying that its clout in the 1960's and 1970's arose because companies were desperate to play catch-up ball and wanted the services offered by the ministry. "We had an obvious foreign competitor," said Chikao Tsukuda, a former ministry official and now a consultant to it—"I.B.M."

Problems with an Activist Industrial Policy MITI's success did not come without problems. Its activism involved government in business decisions. This opened up significant possibilities for graft. In the late 1980s a major scandal erupted in Japan when it was revealed that some Japanese corporations had given many politicians in the ruling Liberal Democratic Party options to buy stock in the companies at low prices.

Such problems are likely to arise under an activist industrial policy. Because government decisions can mean a difference of hundreds of millions of dollars to firms, companies will inevitably spend money to influence those decisions, either legally through lobbying or illegally through bribery and graft. The exposure of the scandals in Japan has already changed the composition of its elected ruling party. Whether the scandals will change Japan's industrial policy remains to be seen.

While the United States has never had an activist industrial policy like Japan's, a close connection has developed among the armed forces, the industries that manufacture weapons, and members of Congress from states and districts that depend heavily on the defense industry. This relationship of mutual benefit, referred to as the **military-industrial complex,** is an activist relationship in that it involves government in the decisions of privately owned defense manufacturers. This involvement often prevents government from making tough economic choices. For example, in 1989 Congress seemed about to cut production of the B-2 Stealth bomber. Northrup, the plane's manufacturer, took out full-page news-

Military-industrial complex The mutually beneficial relationship among the armed services, weapons industries, and government officials.

paper ads, pointing out that parts of the B-2 were produced in 48 states and that thousands of jobs would be lost if the government canceled the contract. Congress gave in, as it has done on many other defense items that are widely regarded as nonessential to national security. With the ending of the Cold War in the early 1990s, many felt that defense spending could be cut substantially. But whenever specific cuts were suggested, the military-industrial complex fought hard against them.

Should the United States Adopt an Activist Industrial Policy?   Any time economic decisions are made on a political basis, waste is inevitable. It's the cost of an activist industrial policy in a democratic government. But there are also benefits. Competition can be wasteful, especially in research. That's why scientific conventions (rules limiting scientists' behavior) exist that support openness and sharing of scientific knowledge. Cooperation by firms with government and universities can lead to more productive research. Even with the problem of wasteful defense spending, the United States has maintained a technological lead in aerospace in large part because of the government's support for that industry. Some economists have argued that the United States wouldn't have remained highly competitive without the defense industry's close connection with, and subsidies by, the government. As with every decision in economics, there are both costs and benefits.

In weighing these costs and benefits, a majority of economists come out on the side of opposing an activist industrial policy for the United States. This includes most conservative economists who generally oppose activist government policies plus a number of liberal economists who are concerned about the politics of an industrial policy. They believe that a formal activist industrial policy would probably lead to more inefficiency and waste as the invisible feet of politics and law extended their influence over the invisible hand of the marketplace, yielding more costs than benefits.

To argue against an activist industrial policy is not to argue against an informal government policy of encouraging research in certain areas. This can be done by fostering connections between universities and business, by directly subsidizing private industry's basic research, or by loosening the antitrust laws. Many economists support such policies in particular cases even as they oppose a general activist industrial policy being extended to all businesses.

KEY POINTS

- There is a debate on whether markets should be judged on the basis of structure or on the basis of performance. **1**
- Antitrust policy is the government's policy toward the competitive process. **2 3**
- Important antitrust laws include the Sherman Antitrust Act, the Clayton Act, and the Federal Trade Commission Act. **2**
- Three types of mergers are horizontal, vertical, and conglomerate. **4**
- Five reasons that two unrelated firms would

want to merge are economies of scope, a good buy, diversification, warding off a takeover bid, and strengthening political-economic influence. **5**
- The increasing internationalization of the relevant U.S. market has changed U.S. policy's focus from antitrust policy to industrial policy. **6**
- Industrial policies have advantages and disadvantages. **7**

KEY TERMS

acquisition *(573)*
Antitrust policy *(565)*
Clayton Antitrust
  Act *(567)*
conglomerate
  merger *(574)*
deacquisition *(576)*

Federal Trade Commission
  Act *(568)*
horizontal merger *(574)*
hostile takeover *(573)*
industrial policy *(579)*
judgment by
  performance *(565)*

judgment by
  structure *(565)*
merger *(573)*
military-industrial
  complex *(580)*
MITI *(570)*
multinationals *(577)*

natural monopoly *(571)*
Sherman Antitrust
  Act *(565)*
takeover *(573)*
vertical merger *(574)*

QUESTIONS FOR THOUGHT AND REVIEW

The number after each question represents the estimated degree of critical thinking required. (1 = almost none; 10 = deep thought.)

1. How would the U.S. economy likely differ today if Standard Oil had not been broken up? *(9)*
2. Colleges require that certain courses be taken at that college in order to get a degree. Is that an example of a tie-in contract that limits consumers' choices? If so, should it be against the law? *(7)*
3. Colleges give financial aid to certain students. Is this price discrimination? If so, should it be against the law? *(7)*
4. Should interlocking directorships be against the law? Why or why not? *(6)*
5. Distinguish the basis of judgment for the Standard Oil and the ALCOA cases. *(2)*

6. If you were an economist for a firm that wanted to merge, would you argue that the two-digit or four-digit industry is the relevant market? Why? *(5)*
7. Has telephone service improved since AT&T was broken up? What does this imply about antitrust laws? *(7)*
8. Under the 1982 Department of Justice guidelines, would a merger be allowed between the number 3 firm in an industry and a firm with 2 percent of the market? The number 4 firm in the industry has 11 percent of the market. *(6)*
9. Should the United States have a policy against conglomerate mergers? Why or why not? *(7)*
10. How would you design an industrial policy to avoid the problems inherent in such a policy? *(9)*

PROBLEMS AND EXERCISES

1. You're working at the Department of Justice. Ms. Ecofame has just brought in a new index, the Ecofame index, which she argues is preferable to the Herfindahl index. The Ecofame index is calculated by cubing the market share of the top 10 firms in the industry.
   a. Calculate an Ecofame guideline that would correspond to the 1982 Department of Justice guidelines.

   b. State the advantages and disadvantages of the Ecofame index as compared to the Herfindahl index.
2. Using a monopolistic competition model, a cartel model of oligopoly, and a contestable market of oligopoly, discuss and demonstrate graphically where possible the effect of antitrust policy.

28

Politics, Economics, and Agricultural Markets

American farmers have become welfare addicts, protected and assisted at every turn by a network of programs paid for by their fellow citizens. If Americans still believe in the virtue of self-reliance, they should tell Washington to get out of the way and let farmers practice it.

Stephen Chapman

After reading this chapter, you should be able to:

1

Explain the good/bad paradox in farming.

2

Give a brief summary of the history of U.S. farm policy.

3

State the general rule of political economy in a democracy.

4

Explain, using supply and demand curves, the distributional consequences of four alternative methods of price support.

5

Argue both sides of the question of agricultural price supports.

Agricultural markets provide good examples of the interaction of the invisible hand (the market) and the invisible foot (politics). Considering the economics of agricultural markets shows us how powerful a tool supply and demand analysis is in helping us understand not only the workings of perfectly competitive markets but also the effects of government intervention in a market. So in this chapter I consider agricultural markets and the effect of government policies on them. But bear in mind that while the focus is on agriculture, the lessons of the analysis are applicable to a wide variety of markets in which the invisible hand and foot interact. As you read the chapter, applying the analysis to other markets will be a useful exercise.

THE NATURE OF AGRICULTURAL MARKETS

In many ways agricultural markets fit the classic picture of perfect competition. First, there are many independent sellers who are generally *price takers*. Second, there are many buyers. Third, the products are interchangeable: farm A's wheat can readily be substituted for farm B's wheat. And fourth, prices can, and do, vary considerably. On the basis of these inherent characteristics, it is reasonable to talk about agricultural markets as competitive markets.

In other ways, however, agricultural markets are far from perfectly competitive. The competitiveness of many agricultural markets is influenced by government programs. In fact, neither the United States nor any other country allows the market, unhindered, to control agricultural prices and output. For example, the U.S. government sets a minimum price for milk; buys up large quantities of wheat and stockpiles it; and licenses tobacco growers, allowing only those with licenses to grow tobacco.

I could have made the list of government programs much longer, because the government has a program for just about every major agricultural market. The point is clear, however: The competitive market in agriculture is not a story of the invisible hand alone. It's the story of a constant struggle between the invisible hand and the invisible foot. Whenever the invisible hand pushes prices down, farmers use their political clout (the invisible foot) to kick them back up.

The Good/Bad Paradox in Agriculture

Good/bad paradox The phenomenon of doing poorly because you're doing well.

1

Agriculture is characterized by what might be called a **good/bad paradox** (the phenomenon of doing poorly because you're doing well). This good/bad paradox shows up in a variety of ways. Looking at the long run, we see that the enormous increase in agricultural productivity over the past few centuries has reduced agriculture's importance in U.S. society and has forced many farmers off the farm. Looking at the short run, we see that when harvests are good, farmers often fare badly financially; when harvests are poor, farmers often do well financially. Let's consider these two cases in some detail.

The Long-Run Decline of Farming
Most countries, the United States included, began their existence as predominantly agricultural societies. When the United States was founded a little more than 200 years ago, 97 percent of the labor force was engaged in farming, but today less than 3 percent of the U.S. labor force works in agriculture.

The decline in the number of farmers isn't the result of the failure of U.S. agriculture. Rather, it's the result of its tremendous success—the enormous increase in its productivity. It used to take the majority of the population to provide food for the United States. Today it takes only a small proportion to produce more food than the U.S. population can consume.

Exhibit 1 shows how success can lead to problems. The long-run price elasticity of demand for wheat is inelastic (i.e., the percent change in quantity is small relative to the percent change in price) as it is for most agricultural products, so the exhibit shows an inelastic demand curve.

In this example, initially farmers are selling quantity Q_0 for price P_0. Their total income is P_0Q_0, shown by rectangles A and B. Now say that increases in productivity shift the supply curve out from S_0 to S_1. Output increases from Q_0 to

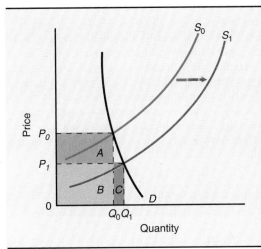

EXHIBIT 1 The Good/Bad Paradox

The good/bad paradox is demonstrated in this graph. At price P_0 the quantity of wheat produced is Q_0. Total income is P_0Q_0. But if the supply of wheat increases from S_0 to S_1 due to increased productivity, the price of wheat will fall from P_0 to P_1 and quantity demanded will increase from Q_0 to Q_1. The increase in farmers' income (area C) is small. The decrease in farmers' income (area A) is large. Overall, the increased productivity has led to a decrease in farmers' incomes.

Q_1 and price falls to P_1. Income falls to P_1Q_1, shown by the B and C rectangles. Farmers have gained the C rectangle but lost the A rectangle. The net effect is the difference in size between the two rectangles. So in this example the net effect is negative.

In short, productivity has increased but income has fallen and many farmers have stopped farming altogether. They've done good by producing a lot, but the result for them is bad. This good/bad paradox will occur whenever the supply curve shifts outward in the inelastic range of the demand curve.

Due to competition among farmers, most benefits of productivity increases in agriculture have gone to consumers, in the form of lower prices. As an example, consider chicken. In the early 1930s, when Herbert Hoover was president of the United States and running for reelection, he promised prosperity to the country by saying there would be "two chickens in every pot." That promise meant a lot because, in today's money, chicken would have cost $8 a pound. By 1992 the price of chicken had fallen to under $2 a pound, only about one-quarter of its price in 1930.

The Short-Run Cyclical Problem Facing Farmers

The long-run good/bad paradox for farmers is mirrored by a short-run good/bad paradox: Good harvests often mean bad times and a fall in income; poor harvests often mean a rise in income.

A fact of life that farmers must deal with is that agricultural production tends to be highly unstable because it depends on weather and luck. Crops can be affected by too little rain, too much rain, insects, frost, heat, wind, hail—none of which can be easily controlled. Say you're an apple grower and you're having a beautiful spring—until the week that your trees are blossoming, when it rains continually. Bees don't fly when it rains, so they don't pollinate your trees. No pollination, no apple crop. There goes your apple crop for this year.

The short-run demand for most agricultural goods is even more inelastic than the long-run demand. Because short-run demand is so inelastic, short-run changes in supply can have a significant effect on price. The result is that good harvests for farmers in general can lower prices significantly, while poor harvests can raise prices significantly. When the short-run price effect overwhelms the short-run quantity effect (as it does when demand is inelastic), farmers face the short-run good/bad paradox.

The Difficulty of Coordinating Farm Production

This good/bad paradox caused by inelastic demand isn't lost upon farmers. They, quite naturally, aren't wild about passing on the gains to consumers instead of keeping the gains themselves. However, because agriculture is competitive, it is not in any one farmer's interest to decrease his or her supply in order to avoid encountering the paradox. Com-

ADDED DIMENSION

THE COST OF A BOX OF
WHEATIES

When people think of agricultural products, they often think of the products they buy, like Wheaties. Doing so gives them the wrong impression of the cost of agricultural products. To see why, let's consider an 18-ounce box of Wheaties which costs you, say, $3.35. If you look at the ingredients, you'll see that you're buying sugar, salt, malt syrup, and corn syrup. So you're buying agricultural products, right? Well, a little bit. Actually, the total cost of those agricultural ingredients is probably somewhere around 25¢, less than one-tenth of the cost of the box of Wheaties. What are you spending the other nine-tenths on? Well, there's packaging, advertising, transporting the boxes, processing the ingredients, stocking the grocery store shelves, and profits. These are important components of Wheaties, but they aren't agricultural components.

The point of this example is simple. Much of our food expenditure isn't for agricultural goods; it's for the services that transform the agricultural goods into the processed foods, convince us we want to eat those foods, and get those foods to us.

petitive farmers take the market price as given. That's the definition of a competitive industry. While it is in the industry's interest to have a "bad year" (to reduce total supply), it is in each individual farmer's interest to have a good year (to increase output) even if the combination of *all* farmers having a good year would cause all farmers to have a bad year.

It is, however, in farmers' joint interest to figure out ways to have continually "bad" years—which are, of course, actually "good" years for them. In other words, it's in their interest to figure out ways to limit the production of all farmers.

In a competitive industry, limiting production is easier said than done. It is difficult for farmers to limit production privately, among themselves, because although they make up only a small percentage of the total U.S. population, there are still a lot of them—2 million. That's too many to coordinate easily.

A Way around the Good/Bad Paradox   The difficulty of organizing privately to limit supply can be avoided by organizing through government. The U.S. political structure provides an alternative way for farmers (and other suppliers) to coordinate their actions and limit supply. Suppliers can organize and get government to establish programs to limit production or hold price high, thereby avoiding the good/bad paradox. And that's what farmers have done, and that's why so many government agricultural programs exist today. Before we consider how these government farm programs work, let's briefly review their history.

HISTORY OF U.S.
FARM PROGRAMS

2

I'll begin the story in the early 1900s when, because of strong growth in U.S. income, there was an increased demand for U.S. farm products, which led to high and growing income for farmers. The eruption of World War I increased demand so much that the war years, 1914–18, are known as the golden age of American farming. The depression of 1920 ended that golden age. In 1921 the U.S. economy improved, but agriculture did not; it remained in a severe slump, marked by high production, low prices, and low farm income.

The reasons for this continued severe slump were various. Two important reasons were the postwar recovery of agricultural production in Europe (which decreased demand for U.S. farm products) and the high tariffs the U.S. government placed on imported manufactured goods during the 1920s (which increased farm costs).

During the war, the number of American farms increased significantly to meet the combined demand from European countries (whose production had fallen significantly as they devoted their resources to war) and from the United States itself (which was experiencing wartime economic boom). After the war, production remained high in the United States but demand fell as European agricultural production increased.

The impact of the low prices U.S. farmers received in the 1920s was intensified by high tariffs on imported manufactured goods. These tariffs squeezed the

THE CARTEL PROBLEM

When facing an inelastic demand, it's in the interest of producers as a whole to limit production, but it's in any one producer's individual interest to produce as much as it profitably can. This difference between what's in the interest of an individual producer and what's in the interest of the group of producers is called the *cartel problem*. Agriculture is simply one example of the cartel problem; there are many other examples, such as oil production and manufacturing.

Producers have several methods to deal with the cartel problem. These methods differ among industries. For example, in the United States, *trusts* (another name for cartels) were formed in manufacturing in which each firm was allocated market share. Production was held down by agreement. These trusts were hard to enforce. Eventually, to eliminate the enforcement problem, many of the firms merged, although the amount of merger activity was limited by the U.S. antitrust laws.

Even if a group of suppliers gain a domestic cartel, they can still face competition from abroad which can undermine the domestic cartel. To be effective, a cartel often must be an international cartel. Luckily for consumers, international cartel agreements are even more difficult to enforce than domestic cartel agreements. One reason many economists support free trade is the competitive pressure free trade creates for domestic producers. It places a limit on domestic cartels.

Profits aren't necessarily a good measure of a cartel's effectiveness. Often its costs will rise as workers and other factors share in the gains. That's what happened in the U.S. manufacturing industries. The firms formed cartels, which led to the formation of unions and the institution of government regulations, which pushed up costs. Thus, even though we don't see U.S. manufacturing firms earning enormous profits, that doesn't necessarily mean that they haven't, to a degree, limited production to raise price.

---

farmers in two ways. First, they increased the prices of goods farmers bought; and second, they further reduced demand for U.S. farm products. Unable to afford the high U.S. tariffs on their exports, the European countries, already financially weakened by the war, couldn't afford to import U.S. agricultural goods. The result of these developments was the good/bad paradox with a vengeance: low prices and high output with a tremendous fall in farm income.

The good/bad paradox is not a textbook concept. It has significant real-world effects. What it meant in the 1920s and 1930s was that a large number of U.S. farmers were going broke. They worked hard and got little or nothing in return. This was the time period captured in John Steinbeck's 1939 novel, *The Grapes of Wrath,* about an Oklahoma farm family forced to leave their land and migrate to California in a futile search for better conditions.

By 1929 the U.S. agricultural sector was extremely weak, but it was to become even weaker. The Great Depression that started in 1929 further devastated agricultural markets. These historical events led many to believe that competition didn't work and that the economic system used by the United States had to be changed. It was a bit like a title fight when one fighter is so bloodied and beaten that the referee steps in and stops the fight. That's what the government did; it said competition wasn't working the way society wanted it to work, and it stepped in to regulate that competition. The Great Depression marked the beginning of many of the U.S. agricultural programs that are still around today.

What would have happened without these programs is unclear. Farmers might have eventually been dominated by a few large **agrifirms** (firms that own huge farms and operate them like big corporations) which could have limited production and smoothed out price fluctuations. But as I said, achieving a private organization that limits production in agricultural markets is extraordinarily difficult. Thus, such a private "solution" to the good/bad paradox never occurred. Instead farmers used their political clout to induce the U.S. government to step in.

In 1929 the government created the Federal Farm Board, which was given a relatively large budget to stabilize and then support agricultural prices. The difference between stabilization and support is the following: To stabilize is to smooth out short-run fluctuations, but not to affect the long-run trend. To support is to try to affect the long-run trend.

Initially the Farm Board focused on stabilizing prices by buying agricultural products directly when the price was low and selling them directly when the price

The Beginnings of Government Agricultural Programs

Agrifirms Large firms that own huge farms and operate them like big corporations.

EXHIBIT 2 The Price of Corn from 1900 to 1990

If there had been no government intervention, the price of corn would have fluctuated around a downward trend as in this diagram.

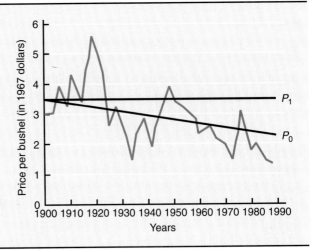

was high. That was done to smooth out price fluctuations. Then direct buying and selling programs were replaced by a variety of other measures designed not only to stabilize but also to support or raise prices above their long-run trend.

Let's assume that you've been hired as an economist for the Federal Farm Board. Your assignment is to determine a price at which the government should buy and sell corn so as to stabilize the market by minimizing future fluctuations in its price at the lowest net cost to the government.

The jagged line in Exhibit 2 is a hypothetical line showing what the price of corn would have been from 1900 to 1990 had there been no stabilization program. It illustrates the price pattern of most agricultural goods. Two aspects of this exhibit are easily recognizable. First, the long-run trend in prices is downward. Second, there are significant short-run fluctuations around that trend.

What price would you choose? Since your object is to stabilize price at the lowest cost to the government, you should choose a price on the P_0 line, which reflects the downward trend of prices. Setting the price at that trend price, you'd expect to buy corn whenever the price falls below the trend line, stopping price from falling further and pushing the price up toward the trend line. If the price of corn rose above the trend line, you'd sell the corn you had bought. A perfect stabilization program would eliminate all price fluctuations, other than the general downward trend of prices.

If you've set the price on the trend line P_0, it's reasonable to expect that the surpluses will roughly equal the shortages. If the government chooses a stabilization price above the trend line, on average, government will accumulate surpluses; if it chooses a price below the trend line, on average, it will have shortages and will have to buy corn from abroad to meet the demand.

So if the government's goal is to minimize fluctuations in price at the lowest possible cost, it should choose a continually decreasing price that builds in the expectations of (1) increases in productivity and (2) a continually falling long-run price. That's what a **price stabilization program** is: a program designed to eliminate short-run fluctuations in prices but to allow prices to follow their long-term trend line.

Farmers aren't against such price stabilization programs. However they're generally more interested in another type of program: a **price support program.** A price support program is one that maintains prices at a level higher than the trend of prices. If price support is your goal, you won't choose a price on trend line P_0; you'll choose a price above it on a price line such as P_1. In a price support system, surpluses and shortages don't net out. Instead when the price trend is downward,

Stabilization and Support for Agricultural Prices

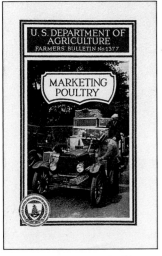

Marketing Poultry—This 1936 Department of Agriculture publication is representative of the major role government has played in agriculture.

Price stabilization program Program designed to eliminate short-run fluctuations in prices but allow prices to follow their long-term trend line.

Price support program Program that maintains prices at a level higher than the trend of prices.

the program generates continual surpluses, which the government must figure out how to manage.

Government programs have been both stabilization and support programs. That is, they've been designed not only to minimize fluctuations in prices, but also to increase income for farmers. Farmers have come to rely on these programs to help them avoid the problems caused by the good/bad paradox.

The Choice of a Parity Price   At the center of the government's price support system has been the idea of a *parity price* that farmers should receive. A **parity price** of, say, corn, is a price of corn that keeps farmers as well off relatively as they were in a specified base year (1912). If farmers received the parity price for corn, the ratio of the prices received by farmers for that corn and prices paid by farmers would always be the same as it was in 1912. For example, say the 1912 price of corn was $3 a bushel and the price paid by farmers for a composite of manufactured goods was $4. If the price of manufactured goods rises to $6 (a rise of 50 percent), the parity price of corn also rises by 50 percent—to $4.50 in this hypothetical example.

> **Parity price** Price that maintains the ratio of prices received and paid by farmers to a base year.

Parity was justified by relatively simple arguments. Farmers argued that if they could exchange a bushel of corn for a shirt in 1912, they should also be able to exchange a bushel of corn for a shirt in 1933. If price parity is maintained, the relative prices of agricultural goods (and hence farmers' relative income) cannot fall. If price parity is maintained, the trend line of agricultural prices will be flat, not downward sloping.

The argument that farmers deserve price parity sounds logical on the surface, but it's flawed for two reasons. It doesn't allow for normal fluctuations in price and it doesn't explain why the base year should be 1912. Why not use 1933 as the base year?

To understand why 1912 was chosen, one must recognize that U.S. government agricultural programs were designed to increase farmers' income—to support as well as stabilize prices. Choosing as the parity level the price ratio that existed during the golden age of agriculture, 1910–14, when relative agricultural prices were at their peacetime, post-1900 high, conveyed a sense that any lower price was unfair. Parity sounds good. Who would be against giving the farmers parity? Had it been called a price support system, the program would have been harder to sell politically.

Not only was a high parity price chosen, but also no downward trend was automatically built into the parity price system. The initial parity price was to be consistently maintained. If it had been maintained, increases in productivity that have occurred over time would have made the programs more and more into support programs, with government subsidies to farmers increasing each year. However the initial parity price has not been maintained. Instead it has become simply a reference price; the actual support price is defined as a percentage or ratio of parity: the **parity ratio** is

> **Parity ratio** Prices received by farmers divided by prices paid by farmers.

$$\text{Parity ratio} = \frac{\text{Index of prices received by farmers}}{\text{Index of prices paid by farmers}}.$$

Exhibit 3 shows the prices farmers paid compared to the prices that farmers received from 1910 to 1990. As you can see, the prices farmers pay has increased more than the prices farmers receive. Dividing the prices received by the prices paid by farmers gives us the actual parity ratio which can be compared to the 100 percent parity ratio that would have existed if parity had been maintained. As you can see, in the early 1990s the actual parity ratio was about 60 percent, which means that farmers received only about 60 percent of parity price.

How high the support price has been held (which parity ratio has been guaranteed) has depended on the political power of farmers. To increase their political power thay have organized a **farm lobby** (an organization of farmers

> **Farm lobby** Organization formed to further political goals that will benefit farmers.

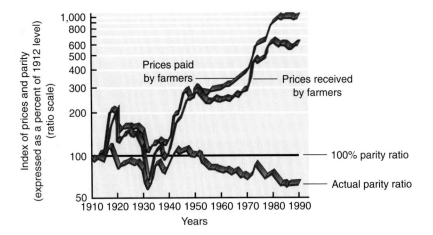

EXHIBIT 3 Parity Price Compared to Actual Price, 1910–1990

The graph shows the actual parity price farmers received from 1910 to 1990 compared to the 100 percent parity price. Parity is a ratio of the prices farmers received to the prices paid by farmers.
Source: U.S. Dept. of Agriculture, and *Business Statistics*, June 1992.

whose purpose is to further political goals that will benefit farmers). Although the farm lobby has not been politically strong enough to achieve full parity with the golden age, it has been able to hold the price farmers get above what the average competitive market price would otherwise have been.

How do we know that this has been the case? We know because surpluses have consistently exceeded shortages. Had the government maintained prices at the average competitive price, the surpluses would be sold in time of shortage. Expressing the support price in terms of a high parity price serves a political purpose. The price support program could always be presented to the public as a limited program, going only part way to parity.

Politics and Parity   If farmers are helped by farm programs, who is hurt? The answer is taxpayers and consumers. One would expect that these broad groups would strongly oppose farm programs because farm programs cost them in two ways: (1) higher taxes that government requires in order to buy up surplus farm output and (2) higher prices for food. It's not easy for a politician to tell her nonfarm constituents, "I'm supporting a bill that means higher prices and higher taxes for you." Nevertheless the farm lobby has been quite successful in seeing that these programs are retained.

Economists who specialize in the relationship between economics and politics (known as *public choice economists*) have suggested that the reasons for farm groups' success involve the nature of the benefits and costs. The groups that are hurt by agricultural subsidies are large, but the negative effect on each individual in that group is relatively small. Large groups that experience small costs per individual don't provide a strong political opposition to a small group that experiences large gains. This seems to reflect a **general rule of political economy** in a democracy:

> When small groups are helped by a government action and large groups are hurt by that same action, the small group tends to lobby far more effectively than the large group. Thus, policies tend to reflect the small group's interest, not the interest of the large group.

General rule of political economy
Small groups that are significantly hurt by a policy lobby more effectively than large groups that are helped by that same policy.

3

This bias in favor of farm programs is strengthened by the historical representation of farmers in Congress. Right from its beginnings in 1787, the U.S. political system has reflected the importance of agriculture. The Constitution gives representation in the Senate equally to all states. Only representation in the House of Representatives is based on a state's population. Since farm states have smaller populations than urban states, this arrangement gives farmers relatively more political power per capita than nonfarmers.

Farmers' strong political representation in Congress establishes a core of lawmakers who favor price supports. That core, combined with the lack of political organization of large groups (consumers and taxpayers), has made it possible for the farm lobby to put together enough votes to maintain farm price support programs. When political pressure does become intense, a bit of obfuscation[1] can be used to get a bill passed. For example, what if, instead of a price support system, one introduced a loan program? Who could oppose making loans to hard-pressed farmers? That's what happened in the early 1930s, when a number of farm loan programs were enacted by Congress.

One group that could and did oppose such a loan program was the Supreme Court. In 1936 the Supreme Court overturned a set of policies that had been established to assist farmers with money raised through taxes on processors of farm commodities. In response Congress quickly passed some slightly different legislation which got around the constitutional problems the Court had described in its 1936 decision. The revised legislation helped farmers, using general revenues rather than new tax revenues, and also established a farm credit program designed to provide low-interest mortgages and loans to farmers.

How a Loan Program Became a Price Support Program   To implement this loan program, the government created the Commodity Credit Corporation (CCC), which had the authority to make loans to farmers using their crops as collateral at, say, $6 per bushel of corn, with $6 being the support price for corn chosen by government. The loans were nonrecourse loans, which meant that if the farmer defaulted, the CCC got the grain and nothing else. It had no recourse—no other way to collect on the loan. It couldn't seize the farm itself, for example. Such nonrecourse loans aren't really loans at all, but are price support payments in disguise. Say, for example, that the government support price for corn was $6 and the market price of corn was $5. No farmer would sell at the market price. Instead farmers would borrow against all of their crop. When the harvest came in, they would default on their loans and forfeit their crops. The lender (in this case the CCC) would in effect become the sole purchaser of corn.

After buying all the corn, the CCC would then sell as much as it could at the market-determined price of $5 and put the excess in storage. In that way the CCC loan program actually worked as a pure price support system with the government holding the surpluses. During the early 1930s the U.S. government bought substantial amounts of crops through the CCC, but when World War II began in Europe in the late 1930s, U.S. farm prices rose above the partial support level set by Congress and the surpluses disappeared.

James Buchanan—Nobel prize, 1986, for work in public choice theory. © *The Nobel Foundation.*

Once the market price went above the parity support level, the CCC could sell all of its surpluses at a profit. Farmers would then sell their crops on the open market rather than deliberately defaulting on loans from the CCC. As you can see in Exhibit 3, World War II brought farmers a prosperity that continued in the years immediately after the war. An important reason for that postwar prosperity was that instead of instituting large tariffs on manufactured goods following the war, the United States embarked upon the Marshall Plan, a system of making large loans to European countries that allowed them, among other things, to continue to buy U.S. agricultural products. Increased exports, combined with the low interest rates of the time, were a boon to U.S. farmers, who continued to do well during the Korean War in the early 1950s.

The superprosperity for farmers ended in the mid-1950s as the Korean War, which had begun in 1950, ended and the U.S. economy slowed down. Once again the parity price support levels were reached. Surpluses began building, and although the price support levels were lowered slightly in 1954, by the end of the 1950s the United States was spending almost $40 billion a year (in 1990 dollars) to purchase surplus grain.

President John F. Kennedy increased farm support prices when he took office in 1961. This would have substantially increased the amount of surplus had the

---

[1] *Obfuscation* is a wonderful word meaning "to make obscure, or to confuse." It comes to us from the Latin word for "to darken."

government not established other programs to take land out of production through a set of *acreage control programs,* sometimes called *land bank programs.* In a land bank program, a farmer who agrees not to produce receives payments from the government.

The 1970s were good times for U.S. farmers. With land prices rising significantly and food prices high, many farmers expanded, financing that expansion by borrowing, using their land as collateral. The good times ended in the late 1970s and early 1980s as interest rates rose substantially, while land and food prices fell. Once again there was a strong push on government to help the farmer. And once again the government came through, although the huge federal budget deficit kept it from being quite as generous as in the past. In the early 1990s farm prices had recovered from the mid-1980s slump, and the cost of the government farm programs was reduced.

The combination of acreage reduction and price support systems has continued through today, although the level of support depends on what political pressures are being applied at a particular time.

HOW A PRICE SUPPORT SYSTEM WORKS IN THEORY

Now that we've briefly reviewed the history of the U.S. government support system for agricultural prices, let's consider more carefully the theory underlying some alternative farm price support options. In doing so, we'll try to understand which options, given the political realities, would have the best chance of being implemented, and why.

Four Price Support Options

In a price support system the government maintains a higher than equilibrium price, as diagrammed in Exhibit 4. At support price P_1, the quantity people want to supply is Q_S, but the quantity demanded at that price is Q_D.

At price P_1 there's excess supply, which exerts a downward pressure on price (arrow *A*). To maintain price at P_1, some other force (arrow *B*) must be exerted; otherwise the invisible hand will force the price down.

4   The government has various options to offset that downward pressure on price:

1. Using legal and regulatory force to prevent anyone from selling or buying at a lower price.
2. Providing economic incentives to reduce the supply enough to eliminate the downward pressure on price.
3. Subsidizing the sale of the good to consumers so that while suppliers get a high price, demanders have to pay only a low price.
4. Buying up and storing, or giving away, or destroying enough of the good so that the total demand (including government's demand) increases enough to eliminate downward pressure on price.

Each of these methods distributes the costs and benefits in a slightly different way. Let's consider each method in detail.

Supporting the Price by Regulatory Measures   Suppose the government simply passes a law saying that from now on the price of wheat will be at least $5 per bushel. No one may sell wheat at a lower price. If the competitive equilibrium price is higher than $5, the law has no effect. When the competitive equilibrium is below the price floor (say, $3.50 per bushel), the law limits suppliers from selling their wheat at that lower price.

The price floor helps some suppliers and hurts others. Those suppliers who are lucky enough to sell their wheat benefit. Those suppliers who aren't lucky and can't find buyers for their wheat are hurt. How many suppliers will be helped and how many will be hurt depends on the elasticities of supply and demand. When supply and demand are inelastic, a large change in price brings about a small change in quantity supplied, so the hurt group is relatively small. When the supply and demand are elastic, the hurt group is large.

EXHIBIT 4   A Price Support System

In a price support system, the government maintains a higher-than-equilibrium price. At support price, P_1, the quantity of product demanded is only Q_D, while the quantity supplied is Q_S. This causes downward pressures on the price, P_1, which must be offset by various government measures.

In Exhibit 5(a) suppliers would like to sell quantity Q_2 but, by law, they can supply only Q_1. They end up with a surplus of wheat, $Q_2 - Q_1$. Demanders, who must pay the higher price, \$5, and receive only Q_1 rather than Q_e, are hurt.

The law may or may not specify who will, and who will not, be allowed to sell, but it must establish some noneconomic method of rationing the limited demand among the suppliers. If it doesn't, buyers are likely, for example, to buy from farmers who are their friends. If individual farmers have a surplus, they'll probably try to dispose of that surplus by selling it on the black market at a price below the legal price. To maintain the support price, the government will have to arrest farmers who sell below the legal price. If the number of producers is large, such a regulatory approach is likely to break down quickly, since individual incentives to sell illegally are great and the costs of enforcing the law are accordingly high.

In understanding who benefits and who's hurt by price floors, it's important to distinguish two groups of farmers: the farmers who had been producing before the law went into effect and the farmers who entered the market afterward. In Exhibit 5(a) the first group supplies Q_e; the second group, which would want to enter the market when the price went up, would supply $Q_2 - Q_e$. Why must the second group be clearly identified? Because one relatively easily enforceable way to limit the quantity supplied is to forbid any new farmers to enter the market. Only people who were producing at the beginning of the support program will be allowed to produce, and they will be allowed to produce only as much as they did before the program went into effect. Restricting production will reduce the quantity supplied to Q_e, leaving only $Q_e - Q_1$ to be rationed among suppliers. This method of restriction, which is said to **grandfather in** existing suppliers, is one of the easiest to enforce and thus one of the most widely used. For example, when supply limitations were placed on tobacco, existing growers were all allowed to grow tobacco on land they were currently using for tobacco production. They could not, however, devote any new land to growing tobacco. (Later the acreage allocations were allowed to be transferred, at a price of course, so that if old land were taken out of tobacco production, new land could be added.)

When it comes to grandfathering groups *out* of production, foreign producers are perhaps the politically easiest targets. To keep the domestic price of a good up, foreign imports must be limited as well as domestic production. U.S. taxpayers might put up with subsidizing U.S. farmers, but they're likely to balk at subsidizing foreign farmers. So most farm subsidy programs are supplemented with tariffs and quotas on foreign imports of the same commodity.

Notice that with an inelastic demand, even though the average farmer is constrained as to how much can be sold, he or she is made better off by that constraint because the total revenue going to all farmers is higher than it would be if supply weren't constrained. The farmer's total revenue increases by rectangle A

Grandfather in To pass a law affecting a specific group but providing that those in the group before the law was passed are not subject to the law.

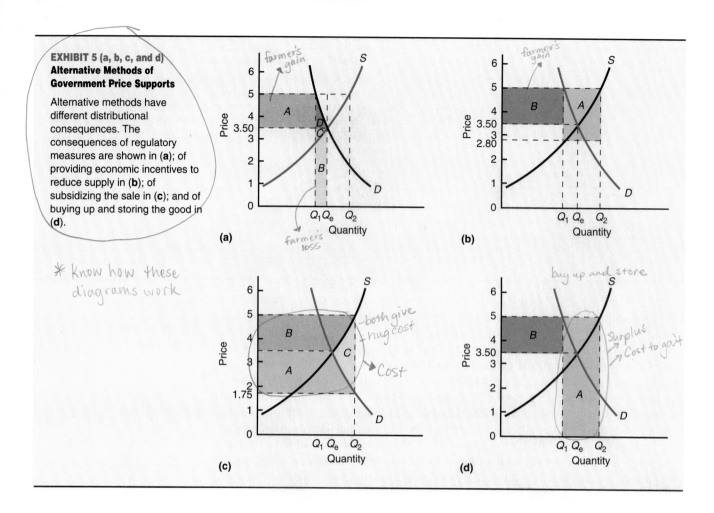

EXHIBIT 5 (a, b, c, and d)
Alternative Methods of Government Price Supports

Alternative methods have different distributional consequences. The consequences of regulatory measures are shown in (a); of providing economic incentives to reduce supply in (b); of subsidizing the sale in (c); and of buying up and storing the good in (d).

✳ know how these diagrams work

in Exhibit 5(a) and decreases by the rectangle composed of the combined areas B and C. Of course, making the farmer better off is not cost-free. Consumers are made worse off because they must pay more for a smaller supply of wheat. There's no direct cost to taxpayers other than the cost of enforcing and administering the regulations.

Notice in the diagram the little triangle made up of areas C and D, which shows an amount of income that society loses but farmers don't get. It's simply wasted. That little triangle is a net loss to society from the restriction. It's called an **excess burden,** and it results whenever the market is prevented from operating freely.

Providing Economic Incentives to Reduce Supply   A second way in which government can keep a price high is to provide farmers with economic incentives to reduce supply.

Looking at Exhibit 5(b), you see that at the support price, $5 per bushel, the quantity of wheat supplied is Q_2 and quantity demanded is Q_1. To avoid a surplus the government must somehow find a way to shift the quantity supplied back from Q_2 to Q_1. For example, it could pay farmers not to grow wheat, as it did in the land bank program. How much would such an economic incentive cost? To reduce the quantity supplied to Q_1, the government would have to pay farmers $2.20 ($5.00 − $2.80) for each bushel of wheat they didn't grow. This amount is shown by the A rectangle.

There is, however, a problem in identifying those individuals who would truly supply wheat at $5 a bushel. Knowing that the government is paying people not to grow wheat, people who otherwise had no interest in growing wheat will pretend that at $5 they would supply the wheat, simply to get the subsidy. To avoid this problem, often this incentive approach is combined with our first option, reg-

Excess burden Loss caused to society when a policy results in society losing income but suppliers failing to get that income.

ulatory restrictions. Farmers who are already producing wheat at Q_e are grand-fathered in; only they are given economic incentives not to produce. All others are forbidden to produce.

When economic incentives are supplied, the existing farmers do very well for themselves. Their income goes up for two reasons. They get the A rectangle from the government in the form of payments not to grow wheat, and they get the B rectangle from consumers in the form of higher prices for the wheat they do grow. Farmers are also free to use their land for other purposes, so their income rises by the amount they can earn from using the land taken out of wheat production for something other than growing wheat. Consumers are still being hurt as before: They are paying a higher price and getting less. In addition, they're being hurt in their role as taxpayers because the lightly shaded area (rectangle A) represents the taxes they must pay to finance the government's economic incentive program. Thus, this option is much more costly to taxpayers than the regulatory option.

Subsidizing the Sale of the Good   A third option is for the government to subsidize the sale of the good in order to hold down the price consumers pay but keep the amount suppliers receive high. Exhibit 5(c) shows how this works. Suppliers supply quantity Q_2 and are paid $5 per bushel. The government then turns around and sells that quantity at whatever price it can get—in this case, $1.75. No direct transfer takes place from the consumer to the supplier. Both are made better off. Demanders get more goods at a lower price. They are benefited by area A. Suppliers get a higher price and can supply all they want. They are benefited by area B. What's the catch? The catch, of course, is that taxpayers foot the entire bill, paying the difference between the $5 and the $1.75 ($3.25) for each bushel sold. The cost to taxpayers is represented by areas A, B, and C. This option costs taxpayers the most of any of the four options.

Buying Up and Storing, Giving Away, or Destroying the Good   The final option is for the government to buy up all the supply that demanders don't buy at the support price. This option is shown in Exhibit 5(d). Consumers buy Q_1 at price $5; the government buys $Q_2 - Q_1$ at price $5, paying the A rectangle. In this case consumers transfer the B rectangle to suppliers when they pay $5 rather than $3.50, the competitive equilibrium price. The government (i.e., the taxpayers) pays farmers rectangle A. The situation is very similar to our second option, in which the government provides suppliers with economic incentives not to produce. However it's more expensive since the government must pay $5 per bushel rather than paying farmers $2.20 per bushel. In return for this higher payment, the government is getting something in return: $Q_2 - Q_1$ of wheat.

Of course, if the government buys the surplus wheat, it takes on the problem of what to do with this surplus. Say the government decides to give it to the poor. Since the poor were already buying food, in response to a free food program they will replace some of their purchases with the free food. This replacement brings about a drop in demand—which means that the government must buy even more surplus. Instead of giving it away, though, the government can burn the surplus or store it indefinitely in warehouses and grain elevators. Burning up the surplus or storing it, at least, doesn't increase the amount government must buy.

Why, you ask, doesn't the government give the surplus to foreign countries as a type of humanitarian aid? The reason is that just as giving the surplus to our own poor creates problems in the United States, giving the surplus to the foreign poor creates problems in the countries involved. To the degree that the foreign poor have any income, they're likely to spend most of it on food. Free food would supplant some of their demand, thus lowering the price for those who previously sold food to them. Giving anything away destroys somebody's market, and when markets are destroyed someone gets upset. So when the United States has tried to give away its surplus food, other foreign countries have put enormous pressure on the United States not to "spoil the world market."

Politics, Economics, and Price Supports

The four price support options I've just described can, of course, be used in various combinations. It's a useful exercise at this point to think through which of the options farmers, taxpayers, and consumers would likely favor and to relate the history of the farm programs to these options.

Which Group Prefers Which Option?   The first option, regulation, costs the government the least, but it benefits farmers the least. Since existing farmers are likely to be the group directly pushing for price supports, government is least likely to choose this approach. If it is chosen, most of the reduction in quantity supplied will probably be required to come from people who might enter farming at some time in the future, not from existing farmers.

The second option, economic incentives, costs the government more than the first option but less than the third and fourth options. Farmers are benefited by economic incentive programs in two ways. They get paid not to grow a certain crop, and they can sometimes get additional income from using the land for other purposes. When farmers aren't allowed to use their land for other purposes, they usually oppose this option, preferring the third or fourth option.

The third option, subsidies on sales to keep prices down, benefits both consumers (who get low prices) and farmers (who get high prices). Taxpayers are harmed the most by this option. They must finance the subsidy payments for all subsidized farm products.

The last option, buying up and storing or destroying the goods, costs taxpayers more than the first two options but less than the third, since consumers pay part of the cost. However it leaves the government with a surplus to deal with. If there's a group who can take that surplus without significantly reducing their current demand, then that group is likely to support this option.

As I discussed in the historical section, the two prevalent farm programs in the United States are (1) the land bank program (in which government supports prices by giving farmers economic incentives to reduce supply) and (2) the nonrecourse loan program (in which government ''buys'' goods in the form of collateral on defaulting loans). Programs that support prices through regulation, our first option, generally haven't been applied to existing farmers. They have often, however, been used to prevent new farmers from entering the market—which isn't surprising since the political impetus for farm programs comes from existing farmers.

The third option, to subsidize the sale of the good, so the farmer gets a high price and the consumer pays a low price, hasn't been used because it would be the most costly to taxpayers. Rather than costing $10 billion or $20 billion a year, as they do now, farm programs involving direct subsidies would likely cost $60 billion to $100 billion a year. In contrast, economic incentive and government purchase programs hide the true costs of price supports better. However direct subsidies are used in a number of developing countries where governments are under strong and conflicting political pressures from both consumers and farmers. Often the subsidies are financed by budget deficits, not taxes, so the taxpayers aren't directly confronted with the bill. (But since there's no such thing as a free lunch, they'll face the bill later when they must pay the interest on the debt.)

Economics, Politics, and Real-World Policies   The actual political debate is, of course, much more complicated than presented here. For example, other pressure groups are involved. Recently farm groups and environmental groups have combined forces and have become more effective in shaping and supporting farm policy. Thus, in the 1990s restrictions on supply in farming are likely to operate in ways that environmentalists would like, such as regulating the types of fertilizer and chemicals farmers can use.

Moreover the three interest groups discussed here—farmers, taxpayers, and consumers—aren't entirely distinct one from another. Their memberships over-

The midwest of the North American continent has some of the best farmland in the world. © *John Eastcott/YVA Momatiuk/The Image Works.*

lap. All taxpayers are also consumers; farmers are both taxpayers and consumers; and so on. Thus, much of the political debate is simply about from whose pocket the government is going to get money to help farmers. Shall it be the consumer's pocket (through higher prices)? Or the taxpayer's (through higher taxes)? That said, the political reality is that consumer and taxpayer interests and the lobbying groups that represent them generally examine only part of the picture—the part that directly affects them. Accordingly politicians often act as if these groups had separate memberships. Politicians weigh the options by attempting to balance their view of the general good with the power and preferences of the special interest groups that they represent or that contribute to their election campaigns.

The final real-world complication that must be taken into account in the 1990s is the international dimension. If you think government is significantly involved in U.S. agriculture, you should see its role in other countries such as the members of the European Common Market and Japan. Our agricultural policy is in part determined by trade negotiations with these other countries. For example, the U.S. government could subsidize U.S. agriculture to keep U.S. agricultural products competitive with the heavily subsidized EEC production. A reduction in EEC subsidies could bring about a reduction in our subsidies.

AN ASSESSMENT OF FARM PRICE SUPPORT PROGRAMS

This chapter's overview of government price support programs and their effects on farmers, consumers, and taxpayers should have given you a sense that for society as a whole the competitive solution would be a much better option than any of the other four approaches that we've discussed. Society would probably be better off, on average, if all the government farm programs were eliminated and replaced with a free market in agricultural goods. There would likely be much larger fluctuations in agricultural prices than there currently are, but the average price paid by consumers and the cost to taxpayers would both be lower.

But given the realities of the agricultural markets, it's unlikely that the competitive solution is a practical one. The inelastic demand for, and the fluctuating supply of, most agricultural goods create enormous pressure for cartelization of the various agricultural markets. In the absence of government programs, it's likely that the pressure would rise for the formation of private cartels—organizations of suppliers whose purpose is to limit supply—to stabilize and support agricultural prices. Had the government support programs not been established, agricultural production in the United States might today be controlled by four or five major firms which could limit supply even more than now. Agricultural prices might be higher and agricultural production lower than they currently are.

Had such private cartelization occurred, these firms would have initially made large profits, as did many of the first large manufacturing companies. The response to such profits would also likely have been similar. Agricultural workers would have organized and demanded safer working conditions and limited hours. They would have established pension systems similar to those that workers in manufacturing industries obtained. That would have significantly increased the costs of agricultural goods. The result might have been lower production and higher prices than we currently have.

To see the differences in the nature of production under our current system of private production and government support programs and under a system of private cartelization of agriculture, let's consider the question of industrial safety. To put the matter bluntly, one reason why U.S. farms are so productive is that farmers work extremely hard and skimp a lot on safety measures. Competition drives farmers to be productive, but it also kills and maims them. The accidental death rate for farmers is almost 50 per 100,000 per year. That's almost twice the death rate in mining (often considered the most dangerous occupation) and five times the national average. In a three-week period in 1989 the following accidents happened:

- A man in Kempton, Indiana, was strangled when his clothes got caught in a corn picker.
- A man in Ventura, Iowa, was buried and suffocated by corn sliding into the center of the steel bin where he was working.
- A woman in Litchfield, Minnesota, was seriously injured when her clothing was caught in the machinery of a harvesting combine.
- A man in Columbus, Nebraska, was crushed by cattle in his farmyard.
- A child suffocated in a corn wagon in Boemer, Nebraska.

If those accidents had happened in any other industry, there would be demands for government intervention and new safety regulations. But not in farming. It wasn't Big Business that was responsible; it was individual farmers making their own decisions. Under a cartelized system, Big Business *would* be held responsible, and there would be a clamor for government-imposed regulations. Such requirements would significantly increase costs and decrease productivity.

Arguments like the one I am making are always tenuous because no one can say for sure what the farm industry would have been like if government programs had never existed. For example, it's possible that, even if there had been large-scale cartelization in agriculture, international competition would have forced that domestic cartel to be competitive.

Because it's unclear what the correct hypothetical comparison is, one must be extremely careful in arguing that our present system is preferable to some hypothetical alternative, just as one must be careful to argue that perfect competition would be preferable to the present situation.

Many economists speak rather harshly about our current government agricultural programs, comparing their waste and inefficiency with the operation of a perfectly competitive market. That comparison is problematic. An alternative to current U.S. farm programs might have been, not perfect competition, but the cartelization of the entire farming industry, resulting in higher prices, lower production, and less efficiency than the existing level.

Thus, while, ideally, perfect competition would be best for our society, policymakers must recognize the reality that competition isn't always the relevant alternative, given the nature of politics and the market. Relevant policy choices must be made between the two most likely alternatives, not between a tidy ideal and a messy reality. Which is the better situation? As usual, there's no easy answer.

This chapter has focused on agricultural markets, but it should be clear that the discussion is about much more than just agriculture; it's about the interrelationship between economics and politics. If individuals are self-interested maximizers, it's reasonable to assume that they're maximizers in all aspects of their lives. What they can't achieve in the economic sphere, they might be able to achieve in the political sphere.

To understand the economic policies that exist, one must consider how people act in both spheres. Considering the economics underlying government policies often leads to useful insights. For example, a military draft can be seen as a mechanism for focusing the costs of defense away from the taxpayer and onto a specific group of individuals—young men. The government's support for the arts can be seen as a transfer from general taxpayers to a specific group of individuals who like the arts. Government support for education can be seen as a transfer from general taxpayers to a specific group of individuals: students and instructors. These groups maintain strong lobbies to achieve their political ends, and the interaction of the various lobbying groups typically strongly influences what policies government will follow.

Economics doesn't tell you whether government intervention or any particular policy is good or bad. That, you must decide for yourself. But what economics can do is pose the policy question in terms of gains and losses for particular groups. Posing the question in that framework often cuts through to the real reasons behind various groups' support for this or that policy. Farmers aren't going to tell you that they support agricultural programs because those programs transfer money from taxpayers and consumers to farmers. Similarly, academics generally aren't going to tell you that the reason they favor government support for education is that those policies transfer money to them.

The economic framework directs you to look beyond the reasons people say they support policies. The economic framework directs you to look for the self-interest. The supply/demand framework provides a neat graphical way to picture the relative gains and losses resulting from various policies, which is why the supply/demand framework is such a powerful tool, even when few industries are actually perfectly competitive.

But as usual there's an *on the other hand.* Just because some groups may support policies for self-serving reasons it is not necessarily the case that the policies are bad, or shouldn't be adopted. Reality is complicated with many more gray answers than black-and-white ones.

KEY POINTS

- Because most agricultural markets have an inelastic demand, they produce a good/bad paradox for farmers. **1**
- The history of the U.S. farm program is one of government intervention to keep prices higher than they otherwise might have been. **2**
- U.S. agriculture is enormously productive and efficient. **2**
- A general rule of political economy in a democracy is that policies tend to reflect small groups' interests, not the interests of large groups. **3**
- Farm price support options are regulations, economic incentives, subsidies, and buying up and storing or destroying. **4**
- In judging a policy, the appropriate comparison is often the counterfactual. What would have happened if that policy had not been introduced? **5**
- Reality is complicated, with many more gray answers than black-and-white ones. **5**

KEY TERMS

agrifirms *(587)*
excess burden *(594)*
farm lobby *(589)*

general rule of political
  economy *(590)*
good/bad paradox *(584)*

grandfather in *(593)*
parity price *(589)*
parity ratio *(589)*

price stabilization
  program *(588)*
price support
  program *(588)*

QUESTIONS FOR THOUGHT AND REVIEW

*The number after each question represents the estimated
degree of critical thinking required. (1 = almost none;
10 = deep thought.)*

1. If the demand for farm products were elastic rather
   than inelastic, would the good/bad paradox still exist?
   Why or why not? *(5)*
2. Demonstrate, using supply and demand curves, the
   distributional consequences of a price support system
   achieved through acreage restriction. *(4)*
3. Which would a taxpayers' group prefer: price support
   achieved through buying up the surplus, or through
   providing economic incentives for not producing?
   Why? *(5)*
4. Say a city is establishing rent controls requiring rents
   to be set below market rents. What alternative methods could it use to ration apartments? *(8)*

5. What's the most costly method of price support to the
   taxpayer? Demonstrate graphically. *(4)*
6. What is the least costly method of price support to the
   taxpayer? Demonstrate graphically. *(4)*
7. Why do tariffs and quotas generally accompany price
   support systems? *(5)*
8. How does the elasticity of supply affect the cost of
   price supports in each of the four options? *(6)*
9. Does the comparatively high accidental death rate for
   farmers say anything about the efficiency of U.S. regulation? If so, what? *(7)*
10. All government intervention in markets makes society
    worse off. True or false? Evaluate. *(8)*

PROBLEMS AND EXERCISES

1. Show graphically how the effects of an increase in supply will differ according to the elasticities of supply and
   demand.
   a. Specifically demonstrate the following combinations:
      1. An inelastic supply and an elastic demand.
      2. An elastic supply and an inelastic demand.
      3. An elastic supply and an elastic demand.
      4. An inelastic supply and an inelastic demand.
   b. Demonstrate the effect of a government guarantee of
      the price in each of the four cases.
   c. If you were a farmer, which of the four combina-
      tions would you prefer?
2. Congratulations. You've been appointed finance minister of Farmingland. The president wants to protect her
   political popularity by increasing farmers' incomes.
   She's considering two alternatives: (a) to bolster agricultural prices by adding government demand to private
   demand and (b) to give farmers financial incentives to
   restrict supply and thereby increase price. She wants to
   use the measure that's least costly to the government.

The conditions of supply and demand are illustrated in
the accompanying diagram. (S_1 is what the restricted
supply curve would look like. P_s is the price that the
president wants to establish.) Which measure would
you advise?

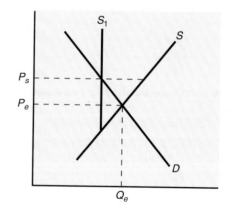

29

Microeconomics,
Social Policy,
and Economic Reasoning

*If an economist becomes certain of
the solution of any problem, he can be equally certain that his
solution is wrong.*

H. A. Innis

After reading this chapter, you should be able to:

1

List three reasons why economists
sometimes differ in their views on
social policy.

2

Explain why liberal and conservative
economists often agree in their views on
social policy.

3

Define cost/benefit analysis.

4

Explain the typical economist's view of
many regulations.

5

State why economists disagree about
whether the minimum wage should be
raised.

6

Explain why teaching a parrot the phrase
supply and demand will not make an
economist.

One of the important jobs that economists do is to give advice to politicians and other policymakers on a variety of questions relating to social policy: How should unemployment be dealt with? How can society distribute income fairly? Should the government redistribute income? Would a program of equal pay for jobs of comparable worth (a pay equity program) make economic sense? Should the minimum wage be increased?

Economists differ substantially in their views on these and other social policy questions. As one pundit remarked, ''If you laid all economists end to end, they still wouldn't reach a conclusion.'' Such comments have a superficial truth to them, but they also are misleading. Economists agree on many issues, and the reasons they disagree often have little to do with economics.

Understanding what economists agree and disagree about, and why, is an important part of understanding economics. Thus, this chapter considers some areas of agreement and disagreement among economists. This analysis will give you a good sense of economic reasoning as it's used in formulating social policy.

ECONOMISTS' DIFFERING VIEWS ABOUT SOCIAL POLICY

■

Economists have many different views on social policy because:

1. Economists' suggestions for social policy are determined by their subjective value judgments (normative views) as well as by their objective economic analyses.

2. Policy proposals must be based on imprecise empirical evidence, so there's considerable room for differences of interpretation not only about economic issues, but also about how political and social institutions work. Economic policy is an art, not a science.

3. Policy proposals are based on various models which focus on different aspects of a problem.

The first and third reasons directly concern the role of ideology in economics, a controversial subject among economists. However, all economists agree that any policy proposal must embody both economic analysis *and* value judgments because the goals of policy reflect value judgments. When an economist makes a policy proposal, it's of this type: ''If A, B, and C are your goals, then you should undertake policies D, E, and F to achieve those goals most efficiently.'' In making these policy suggestions, the economist's role is much the same as an engineer's: he or she is simply telling someone else how to achieve desired ends most efficiently. Ideally the economist is, as objectively as possible, telling someone how to achieve his or her goals (which need not be the economist's goals).

How Economists' Value Judgments Creep into Policy Proposals

Even though responsible economists attempt to be as objective as possible, value judgments still creep into their analyses in three ways: interpretation of policymakers' values, interpretation of empirical evidence, and choice of economic models.

Interpretation of the Policymakers' Values   In practice, social goals are seldom so neat that they can be specified A, B, and C; they're vaguely understood and vaguely expressed. An economist will be told, for instance, ''We want to make the poor better off'' or ''We want to see that middle-income people get better housing.'' It isn't clear what *poor, better off,* and *better housing* mean. Nor is it clear how interpersonal judgments should be made when a policy will benefit some individuals at the expense of others, as real-world policies inevitably do.

Faced with this problem, some academic economists have argued that economists should recommend only policies that benefit some people and hurt no one. Such policies are called **Pareto optimal policies** in honor of the famous Italian economist, Wilfredo Pareto, who first suggested that kind of criterion for judging

Pareto optimal policies   Policies that benefit some people and hurt no one.

social change.[1] It's hard to object to the notion of Pareto optimal policies, because, by definition, they improve life for some people while hurting no one.

I'd give you an example of a real-world Pareto optimal policy if I could, but, unfortunately, I don't know of any. Every policy inevitably has some side effect of hurting, or at least seeming to hurt, somebody. In the real world, Pareto optimal policies don't exist. Any economist who has advised governments on real-world problems knows that all real-world policies make some people better off and some people worse off.

But that doesn't mean that economists have no policy role. In their policy proposals economists try to spell out what a policy's income distributive effects will be, whether a policy will help a majority of people, who those people are, and whether the policy is consistent with the policymaker's value judgments. Doing so isn't easy because the policymaker's value judgments are often vague and must be interpreted by the economist. In that interpretation the economist's value judgment often slips in.

Interpretation of Empirical Evidence   Value judgments further creep into economic policy proposals through economists' interpretations of empirical evidence which is almost always imprecise. For example, say an economist is assessing the elasticity of a product's demand. She can't run an experiment to isolate prices and quantities demanded; instead she must look at events in which hundreds of other things changed and do her best to identify what caused what. In selecting and interpreting empirical evidence a person's values will likely show through, try as one might to be objective. People tend to focus on evidence that supports their position. Economists are trained to be as objective as they can be, but pure objectivity is impossible.

Let's consider an example. Some economists recently proposed that a large tax be imposed on sales of disposable diapers, citing studies that suggested disposable diapers made up between 15 and 30 percent of the garbage in a landfill. Others objected, citing studies that showed disposable diapers made up only 1–2 percent of the refuse going into landfills. I don't know which of these two sets of figures is correct. More studies are necessary, but generally policy debates don't wait for further studies. Economists' value judgments influence which incomplete study they choose to believe is more accurate.

Choice of Economic Models   Similarly with the choice of models. A model, because it focuses on certain aspects of economic reality and not on others, necessarily reflects certain value judgments, so economists' choice of models must also reflect certain value judgments. Albert Einstein once said that theories should be as simple as possible, but not more so. To that we should add the maxim: Scientists should be as objective and as value-free as possible, but not more so.

This book presents the mainstream neo-classical model of the economy. That model directs us to certain conclusions. Two other general models that some economists follow are a Marxian (radical) model and a public choice (conservative) model. Those other models, by emphasizing different aspects of economic interrelationships, would sometimes direct us to other conclusions.

Let's consider an example. Mainstream neo-classical analysis directs us to look at how the invisible hand achieves harmony and equilibrium through the market. Thus, when neo-classical economists look at labor markets, they generally see supply and demand forces leading to equilibrium. When Marxist economists look at labor markets, their model focuses on the tensions among the social

Kenneth Arrow—Nobel prize, 1972, for work in welfare economics.   © *The Nobel Foundation.*

[1] Pareto, in his famous book, *Mind and Society,* suggested this criterion as an analytic approach for theory, not as a criterion for real-world policy. He recognized the importance of the art of economics and that real-world policy has to be judged by much broader criteria.

classes, and they generally see exploitation of workers by capitalists. When public choice economists look at labor markets, they see individuals using government to protect their monopolies. Their model focuses on political restrictions that provide rents to various groups. Each model captures different aspects of reality. That's why it's important to be as familiar with as many different models as possible.

Why Economists Advise Policymakers Who Share Their Value Judgments

2

Usually economists provide advice for policymakers whose values agree with their own. Economists with liberal values usually provide policy recommendations for liberal policymakers; economists with conservative values usually provide policy recommendations for conservative policymakers. Why? Because of the inevitable influence of economists' value judgments on their policy prescriptions. When economists have the same values as policymakers, they can have a better feel for a policy's harmony with the policymakers' worldview.

Let me give you a personal example. I've generally consulted for liberal policymakers even though the policies I've advocated are often classified as conservative. Why? Because my basic values are consistent with most liberals' values: I don't like people to go hungry, and I believe that we, as a society, should do what we can to help the poor. Paradoxically much of my policy advice focuses on how existing government policies to help the poor don't achieve their desired ends, and how stronger reliance on market forces would be more effective in achieving those ends. I've found that I simply can't offer advice to politicians who, deep down, don't share my value judgments about what a just society is.

John Maynard Keynes once said that economists should be seen in the same light as dentists—as competent technicians. He was wrong, and his own experience is a contradiction of that view. In dealing with real-world economic policy, Keynes was no mere technician. He had a definite worldview, which he shared with many of the policymakers he advised. An economist who is to play a role in policy formation must be willing to combine value judgments and technical knowledge.

AGREEMENT AMONG ECONOMISTS ABOUT SOCIAL POLICY

Despite their widely varying values, both liberal and conservative economists agree more often on policy prescriptions than most laypeople think they do. They're economists, after all, and their models focus on certain issues—specifically on incentives and individual choice. All economists believe economic incentives are important, and most economists tend to give significant weight to individuals' ability to choose reasonably. This leads economists, both liberal and conservative, to look at a problem differently than other people do.

Many people think economists of all persuasions look at the world cold-heartedly. That opinion, in my view, of course, isn't accurate, but it's understandable how people could reach it. Economists are taught to look at things in an "objective" way that takes into account a policy's long-run incentive effects as well as the short-run effects. Many of their policy proposals are based upon these long-run incentive effects, which in the short run make the policy look cold-hearted. Economists argue that they aren't being cold-hearted at all, that they're simply being reasonable, and that following their advice will lead to less suffering and more people being helped than following others' advice. They ask, "How can advice that will lead to less suffering be cold-hearted?" This is not to say that all economists' advice will lead to significant long-run benefits and less long-run suffering. Some of it may be simply misguided. You must decide your position on that, but you should decide it knowing economists' defense of their policy suggestion.

Some economists argue that comparing marginal cost and marginal benefit (making efficient decisions) will lead to the most equitable and fairest systems—interpreted as most people would interpret *equitable* and *fairest*. Economists have had problems in getting their ideas fairly expressed in public because their arguments are often long-run arguments, while the press and policymakers usually focus on short-run effects. The problem economists face is similar to the one parents face when they tell their children that they can't eat candy or must do their homework before they can play. Explaining how "being mean" is actually "being nice" to a six-year-old isn't easy.

A colleague of mine, Abba Lerner, was well known for his strong liberal leanings. The government of Israel called on him for advice on what to do about unemployment. He went to Israel, studied the problem, and presented his advice: "Cut union wages." The government official responded, "But that's the same advice the conservative economist gave us." Lerner answered, "It's good advice too." The Israeli Labor government then went and did the opposite; it raised wages, thus holding onto its union support in the short run.

The best way to see the consistency and the differences in economists' policy advice is to consider some examples. Some of the following examples bring out certain characteristics of most economists' policy advice, while others show the differences among economists in values and in empirical interpretations. Let's start with a general consideration of economists' views on regulation.

EXAMPLES OF
ECONOMISTS'
POLICY ADVICE

Economists' Cost/Benefit Approach to Government Regulation

Say that there has been a plane crash in which 200 people died. Newspaper headlines trumpet the disaster while news magazines are filled with stories about how the accident might have been caused, citing speculation about poor maintenance and lack of government regulation. The publicity spreads the sense that "something must be done" to prevent such tragedies. Politicians quickly pick up on this, feeling that the public wants action. They introduce a bill outlawing faulty maintenance, denounce poor regulatory procedures, and demand an investigation of sleepy air controllers. In short, they strike out against likely causes of the accident and suggest improved regulations to help prevent any more such crashes.

Economists differ in their views on government regulation of airlines and other businesses, but economists of all ideological persuasions find themselves opposing some of the supposedly problem-solving regulations proposed by politicians. Considering why they react this way gives you insight into economists' similarity.

"Count-from-1-to-10" Philosophy   One reason economists unite in their opposition to many proposed government regulations is that they believe decisions should be made rationally on the basis of costs and benefits, not on the basis of political expediency.

Their position simply reflects their trained reasonableness. Reasonable people should look at the costs and the benefits of various possible courses of action, and make decisions based on those costs and benefits. After an emotional event like a plane crash, it's difficult to make rational decisions based on costs and benefits. Economists argue that laws enacted quickly in reaction to an emotional event generally will be ill thought out and will reflect the information provided by special interest groups (information that has not necessarily been processed and analyzed by independent observers). Psychologists advise patients not to make major decisions during a time of crisis; economists advise policymakers not to do so either. This advice reflects what we'll call the *count-from-1-to-10* philosophy.

In advising policymakers to stop and count to 10 before recommending new regulations, economists point out that lawmakers have an incentive to act fast—to make it look as if they're doing something when the issue is hot and they're likely to get good press. But by the same reasoning economists have an incentive to act slowly—to advise studying the issue (by hiring economists to do so) and coming to a "rational" conclusion. Whether economists are offering self-serving advice or good advice is for you to decide.

EXHIBIT 1   **The Value of a Human Life**

Basis for calculation	Value of life (in 1987 dollars)
Desire for prompt coronary care	$ 66,000
Automobile air bag purchases	360,000
Smoke detector purchases	373,000
EPA requirement for sulfur scrubbers	500,000
Seat belt usage	541,000
Wage premiums for dangerous police work	850,000
EPA regulation of radium content in water	2,500,000
Wage premiums for dangerous factory jobs	3,200,000
OSHA rules for workplace safety	3,500,000
Premium tire usage	3,600,000
Desire for safer airline travel	11,800,000

Source: Stan V. Smith, Adjunct Professor, DePaul College of Law and President, Corporate Financial Group, Chicago. Used by permission.

A British economics magazine that closely follows economic developments in the world.

The Assignment of a Cost and a Benefit to Everything   A second reason economists often find themselves united with one another but at odds with the general public is that their cost/benefit approach requires them to determine a quantitative cost and benefit for everything, including life. What's the value of a human life? All of us would like to answer, "*Infinite.* Each human life is beyond price." But if that's true, then in a cost/benefit framework, everything of value should be spent on preventing death. People should take no chances. They should drive at 30 miles per hour with airbags, triple-cushioned bumpers, double roll bars—you get the picture.

It would be possible for manufacturers to make a car in which no one would die as the result of an accident. The fact is that people don't want such cars. Many people don't buy those auto safety accessories that are already available, and many drivers ignore the present speed limit. Instead many people want cars with style and speed.

Far from regarding human life as priceless, people make decisions every day that reflect the valuations they place on their own lives. Exhibit 1 presents one economist's estimates of some of these quantitative decisions. These values are calculated by looking at people's revealed preferences (the choices they make when they must pay the costs). To find them, economists calculate how much people will pay to reduce the possibility of their death by a certain amount. If that's what people will pay to avoid death, the cost to them of death can be calculated by multiplying the inverse of the reduced probability by the amount they pay.

For example, say someone will buy a car whose airbags add up to $500 to the vehicle's cost, but won't buy a car whose airbags add more than $500 to its cost. Also say that an airbag will reduce the chance of dying in an automobile accident by 1/720. That means that to increase the likelihood of surviving an auto accident by 1/720, the buyer will pay $500. That also means that the buyer is implicitly valuing his or her life at roughly $360,000 (720 × $500 = $360,000).

Alternatively say that people will pay an extra $36 for a set of premium tires that reduce the risk of death by 1/100,000. As opposed to having a 3/100,000 chance per year of dying in a skid on the highway, people with premium tires all round have a 2/100,000 chance of dying. (3/100,000 − 2/100,000 = 1/100,000) Multiplying 100,000 (the inverse of the reduction in probability) by $36, the extra cost of the set of premium tires, you find that people who buy these tires are implicitly valuing their lives at $3,600,000.[2]

---

[2] For simplicity of exposition I'm not considering other benefits of these decisions such as lowering the chance of injury.

No one can say whether people know what they're doing in making these valuations, although the inconsistencies in the valuations people place on their lives suggest that to some degree they don't, or that other considerations are entering into their decisions. But even given the inconsistencies, it's clear that people are valuing life. Most people are aware that in order to "live" they must take chances on losing their lives. Economists argue that individuals' revealed choices are the best estimate that society can have of the value of life, and that in making policy society shouldn't pretend that life is beyond value.

Placing a value on human life allows economists to evaluate the cost of a crash. Say each life is worth $2 million. If 200 people die in that plane accident and a $200 million plane is destroyed, the cost of the crash is $600 million.

Right after the accident, or even long after the accident, tell a mother and father you're valuing the life of their dead daughter at $2 million and the plane at $200 million, and you'll see why economists have problems with getting their views across. Even if people can agree rationally that a value must be placed on life—that they implicitly give their own lives a value—it's not something they want to deal with emotionally, especially after an accident. Using a cost/benefit approach, an economist must be willing to say, if that's the way the analysis turns out, "It's reasonable that my son died in this accident because the cost of preventing the accident by imposing stricter government regulations would have been greater than the benefit of preventing it."

Economists take the emotional heat for making such valuations. Their cost/benefit approach requires them to do so.

Comparing Costs and Benefits of Different Dimensions   After the marginal cost and marginal benefit data have been gathered and processed, one is ready to make an informed decision. Will the cost of a new regulation outweigh the benefit, or vice versa? Here again economists find themselves in a difficult position in evaluating a regulation about airplane safety. Many of the costs of regulation are small but occur in large numbers. Every time you lament some "bureaucratic craziness" (such as a required weekly staff meeting or a form to be signed assuring something has been done), you're experiencing a cost. But when those costs are compared to the benefits of avoiding a major accident, the dimensions of comparison are often wrong.

For example, say it were discovered that a loose bolt was the probable cause of the plane crash. A regulation requiring airline mechanics to check whether that bolt is tightened and, to ensure that they do so, requiring them to fill out a form each time the check is made, might cost $1. How can one compare $1 to the $600 million cost of the crash? Such a regulation obviously makes sense from the perspective of gaining a $600 million benefit from $1 of cost.

But wait. Each plane might have 4,000 similar bolts, each of which is equally likely to cause an accident if it isn't tightened. If it makes sense to check that one bolt, it makes sense to check all 4,000. And the bolts must be checked on each of the 4,000 flights per day. All of this increases the cost of tightening bolts to $16 million per day. But the comparison shouldn't be between $16 million and $600 million. The comparison should be between the marginal cost ($16 million) and the marginal benefit, which depends upon how much tightening bolts will contribute to preventing an accident.

Let's say that the decreased probability of having an accident because of having checked that bolt daily is .001. This means that the check will prevent one out of a thousand accidents that otherwise would have happened. The marginal benefit of checking a particular bolt isn't $600 million (which it would be if you knew a bolt was going to be loose), but is

$$.001 \times \$600 \text{ million} = \$600,000.$$

That $600,000 is the marginal benefit that must be compared to the marginal cost of $16,000,000.

It's not only the general public that disdains economists' analyses. Sometimes economists disdain them themselves. In 1989 Herbert Stein (a well-known economist who has been, among other things, an economic advisor to a president of the United States) wrote a little piece for *The New York Times* that touched on the empirical problems of implementing cost/benefit analysis.

Stein alluded to a tendency of economists that makes ordinary people think that computer ink and not real blood runs in economists' veins; that where people anatomically locate their hearts, economists have a tidy box of microchips, electronic circuits, a few beeps, and an occasional flashing light. He invented a "newspaper article" announcing that a group of economists had studied the costs and benefits of traffic lights. The group concluded that the cost of installing, operating, and maintaining traffic lights, together with the costs incurred by motorists who lost time, wasted gas, and imposed wear and tear on their engines by stopping at red lights, were worth it in terms of lives saved in car accidents that didn't happen—but only just barely worth it. If the lights cost as little as 3 percent more or if lives were worth as little as 3 percent less, it would be cheaper to compensate accident victims and their families than to spend all that money on traffic lights.

Then, pointing out the human weakness for people to choose data to fit their value judgments, he invented another group of economists. The second group, he said, was very upset that any economic study would come to the conclusion that a social expense was worth the money it cost. In fact, the group was so upset that it was sure the first group must have made a mistake in analyzing its data, so the second group was going to conduct the study over again, convinced that this time it would come out the way their model said it should: Don't install traffic lights because they cost too much compared to the return on mere human life, health, and happiness.

Stein's playful story captures two aspects of economists that we've emphasized in this chapter:

1. Economists' tendency to view everything in a cost/benefit framework.
2. Economists'—and everyone else's—tendency to use empirical evidence selectively (that is, to use it to support positions they favor).

Given these numbers, I leave it to you to decide: Does this hypothetical regulation make sense?

Putting Cost/Benefit Analysis in Perspective   The numbers in our plane crash example are hypothetical. The numbers used in real-world decision making are not hypothetical, but they are often ambiguous. Measuring costs, benefits, and probabilities is difficult, and economists often disagree on specific costs and benefits. That's one reason why economists differ in their views of regulation. In considering any particular regulation, some economists will favor it and some will oppose it. But their reasoning process—comparing marginal costs and marginal benefits—is the same; they differ only on the estimates they calculate.

Economists' Debate on Increasing the Minimum Wage

As a second case study, I'll consider economists' views of the minimum wage. The basic argument in favor of the minimum wage is that it raises poor people's income. The basic economic argument against the minimum wage is that it prevents market forces from working and creates unemployment. How it does so is captured in Exhibit 2. In it you can see how the minimum wage, W_m, set above the equilibrium wage, W_e, increases the gap between the quantity of labor supplied and the quantity demanded and thereby creates unemployment equal to $Q_S - Q_D$. The simple argument against the minimum wage is that it creates this unemployment which hurts poor people.

How does one compare the costs and benefits here? First, we must determine how many, and how much, poor people will be helped or hurt. This depends on the elasticities of supply and demand. For example, say the supply and demand curves are highly inelastic. In that case not many people will lose their jobs because of the minimum wage. However if the supply and demand curves are

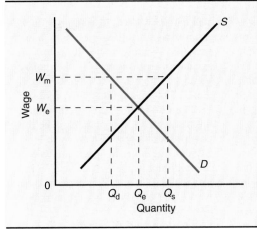

EXHIBIT 2   The Effect of a Minimum Wage

A minimum wage creates a gap between the quantity of labor supplied and the quantity of labor demanded, and hence creates unemployment. It helps those who manage to keep their jobs, increasing their wage from the equilibrium wage, W_e, to the minimum wage, W_m. But it hurts those who find that they can't get a job at the minimum wage, or keep a job they already had if the wage goes up (because the employer will just get along without that employee rather than pay more). This is shown by the distance Q_s-Q_d.

highly elastic, a large number of people will lose their jobs when a minimum-wage law is introduced.

But estimating elasticities isn't sufficient to make a decision on whether a minimum wage is desirable. Another issue that must always be considered is the *general equilibrium* issue. Supply and demand are **partial equilibrium** concepts. They assume "all other things remain equal." But all other things don't remain equal. A minimum wage will cause firms to demand labor-saving machines. This will affect the demand for machines, and the demand for machines will affect the demand for labor. To consider the things that don't remain equal is to consider the general equilibrium issue. **General equilibrium analysis** is the analysis of the simultaneous interaction of all markets. To say that something is a general equilibrium issue is to say that looking at a supply/demand model isn't sufficient. Such general equilibrium considerations make policy debates much more complicated.

You've already had far too many of my interpretations of economists' reasoning, so this time we'll look at the real thing—a debate between economists in *The Christian Science Monitor* concerning the minimum wage. As you read the following two articles, try to decide whether you agree with one or the other. Ask yourself why you agree with one and not the other, and why there's disagreement between the two sides.

Partial equilibrium analysis Analysis that assumes all other things remain equal.

General equilibrium analysis The analysis of the simultaneous interaction of all markets.

The Debate

RAISING WAGE IS NO HELP TO WORKERS

By Richard B. McKenzie and Walter Wessels

The $1.20-an-hour increase in the federal minimum wage over three years that has been passed by the House of Representatives is not as bad as the vast majority of economists say. It is much worse!

Critics of the increase have focused their analysis on the harm done to the sizable number (100,000 to 750,000, depending on the study

Source: *Christian Science Monitor*, May 8, 1989. Courtesy Richard B. McKenzie and Walter Wessells.

cited) of mainly disadvantaged workers who will lose their jobs because of the increase. But the statistical work that we and other economists have done in recent years shows that the increase will even penalize those covered workers who retain their jobs at the higher $4.55 wage rate.

Both proponents and opponents of a minimum-wage increase have misguided the public debate on two counts. First, analysts have failed to recognize that legal wage constraints do not suppress competitive pressures that have kept the wages of workers with limited skills low. Wage constraints only redirect the competitive pressures and, by wiping out tens of thousands of job oppor-

tunities, worsen the competitive bind of workers covered by the wage law.

Second, the overwhelming majority of contemporary workers, even low-paid workers, are not compensated *solely* in terms of so many dollars an hour. Rather, they are paid in "bundles of benefits"—including money, but also including relaxed work demands and a variety of fringe benefits (insurance, rest breaks, flexible schedules, discounts on personal purchases, and on-the-job training, just to name a few).

Although Congress can legislate an increase in workers' money wage, it exerts little control over the many other nonmoney dimensions of employment. And to contain production costs in competitive markets, employers must respond to mandated money-wage increases with decreases in nonmoney benefits—for example, reductions in on-the-job training, the elimination of fringe benefits, and increases in work demands.

Unfortunately, the combination of mandated money-wage increases and reductions in nonmoney benefits makes workers relatively more costly to hire and, thereby, reduces the demand for—and worsens the competitive position of—covered workers. Though still controversial, this new perspective on the effects of minimum-wage laws is supported by a growing body of research:

- Writing in the *American Economic Review*, Nori Hashimoto found that under the 1967 minimum-wage increase, workers on average lost $1.28 worth of training for every $1 increase in the minimum wage.

- Linda Leighton and Jacob Mincer in one study and Belton Fleisher in another came to a similar conclusion: Increases in the minimum wage reduce on-the-job training—and, as a result, cause workers to lose more in future income growth than they gain from the new minimum wage.
- One of the authors of this article (Mr. Wessels) found that an increase in the minimum wage caused retail establishments in New York to increase work demands. In most stores, fewer workers were given fewer hours to do the same work.
- The research of Mr. Fleisher, William Alpert, and L. F. Dunn shows that minimum-wage increases lead to large reductions in fringe benefits and to worsening working conditions.

Given the findings of various studies, we estimate that every $1-an-hour increase in the minimum wage

will cause workers to give up a minimum of $1.20 an hour in employment benefits, making them 20 cents an hour worse off in terms of the money value of their total "payment bundles." This means that the proposed $1.20-an-hour increase in the minimum wage will, on balance, make the covered workers worse off by at least 24 cents an hour. In short, increasing the minimum wage is a political recipe for making many very low-income workers, even those who retain their jobs, worse off.

Richard McKenzie is professor of economics at the University of Missouri, Oxford MS. Walter Wessels is an associate professor of economics at North Carolina State University.

'BAD SIDE' OF A HIGHER WAGE ISN'T SO BAD

By George Ignatin

How can we explain the remarkable compassion that conservatives have suddenly shown toward the working poor in response to efforts to raise the minimum wage? Or some of the statements made by supposedly thoughtful economists? Like Nori Hashimoto's contention that when minimum wages are raised by $1, businesses decrease training by $1.28—as if businessmen, displaying their well-known eleemosynary tendencies, were giving their least skilled workers more training than was profitable to the business.

Which raises the point: How much and what kind of "training" do businesses provide minimum-wage workers? Picture the typical such worker: an usher at a theater, a bag boy at the supermarket, a cashier at a video-rental store. Now picture the training that is done: $1.28 worth an hour, three to eight hours a day; and for six months—as envisioned by President Bush's proposal for a sub-

minimum training wage. This proposal presumes far more training than would occur and is fraught with potential abuse: Minimum-wage jobs have extremely high turnover rates. Most last less than six months. So the President's "training wage" could easily become *the* wage. All new employees would be defined as trainees; after six months, if they lasted that long, they'd be declared trained, and replaced with a new class of trainees.

Three other economists claim that an increase in the minimum wage will be offset by a reduction in benefits. Although we'd expect *some* decrease, they have the gall to count breaks from work as benefits of the job, which makes one wonder why they didn't also count the geographical knowledge obtained by employees in their trips to work.

Most economists agree that an increase in the minimum wage would cost some jobs, but the operative word is "some." The congressional bill would increase the minimum next year by about 15 percent. The best estimates are that this would lead to a decrease in employment of minimum-wage labor by one-quarter to one-fifth of that—say about 3.5 percent—or

about 90,000 workers. If the minimum wage was raised to $4.55 an hour in one jump (a 36 percent increase), employment would fall by 180,000 to 240,000. Although less than 10 percent of minimum-wage workers would be laid off, more than 90 percent would keep their jobs and be paid more.

But it's not quite that simple. One of the more important concepts in economics has to do with substitution effects. When those minimum-wage workers lose their jobs, what do employers do? Sweep the floors and clean the toilets themselves? Historically, they lay off their least productive labor and hire more-productive workers, generally adult women, at slightly higher wages. Three 25-year-old women at $5 or $6 an hour to do the work of four 17-year-olds. They also pay their more highly skilled workers slightly more.

So next year, there would be a transfer of jobs, with 90,000 fewer teens and 60,000 *more* adults working—all at higher wages. And most of the unemployed teens would reenroll in school, and some of them might even improve their future job prospects.

Source: *Christian Science Monitor*, May 8, 1989. Courtesy George Ignatin.

Another thing employers do is substitute capital—machinery—for labor, and this allows workers to be more productive. Unfortunately, many minimum-wage jobs can't be performed efficiently by machines— unless we devise assembly-line hamburger shaper/cookers or motorized wash rags.

Other employers won't lay off anyone; they'll simply absorb the increase and their costs will go up. That's why businesses are opposed to the increase. Especially small businesses (with large numbers of unskilled workers) operating in highly competitive product markets that discourage price increases.

Thus, the ''bad'' side of a minimum wage increase isn't all that bad: For every worker or small businessman who suffers from it, there will be 15 to 30 workers who will benefit.

The US has historically paid the highest wages in the world and until the mid-1970s was highly competitive in world markets. But in the last 15 years, it has tried the competitive method of third-world countries: low wages, small amounts of capital (relative to countries like Japan), and relatively stagnant technology. This method hasn't worked very well.

George Ignatin is associate professor of economics at the University of Alabama at Birmingham.

Ways in Which Economists Differ   Reading this debate should have brought home the point that economists differ, often substantially, about policy. On the surface the economists who wrote these articles seem to disagree about everything. But closer examination of the articles shows that, while their conclusions differ, the assumptions underlying their analysis have much in common. For example, both use a cost/benefit framework. They also both view individuals—low-wage workers and employers—as rational. Where they differ is in their empirical estimates and in their view of the side effects of an increase in the minimum wage.

Let's consider those differences.

Differences in Empirical Estimates   Notice in both articles the wide range of empirical estimates of the effect on employment levels of an increase in the minimum wage to $4.55 an hour. McKenzie and Wessels state that anywhere from 100,000 to 750,000 workers would lose their jobs. Ignatin estimates there would be 180,000 to 240,000 additional unemployed people. Such a wide range of empirical estimates is typical of most economic debates. Even using complicated, sophisticated techniques, economists simply can't provide exact empirical estimates of a given policy's effects. Inevitably there will be disagreements and different views, depending on which estimates one believes.

Making these estimates is an important part of economists' work, and that's why one must, in order to become an economist, study statistics and have a good sense of the economic institutions to know whether one's formal empirical estimates make sense. In making and interpreting empirical estimates, it is important to recognize that much more than formal statistical training is necessary. Notice how Professor Ignatin scorns the formal empirical estimate that workers on average lose $1.28 in training for every $1 increase in the minimum wage. He asks if the reader believes that a ''typical worker'' receives $1.28 in training for each hour worked. He relies on the reader's institutional knowledge of how much training occurs in minimum-wage jobs and strongly suspects that the reader's answer will be no.

One must, of course, be careful in relying on the reader's institutional knowledge. The lost training is in the jobs the workers would have had if the minimum-wage increase hadn't occurred, not in the jobs they actually had. What those potential jobs would have provided in the way of training must be based on projections of future jobs, not on jobs that currently exist.

Differences in Side Effects   A second way in which the economists differ is in the side effects they see stemming from a particular policy. McKenzie and Wessels see employers reducing nonwage benefits of a job in response to having to pay a higher minimum wage. They argue that the minimum-wage increase will make those minimum-wage workers *who retain their jobs* worse off, as well as the ones who lose their jobs.

Ignatin focuses on a different side effect. He points out that the jobs done by the minimum-wage workers would still need to be done, and that more workers would be needed to produce the machines to do these jobs. Although there might be a decrease in the total number of minimum-wage jobs, an increase in the minimum wage would also lead to higher-paying jobs producing and using machines.

Lessons from the Debate   I presented the debate, not only for you to decide who's right and who's wrong, but to show you an example of a real-world economic debate. The presentation is meant to convey to you the need for openness and caution in judging any economic debate.

Openness   Once you get into the real world, policy issues become cloudy. Any debate turns on differences in empirical estimates and on differing views of the side effects of policies, just as does this debate about the minimum wage. Reading only one side of a debate is a way to come to a conclusion about the issue, but it is not a way to come to a *correct* conclusion.

All real-world issues have many sides. To decide a question of economic policy, it's important to read and carefully consider *all* views: radical, liberal, conservative. Each has something to contribute.

Caution   Good economists can write well. Their arguments are, or at least should be, convincing. But good economists exist on all sides of most issues, and after reading all the convincing arguments, the answer you'll arrive at on many issues is "It depends." You, as an introductory student, generally don't have the background or the institutional knowledge to come to a final conclusion.

There's nothing wrong in arriving at an indefinite answer like "It depends." All too often students feel they must decide an economic issue when in fact they don't have sufficient economic information, experience, and training to make an informed judgment. In such cases, caution (admitting that the answer depends on a variety of factors) is well advised. That doesn't mean you don't make tentative decisions—inevitably you must decide without full information. It simply means that you keep an open mind to new evidence and arguments and always are willing to change that decision.

How government can best contribute to quality education is much in debate.
© *Bill Bachmann/The Image Works.*

As a third case study of real-world economic policy I consider a speech that John Chubb, a senior fellow at the Brookings Institution (a Washington, D.C. economic think tank), presented to a group of educators, summarizing some of his work.[3]

I present the speech for a number of reasons. First, Chubb is a good political economist, and his arguments are absorbing. Second, the topic (education) is one that most people are interested in and have some knowledge about. And third, it shows economic analysis applied to a broader issue than those to which it's usually applied in economics textbooks. Economic reasoning has had an enormous impact on the management and organizational structure of many kinds of organizations, and this selection gives you a sense of that influence.

A Political Economist Speaks about How to Make Public Schools Better

MAKING SCHOOLS BETTER

By John Chubb

Most of you are familiar with the state of American education. Just to give you some basic statistics, for roughly 20 years from the mid 1960s until the mid-1980s, the SAT scores of American students dropped sharply. Although scores have been going up for the last few years, they've recently stalled. Our students still are well behind where they were in 1965.

In addition, the dropout rate in the United States is about 25 percent. That is to say, 25 percent of our students are not finishing high school on time. In many of our large cities only half of the students finish high school on time.

Comparing the United States to countries around the world is even more depressing. In math and science, U.S. students rank dead last in any comparison with students from the nations that are our leading competitors. . . .

There is a bit of good news. For the last five years, Americans, mostly at the state level, have been trying very hard to turn things around. . . . [W]hen reports began to come out suggesting various ways to improve our nation's school systems, a lot of skeptics said we could never find that much money. But . . . we have spent far more money than any of the skeptics thought possible.

Between 1981 and 1986 expenditures per pupil for elementary and secondary education went up 40 percent. In real terms we now spend four

times as much per child as we did in 1950. In the first half of the 1980s, teachers enjoyed larger salary increases than any other occupational group in the country. Their salaries are still arguably too low, $29,000 per year, but they have gone up very quickly. We've also spent a good deal of money to reduce the size of classes.

There has been a crackdown on teacher incompetence. Teachers are being asked to take more tests, to demonstrate that they are able. There has been a crackdown on student underachievement. Graduation and promotion requirements are being boosted around the country.

This is very heartening because it is unusual for our political system to act so forthrightly. Clearly, Americans are taking the problem seriously. Unfortunately, the prospects that these reforms will make much of a difference are not very good. That is doubly discouraging because we may be wasting a rare political opportunity to really do something.

Why am I willing to say that what has been taking place is not likely to make much of a difference? The reasons are reflected in the study I did . . . [e]ntitled "What Price Democracy?" . . .

This study included 500 randomly selected high schools nationwide, public and private. Within these high schools it included the principals, 12,000 teachers, and 12,000 students. We've never before had, in this country, a data set that puts together such detailed information on

both students and the schools that they've attended. Large studies usually concentrate on either schools or students. We've combined the two.

The other thing that is virtually unique about this data set is that the students were examined not once, but twice. They were examined when they began high school as sophomores, and again when they graduated. Thus we were able to study not simply changes in the levels of student achievement over time, but how a particular group of students progressed.

We focused on one major issue . . . academic achievement. We used five tests: math, science, reading, writing, and vocabulary, and combined the results into a comprehensive measure of student achievement between sophomore year and graduation.

After determining which students were achieving and which were failing, we sought to uncover the sources of success or failure. First came a bit of bad news: The most important determinant of how students achieve is their aptitude. Bright kids learn more in high school than kids that aren't so bright. There is a certain amount of student achievement that is beyond the reach of school reformers.

But the good news is that the second most important determinant of how well students do is the school they attend. The skeptics of the 1960s and '70s, who doubted that schools could make a difference, were wrong. Schools make a big difference. They are marginally more important than

---

[3] The occasion for the speech was a Manhattan Institute Seminar entitled "Making Schools Better," sponsored by a grant from the Gannett Corporation; it was published by the Manhattan Institute as Manhattan Paper #5. Reprinted with the permission of the Manhattan Institute for Policy Research.

the influence of parents. They are far more important than the influence of peer groups.

The next question naturally is, "What makes the difference between successful and unsuccessful schools?" Let me begin by telling you what doesn't make a difference. Neither expenditures, teacher salaries, class size, graduation requirements, the amount of homework assigned, or any other individual school policy that we looked at matters. There was no correlation between student achievement and any of the variables on which school reformers have been concentrating so much time, effort, and money. That is why there is very little reason to believe that school reform, as it is proceeding, is going to work.

What will work? For any of you who are involved in management, the answer may seem pretty obvious. The thing about schools that really seems to matter is how they're organized. To begin with, good and bad schools have different goals. The schools that are succeeding, whether with poor students or the best students, consciously focus on academic achievement. If you ask personnel in these schools what their goal is, they will say, "academic achievement," or "academic excellence." People in schools that aren't doing so well say things like "the basics," "occupational training," or "citizenship." These goals may well be important. But if you want achievement the school has to focus on achievement.

I should also say that clarity and consensus about goals are as important as what you call the goal. The thing that distinguishes successful schools is that there is a real consensus within those organizations about what they are trying to achieve, whether they say, "the basics," or "academic excellence." . . . The schools in our survey that were succeeding consciously focused on one purpose.

Another important aspect of organization was leadership. The principals of successful and unsuccessful schools were as different as night and day. Successful schools were led by principals whom the teachers said had a vision, knew where they wanted the

school to go, and knew how to take the school in that direction. These are standard qualities of strong leadership. Also, the principals in the good schools were educationally oriented and thought of themselves as educational leaders, not administrators.

When we asked principals of unsuccessful schools why they became principals they would say things like: "I prefer administration to teaching." When asked what their long-term goals were, unsuccessful principals were much more likely to say, "I want to get out of the school, move up into the central office and rise in the administrative hierarchy."

In the successful schools, the principals wanted to stay in the schools. When you asked them why they became principals, they were more likely to say, "Because I wanted to take control of the school. I wanted to control personnel, I wanted to control policy." They wanted to lead, not merely manage.

The other profound organizational difference was that in successful schools [the staff's] sense of professionalism, independence, and responsibility for one's work was enormously higher. Teachers and principals in the successful schools were true professionals. Those in the unsuccessful schools weren't professionals at all. The teachers in successful schools had more independence, they participated more extensively in school decisions, and they had more influence over those decisions. Within their classrooms they were free to tailor their practices to the needs of the students. . . . In the successful schools teachers had discretion. To us, the concept that best summarized the difference between the successful and unsuccessful school organizations was that of a team. In successful schools the organization was held together by consensus and cooperation, not primarily by rules and regulations. The unsuccessful school looked like a classic bureaucracy, held together primarily by rules and regulations—a hierarchy, not a team at all.

If strong leadership, clear goals, professionalism and team spirit are what is important, how do you instill

these somewhat elusive qualities in a school? Can it be done at all?

Many state legislatures believe that it can be done by sending teachers and principals to classes. . . . But if you look around the country at successful school organizations, it doesn't appear that formal management training accounts for much.

We took a careful look at what accounts for effective organization. The key determinant, more important than anything else, turns out to be autonomy. Successful schools were relatively independent of external influence by administrators: superintendents, central office bureaucrats, and union officials. A school that was free to chart its own course was much more likely to develop effective organization and thereby breed academic achievement.

Principals who had greater influence over curriculum, instruction, discipline, and especially hiring and firing, put together effective organizations. It doesn't take much insight to figure out why. If you're a principal and you get to determine who teaches in that school and what the school's resources are, you are much more likely to trust the members of the organization, which, after all, you assembled. You are more likely to treat them as members of the team and grant them the autonomy they need to do their jobs. If you don't have control over personnel, you're less likely to treat people as if they're team members. You distrust them. You believe there is going to be conflict and you regulate. Soon you have an organization that is held together not by a common vision but by rules and regulations, that is, a bureaucracy. . . .

If you don't find autonomy in public schools except under unusual circumstances, you almost always find it in private schools, including religious schools. Private schools are more autonomous and, all things being equal, have more effective organizations and perform better than public schools. . . .

In the course of explaining about autonomy to a reporter, I told him that in New York City they have an enormous central office bureaucracy, staffed by 5,000 people, which is tremendously overbearing and leaves the principals with very little influence over their schools. I contrasted this with the Catholic school system in New York City, which despite the church's reputation for hierarchy has only 50 people in its central office, though the system has almost a quarter of the students the public schools have. [Later] I saw all these numbers and I thought, "Five thousand versus fifty! I better double-check," because [originally I had gathered them from different] sources.

I called the personnel office of the city school system and said, "I have a simple question: How many people work in the central office of the New York City School System?" The first person I reached had no idea, nor did the second or third, but they all promised to transfer me to someone who did.

Thirty-five minutes and many transfers later, I got to a person who said, "Yes, I do know the number, but if you want to know, you'll have to put your request in writing, send it through proper channels and we'll get the information back to you in a month." . . . (Finally I was told . . . it wasn't 5,000, it was 6,000.)

. . . I got someone in [the Catholic school system] central office and said, "I need some basic facts. I need to know the number of students in your school system." She told me. "I need to know the number of teachers in your school system." She told me. "I need to know the number of schools in the system." She told me. So I said, "The last thing I need to know is how many people work in the central bureaucracy of the Catholic school system in New York City."

And she said, "I'm sorry, we don't keep that kind of data."

"Well," I said, "would you have any idea? Is there any way you could get the number for me?"

And she said: "Just a minute—I'll count them." And she counted. There are 25. Twenty-five people running a school system that's a fifth to a quarter of the size of the public school system.

Public and private education are organized in an enormously different fashion. Those differences between the performance of public schools and private schools account for all of the differences between the performance of public schools and most of the differences between good public schools and bad public schools.

The message for reformers [is] . . . if you want schools to be organized more effectively and to teach more successfully, you must give them autonomy. But, as any public school administrator will tell you, you can't just turn over a school to principals and teachers without holding them accountable in some way. You've got to provide autonomy without losing accountability. And once public school administrators begin thinking about accountability, they think about tests and rules and regulations and before you know it the autonomy is done.

The only way to provide autonomy without losing accountability is to go to a different system of accountability. A top-down system will not work. You must build a system of accountability to parents and students rather than to politicians and administrators.

It works in the private sector. Private schools are held accountable to their constituency through the process of competition and choice. Similarly, the surest way to get autonomy and accountability into the public school system is not through regulation or spending, but through a mechanism of choice. There are many ways in which choice systems can be set up. Vouchers, open enrollments, magnet schools, and others.

Lessons from the Speech: Aspects of Economic Reasoning   Chubb's speech shows you economics being applied to the real world. It shows you how economists view issues that are outside the customary realm of economics. While costs and benefits aren't specifically mentioned, they lie behind Chubb's analysis. The speech also shows how economists and other social scientists use statistical data and how they apply economic reasoning in order to understand real-world problems and to propose solutions to them. Let's consider some of these aspects of economic reasoning a bit more carefully.

Economists Focus on Competitive Pressures   Notice that supply/demand analysis does not explicitly show up in the speech, but there's a sense of the strength of competition that supply/demand analysis is designed to convey. For example, Chubb points out that competitive pressures on private schools force them to be accountable—to meet the problems and solve them. Competitive pressures are behind the dynamic laws of supply and demand. That argument is the key to his speech.

Economists Do Not Always Favor the Market Solution   Although the argument concerns competitive pressures, the policies Chubb presents are not only a proposal to "create a market in educational services." At the end of the speech he presents a few ways in which accountability might be achieved: open enrollment, magnet schools, and vouchers. A voucher system, in which students are given vouchers and are allowed to spend those vouchers at whatever school they want, is a type of market solution. The others are not market solutions.

Also notice that Chubb's argument is not an argument for profit over non-profit organizations; it's a comparison of two nonprofit school systems. Despite the fact that we focus on market incentives in introductory courses, economists don't always argue for the market and for profit-making firms over all other types of organizations. What they do argue for is the need to take competitive pressures into account in analyzing any type of organizational structure.

Economists acknowledge that spending more money doesn't necessarily solve problems. Clearly spending money on a problem is often part of the solution, but many economists believe that one should first look at the internal organization of the troubled institution. Notice that Chubb points out that in real terms spending per pupil has increased fourfold since the 1950s and yet, as a result of organizational problems, education is achieving less than it did in the 1950s.

Economists Recognize All the Invisible Forces   Economists recognize that monetary incentives (the invisible hand) aren't the only influence on behavior. In their real-world policy prescriptions they take account of other forces as well. Chubb's argument isn't based on self-interest. He doesn't necessarily call for the privatization and profitization of schools (as some other economists have). The issues he focuses on are autonomy and accountability of teachers and administrators. Autonomy is desirable not only because it allows competitive pressures to operate, but also because it helps engender and foster a team spirit. Accountability is necessary because it makes individuals' incentives consistent with organizational goals.

In their practical work, economists take into account the strength of the invisible handshake. Much of management theory explores how the invisible hand and the invisible handshake can be integrated and made stronger.

Economists Use Empirical Evidence   A fourth point to recognize is that Chubb has collected and uses empirical evidence in his argument. This is another trait of good economic reasoning. In making judgments economists try to present quantitative data to back up their views. Notice that Chubb doesn't simply say that public education is in worse shape than it used to be. He quantifies his assertion by reporting SAT scores, dropout rates, and international comparisons.

The empirical research underlying economists' arguments helps make them persuasive. When the empirical evidence leads to a position different from the one that economic theory would have predicted, an honest economist still presents that evidence. For example, Chubb's evidence suggests that higher salaries haven't made a difference, even though the standard economic model would predict that they would. In this speech to noneconomists, Chubb didn't have any need to explore why his estimate departed from the estimate predicted by the standard model. Chubb's audience wasn't concerned with an issue like why there were deviations from the standard model. In a discussion with economists, though, that finding would have been subject to careful scrutiny.

Quantifying provides a structure for economists' research. They don't simply go and study a problem. They design a quantitative study and use information they gather from the study to structure their analysis of the problem. Of course, quantification by itself isn't sufficient. The empirical evidence must be interpreted, and general, nonquantifiable conclusions must be drawn. Chubb doesn't shy away from doing so.

Economists Tend to Dislike Bureaucracy   Chubb's speech reflects the somewhat negative attitude toward administrators and bureaucracy that many economists share. It follows from their basic view of human nature. Economists see self-interested individuals as trying to build little monopolies in order to make their lives easier.

PAVING THE ROAD TO DISILLUSION WITH GOOD INTENTIONS

S uppose that you are an influential member of the U.S. government and that you and a group of your powerful colleagues are worried about how expensive housing has become. Millions of low-income people are living in run-down houses or apartments or doubling up with friends and relatives. Some even sleep in their cars or spend their lives wandering the streets without any regular place to live at all.

You're in a position to write a law and get it passed. You do enact a law, a "Low-Income Housing Act." You state your purpose: "It is the policy of the United States to assist the States and their subdivisions to remedy the unsafe and unsanitary housing conditions and the acute shortage of decent, safe, and sanitary dwellings for families of low income."

You believe that when this program gets going, old housing will be rehabilitated, new housing will be built, and these units will be made available to low-income families at rents they can afford.

You institute the program and it's initially a success: All available units are rented. But its success creates an incentive problem. Once in such a unit, a family does its best to remain there. That's not what you intended; you intended that as families benefited from this assistance, they would gradually improve their circumstances and income, and move on to homes of their own or the better apartments

available on the open market. This would make room for other low-income families to move in and begin their own move up the economic ladder. But what's the incentive for a family fortunate enough to obtain one of these units? The incentive is to remain a low-income family in order to continue to qualify for the "decent, safe, and sanitary dwelling" where it lives. Given this incentive there's little turnover in these units. When occupants die, relatives and even friends struggle to remain in the units under a provision that permits "remaining occupants" to continue to live there. Another incentive problem is that landlords have no incentive to keep rents below the rent that similar units outside the program command, because as long as the rent doesn't exceed fair market rents in the area, the occupants need pay only 30 percent of their monthly income in rent. Rent increases don't matter to the occupants. They continue to pay only 30 percent of their income, with the government paying the difference.

How can I be so sure about the problems of such a law? Because the law I describe exists in the United States. Called *Section 8 Housing,* it's administered by the U.S. Department of Housing and Urban Development (HUD). In 1989 Congress began a series of investigations into this program's administration and it found that the law was failing because of incentives inherent in the program.

In Chubb's speech we see this view coming out in his discussion of how administrators are more interested in protecting their positions than in educating kids. What stops people from following their own self-interest beyond some limits is competition. Large organizations generally have little competition and, thus, economists are suspicious of them unless they are operating in a highly competitive market structure. Public school administrations generally don't face significant competition, so economists approach public administration with a certain cynicism.

At times that cynicism is unwarranted; many public administrators have a commitment to doing a good job efficiently and fairly. Economists recognize that such administrators exist, but believe that institutional incentives often undercut any commitment to efficiency even in the most committed administrator.

A Qualification   Chubb's speech is an example of good economic reasoning watered down and homogenized for presentation to the lay public. It is, however, an advocacy presentation and not a neutral presentation. For example, his argument doesn't point out some of the costs of the autonomy he recommends for principals and teachers. A critic would point out that often autonomy is used in the wrong way—to line the pockets of administrators, or to make unfair decisions and wasteful expenditures. An economist who wasn't advocating a certain position would have outlined the costs as well as the benefits.

Economics teaches people to be reasonable—sickeningly reasonable, some people would say. I hope that this chapter has given you some sense of what I mean by that. Economists' cost/benefit approach to problems (which pictures a world of individuals whose self-interested actions are limited only by competition) makes them look for the self-interest behind individuals' actions, and for how competition can direct that self-interest into the public interest.

ECONOMISTS,
POLICYMAKERS,
AND POLICY

In an economist's framework,

- Well-intentioned policies often are prevented by individuals' self-seeking activities.
- Policies that relieve immediate suffering often have long-run consequences that create more suffering.
- Politicians have more of an incentive to act fast—to look as if they're doing something—than to take enough time to get something done well that makes sense from a cost/benefit point of view.

Policy for the Real World

I've argued that it's important for economic considerations to be taken into account in decision making, and that people are, over the long haul, rational. But in proposing policies that will work, economists must also keep in mind that, in the short run, people are often governed by emotion, swayed by mass psychology, and are irrational. Politicians and other policymakers know that; the laws and regulations they propose reflect such calculations. Politicians often tell academic economists, "Yes, your arguments are reasonable, but politically I must reflect my constituents' positions. I'd be eaten alive if I followed your advice."

Politicians don't get elected and reelected by constantly saying that all choices have costs and benefits. And so, while policymakers listen to the academic economists they ask for advice, and in private frequently agree with those advisors, in practice they often choose to ignore economists' policy recommendations.

The way economic reasoning influences policy can be subtle. Sometimes one sees an elaborate charade acted out: A politician puts forward a bill that from a cost/benefit viewpoint doesn't make sense but that makes her look good. She hopes the bill won't pass, but she also hopes that presenting the bill will allow enough time to pass so that emotions can cool and a more reasonable bill can be put forward. Other times, compromise bills are proposed that incorporate as much cost/benefit policy as possible, but also appeal to voters' emotional sense. So economists and economic reasoning do influence policy.

Still, all too often (in my view) economists' advice is dumped as irrelevant, and special interest groups' policies are adopted instead. Social policy made in the real world reflects a balancing of cost/benefit analysis and special interest desires. Walking on that political tightrope is an art in which academic economists, in their role as economists, have little training.

When they propose policies, academic economists don't have to deal with such concerns. From their ivory towers they put ideas into the real world and they help students better understand the reasoning behind those ideas. Often the ideas don't have a snowball's chance in Hell of being implemented, but the ideas do make people think and influence *the way* they think. That's the payoff many economists are looking for. You'll understand policy proposals better if you bear in mind that the goal behind them isn't always to get them implemented.

Parrots and Economic Reasoning

As you can see, applying economics is much more than muttering "supply and demand" to explain every situation. Thomas Carlyle, who, as we saw in an earlier introductory quotation, argued that all you have to do is teach a parrot the words *supply and demand,* was wrong. Economics involves the thoughtful use of economic insights and empirical evidence. If this book is giving you a sense of the nature of that thoughtful application along with the core of economic reasoning, then it's succeeding in its purpose.

KEY POINTS

- Economists differ because of different underlying value judgments, because empirical evidence is subject to different interpretations, and because their underlying models differ. **1**
- Value judgments inevitably work their way into policy advice, but good economists try to be objective. **1**
- Economists tend to agree on certain issues because they experience similar training. **2** **3**
- The economic approach to analyzing issues is a cost/benefit approach. **3**

- Economists generally have reservations about regulations. **4**
- Collecting and using empirical evidence is an important part of economics. **5**
- Collecting and interpreting empirical evidence is difficult, which contributes to disagreements among economists. **5**
- Economics involves the thoughtful use of economic insights and empirical evidence. **6**

KEY TERMS

general equilibrium analysis *(609)*

Pareto optimal policies *(602)*

partial equilibrium analysis *(609)*

QUESTIONS FOR THOUGHT AND REVIEW

The number after each question represents the estimated degree of critical thinking required. (1 = almost none; 10 = deep thought.)

1. Could anyone object to a Pareto optimal policy? Why? *(8)*
2. Would it be wrong for economists to propose only Pareto optimal policies? *(9)*
3. Would all economists oppose price controls? Why or why not? *(7)*
4. Should body organs be allowed to be bought or sold? Why or why not? *(8)*
5. In cost/benefit terms, explain your decision to take an economics course. *(6)*

6. How much do you value your life in dollar terms? Are your decisions consistent in that valuation? *(9)*
7. If someone offered you $1,000,000 for one of your kidneys, would you sell it? Why or why not? *(7)*
8. Should the minimum wage be eliminated? Why? *(8)*
9. What did John Chubb find is the most important reason for the difference between a successful school and an unsuccessful school? *(5)*
10. Why might an economist propose a policy that has little chance of adoption? *(4)*

PROBLEMS AND EXERCISES

1. Demonstrate graphically, and explain why, both perfect competition and a perfectly discriminating monopoly lead to a Pareto optimal outcome.
2. Say that the cost of a car crash is $8,000. Assume further that installing a safety device in a car at a cost of $12 will reduce the probability of an accident by .05 percent. The plant makes 1,000 cars each day.

   a. If the preceding are the only relevant costs, would you favor or oppose the installation of the safety device?
   b. What other costs might be relevant?

30

The Role of Government in the Economy

*You've got to distinguish between
a politician using economics and using economics.*

Charles Schultze

After reading this chapter, you should be able to:

1

State four arguments in favor of
government intervention in the economy.

2

Explain what an externality is.

3

State four arguments against government
intervention in the economy.

4

Define a sin tax and state why Milton
Friedman would likely disapprove of it.

5

List three arguments for
and against licensure.

6

Answer just about every question posed to
you with, "It depends on the costs
and benefits."

Should the government intervene in the private affairs of individuals? If the government does intervene, what should the nature of that intervention be? Throughout this book, these questions have been at the bottom of policy discussions. In this chapter I address these questions directly, tying together the policy discussions of the earlier chapters. I consider four justifications for government intervention in markets: to prevent restraints on trade; to offset problems of information and rationality; to correct externalities; and to prevent unfairness.

Most activities of real-world markets contain elements to which each of these reasons might apply. Thus, in most cases there's legitimate debate about whether the government should intervene, and, if it should, what form the intervention should take. Such decisions generally can be made only on the basis of specific knowledge about institutions and normative judgments, both of which are beyond the scope of an introductory economics textbook. What this book can provide you with is a framework for making such decisions. That's the purpose of this chapter.

Before you address the issues of government intervention, you must consider the question: What is government? In the United States we're all fairly clear about what we mean by **government.** It's the combination of federal, state, and local agencies whose officials are elected by the people, or are appointed by officials who are elected by the people. The federal government handles the economic matters of defense, income security, national economic regulation, and macroeconomic stability. State and local governments handle matters of education, roads, welfare, and state and local economic regulation.

Government The combination of federal, state, and local agencies whose officials are elected by the people or appointed by elected officials.

Not all countries are organized like this. Many governments, especially in developing countries, are autocracies in which the leaders are not subject to elections, but hold office on the basis of power or historical precedent. The division of responsibilities among levels of authority also differs. For example, in some countries educational policy is set on the national, rather than the state and local, level.

The discussion in this chapter assumes that the government either is a functioning democracy in which the people elect their leaders or else is a beneficent autocracy in which the unelected leader tries to do what's in the people's best interests. Faced with nonbeneficent autocracies in which the leaders worry only about their own benefit, not society's benefit, and in which the leaders pursue their own self-interests, almost all economists become supporters of government nonintervention or **laissez-faire** (the philosophy that government should intervene in the economy as little as possible).

Laissez-faire The philosophy that government should intervene in the economy as little as possible.

THE ARGUMENTS FOR AND AGAINST GOVERNMENT INTERVENTION

A good way to consider the arguments for and against government intervention is to consider a debate between two imaginary economists: Paul, who favors intervention, and Milton, who opposes it. I, the author, take the role of moderator. There's one rule: Each person will be allowed to present his case without interruption.

As background for the debate, let me state two general insights that form the basis of most economists' support of markets.

1. If two individuals trade in a market, one can presume that they're both better off after the trade; otherwise they wouldn't have traded.

2. If individuals are free to produce whatever goods they want, then when excess profit is being made, more people will enter into the production of that good and consumers will benefit as the price is pushed down.

Both economists in the debate accept these two insights but differ as to how many qualifications they make to them. In the imaginary debate that follows, Milton takes the position that few qualifications should be made. Paul takes the position that many qualifications should be made. The debate begins with Milton having stated the two general propositions, after which he draws the following conclusions:

ADDED DIMENSION

LAISSEZ-FAIRE
IS NOT ANARCHY

Most reasons for government intervention discussed in this chapter are debatable.

There is, however, one governmental role that even the strongest laissez-faire advocates generally accept. That role is for government to set up an appropriate institutional and legal structure within which markets can operate.

The reason there's little debate about this role is that all economists recognize that markets do not operate when there is anarchy. They require institutional structures that determine the rules of ownership, what types of trade are allowable, how contracts will be enforced, and what productive institutions are most desirable.

Before anyone conducts business, he or she needs to know the rules of the game and must have a reasonable expectation that those rules will not be changed. The operation of the modern economy requires that contractual arrangements be made among individuals. These contractual arrangements must be enforced if the economy is to operate effectively.

Economists differ significantly as to what the rules for such a system should be and whether any rules that already exist should be modified. Even if the rules are currently perceived as unfair, it can be argued that they should be kept in place. Individuals have already made decisions based on those rules, and it's unfair to them to change the rules in the middle of the game.

Stability of rules is a benefit to society. When the rules are perceived as unfair and changing them is also perceived as unfair, the government must find a balance between these two degrees of unfairness. Government often finds itself in that difficult position. Thus, while there's little debate about government's role in providing some institutional framework, there's heated debate about which framework is most appropriate.

For an interesting discussion of these issues applied to antitrust law, see Walter Adams and James Brock, *Antitrust Economics on Trial: A Dialogue on the New Laissez-Faire* (Princeton, N.J.: Princeton University Press, 1991).

Milton: *All government intervention can be seen as intervention in free trade among people. Government intervention prevents individuals from making trades that will make them both better off. Thus, government intervention can only hurt society. So let's get the government off our backs.*

Four Arguments for Government Intervention

Paul: *Oh, come on, Milton! I'm not naive. Your argument, while it sounds nice, doesn't stand up to close scrutiny. I can list four arguments for government intervention.*

1. Preventing Restraints on Trade

Paul: *The first insight argues that all agreements freely entered into should be allowed. But what if two people agree to limit supply and prevent others from entering the market? That would violate the second insight since individuals would not be free to produce whatever goods they want. You'll certainly want to amend your argument against intervention to rule out certain agreements that restrain trade. Thus, one argument for government intervention is to defend competition and to prevent restraint of trade.*

2. Correcting Informational and Rationality Problems

Paul: *A second argument for intervention is an informational and rationality argument. Your free trade argument assumes that people are rational and have all the information they need to make a rational decision. What if they aren't or don't? Say two individuals make a trade: A 3-year-old says to a 17-year old, "I'll give you my future inheritance if you'll let me play with your toy." In my view that trade is unfair because the 3-year-old isn't yet able to make rational decisions.*

Milton: *OK, I'll grant you that 3-year-olds don't fit my argument, but I'm talking about adults.*

Paul: *I am too. I only presented the argument about the 3-year-old to establish the point. Let's consider another example where the same principle applies. Let's say that your car breaks down and you have it towed to a garage where the me-*

Paul Samuelson—Nobel prize, 1970, for furthering economic science. © *The Nobel Foundation.*

ADDED DIMENSION

ECONOMIC DEBATES

An intellectual inquiry like economics is a debate of ideas. It's not a set of facts or truths. To understand arguments in economics, one must understand both sides of the arguments and the context within which a particular argument is made.

In a debate of ideas, usually a relatively simple idea is presented first. That simple idea provokes responses that can only be understood if the participants and the audience recognize that the responses are reactions to that initial idea. In order to understand ideas properly, one must know the arguments to which they are a response. These arguments require an understanding of the debate that has preceded them. For example, to understand the externality argument in favor of government intervention, one must understand the basic argument in favor of free trade to which the externality argument is a response.

There are higher and higher levels of arguments. Such higher-level arguments are the grist of academic journals and are one of the reasons many academic arguments seem unintelligible to students who don't know the history of the debate. (Another reason is that sometimes academic arguments are indeed unintelligible.)

I present this chapter as a debate to emphasize, first, that learning economics is like listening in on a conversation in which arguments build on one another and, second, that one can expect that there will always be a rebuttal to any argument. Picturing economics as such an unending clash of ideas gives one a good perspective on many economic issues.

chanic tells you that your differential is sloppy and your clutch is chattering and that they both need to be replaced at a total cost of $1,600. Or suppose a surgeon tells you that for $32,000 you can have a quadruple coronary artery bypass which will make you feel better. Both of these cases have a potential for useful government intervention, because the two sides in each transaction don't have equal access to information, meaning that the trades aren't necessarily fair. It could well be that all your car really needed was a $10 adjustment and that you had no need for bypass surgery. How can you be sure if the mechanic and the surgeon are advising what's best for you or if they just want the money? When both sides of a trade don't have equal access to information, the argument for nonintervention breaks down.

Similarly for rationality. People aren't always rational. Say some fast-talking salesperson convinces a 70-year-old couple to invest all their savings in a partnership to turn water into gold. They might do it voluntarily, but in my view that doesn't make it rational. Government intervention is necessary to prevent such injustices.

3. Correcting for Externalities

Paul: *Let's now consider another case. Say that we agree that I'll produce steel for you. I'll build my plant on land I own, and start producing. Who can complain? It's a fair trade freely entered into by both of us, right? It's fair for the two of us— but what about my plant's neighbors? I suspect that they'll complain, and rightfully so. The resulting smoke will pollute the air they breathe; the sulphur smell will drive all the tourists away; and the factory will be an eyesore. So there's an agreement freely entered into by rational individuals that it may be better for government to prevent because the agreement affects third parties.*

Such third-party effects are called **externalities** *(effects of decisions not taken into account by the decision makers). Externalities provide a potential role for government intervention. I can demonstrate the effect of an externality with the simple supply/demand graph in Exhibit 1.*

The supply curve, S, represents the marginal private cost to society of producing steel. It represents my opportunity cost. The demand curve, D, represents the marginal social benefit to demanders of my steel. When there are no externalities, the marginal private costs and benefits represent the marginal social costs and benefits, so the supply/demand equilibrium (P_0, Q_0) represents the point where the marginal social benefit equals the marginal social cost. At that point society is as well off as possible.

But now consider what happens when there are externalities in production, as in this example. In that case other people must bear part of the cost of our agreement. This means that the marginal social cost is different from the marginal

Externalities Effects of decisions not taken into account by the decision makers.

E xternalities can be positive or negative. A positive externality is the benefit conveyed to third parties by an action in which they were not actors themselves. A negative externality is the harm inflicted on third parties by an action in which they were not actors themselves. An example of a negative externality is the negative effect of pollution on society. An example of a positive externality is the effect on society of the education of its citizens.

When actions have either positive or negative third-party effects, it's not clear that society will be better off or worse off if it follows a laissez-faire policy. Unless the government intervenes, many agreements that produce negative externalities will be allowed and many agreements that produce positive externalities won't take place. Government intervention *may* be able to make individuals take third-party benefits or costs into account.

An extreme case of a positive externality is called a

public good. A *public good* is a good that an individual can consume without diminishing the amount of it that other people consume. Thus, supplying a public good conveys a positive externality not only to one or two individuals but to all individuals in the society. An example of a public good is national defense. Each person in an army who defends the nation provides defense for all in the society.

Many other activities carry with them strong negative externalities. Consider fishing from a lake. Whenever you catch a fish, there's one fewer fish for all other people to catch. You're better off, but other people are worse off. But you're concerned only with your own welfare, so you won't take into account the harm done to other people. Activities like that which deplete or use up a commonly held resource involve significant negative externalities. If we allow everyone to carry on such activity unrestricted—if we follow a policy of laissez-faire—society as a whole will be worse off.

private cost. I represent this case by adding a curve to Exhibit 1 which can be called the marginal social cost curve (to distinguish it from the marginal private cost curve). In my example this marginal social cost curve would include all the marginal costs that my neighbors bear from my production of steel as well as all the marginal private costs associated with that production.

When free trade is allowed, these costs aren't taken into account, and the supply/demand equilibrium is at too high a quantity, Q_0, and too low a price, P_0. The combination of price and quantity that takes into account all social costs and benefits occurs at P_1, Q_1, where the marginal social benefit equals the marginal social cost. Some type of intervention to reduce production from Q_0 to Q_1 and raise price from P_0 to P_1 is needed. Government is the logical agency to make that intervention.

Milton: *I can't let you continue. Your arguments make sense, but they're missing an essential point. And I'm not getting equal time—these boxes are extending the time allotted to Paul. I appeal to the author to let me respond.*

Author: *I'm sorry, Milton, but rules are rules; besides, good teaching requires presentation of all the arguments. So I'll let Paul state his final argument and then turn the pages over to you.*

4. Preventing Unfairness

Paul: *Thank you, Author. I'll try to be brief. My final argument is in some ways the most subtle, but in other ways is the most obvious. It goes like this: Markets operate only when there are property rights—when individuals control the items being traded. If one believes that the distribution of property rights is unfair, one can reasonably oppose the use of the market.*

Let's consider an example. Say a robber walks up to you and makes you an offer you can't refuse: "Your money or your life." You give him your money and in exchange he doesn't kill you. You're better off; he's better off; and no one else is worse off. But such an exchange is not one that, in my view, societies should condone. Put simply, the robber has no right to your life, so it's unfair for him to offer it in exchange for your money. Because the robber unfairly assumed property rights in your life, the result of the trade is unfair (although you're better off than if you hadn't made the trade).

Now let's change the example slightly. Instead of a robber, it's now an employer who makes you an offer you can't refuse: "You work for me on my terms or I'll fire you." The same unfairness argument can be made about this trade. One could argue that it's unfair because no one should have the right arbitrarily to refuse to allow a person to work, unless the terms of employment are "fair."

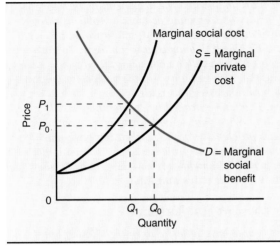

EXHIBIT 1   The Effect of an Externality

When there is a negative externality, the marginal private cost will be below the marginal social cost and the competitive price will be too low to maximize social welfare.

Most Americans don't hold that view; they believe that employment is a fair trade, within limits, as long as other jobs exist that an individual can take. But their concept of unfairness of underlying property rights determines many of their arguments in favor of government intervention, and rightfully so. Say that a firm decides that it doesn't want to hire you because you're black or a woman. Most Americans would argue that the employer has exceeded the limitations of the "fair" employment contract at that point, because a firm shouldn't be allowed to decide whom it will hire on the basis of race or sex.

    What I'm saying is that certain underlying rights—such as the right to employment—must be distributed equally for a society to be considered fair. Similarly with the right to a decent living. If the market doesn't provide that for people, then intervention is needed.

Author: *Before I turn the pages over to Milton, let me restate Paul's four arguments in favor of government intervention.*

Summary: Four Arguments for Government Intervention

1. Agreements to restrain trade should themselves be restricted.
2. When there are informational and rationality problems, government should intervene.
3. When there are externalities, intervention is necessary to see that marginal social costs and marginal social benefits are equal.
4. When property rights are unfair, government should intervene to achieve fairness.

Author: *Now go ahead, Milton.*

Milton: *It's always difficult to argue with Paul because he makes his arguments so clearly and convincingly. And in each of the cases he presents, I must agree that he captures a kernel of the truth. But all of the arguments suffer from a serious flaw. They assume that when the government comes in, it will actually correct a problem without introducing new problems that are even worse. Paul sees government as a group of individuals committed to doing good. That's not the way all governments work, as the author points out in the opening of this chapter. The point the author didn't make, and the point that Paul totally ignored, is that that's not the way even democratic governments operate. In my view all government is a mechanism through which some people—people in government and people with access to government—take advantage of other people.*

    Once one sees government for what it truly is, then the arguments for government intervention fall apart, except for government's role in establishing a proper institutional structure within which markets can operate. But, as the author pointed out, that general role isn't in debate.

Four Arguments against
Government Intervention

The other roles for government are *in debate. The argument against government intervention rests on the difficulty of correcting economic problems through government. Yes, all the problems Paul mentions do exist, and it would be nice if they didn't exist. But it would also be nice if diamonds grew on trees. To make the four arguments in favor of government intervention convincing, Paul would have to show that there's a better way and that the "solution" to the problems won't make the problems worse. Paul hasn't even addressed this issue.*

The reality is that government is often controlled by special interests. It's inefficient, bureaucratic, and oppressive. When you expand government, you make people worse off. So, yes, there are problems with the market, but government's attempts to correct those problems create worse problems. Laws passed in the name of the public good, in fact, generally benefit only a small group. To show you what I mean, let's consider each of the four cases that Paul presents.

1. Preventing Private Restraints on Trade Creates Even More Restraints

Milton: *There's no question that people have a desire to restrain trade, but if we look at the real world we see that the primary way they restrain trade is through governmental restrictions such as licensing requirements, antitrust legislation, and zoning regulations. Allowing government to try to stop private individuals from restricting trade opens up a Pandora's box of new possibilities for restricting trade through government. Not only will somewhat reasonable restrictions be made, totally unreasonable restrictions also will be made. And that Pandora's box need not be opened, because without government enforcement of restrictions, competition will soon break down any private restrictions on trade. The only long-lasting restraints are those imposed by government.*

2. Correcting Informational and Rationality Problems Creates Other Problems

Milton: *There's no doubt that informational problems like the ones Paul describes do exist. They're facts of life. But once again, using government to solve a problem creates worse problems. Say that government passes a law that all cost estimates for auto repairs must be approved as fair before the repairs can be made. Can you imagine how long you'd have to wait for the paperwork to be processed? You'd be waiting months for your car. And all that paperwork would add to your repair costs. Not only would you pay too much to have your car fixed; often you wouldn't get it back for months.*

Here's another example. The Food and Drug Administration "protects" us from unsafe drugs, but in doing so it creates enormous bureaucratic hassles for the manufacturers of all new drugs, many of which would be beneficial. For instance, the FDA prevented a number of experimental drugs from being used on AIDS patients for years, even though their use represented many people's only chance to survive, or at least to survive longer and more comfortably. By the time the FDA approved the drugs, many of the patients were dead.

3. Correcting for Externalities Creates Other Problems

Milton: *I've heard the externality argument hundreds of times, but, I swear, every time I examine a so-called externality, I discover either that it isn't a true externality that can be corrected by government or that the way in which government will correct for the externality will cause more harm than good.*

To see this, let's first consider Paul's Exhibit 1. Is it likely that government will pass a law reducing Paul's production of steel to Q_1 and raise the price to P_1? Or is it more likely that government will simply ban production of steel at Paul's house altogether? If it bans production of a good altogether, quantity will fall to zero. The good won't be available at any price, a result that would be far worse than if the market result had been left alone. Government regulatory agencies aren't designed to do the delicate balancing of benefits and costs necessary to make the marginal changes that Paul's argument calls for. Such refinements require a scalpel, and government intervention is more like a chain saw.

The same problem of government intervention causing more harm than good exists for activities with so-called positive externalities. Government intervention simply creates a possibility for special interests to come in and channel government revenue to support their own interests. In my view, positive externalities generally are the result of a poor specification of property rights. The positive externalities argument is made by some group attempting to use government for its own ends.

Government intervention for positive externalities inevitably means government subsidization, which must be paid for in higher taxes. These higher taxes are likely to offset the good the subsidized externalities might do; that is, higher taxes reduce private incentives to work and to undertake private economic activity. In my view and in the view of most noninterventionists generally, private activity done without government intervention involves as many, or more, positive externalities than do government-supported activities.

For example, in the early 1990s, as the threat from the former Soviet Union significantly diminished, it made sense to close a number of military bases around the country. But political pressure against doing so was intense. One argument used by supporters of keeping these bases open was that they had positive externalities: They created jobs for civilians in the area.

What's wrong with this argument is that in order to pay for these bases, government has to collect taxes, which discourages private activities. The net job creation is essentially zero. As was the case with negative externalities, even when government activities do have clear-cut positive externalities, it's not at all clear that the political process will choose the right amount of the activity. Generally the political process won't produce a decision based on comparing marginal social costs with marginal social benefits. It will make the decision based on marginal political costs and marginal political benefits, which often have little or nothing to do with marginal social costs or benefits.

As an example of how politics guide government's decisions, consider the B-2 (Stealth) bomber, which was kept in production long after most independent observers believed it would serve no useful purpose. Why? Because the Pentagon and defense firms that wanted the bomber built understood how the system operated and saw to it that its components were built in 48 different states. Members of Congress from these states were reluctant to cancel a defense contract that provided jobs for so many of their constituents. Consideration of politics, not cost-effectiveness, almost certainly guided the government's choice.

Finally, let's now consider the argument that Paul sneaked into his presentation in the box on externalities and public goods. That's the argument about the overuse of common resources. I suggest that the overfishing is not an example of market failure. It's an example of what happens when no market exists. Paul's argument was that the lake would be overfished because of individuals' failure to take into account the full social cost of catching fish. I contend that the overfishing occurred because no one owns the lake. If someone owned the lake, that person would take into account the fact that when someone caught a fish, the catch available to others was reduced. To prevent overfishing the owner would charge people for the right to fish and would maximize his or her wealth by seeing to it that enough fish were left in the lake to reproduce for next year's fishing. Or, alternatively, consider air pollution: If the air were owned by private individuals, those individuals would charge others for the right to pollute it and, in doing so, would decrease the amount of pollution.

Even though the air isn't privately owned, people will negotiate ways to reduce or eliminate the negative externalities of air pollution. For example, if Paul's neighbors are so worried about air pollution from the mill he proposes to build on his land, they can get together and buy his property or, at least, pay him not to build the mill. Any other solution is simply a usurping of Paul's property rights.

4. Preventing Unfairness Creates More Unfairness

Milton: *Paul was right in saving the unfairness argument for the end because it's the argument that we market advocates find most difficult to defend against. But it too suffers from a serious flaw. It suggests that some standard of fairness other than the market standard exists by which to judge events.*

I contend that the market is a standard of fairness to which many people, including me, subscribe: People who are more productive and who work harder deserve more material rewards than people who don't work hard. By rewarding productivity and hard work, the market stimulates economic activity and provides benefits for everyone.

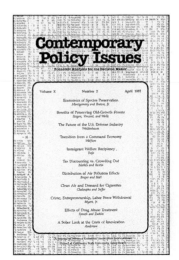

One of the most policy-oriented of the economic journals.

ADDED DIMENSION   THE LIGHTHOUSE AND THE BEES

The debate about externalities, public goods, and differences between marginal social costs and benefits has long been conducted in economics. The examples that have been used are subject to much criticism.

For instance, an early textbook example of a public good that had to be supplied by government rather than privately was the lighthouse. If one person builds a lighthouse so coastal ships can avoid the rocks, the benefit will be there for others to enjoy. So, the textbook argument went, private business wouldn't provide lighthouses because lighthouses were a public good. However, upon searching the real world, people discovered that many private lighthouses existed and that firms had found ways to finance the lighthouses privately. The lighthouse example was dropped from the textbooks.

Another frequent textbook example of marginal social costs differing from marginal private costs has been the case of bees. The textbooks argued: Bees pollinate blossoms and therefore provide a positive externality. Because of this positive externality, there will be too few bees because the benefits they provide—flowers—are external to the beekeeper's decisions—to keep them for their honey.

But when researchers looked into beekeeping, they found a market in bee services. Orchard owners were rent-ing bees from beekeepers in order to pollinate the flowers on their trees. The externality was being paid for and therefore wasn't an externality. The bee example was dropped from the textbooks.

Some opponents of government intervention to correct for externalities use these examples to argue that government shouldn't intervene on the basis of externalities, but that argument is too strong. The existence of private markets doesn't mean that the private market supplies enough of the good or service to make the marginal social cost equal the marginal social benefit. Nor does it mean that there aren't other, better, examples in which there are no markets.

Two lessons should be drawn from these two examples:

1. One should always carefully consider the arguments that textbook writers make and compare those arguments to reality.

2. One should recognize that private sources of solutions to social problems may exist and that before one advocates having government intervene to correct for an externality, one should carefully consider the private alternatives.

Let's consider Paul's example about the employer when he talked about "Preventing unfairness." Why is the employer the employer? Paul didn't answer that. He made it seem as if it was simply happenstance. But more often than not, the employer is the employer because he or she worked harder or was more productive than others. If society limits the gains of hard work and the freedom of people who work hard to do what they want, then society will discourage hard work. When hard work by the productive people is discouraged, society is made worse off.

That's bad, but the negative incentives created by government intervention are even worse. As soon as people see that they can get more rewards from the government than from their own hard work, productivity slows and private economic activity is discouraged. Keeping arguments about fairness out of the government decision-making process helps everyone, the poor as well as the rich. It creates more for everyone as the wealth trickles down from the hard-working rich to the poor. The only workable standard of fairness is the market standard: Them that works gets; them that don't work go without—unless them that works want to help them that don't.

Author: *Paul, before you respond, I'd like to summarize Milton's four arguments against government intervention.*

3 Summary: Four Arguments against Government Intervention

1. Preventing private restraints on trade creates even more restraints.
2. Correcting informational and rationality problems creates even more problems.
3. Correcting for externalities creates other problems.
4. Preventing unfairness creates more unfairness.

Author: *Now, Paul, you can respond, but please be brief.*

Paul's Rebuttals

Paul: *I must admit that there's a certain truth to each of Milton's counterarguments. But, in my view, government isn't nearly so controlled by special interests or so inefficient as Milton would have us believe. For every case of government ineffectiveness, I can point to a case of effective government intervention.*

EXHIBIT 2   **Regulation through Taxing**

If the government sets a tax sufficient to take into account a negative externality, individuals will respond by reducing the quantity of the pollution-causing activity supplied to a level that individuals would have supplied had they included the negative externality in their decision.

As for property rights eliminating the need for government: Who is to establish those rights, if not government? Without government, productive activity would be impossible; people would spend all their time fighting over property rights. Governments use markets to avoid continually making judgments of who should get what. Once the initial property rights are established, the market decides. That method saves enormous political fighting and is good and necessary. But if the initial allocation of property rights leads to results that aren't to society's liking, then it's society's right to modify those property rights. Property rights aren't inalienable rights; they're conferred rights.

What I'm saying is that the market is not above the government. Rather the government is above the market, and a democratic government will see to it that the market's allocation of property rights is within the range of fairness that society finds acceptable. If Milton doesn't agree with society's right to change property rights, then he doesn't agree with democracy. Let me give you an example of the need for government to make decisions about fairness.

Milton says, "Private individuals should own the lakes and the air." But who decides which individuals will be the owners, and who prevents unproductive fights over the allocation of property rights? If the government didn't act to prevent private individuals from usurping common resources, the social structure would break down.

Next let me deal with the argument that government intervention is a chain saw instead of the scalpel that we need. In many cases of past regulation I think Milton is right, but he's right only because economists haven't played a significant role in helping to design the government's intervention.

*All too often the type of government intervention has been administrative or regulatory. One benefit of economics is that it suggests alternatives to regulation. For example, consider pollution. If, rather than regulating the permissible amount of pollution administratively, government taxes pollution—creating activities and subsidizes reduction of pollution, the result can be more precise and appropriate— the scalpel effect. Say that in Exhibit 2 the government determines that the additional marginal social cost of producing steel equals C_2. If government sets a firm's pollution tax on steel production at $t = C_2$, the firm will reduce its output to Q_1 on its own. It's a tribute to economists' influence that such taxes, called **effluent fees**, are now widely used in helping deal with pollution.*

An alternative way in which the government can regulate efficiently is to foster the creation of markets. As I stated, markets don't simply come into existence; they require the definition, establishment, and enforcement of property rights. Pollution provides an example here. In dealing with pollution, governments in certain areas are establishing "pollution rights." All existing firms are required to reduce their pollution by 10 percent. New firms can pollute if they pay existing firms to reduce pollution further, by an amount that will offset the new pollution introduced by the new firms. If an existing firm is willing to reduce its pollution by 20 percent, it can sell some of its entitlements to pollute to new firms and to other existing

Effluent fees Charges imposed by government on pollution.

firms which, with these permits, would be allowed to reduce pollution by less than the required 10 percent. By creating these rights and establishing a market in them, total pollution can be reduced by 10 percent, while each individual firm is still free to decide how much it will reduce pollution. Firms that have a low marginal cost of reducing pollution will reduce more than 10 percent so they can sell the right to pollute to other firms whose cost of reducing pollution is higher.

Such novel plans have problems that must be worked out before they can be widely used, but they demonstrate that government regulation can be made compatible with the market.

Finally let me comment on the ''them that works gets'' philosophy. It isn't so simple. There's nothing necessarily fair about the allocation of abilities. What's fair about Michael Jordan being endowed with his natural abilities and someone else being born a klutz? Should we let people starve simply because their market wage is below the subsistence wage? Society will continue to use the market only if it can adjust the distributional results of the market.

Milton's Rebuttals

Milton: *Paul concedes many of my points and differs from me primarily in judgments. But he gives few justifications for his judgments. Those justifications aren't better than the ones I initially gave, so they don't require a direct rebuttal. It's quite clear that I have a much stronger belief in the sanctity of property rights than does Paul. Because of this belief, I find it necessary to limit government by historical and constitutional constraints, such as existing property rights. I ask Paul to compare the experience of Western market economies with socialist economies if he wants an example of the power of property rights and the market.*

As for interventionist economists improving the situation, I have my doubts. Often they have simply introduced new ways for government to intervene—ways that look as if they are compatible with markets, but actually require enormous government involvement.

The Difficult Decisions

At this point our debate must stop. General arguments are fine, but judging from historical experience, the debate is unending. Both sides of this debate about whether government should intervene in the market have valid points. No one general argument obviously wins out over the others. Decisions about government intervention will need to be made on a case-by-case basis, using a cost/benefit framework. In the remainder of this chapter, we look at two cases to give you an idea of the clash of these ideas in the real world.

THE DRUG LEGALIZATION DEBATE

Let's start by considering two letters that appeared in *The Wall Street Journal* in 1989. In the first, Milton Friedman (a well-known free market economist) advocates the legalization of marijuana. The second is a response by William Bennett, who headed the federal government's office of National Drug Control Policy. After exploring these two views, we'll consider a policy partway between the two: Legalize drugs, but tax them so heavily that their price doesn't fall.

A Drug Policy Alternative

The debate laid out in the Friedman and Bennett letters leaves out a third possibility that some economists support: the legalize-but-tax alternative, a position in between Bennett's and Friedman's. It accepts a government role in controlling the use of drugs, but it uses market incentives to achieve the desired end.

According to this perspective, government should legalize drug consumption but impose enormously high taxes on the sale of drugs. This possibility is sometimes called a **sin tax** approach because it discourages activities society believes are harmful (sinful) for individuals. Thus, the government is making a value judgment about what's good for individuals, but it's using market incentives rather than regulation to achieve its end. How that end could be achieved is shown in Exhibit 3.

When legalized, drugs have a price of P_e and a quantity of Q_e. A law forbidding the sale of drugs should, in principle, reduce the supply to zero. In

Sin tax Tax designed to discourage activities society believes are harmful to individuals.

AN OPEN LETTER TO BILL BENNETT

Dear Bill:

In Oliver Cromwell's eloquent words, "I beseech you, in the bowels of Christ, think it possible you may be mistaken" about the course you and President Bush urge us to adopt to fight drugs. The path you propose of more police, more jails, use of the military in foreign countries, harsh penalties for drug users, and a whole panoply of repressive measures can only make a bad situation worse. The drug war cannot be won by those tactics without undermining the human liberty and individual freedom that you and I cherish.

You are not mistaken in believing that drugs are a scourge that is devastating our society. You are not mistaken in believing that drugs are tearing asunder our social fabric, ruining the lives of many young people, and imposing heavy costs on some of the most disadvantaged among us. You are not mistaken in believing that the majority of the public share your concerns. In short, you are not mistaken in the end you seek to achieve.

Your mistake is failing to recognize that the very measures you favor are a major source of the evils you deplore. Of course the problem is demand, but it is not only demand, it is demand that must operate through repressed and illegal channels. Illegality creates obscene profits that finance the murderous tactics of the drug lords; illegality leads to the corruption of law enforcement officials; illegality monopolizes the efforts of honest law forces so that they are starved for resources to fight the simpler crimes of robbery, theft and assault.

Drugs are a tragedy for addicts. But criminalizing their use converts that tragedy into a disaster for society, for users and non-users alike. Our experience with the prohibition of drugs is a replay of our experience with the prohibition of alcoholic beverages.

In 1972 I wrote a column on "Prohibition and Drugs." The major problem then was heroin from Marseilles; today, it is cocaine from Latin America. Today, also, the problem is far more serious than it was 17 years ago: more addicts, more innocent victims; more drug pushers, more law enforcement officials; more money spent to enforce prohibition, more money spent to circumvent prohibition.

Had drugs been decriminalized 17 years ago, "crack" would never have been invented (it was invented because the high cost of illegal drugs made it profitable to provide a cheaper version) and there would today be far fewer addicts. The lives of thousands, perhaps hundreds of thousands of innocent victims would have been saved, and not only in the U.S. The ghettos of our major cities would not be drug-and-crime–infested no-man's lands. Fewer people would be in jails, and fewer jails would have been built.

Colombia, Bolivia and Peru would not be suffering from narco-terror, and we would not be distorting our foreign policy because of narco-terror. Hell would not, in the words with which Billy Sunday welcomed Prohibition, "be forever for rent," but it would be a lot emptier.

Decriminalizing drugs is even more urgent now than in 1972, but we must recognize that the harm done in the interim cannot be wiped out, certainly not immediately. Postponing decriminalization will only make matters worse, and make the problem appear even more intractable.

Alcohol and tobacco cause many more deaths in users than do drugs. Decriminalization would not prevent us from treating drugs as we now treat alcohol and tobacco: prohibiting sales of drugs to minors, outlawing the advertising of drugs and similar measures. Such measures could be enforced, while outright prohibition cannot be. Moreover, if even a small fraction of the money we now spend on trying to enforce drug prohibition were devoted to treatment and rehabilitation, in an atmosphere of compassion not punishment, the reduction in drug usage and in the harm done to the users could be dramatic.

This plea comes from the bottom of my heart. Every friend of freedom, and I know you are one, must be as revolted as I am by the prospect of turning the United States into an armed camp, by the vision of jails filled with casual drug users and of an army of enforcers empowered to invade the liberty of citizens on slight evidence. A country in which shooting down unidentified planes "on suspicion" can be seriously considered as a drug-war tactic is not the kind of United States that either you or I want to hand on to future generations.

Milton Friedman
Senior Research Fellow
Hoover Institution
Stanford University

reality the law would only decrease the supply somewhat, depending on the degree of enforcement of the law and people's adherence to it.

Assuming that the law prohibiting drug trafficking decreases supply from S_0 to S_1, the equilibrium black market price of drugs is P_b and the black market quantity of drugs sold is Q_b. Notice the large difference between the free market cost of producing Q_b, which is C_b, and the black market price, P_b. The difference (the shaded rectangle) is a cost that reflects the aversion to breaking the law, either because it represents a chance of being caught and punished or because it represents the cost to individuals who find it morally wrong to violate the law.

A RESPONSE TO MILTON FRIEDMAN

Dear Milton:

There was little, if anything, new in your open letter to me calling for the legalization of drugs. As your earlier 1972 article made clear, the legalization argument is an old and familiar one, which has recently been revived by a small number of journalists and academics who insist that the only solution to the drug problem is no solution at all. What surprises me is that you would continue to advocate so unrealistic a proposal without pausing to consider seriously its consequences.

If the argument for drug legalization has one virtue it is its sheer simplicity. Eliminate laws against drugs, and street crime will disappear. Take the profit out of the black market through decriminalization and regulation, and poor neighborhoods will no longer be victimized by drug dealers. Cut back on drug enforcement, and use the money to wage a public health campaign against drugs, as we do with tobacco and alcohol.

Counting Costs

The basic premise of all these propositions is that using our nation's laws to fight drugs is too costly. To be sure, our attempts to reduce drug use do carry with them enormous costs. But the question that must be asked—and which is totally ignored by the legalization advocates—is, what are the costs of *not* enforcing laws against drugs?

In my judgment, and in the judgment of virtually every serious scholar in this field, the potential costs of legalizing drugs would be so large as to make it a public policy disaster.

Of course, no one, including you, can say with certainty what would happen in the U.S. if drugs were suddenly to become a readily purchased product. We do know, however, that wherever drugs have been cheaper and more easily obtained, drug use—and, addiction—has skyrocketed. In opium and cocaine producing countries, addiction is rampant among the peasants involved in drug production.

Professor James Q. Wilson tells us that during the years in which heroin could be legally prescribed by doctors in Britain, the number of addicts increased forty-fold. And, after the repeal of Prohibition—an analogy favored but misunderstood by legalization advocates—consumption of alcohol soared by 350%.

Could we afford such dramatic increases in drug use? I doubt it. Already the toll of drug use on American society—measured in lost productivity, in rising health insurance costs, in hospitals flooded with drug overdose emergencies, in drug caused accidents, and in premature death—is surely more than we would like to bear.

You seem to believe that by spending just a little more money on treatment and rehabilitation, the costs of increased addiction can be avoided. That hope betrays a basic misunderstanding of the problems facing drug treatment. Most addicts don't suddenly decide to get help. They remain addicts either because treatment isn't available or because they don't seek it out. The National Drug Control Strategy announced by President Bush on Sept. 5 goes a long way in making sure that more treatment slots are available. But the simple fact remains that many drug users won't enter treatment until they are forced to—often by the very criminal justice system you think is the source of the problem.

As for the connection between drugs and crime, your unswerving commitment to a legalization solution prevents you from appreciating the complexity of the drug market. Contrary to your claim, most addicts do not turn to crime to support their

Those suppliers who aren't caught make enormous profits. From discussions I've had with individuals exposed to the drug trade, I understand that the pay for low-level suppliers is $50 to $100 an hour, and for high-level suppliers it's in the $1,000 to $10,000 an hour range. The profit to suppliers (the lightly shaded area in Exhibit 3) is large, as you can see. How large depends on the elasticity of the supply and demand curves, how vigorously the law is enforced, and how strongly people feel about breaking the law. The cost of producing the drugs compared to the selling price is likely to be minimal. Most of a black market drug's price is a payment for the seller's risk of getting caught.

Now let's say that instead of prohibiting drug trafficking, the government institutes an extremely high tax of t_1 on drug sales. That tax shifts the after-tax supply curve from S_0 to S_1, just as the law did, so that the price that the consumer pays to receive quantity Q_b is still P_b. Drug users are now presented with a choice: to buy illegally from a black market dealer and risk arrest, or to buy legally from a government-authorized seller at the same price but with no risk of arrest. Faced with that option, most buyers would buy from government-authorized sellers. In response, dealers would be forced to lower prices and some would be squeezed out of the market. As that happened, the government would get more of the revenue that had been going to the dealers.

The extra revenue could be substantial—perhaps as much as $50 or $60 billion if most black market sales at lower prices could be prevented. The government habit. Research shows that many of them were involved in criminal activity before they turned to drugs. Many former addicts who have received treatment continue to commit crimes during their recovery. And even if drugs were legal, what evidence do you have that the habitual drug user wouldn't continue to rob and steal to get money for clothes, food or shelter? Drug addicts always want more drugs than they can afford, and no legalization scheme has yet come up with a way of satisfying that appetite.

The National Drug Control Strategy emphasizes the importance of reclaiming the streets and neighborhoods where drugs have wrought havoc because, I admit, the price of having drug laws is having criminals who will try to subvert them. Your proposal might conceivably reduce the amount of gang- and dealer-related crimes but it is fanciful to suggest that it would make crime vanish. Unless you are willing to distribute drugs freely and widely, there will always be a black market to undercut the regulated one. And as for the potential addicts, for the school children and for the pregnant mothers, all of whom would find drugs more accessible and legally condoned, your proposal would offer nothing at all.

So I advocate a larger criminal justice system to take drug users off the streets and deter new users from becoming more deeply involved in so hazardous an activity. You suggest that such policies would turn the country "into an armed camp." Try telling that to the public housing tenants who enthusiastically support plans to enhance security in their buildings, or to the residents who applaud police when a local crack house is razed. They recognize that drug use is a threat to the individual liberty and domestic tranquility guaranteed by the Constitution.

I remain an ardent defender of our nation's laws against illegal drug use and our attempts to enforce them because I believe drug use is wrong. A true friend of freedom understands that government has a responsibility to craft and uphold laws that help educate citizens about right and wrong. That, at any rate, was the Founders' view of our system of government.

Liberal Ridicule

Today this view is much ridiculed by liberal elites and entirely neglected by you. So while I cannot doubt the sincerity of your opinion on drug legalization, I find it difficult to respect. The moral cost of legalizing drugs is great, but it is a cost that apparently lies outside the narrow scope of libertarian policy prescriptions.

I do not have a simple solution to the drug problem. I doubt that one exists. But I am committed to fighting the problem on several fronts through imaginative policies and hard work over a long period of time. As in the past, some of these efforts will work and some won't. Your response, however, is to surrender and see what happens. To my mind that is irresponsible and reckless public policy. At a time when national intolerance for drug use is rapidly increasing, the legalization argument is a political anachronism. Its recent resurgence is, I trust, only a temporary distraction from the genuine debate on national drug policy.

William J. Bennett
Director
Office of National Drug
Control Policy

could greatly reduce black market sales if it used, say, one-fifth of the tax proceeds to increase the enforcement effort. Illegal dealers would be squeezed on both sides. Their costs would rise and their revenues would fall since they'd have

EXHIBIT 3   The Sin Tax Alternative

If drug consumption is legalized, the government can discourage drug use by imposing high taxes on the sale of drugs. If the use of the drugs is legal and no intervention takes place, along supply S_0 the price is P_e and the quantity consumed is Q_e. By instituting a high tax rate of t_1, the government can cause the supply curve to shift up from S_0 to S_1, raising the price from P_e to P_b and decreasing the quantity supplied from Q_e to Q_b. The government will receive the shaded area in taxes.

to charge 10 or 20 percent less than the legal price to get people to buy their illegal drugs rather than the legal drugs. The remaining tax revenue could be used for drug treatment programs and for educating people about the evils of drugs. How much revenue the government would receive and how effective the tax would be in stopping drug use depends on the elasticities of supply and demand. A good exercise for you is to explain, assuming it could choose, whether the government should prefer elastic or inelastic supply and demand curves.

Many more arguments could be made for and against all three of these positions regarding government intervention in the drug trade. But the discussion should be enough to start you thinking about the myriad options available for dealing with society's problems and about how economics provides a way to consider the costs and benefits of the various options.

THE LICENSURE DEBATE

As the drug trade example demonstrates, all government intervention is not the same. The government can respond to any specific problem or situation in any number of ways, some of which are preferable to others. As a result of political pressure, the important policy debates often concern not *whether* government should intervene, but *how*.

5 In the drug example we looked at taxation as the method of intervention. Now let's consider another example of government intervention—the licensing of doctors—and consider an alternative.[1]

Licensing Doctors

In the early 1800s medical licenses were not required by law in the United States, so anyone who wanted to could set up shop as a physician. The most popular type of medical treatment at the time was heroic therapy, which consisted primarily of bloodletting, blistering, and the administration of massive doses of mineral poisons, such as mercury.[2] The practitioners of two alternative types of medicine—homeopathy (which focused on natural healing) and eclecticism (which combined a variety of approaches) together laid the foundation of modern medicine. These practitioners challenged the status quo by arguing that heroic therapy was not helping people. They pressured Congress to pass licensure laws requiring that all doctors earn a license to practice medicine by receiving training in homeopathy and eclecticism. Ever since it has been illegal to practice medicine without a license.

To get that license, one must go through a pre-med program in college, four years of medical school, and a residency in a hospital for anywhere from one to several years, as well as pass a series of National Medical Board examinations.

Licensing of doctors is justified by the informational and rationality problems discussed before. Since individuals often don't have an accurate way of deciding whether a doctor is good, government intervention is necessary. The informational problem is solved because licensing requires that all doctors have at least a minimum competency. People have the *information* that a doctor must be competent because they see the license framed and hanging on the doctor's office wall.

Sometimes even when people have the information available, they don't use it *rationally*. Without licensing, businesses would be established to sell a whole set of schemes, such as using laetrile to fight cancer or using vitamin C to fight everything. According to scientific research, laetrile does not cure cancer and vitamin C does not cure everything.

A small number of economists, of whom Milton Friedman is the best known, have proposed that licensure laws be eliminated, leaving the medical field unlicensed. While such a proposal is supported by only a few economists, it's

---

[1] The arguments presented here about licensing doctors also apply to dentists, lawyers, college professors, cosmetologists (in some states, cosmetologists must be licensed), and other professional groups.

[2] Bloodletting involved extracting blood from the body, on the theory that the person's problem stemmed from "too much blood." Blistering involved causing blisters to form on the body, on the theory that when they burst, they would expel the poisonous matter that was making the person ill.

instructive to consider their proposal: Let anyone practice medicine who wishes to.

They argue that licensure was instituted as much, or more, to restrict supply as it was to help the consumer. Specifically critics of medical licensure raise these questions:

Why, if licensed medical training is so great, do we even need formal restrictions to keep other types of medicine from being practiced?

Whom do these restrictions benefit: the general public or the doctors who practice mainstream medicine?

What have the long-run effects of licensure been?

Even the strongest critics of licensure agree that in the case of doctors, the informational argument for government intervention is strong. But the question is whether licensure is the right form of government intervention. Why doesn't the government simply provide the public with information about which treatments work and which don't? That would give the freest rein to **consumer sovereignty** (the right of the individual to make choices about what is consumed and produced). As for the rationality argument, critics of licensure simply reject it out of hand. They ask: Who is the government to decide for people what is, or isn't, good for them? If people have the necessary information but still choose to treat cancer with laetrile or treat influenza with massive doses of vitamin C, why should the government tell them they can't?

Consumer sovereignty The right of the individual to make choices about what is consumed and produced.

If the informational alternative is preferable to licensure, why didn't the government choose it? Friedman argues that government didn't follow that path because the licensing was done as much for the doctors as for the general public. Licensure has led to a monopoly position for doctors. They can restrict supply and increase price and thereby significantly increase their incomes. Friedman further argues that the group most hurt by the decision to choose the licensure alternative is the poor, who often can't afford the higher fees licensed doctors charge.

Let's now take a closer look at the informational alternative.

The informational alternative is to allow anyone to practice medicine, but to have the government certify doctors' backgrounds and qualifications. The government would require that doctors' backgrounds be made public knowledge. Each doctor would have to post the following information prominently in his or her office:

The Informational Alternative to Licensure

1. Grades in college.
2. Grades in medical school.
3. Success rate for various procedures.
4. References.
5. Medical philosophy.
6. Charges and fees.

According to supporters of the informational alternative, these data would allow individuals to make informed decisions about their medical care. Like all informed decisions, they would be complicated. For instance, doctors who take only patients with minor problems can show high "success rates," while doctors who are actually more skilled but who take on problem patients may have to provide more extensive information so people can see why their success rates shouldn't be compared to those of the doctors who take just easy patients. But despite the problems, supporters of the informational alternative argue that it's better than the current situation.

Current licensure laws don't provide any of this information to the public. All a patient knows is that a doctor has managed to get through medical school and has passed the medical board exams (which are, after all, only sets of multiple-choice questions). The doctor may have done all this 30 years ago, possibly by the skin of his or her teeth, but, once licensed, a doctor is a doctor for life. (A well-known doctor joke is the following: What do you call the person with the lowest grade point average in medical school? Answer: Doctor.) Thus, the informational alternative would provide much more useful data to the public than the current licensing procedure.

Let's now consider two examples of how the informational alternative would work.

Two Examples of How the Informational Alternative Would Work　Say you're wondering whether that new mole on your arm is cancerous. What do you do? Under our current system, you ask your private physician, or you go to your local hospital and ask. The physician, most likely, won't know. He or she had two or three lectures on skin cancer in medical school and may have seen some in practice, but probably isn't a specialist in cancer. So all you get is a referral to a specialist (cost: $35).

Why not go to the specialist in the first place? By agreement among doctors, specialists usually will see only those patients who have been referred to them by a general physician.[3] Now let's say that you go to the specialist, who looks at the mole and recognizes immediately that it's just a mole (cost: $50). But she orders a biopsy, just to be sure (cost: $20). She's right and you're relieved, but you're also $105 poorer. To find out from the specialist whether the mole was cancerous cost you $105 and about four hours of your time. Many people without insurance won't pay the cost. They'll just hope the mole isn't cancerous.

Consider this hypothetical informational alternative: You go to a person who hasn't been to medical school, but who's been through a special one-year training program in diagnosing malignant carcinomas (skin cancer). The success rate of detection by such persons is 99.8 percent; the fee is $10 if no biopsy is needed, $30 if one is. The process is quick, easy, and inexpensive.

As a second example, consider surgery. This should be the strongest case for licensure. Would you want an untrained butcher to operate on you? Of course not. But opponents of licensure point out that it's not at all clear how effectively licensure prevents butchery. Ask a doctor, "Would you send your child to any board-certified surgeon picked at random?" The honest answer you'd get is "No way. Some of them are butchers." How do they know that? Being around hospitals, they have access to information about various surgeons' success and failure rates; they've seen them operate and know whether or not they have manual dexterity.

Advocates of the informational alternative suggest that you ask yourself, "What skill would you want in a surgeon?" A likely answer would be "Manual dexterity. Her fingers should be magic fingers." Does the existing system of licensure ensure that everyone who becomes a surgeon has magic fingers? No. To become licensed as a surgeon requires a grueling seven-year residency after four years of medical school, but manual dexterity, as such, is never explicitly tested or checked!

The informational alternative wouldn't necessarily eliminate the seven-year surgical residency. If the public believed that a seven-year residency was necessary to create skilled surgeons, many potential surgeons would choose that route. But there would be other ways to become a surgeon. For example, in high school, tests could be given for manual dexterity. Individuals with superb hand/eye coordination could go to a one-year technical college to train to be "heart technicians," who would work as part of a team doing heart surgery.

Clearly open-heart surgery is the extreme case, and most people will not be convinced that it can be performed by unlicensed medical personnel. But what

---

[3] Sometimes the general physician and the specialist are in the same group practice, and they each contribute a percentage of their income to a common pool, which is later divided among the members of the pool. Thus, when the doctors are in a group practice, the referring doctor gets a percentage of the specialist's fee. In such cases it's not even clear that your doctor has an incentive to send you to the most competent specialist!

about minor surgery? According to informational alternative advocates, many operations could be conducted more cheaply and better (since people with better manual dexterity would be doing the work) if restrictive licensing were ended. Or, if you don't accept the argument for human medical treatments, how about for veterinarians? For cosmetologists? For plumbers? Might the informational alternatives work in these professions?

Some Words of Caution about the Informational Alternative   If you were convinced that the informational alternative was preferable to medical licensure, beware. The preceding discussion of licensure and the informational alternative presented only the arguments in favor of that alternative. It highlights the benefits of the informational alternative and the problems with the licensure alternative. I presented the alternatives in a one-sided way to stimulate your thinking, not to convince you that doctors are monopolists concerned only with their own incomes and that eliminating the medical monopoly will solve our country's health care woes. Reality is far more complicated than that. A complete presentation would have discussed problems of the informational alternative and how, if chosen, the alternative could be implemented. In the real world, systems for qualifying professionals have serious problems; arguments can be made against the informational and certification alternatives that would convince you that neither is the answer.

Ultimately one needs an intimate knowledge of the actual practice and institutions to judge whether reforms would really make things better or worse. Therein lies the problem of reform. Just about the only individuals who have detailed knowledge are those who have a vested interest in the current system. So the information you're likely to get about potential reforms may well be biased toward only those reforms that will help the vested interest.

As a textbook writer, I wish I could say that some conclusions can be drawn about whether the government should, or should not, enter into the economy. I certainly have views about particular instances (in case you haven't guessed, I'm a highly opinionated individual), but to lay out arguments and information that would convince a reasonable person to agree with me would take an entire book for each area in which government might intervene.

What I can do in this textbook is to stimulate your interest in discovering for yourself the information and the subtleties of the debates for and against government intervention. Just about every time you read, hear, or are asked the question "Should the government intervene in a market?" the answer is "It depends." If your first impulse is to give any answer other than that one, you may have trouble maintaining the appropriate objectivity when you start considering the costs and benefits of government intervention.

CONCLUSION

6

KEY POINTS

- A laissez-faire policy is not anarchy. **1**
- Possible reasons for government intervention include preventing private restraints on trade, informational and rationality problems, externalities, and unfairness. **1**
- An externality is the result of a market transaction that is not taken into account by the transactors. **2**
- Laissez-faire advocates argue that government intervention usually makes the situation worse, not better. **3**

- Making something illegal creates the possibility of a black market with large returns to breaking the law. **3**
- Taxing an illegal activity is an alternative way of discouraging it. **4**
- Licensure laws are often presented as helping the public, but in fact are often designed to help a particular group. **5**
- In answer to a question "Should the government intervene?" an objective initial response is almost always "It depends." **6**

KEY TERMS

consumer
   sovereignty   *(635)*

effluent fees   *(629)*
externalities   *(623)*

government   *(621)*
laissez-faire   *(621)*

sin tax   *(630)*

QUESTIONS FOR THOUGHT AND REVIEW

The number after each question represents the estimated degree of critical thinking required. (1 = almost none; 10 = deep thought.)

1. State four reasons for a potentially beneficial role of government intervention.   *(1)*
2. Would a laissez-faire advocate support or oppose anti-trust laws? Why or why not?   *(9)*
3. Should the Food and Drug Administration's role in restricting which drugs may be marketed be eliminated? Why or why not?   *(8)*
4. Pollution is often considered an externality. Should the government pass laws that prevent pollution? Why or why not?   *(8)*
5. What would be the sin tax method of controlling pollution?   *(4)*

6. Most redistribution in the United States is from one middle-class group to another middle-class group. What does that suggest about the laissez-faire/government intervention fight?   *(5)*
7. Why would Milton Friedman likely oppose the legalize-and-heavily-tax solution to the addictive drug problem?   *(5)*
8. Why would William Bennett likely oppose the legalize-and-heavily-tax solution to the addictive drug problem?   *(5)*
9. Financial analysts are currently unlicensed. Should they be licensed? Why or why not?   *(6)*
10. An advanced degree is required in order to teach at most colleges. In what sense is this a form of restricting entry through licensure?   *(5)*

PROBLEMS AND EXERCISES

1. The marginal cost, marginal social cost, and demand for a firm are given in the accompanying diagram. The social cost is higher than the private cost due to pollution emitted by the plant.
   a. What is the efficient level of output?
   b. Given the information in the accompanying diagram, if the government wanted to set a fee to force the firm to decrease emissions, what fee would you recommend?
2. Congratulations! You've been made finance minister of Happyland. The president is unhappy that so many of her subjects are taking illegal drugs. You recommend legalizing such drugs and then imposing a tax on them.
   a. Demonstrate graphically the supply/demand equilibrium for the use of illegal drugs before your program is instituted.
   b. What should the minimum amount of tax be if the president wants to keep drug use no higher than its previous level?
   c. Show graphically the government's revenue.

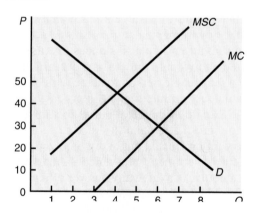

d. Your drug program failed miserably for political reasons. The president fires you but secretly comes to you for advice. She has heard that a cartel is taking over the drug trade and wonders what she should do about it. What advice do you give her?

31

Economics and the Environment

*The attempt to turn a complex
problem of the head into a simple moral question for the heart to
answer is of course a necessary part of all political discussion.*
Frank Colby

After reading this chapter, you should be able to:

1
List four ways in which an economist's
approach to environmental problems differs
from a noneconomist's approach.

2
Say why correlation does not necessarily
imply causation.

3
Explain why economists often oppose
mandatory regulation.

4
Justify the notion of an optimal level of
pollution.

5
Discuss economists' concerns about
voluntary programs.

6
Explain the relation between the free rider
problem and NIMBY.

7
Apply economists' reasoning to an
environmental issue that has not been
discussed in this chapter.

An important area of application of economic reasoning is the environment and resources. In the debate, economists who study and are concerned about these issues often have different views than do other individuals who are concerned about these areas, but who aren't trained in economics. Some of the differences include:

❚1❚

1. Economists' understanding and statement of the environmental problem are likely to differ from those of lay conservationists.
2. Economists often oppose explicit regulation and prohibitions of certain actions (such as the use of styrofoam), preferring alternative incentive-based programs to achieve the same end.
3. Economists are often dubious about voluntary solutions.
4. Economists' methods of paying for environmental programs are likely to differ from lay conservationists' methods.

In this chapter we consider an example of each of these differences to give you some insight into how economists think and how understanding economic principles affects one's understanding of environmental problems. Then we consider a case study of a mandatory recycling program, the economic analysis of that program, and, finally, alternatives to it.

ECONOMISTS' INTERPRETATION OF THE PROBLEM

One important difference between economists and laypeople is a result not so much of economists' economic training as of their statistical training. Having worked with statistics, economists know the difficulty of reaching definite conclusions about what's happening or will happen on the basis of what has happened in the past.

The Empirical Debate about Global Warming

Global warming theory The theory that the earth is now going through a period of warming due to the rise of carbon dioxide gases caused by the burning of fossil fuels.

Let's consider this difference in relation to the **global warming theory** (the theory that the earth is now going through a period of warming due to the rise in carbon dioxide gases caused by the burning of fossil fuels). The problem of global warming and the policies we should use to deal with it have been much in the news in the 1990s. Before one can discuss what policies to use to deal with global warming, one must answer the question: Is the global warming theory correct? It's not all that easy a question to answer.

Is the Global Warming Theory Correct?   The temperature measurements on global warming in the Northern Hemisphere have been on an upward trend over the last 100 years, as we see in Exhibit 1(a). There's no debate about that. There's also no debate about the recent increase in carbon dioxide gas in the atmosphere. But to a statistician, and hence to an economist who's trained as a statistician, those facts don't necessarily mean that the global warming theory is correct.

Correlation Term in statistics meaning the joint movement of data points.

Causation Term in statistics meaning that a change in one data point causes another data point to change.

❚2❚

Correlation Does Not Imply Causation   Early on in any statistics course, all economists, like all scientists, learn that **correlation** (the joint movement of data points) does not imply **causation** (that the change in one of those data points caused the other data point to change). If the global warming theory is correct, a number of conditions are necessary. These include: (1) future temperatures must not be expected to fall unless carbon dioxide in the atmosphere falls and (2) temperatures must be expected to continue to rise as long as carbon dioxide in the atmosphere continues to rise.

For example, if in the 1990s temperatures fall even as carbon dioxide in the atmosphere increases, the global warming theory will be shown incorrect. But even if temperatures continue to rise, the theory *won't* be *proven* correct (a theory can *never* be proven correct); it can only be corroborated. (**Corroboration** means that the data are more consistent with this theory than with any other theory, so it makes sense to use the theory.) We generally treat a corroborated theory as correct even though we're not sure it's correct.

Corroboration Term in statistics meaning the data are more consistent with one theory than with any other theory.

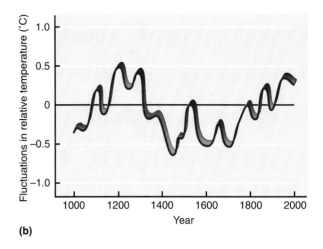

(a)   (b)

EXHIBIT 1 (a and b)   Global Warming Statistics

When we look at recent data, (a), the global warming theory seems reasonable. But when we look at long-run data, (b), we see enormous fluctuations in temperature long before the appearance of the causes identified by the global warming theory.
Source: Adapted by permission from *The Changing Atmosphere* by John Firor © Yale University Press, New Haven, CT, 1990.

Deciding whether the global warming theory is corroborated is a difficult statistical question with no definitive answer. It requires interpretation and integration of data from many sources. Statisticians are still debating this issue. The current state of the debate is that interpretation of the data depends on one's prior belief.[1] If one believes that it's reasonable to assume that a qualitative change in the model has taken place, then the data are consistent with the global warming theory. Statisticians who believe that the burning of fossil fuel since the 1860s is likely to have produced a qualitative change in the nature of our weather system would take this view. If, however, one presently believes:

1. That no qualitative change in the system generating these data has taken place;

2. That the general temperature pattern is subject to significant long-run cyclical fluctuations; and

3. That potential measurement problems exist—specifically (1) that the instruments measuring temperature aren't completely representative of global conditions but are instead representative of conditions close to inhabited areas and (2) that the precision of the instruments in early years had problems,

Nicholas Georgescu-Roegen—One of the earliest environmental economists.

then the data are inconclusive. A few statisticians believe this and the debate between the two groups of statisticians remains unresolved.

The Ambiguity of Formal Statistical Results   Like statisticians, economists who focus on this area differ in their assessments of what can be drawn from the data, but they're all far more careful about drawing inferences from the data than is the typical layperson. Each year of new data provides more information. However, as you can see in Exhibit 1(b) (which shows estimated fluctuations in temperatures over hundreds of years), temperatures have fluctuated even before any carbon fuels were burnt. We have no satisfactory explanation why. Given our lack of

[1] In high-level statistical theory there's a debate between Bayesian statisticians (who believe that all statistics must be interpreted through a person's prior beliefs) and Classical statisticians (who believe that purely objective statistical estimates, not based in any way on prior beliefs, can be made). Most statisticians accept that in areas where there's much ambiguity (such as in global warming) and where precise data are so limited, it's impossible to be totally objective. This doesn't mean that the scientists are doing bad science; it only means that the data are limited. The fact that data are limited doesn't mean the policy question shouldn't be addressed. Often policy problems must be addressed long before adequate data are available.

knowledge of the reasons for these earlier fluctuations, even another hundred years of data will be unlikely to decide the issue conclusively. Still by the turn of the century it's possible that the group believing the global warming theory is corroborated or the group believing the data are inconclusive will have strengthened its case significantly.

In an article discussing global warming, the magazine *The Economist* summarizes the data's ambiguity. It concludes that it's very possible that future effects on climate "will be unlike any seen before." The writers continue:

> This is not good news for computer modelers. Climate models are derived from weather forecasting programs that are designed to provide tomorrow's weather when told about today's. As such, they may have many assumptions built into them that have nothing to do with the underlying mechanisms governing the weather and climate. They can be inspired fudges. (*The Economist,* April 7, 1990, p. 100.)

This ambiguity of formal statistical results isn't an exception; it's the rule in economics and business. But in the real world decisions must be made before statistically conclusive evidence is in. That's where the art of economics comes into play. One must use one's judgment, accepting that it might be wrong. Based on such judgment, not formal statistical proof, many economists believe that global warming is taking place.

Statistical Inference and Policy   Given that most economists believe the global warming theory is correct, the next question is what to do about it. Here again the economist's statistical training enters in. Economists recognize that averages aren't enough. Even if the average temperature has risen, the problem presented by that rise depends on how average temperature has risen. Advocates of the global warming theory's correctness claim that, based on a computer projection, a two- or three-degree increase in temperature will cause enormous problems for agriculture and create desert areas in much of the world. But that conclusion depends on when in the year the temperature rises.

Some economists point out that the data collected to date have suggested the rise in the average is occurring by winters becoming milder and summer temperatures remaining almost unchanged. Moreover the warming is greater in polar regions than it is near the equator. Since such an asymmetrical change in temperature wouldn't create deserts, but would extend the growing season in a number of areas (reducing the cost of growing agricultural goods), it's not at all clear that such global warming will have dire negative effects on the economy. In fact a few economists even suggest that in certain circumstances such a global warming may benefit society.

For those economists who accept that global warming will present a problem the next question is what to do about it. Many economists such as William Nordhaus (a professor at Yale who did a study of policy to deal with global warming) advocate a tax on the use of carbon fuels. We'll discuss economists' policy proposals shortly.

I emphasize these interpretative statistical problems here because before discussing policy, we must recognize how important data interpretation is. Much real-world applied economics is slogging through data, bringing one's statistical training to bear on that data so that one can understand what the problem is. If you don't understand statistical inference, you are likely to go off to solve the wrong problem.

How Limited Are Our Natural Resources?

Before moving on, let's consider another debate in which many economists have questioned the conventional wisdom based on their empirical and statistical training. That debate concerns the extent to which the world's resources are limited.

Proven Reserves   The layperson's conventional wisdom is that the world is running out of resources. After all, resources are fixed and, once used up, they're gone. To support this view, statistics are often cited that we have only, say, 20 years of copper left, 30 years of fossil fuel, and so on. Economists have two problems with these statistics. The first is that the available statistics don't tell us how large existing reserves of any resource are. The statistics we have concern **proven reserves** (reserves that have been discovered and are recoverable), assuming current technology and prices. The calculation of proven reserves changes over time as more resources are discovered. As reserves run low, new exploration may well find more reserves.

Proven reserves Resource reserves that have been discovered and documented to date.

As an example, consider the case of copper. In 1950 proven reserves were said to be enough for 27.9 production years. Thus, in 1950 one might have predicted that copper reserves would run out by 1980. That didn't happen. In 1980 proven reserves of copper were said to be enough for 38 production years, an increase of about 10 production years. Using these data some cynical economists facetiously argue that if the trend continues, eventually the world will be swamped with copper. That obviously won't happen, but it's not clear from the statistics we have now that we should be concerned about running out of copper in the near, or even distant, future.

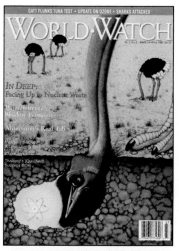

A strongly proenvironment magazine published by the Worldwatch Institute.

The Invisible Hand at Work   A second problem economists have with these long-run projections about running out of resources is that the use of any resource depends upon its price. As the price rises, people use less of the resource (the law of demand) and spend much more time, energy, and money on finding alternatives. Rising price brings about technical change. If people expect resources to be in short supply in the future, the price of those resources will go up now, causing people to conserve. That's the market's way of conserving resources.

The fact that the price of a particular resource isn't going up now suggests that maybe the problem isn't viewed as that great by the people who produce, buy, and sell the resource. Economists point out that this group of people has the most information about future supplies and demand. Hence economists believe the current price tends to be a good signal about future shortages. If the current price isn't high or rising, then there are probably strong empirical data to support the view that we are *not* going to run out of that resource in the foreseeable future. If the price is high and rising, then one would expect that people will be undertaking more and more conservation measures without any regulatory policies to induce them to do so. The invisible hand does the work. The higher price gives them an incentive to choose to conserve. But the real price of most minerals hasn't risen. In fact, real prices of most minerals have fallen over time.

Many empirical studies suggest relative scarcity declining over time. How can scarcity decline? Remember back in the first chapter when I first discussed resources and scarcity. Available resources depend upon technology—and if technology increases faster than resources are used, relative scarcity declines.

Once again, my purpose in discussing the issue of limited resources is not to argue which view is right, but simply to point out how careful one must be in interpreting empirical evidence before discussing policy proposals.

But let's now suppose that one has come to the conclusion that there's a problem—say that we've concluded that people are using too much oil. Having come to that conclusion, let's now specifically consider the policies to which an economist and a layperson might naturally gravitate.

ALTERNATIVE POLICY APPROACHES

Economists and Direct Regulation
3

One difference is that a layperson is likely to favor a program of **direct regulation,** in which the amount of oil people are allowed to use is directly limited by the government. Economists are likely to oppose that solution because it does not

Direct regulation   Program in which the amount of a resource people are allowed to use is directly limited by the government.

Efficiently   At the lowest cost possible in total resources, without consideration as to who pays those costs.

Externality   A result of a decision that is not taken into account by the decision maker.

Market incentive program   Program that makes the price of a resource reflect a negative externality.

Inefficient   More costly than necessary.

Tax incentive program   Any program in which a tax is used to create incentives for individuals to structure their activities in a way that is consistent with particular desired ends.

Marketable certificate program   A program that formalizes rights by issuing certificates and allowing trading of those rights.

achieve the desired end as **efficiently** (at the lowest cost possible in total resources without consideration as to who pays those costs) and fairly as possible. As we discussed in the last chapter, for an economist, coming to the conclusion that too much oil is being consumed would imply that for some reason the consumption of oil involves a negative **externality** (the result of a decision that is not taken into account by the decision maker).

As an alternative to direct regulation, economists will likely favor some type of a **market incentive program** (a program that makes the price of oil reflect the negative externality).

The reason for this difference between the layperson's and the economist's view of policy is the same reason that we discussed in the last chapter: Regulation does not get people to equate the marginal costs of reducing oil consumption with the marginal benefits.

Let's consider an example. Say we have two individuals, Mrs. Thrifty using 10 gallons of gasoline (which is made from oil) a day and Mr. Big using 20 gallons of gas a day. Say we have decided that we want to reduce these two individuals' daily gas consumption by 10 percent, or 3 gallons. The regulatory solution might require everyone to reduce consumption by some amount. Likely direct regulatory reduction strategies would be to require an equal quantity reduction (each consumer reducing consumption by 1.5 gallons) or to require an equal percentage reduction (each consumer reducing consumption by 10 percent).

Economists' problem with this direct regulatory solution is that it doesn't take into account the costs to individuals of reducing consumption. Say, for example, that Mrs. Thrifty could easily (i.e., almost costlessly) reduce consumption by three gallons while Mr. Big would find it very costly to reduce consumption by even .5 gallons. In that case either regulatory solution would be **inefficient** (more costly than necessary). It would be less costly to have Mrs. Thrifty undertake the entire reduction. Economists would prefer a policy that would automatically make the person who has the lower cost of reduction *choose* (as opposed to being *required*) to undertake the most reduction. In this case the policy should get Mrs. Thrifty to *choose* to undertake the majority of the reduction.

Two types of policies would get Mrs. Thrifty to undertake the largest share of the reduction, and economists generally favor these alternative policies if they are administratively feasible. One is to create a tax incentive to achieve the desired reduction; the other is to create a type of property right embodied in a permit or certificate and to allow individuals to trade these property rights freely. Let's consider each separately.

Tax Incentives to Conserve   Let's say that the government imposes a 50¢ per gallon tax on gasoline consumption. This would be an example of a **tax incentive program** (a program using a tax to create incentives for individuals to structure their activities in a way that is consistent with the desired ends). Since Mrs. Thrifty can almost costlessly reduce her gasoline consumption, she will likely respond to the tax by reducing gasoline consumption by, say, 2.75 gallons. She pays only $3.63 in tax but undertakes most of the conservation. Since Mr. Big finds it very costly to reduce his consumption of gasoline, he will likely respond by reducing gasoline consumption by very little—say by .25 gallons. He pays $9.88 in tax but does little of the conservation.

In this example, the tax has achieved the desired end in a more efficient manner than the regulatory solution would—the person for whom the reduction is least costly cuts consumption the most. Why? Because the incentive to reduce is embodied in the price, and individuals are forced to choose how much to change their consumption. The solution also has a significant element of fairness about it. The person who conserves the most pays the least tax.

Marketable Certificates and Conservation   A second method of incorporating the incentive into the individual's decision is a **marketable certificate program** (a program

ADDED DIMENSION

MARKETABLE PERMITS
FOR POLLUTION

Marketable permits are being used more and more to deal with environmental issues. In many areas air quality permits are required of firms before they may begin production. The only way a new firm may start production is if it buys permits from existing firms, which are allowed to sell permits only if they decrease air pollution by the amount of the permit.

Another example of the use of marketable permits is a program instituted in California to deal with a drought. The only way a construction firm is allowed to build a new house is if it reduces existing water usage by a specific amount. To do this the firm goes around to existing home owners, offering to put in water-saving devices for free. In some areas more than 60 percent of the existing homes have introduced these water-saving devices, which were paid for by the construction firms and hence, indirectly, by the new home buyers.

requiring everyone to certify that they have reduced total consumption—not necessarily their own individual consumption—by a specified amount, say 1.5 gallons). Such a program would be close to the regulatory solution but it involves a major difference. If individuals choose to reduce consumption by more than the required amount, they will be given a marketable certificate which they can sell to someone who has chosen to reduce consumption by less than that amount. By buying that certificate, the person who has not personally reduced consumption by the 1.5 gallons will have met the program's requirements. Let's see how the program would work with Mr. Big and Mrs. Thrifty.

In our example, Mr. Big finds it very costly to reduce consumption while Mrs. Thrifty finds it easy. So we can expect that Mr. Big won't reduce consumption much and will instead buy certificates from Mrs. Thrifty, who will choose to undertake significant reduction in her consumption to generate the certificates, assuming she can sell them to Mr. Big for a high enough price to make that reduction worth her while. So, as was the case in the tax incentive program, Mrs. Thrifty undertakes most of the conservation, but she reaps a financial benefit for it.

Obviously there are enormous questions about administrative feasibility of these types of proposals, but what's important to understand here is not the specifics of the proposals, but instead, the way in which the economists' policies are *more efficient* than the regulatory policy. As I stated before, *more efficient* means *less costly* in terms of resources with no consideration paid to who is bearing those costs. Incorporating the incentive into a price and then letting individuals choose how to respond to that incentive lets those who find it least costly undertake most of the adjustment.

More and more, governments are exploring economists' policies for solving problems. Sin taxes (discussed in the preceding chapter) are an example of the tax incentive approach. Marketable pollution rights discussed in the accompanying box are an example of the marketable certificate approach. You can probably see more examples discussed in the news.

The Optimal Amount of Pollution   An **optimal policy** is one in which the marginal cost of undertaking the policy equals the marginal benefit of that policy. If a policy isn't optimal (that is, the marginal cost exceeds the marginal benefit or the marginal benefit exceeds the marginal cost), resources are being wasted because the savings from a reduction of expenditures on a program will be worth more than the gains that would be lost from reducing the program, or the benefit from spending more on a program will be worth more than the cost of expanding the program.

Let's consider an example of this latter case. Say the marginal benefit of a program significantly exceeds its marginal cost. That would seem good. But that would mean that we could expand the program by decreasing some other program or activity whose marginal benefit doesn't exceed its marginal cost, with a net gain

Optimal policy Policy whose marginal cost equals its marginal benefit.

in benefits to society. To spend too little on a beneficial program is as inoptimal as spending too much on a nonbeneficial program.

4   This concept of optimality carries over to economists' view of most problems. For example, some environmentalists would like to completely rid the economy of pollution. Most economists believe that doing so is costly and that since it's costly, one would want to take into account those costs. That means that society should reduce pollution only to the point where the marginal cost of reducing pollution equals the marginal benefit. That amount of pollution at which the marginal benefit of reducing pollution equals the marginal cost is called the **optimal level of pollution.** To reduce pollution below that level would make society as a whole worse off.

Optimal level of pollution Amount of pollution at which the marginal benefit of reducing pollution equals the marginal cost.

Economists Are Dubious of Voluntary Solutions

A second point upon which economists often differ from laypeople is in their view of the effectiveness of voluntary solutions. Say that one has decided that energy reduction is a desired goal. Often the first policy presented to achieve the desired end is the voluntary one: ask everyone to save energy, leaving individuals free to choose whether to save or not. Since it involves free choice, economists don't oppose this solution, but they often do question whether it will work in a large group.

5   To see why, let's consider Mr. Big and Mrs. Thrifty again. Say the government simply asks them to reduce their consumption voluntarily. Let's say that Mrs. Thrifty has a social conscience and undertakes most of the reduction while Mr. Big has no social conscience and does not reduce consumption significantly. Then it seems that this is a reasonably efficient solution. But what if the costs were reversed and Mr. Big had the low cost of reduction and Mrs. Thrifty had the high cost? Then the voluntary solution would not be so efficient.

The potential lack of efficiency is not the main reason economists generally are dubious about voluntary solutions. After all, when people do something voluntarily, they are choosing to do it and, assuming they are rational, it must make them better off, or they wouldn't choose to do it. So one could argue that even in the case where Mrs. Thrifty has a high cost of reduction *and* voluntarily undertakes most of the reduction, she also has a high benefit from reducing her consumption, so the person who is undertaking the reduction is getting the benefit.

Within the economists' model of rational decision makers, the preceding reasoning is correct, but most economists are quite willing to admit that this model of rational decision makers is insufficient to capture people's complex motives and psychology. Most economists fully recognize that people have a social conscience in varying degrees and do things for the good of society as well as for their own good. However economists point out that a person's social conscience and willingness to do things for the good of society generally depend on that person's belief that others will also be helping.

Free rider problem The unwillingness of individuals to share in the cost of a public good.

If a socially conscious person comes to believe a large number of other people won't contribute, he or she will often lose that social conscience: Why should I do what's good for society if others won't? This is another example of the **free rider problem** (individuals' unwillingness to share in the cost of a public good) which economists believe will often limit, and eventually undermine, social actions based on voluntary contributions. The free rider problem and its likely effect on social consciousness are the most important reasons why economists are skeptical of voluntary solutions. They believe a small number of free riders will undermine the social consciousness of many in the society and that eventually the voluntary policy will fail.

There are exceptions. During times of war and extreme crisis, voluntary programs are often successful. For example, upon the advice of economists, during World War II the war effort was in part financed through successful voluntary programs. But for other social problems that are long run and that involve individuals accepting significant changes in their actions, generally the results of voluntary programs haven't been positive. Economists don't oppose such voluntary programs; they simply don't have much faith in them.

A third way in which economists' approach to environmental policy differs from environmentalists' approach is in how to pay for any environmental program. Most environmentalists see taxes only as a way to collect the money to pay for an environmental program. Economists see taxes and other policies to affect prices as a central part of the program. In fact, for an economist the incentive embodied in the price is the single most important part of a policy.

How to Pay for Conservation

Let's consider what this difference means. Say that the problem is too much pollution. Immediately an economist's training directs him or her to look at the price of polluting and how that price can be raised. If there is too much use of carbon fuel, an economist immediately looks at the price of carbon fuel and how it can be raised. Moreover, as we discussed, the economist, in deciding whether there's a problem, looks at the price and tries to reason out whether there's an externality that makes the price too low. In many cases the externality is easy to find. For example, when people pollute they don't pay for the cost of that pollution, so there is an argument that pollution is an externality and the price of polluting is too low. If there is no such externality argument, then an economist will likely conclude that there is no problem.

In most environmental issues, it is relatively easy to conclude that there is a negative externality. Thus, economists often agree with environmentalists: There is a social environmental problem that the current market structure doesn't solve. But the answer to that problem for an economist is seldom direct regulation nor is it voluntary conservation paid for by some type of tax. Rather the economist's answer is *to find a program that makes the price people pay reflect the cost of the externality*.

Many examples presented in this book concern the federal government and national problems. While many of the environmental issues are national and even international—such as ozone depletion and global warming—others are local.

A CASE STUDY: A MANDATORY RECYCLING PROGRAM

In the remainder of this chapter we consider a local case—one you might read about in a small-town paper. That case is a mandatory recycling program instituted by a small town. We'll consider the chosen policies and some alternative policies an economically trained environmentalist might have suggested.

The case begins with trash. It seems that the people of Vermont, a state that used to boast that it had more cows than people, were generating more trash than the existing Vermont landfills could handle. This wasn't the result of a sudden decrease in the amount of land. Rather, as people became more environmentally conscious, their concerns about the potential polluting effects of landfills increased and landfills became much more regulated. In fact, they became unacceptable to most neighborhoods. **NIMBY (Not In My Back Yard)** became the political ''in'' word.

NIMBY A short way to express "Not In My Back Yard" when a community objects to a proposed development in its neighborhood.

It was decided that something must be done to reduce the amount of trash, and many Vermont communities instituted recycling programs. This is the story of the path one Vermont community followed.

The first problem they had was setting up the administrative apparatus to plan and organize the recycling program. What area would it cover? The decision: A regional solid waste management area was established for the county and a recycling coordinator was appointed. Within that regional area the largest town was selected for an initial recycling program.

The largest town, which we'll call Big Town (population 8,293), then appointed its own recycling coordinator, a part-time employee who was a recent graduate of a local college who had majored in political science and was a strong environmentalist. Working with town planners, Big Town's recycling coordinator designed the program. Her first decision was that the plan would be mandatory. It was felt that a voluntary program wouldn't achieve anywhere near the amount of desired recycling. Big Town then enacted an ordinance making the recycling of certain items mandatory for all residents.

The second decision she had to make was what would be recycled. What was there a market for? Likely candidates included certain plastics, newspapers and magazines, glass, metal containers, and cardboard. Unfortunately upon checking the second-hand market she found that the price that could be obtained for selling most of these recycled items was very low and that no regional market existed at all for magazines and cardboard. Moreover recycling firms would take the items only if they were "uncontaminated," which meant that not only would paper have to be separated from plastic but that various types of plastic and various types of paper would have to be subdivided into different kinds of paper and different kinds of plastic. For example, one could not simply recycle "paper." One would have to separate at least four different types: newspaper, glossy magazines and catalogs, colored stationery, and white stationery. For another example, only a few of the many kinds of plastic would be acceptable to recycling firms, and it would be costly to determine which types were recyclable and which were not. All this sorting would add enormously to the cost of recycling. In short the cost of sorting trash would be so high that it would far exceed the payment the town would receive from recycling firms.

This led to a third decision: that householders would have to separate their trash themselves. This, in turn, meant that ordinary garbage trucks could not pick up the trash because the separated trash would have to be placed in individual compartments in the truck, and ordinary trucks aren't built that way. Therefore special new trucks had to be bought at a cost of about $80,000 per truck. Because no trash collection firm was willing to buy such trucks, Big Town had to find some way to pay for the trucks if there was to be any recycling.

The job of collecting recycled trash was put out to bid. Only one local trash collector was willing to take on the job. Not surprisingly that company won the bid.

The final agreement was that this company would collect the separated trash once every two weeks and would be paid a $4 monthly pickup fee by every household, regardless of whether the household used the service. Big Town would borrow the money to buy the truck for the collector and the collector would pay the town for its use in installments.

This $4 per month recycling fee was in addition to the fees that people were already paying private companies to pick up their trash. So at the initiation of the recycling program, people were faced with two trash fees: one for the regular trash and one for the separated trash.

Since there were about 2,600 households, this fee meant that the firm received about $10,400 per month (about $125,000 per year). From that it had to repay Big Town for the truck, pay for the labor to pick up the recycled items, and get rid of the recyclable items. (The administrative cost of the program, including the Big Town coordinator's salary, also had to be paid for. This cost was incorporated in the property tax rate payable to the town.)

The remaining problem was compliance: how to enforce the requirement that people recycle. This was done by providing a fine of up to $1,000 for each failure to recycle. Thus, households that put recyclable material in the regular trash instead of the separated trash risked a heavy fine. The final design of the program was as follows:

1. Every residential building had to separate its trash according to rules published by the Big Town coordinator.
2. Each household was provided with a blue plastic box into which it would sort its recyclable trash. The householder then had to carry the recyclable trash to curbside before 7 A.M. on pickup day. Pickup was once every two weeks, with the exact day depending on the neighborhood.

The *Eight-Penny News*, a newspaper for light contractors, ran an article about the Gyp Chipper—a 500-pound, 4' × 4' machine that "eats wallboard at the rate of 10,000 pounds an hour and costs $8000." Wallboard (also called *plasterboard*) is the covering on most walls in houses, and when any remodeling is done the old wallboard needs to be discarded. How much is discarded? Approximately 3 million tons a year—about 1 percent of the U.S. waste stream.

The article was written for contractors. It addressed the issue of whether it would be worthwhile to buy the machine and whether recycling wallboard would be in the interest of the construction tradespeople, called *drywallers,* who worked with wallboard. The bottom line of the article was that at "$60 a ton tippage fee (the landfill cost), it probably wasn't in their interest to recycle, but at $100 or $200 a ton it would be relatively easy to convince drywallers that recycling beats throwing away whole truckloads of wallboard."

3. The recycling trash collector inspected each bin and left behind any items that didn't fit the rules. For example, only plastic bottles whose bottoms bore a raised symbol including the number 2 were acceptable. If items were rejected, the collector left a notice stating the reason.

4. The recycling collector kept records of people who were not putting out the blue bins so that the town could make investigations and impose any fines that appeared justified.

5. Householders had to pay a flat $4 a month to the recycling trash collector, no matter how many or how few recyclable items they had or even if they had no recyclable items at all. They could obtain any number of additional blue bins they needed, the only limitation being that they had to pay $5 for each additional one. (The first bin was free of charge because funds to pay for these had been provided by a local civic organization.)

6. It was up to the recycling collector to dispose of what was collected. If it could sell the items, it could keep the money.

The initiation of the program brought significant complaints from various groups. One group was composed of competing trash collectors whose customers were generating less trash and were therefore opting to save money by requesting fewer collections. These competing collectors were also losing business to the collector who won the bid to pick up the separated trash. This collector would give a discount to the customers who also hired this company to pick up their regular trash, giving people an incentive to switch to this company. Another group complaining about the program were residents of households who generated almost no recyclable trash yet had to pay for its collection. There were documented instances of elderly women who put out nothing but one tin can in two weeks. A third group who complained were apartment house landlords who were responsible for paying the monthly fee and/or fines but who could not force their tenants into individual compliance. A final group who complained were civil libertarians who claimed that it was illegal to search people's regular trash to be sure no recyclable items were being put into it.

Despite the complaints, the program was considered successful by most citizens. Compliance was high (about 95 percent of households), and total trash going into the landfill was reduced by one-fifth—2,000 tons out of a total annual trash generation of about 10,000 tons. In the view of the environmentally conscious organizers of the program, at least the people of Big Town were doing something to deal with the environmental problem, and that made the program successful.

An Economist's Cost/Benefit View of the Program

This view of the program's success wouldn't be shared by all. Specifically most economists, even ones who strongly support environmental issues, would have a number of problems with it.

The first problem concerns whether a recycling program made sense at the time it was instituted. Recycled items sold for anywhere from $10 to $70 a ton delivered to the recycling plant. Unfortunately there were no such plants nearby. Essentially, the delivery costs, even after the items were separated, roughly equaled the value of the recycled material! This rough equality of costs presents a major problem to an economist. The first question any economist asks about a program is whether program costs exceed the benefits. Since the delivered value of the recycled material is essentially zero, there's a significant concern about the benefit of recycling.

Deciding costs and benefits necessarily involves judgment. For example, in the publicity literature the recycling program distributed, the organizers stated that program costs were covered by the saved tipping fees (fees charged by the landfill). But for individuals, this was questionable, since the recycling program cost them $48 per year per household in direct payments but, for most people, did not reduce their trash costs significantly. Moreover some administrative costs were part of the general town budget and not separable, so one couldn't attribute the proper amount to the recycling program. What makes it hard to come to any definite conclusion about these direct costs is that trash removal fees were rising anyhow, and the appropriate comparison is how much they would have been otherwise. So even for "direct costs" there is ambiguity.

But there is even more ambiguity in costs since for economists the comparison of direct costs and benefits is not sufficient. Because of the way the program was set up, many program costs were passed on to individuals who have to separate their trash and spend time determining what goes where. Although these costs involve no direct payment, they are included in **opportunity costs** (the costs of forgone resources). These opportunity costs of the time it takes to separate the trash do not show up when officials calculate the cost of the program, but they are still costs. If we assume that it takes an hour per week for a household to separate its trash, then each household spends a total of 52 hours a year separating trash. How should that time be valued? The time should be valued at its opportunity cost, but that opportunity cost isn't directly measurable. Some people dislike separating trash, so they would place a high opportunity cost on their time. Others might enjoy it (they are contributing to recycling); for them the opportunity cost is zero. In fact, for them, taking part in the program can be seen as a benefit.

Opportunity costs Costs of forgone resources.

How does it all net out? It would take an enormous study to figure that out, and even that study probably would not come to a conclusive result. But let us say for the sake of argument that the study concluded that the appropriate value was $2 per hour. Using this number, we arrive at a cost of $104 per year ($52 \times \$2 = \$104$). Thus, the yearly cost of the recycling program would be $152 ($48 to the collector and $104 in householder's time) per household. The administrative costs in the first year were approximately $20,000. There are about 2,600 households in the town, so, given these assumptions, the yearly cost of mandatory recycling is ($152 \times 2,600$) + $20,000 = $395,200 + $20,000 = $415,200.

For this yearly expense, approximately 2,000 tons of trash is processed through the recycling program each year. Since the landfill cost of 2,000 tons of trash is approximately $118,880 ($59.44 per ton for the town in our cash study), this suggests that, if that landfill cost is the appropriate cost, the costs of this program significantly exceed the benefits. Of course, assuming the landfill cost is the appropriate cost is a big *if*. Supporters of the program see landfills as much more expensive than the actual costs, which, if true, would increase the benefits of recycling significantly.

There are also other possible benefits. For example, one could argue that separating trash is creating an environmentally aware community and is building environmentally sound habits into the population. Therefore, the argument would run, the program has significant positive external effects which should be considered.

Until recently landfills were the primary means of waste disposal in the United States. © *Jim Sculley/The Image Works.*

As you can see, cost/benefit studies aren't conclusive, especially when done in a way as cursory as this one. But even a much more thorough study still wouldn't be definitive; it would reflect the assumptions put in.

Despite the ambiguity, as cost/benefit studies go, this one isn't highly favorable to the program unless one is willing to make some strong assumptions about the program's external benefits and about the value of people's time. But if these external benefits exist—if the social and landfill costs significantly exceed the actual costs paid—then for an economist the natural solution is not mandatory recycling, but is, instead, figuring out a way to get the private costs of the landfill to equal their social costs.

How would an economist handle the problem? That's unclear, but what is clear is that an economist would look much more carefully into costs and would try to build price incentives into the program. For example, if the landfill costs are only $59.44 per ton, then the entire program is called into question; but if the landfill costs were $250 per ton, the program would make sense since the savings on 2,000 tons would then be $500,000, not $118,880.

To decide whether there are significant external effects, an economist would ask whether landfill costs are for some reason not being determined by market pressures, or whether landfills create an externality that is not being taken into account in the price of the landfill. If either of those is the case, an economist would look for a program that would incorporate the externality into the price. Perhaps a preferable program would be to push landfill prices up to a price that included the externality. Big Town's recycling program does not incorporate the price of the externality into the price the consumer pays. The Big Town program is financed with a flat $4 fee per month for every household. That flat fee is paid regardless of how much or how little recycling the household does. Thus, the fee provides no price incentive for recycling or for refraining from using the resources in the first place.

Now it's quite clear that one of the main pressures for recycling has been the decrease in the number of areas willing to accept landfills. But in that search for landfills, no one explored the possibility of allowing the price of landfills to rise by almost 300 percent and seeing how many areas might be willing to accept environmentally sound landfills at that much higher price.

It's likely that if areas were to receive large payments to accept a landfill voluntarily, as opposed to the landfill site being administratively chosen, many

■f the price is perfectly flexible, shortages can't exist. For an economist, the term *shortage* conveys a situation in which the price cannot rise to a level to equate the quantity supplied and the quantity demanded. Below, we consider how a shortage of landfills can occur.

As we've drawn it, you can see that at $50 per ton of trash dumped, the quantity of landfills demanded significantly exceeds the quantity of landfills supplied, but at $200 per ton of trash dumped (with a large portion of that going to the town that allows the landfill), the supply and demand are equal. Why? Because the higher cost of getting rid of trash reduces the amount of trash and hence lowers the need for landfills and gets many more areas willing to accept landfills. Thus, supply and demand analysis suggests that NIMBY is not a necessary state of the world; it is simply a state that is characterized by too low a price of landfills and waste disposal.

more areas would be willing to accept landfills. True, the cost of landfills would be higher, but that higher cost would create stronger incentives to recycle. Individuals would choose to recycle, not be forced to recycle by the threat of a fine. Thus, economists would look much more carefully at a policy that would raise the landfill cost to a level where the NIMBY pressure would be much weaker than it currently is. Currently most communities with landfills get nothing or only a minimal fee when other communities dispose of their trash in the landfill. Suppose a community with no landfill were to be charged $250 per ton of landfill accepted, with $200 of that fee going to the community that is willing to have a landfill within its borders. At $250 per ton of landfill accepted, communities that were willing to have a landfill facility could fund their services—such as schools, police, fire, streets, and street lights—even as they lowered or even eliminated their property taxes. Since a $250 landfill fee was necessary for the benefits of the mandatory recycling program to exceed the costs, if the market-determined landfill prices did not rise to that level, then an economist would seriously consider whether a mandatory recycling program made economic sense at this time.

The Economist's Perspective on Environmental Problems

A second way in which an economic environmentalist's solution would likely differ from a noneconomic environmentalist's solution is that the economist would look at the problem from a broader perspective. He or she would likely say that environmentally sound recycling is only part of the issue; the real issue is the total amount of trash generated. For example, say that total trash were reduced by 20 percent through lower consumption of items that create trash rather than through recycling. Wouldn't that achieve the same end? Using such reasoning, an economist is likely to argue that the problem shouldn't be seen as a problem of recycling, but as a problem of trash generation. Why is trash generation the problem? Because when individuals buy goods they *do not* pay the cost of disposing of those goods.

To see why this is the approach to which economists are directed, think back to our discussion of how economists view problems. They look for a reason why individual decisions might involve an externality (a result of a decision that's not taken into account by the decison maker). If there's an externality of too much trash, it is that people are not taking into account the cost of getting rid of products when they make decisions about buying the products. Thus, the externality view focuses the analysis on trash generation and not on recycling because recycling is only one of many methods to reduce the amount of trash.

What's the economist's answer to this problem? Since trash generation involves an externality, the answer is that the externality's cost must be integrated into the good's initial price. Doing so will give people incentive to create less trash by seeing to it that the price of those goods that create trash includes the cost of getting rid of that trash. Thus, rather than support a mandatory recycling program, an economist would be more likely to support (1) a ''trash tax'' in which the price of items sold must include the cost of disposing of the items or (2) a ''disposal requirement'' on goods.

Let's consider how these economists' policies might work in regard to newspapers (a significant component of trash). We first look at the trash tax.

A Trash Tax   A trash tax of, say, 10¢ per pound of newspaper would increase the price of newspapers significantly, causing people to demand fewer newspapers and/or publishers to print fewer pages in their newspapers. Here the reduction in trash wouldn't take place through recycling; it would take place through a reduction in newspapers demanded and/or newspaper pages supplied. This approach has an added benefit. The tax money that is generated could then be used to fund environmental programs that create environmental consciousness.

A Disposal Requirement   Alternatively the government could simply pass a law requiring newspapers to cut the volume of newspapers they generate by 10 percent. In other words, newspaper publishers would be responsible for insuring that 10 percent of their papers are either recycled or eliminated. The program would allow some newspapers to exceed a 10 percent reduction. Such newspaper firms would be given disposal certificates for the tonnage they saved in excess of 10 percent. These certificates would be marketable, which means that the firms could sell the certificates to other firms who reduced their trash generation by less than 10 percent. Under this program firms would have two ways to meet the law's requirements. They could either directly meet the requirement by reducing the trash they generate by 10 percent or they could indirectly meet the requirement by buying the necessary disposal certificates from other firms that had reduced their trash generation by more than 10 percent.

This program would give newspapers a strong incentive to see that their newspapers are recycled directly. It might cause newspaper carriers to collect old newspapers when they delivered new ones. This program would also stimulate the development of a computer newspaper that would involve no paper whatsoever. People would simply wake up in the morning and flip on their computer screen or TV to get the latest headlines and the accompanying stories.

A Final Word

Obviously there's much more to be discussed about economists' approach to recycling and various alternative programs, but this brief discussion should give you a sense of economists' approach and convince you that *to be an economist does not mean that one cannot be an environmentalist*. But it should also give you a sense that an environmentalist economist's approach to an environmental problem could differ significantly from the approach of an environmentalist untrained in economics.

CONCLUSION

Environmental issues are enormously complicated and require intense study before one can come up with a viable way of dealing with the problems. There are major difficulties with the economists' solutions presented here. I did not discuss those difficulties because (1) it would have made the chapter too long and (2) it would have taken some of the sharp edge off of the arguments—and I wanted the arguments to cut deeply and make you think.

Usually we economists see only a few environmentalists taking our courses, and those we do see take one or two courses at most. Thus, the discussions about environmental problems at the local level generally involve little economic sensibility because so few of the community members have had significant education in economics. (At the national level that isn't true. Economists play a major role in the federal Environmental Protection Agency.)

Economists are seen by many laypeople as opposed to environmentalism. That isn't the case. There's no fundamental difference between environmentalists and economists in terms of beliefs or concerns about the environment. What difference there is involves initial approach. An environmental economist's initial thoughts are likely to focus on market incentives, while an environmentalist untrained in economics is likely to distrust the market's effectiveness and therefore favor regulatory approaches.

To emphasize how economic training can affect one's view of environmental problems, this chapter's approach has been to contrast the two views, showing the advantages of the economist's approach and the disadvantages of the regulatory approaches. But the decision to write the chapter this way creates a problem in making some people believe that the economic answer is obviously the correct answer. It isn't. The economist's approach, like the regulatory environmentalist's approach, has disadvantages. For example, if landfill prices rose significantly, people would likely burn their own trash or dump it illegally. Similarly a trash tax would involve significant administrative problems. So you should not come away from this chapter believing that economics has all the answers or even that economic approaches are preferable to regulatory approaches (although I believe that the economic approach is preferable). Instead I'd like you to come away from this chapter believing that economic approaches to environmental issues are worth considering and that it is important to keep an open mind in approaching environmental problems.

KEY POINTS

- There is no contradiction in being both an economist and an environmentalist, but an economic environmentalist's approach to solving environmental problems often differs from a lay environmentalist's approach. **1**
- Economists often question ''statistical proof'' that laypeople accept without question. **2**
- Economists generally prefer incentive-based programs to direct regulatory programs because incentive-based programs are more efficient. **1 3**
- An optimal policy is one in which the marginal cost of undertaking the policy equals its marginal benefit. **4**
- Economists are often dubious about voluntary solutions. **5**
- NIMBY suggests that some prices are not free to fluctuate. **6**
- All policies have problems and advantages. It is important to consider both before deciding on a policy. **7**

KEY TERMS

causation *(640)*
correlation *(640)*
corroboration *(640)*
direct regulation *(644)*
efficiently *(644)*
externality *(644)*

free rider problem *(646)*
global warming
  theory *(640)*
inefficient *(644)*
market incentive
  program *(644)*

marketable certificate
  program *(644)*
NIMBY *(647)*
opportunity costs *(650)*
optimal level of
  pollution *(646)*

optimal policy *(645)*
proven reserves *(643)*
tax incentive
  program *(644)*

QUESTIONS FOR THOUGHT AND REVIEW

The number after each question represents the estimated degree of critical thinking required. (1 = almost none; 10 = deep thought.)

1. Many environmentalists agree that the data supporting the global warming theory are questionable but argue that if the theory is correct, unless we start doing something about global warming now, it will be too late to do anything about it. Would you expect an economist to accept this argument? Why or why not? *(7)*

2. A friend tells you that by historical standards the price of gold is low, so now is a great time to buy gold. Would you agree? Why or why not? *(5)*

3. Explain why a market incentive program is more efficient than a direct regulatory program. *(6)*

4. It is sometimes said that there is a trade-off between fairness and efficiency. Explain one way in which that is true and one way in which it is not true. *(8)*

5. How would an economist likely respond to the statement "There is no such thing as acceptable pollution"? *(5)*

6. State two reasons why an economist generally opposes a solution based upon voluntary action that is not in people's self-interest. *(4)*

7. Say that the government placed a high tax on the use of oil. Would that significantly reduce the amount of pollution coming from the use of oil? Why or why not? *(4)*

8. Say that the government placed a high tax on the use of oil. Would that significantly reduce the total amount of pollution in the environment? *(8)*

9. If the price of landfills rose significantly, what problems do you see arising in the disposal of trash? *(7)*

10. How does your community deal with trash? What would an economist think of that method? *(9)*

PROBLEMS AND EXERCISES

1. There's a gas shortage in Gasland. You're presented with two proposals that will achieve the same level of reduction in the use of gas. Proposal A would force everybody to reduce their gas consumption by 5 percent. Proposal B would impose a 50¢ tax on the consumption of a gallon of gas which would also achieve a 5 percent reduction. Demand curves for two groups are shown below.
   a. Show the effect of both proposals on each group.
   b. Which group would support a regulatory policy? Which would support a tax policy?

2. The marginal cost, marginal social cost, and demand for fish are represented by the above curves. Suppose that there are no restrictions on fishing.
   a. Assuming perfect competition, what is the catch going to be, and at what price will it be sold?
   b. What are the socially efficient price and output?
   c. Some sports fishers propose a ban on commercial fishing. As the community's economic advisor, you're asked to comment on it at a public forum. What do you say?

3

Factor Markets

32

Who Gets What? The Distribution of Income

"God must love the poor," said
Lincoln, "or he wouldn't have made so many of them." He must
love the rich, or he wouldn't divide so much mazuma among so
few of them.
H. L. Mencken

After reading this chapter, you should be able to:

1
State what a Lorenz curve is.

2
Explain what has happened to the U.S.
Lorenz curve over time.

3
State the official definition of *poverty*.

4
Summarize the statistical findings on
income and wealth distribution.

5
Explain three problems in determining
whether an equal distribution is fair.

6
List three side effects of
redistributing income.

7
Summarize U.S. expenditure programs to
redistribute income.

In 1988 Michael Milken, the junk bond king who has since been convicted of insider trading, earned $550 million; that's $10,576,923 per week. Assuming he worked 70 hours per week (you have to work hard to earn that kind of money), that's $151,099 per hour.

In 1992 the average doctor earned $150,000; that's $2,885 per week. Assuming she worked 70 hours per week (she's conscientious, makes house calls, and spends time with her hospitalized patients), that's $41 per hour.

In 1992 Joe Smith, a cashier in a fast-food restaurant, earned $19,235, or $370 per week. His base wage was the minimum wage; that's $4.35 per hour. (But to earn enough for his family to be able to eat, he worked a lot of overtime, for which he was paid time and a half, or $6.53 per hour.) So he made $370 per week, by working 70 hours a week.

In 1992 Nguyen, a peasant in Vietnam, earned $260; that's $5 per week. Assuming he worked 70 hours per week (you have to work hard at that rate of pay just to keep from starving), that's 7¢ per hour.

Are such major differences typical of how income is distributed among people in general? Are such differences fair? And if they're unfair, what can be done about them? This chapter addresses such issues.

WAYS OF CONSIDERING THE DISTRIBUTION OF INCOME

There are several different ways to look at income distribution. In the 1800s economists were concerned with how income was divided among the owners of businesses (for whom profits were the source of income), the owners of land (who received rent), and workers (who earned wages). That concern reflected the relatively sharp distinctions among social classes that existed in capitalist societies at that time. Landowners, workers, and owners of businesses were distinct groups. Few individuals moved from one group to another. Time has changed that; the social divisions that were once important have faded. Today workers, through their pension plans and investments in financial institutions, are owners of over 25 percent ($2.5 trillion worth of stock equity) of all the shares issued on the New York Stock Exchange. That percentage will likely rise to over 50 percent by the year 2000. Landowners as a group receive only a small portion of total income. Companies are run not by capitalists, but by managers who are, in a sense, workers. In short, the social lines have blurred.

But this blurring of the lines between social classes doesn't mean that we can forget the question: "Who gets what?" It simply means that our interest in who gets what has a different focus. We no longer focus on classification of income by source. Instead we look at the relative distribution of total income. How much income do the top 5 percent get? How much do the top 15 percent get? How much do the bottom 10 percent get? This relative division is called the **size distribution of income.**

Size distribution of income The relative division or allocation of total income among income groups.

A second distributional issue economists are concerned with is the **socioeconomic distribution of income** (the allocation of income among relevant socioeconomic groupings). How much do blacks get relative to whites? How much do the old get compared to the young? How much do women get compared to men?

Socioeconomic distribution of income The relative division or allocation of total income among relevant socioeconomic groups.

The next three sections consider these distributional categories. Then the last three sections of the chapter ask whether the distribution of income is fair and, if it isn't, what can be done to change it?

THE SIZE DISTRIBUTION OF INCOME

The U.S. size distribution of income measures aggregate family income, from the poorest segment of society to the richest. It ranks people by their income and tells how much the richest 20 percent (a quintile) and the poorest 20 percent receive. For example, the poorest 20 percent might get 5 percent of the income and the richest 20 percent might get 40 percent.

The Lorenz Curve

Exhibit 1(a) presents the size distribution of income for the United States in 1990. In it you can see that the 20 percent of Americans receiving the lowest level of

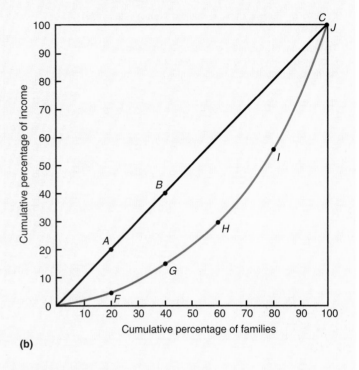

Income quintile	Percentage of total family income	Cumulative percentage of total family income
Lowest fifth	3.9	3.9
Second fifth	9.6	13.5
Third fifth	16.0	29.5
Fourth fifth	24.1	53.6
Highest fifth	46.4	100.0

(a)

(b)

EXHIBIT 1 (a and b)   A Lorenz Curve of U.S. Income (1990)

If income were perfectly equally distributed, the Lorenz curve would be a diagonal line. In (**b**) we see the U.S. Lorenz curve based on the numbers in (**a**) compared to a Lorenz curve reflecting a perfectly equal distribution of income.
Source: U.S. Bureau of the Census, *Current Population Reports, 1992.*

income got 3.9 percent of the total income. The top 20 percent of Americans received 46.4 percent of the total income. The ratio of the income of the top 20 percent compared to the income of the bottom 20 percent was about 12:1.

A **Lorenz curve** is a geometric representation of the size distribution of income among families in a given country at a given time. It measures the percentage of *families* on the horizontal axis arranged from poorest to richest and the cumulative percentage of *family income* on the vertical axis. Since the exhibit presents cumulative percentages (all of the families with income below a certain level) both axes start at zero and end at 100 percent.

A perfectly equal distribution of income would be represented by a diagonal line like the one in Exhibit 1(b). That is, the poorest 20 percent of the families would have 20 percent of the total income (point *A*); the poorest 40 percent of the families would have 40 percent of the income (point *B*); and 100 percent of the families would have 100 percent of the income (point *C*). An unequal distribution of income is represented by a Lorenz curve that's below the diagonal line. All real-world Lorenz curves are below the diagonal because income is always distributed unequally in the real world.

The colored line in Exhibit 1(b) represents a Lorenz curve of the U.S. income distribution presented in Exhibit 1(a)'s table. From Exhibit 1(a) you know that in 1990 the bottom 20 percent of the families in the United States received 3.9 percent of the income. Point *F* in Exhibit 1(b) represents that combination of percentages (20 percent and 3.9 percent). To find what the bottom 40 percent received, you must add the income percentage of the bottom 20 percent and the income percentage of the next 20 percent. Doing so gives us 13.5 percent (3.9 plus 9.6 percent from column 2 of Exhibit 1(a)). Point *G* in Exhibit 1(b) represents the combination of percentages (40 percent and 13.5 percent). Continuing this process

Lorenz curve A geometric representation of the size distribution of income among families in a given country at a given time.

1

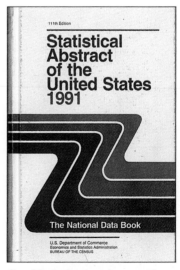

One of the best sources for economic and social statistics.

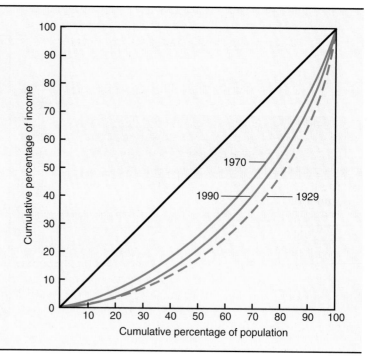

EXHIBIT 2   Lorenz Curve for United States: 1929, 1970 and 1990

The amount of inequality of income distribution has fluctuated in the United States. Until about 1970, it decreased; since then it has increased.

for points *H*, *I*, and *J*, you get a Lorenz curve that shows the size distribution of income in the United States in 1990.

U.S. Income Distribution over Time

Lorenz curves are most useful in visual comparisons of income distribution over time and between countries. Exhibit 2 presents Lorenz curves for the United States in 1929, 1970, and 1990. They show that from 1929 to 1970 the size distribution of income became more equal. (The curve for 1970 is closer to being diagonal than the curve for 1929.) Income of the bottom fifth of families rose by a much higher proportion than did income of the top fifth. That was a continuation of a trend that had begun in the 1920s. In the 1970s that trend stopped and began to reverse. As you can see, from 1970 to 1990 income distribution became less equal. (The curve for 1990 is further from being diagonal than is the curve for 1970.) The income of the bottom fifth of families fell by over 10%, while the income of the top fifth rose significantly.

Important reasons for the initial increase in equality are the redistribution measures instituted by the U.S. government between the 1930s and the 1970s, including welfare programs, unemployment insurance, social security, progressive taxation (taxation of higher income at higher rates, lower income at lower rates), and improved macroeconomic performance of the economy.

The trend back toward greater inequality in the 1970s and 1980s was caused by a fall in the real income of the poor. This was due to wage increases that didn't keep up with price increases during that period, a movement away from progressive taxation, and a reduction in government funding for some social programs in the 1980s.

Defining Poverty

Much of the government's concern with income distribution has centered on the poorest group—those in poverty. It's tough to say exactly where poverty begins. If poverty were defined as some absolute amount of real income and that amount had been determined 50 or 60 years ago, few in the United States would be in poverty in the 1990s. Most poor families today have real incomes higher than did the middle class 50 or 60 years ago. If a relative concept of poverty were chosen, whether a family would be classified as being in poverty would depend on what percentage of the average income it received. Poverty would then be impossible to eliminate, because some proportion of people would always be classified as poor.

The Official Definition of *Poverty*   The United States has adopted an official definition of **poverty** that is primarily an absolute measure but includes aspects of a relative definition. The U.S. official poverty line is drawn at three times the United States Department of Agriculture's minimum food budget, on the theory that an average family spends one-third of its income on food. If that minimum food budget is recalculated to account for rising standards of living, then the measure is a relative one. If the definition is held constant and only adjusted for changes in the prices of the foods selected in the original standard-of-living choice, then the measure is an absolute one.

The definition is currently not adjusted for rising standards of living, so it would seem to be an absolute measure of poverty. However it is adjusted by the rate of inflation rather than by the rise in the price of the originally selected foods. But food prices have risen by less than the rise in the general price level, so the index of poverty has gone up by more than it would have had that fixed ratio of food to income remained constant, so the definition includes aspects of relativity.

The minimum food budget includes four eggs, $1\frac{1}{2}$ pounds of meat, 3 pounds of potatoes, about 4 pounds of vegetables, and other foods that cost a total of about $21.50 per person per week. If one triples that amount to $64.50 (since food is said to require one-third of a family's income) and multiplies by 52 (the number of weeks in a year), one arrives at a poverty level of about $3,350 per person per year or about $13,400 for a family of four. That's not a lot of money in today's society, even if the measure has some relativity in it.

A number of other issues regarding poverty are debated. Considering them briefly will give you a good sense of the types of statistical and data problems that economists must consider as they analyze the economy. U.S. poverty figures include the after-tax income of the poor and the cash assistance that the poor receive. However they don't include *in-kind* (noncash) *transfers*, such as food stamps and housing assistance. Nor do they take underreporting of income into account. If one makes adjustments for in-kind transfers and underreporting of income, the number of people said to be in poverty decreases to about 60 percent of the number calculated without the adjustments. Moreover, since in-kind transfers grew enormously in the 1970s, the official poverty rate underestimates the decline in poverty during that period. So, as is the case with most economic statistics, poverty statistics should be used with care.

As Exhibit 3 shows, using the official poverty measure, the number of people in poverty decreased in the 1960s and then, after remaining approximately the

3

Poverty Defined by the U.S. government as three times an average family's minimum food expenditures as calculated by the U.S. Department of Agriculture.

	Number of people (in millions)	Percentage of population	Poverty income of family of 4 (in dollars)
1960	39.9	22.2	3,022
1970	25.4	12.6	3,968
1975	25.9	12.3	5,500
1980	29.3	13.0	8,414
1985	33.1	14.0	10,989
1986	32.4	13.6	11,203
1987	32.2	13.4	11,611
1988	31.7	13.0	12,092
1989	31.5	12.8	12,674
1990	33.6	13.5	13,359
1991	35.7	14.2	13,924

EXHIBIT 3   Number and Percentage of Persons in Poverty, 1960–1991

Source: U.S. Bureau of the Census, *Current Population Report, 1991* and *Social Security Bulletin,* 1993.

In 1992, the problems of poverty and racism erupted into violence in Los Angeles. *Reuters/Bettmann.*

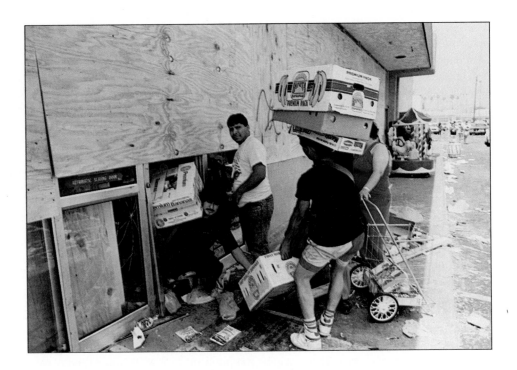

same for about 10 years, began increasing in the late 1970s. It remained over 30 million in the 1980s. Then in the early 1990s, with the recession, it rose even more. This poverty contributed to the Los Angeles riots in 1992.

The adjustments just discussed reduce the total number in poverty and some of the percent changes from year to year, but they do not modify the central conclusion that the number of people in poverty remained high in the 1980s and increased in the early 1990s. That rise has led some to question the fairness of the U.S. economy.

Alternative Views on the Increase in Poverty   People who favor policies aimed at achieving equality of income argue that this increase in poverty is a significant cost to society. One reason is that society suffers when some of its people are in poverty, just as the entire family suffers when one member doesn't have enough to eat. Most people derive pleasure from knowing that others are not in poverty. A second reason society as a whole benefits from a decrease in poverty is that the incentives for crime are decreased. As people's incomes increase, they have more to lose by committing crimes, and, therefore, fewer crimes are committed. In short, poverty breeds problems for society. Eliminating poverty helps to eliminate those problems. Those who favor equality of income argue that the increased poverty in the late 1970s and 1980s represents a failure of the economic policies of that period.

Others respond that the widening gap between rich and poor is not the result of government tax and spending policies. It has more to do with demographic changes. For example, the number of single-parent families increased dramatically during this period, while rapid growth of the labor force depressed wages for young, unskilled workers.

Advocates of reducing poverty respond that this argument is unconvincing. They argue that the tax cuts of the 1980s favored the rich while decreased funding for government programs hurt the poor. To compensate, they argue, free day care should be provided for children so that heads of single families can work full-time, and the low wages of the working poor should be supplemented by government. They hold that demographic changes are not a valid excuse for ducking a question of morality.

Why does poverty exist? That's a tough question to answer in a whole book, let alone a box. So instead of explaining why poverty exists, I'll simply list some factors that contribute to poverty, leaving it to you to figure out how important each factor is.

Suggested causes of poverty include low ability, lack of initiative, lack of access to education, deprived childhood, lack of luck, discrimination, and statistical mistakes.

This group of causes is self-explanatory except for "statistical mistakes," but the following editorial from The Wall Street Journal should give you a good, partisan, idea of what statistical mistakes mean.

Poverty Explained

In Washington, the poverty debate now centers on one crucial issue: How to blame the other guy. The Democratically controlled Ways and Means Committee recently produced a study, smilingly called "nonpartisan," that implicitly blamed the Reagan administration for recent increases in the poverty rate. To do so, it had to count 1979 and 1980 as Reagan administration years. Then it could show that poverty indeed increased between 1979 and 1987. The New York Times ran a front-page opinion piece based on this report and headlined, "Forces in Society, and Reaganism, Helped Dig Deeper Hole for Poor."

The Republican Study Committee screamed bloody murder. It used the Ways and Means data to show that between 1982 and 1987, years when Reagan budgets were actually in place, real income for those in the poorest fifth of the nation actually increased 4.1%. It was in the Carter years, it says, that the poor got poorer.

The fuss is all good politics. But it has nothing to do with poverty. Poverty trends are complex and deep; they simply can't be pegged to inauguration schedules.

Here is what really happened. Through the postwar era, the number of people living in poverty declined until about 1973. Then, remarkably, the poverty rate leveled off and began to increase. Since then, it has been fluctuating around a higher plateau. The years between 1979 and 1983 were brutal on the poor. Since 1984, the situation has been somewhat better.

The crucial question really is what happened around 1973 to cause the long decline in poverty to reverse itself. That is what honest poverty experts generally debate, some arguing that Great Society programs caused the change, some that the cultural revolution of the 1960s was responsible, others saying there had been a more fundamental change in the U.S. economy. Meanwhile it has become nothing short of hilarious to watch the political operatives in newspapers, magazines and on Capitol Hill pretend that troubling poverty trends started with Ronald Reagan.

To play their political games, the partisans rely on statistics and categories that are quaintly archaic. Back in the '60s and '70s, it was believed that poverty was a problem of scarcity. If government could divert resources to the poor, then they would be pushed out of poverty. Economists dominated the poverty debate, talking about income quintiles, and amassing data from little green books.

With the recognition of the underclass around 1982, it became obvious that behavior, not merely income level, had a lot to do with who was poor. Sociologists began to dominate discussion, and a welfare consensus emerged around the need for developing good work habits, sexual self-restraint and individual accountability. Even the liberal Ford Foundation has acknowledged that family breakdown is a major cause of social problems.

Savvy experts stopped relying on income quintiles because they tell you nothing about how poor people behave. When the Ways and Means Committee comes out and focuses on poverty rates and income distribution, it is a bit like watching a 20-year-old rerun of Dick Clark's "American Bandstand." It's hard to believe people really talked that way.

Here's a hoary old chestnut that stands as the centerpiece of the Ways and Means report: "The rich are getting richer and the poor are getting poorer." This formulation has always appealed to envy, but not much to common sense. In the first place, it's never been clear what the first observation has to do with the second. It is incoherent to pretend that the poor are getting poorer *because* the rich are getting richer. The economy is not finite. In fact, members of the working poor usually get richer only when the entire economy, including the rich, does better. To introduce the rich into talk of how the poor are doing is merely a lame effort to transform the problem into a pseudo-Marxian class struggle.

The more fundamental problem with the saying is that it pretends there is such a thing as "the poor." The obsolete economic perspective on poverty picks an income level and then lumps everybody under it as "the poor." In reality, 41% of this group own their own homes; many, however, are drug addicts living in the street. Some 11% have completed college, but many have virtually no marketable skills. Almost 40% of poor families have both parents in the home; the other 60% are female headed. The differences are profound, and they have to do with situation, not income.

It's time to stop defining poor people by how much they make, and to start defining them by behavior—by education, by job history, by family status. In the 1980s, we have arrived at a more realistic perception of poverty, but statistical measures haven't caught up. Until they do, we will be inundated by silly, partisan reports and nonsensical news articles.

Source: *The Wall Street Journal*, July 29, 1989. Reprinted with permission of THE WALL STREET JOURNAL © 1989 Dow Jones & Company, Inc. All rights reserved worldwide.

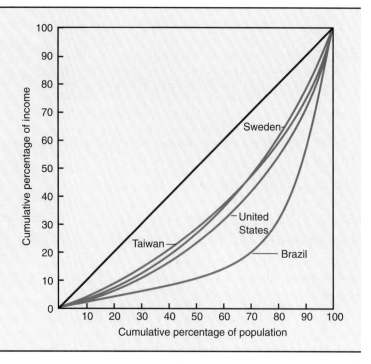

International Dimensions of
Income: The Income
Distribution Question

When considering income distribution, one usually is looking at conditions within
a single country. For example, the richest 5 percent of the U.S. population gets
approximately 30 times what the poorest 5 percent of the American people get.

   There are other ways to look at income. One might judge income inequality in
the United States relative to income inequality in other countries. Is the U.S.
distribution of income more or less equal than another country's? One could also
look at how income is distributed among countries. Even if income is relatively
equally distributed within countries, it may be unequally distributed among countries. Finally one can ask about the total level of world income. If the poorest
people in the world had income of $100,000 per year, would it matter that some
people had income of $300,000 a year?

Comparing U.S. Income Distribution with That in Other Countries   Exhibit 4 gives us a sense
of how the distribution of income in the United States compares to that in other
countries. We see that the United States has significantly more income inequality
than Sweden, but significantly less than Brazil (or most other developing and
newly industrialized countries). An important reason why the United States has
more income inequality than Sweden is that Sweden's tax system is more progressive. Until recently (when Sweden's socialist party lost power) the top marginal tax rate on the highest incomes in Sweden was 80 percent, compared to
about 33 percent in the United States. Given this difference, it isn't surprising that
Sweden has less income inequality. In a newly industrialized country like Brazil,
where a few individuals earn most of the income and, to a large degree, control the
government, the government is not likely to begin redistributing income to
achieve equality.

Income Distribution among Countries   When one considers the distribution of world
income, the picture becomes even more unequal than the picture one sees when
considering the distribution of income within countries. The reason is clear:
Income is highly unequally distributed among countries. The average per capita
income of the richest 5 percent of the countries of the world is more than 100 times
the average income of the poorest 5 percent of the countries of the world. Thus, a
Lorenz curve of world income would show much more inequality than the Lorenz

THE GINI COEFFICIENT

A second measure economists use to talk about the degree of income inequality is the Gini coefficient of inequality. The Gini coefficient is derived from the Lorenz curve by comparing the area between the (1) Lorenz curve and the diagonal (area *A*) and (2) the total area of the triangle below the diagonal (areas *A* and *B*). That is,

Gini coefficient = Area *A*/(Areas *A* + *B*).

A Gini coefficient of zero would be perfect equality since area *A* is zero if income is perfectly equally distributed. The highest the Gini coefficient can go is 1. So all Gini coefficients must be between zero and one. The lower the Gini coefficient, the closer income distribution is to being equal.

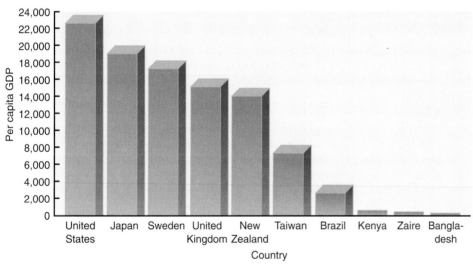

EXHIBIT 5   Per Capita GDP in Various Countries, 1991

Income is unequally distributed among the countries of the world.
Source: *The World Fact Book*, 1992.

curve for a particular country. Worldwide, income inequality is enormous. A minimum level in the United States would be a wealthy person's income in a poor country like Bangladesh.

To give you a better picture of income distribution problems, you need to consider not only the division of income, but also the total amounts of income in various countries. Exhibit 5 presents per capita GDP for various countries. Looking at the enormous differences of income among countries, we must ask which is more important: the distribution of income or the absolute level of income. Which would you rather be: one of four members in a family that has an income of $3,000 a year, which places you in the top 10 percent of Bangladesh's income distribution, or one of four members of a family with an income of $12,000 (four times as much), which places you in the bottom 10 percent of the income earners in the United States?

The Total Amount of Income in Various Countries

THE DISTRIBUTION OF WEALTH

Wealth The value of assets an individual owns.

Income Payments received plus changes in value of one's assets in a specified time period.

A Lorenz Curve of the Distribution of Wealth

4

Capital gain Increase in the value of one's assets in a specified time period.

In considering equality, two measures are often used: *equality of wealth* and *equality of income*. Because of space limitations, my focus will be on income, but I want to mention wealth. **Wealth** is the value of the things individuals own. It is a *stock* concept representing the value of assets such as houses, buildings, and machines. For example, a farmer who owns a farm with a net worth of $1 million is wealthy compared to an investment banker with a net worth of $225,000.

Income, in contrast, is a *flow* concept. It's a stream through time. That farmer might have an income of $20,000 a year while the investment banker might have an income of $80,000 a year. The farmer, with $1 million worth of assets, is wealthier than the investment banker, but the investment banker has a higher income than the farmer.

Exhibit 6(a) presents the distribution of wealth in the United States. Exhibit 6(b) compares the Lorenz curve for wealth in the United States with the Lorenz curve for income in the United States. You can see that wealth in the United States is more unequally distributed than income. The reason is twofold. First, wealth generates income. Wealthy people receive income from their investments as well as from any job they have. Some individuals with little wealth may have high income, but most individuals with large amounts of wealth do have high incomes.

Second, wealth is more unequally distributed than income because much of the income that the wealthy have doesn't show up as income. When an asset such as a stock or a house appreciates (goes up in value), the owner of those assets has an income of the amount of that appreciation. That type of income is called a **capital gain.** Capital gains are income, but the income distribution figures do not include income in the form of capital gains, since they are hard to measure. Thus, income distribution figures significantly understate the income of wealthy individuals.

Wealth quintile	Percentage of total household wealth
Bottom fifth	−0.2
Second fifth	0.2
Third fifth	2.7
Fourth fifth	13.3
Top fifth	84.3

(a)

(b)

EXHIBIT 6 (a and b)   Wealth Distribution in the United States and Wealth Compared to Income

Wealth is much more unequally distributed than income in the United States. In fact, the lowest 40 percent of the population have 0 percent of the wealth; they have borrowed as much as they own.
Source: U.S. Bureau of the Census and Edward N. Wolff, New York University (with permission).

Wealth (in billions)			
Americans		Non-Americans	
Walton family	$8.7	Taikichiro Mori (Japan)	Over $10 billion
Warren Edward Buffett	$3.5	Yoshiaki Tsutsumi (Japan)	
John Werner Kluge	$3.2	Brenninkmeyer family (Holland)	
Henry Ross Perot	$3.0	Eitaro Itoyama (Japan)	
Samuel Irving Newhouse, Jr.	$2.6	Hans and Gad Rausing (Sweden)	Over $5 billion
Donald Edward Newhouse	$2.6	Reichmann family (Canada)	
Henry Lea Hillman	$2.5	Kyuk-ho Shin (Korea)	
Sumner Murray Redstone	$2.5	Hirotomo Takei (Japan)	
Ted Arison	$2.5	Kenneth Roy Thomson (Canada)	
Lester Crown	$2.4	Kitaro Watanabe (Japan)	

EXHIBIT 7   Ten Wealthiest Americans and Non-Americans: 1989

Source: Harold Seneker, "A Wealth of Billionaires," Excerpted by permission of FORBES magazine, *July 24, 1989.* © Forbes Inc., 1989.

How Much Wealth Do the Wealthy Have?

Relative comparisons such as those depicted by Lorenz curves don't give you a sense of how much wealth it takes to be "wealthy." Exhibit 7 does that.

It presents a list of some of the wealthiest families in the United States and in the world in 1989. Most of us have little hope of joining either group; in fact, most of us have little possibility of becoming one of the top 5 percent of the wealthholders in the United States, which would require total wealth of at least $3 million. Once there was a time that people's ultimate financial goal was to be a millionaire. In the 1990s, thanks to inflation, the ultimate financial goal for the wealthiest people is to be a billionaire. The millionaire's club is no longer highly exclusive.

Of course, people on the list don't always stay there. Sam Walton died in 1992, leaving his fortune to his family. The Reichmann family had a major financial setback in 1992 and lost billions, and most of the Japanese billionaires lost billions in the fall of the Japanese stock market. Today, some of these people and families might only be multi-millionaires. (It's tough to stay a billionaire.)

SOCIOECONOMIC DIMENSIONS OF INCOME INEQUALITY

The size distribution of inequality is only one of the dimensions that inequality of income and wealth can take. As I mentioned before, the distribution of income according to source of income (wages, rents, and profits) was once considered important. Today's focus is on the distribution of income based on race, ethnic background, geographic region, and other socioeconomic factors such as gender and type of job.

Income Distribution according to Socioeconomic Characteristics

Exhibit 8 gives an idea of the distribution of income according to socioeconomic characteristics.

You can see that income differs substantially by type of job, leading some economists to argue that a new professional/nonprofessional class distinction is arising in the United States. There are also substantial differences between the incomes of women and men and between whites and blacks. Some of these variations are explained by sociological and cultural differences, but a substantial fraction of that variation is the result of **discrimination** (differential treatment of individuals because of physical or social characteristics).

Discrimination Differential treatment of individuals because of physical or social characteristics.

What Are the Causes of Discrimination?

Discrimination exists in all walks of life: Women are paid less than men, and blacks are often directed into lower-paying jobs. Economists have done a lot of research in order to understand the facts about discrimination and what can be done about it. The first problem is to measure the amount of discrimination and get an idea of how much discrimination is caused by what. Let's consider discrimination against women.

EXHIBIT 8   Various Socioeconomic Income Distribution Designations

Mean Income, 1990		
By Occupational Category	Male	Female
Managerial and professional specialty occupation	$43,634	$24,217
Technical, sales and administrative support occupations	$27,324	$14,080
Service occupations	$13,926	$7,490
Farming, forestry, and fishing occupations	$12,127	$6,592
Precision production, craft, and repair occupations	$23,961	$14,835
Operators, fabricators, and laborers	$18,244	$11,492
Armed forces	$22,408	$19,528
Average of all workers	$26,421	$15,075

By Region, 1990	Median Household Income
Northeast	$32,676
Midwest	$29,897
South	$26,942
West	$31,761

Mean Income				
By Sex	1970	1980	1985	1990
Male	$7,537	$15,340	$20,652	$27,866
Female	$3,138	$6,772	$10,584	$19,816

By Race, 1990	Median Household Income
White	$31,231
Black	$18,676
Hispanic	$22,330

Source: U.S. Bureau of the Census, *Current Population Reports, Consumer Income 1992.*

Gunnar Myrdal—Nobel prize, 1974, for his work on the interdependence of economic, social, and political forces.
© *The Nobel Foundation.*

On average, women receive somewhere around 60 percent of the pay that men receive to do the same kind of job. That suggests that discrimination is occurring. The economist's job is to figure out how much of this is statistically significant, and, of that portion that is caused by discrimination, what is the nature of that discrimination.

Analyzing that data, economists have found that somewhat more than half of this difference can be explained by other causes, such as lengths of time on the job. But that still leaves a relatively large difference that can be attributed to discrimination.

Is it demand-side workplace discrimination by employers? Or is it supply-side sociological discrimination which occurs in the general social interactions between men and women? It's clear what demand-side workplace discrimination by employers is: When an employer hires a man rather than an equally qualified woman, or pays a woman less for doing a job than the employer pays a man for that job, that's demand-side discrimination.

Supply-side sociological discrimination is more complicated. For example, sociologists have found that in personal relationships women come out on the short end. For instance, women tend to move to be with their partners more than men move to be with their partners. In addition, women in two-parent relationships do much more work around the house and take a greater responsibility for child rearing than men do even when both the man and the woman are employed.

These observations suggest that there is sociological supply-side discrimination. Such discrimination can lead to the same pay statistics as can demand-side discrimination. The more an employer can count on an employee's total dedication to the job, the more likely the employer is to pay that employee a high wage. When a woman gives up a promotion possibility because it would require her to move away from her partner, or resigns a good job to move to be with her partner, she's lowering her average pay. Similarly when she misses a key meeting to stay with a sick child who has a 104° temperature, she may be behaving admirably, but she is lowering her advancement and pay possibilities. The fact that women, on average, take personal relationships more seriously than do men means that women, on average, will be paid less than men even if there is no demand-side discrimination.

How important are these sociological observations? In discussing discrimination I ask the members of my class to state if they expect their personal relationships with their partners to be fully equal. The usual result is the following: 80 percent of the women expect a fully equal relationship; 20 percent expect their partner to come first. Eighty percent of the men expect their careers to come first; 20 percent expect an equal relationship. I then point out that somebody's expectations aren't going to be fulfilled. Put simply, most observers believe that supply-side discrimination that occurs in interpersonal relationships is significant.

Economists have made adjustments for these sociological factors, and have found that supply-side factors explain a portion of the lower pay but that work-place discrimination also explains a portion. How big a portion to attribute to demand–side factors and how big a portion to attribute to supply-side factors is undetermined, even though it has been subject to considerable debate. One reason for this continued debate is that the two types of discrimination interact. Say a firm doesn't have an inherent bias against women but expects that women will be less-committed employees. The firm will likely assign women to the less critical jobs. The firm is discriminating against women, but that discrimination is a reflection of its expectation of supply-side discrimination.

A final point: Even if women *in general* are less likely than men to be "fully committed employees," that does not mean that any *individual* woman will be less committed. The question of whether it is appropriate to accept discrimination against particular individuals on the basis of group characteristics is a normative issue that society, not economists, must resolve. What economists can do is to identify the nature of the discrimination and point out the consequences of policies intended to eliminate it.

The supply-side/demand-side distinction is important in deciding what to do about discrimination. If the primary cause is on the supply side, it can be strongly argued that if one wants to end discrimination, the fight is best directed at the discrimination that occurs in male/female relationships. Why do women allow themselves to be "exploited" by men, and can that exploitation be reduced? If the discrimination is on the demand side because employers are reluctant to hire women, equal opportunity laws will be more successful than if the discrimination is on the supply side.

As you can see from this brief summary, discussions of discrimination quickly get complicated and intertwined with normative issues. Pointing out that seemingly simple issues are actually very complicated is something that economists often do. It's a logical conclusion of economic thinking.

Deciding What to Do about Economic Discrimination

Early economists focused on the distribution of income by wages, profits, and rent because that division corresponded to their class analysis of society. Land-owners received rent, capitalists received profit, and workers received wages. Tensions among these classes played an important part in economists' analyses of the economy and policy.

As class divisions by income source have become blurred, they've become only a tiny part of mainstream economists' analysis of the economy. That doesn't mean that other types of socioeconomic classes no longer exist. They do. The United States has a kind of upper class. In fact, there is a company in the United States that publishes the *Social Register,* which contains the names and pedigrees of about 35,000 socially prominent people who might be categorized "upper-class." Similarly, it is possible to further divide the U.S. population into a middle class and a lower class.

The difference today is that class divisions are no longer determined by income source. For example, upper-class people do not necessarily receive their

Income Distribution according to Class

Class levels	Upper class	Upper middle class	Middle class	Lower middle class	Lower class
Approximate percentage of population	4	12	33	33	18
Likely occupation	Independently wealthy Lawyers Professors Doctors Accountants	Small busness people Teachers Social workers Managers of small firms	Administrative Clerical Chain store managers Technicians Salespeople	Unskilled labor Industrial workers	Unskilled labor Unemployed
Likely education	17 or more years of school, college, and beyond	Around 15 years College	High school and some college	10 to 12 years	Elementary school
Religious affiliation	Jewish Episcopalian Congregational A few Roman Catholics	Congregational Jewish Some Catholics	Methodist Baptist Many Catholics	Methodist Many Catholics	Baptist Pentecostal Extreme fundamentalist groups
Approximate annual income (some overlap between classes)	Over 100,000 Some extremely high Much inherited wealth	Between 50,000 and 100,000 Most earned income by salary	Between 20,000 and 50,000 Salary Some wages	12,000 to 20,000 Hourly wages	Under 13,000 Poverty programs and welfare
Residential neighborhood	Very elite neighborhood Expensive houses	Good neighborhoods Moderately expensive homes	Private homes, medium sized Some tract homes	Apartments Small tract homes	Slum areas Poor apartments
Leisure time activities	Music, cultural events Travel "Serious" reading Elite clubs Active sports (tennis, golf, sailing)	Cultural events Formal parties Travel Family outings Racquetball	Visiting friends Television Movies Some "light" reading	Visiting relatives Television Detective novel Observer sports (baseball, football) Bowling	Television Visiting relatives Bowling
Newspaper reading	*Wall Street Journal* *New York Times*	*Wall Street Journal* *New York Times*	Local paper *USA Today*	Local paper *National Enquirer*	Local paper *National Enquirer*

EXHIBIT 9   Socioeconomic Class Divisions

Social scientists disagree about how many classes there are in the United States because there are no sharp breaks between them. This chart presents one possible method of division and the characteristics of each class.
Source: Adapted from a Bureau of the Census chart.

income from rent and profits. Today we have ''upper-class'' people who derive their income from wages and ''lower-class'' people who derive their income from profits (usually in the form of pensions, which depend upon profits from the investment of pension funds in stocks and bonds). Nowadays in the United States classification is based on characteristics other than source of income. Upper-class people don't bowl and lower-class people don't like opera—or so the classes have been stereotyped.

Exhibit 9 gives you an idea of the socioeconomic divisions and income of the various classes. In it you can see that income isn't the only determinant of class.

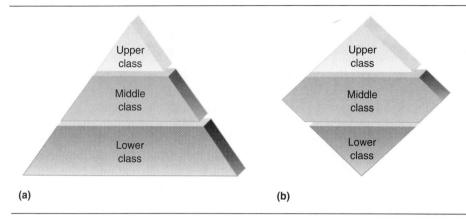

Other characteristics, like your education, what you read, and your job or career, contribute to your class designation.

The Importance of the Middle Class   What has made the most difference in today's class structure in the United States compared to its class structure in earlier periods and to the structure in today's developing countries is the tremendous growth in the relative size of the middle class. Economists used to see the class structure as a pyramid—and still do in developing countries. From a base composed of a large lower class the pyramid tapered upward through a medium-sized middle class to a peak occupied by the upper class (Exhibit 10(a)). A few upper-class individuals were supported by some middle-class people, while both of those classes rested on a large number of lower-class individuals. The class structure is still pyramidal in developing countries. In the United States and other developed countries the pyramid has bulged out into a diamond, as shown in Exhibit 10(b). The middle class has become the largest class while the upper and lower classes are smaller in relative terms.

This enormous increase in the relative size of the middle class in developed countries has significantly blurred the distinction between capitalists and workers. In early capitalist society the distributional fight (the fight over relative income shares) was largely between workers and capitalists. In modern capitalist society the distributional fight is among various types of individuals. Union workers are pitted against nonunion workers; salaried workers are pitted against workers paid by the hour. The old are pitted against the young; women are pitted against men; blacks are pitted against Hispanics and Asians, and all three groups are pitted against whites.

Distributional Questions and Tensions in Society   While mainstream economists tend to focus on the size distribution of income, nonmainstream economists tend to emphasize class and group structures in their analysis. Radical economists emphasize the control that the upper class has over the decision process and the political process. Conservative economists emphasize the role of special interests of all types in shaping government policy. Both radical and conservative analyses bring out the tensions among classes in society much better than does the mainstream, classless analysis.

When people feel they belong to a particular class or group, they will often work to further the interests of that class or group. They also generally have stronger feelings about inequalities among classes or groups than when they lack that sense of class or group identity. Using a classless analysis means overlooking the implications of class and group solidarity in affecting the tensions in society.

Those tensions show up every day in political disputes over the tax system, in the quiet fuming of individuals as they see someone else earning more for doing the same job, and in strikes and even riots. Such tensions often underlie the economic relationships of all countries; in many developing countries they break out into the open as armed insurrections or riots over food shortages (or soap shortages or cigarette shortages, as we saw in the former USSR in the early 1990s).

Those tensions have been kept to a minimum in American society. A majority of Americans believe that income distribution is sufficiently fair for them to accept their share more or less contentedly. To remedy the unfairness that does exist, they don't demand that the entire system be replaced. Instead they work for change within the present system. They look to affirmative action laws, comparable-pay laws, minimum-wage laws, and social welfare programs for any improvement they perceive to be necessary or desirable. There's much debate about whether these government actions have achieved the desired ends, but the process itself reduces tensions and has worked toward the maintenance of the entire system.

People's acceptance of the U.S. economic system is based not only on what the distribution of income is but also on what people think it should be, what they consider fair. It is to that question that I now turn.

INCOME DISTRIBUTION AND FAIRNESS

Philosophical Debates about Equality and Fairness

Judgments about whether the distribution of income is fair or should be changed are normative ones, based on the values one applies to the situation. Value judgments necessarily underlie all policy prescriptions.

Depending on one's values, any income distribution can be justified. For example, Friedrich Nietzsche, the 19th-century German philosopher, argued that society's goal should be to support its supermen—its best and brightest. Lesser individuals' duty should be to work for the well-being of these supermen. Bertram de Juvenal, a 20th-century philosopher, has argued that a high level of income inequality is necessary to sustain the arts, beauty, education, and civilization. He and others say that a world of equally distributed income would be a world without beauty. Even if we don't personally own beautiful, expensive homes or aren't devoted opera fans, these philosophers argue, our lives are improved because some people do own such homes and because opera performances exist. Inequality creates diversity in our lives, and that diversity enriches the lives of everyone.

Other philosophers disagree strongly. They argue that equality itself is the overriding goal. That view is embodied in the U.S. Declaration of Independence: "We hold these truths to be self-evident, that all men are created equal." And for many people the inherent value of equality is not open to question—it is simply self-evident. Believing that equality is an overriding goal does not necessarily imply that income should be equally distributed. For example, John Rawls (a Harvard University professor who believes that equality is highly desirable and that society's goal should be to maximize the welfare of the least well-off) agrees that to meet that goal some inequality is necessary. Rawls argues that if, in pursuing equality, you actually make the least well-off worse off than they otherwise would have been, then you should not pursue equality any further. For example, say under one policy there will be perfect equality and everyone receives $10,000 per year. Under another policy, the least well-off person receives $12,000 per year and all others receive $40,000. Rawls argues that the second policy is preferable to the first even though it involves more inequality.

Economists, unlike philosophers, are not concerned about justifying any particular distribution of income. In their objective role, economists limit themselves to explaining the effects that various policies will have on the distribution of income; they let the policymakers judge whether those effects are desirable.

However in order to judge economic policies, you, in your role as a citizen who elects policymakers, must make certain judgments about income distribution because all real-world economic policies have distribution effects. Accordingly a brief discussion of income distribution and fairness is in order.

Fairness and Equality

The U.S. population has a strong general tendency to favor equality—equality is generally seen as fair. Most people, including me, share that view. However there are instances when equality of income is not directly related to people's view of fairness. For example, consider this distribution of income between John and Fred:

John gets $50,000 a year.

Fred gets $12,000 a year.

Think a minute. Is that fair? The answer I'm hoping for is that you don't yet have enough information to make the decision.

Here's some more information. Say that John gets that $50,000 for holding down three jobs at a time, while Fred gets his $12,000 for sitting around doing nothing. At this point, many of us would argue that it's possible that John should be getting even more than $50,000 and Fred should be getting less than $12,000.

But wait! What if we discover that Fred is an invalid and unless his income increases to $15,000 a year he will die? Most of us would change our minds again and argue that Fred deserves more, regardless of how much John works.

But wait! How about if, after further digging, we discover that Fred is an invalid because he squandered his health on alcohol, drugs, and fried foods? In that case some people would likely change their minds again as to whether Fred deserves more.

By now you should have gotten my point. Looking only at a person's income masks many dimensions that most people consider important in making value judgments about fairness.

When most people talk about believing in equality in income, they mean they believe in equality of opportunity for comparably endowed individuals to earn income. If equal opportunity of equals leads to inequality of income, that inequality in income is fair. Unfortunately there's enormous latitude for debate on what constitutes equal opportunity of equals.

In the real world, needs differ, desires differ, and abilities differ. Should these differences be considered relevant differences in equality? You must supply the answers to those questions before you can judge any economic policy because to make a judgment on whether an economic policy should or should not be adopted, you must make a judgment about whether a policy's effect on income is fair. In making those judgments most people rely on their immediate gut reaction. I hope what you have gotten out of this discussion about John and Fred and equality of opportunity is the resolve to be cautious about trusting your gut reactions. The concept of fairness is crucial and complicated, and it deserves deeper consideration than just a gut reaction.

Let's now say that we have considered all the issues discussed so far in this chapter and have concluded that some redistribution of income from the rich to the poor is necessary if society is to meet our ideal of fairness. How do we go about redistributing income?

To answer that question, we must consider what programs exist and what their negative side effects might be. The side effects can be substantial and they can subvert the intention of the program so that far less overall money is available for redistribution and equality is reduced less than one might think.

Three important side effects that economists have found in programs to redistribute income are:

1. The incentive effects of a tax may result in a switch from labor to leisure.
2. The effects of taxes may include attempts to avoid or evade taxes, leading to a decrease in measured income.
3. The incentive effects of distributing money may cause people to make themselves look as if they're more needy than they really are.

5

Fairness as
Equality of Opportunity

THE PROBLEMS OF
REDISTRIBUTING INCOME

Three Important Side Effects of
Redistributive Programs

6

Appendix A provides a numerical example of each of these, showing that these effects can be substantial and make income redistribution costly in terms of reduced total income.

All economists believe that the incentive effects of taxation are important and must be taken into account in policy making. But they differ significantly in the importance they assign to incentive effects, and empirical evidence doesn't resolve the question. Some economists believe that incentive effects are so important that little taxation for redistribution should take place. They support what has come to be known as the **trickle-down theory** (the theory that the poor are better off when the rich do well). The reasoning behind the theory goes as follows: When the rich do well the total pie is increased so much that the benefits that *trickle down* to the poor are greater than the proceeds they would get from redistribution. For example, supporters of the trickle-down theory argue that the growth in capitalist economies was made possible by entrepreneurs. Because those entrepreneurs invested in new technology, there was more growth in society. Moreover these entrepreneurs paid taxes. The benefits resulting from entrepreneurial action trickled down to the poor, making them better off. The fact that some of those entrepreneurs became rich is irrelevant because all society was better off due to their actions.

Other economists believe that there should be significant taxation for redistribution. While they agree that sometimes the incentive effects are substantial, they see the goal of equality overriding these effects.

Trickle-down theory The belief that giving benefits to the rich will expand aggregate output and thereby help the poor.

Politics, Income Redistribution, and Fairness

We began this discussion of income distribution and fairness by making the assumption that our value judgments determine the taxes we pay—that if our values led us to the conclusion that the poor deserved more income, we could institute policies that would get more to the poor. Reality doesn't necessarily work that way. Often politics, not value judgments, plays the central role in determining what taxes individuals will pay. The group that has the most votes will elect lawmakers who will enact tax policies that benefit that group at the expense of groups with fewer votes.

On the surface the democratic system of one person/one vote would seem to suggest that the politics of redistribution would favor the poor, but it doesn't. One would expect that the poor would use their votes to make sure income was redistributed to them from the rich. Why don't they? The answer is complicated. One reason is that many of the poor don't vote because they reason that "one vote won't make much difference." As a result poor people's total voting strength is reduced. A second reason is that the "poor" aren't seen by most politicians as a solid voting block. There's no organization of the poor that can deliver votes to politicians. A third reason is that those poor people who do vote often cast their votes with other issues in mind. An anti–income-redistribution candidate might have a strong view on abortion as well, and for many the abortion view is the one that decides their vote.

A fourth reason is that elections require financing; much of that financing comes from the rich. The money is used for advertising and publicity aimed at convincing the poor that voting for a person who supports the rich is actually in the best interests of the poor. Poor people are often misled by that kind of publicity, but not necessarily because they are dumb. In my view they do as well as anyone else could in processing the information they receive. The trouble is that information on the redistributive effect of a policy is often biased.

The issues are usually sufficiently complicated that a trained economist must study the information about them for a long time to determine which arguments make sense. Reasonable-sounding arguments can be made to support just about any position, and the rich have the means to see that the arguments that support their positions get the publicity.

EXHIBIT 11   **Rates of Personal and Corporate Income Tax, 1992**

Federal Individual Income Tax		
Joint return	Single taxpayer	Rate
$0–$34,000	$0–$20,350	15%
$34,001–$82,150	$20,351–$49,300	28%
$82,151–$149,999	$49,301–$99,999	34%
$150,000 and above	$100,000 and above	28%

Federal Corporation Taxes	
Taxable income	Percentage rate
$0–$50,000	15%
$50,001–$75,000	25%
$75,001–$100,000	34%
$100,001–$335,000	39%
$335,001 and above	34%

Source: Internal Revenue Service, *Statistics of Income Bulletin*, 1992.

The preceding discussion provided you with a general sense of the theoretical difficulty of redistributing income. In this section I give you a sense of how income redistribution policies and programs have worked in the real world. As you've seen, there are two direct methods through which government redistributes income: taxation (policies that tax the rich more than the poor) and expenditures (programs that help the poor more than the rich).

The U.S. federal government gets its revenue from a variety of taxes. The three largest sources of revenue are the personal income tax, the corporate income tax, and the social security tax. Exhibit 11 shows the 1991 rates for corporate and personal income taxes.

State and local governments get their revenue from state income taxes, sales taxes, and property taxes. The rates vary among states.

Tax systems can be progressive, proportional (sometimes called *flat rate*), or regressive. A **progressive tax** is one in which the average tax rate increases with income. It redistributes income from the rich to the poor. A **proportional tax** is one in which the average rate of tax is constant regardless of income level. It is neutral in regard to income distribution. A **regressive tax** is one in which the average tax rate decreases with income. It redistributes income from poor to rich.

In the early 1940s the federal personal income tax was made highly progressive, with a top tax rate of 90 percent on the highest incomes. The degree of progressivity went down significantly through various pieces of legislation after World War II until 1986, when the income tax system was amended to provide for an initial rate of 15 percent and a top rate of 34 percent. The changes did not reduce the actual progressivity of the personal income tax as much as they seemed to, because the 1986 reforms eliminated many of the loopholes in the U.S. Tax Code. Some loopholes had allowed rich people to legally reduce their reported incomes and to pay taxes on those lower incomes at lower rates.

Whereas the personal income tax is progressive, the social security tax is initially proportional. All individuals pay the same tax rate on wage income (7.65 percent for employer; 7.65 percent for employee; 15.3 percent for self-employed) up to a cap of about $53,000. Above that income cap, no social security tax is due, so the social security tax becomes regressive: Higher-income individuals pay a lower percentage of their total income than lower-income individuals.

REAL-WORLD POLICIES AND PROGRAMS FOR INCOME REDISTRIBUTION

Taxation to Redistribute Income

Progressive tax Average tax rate increases with income.

Proportional tax Average tax rate is constant with income.

Regressive tax Average tax rate decreases with income.

EXHIBIT 12   Effective Rates of Federal, State, and Local Taxes, 1985

Population deciles	Percentage of total income
Bottom tenth	21.9
Second tenth	21.3
Third tenth	21.4
Fourth tenth	22.5
Fifth tenth	23.1
Sixth tenth	23.5
Seventh tenth	23.7
Eighth tenth	24.6
Ninth tenth	25.1
Top tenth	25.3

Source: Joseph Pechman, "Who Paid the Taxes 1966–1985?" (Washington, D.C.: Brookings Institution, 1985). Used by permission.

State and local governments get most of their income from the following sources:

1. Income taxes, which are generally somewhat progressive.
2. Sales taxes, which tend to be proportional (all people pay the same tax rate on what they spend) or slightly regressive. (Since poor people often spend a higher percentage of their incomes than rich people, poor people pay a higher average tax rate as a percentage of their income than rich people.)
3. Property taxes, which are taxes paid on the value of people's property (usually real estate, but sometimes also personal property like cars). Since the value of people's property is related (although imperfectly related) to income, the property tax is considered to be roughly proportional.

When all the taxes paid by individuals to all levels of governments are combined, the conclusion that most researchers come to is that little income redistribution takes place on the tax side. The progressive taxes are offset by the regressive taxes, so the overall tax system is roughly proportional. That is, on average the tax rates individuals pay are roughly equal. Estimates of the effective tax rates for various income groups are presented in Exhibit 12. In it you can see that lower-income individuals pay approximately 22 percent of their total income in taxes; higher-income individuals pay about 25 percent. Recent changes in the tax laws have not changed these figures significantly.

Expenditure Programs to Redistribute Income

Since taxes don't redistribute income significantly, if the government does redistribute income, it must do so through expenditure programs. Exhibit 13 presents the federal government's expenditures on some programs that contribute to redistribution.

Social security Social insurance program that provides financial benefits to the elderly and disabled and to their eligible dependents and/or survivors.

Social Security
The program that redistributes the most money is the **social security** system. It was established on a small scale during the Great Depression in 1935, but it has grown enormously since then. Almost all workers in the United States, including the self-employed, pay social security tax on their income. When you get your paycheck, this deduction is probably designated "FICA," which stands for Federal Insurance Contribution Act. This money goes into the social security trust fund, from which benefits are payable to eligible persons who are elderly or disabled, to certain of their dependents, and to surviving dependents of deceased workers. Social security also has a multibillion-dollar medical insurance component called **Medicare.**

Medicare Medical insurance component of the social security program.

The population is aging, the death rate is going down, and the birth rate has been low. These demographic facts mean that fewer and fewer active workers are

EXHIBIT 13   Expenditures on Government Programs to Redistribute Income, 1989

Program classification	Total (in billions)	Percentage* Federal	Percentage* State and local
Social insurance (including programs such as social security and unemployment insurance)	$468	83%	17%
Public aid (including programs such as Public Assistance and Supplemental Security Income)	$127	62%	38%
Health and medical programs (including Medicare and Medicaid)	$57	44%	56%
Veterans programs	$30	99%	1%
Education	$238	7%	93%
Housing	$18	85%	15%
Other social welfare	$17	53%	47%

* Estimate based on past division.

Source: *Social Security Bulletin, 1992.*

contributing to the fund while more and more people are becoming eligible for benefits. A social security crunch can be expected by the year 2020. Medical expenses in the United States are increasing at a rapid rate, and the medical insurance part of the fund may be in difficulty even sooner—perhaps by 2010.

The amount of an individual's social security retirement, disability, or survivors' monthly cash benefits depends on a very complex formula, which is skewed in favor of lower-income workers. The program is not a pension program that pegs benefits to the amount paid in. Many people will get much more than they paid in; some who never paid anything in will get a great deal; and a few who paid in for years will get nothing. (No benefits are payable if you die before you retire and leave no survivors eligible for benefits due to your work.) On the whole, the program has been successful in keeping the elderly out of poverty. In addition, social security benefits have helped workers' survivors and the disabled.

In the early 1990s there were about 40 million recipients of cash social security benefits, many of whom also received Medicare health insurance payments. Total benefits paid in 1990 came to $244.7 billion.

Public Assistance   **Public assistance** programs (more familiarly known as *welfare payments*) exist in every state of the union, although the amount paid varies greatly from state to state. The main kinds of public assistance are:

Public assistance ("welfare") Means-tested social programs targeted to the poor and providing financial, nutritional, medical, and housing assistance.

Aid to Families with Dependent Children (AFDC). Provides financial assistance to needy families with children under age 19.

Food stamps. Provides nutritional assistance in the form of coupons redeemable at most food stores.

Medicaid. Medical assistance for the poor, paid for by the individual states. It's different from, and usually more generous than, Medicare.

General assistance. State assistance to poor people when emergencies arise that aren't taken care of by any of the other programs.

By far the largest proportion of payments goes to needy families with dependent children, especially since these families are usually so poor that, in addition to qualifying for AFDC, they meet the eligibility requirements for food stamps and Medicaid.

A common complaint about welfare recipients is that they should get a job. A little research reveals that this criticism is misplaced. About 70 percent of the recipients are children, and many of the adults receiving welfare are too disabled to work. Moreover most welfare programs conduct job training and other programs designed to help recipients who are able to work get off the welfare rolls. In 1990 about $127 billion was paid in public aid (including the value of food stamps).

Supplemental Security Income   Hundreds of thousands more people would be receiving public assistance if it weren't for **Supplemental Security Income (SSI),** a federal

Supplemental Security Income (SSI) Federal program that pays benefits, based on need, to the elderly, blind, and disabled.

EXHIBIT 4   Distribution of Income before and after Taxes and Transfers

Although little redistribution takes place through the tax system, significant redistribution occurs through the transfer system, making the after-tax and transfer distribution of income more equal than the before-tax distribution of income.
Source: U.S. Bureau of the Census.

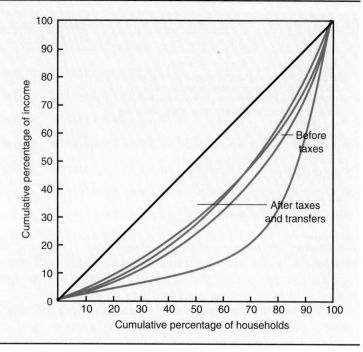

program administered through Social Security Administration offices. Unlike social security benefits, SSI pays benefits to the elderly, blind, and disabled based solely on the basis of need. Again unlike social security, the recipients pay nothing toward the cost of the program. To be eligible, though, people must have very low incomes and almost no resources except a home, if they are fortunate enough to own one, a wedding ring and engagement ring, and an automobile. In 1990 about $15.2 billion was paid in SSI benefits.

Unemployment compensation Short-term financial assistance, regardless of need, to eligible individuals who are temporarily out of work.

Unemployment Compensation   **Unemployment compensation** is limited financial assistance to people who are out of work through no fault of their own and have worked in a covered occupation for a substantial number of weeks in the period just before they became unemployed. These programs are administered by the states, even though they are largely funded by the federal government, which in turn gets the money from a tax on employers. Employees do not have anything deducted from their paychecks for unemployment compensation. The amount and duration of benefit payments varies from state to state. Unemployment compensation is not a long-term program, because it was designed to tide a person over who is temporarily out of work because of a lay-off or the seasonal nature of his or her occupation. A person can't just quit a job and live on unemployment benefits. While receiving unemployment benefits, people are expected to actively search for work.

Normally a person can receive unemployment benefits for only about six months in any given year, and the amount of the benefit is always considerably less than the amount the person earned when working. Lower-income workers receive unemployment payments that are more nearly equal to their working wage than do higher-income workers, but there is no income eligibility test. In 1990 about $18 billion was paid in unemployment benefits, in 1991, $27 billion; and in 1992, $36.7 billion.

Housing Programs   Federal and state governments have many different programs to improve housing or to provide affordable housing. While many of these programs are designed to benefit "low-income" persons, there are also programs for "moderate-income" persons and "lower-income persons" (people whose incomes are lower than "moderate" but higher than "low").

The federal agency overseeing most of these programs, the Department of Housing and Urban Development (HUD), has been criticized for abuse and mismanagement. Hundreds of millions of dollars that could have benefited the poor went instead to developers of housing and other projects, to consultants, and to others who skimmed off money before—or instead of—building or rehabilitating housing. In part because of these problems, federal funding for housing was steadily reduced during the 1980s. In 1990 about $18 billion was allocated to federal housing programs.

Overall Effect of Income Redistribution Programs   While the tax system has not proven to be an effective means of redistributing income, the government expenditure system has been quite effective. Exhibit 14 shows Lorenz curves before and after analyzing the effect of both taxes and government programs on the redistribution of income. As you can see, the after-transfer income is significantly closer to being equally distributed. But because of the incentive effects of collecting and distributing the money, that redistribution has come at the cost of a reduction in the total amount of income earned by the society. The debate about whether the gain in equality of income is worth the cost in reduction of total income is likely to continue indefinitely.

Much more could be said about the issues involved in income redistribution. But limitations of time and space pressure us to move on and look at income distribution from different perspectives. The next chapter considers a primary source of income—wage income—and the economic forces that determine what wages will be. It gives you a sense of how supply and demand in factor markets, in conjunction with historical and social forces, determine wages. The final chapter in this section looks at nonwage income (profits, rent, and interest) and shows how some people in capitalist countries get rich quick. Combined, these chapters will give you a good introduction to the topic of income distribution.

CONCLUSION

KEY POINTS

- The Lorenz curve is a measure of the inequality of income. **1** **2**
- There are alternative views about government's role in reducing poverty. **3**
- Wealth is distributed less equally than income. **4**
- Fairness is a philosophical question. Each person must judge a program's fairness for him or herself. **5**
- Income is difficult to redistribute because of in-

centive effects of taxes, avoidance and evasion effects of taxes, and incentive effects of redistribution programs. **6**
- On the whole, the U.S. tax system is roughly proportional, so it is not very effective as a means of redistributing income. **7**
- Government expenditure programs are more effective than tax policy in reducing income inequality in the United States. **7**

KEY TERMS

capital gain *(668)*
discrimination *(669)*
income *(668)*
Lorenz curve *(661)*
Medicare *(678)*
poverty *(663)*
progressive tax *(677)*

proportional tax *(677)*
public assistance ("welfare") *(679)*
regressive tax *(677)*
size distribution of income *(660)*

social security *(678)*
socioeconomic distribution of income *(660)*
Supplemental Security Income (SSI) *(679)*

trickle-down theory *(676)*
unemployment compensation *(680)*
wealth *(668)*

QUESTIONS FOR THOUGHT AND REVIEW

The number after each question represents the estimated degree of critical thinking required. (1 = almost none; 10 = deep thought.)

1. Why are we concerned with the distribution of income between whites and blacks, but not between redheads and blonds? *(8)*
2. The Lorenz curve for Bangladesh looks like this:

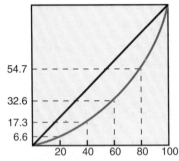

   How much income do the top 20 percent of individuals in Bangladesh receive? *(2)*
3. If one were to draw a Lorenz curve for lawyers, what would it represent? *(5)*
4. Should poverty be defined absolutely or relatively? Why? *(6)*
   relative to people around them

5. Some economists argue that a class distinction should be made between managerial decision makers and other workers. Do you agree? Why or why not? *(8)*
6. If a garbage collector earns more than an English teacher, does that mean something is wrong with the economy? Why or why not? *(8)*
7. Is it ever appropriate for society to:
   Let someone starve?
   Let someone be homeless?
   Forbid someone to eat chocolate? *(8)*
8. If you receive a paycheck, what percentage of it is withheld for taxes? What incentive effect does that have on your decision to work? *(5)*
9. Give four reasons why women earn so much less than men. Which reasons do you believe are most responsible for the difference? *(6)*
10. There are many more poor people than there are rich people. If the poor wanted to, they could exercise their power to redistribute as much money as they please to themselves. They don't do that, so they must see the income distribution system as fair. Discuss. *(6)*

PROBLEMS AND EXERCISES

1. The accompanying table shows income distribution data for three countries.

| | Percentage of total income | | |
Income quintile	India	South Korea	Mexico
Lowest 20%	7	5.7	2.9
Second quintile	9.2	11.2	7.0
Third quintile	13.5	15.1	12
Fourth quintile	20.5	22.4	20.4
Highest 20%	49.8	45.6	57.7

   a. Using this information, draw a Lorenz curve for each country.
   b. Which country has the most equal distribution of income?
   c. Which country has the least equal?

   d. By looking at the three Lorenz curves, can you tell which country has the most progressive tax system? Why or why not?
2. In Taxland, a tax exemption is granted for the first $10,000 earned per year. Between $10,000.01 and $30,000, the tax rate is 25 percent. Between $30,000.01 and $50,000, it's 30 percent. Above $50,000, it's 35 percent. You're earning $75,000 a year.
   a. How much in taxes will you have to pay?
   b. What is your average tax rate? Your marginal tax rate?
   c. Taxland has just changed to a tax credit system in which, in lieu of any exemption, eligible individuals are given a check for $4,000. The two systems are designed to bring in the same amount of revenue. Would you favor or oppose the change? Why?

A Numerical Example of the Problems of Redistributing Income

To give you a better sense of the problems of redistributing income, let's consider a numerical example. In this appendix we'll once again consider our John and Fred example. This time we'll say that John and Fred are each working, one job apiece, and that they're roughly equal in ability and needs. Because they're equals, we've decided that, according to our values, it's unfair that John earns more than four times as much as Fred. We believe that Fred should get more than the $12,000 he's currently getting and John should get less than $50,000. We decide that ideally the income ratio between these two should be one to one. Each should get $31,000:

$$\$12,000 + \$50,000 = \$62,000/2 = \$31,000.$$

One way to accomplish this end would be to institute a tax on John and give the proceeds to Fred. But in the United States, by law a tax must treat people who are equally situated equally, so our government cannot simply impose a tax on John and give the proceeds to Fred. Instead, in order to treat equals equally, the government must relate the tax to income rather than to individuals. The tax must be such that two people earning the same amount pay the same amount of tax.

Incentive Effects of Taxation

Let's say we impose a tax of 40 percent on everyone's income, hoping that the tax will bring in $20,000 from John and $4,800 from Fred for total revenue of $24,800 available for redistribution. But will our hopes be met? Probably not. Taxes have incentive effects. Both John and Fred, faced with a 40 percent tax rate, will reduce the amount of income that they earn, preferring instead to take more leisure than before. If the government is going to tax away 40 percent of your hard-earned dollars, why work so hard?

Say John reduces his income by 30 percent and Fred reduces his by 20 percent. John's after-tax income is $21,000. (He reduced his income from $50,000 to $35,000, of which the 40 percent tax takes $14,000.) Fred's after-tax income is $5,760. (He reduced his income from $12,000 to $9,600, of which the 40 percent tax takes $3,840). Now society's total income (John's plus Fred's) falls from $62,000 to $44,600, so our total tax revenue isn't the $24,800 we hoped for, but only $17,840. As government collects tax revenue to redistribute, incentive effects shrink the total amount of income earned by the society.

Incentive Effects of Distributing Income

The next problem is how to give out the revenue we've collected for redistribution. Since our goal is to redistribute the money to Fred, we might simply give it all to Fred. But doing so would violate the law requiring equal treatment of equally situated individuals, so our redistribution system must be related to income levels and not to the characteristics of particular individuals. Let's say we decide to give the proceeds to persons who have less than $20,000 in after-tax income. We distribute this $17,840 to Fred, pulling his after-tax income up to $5,760 + $17,840 = $23,600, a level slightly higher than John's after-tax income.

But now John, seeing what we've given Fred, figures out a way to work "off the books." He works out a deal so that he's paid $5,000 of his income in cash under the table. He takes a chance by breaking the law and failing to report this $5,000 on his income tax return. That means it looks as if he's earning only $18,000 in after-tax income. He's below the $20,000 cutoff, so he can share in our income redistribution program and get back some of the tax money we collected from him. (His pretax income is still $35,000, but $5,000 of it isn't reported to the government, so he pays the 40 percent tax on only $30,000, which means that his tax is $12,000 and he's left with reported after-tax income of $18,000.) If working off the books doesn't accomplish this goal, he can simply choose to work less in order to make his after-tax income fall below the $20,000 cutoff.

Thus, there's an incentive effect of redistributing income as well as an incentive effect of collecting the money to be redistributed. As income is redistributed, individuals have an incentive to make it look as if they earn less income than they do, or to actually earn less income, in order to get a share of the redistributed income.

The negative incentive effects of redistribution further reduce the size of the income pie. In this case, if John reduces his before-tax income to $30,000, his 40 percent tax is only $12,000—and now the redistribution pot is only $15,840 ($12,000 from John and $3,840 from Fred). At the same time, the number of people eligible to share in the redistribution has doubled. Before only Fred was eligible; now both John and Fred are eligible. Now Fred receives only $7,920 from the government instead of $17,840. So his total before-tax income is $9,600 + $7,920 = $17,520. If John got his reported taxable income down to $30,000 by taking $5,000 under the table, this means that John's after-tax income is $30,920:

    $30,000 total reported income
    − 12,000 taxes

      18,000 after-tax income
    + 5,000 under-the-table income

      23,000
    + 7,920 half share of redistribution pot
    $30,920

The effect of our redistribution program on the total income in our two-person society is an aggregate reduction in income from $62,000 to $39,600 of total reported income (assuming John does take that $5,000 under the table). The initial inequality of measured income was approximately 4.2:1 (John's $50,000 to Fred's $12,000). The higher-income person earned four times as much as the lower-income person. Now the inequality of measured before-tax income is approximately 3:1 (John's reported $30,000 to Fred's $9,600), an improvement from the 4:1 it was before. The inequality of after-tax income is $18,000 (John) to $5,760 (Fred), which is also approximately a 3:1 ratio.

The absolute increase in Fred's income is $1,680 (his income is now $5,760 after-tax income plus $7,920 in redistribution proceeds), and the absolute decrease in John's income is $19,080. The net after-tax, after-redistribution positions are:

    John: $30,920
    Fred: $13,680.

That's approximately a ratio of 2.3:1. Clearly some improvement in equality has been achieved (from 4.2:1 to 2.3:1), but it has come at a high cost in total income of the society, which has fallen from $62,000 to $44,600.

33

Work and the Labor Market

Work banishes those three great evils: boredom, vice, and poverty.

Voltaire

After reading this chapter, you should be able to:

1

Apply rational choice theory to the supply of labor.

2

Explain why an increase in the marginal tax rate is likely to reduce the quantity of labor supplied.

3

Determine a firm's derived demand for labor.

4

Explain why a monopolist's demand for labor will be lower than a competitive firm's demand for labor.

5

Define *monopsonist* and *bilateral monopoly*.

6

Discuss real-world characteristics of labor markets in terms of the invisible forces.

Most of us earn our living by working. We supply labor (get a job) and get paid for doing things that other people tell us they want done. Even before we get a job, work is very much a part of our lives. We spend a large portion of our school years preparing for work. Probably many of you are taking this economics course because you've been told that it will help to prepare you for a job—or that it will get you more pay than you're getting in your present job. For you, this course is investment in "human capital." If work isn't already familiar to you, once you get out of school (unless you're sitting on a hefty trust fund or marry somebody who is), work in the marketplace will become very familiar to you.

Your job will occupy at least a third of your waking hours. To a great extent, it will define you. When someone asks, "What do you do?" you won't answer, "I clip coupons, go out on dates, visit my children . . ." Instead you'll answer, "I work for the Blank Company" or "I'm an economist" or "I'm a teacher." Defining ourselves by our work means that work is more than the way we get income. It's a part of our social and cultural makeup. If we lose our jobs, we lose part of our identity.

There's no way I can discuss all the social, political, cultural, and economic dimensions of work and labor in one chapter, but it's important to begin by at least pointing them out in order to put my discussion of labor markets in perspective. A **labor market** is a factor market in which individuals supply labor services for wages to other individuals and to firms that need (demand) labor services. The labor market is a market in which social and political pressures are particularly strong, and we can understand the nature of labor markets only by considering how the three invisible forces interact to determine our economic situation.

To do that, I first ask the question: What would labor markets be like if only economic forces—the invisible hand—operated on them? I examine how the other invisible forces interact with economic forces to produce existing labor market institutions. Finally, I consider the implications of the analysis for you and your future in the job market.

Labor market Factor market in which individuals supply labor services for wages to firms that demand labor services.

THE INVISIBLE HAND AND THE LABOR MARKET

If the invisible hand were the only force that was operating, wages would be determined entirely by supply and demand. There's more to it than that, as you'll see, but it shouldn't be surprising to you that my discussion of the invisible hand and the labor market is organized around the concepts of supply and demand.

The Supply of Labor

The labor supply choice facing an individual (that is, the decisions of whether, how, and how much to work) can be seen as a choice between nonmarket activities and legal market activities. Nonmarket activities include sleeping, dating, studying, playing, cooking, cleaning, gardening, and black market trading. Legal market activities include taking some type of paid job or working for oneself, directly supplying products or services to the consumer. Many considerations are involved in individuals' choice of whether and how much to work and what kind of job to work at. Social background and conditioning are especially important, but the factor economists focus on is the **incentive effect** (how much a person will change his or her hours worked in response to a change in the wage rate). The incentive effect is determined by the value of supplying one's time to legal market activities relative to the value of supplying one's time to nonmarket activities. The normal relationship is:

Incentive effect How much a person will change his or her hours worked in response to a change in the wage rate.

1

The higher the wage, the higher the quantity of labor supplied.

This relationship between the wage rate and the quantity of labor supplied is shown in Exhibit 1. The wage rate is measured on the vertical axis; the quantity of labor supplied is measured on the horizontal axis. As you can see, its upward slope indicates that as the wage rate increases, the quantity of labor supplied increases. Why is that the normal relationship? Because work involves opportunity cost. By working one hour more, you have one hour less to devote to

EXHIBIT 1   The Supply of Labor

The supply of labor is generally considered to be upward sloping because the opportunity cost of work increases as wages get higher.

nonmarket activities. Alternatively if you devote the hour to nonmarket activities, you lose one hour's worth of income from working.

Say, for example, that by working you would have made $10 per hour. If you decide to work two hours less, you'll have $20 less to spend, but two hours more available for other activities (including spending the smaller amount of money). When the wage rises, say to $12 per hour, an hour of leisure has a higher opportunity cost. As the cost of leisure goes up, you buy less of it, meaning that you work more.

As I noted in my general discussions of supply and demand, the incentive effects represented by the market supply curve come from individuals' either/or decisions to enter, or leave, the labor market; and from individuals' decisions to work more, or fewer, hours. Given the institutional constraints in the labor market which require many people to work a fixed set of hours if they work at all, much of the incentive effect of higher wages works on the either/or decisions of individuals. This increases the labor force participation rate rather than adjusting the number of hours worked. For example, when wages rise, retired workers may find it worthwhile to go back to work and many teenagers may choose to find part-time jobs.

Real Wages and the Opportunity Cost of Work   The upward-sloping supply curve of labor tells you that, other things equal, as wages go up, the quantity of labor supplied goes up. But if you look at the historical record, you see real wages in the United States increasing and the average number of hours worked per person falling. This difference is partly explained by the income effect, which is discussed below. Higher incomes make people richer, and richer people choose more leisure.

Given that people are far richer today than they were 50 or 100 years ago, it isn't surprising that they work less. What's surprising is that they work as much as they do—eight hours a day rather than the four, or so, hours a day that would be enough to give people the same income that they had a century ago.

The explanation of why people haven't reduced their hours of work more substantially can be found in the type of leisure taken. A century ago, conversation was an art. People could use their time for long, leisurely conversations. Letter writing was a skill all educated people had, and cooking dinner was a three-hour event. Leisure was time-intensive. If today people were satisfied with leisure consisting of long conversations, whittling, and spending quality time with their families rather than skiing, golfing, or travelling, they could get by with working perhaps only four or five hours per day instead of eight hours. But that isn't the case.

Today leisurely dinners, conversations about good books, and witty letters have been replaced by "efficient" leisure: a fast-food supper, a home video, and the instant analysis of current events. Microwave ovens, frozen dinners, Pop-Tarts, cellular telephones, fax machines—the list of gadgets and products de-

Theodore Schultz—Nobel prize, 1979, for work on human capital. © *The Nobel Foundation.*

Because labor income is such an important component of most people's total income, other things often do not stay equal, and at times the effect can seem strange. For example, say that you earn $10 an hour and you decide to work eight hours per day. Suddenly demand for your services goes up and you find that you can receive $40 an hour. Will you decide to work more hours? According to the rational choice rule, you will, but you might also decide that at $40 an hour you'll work only six hours a day—$240 a day is enough; the rest of the day you want leisure time to spend your money. In such a case a higher wage means working less.

Does this violate the rational choice rule? The answer is no, because other things—specifically your income—do not remain equal. The higher wage makes you decide to work more—as the rational choice rule says; but the effect of the higher wage is overwhelmed by the effect of the higher income that allows you to decide to work less.

To distinguish between these two effects, economists have given them names. The decision, based on the rational choice rule, to work more hours when your pay goes up is called the *substitution effect*. You substitute work for leisure because the price of leisure has risen. The decision, based on the fact that you're richer and therefore can live a better life, to work fewer hours when your pay goes up is called the *income effect*.

It's possible that the income effect can exceed the substitution effect, and a wage increase can cause one to work less, but that possibility does not violate the rational choice rule, which refers to the substitution effect only. For those of you who didn't make a deal with me in the chapter on demand, a good exercise is to show the income and substitution effects with indifference curves and to demonstrate how it might be possible for an increase in the wage to lead to a decline in hours of work.

signed to save time is endless. All these gadgets that increase the "efficiency" of leisure (increase the marginal utility per hour of leisure spent) cost money, which means people today must work more to enjoy their leisure! In the United States, one reason people work hard is so that they can play hard (and expensively).

The fast pace of modern society has led a number of people to question whether we, as a society, are better off working hard to play hard. Are we better off or simply more harried? Economists don't try to answer this normative question; but they do point out that people are choosing their harried life-style, so to argue that people are worse off, one must argue that people are choosing something they don't really want. That may be true, but it's a tough argument to prove.

The Supply of Labor and Nonmarket Activities   In addition to leisure, there are other nonmarket activities in which labor supply issues and market incentives play an important role. For example, there's a whole set of illegal activities, such as selling illegal drugs, which are alternatives to taking a legal job. Let's say that an 18-year-old street kid figures he has only two options: Either he can work at a $4.35-an-hour job or he can deal drugs illegally. Dealing drugs involves enormous risks of getting arrested or shot, but it also means earning $50 or $75 an hour. Given that choice, many risk takers opt to sell drugs. When an emergency room doctor asked a shooting victim in New York City why he got involved in selling drugs, he responded, "I'm not going to work for chump change. I make $2,000 a week, tax-free. What do they pay you, sucker?" The doctor had to admit that even he wasn't making that kind of money.

For middle-class individuals who have prospects for good jobs, the cost of being arrested can be high—an arrest can destroy their future prospects. For poor street kids with little chance of getting a good job, an arrest makes little difference to their future. For them the choice is heavily weighted toward selling drugs. This is especially true for the entrepreneurial types—the risk takers—the movers and shakers who might have become the business leaders of the future. I've asked myself, had I been in their position, what decision I would have made. And I suspect I know the answer.

Prohibiting certain drugs leads to high income from selling those drugs and has significant labor market effects. The incentive effects that prohibition has on the choices facing poor teenagers in their choice of jobs is a central reason why some economists support the legalization of currently illegal drugs.

Income Taxation, Work, and Leisure   It is after-tax income, not before-tax income, that determines how much you work. Why? Because after-tax income is what you give up by not working. The government, not you, forgoes what you would have paid in taxes if you had worked. This means that when the government raises your **marginal tax rate** (the tax you pay on an additional dollar) it reduces your incentive to work. The reason is that leisure and other nonmarket activities aren't taxed, so their relative price goes down. When the marginal tax rate gets really high—say 60 or 70 percent—it can significantly reduce individuals' incentive to work and earn income.

Marginal tax rate Tax rate on an additional dollar of income.

One main reason why the U.S. government reduced marginal income tax rates in the 1980s was to reduce the negative incentive effects of high taxes. Whereas in the 1950s and 1960s the highest U.S. marginal income tax rate was 70 percent, in the 1990s the highest marginal income tax rate is 34 percent. European countries, which have significantly higher marginal tax rates than the United States, are currently struggling with this problem of providing incentive for people to work. The lack of incentive to work due to high marginal tax rates has even acquired a European name. It's called the **Dutch disease** because so many Dutch citizens were deciding that, given their country's high marginal tax rate and the guaranteed welfare and medical benefits they receive whether they work or not, they would not work.

Dutch disease Decision not to work because marginal tax rates are so high while welfare and medical benefits are guaranteed whether one works or not.

Reducing the marginal tax rate in the United States hasn't completely eliminated the problem of negative incentive effects on individuals' work effort. The reason is that the amounts one receives from many other programs are tied to earned income. When your earned income goes up, your benefits from these other programs go down. Say, for example, that you're getting welfare and you're deciding whether to take a $5 an hour job. Income taxes and social security taxes reduce the amount you take home from the job by 20 percent, to $4 an hour. But you also know that the Welfare Department will reduce your welfare benefits by 50¢ for every dollar you take home. This means that you lose another $2 per hour, so the marginal tax rate on your $5 an hour job isn't 20 percent; it's 60 percent. By working an hour, you've increased your net income by only $2. When you consider the transportation cost of getting to and from work, the expense of getting new clothes to wear to work, and other job-associated expenses, the net gain in income is often minimal. Your implicit marginal tax rate is almost 100 percent! At such rates, there's an enormous incentive either not to work or to work off the books (get paid in cash so you have no recorded income that the tax agent can trace).

The negative incentive effect can sometimes be even more indirect. For example, college scholarships are generally given on the basis of need. A family that earns more gets less in scholarship aid; the amount by which the scholarship is reduced as a family's income increases acts as a marginal tax on individuals' income. Why work hard to provide for yourself if there's a program to take care of you if you don't work hard? Hence, the irony in any need-based assistance program is that it reduces people's incentive to prevent themselves from being needy. These negative incentive effects on labor supply that accompany any need-based program present a public policy dilemma for which there is no easy answer.

The Elasticity of the Supply of Labor   Exactly how these various incentives affect the amount of labor an individual supplies is determined by the elasticity of the individual's supply curve of labor. Exhibit 2 shows two possible supply curves of

EXHIBIT 2 (a and b)   Inelastic and Elastic Supply of Labor

The elasticity of an individual's supply of labor determines to what extent various incentives affect the amount of labor an individual supplies. In (**a**), the individual has a highly inelastic supply of labor curve: a 30 percent drop in wages would make him work one hour less, whereas an individual with an elastic supply of labor curve, as in (**b**), would work one hour less if his wage were to drop only 6.7 percent.

labor.[1] The supply curve of labor in Exhibit 2(a) is inelastic. (The percent change in quantity supplied divided by the percent change in wage is less than one.) The incentive effects cause little change in the number of hours an individual works. The supply curve in Exhibit 2(b) is elastic; the incentive causes a large change in the number of hours of labor supplied.

The elasticity of the market supply curve is determined by the elasticity of individuals' supply curves and by individuals entering and leaving the labor force. If a large group of people are willing to enter the labor market when wages rise, then the market labor supply will be highly elastic even if individuals' supply curves are inelastic.

The elasticity of supply also depends on the type of market being discussed. For example, the elasticity of labor supply facing one firm in a small town will likely be far greater than the elasticity of the labor supply of all firms in that town. If only one firm raises its wage, it will attract workers away from other firms; if all the firms in town raise their wages, any increase in labor must come from increases in labor force participation, increases in hours worked per person, or in-migration (the movement of new workers into the town's labor market).

Existing workers prefer inelastic labor supplies because that means an increase in demand for labor will raise their wage. Employers prefer elastic supplies because that means an increase in demand for labor doesn't require large wage increases. These preferences can be seen in news reports about U.S. immigration laws, their effects, and their enforcement. Businesses such as restaurants often oppose strict immigration laws. Their reason is that jobs such as janitor, chambermaid, and busperson are frequently filled by new immigrants or illegal aliens who have comparatively low wage expectations.

Because of the importance of the elasticity of labor supply, economists have spent a great deal of time and effort estimating it. Their best estimates of labor

---

[1] My discussion of supply curves focuses on the incentive effect. Since wages are an important determinant of one's income, there can also be an income effect of changes in the wage: Higher wages make one richer. That income effect can also influence the elasticity of the measured supply curve. For example, higher income might lead one to work less. In certain instances, the income effect can actually make the supply curve of labor backward bending.

supply elasticities to market activities are about 0.1 for heads of households and 1.1 for secondary workers in households. These elasticity figures mean that a wage increase of 10 percent will increase the supply of labor by 1 percent for heads of households (an inelastic supply) and 11 percent for secondary workers in households (an elastic supply). Why the difference? Institutional factors. Hours of work are only slightly flexible. Since most heads of households are employed, they cannot significantly change their hours worked. Many secondary workers in households are not employed, and the higher elasticity reflects new secondary workers entering the labor market.

When individuals are self-employed (work for themselves), the demand for their labor is the demand for the product or service they supply—be it cutting hair, shampooing rugs, or filling teeth. You have an ability to do something; you offer to do it at a certain price; and you see who calls. You determine how many hours you work, what price you charge, and what jobs you take. The income you receive depends upon the demand for the good or service you supply and your decision about how much labor you want to supply. In analyzing self-employed individuals, one can move directly from demand for the product to demand for labor.

The Derived Demand for Labor

When a person is not self-employed, determining the demand for labor isn't as direct. It's a two-step process: Consumers demand products from firms; firms, in turn, demand labor and other factors of production to produce those products. The demand for labor by firms is a **derived demand;** it's derived from the consumer's demand for the goods that the firm sells. Thus, you can't think of demand for a factor of production such as labor separately from demand for goods. Firms translate consumers' demands into a demand for factors of production.

Derived demand The demand for factors of production by firms, which depends upon consumers' demands.

Factors Influencing the Elasticity of Demand for Labor   The elasticity of the derived demand for labor, or for any other factor of production, depends upon a number of factors. One of the most important is (1) *the elasticity of demand for the firm's good*. The more elastic the final demand, the more elastic the derived demand. Other factors influencing the elasticity of derived demand include: (2) *the relative importance of the factor in the production process* (the more important the factor, the less elastic is the derived demand); (3) *the possibility of, and cost of, substitution in production* (the easier substitution is, the more elastic is the derived demand); and (4) *the degree to which the marginal productivity falls with an increase in the factor* (the faster productivity falls, the less elastic is the derived demand).

Each of these relationships follows from the definition of *elasticity* (the percent change in quantity divided by the percent change in price) and a knowledge of production. To be sure you understand, ask yourself the following question: "If all I knew about two firms was that one was a perfect competitor and the other was a monopolist, which firm would I say is likely to have the more elastic derived demand for labor?" If your answer wasn't automatically "the competitive firm" (because its demand curve is perfectly elastic and hence more elastic than a monopolist's), I would suggest that at this point you review the discussion of factors influencing demand elasticity in the chapter on demand and relate that to this discussion. The two discussions are similar and serve as good reviews for each other.

Labor as a Factor of Production   The traditional factors of production are land, labor, capital, and entrepreneurship. When economists talk of the labor market, they're talking about two of these factors: labor and entrepreneurship. **Entrepreneurship** is a type of creative labor. The reason for distinguishing between labor and entrepreneurship is that an hour of work is not simply an hour of work. If high degrees of organizational skill, concern, and creativity are exerted (which is what economists mean by *entrepreneurship*) one hour of such work can be the equivalent of days, weeks, or even years of simple labor. That's one reason that pay

Entrepreneurship Labor services that involve high degrees of organizational skills, concern, and creativity.

often differs between workers for doing what seems to be the same job. It's also why one of the important decisions a firm makes is what type of labor to hire. Should the firm try to hire high-wage entrepreneurial labor or low-wage non-entrepreneurial labor?

We'll talk about the other two factors of production (land and capital) in the next chapter, but you should note that the formal analysis of the firm's derived demand presented in this chapter as the derived demand for labor is quite general and carries over to the derived demand for capital and for land. Firms translate consumers' demands for goods into derived demands for any and all of the factors of production.

The Firm's Decision to Hire   What determines a firm's decision to hire someone? The answer is simple. A profit-maximizing firm hires someone if it thinks there's money to be made by doing so. Unless there is, the firm won't hire the person. So for a firm to decide whether to hire someone, it must compare the worker's **marginal revenue product** (the marginal revenue it expects to earn from selling the additional worker's output) with the wage that it expects to pay the additional worker. For a competitive firm (for which $P = MR$), that marginal revenue product equals the worker's **value of marginal product**—the worker's **marginal physical product (MPP)**—which is the additional units of output that hiring an additional worker will bring about—times the price (P) at which the firm can sell the additional product.

$$\text{Marginal revenue product} = \text{MPP} \times P.$$

Say, for example, that by hiring another worker a firm can produce an additional six widgets an hour which it can sell at $2 each. That means the firm can pay up to $12 per hour and still expect to make a profit. Notice that a key question for the firm is: How much additional product will we get from hiring another worker? A competitive firm can increase its profit by hiring another worker as long as the value of the worker's marginal product (which also equals her marginal revenue product) (MPP $\times$ P) is higher than her wage.

To see whether you understand the principle, consider the example in Exhibit 3(a). Column 1 shows the number of workers, all of whom are assumed to be identical. Column 2 shows the total output of those workers. Column 3 shows the marginal physical product of an additional worker. This number is determined by looking at the change in the total product due to this person's work. For example, if the firm is currently employing 30 workers and it hires one more, the firm's total product or output will rise from 294 to 300, so the marginal product of moving from 30 to 31 workers is 6.

Notice that workers' marginal product decreases as more workers are hired. Why is this? Remember the assumption of fixed capital: More and more workers are working with the same amount of capital and there is diminishing marginal productivity.

Column 4 shows the average output per worker (**labor productivity**), a statistic commonly referred to in economic reports. It's determined by dividing the total output by the number of workers. Column 5 shows the additional worker's marginal revenue product, which, since the firm is assumed to be competitive, is determined by multiplying the price the firm receives for the product it sells ($2) by the worker's marginal physical product.

Column 5, the marginal revenue product, is of central importance to the firm. It tells the firm how much additional money it will make from hiring an additional worker. That marginal revenue product represents a competitive firm's demand for labor.

Exhibit 3(b) graphs the firm's derived demand for labor, based on the data in column 5 of Exhibit 3(a). The resulting curve is the firm's **derived demand curve for labor.** It shows the maximum amount of labor, measured in labor hours, that a firm will hire. To see this, let's assume that the wage is $9 and that the firm is hiring 30 workers. When there are 30 workers, workers' marginal revenue product

Marginal revenue product (MRP) The additional revenue a firm receives when it has an additional worker.

Value of marginal product Marginal physical product times the price that the firm can sell that product for.

Marginal physical product (MPP) Additional units of output that hiring an additional worker will bring about.

Labor productivity Average output per worker.

3

Derived demand curve for labor A demand curve showing the maximum amount of labor, measured in labor hours, that a firm will hire.

(1)	(2)	(3)	(4)	(5)
Number of workers	Total product per hour	Marginal physical product per hour	Average product per hour	Marginal revenue product (MRP)
27	270		10	
		9.00		18
28	279	8.50	9.96	17
		8.00		16
29	287	7.50	9.90	15
		7.00		14
30	294	6.50	9.80	13
		6.00		12
31	300	5.50	9.68	11
		5.00		10
32	305	4.50	9.53	9
		4.00		8
33	309	3.50	9.36	7
		3.00		6
34	312	2.50	9.18	5
		2.00		4
35	314	1.50	8.97	3

(a)

(b)

EXHIBIT 3 (a and b)   Determining How Many Workers to Hire and the Firm's Derived Demand for Labor

The marginal revenue product is any firm's demand curve for labor. Since for a competitive firm $P=MR$, a competitive firm's derived demand curve is its value of the marginal product curve ($P \times MPP$). This curve tells us the additional revenue the firm gets from having an additional worker. From the chart in (**a**) we can see that with 28 workers the marginal product per hour for each worker is 8.5. If the product sells for $2, then the value of the marginal product is $17, which is one point on the demand curve for labor (point *A* in (**b**)). When there are 35 workers, the value of the marginal product decreases to $3. This is another point on the firm's derived demand curve (point *B* in (**b**)). By connecting the two points, as I have done in (**b**), you can see that the firm's derived demand curve for labor is downward sloping.

of $13 exceeds their wage of $9, so the firm can increase profits by hiring another worker. Doing so increases output and profits, since the additional revenue the firm gets from increasing workers from 30 to 31 is $12 and the additional cost the firm incurs is the wage of $9.

Now say the firm has hired 5 additional workers so it has 35 workers. As the firm hires more workers, the marginal product of workers declines. As you can see from the graph in Exhibit 3(b), the marginal revenue product of workers when there are 35 workers is $3. Since the workers' marginal revenue product of $3 is less than their wage of $9, now the firm can increase profits by laying off some workers. Doing so decreases output but increases profit, because it significantly increases the average product of the remaining workers.

Only when workers' wage of $9 equals the marginal revenue product does the firm have no incentive to change the number of employees. In this example, the wage ($9) equals workers' marginal revenue product at 32 workers. When the firm is hiring 32 workers, either hiring another worker or laying off one worker will decrease profits. Since the marginal revenue product curve tells the firm, given a wage, how many workers it should hire, *the marginal revenue product curve is the firm's demand curve for labor*.

The fact that the demand for labor curve is downward sloping means that as more workers are hired, workers' marginal product falls. This might tempt you to think that the last worker hired is inherently less productive than the first worker hired. But that simply can't be because, by assumption, the workers are identical. Thus, the marginal product of any worker must be identical to the marginal product of any other worker, given that a specified number of workers are working. What the falling marginal product means is that *when 30 rather than 25 workers are working,* the marginal product of any one of those 30 workers is less than the marginal product of any one of 25 of those workers when only 25 are working. When the other inputs are constant, hiring an additional worker lowers the marginal product not only of the last worker but also of any of the other workers.

To understand what's going on here you must remember that when marginal product is calculated, all other inputs are held constant—so if a firm hires another worker, that worker will have to share machines or tools with other workers. When you share tools, you start running into significant bottlenecks, which cause production to fall. That's why the marginal product of workers goes down when a new worker is hired. This assumption that all other factors of production are held constant is an important one. If all other factors of production are increased, it is not at all clear that workers' productivity will fall as output increases.

Why does a firm hire another worker if doing so will lead to a fall in other workers' productivity and, possibly, a fall in the average productivity of all workers? Because the firm is interested in total profit, not productivity. As long as hiring an extra worker increases revenue by more than the worker costs, the firm's total profit increases. A profit-maximizing firm would be crazy not to hire another worker, even if by doing so it lowers the marginal product of the workers.

Factors Affecting the Demand for Labor   There are many technical issues that determine how the demand for products is translated through firms into a demand for labor (and other factors of production), but we need not go into them in detail. I will, however, state four general principles and give examples of each. The four general principles are:

1. Changes in the demand for a firm's product will be reflected in changes in its demand for labor.
2. The structure of a firm plays an important role in determining its demand for labor.
3. A change in the other factors of production that a firm uses will change its demand for labor.
4. A change in technology will change its demand for labor.

Let's consider each of these principles in turn.

Changes in the Firm's Demand   The first principle is almost self-evident. An increase in the demand for a product leads to an increase in demand for the laborers who produce that product. The increase in demand pushes the price up, raising the marginal revenue product of labor (which, you'll remember, for a competitive firm is the price of the firm's product times the marginal physical product of labor). The implications of this first principle, however, are not so self-evident. Often people think of firms' interests and workers' interests as being counter to one another, but this principle tells us that in many ways they are not. What benefits the firm also benefits its workers. Their interests are in conflict only when it comes to deciding how to divide up the total revenues among the owners of the firm, the workers, and the other inputs. Thus, it's not uncommon to see a firm and its workers fighting each other at the bargaining table but also working together to prevent imports that might compete with the firm's product or to support laws that may benefit the firm.

An example of such cooperation occurred when union workers at a solar energy firm helped fight for an extension of government subsidies for solar energy. Why? Because their contract included a clause that if the solar energy subsidy bill passed, the union workers' wages would be significantly higher than if it didn't. This cooperation between workers and firms has led some economists to treat firms and workers as a single entity, out to get as much as they can as a group. These economists argue that it isn't helpful to separate out factor markets he economic model of labor markets assumes that marginal productivities can be determined relatively easily. In reality they can't. They require guesses and estimates which are often influenced by a worker's interaction with the person doing the guessing and estimating. Thus, social interaction plays a role in determining wages. If you get along with the manager, his estimate of your marginal productivity is likely to be higher than if you don't. And for some reason, managers' estimates of their own marginal productivity tend to be high. In part because of difficulties in estimating marginal productivities, actual pay can often differ substantially from marginal productivities.

and goods markets. They argue that bargaining power models, which combine factor and goods markets, are the best way to analyze at what level wages will be set. In other words, the cost of labor to a firm should be modeled as if it is determined at the same time that its price and profitability are determined, not separately.

The Structure of the Firm and its Demand for Labor   The way in which the demand for products is translated into a demand for labor is determined by the structure of the firm. For example, let's consider the difference between a monopolistic industry and a competitive industry. For both, the decision about whether to hire is based on whether the wage is below or above the marginal revenue product. But the firms which make up the two industries calculate their marginal revenue products differently.

The price of a competitive firm's output remains constant regardless of how many units it sells. Thus, its marginal revenue product equals the value of the marginal product. To calculate its marginal revenue product we simply multiply the price of the firm's product by the worker's marginal physical product. For a competitive firm

Marginal revenue product of a worker = Value of the worker's marginal product = MPP × Price of product.

Marginal revenue product of a worker = Value of the worker's marginal product = MPP × Price of product.

The price of a monopolist's product decreases as more units are sold since the monopolist faces a downward-sloping demand curve. The monopolist takes that into account. That's why it focuses on marginal revenue rather than price. As it hires more labor and produces more output, the price it charges for its product will fall. Thus, for a monopolist

4

Marginal revenue product of a worker = MPP × Marginal revenue.

Marginal revenue product of a worker = MPP × Marginal revenue.

Since a monopolist's marginal revenue is always less than price, a monopolistic industry will always hire fewer workers than a comparable competitive industry will, which is consistent with the result we discussed in the chapter on monopoly: that a monopolistic industry will always produce less than a competitive industry will, other things equal.

To ensure that you understand the principle, let's consider the example in Exhibit 4, a table of prices, wages, marginal revenues, marginal physical products, and marginal revenue products for a firm in a competitive industry and a monopolistic industry. A firm in a competitive industry will hire up to the point where the wage equals MPP × P (columns 5 × 3). As you can see, this occurs at six workers. Hiring either fewer or more workers would mean a loss in profits for a firm in a competitive industry. Now let's compare the competitive industry with an equivalent monopolistic industry. Whereas the firm in the competitive industry did not take into account the effect an increase in output would have on prices, the monopolist will do so. It takes into account the fact that in order to sell the additional output of an additional worker, it must lower the price of the good. The relevant marginal revenue product for the monopolist appears in column 7. At six workers, the worker's wage rate of 2.85 exceeds the worker's marginal revenue product of 2, which means that the monopolist would hire fewer workers.

1 Number of workers	2 Wage	3 Price P	4 Marginal revenue (monopolist) MR	5 Marginal physical product MPP	Marginal revenue product	
					6 Competitive (MPP × P)	7 Monopolist (MPP × MR)
5	2.85	1.0	0.75	5	5	3.8
			0.70	4		
6	2.85	.95	0.65	3	2.85	2
			0.60	2		
7	2.85	.9	0.55	1	.9	0.55
			0.50	0		

As a second example of how the nature of firms affects the translation of demand for products into demand for labor, consider what would happen if workers controlled the firms rather than independent profit-maximizing owners controlling the firm. You saw before that whenever another worker is hired, other inputs constant, the marginal physical product of all similar workers falls. That can contribute to a reduction in existing workers' wages. The profit-maximizing firm doesn't take into account that effect on existing workers' wages. It wants to hold its costs down. If existing workers are making the decisions about hiring, they'll take that wage decline into account. If they believe that hiring more workers will lower their own wage, they have an incentive to see that new workers aren't hired. Thus, like the monopolist, a worker-controlled firm will hire fewer workers than a competitive profit-maximizing firm will.

There aren't many worker-controlled firms in the United States, but a number of firms include existing workers' welfare in their decision processes. Moreover, with the growth of the team concept of production discussed in the chapter on production, existing workers' input into managerial decision making is increasing. In many U.S. firms workers have some say in whether additional workers will be hired and at what wage they will be hired. Others firms have an implicit understanding or a written contract with existing workers which restricts hiring and firing decisions. Some firms, like IBM, have never laid off a worker; if they have to reduce their work force, they create early retirement incentives.

Why do firms do such things? To be seen as a "good employer," which makes it easier for them to hire in the future. Given the strong social and legal limitations on firms' hiring and firing decisions, one cannot simply apply marginal productivity theory to the real world. One must first understand the institutional and legal structures of the labor market. However the existence of these other forces doesn't mean that the economic forces represented by marginal productivity don't exist. Rather, it means that firms struggle to find a wage policy that accommodates both economic and social forces in their wage-setting process. For example, in the 1980s a number of firms (such as airline firms) negotiated two-tier wage contracts. They continued to pay their existing workers a higher wage, but paid new workers a lower wage, even though old and new workers were doing identical jobs. These two-tier wage contracts were the result of the interactions of the social and market forces.

Changes in Other Factors of Production   A third principle determining the derived demand for labor is the amount of other factors of production that the firm has. Given a technology, an increase in other factors of production will increase the marginal physical product of existing workers. For example, let's say that a firm buys more machines so that each worker has more machines with which to work. The workers' marginal physical product increases and the cost per unit of output for the firm decreases. The net effect on the demand for labor is unclear; it depends on how much the firm increases output, how much the firm's price is affected, and how easily one type of input can be substituted for another—or whether it must be used in conjunction with others.

While we can't say what the final effect on demand will be, we can determine the firm's cost minimization position. When a firm is using resources as efficiently as possible, and hence is minimizing costs, the marginal product of each factor of production divided by the price of that factor must equal that of all the other factors. Specifically, the **cost minimization condition** is:

$$\mathrm{MP}_1/w = \mathrm{MP}_c/P_c = \mathrm{MP}_x/P_x$$

> **Cost minimization condition** The ratio of marginal product to the price of an input is equal for all inputs.

where

w = Wage rate
1 = Labor
c = Capital
x = Any other input.

If this cost minimizing condition is not met, the firm could hire more of the input with the higher marginal product and less of other inputs, and produce the same amount of output at a lower cost.

Let's consider a numerical example. Say the marginal product of labor is 20 and the wage is \$4 while the marginal product of capital is 30 and the price of capital is \$4. You're called in to advise the firm. You say, "Fire one worker, which will decrease output by 20 and save \$4; spend that \$4 on capital, which will increase output by 30." Output has increased by 10 while costs have remained constant. As long as the marginal products divided by the prices of the various inputs are unequal, you can make such recommendations to lower cost.

Changes in Technology Our fourth and final principle governing the demand for labor concerns the effect of changes in technology. What effect will a change in technology have on the demand for an input? This question has often been debated, and it has no unambiguous answer. What economists do know is that the simple reasoning often used by laypeople when they argue that the development of new technology will decrease the demand for labor is wrong. That simple reasoning is as follows: "Technology makes it possible to replace workers with machines so it will decrease the demand for labor." This is sometimes called *Luddite reasoning* because it's what drove the Luddites to go around smashing machines in early-nineteenth-century England.

What's wrong with Luddite reasoning? First, look at history. Technology has increased enormously, yet the demand for labor has not decreased; instead it has increased as output has increased. In other words, Luddite reasoning doesn't take into account the fact that total output can change. A second problem with Luddite reasoning is that labor is necessary for building and maintaining the machines, so increased demand for machines increases the demand for labor.

Luddite reasoning isn't *all* wrong. Technology can sometimes decrease the demand for certain types of skills. The computer has decreased demand for calligraphers; the automobile reduced demand for carriage makers. New technology changes the types of labor demanded. If you have the type of labor that will be made technologically obsolete, you can be hurt by technological change. However technological change hasn't reduced the overall demand for labor; it has instead led to an increase in total output and a need for even more laborers to produce that output.

In the 1990s we're likely to see an enormous increase in the use of robots to do many repetitive tasks that blue collar workers formerly did. Thus, demand for manufacturing labor will likely decrease, but it will be accompanied by an increase in demand for service industry labor—designing and repairing robots and designing activities that will fill up people's free time.

In the early 1800s a group of British textile workers revolted against the introduction of a machine to produce cloth called a *wide frame,* which they said resulted in an inferior product. By all accounts, the wide frame produced textiles faster and reduced demand for textile workers. Angered by the introduction of these machines, a group of textile workers masked themselves and went around breaking up wide frame machines. They threatened any employee who used a wide frame. They were known as *Luddites* in memory of Ned Ludd, a worker who, 30 years earlier, had attacked stocking frames because he thought those devices were replacing workers in the manufacture of stockings.

In 1812, after a number of people had been killed, the British government stepped in and ended the movement, hanging some of the Luddite leaders and sending others to the colonies (which in those days was regarded as a severe punishment). By the 1820s the wide frame was used throughout the British textile industry. But the term *Luddite* has remained part of the English language and is used to describe people who, in fear of losing their jobs, strongly oppose the introduciton of new technology.

The Supply of and Demand for Labor

Exhibit 5(a) puts the supply of and demand for labor on the same graph. The equilibrium wage occurs at the point where the quantity of labor supplied equals the quantity of labor demanded. The equilibrium wage is W_0 and the equilibrium quantity of labor is L_0.

Supply and demand forces strongly influence wages, but they do not fully determine wages. Real-world labor markets are filled with examples of suppliers or demanders who resist these supply and demand pressures through organizations such as labor unions, professional associations, and agreements among demanders. But, as I've emphasized throughout the book, supply and demand analysis is a useful framework for considering such resistance.

For example, say that you're advising a firm's workers on how to raise their wages. You point out that if workers want to increase their wages, they must figure out some way either to increase the demand for their services or to limit the labor supplied to the firm. One way to limit the number of workers the firm will hire (and thus keep existing workers' wages high) is to force the firm to pay an above-equilibrium wage, as in Exhibit 5(b). Say that in their contract negotiations the workers get the firm to agree to pay a wage of W_1. At wage W_1, the quantity of labor supplied is L_1 and the quantity of labor demanded is L_2. The difference, $L_1 - L_2$, represents the number of people who want jobs at wage W_1 compared to the number who have them. In such a case jobs must be rationed. Whom you know, where you come from, or the color of your skin may play a role in whether you get a job with that firm.

As a second example, consider what would happen if U.S. immigration laws were liberalized. If you say the supply curve of labor would shift outward and the wage level would drop, you're right, as shown in Exhibit 6. In it the supply of labor increases from S_0 to S_1. In response, the wage falls from W_0 to W_1 and the quantity of labor demanded increases from L_0 to L_1.

In analyzing the effect of such a major change in the labor supply, however, remember that supply and demand are partial equilibrium tools and that they're relevant only if the change in the supply of labor doesn't also affect the demand for labor. In reality, a change in U.S. immigration laws might increase the demand for products, thereby increasing the demand for labor and raising wages. Looking at the overall effects of a change, rather than just at the partial equilibrium effects, often makes the final result less clear-cut. That's why it's important always to remember the assumptions behind the model you're using. Those assumptions often add qualifications to the simple ''right'' answer.

I hope I've given you a sense of how supply and demand analysis can be applied to the labor market. It's applied to the labor market just as it is to any other market: It leads one to consider the incentives of the relevant decision

(a)

(b)

EXHIBIT 5 (a and b)   The Supply of and Demand for Labor
When the supply and the demand curves for labor are placed on the same graph, the equilibrium wage, W_0, is where the supply equals demand as in (**a**). At this wage, L_0 laborers are supplied. We see the effect of an above-equilibrium wage: In order for workers to increase their wages, they must increase the demand for their services or limit the quantity of workers supplied. If they force the firm to pay them W_1 wages instead of the equilibrium wage, there will be more workers supplied (L_1) than demanded (L_2). With an excess supply of labor, jobs must be rationed.

EXHIBIT 6   The Effect of an Increase in the Supply of Labor

With an increase in the supply of labor—for example, because of liberalization in the immigration laws—the supply of labor curve shifts outward from S_0 to S_1. Assuming the demand for labor remains the same, the increase in the supply of labor will cause the wage level to drop from W_0 to W_1.

makers, to pinpoint each decision maker's best strategy, and then to see how the various strategies interact within the framework of supply and demand.

Whenever you look at labor markets, thinking about supply, demand, incentives, and strategies is an important first step in figuring out what's going on. However it's only a first step. As was stated in the introduction to this chapter, the invisible handshake and invisible foot play key roles in determining the wages people receive. In the remainder of this chapter, we discuss some of these issues.

Just as product markets can be imperfectly competitive, so too can labor markets. For example, there might be a **monopsony** (a market in which only a single firm hires labor). Alternatively laborers might have organized together in a union that allows workers to operate as if there were only a single seller. In effect the union

Imperfect Competition and the Labor Market   **5**

Monopsony   A market in which only a single firm hires labor.

EXHIBIT 7   Monopsony, Union Power, and the Labor Market

A monopsonist hires fewer workers and pays them less than would a set of competitive firms. The monopsonist determines the quantity of labor, Q_m, to hire at the point where the marginal factor cost curve intersects the demand curve. The monopsonist pays a wage of W_m. A union has a tendency to push for a higher wage, W_u, and a lower quantity of workers, Q_u.

Bilateral monopoly A market in which there are only a single seller and a single buyer.

could operate as a monopoly. Alternatively again, there might be a **bilateral monopoly** (a market with only a single seller and a single buyer). Let's briefly consider these three types of market imperfections.

Monopsony   When there's only one buyer of labor services, it makes sense for that buyer to take into account the fact that if it hires another worker, the equilibrium wage will rise and it will have to pay more for all workers. The choice facing a monopsonist can be seen in Exhibit 7. In it the supply curve of labor is upward sloping so that the **marginal factor cost** (the additional cost to a firm of hiring another worker) is above the supply curve since the monopsonist takes into account the fact that hiring another worker will increase the wage rate it must pay to all workers.

Marginal factor cost The additional cost to a firm of hiring another worker.

Instead of hiring Q_c workers at a wage of W_c, as would happen in a competitive labor market, the monopsonist hires Q_m workers and pays them a wage of W_m. (A good exercise to see that you understand the argument is to show that where there's a monopsonist, a minimum wage simultaneously can increase employment and raise the wage.)

Union Monopoly Power   When a union exists it will have an incentive to act as a monopolist, restricting supply so as to increase its members' wage. To do so it must have the power to restrict both supply and union membership. The equilibrium wage and employment would depend on who is allowed to be a union member and what methods of redistributing income among union members exist. But there would be a strong tendency for the union to act like a monopolist and to move to an equilibrium somewhat similar to the monopsonist case, except for one important difference. The wage the union would set wouldn't be set below the competitive wage; instead the wage would be above the competitive wage at W_u, as in Exhibit 7. Faced with a wage of W_u competitive firms will hire Q_u workers. Thus, with union monopoly power, the benefits of restricting supply accrue to the union members, not to the firm as it did in the monopsonist case.

Bilateral Monopoly   As our final case, let's consider a bilateral monopoly in which a monopsonist faces a union with monopoly power. In this case, we can say that the equilibrium wage will be somewhere between the monopsonist wage, W_m, and the union monopoly power wage, W_u, and the equilibrium quantity will be somewhere between Q_u and Q_m in Exhibit 7. Where in that range the wage and equilibrium quantity will be depends on the two sides' negotiating skills and other noneconomic forces.

Let's now consider some real-world characteristics of labor markets. For example:

1. English teachers are paid close to what economics teachers are paid even though the quantity of English teachers supplied significantly exceeds the quantity of English teachers demanded, while the quantity of economics teachers supplied is approximately equal to the quantity demanded.

2. On average, women earn about 65 to 70 cents for every $1 earned by men.

3. The relative pay of many kinds of jobs seems to fall into a pattern in which one is always the same percentage of another. This pattern is called a *wage contour*, and it often remains constant despite shifts in supply and demand among the various jobs.

4. Certain types of jobs are undertaken primarily by members of a single ethnic group. For example, Mohawk Indians make up a large percentage of construction workers on high-rise buildings. They have an uncanny knack for keeping their balance on high, open building frames.

5. Firms often pay higher than "market" wages.

6. Firms often don't lay off workers even when there is a decrease in the demand for their product.

7. Wages don't fluctuate very much as unemployment rises.

8. It often seems that there are two categories of jobs: dead-end jobs and jobs with potential for career advancement. Once in a dead-end job, a person finds it almost impossible to switch to a job with potential.

9. The rate of unemployment among blacks is approximately twice as high as the rate among whites.

Supply and demand analysis alone doesn't explain these phenomena. Each of them can, however, be explained as the result of a combination of invisible forces. Thus, to understand real-world labor markets it is necessary to broaden the analysis of labor markets to include other invisible forces that limit the use of the market. These include the invisible handshake (which creates social limitations on the self-seeking activities of firms and individuals) and the invisible foot (which creates legal limitations on the self-seeking behavior of firms and individuals). Let's consider a couple of the central issues of interaction among the invisible forces and see how they affect the labor market.

People generally have an underlying view of what's fair. That view isn't always consistent among individuals, but it's often strongly held. The first lesson taught in a personnel or human resources course is that people aren't machines. They're human beings with feelings and emotions. If they feel good about a job, if they feel they're part of a team, then they will work hard; if they feel they're being taken advantage of, they can be highly disruptive.

On some assembly line jobs, effort is relatively easy to monitor so individuals can be—and in the past often were—treated like machines. Their feelings and emotions were ignored. Productivity was determined by the speed of the assembly line; if workers couldn't or wouldn't keep up the pace, they were fired.

Most modern jobs, however, require workers to make decisions and to determine how best to do a task. Today's managers are aware that workers' emotional state is important to whether they make sound decisions and do a good job. So most firms, even if they don't really care about anything but profit, will try to keep their workers happy. It's in their own interest to do so. That might mean paying workers an above-average wage, not laying them off even if layoffs would make sense economically, providing day care so the workers aren't worried about their children, or keeping wage differentials among workers small to limit internal rivalry. Such actions can often make long-run economic sense, even though they might cost the firm in the short run.

THE OTHER INVISIBLE FORCES AND THE LABOR MARKET

Fairness and the Labor Market

ADDED DIMENSION DEMOCRACY IN THE WORKPLACE

In the United States slavery is illegal. One cannot sell oneself to another, even if one wants to. It's an unenforceable contract. But work, which might be considered a form of partial slavery, is legal. We can sell our labor services for a specific, limited period of time. Is there any inherent reason that such partial slavery should be seen as acceptable? The answer to that question is complicated. It deals with the rights of workers, and is based on value judgments. You must answer it for yourself. I raise it because it's a good introduction to Karl Marx's analysis of the labor market (which deals with alienation) and to some recent arguments about democracy in the workplace.

Marx saw selling one's labor as immoral, just as slavery was immoral. He believed that capitalists exploited workers by alienating them from their labor. The best equivalent I can think of is the way most people today view the selling of sex. Most people see selling sex as wrong because it alienates a person from his or her body. Marx saw all selling of labor that same way. A labor market makes one see oneself as an object, not as a human being.

The underlying philosophical issues of Marx's concern are outside of economics. Most people in the United States don't agree with Marx's philosophical underpinnings. But it's nonetheless a useful exercise to think about this issue and ask yourself whether it helps explain why we somehow treat the labor market as different than other markets and limit by law the right of employers to discriminate in the labor market.

Some of Marx's philosophical tenets are shared by the modern democracy-in-the-workplace movement. In this view, a business isn't owned by a certain group, but is an association of individuals who have come together to produce a certain product. For one group—the owners of stock—to have all the say as to how the business is run, and

for another group—the regular workers—to have no say, is immoral in the same way that not having democracy in deciding on government is immoral. According to this view, work is as large a part of people's lives as is national or local politics, and a country can call itself a democracy only if it has democracy in the workplace.

As with most grandiose ideas, this one is complicated, but it's worth considering because it's reflected in certain laws. Consider, for example, the 1989 federal law that limits firms' freedom to close plants without giving notice to their workers. The view that workers have certain unalienable rights played a role in passing that law.

For those of you who say, "Right on!" to the idea of increasing workers' rights, let me add a word of caution. Increasing workers' rights has a cost. It makes it less likely that firms and individuals who can think up things that need doing will do so, and thus will decrease the number of jobs available. It will also enormously increase firms' desire to discriminate. If you know you must let a person play a role in decisions once you hire that person, you're going to be much more careful whom you hire.

None of these considerations mean that democracy in the workplace can't work. There are examples of somewhat democratic "firms." Universities are run as partial democracies, with the faculty deciding what policies should be set. (There's serious debate about how well universities are run.) But as soon as you add worker democracy to production, more questions come up: What about consumers? Shouldn't they, too, have a voice in decisions? What about the community within which the firm is located?

Economics can't answer such questions. Economics can, however, be used to predict and analyze some of the difficulties such changes might bring about.

Views of fairness also enter into wage determination through political channels. Social views of fairness influence government, which passes laws to implement those views. Minimum wage laws, comparable worth laws, and antidiscrimination laws are examples.

Job Discrimination and the Labor Market

Discrimination is an important noneconomic factor that helps explain why labor markets don't operate as supply and demand analysis suggests they should. Managers, like many other people, have prejudices that are reflected (consciously or unconsciously) in their hiring decisions. When one group (in our society, white males) controls the hiring for most of the jobs, their prejudices can, and do, affect their hiring decisions. Whether prejudice should be allowed to affect the hiring decision is a normative question for society to settle.

In answering these normative questions our society has passed laws making it illegal for employers to discriminate on the basis of race, religion, sex, age, disability, or national origin. The reason society has made it illegal is its ethical belief in equal opportunity for all, or at least most, individuals. (Homosexuals still aren't protected by federal legislation assuring them equal opportunities.)

Economics cannot provide answers to the normative questions of whether society should allow discrimination. Economics can, however, provide insight into how discrimination, and society's attempts to eliminate it, will affect the economy, so that if society passes laws that prevent market forces from operating, it realizes the cost of doing so.

In analyzing discrimination, it's important to distinguish three types. One type of discrimination is based on individual characteristics that will affect job performance. For example, restaurants might discriminate against applicants with sourpuss personalities. Another example of this might be a firm trying to hire young salespeople because its clients like to buy from younger rather than older employees. A second type of discrimination is based on correctly perceived statistical characteristics of a group. A firm may correctly perceive that young people in general have a lower probability of staying on a job than do older people and therefore discriminate against younger people. A third type of discrimination is based on individual characteristics that don't affect job performance or are based on incorrectly perceived statistical characteristics of groups. A firm might not hire people over 50 because the supervisor doesn't like working with older people, even though older people may be just as productive as younger people.

Of the three types, the third will be easiest to eliminate; it doesn't have an economic motivation. In fact discrimination based on individual characteristics that don't affect job performance is costly to a firm, and market forces will work toward eliminating it. An example of the success of a firm's policy to reduce discrimination is the decision by McDonald's to create a special program to hire the learning-disabled. This group makes good employees. They have lower turnover rates and follow procedures better than do many of the other people McDonald's hires who view the job as temporary. Moreover, through advertising, McDonald's helped change people's negative view about being served by a special person into a positive view of such service. So in this case market forces and political forces are working together.

If the discrimination is of either of the first two types and is based on characteristics that do affect job performance, either directly or statistically, the discrimination will be harder to eliminate. Not discriminating can be costly to the firm, so political forces to eliminate discrimination will be working against market forces to keep discrimination.

Whenever discrimination saves the firm money, it will have an economic incentive to use subterfuges to get around an antidiscrimination law. These subterfuges will make the firm appear to be meeting the law, even when it isn't. For example, a firm will find another reason to explain why it isn't hiring an older person and will avoid using age as the reason.

Now that we've briefly considered how noneconomic forces can influence labor markets, let's turn our attention to real-world labor markets so you can have a sense of how they developed and how they might affect you.

Labor Markets in the Real World

Labor markets as we now know them developed in the 1700s and 1800s. Given the political and social rules that operated at the time, the invisible hand was free to push wage rates down to subsistence level. Work weeks were long and working conditions were poor. Laborers began to turn to other ways—besides the market—of influencing their wage. One way was to use political power to place legal restrictions on employers in their relationship with workers. A second way was to organize together—to unionize. Let's consider each in turn.

Evolving Labor Laws Over the years government has responded to workers' political pressure with a large number of laws that limit what can and what cannot be done in the various labor markets. For example, in many areas of production laws limit to eight the normal number of hours a person can work on one job in a day. The laws also prescribe the amount of extra pay an employee who works more than the normal number of hours must receive. (Generally it's time-and-a-half.)

Similarly the number and length of coffee breaks workers get are defined by law (one 15-minute coffee break every four hours). Child labor laws mandate that a person must be at least 16 in order to be hired. The safety and health conditions

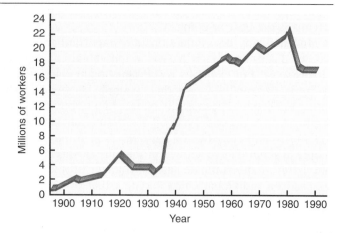

EXHIBIT 8   Change in Union Membership, 1895–1990

The graph shows union membership from 1895–1990. As can be seen, after the Depression in the 1930s, unions grew in importance. In the 1980s the importance of unions declined, even though the labor force was growing significantly.
Source: Bureau of Labor statistics.

under which a person can work are regulated by laws. (For example, on a construction site all workers are required to wear hard hats.) Workers can be fired only for cause, and employers must show that they had cause to fire a worker. (For example, a 55-year-old employee cannot be fired simply because he or she is getting old.) Employers must not allow sexual harassment in the workplace. (Bosses can't make sexual advances to employees and firms must make a good-faith attempt to see that some employees don't sexually harass other employees.)

Combined, these laws play an enormously important role in the functioning of the labor market.

Unions and Collective Bargaining   Some of the most important labor laws concern workers' right to organize together in order to bargain collectively with employers. These laws also specify the tactics workers can use to achieve their ends. In the latter part of the 1800s workers had few rights to organize themselves. The Knights of Labor was formed in 1869, and by 1886 it had approximately 800,000 members. But a labor riot in 1886 turned public opinion against these workers and led to the organization's breakup. In its place the American Federation of Labor developed and began to organize strikes to achieve higher wages. Business opposed unions' right to strike, and initially the government supported business. Police and sometimes the army were sent in to break up strikes. Under the then-existing legal structure of the economy, unions were seen as monopolistic restraints on trade and an intrusion into management rights.

In the 1920s and 1930s society's view of unions changed, and laws such as the National Labor Relations Act and Wagner Act were passed which guaranteed workers the right to form unions, to strike, and to engage in collective bargaining. As Exhibit 8 shows, from 1935 to 1980 unions grew significantly in size and importance.

Businesses weren't happy with unions' increasing strength, and in 1947 they managed to get the Taft-Hartley Act passed. That act placed limitations on union activities. It allowed states to pass "right-to-work" laws forbidding union membership to be made a requirement for continued employment. Moreover it made **closed shops** illegal. In a closed shop the union controls hiring; before anyone can be hired he or she must be a member of the particular union. In **union shops,** which federal law does permit, individuals are required to join a union after working for the firm for a period of time. A number of states have right-to-work laws that make union shops illegal. The Taft-Hartley Act also outlawed *secondary boycotts*. In a secondary boycott, in order to strengthen its bargaining position, a union gets other unions to refuse to buy a firm's products, even if members of the other unions aren't employed by that firm.

As we see in Exhibit 8, since the 1980s the number of workers in unions has been declining. Moreover when the growth of the labor force is taken into

Closed shop A firm in which the union controls hiring.

Union shop A firm in which all workers must join the union.

In the late 1800s, many workers worked in sweatshops; they often had quotas that required them to work 60 or more hours a week. Fines were imposed for such indiscretions as talking or smiling. *The Bettmann Archive.*

account, the relative decline in labor union membership is even more significant. Unions don't have the political or economic clout they once had.

Part of the reason, ironically, is their success. By pressuring the government to pass laws that protected workers, unions made themselves less necessary. Another part of the reason is the changing nature of production in the United States. Labor unions were especially strong in manufacturing industries. As manufacturing has declined in importance in the United States and the service sector has increased in importance, the base of union membership has been reduced. Unions have somewhat compensated for this change by pushing unionization drives among public sector workers (that is, government employees), and this sector has seen the largest increase in union membership. These unions are becoming strong and will likely be exerting their influence in the 1990s.

This chapter is meant to give you a sense of how the labor market works. But what does it all mean for those of you who'll soon be getting a job or are in the process of changing jobs? I'll try to answer that question in this section.

THE LABOR MARKET AND YOU

Exhibit 9 shows a variety of potentially useful statistics about the labor market. Let's consider how some of them might affect you. For example, consider relative pay of jobs requiring a college degree compared to jobs requiring only high school degrees. Jobs requiring a college degree earn significantly more, on average, than do jobs only requiring a high school degree. In recent years the income gap between the two groups has noticeably increased. So the answer to the question of whether it's worthwhile to stick college out for another couple of years and get a degree is probably yes.

Next, consider the salaries of Ph.D.s compared to the salaries of MBAs. A *Ph.D.* is a person who has gone to graduate school after college, usually for a number of years, and earned an advanced degree called a **D**octorate of **Phi**losophy—even though there are many subjects besides philosophy (such as economics) in which one can earn a Ph.D. As you can see, Ph.D.s' starting salaries are considerably lower than salaries of MBAs and professionals with other kinds of advanced degrees. Does this mean that Ph.D.s are discriminated against? Not

EXHIBIT 9 (a,b,c,d) Some Useful Labor Information

Some Typical Starting Salaries of BAs: 1993

	Private or state	U.S. government
Budget analyst	$24,000	$17,000
Management analyst	22,000	17,000
Regional planner	15,000	17,000
Physician assistant	32,000	—
Secretary	15,000	13,500
Secondary school teacher	18,000	—
Economist	19,000	17,000
Janitor	13,000	13,000
Retail sales (salary and commission)	14,000	—
Insurance sales	19,000	—

Sources: Author's estimates based on *Occupational Outlook Handbook* and U.S. Dept. of Labor Statistics (pay varies significantly by region).

(a)

Average Weekly Earnings in Selected Fields, 1992

Manufacturing	$469
Transportation and public utilities	523
Wholesale trade	435
Retail trade	206
Finance, insurance, and real estate	387
Services	343

Source: U.S. Dept. of Labor, *Monthly Labor Review,* February 1993.

(b)

Predicted Change in Employment 1990–2005

Occupational group	Expected change
Total	+20%
Technicians	+37
Professional specialties	+32
Service	+29
Managerial	+27
Marketing and sales	+24
Transportation	+21
Construction	+20
Mechanics	+16
Administrative support	+13
Laborers	+8
Farming and forestry	+5
Production	−4

Source: Bureau of Labor Statistics, *Occupational Outlook Handbook,* 1992.

(c)

Starting Salaries for Selected Professional Degrees, 1993*

Law (3 years)	
High-ranked school	$70,000
Intermediate-ranked school	40,000
Low-ranked school	27,000
Engineering	
Bachelor's degree	35,000
Master's degree	47,000
Business (2 years)	
Bachelor's degree	25,000
Master's (MBA) degree	43,000
M.D. (4 years and internship)	110,000
Ph.D. (5 years)	
in economics	40,000
in humanities	33,000

* These figures are rough estimates based on data from the Dept. of Labor and informal surveys.

Source: U.S. Department of Labor.

(d)

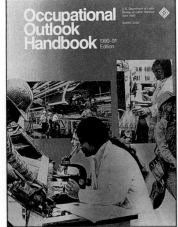

An excellent Department of Labor publication for checking the outlook for various careers.

necessarily. It's possible that Ph.D.s' lower pay suggests that Ph.D.s derive a "psychic income" from their work in addition to the amount of money they earn.

Since Ph.D.s are often quite smart, their willingness to accept psychic income as a substitute for higher pay suggests that there's much more to consider in a job than the salary. What's most important about a job isn't the wage, but whether you like what you're doing and the life that job is consistent with. (Of course, their lower salaries also could imply that Ph.D.s really aren't so smart.)

So my suggestion to you is definitely to finish college, especially if you enjoy it. (And with books like this, how can you help but enjoy it?) But go to graduate school only if you really enjoy learning. In picking your job, first and foremost pick a job that you enjoy (as long as it pays you enough to live on). Among jobs that you like, choose a job in a field in which the supply of labor is limited, or the demand for labor is significantly increasing. Either of those trends is likely to lead to higher wages. After all, if you're doing something you like, you might as well get paid as much as possible for it.

Jobs in which the supply will likely be limited are those on which the invisible foot has placed restrictions on entry or those requiring special abilities. If you have some special ability, try to find a job you enjoy in which you can utilize that ability. You might also look for a job in which entry is restricted, but beware: Jobs that are restricted in supply must be rationed, so while such jobs pay higher wages, you may need personal connections to obtain one of them.

I'm sure most of you are aware that your choice of jobs is one of the most important choices you'll be making in your life. So I'm sure you feel the pressure. But you should also know that a job, unlike marriage, isn't necessarily supposed to be for life. There's enormous flexibility in the U.S. labor market. Many people change jobs six or seven times in their lifetime. So while the choice is important, a poor choice can be remedied, so don't despair if the first job you take isn't perfect. Good luck.

KEY POINTS

- Incentive effects are important in labor supply decisions. **1 2**
- The demand for labor by firms is a derived demand determined by labor's marginal revenue product. **3**
- A firm's demand for labor is affected by the demand for a firm's product, the firm's internal structure, substitutes available to consumers, and technology. **4**
- A monopsony is a market in which only a single firm hires labor; a bilateral monopoly is a market

in which there is a single seller and a single buyer. **5**
- In the labor market the invisible handshake and the invisible foot are very active. **6**
- Labor laws have evolved and will continue to evolve. **6**
- Since the 1980s labor unions have been declining in importance. **6**
- To be happy, finish college and choose a job you enjoy. **6**

KEY TERMS

bilateral monopoly *(700)*
closed shop *(704)*
cost minimization condition *(697)*
derived demand *(691)*
derived demand curve for labor *(692)*

Dutch disease *(689)*
entrepreneurship *(691)*
incentive effect *(686)*
labor market *(686)*
labor productivity *(691)*
marginal factor cost *(700)*

marginal physical product (MPP) *(692)*
marginal revenue product (MRP) *(692)*
marginal tax rate *(689)*

monopsony *(699)*
union shop *(704)*
value of marginal product *(692)*

QUESTIONS FOR THOUGHT AND REVIEW

The number after each question represents the estimated degree of critical thinking required. (1 = almost none; 10 = deep thought.)

1. Why are the invisible handshake and invisible foot more active in the labor market than in most other markets? *(4)*
2. Welfare laws are bad, not for society, but for the people they are meant to help. Discuss. *(8)*
3. Which would you choose: selling illegal drugs at $75 an hour (20 percent chance per year of being arrested) or a $6-an-hour factory job? Why? *(9)*
4. If the wage goes up 20 percent and the quantity of labor supplied increases by 5 percent, what's the elasticity of labor supply? *(3)*
5. A competitive firm gets $3 per widget. A worker's average product is 4 and marginal product is 3. What is the maximum the firm should pay the worker? *(5)*

6. How would your answer to Question 5 change if the firm were a monopolist? *(6)*
7. Why might it be inappropriate to discuss the effect of immigration policy using supply and demand analysis? *(5)*
8. Comparable worth laws require employers to pay the same wage scale to workers who do comparable work or have comparable training. What likely effect would these laws have on the labor market? *(9)*
9. Why is unemployment nearly twice as high among blacks as among whites? What should be done about the situation? *(9)*
10. My brother was choosing between being a carpenter and being a plumber. I advised him to take up plumbing. Why? *(6)*

PROBLEMS AND EXERCISES

1. Fill in the following table.

Number of workers	TP	MPP	AP	MRP
0				
1	10			
2	19			
3		8		
4			8.5	
5				11

2. Your manager comes in with three sets of proposals for a new production process. Each process uses three inputs: land, labor, and capital. Under Proposal A, the firm would be producing an output where the MPP of land is 30, labor is 42, and capital is 36. Under Proposal B, at the output produced the MPP would be 20 for land, 35 for labor, and 96 for capital. Under Proposal C, the MPP would be 40 for land, 56 for labor, and 36 for capital. Inputs' cost per hour is $5 for land, $7 for labor, and $6 for capital.
   a. Which proposal would you adopt?
   b. If the price of labor rises to $14 how will your answer change?

34

Nonwage Income
Rent, Profits, and Interest

The first man to fence in a piece of land, saying "This is mine," and who found people simple enough to believe him, was the real founder of civil society.

Jean-Jacques Rousseau

After reading this chapter, you should be able to:

1

Define *rent* and explain why landowners will bear the entire burden of a tax on land.

2

Explain rent seeking and its relationship to property rights.

3

Differentiate between normal profits and economic profits.

4

Summarize the reasons an entrepreneur searches out market niches.

5

Define *interest* and demonstrate how it is used in determining present value.

6

Use the annuity rule and the rule of 72 to determine present value.

7

Explain the marginal productivity theory of income distribution.

The four traditional categories of income are wages, rent, profits, and interest. Wages are discussed in the last chapter. They are determined by economic factors (the forces of supply and demand) with strong influences by political and social forces, which often restrict entry or hold wages at non–market-clearing levels.

The same holds true for nonwage income: rent, profits, and interest. These forms of income are determined by the forces of supply and demand. But, as we have emphasized throughout the book, supply and demand are not necessarily the end of the story. Supply and demand determine price and income, given an institutional structure that includes **property rights** (the rights given to people to use specified property as they see fit) and the **contractual legal system** (the set of laws that govern economic behavior) of the society. If you change property rights, you change the distribution of income. Thus, in a larger sense, supply and demand don't determine the distribution of income; the distribution of property rights does.

The system of property rights and the contractual legal system that underlie the U.S. economy evolved over many years. Many people believe that property rights were unfairly distributed to begin with; if you believe that, you'll also believe that the distribution of income and the returns to those property rights are unfair. In other words you can favor markets, but object to the underlying property rights. Many political fights about income distribution concern fights over property rights, not fights over the use of markets.

Such distributional fights have been going on for a long time. In feudal times much of the land was held communally; it belonged to everyone, or at least everyone used it. It was common land—a communally held resource. As the economy evolved into a market economy, that land was appropriated by individuals and these individuals became landholders who could determine the use of the land and could receive rent for allowing other individuals to use that land. Supply and demand can explain how much rent will accrue to a landholder; it cannot explain the initial set of property rights.

The type of issues raised by looking at the underlying property rights are in large part academic for Western societies. The property rights that exist, and the contractual legal system under which markets operate, are given. You're not going to see somebody going out and introducing a new alternative set of property rights in which the ownership of property is transferred to someone else. The government may impose shifts at the margin; for example, new **zoning laws** (laws that set limits on the use of one's property) will modify property rights and create fights about whether society has the right to impose such laws, but there will be no wholesale change in property rights. That's why most economic thinking simply takes property rights as given.

But taking property rights as given isn't a reasonable assumption for the developing countries or the formerly socialist countries now in the process of establishing markets. They must decide on what structure of property rights they want. Who should be given what was previously government land and property? Who should own the factories? Do those societies want land to be given to individuals in perpetuity, or do they want it given to individuals for, say, 100 years? As these questions have been raised, economists have redirected their analysis to look more closely at the underlying legal and philosophical basis of supply and demand. As they do so they are extending and modifying the economic theory of income distribution, as we'll discuss shortly.

Despite these changes that are taking place, it's helpful to consider the three traditional income categories besides wages (rent, profits, and interest) because doing so provides useful insight into forces that make our economy work and that determine who gets what.

Property rights The rights to use specified property as one sees fit.

Contractual legal system The set of laws that govern economic behavior.

Zoning laws Laws that set limits on the use of one's property.

RENT

Rent The income from a factor of production that is in fixed supply.

Rent is the income from a factor of production that is in fixed supply. Traditionally rent was associated with land, which was assumed to be a totally fixed factor of production. When the supply of a factor is fixed all we need to know to determine

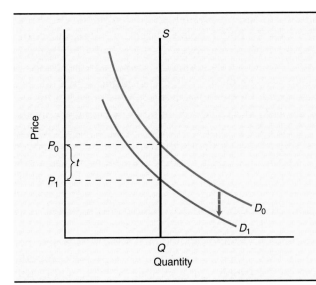

EXHIBIT 1   Rent

A tax on any factor with a perfectly inelastic supply will fall only on the supplier. A tax of t will shift the demand curve down from D_0 to D_1, leaving the after-tax price that the demander pays constant but lowering the after-tax price that the supplier receives by t from P_0 to P_1.

what the price of land (rent) will be is the amount of land there is and the demand curve. Exhibit 1 shows how the price of land is determined. In it you can see that since the supply of land is perfectly inelastic, the level of demand determines the rent on land.

The Effect of a Tax on Land

To check whether you understand the concept of rent, let's try a couple of questions. Say the government places a tax on the user of land. What will that tax do to the quantity of land supplied; what will that tax do to the price of the land; and who will end up bearing the burden of that tax? (Before proceeding, think, and try to answer these questions.)

The answers you should have given are that the quantity of land supplied will not change; the price of the land will not change, and the owner of the land will bear the entire burden of the tax even though the user of the land will actually pay the tax. In technical terms, the tax shifts the demand curve for land down from D_0 to D_1. Now the user simply pays part of the rental payment (t) to the government. So if the landowner were getting $100 per year in rent, after a tax of $30 per year the landowner would get only $70 per year. This follows immediately from the diagram: Given the quantity of land supplied, demanders will pay no more than the equilibrium price. By assumption, suppliers will supply the same amount of land regardless of the price they receive so they must bear the entire burden of the tax. If they didn't, the price of land would have to rise and it cannot; demanders won't pay more for that quantity.

If you've followed the analysis, the preceding conclusion was obvious, but now let's extend it to the real world. Say the government increases the property tax. Should people who rent apartments worry that such a tax is going to raise rents? The analysis tells us no, they shouldn't; in reality, they do worry about it a lot. Part of the reason is that the assumptions don't fit reality. The supply of land isn't perfectly inelastic; new land can be created by landfills and land can be converted from useless land to useful land by a variety of methods. The supply of apartments is even more elastic since rental apartments have other uses. So the consumers are partially right.

But the model is partially right too because even taking these provisos into account, most economists see the supply of apartments as rather inelastic. And as long as the supply of apartments is less elastic than the demand for apartments, most of the property tax will fall on the apartment owner and most of an increase in the property tax won't be passed on to the consumer. It can look as if it's being passed on since actual rents are determined only at periodic intervals, and often

Henry George—A 19th-century economist who advocated the land tax.

the actual rent paid can deviate from the supply/demand determined rent. Property owners often find it convenient to blame raises in rent on increased costs, even though they would have increased rent even if there had been no tax. Blaming the government is much easier than saying, "Look, apartments are in tight supply. Somebody else will pay me more, so I'm increasing your rent."

The inelastic supply of land and the knowledge that ultimately most of the tax on land will be paid by the owner of land has led to a number of taxing proposals. One such proposal was put forward by Henry George, who argued that the government should replace all other taxes with a land tax. His proposal enjoyed significant political influence in the late 19th century; an economic institute dedicated to his ideas still exists today.

Quasi Rents

Quasi rent Any payment to a resource above the amount that the resource would receive in its next-best use. Also called *producer surplus.*

The concept of rent was extended in the 1900s to include any payment to a resource above its opportunity cost—that is, above the amount it would receive in its next-best use. This broader concept of rent is shown in Exhibit 2. In it you can see that the supply curve is upward sloping. Equilibrium is at price P_0 and quantity Q_0. Consider a person on the supply curve at point A. That person will receive price P_0, but would have been willing to supply his or her resource at S_0. The difference, $P_0 - S_0$, is the person's rent. (Sometimes this difference is called **quasi rent** or *producer surplus* to distinguish it from pure rent, in which the opportunity cost of supplying the factor is zero.)

Let's consider an example: Michael Jordan. The demand for his services as a basketball player is high so he earns a multimillion dollar salary. His salary likely significantly exceeds his opportunity cost (the wage he could get at the next-best job). The difference between the two would be the quasi rent component of his salary.

This broader concept of rent applies to all types of income. For example, wage income can include a considerable rent component, as can profits and interest. As long as a supply curve is upward sloping, some suppliers are receiving some rent.[1]

Rent Seeking and Institutional Constraints

2

Rent seeking Restricting supply in order to increase the price.

The broadened definition of rent led to the insight that if individuals could somehow restrict supply, the rent they received would be higher. Restricting supply in order to increase the price suppliers receive is called **rent seeking.** The concept of rent seeking ties back into our earlier discussion of property rights. If you own something, you can get a rent for owning it. Thus, rent seeking is an attempt to create either ownership rights or institutional structures that favor you. Rent seeking is an activity in which self-interest doesn't necessarily lead to societal interest. The property rights you get might simply take away property rights from another person.

Let's consider an example: high-resolution television. For technical reasons every country must choose a design (the number and structure of dots per inch on a television) for broadcasting. The United States is currently making such a decision for the late 1990s when large-screen television will probably be standard. If a firm can get the law defined in a way that favors its design, rather than a competitor's, it will receive a rent. Thus, firms are expending great effort and money on lobbyists to get their design adopted. When they do so they are rent seeking.

Alternatively if a group of individuals (workers and firms) can get a tariff imposed on goods that are similar to those that they produce, they'll be able to receive a higher price for their good; a component of that price will be rent, which is why the activity of getting that tariff adopted is another example of rent seeking.

---

[1] One could also say that as long as the demand curve is downward sloping, some demander is receiving rent. One doesn't say that, however. The difference between what a demander would be willing to pay and what the demander actually pays is called *consumer surplus.* As was discussed in earlier chapters, consumer surplus is the demand-side equivalent of rent.

EXHIBIT 2   Quasi Rent

Quasi rent is the payment to a supplier above his or her opportunity cost. In this example an individual represented by point A on the supply curve would be willing to supply the good at S_0 but the market equilibrium price is P_0. The difference $P_0 - S_0$ is his or her quasi rent.

Of course, it is a legitimate activity for people to try to structure property rights to benefit themselves. Sometimes it can have positive social consequences so there's no easy answer about what is the appropriate social policy to deal with rent seeking. All rent seeking isn't bad, but there's no simple way to separate the bad from the good.

Let's consider a final hypothetical example from the biotechnology field, which demonstrates one of the problems in making value judgments about rent seeking. Say a firm has created a new organism (a new life form) that eats nuclear waste and transforms it into humus soil. (OK, so I'm a dreamer; it could happen.) The firm will likely spend enormous amounts of money on trying to ensure that it will "own" that life form, because otherwise it won't make any income from it. In other words it will engage in rent seeking. But the rent seeking has a positive side. Unless a firm can expect to own the life form, it is unlikely to expend money on developing such a life form. Society may well be better off if property rights in such life forms exist.

PROFIT

A second component of nonwage income is profit. **Profit** is a return on entrepreneurial activity and risk taking. As discussed in earlier chapters, profits are generally divided into normal profits and economic profits. **Normal profits** are payments to entrepreneurs as the return on their risk taking. They are an amount that an entrepreneur could get if he or she supplied entrepreneurship to the market. It is the marginal entrepreneur—the entrepreneur whose opportunity cost equals his or her expected gain—who receives a normal profit. Others receive a quasi rent in addition to profit. Because normal profits include returns on risk taking, profits aren't normally normal. Sometimes normal profits are high; sometimes they're nonexistent; and sometimes they're negative (that is, there are losses). Normal profits should be judged in reference to expectations, not in reference to what they actually are in any one year.

Profit The return on entrepreneurial activity and risk taking.

Normal profits Amount that an entrepreneur could get by supplying entrepreneurship to the market.

Profit, Entrepreneurship, and Disequilibrium Adjustment

Economic profits are a return on entrepreneurship above and beyond normal profits. Economic profits are a sign of disequilibrium and are a signal to other entrepreneurs that it may be worthwhile to enter that market. Economic profits are the driving force of the invisible hand. The expectation of economic profit leads to innovation and creates incentives for entrepreneurs to enter into new markets. As entrepreneurs enter, they drive the price to an equilibrium price and eliminate economic profits. In this way the expectations of profits are the dynamic force in the economy, unleashing the competitive forces that will eliminate the profits.

Economic profits Return on entrepreneurship above and beyond normal profits.

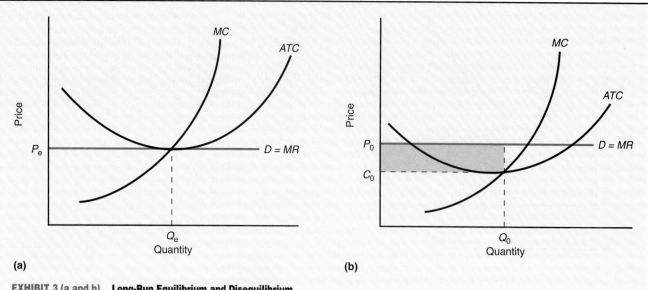

EXHIBIT 3 (a and b)   Long-Run Equilibrium and Disequilibrium

In a competitive market all profit is competed away in long-run equilibrium as it is in (**a**): *P=MC=ATC*. When there is a market niche, profit can remain and price can deviate from *ATC*, leaving profit of the shaded area in (**b**).

To drive this important point home, let's relate this discussion of profit to our earlier analysis. One of the lessons you have learned (or should have learned) from the theoretical analysis of supply and demand is that competition drives the price in a market down to equal average total costs. In the long run, suppliers make normal returns on their investments—that is, zero economic profits. To remind you of that point, I show a firm in long-run equilibrium in Exhibit 3(a).

Equilibrium isn't something that just exists. It's brought about by competition—by other suppliers entering into the market. Entrepreneurs avoid highly competitive markets that are in equilibrium. Why? Because there aren't a whole lot of profits to be made in such markets. What they look for are not-so-competitive markets—markets in disequilibrium with price greater than average cost. In disequilibrium you *can* make a lot of profits. Consider Exhibit 3(b). It represents a market in disequilibrium. Notice that the price is P_0 but the costs per unit are only C_0, which means that the supplier makes an economic profit represented by the shaded rectangle.

Market Niches, Profit, and Rent

4

Market niche An area in which competition is not working.

What kind of markets are in disequilibrium? Ones in which competition isn't working or is working slowly. An area in which competition is not working is called a **market niche.** Entrepreneurs search for market niches. The best type of market niche to have is a monopoly, in which you're the sole supplier and you face no competition. Such pure monopolies are rare, but temporary disequilibrium is not rare. In fact, the competitive conditions that push economic profit all the way down to zero often don't exist. For example, if no one knows you're making a profit, competitors won't enter the market to drive the price down; a disequilibrium can continue indefinitely. Bright entrepreneurs who have found a profitable market niche don't advertise the fact.

Often after an entrepreneur has made an innovation and is enjoying his above-normal economic profits, his income can look a lot like rent. This leads some people to think that society can simply tax it away with no consequence; the entrepreneur's actions won't change. That's true—if one considers those above-normal profits without historical perspective. But with historical perspective, there is a major difference. One of the driving forces behind the entrepreneur was probably the expectation of future profit. That's an important reason why she did her entrepreneurial thing.

ADDED DIMENSION

WHERE TO FIND
A MARKET NICHE

■any kinds of market niches exist, and competition works because people search out these market niches and exploit them. In doing so, they eliminate the niches. That's what competition is.

The most likely place to find a temporary market niche may be at your current job. Say you're working for a construction firm and notice that the firm is having trouble reaching high places where it needs to work. The firm doesn't often work on high places, so it isn't worthwhile for it to buy an aerial lift truck; but when it does need to work up high, it could save enormous amounts of time and money if it had such a lift. You check out other construction firms and find they're in a similar situation. You quit your job, buy an aerial lift truck, and start your own firm, renting out your services. For a while, at least, you'll have a market niche.

That is the strategy I followed with this book. Most of the other introductory economics textbooks I read were staid and boring. I believed there was room in the market for a book with pizzazz—a book in which the author wouldn't be afraid to allow his true style to show through. This book exists in part because of market incentives that led me to exploit a market niche. It's the invisible hand at work.

But market incentives aren't the only reason I wrote this book. I wrote this book because I didn't like the way I was taught introductory economics. Given my ego, I thought I could do better—that I could make economics come alive. The desire to "do it right" was the most important reason I wrote this book. (That isn't to say that the expectation of profit didn't play a role.)

The lesson is simple: To understand the economy it's important to remember that while the profit motive drives people, so too do other motives.

It's true that after she's done her entrepreneurial thing, if you take what she got for doing it away from her, it won't change the past. But it will most likely change the future. Other entrepreneurs will draw the inference that their profits will be taken away from them and they won't do their entrepreneurial thing. But entrepreneurial activity is what drives the economy to equilibrium and is what leads to many of the innovations in the economy. If entrepreneurial incentives are removed, society may well be worse off.

The third traditional component of nonwage income is interest. **Interest** is the income paid to savers—individuals who produce now but don't consume now. Instead they lend out the proceeds of their production, allowing others to invest or consume now. In return they get a promise to pay back that loan, together with whatever interest they negotiated. Whereas profits and rents accrue to the individuals who are supplying some resource to the economy, interest is what businesses and entrepreneurs pay to those who make loans to them. High profits encourage entrepreneurial action; high interest rates discourage it.

All economists agree that the interest rate is determined by the supply of and demand for something, but they don't agree on what that something is. Classical economists see the interest rate as determined by the supply of and demand for savings; that is, the interest rate depends primarily upon how much people want to save and how much they want to borrow. Keynesian economists see the interest rate as determined by the supply of and demand for money: how much money is in the economy and how much money people want to hold.

These two theories agree that in macroequilibrium the supply of and demand for both savings and money will be equated by the interest rate. But they disagree about how that equilibrium is brought about. Keynesians believe the aggregate level of income fluctuates to bring about equilibrium of the two interest rates. Classical economists believe a price level change, which causes the real money supply to change, brings about aggregate equilibrium.

There's no way I have time to do justice to either of these theories; all theories of interest rates are complicated. But one aspect of the interest rate is absolutely essential: its role in allowing us to determine the present value of future income flows and the future values of income in the present.

INTEREST ▣

Interest The income paid to savers—individuals who produce now but do not consume now.

Individuals use publications such as this one to determine how to get the highest return on their investments.

Present Value

Present value Method of translating a flow of future income or savings into its current worth.

Present value is a method of translating a flow of future income or savings into its current worth. For example, say a smooth-talking, high-pressure salesperson is wining and dining you. "Isn't that amazing?" the salesman says. "My company will pay $10 a year not only to you, but also to your great-great-great-grand-children, and more, for 500 years—thousands of dollars in all. And I will sell this annuity—this promise to pay money at periodic intervals in the future—to you for a payment to me now of only $800, but you must act fast. After tonight the price will rise to $2,000."

Do you buy it? My rhetoric suggests that the answer should be no—but can you explain why? And what price *would* you be willing to pay?

To decide how much an annuity is worth, you need some way of valuing that $10 per year. *You can't simply add up the $10 five hundred times.* Doing so is wrong. Instead you must *discount* all future dollars by the interest rate in the economy. Discounting is required because a dollar in the future is not worth a dollar now.

If you have $1 now, you can take that dollar, put it in the bank, and in a year you will have that dollar plus interest. If the interest rate you can get from the bank is 5 percent, that dollar will grow to $1.05 a year from now. That means also that if the interest rate in the economy is 5 percent, if you have 95¢ now, in a year it will be worth $.9975. (5% × $.95 = $.0475.) Reversing the reasoning, $1 one year in the future is worth 95¢ today. So the present value of $1 one year in the future at a 5 percent interest rate is 95¢.

A dollar *two* years from now is worth even less today. Carry out that same reasoning and you'll find that if the interest rate is 5 percent, $1 two years from now is worth approximately 90¢ today. Why? Because you could take 90¢ now, put it in the bank at 5 percent interest, and in two years have $1.

Carrying out such reasoning for every case would be a real pain. But luckily, there's a formula and a table that can be used to determine the present value (PV) of future income. The formula is

$$PV = A_1/(1 + i) + A_2/(1 + i)^2 + A_3/(1 + i)^3 + \ldots + A_n/(1 + i)^n$$

where

A_n = the amount of money received n periods in the future
  i = the interest rate in the economy (assumed constant).

Solving this formula for any time period longer than one or two years is complicated. To deal with it, people either use a business computer or a present-value table like that in Exhibit 4(a).

Exhibit 4(a) gives the present value of a single dollar at some time in the future at various interest rates. Notice a couple of things about the chart. The further into the future one goes and the higher the interest rate, the lower the present value. At a 12 percent interest rate, $1 fifty years from now has a present value of essentially zero.

Exhibit 4(b) is an annuity chart; it tells us how much a constant stream of income for a specific year is worth. Notice that as the interest rate rises, the value of an annuity falls. At an 18 percent interest rate, $1 per year for 50 years has a present value of $5.55. To get the value of amounts other than $1, one simply multiplies the entry in the table by the amount. For example, $10 per year for 50 years at 18 percent interest is 10 × $5.55, or $55.50.

As you can see, the interest rate in the economy is a key to present value. *You must know the interest rate to know the value of money over time.* The higher the current (and assumed constant) interest rate, the more a given amount of money in the present will be worth in the future. Or alternatively, the higher the current interest rate, the less a given amount of money in the future will be worth in the present.

6 **Some Rules of Thumb for Determining Present Value**   Sometimes you don't have a present-value table or a business computer handy. For those times, there are a few rules of

EXHIBIT 4 (a and b)   Sample Present-Value and Annuity Tables

The present value of a future dollar converts a known future amount into a present amount.

Interest Rate

Year	3%	4%	6%	9%	12%	15%	18%
1	0.97	0.96	0.94	0.92	0.89	0.87	0.85
2	0.94	0.92	0.89	0.84	0.80	0.76	0.72
3	0.92	0.89	0.84	0.77	0.71	0.66	0.61
4	0.89	0.85	0.79	0.71	0.64	0.57	0.52
5	0.86	0.82	0.75	0.65	0.57	0.50	0.44
6	0.84	0.79	0.70	0.60	0.51	0.43	0.37
7	0.81	0.76	0.67	0.55	0.45	0.38	0.31
8	0.79	0.73	0.63	0.50	0.40	0.33	0.27
9	0.77	0.70	0.59	0.46	0.36	0.28	0.23
10	0.74	0.68	0.56	0.42	0.32	0.25	0.19
15	0.64	0.56	0.42	0.27	0.18	0.12	0.08
20	0.55	0.46	0.31	0.18	0.10	0.06	0.04
30	0.41	0.31	0.17	0.08	0.03	0.02	0.01
40	0.31	0.21	0.10	0.03	0.01	0.00	0.00
50	0.23	0.14	0.05	0.01	0.00	0.00	0.00

(a)

The present value of a yearly stream of income converts a known stream of income into a present amount.

Interest Rate

Number of years	3%	4%	6%	9%	12%	15%	18%
1	0.97	0.96	0.94	0.92	0.89	0.87	0.85
2	1.91	1.89	1.83	1.76	1.69	1.63	1.57
3	2.83	2.78	2.67	2.53	2.40	2.28	2.17
4	3.72	3.63	3.47	3.24	3.04	2.85	2.69
5	4.58	4.45	4.21	3.89	3.60	3.35	3.13
6	5.42	5.24	4.92	4.49	4.11	3.78	3.50
7	6.23	6.00	5.58	5.03	4.56	4.16	3.81
8	7.02	6.73	6.21	5.53	4.97	4.49	4.08
9	7.79	7.44	6.80	6.00	5.33	4.77	4.30
10	8.53	8.11	7.36	6.42	5.65	5.02	4.49
15	11.94	11.12	9.71	8.06	6.81	5.85	5.09
20	14.88	13.59	11.47	9.13	7.47	6.26	5.35
30	19.60	17.29	13.76	10.27	8.06	6.57	5.52
40	23.11	19.79	15.05	10.76	8.24	6.64	5.55
50	25.73	21.48	15.76	10.96	8.30	6.66	5.55

(b)

thumb and highly simplified formulas for which you don't need either a present-value table or a calculator. Let's consider two of them: the infinite annuity rule and the rule of 72.

The Annuity Rule   To find the present value of an annuity that will pay $1 for an infinite number of years in the future when the interest rate is 5 percent, we simply divide $1 by 5 percent (.05). Doing so gives us $20. So at 5 percent, $1 a year paid to you forever has a present value of $20. Our general **annuity rule** for any annuity is

$$PV = X/i.$$

That is, the present value of an infinite flow of income, X, is that income divided by the interest rate, i.

Most of the time, people don't offer to sell you annuities for the infinite future. A typical annuity runs for 30, 40, or 50 years. However the annuity rule is still useful. As you can see from the present-value table, in 30 years at a 9 percent interest rate, the present value of $1 isn't much (it's 8¢) so we can use this infinite flow formula as an approximation of long-lasting, but less than infinite, flows of future income. We simply subtract a little bit from what we get with our formula. The longer the time period, the less we subtract. For example, say you are wondering what $200 a year for 40 years is worth when the interest rate is 8 percent. Dividing $200 by .08 gives $2,500, so we know the annuity must be worth a bit less than $2,500. (It's actually worth $2,411.)

The annuity rule allows us to answer the question posed at the beginning of this section: How much is $10 a year for 500 years worth right now? The answer is that it depends on the interest rate you could earn on a specified amount of money now. If the interest rate is 10 percent, the maximum you should be willing to pay for that 500-year $10 annuity is $100:

$$\$10/.10 = \$100.$$

If the interest rate is 5 percent, the most you should pay is $200. ($10/.05 = $200.) So now you know why you should have said no to that supersalesman who offered it to you for $800.

The Rule of 72   A second rule of thumb for determining present values of shorter time periods is the **rule of 72.** The rule of 72 states:

Annuity rule Present value of any annuity is the annual income it yields divided by the interest rate: PV = X/i.

Rule of 72 A certain amount of money will double in value in the number of years obtained when one divides 72 by the interest rate.

The number of years it takes for a certain amount to double in value is equal to 72 divided by the rate of interest.

Say, for example, that the interest rate is 4 percent. How long will it take for your $100 to become worth $200? Dividing 72 by 4 gives 18. So the present value of $200 at a 4 percent interest rate 18 years in the future is about $100. (Actually it's $102.67.)

Alternatively say that you will receive $1,000 in 10 years. Is it worth paying $500 for that amount now if the interest rate is 9 percent? Using the rule of 72, we know that at a 9 percent interest rate it will take about eight years for $500 to double:

$$72/9 = 8$$

so the future value of $500 is more than $1,000. It's probably about $1,200. (Actually it's $1,184.) So if the interest rate in the economy is 9 percent, it's not worth paying $500 now in order to get that $1,000 in 10 years. By investing that same $500 today at 9 percent, you can have $1,184 in 10 years.

The Importance of Present Value   Many business decisions require such present-value calculations. In almost any business you'll be looking at flows of income in the future and comparing them to present costs or to other flows of money in the future. That's why understanding present value is a necessary tool.

THE MARGINAL PRODUCTIVITY THEORY OF INCOME DISTRIBUTION

Marginal productivity theory   The theory that factors of production are paid their marginal revenue product.

7

Society's view of individuals who receive their income from investments has often been less than admiring, as seen in the 18th-century etching by Brichet of "The Financier." *Bleichroeder Print Collection, Baker Library. Harvard Business School.*

We've completed our brief survey of rent, profit, and interest. Let's now consider how these categories of income combine with wage income to fit into a theory of income distribution.

The traditional economic theory of the distribution of income is **marginal productivity theory.** This theory states that factors are paid their marginal revenue product (what they contribute at the margin to revenue). We saw how marginal revenue product of labor was determined in the last chapter. In marginal productivity theory that same reasoning is used to explain the income going to the other three factors. If that factor is entrepreneurship, then the income the person receives can be called *profit;* if that factor is a fixed factor, the income the person receives can be called *rent;* if the factor is current production that is not consumed, the income that person receives can be called *interest.* Marginal productivity theory essentially says that supply and demand determines who gets what.

Modern economists are in the process of extending this functional theory. One extension is to look at the theory of income distribution more abstractly than did early Classical economists. Modern-day economists focus their analysis on what "unspecified" factors of production will be paid, not on what labor or capital or entrepreneurs will be paid. Whether an unspecified factor income is interest, rent, profit, or wages doesn't matter to the analysis since the forces of supply and demand are the same in each case. Modern economists argue that what factors will be paid depends upon (1) the supply of that factor and (2) the derived demand for that factor, which in turn depends upon the marginal productivity of that factor. Thus, they still use the marginal productivity theory, but they use it more abstractly.

Modern-day economists stopped looking at the functional distribution of income among rent, profit, interest, and wages and started to look at the issue more abstractly because the social reality had changed. The marginal productivity theory of the functional distribution of income was developed to reflect a social reality that had distinct classes of people. One class represented the workers; another represented a group of gentrified landowners who received rent; another represented a group of energetic industrialists; and the fourth represented a group who controlled much of the financial wealth of the society. The wage, rent, profit, and interest categories fit that social reality nicely. Modern society is much more complicated and far less class-oriented, which means that the wage/rent/profit/interest components of income are often mixed. When the president of a huge corporation earns $10,000,000 a year, few economists would see that as wage

T he failure to understand the concept of present value often shows up in the popular press. Here are three examples.

THE PRESS AND PRESENT VALUE

Headline: **COURT SETTLEMENT IS $40,000,000**

Inside story: The money will be paid out over a 40-year period.

Actual value: $11,925,000 (8 percent interest rate)

Headline: **DISABLED WIDOW WINS $25 MILLION LOTTERY**

Inside story: The money will be paid over 20 years.

Actual value: $13,254,499 (8 percent interest rate)

Headline: **BOND ISSUE TO COST TAXPAYERS $68 MILLION**

Inside story: The $68 million is the total of interest and principal payments. The interest is paid yearly; the principal won't be paid back to the bond purchasers until 30 years from now.

Actual cost: $20,000,000 (8 percent interest rate)

Such stories are common. Be on the lookout for them as you read the newspaper or watch the evening news.

income. Even the terminology describing income forms that modern economists use is different. They often don't talk about labor income as wage income. Instead they call labor *human capital* to emphasize the profit and rent component of wages.

A second extension modern economists are making to the marginal productivity theory of the functional distribution of income is that they are looking behind it. Marginal productivity theory explains the distribution of income, *given property rights*. It does not explain why property rights are what they are. As we discussed in the beginning of this chapter, modern economists are going beyond the marginal productivity theory of income and are trying to explain why property rights are what they are. This doesn't mean that modern economists don't accept marginal productivity theory; it simply means that they are trying to get at a deeper understanding of the distribution of income.

Despite the fact that the theory of income distribution is currently being expanded and the traditional categories of factors are being given less importance, there is still much to be gained from a knowledge of the traditional theory of income distribution. For example, it tells us that factors in inelastic supply will bear the burden of a large portion of any tax on users of that factor. Similarly it highlights some key elements of the economic forces that determine who gets what—how the forces of supply and demand work. The trick is to understand that and simultaneously to understand the role that political and social forces play in determining what the underlying property rights are, and how those forces interact with economic forces. These questions are high on modern economists' research agendas. Their analysis of rent seeking will likely yield new insights in the years to come.

CONCLUSION

KEY POINTS

• Rent is the income paid to a factor of production that is perfectly inelastic in supply.   **1**

• Rent seeking is an attempt to create ownership rights and institutional structures that favor you.   **2**

• Normal profits are payments to entrepreneurs and the return on their risk taking. Economic profits are a return on entrepreneurship above and beyond normal profits.   **3**

• Entrepreneurs search out market niches in order

to earn above-normal profits. Successful search by entrepreneurs tends to eliminate those above-normal profits. **4**

• Interest is the income paid to savers—individuals who produce now but do not consume now. **5**

• The annuity rule and the rule of 72 are useful rules of thumb for determining present value. **6**

• The marginal productivity theory of distribution is the theory that factors of production are paid their marginal revenue product. **7**

KEY TERMS

annuity rule *(717)*
contractual legal
  system *(710)*
economic profits *(713)*
interest *(715)*

marginal productivity
  theory *(718)*
market niche *(714)*
normal profits *(713)*
present value *(716)*

profit *(713)*
property rights *(710)*
quasi rent *(712)*
rent *(710)*
rent seeking *(712)*

rule of 72 *(717)*
zoning laws *(710)*

QUESTIONS FOR THOUGHT AND REVIEW

The number after each question represents the estimated degree of critical thinking required. (1 = almost none; 10 = deep thought.)

1. List the four traditional categories of income and explain why they have become less important to modern economic analysis. *(2)*
2. Some people argue that zoning laws are immoral. Based on your understanding of property rights, explain how they likely justify this position. *(8)*
3. Which would an economist normally recommend taxing: an elastic or an inelastic supply? Why? *(4)*
4. Differentiate normal profits from economic profits. *(3)*
5. Explain two reasons why the formerly socialist countries will probably have a hard time generating significant entrepreneurial activity. *(6)*

6. "In perfect competition no one would get rich quick, but the economy would stagnate." Evaluate this statement. *(8)*
7. A salesperson calls you up and offers you $200 a year for life. If the interest rate is 7 percent, how much should you be willing to pay for that annuity? *(3)*
8. The same salesperson offers you a lump sum of $20,000 in 10 years. How much should you be willing to pay? (The interest rate is still 7 percent.) *(4)*
9. Define *human capital* and explain why modern economists' use of the term makes the functional distribution of income analysis less useful. *(5)*
10. "If all people were paid their marginal product, there would be true justice in the economy." Evaluate this statement. *(9)*

PROBLEMS AND EXERCISES

1. Demonstrate graphically how the price of land is determined.
   a. Show the effect of a tax on that land.
   b. Explain why that tax won't cause the price of land to rise.
   c. Based on this analysis, would you support more extensive use of land and property taxes in the United States? Why?
2. What is the present value of a cash flow of $100 per year forever (a perpetuity), assuming:

   The interest rate is 10 percent.
   The interest rate is 5 percent.
   The interest rate is 20 percent.
   a. Working with those same three interest rates, what are the future values of $100 today in one year? How about in two years?
   b. Working with those same three interest rates, how long will it take you to double your money?

4

INTERNATIONAL ECONOMICS

In earlier chapters international considerations have appeared continuously. It could hardly be otherwise. So why have a separate section on international economics? There are two reasons. First, over the past 20 years international issues have become increasingly important for the U.S. economy. Second, raising international issues in the context of the microeconomic and macroeconomic discussions is different than raising microeconomic and macroeconomic considerations in an international context. The different perspective amplifies and reinforces the information presented earlier. So in this section I survey international issues as they would be presented in an international economics course.

Let me start by amplifying your sense of the importance of international issues. The statement in the first paragraph that "over the past 20 years international issues have become increasingly important for the U.S. economy" would be correct even if the reference period went back as far as the late 1800s. The late 1800s and the first 40 years of the 1900s was an isolationist period for the United States in which the country turned inward in both economic and foreign policies.

The statement would not be correct if the reference period were earlier than the late 1800s. In the 1600s, 1700s, and most of the 1800s international trade was vital to the American economy—even more vital than now. The American nation grew from colonial possessions of England, France, and Spain. These "new world" colonial possessions were valued for their gold, agricultural produce, and natural resources. From a European standpoint, international trade was the colonies' reason for being.[1]

A large portion of the U.S. government's income during much of the 1800s came from tariffs. Our technology was imported from abroad and international issues played a central role in wars fought here. (Many historians believe that the most important cause of the U.S. Civil War was difference of views about tariffs on manufactured goods. The South opposed them because it wanted cheap manufactured goods while the North favored them because it wanted to protect its manufacturing industries.) Up until the 1900s no one would have studied the U.S. economy independently of international issues. Not only was there significant international trade; there was also significant immigration. The United States is a country of immigrants.

Only in the late 1800s did the United States adopt an isolationist philosophy in both politics and trade. So in reference to that isolationist period, the U.S. economy has become more integrated with the world economy. However in a broader historical perspective, that isolationist period was an anomaly, and the 1990s is simply returning international issues to the key role they've usually played.

A second important insight is that international trade has social and cultural dimensions. While much of the following four chapters will deal with specifically economic issues, we must also remember the cultural and social implications of trade.

Let's consider an example from history. In the Middle Ages, Greek ideas and philosophy were lost to Europe when hordes of barbarians swept over the continent. These ideas and that philosophy were only rediscovered in the Renaissance as a by-product of trade between the Italian merchant cities and the Middle East. (The Greek ideas that had spread to the Middle East were protected there from European upheavals.) *Renaissance* means rebirth: a rebirth in Europe

---

[1] The American Indian standpoint was, I suspect, somewhat different.

of Greek learning. Many of our traditions and sensibilities are based on those of the Renaissance, and that Renaissance was caused, or at least significantly influenced, by international trade. Had there been no trade, our entire philosophy of life might have been different.

Fernand Braudel, a French historian, has provided wonderful examples of the broader implications for trade. For instance, he argued that the effects of international trade, specifically Sir Walter Raleigh's introduction of the potato into England from South America in 1588, had more long-run consequences than did the celebrated 1588 battle of the English navy and Spanish Armada.

Another example, which Braudel did not live to see, is the major change in socialist countries in the 1990s. Through the 1960s China, the Soviet Union, and the Eastern European countries were relatively closed societies—behind the Iron Curtain. That changed in the 1970s and 1980s as these socialist countries opened up trade with the West as a way to speed their own economic development. That trade, and the resulting increased contact with the West, gave the people of those countries a better sense of the material goods to be had in the West. That trade also spread Western ideas of the proper organization of government and the economy to these societies. A strong argument can be made that along with trade came the seeds of discontent which changed those societies and their economies forever.

The international economics presented in the following chapters does not focus on these broader cultural issues. International economics is about relatively technical issues such as exchange rate determination and reasons for trade. But keep in the back of your mind these broader implications as you go through the various components of international economies. They add a dimension to the story that otherwise might be forgotten.

Chapter 35 presents the underlying theory of international trade. It asks why countries trade and why they also often place limitations on trade. After reading it, you should have a much better sense of when there are, and when there are not, possibilities for trade between countries.

Chapter 36 considers financial aspects of international trade. It looks carefully at exchange rates and the balance of payments, and gives you a sense of how exchange rates are determined in practice. After reading it, you should be able to explain the forces that influence exchange rates and understand why exchange rates are so hard to predict.

Chapter 37 looks at the problems of developing countries and asks questions like: What can a country do to develop? After reading Chapter 37 you should have a better sense of why that one is such a difficult question.

Finally, in Chapter 38, I consider the transformations socialist and formerly socialist countries are currently undergoing. I look at how central planning works and discuss problems with a system of central planning. This chapter should give you a good sense of why these changes are occurring.

And that's it. After Chapter 38 I'm out of time, but I hope that isn't the end of your consideration of things economic. The coming decades will create new chapters in economics, waiting to be opened. I strongly hope that you'll stay tuned and think back every so often to the insights and ideas you've discovered in this book.

35

International Trade

*One of the purest fallacies is that
trade follows the flag. Trade follows the lowest price current. If a
dealer in any colony wished to buy Union Jacks, he would order them
from Britain's worst foe if he could save a sixpence.*

Andrew Carnegie

After reading this chapter, you should be able to:

1

List the primary trading partners of the
United States.

2

Explain the principle of absolute advantage.

3

Explain the principle of comparative
advantage.

4

List three determinants of the terms
of trade.

5

Explain three policies countries use to
restrict trade.

6

Discuss why countries impose
trade restrictions.

7

Summarize why economists generally
oppose trade restrictions.

Many goods we use every day aren't made in the United States: cars, clothes, televisions—the list is endless. These goods are imported from other countries. Almost every day we hear calls from some sector of the economy to restrict foreign imports in order to save U.S. jobs and protect U.S. workers from unfair competition. Economists generally oppose these restrictions; economists favor free trade. In this chapter I consider why countries trade, why economists generally favor free trade, and why, despite what economists tell them, countries impose trade restrictions.

PATTERNS OF TRADE

Increasing but Fluctuating World Trade

Before I consider these issues, let's look at some numbers relevant to international trade to get a sense of the nature and dimensions of international trade.

In 1928 total world trade was about $245 billion (in 1980 dollars). U.S. gross domestic product was about $430 billion, so world trade as a percentage of U.S. GDP was almost 60 percent. In 1935 that ratio had fallen to less than 30 percent. In 1950 it was 20 percent. Then it started rising. In 1990 it was once again approximately 60 percent. As you can see, the level of world trade has fluctuated significantly.

In terms of dollar amounts, the fluctuations in international trade over the years are even greater. In constant 1980 dollars, world trade fell from $245 billion in 1928 to $110 billion in 1935. It then rose again, to about $2 trillion, by 1990. The conclusion: International trade has been growing, but with significant fluctuations in that growth. Sometimes international trade has grown rapidly; at other times it has grown slowly or has even fallen.

In part, fluctuations in world trade result from fluctuations in world output. When output rises, international trade rises; when output falls, international trade falls. Fluctuations in world trade are also in part explained by trade restrictions that countries have imposed from time to time. For example, decreases in world income during the depression caused a large decrease in trade, but that decrease was exacerbated by a worldwide increase in trade restrictions during the 1930s.

Differences in Importance of Trade

The importance of international trade to countries' economies differs widely, as we can see in Exhibit 1, which presents the importance of the shares of exports and imports for various countries. Among the countries listed, the Netherlands has the highest amount of exports compared to GDP; the United States has the lowest.

The Netherlands' imports are also the highest as a percentage of GDP. The United States has the lowest. The relationship between a country's imports and its exports is no coincidence. For most countries, imports and exports roughly correspond, though in any particular year that correspondence can be rough indeed. For the United States in recent years, imports have generally significantly exceeded exports. But that situation can't continue forever, as I'll discuss.

Total trade figures provide us with only part of the international trade picture. We must also look at what types of goods are traded and with whom that trade is conducted. Exhibit 2 breaks U.S. international trade down into its various components. Notice that the United States both imports and exports significant amounts of manufactured goods. This isn't unusual, since much of all international trade is in manufactured goods.

■ Exhibit 3 shows the regions with which the United States trades. Exports to Canada and Western Europe made up a large percentage of total U.S. exports in 1990. Regions from which the United States imports major quantities include Canada, Western Europe, Japan, and Southeast Asia. Notice how the relative share of imports from Japan to total U.S. imports has increased over the years, while the percent share of U.S. exports to Japan has remained the same.

	GDP*	Exports*	% GDP	Imports*	% GDP
U.S.	5673.0	428.1	8	499.4	9
Canada	521.5	124.0	24	118.0	23
Netherlands	249.6	131.5	53	125.9	50
Germany‡	1235.8	324.3	26	346.5	28
United Kingdom	915.5	186.4	20	211.9	23
Italy	965.0	209.0	22	222.0	23
France	1033.7	209.5	20	232.5	22
Japan	2360.7	314.3	13	236.6	10

EXHIBIT 1   Relation of Exports and Imports to GDP in Selected Countries, 1992

* Numbers in billions.

‡ Figures are for Western Germany not applicable to Federal Republiz of Germany.

Source: *The World FactBook, 1992.*

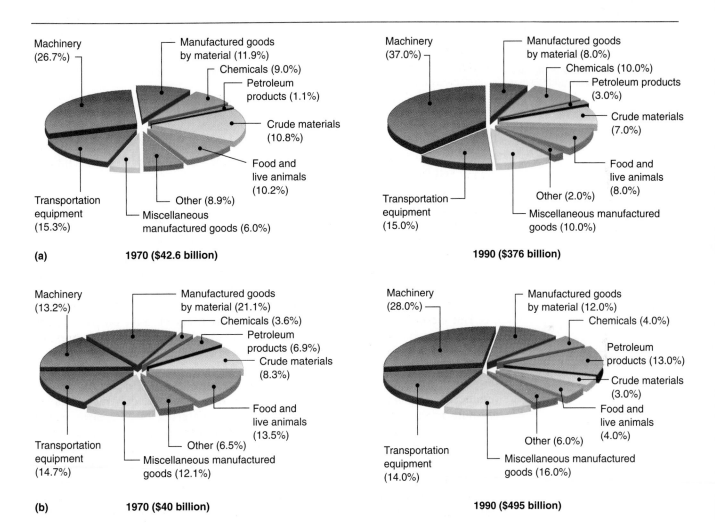

(a)   1970 ($42.6 billion)

1990 ($376 billion)

(b)   1970 ($40 billion)

1990 ($495 billion)

EXHIBIT 2 (a and b)   U.S. Imports and Exports by Commodity

The pie charts show the relative shares of each commodity group in exports (**a**) and imports (**b**). Notice how much of U.S. trade consists of machinery, manufactured goods, and transportation equipment. This is not unusual, because much of all international trade is in manufactured goods.

Source: U.S. Department of Commerce, *Survey of Current Business.* (Some 1990 data are estimated because of a change in classification system.)

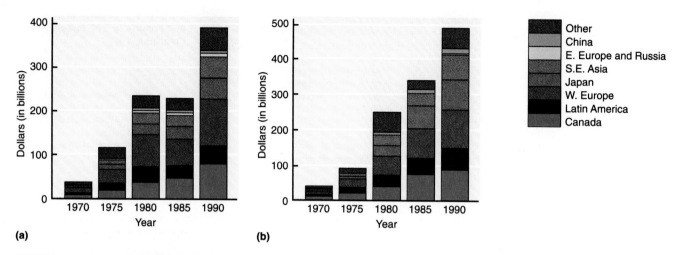

(a)   **(b)**

EXHIBIT 3 (a and b)   **U.S. Exports and Imports by Region**

U.S. exports (**a**) and imports (**b**) have increased significantly over time. Major regions that trade with the United States include Canada, Western Europe, Japan, and Southeast Asia.

WHY DO NATIONS TRADE?

The Principle of Absolute Advantage

Principle of absolute advantage A country that can produce a good at a lower cost than another country has an absolute advantage in the production of that good.

International trade exists for the same reason that all trade exists: Party A has something that party B wants and party B has something that party A wants. Both parties can be made better off by trade.

Trade between countries in different types of goods is relatively easy to explain. For example, trade in raw materials and agricultural goods for manufactured goods can be easily explained by the **principle of absolute advantage:**

A country that can produce a good at a lower cost than another country can is said to have an absolute advantage in the production of that good. When two countries have absolute advantages in different goods, there are gains of trade to be had.

The principle of absolute advantage explains trade of, say, oil from Saudi Arabia for food from the United States. Saudi Arabia has millions of barrels of easily available oil, but growing food in its desert climate and sandy soil is expensive. The United States can grow food cheaply in its temperate climate and fertile soil, but its oil isn't as easily available or as cheap to drill for. Because it can produce a certain amount of oil with fewer resources, Saudi Arabia has an absolute advantage over the United States in producing oil. Because it can produce a certain amount of food with fewer resources, the United States has an absolute advantage over Saudi Arabia in producing food. When each country specializes in the good it has an absolute advantage in, both countries can gain from trade.

In Exhibit 4, I consider a hypothetical numerical example which demonstrates how the principle of absolute advantage can lead to gains from trade. For simplicity, I assume constant opportunity costs.

Exhibits 4(b) and (d) show the choices for the United States; Exhibits 4(a) and (c) show the choices for Saudi Arabia. In Exhibits 4(a) and (b) you see that the United States and Saudi Arabia can produce various combinations of food and oil by devoting differing percentages of their resources to producing each. Comparing the two tables and assuming the resources in the two countries are comparable, we see that Saudi Arabia has an absolute advantage in the production of oil and the United States has an absolute advantage in the production of food.

For example, when the United States and Saudi Arabia devote equal amounts of resources to oil production, Saudi Arabia can produce 10 times as much as the

Saudi Arabia

Percentage of resources devoted to oil	Oil produced (barrels)	Food produced (tons)	Row
100	1,000	0	A
80	800	20	B
60	600	40	C
40	400	60	D
20	200	80	E
0	0	100	F

(a)

United States

Percentage of resources devoted to oil	Oil produced (barrels)	Food produced (tons)	Row
100	100	0	A
80	80	200	B
60	60	400	C
40	40	600	D
20	20	800	E
0	0	1,000	F

(b)

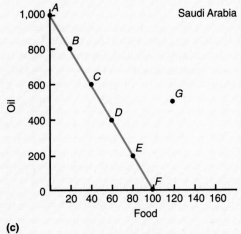

(c)

(d)

EXHIBIT 4 (a, b, c, and d)   Absolute Advantage: The United States and Saudi Arabia

Looking at tables (a) and (b), you can see that if Saudi Arabia devotes all its resources to oil, it can produce 1,000 barrels of oil, but if it devotes all of its resources to food, it can produce only 100 tons of food. For the United States, the story is the opposite: devoting all of its resources to oil, the United States can only produce 100 barrels of oil—10 times less than Saudi Arabia—but if it devotes all of its resources to food, it can produce 1,000 tons of food—10 times more than Saudi Arabia. Assuming resources are comparable Saudi Arabia has an absolute advantage in the production of oil, and the United States has an absolute advantage in the production of food. The information in the tables is presented graphically in (c) and (d). These are the countries' production possibility curves without trade. Each point on each country's curve corresponds to a row on that country's table.

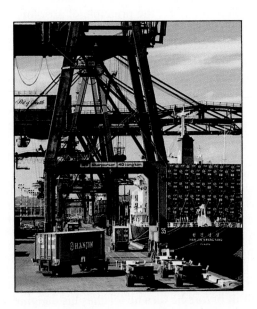

International trade means that huge amounts of goods are shipped through ports. Here U.S. exports are being loaded onto a South Korean shipping line in Seattle.   © *Bob Daemmrich/The Image Works.*

EXHIBIT 5   Distribution of Production among the United States, Saudi Arabia, and I. T.

	Oil (barrels)	Food (tons)
Total production	1000	1000
U.S. consumption	80	500
Saudi consumption	500	120
I. T.'s profit	420	380

United States can. Alternatively, when the United States devotes 60 percent of a given amount of resources to oil production, it gets 60 barrels of oil. But when Saudi Arabia devotes 60 percent of that same amount of resources to oil production, it gets 600 barrels of oil. The information in the tables is presented graphically in Exhibits 4(c) and (d). These graphs represent the two countries' production possibility curves without trade. Each combination of numbers in the table corresponds to a point on the curve. For example, point *B* in each graph corresponds to the entries in row B, columns 2 and 3, in the relevant table.

Let's assume that without any international trade the United States has chosen point *C* (production of 60 barrels of oil and 400 tons of food) and Saudi Arabia has chosen point *D* (production of 400 barrels of oil and 60 tons of food).

Now I. T. (International Trader), who understands the principle of absolute advantage, comes along and offers the following deal to Saudi Arabia:

> If you produce 1,000 barrels of oil and no food (point *A*) and give me 500 barrels of oil while keeping 500 barrels for yourself, I guarantee you 120 tons of food, double the amount of food you're now getting. I'll put you on point *G,* which is totally above your current production possibility curve. You'll get more oil and more food. It's an offer you can't refuse.

I. T. then flies off to the United States, to whom he makes the following offer:

> If you produce 1,000 tons of food and no oil (point *F*) and give me 500 tons of food while keeping 500 tons for yourself, I'll guarantee you 80 barrels of oil, double the amount you're now getting. I'll put you on point *H,* which is totally above your current production possibility curve. You'll get more oil and have more food. It's an offer you can't refuse.

Both countries accept; they'd be foolish not to. So the two countries' final consumption positions are as shown in Exhibit 5. For arranging the trade, I. T. makes a handsome profit of 380 tons of food and 420 barrels of oil.

I. T. has become rich because he understands the principle of absolute advantage. Unfortunately for I. T., the principle of absolute advantage is easy to understand, which means that he will quickly face competition. Other international traders come in and offer the countries even better deals than I. T. offered, squeezing his share. With free entry and competition in international trade, eventually I. T.'s share is squeezed down to his costs plus a normal return for his efforts.

Now obviously this hypothetical example significantly overemphasizes the gains a trader makes. Generally the person arranging the trade must compete with other traders and offer both countries a better deal than the one presented here. But the person who first recognizes a trading opportunity often makes a sizable fortune. The second and third persons who recognize the opportunity make smaller fortunes. Once the insight is generally recognized, the possibility of making a fortune is gone. Traders still make their normal returns, but the instantaneous fortunes are not to be made without new insight. In the long run, benefits of trade go to the countries, not the traders.

I. T. realizes this and spends part of his fortune on buying a Greek island, where he retires to contemplate more deeply the nature of international trade so he can triple his remaining fortune. He marries, has a daughter whom he names I. T. Too, and dies. But before he dies he teaches his daughter about international

Edward Leamer, an economist who has made significant contributions to empirically applying international trade theory. *Philip Channing.*

Germany				Algeria		
	% of resources devoted to autos	Autos produced	Food produced		% of resources devoted to autos	Autos produced	Food produced
A	100	100	0	A	100	20	0
B	80	80	40	B	80	16	1
C	60	60	80	C	60	12	2
D	40	40	120	D	40	8	3
E	20	20	160	E	20	4	4
F	0	0	200	F	0	0	5
		(a)				(b)	

EXHIBIT 6 (a and b) Germany's Comparative Advantage over Algeria in the Production of Autos and Food

trade and how new insights can lead to fortunes. His dying words to his daughter are, "Keep searching for that new insight."

The Principle of Comparative Advantage

Many years pass. I. T. Too grows up, and one day, while walking along the beach, contemplates the possibilities of trade between Germany and Algeria in automobiles and food. No other traders have considered trade between these two countries because Germany is so much more productive than Algeria in *all* goods. No trade is currently taking place because Germany has an absolute advantage in production of both autos and food. Assuming the resources in the two countries are comparable, this case can be seen in Exhibit 6.

But I. T. Too is bright. She remembers what her father taught her about opportunity costs back in her first economics lesson. She reasons as follows: Germany's opportunity cost of producing an auto is 2/1. That means Germany must give up 2 tons of food to get 1 additional auto. For example, if Germany is initially producing 60 autos and 80 tons of food, if it cuts production of autos by 20, it will increase its food output by 40. For each car lost, Germany gains 2 tons of food. When Algeria cuts its production of autos by 4, it gains 1 ton of food. Algeria's opportunity cost of producing another auto is 1/4. It must give up 1 unit of food to get an additional 4 autos.

I. T. Too further reasons that if Algeria needs to give up only $\frac{1}{4}$ unit of food to get an auto while Germany needs to give up 2 tons of food to produce 1 auto, there are potential gains to be made, which can be split up among the countries and herself. Then, like her father before her, she can make the countries offers they can't refuse. She walks the beach mulling the following: "*Absolute advantage* is not necessary for trade; *comparative advantage* is." A smile comes over her face; she understands. Flying happily over the Mediterranean Sea, she formulates her insight precisely. She calls it the **principle of comparative advantage:** *As long as the relative opportunity costs of producing goods (what must be given up in one good in order to get another good) differ among countries, there are potential gains from trade, even if one country has an absolute advantage in everything.*

It is comparative advantage, not absolute advantage, that forms a basis of trade. If one country has a comparative advantage in one good, the other country must, by definition, have a comparative advantage in the other good.

Having formulated her idea, she applies it to the Germans and Algerians. She sees that, unexpectedly, Germany has a comparative advantage in producing food and Algeria has a comparative advantage in producing cars. With this insight firmly in mind, she leaves her island, flies to Germany, and makes the Germans the following offer:

> You're currently producing and consuming 60 autos and 80 tons of food (row *C* of Exhibit 6(a)). If you'll produce only 48 autos but 104 tons of food and give me 22 tons of food, I'll guarantee you 13 autos for those 22 tons of food. You'll have more autos (61) and more food (82). It's an offer you can't refuse.

Principle of comparative advantage As long as the relative opportunity costs of producing goods differ among countries, there are potential gains from trade, even if one country has an absolute advantage in everything.

In case you were wondering, I. T. Too didn't really formulate the principle of comparative advantage. It first appeared in a book called *Principles of Economics* written by an extraordinarily bright stockbroker, David Ricardo, in 1817. Thus, it's often called the *Ricardian principle of comparative advantage.*

As with many other principles of economics, the true lineage of this principle is subject to dispute. Ideas are often "in the air" long before they get into print, and the person to whom history attributes them may not be the person who formulated them. After some superb detective work, in 1976 William Thweat discovered that Ricardo's good friend, economist James Mill, and not Ricardo himself, was the first to write about comparative advantage and so deserves to be called the discoverer of the principle of comparative advantage. Not all historians agree with Thweat, but all agree that it was one of those two, not I. T. Too.

EXHIBIT 7   Final Consumption for Both Countries

	Autos	Food
Total production	68	104
German consumption	61	82
Algerian consumption	5	5
I. T. Too's profit	2	17

She then goes to Algeria and presents the Algerians with the following offer:

You're currently producing 4 tons of food and 4 automobiles (row *E* of Exhibit 6(b)). If you'll produce only automobiles (row *A*) and turn out 20 autos, keeping 5 for yourself and giving 15 of them to me, I'll guarantee you 5 tons of food for the 15 autos. You'll have more autos (5) and more food (5). It's an offer you can't refuse.

Neither Germany nor Algeria can refuse. They both agree to I. T. Too's offer. The final position appears in Exhibit 7.

I. T. Too then proceeds to visit various other countries, making similar offers. They accept the offers because it's in their interest to accept them. Countries (and people) trade because trade benefits them.

As was the case with her father, her initial returns are the greatest. Then, as other people recognize the principle of comparative advantage and offer the countries better deals than hers, her share shrinks until her return just covers her opportunity cost and the costs of transporting the goods. But because the principle of comparative advantage is more difficult to understand than the principle of absolute advantage, the competing traders enter in much more slowly. Her above-normal returns last longer than did her father's, but eventually they're competed away. When the gains decline to only normal levels, she sells out and retires.

Dividing Up the Gains from Trade

The principle of comparative advantage is powerful. It determines when there are gains of trade to be made. It doesn't determine how those gains of trade will be divided up among the countries involved and traders like I. T. Too. I can, however, offer some insights into how those gains are likely to be divided up. I've already noted the first insight:

The more competition that exists in international trade, the less likely it is that the trader gets the gains of trade; more of the gains from trade will go to the citizens in the two countries.

■ This insight isn't lost upon trading companies. Numerous import/export companies exist whose business is discovering new possibilities for international

ADDED DIMENSION

COUNTERTRADE

Many countries place restrictions on imports and allow a trader to sell foreign goods in a country only if the trader finds someone to buy an equal amount of the country's exports. Such restrictions are called *countertrade restrictions*. Thus, to sell your goods to a foreign country, you may find yourself selling that country's goods to your own country. For example, a U.S. hospital supply firm that sells its goods to China might sell Chinese textiles in the United States, while a U.S. heavy equipment firm that sells machinery to Africa might sell African coffee beans in the United States.

To meet the needs of these various firms, "countertrading" firms have sprung up, which buy the countertrade goods (at a discount, of course) and sell them in the United States.

trade. Individuals representing trading companies go around hawking projects or goods to countries. For example, in 1989 at the end of the Iran/Iraq war, what the business world calls the *import/export contingent* flew in to Iraq with offers of goods and services to sell. Many of these same individuals had been in Saudi Arabia when the oil price rose in the 1970s, and in the Far East when China opened its doors to international trade in the 1980s. In the early 1990s this same group flocked to what had been the Soviet Union.

Selling U.S. goods is often easy for such U.S. traders. The problem generally is arranging financing. The goods must be paid for in the currency of the country doing the exporting, not in the currency of the country doing the importing. Thus, often firms that are doing the selling must also arrange financing for the trade. I'll discuss problems of financing trade in the next chapter.

A second insight is:

> Once competition prevails, smaller countries tend to get a larger percentage of the gains of trade than do larger countries.

The reason, briefly, is that more opportunities are opened up for smaller countries by trade than for larger countries. The more opportunities, the larger the relative gains. Say, for instance, that the United States begins trade with Mali, a small country in Africa. Enormous new consumption possibilities are opened up for Mali—prices of all types of goods will fall. Before international trade began, cars were probably extraordinarily expensive in Mali, while fish were cheap. With international trade, the price of cars in Mali falls substantially, so Mali gets the gains. Because the U.S. economy is so large compared to Mali's, the U.S. price of fish doesn't change noticeably. Mali's fish are just a drop in the bucket. The price ratio of cars to fish doesn't change much for the United States, so it doesn't get much of the gains of trade. Mali gets almost all the gains from trade.

There's an important catch to this gains-from-trade argument. The argument holds only "once competition among traders prevails." That means that Mali residents are sold cars at the same price (plus shipping costs) as U.S. residents. International traders in small countries often have little competition from other traders and keep large shares of the gains from trade for themselves. In the preceding examples, Germany and Algeria didn't get a large share of the benefits. It was I. T. Too who got most of the benefits. Since the traders often come from the larger country, the smaller country doesn't get the benefits of the gains from trade; the larger country's international traders do.

A third insight is:

> Gains from trade go to countries that produce goods that exhibit economies of scale.

Trade allows an increase in production. If there are economies of scale, that increase can lower the average cost of production of a good. Hence an increase in production can lower the price of the good in the producing country. The country producing the good with the largest economies of scale has its costs reduced by more, and hence gains more from trade than does its trading partner.

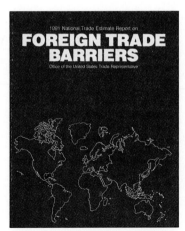

One of the many U.S. government publications that give specific information about international trade.

TRADE RESTRICTIONS

In the previous examples I. T. Too had a relatively easy time persuading the countries to trade. All she had to do was show them that there were gains from trade to be made. Like any good trader, she didn't emphasize the potential difficulties that trade presents. In reality, international trade creates significant problems. That's why almost no country in the world allows free trade, but instead imposes a variety of trade restrictions. We briefly consider the nature of those policies to reduce trade.

Varieties of Trade Restrictions

5

Countries can use a variety of policies to restrict trade. These include tariffs, quotas, voluntary restraint agreements, embargoes, regulatory trade restrictions, and nationalistic appeals. I'll consider each in turn.

Tariff   Tax on internationally traded goods.

Tariffs   **Tariffs,** also called *customs duties,* are taxes governments place on internationally traded goods—generally imports. Tariffs are the most-used and most familiar type of trade restriction. Tariffs operate in the same way a tax does: They make imported goods relatively more expensive than they otherwise would have been and thereby encourage the consumption of domestically produced goods. On average, U.S. tariffs raise the price of imported goods by 5 percent. Exhibit 8 presents tariff rates on various goods imposed by the United States, the European Community, and Japan.

Probably the most infamous tariff in U.S. history is the Smoot-Hawley Tariff of 1930, which raised tariffs on imported goods an average of 60 percent. It was passed in an attempt to stop the Great Depression in the United States and protect American jobs. It didn't work. Other countries responded with similar tariffs. As a result of these trade wars, international trade plummeted from $60 billion in 1928 to $25 billion in 1938, unemployment worsened, and the international depression deepened. These effects of the tariff convinced many, if not most, economists that free trade is preferable to trade restrictions. The dismal failure of the Smoot-Hawley Tariff was the main reason the **General Agreement on Tariffs and Trade (GATT),** the regular international conference to reduce trade barriers, was established.

Quota   Quantity limit placed on imports.

Quotas   **Quotas** are quantity limits placed on imports. Their effect in limiting trade is similar to a tariff's effect. One big difference is in who gets the revenue. With a tariff, the government gets the revenue; with a quota, revenues accrue to producers of the protected good. For example, if the United States places quotas on foreign textiles, foreign producers of textiles will receive the proceeds of the resulting higher price. If the United States places a tariff on textile imports, the prices will also rise, but the U.S. government will receive the revenue.

A second big difference is that under a quota, any increase in domestic demand will be met by the less efficient domestic producers (who would otherwise lose in the competition) since a quota places strict numerical limitations on what can be imported. Under a tariff, part of any increase in domestic demand will be met by more efficient foreign producers since a tariff places a tax on imports but does not restrict their quantity. Needless to say, producers prefer quotas to tariffs.

Voluntary Restraint Agreements   Imposing new tariffs and quotas is specifically ruled out by GATT, but foreign countries know that GATT is voluntary and that, if a domestic industry brought sufficient political pressure on its government, GATT would be forgotten. To avoid the imposition of new tariffs on their goods, countries often voluntarily restrict their exports. That's why Japan has agreed informally to limit the number of cars it exports to the United States.

The effect of such voluntary restraint agreements is identical to the effect of quotas: They directly limit the quantity of imports, increasing the price of the good and helping domestic producers. For example, when the United States encouraged Japan to impose ''voluntary'' quotas on exports of its cars to the United States, Toyota benefited from the quotas because it could price its limited

EXHIBIT 8   Tariff Rates: United States, European Community, and Japan

Industry	United States	European Community	Japan
Agriculture, forestry, and fisheries	1.8%	4.9%	18.4%
Food, beverages, and tobacco products	4.7	10.1	25.4
Textiles	9.2	7.2	3.3
Wearing apparel	22.7	13.4	13.8
Leather products	4.2	2.0	3.0
Footwear	8.8	11.6	15.7
Wood products	1.7	2.5	.3
Furniture and fixtures	4.1	5.6	5.1
Paper and products	.2	5.4	2.1
Printing and publishing	.7	2.1	.1
Chemicals	2.4	8.0	4.8
Petroleum and related products	1.4	1.2	2.2
Rubber products	2.5	3.5	1.1
Nonmetallurgical mineral products	5.3	3.7	.5
Glass and glass products	6.2	7.7	5.1
Iron and steel	3.6	4.7	2.8
Nonferrous metals	.7	2.1	1.1
Metal products	4.8	5.5	5.2
Nonelectrical machinery	3.3	4.4	4.4
Electrical machinery	4.4	7.9	4.3
Transportation equipment	2.5	8.0	1.5
Miscellaneous manufactures	4.2	4.7	4.6

Source: General Agreement *on* Tariffs and Trade *(GATT)*.

supply of cars higher than it could if it sent in a large number of cars, so profit per car would be high. Since they faced less competition, U.S. car companies also benefited. They could increase their prices because Toyota had done so.

Embargoes   An **embargo** is an all-out restriction on import or export of a good. Embargoes are usually established for international political reasons rather than for primarily economic reasons.

Embargo All-out restriction on import or export of a good.

An example is the U.S. embargo of trade with Iraq. The U.S. government hoped that the embargo would so severely affect Iraq's economy that Saddam Hussein would lose political power. It did make life difficult for Iraqis, but it didn't bring about the downfall of the Hussein government.

Regulatory Trade Restrictions   Tariffs, quotas, and embargoes are the primary *direct* ways in which international trade is restricted. There are also indirect methods that restrict trade in not-so-obvious ways; these are called **regulatory trade restrictions** (government-imposed procedural rules that limit imports). One type of regulatory trade restriction has to do with protecting the health and safety of a country's residents. For example, a country might restrict import of all vegetables grown where certain pesticides are used, knowing full well that all other countries use those pesticides. The effect of such a regulation would be to halt the import of vegetables.

Regulatory trade restrictions Government-imposed procedural rules that limit imports.

A second type of regulatory restriction involves making import and customs procedures so intricate and time consuming that importers simply give up. For example, France requires all imported VCRs to be individually inspected in Toulouse. Since Toulouse is a provincial city, far from any port and outside the normal route for imports after they enter France, this inspection process can take months.

Some regulatory restrictions are imposed for legitimate reasons; others are designed simply to make importing more difficult and hence protect domestic producers from international competition. It's often hard to tell the difference. A good example of this difficulty occurred in 1988 when the EEC disallowed all imports of meat from animals that had been fed growth-inducing hormones, as the accompanying box details.

Trade restrictions, in practice, are often much more complicated than they seem in textbooks. Seldom does a country say, "We're limiting imports to protect our home producers." Instead the country explains the restrictions in a more politically acceptable way. Consider the fight between the European Economic Community and the United States over U.S. meat exports. In 1988 the EEC, in line with Community-wide internal requirements, banned all imports of any meat from animals treated with growth-inducing hormones, which U.S. meat producers use extensively. The result: the EEC banned the meat exported from the United States.

The EEC claimed that it had imposed the ban only because of public health concerns. The United States claimed that the ban was actually a trade restriction, pointing out that its own residents ate this kind of meat with confidence because a U.S. government agency had certified that the levels of hormones in the meat were far below any danger level. The United States retaliated against the EEC by imposing 100 percent tariffs on Danish and West German hams, Italian tomatoes, and certain other foods produced by EEC member nations. The EEC threatened to respond by placing 100 percent tariffs on $100 million worth of U.S. walnuts and dried fruits, but instead entered into bilateral meetings with the United States. Those meetings allowed untreated meats into the EEC for human consumption and treated meats that would be used as dog food. In response, the United States removed its retaliatory tariff on hams and tomato sauce, but retained its tariffs on many other goods. In 1992 talks were still continuing.

Which side is right in this dispute? The answer is far from obvious. As I said, trade restrictions are more complicated in reality than in textbooks.

Nationalistic Appeals   Finally nationalistic appeals can help to restrict international trade. "Buy American" campaigns and Japanese xenophobia[1] are examples. Many Americans, given two products of equal appeal except that one is made in the United States and one is made in a foreign country, would buy the U.S. product. To get around this tendency, foreign and U.S. companies often go to great lengths to get a MADE IN U.S.A. classification on goods they sell in the United States. For example, components for many autos are made in Japan but shipped to the United States and assembled in Ohio or Tennessee so that the finished car can be called an American product. Americans aren't the only nationalistic people on the international trade scene. Preference for Japanese goods is deeply ingrained in Japanese culture. Faced with U.S. demands that Japan reduce its trade surplus, and with threats of retaliation if it doesn't, the Japanese government has attempted to change its people's cultural bias and to encourage consumption of U.S. goods.

Reasons for Trade Restrictions

6

As you can see, there are many ways to restrict trade. But if trade makes sense, as it did in our example of I. T., why do countries restrict trade? Reasons for restricting trade include:

1. Unequal internal distribution of the gains from trade.
2. Haggling by companies over the gains from trade.
3. Haggling by countries over trade restrictions.
4. Specialized production: learning by doing and economies of scale.
5. Macroeconomic aspects of trade.
6. National security.
7. International politics.
8. Increased revenue brought in by tariffs.

I consider each of these obstacles to free trade in turn.

---

[1] *Xenophobia* is a Greek word meaning "fear of foreigners." Pronounce the *X* like *Z*.

Unequal Internal Distribution of the Gains from Trade   In the first example of trade discussed in this chapter, I. T. persuaded Saudi Arabia to specialize in the production of oil rather than of food, and persuaded the United States to produce more food than oil. That means, of course, that some U.S. oil workers will have to become farmers, and in Saudi Arabia some farmers will have to become oil producers. Often people don't want to make radical changes in the kind of work they do—they want to keep on producing what they're already producing. So when these people see the same kinds of goods that they produce coming into their country from abroad, they lobby to prevent the foreign competition. Often they're successful. A good example is the "voluntary" quotas placed on Japanese cars discussed earlier. These quotas saved U.S. jobs, but forced consumers to pay higher prices for cars. Economists have estimated that it cost consumers about $100,000 for each job saved.

The Costs of Change   Had I. T. been open about the difficulties of trading, he would have warned the countries that change is hard. It has very real costs that I. T. didn't point out when he made his offers. But these costs of change are relatively small compared to the gains from trade. Moreover they're short-run, temporary costs, whereas gains from trade are permanent, long-run gains. Once the adjustment has been made, the costs will be gone but the benefits will still be there.

For most goods the benefits for the large majority of the population so outweigh the small costs to some individuals that, decided on a strict cost/benefit basis, international trade is still a deal you can't refuse. With benefits so outweighing costs, it would seem that transition costs could be forgotten. But they can't.

Benefits of trade are generally widely scattered among the entire population. In contrast, costs of free trade often fall on specific small groups of people who loudly oppose the particular free trade that hurts them. Though the benefits of free trade to the country at large exceed the costs of free trade to the small group of individuals, the political push from the few (who are hurt) for trade restrictions exceeds the political push from the many (who are helped) for free trade. The result is trade restrictions on a variety of products. You'll likely see TV ads supporting such restrictions under the heading SAVING U.S. JOBS. But you'll see few ads in favor of free trade to keep prices low for consumers.

It isn't only in the United States that the push for trade restrictions focuses on the small costs and not on the large benefits. For example, the European Economic Community places large restrictions on food imports from nonmember nations. If the EEC would remove those barriers, food prices in EEC countries would decline significantly. For example, meat prices would probably fall by 65 percent. Consumers would benefit, but farmers would be hurt. The farmers, however, have the political clout to see that the costs are considered and the benefits aren't. The result: The EEC places high duties on foreign agricultural products.

Trade Adjustment Assistance   Trade restrictions make the international trader's life more difficult but they also open up new possibilities. To see these possibilities, let's go back to I. T. Too. She has died and her son, I. T. Too II, has frittered away the entire family fortune and now must rely on his wits. Like his ancestors, he has good insights. He analyzes the problem as follows:

> Trade will make most members of society better off, but will make a particular subgroup in society worse off. Because of the country's political dynamics, this subgroup can prevent free trade. If I structure a program so that it transfers some of society's gains to individuals who are made worse off by trade, I can eliminate their opposition and thereby make society better off.

Such programs are called **trade adjustment assistance programs.** Using this analysis, he presents the countries with the following deal:

Trade adjustment assistance programs Programs designed to compensate losers for reductions in trade restrictions.

Given that adjustment costs of trade are small, here's what I'll do. I'll pay the adjustment costs of those people who are hurt by the trade—costs I've calculated to be only 1/20 of the gains. I'll then have eliminated the opposition to free trade. For doing this, all I want for myself is 1/10 of the gains from trade, leaving 17/20 of the gains going to society. Now isn't this a deal you can't refuse?

Unfortunately for I. T. Too II, it's a deal more countries *can* refuse. Here's why.

Governments have tried to use trade adjustment assistance to facilitate free trade, but they've found that it's enormously difficult to limit the adjustment assistance to those who are actually hurt by international trade. As soon as people find that there's assistance for people injured by trade, they're likely to try to show that they too have been hurt and deserve assistance. Losses from free trade become exaggerated and magnified. Instead of only 1/20 of the gains from trade being needed for trade adjustment assistance, much more is demanded—often even more than the gains.

Telling people who claim to be hurt that they aren't really being hurt isn't good politics. That's why offering trade adjustment assistance as a way to relieve the pressure to restrict trade is a deal many governments can refuse. I. T. Too II must return home to go on public welfare and contemplate further the nature of international trade.

Haggling by Companies over the Gains from Trade   Many naturally advantageous bargains aren't consummated because each side is pushing for a larger share of the gains from trade than the other side thinks should be allotted. This is another example of the prisoner's dilemma.

To see how companies haggling over the gains of trade can cause restriction on trade, let's reconsider the original deal that I. T. proposed. I. T. got 380 tons of food and 420 barrels of oil. The United States got an additional 100 tons of food and 20 barrels of oil. Saudi Arabia got an additional 100 barrels of oil and 60 tons of food. Suppose the Saudis had said, "Why should we be getting only 100 barrels of oil and 60 tons of food when I. T. is getting 420 barrels of oil and 380 tons of food? We want an additional 300 tons of food and another 300 barrels of oil, and we won't deal unless we get them." Similarly the United States might have said "We want an additional 300 tons of food and an additional 300 barrels of oil, and we won't go through with the deal unless we get them." If either the U.S. or the Saudi Arabian company that was involved in the trade for their country (or both) takes this position, I. T. might just walk—no deal. The potential for gains from trade is there, but tough bargaining positions can make it almost impossible to achieve them.

Such bargaining problems occur often. The side that drives the hardest bargain gets the most gain from the bargain, but it also risks making the deal fall through. Such strategic bargaining goes on all the time. **Strategic bargaining** means demanding a larger share of the gains from trade than you can reasonably expect.[2] If you're successful, you get the lion's share; if you're not successful, the deal falls apart and everyone is worse off.

Strategic bargaining Demanding a larger share of the gains of trade than you can reasonably expect.

Haggling by Countries over Trade Restrictions   Another type of trade bargaining that often limits trade is bargaining between countries. Trade restrictions and the threat of trade restrictions play an important role in that kind of haggling. Sometimes countries must go through with trade restrictions that they really don't want to impose, just to make their threats credible.

Once one country has imposed trade restrictions, other countries attempt to get those restrictions reduced by threatening to increase their own restrictions.

---

[2] Here's an example: You're buying a house. You're willing to pay $80,000, but you'd prefer to pay less. The seller is asking $85,000, but you believe the seller will accept considerably less. So what do you offer? There's no one right strategy. If you offer $75,000 and refuse to go higher, you're using strategic bargaining.

Again, to make the threat credible, sometimes countries must impose or increase trade restrictions simply to show they're willing to do so.

Ultimately strategic bargaining power depends on negotiators' skills and the underlying gains from trade that a country would receive. A country that would receive only a small portion of the gains from trade is in a much stronger bargaining position than a country that would receive significant gains. It's easier for the former to walk away from trade.

The United States is currently using such strategic bargaining in its attempt to get Japan to lower its restrictions on imports of U.S. goods. The U.S. Congress often threatens to restrict imports from Japan significantly if Japan doesn't ease its trade restrictions against U.S. goods. Since Japan depends heavily on exports to the United States, she takes such threats seriously. For example, in the late 1980s Japan's prime minister went on TV and asked Japanese people to buy U.S. goods. Japan also changed some of its laws governing industrial organization to make selling goods in Japan easier for U.S. companies.

Specialized Production: Learning by Doing and Economies of Scale My discussion of absolute and comparative advantage took it as given that one country was more productive than another country in producing certain goods. But when one looks at trading patterns, it's often not at all clear why particular countries have a productive advantage in certain goods. There's no inherent reason for Switzerland to specialize in the production of watches or for South Korea to specialize in the production of cars. Much in trade cannot be explained by inherent resource endowments.

If they don't have inherent advantages, why are countries and places often so good at producing what they specialize in? Two important explanations are that they *learn by doing* and that *economies of scale* exist.

Learning by Doing **Learning by doing** means that you become better at a task the more often you perform it. Take watches in Switzerland. Initially production of watches in Switzerland may have been a coincidence; the person who started the watch business happened to live there. But then people in the area became skilled in producing watches. Their skill made it attractive for other watch companies to start up. As additional companies moved in, more and more members of the labor force became skilled at watchmaking, and word went out that Swiss watches were the best in the world. That reputation attracted even more producers so Switzerland became the watchmaking capital of the world. Had the initial watch production occurred in Austria, not Switzerland, Austria might be the watch capital of the world.

> **Learning by doing** You become better at a task the more often you perform it.

When there's learning by doing, it's much harder to assign comparative advantage to a country. One must always ask: Does country A truly have a comparative advantage, or does it simply have more experience? Once country B gets the experience, will country A's comparative advantage disappear? If it will, then country B has a strong reason to limit trade with country A in order to give its own workers time to catch up as they learn by doing.

Economies of Scale In determining whether an inherent comparative advantage exists, a second complication is **economies of scale.** There are economies of scale when costs per unit output go down as output increases. Many manufacturing industries (such as steel and autos) exhibit economies of scale. The existence of significant economies of scale means that it makes sense (i.e., it lowers costs) for one country to specialize in one good and another country to specialize in another good. But who should specialize in what is unclear. Producers in a country can, and generally do, argue that if only the government will establish barriers, they'll be able to lower their costs per unit and eventually sell at lower costs than foreign producers.

> **Economies of scale** Costs per unit output go down as output increases.

A number of countries follow trade strategies to allow them to take advantage of economies of scale. For example, in the 1970s and 1980s Japan's government consciously directed investment into automobiles and high tech consumer products and significantly promoted exports in these goods to take advantage of economies of scale.

Most countries recognize the importance of learning by doing and economies of scale. A variety of trade restrictions are based on these two phenomena. The most common expression of the learning-by-doing and economies-of-scale insights is the **infant industry argument,** which countries use to justify many trade restrictions. They argue, "You may now have a comparative advantage, but that's simply because you've been at it longer, or are experiencing significant economies of scale. We need trade restrictions on our _____ industry to give it a chance to catch up. Once an infant industry grows up, then we can talk about eliminating the restrictions."

Infant industry argument With initial protection an industry will be able to become competitive.

Macroeconomic Aspects of Trade   The comparative advantage argument for free trade assumes full employment. When countries don't have full employment, imports can decrease domestic aggregate demand and increase unemployment. Exports can stimulate aggregate domestic demand and decrease unemployment. Similarly imports can decrease domestic economic activity. Thus when an economy is in a recession, there is a strong macroeconomic reason to limit imports and encourage exports. These macroeconomic effects of free trade play an important role in the public's view of imports and exports. When a country is in a recession, pressure to impose trade restrictions increases substantially.

National Security   Countries often justify trade restrictions on grounds of national security. These restrictions take two forms:

1. Export restrictions on strategic materials and defense-related goods.
2. Import restrictions on defense-related goods. For example, in a war we don't want to be dependent on oil from abroad.

For a number of goods, national security considerations make sense. For example, the United States restricts the sale of certain military items to countries that are likely to be fighting the United States some day. The problem is where to draw the line about goods having a national security consideration. Should countries protect domestic agriculture? All high technology items, since they might be useful in weapons? All chemicals? Steel? The national security argument has been extended to a wide variety of goods whose importance to national security is indirect rather than direct. When a country makes a national security argument for trade, one must be careful to consider whether a domestic political reason may be lurking behind that argument.

International Politics   International politics frequently provides another reason for trade restrictions. The United States forbids trade with Cuba to punish that country for trying to extend its Marxist political and economic policies to other Latin American countries. Until 1991 the United States restricted exports to and imports from the Union of South Africa because it disapproved of South Africa's racist apartheid policies. U.S. grain exports to the Soviet Union were stopped in 1979 to protest the Soviet invasion of Afghanistan. The list can be extended, but you get the argument: Trade helps you, so we'll hurt you by stopping trade until you do what we want. So what if it hurts us too? It'll hurt you more than us.

Increased Revenue Brought in by Tariffs   A final argument made for one particular type of trade restriction—a tariff—is that tariffs bring in revenues. In the 19th century tariffs were the U.S. government's primary source of revenue. They've receded in importance as a revenue for developed countries because those countries have instituted other forms of taxes. However tariffs remain a primary source of revenue for many developing countries. They're relatively easy to collect and are paid by people rich enough to afford imports. These countries justify many of their tariffs with the argument that they need the revenues.

Each of the preceding arguments for trade restrictions has some validity, but most economists discount them and support free trade. The reason is that in their considered judgment the harm done by trade restrictions outweighs the benefits.

Economists' first argument for free trade is that, viewed from a global perspective, free trade increases total output. From a national perspective, economists agree that particular instances of trade restriction may actually help one nation, even as most other nations are hurt. But they argue that the country imposing trade restrictions can benefit *only if the other country doesn't retaliate* with trade restrictions of its own. Retaliation is the rule, not the exception, however, and when there is retaliation, trade restrictions cause both countries to lose.

A second reason most economists support free trade is that trade restrictions reduce international competition. International competition is desirable because it forces domestic companies to stay on their toes. If trade restrictions on imports are imposed, domestic companies don't work as hard, and they become less efficient. For example, in the 1950s and 1960s the United States imposed restrictions on imported steel. U.S. steel industries responded to this protection by raising their prices and channeling profits from their steel production into other activities. By the 1970s the U.S. steel industry was a mess, internationally uncompetitive, and using outdated equipment to produce overpriced steel. Instead of making the steel industry stronger, restrictions made it a flabby, uncompetitive industry.

Economists dispose of the infant industry argument by reference to the historical record. In theory the argument makes sense. But very few of the infant industries protected by trade restrictions have ever grown up. What tends to happen instead is that infant industries become dependent on the trade restrictions and use political pressure to keep that protection coming. As a result, they often remain immature and internationally uncompetitive forever. Most economists would support the infant industry argument only if the trade restrictions included definite conditions under which the restrictions would end.

Most economists agree with the national security argument for export restrictions on goods that are directly war related. Selling bombs to Iraq, with whom the United States was at war in early 1991, doesn't make much sense (although it should be noted that the United States did exactly that throughout the 1980s when the United States supported Iraq in its war with Iran). Economists point out that the argument is often carried far beyond goods directly related to national security. For example, in the 1980s the United States restricted exports of sugar-coated cereals to the Soviet Union for reasons of national security. Sugar-frosted flakes may be great, but they were unlikely to help the Soviet Union start a war. Another argument that economists give against the national security rationale is that trade restrictions on military sales can often be evaded. Countries simply have another country buy the goods for them. Such third-party sales—called *transshipments*—are common in international trade and limit the effectiveness of any absolute trade restrictions for national security purposes. Economists also argue that by fostering international cooperation, international trade makes war less likely—a significant contribution to national security.

Economists' final argument against trade restrictions is: Yes, some restrictions might benefit a country, but almost no country can limit its restrictions to the beneficial ones. Trade restrictions are addictive—the more you have, the more you want. Thus, a majority of economists take the position that the best response to such addictive policies is "just say no."

Why Economists Generally Oppose Trade Restrictions

E ven though most economists support free trade, they admit that in bargaining it may be necessary to adopt a strategic position. A country may threaten to impose trade restrictions if the other country does so. When such strategic trade policies are successful, they end up eliminating or reducing trade restrictions.

The problem with strategic trade policies is that they can backfire. One rule of strategic bargaining is that the other side must believe that you'll go through with your threat. Thus, strategic trade policy can lead a country that actually supports free trade to impose trade restrictions, just to show how strongly it believes in free trade. Even though most economists support free trade, they admit that in bargaining it may be necessary to adopt a strategic position. A country may threaten to impose trade restrictions if the other country does so. When such strategic trade policies are successful, they end up eliminating or reducing trade restrictions.

Free Trade Associations

Free trade association Group of countries that allows free trade among its members and puts up common barriers against all other countries' goods.

Most politicians feel a strong push from constituents to impose trade barriers. Even politicians who accept free trade in principle support restrictions in practice. They have, however, found it possible to support a limited type of free trade in which a few countries agree to have free trade with each other. A **free trade association** (or *customs union*) is a group of countries that allows free trade among its members and, as a group, puts up common barriers against all other countries' goods.

Common Markets The **European Economic Community** (Common Market) is the most famous free trade association. All barriers to trade among the EEC's 12 member countries were removed in 1992. During the 1990s more European countries, such as Sweden, can be expected to join the EEC. In 1988 the United States and Canada agreed to enter into a similar free trade union, and they, together with Mexico, are moving toward free trade in the 1990s.

Economists have mixed reactions to free trade associations. They see free trade as beneficial, but are concerned about the possibility that these customs unions will impose significant trade restrictions on nonmember countries. They also believe that bilateral negotiations between member nations will replace multilateral efforts among members and nonmembers. Whether the net effect of these bilateral negotiations is positive or negative remains to be seen.

GATT Devastating trade wars took place during the 1930s. As a result, international trade fell by over 75 percent. This decline contributed to the worldwide Great Depression. Following that experience, countries organized to try to promote free trade among themselves. The most visible result—the General Agreement on Tariffs and Trade (GATT) established in 1947—had as its central goal the elimination of tariffs.

GATT created a mechanism for the 96 subscribing countries to establish multilateral regulations for eliminating trade barriers. Member countries meet every five years to work toward this end. Initially GATT focused on tariffs on manufactured goods, but has increasingly included trade in services and agricultural goods as trade in these activities has expanded.

Most-favored nation Country that will pay as low a tariff on its exports as will any other country.

One of the goals of GATT was to equalize a country's trade barriers so that it did not discriminate against one specific country. The term **most-favored nation** refers to a country that will be charged as low a tariff on its exports as any other country. Thus, if the United States lowers tariffs on goods imported from Japan, which has most-favored nation status with the United States, it must lower tariffs on those same types of goods imported from any other country with most-favored nation status.

Trade negotiations are never easy. Here's the type of problem that continually occurs in trade negotiations: In the 1988 Round (as GATT meetings are called), a dispute arose over agricultural policy. The United States argued that the

ADDED DIMENSION

DUMPING

G ATT allows countries to impose trade restrictions on imports if they can show that the goods are being dumped. *Dumping* is selling a good in a foreign country at a lower price than in the country where it's produced. On the face of it, who could complain about someone who wants to sell you a good cheaply? Why not just take advantage of the bargain price? The first objection is the learning-by-doing argument. To stay competitive, a country must keep on producing. Dumping by another country can force domestic producers out of business. Having eliminated the competition, the foreign producer has the field to itself and can raise the price. Thus, dumping can be a form of predatory pricing.

The second argument against dumping involves the short-term macroeconomic and political effects it can have on the importing country. Even if one believes that dumping is not a preliminary to predatory pricing, it can displace workers in the importing country, causing political pressure on that government to institute trade restrictions. If that country's economy is in a recession, the resulting unemployment will have substantial macroeconomic repercussions, so pressure for trade restrictions will be amplified.

EEC's subsidies to farmers should be reduced, and that tariffs on farm exports from the United States to the EEC should be reduced or eliminated. When the EEC hesitated to go along with these proposals, there was a temporary breakdown of the talks which continued into 1992. Such breakdowns demonstrate the fragility of all free trade agreements. They can quickly be replaced by trade wars which hurt all countries.

International trade will become more and more important for the United States. With international transportation and communication becoming easier and faster, and with other countries' economies growing, the U.S. economy will inevitably become more interdependent with the other economies of the world. As international trade becomes more important, the push for trade restrictions will likely increase. Various countries' strategic trade policies will likely conflict, and the world will find itself on the verge of an international trade war which would benefit no one.

Concern about that possibility leads most economists to favor free trade. As often happens, economists advise politicians to follow a policy that is politically unpopular—to take the hard course of action. Whether politicians follow economists' advice or whether they follow the politically popular policy will play a key role in determining the course of the U.S. economy in the 1990s.

CONCLUSION

KEY POINTS

- The primary trading partners of the United States are Canada, Western Europe, and Japan. **1**
- According to the principle of absolute advantage, a country that can produce a good more cheaply than another country can is said to have an absolute advantage in the production of that good. When two countries have absolute advantages in different goods, there are gains from trade to be had. **2**
- According to the principle of comparative advantage, as long as the relative opportunity costs of producing goods (what must be given up in one good in order to get another good) differ among

countries, there are potential gains from trade, even if one country has an absolute advantage in everything. **3**
- Three insights into the terms of trade include:
  1. The more competition exists in international trade, the less the trader gets and the more the involved countries get.
  2. Once competition prevails, smaller countries tend to get a larger percentage of the gains from trade than do larger countries.
  3. Gains from trade go to countries that produce goods that exhibit economies of scale. **4**

· Trade restrictions include: tariffs, quotas, embargoes, voluntary restraint agreements, regulatory trade restrictions, and nationalistic appeals. ▮5
· Reasons that countries impose trade restrictions include: unequal internal distribution of the gains from trade; haggling by companies over the gains from trade; haggling by countries over trade restrictions; learning by doing and economies of scale; macroeconomic aspects of trade; national security; international political reasons; and increased revenue brought in by tariffs. ▮6
· Economists generally oppose trade restrictions because of their knowledge of history and their understanding of the advantages of free trade. ▮7

KEY TERMS

economies of scale *(739)*
embargo *(735)*
European Economic
 Community (EEC) *(742)*
free trade
 association *(742)*
General Agreement on
 Tariffs and Trade
 (GATT) *(734)*

infant industry
 argument *(740)*
learning by doing *(739)*
most-favored nation *(742)*
principle of absolute
 advantage *(728)*
principle of comparative
 advantage *(731)*

regulatory trade
 restrictions *(735)*
quota *(734)*
strategic bargaining *(738)*
tariff *(734)*

trade adjustment
 assistance
 programs *(737)*

QUESTIONS FOR THOUGHT AND REVIEW

The number after each question represents the estimated degree of critical thinking required. (1 = almost none; 10 = deep thought.)

1. With which countries does the United States trade most? *(2)*
2. Are these countries the ones you would expect the United States to trade with, based on the law of comparative advantage? Why? *(7)*
3. Textland can produce, at most, 40 olives, 20 pickles, or some combination of olives and pickles such as the 20 olives and 10 pickles it's currently producing. Happyland can produce, at most, 120 olives, 60 pickles, or some combination of olives and pickles such as the 100 olives and 10 pickles it's currently producing. Is there a basis for trade? If so, offer the two countries a deal they can't refuse. *(6)*
4. Would your answer to Question 3 differ if you knew that there were economies of scale in the production of pickles and olives rather than the production possibilities described in the question? Why? If your answer is yes, which country would you have produce which good? *(9)*
5. Widgetland has 60 workers. Each worker can produce 4 widgets or 4 wadgets. It's considering producing only widgets. Wadgetland also has 60 workers. Each can produce 3 widgets or 12 wadgets. Its residents consume wadgets but never buy widgets. Is there a basis for trade? If so, offer the countries a deal they can't refuse. *(7)*
6. Why do smaller countries usually get most of the gains from trade? What are some reasons why a small country might not get the gains of trade? *(6)*
7. Demonstrate diagrammatically how the effects of a tariff differ from the effects of a quota. *(6)*
8. If you were economic advisor to a country that was following your advice about trade restrictions and that country fell into a recession, would you change your advice? Why, or why not? *(7)*
9. The U.S. trade balance improved significantly in early 1991. What would you say is the primary reason for that improvement? *(6)*
10. Mexico exports many vegetables to the United States. These vegetables are grown using chemicals that are not allowed in U.S. vegetable agriculture. Should the United States restrict imports of Mexican vegetables? Why, or why not? *(7)*

PROBLEMS AND EXERCISES

1. Suppose that two countries, Machineland and Farmland, have the following production possibility curves:

 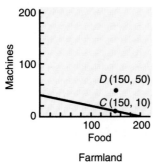

Machineland   Farmland

a. Explain how these two countries can move from points *A* and *C* where they currently are to points *B* and *D*.

b. If possible, state by how much *total production* for the two countries has risen.

c. If you were a trader, how much of the gains from trade would you deserve for discovering this trade?

d. If there were economies of scale in the production of both goods, how would your analysis change?

2. The world price of textiles is P_w as in the accompanying figure of the domestic supply and demand for textiles.

The government imposes a tariff, *t*, to protect domestic producers.

a. Shade in the gains to producers from this tariff.

b. Shade in the revenue to government.

c. Shade in the costs to producers.

d. Are the gains greater than the costs? Why?

36

International Finance

*A foreign exchange dealer's office
during a busy spell is the nearest thing to Bedlam I have struck.*
Harold Wincott

After reading this chapter, you should be able to:

1
Describe the balance of trade and the
balance of payments.

2
Explain why a country might have
simultaneously a balance of trade surplus
and a balance of payments deficit.

3
Discuss how real-world exchange rates
are set.

4
Explain why many developing countries
have nonconvertible currencies.

5
Differentiate fixed, floating, partially
floating, and nonconvertible exchange rates,
and discuss the advantages and
disadvantages of each.

6
Give a brief history of the gold standard.

As I have emphasized throughout the book, in the 1990s economic questions must be considered in an international setting. Earlier chapters introduced international financial issues such as exchange rates and the balance of payments. This chapter expands on those discussions and presents the central issues of international finance.

Let's first review two conclusions of our earlier analysis. In the short run:

Expansionary monetary policy pushes down the exchange rate and increases the trade deficit; contractionary monetary policy does the opposite.

Expansionary fiscal policy has an ambiguous effect on the exchange rate, but like expansionary monetary policy, it increases the trade deficit; contractionary fiscal policy does the opposite.

You should be able to work through the reasons expansionary monetary and fiscal policies have those effects. If not, you will benefit from a review of earlier chapters.

The best door into an in-depth discussion of international financial issues is a discussion of **balance of payments** (a country's record of all transactions between its residents and the residents of all foreign nations).[1] These include buying and selling of goods and services (imports and exports), interest and profit payments from previous investments, together with all the capital inflows and outflows. Exhibit 1 presents the 1987 and 1990 balance of payments account for the United States. It records all payments made by foreigners to U.S. citizens and all payments made by U.S. citizens to foreigners in those years.

In the balance of payments accounts, flows of payments into the United States have a plus sign. Goods the U.S. exports must be paid for in dollars, so they have a plus sign; they involve a flow of payments into the United States. Similarly U.S. imports must be paid for in foreign currency; they involve a flow of dollars out of the United States and thus, they have a minus sign. Notice that the bottom line of the balance of payments is $0. By definition the bottom line (which includes *all* supplies and demands for currencies, including those of the government) must add up to zero.

As you can see in Exhibit 1, the balance of payments account is broken down into the *current account,* the *capital account,* and the *official transactions account.* The **current account** (lines 1–13) is the part of the balance of payments account in which all short-term flows of payments are listed. It includes exports and imports, which are what one normally means when one talks about the trade balance. The **capital account** (lines 14–17) is the part of the balance of payments account in which all long-term flows of payments are listed. If one buys a German stock, or if a Japanese company buys a U.S. company, the transaction shows up on the capital account.

The government can influence the exchange rate by buying and selling currencies, or by buying and selling other international reserves, such as gold. Such buying and selling is recorded in the **official transactions account,** line 20 of Exhibit 1. To get a better idea of what's included in the three accounts, let's consider each of them more carefully.

At the top of Exhibit 1, the current account is composed of the merchandise (or goods) account (lines 2–5), the services account (lines 6–9), the net investment income account (line 10), and the net transfers account (lines 11 and 12).

THE BALANCE OF PAYMENTS

Balance of payments A country's record of all transactions between its residents and the residents of all foreign nations.

1

Current account The part of the balance of payments account that lists all short-term flows of payments.

Capital account The part of the balance of payments account that lists all long-term flows of payments.

Official transactions account The part of the balance of payments account that records the amount of dollars a nation buys.

The Current Account

---

[1] These records are not very good. Because of measurement difficulties many transactions go unrecorded and many numbers must be estimated, leaving a potential for large errors.

EXHIBIT 1   The Balance of Payments Account, 1987, 1992

		1987		1992	
1.	**Current account**				
2.	Merchandise				
3.	Exports	+251		+440	
4.	Imports	−410		−536	
5.	Balance of trade		−159		− 96
6.	Services				
7.	Exports	+ 93		+175	
8.	Imports	− 85		−120	
9.	Balance on services		+ 8		+ 55
10.	Net investment income	+ 11		+ 10	
11.	Net transfers	− 23		− 31	
12.	Invest. trans. balance		− 12		− 21
13.	**Balance on current account**		−163		− 62
14.	**Capital account**				
15.	Capital inflows	+230		+120	
16.	Capital outflows	− 72		− 45	
17.	**Balance on capital account**		+158		+ 75
18.	Current and capital balance		− 5		+ 13
19.	Statistical discrepancy		− 4		− 13
20.	**Official transactions account**		+ 9		0
21.	**Totals**		0		0

Source: *Economic Indicators*, April 1993 and *Federal Reserve Bulletin*, May 1993.

1

Balance of trade The difference between the amount of goods a nation exports and the amount of goods it imports.

Starting with the merchandise account, notice that in 1987 the United States imported $410 billion worth of goods and exported $251 billion worth of goods. The difference between the two is sometimes called the **balance of trade.** Looking at line 5, you can see that the United States had a balance of trade deficit of $159 billion in 1987 and $96 billion in 1992.

The trade balance is often discussed in the press as a summary of how the United States is doing in the international markets. It's not a good summary. Trade in services is just as important as trade in merchandise, so economists pay more attention to the combined balance on goods and services. Notice that in both 1987 and 1992 most of the U.S. trade deficit resulted from an imbalance in the merchandise account. The service account worked in the opposite direction. It was slightly positive in 1987; in 1992 the services account reduced the trade deficit by $55 billion. Such services include tourist expenditures and insurance payments by foreigners to U.S. firms. For instance, when you travel in Japan, you spend yen, which you must buy with dollars; this is an outflow of payments or a negative contribution to the services account.

There is no reason that the goods and services sent into a country must equal the goods and services sent out in a particular year, even if the current account is in equilibrium, because the current account also includes payments from past investments and net transfers. When you invest, you expect to make a return on that investment. The payments to foreign owners of U.S. capital assets is a negative contribution to the U.S. balance of payments. The payment to U.S. owners of foreign capital assets is a positive contribution to the U.S. balance of payments. These payments on investment income are a type of holdover from past trade and services imbalances.

The final component of the current account is net transfers, which include foreign aid, gifts, and other payments to individuals not exchanged for goods or services. If you send $100 to your aunt in Mexico, it shows up with a minus sign here.

Adding up the pluses and minuses on the current account, we arrive at line 13, the current account balance. Notice that in 1987 the United States ran a $163

Ragnar Frisch—Nobel prize, 1969, for work on statistical methods in economics. © The Nobel Foundation.

billion deficit on the current account and in 1992 the United States had a deficit of $62 billion (line 13). That means that in the current account the supply of dollars greatly exceeded the demand for dollars. If the current account represented the total supply of and demand for dollars, the value of the dollar would have fallen. But it doesn't. There are also the capital account, statistical discrepancies, and the official transactions account.

The capital account measures the flow of payments between countries for assets such as stocks, bonds, and real estate. As you can see in Exhibit 1, in 1987 there was a significant inflow of capital into the United States in excess of outflows of capital from the United States. Capital inflows (payments by foreigners for U.S. real and financial assets) were $158 billion more than capital outflows (payments by U.S. citizens for foreign assets). In 1992 there was a smaller inflow of $75 billion (line 17). To buy these U.S. assets foreigners needed dollars, so these net capital inflows represent a demand for dollars. This demand for dollars to buy capital goods went a long way toward balancing the excess supply of dollars on the current account. In 1987 they were $5 billion short, and in 1992 they were $13 billion in surplus. Actually in 1987 there was a larger $9 billion shortfall, and in 1992 there was a balance of the two accounts. The reason is significant statistical discrepancies, as we see in line 19. In 1987 there was a −$4 billion discrepancy and in 1992 there was −$13 billion discrepancy. These discrepancies arise because many international transactions, especially on the capital account, go unrecorded and hence must be estimated. With these discrepancies taken into account, in the absence of government policy there would have been downward pressure on the value of the dollar in 1987. Because of the importance of capital flows, when you think about what's likely to happen to a currency's value, it's important to remember both the demand for dollars to buy goods and services and the demand for dollars to buy assets.

The Capital Account

There is, of course, a difference between demand for dollars to buy currently produced goods and services and demand for dollars to buy assets. Assets earn profits or interest, so when foreigners buy U.S. assets, they earn income from those assets just for owning those assets. The net investment income from foreigners' previous asset purchases shows up on line 10 of the current account. It's the difference between the income U.S. citizens receive from their foreign assets and the income foreigners receive from their U.S. assets. If assets earned equal returns one would expect that when foreigners own more U.S. capital assets than U.S. citizens own foreign capital assets, net investment income should be negative. And when U.S. citizens own more foreign capital assets than foreigners own U.S. capital assets, net investment income should be positive. Why is this? Because net investment income is simply the difference between the returns on U.S. citizens' assets held abroad and foreign citizens' assets held in the United States.

2

In the 1980s the inflow of capital into the United States greatly exceeded the outflow of capital from the United States, and this trend has continued into the early 1990s. As a result the amount foreigners own in the United States now exceeds the amount U.S. citizens own abroad by well over $500 billion. So one would expect that U.S. investment income would be negative. But looking at Exhibit 1 we see that was not the case. The reason? Foreigners' returns have been low. For example, the Japanese bought a lot of real estate at very high prices and have been losing money on those investments. But one cannot expect this trend to continue. In the 1990s net investment income will likely become negative.

The current account and the capital account measure the private and non-U.S. government supply of and demand for dollars. The net amount of these two accounts is called the *balance of payments surplus* (if demand for a currency exceeds supply), or *deficit* (if supply of a currency exceeds demand). In 1987 the

The Official Transactions Account

private supply of dollars exceeded the private demand by $9 billion while in 1992 the private demand for dollars equalled the private supply of dollars. In 1987 the United States had a balance of payments deficit; in 1992, the United States was in equilibrium balance of payments.

A balance of payments deficit will put downward pressure on the value of a country's currency. If a country wants to prevent that from happening, it can buy its own currency. The third component of the balance of payments account, the official transactions account, records the amount of dollars that the United States bought. As you can see on line 20 of Exhibit 1, in 1987 the government entered into the foreign exchange market and bought $9 billion worth of U.S. dollars, using $9 billion of foreign reserves that it had. In 1992 it did not enter the market. When a government buys its own currency to hold up the currency's price, we say that the government has supported its currency. It's holding the exchange rate higher than it otherwise would have been. If it sells its currency, it's attempting to depress the value of the currency.[2]

Now let's return to the point made at the beginning of the chapter: As long as a currency is freely exchangeable for another currency, the three accounts (current, capital, and official transactions) must sum to zero. Why is this? Because that's what it means to be freely exchangeable. Whenever anybody wants, they can take their currency and trade it for another. The supply must equal the demand.

The concepts *balance of payments* and *surplus* or *deficit* refer to the balance of payments not counting a country's official reserve transactions. Thus, if a currency is freely exchangeable, any deficit in the balance of payments must be offset by an equal surplus in the official reserve transactions and any surplus must be offset by an equal deficit. This means that the supply of and demand for a freely exchangeable currency must sum to zero by definition.

EXCHANGE RATES

The balance of payments has two sides: the flow of goods or assets and the flow of money to pay for those goods. International finance is more complicated than domestic finance because international finance always involves two financial transactions: the exchange of a real good or asset for money and the exchange of money of one country for the money of another country. For international trade to take place, one must be able to exchange currencies. If either of these financial transactions is difficult or costly, trade is impeded.

Nonconvertible currency A currency that cannot be freely exchanged with currencies of other countries.

As I will discuss later, a number of countries' currencies cannot be freely exchanged today. These countries have what are called **nonconvertible currencies.** International trade is greatly impeded by that lack of free exchange. The former Soviet Union is an example of a country whose currency did not trade freely. In the 1980s as the Soviet Union attempted to expand its international trade, it looked for ways to make its currency (the ruble) convertible (exchangeable) into other currencies.

Thinking about the problem of trade with nonconvertible currencies gives one a deeper appreciation of the role of money in an economy. Money makes an economy operate efficiently—but only if everyone agrees to the monetary convention. You accept dollars because you know that someone else will accept dollars who in turn knows that someone else will accept dollars. Dollars have no inherent value, but they acquire value because our government declares that dollars are legal tender and that it will accept only dollars in payments of taxes, and because people believe that dollars have value. Hence dollars do have value.

In the international sphere there is no legally mandated monetary convention, so a foreign exchange market in which one currency can be exchanged for another must be set up. That foreign exchange market is a system of formal or informal

---

[2] Support for the dollar can also come from foreign central banks. In 1987 foreign central banks bought $45 billion and in 1990 bought $32 billion worth of dollars, thereby playing a big role in holding the value of the dollar higher than it otherwise would have been.

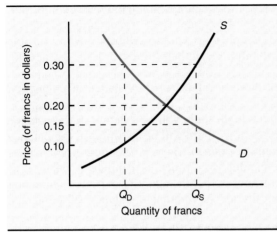

EXHIBIT 2   The Supply and Demand for Francs

As long as one keeps "quantities and prices of what" straight, the standard, or fundamental, analysis of the determination of exchange rates is easy. Exchange rates are determined by the supply and demand for a country's currency. Just remember that if you're talking about the supply and demand for francs, the price will be measured in dollars and the quantity will be in francs, as in this exhibit. If you're talking about the supply of and demand for dollars, the quantity will be in dollars, but the price of dollars will be measured in another currency. Otherwise the price of a dollar would be a dollar.

international monetary markets governed by a set of internationally agreed upon conventions. These conventions provide the framework within which international financial affairs are conducted.

Supply and demand are the two central forces of economics, and so it shouldn't be surprising that our initial discussion of the determination of exchange rates uses supply and demand curves.

At first glance, the analysis of foreign exchange rates seems simple: You have an upward-sloping supply curve and a downward-sloping demand curve. But what goes on the axes? Obviously price and quantity, but what price? And what quantity? Because you're talking about the relative prices of currencies—that's basically what exchange rates are—you have to specify which currencies you're using.

In Exhibit 2 I present the supply and demand for French francs in terms of dollar prices. Notice that the quantity of francs goes on the horizontal axis and the dollar price of francs goes on the vertical axis.

The first point to recognize is that when you are comparing the currencies of only two countries, the supply of one currency is equal to the demand for the other currency. To demand one currency, you must supply the other. In Exhibit 2 we are assuming that there are only two countries: the United States and France. This means that the supply of francs is the equivalent of a demand for dollars. The demand for dollars comes from the French who want to buy U.S. goods or assets. To do so, they supply francs to buy dollars. Let's consider an example showing why. Say a French person wants to buy an IBM computer made in the United States. She has francs, but IBM wants dollars. So, in order to buy the computer, she or IBM must somehow exchange francs for dollars. She is *supplying* francs and *demanding* dollars.

The supply curve of francs is upward sloping because the more dollars French citizens get for their francs, the cheaper U.S. goods and assets are for them. Say, for example, that the dollar price of one franc rises from 15¢ to 20¢. That means that the price of a dollar to a French person has fallen from 6.67 francs to 5 francs. For a French person, a good that cost $100 now falls in price from 667 francs to 500 francs. U.S. goods are cheaper, so the French buy more U.S. goods and more dollars, which means they supply more francs.

The demand for francs comes from Americans who want to buy French goods or assets. The demand curve is downward sloping because the lower the dollar price of francs, the more francs U.S. citizens want to buy, for the same reasons I just described.

Equilibrium is where the quantity supplied equals the quantity demanded. In my example, equilibrium occurs at a dollar price of 20¢ for one franc. If the price of francs is above or below 20¢, quantity supplied won't equal the quantity

Supply, Demand, and Fundamental Analysis of Exchange Rates

demanded and there will be pressure for the exchange rate to move to equilibrium. Say, for example, that the price is 30¢. The quantity of francs supplied will be greater than the quantity demanded. People who want to sell francs won't be able to sell them. To find buyers, they will offer to sell their francs for less. As they do, the price of francs falls.

The supply/demand framework directly relates to the balance of payments. When quantity supplied equals quantity demanded, the balance of payments is in equilibrium. If the exchange rate is too high, there will be a deficit in the balance of payments; if the exchange rate is too low, there will be a surplus in the balance of payments. Thus, in Exhibit 2 when the price of francs is 30¢, quantity of francs supplied exceeds the quantity demanded so France is running a balance of payments deficit. When the price of francs is 15¢, the quantity of francs demanded exceeds the quantity supplied, so France is running a balance of payments surplus.

Supply/Demand, Traders, and Exchange Rates   It would appear from Exhibit 2 that the determination of exchange rates is a relatively simple process: All one need do is determine the supply and demand curves and decide where equilibrium occurs. And in some ways, it is relatively easy. But in other ways it isn't; if it were as simple as determining supply and demand curves and equilibrium, the quotation at the head of this chapter about the bedlam in a foreign exchange dealer's office wouldn't have been appropriate and governments would not agonize over exchange rates as they do. There's more to the story of exchange rates than is told in those two curves.

The reason is that the curves in Exhibit 2 reflect long-run considerations; they reflect the effect of normal market forces on the supply and demand for currency. It was normal market forces that we used to justify the shapes of the curves. An analysis of curves based on normal market forces like that in the discussion of Exhibit 2 is often called **fundamental analysis** because the forces described there are the forces one arrives at by applying normal or fundamental economic analysis to the exchange rates. The normal market forces are the forces that will determine exchange rates in the long run—say in two, three, or four years.

Most movements in exchange rates that are discussed in the newspapers are influenced by these normal market forces, but are not driven by the normal economic forces. Thus, the short-run analysis of exchange rates (what will happen to the exchange rate in the next week, month, or year) is not directly based on fundamental analysis but upon a variety of effects that influence traders' decisions whether to buy, sell, or hold a currency. Those decisions depend much more on a variety of forces that cause *shifts in* the supply and demand curves for a country's currency than on forces governing the shapes of the supply and demand curves. (Technical reasons why this is the case appear in Appendix A.)

In the real world, shifts in the supply of and demand for currencies are extremely important, and the exchange rate fluctuations necessary to keep the balance of payments in equilibrium in the short run are large. As we will see, such large shifts in exchange rates cause problems and lead to attempts to reduce exchange rate fluctuations. But before we consider this problem, let's consider the forces that cause supply of and demand for currencies to shift.

Forces That Cause Shifts in the Supply of and Demand for Currencies   The major forces that can cause shifts include changes in a country's income, changes in a country's prices, changes in interest rates, and changes in expectations. Let's consider each in turn.

Changes in a Country's Income   The demand for imports depends on the income in a country. When a country's income falls, demand for imports falls. Hence demand for foreign currency to buy those imports falls, which means that the supply of the

Fundamental analysis Analysis of curves describing fundamental forces that will be operating in the long run.

■3

s you can see on the graph, the dollar's value has fluctuated considerably since 1967. A good exercise to see if you understand the dollar is to try to choose which factors caused the fluctuation.

Let's start with 1971. During that time the United States had relatively large inflation compared to other countries, so the value of the dollar fell. The sudden fluctuations in 1972 and 1973 probably reflected expectational bubbles—in which speculators were more concerned with short-run than long-run fundamentals—while the dollar's low value in 1979 and 1980 reflected high inflation, relatively low real interest rates, and the booming U.S. economy. The rise of the dollar in the early 1980s reflects higher interest rates and the falling U.S. inflation rate, although the rise was much more than expected and probably reflected speculation, as does the sudden fall in the dollar's value in 1985.

As you can see, after the fact we economists are pretty good at explaining the movements in the exchange rates.

Alas, before the fact we aren't so good because often speculative activities make the timing of the movements unpredictable.

country's currency to buy the foreign currency falls. That's why in our presentation of the Keynesian model we said that imports depend on income.

How important is this relationship? Very important. For example, in early 1991 the U.S. economy went into recession and as it did, the trade deficit was reduced and the supply of dollars was also reduced significantly. This decrease in the supply of dollars tended to push up the price of U.S. dollars relative to foreign currencies.

Changes in a Country's Prices The United States's demand for imports and foreign countries' demand for U.S. exports depend on prices of U.S. goods compared to prices of foreign competing goods. If the United States has more inflation than other countries, foreign goods will become cheaper, U.S. demand for foreign currencies will tend to increase, and foreign demand for dollars will tend to decrease. This rise in U.S. inflation will shift the dollar supply outward and the dollar demand inward.

Changes in Interest Rates People like to invest their savings in assets that will yield the highest return. A rise in U.S. interest rates relative to those abroad will increase demand for U.S. assets as long as that rise is a rise in the real interest rate—that is, as long as the rise isn't accompanied by a rise in inflation. As a result of a rise in the U.S. interest rate, demand for dollars will increase, while simultaneously the supply of dollars will decrease as fewer Americans sell their dollars to buy foreign assets. A fall in the U.S. interest rate or a rise in foreign interest rates will have the opposite effect.

Changes in Expectations If the value of a currency falls, the holders of that currency and of assets denominated in that currency lose; if the value of a currency rises, the holders of that currency and of assets denominated in that currency gain. So everyone tries to hold currencies whose value will rise and get rid of currencies whose value will fall. Thus, expectations of whether a currency will rise or fall can cause large shifts in the supply and demand. Expectations can even be self-fulfilling. For example, the expectation of a rise in the dollar's value will increase the demand for dollars and decrease the supply, which will cause a rise in the value of the dollar. The dollar rises because it is expected to rise.

Stability and Instability in Foreign Exchange Markets

Given that these large shifts in the supply and demand for currencies are constantly occurring, one might expect that there would be enormous shifts in exchange rates. But that doesn't often happen. Usually exchange rates are rather stable for two reasons. First, government enters into exchange markets to maintain stability. When people buy, the government sells; and when people sell, the government buys. Government action counters the shifts.

A second reason is that foreign exchange traders and speculators stabilize the rates. Traders know that eventually market forces will be strong and will lead to fundamental forces that will control the exchange rates, and they base their expectations on those fundamentals. Which of these two reasons is more important is debatable. Since that debate centers on whether private traders or government are better at stabilizing exchange rates, we need to look behind the supply and demand curves for currencies, at the traders who make the markets work.

Exchange Rate Markets, Traders, and the Spread   International currency traders are interested in making money. They buy and sell currencies. If they buy low and sell high, they make a profit. If they buy high and sell low, they lose money. The currency trader is constantly on the phone offering to buy a currency at one rate and to sell it at another rate.

Spread The difference between the price at which traders buy and sell a currency.

The **spread** is the difference between the price at which they buy a currency and the price at which they sell it. To see how the spread works, let's consider a trader of francs and dollars. She might post the following rates:

Today's Rates

Sell: $1 . . . . 4.5 francs
Buy: $1 . . . . 4.4 francs
Sell: 1 franc . . . . 23¢
Buy: 1 franc . . . . 22¢

The spread is 1¢ for every franc traded and 10 centimes (100 centimes equals one franc) for every dollar traded. The greater the spread, the greater the profit per transaction but the smaller the number of transactions that are likely to go through that trader. Traders get known as aggressive or nonaggressive. Aggressive traders have the smallest spread. They buy high and sell cheap, relying on volume for their profit.

How does an international currency trader choose what rates she will set? The answer is that she must choose a rate that brings her about the same amount of dollars that other people want to buy. That is, she must choose a rate for which the quantity of dollars supplied roughly equals the quantity of dollars demanded.

Thus, after a trader sets her rates, she will see how many dollars her advertised rates are bringing in, and how many dollars are going out. If fewer dollars are coming in than going out, she'll raise the price of dollars in terms of French francs. Instead of 4.5 francs to the dollar, she'll make it 4.6 francs to the dollar. Dollars become more expensive in terms of francs; francs become cheaper in terms of dollars. International traders hope that if everything goes right, that change will bring the two currencies into equilibrium. Traders set exchange rates to equate supply and demand for dollars.

The Short-Run Determination of Exchange Rates   Most currency traders will have taken an introductory economics course, so they'll look at the factors that cause shifts in supply and demand and think about the general long-run direction of exchange rates. As stated before, they call the analysis of the long-run determinants of

ADDED DIMENSION

ARBITRAGE

■ nternational currency traders often deal in a variety of currencies, and when they do they must be continually on the lookout for discrepancies among the exchange rates for various countries. For example, let's say a trader opens an office with several windows and sets up the following exchange rates:

Window 1: $1 = 4.5 francs or 1 franc = 22.5¢
Window 2: $1 = 707.9 won or 1 won = 0.14¢
Window 3: 1 won = 0.005 francs or 1 franc = 200 won.

Enter Mr. Arbitrage, who's always keeping his eye on international currency traders. Mr. Arbitrage goes up to window 1 and says, "I'll buy $1,000 worth of French francs." He receives 4,500 francs. He then goes to window 3 and says, "I'd like to buy Korean won for these 4,500 French francs, please." Handing over 4,500 francs, he receives 900,000 won. He then goes to window 2 and says, "I'd like to exchange these 900,000 won for dollars, please." He hands over 900,000 won, for which he receives $1,260. Next he takes the $1,260 back to window 1 and says, "I'd like to buy French francs, please." At this point the currency trader should know that she's goofed: In setting the exchange rates she has forgotten the principle of arbitrage. *Arbitrage* is the buying of a good in one market at a low price and selling that good in another market at a higher price. It limits the exchange rates a currency trader can set in various markets and still make a profit. Specifically the roundabout exchange rates must be identical to the direct exchange rates. Recognizing this, she changes the exchange rate between won and francs so that 1 won = 0.0063 francs and no arbitrage profits are to be made.

Our little story and example make it look as if arbitrage is simple. But remember, there are hundreds of currencies and with even as few as 50 currencies there are many thousands of possible roundabout exchange rates. The table shows some of them.

Key Currency Cross Rates Late New York Trading Mar. 11, 1992									
	Dollar	Pound	Swiss franc	Guilder	Yen	Lira	German mark	French franc	Canadian dollar
Canada	1.1958	2.0645	.79350	.63940	.00896	.00096	.71928	.21181	....
France	5.6455	9.747	3.7462	3.0187	.04232	.00453	3.3958	....	4.7211
Germany	1.6625	2.8703	1.1032	.88894	.01246	.00133	....	.29448	1.3903
Italy	1245.8	2150.8	826.64	666.11	9.338	....	749.32	220.66	1041.8
Japan	133.40	230.32	88.520	71.329	....	.10708	80.241	23.629	111.56
Netherlands	1.8702	3.2289	1.2410	....	.01402	.00150	1.1249	.33127	1.5640
Switzerland	1.5070	2.6018	....	.80580	.01130	.00121	.90647	.26694	1.2602
U.K.	.57921	....	.38434	.30970	.00434	.00046	.34839	.10260	.48437
U.S.	....	1.7265	.66357	.53470	.00750	.00080	.60150	.17713	.83626

Real-world arbitragers have computers that constantly monitor these exchange rates. If they find a difference, they buy and sell quickly, keeping the people who set exchange rates on their toes to set all exchange rates so that arbitragers can't make money by arbitraging markets.

Foreign exchange markets have become sophisticated and the spread is small. Computers programmed to spot any potential for arbitrage monitor exchange rates and keep exchange rates among currencies in line so that roundabout trading does not bring about long-term profits for arbitragers. Arbitragers, like others in a competitive market, cover their costs (which include normal profits) but don't make so much profit that they attract others into the business.

exchange rates *fundamental analysis*. But traders recognize that in the very short run the quantities of currencies supplied and demanded aren't significantly influenced by exchange rates, but are significantly influenced by expectations. They expect that supply and demand for currencies will shift enormously, which means the equilibrium price will fluctuate widely. Traders' time horizon is the very short run (minutes, hours, or days). Thus, you'll seldom hear currency traders talking about fundamentals of exchange rate determination. They're far more concerned with the short-run factors that shift demand, especially expectations.

Currency traders are active in markets for most of the major currencies. The spreads are extremely narrow. The traders are constantly buying or selling—listening for trade figures, rumors on the street, and interest rate policy changes by government. They don't limit themselves to buying and selling for customers. They can buy for their own accounts, speculating on whether a currency is about to go up or down. Often a trader has millions of dollars riding on whether a currency will go up or down a single percentage point.

Traders see only a small part of a currency's supply and demand—the part that flows through their offices as they buy and sell. Given their very limited observations, they have to guess what's going on. They're making judgments not about shifts in demand, but about their belief about other traders' beliefs about . . . . Rumors can, and do, drive international currency markets wild.

Predicting how much of a foreign currency all the people in a country will want in the short run is a complicated task. If a currency trader predicts wrong, she gets stuck with some currencies that nobody wants. When the spread is wide, she can afford a few losses, but when the bid/ask spread is narrow, she must predict very carefully and must try to make sure that she chooses a rate for which the supply of and demand for various currencies flowing through her office are equal.

Government's Role in Determining Exchange Rates

So far I haven't discussed government's role in exchange rate determination. Where does government policy come in?

Every country has goals for its international exchange rate and trade balance, and uses monetary and fiscal policies to achieve those goals. Through these policies governments can influence income and, hence, the current account and interest rates and, hence, the capital account. This means that through monetary and fiscal policies government can indirectly affect a country's balance of payments and, hence, exchange rates.

In addition to monetary and fiscal policies, countries can use other economic policies to influence the exchange rate. A government might simply pass a law flatly specifying what the exchange rate will be. Alternatively a government can

LIMITS ON TRADERS' SPECULATION

When many U.S. banks first got seriously involved in international currency markets in the 1970s, traders had relatively loose limits on the speculative positions they could take. A *speculative position* is the net amount of a currency a trader holds from buying or selling currency for his or her own account in the hope that its value will rise or fall. Speculative positions can be either long or short. Holding a currency in the hope that its price will rise is a *long position;* selling a currency you don't have but will buy when you must supply it, in the hope that its price will have fallen, is a *short position.* Some traders lost millions of dollars for their banks in a short time. In the famous case of Franklin National Bank, the losses in trading currencies brought the bank under—that is, it went bankrupt and had to be bailed out by the Federal Deposit Insurance Corporation.

In response to such problems, most banks instituted stringent controls over the positions that traders could take.

Most traders weren't allowed to have unauthorized positions at the end of each trading day.

Who are these foreign exchange traders? Usually they're not Ph.D. economists or even MBAs; such people often don't have the guts or personality to be traders. Instead traders are often people who are directly out of high school or college, people who have been discovered to have an ability to make split-second correct decisions (to buy or sell); who have few regrets ("If only I'd . . ."); and who want to earn about $60,000 a year to start. They're a bungee-type group. (Bungee is a sport in which you tie one end of an elastic rope to a rock or a tree and the other end to your feet and dive off a cliff, hoping the rope will stop you right before you hit the ground. If you're successful, you yo-yo up and down for two or three minutes). Bungee is a trader's hobby. I prefer gardening.

---

directly affect its currency's exchange rate by means of capital control policies and exchange rate policies. Still another possibility is for it to use trade policies, such as quotas and tariffs, to influence the trade balance. I discussed trade policies in the last chapter. In this chapter I consider setting exchange rates by legal mandate, exchange rate policies, and capital control policies.

Exchange Rates Set by Law: Nonconvertible Currency and Capital Controls   A government can simply pass a law outlawing international currency trading and prohibiting the buying and selling of foreign currencies except at a rate determined by the government. Many developing countries set their exchange rates in this manner. When governments do so, they make international trade difficult, because their currencies can't be freely exchanged with other currencies—that is, their currencies are *nonconvertible*.

Nonconvertible currencies' exchange rates don't fluctuate in response to shifts in supply and demand. Often the only legal way to deal in such currency is to buy it from the government and sell to the government. It is illegal to trade nonconvertible currencies privately or even to carry large amounts of nonconvertible currency out of the country. Such prohibitions against currency flowing freely into and out of a country are called **capital controls.** If one country's currency can't be exchanged for another's at anything reflecting a market price, it's very difficult to buy each other's goods.

> **Capital controls** A government's prohibitions on its currency freely flowing into and out of the country.

If nonconvertible currencies make trade so difficult, why do countries use them? The answer is: to avoid making the economic adjustments that international considerations would otherwise force upon them. Say that a country is running a large balance of payments deficit and the value of its currency is falling. This fall is pushing up the price of imports, causing inflation, and making its assets cheaper for foreigners.

Foreigners can come in and buy up the country's assets at low prices. The country can avoid this political problem simply by passing a law that fixes the exchange rate at a certain level. This action indirectly limits imports, since most foreign firms won't sell their goods at the official exchange rate. They don't want the country's currency at the official exchange rate. It also limits exports since the price of a country's exports is held high. The government can and often does give favored firms special dispensation to import or export. Thus, having a nonconvertible currency enables the government to control what can and can't be imported and exported. Generally when there's a nonconvertible currency, there is a large incentive for people to trade currencies illegally in a black market.

Exchange rate policy Government policy of buying and selling a currency to affect its price.

Exchange Rate Policy and Government Intervention in the Currency Market   Even if a government doesn't establish a nonconvertible currency, it can still directly affect the exchange rate. The government can buy and sell currencies, just like an individual trader. If it buys or sells enough of a particular currency, it can affect that currency's relative price (its exchange rate). So an **exchange rate policy** is a policy in which the government buys and sells a currency in order to affect its price.

Say the Federal Reserve wants to raise the value of the U.S. dollar. If it buys lots of dollars (paying for them with other currencies), it will increase the demand for dollars, which will push the price of dollars up. If it wants to lower the price of dollars (in terms of other currencies), it can sell dollars and buy other currencies.

Think back to the U.S. balance of payments as summarized in Exhibit 1. When the United States bought $9 billion worth of dollars in 1987, paying for them from its reserves, it was using exchange rate policy to support the value of the dollar.

Since the United States can create all the dollars it wants, it's easier for the United States to push the value of its currency down by selling dollars than to hold it up. In contrast, it's easier for another country (say, Japan) to push the value of the dollar up (by pushing the value of the yen down). Thus, if the two countries can decide which way they want their exchange rates to move, they have a large incentive to cooperate. Of course, cooperation requires an agreement on the goals. One role of the various international economic organizations discussed in Chapter 5 is to provide a forum for reaching agreement on exchange rate goals and a vehicle through which cooperation can take place.

The Effect of Exchange Rates on the Balance of Goods and Services and Balance of Payments   A government's exchange rate goal can be an end in itself, or it can be a means to an end. A decrease in a country's exchange rate—that is, a decline in its currency's value relative to that of another country's currency—pushes the price of imports up and the price of exports down. Thus, it tends to decrease the *quantity* of imports coming into a country and to increase the *quantity* of exports going out of a country. It also makes a country's assets cheaper to foreigners. These changes in quantity *eventually* improve the balance of trade and hence the balance of payments.

I emphasize the words *eventually* and *quantity* to highlight a paradox that often occurs when exchange rates change. Often initially a fall in the exchange rate doesn't decrease the balance of trade deficit and the balance of payments deficit; it increases them. This phenomenon has occurred so often that it has acquired a name, the **J-curve.** I'll explain why it's called that in a moment.

J-curve Curve describing the rise and fall in the balance of trade deficit following a fall in the exchange rate.

Why do deficit increases initially occur when a country's exchange rate falls? To answer that question, remember that a country's imports and exports are determined by two variables: price multiplied by quantity. When a country's exchange rate falls, the *quantity* of imports tends to decrease and the *quantity* of exports tends to rise but the *price* of imports tends to rise and the *price* of exports tends to fall. In the short run these price effects tend to predominate over the quantity effects, so the balance of payments and balance of trade deficits get larger. Eventually, however, the quantity effects tend to predominate over the price effects, so the balance of trade and balance of payments deficits get smaller.

If one were graphing what happens to the balance of trade and balance of payments after an exchange rate falls, the graph would look something like Exhibit 3.[3] The fall in the exchange rate occurs at time T_0, and initially the balance

---

[3] The relationship between the J-curve and the short-run supply of and demand for a currency is presented in Appendix A.

EXHIBIT 3   The J-Curve

Generally, a depreciation of the currency does not initially improve the balance of trade deficit; it makes it worse. Eventually it starts to get better, and eventually, eventually, a depreciation will eliminate a trade deficit. Tracing out the time path of the balance of trade gives one a curve that looks like a J.

of trade and hence the balance of payments worsen. The balance of trade keeps worsening until time T_1, whereupon it starts to improve. At time T_2, it's back where it was to begin with, and thereafter it substantially improves. The curve looks like a "J"—hence the name *the J-curve*.

Let's go through a numerical example to place the J-curve concept into your deep memory. Say that at an exchange rate of 2.5/1 (2.5 German marks to $1.00), the United States is importing 40 Mercedes at $50,000 (125,000 German marks) each, and is exporting to Germany 200,000 videos at $9 (22.5 German marks) each. Imports are $2,000,000 (40 × $50,000) and exports are $1,800,000 (9 × $200,000). The United States thus has a $200,000 trade deficit with Germany. Now say that the value of the dollar falls to 2.27/1 and the price of Mercedes to U.S. citizens goes to $55,000. In response the quantity imported falls to 39. The price of videos falls to $8.20 and the quantity exported rises to 210,000. Let's now calculate the trade balance:

$$\text{Imports } (\$55,000 \times 39) = \$2,145,000$$
$$\text{Exports } (\$8.20 \times 210,000) = \underline{\$1,722,000}$$
$$\text{Trade deficit} \qquad \$ \ \ 423,000$$

In response to a *fall* in the relative value of the dollar, the trade deficit has increased from $200,000 to $423,000.

This result was dependent on the numbers I chose. Experience suggests that eventually the quantity effect is much larger than this example indicates, and a fall in the value of a currency improves a country's trade balance, but that *eventually* can be as long as five to seven years. This possibility presents policymakers with a serious long-run/short-run dilemma in using exchange rate policy to achieve government's balance of trade and payments goals. Escaping that dilemma is one reason that many developing countries use nonconvertible currencies. Politically, often they can't afford to make their balance of payments deficit larger in the short run in order to achieve a long-run improvement.

The J-curve phenomenon—which suggests that normal market forces don't operate to keep the exchange rate in short-run equilibrium—is the reason that in our earlier discussion we separated the short-run determination of the exchange rate from the long-run determination of exchange rates. Fundamental analysis only works in the long run. In the short run, normal market forces don't determine exchange rates.

Understanding the limited, and possibly even perverse, short-run effect of normal market forces on achieving equilibrium is important to understanding why most governments don't leave determination of the exchange rate to the market, but instead play varying roles in its determination. We now turn to a consideration of three alternative exchange rate regimes and how they affect short-run determination of exchange rates.

FLEXIBLE, PARTIALLY FLEXIBLE, AND FIXED EXCHANGE RATES

5

Flexible exchange rate Determination of exchange rates is left totally up to the market.

Partially flexible exchange rate The government sometimes affects the exchange rate and sometimes leaves it to the market.

Fixed exchange rate The government chooses an exchange rate and offers to buy and sell currencies at that rate.

When governments do not enter into foreign exchange markets at all, but leave the determination of exchange rates totally up to currency traders, the country is said to have a **flexible exchange rate.** The price of its currency is allowed to rise and fall as market forces dictate. When governments sometimes buy or sell currencies to influence the exchange rate, while at other times they let private market forces operate, the country is said to have a **partially flexible exchange rate.** A partially flexible exchange rate is sometimes called a *dirty float* because it isn't purely market determined or government determined.

If the government chooses a particular exchange rate and offers to buy and sell currencies at that price, it is imposing a **fixed exchange rate.** For example, suppose the U.S. government says it will buy francs at 20¢ and sell dollars at 5 francs. In that case we say that the country has a fixed exchange rate of 5 francs to the dollar.

Notice that in principle any trader could establish a fixed exchange rate by guaranteeing to buy or sell a currency at a given rate. Any "fix," however, is only as good as the guarantee, and to fix an exchange rate the trader would require many more resources than she has; only governments have sufficient resources to fix an exchange rate, and often even governments run out of resources. To maintain a fix they must borrow other currencies to prevent the price of their currency from falling.

History of Exchange Rate Systems

A good way to give you an idea of how the various systems work is to present a brief history of international exchange rate systems.

6

Gold standard System by which the value of a country's currency is fixed in relation to the price of gold.

The Gold Standard: A Fixed Exchange Rate System Governments played a major role in determining exchange rates until the 1930s. Beginning with the Paris Conference of 1867 and lasting until 1933 (except for the period around World War I), most of the world economies had a system of relatively fixed exchange rates under what was called a **gold standard.** Under a gold standard, the amount of money a country issued had to be directly tied to gold, either because gold coin served as the currency in a country (as it did in the United States before 1914) or because countries were required by law to have a certain percentage of gold backing their currencies. Gold served as currency or backed all currencies. Each country participating in a gold standard agreed to fix the price of its currency relative to gold. That meant a country would agree to pay a specified amount of gold upon demand to anyone who wanted to exchange that country's currency for gold. To do so, each country had to maintain a stockpile of gold. When a country fixed the price of its currency relative to gold, it fixed its currency's price in relation to other currencies, as a result of the process of arbitrage.

Under the gold standard, a country made up a difference between the quantity supplied and the quantity demanded of its currency by buying or selling gold to hold the price of its currency fixed in terms of gold. How much a country would need to buy and sell depended upon its balance of payments deficit or surplus. If the country ran a surplus in the balance of payments, it was required to sell its currency—that is, buy gold—to stop the value of its currency from rising. If a country ran a deficit in the balance of payments, it was required to buy its currency—that is, sell gold—to stop the value of its currency from falling.

The gold standard enabled governments to prevent short-run instability of the exchange rate. If there was a speculative run on its currency, the government would buy its currency with gold, thereby preventing the exchange rate from falling.

Gold specie flow mechanism Long-run adjustment mechanism under the gold standard in which gold flows and price level changes bring about equilibrium.

But for the gold standard to work, there had to be a method of long-run adjustment; otherwise countries would run out of gold and would no longer be able to fulfill their obligations under the gold standard. That long-run adjustment mechanism was called the **gold specie flow mechanism.** Here's how it worked: Since gold served as reserves to a country's currency, a balance of payments *deficit* (and hence a downward pressure on the exchange rate) would result in a flow of gold out of the country and hence a decrease in the country's money supply. That decrease in the money supply would contract the economy, decreasing imports, lowering the country's price level, and increasing the interest rate, all of which would work toward eliminating the balance of payments deficit.

Similarly a country with a balance of payments *surplus* would experience an inflow of gold. That flow would increase the country's money supply, increasing income (and hence imports), the price level (making imports cheaper and exports more expensive), and lowering the interest rate (increasing capital outflows). These would work toward eliminating the balance of payments surplus.

Thus, the gold standard determined a country's monetary policy and forced it to adjust any international balance of payments disequilibrium. Adjustments to a balance of payments deficit were often politically unpopular; they led to recessions, which, because the money supply was directly tied to gold, the government couldn't try to offset with expansionary monetary policy.

The gold adjustment mechanism was called into play in the United States when the Federal Reserve in late 1931, in response to a shrinking U.S. gold supply, decreased the amount of money in the U.S. economy, deepening the depression that had begun in 1929. The government's domestic goals and responsibilities conflicted with its international goals and responsibilities. That conflict led to partial abandonment of the gold standard in 1933. At that time the United States made it illegal for individual U.S. citizens to own gold. Except for gold used for ornamental and certain medical and industrial purposes, all privately owned gold had to be sold to the government. Dollar bills were no longer backed by gold in the sense that U.S. citizens could exchange dollars for a prespecified amount of gold. Instead dollar bills were backed by silver, which meant that any U.S. citizen could change dollars for a prespecified amount of silver. In the late 1960s that changed also. Since that time, for U.S. residents, dollars have been backed only by trust in the soundness of the U.S. economy.

Gold continued to serve, at least partially, as international backing for U.S. currency. That is, other countries could still exchange dollars for gold. However in 1971, in response to another conflict between international and domestic goals, the United States totally cut off the relationship between dollars and gold. After that a dollar could be redeemed only for another dollar, whether it was a U.S. citizen or a foreign government who wanted to redeem the dollar.

The Bretton Woods System: A Fixed Exchange Rate System   As World War II was coming to an end, the United States and its allies met to establish a new international economic order. After much wrangling they agreed upon a system called the **Bretton Woods system,** named after the resort in New Hampshire where the meeting was held.

Bretton Woods system An agreement which governed international financial relationships from the period after World War II until 1971.

The Bretton Woods system established the International Monetary Fund (IMF) to oversee the international economic order. The IMF was empowered to arrange short-term loans between countries. The Bretton Woods system also established the World Bank, which was empowered to make longer-term loans to developing countries. Today the World Bank and IMF continue their central roles in international financial affairs.

The Bretton Woods system was based upon mutual agreements about what countries would do when experiencing balance of payments surpluses or deficits. It was essentially a fixed exchange rate system. For example, under the Bretton Woods system the exchange rate of the dollar for the British pound was set at a bit over $4 to the pound.

The Bretton Woods system was not based on a gold standard. When countries experienced a balance of payments surplus or deficit, they did not necessarily buy or sell gold to stabilize the price of their currency. Instead they bought and sold other currencies. To ensure that participating countries would have sufficient reserves, they established a stabilization fund from which a country could obtain a short-term loan. It was hoped that this stabilization fund would be sufficient to handle all short-run adjustments that did not reflect fundamental imbalances.

In those cases where a misalignment of exchange rates was determined to be fundamental, the countries involved agreed that they would adjust their exchange rates. The IMF was empowered to oversee an orderly adjustment. It could authorize a country to make a one-time adjustment of up to 10 percent without getting formal approval from the IMF Board of Directors. After a country had used its one-time adjustment, formal approval was necessary for any change greater than 1 percent.

The Bretton Woods system reflected the underlying political and economic realities of the post–World War II period in which it was set up. European economies were devastated; the U.S. economy was strong. To rebuild, Europe was going to have to import U.S. equipment and borrow large amounts from the United States. There was serious concern over how high the value of the dollar would rise and how low the value of European currencies would fall in a free market exchange. The establishment of fixed exchange rates set limits on currencies' relative movements; the exchange rates that were chosen helped provide for the rebuilding of Europe.

In addition the Bretton Woods system provided mechanisms for long-term loans from the United States to Europe that could help sustain those fixed exchange rates. The loans also eliminated the possibility of competitive depreciation of currencies, in which each country tries to stimulate its exports by lowering the relative value of its currency.

Special Drawing Rights (SDRs) IOUs of the IMF.

One difficulty with the Bretton Woods system was a shortage of reserves and international liquidity. To offset that shortage, the IMF was empowered to create a type of international money called **Special Drawing Rights (SDRs).** But SDRs never became established as an international currency and the U.S. dollar soon began serving as a **reserve currency** (a currency in which countries hold their liquid financial assets) for individuals and countries. To get the dollars to foreigners, the United States had to run a deficit in the current account. Since countries could exchange the dollar for gold at a fixed price, the use of dollars as a reserve currency meant that under the Bretton Woods system the world was on a gold standard once removed.

Reserve currency A currency in which countries hold reserves.

The number of dollars held by foreigners grew enormously in the 1960s. By the early 1970s those dollars far exceeded in value the amount of gold the United States had. Most countries accepted this situation; even though they could legally demand gold for their dollars, they did not. But Charles de Gaulle, the nationalistic president of France, wasn't pleased with the U.S. domination of international affairs at that time. He believed France deserved a much more prominent position. He demanded gold for the dollars held by the French central bank, knowing that the United States didn't have enough gold to meet his demand. As a result of his demands, on August 15, 1971, the United States ended its policy of exchanging gold for dollars at $35 per ounce. With that change the Bretton Woods system was dead.

The Present System: A Partially Flexible Exchange Rate System

International monetary affairs were much in the news in the early 1970s as countries groped for a new exchange rate system. The makeshift system finally agreed upon involved partially flexible exchange rates. Most Western countries' exchange rates are allowed to fluctuate, although at various times governments buy or sell their own currencies to affect the exchange rate.

Under the present partially flexible exchange rate system, countries must continually decide when a balance of payments surplus or deficit is a temporary phenomenon and when it is a signal of a fundamental imbalance. If they believe the situation is temporary, they enter into the foreign exchange market to hold their exchange rate at what they believe is an appropriate level. If however they believe that the balance of payments imbalance is a fundamental one, they let the exchange rate rise or fall.

While most Western countries' exchange rates are partially flexible, certain countries have agreed to fixed exchange rates of their currencies in relation to rates of a group of certain other currencies. For example, European Common Market countries maintain almost fixed exchange rates among their currencies, although this group of EEC currencies can float relative to other currencies. (They allow their currencies' values to fluctuate, but only within a narrow range.) Other currencies are fixed relative to the dollar.

Deciding what is, and what is not, a fundamental imbalance is complicated, and such decisions are considered at numerous international conferences held under the auspices of the IMF or governments. A number of organizations such as G-5 (Group of Five) and G-7 (Group of Seven), which were introduced in Chapter 5, focus much of their discussion on this issue. Often the various countries meet and agree, formally or informally, on acceptable ranges of exchange rates. Thus, while the present system is one of partially flexible exchange rates, the range of flexibility is limited.

Now that I've summarized the history of exchange rate systems, let's consider the advantages and disadvantages of each of the three exchange rate systems.

Advantages and Disadvantages of Alternative Exchange Rate Systems

5

Fixed Exchange Rates   The advantages of a fixed exchange rate system are:

1. Fixed exchange rates provide international monetary stability.
2. Fixed exchange rates force governments to make adjustments to meet their international problems.

The disadvantages of a fixed exchange rate system are:

1. Fixed exchange rates can become unfixed. When they're expected to become unfixed, they create enormous monetary instability.
2. Fixed exchange rates force governments to make adjustments to meet their international problems. (Yes, this is a disadvantage as well as an advantage.)

Let's consider each in turn.

Fixed Exchange Rates and Monetary Stability   To maintain fixed exchange rates, the government must choose an exchange rate and have sufficient reserves to support that rate. If the rate it chooses is too high, its exports lag and the country continually loses reserves. If the rate it chooses is too low, it is paying more for its imports than it needs to and is building up reserves, which means that some other country is losing reserves. A country that is continually gaining or losing reserves must eventually change its fixed exchange rate.

The difficulty is that as soon as the country gets close to its reserves limit, foreign exchange traders begin to expect a drop in the value of the currency, and they try to get out of that currency because anyone holding that currency when it falls will lose money. False rumors of an expected depreciation or decrease in a country's fixed exchange rate can become true by causing a ''run on a currency,'' as all traders sell that currency. Thus, at times fixed exchange rates can become highly unstable because expectation of a change in the exchange rate can force the change to occur. As opposed to small movements in currency values, under a fixed rate regime these movements occur in large, sudden jumps.

Fixed Exchange Rates and Policy Independence   Maintaining a fixed exchange rate places limitations on a central bank's actions. In a country with fixed exchange rates, the central bank must ensure that the international supply of and demand for its currency are equal at the existing exchange rate. Say, for example, that the United States and the Bahamas have fixed exchange rates: $1 B = $1 U.S. The Bahamian

Major fluctuations in exchange rates can cause problems for international trade. Say, for instance, that a firm decides to build a plant in the United States because costs in the United States are low. But say the value of the dollar then rises significantly; the firm's costs rise significantly too, making it uncompetitive. Or let's take a recent real-world example: Korean companies decided to make a major drive to sell Korean VCRs in the United States. They decided on a low-price strategy, which was justified by their cost advantage. Their export drive was a success, but the value of the Korean won relative to the dollar rose significantly. The result was that in 1989 Korean VCR companies were losing money on each VCR they sold in the United States. They kept the price low, hoping that the won would fall in value. (In other words, their average variable costs were less than the price; their average total costs were greater than the price.)

central bank decides to run an expansionary monetary policy, lowering the interest rate and stimulating the Bahamian economy. The lower interest rates will cause financial capital to flow out of the country and the higher income will increase imports. Demand for Bahamian dollars will fall. To prop up their dollar and to maintain the fixed exchange rate, the Bahamas will have to buy their own currency. They can do so only as long as they have sufficient reserves of other countries' currencies.

Because most countries' international reserves are limited, a country with fixed exchange rates is limited in its ability to conduct expansionary monetary and fiscal policies. It loses its freedom to stimulate the economy in response to a recession. That's why, when a serious recession hits, many countries are forced to abandon fixed exchange rates. They run out of international reserves, and choose expansionary monetary policy to achieve their domestic goals over contractionary monetary policy to achieve their international goals.

Flexible Exchange Rates   The advantages and disadvantages of flexible exchange rates are the reverse of those of fixed exchange rates.

The advantages are:

1. Flexible exchange rates provide for orderly incremental adjustment of exchange rates, rather than large, sudden jumps.
2. Flexible exchange rates allow government to be flexible in conducting domestic monetary and fiscal policies.

5 The disadvantages are:

1. Flexible exchange rates allow speculation to cause large jumps in exchange rates that do not reflect market fundamentals.
2. Flexible exchange rates allow government to be flexible in conducting domestic monetary and fiscal policies. (This too is a disadvantage as well as an advantage.)

Let's consider each in turn.

Flexible Exchange Rates and Monetary Stability   Advocates of flexible exchange rates argue as follows: Why not treat currency markets like any other market and let private market forces determine a currency's value? There is no fixed price for TVs; why should there be a fixed price for currencies? The opponents' answer is based on the central role that international financial considerations play in an economy and the strange shapes and large shifts that occur in the short-run supply and demand curves for currencies.

As you saw in the discussion of the J-curve, short-run changes in the exchange rate do not necessarily improve the balance of payments. This suggests that the short-run supply of and demand for currencies may be a little bit strange. As opposed to sloping up and sloping down nicely (as normal supply and demand

The British newspaper is one of the best sources for up-to-date news on international finance.

curves do), short-run supply and demand curves for currencies often slope in a way that makes the invisible hand push the wrong way: Supply curves are likely to bend backward and demand curves are likely to fall backward.

With supply and demand curves that slope the wrong way and shift around all the time, there's no guarantee that a fall in the exchange rate will help achieve equilibrium. As you saw with the J-curve, it can take the economy further from equilibrium. If equilibrium is to be achieved, it must be achieved because speculators enter in and buy an undervalued currency in expectation of its future rise. Thus, two arguments against flexible exchange rates are that they don't necessarily help achieve equilibrium in the short run and that they allow far too much fluctuation in exchange rates, making trade difficult.

Flexible Exchange Rates and Policy Independence   The policy independence arguments for and against flexible exchange rates are the reverse of those given for fixed exchange rates. Individuals who believe that national governments should not have flexibility in setting monetary policy argue that flexible exchange rates don't impose the discipline on policy that fixed exchange rates do. Say, for example, that a country's goods are uncompetitive. Under a fixed exchange rate system, the country would have to contract its money supply and deal with the underlying uncompetitiveness of its goods. Under a flexible exchange rate system, the country can maintain an expansionary monetary policy, allowing inflation simply by allowing the value of its currency to fall.

Advocates of policy flexibility argue that it's stupid for a country to go through a recession when it doesn't have to; flexible exchange rates allow countries more flexibility in dealing with their problems. True, policy flexibility may lead to inflation, but inflation is better than a recession.

Partially Flexible Exchange Rates   Faced with the dilemma of choosing between these two unpleasant policies, most countries have opted for a policy in between the two: partially flexible exchange rates. With such a policy they try to get the advantages of both a fixed and a flexible exchange rate.

When policymakers believe there is a fundamental misalignment in a country's exchange rate, they will allow private forces to determine it—they allow the exchange rate to be flexible. When they believe that the currency's value is falling because of speculation, or that too large an adjustment in the currency is taking place, and that that adjustment won't achieve their balance of payment goals, they step in and fix the exchange rate, either supporting or pushing down their currency's value.

If policymakers are correct, this system of partial flexibility would work smoothly and would have the advantages of both fixed and flexible exchange rates. If policymakers are incorrect, however, a partially flexible system has the disadvantages of both fixed and flexible systems.

Which view is correct is much in debate. Most foreign exchange traders that I know tell me that the possibility of government intervention increases the amount of private speculation in the system. In private investors' view, their own assessments of what exchange rates should be are better than those of policymakers. If private investors knew the government would not enter in, private speculators would focus on fundamentals and would stabilize short-run exchange rates. When private speculators know government might enter into the market, they don't focus on fundamentals; instead they continually try to outguess government policymakers. When that happens, private speculation doesn't stabilize; it destabilizes exchange rates as private traders try to guess what the government thinks.

Many of my economics colleagues who work for the Fed aren't convinced by private investors' arguments. They maintain that some government intervention helps stabilize currency markets. I don't know which group is right.

CONCLUSION

Even though you've stayed with me through the chapter's in-depth introduction to international finance, you still won't be able to predict exchange rates. Nobody can do that. But at least I hope you know why you can't. The most honest prediction that one can make is that exchange rates are likely to be highly volatile—unpredictable in the short run and even unpredictable in the long run as new short-run phenomena develop. To make even a reasonable guess about what will happen in such markets, you will likely need a psychologist (who can tell you what other people are thinking, what other people think you're thinking, what other people think you think you're thinking, and so on), and perhaps also a psychiatrist to handle the mental marshmallow you might become if you get into international currency markets. Being an international currency trader isn't for most people; when my students suggest that they'd like to become international currency traders, I suggest they go into a more pleasant, less stressful field—like, say, air traffic control.

Our story has a moral, however. The moral is that in many so-called economic phenomena, noneconomic criteria play a significant role in what happens; in the short run they swamp the long-run economic forces. Economists can predict which types of markets will have these fluctuations (foreign exchange markets are definitely one type), but they can't predict exactly how prices will fluctuate in these markets.

KEY POINTS

· The balance of payments is made up of the current account, the capital account, and the official transactions account. **1**
· In 1988 the United States became a net debtor nation. In the early 1990s it is the largest debtor nation in the world. **2**
· Exchange rates in a perfectly flexible exchange rate system are determined by the supply of and demand for a currency. **3**
· When a country sets an exchange rate by law, it has a nonconvertible currency. **3**
· It is easier technically for a country to bring the value of its currency down than it is to support its currency. **3**
· In many so-called economic phenomena, noneconomic criteria play a significant role in what happens. **4**
· Often, in the short run, a fall in a country's exchange rate can increase a balance of payments and balance of trade deficit. In the long run, a fall tends to improve those balances. **5**
· Flexible, partially flexible, and fixed exchange rates have advantages and disadvantages. **5 6**

KEY TERMS

balance of payments *(747)*
balance of trade *(748)*
Bretton Woods system *(761)*
capital account *(747)*
capital controls *(757)*
current account *(747)*
exchange rate policy *(758)*

fixed exchange rate *(760)*
flexible exchange rate *(760)*
fundamental analysis *(752)*
gold specie flow mechanism *(760)*

gold standard *(760)*
J-curve *(758)*
nonconvertible currency *(750)*
official transactions account *(747)*

partially flexible exchange rate *(760)*
reserve currency *(762)*
Special Drawing Rights (SDR's) *(762)*
spread *(754)*

QUESTIONS FOR THOUGHT AND REVIEW

The number after each question represents the estimated degree of critical thinking required. (1 = almost none; 10 = deep thought.)

1. If a country is running a balance of trade deficit, will its current account be in deficit? Why? *(3)*
2. When someone sends 100 British pounds to a friend in the United States, will this transaction show up on the capital or current account? Why? *(3)*
3. Support the statement: "It is best to offset a capital account surplus with a current account deficit." *(7)*
4. Support the statement: "It is best to offset a capital account deficit with a current account surplus." *(5)*
5. Which is likely to have the larger spread: South Korean won or U.S. dollars? Why? *(7)*
6. What are the advantages and disadvantages of a non-convertible currency? *(5)*
7. What is the J-curve and why might its existence provide an argument for a country having a nonconvertible currency? *(6)*
8. Explain how an international financial adjustment would occur under a gold standard. *(6)*
9. Which is preferable: a fixed or a flexible exchange rate? Why? *(7)*
10. Demonstrate how the J-curve phenomenon might lead to a backward-bending supply curve. *(9)*

PROBLEMS AND EXERCISES

1. Draw the fundamental analysis of the supply and demand for British pound sterling in terms of dollars. Show what will happen to the exchange rate with those curves in response to each of the following events:
   a. The U.K. price level rises.
   b. The U.S. price level rises.
   c. The U.K. economy experiences a boom.
   d. The U.K. interest rates rise.
2. At an exchange rate of Rs20 to $1 (Rs is the sign for rupees), Pakistan is exporting 100,000 bales of cotton to the United States at $5 (or Rs100) each. It's importing 60 cars from the United States at $10,000 (Rs200,000) each. Now say that the value of the rupee falls to Rs22 to $1. Pakistan's exports rise to 103,000 bales of cotton while car imports fall to 58.
   a. What has happened to the trade balance?
   b. What will likely happen in the long run?
   c. What would happen if Pakistani exporters raised their price for cotton so that they were getting the same revenue as before the rupee's fall in value?
   d. How would that response affect what would happen in the long run?

The Analytic Foundations of the J-Curve

In fundamental analysis one would expect that a fall in a country's exchange rate would increase the quantity demanded and decrease the quantity supplied. In the long run this is the case, but in the short run it is not. To see why, think of the problem from a U.S. exporter's point of view. Say the value of the dollar falls by 10 percent. Eventually the exporter would like to export more, but increasing exports takes time. It often requires building up a foreign sales staff, increasing advertising, and setting up or expanding foreign exchange centers. Even shipping goods and processing them through customs can take weeks or months. So in the short run a rise or fall in an exchange rate is unlikely to change the amount he exports significantly. The same analysis exists for importers. The shift in the exchange rate is unlikely to cause a significant change in their actions either.

What this means technically in terms of supply and demand curves is that short-run supply and demand curves will be highly inelastic and that it takes large fluctuations in exchange rates to maintain an equilibrium in the supply and demand for currencies.

To show this, I present highly inelastic supply and demand curves for dollars in Exhibit A1. As you can see, there's still an equilibrium, but when supply and demand are highly inelastic, a small shift in either supply or demand can mean an enormous change in the exchange rate. For example, say the demand for dollars shifts a small amount from D_0 to D_1. At demand D_0 one franc costs 20¢; at demand D_1 one franc costs 40¢. The price of French goods has doubled in response to a small shift in the demand for currencies.

As if highly inelastic supply and demand curves weren't bad enough, it is also possible, and even likely, that supply and demand curves for currencies have the wrong shape: Supply curves bend backward and demand curves fall backward!

To see that this is the case, let's consider more carefully the effects of a changing value of a currency.

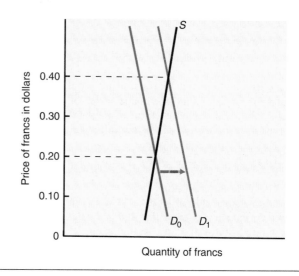

Specifically, let us consider what the shape of supply and demand curves would be in the numerical example of the J-curve in the text. Remember that the J-curve phenomenon means that a fall in a currency's value often worsens the balance of payments in the short run. Relating that J-curve observation to the supply and demand for currencies is a helpful exercise that explains why short-run exchange rate determination is often not governed by fundamental economic forces.

In the example presented in the text, when the dollar's value fell, fewer dollars were spent on U.S. exports, so the quantity of dollars demanded decreased. This suggests that the short-run demand for dollars isn't normally shaped; instead as the price of dollars in terms of French francs falls from 30¢ to 20¢, the quantity of dollars demanded *decreases* so demand for dollars is backward falling. By similar reasoning, using the numbers presented in the text, the supply of dollars is also backward bending! So, if the J-curve phenomenon holds in the short run (as past empirical estimates suggest it does), the short-run supply and demand for dollars are not only highly inelastic; the curves slope the wrong way and in the short run a fall in the relative value of a currency will worsen, not improve, a country's balance of payments deficit.

In Exhibit A2 I give an example in terms of German marks. As you can see, at the 2.5/1 rate the United States has a balance of payments deficit, meaning that the quantity of dollars supplied exceeds the quantity of dollars demanded. Now say the exchange rate falls from 2.5/1 to 2.27/1. In that event, as you can see, the difference between the quantity supplied and the quantity demanded (the excess supply of dollars), or the balance of payments deficit, doesn't decrease; it increases!

In summary, if supply and demand curves don't have normal shapes (as they don't in foreign exchange markets), the invisible hand does not guide markets to resolve disequilibrium effectively. In fact, if the exchange rate kept falling, and the curves had the shape suggested by the J-curve, the balance of payments deficit would simply get larger and larger as the value of the dollar fell. That, of course, wouldn't happen. Instead one of two things would happen. One possibility is that speculators would enter in on the expectation of a future rise in the value of the dollar. Remember, the J-curve effect means only the short-run supply and demand curves are strange; in the long run, supply and demand have normal shapes. If private speculators recognize that eventually the price of

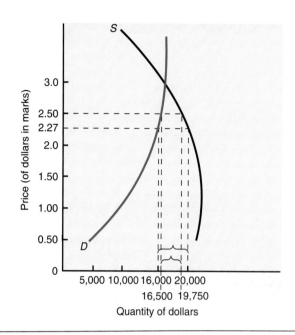

a currency will rise, they'll buy the currency now and the price *will* rise. Such speculation would tend to stabilize the value of the dollar. A second possibility is that government would enter in and either make its currency nonconvertible or buy its currency to stop the fall in value. Differing views about which of these is the better choice underlie differing views about what a government's exchange rate policy should be.

37

Growth and Economics of Developing Countries

*It is always depressing to go back
to Adam Smith, especially on economic development, as one realizes
how little we have learned in nearly 200 years.*

Kenneth Boulding

After reading this chapter, you should be able to:

1

State some comparative statistics on rich
and poor countries.

2

List seven problems facing
developing countries.

3

Explain how the market can function in
inappropriate ways when there is no well-
developed public morality.

4

Explain why it is so difficult for developing
countries to generate investment.

5

State the arguments for and against a
country repudiating its debt.

6

Summarize three debates about strategies
for growth.

7

Defend the position that economic
development is a complicated problem.

There are approximately 5 billion people in the world. Of these, 3.8 billion (about 75 percent) live in developing, rather than developed, countries. Per capita income in developing countries is around $500 per year; in the United States per capita income is about $22,000.

These averages understate the differences between the poorest country and the richest. Consider the African country of Chad—definitely one of the world's poorest. Its per capita income is about $200 per year—less than 1/100 of the per capita income in the United States. Moreover income in Chad goes primarily to the rich, so Chad's poor have per capita income of significantly less than $200.

Before I consider the obstacles to economic development, let's consider how a person lives on that $200 per year as many people in the world do. To begin with, that person can't:

DEVELOPMENT: PRELIMINARY CONSIDERATIONS

Go out for Big Macs.

Use Joy perfume (or any type of perfume).

Wear designer clothes.

And that person must:

Eat grain—usually rice or corn—for all meals, every day.

Mix fat from meat—not meat itself—with the rice on special occasions (maybe).

Live in one room with 9 or 10 other people.

Work hard from childhood to old age (if there is an old age). Those too old to work in the fields stay at home and care for those too young to work in the fields. (But children go out to work in the fields when they're about six years old.)

Go hungry, because no matter how many family members can work in the fields, probably the work and soil don't yield enough to provide the workers with an adequate number of calories per day.

In a poor person's household it's likely that a couple of the older children may have gone into the city to find work that pays money wages. If they were lucky and found jobs, they can send money home each month. That money may be the

A view of the difficult life in a developing country—washing clothes and children in Rio de Janeiro, Brazil.
© *McGlynn/The Image Works.*

ADDED DIMENSION

WHAT TO CALL
DEVELOPING COUNTRIES

▮n this chapter, following common usage, I call low-income countries *developing countries*. They have not always been called *developing*. In the 1950s they were called *backward*, but it was eventually realized that *backward* implied significant negative value judgments. Then these countries were called *underdeveloped*, but it was eventually realized that *underdeveloped* also implied significant negative value judgments. More recently they have been called *developing*, but eventually everyone will realize that *developing* implies significant negative value judgments. After all, in what sense are these countries "developing" any more than is the United States? All countries are evolving or developing countries. Many so-called developing countries have highly refined cultures which they don't want to lose; they may want to develop economically, but not at the cost of cultural change.

What should one call these countries? That remains to be seen, but whatever one calls them, bear in mind that language can conceal value judgments.

only cash income their family back in the fields has. The family uses the money to buy a few tools and cooking utensils.

The preceding is, of course, only one among billions of different stories. Even Americans and Europeans who are classified as poor find it hard to contemplate what life is really like in a truly poor country.

Don't Judge Society by Its Income Alone

Poor people in developing countries survive and often find pleasure in their hard lives. There are few suicides in the poorest countries. For example, the U.S. suicide rate is approximately 13 per 100,000 people. In Costa Rica it's 4.9; in Mexico it's 1.4; and in Peru it's .5. Who has time for suicide? You're too busy surviving. There's little ambiguity and few questions about the meaning of life. Living! That's what life's all about. There's no "Mom, what am I going to do today?" You know what you're going to do: survive if you can. And survival is satisfying.

Often these poor societies have elaborate cultural rituals and networks of intense personal relationships, which provide individuals with a deep sense of fulfillment and satisfaction.

Are people in these societies as happy as Americans are? If your immediate answer is no, be careful to understand the difficulty of making such a judgment. The answer isn't clear-cut. For us to say, "My God! What a failure their system is!" is wrong. It's an inappropriate value judgment about the relative worth of cultures. All too often Americans have gone into another country to try to make people better off, but have ended up making them worse off.

An economy is part and parcel of a culture. You can't judge just an economy; you must judge the entire culture. Some developing countries have cultures that, in many people's view, are preferable to ours. If one increases a country's income but takes away its culture in doing so, one may well have made its people worse off.

That said, we're ready to consider whether people in developing countries would be better off if they had more income. Most people in developing countries would definitely answer yes!

Even culturally sensitive people agree that economic growth within the context of a developing country's culture would be a good thing, if only because those countries exist simultaneously with market economies. Given market societies' expansionary tendencies, without economic growth, cultures in poor countries would simply be overrun and destroyed by the cultures of market societies. Their land would be taken, their agricultural patterns would be changed, and their traditional means of subsistence would be destroyed. So generally the choice isn't between development and preservation of the existing culture (and its accompanying ancient ways to which the poor have adjusted). Rather, the choice is

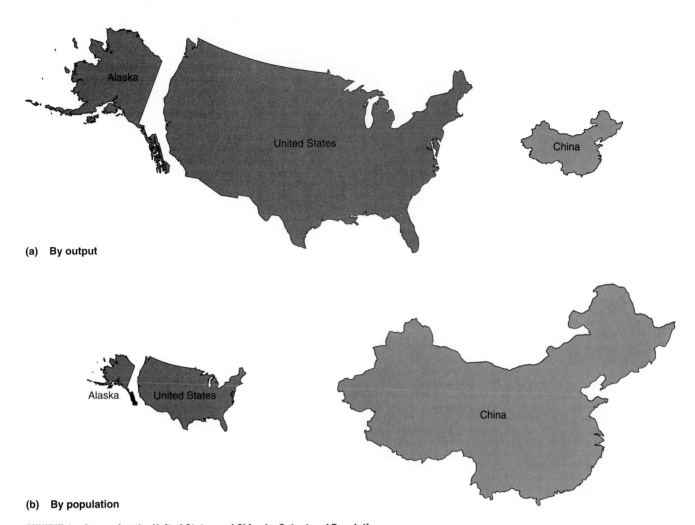

(a) By output

(b) By population

EXHIBIT 1   Comparing the United States and China by Output and Population

The areas of China and the United States are approximately equal. If, however, we were to scale their sizes in accordance with their relative outputs, as in (**a**), the United States would be shown double in size and China would be shown reduced to one fifth of its size. If we scaled their sizes in accordance with population, as in (**b**), it is China that would increase its size, more than doubling, while the size of the United States would be cut in half.

between development (with its attendant wrenching cultural transitions) and continuing poverty (with exploitation by developed countries and its attendant wrenching cultural transitions).

Exhibit 1 gives you a sense of the uneven distribution of production among rich and poor countries.

Some Comparative Statistics on Rich and Poor Nations

The low average income in poor countries has its effects on people's lives. Life expectancy is about 50 years in most very poor countries (compared to about 75 years in the United States). In poor countries most people drink contaminated water, consume about half the number of calories the World Health Organization has determined is minimal for good health, and do physical labor (often of the kind done by machine in developed countries). Exhibit 2 compares developing countries, middle-income countries, and developed countries.

As with all statistics, care must be taken in interpreting the figures in Exhibit 2. For example, the income comparisons were all made on the basis of current exchange rates. But relative prices between rich and poor countries often differ substantially; the cost of goods relative to total income tends to be much lower for people in developing countries than for those in developed countries.

EXHIBIT 2   Statistics on Developing, Middle-Income, and Developed Countries

	Country	Population per physician	Daily calorie supply	Life expectancy (m)	Infant mortality (per 1,000)	Labor force in agriculture (%)	Labor force in industry (%)	Literacy rate	People per TV receiver	GDP per capita ($)
Developing	Bangladesh	6,166	2,021	55	112	74	11	35	315	200
	Ethiopia	36,660	1,667	50	112	80	8	62	503	130
	Haiti	6,039	2,013	53	104	66	9	53	234	440
Middle-Income	Brazil	684	2,751	62	67	31	27	81	4	2,300
	Iran	2,992	3,181	64	64	33	21	54	23	1,500
	South Korea	1,066	2,852	67	23	21	27	96	5	6,300
	Thailand	4,883	2,316	67	35	62	13	93	11	1,630
Developed	Japan	609	2,956	77	4	7	33	99	1.8	19,000
	Sweden	320	2,960	75	6	3	21	99	2.4	17,200
	United States	404	3,671	72	10	4	28	98	1.3	22,470

Sources: *U.N. Statistical Yearbook*, 1992 and *The World Factbook*, 1992.

Purchasing power parity Method of comparing income by looking at the domestic purchasing power of money in different countries.

To allow for these differences, some economists have looked at the domestic purchasing power of money in various countries and have adjusted the comparisons accordingly. Rather than working with exchange rates, they compare what a specified market basket of consumer goods will cost in various countries and use these results to compare currencies' values. This is called the **purchasing power parity** method of comparing income of countries. Making these adjustments, the World Bank found that income differences among countries are cut by half. In other words, when one uses the World Bank's purchasing power parity method of comparison, it's as if the people in developing countries had twice as much income as they had when the exchange rate method was used.

A similar adjustment can be made with the life expectancy rates. A major reason for the lower life expectancies in developing countries is their high infant mortality rates. Once children survive infancy, however, their life expectancies are much closer to those of children in developed countries. Say a country's overall life expectancy is 50 years and that 15 percent of all infants die within their first year. As a person grows older, at each birthday the person's life expectancy is higher. So if a child lives to the age of 3 years, then at that point the child has an actual life expectancy of close to 60 years, rather than 50 years.

Developing Countries Focus on Growth

Before the Industrial Revolution, when Western countries had low incomes compared to today's income in developing countries, Western economists focused on one question: What makes a society grow? By *growth* they meant growth of material production. It isn't surprising that the focus of the economics of developing countries is material growth: how to achieve and maintain growth in per capita income.

The record for most countries in achieving growth isn't good. Only a small number of countries have moved out of the "developing country" ranks. One group that has moved out is the oil-producing countries. Another group of countries, called the **Asian tigers** (for example, Taiwan, South Korea, Singapore, and Hong Kong[1]) have achieved substantial economic growth and are no longer considered developing countries. They've become middle-income countries. The Asian tigers are an exception. Considered as a group, developing countries

Asian tigers Group of Asian countries that have achieved so much economic growth that they are no longer considered developing countries.

---

[1] Hong Kong isn't an independent country. Currently it's administered by Great Britain. In 1997 it's scheduled to be returned to China. However at present economically it behaves very much like an independent country.

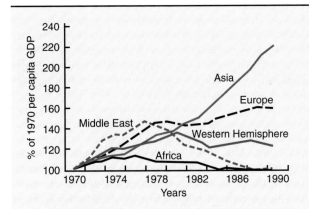

EXHIBIT 3   Growth Rates—Groupings of Countries

Since the late 1970s, African and Middle Eastern economic growth has essentially come to a halt. Only the Asian tigers have grown faster than Europe or the Western Hemisphere.
Source: *World Economic Outlook* (Washington, D.C. : IMF).

haven't done well compared to developed countries. While from 1950 until 1990 developing countries' average overall growth rates were slightly higher than growth rates of industrial market countries, their per capita growth rates were much lower. But to catch up with developed countries, the developing countries would have to grow at a faster rate than the developed countries. For example, if developing countries grew 4 percent a year and developed countries grew 3 percent, after 24 years developing countries' income would have increased 156 percent while developed countries' income would have increased 103 percent. As opposed to having $\frac{1}{18}$ of a developed country's per capita income, a developing country after 24 years of growth would have improved to the point of having $\frac{1}{14}$ of a developed country's per capita income. But even that small gain isn't occurring. As you can see from Exhibit 3, in the 1980s the growth rate of most developing countries except those in Asia—both per capita and overall—slowed. Per capita income fell in a number of countries. Unless this trend changes, the relative income gap between developed and developing countries will become increasingly wide.

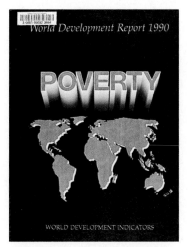

One of the best sources of information about development issues is the *World Development Report,* published by the World Bank.

What stops countries from developing economically? Economists have discovered no magic potion that will make a country develop. We can't say, "Here are steps 1, 2, 3, 4. If you follow them you'll grow, but if you don't follow them you won't grow."

What makes it so hard for developing countries to devise a successful development program is that social, political, and economic problems blend into one another and cannot be considered separately. The institutional structure that we take for granted in the United States often doesn't exist in those countries. For example, economists' analysis of production assumes that a stable government exists that can enforce contracts and supply basic services. In most developing countries, that assumption can't be made. Governments are often anything but stable; overnight a coup d'état can bring a new government into power, with a whole new system of rules under which businesses have to operate. Imagine trying to figure out a reasonable study strategy if every week you had a new teacher, who emphasized different things and gave totally different types of tests from last week's teacher. Firms in developing countries face similar problems.

While economists can't say, "Here's what you have to do in order to grow," we have been able to identify some general obstacles that all developing countries seem to face: These problems include:

1. Political instability.
2. Corruption.

OBSTACLES TO ECONOMIC DEVELOPMENT

3. Lack of investment.
4. Excessive debt.
5. Inappropriate education.
6. Overpopulation.
7. Unemployment and inflation.

I consider each in turn.

Political Instability

A student's parents once asked me why their son was doing poorly in my economics class. My answer was that he could not read and he could hardly write. Until he could master those basics, there was no use talking about how he could better learn economics. Roughly the same reasoning can be applied to the problem of political instability in developing countries. Unless a country achieves political stability (acceptance within a country of a stable system of government) it's not going to develop economically, no matter what it does.

All development strategies require the existence of a stable government if they are to succeed. A mercantilist or a socialist development strategy requires an elaborate government presence. A market-based strategy requires a much smaller government role, but even with markets, a stable environment is needed for a market to function and for contracts to be made with confidence. Many developing countries don't have that stability. Politically they haven't established a tradition of orderly governmental transition. Coups d'état or armed insurrections always remain possible, and economies can fluctuate from a Marxist regime one month to a capitalist regime the next to a nonaligned regime the third month. In Burma, for example, prodemocratic civilian demonstrations in 1988 forced the authoritarian government then in power to announce plans for free elections. Those plans were scuttled in 1989 when the army took control, imposed martial law, announced that the country was being renamed Myanmar, and left the situation so unclear that no one could predict what the future of the Burmese (or Myanmarese) government would be.

Even countries whose governments aren't regularly toppled face threats of overthrow, and those threats are sufficient to prevent individual economic activity. To function, an economy needs some rules—any rules—that will last.

The lack of stability is often exacerbated by social and cultural differences among groups within a country. Political boundaries often reflect arbitrary decisions made by former colonial rulers, not the traditional cultural and tribal boundaries that form the real-life divisions. The result is lack of consensus among the population as a whole as well as intertribal suspicion and even warfare. For example, Nigeria is a federation established under British colonial rule. It comprises three ethnic regions: the northern, Hausa Fulan, region; the western, Yoruba, region; and the eastern, Ibo, region. These three regions are culturally distinct and so are in continual political and military conflict. Nigeria has experienced an endless cycle of military coups, attempts at civilian rule, and threats of secession by the numerically smaller eastern region. Had each region been allowed to remain separate, economic development might have been possible; but because the British lumped the regions together and called them a country, economic development is next to impossible.

The Influence of Political Instability on Development
Do these political considerations affect economic questions? You bet. As I will discuss shortly, any development plan requires financial investment from somewhere—either external or internal. Political instability closes off both sources of investment funds.

Any serious potential investor takes political instability into account. Foreign companies considering investment in a developing country hire political specialists who analyze the degree of risk involved. Where the risk is too great, foreign companies simply don't invest.

Political instability also limits internal investment. Income distribution in many developing countries is highly skewed. There are a few very rich people and an enormous number of very poor people, while the middle class is often small. Whatever one's view of the fairness of such income inequality, it has a potential advantage for society. Members of the wealthy elite in developing countries have income to spare, and their savings are a potential source of investment funds. But when there is political instability, that potential isn't realized. Fearing that their wealth may be taken from them, the rich often channel their investment out of their own country so that should they need to flee a revolution, they'll still be able to live comfortably. Well-off people in developing countries provide major inflows of investment into the United States and other Western countries.

Ferdinand Marcos, former president of the Philippines, was reported to have $10 billion worth of assets scattered around the developed countries of the world. Had he invested those billions in the Philippines, he most likely would have lost all that money when he was deposed in 1986. Marcos, having placed his wealth abroad—often hiding its ownership—didn't lose it, or at least he didn't lose all of it, after being deposed. So the Philippines lost twice from Marcos's actions. First, he took money that didn't belong to him; and second, he deprived the Philippines of much-needed investment capital.

Political Instability and Unequal Distribution of Income   The highly skewed distribution of income in most developing countries contributes in another way to political instability. It means that the poor majority has little vested interest in maintaining the current system. A coup? Why not? What have they got to lose? The economic prospects for many people in developing countries are so bleak that they are quite willing to join or at least support a guerilla insurgency that promises to set up a new, better system. The resulting instability makes development almost impossible.

Bribery, graft, and corruption are ways of life in most developed countries. In Egypt it's called *baksheesh* (meaning "gift of money"); in Mexico it's called *la mordida* ("the bite"). If you want to park in a parking spot in Mexico City, you'd better pay the policeman, or your car will get a ticket. If you want to take a photograph of the monument to Rameses II in front of the Cairo railroad station, you'd better slip the traffic officer a few bucks, or else you may get run over.

Corruption

3

Without a well-developed institutional setting and a public morality that condemns corruption, market forces function in a variety of areas that people in developed countries would consider inappropriate. In any country the government has the right to allow imports, to allow development, to determine where you can park your car, to say whether you can take photographs of public buildings, to decide who wins a lawsuit, and so forth. In developing countries, however, those rights can be, and often are, sold. The litigant who pays the judge the most wins. How about the right to import? Want to import a new machine? That will be 20 percent of the cost, please.

Such graft and corruption quickly become institutionalized, so that all parties involved feel that they have little choice but to take part. Government officials say that graft and bribery are built into their pay structure, so unless they take bribes, they won't have enough income to live on. Businesspeople say that if they want to stay in business they have to pay bribes. Similarly workers must bribe business in order to get a job, and labor leaders must be bribed not to cause trouble for business.

I'm not claiming that such payments are wrong. Societies decide what is right and wrong; economists don't. The term *bribery* in English has a pejorative connotation. In many other languages the terms people use for this type of activity don't have such negative connotations.

But I *am* claiming that such payments—with the implied threat that failure to pay will have adverse consequences—make it more difficult for a society's economy to grow. Knowing that those payments must be made prevents many people from undertaking actions that might lead to growth. For example, a friend of mine wanted to build a group of apartments in the Bahamas, but when he discovered the payoffs he'd have to make to various people, he abandoned the whole idea.

Limiting an activity makes the right to undertake that limited activity valuable to the person doing the limiting. When bribery is an acceptable practice, it creates strong incentives to limit an ever-increasing number of activities—including many activities that could make a country grow.

Lack of Investment

Even if a country can overcome the political and social constraints on development, there are also economic constraints. If a country is to grow it must somehow invest, and funds for investment must come from savings. These savings can be either brought in from abroad (as private investment or foreign government aid) or generated internally (as domestic savings). Each source of investment capital has its problems.

Investment Funded by Domestic Savings In order to save, a person must first have enough to live on. With per capita incomes of $200 per year, poor people in developing countries don't have a whole lot left over to put into savings. Instead you rely on your kids, if they live, to take care of you in your old age. As for the rich, the threat of political instability often makes them put their money into savings abroad, as I discussed before. For the developing country, it's as if the rich didn't save. In fact, it's even worse because when they save abroad, the rich don't even spend the money at home as do poor people, so the rich don't generate even as much as the first-round income multiplier effects in their home country.

That leaves the middle class (small as it is) as the one hope these countries have for domestic savings. For them, the problem is: Where can they put their savings? Often these countries have an underdeveloped financial sector; there's no neighborhood bank, no venture capital fund, no government-secured savings vehicle. The only savings vehicle available may be the government savings bond. But savings bonds finance the government deficit, which supports the government bureaucracy, which is limiting activities that could lead to growth. Few middle-class people invest in those government bonds. After all, what will a government bond be worth after the next revolution? Nothing!

Some governments have taxed individuals (a type of forced savings) and channeled that money back into investment. But again, politics and corruption are likely to enter in. Instead of going into legitimate productive investment, the savings—in the form of "consulting fees," outright payoffs, or "sweetheart contracts"—go to friends of those in power. Before you get up on your high horse and say, "How do the people allow that to happen?" think of the United States, where it's much easier to prevent such activities but where scandals in government spending are still uncovered with depressing regularity. On the day I'm writing this, the newspapers report hundreds of millions of dollars misspent by the U.S. Department of Housing and Urban Development to benefit friends of politicians.

Investment Funded from Abroad The other way to generate funds for investment is from external savings, either foreign aid or foreign investment.

Foreign Aid The easiest way to finance development is with **foreign aid** (funds that developed countries loan or give to developing countries). The problem is that

Country	Development aid 1990 (millions of U.S. dollars)	% of GDP
United States	11,394	0.21
France	9,380	0.79
United Kingdom	2,638	0.27
Japan	9,069	0.31
Germany	6,320	0.42
Italy	3,395	0.32
Austria	394	0.25
Sweden	2,012	0.90
Canada	2,470	0.44

EXHIBIT 4   Foreign Aid Given by Major Countries, 1990

Source: The World Bank, *World Development Report 1992.*

foreign aid generally comes with strings attached; funds are earmarked for specific purposes. For example, most foreign aid is military aid; helping a country prepare to fight a war isn't a good way to help it develop.

As you can see in Exhibit 4, the United States gives about $11 billion (about $45 per U.S. citizen) per year in foreign aid. For the 2.5 billion people in developing countries, total foreign aid from all countries comes to $4.50 per person. That isn't going to finance a lot of economic development, especially when much of the money is earmarked for military purposes.

Foreign aid Funds that are loaned or given to developing countries by developed countries.

Foreign Investment   If a multinational company believes that a country has a motivated, cheap work force, a stable government supportive of business, and sufficient **infrastructure investment** such as transportation and energy facilities, it has a strong incentive to invest in the country. That's a lot of ifs, and generally the poorest countries don't measure up. What they have to offer instead are raw materials that the multinational corporation can develop.

Infrastructure investment A country's investment in facilities such as transportation and energy.

Countries at the upper end of the group of developing countries (such as Mexico and Brazil) may meet all these requirements, but large amounts of foreign investment often result in political problems as citizens of these countries complain about imperialist exploitation, outside control, and significant outflows of profits. Developing countries have tried to meet such complaints by insisting that foreign investment come in the form of joint development projects under local control, but that cuts down the amount that foreign firms are willing to invest.

When the infrastructure doesn't exist, as is the case in the poorest developing countries, few firms will invest in that country, no matter how cheap the labor or how stable the government. Firms require infrastructure investment such as transportation facilities, energy availability, and housing and amenities for their employees before they will consider investing in a country. And they don't want to pay to establish this infrastructure themselves.

In the 1970s developing countries could look to foreign banks for loans to finance development projects by private domestic firms. Governments of the developing countries would provide guarantees that the loans would be repaid. Had the loans gone for productive investments that paid a return greater than the principal and interest on the loans, these investments would have been helpful. But, in reality, as a result of political corruption and economic mismanagement, the investments were often unproductive. Returns on the investments didn't even cover the interest payments, let alone the principal. The governments that had guaranteed the loans found themselves responsible for repaying the loans without the wherewithal to do so. They found themselves in a debt crisis.

In 1990 Latin American countries owed over $400 billion, much of it to U.S. banks, while all the developing countries combined had about $1.4 trillion in outstanding debt. That meant that they had to pay about $140 billion in interest

Excessive Debt

each year. Many countries' annual interest was more than they could afford to pay from their export earnings. These developing countries had to have a large trade surplus simply to pay the interest on their debt. Meanwhile no payments had been made on the principal, and as long as that debt remained unpaid, no money could be devoted to development.

Managing the Debt Crisis　　There's a saying in banking, "If you owe the bank a million, you're in trouble; if you owe the bank a billion, your trouble is the bank's trouble." When a lender will go broke if a borrower defaults, the lender will try as hard as it can to work something out. Accordingly the 1980s was a period of intense negotiation designed to prevent developing countries from defaulting on their loans. The U.S. government, other Western governments, and the International Monetary Fund were active in these negotiations.

Default was prevented by (1) restructuring the debt, (2) lending the countries even more money so they could pay the interest on the debts, (3) writing off some of the old loans (essentially forgiving them), and (4) lowering the interest rate on the remaining loans.

The process of restructuring went like this: The U.S. government lent money to the IMF, which lent money to the debtor government, which used the money to pay off some of its debt to the lending banks. In short, the U.S. government's money went to U.S. banks. Why the roundabout process? Politics. Politically it was easier for the United States to lend money to the IMF than directly to the banks, even though—also for political reasons—the U.S. government was making the loan as much to help the U.S. banks as it was to help the developing country.[2] Politically it was easier for the IMF to pressure the government of a developing country to put its fiscal affairs in order than it would have been for that developing country's government to do it on its own. If a government can blame the necessity of making hard decisions on someone else, it is more likely to survive after making those decisions. The basis for such IMF loans is called **conditionality**—the loans are made on the condition that the developing country establish "responsible monetary and fiscal policies" (meaning lower inflation, reduced deficit, and reduced consumption).

At times conditionality can be helpful to a developing country. At other times, however, conditionality can bring a government down. Consider what conditionality means in practice: Government budgets are cut, resulting in cutbacks of government-supported health care and welfare payments; prices of imported goods rise enormously; and the population's real income often falls drastically. The people may find the costs of conditionality too high and throw out the government that imposed them.

In return for making loans, the U.S. government also called for some direct restructuring: changing some of the debt to equity. As discussed in earlier chapters, equity requires no fixed payment, but it does confer ownership rights and the owners receive profits, if there are any. Debt requires a fixed payment but doesn't confer ownership rights. By exchanging debt for equity, the developing country's payments are reduced but ownership of the companies to which the debtor country has distributed the borrowed funds is transferred to foreigners. Politically making this transfer is difficult for developing countries, even though it reduces their interest payments. They are accused of selling off their country to the banks, and very few debt/equity swaps have occurred as of the early 1990s.

Negotiations on international debt restructuring are still going on. Because the problems are so severe and widespread, and because the lending countries have many problems of their own, it is unlikely that completely satisfactory solutions will be achieved any time soon.

Conditionality　Requirement of IMF loans that the developing country establish responsible monetary and fiscal policies.

---

[2] It should be mentioned that politics often played a role in the initial loan. In the 1970s the U.S. government strongly encouraged banks to make loans to developing countries. Thus many people (including most bankers) felt the government had a moral obligation to help the banks.

The Debt Repudiation Strategy   One strategy some economists urge is simply to have the developing country repudiate the debt: to say it was guaranteed by corrupt former officials and that fraud was involved. The country should just make a new start, declaring that it owes nothing. For obvious reasons this strategy is extraordinarily tempting. In the late 1980s a number of Latin American countries threatened to repudiate their debt, at least partially.

5

Apart from the moral argument that a debt must be repaid, the major argument against repudiation is that it will destroy the country's ability to get loans in the future. The counterargument is that the country already has so much debt that it won't be able to get new credit anyway, so why worry about obtaining future loans? If they repudiate their debt, they won't need much in the way of loans since they can use the interest they were paying on the debt to finance internal development. Moreover if all the developing countries were to get together on repudiation, forming a debtors' cartel, the banks would be unable to single out one or two countries that had repudiated and, according to many observers, would start making loans to them again in a year or two.

Worry about total repudiation increases banks' willingness to give developing countries leeway in repaying loans. This worry also makes those existing loans to developing countries, which can be sold on the secondary market just like bonds, sell for varying amounts. Some sell for only about 15¢ to 30¢ on the dollar. (Each dollar of the loan amount is sold at anywhere between 15¢ and 30¢.) Clearly the market gives a low probability that such loans will ever be paid off.

Inappropriate Education

The right education is a necessary component of any successful development strategy. The wrong education is an enormous burden. Developing countries tend to have too much of the wrong education and too little of the right education.

Often educational systems in developing countries resemble Western educational systems. The reason is partly the colonial heritage of developing countries and partly what might be described as an emulation factor. The West defines what an educated person is, and developing countries want their citizens to be seen as educated. An educated person should be able to discuss the ideas of Vladimir Nabokov, the poetry of Lord Byron, the intricacies of chaos theory, the latest developments in fusion technology, the nuances of the Keynesian/New Classical debate, and the dissociative properties of Andy Warhol's paintings. So saith Western scholars; so be it.

But, put bluntly, that type of education is almost irrelevant to economic growth and may be a serious detriment to growth. When the United States was a developing country with a high rate of growth in the early 1800s, as much as 80 percent of the population was illiterate.

But developing countries' current educational practices may be worse than irrelevant. When the U.S. economy developed, travel opportunities were limited so bright, dynamic individuals, unless they were rich, had to stay home. Except for the elite, students received their instruction from people from their own culture, so their education had a close connection to their own culture.

That isn't what happens in developing countries. Their educational systems often reflect Western culture, not their own cultures. The best students qualify for scholarships abroad; and their education in a different tradition alienates them from their culture. It makes them long for discussion and interaction with other "educated people." In my studies in Europe and the United States, I've come to know a large number of the best and the brightest students from developing countries. They're superb students and they do well in school. But as they near graduation, most of them face an enormously difficult choice. They can return to their home country—to material shortages, to enormous challenges for which they have no training, and to an illiterate society whose traditional values are hostile to the values these new graduates have learned. Or they can stay in the West, find jobs relevant to their training, enjoy an abundance of material goods,

Arthur Lewis—Nobel prize, 1979, for work on economic development. © *The Nobel Foundation.*

Brain drain The outflow of the best and brightest students from developing countries to developed countries.

and associate with people to whom they've now learned to relate. Which would you choose?

The choice many of them make results in a **brain drain** (the outflow of the best and brightest students from developing countries to developed countries). Many of these good students don't return to the developing country. Those that do go home take jobs as government officials, expecting high salaries and material comforts far beyond what their society can afford. Instead of becoming the dynamic entrepreneurs of growth, they become impediments to growth.

There are, of course, many counterexamples to the arguments presented here. Many developing countries try to design their education system to fit their culture. And many of the dynamic, selfless leaders who make it possible for the country to develop do return home. As with most issues there are both positive and negative attributes to the way something is done. I emphasize the problems with educational systems in developing economies because the positive attributes of education are generally accepted. Without education, development is impossible. The question is simply how that education should be structured.

Overpopulation

Two ways a country can increase per capita income are:

1. Decrease the number of people in the country (without decreasing the total income in the country).
2. Increase the income (without increasing the population).

In each case the qualifier is important, for income and population are related in complicated ways: People earn income; without people there would be no income. But often the more people there are, the less income per person there is, because the resources of the country become strained.

A country's population can never be higher than its natural resources can support. But that doesn't mean that overpopulation can't be an obstacle to development. Nature has its own ways of reducing populations that are too large: Starvation and disease are the direct opposite to development. That control system works in nature, and it would work with human societies. The problem is that we don't like it.

Thomas Carlyle gave economics its nickname, *the dismal science,* commenting on the writings of Thomas Malthus, who, in the early 1800s, said that society's prospects are dismal because population tends to outrun the means of subsistence. (Population grows geometrically—that is, at an increasing rate; the means of subsistence grow arithmetically—that is, at a constant rate.) The view was cemented into economic thinking in the law of diminishing marginal productivity: As more and more people are added to a fixed amount of land, the output per worker gets smaller and smaller.

Through technological progress, most Western economies have avoided the fate predicted by Malthus because growth in output has exceeded growth in population. In contrast, many developing economies have not avoided the Malthusian fate, because diminishing marginal productivity has exceeded technological change, and the economic growth developing countries do have isn't enough to offset the increase in population. The result is a constant or falling output per person.

That doesn't mean that developing countries haven't grown economically. They have. But population growth makes per capita growth small or nonexistent.

Population grows for a number of reasons, including:

1. As public health measures are improved, infant mortality rates and death rates for the population as a whole both decline. (Fewer people die each year.)
2. As people get more income, they believe they can afford to have more kids.
3. In rural areas children are useful in working the fields.

What to do? Should the government reduce the population growth rate? If it should, how can it do so? Various measures have been tried: advertising campaigns, free condoms, forced sterilization, and economic incentives. For example, in China the government has tried imposing severe economic penalties on couples who have more than one child while providing a free television set to couples who agreed not to have more than one child.

China's vigorous population control campaign has had a number of effects. First, it created so much anger at the government that in rural areas the campaign was dropped. Second, it led to the killing of many female babies because, if couples were to have only one baby, strong cultural and economic pressures existed to see that the baby was a male. Third, it led to an enormous loss of privacy. Dates of women's menstrual periods were posted in factories and officials would remind them at appropriate times that they should take precautions against getting pregnant. Only a very strong government could impose such a plan.

Even successful population control programs have their problems. In Singapore a population control campaign was so successful among educated women that the government became concerned that its "population quality" was suffering. It began a selective campaign to encourage college-educated women to have children. They issued "love tips" to men (since some college-educated women complained that their male companions were nerds and had no idea how to be romantic) and offered special monetary bonuses to college-educated women who gave birth to children. As you might imagine, the campaign provoked a backlash, and it was eventually dropped by the government.

Individuals differ substantially in their assessment of the morality of these programs, but even if one believes that population control is an appropriate government concern, it does not seem that such programs will be successful, by themselves, in limiting population growth.

It is true that birth control programs have enabled developing countries to slow their population growth, but so far their overall effect hasn't been what planners had hoped. Summarizing past attempts, in 1989 Ashish Bose (head of the Population Research Center of Delhi University in India) stated, "Looking back, high tech, money, and the bureaucracy—all these have failed."

Some people, like social scientist Julian Simon, believe that all such attempts to control population are misplaced. People are the ultimate resource, he argues, and it is inconceivable that a society can have too many people. People will design technologies that will allow ever-increasing numbers to exist in a society.

In my discussion of developing countries, I do not focus on the distinction between micro problems and macro problems. Developing countries' problems are so immense and so tied together with social and cultural issues that the macro/micro division isn't useful. That doesn't mean that developing countries don't have macro problems of inflation and unemployment. They do, but these problems have different dimensions than they do in developed countries.

Unemployment and Inflation

Unemployment Take the problem of unemployment. Many developing countries have a large nonmarket economy. Subsistence farmers, for example, aren't technically unemployed, but often there are so many people on the land that their marginal product is minimal or even negative. Similarly without a significant economic infrastructure (such as roads, utilities, and public transportation), jobs are often available only sporadically, depending on whether and when a local farmer needs additional workers. And without good roads and transportation systems, job seekers are unable to get to jobs, even if jobs exist. It's an open question whether these people should be considered unemployed.

In many developing countries the only nonsporadic work is for the government, and the primary available statistics on unemployment are for government employment. In such cases one would hardly want, or be able, to talk of an

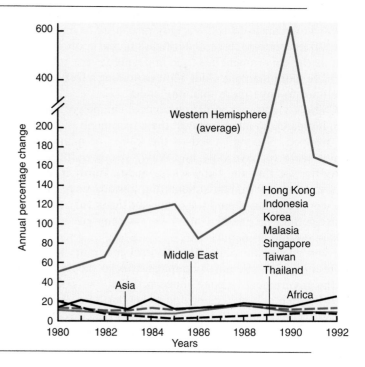

EXHIBIT 5   Inflation Rates of Developing Countries in Various Developing Regions

Inflation is a problem of many developing countries, especially in Latin and South America, which are indicated in the figures for the Western Hemisphere.
Source: *World Economic Outlook* (Washington, D,C.: IMF), 1992.

unemployment problem. The problem is one of misemployment and lack of institutional infrastructure.

Inflation   Similar problems exist in discussing the inflation problem. In developing countries there is significant inflation, as can be seen in Exhibit 5.

By comparison with developing countries' standards, the U.S. inflation rate wouldn't be seen as inflation at all, but only as background noise in the price level. Thus, talking about inflation as a macroeconomic problem of developing countries would seem to make sense. But it doesn't.

In the United States there's significant debate about the cause and nature of inflation. But in developing countries there's much less debate about the cause. Economists of all persuasions agree that inflation occurs because the government is printing too much money. Large inflations can continue only if the government prints large amounts of money. The debate in such situations is a political one, concerning why the government prints too much money and what the political consequences of *not* doing so would be. Often in developing countries, the government's sources of tax revenue are limited. If it tried to collect more taxes, it would be booted out of office. Similarly its ability to cut expenditures is limited. If it cut expenditures, it would be booted out of office. With new tax sources unavailable and with no ability to cut expenditures, the government uses its only other option to meet its obligations—it prints more money.

Developed countries face such political problems too, but in less extreme form. Developed countries have another alternative: to borrow by selling government bonds. Developing countries with unstable governments don't have that option because no one wants to buy their bonds (unless they can talk the World Bank into helping them).

Printing too much money causes inflation, which debases the currency, creating inflation-based tax revenue for the government. The country's fixed-interest-rate debt is wiped out and the government is bailed out. But the bailout is only temporary. Inflation makes bond finance even harder; soon the only kinds of bonds the government can sell are bonds denominated in another currency and indexed bonds (bonds whose face value rises with inflation). Both these types of bonds wipe out much of the gain to the government from further inflation. With indexed bonds, in fact, further inflation increases government debt astronomically and leads to hyperinflation and destruction of the government's currency.

The fact that inflation is only a temporary solution doesn't stop developing countries' leaders from using it. They don't have time for the luxury of long-run solutions and are often simply looking for policies that will hold their governments together for a month at a time.

Even those developing countries with relatively stable governments often face cultural fights within the country. Take India, for example. Until the early 1990s the government was stable, but various factions were committed to seceding from the country or to limiting the government's effectiveness. These fights led to assassinations of leaders and enormous political conflict. Dealing with these conflicts takes time and resources that the government might have used to deal with economic problems.

Another factor that limits the macroeconomic options of developing countries is that the nature of monetary policy and fiscal policy is substantially different for them than for developed countries. International trade balances (imports and exports) dominate developing countries' national income accounts, and the political constraints on taxing and on reducing spending make contractionary fiscal policy impossible.

Similarly with monetary policy. Lack of an established government bond market rules out open market operations as an option, so developing countries' national banks must use other tools to affect the money supply. Moreover the predominance of international monetary flows (as discussed in the previous chapter) severely restricts central banks' ability to conduct an independent monetary policy. Because of these limitations, developing countries' national banks often act as facilitators of international trade rather than as control agencies in charge of monetary policy. That is, they buy and sell foreign currencies instead of carrying out domestic monetary policy.

The limitations on macro policy discussed here exist in varying degrees in all countries. But in developing countries the limitations become so large that they preclude serious consideration of the kinds of policy options available to developed countries.

While developing countries' problems seem overwhelming, development economists have nonetheless offered a variety of strategies for growth. These strategies have been much debated, and a brief discussion of three areas of debate is appropriate at this point. All three presume that development money is available; the debate involves how best to spend it.

In deciding how to spend your development money, do you follow an **unbalanced growth plan,** focusing on one sector of the economy and hoping that that will generate development in other sectors? Or do you adopt a **balanced growth plan,** spreading the money around and trying to spur development in all sectors simultaneously? With a balanced growth plan, you risk spreading the money so thin that nothing substantial can be accomplished. With an unbalanced growth plan, you risk creating an oasis of development that the economy cannot sustain for long. The debate has sometimes been likened to a debate about how you should pull yourself up by your own bootstraps. Should you pull one side first? Or should you pull both sides together? And how can you pull yourself up at all if you are standing on the very surface you're trying to lift?

Balanced versus
Unbalanced Growth

Unbalanced growth plan Encouraging growth primarily in just one sector of the economy with the hope that growth will spread to other sectors.

Balanced growth plan Spreading development money simultaneously among all sectors of a country's economy.

■6

Most developing countries' economies depend on agriculture. Developed countries' economies depend on industry. If you have some development money, do you spend it on agriculture, where most of your production takes place, or do you spend it on developing an industrial base for growth?

The argument for spending the money on industry is that such expenditures will allow you to decrease imports and will encourage further industrial growth so the developing country can become like the developed countries. Advocates of this position contend that agriculture is a dead-end path.

The argument for spending the money on agriculture instead of industry is that agriculture is already built into the culture of that society, so gains in a congenial area (agriculture) are much more likely to occur than are gains in an unfamiliar area (industry).

Infrastructure versus Directly Productive Investment

As I stated before, most developing countries do not have the infrastructure necessary for most kinds of production. Should you invest your development money in the infrastructure, which is indirectly productive, or in directly productive activities like building a mill or providing a fertilizer subsidy? Infrastructure investment shows no immediate monetary return. If it is to show a return, it must increase private investment which in turn generates a short-run monetary return; if private investment isn't forthcoming, the money spent on infrastructure is wasted. Thus, there is a strong incentive to use the money in directly productive investment. But directly productive investment often cannot compete internationally unless the infrastructure is in place.

MISSION IMPOSSIBLE

7

At this point in my course I inevitably throw my hands up and admit that I don't know what makes it possible for a country to develop. Nor, judging from what I have read, do the development experts. The good ones (that is, the ones I agree with) admit that they don't know; others (that is, the ones I don't agree with) simply don't know that they don't know.

My gut feeling is that there are no definitive general answers that apply to all developing countries. The appropriate answer varies with each country and each situation. Each proposed solution to the development problem has a right time and a right place. Only by having a complete sense of a country, its history, and its cultural, social, and political norms can one decide whether it's the right time and place for this or that policy.

KEY POINTS

- One must be careful in judging economies. **1**
- Developing countries' growth rates in the past few years have been lower than developed countries' growth rates. **1**
- Seven obstacles to economic development are political instability, corruption, lack of investment, excessive debt, inappropriate education, overpopulation, and stagflation (unemployment and inflation). **2**
- Without an appropriate infrastructure governments can sell rights to all kinds of things and thereby limit development. **3**

- Generating sufficient investment is a difficult problem for developing countries. **4**
- Repudiation of debt is a good short-run solution, but it presents long-run problems. **5**
- Three debates about strategies for growth include the balanced/unbalanced growth debate, the agriculture/industry debate, and the infrastructure/directly productive investment debate. **6**
- Optimal strategies for growth are country-specific. **7**

KEY TERMS

Asian tigers *(774)*
balanced growth
 plan *(785)*
brain drain *(782)*

conditionality *(780)*
foreign aid *(778)*
infrastructure
 investment *(779)*

purchasing power
 parity *(774)*

unbalanced growth
 plan *(785)*

QUESTIONS FOR THOUGHT AND REVIEW

The number after each question represents the estimated degree of critical thinking required. (1 = almost none; 10 = deep thought.)

1. If you suddenly found yourself living as a poor person in a developing country, what are some things that you now do that you would no longer be able to do? What new things would you have to do? *(2)*
2. What is wrong with saying that people in developing countries are worse off than people in the United States? *(3)*
3. Does the fact that suicide rates are lower in developing countries than in the United States imply that Americans would be better off living in a developing country? Why? *(5)*
4. Why are investment and savings so low in developing countries? *(5)*
5. If developing countries are so unstable and offer such a risky environment for investment, why do foreigners invest any money in them at all? *(5)*
6. If you were a foreign investor thinking of making an investment in a developing country, what are some things that you would be concerned about? *(4)*
7. Should developing countries send their students abroad for an education? *(5)*
8. How does corruption limit investment and economic growth? *(6)*
9. Should a country control the size and makeup of its population? Why? *(7)*
10. If a person stated, ''The reason a developing country has high inflation is that it's increasing its money supply,'' how would you respond? *(6)*

PROBLEMS AND EXERCISES

1. Interview a foreign student in your class or school. Ask about each of the seven obstacles to economic development and how her country is trying to overcome them.
2. Spend one day living like someone in a developing country. Eat almost nothing and work lifting stones for 10 hours. Then, that same evening, study this chapter and contemplate the bootstrap strategy of development.

38

Socialist Economies in Transition

May you live in interesting times.
Ancient Chinese toast

After reading this chapter, you should be able to:

1

Define *socialism*.

2

Give a brief historical description of the
background of socialism.

3

Summarize how a centrally planned
economy works.

4

State the major problems of a centrally
planned economy.

5

Summarize some transition problems
socialist countries are experiencing.

Chapter 3 introduced you to the two most prominent forms of economic organization of society: capitalism and socialism. Most of this book has considered the operations and institutions of capitalist economies, and has discussed how economic forces work within market situations. However, as emphasized throughout this book, economic forces are at work in *all* situations. A market is simply an institution in which economic forces are allowed to predominate over political and social forces.

In this final chapter we switch gears and look at what happens when markets aren't used. We do that by considering the operation of economic forces in socialist economies and how those forces fit into the transition that most socialist economies have recently been experiencing. Considering these not only gives you insight into a current economic debate that's much in the news; it also provides a summary for much of this book because it concerns the advantages and disadvantages of markets.

Before we consider these issues, it's helpful to consider the historical roots of socialism, how and why it developed, and what in theory it was meant to accomplish. We do that by building on our discussion of the history of socialism in Chapter 3. Having done that, we'll consider how socialism has worked in practice—and how that practice differed from theory. Finally we'll consider the ongoing transition of socialist economies and the problems these economies face.

The theory of modern socialist economies originated when a group of writers in the 1800s reacted to the excesses of unregulated capitalism. Looking at what the Industrial Revolution had wrought—the 10-hour work day, child labor, poor working conditions, a highly unequal distribution of income, unemployment, and starvation—they argued that there must be a better way to organize economic society.

The doctrine of socialism itself began in the early 19th century with the work of Louis Blanc, a French historian and government official. Blanc focused on the belief that everyone who was willing and able to work should have a job. Over time, the emphasis in socialism changed from creating an economy in which everyone had a job, to creating an economy that redistributed income from the rich to the poor, and finally to creating an economy in which the government controlled production.

As the emphasis shifted, the definition of *socialism* evolved, and with the current reforms, that definition continues to evolve. However, since a generally accepted new definition hasn't yet emerged from the current turmoil in socialist economies, we'll use the traditional definition that was generally accepted in the 1980s: **Socialism** is an economic system based upon government ownership of the means of production. Under socialism individuals are encouraged to act for society's benefit; government planning, rather than the market, is relied upon to coordinate economic activity; and distribution of production is determined by need.

The early socialist thinkers vigorously disputed how socialist theory was to be put into practice. One group believed that once socialism was understood by the general public, democratic governments would bow to the wishes of the majority of voters and adopt a socialist system.

Many of this group of 19th-century socialists, such as Comte Henri de Saint-Simon, Charles Fourier, and Robert Owen, preached universal love. They developed concepts of ideal social and economic arrangements and appealed to people's higher nature to adopt them. This strain of socialism came to be known as **utopian socialism.** Some utopian socialists started communities as demonstration projects of the world-to-be, believing that when everyone saw how wonderful life under socialism was, all society would vote to change over to socialism. These

THE HISTORICAL ROOTS OF SOCIALISM

Socialism An economic system based upon government ownership of the means of production.

Utopian Socialism

Utopian socialism Ideal state where social and economic arrangements appeal to people's higher nature.

THE SEARCH FOR UTOPIA

If only the world were wonderful, or at least better than it is. How many times have you thought that? Probably many, and you're not alone. Sir Thomas More in 1515 wrote a book about such a wonderful society, which he called *Utopia*. Ever since, dream worlds have gone by the name *Utopia*.

In the 18th and early 19th centuries there were many dreamers of Utopia. Democracy had been ushered in and new, better, forms of government were taking hold. Why not a better economy too? Not an economy in which people starved; not an economy in which people were held under the "gun" of competition—but a society of cooperation, of concern for others, and of love.

If it sounds wonderful to you, it also sounded wonderful to numerous individuals in the early 1800s, including Robert Owen, owner of a large, successful cotton mill in Manchester, England. Owen believed sufficiently in his ideas to put his money where his mouth was. To demonstrate the superiority of his utopian ideas, he bought a mill in New Lanark, near Manchester, and instead of paying low wages and tolerating unsanitary conditions, he took a strong

interest in the workers' welfare. He provided decent housing, education, and low-cost goods for his workers at the company store. The mill was a success.

Owen then expanded his mission, recommending that entire towns adopt a "cooperative," not a "competitive," structure. He suggested villages of "unity and cooperation" of about 1,200 inhabitants, with each village offering a public kitchen and dining room. Parents would care for their children until the age of three, after which children would be raised by the community so that they would be imbued with the appropriate cooperative social attitude. He believed that once society saw how wonderful these communities were, all societies would voluntarily adopt the structure and soon the whole world would embrace his ideas.

To implement his plans he moved to the United States and set up a model project—New Harmony, Indiana—in 1825. Life in New Harmony was anything but harmonious. In three years Owen was broke and the project was dead— killed by internal fights and arguments. Other similar communities suffered the same fate. The experiment in voluntary socialism was a failure.

communities generally failed, and utopian socialism became synonymous with wild-eyed dreams of economic impossibilities.

Democratic Socialism

Democratic socialism A socialist system that operates within the existing democratic framework.

While utopian socialism is dead, **democratic socialism** (which is voted in, and can be voted out) is not. Democratic socialists operate within existing democratic frameworks and, when elected to public office, introduce socialist policies into the economy. They take over major businesses and institute redistribution and social welfare policies. In a number of Western European countries socialist parties have controlled their economy and, when in power, have implemented socialist principles. In the early 1990s France, for example, was governed by the French socialist party.

As was discussed in Chapter 3, capitalist countries have adopted many social welfare programs advocated by socialists. In many Western European countries socialists have become simply one more political party competing in elections with other political parties. These socialist parties sometimes seem more market-oriented than other parties. They propose policies on the basis of what they think will work and will get them elected, not strictly on the basis of ideology.

Revolutionary Socialism and the Emergence of Communism

A second group of early socialist thinkers argued that existing governments were not truly democratic and would prevent the voluntary development of socialism even if such a development was in society's best interest. The vested interests controlling capitalist societies would prevent socialism because it took away their privileges. Socialism, therefore, would have to be established by revolution. Karl Marx and his brand of socialism (communism) fall within this group. Marx foresaw a revolutionary—not a voluntary, evolutionary—change to socialism.

Marx viewed capitalism as a historical stage in the progression toward communism. He believed that capitalism would end as a nation's oppressed workers united, overthrew the existing government, and established a socialist nonoppressive state. Living under socialism would change people's basic beliefs. People would no longer be interested primarily in themselves but would instead be interested in what was good for society. When that happened, the state could, as Marx expressed it, "wither away" and socialism could become true communism in which all people were concerned with what is good for society, not what is good for themselves.

However, that is not what occurred when the first socialist state was established. Contrary to Marx's prediction, the first socialist state developed in Russia, not in an industrial country. The Russian revolution of 1917 was a revolution not of the proletariat (the working class), but of a small group of dedicated communists, the Bolsheviks. They were able to take over Russia as a result of the incompetence of the established Czarist regime, the devastation of World War I, and their own political skill.

While Marx's writings provided the impetus for the Russian Revolution and gave the revolutionaries a vision of what a socialist economy should be like, his work did not provide much help in the actual running of the economy. When the communists took over, the country's economy was in shambles. Reality forced them to be pragmatic during the initial development of the Russian economic system. There was little time for grand theorizing; instead it was a matter of doing whatever worked.

The main economic features of the former Soviet socialist economy—rigid central planning, state ownership of the means of agricultural and industrial production, collective farms, and state control of wages and prices—all developed in the 1920s and early 1930s, a period of enormous economic crisis, not only in the former Soviet Union but in many Western economies as well.[1]

In understanding the former Soviet Union's economic organization and the meaning of recent economic reforms, it's important to recognize that Marx didn't see capitalism as all bad. He acknowledged that capitalism had created wealth beyond the imagination of individuals who lived in feudal and mercantilist societies. He saw capitalism as an "engine of growth" which had extracted surplus, or savings, from society and had channeled that surplus into investment. In Marx's view, investing (causing growth) was the historical purpose of the capitalist class, and capitalists had fulfilled their role effectively. Their very success would cause the demise of capitalism. As businesses got bigger and bigger by exploiting labor, the workers would form a coherent class (the proletariat) who would eventually revolt and overthrow the capitalists and undermine the capitalist system. Capitalism would produce, as Marx put it, "its own grave-diggers."

Since the communist revolution and the initial introduction of socialism occurred in Russia, and not in the more developed Western economies as Marx had predicted, the job of extracting surplus from workers (which Marx had argued was the reason for the capitalist stage of economies) had not yet been done. Communist leaders found themselves in a dilemma: Because capitalism hadn't done the dirty work, Russia would have to do it. And it did. Russia's new communist leaders found it necessary to extract surplus for investment, and some of their first actions, once in power, were to do so from wherever they could—primarily from the peasants. The communists forced peasants to sell all their grain to the state at a low price, and distributed that grain at a higher price. Needless to say, the peasants strongly objected to this arrangement. The government repressed their revolt, however, and gained even tighter control over the surplus by setting up collective farms owned jointly by all members of the farm and requiring individuals to work on them. A similar extraction of surplus from the peasants occurred in China when communists took over that country after World War II.

The Transition to Pure Communism

---

[1] After their 1917 revolution Russia and 14 other republics were combined into the USSR (the Union of Soviet Socialist Republics). In the early 1990s that union came apart—in part because of the economic problems of socialism and in part because of social and cultural differences among republics.

As communism undergoes change, it becomes difficult to determine what communism actually is. One way to decide is to look at its roots. In the *Communist Manifesto* (1848) Karl Marx and Friedrich Engels set forth the principles of modern communism. They said that communism means:

1. Abolition of property in land and application of all rents of land to public purposes.
2. A heavy progressive or graduated income tax.
3. Abolition of all rights of inheritance.
4. Confiscation of the property of all emigrants and rebels.
5. Centralization of credit in the hands of the state, by means of a national bank with state capital and an exclusive monopoly.
6. Centralization of the means of communication and transport in the hands of the state.
7. Extension of factories and instruments of production owned by the state; the bringing into cultivation of waste lands; and the improvement of the soil generally in accordance with a common plan.
8. Equal obligation of all to work. Establishment of industrial armies, especially for agriculture.
9. Combination of agriculture with manufacturing industries; gradual abolition of the distinction between town and country by a more equitable distribution of the population over the country.
10. Free education for all children in public schools; abolition of child factory labor; combination of education with industrial production.

Communist Manifesto Principles of communism as set forth in a book written by Karl Marx and Friedrich Engels in 1848.

Large collective farms were set up to keep the peasants under government control. The moves were consistent with Marx's guidelines in the *Communist Manifesto.*

The communists in both China and Russia faced similar problems in running industry. Not surprisingly many of the capitalists and managers at the time of the communist takeover didn't trust the communists. Many managers and capitalists left the country; many who stayed tried to sabotage production. The communists responded by taking over all large businesses and directing production from above. As was the case with agriculture, this was done for both political and economic reasons. They wanted political control of production to be in the hands of the central government.

Having taken over the management of agricultural and industrial enterprises and eliminated market prices, the Russian communists were left with the problem of how to coordinate the production and distribution of goods and services. Something had to replace the market as a coordinating mechanism. That something was command and control. It was at this time that a socialist economy became synonymous with a **centrally planned economy** in which a central planning board decides *what* will be produced, *how* production will take place, and *for whom* it will be produced.

Centrally planned economy An economy in which a central planning board decides *what, how,* and *for whom.*

Socialism's Rise and Decline since World War II

Until World War II the former Soviet Union was the only socialist state. However in the economic and political chaos that followed the war, a number of governments in Eastern Europe established socialist economic systems. The establishment of communist-dominated socialist economies was not voluntary. The former Soviet Union dominated Eastern Europe after the war and, through its military power, saw to it that one-party communist rule was established in its European satellite states including East Germany, Hungary, Poland, and Czechoslovakia, among others. In 1949 communists came to power in China. Then in the 1950s and 1960s a number of other countries including Cuba, Angola, North Korea, and Vietnam developed socialist economies controlled by one-party communist governments.

In the late 1980s that changed considerably as various countries began experiencing internal revolts and change. The Soviet Union fell apart into 15 separate states, most of which were attempting to establish market economies; Eastern European countries also tried to institute market economies. China, the last remaining large socialist economy, significantly modified its economic system. The economic question most socialist economies were concerned about in the early 1990s was not *if,* but *how fast* the transition to a market economy should occur.

To understand why these enormous transitions in socialist economies took place, and what these countries were changing from, let's take an in-depth look at how central economic planning was supposed to work in a socialist economy and at the problems that it had in practice.

In a centrally planned economy, central planners decide the general directions the economy will take. They make the *what, how,* and *for whom* decisions. Should the economy focus on producing consumer goods? Machinery? Agriculture? Military hardware? The government's central planners decide. In communist-dominated socialist economies like the former Soviet Union, China, or in pre-1990 Eastern Europe, the power behind the central planners was the Communist party. The Communist party nominated candidates for office. The public then ratified the choices by voting in elections in which the Communist party candidates were the only candidates. Thus, these systems were political systems as well as economic systems in which the Communist party was like an autocracy, being a government composed of a small group of people with nearly unlimited power, not of a popularly elected set of officials.

A centrally planned economy differs from a market economy like that of the United States. That difference is not, however, that in one there is planning and in the other there is not. The difference lies in who does the planning, how many planners there are, and what motives guide planners' decisions. A centrally planned economy has one central agency for economic planning while a market economy has many planners. Since the idea of planning in a market economy may be a bit unusual to you, let's consider who does the planning in the United States. For the 25 percent of U.S. output controlled by the various branches of government (the public sector), the government is the planner, and its decisions are periodically ratified by the public through regularly scheduled elections. In the rest of the economy (the private sector) the planners are business executives, and their decisions are guided by the profit motive, which in turn reflects consumer sovereignty. The multitude of planners in a market economy makes it difficult to say exactly who decides *what, how,* and *for whom* to produce. So normally economists say, "The market decides," but it's important to remember that planning does take place in a market economy. Exhibit 1 summarizes the differences in planning in market and centrally planned economies.

Until the 1990s the former Soviet Union was the prototypical example of central planning. To understand the forces that led the republics of the former Soviet Union to decide to change to a market economy, it is important to see how the centrally planned system was supposed to work. That's what we consider in this section.

In theory the Communist party was the representative of the people's will. The Communist party representatives were the ones whose views were expressed in the planning. In the Soviet government the committee that represented the Communist party was the Politburo. The Politburo was part of the Presidium of the Supreme Soviet, the central decision-making body in the Soviet Union. This Politburo was responsible for formulating five-year plans for the nation's economy. The Politburo also apointed ministers (administrative heads of a government ministry or department) to oversee activity in the various sectors of the economy. These ministers, who were part of the central Soviet government, met to translate the general directives of the government's five-year plan into more specific objectives, which were spelled out in one-year plans.

HOW A CENTRALLY PLANNED ECONOMY WORKS

Planning in a Centrally Planned Economy and in a Market Economy

How a Centrally Planned Economy Worked in Practice

3

EXHIBIT 1 Planning in a Centrally Planned and in a Market Economy

All economists must plan. The difference between a market economy and a centrally planned economy is in who does the planning and what the planners' motivations are.

	Centrally planned	Market
Who	• Central planners	• Government • Private business • Nonprofit business
Why	• Ideally, good of society In reality?	• Government and nonprofit • Ideally, good of society In reality? • Private business profit motive (fill consumer desires and make a profit)

A general directive issued by the Politburo was something like the following: "Over the next five years the focus of the economy will be on producing more machinery. Production in machinery will increase 8 percent per year. We will increase agricultural goods by 4 percent per year and consumer goods by 5 percent." The Council of Ministers then met and decided what kinds of machinery would be produced and what crops would be focused on in each of those five years.

Even when these decisions had been made, many more specifics needed to be added before the plans were meaningful enough to be carried out. For example, managers and workers needed to know not only how many tractors to produce, but also: What horsepower? What size tires? What kind of steel? What inputs will be available? The task of translating the Council of Ministers' general plans into concrete plans fell to **Gosplan** (the State Planning Commission), which was made up of civil servants who specialized in economics. How extensive was planning in a centrally planned economy? In 1987 Gosplan set quotas and prices for over 200,000 commodities and controlled the operation of over 37,000 enterprises.

The general structure of the former Soviet planning system is shown in Exhibit 2. As you can see, Gosplan was located between the Council of Ministers and the planning commissions of the various Soviet republics and regions. Together with **Gosbank,** which handled the financial aspects of planning, Gosplan was in charge of seeing that the central planners' directives were carried out.

An individual official in Gosplan was assigned a certain group of factories or production units, usually all in the same region of the country. This individual knew the capabilities of the factories in the region and on the basis of that knowledge he or she set production quotas for each factory.

For example, say the government's five-year plan emphasized plenty of bread to go around. To fulfill this plan, bread output was to be increased by 40 percent over five years. The Council of Ministers would translate that goal into an increase in the output of bread of, say, 7 percent per year, which, compounded over five years, would achieve more than the 40 percent desired growth. Gosplan translated those targeted increases into specific production quotas for regions containing groups of firms—8 percent for one region, 3 percent for another, and so on.

Having worked out the general one-year plan for groups of firms, Gosplan transmitted the plan to the Planning Commissions of the country's various republics and their regions. These planning commissions translated the plans into directives for the managers of individual factories. Thus, a bakery manager was given a set of directives specifying what he or she would be required to produce

Gosplan Former Soviet economic planning agency.

Gosbank Former Soviet institution in charge of the financial elements of the central plan.

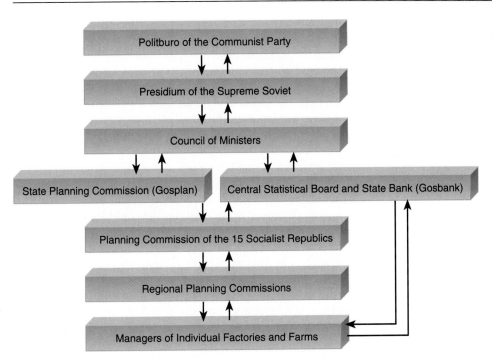

EXHIBIT 2 **The Structure of the Central Planning System in the Soviet Union in the 1980s**

Before its breakup the former Soviet Union had a complicated planning structure controlled by the Communist party. That structure was built into its economic system, and the republics of the former Soviet Union will spend much of the 1990s trying to untangle it.

over the next year and what inputs would be available in order to meet the goal. The directive would have read as follows: "Next year you will produce 4,000,000 loaves of white bread, 2,000,000 loaves of rye bread, 1,000,000 loaves of whole wheat bread, and 1,000,000 loaves of pumpernickel. To do so, you will be allocated 400 workers, 1 plant, and 4,000,000 pounds of grain."

This one-year directive was subdivided into monthly, weekly, and even daily input and output levels. Managers' performances were judged according to how close they came to meeting their assigned goals. Under actual conditions the plans would have been much more detailed than the hypothetical directive I've constructed, but the example gives you the general idea.

Counterplanning   The preceding description may make it seem as if, in a central planning system, the various planning agencies in Exhibit 2 would continually be telling the agencies below them what to do. That was true, but the information flowed both ways. Long before a final directive was issued, the higher-level planners conferred extensively with lower-level planners (the minister, the Gosplan specialist, the regional planning commission, and the plant manager). They would go over what was feasible. After talking with the lower-level planning group, the higher-level planning group would usually show the lower-level group a draft plan.

Each lower-level group had a chance to point out that it wasn't allocated the inputs necessary to achieve the output quota or that the output quota was unrealistic. They could suggest modifications to the plan. This process of modifying the plan from below was known as **counterplanning.** Counterplanning let individuals at lower levels of the hierarchy influence decisions of those at higher levels and thereby affect the decision made by the highest level of central planners.

Counterplanning Process that lets individuals low in the hierarchy influence the planning decisions of those above them in the hierarchy.

Coordinating the Plans: Material Balances   Directing and issuing detailed plans for an entire economy was a complicated procedure. The planners had to ensure that the output of firms whose products were used in the production of other products matched the inputs that the planners had assigned to the manufacturers of those other products. This coordination of directives was achieved through a system called *material balances*.

Material balance Process by which central planners adjust incoming and outgoing quantities of materials until supply equals demand (at least on paper).

Using the **material balance** approach, essentially the planning board added up what was coming in, subtracted what was going out, and kept adjusting incoming and outgoing quantities of materials until they were equal—until the materials balanced. Hence the name *material balance*. The process wasn't easy. It was like trying to put a Rubik Cube back in the pattern it had when it came out of the box. One kept trying various combinations of inputs and outputs until one got everything to fit.

To aid in this complex process of making inputs and outputs balance, economists designed and perfected some mathematical tools. These tools were important tools not only to planned economies; they are still important tools to Western business firms. The tools include linear programming, designed by Leonid Kantorovich (a Soviet economist) and input-output analysis, designed by Wassily Leontief (a Russian-born American economist who was interested in analyzing centrally planned economies). The two men won Nobel prizes for their work, Kantorovich in 1975 and Leontief in 1973. The material balance approach, assisted by tools such as input-output analysis and linear programming, was the most widely used system for coordinating centrally planned economic systems, and a variant is still being used in China.

Deciding What to Produce

Now that you've been introduced to the technical planning apparatus, let's consider planners' motivation in deciding what and how much of something to produce next year. There are no simple answers to these questions. The planners could, if they desired, decide how much would be wanted by consumers next year in about the same way a firm in the United States decides. Alternatively they could look at what was produced one year, estimate how much demand for the product would increase the next year, and base their production decisions on that estimate. Or they could base their decision on other criteria.

But whatever criteria they choose, there's a big difference in the motivation behind planning in a socialist economy and in a capitalist economy. In a capitalist economy a firm makes its profits by producing *what* and *how much* is wanted by consumers. To stay in business, firms must take the consumers' desires into account. Central planners in a socialist economy don't have to take consumers' desires into account. Socialist planners might realize that Twinkies will be wanted by consumers but the planners might believe that Twinkies aren't good for people, so their decision might be to produce whole-wheat bread instead.

Central planners could follow any set of principles they wanted to in determining what output levels to assign the producers of various goods. Exhibit 3 presents a production possibility curve showing the range of choices that societies could make between investment goods and consumer goods. In the 1970s and 1980s Soviet planners chose a point like *A*, focusing on investment goods (heavy equipment, large machines, space exploration, and military goods such as tanks and planes), having decided that these goods were what their society needed. Consumer goods (cars, household appliances, clothing) were given short shrift. Most market economies, in which the profit motive directs firms to produce what they think people want, choose a point like *B*, which includes more consumer goods.

The reason socialist planners chose a point like *A* was that higher production of investment goods was supposed to lead to faster growth, which would make up for the lower level (relative to Western developed countries) at which the former Soviet Union and other socialist countries started out. It's as if your economics instructor told you to work harder at the beginning of the term because it will pay off at the end. This strategy can be successful, but socialist economies, for reasons that I'll discuss later, didn't grow faster than the United States and other

Leonid Kantorovich—Nobel prize, 1975, for work on linear programming and economic planning. © *The Nobel Foundation.*

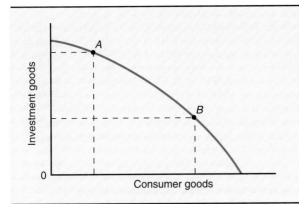

EXHIBIT 3   Choice between Investment Goods and Consumer Goods

One of the reasons socialist economies had shortages of consumer goods is that the planners made a conscious decision to emphasize investment goods, choosing a position like *A* over *B*.

market economies. They grew more slowly. The payoff for choosing investment goods over consumer goods didn't come, and that missing payoff was a significant factor in the demise of socialist planned economies.

Central planners had not only to decide what goods to produce; they also had to decide what prices to charge for those goods. In a market economy most prices are set by suppliers at a level that covers costs of production and provides them with a profit margin that they feel is appropriate. If suppliers set their prices too high, consumers will buy from other suppliers; if suppliers set their prices too low, they won't cover their costs and they'll lose money.

Pricing in a Centrally Planned Economy

In a market economy suppliers are free to adjust their prices to make the quantity demanded equal the quantity supplied. If demand is lower than expected, firms will lower their prices to stimulate an increase in the quantity demanded. If demand is high, prices will tend to rise, encouraging consumers to economize on the good, and producers to increase their production. That's what's meant by *market-determined prices*.

In a centrally planned economy, prices are determined by the central planners, not by the market. The prices that central planners set influence the quantity demanded of various goods. When planners set a low price, the quantity demanded will be high; when they set a high price, the quantity demanded will be low. That's the same as in a capitalist economy.

What are different are the criteria that central planners use to set prices. To some degree, they set prices to cover costs (not including profits, since socialist producers aren't supposed to earn profits), but they can also set prices at the level they believe is fair or at the level they believe is the social worth of a product—in short, at whatever level they want.

How did central planners actually decide where to set prices? The general approach to pricing taken by socialist countries was to price necessities (like basic foods) low and luxuries (like washing machines and cars) high, independent of costs. For example, in the late 1980s Soviet rents were set at the U.S. equivalent of $80 a month for a one-bedroom apartment in Moscow. Compare this to the usual $1,000 monthly rent for a one-bedroom apartment in New York City at that time. Medical care was free. Bread and potatoes were priced far below what it cost to produce them. Exhibit 4 shows prices of selected goods in East and West Germany in 1988, before the two nations were reunited. After unification, East Germany's prices were changed to reflect those of West Germany.

The ability to set prices at whatever level they wanted didn't free central planners from economic forces. The laws of supply and demand still operated. There were surpluses of goods whose prices were set too high relative to the quantity supplied. There were shortages of goods whose prices were set too low relative to the quantity supplied.

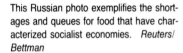

EXHIBIT 4   Prices (in dollars) in East and West Germany before Unification

Item	West Germany (D-mark)	East Germany (OstMark)
Coffee (1 pound)	$3.39	$13.33
Color TV set	$600	$2,000
Electricity (1 kwh)	17¢	3¢
Monthly rent	$200	$30
Potatoes (10 pounds)	$1.80	30¢
Refrigerator	$250	$570
Rye bread (1 kg)	75¢	10¢
Washing machine	$400	$1,000

Sources: Based on information collected by Deutsche Bank, World Bank, and estimates by author.

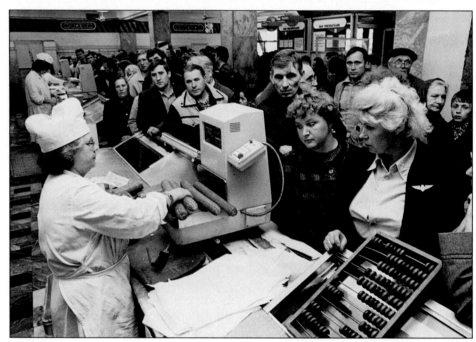

This Russian photo exemplifies the shortages and queues for food that have characterized socialist economies. *Reuters/Bettman*

Most socialist economies suffered from consistent shortages of most goods. Getting an apartment required a wait of five years or even longer. Getting a car required a still longer wait. This suggests that the prices the planners chose (even the relatively high prices) were too low relative to demand. This was one of people's big complaints with the centrally planned economies—a consistent shortage of goods.

When there are shortages of goods, an alternative rationing system must be established to determine who gets what. In socialist countries that rationing system generally involved being a member of the Communist party or being in the in-group. Officials received "gifts," were put at the top of waiting lists, and were notified by distributors when scarce goods came in so that they could shop ahead of other people. In Romania, for example, before the revolution that broke out at the end of 1989, the communist leadership could get pretty much whatever consumer goods it wanted. That inequality went against the goals of communism, and the people's resentment of it was one cause of the uprisings against communism and socialism in the late 1980s and early 1990s. We'll cover this issue in more depth when we discuss reforms.

The Role of Markets in Centrally Planned Economies

Market economies have always had certain sectors in which markets aren't officially allowed. For example, addictive drugs, votes, and sex can't legally be bought and sold. Centrally planned economies, similarly, always had certain sectors in which markets were legal. For example, central planners always allowed some food items and some repair services to be bought and sold in a market.

Where markets aren't legal they often spring up anyway and operate as gray or black markets. Thus, the United States has black markets in addictive drugs, while the centrally planned Soviet Union of the late 1980s had black markets in Western rock records.

Up until the mid-1980s socialist governments tried to eliminate black markets, but in the 1990s the remaining socialist countries, such as China, have condoned the black markets, turning them into gray markets, or even encouraged them— turning them into legal markets. For example, China now has numerous independent businesspeople.

The legalization of markets and market forces in China and other centrally planned economies represents a major change in the nature of socialist economies—one in some ways comparable to the extension of the government *into* market economies during the 1930s and 1940s. Whether markets and socialism are compatible, given the historical tension between the two, remains to be seen.

THE PROBLEMS OF CENTRAL PLANNING

While the speed of the change in socialist economies surprised many economists, the economic problems of central planning that played a big role in bringing about the recent changes did not. Most economists have never liked central planning. Two important reasons are: (1) their belief that central planning doesn't achieve the economic goals that it is meant to achieve and (2) their belief that central planning is inconsistent with a democratic political system. Considering these two beliefs provides a nice summary of many of the ideas in this book.

Central Planning Doesn't Achieve Its Economic Goals

4

Economists have identified five problems that tend to undermine central planning:

1. Nonmarket pricing and perverse incentives.
2. Inability to adjust prices quickly.
3. Lack of information about demand.
4. Ambiguous directives.
5. Inability to adjust plans quickly to changing situations.

Let's look at each of these problems in turn.

Nonmarket Pricing and Perverse Incentives In a market economy, prices reflect costs—a central lesson of the economic analysis of production. The advantage of having prices reflecting costs was a central lesson of microeconomic theory. Prices that reflect costs make people's decisions about what to consume and what to produce reflect productivity cost. The result is efficient use of resources.

Central planners can override the market and choose prices that don't reflect costs. However, as discussed in the chapter on consumer choice, when prices don't reflect costs, consumers have an incentive to use goods in a manner that reflects the price to them and not the costs to the society. Economists call an incentive to use goods in a manner that doesn't reflect the cost to society a **perverse incentive.**

Perverse incentive Incentive to use goods in a manner that does not reflect that use's cost to society.

Let's say that the economic planners decide that everyone in the society deserves inexpensive bread, so they lower the price of bread from 50¢ to 5¢ for a 16-ounce loaf. Say that last year at 50¢ a loaf people consumed 1 million loaves, so planners figure this year at 5¢ a loaf 2 million loaves will be consumed. After all, how much bread can people eat? In principle, that's plenty of bread, but most likely the outcome will be a shortage of bread to eat. Why? Because at 5¢ a loaf, self-interested people will discover lots of other things one can do with bread besides eat it themselves. For example, after the fall in price, a pig farmer might buy four loaves of bread a week for his family and 7,000 loaves a week for his pigs. At 5¢ a loaf, it pays him to feed bread, rather than oats or corn, even though the equivalent amount of oats or corn would be better for the pigs and less costly to society. Pig farming will increase enormously. If the cost to society of producing a loaf of bread is 40¢ and the cost of producing oats or corn of equal feed value is 20¢, the 5¢ price of bread not only creates a shortage of bread for people to eat, but also subsidizes pig farmers. Moreover society will be losing 35¢ (the 40¢ it costs minus the 5¢ it gets for the bread) for each loaf of bread fed to pigs while gaining only 20¢ of value in additional output of pigs. The net loss to society will be 15¢ per loaf (the opportunity cost of the oats or corn).

If central planners have a high degree of control over which, and how, inputs are used, they can stop such "inappropriate" uses of bread simply by forbidding them. But unless people are not self-interested, policing and enforcing those additional rules require an enormous amount of central control, which requires a large, costly bureaucracy and causes other problems.

Central planners must direct individuals to do what is consistent with their plan, and must enforce their directives. The market, in contrast, uses economic incentives to guide people to do what is in society's interest.

Inability to Adjust Prices Quickly   Centrally planned pricing decisions are also not consistent with quick adjustment of prices. The reason is that the information about what is selling fast and what isn't doesn't get back to the central planners rapidly enough. Why? Sales information is often delayed by the need to flow through three or four levels of bureaucracy: A salesperson must tell his boss, who must tell the regional director, who must tell the central planning assistant director—all by memo, and memos simply don't travel very fast. It's a law of nature that administrative decisions aren't made quickly. Large firms in the United States have the same problems; they tend to adjust their prices more slowly than do small firms.

The result of central planning's inability to adjust prices quickly is a surplus of some items whose price is too high and a shortage of other goods whose price is too low. Shortages and surpluses were especially apparent in specialized consumer goods such as fashionable clothing (for example, stone-washed jeans), household appliances, and novelty items. In the United States, you can walk into stores and get almost anything you want, whenever you want. As long as some person can predict a demand and make a profit filling that demand, the demand will be filled. In the centrally planned former Soviet Union "frivolous needs" received a low priority, resulting in chronic shortages of all types of consumer goods.

China is currently changing its planning focus toward more consumer goods while simultaneously allowing more market production of consumer goods. Economic theory predicts that the market will do much better than the planners. The reason is that predicting demand for consumer items is always difficult, and central planning makes it even more difficult. In a market economy, surpluses are dealt with by running sales: "CLEARANCE SALE! TAKE 60% TO 70% OFF ALL RED-TAGGED ITEMS!" At some price suppliers in a market economy will find demanders for those purple trousers or those dresses with last year's length.

Socialist retail firms will have trouble running sales because the need to get approval prevents them from changing prices quickly enough. So the planners' retail stores may find themselves with empty racks for jeans but overflowing racks of purple trousers.

Lack of Accurate Information about Demand   The problems caused by the planners' inability to adjust prices are amplified by their lack of information about what products are desired. In a centrally planned economy producers have little incentive to tell the planners that their plans will create a surplus or a shortage; nor do they have an incentive to see that their goods sell. When producers are judged by their ability to meet their production quotas, not by whether their goods sell, they don't provide planners with information about what sells. Instead they provide information that will encourage planners to set production targets that are easy to meet.

The result of such misleading feedback has been the production of lots of undesirable and unwanted goods and severe shortages of desired goods. In most centrally planned economies, consumers walked around with lots of cash and shopping bags. When they saw something they needed or liked in a store, they got in line to buy large quantities for themselves and their friends—which worsened the shortage for other consumers.

Ambiguous Production Directives   Another problem that centrally planned economies had is that production directives were inevitably ambiguous. To be unambiguous, a directive must give all relevant specifications of a product. One can't simply say, "Produce 4 million tons of screws." One must specify size, quality, type of material to be used, and number of threads. One perhaps apocryphal story concerns a directive for chandeliers that specified only the overall weight. To meet the directive, the plant simply built one gigantic chandelier made of lead, for which no truck large enough to move it could be found. The plant met its quota, but did not produce anything useful or desirable.

This problem is a general one of administrative control and isn't confined to centrally planned economies. At General Motors, for example, until recently managers were often given quantitative goals that left out certain qualitative specifications. In the 1970s the basic goals were to produce lots of cars quickly and cheaply. The result: low-quality cars and the decline of the U.S. auto industry.

Inability to Adjust Plans Quickly   Another problem for centrally planned economies is that they do not adjust plans very well. In any economy, things never develop in quite the way they're expected to. Inevitably there are emergencies, breakdowns, and changes in priorities that require changes in the plan.

In market economies, decisions about adjusting plans are made by individuals and firms, using the information available to them. Firms react to market incentives. If there's a significant shortage of a good, its price rises and, as it does, some individual or firm has a monetary incentive to provide it. If an automobile manufacturer in a market economy finds that its steel supplies aren't being delivered on schedule, it calls other suppliers to round up an alternative supply. The market provides both the *information* needed to adjust the plan and *incentives* to do so.

In a centrally planned economy, all information about the need to adjust plans must go through a central office. Say an auto plant in a centrally planned economy found that steel supplies were falling short. The managers would have to call the next level of the central planning office, which in turn would have to call the next level, which would have to call the steel producers and try to find out what was going wrong. Once a decision to adjust the plans was made, the same bureaucratic procedure was followed in reverse. The producer called the subplanner, the subplanner called the planner, and so on. By the time the information led to a change in direction, most likely everyone had said, "The hell with it." Your own experiences in dealing with some large U.S. firm or bureaucratic institution may have been merely frustrating, but centrally planned economies would have driven you crazy.

In principle, planners could have built into their plans a method of adjustment—their plans could have been contingent plans. But, in practice, merely specifying the dimensions of the product made the plans so complicated that formulating contingent plans was out of the question. There were hundreds of possible contingencies, and specifying plans for them was impossible. In short, information about what adjustment to make wasn't efficiently transmitted among producers and planners in a centrally planned economy. This was the lesson of microeconomic theory: *Market prices transmit information efficiently.*

Even if such information were efficiently transmitted in a centrally planned economy, there would still be a lack of incentive to proceed with the adjustments. It isn't easy to adjust production plans in any economy. In a market economy, competition—the threat of losing business—keeps suppliers on their toes; they have to adjust to the changing whims of consumers because if they don't, they won't make a profit. In a centrally planned economy, the profit motive doesn't exist, so it couldn't serve as an incentive to adjust plans.

Let's consider a car production manager in a centrally planned economy who discovers that delivery of steel supplies is falling behind. The question he asks is "Can I cover my backside?" The answer: "Yes, I can blame the steel company for not meeting its plan." Since the manager can't be blamed—or fired—for the steel shortages, he or she has little *incentive* to find an alternative source of steel. The problem becomes even more difficult with consumer goods. Meeting consumer demands is tough work. Being nice to the fickle, frivolous consumer takes effort—and unless one is profiting significantly from making that effort, being nice isn't worth it. It's not from benevolence that Kmart meets your whims; it's from Kmart's self-interest. And in centrally planned economies, meeting consumer whims isn't directly in producers' self-interest.

Again, China is currently heeding the lessons from the former Soviet Union. It is directing its retail employees to be friendly and to meet customers' whims. Chinese planners are now trying to produce what they believe the people want. Economic theory predicts that they will have trouble doing so, and will be outcompeted by firms operating in the market—if they continue to allow such firms to exist.

Central Planning, Bureaucracy, and Markets

It's important to go over these problems with central planning, not only because they provide an understanding of why socialist countries are moving away from central planning and from socialism itself, but also because you'll see many examples of such problems in the United States.

Many larger U.S. firms face the same inefficient transmission of information and lack of incentives to adjust plans that centrally planned economies do. In fact, the difference between them, as far as these problems of unresponsiveness are concerned, is just a matter of size. The Soviet or Chinese planner would deal with a supermega company consisting of the entire economy, while U.S. managers face only the particular company they work for. Like their socialist counterparts, U.S. executives are removed from the flow of information needed for them to know what consumers want. They too often lack the incentives to meet consumer demands. The managers are often more interested in office politics and internal management promotion criteria than they are in meeting consumer demands. The reason is that in large firms the profit motive exists for the *firm* but isn't translated to the individual employee.

Because of this similarity, much of the training and many of the tools used in socialist planning are identical to those taught in business schools and used in management. That training and the tools focus on how incentives within the system can be structured so that the system achieves the desired goals.

Even with training, large businesses in the United States aren't especially responsive to consumers. That's why small firms and businesses are constantly springing up, to fill in the gaps left by the large firms. These small firms keep the large firms alert to consumer demands. If the large firms don't meet those demands, they'll lose their market to small firms and go out of business.

Why do bureaucracies exist if they have such problems? The reason is simple: Markets have their problems too. Market economies have firms (which are essentially bureaucratic command and control organizations) because setting up

ADDED DIMENSION

P lanned economies are often presented as the antithesis of market economies. However, while considering planned economies, remember that market economies have within them large organizations that run by plans—not by market. For example, in the United States General Motors had sales in 1990 of $126 billion, sales larger than those of all but five or six countries of the world. GM is a planned economy unto itself.

Markets could exist to coordinate activities within these firms, but they don't. Imagine, for a moment, that the United States didn't have any antitrust laws and that one of the conglomerate companies, call it Super Pac Company,

began buying more and more firms until eventually it owned all the firms in the United States. While its theoretical goals might be different, Super Pac Company would want to earn profit for its owners rather than provide a good life for its workers. Its organizational problems would be exactly the same as the problems facing a socialist planner.

Thus, the economics of socialist countries is, in a sense, managerial economics. The problems managers of large U.S. firms and central planners face are similar: how to coordinate and motivate individuals without the use of the market.

markets and negotiating about prices for every transaction would simply be too time consuming. Imagine the complexities if each day firms had to negotiate pay with workers, or students had to negotiate with every teacher how much they would pay for each lecture. Instead institutions and contracts develop that take some of those decisions out of the market. For example, you pay tuition for a semester, not an amount per teacher and lecture; classes are then allocated by nonmarket mechanisms. Institutions, bureaucracies, and administrative controls exist because "the market" isn't the answer to every problem.

The difficulty, of course, is to find the middle ground between market control and coordination, and administrative control and coordination. Pinpointing that middle ground is a judgment call. Most economists are willing to make that judgment call against central planning in a large country, but similarly most economists believe that some large institutions and government coordination are necessary. The debate is about the appropriate mix.

Economic efficiency is not an end in itself. It has a meaning only in relation to its contribution to the goals of society. If economic efficiency violates other goals of society, then one might say, "To hell with economic efficiency." I point this out because a second argument some economists use against central planning is that it's inconsistent with democratic institutions (to which they have an ideological commitment) and that it violates the rights of individuals. If one agrees with this argument, one would oppose central planning even if it were efficient.[2]

The ideological argument against central planning is that it gives too much economic power to the central planners and thus is inconsistent with true democracy. Holders of this view argue that unless various groups in society have economic power, government will become oppressive, trample on individual rights, and destroy democracy. To give as much economic power to a small group of individuals as central planning gives can only lead to corruption. As 19th-century historian Lord Acton said, "Power corrupts, and absolute power corrupts absolutely." Proponents of this view argue that this is what happened in many socialist countries. When it was first established, the Communist party in most socialist countries may have had society's goals in mind, but by the 1980s the parties had their own welfare, not society's, in mind. Thus, the parties had failed, even on the terms that they set out for themselves.

One example of this failure was the almost total lack of concern for the environment in these countries. Water, land, and air were far more polluted than in the United States. Environmental concerns involve externalities that the mar-

Central Planning Is Inconsistent with Democracy

---

[2] I should point out that the argument also works in reverse: If one believes that capitalism and a market system violate individuals' rights, then one could oppose the market even though it is more efficient.

ket alone cannot effectively handle. So one would have expected that a socialist government would be able to internalize the externalities and deal more effectively with environmental problems than has the United States. Yet, by all accounts, they did not.

Another example concerns the distribution of income. One of the Communist party's goals was the equal distribution of income among the people, but, as Abram Bergson (an economist at Harvard) has pointed out, the actual distribution of income was no more equal in the former Soviet Union and most other socialist countries than it was in the United States.

So not only did their economies provide fewer goods than are provided in market economies, those fewer goods were not more equally divided. As we discussed, many goods in those countries were rationed, but somehow Communist party members were able to get these scarce, rationed goods that nonmembers could not. Many high-level communist leaders lived in palatial homes while ordinary citizens were crammed into tiny apartments. There were even tales of government leaders having billions of dollars stashed away in foreign bank accounts. In the early 1990s the perception that Communist party members were being treated "more fairly" than others played a major role in the overthrow of communist-dominated socialist governments. Once those governments were out of power, it quickly became apparent how badly the communist parties had failed. In free elections, large majorities in most of the formerly socialist countries voted to eliminate socialism entirely, and the countries adopted market economies.

SOCIALIST ECONOMIES IN TRANSITION

5

Transition Problems

In the early 1990s political and economic changes in Eastern Europe, the Soviet Union, and China have come so fast and so erratically that it's impossible to provide an up-to-date survey in a textbook. It is possible, however, to provide a brief background of the changes and some of the problems these countries will be experiencing.

The choices these countries face aren't pleasant. They're much larger choices than the choice of an economic system. They're choices that have political and social elements as well. For example, the republics of the former Soviet Union and Eastern European countries are combinations of distinct nationalities with their own customs and allegiances. Many of these groups want political independence. The fights about the economic system will be interrelated with these political fights. As we discussed in the previous chapter on developing countries, such political and social upheavals make it impossible for any economic system to operate effectively. So one complex problem they face is political and social instability. Markets aren't going to solve this problem.

A second problem they face is lack of a consensus as to which direction to follow. Some groups favor maintaining a centrally planned system. Others favor moving totally to a market economy. Still others favor what they call *a third way,* an as yet undefined economic system that would supposedly provide the best of both worlds. The uncertainty accompanying these potential alternative directions will make it almost impossible for any economic system to operate. Central planning doesn't work because managers at the firm level no longer see their personal and professional futures tied to fulfillment of the centrally directed plan. But neither does the market, since a well-functioning market requires the existence of a legal structure that can see that contracts are carried out, a well-defined structure of private property, and a populace with entrepreneurial skills. And who knows what the third way requires.

In the early 1990s most of the formerly socialist countries were trying to establish market economies. But the economic and political chaos in those nations made progress unlikely. Those who expected an easy transition to a market economy were quickly proved wrong. Complicated market systems require complicated legal arrangements.

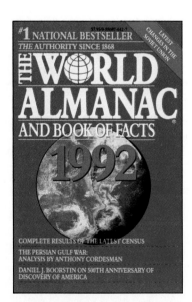

Almanacs are excellent sources of recent economic statistics.

ECONOMISTS' ADVICE IN THE TRANSITION: TANSTAAFL

Like many other Western economists, the author of this book made the trip over to the formerly socialist countries. I spent two months in Bulgaria trying to understand what was going on and discussing the country's economic problems with the people there. I had an office in the former Karl Marx University (now the National Institute of International Economics), right next to the office of the university's chief administrator.

I taught classes about Western banking systems, markets, and international financial systems. Bulgarian newspaper, radio, and television reporters came to me asking what the answers were. I went over the problems and took positions on many of the controversial issues facing the Bulgarian government. But in giving my advice, I made clear to my questioners that it was contingent advice—that my knowledge of their institutions and social structure wasn't deep enough to come to conclusions. I emphasized that my training allowed me to help them understand what markets could and could not do, but it did not allow me to tell them, "This is what you should do." That, they had to decide for themselves.

But wherever I went, I told the story of King Tanstaafl. I became known as the Tanstaafl professor. If the Bulgarians learn that lesson, they will do ok, because that is the most important lesson the West has for them.

Uncertainty associated with the transition makes most economists pessimistic about the short-term prospects for the group of economies that were formerly centrally planned, regardless of which direction these economies follow.

As formerly socialist countries are discovering, the transition to a non–centrally planned economy is a rocky one. I could list many more problems and decisions that they're facing, but this brief discussion should give you a sense of the enormity of the transition problem. There are potential answers for each difficulty, but for each answer there are additional problems.

In this last paragraph of the last chapter of this book I wanted to present a grand summary of the problems of socialist countries that would simultaneously provide a grand summary of the entire book. I struggled with such a grand summary for quite a while, and none of my attempts were all that grand. Then I thought about it some more and decided that this is not the place for a grand summary. This book is an introduction to your economic study, not an end to it. Introductory economics has no grand summary. What it does have is a number of important insights and ideas that I hope you've gained as you've worked your way through the chapters. If you want the grand summary, which I hope you do, you'll have to take more economics courses. It's the right thing to do.

What Is the Future?

KEY POINTS

- Socialism is an economic system based upon collective ownership. Under socialism individuals are encouraged to act for society's benefit. With recent reforms, this definition is likely to change. **1**
- Socialism did not evolve from capitalism. It arose in feudal Russia at a time when that country was in a war crisis. At that time socialism became synonymous with a planned economy. **2**
- In a centrally planned economy, central planners make the *what, how,* and *for whom* decisions. **3**
- Planned economies have been plagued by shortages of consumer goods. These shortages have been partly due to conscious decisions since central planners have generally chosen investment over consumption goods. **4**
- Five problems of centrally planned economies are:

  1. Nonmarket pricing and perverse incentives.
  2. Inability to adjust prices quickly.
  3. Lack of information about demand.
  4. Ambiguous directives.
  5. Inability to adjust plans quickly to changing situations. **4**

- Transforming socialist economies will be a difficult process. Whether the transformation will succeed is an open question. **5**

KEY TERMS

centrally planned
  economy *(792)*
Communist
  Manifesto (792)

counterplanning *(795)*
democratic
  socialism *(790)*
Gosbank *(794)*

Gosplan *(794)*
material balance *(796)*
perverse incentive *(799)*

socialism *(789)*
utopian socialism *(789)*

QUESTIONS FOR THOUGHT AND REVIEW

*The number after each question represents the estimated
degree of critical thinking required. (1 = almost none;
10 = deep thought.)*

1. If people are inherently good, socialism is the best
economic system; if people are inherently bad, capitalism is the best economic system. True or false?
Why? *(7)*
2. Contrast the ways a capitalist country and a socialist
country would respond to an increase in demand for
shoes. *(5)*
3. Socialist countries are fairer than capitalist countries
because they price luxuries high and necessities low.
True or false? Why? *(7)*
4. Perverse incentives are not only a problem of socialist
economies; they are a problem of all bureaucracies organized around administrative control. Give an
example of a perverse incentive you see in the United
States. *(6)*

5. How would you redesign the bureaucratic structure
that caused that perverse incentive? *(8)*
6. What problems would your redesign cause? *(8)*
7. If your redesigned structure would improve the efficiency of the bureaucratic structure, why hasn't the
bureaucratic structure been redesigned? *(8)*
8. Market socialism is doomed to failure because prices
provide information as well as coordinate action. True
or false? Why? *(8)*
9. Some socialist reformers have talked about a "third
way" that is neither socialism nor capitalism. What
might be some characteristics of that "third
way"? *(9)*
10. A centrally planned economy is inconsistent with a
democratic society. True or false? Why? *(6)*

PROBLEMS AND EXERCISES

1. In a centrally planned economy the government fixes
the apartment rents at $50 per month even though the
equilibrium price is $100 per month.
  a. Show the likely result with supply and demand
curves.
  b. Say the central planners recognize the problem and
decide to eliminate the shortage by charging the
equilibrium price. Show the likely result.
  c. If they do charge the equilibrium price, will the eco-

nomic system be equivalent to a market system?
Why?
2. Research the recent economic reforms in China, Bulgaria, and Latvia.
  a. Which country is doing best?
  b. What are the reasons for this?
  c. Would a different reform path have changed the results? Why?

Index

Index

Note: Page references in **bold face** indicate definitions in margin of text.

This new printing of *ECONOMICS* offered us the opportunity to provide you with the most current information, so we seized it. Listed below are the pages where we checked sources and updated data when necessary.

81 (Ex. 1)	87 (Ex. 4)	89 (Ex. 5)
93 (Ex. 8 & text)	94 (Ex. 9a)	95 (Ex. 9b & text)
96 (Ex. 10)	97 (Ex. 11)	113 (Ex. 3)
116 (Ex. 5)	120 (Ex. 6)	137 (Ex. 1)
138 (Ex. 2)	145 (text)	146 (Ex. 5)
147 (text)	149 (Ex. 6)	151 (Ex. 8)
165 (Ex. 3 & text)	166 (Ex. 5 & Ex. 6)	167 (text)
168 (Ex. 7 & text)	169 (Ex. 8 & text)	170 (Ex. 10 & text)
173 (text)	377 (time line)	549 (Ex. 1)
576 (Ex. 2)	590 (Ex. 3)	663 (Ex. 3)
667 (Ex. 5)	670 (Ex. 8)	677 (Ex. 11)
679 (Ex. 13)	680 (text)	706 (Ex. 9)
727 (Ex. 1)	748 (Ex. 1 & text)	749 (text)
750 (text)	774 (Ex. 2)	784 (Ex. 5)

Economic Report of the President